900 1950 015

LIU CIXIN'S *The Three-Body Pi*

GAO XINGJIAN NOBEL PRIZE 2000 ●

HANDOVER OF HONG KONG 1997 ●

HOU HSIAO-HSIEN'S *A City of Sadness* RELEASED 1989 ●

TIANANMEN INCIDENT 1989 ●

LIFTING OF MARTIAL LAW IN TAIWAN 1987 ●

━━━━━ 1966 – 1976 CULTURAL REVOLUTION

● 1958 MAO ZEDONG'S GREAT LEAP FORWARD

● 1949 FOUNDING OF THE PEOPLE'S REPUBLIC OF CHINA

━━ 1946 – 1949 CHINESE CIVIL WAR

● December 1937 NANJING MASSACRE

━━━━ 1937 – 1945 SECOND SINO-JAPANESE WAR

● 1931 DEATH OF XU ZHIMO IN A PLANE CRASH

1920 ├──────────────┤ EILEEN CHANG ├──────────────┤ 1995

● May 4, 1919 MAY FOURTH MOVEMENT

● 1911 FOUNDING OF THE REPUBLIC OF CHINA AND OVERTHROW OF QING DYNASTY

1902
├──────────────┤ SHEN CONGWEN ├──────────────┤ 1988

● 1902 "DIVISION OF LITERATURE"

1900 BOXER REBELLION

──────────┤ LIN YUTANG ├──────────────┤ 1976

━━━━━━━━━━━━━━━ 1895 – 1945 COLONIZATION OF TAIWAN BY JAPAN

──────┤ HU SHI ├──────────┤ 1962

─┤ LU XUN ├────────┤ 1936

───┤ 1907

──────────┤ 1929

────────┤ 1927

──┤ 1909

──────┤ 1924

900 1950 2000 2015

A NEW LITERARY HISTORY OF MODERN CHINA

A NEW LITERARY HISTORY OF

Modern China

Edited by DAVID DER-WEI WANG

THE BELKNAP PRESS OF HARVARD UNIVERSITY PRESS

CAMBRIDGE, MASSACHUSETTS · LONDON, ENGLAND · 2017

Library of Congress Cataloging-in-Publication Data

Names: Wang, Dewei, editor.
Title: A new literary history of modern China / edited by David Der-wei Wang.
Description: Cambridge, Massachusetts : The Belknap Press of Harvard University Press,
    2017. | Includes bibliographical references and index.
Identifiers: LCCN 2016046104 | ISBN 9780674967915 (alk. paper)
Subjects: LCSH: Chinese literature—History and criticism. | Literature and Society—
    China—History.
Classification: LCC PL2258 .N49 2017 | DDC 895.109—dc23
LC record available at https://lccn.loc.gov/2016046104

CONTENTS

ACKNOWLEDGMENTS

This volume represents the collective effort of more than 140 scholars, writers, and translators in the Chinese, Sinophone, and Sinological worlds. I wish to express my deepest gratitude to them—contributors from China, Taiwan, Hong Kong, Japan, Singapore, Malaysia, Australia, the United Kingdom, Germany, Holland, France, Sweden, Canada, and the United States—for their willingness to participate in a highly unconventional project. This project would not have come into being without the benefit of their critical and imaginative input, as well as their ingenious writing.

I also extend my heartfelt thanks to the members of the Editorial Board, Professors Kirk Denton, Michel Hockx, Theodore Huters, Carlos Rojas, Xiaofei Tian, Jing Tsu, Ban Wang, and Michelle Yeh, for their strongest support at every stage of editorial work. They have always illuminated me with their thoughts and scholarship. Their conscientiousness and generosity of time and wisdom are deeply appreciated.

Special thanks go to the assistant editors of the volume, Jingling Chen, Kyle Shernuk, and Dylan Suher, for undertaking research assistance, reading the manuscript, and offering editorial suggestions. They are promising scholars of the field and their dedication and insight have taught me again the power and pleasure of literature. I would also like to thank other young scholars—Dingru Huang, Jessica Tan, Tu Hang, Huanruo Wang, and Ying Lei—who have been involved in the project at various stages.

Dr. Lindsay Waters, executive editor for the humanities at Harvard University Press, has been extremely perceptive and patient in helping me prepare the volume. I thank him and his colleagues, Heather Hughes, Shan Wang, and Amanda Peery, as well as John Donohue and Ashley Moore of Westchester Publishing Services for their editorial expertise and professionalism.

Due to format constraints, sources are not referenced in footnotes but are often mentioned in the text itself. More source details are provided in select bibliographies at the ends of the essays. To all references the authors of these essays are deeply indebted.

Two leading senior scholars passed away as this volume was being prepared. Professor C. T. Hsia (1921–2013) pioneered modern Chinese literary studies in Western academia, and his *A History of Modern Chinese Fiction* (1961) remains the most provocative work to date. Professor Patrick Hanan (1927–2014) was one of the most erudite scholars in late imperial and early modern Chinese literature, and a first-rate Sinologist. I was extremely fortunate to have been able to work with both of them, enjoying their guidance and friendship, at Columbia University and at Harvard University. Hsia's contribution to the field is a topic within this volume, and Hanan wrote the final piece of his career for it.

This book is dedicated to my mentor, Professor Arthur E. Kunst (1934–2013). His scholarship, cosmopolitan mind, and passion for literature and life are remembered forever.

A NEW LITERARY HISTORY OF MODERN CHINA

INTRODUCTION

Worlding Literary China

David Der-wei Wang

A New Literary History of Modern China is a collective project that introduces the "long" modern period of Chinese literature from the late eighteenth century to the new millennium. The volume, with 161 essays contributed by 143 authors on a wide spectrum of topics, is intended for readers who are interested in understanding modern China through its literary and cultural dynamics. At the same time, it takes up the challenge of rethinking the conceptual framework and pedagogical assumptions that underlie the extant paradigm of writing and reading literary history.

The past two centuries have been an era of constant turmoil for China. The nation has been wracked by military and political upheavals, from the first Opium War (1839–1842) to the Taiping Rebellion (1850–1864), the Boxer Rebellion (1900), the first and second Sino-Japanese Wars (1894–1895; 1937–1945), the founding of the Republic of China (1911–) and the People's Republic of China (1949–), the Cultural Revolution (1966–1976), and the Tiananmen Incident (1989). Chinese society has undergone cataclysmic social changes, running the gamut from advancements in technology and commerce to a revolution in epistemology. Modern China has been the site of drastic contestations between indigenous innovations and foreign stimuli, radical provocations and conciliatory responses. Now, in the new century, another drastic change is taking place in China amid calls for its "peaceful rise" and the global dissemination of the "Chinese Dream."

This was also a period that saw literature conceptualized, practiced, circulated, and assessed in ways without precedent in Chinese history. Imported printing technology, innovative marketing tactics, increased literacy, widening readership, a boom in the diversity of forms of media and translation, and the advent of professional writers all created fields of literary production and consumption that in the preceding centuries would hardly have been imaginable. Along with these changes, Chinese literature—as an aesthetic vocation, scholarly discipline, and cultural institution—underwent multiple transformations to become "literature" as we understand the word to mean today. The shifting definition of literature was indeed one of the most acute symptoms of Chinese modernity.

The World of Chinese Literature

According to conventional wisdom, literary history is a coherent narrative of canonical figures, masterpieces, and notable movements and events, and an articulation of national characteristics. Such a concept was introduced to China at the turn of the twentieth century and still remains dominant in Sinology in general. In fact, the institution of literary history has had profound political implications for modern Chinese literature. This volume seeks to explore new ways to engage the roots and ramifications of modern Chinese literary history. It proposes that we rethink issues such as the periodization of "modern" Chinese literature, the conceptualization of Chinese "literature," the feasibility of "literary history," and, more controversially, the meaning of "Chinese" literary history.

To begin with, according to the extant paradigm, the May Fourth Movement—a nationwide cultural and political campaign begun on May 4, 1919, that called for self-rejuvenation in response to China's setbacks in post–World War I international politics—was the turning point in China's search for literary modernity. By contrast, the late Qing era (that is, the last decades of the Qing dynasty [1644–1911]) is seen as a transitional moment between the collapse of the old sociopolitical and literary order and the establishment of a new one. Scholars have taken issue with this paradigm in recent years, suggesting that the conception, production, and dissemination of literature during the late Qing possessed a vigor and variety that exceeded the narrow confines prescribed by May Fourth discourse.

What makes Chinese literature since the nineteenth century "modern"? One way to answer this question is to consider the historical context in which this inquiry is grounded. In the storyline drawn by political scientists and (literary) historians, China's literary initiation into the modern was a process of inscribing, and being inscribed by, developments such as the advent of Western powers; the call for constitutional democracy and vernacularism; the discovery of psychologized and gendered subjectivities; the industrialization of military, economic, and cultural production; the rise of an urban landscape; and, above all, the valorization of the forward movement of historical time as an evolutionary or revolutionary sequence. These phenomena first developed in Europe, but, as they reached non-Western civilizations such as China, they gained global relevance and took on local urgency.

This imagined scenario describes the *conditions* that gave rise to modern Chinese literature, but falls short of explaining the distinctive modernity that characterizes Chinese literature alone. Literary modernity may arise in response to the shared global phenomena of political and technological modernization, but it need not repeat the same predetermined order or content. As a collective reimagining of the function of literature vis-à-vis the invention of a modern China, this volume addresses the following questions: How has modernity manifested itself in the specific regional context of China? Is modernity an imported conceptual and empirical entity, and therefore a product of cross-cultural translation and transaction, or is it a native force of self-renewal arising in response to external stimuli? Can terms commonly associated with "modern," such as "novelty," "creativity," and "rupture," shed new light on a literary tradition that has valued convention, derivativeness, and "reactionary reform"? Finally, to what extent did the Chinese experience contribute to the global circulation of modernities?

With these questions in mind, *A New Literary History of Modern China* proposes to view Chinese literary modernization not as a monolithic process, with each stage inevitably leading toward a higher one in accordance with a certain timetable, but as a process with multiple entry points and ruptures.[1] As demonstrated by the essays in the volume, the advent of the modern at any given historical juncture resulted in a fierce competition of new possibilities, and the winners of this competition were not necessarily the best of those possibilities. For instance, Chinese literary modernization used to be attributed to the rise of vernacular literature; recent scholarship indicates nevertheless that a domestic transformation of the classical concept of "literariness" (*wen*) and the culture of translation fostered by missionaries might have played equally important roles. Many innovations, whatever their capacity for generating more positive outcomes, nevertheless perished due to the contingencies of history. To say that the end of this process is not necessarily the "best of all possible worlds," however, does not mean that the very idea of literary modernization is meaningless. Rather, it simply means that there is no one set path of literary evolution and that no outcome could have been predicted from the outset; indeed, no discrete constituent factor could ever be replicated were the process repeated, because any pathway to the realization of the modern proceeds through countless mutable and amorphous stages.

Second, Chinese "literature" as we understand it in academia today is a phenomenon that arose in late imperial China and gradually became institutionalized at the turn of the twentieth century. In 1902, at the order of Cixi (1835–1908), the Empress Dowager and then de facto ruler of China, the politician and educator Zhang Baixi (1847–1907) proffered several regulations to reform the recently founded Imperial University of Peking. Via these regulations, Zhang introduced *wenxue ke*, literally "division of literature," which covered the following programs: Confucius Studies, History, Ancient Thought, Archival Studies, Foreign Languages, Philology, and Literary Works (*cizhang*). While similar in some ways to the liberal arts, *wenxue ke* reflected the traditional paradigm of Chinese "literature," one that comprised several different fields of humanistic learning. The prototype of "literature" in modern terms was the program of Literary Works. The core curriculum of Literary Works featured courses such as Methodology of Literary Study, Etymology, Phonology, Literary Trends across Dynasties, and Classical Treatises on Writing. Combining traditional Chinese philological study and the Western Romantic appeal to aesthetic taste, the program paved the way for the eventual institutionalization of literature as an exercise and appraisal of rhetorical forms and fictional narratives.

Nevertheless, though it has adopted the Western system of generic classification with categories such as fiction, prose, poetry, and drama, and though it experiments with modern discourses ranging from realism to postmodernism, modern Chinese literature continues an implicit dialogue with the traditional concepts of *wen* and *wenxue*. That is to say, writers and readers of Chinese literature tend to associate literary exercises not only with the endeavor of using the word to represent the world, but also with the continued process of illuminating a cosmic pattern, a process that purportedly emanates from the mind and finds manifold manifestations—in corporal, artistic, sociopolitical, and natural terms—in the world. Thus, instead of merely playing with the dialectic of truth versus fiction, modern Chinese literature implants itself at every level of human experience, forming an ever-amplifying orbit of manifestations that are imaginatively evoked and historically embedded.

This understanding of literature is deeply imbricated in the ancient poetics of *wen*, a classical Chinese term that can mean "ornamentation," "pattern," "sign," "artistic inscription," "cultural upbringing," "civilization," and "a sign of the movement of the cosmos." By extension, *wenxue*, or "literature," refers to the art of registering, and being registered by, the incessant metamorphosis, from era to era and from region to region, of forms, thoughts, and attitudes regarding *wen*.[2] In Stephen Owen's words,

> If literature (*wen*) is the entelechy of a previously unrealized pattern, and if the written word (*wen*) is not a sign but a schematization, then there can be no competition for dominance. Each level of *wen*, that of the world and that of the poem, is valid only in its own correlative realm; and the poem, the final outward form, is a stage of fullness.[3]

Beyond the familiar canon of *literature as representation*, we need to include the tradition of *literature as manifestation*, on both textual and contextual levels, in a history of modern Chinese literature. Therefore, in addition to familiar genres, this volume features a diverse lineup of forms, from presidential speeches to pop song lyrics, from photographs to films, and from political treatises to prison house jottings—forms that not only represent the material world, but can also shape it and complete it. All of these forms "manifest" in one way or another the evolving and changing concept and "pattern" of *wen* in modern China, a concept that has evolved in terms of both what it aims to enact within the world and how it aims to enact it. As Owen puts it, "The process of manifestation must begin in the external world, which has priority without primacy. As a latent pattern follows its innate disposition to become manifest, passing from the world to mind to literature, a theory of sympathetic resonance is involved."[4]

Such a belief in *wen* as a manifestation of the heart and the world explains why literature was taken so seriously in China throughout the modern century: in the 1900s, when Liang Qichao (1873–1929) promoted a literary reform as the foundation of national reform; in the 1920s, when post–May Fourth radicals debated not only literary revolution but literature *as* revolution; in the 1940s, when Mao Zedong (1893–1976) made literature a key principle of communist revolution; in the 1960s, when literature became the key to the "revolution fought in the deepest niche of the soul" during the Cultural Revolution; and in the 1990s, when the nation was engulfed in a frenzy for the Nobel Literature Prize.

Third, *A New Literary History of Modern China* seeks to engage with the institution of "literary history" as a humanistic discipline in modern China. Although there was a cornucopia of historical accounts recording literary figures, activities, and accomplishments in dynastic China, the writing of Western-style literary history did not take place until 1904. When the Imperial University of Peking established its Literature Program, a young teacher named Lin Chuanjia (1877–1922) was commissioned to write a *History of Chinese Literature* for the purposes of teaching. Modeled after the Japanese scholar Sasagawa Rinpū's (1870–1949) *History of Chinese Literature* (1898), which was in turn inspired by European literary histories, Lin's history is an eclectic undertaking that comprises genre classification, philological inquiry, and chronological periodization. He highlights the vicissitudes of intellectual history from Confucius onward and describes the transformations of classical prose, paying little attention to poetry, vernacular fiction, and drama. The same year also saw the publication of the *History of Chinese Literature* written by Huang Ren (1866–1913), a scholar at Soochow University. Huang's history, by way of contrast, takes the form of a quasi-encyclopedic narrative of bygone literary events.

During the Republican era (1911–1949), classical literature was the dominant subject of literary historiography, and modern literature was rarely taught in schools. Although May Fourth leaders such as Hu Shi (1891–1962) and Zhou Zuoren (1885–1967) published books on Chinese literary history during the 1920s and 1930s, new literature represented only a small part of their investigations. From the 1930s onward, new literature attracted more attention from leftist historians such as Wang Zhefu and Li Helin (1904–1988), yet in general it remained marginal in the discourse prior to 1949. In 1951, a young scholar and Communist Party member, Wang Yao (1914–1989), published *A Draft History of New Chinese Literature*, the first major modern Chinese literary historiography. Since the publication of Wang's work, hundreds of histories of modern Chinese literature have been published in China, a level of production of literary historiography unparalleled by any other country in the world.

The upsurge of modern Chinese literary historiography after 1949, to be sure, is related to the ideological agenda of the Communist regime. According to communist ideology, literary development parallels political development; as the allegorical other of politics, new, robust literature is said to replace old, feudalistic literature on the path to the socialist telos. But this ideology alone does not explain why literature and literary history matters so much to the new regime and the Chinese public. As I have discussed, although it has been deeply influenced by the Western impulse to develop systems of representation, modern Chinese literary practice still reflects the time-honored concept of *wen*. Despite its anti-traditional platform, the Communist regime uncannily has held on to this concept. As a matter of fact, the regime seems to have continued to implement the concept of *wen* in everyday life and even in the realization of national projects. The regime therefore cannot treat literature as merely a linguistic, fictitious representation of the world, and instead must view it as an integral part of the process by which ideology becomes rooted in one's heart and blossoms into an ideal polity. By corollary, literary history, as a chronicle of the zeitgeist, is subject to careful writing, reading, and revision.

With this ideology in mind, we must rethink the intertwined relationship between literature *and* history in traditional Chinese thought. Scholars have long pointed out that the "representability" of historical experience was a contested issue among ancient Chinese historians.[5] Narrating history—fleshing out the figures and events under treatment—requires not only archival data and a theoretical framework, but also rhetorical expertise and personal integrity. According to the *Analects*, Confucius said that "when there is a preponderance of acquired refinement (*wen*) over native substance (*zhi*), the result will be ornamentation as performed by historians and bureaucrats (*shi*)."[6] Contrary to the conventional wisdom that favors history as more reliable than literature, the sage seems to suggest that historical discourse tends to be more exaggerated and insubstantial than literary engagement, and that both history and literature should be modulated in such a way as to illuminate the world truthfully. Thus, the arch-historian Sima Qian (135?–86 BCE) is said to have created in his work the ideal juncture between the represented and representation, and between objective facts and palpable truth. With Sima's *Records of the Grand Historian* in mind, Shen Congwen (1902–1988), the greatest writer of lyricism and nativist literature in modern China, concludes that a great history must be a *literary* history.[7]

Ever since the ninth century, the concept of "poetry as history" (*shishi*) has become a fundamental idea within Chinese poetics. The ninth-century Tang literatus Meng Qi (fl. ninth century) commented, "When a poetic incantation is occasioned by an event, it is precisely where deep feelings concentrate" (*chushi xingyong, yousuo zhongqing*).[8] Meng considers both the circumstantial and emotive functions of feeling (*qing*), thereby articulating the reciprocal relationship between historical experience and poetic mind. Accordingly, when Du Fu (712–770), the "Sage of Poetry," is honored in traditional Chinese historiography as the arch-practitioner of "poetry as history," the title refers not only to his skill in rendering mimetic accounts of historical events, but also to his poetic vision, which resonates with human and cosmic movements. The discourse of "poetry as history" reached a climax in the mid-seventeenth century, coinciding with the cataclysmic decline of the Ming dynasty (1368–1644). Hence, to slightly paraphrase the Ming loyalist Huang Zongxi (1610–1695), "Where history collapses, poetry arises."[9]

The structural framework of *A New Literary History of Modern China* has been influenced by a variety of Western theories, ranging from Walter Benjamin's "constellation," to Mikhail Bakhtin's "heteroglossia," Michel Foucault's "genealogy," and Gilles Deleuze's "assemblage." However, it is the mutual illumination between *wen* (literature) and *shi* (history) that underlies my editorial vision. How modern writers reflected on, and how modern literature came to reflect, this dialogic remains a central concern of this volume. Through the essays, I intend to configure a world in which literature of myriad attitudes, styles, and levels is brought to bear on history, and history is similarly brought to bear on literature. Each essay in this history is identified by a date and a corresponding event. These events are of very different sorts: the publication of a particular work; the establishment of a specific institution (a society, a magazine, a publishing house); the first use of a notable stylistic, thematic, or technological innovation; a debate or controversy over a specific issue; a political action; a romance; a scandal.… The purpose of each essay is to elicit the historical significance of that event, as represented through literary texts or experiences, be it in terms of its particular circumstances, its long-term relevance, or its contemporary resonance or dissonance.

Moreover, insofar as "poetry as history" compels one to treat even a fantastic work as "a unique factual account of an experience in historical time, a human consciousness encountering, interpreting, and responding to the world," I encouraged the contributors, some of whom are renowned creative writers, to adopt whatever form they felt best expressed their historical "feeling."[10] For instance, Ha Jin writes a story about how Lu Xun (1881–1936) composed "A Madman's Diary," the harbinger of modern Chinese fiction; Uganda Sze Pui Kwan personifies Sir Thomas Wade (1818–1895), whose audience with the Tongzhi Emperor (r. 1862–1874) helped institutionalize the practice of translation in early modern China. Ari Larissa Heinrich's contemplation of Qiu Miaojin (1969–1995) and queer writing leads him to compose a piece that can be read with any paragraph as the starting point. By combining selectivity and intensity of focus with a flexible frame of inquiry, I hope to produce a constellation of essays that will each illuminate a singular cultural-historical moment and a literary mind, and that collectively will resonate with one another in such a way as to provide a more nuanced reading of the *literary* rendition of history.

Finally, we come to the subject of literary history and national representation. Chronologically, this volume covers literature through a series of political regimes, from the late Ming dynasty to the Qing dynasty, and then from the Republic of China (ROC) to the People's Republic of China (PRC). Although "China" is the umbrella term used to refer to all of these political regimes, we must keep in mind that "China" as a political, racial, and cultural entity has been defined differently at different points in history. According to historians Cho-yun Hsu and Ge Zhaoguang, the earliest usage of the Chinese equivalent to "China," *zhongguo*, dates as far back as the Zhou dynasty (1046–256 BCE), when it referred to the spatial position "right in the middle of" a social and geographical domain. "China" gradually came to apply to the nation as a whole during the Song dynasty (960–1279), when "barbarian" regimes in the north intensified the Song court's awareness of territorial rule.[11] "China" was invoked to represent both the Ming and the Qing; it was not until the early twentieth century that "China" became associated with political sovereignty and nationhood in the modern sense. The ROC was founded in 1911 after the revolution to overthrow the Qing. The PRC was founded in 1949 after the victory of the Communists in the Chinese Civil War (1946–1949). The ROC government withdrew to Taiwan, where it continues to exist to this day.

Therefore, when we discuss the literary history of modern China, there are at least four layers of meaning that compose the term "China" that we must consider: China as a historical process, as a cultural and intellectual lineage, as a political entity, and as an "imagined community." Since the Great Divide in 1949, modern Chinese literature has bifurcated into two traditions, each with a distinct national agenda. For all the ideological antagonism between the two traditions, there were striking similarities between Nationalist and Communist governance of literary activities during the 1950s. However, the sixties saw the unlikely advent of modernism in the literary scene of Taiwan, followed by the nativist debate over whether "China" should be located in exile in Taiwan or on the mainland (to be restored eventually by the nationalists). Meanwhile, the Cultural Revolution pushed Chinese socialist literature to the extremes of collectivity. Literature in both Chinese communities underwent a shakeup in the eighties. As various movements have come and gone in both the mainland and Taiwan, "China" has been postsocialized, decolonized, postmodernized, deconstructed, gendered, and even de-Sinicized. For advocates of Taiwanese independence, "China" has become a politically incorrect signifier. By contrast, as nationalism gains new momentum on the mainland, the government has coined the surprisingly literary term "Chinese Dream"—uncannily resonating with the familiar "American Dream"—in order to consolidate public feeling.

In 1971, C. T. Hsia (1921–2013) coined the term "Obsession with China" to describe the ambivalent attitude of modern Chinese literati toward the challenges of Chinese modernity. Hsia holds that modern Chinese literati are so obsessed by national crises as to turn their repugnance for the status quo into a masochistic mentality. These literati see any given social or political malaise as a sickness unique to China, and thus grapple with Chinese modernity only negatively, by denouncing it.[12] To remedy this syndrome, Hsia calls for a cosmopolitanism characterized by interaction with Western literature. Hsia authored *A History of Modern Chinese Fiction* (1961), which remains to date the most influential book of modern Chinese literary history in the English-speaking world. Although it has been criticized, particularly among leftist circles, for endorsing Cold War ideology, Western liberal humanism, and New Criticism, one cannot overlook its polemical power. Now, almost half a century after Hsia's critique, the "Obsession with China" still casts a shadow over Chinese discourse, but the phenomenon has developed in unexpected ways. Whereas writers and readers on the mainland have turned their "obsession" into something more complex—from fanaticism to cynicism, from passion to nonchalance—their radical counterparts in Taiwan have come to love hating everything about China, such that, in an ironic way, they reinstate the classic symptoms of "obsession" with China.

A New Literary History of Modern China seeks to record the changing imaginaries of China by assessing the enunciative endeavors, ranging from classical treatises to avant-garde experiments, from foreign thoughts to native ruminations, that have informed Chinese literary discourse, and also to identify the historical factors that have affected the interplay of Chinese (post)modernities. More significantly, it recognizes the fact that modern Chinese literature is not merely a national project, with distinct linguistic, discursive, and cultural characteristics, but also part of a transnational endeavor that defines the nation in relation to other political and cultural entities. At a time when both mainland China and Taiwan are developing literary histories hemmed in by ideological guidelines and cultural provincialism, we need additional perspectives in order to expose the limitations of Chinese national literatures. As will be elaborated in the rest of this introduction, I argue that this volume, by involving contributors from various communities in greater China and beyond, and by covering subjects that transcend conventional national and generic boundaries, can contribute to a vision of literary China more complex than those sanctioned by either the PRC or the ROC.

Worlding Literary China

A New Literary History of Modern China is the fourth volume in Harvard University Press's series of national literary histories, following *A New History of French Literature*, edited by Denis Hollier (1989); *A New History of German Literature*, edited by David Wellbery (2004); and *A New Literary History of America*, edited by Greil Marcus and Werner Sollors (2009). All three previous volumes seek to revise the traditional formula of writing and reading literary history, one that places masters, canonical works, and crucial events into a linear sequence informed by politics. Instead, these volumes feature a series of entries based on seemingly arbitrary dates and data, and generate from them a web of mutually illuminating timelines and meanings. By combining both the pointillism of the chronicle and the comprehensiveness of *grand récit*, this revisionist endeavor has been received with much critical acclaim.

These three volumes differ, nevertheless, in their visions of literary history. Both *A New History of French Literature* and *A New History of German Literature* begin in the eighth century CE and move forward to trace the multiple literary representations of societies that predate the emergence of the modern French and German nations. But whereas *A New History of French Literature* recognizes the role of contingency and playfully deconstructs the grand narrative of history, *A New History of German Literature* tries to identify a set of "framing conditions"—such as mediality, time, linguistic-national identity, and communication—so as to reinstate the thematic structure in historical inquiry.

A New Literary History of America begins in the sixteenth century but focuses mostly on the nineteenth and twentieth centuries. It tells the story of an imagined nation that in many ways preceded the emergence of recognizable American society. To quote Marcus and Sollors, unlike its French or German counterpart, American literature was not "inherited but invented, as if it were a tool or a machine, or discovered, as if it were a gold strike or the next wonder of the Louisiana Purchase." Thus, "no tradition has ever ruled and no form has ever been fixed."[13] The volume introduces a multitude of representations of the American experience—ranging from political speeches to poetic articulations, from constitutional negotiations to novelistic adventures—and frames them as literature.

While following compositional principles of the three previous volumes, *A New Literary History of Modern China* makes a few conceptual and structural innovations that respond to both the distinct characteristics of modern Chinese literary culture and developments in literary studies in the past few decades. One of the most salient features of this new volume is that it presents not Chinese literary history in its entirety but only *modern* Chinese history. Thus it has to engage at the outset in reconciling—indeed, rethinking—the temporal and conceptual frameworks proposed by the French, German, and American literary histories. In light of the lineage of Chinese literary culture spanning more than three thousand years, it has to account for the ways in which the moderns inherit or abandon the resources of tradition. On the other hand, in view of China's drastic sociopolitical transitions during the modern era, from a dynastic monarchy to a republic and then a socialist nation-state, it has to deal with the way in which literature is continually reinvented in response to each emerging ethos.

The key concept for this immense display of topics, figures, objects, and events has been the idea of "worlding literary China." "Worlding" is a term originally coined by Martin Heidegger (1889–1976).[14] By turning the noun "world" into an active verb, Heidegger calls attention to the way in which the world is constructed and exists eternally in a constantly shifting state of becoming. Worlding is a complex and dynamic process of ever-renewing realities, sensations, and perceptions through which one incessantly works to access "the Open of the world."[15] Insofar as worlding is always already a flux of unfolding experience, it suggests a world as familiar as it is forever fresh. Importantly, Heidegger stresses that worlding is not a task in which we engage volitionally, but emerges automatically in response to specific phenomena, or "things": "If we let the thing be present in its thinging from out of the worlding world, then we are thinking of the thing as thing."[16]

The concept of "worlding" has been adopted by critics in recent years to describe projects ranging from urban planning to comparative literature and medicinal studies.[17] The term is often used, however, merely to refer to global or transnational projects, a far cry from the Heideggerian definition. In his study of contemporary China, Arif Dirlik describes the end of revolutionary politics and the rise of cultural nationalism since 1978. He places these developments within a global context, ultimately making a case methodologically for "worlding" China: bringing China into the world and the world into China.[18] Lisa Rofel takes up the recently recanonized term *tianxia* (under heaven) and proposes strategies for cosmopolitan, socialist "worldings."[19]

My approach is inspired by but not limited to these scholars' adaptations of the term. While examining the "making" and "becoming" of literature in the context of China encountering the world through the past two centuries, I call attention to the subtle reverberations between *wen* (the literary; literariness) and the Heideggerian concept of worlding. "Worlding" describes the conditions of being-in-the-world in relation to the foregrounding and evolvement of things as such. The conditions are less fixed essences than conduits of differences between verbal, written, and mental concepts. According to Heidegger, it is poetry that brings the world and things together in a topology of being, "gathering into a simple onefold of their intimate belonging together."[20] As discussed previously, *wen* points to a multitude of artifacts, locations, or encounters that manifest the world over time. *Wen* is not a sign so much as an articulation of the meaning of the world through a set of correlating ideas, objects, or doings. To be sure, Heideggerian philosophy and traditional Chinese literary thought differ greatly in their conception of what constitutes the "world," let alone the meaning and practice of literature.[21] My point is that the concept of worlding nevertheless may help us to understand Chinese literary modernity in the broader sense of *wen*, as a vehicle "bringing the world home," and, more importantly, as an agency that continuously opens up new configurations of the world.[22]

With this argument in mind, *A New Literary History of Modern China* introduces the following four themes of worlding Chinese literature: architectonics of temporalities, dynamics of travel and transculturation, contestation between *wen* and mediality, and remapping of the literary cartography of modern China.

Architectonics of Temporalities

Readers of this volume will first be struck by the conflation of, and conflict between, two historiographical schemes in the volume. On the one hand, the volume introduces the significant figures, works, discourses, and movements that have constituted modern Chinese literature in chronological order. On the other hand, it also features a series of dates, events, and encounters of relatively lesser significance, making them points of reference to more significant historical phenomena. Alternating between presenting time as a causal sequence and time as a contingent or coincidental arrangement of events, the volume encourages the readers to observe—and imagine—the kaleidoscopic organization of temporalities that inform the literary dynamics of modern China.

As mentioned previously, the current paradigm of Chinese literature sees May Fourth as the point where modern Chinese literature began. Following this paradigm, literary history is streamlined into a linear, progressive agenda, with thematic axes of revolution versus reaction, enlightenment versus tradition. Insofar as the Western model of modernity is treated as the authentic, original gold standard against which all other modernities are measured, its Chinese counterpart is always already beset by a defeated sense of "belated modernity." This volume instead argues that even at its earliest stages, modern Chinese literature had complex conceptions of the modern that existed independently from the conceptions offered by the West. Along the same line, "Western" modernity has to be understood as a diversity of experimentations rather than a unified phenomenon. To be sure, May Fourth writers set in motion a series of epochal shifts that late Qing literati would not have been able to imagine. But May Fourth claims to modernity may equally have obscured, or even eliminated, much of the potential that existed within the late Qing or earlier times; in different circumstances, these possibilities could have given rise to other, richer configurations of literary modernity for China.

For instance, the volume questions the "beginning" of modern Chinese literature by offering two dates in place of May 4, 1919: 1635, when the Confucian scholar–cum–Catholic convert Yang Tingyun (1562–1627) set out to redefine *wenxue* according to concepts inherited from both Jesuit cultivation and classical Chinese learning; and 1933, when Zhou Zuoren and Ren Fangqiu (1909–2000) traced the origin of Chinese literary modernization to the early seventeenth century. As such, the "beginning" of modern Chinese literature suggests both a moment of genesis and a retroactive discovery. Another possible beginning point is 1792. That year witnessed two apparently unrelated events: Lord George Macartney's (1737–1806) diplomatic mission to China, and the publication of Cao Xueqin's (1715–1763) novel *Dream of the Red Chamber*. However, when juxtaposed, the two events shed new light on each other. As Andrew Schonebaum describes in his essay, whereas the Macartney mission (1792–1794) raised the problems and promises of modernity, particularly of foreigners in China, *Dream of the Red Chamber* created a world that encapsulates late imperial Chinese culture at its most intricate, one that signals the beginning of the ending of a civilization; hence the rise of anticipatory nostalgia.

Reexamining May 4, 1919, the canonical date of Chinese literary modernization, reveals a multitude of ironies. According to Michel Hockx, the day turned out to be one without much significance for someone like Lu Xun, the champion of New Literature, and a very significant day for writers of popular (and occasionally pulpy) Mandarin Ducks and Butterflies fiction, who have been marginalized in conventional literary history as apolitical spectators. Time reveals its "thick," synchronic dimension in a year such as 1935, when cartoonist Zhang Leping's (1910–1992) comic strip about the vagabond boy Sanmao became immensely popular; Qu Qiubai (1899–1935), once the leader of the Chinese Communist Party, was executed, leaving a memoir intriguingly entitled *Superfluous Words*; movie star Ruan Lingyu (1910–1935) committed suicide and became a media sensation; and the peasants of Ding County, in Hebei Province, staged an outdoor avant-garde theater production. Time allows for the hindsight of archaeology. In 1970, the Angel Island poetry was excavated, bringing to light the untold stories of Chinese laborers in the United States during the late nineteenth and early twentieth centuries. Time continues the mysterious cycle of fate. In 1927, the aesthetician Wang Guowei (1877–1927) committed suicide by drowning, and his colleague Chen Yinke (1890–1969) penned his famous epitaph in response: "This spirit of independence and the freedom of thought." Forty-two years later, Chen himself died tragically during the Cultural Revolution, his words for Wang turning out to be a foreboding self-elegy. Finally, we look forward in time through visions of the future. In 2066, according to the science fiction writer Han Song (1965–), Martians take over both China and the United States, rendering moot all quests for national glory.

More polemically, many essays in this volume highlight the dialogue between modern literary culture and the classical tradition. Despite the iconoclastic rhetoric of modern Chinese literature, from the May Fourth era to the Cultural Revolution, tradition haunts the modern Chinese mind. Whether inheriting or dispensing with the resources of the classical tradition, through its ingenious appropriations or impassioned negations, the modern is intimately intertwined with the past. His indebtedness to Friedrich Nietzsche and Max Stirner aside, Lu Xun expressed his modernist angst by revisiting the abysmal pathos of both Qu Yuan (340–278 BCE) and Tao Qian (365–427). Wang Guowei strove to cope with his existential crisis not only in terms of Immanuel Kant's and Arthur Schopenhauer's philosophy, but also through the concept of a "mental vista" (*jingjie*), which originates in Buddhist thought. Zhu Guangqian's (1897–1986) career path took him from Nietzsche to Benedetto Croce, Karl Marx, and Giambattista Vico, all the while pondering how to modernize the classical concept "fusion of sentiments and scenes" (*qingjing jiaorong*). In the leftist camp, Qu Qiubai demonstrated a strong penchant for lyricism and Buddhism despite his commitment to Anatoly Lunacharsky and Georgi Plekhanov, and Hu Feng's (1902–1985) avant-garde "subjective fighting spirit" carried traces of both Mencian concepts of mind and György Lukács's Hegelian / Marxian revolutionism.

It is not until recent decades that writers and readers finally came to terms with a startling paradox: many of the putatively modern writers enacted the least modern of modernities, while select "conservative" writers made use of the most unconventional conventionalities. The rediscovery of Eileen Chang (1920–1995) sheds light not only on the sensibilities of the "Shanghai Modern," but also on the aesthetics of decadence that anticipated fin-de-siècle postmodernism. Chen Yinke, often regarded as the most talented historian of modern China, took a literary turn in his last years; he embedded a metaphorical discourse in his scholarship, calling for an "esoteric interpretation" of history. At a time when "modern" and even "postmodern" are transforming into historical periods, one comes to realize all the more acutely that tradition is not a prescribed program but a succession of inventions, anti-inventions, and noninventions.

Dynamics of Travel and Transculturation

A New Literary History of Modern China contends that modern Chinese literature is part of the global circulation of discourses and practices of modernity. This circulation comes about through travel, both in the sense of physical mobility and conceptual, affective, and technological transmutation through space and time. More than half of the essays in the volume touch on travel and transculturation, bringing into full relief the concept of "worlding Chinese literature." Whereas Qiu Jin (1875–1907), the first "Chinese feminist," traveled to Japan and was politically radicalized, by way of contrast, the Taiwanese essayist Sanmao (1943–1991) settled in the deserts of Western Sahara in 1973, as part of an effort to develop her own individual identity. Qu Qiubai took a cross-Siberia train ride to Moscow in 1920 in order to be properly "baptized" as a Communist; W. H. Auden

(1907–1973) and Christopher Isherwood (1904–1986) arrived in China in 1938 to witness the Chinese crusade against Japanese aggression. Some travels had profound cultural consequences. For instance, in 1807, British missionary Robert Morrison (1782–1834) arrived in Guangzhou, only to be turned away and end up in Malacca, where he began his enterprise of translating the Bible into Chinese, a project that inaugurated "translated" Chinese modernity. In 1987, Gao Xingjian (1940–) exiled himself to France, where he continued to write and eventually won the Nobel Prize in 2000.

To these writers, travel became both the impetus for and subject of writing, enabling them to register in various genres and styles a world yet to be fully presented to the majority of Chinese people. Meanwhile, travel took on a different dimension as a result of historical contingencies, from the "Long March" to massive exile to immigration. Eighty million Chinese people were forced into exodus during the Second Sino-Japanese War; five million fled overseas in the Civil War; sixteen million were sent down to the countryside during the Cultural Revolution. For these Chinese people, travel was not a romantic subject but the tragic consequence of historical turmoil. There are cases in which objects travel, too, tracing unexpected trajectories of experience. For one generation of Chinese writers exiled to Taiwan after 1949, food of their home regions triggers a Proustian memory of their bygone days on the mainland. In 1948, a Shanghai high school girl named Nana Hsu daydreamed in her literature class and scribbled on the margins of her textbook. The same textbook turned up miraculously in 2011, testifying to the ups and downs of not only Nana but also the transformation of "literature" as such through the tumultuous decades.

Travel leads to transculturation: the linguistic, cultural, and intellectual interactions between continents, nations, societies, institutions, and communities. Essays in this volume pay particular attention to the relationship between global impacts and local responses, and between state force and popular resistance. News about the downfall of the Ming dynasty (1644) circulated fast in Europe, inspiring two Dutch plays as early as 1666. In the new millennium, the nationalist-tinged Japanese web comic *Axis Powers Hetalia* garnered a Chinese fan base, and that same fan base produced a parody, *One Born a Dragon*, in the name of patriotism. In the heyday of the New Culture Movement, Hu Shi underwent an intellectual metamorphosis as a result of not only his study at Cornell and Columbia Universities, but, according to a recent discovery, his romantic ties to Edith Williams. Hu's time in America was thus both an intellectual baptism and a sentimental education. In Yan'an, from 1940 to 1942, Zhou Libo (1908–1979) taught Western masterpieces by writers from Aleksandr Pushkin to Johann Wolfgang von Goethe and Honoré de Balzac, thus introducing world literature in a revolutionary light. But the West was not merely a source of inspiration for Chinese artists and writers; they, in turn, inspired Western modernists. Mei Lanfang (1894–1961), the king of Peking opera, was a major influence for European film and theater workers, such as Sergei Eisenstein, Konstantin Stanislavsky, and Bertolt Brecht, and America's Denishawn Dancers. Transculturation can also entail violence. In 1930, hundreds of Japanese settlers were beheaded in a riot launched by Tayal aboriginals in Taiwan, then a Japanese colony. As the novelist Wuhe (1951–) tells us, whether the bloody incident should be understood as an anticolonial uprising or an action in the context of aboriginal headhunting rituals remains a subject for debate.

Harvard University played a meaningful role in facilitating transcultural China. Chen Yinke, Lin Yutang (1895–1976), and Wu Mi (1894–1978) were all educated at Harvard during the 1910s and 1920s. Wu later introduced his mentor Irving Babbitt's (1865–1933) new humanism to China, promoting an alternative modernity to a country inundated with radical calls to arms. I. A. Richards (1893–1979) first visited China in 1927, and remained fascinated with the nation until the end of his life. During his residence in Beijing, he was a major influence for a group of the best Chinese poets and critics. Harvard hosted Hu Shi as a visiting professor in 1944, and Eileen Chang as a residential writer (at Radcliffe College) in 1967–1968. The great Czech Sinologist Jaroslav Průšek (1906–1980) taught at Harvard right before the Prague Spring broke out.

The most important medium of transculturation is, without a doubt, translation, through which China and other civilizations encounter and generate new forms of knowledge, feeling, and power exchange. Translation made a formal entry into Chinese discourse when Thomas Wade (1818–1895), in an audience with the Tongzhi Emperor in 1873, offered to set up what became known as "the Interpreters' College." Throughout the twentieth century, from Lin Shu's (1852–1924) entrepreneurial, collaborative "translation" of foreign literature to Guo Moruo's (1892–1978) leftist rendition of Goethe's *Faust*, from the wild popularity of Soviet fiction during the early years of socialist China to the fever of consuming Western avant-garde literature in the post–Cultural Revolution era, translation has been the venue where language has been refashioned and thoughts negotiated. Sherlock Holmes, Baron Münchhausen, Shakespeare, and even Socrates arrived in China during this modern century. Whereas *The Brothers Karamazov* confronted the post–May Fourth youth with the ethical dilemmas of patricide and punishment, Pavel Korchagin, from Nicolai Ostrovsky's *How the Steel Was Tempered*, captured the hearts of millions of Chinese socialist readers with his selflessness and dedication. Franz Kafka, Ernest Hemingway, Gabriel García Márquez, and, later, Haruki Murakami liberated another generation of readers from their ideological shackles in the aftermath of the Mao era.

Above all, transculturation has made a remarkable impression on the discourse of Chinese literary historiography, from its institutional mechanisms to its stylistics of writing. As mentioned previously, "literature" underwent a drastic redefinition at the turn of the twentieth century, as a result of the importation of Western aesthetic education. The very concept of literature has been an object of contestation among competing political agendas and cultural values during the post–May Fourth era, the Yan'an era, the Cultural Revolution, and the New Era. Seven essays in the volume introduce key transcultural encounters that affected the field of modern Chinese literature: in 1904, when a vision of literature adapted from both Chinese and non-Chinese models was institutionalized; in 1906, when Zhang Taiyan (1868–1936) promoted a revolutionary view of literature by restoring the ancient concept of *wen*; in 1932 and 1934, when the "modern origin" of Chinese literature were traced back to the late Ming; in 1942, when Mao yoked literature to politics; in 1952, when the first official version of modern Chinese literary history came under severe attack from the party; in 1963, when C. T. Hsia and Jaroslav Průšek engaged in a debate over the methodology and ideology of modern Chinese literary studies; and in 1988, when the "rewrite literary history" campaign ignited debates over not only the definition of literature, but also the definition of history.

Contestation of *Wen* and Mediality

Readers more familiar with a conventional definition of literature that limits the concept to fiction, poetry, drama, and prose will find in *A New*

Literary History of Modern China a scope of literature that is far broader than expected. Indeed, we have tried to rethink boundaries of genre by looking into the question: What makes Chinese literature modern? Thus, besides the traditional genres just listed, this volume features essays that look into letters, jottings, diaries, manifestoes, public speeches, comic strips, textbooks, folk theaters, traditional operas, minority ballads, films, pop songs, and even pageants. As readers move toward the end of the volume, they will find discussions of animation, comics, and Internet fandom.

In these forms, the indigenous and the foreign, the popular and the elite, the hegemonic and the subversive are brought into play. These forms are not just aesthetic constructs but medial conduits through which the structure of the feeling of a period is formed. For instance, just as the advent of newspaper supplements, fiction magazines, and pictorials in the late nineteenth century fostered a mediasphere that transformed the production and consumption of literature, the Internet boom at the turn of the twenty-first century gave rise to a new media ecology in which literature was created and circulated in ways unimaginable decades before.

Some readers may feel that featuring so many textual and media forms risks shunting aside traditional considerations of literature in favor of a postmodernist carnival. I disagree. Although the volume adopts a pointillistic method and refers to a diverse set of media at the same time, it seeks to introduce a critical inquiry into the persistence of *wen*—as a pattern, a linguistic register, a sign system of sensory data, and a textual display—in modern times, and as such contribute a Chinese dimension to contemporary media discourse. Through the exercise of *wen*, the relationships between the author, the text, and the world begin to manifest themselves. Let us rethink Liu Xie's (465–ca. 522) argument in *Literary Mind and Carving the Dragon* (*Wenxin diaolong*), arguably the most important text of literary thought in ancient China:

There are three basic principles in the Way of setting forth pattern (*wen*). The first is the pattern of shapes, which is constituted of the five colors. The second is the pattern of sounds constituted of the five tones. The third is the pattern of the affections constituted of the five "natures." A mixture of five colors forms the pattern of imperial brocade. The conjunction of five sounds forms the Shao-xia [a legendary piece of ceremonial music]. The five natures come forth and they are pieces of language.[23]

Liu highlights the transfiguring power of *wen* by linking the animate and inanimate worlds, and semiotic and somatic forms. To adapt Liu's conceptualization of *wen* for our own era, the "shapes," "sounds," and "affections" of modern *wen* are manifested in the media chain from the textual to the audiovisual, from the bodily to the digital.

In order to pursue the medial implications of *wen*, this volume contains essays structured around not only dates, events, or texts, but also objects with graphic implications. The Chinese typewriter invented by Lin Yutang, the Chinese costumes and fabrics studied by Shen Congwen, and the first computer purchased by the poet Hsia Yü (1956–) are used to expand the set of associations around what literature / *wen* is and is about. Furthermore, though the individual essays are relatively brief and specific, each tells a story and places it in a broader historical context. As such, each essay does not merely highlight a form (or set of forms) of mediation, but also turns itself into a medial point through which a new linkage is manifested, and a new history unfolds.

One such unlikely linkage is between the discovery of "oracle bones" and the invention of literary modernity. In 1899, a late Qing official purchased pieces of medicinal "dragon bones" only to realize that they were animal bones inscribed with the earliest Chinese characters identifiable to date. But the fact that the bones—as well as the history they represent— were not discovered until the turn of the modern century synchronized, so to speak, the temporalities of past and present. In her essay, Andrea Bachner contemplates this paradoxical synchronicity as she discusses a 1995 story by the Chinese Malaysian writer Ng Kim Chew (1967–). In the story, a Chinese Malaysian scholar performs a nocturnal ritual of killing tortoises and producing "oracle bones," so as to communicate with the dead and the missing. Thus, through the medium of the oracle bone inscriptions, the essay brings to light the linkage between premodern augural technology and postmodern medial haunting, late Qing archaeological discovery and fin-de-siècle diasporic nostalgia.

We also consider the phenomenon of re-mediation, which results from the circulation of and interaction between multiple media forms. On International Women's Day in 1935, the silent movie star Ruan Lingyu committed suicide, closing her suicide note with the line "Gossip is a fearful thing." A ghostly epitaph, the handwritten line would be reproduced in newspapers, inscribed on banners at her funeral, and circulated and contested for years to come. As Kristine Harris points out, the charged phrase was already deeply embedded in Chinese culture, from *The Book of Songs* to the Qing play *The Palace of Everlasting Life*. But these words meant even more in an era of modern media, "when motion pictures, the emergent periodical press, serialized novels, vernacular fiction, teahouse storytelling, new-style operas, and spoken drama all jostled for attention." The story of Ruan finds its sequel in the story of Teresa Teng (1953–1995), a Taiwanese pop singer who won transnational popularity in East Asia in the 1980s. Teng's soft, soothing voice, broadcast in private, literally re-formed the sonic culture of socialist China, such that she was nicknamed Little Deng (Teng), a nickname that implicitly contrasted her to Old Deng—Deng Xiaoping (1904–1997). Teng adopted a traditional Chinese lyrical style, a style she accentuated by featuring songs inspired by classical Chinese poetry and song lyrics. Teng died a sudden death in 1995, but she made a digital comeback in 2013, when she appeared as a three-dimensional hologram of her youthful figure and enchanted another generation of fans.

Last but not least, while acknowledging the uncanny autonomy of media in modern Chinese literary culture, I argue that human agency is still the key nexus in the network of *wen*. When Lu Xun imagined a Mara poet who could "pluck the heart" of the Chinese people, when Mao mandated a "national form" through which the proletariat could be reached, they both sought to refashion the Chinese body and soul through literature. Bodily investment in literature was not, however, confined to the official discourse. One recalls the case of Lin Zhao (1932–1968): jailed in the 1960s for her antirevolutionary thought, she ended up writing on her stained shirt, in her own blood, to protest political oppression. Lin was executed in 1968. She turned her corporal existence and annihilation into a theater of cruelty. Where blood is mixed with ink, literature demonstrates its primitive power. Or consider the case of Chu Hsi-ning (1926–1998), who wrote and rewrote his family saga nine times, refashioning and re-creating it until the end of his life. And no one could be more demonstrative of the power of literature to physically move people than Cui Jian (1961–), "the first rock-and-roll singer" of socialist China, singing

"Nothing to My Name" to, and with, more than a million demonstrators on Tiananmen Square one May afternoon in 1989.

TOWARD A NEW LITERARY CARTOGRAPHY

In this final section, I take the geographical locale in which this volume was conceived and produced seriously, and reflect on the mapping of modern Chinese literary history from an overseas perspective. As mentioned previously, a considerable number of Chinese writers were shaped as writers by their encounters with the foreign, both imaginary encounters and actual adventures abroad. Their "Obsession with China" was always already imbued with their fantasies of, as well as anxieties about, the world outside China. Yu Dafu (1896–1945), for instance, was driven to his notorious patriotic cries by the experience of being a frustrated student in Japan. Lin Yutang's long-term sojourn in Europe and America enabled him to write about the Chinese experience from a cosmopolitan perspective. Eileen Chang first achieved popularity in wartime Shanghai by writing about Hong Kong; she fled Shanghai to Hong Kong after the Communist Revolution, finally finding refuge in the United States. Many modern Chinese writers shaped the spatial imaginary of the mainland from the vantage points of expatriatism, exile, and diaspora.

What is more controversial is the recently introduced concept of "Sinophone literature": Chinese-language literature produced in the regions of "greater China," such as Taiwan, Hong Kong, and the Chinese communities in countries such as Malaysia and Singapore, as well as by Chinese-speaking subjects in diaspora. In contrast to the term "overseas Chinese literature," which connotes a geopolitically peripheral position in relation to literature originating on the Chinese mainland, "Sinophone literature" refers to a heterogeneous body of articulations related to, but not necessarily subject to, the dominant discourse of China. The "Han language," the predominant language of the Chinese people, serves as the common denominator of Sinophone literature. Nevertheless, this language comprises numerous dialects and topolects, and constitutes only one branch of the Sinitic language family.

In her pioneering work on the issue, Shu-mei Shih argues for a Sinophone literature that highlights both writings produced in overseas Chinese-speaking communities and minority literatures on the mainland. As such, her vision of literature is opposed to the hegemony of the PRC literature.[24] In contrast to such a "resistance" approach, Jing Tsu argues for the theoretical framework of "literary governance," which refers to the "imposed or voluntary coordination between linguistic [and political] antagonisms and the idea of the 'native speaker'" that "produce national literature as a common interest as well as a source of strife."[25] Tsu calls attention to the ironic fact that globalization has increased rather than decreased the value of nation and national literature.

I welcome Shih's and Tsu's critiques, but think neither goes far enough in its engagement with China to realize the full potential of the concept of the Sinophone. While exuberant in their depictions of the heteroglossia of the diasporic communities, they leave "China," the source of their Sinophone polemics, intact. I suggest that if Sinophone studies is to successfully intervene in the current paradigm of Chinese literature, it must expand its domain from overseas to China proper. Instead of merely critiquing the hegemony of national language and literature, Sinophone studies must also account for the generative power of "linguistic nativity" *within* the national territory of China. The result is a discovery of multiplying individual voices, regional soundings, dialectical accents, and local expressions that are in constant negotiation with official linguistic and literary mandates. The Han Chinese language, however standardized by the state, is no monolithic language but comprises a diverse and lively set of complex voices. And a corollary to this principle is that so-called standard Chinese literature, despite the restrictions of the state, is capable of alternative expressions and experimentations.

A New Literary History of Modern China features essays that deal with literature by writers from "greater China," as well as from the broader Sinosphere. Literary phenomena, such as the Angel Island poetry produced by Chinese laborers in the United States or the circulation of the leftist guerrilla novel *Hunger* in the jungles of northern Malaysia, point to the immense space in which Chinese experiences have taken place. This volume pays attention to minority literatures produced by Tibetans, Muslims, and Taiwanese aboriginal cultures, among others. To avoid the pitfall of tokenism, it looks into specific cases in which "literature" is invoked to challenge conventional geopoetics. Cases in point include modern, bilingual Tibetan verse and the postmodern forms of southwestern minority poetry. The volume introduces the historical account of Zhang Chengzhi (1948–), a Han Chinese writer with a purportedly Muslim origin. Zhang was one of the first students to call himself a "Red Guard" during the Cultural Revolution. He later transferred his fervor to the Jahrinya school of Islam, a sect that spread throughout northwestern China during the late Qing, and has vowed to write on its behalf. By way of contrast, the volume introduces the mythological narrative of Alai (1959–), a Rgyalrong Tibetan writer with a Muslim paternal background. Often labeled a leading writer of Tibetan culture, Alai has nevertheless shunned any easy identity politics by declaring, "I don't represent."

Finally, this volume introduces the imaginary spaces of China. In *Flowers in the Mirror*, the writer Li Ruzhen (1763–1830) ushered his readers into the fantastic maritime world of the Tang dynasty before the Opium Wars. In *Atlas*, the Hong Kong writer Kai-cheung Dung (1967–) set out to map the mysterious V (for Victoria) City on the eve of the 1997 handover of Hong Kong to the PRC. Shen Congwen's West Hunan and Mo Yan's (1955–) Gaomi County are Chinese counterparts to William Faulkner's Yoknapatawpha County or García Márquez's Macondo Town. In Han Song's *2066: Mars over America*, the year 2066 marks a turning point in the Sino-American relationship. By then, America has crumbled as a result of both economic and political disasters while China has become a superpower, ruled by the artificial intelligence program "Amando," an entity that collapses when mysterious Martians descend on Earth. The reference to Mars (in Chinese, literally "Fire Star") in Han's title brings to mind *Red Star over China* (1937) by Edgar Snow (1905–1972), the first English account of life in Yan'an. By playing with Snow's title, Han prompts us to rethink the geopolitics of utopia—or dystopia—in terms of socialist (China), capitalist (the United States), and extraterrestrial space.

Together with more than 140 scholars, I have worked out a literary history that may raise many eyebrows. By way of conclusion, let me stress again that *A New Literary History of Modern China* is by no means a "complete" history in the conventional sense; rather, it takes into consideration seriously the Quixotic attempt of any historiographical attempt vis-à-vis inexhaustible data and experience. It creates more interstices than it can fill. As such, it invites readers to imagine the vast space implied in the concept of modern Chinese literature, ponder its shifting boundaries vis-à-vis history, and, more importantly, explore its horizons as part of a process of worlding.

Accordingly, the Sinophone intervention represents yet another attempt to broaden the scope of modern Chinese literature. It does not seek to overwrite the extant imaginary of "China," but rather seeks to tease out its complexity. Is it not a paradox that critics can subscribe to a "politics of marginality" and pontificate about a "clash of empires" and "global contextualization," all the while rigidly marginalizing forms of Chinese modernity and historicity that do not emerge within some preconceived mainstream? If one of the most important lessons one can learn from modern Chinese literature and history is the tortuous nature of Chinese writers' attempts to grapple with a polymorphous reality, then this knowledge can be appreciated in full only through a criticism and literary history equally exempt from formulaic dogma and ideological blindness. One must genuinely believe that Chinese and Sinophone writers have been, and still are, capable of complex and creative thought, even at moments of political suppression and personally motivated reticence. The volume argues that any critical endeavor in the name of "modernity" must be unafraid to look squarely at this historical reality—a reality of contested modernities.

NOTES

1. In the People's Republic of China especially, "contemporary literature" (*dangdai wenxue*) is invoked to describe literature produced after 1949, when China supposedly achieved its final stage of historical development. This is contrasted with ideas of "early modern literature" (*jindai wenxue*) and "modern literature" (*xiandai wenxue*), which are used to refer to literature of the late Qing (1840s–1910s) and the May Fourth (1919–1949) periods, respectively. This periodization, with each period representing a more advanced stage in the development of literature, has been used to embed a progressive, revolutionary agenda in the most basic historiography of modern Chinese literature.

2. Literally, *wenxue* means the "study of *wen*," a term later adopted to refer to the translation of literature.

3. Stephen Owen, *Traditional Chinese Poetry and Poetics: Omen of the World* (Madison, WI, 1985), 21.

4. Ibid.

5. See, for instance, Wai-yee Li's discussion in *The Readability of the Past in Early Chinese Historiography* (Cambridge, MA, 2007).

6. Confucius, *The Analects*, trans. D. C. Lau (New York, 1979), 83; translation modified.

7. See my discussion in *The Lyrical in Epic Time: Chinese Intellectuals and Artists through the 1949 Crisis* (New York, 2015), chapter 2.

8. See Zhang Hui's discussion in *Zhongguo "lishi" chuantong* [The tradition of "poetry as history" in China] (Beijing, 2012), chapter 1.

9. [Poetry is composed after the demise of history]. Huang Zongxi, "Wan Lü'an xiansheng shixu" [Preface to the poetry of Mr. Wan Lü'an], in *Nanleiji and Zhuanzhangji* [Collection of works by Mr. Nanlei [Huang Zongxi]: Compendium of works in honor of the venerable], vol. 10 (Hangzhou, China, 1993), 47. My translation slightly alters the original meaning of Huang's statement, which emphasizes more the innate power of poetry in manifesting history, and the bilateral ties between poetry and historiography.

10. Owen, *Traditional Chinese Poetry and Poetics*, 15.

11. Chu-yun Hsu, *Huaxia lunshu: Yige fuza gongtongti de bianhua* [A discourse of hua-xia: Changes of a heterogenetic community] (Taipei, 2015); Ge Zhaoguang, *Zhaizi Zhongguo: Chongjian guanyu "Zhongguo" de lishi lunshu* [Here China resides: Reconstructing a historical discourse about "China"] (Taipei, 2011).

12. C. T. Hsia, "Obsession with China: The Moral Burden of Modern Chinese Literature," appendix 1 of *A History of Modern Chinese Fiction*, 2nd ed. (New Haven, CT, 1971), 533–554.

13. Greil Marcus and Werner Sollors, "Introduction," in *A New Literary History of America* (Cambridge, MA, 2012), xxiii.

14. Martin Heidegger, "The Turning," in *The Question Concerning Technology and Other Essays*, trans. William Lovitt (New York, 1977), 45. "May world in its worlding be the nearest of all nearing that nears, as it brings the truth of Being near to man's essence, and so gives man to belong to the disclosing bringing-to-pass that is a bringing into its own."

15. Martin Heidegger, "The Origin of the Work of Art," in *Poetry, Language, Thought*, trans. Albert Hofstadter (New York, 1971), 44.

16. Martin Heidegger, "The Thing," in *Poetry, Language, Thought*, 178.

17. Ananya Roy and Aihwa Ong, eds., *Worlding Cities: Asian Experiments and the Art of Being Global* (London, 2011); Pheng Cheah, "What Is a World? On World Literature as World-Making Activity," *Daedalus* 137, no. 3 (2008): 26–39; Mei Zhan, *Other-Worldly: Making Chinese Medicine through Transnational Frames* (Durham, NC, 2009).

18. Arif Dirlik, *Culture and History in Postrevolutionary China: The Perspective of Global Modernity* (Hong Kong, 2012).

19. Lisa Rofel, "China's *Tianxia* Worldings: Socialist and Post-Socialist Cosmopolitanism," in *Culture, International Relations, and World History: Rethinking Chinese Perceptions of World Order*, ed. Ban Wang (Durham, NC, forthcoming).

20. Albert Hofstadter, "Introduction," in Heidegger, *Poetry, Language, Thought*, x.

21. For a comparative and contrastive study of Heideggerian philosophy and its Chinese counterparts, see, for instance, Zhang Xianglong, *Haideger sixiang yu Zhongguo tiandao: Zhongji shiyu de kaiqi yu jiaorong* [Heideggerian thought and the Chinese way of heaven: The opening and fusion of eternal visions] (Beijing, 2011).

22. I am referring to Theodore Huters's book title *Bringing the World Home* (Honolulu, 2005). Huters's book deals with early modern Chinese writers' and literati's creative appropriation and approximation of Western literary and conceptual models, such that they opened up a new view of China in the world context.

23. Owen, *Readings in Chinese Literary Thought* (Cambridge, MA, 1992), 241.

24. Shu-mei Shih, *Visuality and Identity: Sinophone Articulations across the Pacific* (Berkeley, CA, 2007).

25. Jing Tsu, *Sound and Script in Chinese Diaspora* (Cambridge, MA, 2011), 2.

1635

Yang Tingyun defines *wenxue* as literature.

1932 · 1934

Zhou Zuoren and Ji Wenfu trace the origin of modern Chinese literature and thought to the late Ming dynasty.

The Multiple Beginnings of Modern Chinese "Literature"

The modern concept of *wenxue*—the Chinese word we now translate as "literature"—first appeared not in the polemical works of literary reformists Kang Youwei (1858–1927) and Liang Qichao (1873–1929) at the end of China's last dynasty (the Qing, 1644–1911), nor on the banners of the modernizing revolutionaries of the May Fourth Movement (1919). Before the turn of the twentieth century, when "modern" literature became a popular slogan, there were already many moments in which attempts at renewing Chinese literature surfaced. One such moment can be traced to the early seventeenth century, when the Confucian scholar-official and Catholic convert Yang Tingyun (1562–1627) composed a religious pamphlet. Born to a devoutly Buddhist family in Hangzhou, a flourishing center of culture during the Ming dynasty (1368–1644), Yang was a scholar who had reached the top ranks of Ming officialdom. In 1611, after witnessing two Jesuit priests administer Catholic last rites for a friend's father, Yang was so moved as to convert to Catholicism, and he devoted the rest of his life to proselytizing his new faith through polemical tracts. In the pamphlet *A Sequel to the Removing of Doubt*, published posthumously in 1635, Yang informs his readers that Western education begins with *wenxue*, whose loose English equivalent is "literature." For Yang, *wenxue* encompasses not only poetry and prose but also historiographies and argumentative essays, in addition to the proverbial sayings of ancient sages.

Yang's 1635 booklet expanded upon an existing usage of *wenxue* in Chinese history, but it broadened the definition of the term dramatically. *Wenxue* first appears in the ancient Confucian text *Analects* as one of the four principal fields of study in Confucianism. In the *Analects*, *wenxue* refers to the task of integrating the lessons of Confucian texts into one's conduct. In subsequent ages, the practice of *wenxue* was taken to include a wide range of cultural and intellectual subjects, from scholarly undertakings to cultural edification, from the "patterned" manifestation of human and natural movements to the practice of linguistic education, from aesthetic exercise to pedagogical discipline.

The late Ming was marked by a drastic revolution in thought concerning many of the topics under the wide umbrella of *wenxue*. Thinkers like Li Zhi (1527–1602) challenged neo-Confucian orthodoxy and called for "free expression." Yuan Hongdao (1568–1610) took issue with the antiquarian literary aesthetics of the time through poetry inspired by personal experience. Other writers and editors, such as Xu Wei (1521–1593), Ling Mengchu (1580–1644), and Feng Menglong (1574–1645), made great strides in the traditionally maligned genres of fiction and drama, and to that effect they can be regarded as forerunners of literary modernization. In part, their innovations were a reaction to the turmoil of the late Ming society as a result of the increasingly weakened imperial reign, a booming urban economy, the advent of foreign missionary culture, and the radical, individualistic turn of Confucian thought.

Although entrenched in the Confucian tradition, Yang was heavily engaged in late Ming cultural and intellectual reinvention. But his understanding of *wenxue* was broadened through his encounter with the Jesuits, who brought Western literary concepts to China. By way of contrast, browsing through early Catholic missionary works such as the *Introduction to Western Learning* (1623) by the Jesuit priest Giulio Aleni (1582–1649), an associate of Yang's, we already witness the expression *wenyi zhixue*, or "the study of the art of writing," employed to include the study of *shi* (poetry) and *ci* (song lyrics), which traditional scholars kept distinct from the practice of *wenxue*. The term *wenyi*, literally meaning "the art of composition," first appears in the Confucian classic *The Book of Rites* (ca. 43 BCE), but Aleni's usage of *wenyi zhixue* is clearly influenced by the *Ratio studiorum*, the set curriculum of European Jesuit schools. Yang incorporated Aleni's Jesuit conception of *wenyi zhixue* into the conventional Chinese discourse of *wenxue*, thus charging the term with a new categorical purpose.

"Literature" in both Chinese and Western paradigms underwent continued transformation between the seventeenth and twentieth centuries. Although Yang's pamphlet had fallen into oblivion by the twentieth century, it had its influence during the Qing dynasty. In the aftermath of the first Opium War (1839–1842), Catholic writings by figures like Yang found renewed popularity among Chinese scholar-officials. One of those scholar-officials well versed in Catholic writings was Wei Yuan (1794–1857). In *Illustrated Treatise on the Maritime Nations*, a hundred-volume atlas containing detailed maps and histories of Western nations, as well as explanations of Western technology, Wei remarks that Rome became a great empire partially because it absorbed the best of *wenxue* traditions of Greece. Wei's usage of *wenxue*, with its focus on belles lettres, closely parallels that of Yang's, and he expands the usage to include not just the study of literature but also literary creation itself.

Wei's and like-minded intellectuals' efforts to renew the meaning of *wenxue* found a counterpart among a set of missionaries. Like the Jesuits, these missionaries felt compelled to explain the Western concept of literature to the Chinese. In 1837, the German missionary Karl F. A. Gützlaff (1803–1851) published an essay, "Poetry," in the Chinese-language magazine *Eastern Western Monthly Magazine* in which he juxtaposed Li Bai (701–762), the poet of Chinese poets, with Homer and John Milton as world literary giants. In the essay, Gützlaff employs *wenxue* in the same way Yang used it during the late Ming. Through his introduction of Homer, Gützlaff inaugurated the modern Chinese learning of Western literary works.

During the mid-nineteenth century, the writings of Protestant missionaries developed and reinforced this new definition of *wenxue*. In 1857, the *Shanghai Serial*, the first Chinese-language monthly magazine in late Qing China, began laying a foundation for the contemporary Western definition of literature in China. From 1857 to 1859, this journal featured in every issue a column by the British missionary Joseph Edkins (1823–1905) that introduced works of Western literature. This column offered discussions on the similarities and differences between the Chinese and Western concepts of *wenxue*, and highlighted the historical contexts in which literary cultures became distinct from one another. Edkins's first essay, in the inaugural issue of *Shanghai Serial*, was entitled "Greece: The Origin of Western *Wenxue*"; it demonstrates the newly charged geographical connotations of *wenxue* of China in relation to the world.

Edkins's major contribution to Chinese literary history lies in his translation of "epic poet" as *shishi*, or "poetic historian." *Shishi* had been

a sanctioned term for the lyrical poet with an acute historical consciousness. The way Edkins used, or misused, it nevertheless helped introduce
the narrative component embedded in Western "epic" to a Sinitic tradition
predicated on poetry. Edkins compares Homeric epics with the poems of
Du Fu (712–770), the "Sage of Chinese Poetry," a task at which a modern scholar would balk as a superficial analogous reading. Still, Edkins's
endeavor led to the reformulation of the literary canon. He widened the
Chinese literary repertoire by including traditional "low" genres such as
drama and narrative fiction. He went so far as to praise the vernacular
drama of the Yuan dynasty (1271–1368), as well as popular literature of
subsequent ages; as such, he anticipated the May Fourth radical reap-
praisal of Chinese literary tradition that happened seventy years after.

In the subsequent issues of *Shanghai Serial*, Edkins turned his attention
to the genres of rhetoric, history, and devotional literature. He identified
the parliamentary system in Europe as the reason why rhetoric flourished
in the West and was neglected as a genre in the East. He then profiled a
series of orators in Western antiquity, such as Plato and Cicero. Edkins's
column also featured the histories of Herodotus and Thucydides. Finally,
Edkins introduced devotional literature, a genre foreign to the late Qing
Chinese literati. Devotional literature, in its Western sense, conveys the
especially Christian values of piety, reverence, and veneration, and represents a new literary outlook (a subject that will be discussed later in this
volume in the essays on the translations and original novels produced by
Protestant missionaries in China). Particularly in light of his inclusion of
devotional literature, Edkins's goal in his series of columns was to shape
and create a literary tradition with the core purpose of guiding people to
believe in God. Such a tradition was unprecedented in China.

The extant paradigm of modern Chinese literary history has addressed
predominantly innovations in the indigenous context. To be sure, one
cannot stress enough the contributions made by Chinese literati. The
cases of Aleni, Gützlaff, and Edkins are described here only to highlight
the long and sprawling process of Chinese literary modernization, as well
as its transcultural and translational nature. In any case, by the end of the
nineteenth century, the stage was set for the advent of modern Chinese
literature. The meaning of *wenxue* was no longer confined to the study
of Confucian classics or traditional forms of cultural edification. Rather,
wenxue came across as a venue of contested forms, agendas, and functions:

both elite and vernacular, both conservative and radical, both indigenous and foreign. If the Confucian teaching of *wen* as that which carries an insurmountable power of didacticism and edification still looms, it derives a new raison d'être from foreign and popular sources. It is in this context that Kang Youwei and Liang Qichao, two leaders of the late Qing Reform Movement, came to propagate *wenxue* for their national cause, to the extent of making literature the sole strategy for rescuing China.

In March 1932, Zhou Zuoren (1885–1967), one of the most vociferous leaders of the May Fourth New Literature Movement, gave a talk in Beijing on the origin of modern *wenxue*, and published *The Origin of Chinese New Literature* shortly afterward. Zhou admired the late Ming literati of the Gong'an and Jingling schools and their emphasis on so-called human emancipation, and he pointed out that "this literary movement [in the late Ming] widely resembles the one that has been inaugurated since the Republican era." Zhou held Yuan Hongdao in particularly high regard. He found modernist echoes in Yuan's advocacy for a literature based on one's individual temperament and a concept of literature that evolves with time.

Zhou was not alone in discovering the origin of Chinese literary modernity in a premodern moment. In 1934, Ji Wenfu (1895–1963), an intellectual historian committed to Marxism, published *The Leftist School of the Wang Yangming Thought*, in which he traced the origin of modern Chinese literature and thought to the late Ming, when the radical vein of the Wang Yangming (1472–1529) school of Confucianism thrived. Zhou and Ji, however, differ from each other in that whereas the former finds in the late Ming era the origin of the May Fourth liberal discourse of humanism, the latter finds in the same late Ming era an incipient sign of socialist revolutionary momentum. Both represent a modern intervention with history in terms of intended anachronism. More fundamentally, both betray an understanding of literature and literary history as a hybrid entity of both Chinese and non-Chinese elements. Later scholars built on Zhou's and Ji's efforts when seeking to bridge the modern and premodern periods. For instance, Ren Fangqiu (1909–2000) offers insight on Yuan's literary views and praises Li Zhi for attempting to break free from the shackles of Confucianism and advocating for freedom of thought.

Although deeply immersed in the May Fourth discourse of radical antitraditionalism, Zhou and Ji understood that literary history comprises as many breaks as continuities. The fact that they sought to trace the beginning of modern Chinese literature to the late Ming era reminds us that modernity is always overdetermined: before "the Chinese modern" came into being at the turn of the twentieth century, there had existed many moments of innovations and self-renewals in history. Accordingly, one may take Zhou's and Ji's (anachronistic) inquiry into Chinese literary modernity one step further, by tracing the Ming literati's principles of "individual emancipation" and "literary evolution" to even earlier historical moments. For instance, the Seven Sages of the Bamboo Grove—a group of literary luminaries of the third and fourth centuries known for their eccentric deeds and recalcitrant temperaments—may well serve as another possible source of inspiration for Chinese moderns. Above all, one recalls Liu Xie (465–ca. 522), author of *Literary Mind and Carving the Dragon*, the foundational work of traditional Chinese poetics, who contemplates the dynamics of literary evolvement in a chapter entitled "Literary Development and Time."

The story about the "beginning" of modern Chinese literature, therefore, must be a narrative with open endings. If the modern literary history conceived by Zhou Zuoren and Ji Wenfu is still informative to us today, it is because it points to the multiple trajectories of *wenxue* or literature as drawn out by figures from Yang Tingyun to Giulio Aleni, from Li Zhi to Yuan Hongdao, from Karl Gützlaff to Joseph Edkins, and from Kang Youwei to Liang Qichao, among others. In this sense, the dates 1635, 1932, and 1934 represent no more than three of the entry points to the immense constellation of Chinese literature.

BIBLIOGRAPHY: Sher-shiueh Li, *European Literature in Late Ming China: Jesuit Exemplum, Its Source and Its Interpretation*, rev. ed. (in Chinese) (Beijing, 2010). Sher-shiueh Li, *Transwriting: Translated Literature and Late-Ming Jesuits* (in Chinese) (Hong Kong, 2012).

SHER-SHIUEH LI

1650 · JULY 22

Dutch papers report the fall of the Ming.

Dutch Plays, Chinese Novels, and Images of an Open World

On April 25, 1644, the three-hundred-year-old Ming dynasty ended as its last ruler, the Chongzhen Emperor (r. 1628–1644), committed suicide by hanging himself on Coal Hill, just north of the Imperial Palace in Beijing. Word about the events soon spread throughout the empire, sometimes through unexpected channels. Recalling how the news first arrived in southern China, Yao Tinglin (1628–after 1697) wrote how "within two months a novel which recounted the fall of the capital in detail, *The Eradication of the Rebel Prince*, was for sale." Yet news of the empire's demise did not stop at China's borders. By July 22, 1650, reports of Chongzhen's suicide had been carried across the globe to Holland by sailors of the Dutch East India Company (Vereenigde Oost-Indische Compagnie; VOC). In 1654, the Jesuit Martino Martini (1614–1661), returning from China after fourteen years, published a full-length account of the fall, *About the Tartar War*. By 1666, not one but two Dutch authors were inspired by the recent events in China to write tragedies about the last night of Ming-dynasty rule.

The story of the fall of the Ming was written across the globe: in Chinese novels, Jesuit histories, and Dutch plays. In Europe, the story contributed to a new image of the globe as a single, interconnected community linked through the free sharing of goods, people, and information. This European narrative revolved around the ideal of openness, an ideal established by depicting China as the peripheral, Oriental other: a landlocked empire, closed off from the world geographically, economically, and epistemologically. Ironically, seventeenth-century European texts based this image on popular Chinese narratives spread by novels such as *The Eradication of the Rebel Prince*, which presented Chongzhen's reign as isolated and lacking in open interaction. In these Chinese narratives, however, Chongzhen's seclusion functioned not as a generic symbol of "China's global isolation," but rather as a telltale sign of a last emperor's inability to communicate clearly with his subjects.

The role the fall of the Ming played in European narratives of an open world can be seen in a poem penned by Johannes Antonides van der Goes

Romeyn de Hooghe (1645–1708), *De Ystroom*, book II (1671). Collection of the author.

(1748–1784), *De Ystroom* (The river Y). *De Ystroom* rhapsodizes about the river Y (on which Amsterdam is located), as well as the economic and political power the river has brought the city and the young Dutch republic. Guided by a single metaphor, water, the poem suggests an aquatic economy of trade to explain the recent Dutch prominence within the world. It is not the actual possession of places, but rather the ability to freely navigate the oceanic connections between places that generates the republic's wealth.

The idea of a globe connected through open waters is illustrated in the print that accompanies the poem. At the heart of the emblem, underneath a globe unveiled by Mercury, patron of messengers and merchants (as well as thieves), sits the god Y River on his throne, surrounded by other deities, each representing a region of the world: Poland, Spain, Gibraltar, and finally the Maiden of China. All these regions offer their riches to add to the glory of the Dutch god at the center. China, the female on the left side of the Y River, generously empties her chest of gold straight into the Y god's lap.

By including China, the print highlights how even the most distant parts of the world have opened to the seafaring Dutch. For decades Ming emperors had resisted any attempt by the VOC to engage in trade. Expelled from Ming shores in the 1620s, the VOC had only been able to establish a colony just beyond the purview of the Ming empire—the lush, if sparsely inhabited, island Taiwan. Though before long the VOC was bringing in Chinese colonists to develop sugar plantations, even this small Dutch colonial outpost was to be lost. In 1662, the Ming loyalist Zheng Chenggong (also named Koxinga; 1624–1662) drove the VOC from Taiwan and established a new headquarters for the loyalist remnants of the Ming on the island, thereby bringing Taiwan fully within the orbit of mainland China's imperial attention for the first time. If the fall of the Ming eventually was to end Dutch colonial adventures on China's periphery (and push China's borders beyond the Taiwan Straits in the process), in 1651 the empire's demise instead seemed to promise the VOC the much-sought inroad into China. In that year, the Jesuit Martini had arrived at the VOC headquarters on Java with the happy news that "the Great Cham of Tartary had conquered the empire of Sina and in the City of Kanton had opened the gates to free trade to all foreign people." A mission to the Tartar Cham soon followed.

In *De Ystroom* the promise of a self-enclosed empire now unlocking itself for an acquisitive Europe becomes a simple economic message:

Now that Sina no longer refuses to deposit her riches
And offers Atlas's golden harvest with a generous hand

Johan Nieuhof (1618–1672), *An Embassy of the Dutch East India Company to the Tartar Cham*, frontispiece (1665). Courtesy of Leiden University Library, RG31.

Though she herself sighs tightly bound,
And the royal court in Beijing, felled by the Tartar Axe,
Proves how with great clamor the mighty fall
From the highest apex, as the country with embarrassment
Saw hanging the greatest emperor from a tree
His dying face, painted with lead rouge,
Now the royal saffron river and the Kang, their mouths once closed
Freely lift their head towards the sun,
Empty their harvest in the harbor of Canton,
And with a wealth of treasures honor us.

In these lines, the Yellow River and the Yangtze serve *De Ystroom*'s principal metaphor of water flowing freely, just as the generic images of the fall of the Ming here spell one single lesson: the whole world, even the empire of China, has opened up to "deposit her riches" in the coffers of the Dutch.

Another Dutch author, Joost van den Vondel (1587–1679), depicted China in need of opening up not to global trade, but rather to the Christian faith. China, according to Van den Vondel, crucially lacked knowledge, and Van den Vondel's play, *Zungchin, or the Demise of China*, blames the fall of the Ming on the emperor Zungchin's (Chongzhen) ignorance of the world around him. The many walls China's emperor has built around himself do not protect him from rebellion; instead, they isolate him from everything happening outside. The emperor does not know that the rebel Lykungzus (Li Zicheng; 1605?–1645?) has infiltrated Beijing and bribed the imperial troops to open the gates and shoot only blanks at the rebel army. Similarly, the emperor fails to recognize that his military council has been bought and now betrays him. Finally, in the fourth act, the emperor's lack of communication with the world comes to a tragic climax. As rumors increasingly begin to swirl around the palace, Chongzhen's treacherous eunuchs do not tell him that the imperial elephants have been poisoned and that the outer palace walls have been taken. The emperor can no longer escape. Trapped within his high walls, deluded by misinformation, Chongzhen commits suicide, hanging himself from a plum tree.

Ultimately, however, Van den Vondel suggests that the emperor's lack of knowledge is not of a secular nature but rather of a religious one. True knowledge can only be found through the Catholic faith. Hence a key role

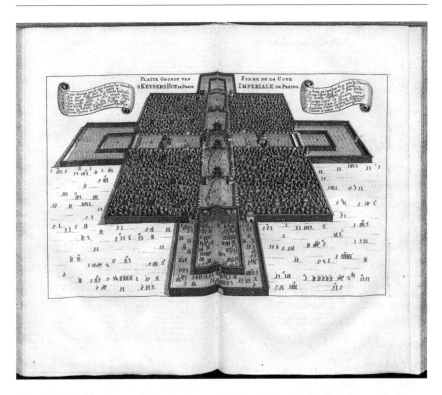

Johan Nieuhof (1618–1672), *An Embassy of the Dutch East India Company to the Tartar Cham,* map of the Imperial Palace in Beijing (1665). Courtesy of Leiden University Library, RG31.

in the tragedy is reserved for Jesuit priests like Adam Schall (1592–1666), who appears in the first act, or the ghost of Saint Xavier (1506–1552), who in the last act descends on the stage amid a choir of angels, foretelling how China will be saved once it opens to the grace of God. Van den Vondel's message of China, as of yet closed, but awaiting the Creator's opening touch, is most firmly worded when, inspired by Martini's recently published *Novus Atlas Sinensis,* Van den Vondel has a chorus rhapsodize about China's famous Great Wall. No man-made structure, they tell us, can ever hope to protect the empire. Only opening oneself up to the Christian faith can safeguard against misfortune.

Van den Vondel derived his tragically ill-informed Chongzhen from Martini, whose works on Chinese geography, history, and the recent "Tartar War" had taken the European book market by storm. Notably, Martini's Chongzhen bears a striking resemblance to the image of the

Martino Martini, *Novus Atlas Sinensis*, frontispiece (1655). Courtesy of the Beinecke Library at Yale University.

Ming emperor popularized in Chinese sources published shortly after the fall of Beijing. Though it is impossible to pinpoint any specific text—Martini never identifies his sources—the striking resemblance suggests that Martini, who read Chinese fluently, based the idea of Chongzhen as inaccessible on the rumors, popular histories, and novels circulating in China at the time. Crucially, however, these Chinese texts present Chongzhen's lack of openness not as a perennial characteristic of a Chinese empire that refuses to open itself to the West, but rather as the flaws of a final ruler disobeying a long-standing governing principle of the Ming: the direct and unobstructed communication between ruler and subject. As Yongle (r. 1402–1424), the emperor responsible for first moving the Ming capital to Beijing, reputedly had stated, "Stability depends on superior and inferior communicating; there is none when they do not. From ancient times, many a state has fallen because a ruler does not know the affairs of the people."

Particularly telling in this regard is the Chinese novel mentioned earlier, *The Eradication of the Rebel Prince*, a text crucial in popularizing the view of Chongzhen as "uncommunicative." The novel includes many details suggestively similar to Martini's and Van den Vondel's accounts: a fifth column betraying the emperor from within the city walls; the imperial artillery firing nothing but blanks; the emperor killing his own daughter with his sword; Chongzhen's final letter, written in blood, accusing his fickle ministers. Indeed, the novel singularly misprints "plum" for "coal" when it tells how Chongzhen hung himself on "Plum [Coal] Mountain," a detail that may well explain the *plum* tree found in Martini's account and Van den Vondel's play. Most importantly, the novel, like Martini and Van den Vondel, portrays Chongzhen as isolated within the high walls of his palace. It does so, however, not to symbolize China's isolation from the world, but rather to emblematize Chongzhen's separation from his subjects, something the novel illustrates dramatically when it portrays the emperor, on the final night of Ming rule, ringing the bell summoning officials to court. None appear in response.

If European texts borrow the image of the Chongzhen Emperor as isolated, they also mirror Chinese narratives when they portray the reinstatement of imperial order as an exercise of "open" rhetoric, a restoration of direct communication between emperor and subjects. *Trazil, or China Overwhelmed*, Van der Goes's tragedy about the fall of the Ming,

Martino Martini, *Historie van den Tartarischen Oorloch* (1654). Courtesy of Leiden University Library, RG31.

stages such unimpeded imperial speech when the newly crowned emperor Xunchi (Shunzhi; r. 1643–1661) addresses a host of Tartar warriors. It is a scene reminiscent of Martini's *About the Tartar War*, which includes a similar moment of "Chinese / Tartar / European" rhetoric.

The idealized image of neoclassical public rhetoric, much like the figure of a four-foot, childlike Shunzhi or the image of Tartar nobles dressed in medieval scholastic robes, may at first seem a complete misrepresentation of historical reality. Yet the European image of an orating emperor is no mere Orientalizing fantasy. Rather, it resonates with late Ming ideals of rhetoric, ideals that demanded unimpeded communication between ruler and subject. For instance, the Chinese novel *The Marvelous Tale of Establishing the Dynasty*, an update of the earlier *Eradication of the Rebel Prince* published in 1651, the year Martini left China, does not present the emperor Shunzhi and his regent Dorgon (1612–1650) as barbarian

Xiwu Iandaoren, *The Eradication of the Rebel Prince* (1645). Courtesy of the Naikaku Bunko Library, Tokyo.

conquerors skilled in "Tartar" ways of horseback riding. Instead, the final chapter portrays them as enlightened rulers whose edicts address their Chinese subjects in the rhetorical forms and with the ethical ideas that any seventeenth-century Chinese scholar would recognize from his primers of neo-Confucian thought.

Indeed, the image painted in the final chapter of *The Marvelous Tale* perfectly matches the illustration found in the earlier novel, which, despite showing a Han Chinese emperor as final victor instead of a Manchu ruler, ends on a similar note: order is restored once ruler and subject can communicate "openly" once more. Certainly, seventeenth-century Dutch ideals of public oratory and early modern Chinese displays of "open" imperial speech differed in terms of both content and form. Yet in terms of function, such displays of "public speech" were remarkably similar: they helped define seemingly universal communities whose boundaries were drawn through the mastery of prescribed rhetorical forms that celebrated "open" communication.

In the seventeenth century, a new vision of the world began to develop in Europe that is still with us today: the world as an open community brought together through a liberal exchange of goods, people, and ideas. In the construction of this vision, China easily came to represent the exception—a closed empire that had to be unlocked to enter into communion with the rest of the globe. This essay has sought to question this image of an isolated China and to raise other questions about this ideal of openness. Does "open" exchange guarantee "equal" exchange? Does the request to open up represent an invitation or an imposition? Are there alternatives to the liberal definition of the term "openness"? Might the debates that raged within late Ming China about unimpeded imperial communication offer such an alternative? Can we imagine a world order that does not impose its singular view of openness on others? And finally, are the differences between a "closed China" and an "enlightened West" really all that great, or do we overemphasize these differences to delineate boundaries and reinstate order in our increasingly interconnected world?

PAIZE KEULEMANS

1755

> "In both ancient and modern times there have generally been three paths to learning: application to moral philosophy (*yili*), to evidential studies (*zhishu*), and to writing (*wenzhang*). Application to letters is equal [to the other two], but subsidiary (*deng er mo*)."

The Revival of Letters in Nineteenth-Century China

In a letter he wrote to a friend in 1755, Dai Zhen (1724–1777), perhaps the most respected scholar of his age, set forth his ideas on the taxonomy of learning. While he cast learning in the trivium standard at the time of moral philosophy (*yili*), evidential research (*zhishu*, a term much less common than the more widely used *kaozheng*), and writing (*wenzhang*), he did not see them as equal and relegated writing to a position inferior to the other two. And even as he stressed that *yili* was the most important element of the triad, Dai was clear enough that the stylistics of prose were not something over which one need show great concern. This is by no means to say that writing was not a constant and vital part of the concerns of the educated elite—it was, after all, the only path to success in the imperial examination, and regulated verse had for a time been restored to the examination curriculum in the 1750s—but rather that, in Dai's view, writing and its mechanics should not take precedence over moral or political contemplation and argument. It was, in other words, not worthy of serious contemplation in and of itself. Qian Daxin (1728–1804), a scholar closely associated with a more purist pursuit of historical and philological research, was even more emphatic, consigning writing to a role verging on the merely functional. As he wrote in praise of Qin Huitian (1702–1764), a scholar he much admired, "When he came to express himself in writing, his writing was luminous, far-reaching and abundant; it went only as far as expressing what he wished to say." The philologist Duan Yucai (1735–1815) expressed the real agenda of the evidential movement, which was to place empirical research at the forefront of all intellectual effort, in his 1792 preface to his edition of Dai Zhen's work. In explicit contrast to Dai, he wrote, "I would say that moral philosophy and letters can only be attained through research."

In contrast to this utilitarian perspective on writing, the man of letters Yao Nai (1732–1815), who, like those he regarded as his predecessors, as well as many of his disciples, hailed from the town of Tongcheng in Anhui Province, regarded writing as the very fount of correct perception and the key to apprehension of the Way. As he wrote in a famous letter to Lu Xiefei (1732–1794),

> I have heard that the Dao of heaven and earth consists in nothing but the yin and the yang, the gentle and the strong. Writing [*wen*] is the finest essence of heaven and earth, and the manifestation of the yin and the yang, the gentle and the strong.... If one has obtained the beauty of the yang and the strong, then one's writing will be like thunder, like lightning, like a strong wind emerging from the valley, like lofty mountains and steep cliffs, like a great river flooding, like galloping steeds.... If one has obtained the beauty of the yin and the gentle, then one's writing will be like the sun just beginning to rise, like a cool breeze, like clouds, like vapor, like mist, like secluded woods and meandering streams.

While the main point of the letter was to set forth the stylistic elements of good prose, which he saw as embodied in "ancient-style prose" (*guwen*), an unencumbered, plain style in the tradition of the Grand Historian Sima Qian (135?–86 BCE), Yao makes it clear that behind his rhetorical concerns lay a conviction that good writing was in effect the true manifestation of the Dao. Yao thus effects a union of aesthetics and didacticism quite beyond the scope of the more practical *wen* envisioned by Dai and Qian Daxin, in effect placing it higher than *yili* on the scale of moral cultivation, even if correct moral apprehension remains the ultimate goal. But while it is easy to see that Yao is advocating a heightened sense of the aesthetic in ordinary prose writing, it should be equally clear that he simultaneously opens the way to augmenting the role of ideology in the aesthetic appreciation and mechanics of prose composition.

Behind these sharply divergent views on the nature and function of writing lay a more fundamental debate, one that concerned the very basis of learning and its relationship to political practice and moral philosophy. The eighteenth-century enthusiasm for evidential research had originally centered on an effort to provide orthodox Confucian ideas with a solid empirical basis through the verification and thus firmer understanding of the import of canonical texts; it was meant to dig beneath what its leaders saw as the stale commonplace assumptions originally established in the Song dynasty that had come to characterize contemporary Confucianism, the state ideology infused into both education and the examination system by which government officials were selected. The determination to reject Song orthodoxy by resorting to what they regarded as a sounder substrate of empirical research undertaken a thousand years earlier in the Han dynasty resulted in this new endeavor gaining the popular moniker "Han learning" (*Hanxue*). While it was generally acknowledged that great achievements had been made in historical understanding and scholarly methodology by the leading lights of the evidentiary movement, by the end of the eighteenth century even some who had been stalwarts of the movement came to have misgivings about the effects of exclusively focusing on turning up new evidence: the idea that conducting esoteric research into archaic institutions and questioning the veracity of certain portions of the canon contributed to the general health of the realm began to give way to the view that such research was too preoccupied with its own agenda and atomized rather than unified the range of applied knowledge.

Yao had been one of the initial skeptics concerning an excessive empiricism, having resigned from a post on the commission compiling the imperial Complete Library of the Four Treasuries out of frustration with the philological bent of its general editorial policies as early as 1774, and leaving Beijing the following year. Yao subsequently developed a marked antipathy to the Han learning and its acolytes in Beijing, and spent the rest of his life as an educator in the provinces, where he acquired numerous loyal students, who were eventually able to propagate widely his doctrine of proper Song-school moral philosophy being embodied in mastery of *guwen*. The turn away from evidentiary studies is probably best exemplified by *A Polemic on Han Learning*, a book by Yao's student Fang Dongshu (1772–1851) that was a thorough denunciation of the work of notably evidential scholars such as Dai and Qian. Most noteworthy, perhaps, is that when eventually published in 1831, it bore the imprimatur of Ruan Yuan (1764–1849), with little doubt the most powerful and influential scholar-official of his day and someone much noted for his own evidential research.

Rejecting the centrifugal tendencies of *kaozheng*, however, did not automatically clear the way for a return to the Song-learning moral platitudes that the evidentiary movement had sought to move beyond: the mountains of evidence compiled by eighteenth-century scholars rendered a return to a purely speculative moral philosophy impossibly naive, which is where the call for renewed attention to the power of writing came to play a vital role—the painstaking discipline called for in prose composition, combined with the moral sense it was meant to embody, distinguished it from both the dry objectivity of classical studies and the insubstantiality of moral speculation unmoored in confirmed textual validity. This sense of a new rigor allowed the emphasis on the moral authority of *guwen* to escape the suspicion of being merely a retrograde retreat to an outmoded Song orthodoxy. As Fang wrote in a letter to Yao Ying (1785–1853), another of Yao Nai's disciples, "To inspire the good in people and to stifle the perversity, to mold the deportment of the gentry, nothing in the universe can match *wen* for conveying virtue and merit so as to stir the world and pass on that [merit and virtue] without exhausting it." For all the emphasis on punctiliousness of style, however, for many scholars of the time, writing in *guwen* was like the prose spoken by Moliere's bourgeois gentleman: they found they had been writing it all their lives, as Jiao Xun (1763–1818) noted in a bemused letter to a friend. In other words, the Tongcheng call for a radical departure ended up being more readily achievable than it might initially have sounded, as the core of their style was essentially the orthodox style of the time. Perhaps not as paradoxical as it sounds, however, the more adepts there were at *guwen*, the more its more stringent advocates like Fang lamented that the new converts were far from grasping its essentials.

Guwen was not the only idea concerning the importance of writing to catch on at this time. The same Ruan Yuan who had sanctioned Fang's polemic against the Han learning came to espouse his own theory of prose, a revival of parallel prose (*pianti wen*), an ornamental form of prose in rhyme, the writing of which had become increasingly popular toward the end of the eighteenth century. It is noteworthy here that parallel prose had enjoyed a vibrant existence in Chinese letters, prior to the late Tang and Song dynasty *guwen* masters having effectively marginalized it almost a thousand years before. It is thus no coincidence that the leading lights of the parallel prose revival came out of the evidentiary school, one way, perhaps, of holding on to their rejection of Song learning. While the emphasis on the importance of prose style was something the two schools had in common, there was one quite substantial difference: whereas *guwen* was implicitly meant to apply to all prose writing, the apostles of parallel prose revived the distinction between two divergent styles, one labeled *wen*, refined writing, and the other *bi*, a plain style they deemed subject to verbosity and endless argumentation. Ruan defined *wen* as *wenzhang*, something that incorporated "deep thought and literary elegance." Thus, while Tongcheng writers sought to put all prose on a single, albeit high-minded, plane, Ruan and those who followed what came to be known as the "*Wenxuan* school"—named after Xiao Tong's (501–531) sixth-century anthology notable for its parallel prose—set off two different types of writing, the more exalted of which seems to overlap substantially with modern notions of "literature." Whether this was actually Ruan's intention or not, his theory opens a space for a writing quite beyond utility, thus foreshadowing Wang Guowei's (1877–1927) radical call for a completely different space for literature in 1906.

Throughout the remaining century of the Qing, these two schools remained the focus of attention for discussion of prose rhetoric, with each school having its peaks and valleys. Many of the most active intellectuals in Beijing during the 1840s, for instance, were adepts of the Tongchengs, while the period after 1895 saw a resurgence of parallel prose. But behind each of these resurgences lay a more or less explicit political agenda that the prose was meant to support. There was thus a sustained struggle over what writing should be, between those striving to preserve the medium as the central portion of a unified field of knowledge and those seeking to elevate letters by splitting them off from ordinary knowledge. In the final analysis, however, these movements represented two sides of the same coin: they both sought to invest prose writing with a weight that could be used to buttress a political and social order that almost everyone sensed to be increasingly threatened as the Qing dynasty drew to a close. This heightened sense of the vital cultural importance of writing inevitably had profound implications for the new field of "literature" (*wenxue*), a term brought to China from Japan after 1895 to signify a unified belles lettres that for the first time in Chinese history put poetry and fiction, whether in the classical or vernacular language, in the same category. Thus, the politicization of literature that became one of the most salient features of modern China had roots in Qing dynasty debates over the nature and function of writing.

THEODORE HUTERS

1792

Dream of the Red Chamber and the Macartney mission to China.

Legacies in Clash:
Anticipatory Modernity versus Imaginary Nostalgia

"We have never valued ingenious articles, nor do we have the slightest need for your country's manufactures," reads an edict from the Qianlong Emperor (r. 1736–1795) to King George III (r. 1760–1820) in response to Lord George Macartney's (1737–1806) diplomatic mission to China.

The year 1792 witnessed two events that profoundly anticipated the Chinese modern experience: Macartney's diplomatic mission and the publication of Cao Xueqin's (1715–1763) novel *Dream of the Red Chamber*, also known as *The Story of the Stone*. These two events both began and were emblematic of the essential and fraught trends in Chinese thought for the centuries that followed. The Macartney mission (1792–1794) raised the problems and promises of modernity, of foreigners in the central kingdom, and of a national self-reflexiveness bordering on obsession. *Dream of the Red Chamber* (published in 1791–1792), by contrast, created a world that encapsulated late imperial Chinese culture at its height, populated by young men and women bubbling over with feelings, which led its readers to a profound nostalgia for a lifestyle and lost culture that most of them, by dint of the era or status of their birth, never experienced.

Chinese foreign policy had not changed much in response to the diplomatic or Christian missions that had been sent since the late sixteenth century. It held that China was the "central" kingdom and that other countries were, by definition, peripheral. The court of Qianlong showed little interest in precise information or detailed study of foreign countries. Chinese descriptions of foreign countries in all manner of texts continued to depict an exotic blend of mystical tales and fantasy, in which foreigners were often likened to animals or birds and were described in patronizing or deliberately belittling language. Arriving at the Chinese court, Macartney and his retinue of almost one hundred were banqueted, hosted with formality and courtesy, and dismissed. In his audience with the emperor in September 1793, Macartney requested the establishment of a diplomatic residence in Beijing, an end to the restrictive Guangzhou trading system, the opening of new ports for trade, and the fixing of fair tariffs. All of his requests were denied. Qianlong sent along an edict with Macartney to George III explaining that China would not increase its foreign commerce because it needed nothing from other countries.

Western powers would not long abide Chinese diplomacy that consistently referred to them as barbarians presenting tribute, and, more, they would not long abide a trade deficit that saw the worlds' silver sunk into such a country in return for silk, porcelain, and tea. Britain began selling opium to China in the middle of the eighteenth century to rectify the deficit.

Macartney's private observation that China's navy was weak in comparison to Britain's was prescient. China was summarily humiliated during the Opium Wars (1839–1842, 1856–1860) and forced to sign unequal treaties. Consequently, China was made into a semicolonial state with a British colony at Hong Kong (Portugal had leased Macau centuries earlier) and concessions to one or another of ten countries in at least fifteen major cities (nine in Tianjin alone). The tensions caused by these humiliations resulted in unrest and rebellion, most notably the Taiping (1850–1864) and Boxer (1900) Rebellions, both of which were eventually put down with the aid of Western forces.

Late Qing reformers became keen to study Western technology and culture, and to travel abroad. Backlashes against these impulses also caused many to long for traditional culture and a time when China truly was the central kingdom. The transculturation between modernity and tradition is powerfully illustrated in responses to the novel *Dream of the Red Chamber*, rivaled in world literature perhaps only by *Don Quixote* as the embodiment of a nation's cultural identity.

Editions of *Dream of the Red Chamber* today, Chinese and English alike, state on their title pages that the novel is the work of Cao Xueqin and supplemented by Gao E (ca. 1738–ca. 1815). Very little is known about Cao, other than that he came from a powerful family that fell out of favor with the emperor. His name occurs in the work's first chapter, but only as one of a series of names, some patently fantastic and others merely unknown, of people who are said to have rewritten or edited earlier versions of the book. Early manuscript copies of the novel do not include an author's name, and the first edition to reach a wider public, Gao E and Cheng Weiyuan's movable-type printing of 1792, notes in its preface, "No one knows for sure who wrote this book."

Dream's protagonist, Jia Baoyu, is an eccentric young man who grows up in a wealthy household among many female cousins and maids during the moral and financial decline of his powerful family. *Dream* is one of the earliest, if not *the* earliest, work of full-length fiction in the Chinese tradition to place feelings in a position of central importance. The process by which Baoyu attains enlightenment—through attachment to his girl cousins, the experience of their loss, and ultimately his detachment from worldly things—is called into question by the novel's existence, since it supposedly was written as a record of these young women so they would not be lost to memory. The irony of enlightenment through attachment and desire is applied to the experience of reading fiction as well. The reader of *Dream* must work through a contemplation of Form or Appearance, and the feelings they engender, to reach some kind of truth, which is knowledge of the Void—the truth that everything in the phenomenal, human world is empty and transient. In this regard, the novel is either jesting at or lamenting the inescapable realization that Buddhist detachment and fictional aesthetics constantly undermine each other.

One of *Dream*'s alternate titles, *The Twelve Beauties of Jinling*, recalls the mostly sad fates predicted for the major heroines in the registers of the "ill-fated fair" that Baoyu reads in a dream. *Dream* creates, in the image of the Grand View Garden, in which Baoyu and his many female cousins and all of their maids reside, an idealized world of female beauty, taste, literary talent, sensitivity, and morality. Yet it also claims that it is a true record of real people and places recalled from childhood.

Many readers are drawn to the material culture in the novel and the lovingly detailed descriptions of lavish objects in the Jia household. Textiles, paintings, furniture, unusual trinkets—all have complicated modes of signifying, and all involve matters of taste, wealth, culture, and connoisseurship. *Dream*, in its encyclopedic inclusiveness, summarizes late imperial Chinese culture in a sense, but more than that, it challenges that culture. It questions the ways in which systems of order construe or confine the self; the meanings of roles and their subversion; the claims of emotions, desire, and artistic imagination to tradition and autonomy; and the tyranny of order and harmony over individual complexity and internal conflict. The complex representation of self and society in *Dream*, its nostalgia for and idealization of a lost world, captures the modern Chinese reader's feelings about traditional Chinese culture. At the same time, however, *Dream's* ironic, critical self-reflexivity suggests the burden of modernity.

The line between high and low culture was constantly shifting in the reproduction, transmission, appropriation, and consumption of *Dream*. Most Chinese universities have more than one "Redologist" among their faculty, and an extravagant fifty-episode television series of *Dream* aired in 2010, preceded by the "*Red Chamber* Casting Contest," in which millions of viewers voted on which of the 236,000 contestants they wanted to play the lead roles. *Dream* has infiltrated the Chinese language, with families referring to their spoiled only sons as their "little Jia Baoyu," and many girls being characterized as either a self-centered Daiyu or a dutiful Baochai. When Wang Li (1900–1986), a towering figure in modern Chinese linguistics, wrote his famous and influential *Modern Chinese Grammar* (1943), his examples were taken almost exclusively from *Dream*.

On the one hand, *Dream* and its cultural influence survived the turbulent changes during the final decades of the nineteenth century and the early twentieth century because it constituted part of the rising mass culture associated with urban entertainment, magazines, modern commercial publishing, and popular professional writers. On the other hand, *Dream* became firmly fixed in the literary canon after the May Fourth Movement (1919) because of modern intellectuals' quest for an equivalent tradition to that of the modern European novel. In the 1950s, Mao Zedong (1893–1976) launched his literary purge by condemning, among others, Yu Pingbo (1900–1990) for his politically incorrect interpretation of *Dream*. In communist discourse, the novel was taken either as an exemplar of feudalistic decadence or as an allegory of youthful revolt against tradition. *Dream* and its cultural influences rely on and are emblematic of a convergence of the social, cultural, and technological changes that defined and redefine modern China.

Popular interpretations, such as Liu Xinwu's (1942–) televised lectures (2005 and 2007) that resuscitated a traditional *Da Vinci Code*–esque approach, read the novel as an extended historical allegory of one emperor's court or another and draw on the recent popularity of television period dramas set in the Qing dynasty. The nostalgia for this lost world, and indeed for lost youth and innocence, is perhaps not as dire as it was a century ago, when foreign influence, modernity, and revolution forcibly put the past beyond reach. Now, interest in *Dream*, traditional culture, and Qing history is a hobby, or even kitsch. Yearnings for the past encapsulated by *Dream* are ameliorated by a trip to the Grand View Garden theme park in Beijing (modeled more closely on the 1987 television series than the novel), where you can dress up as your favorite character or view a sensorama film allowing you to experience Baoyu's famous dream visit to the land of illusion. This impulse to experience *Dream* is not new: Beijing and Shanghai brothels from the last decades of the nineteenth century through the 1920s and 1930s featured prostitutes who took the names of its female characters.

Abridgments and stage adaptations made *Dream* more widely available to the marginally literate or illiterate, but the many "sequels" (not authored by Cao) attest to the original's abiding influence on literary culture. The first sequel was published in 1796, just four years after *Dream's* publication; two sequels appeared in 2006; and at least fifty-six were published in between. Works that might be called fan fiction are still popular, such as the 2004 *Murder in the Red Chamber*, which recasts the main characters not in a poetry club, but in a mystery club (a move that also ignited nationalist outrage since it was a Japanese author who dared appropriate these hallowed characters for his story). Most sequels try in one way or another to rewrite the ending of *Dream*—to eliminate traumatic antinomies, improve on the selfish and eccentric characters of Baoyu and Daiyu, or wishfully ameliorate their tragic romance.

Late Qing literature is marked by (at least) two recurrent themes: belief in the transformative power of overseas study, and a fascination with conjuring utopian civilizations that either critique or resolve tensions in society. Both of these impulses find expression in two novels of the same title, *The New Story of the Stone*. Wu Jianren's (1866–1912) 1908 novel first finds Jia Baoyu traveling to the Barbarous World, where he witnesses the atrocities of the Boxer Rebellion and gets arrested for spreading democratic ideas. He then stumbles upon the Civilized World, a utopia strong in military power, political structure, scientific advancement, and moral cultivation. Baoyu's journey culminates in his visit to the venerable ruler of this world, Dongfang Qiang (literally "Eastern Strength"), who explains his utopia as one based on the Confucian notion of *ren*, or benevolence. The novel by Nanwu Yeman (1909) casts Daiyu as the protagonist. She did not die the day Baoyu married Baochai; rather, she fled the Grand View Garden and found her way to America to study. She eventually earned a doctorate in English and philosophy, shed her former persona, as well as her Chinese dress, and became a professor at the School of the Commonwealth in Tokyo. In order to be near her, Baoyu enrolled at that school and became an overseas Chinese student.

The "Obsession with China" that C. T. Hsia (1921–2013) claims characterizes modern Chinese literature consists of looking backward and looking abroad in order to create a vision of the future. Moreover, the coincidence of Macartney's visit and the publication of *Dream* generates a double vision regarding the way we narrate, imagine, and reflect on Chinese modernity. The desires to "travel," in the broad sense, into the glorious past or into a utopian modernity, are powerful impulses in modern Chinese literature, and both desires are, in large part, legacies of the events of 1792.

BIBLIOGRAPHY: Wai-yee Li, "Full-Length Vernacular Fiction," in *The Columbia History of Chinese Literature*, ed. Victor H. Mair (New York, 2001), 620–658. Helen Henrietta Macartney Robbins, *Our First Ambassador to China; An Account of the Life of George, Earl of Macartney, with Extracts from His Letters, and the Narrative of His Experiences in China, as Told by Himself, 1737–1806* (London, 1908). Shang Wei, "The *Stone* Phenomenon," in *Approaches to Teaching The Story of the Stone (Dream of the Red Chamber)*, ed. Andrew Schonebaum and Tina Lu (New York, 2012), 390–412.

ANDREW SCHONEBAUM

1807 · SEPTEMBER 6

Robert Morrison sets foot in Guangzhou.

Robert Morrison's Chinese Literature and Translated Modernity

On January 31, 1807, twenty-five-year-old Robert Morrison (1782–1834), of the London Missionary Society, embarked on his arduous voyage to China by way of the United States, finally setting foot in Guangzhou on September 6, 1807. Owing to the Qing government's prohibition of Christianity, it was as a translator for the East India Company that the founder of the Protestant missions to China obtained the necessary legal status to remain on Chinese soil.

The year before departing for China, Morrison commenced his life-long study of the Chinese language in the British Museum by copying Jean Basset's (1662–1707) partial translation of the Chinese Catholic Bible, with the assistance of Yong Sam-tak, a Chinese man whom he met in London. On the basis of Basset's Bible, Morrison completed and published the first Chinese translation of the New Testament in 1813 and the entire Bible ten years later. While this was being acclaimed as an epochal achievement for Chinese Christianity, the event also contributed to the rise of Chinese linguistic, literary, and cultural modernity in the early nineteenth century.

Residing in Guangzhou and Macao for almost three decades, Morrison, forbidden to evangelize publicly, dedicated himself to the literary enterprise. In conscientious pursuit of the best style for the Chinese Bible and other theological works, Morrison spoke favorably of Ming-Qing vernacular fiction, particularly *Romance of the Three Kingdoms*. The Mandarin paraphrasing of *The Sacred Edict*, sixteen maxims decreed by the Kangxi Emperor (r. 1662–1722) in 1670, was also influential in shaping the style of Morrison's Chinese publications.

In violation of the Qing imperial edict (1812) decreeing the printing of Christian books a capital crime, one of Morrison's Chinese assistants even carried poison in preparation for death. It was in such high-risk conditions that Morrison, in addition to his Chinese Bible, produced the first Chinese translation of *The Westminster Shorter Catechism* (1812) and portions of *The First Homily of the Church of England* (1812) and *The Book of Common Prayer* (1818), along with scores of hymns commonly sung in Christian countries (*Hymns for Nurturing the Spirit*, 1818). Other than rendering Western works into Chinese, Morrison composed several original literary works, such as *Tour of the World* (1819) and *Domestic Instructor* (1832).

Previous literary historians seem to have overlooked the fact that experiments with Chinese vernacular modernity can be traced to missionaries' literary engagements in the Sinophone world of Southeast Asia. Morrison's prolific translations and writings imported new elements of lexicon, syntax, literary forms, and cultural-religious concepts into the Chinese language. At the lexical level, neologisms were not uncommon in Morrison's translations and often made for the most effective conveyance of foreign terms and ideas. Some notable examples include *mushi* ("master of the herd" or pastor) and *geli* ("rite of cutting" or circumcision) in *Domestic Instructor*, and *shijie mori* ("last day of the world" or doomsday) in *Tour of the World*. Apart from coining new words and phrases, Morrison employed transliteration for the biblical vocabulary with prominent Judaic or Christian colors, for instance "Christ," "Pascal," "talentum," and "diabolos." Many of Morrison's neologisms, like *shijie mori*, are now commonly used in contemporary Chinese.

Modeling inflectional languages' use of agent suffixes such as -er, -ist, or -ian, Morrison lavishly adopted the agentive ending particle *zhe* in his Chinese translations, for instance, *shuzhe* for "redeemer" (*Westminster Shorter Catechism*), *daozhe* for "comforter" (John 14:16), and *laozhe* for "elders" (Matthew 26:3). It is noteworthy that Morrison added the *zhe* ending to Basset's translation of *shanmu* for "good shepherd" (John 10:11). While the particle *zhe* is also found in classical Chinese, its extensive use is characteristic of contemporary Chinese language practices. Morrison was also conscientious in reproducing the plural suffix in the source texts by adding the particle *bei*, and occasionally *men*, to indicate plurality. For instance, the word "saints" was translated as *shengbei* (Ephesians 4:12), "scribes" as *shushibei* (Matthew 26:3), and "we" (John 1:45) as *women*. Morrison's strict observance of highlighting the grammatical number minimized the ambiguity involved in Chinese writing.

In addition to these lexical features, Morrison also introduced new syntactic structures into the Chinese language, which does not overtly reflect any modification to person, tense, or voice. Passive voice in classical Chinese is normally expressed by word order, by putting the object in front of the verb, instead of reliance on passive markers. Morrison, however, frequently translated the passive voice of the source texts into Chinese by resorting to the passive auxiliary *bei*, to indicate that the subject is the object of the action. For instance, the phrase "be betrayed" (Matthew 17:22) was translated as *bei maifu*, "was transfigured" (Matthew 17:2) as *bei bianguo*, and "be crucified" (Matthew 26:2) as *bei ding shizijia*. The passive sentence with the marker *bei* has become a standard syntactic structure in modern Chinese since the early twentieth century.

Morrison's translation of the Apostles' Creed in *The Westminster Shorter Catechism* demonstrates the syntactic rule of ellipsis in English, which allows for the omission of part of a sentence for reasons of economy.

The rule of ellipsis, however, is not applicable to Chinese; it normally requires the repetition of the verb, or even the subject, in parallel clauses. Morrison resorted to the repetition of the Chinese word *yu*, which is approximate to the English preposition "in," "on," or "at," for each noun phrase he desired to omit. In so doing, Morrison introduced to the Chinese language certain European grammatical structures, particularly the rule of ellipsis, the formation of abstract nouns, and the extensive use of long premodifiers, all of which laid the groundwork for the modernization of Chinese in the early twentieth century.

Apart from the introduction of new lexical and syntactic structures, Morrison imported new literary forms to Chinese via his translations. In rendering *The First Homily of the Church of England*, Morrison was meticulous about the re-creation of the rhythmic momentum characteristic of this genre. A homily refers to a Christian commentary in the form of a sermon delivered after the reading of the scriptures during the liturgy. For instance, in translating "Let us night and day muse, and have meditation and contemplation in them (Psa. i.); let us ruminate, and, as it were, chew the cud, that we may have the sweet juice, spiritual effect, marrow, honey, kernel, taste, comfort, and consolation of them," Morrison attempted to reproduce the rhyme pattern, parallel structure, and aura of the scripture by ending the introductory clauses with the particle *zhi* and repeating the possessive pronoun *qi*, in order to capture the poetics and rhetorical beauty of the latter phrases.

Another example is Morrison and his Chinese assistants' rendering of *Hymns for Nurturing the Spirit*, which consists of thirty hymns. In hymn 27, there is a translation of "All people that on earth do dwell" from *The Scottish Psalter* (1635). Its first stanza is "All people that on earth do dwell, / Sing to the Lord with cheerful voice. / Him serve with fear, His praise forth tell; / Come ye before Him and rejoice." With a view to retaining the original melody for the purpose of Christian worship, the translated hymn reproduced the long meter (8, 8, 8, 8) of the original doxology. In the history of classical Chinese literature, poems with eight characters or syllables per line were quite exceptional, while monosyllabic words were dominant. Morrison's translation, however, relinquished the standard meters and rhyme patterns of traditional Chinese poetry and freely used bisyllabic and polysyllabic words. Such attempts opened up new possibilities of poetry writing for modern Chinese literature, which preceded similar avant-garde experiments undertaken by May Fourth poets.

Prior to the first Opium War (1839–1842), scores of Protestant missionaries were stationed in Southeast Asia to prepare for the opening up of China by undertaking the production of biblical texts in the local languages. The majority of their Chinese works, including many of Morrison's, were published by missionary presses in Malacca, Singapore, and Batavia. The missionaries formed a network of proselytizing dialogues and intertextual influences. Morrison's stylistic advocacy and literary experimentation became a great source of inspiration for his fellow missionaries, especially William Milne (1785–1822), Karl F. A. Gützlaff (1803–1851), and Liang Fa (1789–1855), China's first indigenous evangelist.

Modeled on Morrison's use of a fictional framework, Milne produced the first Protestant missionary novel in Chinese, *Two Friends* (1819). Adopting a familiar Chinese setting and nonconfrontational tone, this vernacular novel revolves around twelve dialogues between a Christian and his non-Christian friend concerning such religious themes as sin, everlasting life, and resurrection. Repeatedly revised in different dialects and reprinted until the late 1930s, *Two Friends* emerged as the most widely distributed and well-received Chinese missionary novel, and is the arguable origin of modern vernacular Chinese fiction.

Inspired by Milne's pioneering attempt, Gützlaff dedicated himself to the composition of a sizable number of vernacular Christian novels, notably *Doctor of Redemption* (1834) and *Orthodoxy and Heresy Compared* (1838), possessing vivid features of vernacular fiction peppered with nascent narrative strategies. While the works of Milne, Gützlaff, and Liang made profuse references to Morrison's Chinese Bible, Morrison's hymns were frequently quoted or modified by Gützlaff to serve as the opening poems to his novels. Morrison's writings not only had a far-reaching impact on the literary endeavors of the next generation of missionaries, but also indirectly engendered the Taiping Rebellion due to Hong Xiuquan's (1814–1864) reading of the works of Liang and Gützlaff. It is worth pointing out that Gützlaff's revision of Morrison's Bible was officially adopted by Hong in his Taiping Heavenly Kingdom.

Morrison's literary legacy facilitated Chinese cultural modernity by introducing Chinese readers to Western learning and novel worldviews. From the first-person perspective of a Chinese who traveled round the globe, *Tour of the World* presents Chinese readers with Western geographical concepts, political systems, and theories about the origin of the world. The miscellaneous text *Domestic Instructor* depicts a wide range of modern knowledge about such topics as the French Revolution, the Napoleonic Wars, and Western astronomy. In response to the worsening Anglo-Chinese relations before the Opium Wars, Morrison was commissioned by Charles Majoribanks (1794–1833) of the East India Company to translate the latter's *Brief Account of the English Character*, rendered as *Dayingguo renshi lüeshuo* (1832). With a succinct portrayal of the character and culture of the British people and a petition for more equal Anglo-Chinese trading relations, this politically loaded work was extensively circulated in the coastal regions of China and even reached the Daoguang Emperor (r. 1821–1850) through his local officials. The aforementioned fields of secular knowledge were ingeniously embedded in the underlying assumption that Christianity constituted one of the pillars of European civilization, and thus broadened the Chinese horizons of world history and politics. It also deserves to be noted that some of Morrison's works, for instance, *The Westminster Shorter Catechism*, were used as textbooks in the Anglo-Chinese College in Malacca, which helped shape the religious mind set and ways of expression of the students, some of whom, such as He Jinshan (1817–1871), subsequently emerged as religious and social leaders in Chinese communities.

Not only the precursor of the missionary movement, Morrison also served as a mediator between Chinese and Western cultures by introducing the Chinese language and culture to the Western world. He composed in English a Chinese grammar and several treatises on Chinese culture and society, and translated works of traditional Chinese literature into English, including selections of *Dream of the Red Chamber* as early as 1813. His magnum opus was the six-volume *Dictionary of the Chinese Language* (1815–1822). This first Chinese-English dictionary arranged the Chinese characters alphabetically, instead of using the standard contemporary practice of ordering them according to their radicals. Morrison demonstrated the pronunciation of Chinese characters by romanized letters, offering such phonetic details as tones and aspirations shown by diacritical marks. Predating by many decades both the Wade-Giles and Hanyu Pinyin systems, Morrison's romanization recorded the phonological features of Chinese characters in a precise and systematic manner, which made the Chinese language readily accessible to Western learners.

Due to the fact that the scaffold of classical Chinese might fail to fully support foreign linguistic structures and culture-specific concepts, Morrison and his fellow missionary writers realized the need to search for, if not create, new linguistic modes and means in vernacular Chinese during the process of translating Western works. The translational enterprise of these missionaries not only heralded the evolution of the classical Chinese language into modern vernacular forms, but also functioned as a medium and catalyst for literary innovation and cultural transformation in China during the late nineteenth and early twentieth centuries—a fact that has long been obscured on nationalist and ideological grounds.

BIBLIOGRAPHY: Richard R. Cook, "Overcoming Missions Guilt: Robert Morrison, Liang Fa, and the Opium Wars," in *After Imperialism: Christian Identity in China and the Global Evangelical Movement*, ed. Richard R. Cook and David W. Pao (Eugene, OR, 2011), 35–45. Patrick Hanan, "The Missionary Novels of Nineteenth-Century China," *Harvard Journal of Asiatic Studies* 60, no. 2 (December 2000): 413–443. John T. P. Lai, *Negotiating Religious Gaps: The Enterprise of Translating Christian Tracts by Protestant Missionaries in Nineteenth-Century China* (Sankt Augustin, Germany, 2012). Elizabeth Armstrong Morrison, *Memoirs of the Life and Labours of Robert Morrison* (London, 1839). J. Barton Starr, "The Legacy of Robert Morrison," *International Bulletin of Missionary Research* 22, no. 2 (April 1998): 73–76.

JOHN T. P. LAI

1810

The Korean legate Kim Chŏng-hŭi arrives in tense Beijing.

Gongyang *Imaginary and Looking to the Confucian Past for Reform*

Arriving in Beijing in 1810, Kim Chŏng-hŭi (1786–1856), the Korean legate of the Chosŏn dynasty (1392–1897), sent letters back to Seoul (then Hanseong) writing that the Qianlong Emperor (r. 1736–1795) was a wise ruler, but his reign was compromised by what was then known as the "Heshen affair." Kim's tributary mission arrived a decade after the Jiaqing Emperor (r. 1796–1820) eliminated Heshen (1750–1799), a politician and a Qianlong favorite whose massive corruption was unprecedented. Kim befriended many anti-Heshen partisans. His Korean teacher, Pak Che-ga (1750–1805), had praised the exiled Changzhou scholar-official Hong Liangji (1746–1809) for his philology and commended him as a gifted essayist writing in the commentarial tradition of Master Gongyang (a native of the feudal state of Qi during the Warring States period of 475–221 BCE).

Gongyang's commentary on Confucius's *Spring and Autumn Annals,* a historical chronicle of the affairs of the state of Lu from 722 to 481 BCE, dated to the early second century BCE. Pak's linking of Hong to Confucius through the *Gongyang Commentary* suggested that Hong accepted the ideology of the Gongyang school: that Confucius encoded the "literary and figurative meanings" of political events in the *Annals* and that the *Gongyang Commentary* decoded them. The commentary criticized those who threatened the universal rule of the sage-kings. Hong had used it to combat political corruption during the Heshen era.

Pak's visit to Beijing in 1790 put him in touch with an unexpected "opposition" centered on the scholarly lineage of the Grand Secretary Zhuang Cunyu (1719–1788), based in Changzhou, a city on the banks of the Yangtze in the heart of the prosperous Jiangnan region, and a center of culture during the late Qing.

Kim Chŏng-hŭi personally knew Zhuang's grandsons, Zhuang Shuzu (1750–1816) and Liu Fenglu (1776–1829), early nineteenth-century Changzhou champions of "New Text" classicism, which privileged as authentic those portions of the Confucian canon that had allegedly been compiled from scraps and from memory after the Qin dynasty proscribed Confucianism in the "burning of the books" in 213 BCE. These texts were written down in contemporary-style "clerical" script and hence called "New Texts." They contrasted with the Old Texts, literally called "ancient-style script," as they had been written in the more ancient "large seal" forms of calligraphy. These Old Texts had supposedly been hidden during the burning of the books and then rediscovered. Qing scholars from the Zhuang and Liu lineages in Changzhou were the first to stress the *Spring and Autumn Annals* as the embodiment of Confucius's holistic vision and not merely the court chronicles of the state of Lu, as claimed by the more historically oriented *Zuo Commentary*, one of the three commentaries on the *Spring and Autumn Annals*.

New Text scholars contended that Confucius authored the *Annals* to criticize his time. The *Gongyang Commentary* contained guidelines for acknowledging Confucius as a charismatic who should have received the Mandate of Heaven. Because Confucius did not receive the mandate, he chronicled his times in order to "praise or blame" the era of the Zhou dynasty. Others rejected the orthodoxy of Old Text sources such as *Zuo Commentary*. They charged that imperially sponsored scholars such as Liu Xin (ca. 50 BCE–23 CE) fabricated the Old Texts during the Han interregnum (9–23) of the so-called Han usurper Wang Mang (45 BCE–23 CE). Liu Fenglu later explained,

> Thinking that it would be better to put them into effect rather than rely on empty words, [Confucius's wisdom] was broad and deep, discriminating and clear. He cited histories and records, imbuing them with the mind of a king. Mencius said "the *Annals* represent the affairs of the Son of Heaven."

New Text advocates like the Zhuangs and Lius turned to the *Gongyang* because it was the only New Text commentary that survived intact from the Former Han (206 BCE–9 CE) chief minister Dong Zhongshu (179–104 BCE). According to the *Gongyang*, Confucius composed the *Annals* using particular terminology that demonstrated the historical judgment he attached to events. Dong expanded on the theory provided in the *Gongyang*: "Regarding what he witnessed, Confucius used terminology that concealed; regarding what he heard, he expressed sorrow for calamities; regarding what he read in transmitted records, he set his compassion aside [and wrote dispassionately]. This is in accordance with the feelings [appropriate to each situation]." Dong's theory of epochs was embedded in a notion of cyclical change "according to three ages," which correlated with the interactions of yin and yang and the traditional Chinese theory of the five evolutive phases of wood, fire, earth, metal, and water. Political theory and the world of rulers and officials were intertwined with the workings of heaven:

> The method of the *Annals* is to cite events of the past in order to explain those of the future. For this reason, when a phenomenon occurs

in the world, look to see what comparable events are recorded in the *Annals*; find out the essential meaning of its subtleties and mysteries in order to preserve the significance of the event; and comprehend how it is classified in order to see what causes are implied.

Dynastic change, according to Dong's political theory, brought with it institutional change. For each of the three epochs there was an appropriate institutional framework. Institutions, like dynasties, changed cyclically according to the five phases and yin-yang. The "three unities" of Xia, Shang, and Zhou evolved through time and space, bringing along institutional change in their wake:

> Ancient kings, after receiving [heaven's] mandate, which made them kings [of new dynasties], changed the institutions, titles, and beginning of the year [that had been in force]....Thus there was a single rule [for all] to respond to....This was the way in which heaven's sequences were made clear.

By "differentiating outer barbarians from inner Chinese," the *Annals* proffered a cultural vision of concentrically arranged inner and outer groups of peoples, which informed the tribute system at the heart of ancient foreign affairs. Inner regional states of the Zhou dynasty (1046–256 BCE) had priority over the surrounding tribes and peripheral barbarians. This New Text view of foreign affairs, for example, served as the underlying framework for Liu Fenglu's resolution of diplomatic conflicts while serving in the Ministry of Rites. The *Gongyang Commentary*, a New Text, provided support for the Former Han portrayal of Confucius as a visionary and "uncrowned king."

Until the nineteenth century, the *Zuo Commentary* authorized the Later Han Old Text school's portrayal of Confucius as a respected teacher and transmitter of learning. This ran counter to the Changzhou New Text scholars' vision of Confucius as a charismatic visionary. Changzhou scholars called the *Zuo Commentary* into question. They set New Text scholarship on a course that ultimately pitted political discourse against classical philology. Standing for new forms of belief, New Text studies championed pragmatism and the imperative of change, not just philological niceties.

Zhuang Cunyu's dissent coincided with 1780s court politics. In the 1790s, Zhuang Shuzu passed on his Han-focused philology and New Text scholarship to Liu, who had first studied with his grandfather Cunyu. Wei Yuan (1794–1857) and Gong Zizhen (1792–1841), although lesser figures in their times, carried on the Changzhou tradition in the nineteenth century. Liu's New Text scholarship combined Zhuang Cunyu's *Gongyang* scholarship and Zhuang Shuzu's philology. Wei's "Draft Essays from the Hall of Ancient Subtleties" survive in the Rare Books Section of the National Library in Beijing. They include two versions of the preface Wei penned for the 1820s publication of Zhuang Cunyu's collected essays. In both drafts of the preface, Wei charted Zhuang's career as a "true scholar of the Han Learning."

One version, never published, contained a politically charged statement at the end of the preface. Wei described how, during Zhuang Cunyu's last years, he served as a grand secretary with the erstwhile palace guard turned imperial favorite, Heshen. Wei wrote that Zhuang and Heshen did not get along and that Zhuang's classical studies written during those depressing years were filled with grief and disappointment over Heshen's growing power. In the printed edition of Wei's preface, the Heshen reference was dropped. Members of the Zhuang lineage likely saw to it that this delicate matter was excised. Zhuang's writings reveal, however, that he expressed his critique of Heshen by encoding it within the veil of classical allusions, particularly Confucius's "praise and blame" tradition. The Zhuangs easily could have printed his works earlier. Instead, they remained unpublished for almost forty years after Zhuang's death.

A confidant of the Zhuang lineage, Yun Jing (1757–1817), embodied Changzhou *Gongyang* theories and New Text studies. In his essay series entitled "Successive Reforms during the Three Dynasties," Yun presented ancient-style prose as a medium of political expression and New Text as a vision of institutional change.

The opening salvo in Yun's essays demonstrated the radical conceptual shifts he had incorporated in his historiography and prose. His efforts to "accord with human feelings" resonated with the contemporary reevaluation of human aspirations. Yun tested the limits of classical ideals. Historical realities took precedence over political and moral abstractions. Drawing on Liu Zongyuan's (773–819) views of historical inevitability and the *Gongyang* focus on change during the "three epochs," Yun cited institutional reforms initiated by the sages to show that it was both legitimate and necessary to change in accord with the times. Half a century before Kang Youwei (1858–1927), New Text ideology legitimated political change.

The radicalism of the Changzhou New Text scholars was not limited to content, but also extended to form. Together with scholars in the Tongcheng tradition in Anhui, Changzhou littérateurs defended Song-Ming ancient-style prose at a time when Qing scholars elsewhere increasingly turned to the parallel-prose styles of the Han dynasties. Yanghu ancient-style prose—a precursor of the literati clubs in vogue during the nineteenth century—included among its adherents a diverse collection of local literati, for whom literary achievement meshed with classical studies. Preeminent as stylists, Zhang Huiyan (1761–1802) and Yun had contacts with other Changzhou literati, and these contacts evolved into a literary fellowship concerned with the deleterious effects of the Heshen era.

The overlap between literature and New Text required classical erudition delivered in parallel prose and the stylistic complexity of ancient-style prose. The lyric again became a poetic vehicle for political expression; Zhang deployed lyric poetry as a repository of "esoteric meanings," through which worthy men disguised their critical views of contemporary events. Appropriating the "praise and blame" poetics read into Confucius's *Annals* and *The Book of Songs* (a collection of 305 songs dated by rough estimation to the first four hundred years of the first millennium BCE) by Former Han New Text scholars, Zhang's lyric poetry conveyed indirect criticism of political affairs. The *Annals* and *The Book of Songs* had allegorized the Zhou dynasty's decline. So too the works of lyric poets allegorized their society. In effect, Zhang was simultaneously writing and reading into lyric poetry what Zhuang Cunyu had discovered in the *Gongyang*. In the hands of determined scholar-officials, the written legacy provided contemporary leverage for criticizing the affairs of any age.

The Zhuangs and Lius passed on their *Gongyang* studies within the protected environment of their lineages to the end of the Jiaqing reign in 1820. Subsequently, Liu Fenglu made their views public. Unheralded and unread in twentieth-century scholarly circles, the Changzhou scholars brought to virtual completion the political implications of *Gongyang* teachings. Classical scholarship and political discourse were reunited.

The intellectual, social, and political winds of change that New Text scholars transmitted were picked up by Kang Youwei and others. In the late nineteenth century, first Liao Ping (1852–1932) and then Kang drew on the New Text scholarship of the Changzhou school and its various followers to evoke an alternative, modern Chinese political and cultural imaginary.

A Cantonese scholar, and prominent voice for reform in the late Qing, Kang wrote his philological tour de force, *On the Spurious Classics of Xin Dynasty Learning*, in 1891. Based on this deconstructionist account, which challenged the authenticity of the entire classical canon and blamed its forging on Liu Xin and Wang Mang, Kang constructed a politically perilous interpretation of Confucius as a social reformer in his influential *Study of Confucius as Institutional Reformer*, which was published in 1897 but banned for political reasons in 1898 and again in 1900.

According to Kang, Confucius was a visionary and had enunciated a concept of progress that Old Text scholars had covered up. This reinterpretation invested Kang's modern ideal of "institutional reform" with classical trappings. A strong believer in constitutional monarchy, Kang wanted a reformed imperial China on the model of Meiji Japan. In his masterpiece, the *Book of the Great Society*, he called for an end to private property and the family in the name of a future cosmopolitan utopia. Kang's alternative expressions of legitimate classical learning challenged classical orthodoxy, replacing it with a Western-inspired nativist democracy rooted in ancient China. These simultaneously apocalyptic, millenarian, and millennial ideas influenced both the reformers, such as Liang Qichao (1873–1929), and the future revolutionaries, such as Mao Zedong (1893–1976), who followed.

In contemporary times, the *Gongyang* has stimulated traditionalists such as Jiang Qing (1953–). They contend that China should revive its own ancient political conventions—the "kingly way" that "harmonizes heaven, earth, and humanity"—instead of westernizing the Chinese political tradition. In doing so, Jiang and others seek to reestablish the cosmological gulf between Western forms of government and ancient classical models. Kang Youwei had sought their equivalence.

BIBLIOGRAPHY: Benjamin Elman, *Classicism, Politics, and Kinship: The Ch'ang-chou School of New Text Confucianism in Late Imperial China* (Berkeley, CA, 1990). Jiang Qing,

A Confucian Constitutional Order: How China's Ancient Past Can Shape Its Political Future, ed. Daniel A. Bell and Ruiping Fan, trans. Edmund Ryden (Princeton, NJ, 2013). Susan Mann (Jones), "Hung Liang-chi (1746–1809): The Perception and Articulation of Political Problems in Late Eighteenth-Century China," PhD diss., University of Chicago, 1971.

Benjamin A. Elman

1820

"This girl, in my opinion, is suffering from homesickness."

Flowers in the Mirror *and Chinese Women:* *"At Home in the World"*

Completed in 1820, Li Ruzhen's (1763–1830) novel *Flowers in the Mirror* is a peculiarly untimely work. Ostensibly set in China's distant past—when Empress Wu Zetian (r. 684–705), the former consort of the Tang emperors Taizong (r. 626–649) and Gaozong (r. 649–683), seized power and established her own short-lived dynasty, the Zhou (690–705), thereby becoming the only woman ever to rule China under her own name—the novel at the same time anticipates the women's liberation and national strengthening movements that only began to gain significant traction in China several decades after the novel's completion.

Flowers in the Mirror opens with the protagonist, Tang Ao, being forced into exile after having been falsely accused of plotting a rebellion against the empress. Tang Ao therefore spends the majority of the novel traveling through the South China Sea visiting a series of fantastic island nations, each of which is loosely modeled on those described in the Chinese mythological text *The Classic of Mountains and Seas,* wherein each fictional country is defined by an unusual quality that illustrates a different facet of contemporary Chinese society. The residents of the novel's Country of Forked-Tongued People, for instance, are distinguished by their possession of an invaluable rhyme scheme that allows them to effortlessly master any new foreign language by breaking new words into their constituent phonemes. Inspired by a six-volume treatise on Chinese phonetics that Li himself had published in 1805, the novel's fictional rhyme scheme reflects both the traditional significance of language and philology in China and the growing importance of foreign languages and translation practices.

Tang Ao's local interpreter among the Forked-Tongued has a daughter who suffers from an illness that causes her abdomen to swell up as tight as a drum, and the interpreter therefore asks Tang Ao and his companions to take her with them to find a cure. After they acquire the requisite medicinal herbs, Tang Ao and his companions try to return Melody Orchid to her father, but discover that her symptoms recur as soon as she reenters the coastal waters of her natal island. It is this relapse that prompts Tang Ao's brother-in-law, Merchant Lin, to remark that "This girl, in my opinion, is suffering from homesickness," meaning not that she feels an excessive longing for home, but rather that it is the physical space of her home itself that is making her ill.

The suspicious abdominal swelling that drives Melody Orchid's father to send her off with another man is symptomatic of an exogamic kinship structure, in which Chinese women were traditionally expected to leave their natal home and marry into that of their husband. The sequence, accordingly, reflects allegorically on the way in which Chinese society has traditionally been predicated on a compulsory circulation of women between male patrilines. Within the context of the novel itself, meanwhile, Melody Orchid's expulsion from her home mirrors Tang Ao's state of having been exiled from his homeland, and together these two elements succinctly capture the work's more general fascination with issues of gender and gender inversion. Examples include not only Wu Zetian's accession to the throne at the beginning of the novel and a special women's-only session of the imperial civil service exams at the end, but also the work's famous description of the Country of Women, in which social positions traditionally reserved for men are held by women, while those positions conventionally assigned to women are instead given to men. The Country of Women happens to be the next place Tang Ao and his companions visit after leaving Melody Orchid's island for good, but soon after they arrive, the nation's (female) sovereign takes a liking to Merchant Lin and resolves to keep him as her consort. Merchant Lin is taken to the imperial harem and the narrative describes in detail the indignities to which he is subjected as he is refashioned into a feminine subject, focusing in particular on the excruciating agony he endures when they try to bind his feet. As one of the earliest Chinese descriptions to focus on the physical pain caused by foot-binding, this passage effectively anticipates a critique of foot-binding that would only begin to gain influence in China at the end of the nineteenth century.

Tang Ao's voyages while in exile may be viewed not only as an allegorical illustration of the processes of exogamic displacement, but also more literally as a reflection of China's growing determination to learn from foreign societies and cultures. In particular, China's defeat in the first Opium War (1839–1842) dramatically underscored the nation's comparative military weakness, and impressed many Chinese intellectual and political figures with the need to look abroad for intellectual resources with which to strengthen the nation. In fact, it was in the immediate shadow of the war that the scholar Wei Yuan (1794–1857) compiled and published the first modern world geography in Chinese: *Illustrated Treatise on the Maritime Nations* (the work was first released in 1844, with significantly expanded editions being released in 1846 and 1852). Organized taxonomically by geographical sea region, Wei's *Illustrated Treatise* could be viewed as an updated version of *The Classic of Mountains and Seas*, except that rather than consisting of mythological accounts of fictional lands, the *Illustrated Treatise* instead consists of translations and summaries of Western-language texts describing the geographical and material conditions, as well as technological achievements, of a wide array of foreign nations.

In his preface, Wei explains that the work's primary objectives are "to use barbarians to fight barbarians; to use barbarians to pacify barbarians; and to study barbarians' skills in order to subdue the barbarians." While the first two of these objectives refer to a desire to deploy different groups of "barbarians" against one another (the term Wei uses for "barbarian," *yi*, began to fall out of fashion in official discourse in the 1860s, having been deemed to be too pejorative), the third point instead underscores the need for China to acquire foreign knowledge in order to use it against the foreigners themselves. The logic is that by learning about foreign societies and cultures and mastering what they have to offer, China could thereby reaffirm its underlying identity and strength. Or, to paraphrase the "Chinese learning as substance / Western learning as function" formulation popularized several decades later by the reformer Zhang Zhidong (1837–1909), Wei's argument was that by adopting Western learning for its practical function, it would thereby be possible to fortify Chinese learning and, with it, the Chinese nation. In other words, one must *learn from* foreigners in order to subdue them.

Wei's emphasis on the importance of learning from foreigners became a key driving force in late imperial politics and society. Consequently, during the final decades of the Qing dynasty, a concerted effort was made to translate vast amounts of Western learning into Chinese, including a wide array of scientific, medical, political, philosophical, and literary subjects. One body of scholarship that became particularly influential in China during this period was that of social Darwinism, the writings of which approached geopolitics through the lens of a racial hierarchy that placed whites at the top, followed by the so-called yellow, black, and red races. This racialized vision appealed to many Chinese intellectuals, and inspired the influential late Qing scholar Kang Youwei (1858–1927) to propose that Chinese men be encouraged to intermarry with white women in order to improve the overall racial stock of the nation. Kang's suggested racial alchemy reflected a conviction—to paraphrase Wei—that one must *inherit from* foreigners in order to subdue them.

An ironic twist on Kang's advocacy of racial interbreeding can be found in the figure of Sai Jinhua (1872–1936), a courtesan credited with having used her sexually intimate relationship with Count Alfred von Waldersee (1832–1904), the supreme commander of the allied forces in China, to help save Beijing at the end of the Boxer Rebellion (1900). The Boxers, who hailed from rural Shandong, gradually moved north to Beijing, where they proceeded to attack the foreign concessions and, with the support of the Qing Imperial Army, keep the foreigners there under siege for nearly two months. Foreign forces under Waldersee's command eventually succeeded in overpowering both the Boxers and the Imperial Army, but then proceeded to continue looting and ransacking the rest of the capital. It was at this point that Sai is reputed to have intervened with Waldersee, whom she had previously met while in Europe, convincing him to order the troops under his command to stand down. By saving the capital from further devastation, Sai came to be celebrated as a savior of the nation. While Kang recommended that Chinese men marry white wives, in Sai we instead find a Chinese woman being celebrated for the leverage she herself was able to acquire as a result of sleeping with a white man. The lesson of Sai's example was—to again paraphrase Wei—that one must *love* foreigners in order to subdue them.

Sai's exploits inspired a variety of literary works, one of the most influential of which was Zeng Pu's (1872–1935) roman à clef, *Flowers in a Sinful Sea*. The novel opens during the 1880s when Sai first meets her husband, the Chinese civil servant Hong Jun (1839–1893), and then travels with him to Europe, where she is introduced to Waldersee. If *Flowers in the Mirror* was a very untimely work, *Flowers in a Sinful Sea* was a rather timely one. Conceived in the immediate shadow of the Boxer Rebellion, the novel narrates what is essentially a history of the present. Furthermore, several pivotal moments in the work's history resonate with those of other works dealing with closely related concerns. For instance, chapters 21–30 of *Flowers in a Sinful Sea* (which is to say, the final installment that Zeng completed before his death in 1935) were first published as a stand-alone volume in 1928, which happened to be the centennial anniversary of the first printed edition of Li Ruzhen's *Flowers in the Mirror*; and the initial serialization of the first twenty chapters of the work was completed in 1906, which happened to be the same year as the publication of Liang Qichao's (1873–1929) biography of Kang (which contained the first published version of Kang's advocacy of racial interbreeding).

Perhaps the most revealing historical coincidence, however, may be found in the *prehistory* of *Flowers in a Sinful Sea*. It turns out that Zeng originally got the idea for the work from a fellow author named Jin Song-cen (1874–1947), who first came up with the idea for a roman à clef centered on the figure of Sai. Before handing his outline of the projected sixty-chapter novel over to Zeng, Jin wrote drafts of the first six chapters, of which he published the first two, in 1903. That also happened to be the same year that Jin published a book-length treatise entitled *The Women's Bell*, which is regarded as the first major tract on women's rights in China. *The Women's Bell* recommends that women become more involved in national affairs, and that they be allowed to choose their marriage partners, have an education, and study and travel abroad. Writing on the very eve of the fall of the Qing dynasty and the establishment of the Republic of China, Jin finally made explicit the necessary linkage between women's liberation and national strengthening that Li Ruzhen's novel had prophetically anticipated nearly a century earlier.

To the extent that the structural forces that drive Melody Orchid from her home and Tang Ao from his homeland in *Flowers in the Mirror* figuratively anticipate the broader geopolitical conditions that will inspire several generations of late Qing Chinese intellectuals and politicians to look abroad for ways of addressing sociopolitical challenges back home, in Jin's 1903 manifesto—which could be translated more literally as "The Bell of the Women's World"—this process returns full circle, with the text's eloquent affirmation of the need for Chinese women to be *at home in the world*.

BIBLIOGRAPHY: Jin Tianhe, "The Women's Bell," trans. Michael Hill, in *The Birth of Chinese Feminism: Essential Texts in Transnational Theory*, ed. Lydia Liu, Rebecca Karl, and Dorothy Ko (New York, 2013), 207–286. Li Ju-chen, *Flowers in the Mirror*, trans. and ed. Lin Tai-yi (Berkeley, CA, 1965). Carlos Rojas, *The Naked Gaze: Reflections on Chinese Modernity* (Cambridge, MA, 2008), 54–81. David Der-wei Wang, *Fin-de-Siècle Splendor: Repressed Modernities of Late Qing Fiction, 1849–1911* (Stanford, CA, 1997), 53–117; Zeng Pu, *A Flower in a Sinful Sea*, trans. Rafe de Crespigny and Liu Ts'un-yan, in "Special Issue on Middlebrow Fiction," *Renditions* 17–18 (Spring / Autumn 1982): 137–187.

CARLOS ROJAS

1820 · BEIJING

"Mind's medicine, mind's brilliance are both the mind's disease."

Utter Disillusion and Acts of Repentance in Late Classical Poetry

Throughout the imperial period, serving in the civil bureaucracy was the only fully respectable profession for a male of the Chinese gentry. A finely graded hierarchy of status, with small rewards leading upward and small demerits leading downward, was China's gift to the world and the best way ever devised for a polity to control an adult male population, both granting them power over others and continually reminding them of the polity's ability to withdraw or diminish that power. The gateway to the bureaucracy was the civil service examination, in which there were always far more aspirants than successful examinees. For those who passed, loyalty to the system was sustained by a sea of failure around them; and for those who failed, they could, like lottery addicts, always try again.

Someone who failed the examination could decide to become a "recluse" (often temporary), hope to have his talents recognized by a more sympathetic examiner, or, more practically, build his social network to influence the outcome next time around. One was not supposed to respond with a howl of indignation that the universe was against him, as Meng Jiao (751–814) did in 792 or 793.

> Even eating sweet greens, my guts hurt;
> I force a song, there's no joy in the sound,
> as soon as I go out the door there's a stumbling block—
> who claims that Heaven and Earth are broad?

For this response Meng was censured for a millennium. As a Song critic complained, Meng's poetry "makes a person unhappy." From this we can infer what classical poetry was supposed to do.

Somewhat over a thousand years later, in 1820, the proportion of aspirants to successful examinees was vastly greater, with a large male elite population stalled at various stages in a more complex hierarchy of examinations. Even the *jinshi*, the main civil service examination, was not enough; for a good entry-level position in the bureaucratic hierarchy, one needed to pass the palace examination. Moreover, the content of the examination had become such that one could be too intelligent to even hope to pass.

Gong Zizhen's (1792–1841) maternal grandfather had told him to do something serious with his life—such as becoming a classical philologist, as his grandfather himself was—and not to spend time on literature. Gong wanted to change the world, but in the vast ocean of underemployed male intellectuals in early nineteenth-century China, his chances of having even a feather's worth of impact on the tottering Qing polity were very small indeed. After an 1820 failure, Gong would eventually pass the exam in 1829 at the age of thirty-eight, but, not succeeding in the palace examination, he would continue his disaffection in a sinecure in the cabinet. Like so many in his time, he fed off a system that had nothing meaningful for him to do.

He proposed "reforms," from making the Western Territories (now Xinjiang) into a province to restoring some dignity to officialdom in the imperial system. But more profound than his political agenda, we see in his work and in the work of some of his contemporaries a sense that something was more fundamentally wrong with Chinese society and the Chinese polity than could be fixed by a change of dynasties or a return to the moral standards of antiquity. The old values no longer held, and once you could see outside that structure of old values, you could never go back. For such writers the essential condition of writing in the classical language was irony. In Charles Baudelaire's "L'Heautontimoroumenos" (The self-tormentor) of 1855, the French poet speaks in the voice of a Roman dramatist. Although Baudelaire writes the poem in French, he conveys what the Roman writer feels while writing in Latin:

> Ne suis-je pas un faux accord
> Dans la divine symphonie,
> Grâce à la vorace Ironie
> Qui me secoue et qui me mord?
>
> Am I not a dissonance
> In the divine symphony,
> Thanks to voracious Irony
> who helps me and bites me?

The poet invokes the "divine symphony" to place himself as a dissonance within it; he needs an imagined world of "healthy" values in which to be the disease. Baudelaire is also the most common European poet with which to begin the standard narrative of literary "modernism."

After this examination failure, Gong wrote two poems, entitled "Act of Repentance" and "Another Act of Repentance." Since he is repenting his writing, to do so twice in writing is a noteworthy redundancy. Later in his life he would repeatedly "renounce poetry" with an ironic awareness that he was subverting his vow in the very act of making it.

"Another Act of Repentance"

> The Buddha tells of kalpa fires
>   that melt everything away,
> what is it then that like breakers
>   rages a thousand years?
> In essays on making the government work
>   I polish the daylight away,
> hidden flashes of uncontrolled wit
>   come back in the middle of night.

It comes in such a surging flood
   I have to swing my sword,
it goes away still hanging on,
   one could play it on the flute.
Mind's medicine, mind's brilliance
   are both the mind's disease—
I'm determined to take all my parables
   and burn them in the lamp.

"An act of repentance" is a Buddhist term that loses little in translation: it is acknowledging transgression and openly repenting. A strange repentance it is, opening with the kalpa fires that burn the earth bare at the end of a Buddhist eon, reminding the believer of the meaninglessness in all the striving, pains, and joys of life. Gong cancels even that lesson with the raging of the mind that outlasts the kalpa and will not subside.

When serving as an official, much of what one did to "make the government work" was writing. Not serving, one wrote to persuade others how to make the government work and to demonstrate that the writer had the political talent to do so if given the opportunity. If those writings were unrecognized or unheeded, as Gong's writings were, there was a stock set of responses: despair, withdrawal, or rage. Gong was indeed a brilliant, if eccentric, writer of political prose. But he sees those writings not in terms of their supposed purpose, but as the mere traces of the restless mind, a passion without real object that consumes his days and will not let him rest at night. They are his opium, both the medicine for the brilliant, restless mind and the disease itself. With his favorite figures, the sword and the flute, he describes writing as a seizure that comes with violence, turning into music and trailing away.

The "act of repentance" of the title is not only a purely Buddhist term, it is also a level of Buddhism that was far from the Buddhism popular among intellectuals. Yet in repentance he describes his obsession with writing and his pleasure in his own intelligence with such gusto that it is hard to see "repentance." His only solution is to burn his writings, but he saved so much of his work before 1820, it is equally hard to credit any claim of ascesis here. But even if he had burned it all, he has left this brilliant poem to index the loss. Almost every statement in the poem cancels itself out. This is a poem *in* the classical language, but it is not "classical poetry" anymore. He too is Baudelaire's "self-tormentor," who is both "the blade and the wound."

Is writing to help the nation all vanity, or serious intention, or self-gratifying pleasure in writing? This is Baudelaire's "irony"—you can't believe anything in particular, because you know too many things are true. By his own account and the accounts of others, Gong was a brilliant political writer, a serious classical scholar, a Buddhist at heart, a disappointed aspirant to office, and a lover (whose death, in the popular imagination, was improbably tied to an affair with a Manchu poetess who was the concubine of a Qing prince of the blood). He is so many characters—all strangely unified in his poetry—that he is no one in particular. He was thought of as a "madman," but a sharply intelligent irony is a disability for the Chinese category *kuang*, involuntary, eccentric excess—imperfectly translated as "madman."

China has strict dates for the "recent" (*jindai*, marked by the outbreak of the Opium Wars in 1839) and the "modern" (*xiandai*, following the student movement of May 4, 1919). Gong is not allowed to belong to either—though he is permitted to "anticipate." His is writing in the old classical language, but he no longer belongs to the world of that language. We can recognize in him a basic split in subsequent literature in the classical language: it tends to be either banal nostalgia, pretending everything is still the same, or ironic, writing in between an old language, with its baggage of values and self-imposed restrictions, and a new intellectual world. In 1820 the social and material world had not yet changed, but the intellectual world—the range of what one could think and say—had changed profoundly. One of the tasks of "modern" poetry may be to say what cannot be said. We should recall that Baudelaire, taken by many as the icon of the "modern" poet, wrote in perfect classical forms of what those forms could not contain.

We could tell an alternative story of Chinese poetic modernity here. It begins in a profound rift between the literary language, with its oppressive legacy, and a new intellectual world. It is *not* "classical poetry" any longer; like Baudelaire's work, it is poetry in a classical language that is increasingly not "at home" anymore. In such a story "modernity" is not the new intellectual world itself but the rift between received literary language and the world it fails to represent. In this story of modernity, the new vernacular poetry that appeared a century later was the attempt to heal the rift by instituting a new language for poetry. Let me suggest that this vernacular poetry too became great only in failing to heal the rift.

The vast majority of poems in the classical language after 1820 are banal—but most poems later in the vernacular "new poetry" are also banal, not just in Chinese but in every literature. Modernity is less tolerant of mere accomplishment than traditional poetry. Poetic modernity is not a form or a register of language any more than it is a particular date: it is a changed relation to the world and to the language through which the world is represented.

BIBLIOGRAPHY: Gong Zizhen, *Gong Zizhen quanji* (Shanghai, 1975). Fan Kezheng, *Gong Zizhen nianpu kaolue* (Beijing, 2004). Shirleen S. Wong, *Kung Tzu-chen* (Boston, 1975).

STEPHEN OWEN

1843 · THE SECOND HALF OF JUNE

"We have always followed one path—when will it lead to glory?"

In Search of a Chinese Utopia: The Taiping Rebellion as a Literary Event

In the second half of June 1843, a young man from a Guangxi peasant family, Hong Xiuquan (1814–1864), had a sword cast with his name engraved on it. Eight years later, Hong would become the Heavenly King of the Taiping Tianguo (1851–1864), or Taiping Heavenly Kingdom, the first Christian-utopian political entity in Chinese history. In having the sword cast, Hong re-created a famous historical episode concerning the founder of the Han dynasty (206 BCE–220 CE), Liu Bang (247–195 BCE), who also rose from humble origins. In this episode, Liu and his followers were crossing a swamp and came across a large serpent lying in their path. Refusing to turn back, Liu slashed the serpent in half with his sword. Beginning with Sima Qian's (135?–86 BCE) related entry in *Records of the Grand Historian*, the event has been interpreted as Liu, the son of the Red Emperor, defeating the son of the White Emperor, who had assumed the form of the serpent. By the late imperial period, this story had been adapted into a frequently staged play, wherein Liu is represented as the inheritor of the Mandate of Heaven.

The similar record concerning Hong is preserved in the account of a Swedish missionary, Theodore Hamberg (1819–1854), who heard the story from Hong Ren'gan (1822–1864), Hong Xiuquan's cousin and the second most important leader of the Heavenly Kingdom. Was Hong Xiuquan consciously emulating Liu, the Gaozu Emperor? In 1848, when Feng Yunshan (1822–1852), an important leader of the Taiping movement, was imprisoned on charges of plotting a rebellion in religious disguise, Hong wrote this line to express his agony and longing: "We have always followed one path—when will it lead to glory?" In this five-character poem, which stylistically imitates the famous "Song of the Great Wind," allegedly composed by Liu, Hong further demonstrated a perceived connection to his historical role model.

The evil serpent, the sacred sword, and heavenly glorification are the foundational pillars of the world Hong envisioned. In 1837, like the majority of examinees, Hong failed the provincial civil service examination. After this fourth failure, he experienced a nervous breakdown and had a series of bizarre dreams. A decade later, he published his dreams. In one of them, angels received him in heaven and led him to the Heavenly Father, that is, the Supreme Lord and Great God, and the Heavenly Elder Brother, Christ. The Heavenly Father bestowed on him a sword and a golden seal so that he might chase the demonic serpent out of heaven. Hong successfully accomplished this mission. He then returned to the highest level of heaven and enjoyed the company of his Heavenly Family in the celestial realm until the Heavenly Father sent him down to awaken the people on earth. In reality, Hong's mental breakdown lasted for forty days, after which he gradually recovered and returned to his daily routine, teaching and preparing for the next examination.

However, six years later, in 1843, an accidental rereading of a pamphlet he owned brought him great turmoil, and this time the turbulence extended to the entirety of China and beyond. As a result of this experience, Hong recalled the unusual dreams he had had years ago and came to the conclusion that he had been exposed to a cosmogony unknown in Chinese tradition. He believed he was God's second son sent down to earth, armed with the sacred sword, with a mission to drive the serpent demon, that is, the Manchu ruler, out of the human realm. Eventually, the

Taiping Rebellion he led evolved into one of the most destructive wars in human history, causing the loss of tens of millions lives.

During the mid-nineteenth century, natural disasters were prevalent in areas along the Yellow and Yangtze Rivers, and this already difficult situation was exploited and intensified by uprisings staged by local bandits and secret societies. The Qing government, however, was incapable of controlling such scenarios, mostly because of corruption and bureaucratic incompetence. By the end of the 1850s, the Qing government had lost two wars with Britain, but the conservative court was reluctant to make any substantial changes in order to face their Western challenger. In the Guangxi and Guangdong Provinces, where Hong and his Society of God Worshippers rose to prominence, things were further complicated by the conflict between the Hakka people and local residents, as well as by the proselytizing efforts of Western missionaries. Collectively, these conditions gave rise to the Taiping Rebellion.

The Taiping Rebellion was not only a political movement, but also a literary event. It generated countless literary possibilities, such as propaganda literature and political novels, as well as producing creative amalgamations of Chinese and Western sources that later served as inspiration for a uniquely Chinese vision of utopia. Eventually, this event amounted to a drastic shakeup of Chinese literary culture, particularly in terms of cultural production and ideological contestation, and anticipated twentieth-century China's forthcoming literary form, the political manifesto.

This literary event was facilitated, if not made possible, by the joined force of Western lithographic printing technology and traditional woodblock printing technology. The coexistence of these printing technologies in the nineteenth century brought about an ideological battle between Christianity and traditional Chinese systems of belief, such as Buddhism, Daoism, and Confucianism. Ever since Protestant missionaries' arrival in East Asia, despite the strict Qing ban on printing and disseminating Christian texts, they had actively printed pamphlets in Malacca and Singapore with lithographic printing technology. They then transported and disseminated the pamphlets in coastal provinces such as Guangdong. One of the texts they produced—*Good Words to Admonish the World*, written by the first Chinese evangelist, Liang Fa (aka Liang Afa) (1789–1855)—served as an inspiration for Hong and his Taiping Heavenly Kingdom. During their rebellion, the Taiping troops captured the city of Nanjing, one of the printing centers in late imperial China. Because the woodblock printing required only a limited amount of expertise and capital to operate, Hong immediately began printing Taiping propaganda and disseminating the texts on a large scale. Meanwhile, he issued decrees to destroy Confucian, Buddhist, and Daoist texts and forbid their printing. As the military forces of the Qing government and the Taiping rebels gained and lost control over local counties in turn, the rebellion simultaneously generated a cycle of printing and destroying propaganda. This cycle was further intensified by local gentries and elites, who took it upon themselves to also print and spread traditional orthodox religious beliefs, like those of Confucianism and Buddhism, as a means of resisting Taiping ideology.

Despite the resilience of indigenous religious beliefs, Taiping ideology swayed many with its powerful message, in some ways foreshadowing the overthrow of the Qing dynasty at the turn of the twentieth century. Although nineteenth-century Protestant missionaries primarily preached among commoners, their transmission of the Bible was awkward and their communication with the masses hindered by cultural and linguistic barriers. Their Chinese peers, such as Liang, also did not succeed in making Christian messages more accessible to ordinary people. Compared with the preachers of orthodox Christianity, the Taiping rebels used colloquial language and vivid visual descriptions of the celestial realm as a routine part of their religious discourse. In turn, they created a Chinese brand of utopia, a strategy that appealed to both the illiterate and the semiliterate.

The case in point is the founding document of the Taiping movement, the *Taiping Heavenly Chronicle*. In this piece, Hong borrows his style from the Old and New Testaments, particularly the book of Revelation, to create a mystical aura and a dynamic narrative flow. But the Taiping discourse is also suffused with symbols derived from the discourse of popular imagination that permeates Chinese vernacular literature and popular religion. Such an intuitive appropriation of traditional tropes and images sugarcoats Christianity, presenting it as less foreign and even approachable. In the *Chronicle*, the mise-en-scène of the heavenly battle is reminiscent of those struggles between figures claiming supernatural powers in works of Chinese vernacular fiction, such as *The Investiture of the Gods* and *Journey to the West*. The seal in the *Chronicle*, unlike the ones symbolizing the disasters to befall humanity in the book of Revelation, is represented as the talisman that exorcises evil, just like the magical weapons used to vanquish demons in Chinese popular culture.

Other critical symbols in the *Chronicle* are the serpent, named Yanluo, and the Dragon Demon of the Eastern Sea, both names curiously derived from popular religion and folkloric tradition. In Chinese mythology and history, the serpent is sometimes referred to as a "small dragon"; it symbolizes imperial power and embodies the Mandate of Heaven. In the Christian tradition, however, the serpent is commonly perceived as an incarnation of the devil that seduces Adam and Eve, degrading them from celestial residents to sinful outcasts. Hong identifies with the Christian tradition and goes even further to portray the serpent as a full-fledged character with emotions and schemes of his own. However, Hong's heavenly battle with the Satan-cum-serpent brings to mind the story of Liu's slaying the serpent and claiming the Mandate of Heaven. By combining the symbolic value of the serpent from both traditions, Hong attempts to claim legitimacy according to both the imported Christian idea of Satan and the Confucian concept of the Mandate of Heaven.

Although Hong negates the validity of Confucianism outright, his writings imply that he should assume authority based on the Confucian concept of the Mandate of Heaven, as well as ethical principles such as loyalty and filial piety. In the *Chronicle*, one episode can be read as an allegory of the overall place of Confucianism in Taiping ideology. On the highest level of heaven, God shows his son, Hong, the Old Testament, the New Testament, and the Confucian classics. He tells Hong that the Confucian classics are full of mistakes and perpetuate malicious thoughts in the human realm. Confucius, terrified and speechless, is lashed and forbidden to enter into the human realm forever. Curiously, despite the harmful thoughts Confucius spreads, he is not demonized but pardoned because of his potential to rectify wrongs. As it turns out, in all Taiping propaganda, loyalty to the Heavenly King is closely connected with faith in God; obedience is lauded and doubt reprimanded. The earliest Taiping propaganda, such as the *Ballad to Investigate the Dao and Save the World* and *Admonishment to Investigate the Dao and Awaken the World*, forthrightly urges people to respect and take care of their elders, thus explicitly promoting filial piety.

Despite Hong's firm belief in Christianity, there is a fundamental chasm between his understanding of Christianity and its Western incarnations.

The core father-son relationship between God and Christ, from which Hong also derives his legitimacy, is formally approximate to the kinship ties upheld by Confucian discourse. Clearly, Hong's understanding of this relationship diverges from the Christian theological notion of the Trinity, which defines God as three consubstantial manifestations: the Father, the Son, and the Holy Spirit. The concept of the Trinity, indeed, was beyond Hong's grasp because he received no guidance from the British missionary Issachar J. Roberts (1802–1871), who exposed him for the first time to the Old and New Testaments in 1847, and was mostly disconnected from Western missionaries since that time. In 1861, when challenged by a missionary traveling in the Taiping Heavenly Kingdom, Hong was outraged and vehemently contradicted the missionary. In his later years, as the Taiping Heavenly Kingdom was trapped in successive wars against the Qing military forces, Hong spent an increasing amount of time inside the palace compound to study the Old and New Testaments; he was comparing the "proper" Christian content to Confucian standards while at the same time deleting content related to Confucianism from previously published articles of propaganda. Such a redacted Taiping ideology, however, failed to constitute an effective discourse for stabilizing the Taiping Heavenly Kingdom. The glamour of the Kingdom receded as its realm was tainted by ceaseless war and haunted by the ghosts of those killed in battles. Nevertheless, drawing from Western inspiration, Hong invented a new discourse of utopia that diverged from all previous utopian visions in the Chinese tradition, anticipating the future utopian discourses to appear in modern China, all of which would feature a mixture of Western and traditional Chinese ideologies.

"We have always followed one path—when will it lead to glory?"

BIBLIOGRAPHY: Theodore Hamberg, *Taiping tianguo qiyi ji*, trans. Jian Youwen (Beijing, 1935). Luo Ergang, *Taiping tianguo shi congkao* (Shanghai, 1992). Sima Qian, *Shi ji* (Beijing, 2013). Jonathan D. Spence, *God's Chinese Son: The Taiping Heavenly Kingdom of Hong Xiuquan* (New York, 1996). Taiping tiangguo lishi bowuguan [Taiping Heavenly Kingdom History Museum], ed., *Taiping tianguo yinshu* (Nanjing, 1979).

HUAN JIN

1847 · JANUARY 4

"What am I going to do with my education?"

My Life in China and America *and Transpacific Translations*

On January 4, 1847, a young man named Yung Wing (1828–1912) from southern China boarded the *Huntress* at Guangzhou's Whampoa Port to follow his teacher, an American priest, to the United States. The ship first sailed southwest through the Cape of Good Hope to reach the Island of Saint Helena, then northwest to New York. From there he took the train to New Haven, Connecticut, where eight years later he would become the first Chinese to graduate from Yale University. While on the *Huntress*, he could not have known what this journey would mean for himself and his country, nor could he foresee that his work and life would hinge on the transpacific translations of ideas and institutions, a truth to which his autobiography would later attest.

In homage to the first students who crossed the Pacific, Ha Jin (1956–), following their paths more than a century later, writes,

> None of them knew
> That this was just a beginning—
> That their children would travel
> The same seas.

Indeed, Yung and his followers were the first of many to come, bearing the burden of China's modern transformation—as their extraordinary journeys and struggles became ordinary tales of diaspora, modernity, nationalism, and globalization—and pushing modern Chinese literary history beyond its putative borders.

With the support of kindhearted missionaries in New England, Yung received a solid humanist education. He was expected to apply his education to the service of God in China. His notion of service, however, was not limited to the evangelical kind. "What am I going to do with my education?" he asked. Intending his Yale education to bring radical social change in China, Yung instead wished to serve China by making Western education available to Chinese, to make China regenerated, enlightened, and powerful.

But China was not so easily changed, especially in the 1850s and 1860s, when the Qing government held fast to traditional values and knew little about the West. Thus, Yung's first challenge was how to render his diploma meaningful. He told his mother that Yale is "one of the leading colleges in the United States" and that the AB degree he graduated with is analogous to the Chinese title of *xiucai,* one of the titles awarded to successful candidates in the imperial civil service examination. The need for this kind of translation reflects the lack of East-West communications at the time. Consequently, his employment prospects were limited to serving as a translator in the treaty ports, a job he did not relish. Though reluctant, he worked as a translator on many occasions—including translating obituaries at one point—just to make ends meet, but it was also this experience that made Yung realize the need for greater cross-cultural education and communication.

The turning point came in 1863, when Viceroy Zeng Guofan (1811–1872), the most powerful politician in China at the time, recruited Yung into the modernization movement and honored him with his first official title. Nonetheless, it was not until he was assigned—again as a translator—to settle compensations for the Tianjin Massacre of 1870, in which French missionaries were killed by Chinese mobs, that his plan of establishing the Chinese educational mission received a hearing. In desperate need of talents familiar with Western ideas and practices, the Qing government finally approved his proposal in 1872 and sent the first contingent of thirty young male students—between the tender ages of twelve and fifteen—to study in America. Three more groups followed before the mission was aborted in 1881, but that would not hold off the student migration for long. After the civil service examination system was abolished in 1905 and the Qing dynasty toppled in 1911, the tide of Western learning breached the Great Wall of China, and student migration to the West became unstoppable. Yung thus became known as a model modern Chinese intellectual, patriotic and cosmopolitan, while hailed, on the other side of the Pacific, as an Asian American founding father for breaking ground on the racial frontiers and forging a transpacific career.

The story of Yung's life—including his interracial marriage, his investigation of the Chinese coolies in Peru, his sojourn in Taiwan, and his participation in the Hundred-Day Reform of 1898—is documented in his autobiography, *My Life in China and America,* written in English and published in New York in 1909. Of particular importance in this narrative is his aptitude for American culture, devout sense of patriotism, and the disappointing end of the educational mission in 1881. On the surface, the mission was terminated because Chinese students were denied admission to the military and naval academies in West Point and Annapolis, a rejection that infringed upon the privileges granted to Chinese citizens by the Burlingame Treaty of 1868 and were later formally annulled by the passage of the Chinese Exclusion Act in 1882. The more fundamental reason, however, is that conservative Chinese officials worried that the students had been so westernized that they had become "fake foreign devils"—rebellious and disrespectful of Chinese rules and customs. Their concern was well founded. Yung believed that the core of Western learning was not its machinery and science, but the potential of its liberal education to remold the minds of the Chinese people. Despite his efforts to save the mission by enlisting American supporters to write a public letter of protest, the program was ultimately terminated, leaving faint memories and a few students stranded in the United States. The resulting feelings of disappointment and hurt, conjured by racism, conservatism, and cross-cultural misunderstanding, became the unfortunate themes of Yung's life and time, and a lesson that students after him would continue to ponder.

Except for a handful of friends, *My Life in China and America* went unnoticed in the United States for nearly a century, until Asian American scholars rediscovered it in the 1990s with notable ambivalence. Frank Chin (1940–) interpreted the text as a form of confessional writing and evidence of a "racist love" that compromises Chinese American subjectivity. Amy Ling (1939–1999) also criticized the book for conforming to white tastes. Later scholars, however, reclaimed the work as a "recovered legacy" of Asian America, translating Yung's Chinese patriotism and elite education into a form of antiracist masculinity and resistance, despite his obvious signs of assimilation. As its varied reception indicates, it is a book that is both hated and loved for its transcultural and transnational qualities.

In China and Taiwan, the book has experienced a more treacherous afterlife. Translated by Xu Fengshi and edited by Yun Tieqiao (1878–1935) into vernacular Chinese, *My Life in China and America* made its Chinese debut in 1915 when published in the popular literary journal *Short Story*

Monthly under the title *Xixue dongjianji*, literally meaning "A chronicle of Western learning advancing east." The translation is identified as the "self-narrative of Mr. Rong Chunfu" and was published in eight installments from January to August that year. That the text was placed in the fiction section indicates a very loose definition of fiction in the early Republican era. Framing the text as fiction also shows a nativizing tactic of translation popular in *Short Story Monthly* that seeks to make translation appear to have been written in Chinese. While a photo of Yung is attached to authenticate the narrative, the editor and translator conveniently omitted the preface and the appendix to facilitate the allegorical readings suggested by the Chinese title. Although an unfaithful rendition, the title *A Chronicle of Western Learning Advancing East* accentuated the zeitgeist of the time and "translated" the text from a self-narrative into the national narrative of China's quest for modernity in the West.

In 1915, the Commercial Press also printed the translated text as a single volume. Like its English counterpart, however, the Chinese edition also faded from people's memories. Between the 1910s and 1940s, China was mired in a series of civil wars, increasing social unrest, and foreign invasion, an era when Western-educated students ceased to be a novelty and played crucial roles in China's transformation. The text went unnoted in China after 1949, but it was twice reprinted in Taiwan in the 1960s, although it only received scant attention. It was not until 1981, when Zhong Shuhe (1931–) included the text in an important book series called From East to West: Chinese Travelers before 1911, that *A Chronicle of Western Learning Advancing East* received its due attention and Yung was elevated to the status of Liang Qichao (1873–1929).

The text has since been considered a pioneering work that documents the "peaceful rise" of a modern and global China. Zhong Shuhe explains, "[Yung Wing's] life is worthy of our remembering, for his is the life of a first generation, Western-educated Chinese intellectual dedicated to the modernization of China." During the 1960s, however, it was the same accomplishments that caused Yung to be criticized as an "accomplice of Western imperialism" because he intended "radical, wholesale, capitalist transformation" for China. Yung's reputation was once more revised in 1978, and he has since been hailed as a model patriotic intellectual, bravely standing at the crossroads of East and West and exploring means for national survival. These later invocations of Yung's legacy resonate with contemporary discourse on Chinese modernity, as defined by China's "linking up with the world," and are indicative of the advent of a new era in Chinese history, one where the West ceases to be the enemy and the diaspora becomes a projection of China's global nature.

As a result of his posthumous rise to fame, two vernacular translations of *A Chronicle of Western Learning Advancing East* appeared in 1991 and 2003 under titles more faithful to their English source. An annotated version that included the introduction and commentaries was also published in 1998. At the same time, an increasing number of studies and biographies, abridged and elaborate, appeared during the first decade of the twenty-first century, and explored his influence on the modernization of China's education, finance, and "national revival." Moreover, his hometown, Zhuhai, initiated a campaign to celebrate southern China's links to the West and the Chinese diaspora by building a memorial, a museum, and several schools, all in Yung's name. This interest in Yung, in the meantime, also generated a renewed interest in the Chinese educational mission and resulted in several related publications and documentaries, most notable of which is the 2004 five-episode documentary called *Youtong* (Boy students) commissioned by China Central Television. This Yung fever in the new millennium is possible because his visions remain appealing to Chinese faced with a neoliberal and globalized world, and appropriable for nationalists who are invested in the fantasy of patriotism and the mandate of China's rise to global authority.

However, despite its resurgence and historical importance, *A Chronicle of Western Learning Advancing East* has yet to be inducted into the pantheon of modern Chinese literature, even when more obscure texts—such as Chen Hengze's (1890–1976) "One Day" and Qiu Jin's (1875–1907) *Jingwei Stone*—have been recuperated by the feminist scholarship that has made headway in the study of Chinese autobiography. The truth is that insofar as modern Chinese literature is confined to the May Fourth imagination that, though informed by translation, doggedly focuses on "Chinese vernacular production," *A Chronicle of Western Learning Advancing East* would be an unlikely candidate. Even though it could be read as one of the earliest modern Chinese autobiographies, such as Liang Qichao's *Self-Narrative at Thirty*, or as one of the first examples of "overseas student literature" with a lineage traceable to such obscure late Qing popular fictions as *The New Story of the Stone* and *The Bitter Student*, *A Chronicle of Western Learning Advancing East* is by definition *not* a vernacular literary production, but a work of translation. For May Fourth intellectuals, the idea to regard a translated text, even though it was written by a Chinese, as representative of the national culture would be simply uncanny.

For this precise reason, *A Chronicle of Western Learning Advancing East* poses several critical questions for our conception of modern Chinese literature. As a transpacific translated text, it not only reminds us of the role translation plays in the formation of modern Chinese literature, but also suggests the transpacific context of racism and imperialism behind it. That it was once considered fictional, yet often read for its historical value, suggests that we have not come to terms with its performative characters and allegorical politics. Its reemergence in the age of neoliberal globalization, in addition, compels us to reconsider the meaning of "overseas student writing" as an ironic expression of the Chinese obsession with the West, particularly the United States, as a land of opportunity and a racist country. In effect, that Yung ended up staying in New England foreshadows the intersection of overseas student literature with narratives of assimilation and diaspora, thus expanding the territory of modern Chinese literature and bringing back the question of intellectual independence that Hu Shi (1891–1962) discussed in his "Treatise against Studying Abroad." The implication of Yung's life in translation must be grasped in these trying contexts.

Surely, even on his deathbed at home in Hartford, Connecticut, in 1912, Yung would not have foreseen the fall and rise of his homeland, nor would he have imagined that his life in translation would become an allegory of Chinese modernity. As a transnational patriot, he rests in peace on the frontiers of China and America, neither as an outcast nor as an exile, but as a forerunner of transpacific dreams, where norms are to be transgressed and culture hybridities embraced to construct a modernity that is at once national and global.

BIBLIOGRAPHY: Thomas LaFargue, *China's First Hundred* (Pullman, WA, 1942). Amy Ling, "Yan Phou Lee on the Asian American Frontier," in *Re / collecting Early Asian America: Essays in Cultural History*, ed. Josephine Lee, Imogene L. Lim, and Yuko Matsukawa (Philadelphia, 2002), 273–287. Edward J. M. Rhoads, "In the Shadow of Yung Wing: Zeng Laishun and the Chinese Educational Mission to the United States," *Pacific Historical Review* 74, no. 1 (2005): 19–58.

CHIH-MING WANG

1852

Jiang Shi returns from a short trip in south China.

1885

Huang Zunxian returns from an eight-year sojourn in Japan and the United States.

Two Chinese Poets Are Homeless at Home

Whose house was it by the river? A yellow ox was tied to the
    front gate.
An old woman stood outside,
Fingering the markings on the arm of a steelyard.
Standing next to her, a man was counting money,
Having set down his bamboo basket.
What was in the bamboo basket?
A fish flapping its red tail.
A dog came over, its tongue hanging out,
Its eyes peeking into the basket.
An old man was there, he knew what it wanted,
He beat the dog away, its barking scared the kids.
The kids began to cry and would not stop;
A peddler happened to come by, selling malt sugar.
The old man bought some and gave to the kids,
It was not much, the kids fought over it.
But soon enough they resumed playing,
One of them rode the dog along the wall.
He acted as if he were riding a horse,
Mouthing the cracking sound of a whip.
In a little while, the old man and woman disappeared,
The gate was closed, all was quiet.
The yellow ox vanished as well,
Though one could still hear it moo.
Suddenly the light of a lamp leaked out,
A bright flash like lightning.
The kids were called back into the house,

I knew the fish was done.
I was cooking dinner on the shore,
My heart had a lone clarity in the twilight.
I wrote down this scene and returned;
There was no need to speak of how I felt.

Thus wrote Jiang Shi (1818–1866), who, after a failed attempt to seek patronage, was returning home from Dangtu, a place less than two hundred miles from his hometown, Suzhou. His poem sketches a scene viewed from the river shore, where the poet moors his boat and prepares dinner on a campfire. Traditional Chinese poetics prizes the expression of feelings and advocates the aesthetics of "suffusing a scene with feelings"; and yet, Jiang explicitly separates scene from feelings by setting them apart in the last couplet of the poem. What are we to make of the scene? Supposedly "objective," matter-of-factly observed and recorded? Or, a scene that is so saturated with feelings that there is no need to speak of them further? The happenings are so mundane, even humdrum; but once they are captured on paper, they acquire an almost mystic quality. What in the scene strikes the poet so much that he has to reproduce those micro-events, step by step, in verse?

Jiang was born into a minor gentry family in Jiangsu, a scenic, sophisticated southeastern province. He tried his luck, like every male member of his social class, at the civil service examination more than once, but never passed. He spent most of his life traveling and eked out a living by seeking patronage through personal connections. In the last years of his life, he was caught up in the Taiping Rebellion (1850–1864), one of the largest civil wars in human history, an event that dealt a fatal blow to the already weakening Qing empire. In this poem written in 1852, however, the riverside family seems to live in perfect peace, interrupted only by the ox lowing, the dog barking, and the children crying or laughing.

Everything, everyone, begins with home. For Jiang, the man constantly on the move, the everyday scene of family life watched from the outside signifies an ideal and idealized home space that he could never enter: in the descending darkness, he is illuminated by the flash of light leaking out from the momentarily opened gate, but remains forever shut out. While each of the micro-events—buying fish, chasing away a food-eyeing dog, calling children to dinner, and so on—is so commonplace, their presentation as a narrative sequence accentuates the historical specificity of the happenings and endows them with a realness that is moving in its anonymity and ephemerality. There is a glint of irony in the description of the child riding the dog and pretending it is a horse: the child's implicit desire to go away and pursue a life of action and excitement is contrasted with the traveling poet's yearning for home as he endures the inconvenience of cooking his own dinner, companionless, on a campfire.

Writing in the boat, the poet is in between worlds: neither there nor here, his is a suspended existence. The home beckons, conferring a lone clarity in the twilight. In many ways, Jiang's poem sums up an age-old theme in classical Chinese poetry: the farming community and social class from which the elite traveler excludes himself and onto which he projects a romantic fantasy becomes a spiritual home and an object of eternal desire.

The "return" at the end of Jiang's poem contains a double reference: a return to his boat and a return home. There is little sense of the changing contexts of home here: reading it, one would hardly know that not only was the Qing empire teetering on the edge of downfall, but the traditional social order was also coming to an end, both in China and globally. What if, when one finally comes home, home is no longer the same as before? There is no place like home, but you cannot go home again.

> My family sat around a single lamp,
>   having an intimate chitchat;
> hidden behind the drawn curtains,
>   a door not yet closed.
> My little daughter caressed my beard,
>   asking me this and that;
> then she tugged at her mother's sleeves,
>   who had fallen silent.
> "The shining sun must be very close—
>   one can see it just by lifting one's head;
> you say the ocean is big, but what if
>   I cup it with both hands?"
> I was about to unroll the Earth map
>   and point at it for her to see—

a breeze slipped into the curtains,
    flames flickered, and a moth fell.

This poem, entitled "Little Daughter," was written by Huang Zunxian (1848–1905), arguably the last great poet of imperial China. Huang is often credited with launching a "poetic revolution," a phrase coined by Liang Qichao (1873–1929), an influential reformer and an admirer of Huang's just before the dawn of the twentieth century. Although Liang never applied the phrase directly to Huang's poetry, his description of Huang's poetry as having "opened up a new realm" is clearly in line with his vision of a "poetic revolution," which meant writing about new ideas with classical forms. In Huang's case, this would seem to refer to his poetic evocation of his extensive overseas experience as a diplomat.

Huang wrote "Little Daughter" in 1885, after he came home from an eight-year stay overseas as an attaché, first in Japan, then in San Francisco. Home exists, some would argue, only when it is left behind or lost. It certainly changes its meaning with displacement. Jiang is a passerby standing outside an enclosed family space envisioning and coveting the cooked fish within, much in the same way as the dog peers into the basket craving something it cannot have; Huang, however, writes from inside that family space, similarly delineated by lamplight, walls, and a door. The curtains are drawn to fend off any curious peeping, but the door is "not yet closed," leaving a crack, an opening into the intimate domestic sphere.

The poem is built around the tension between large and small, faraway and close at hand, home and abroad. The word "little" appears twice, once in the title and once in the poem, each time describing the poet's daughter. Her "littleness"—the Chinese word for it, like the English word, can indicate both size and age—is highlighted in her innocent question: "You say the ocean is big, but what if I cup it with *both* hands?" (italics added). The immensity of the ocean, accentuated by the little girl's lack of grasp of its size, becomes the spatial figure of the poet's prolonged absence from home and of his painful inability to communicate his experience to his family. He turns to a visual aid: a world map, literally an "Earth map," he has brought back with him. But his attempt to explain is interrupted: through the open door, a wind blows in and stirs the lamp flames, and a moth meets its fiery little death.

Like a sonnet, the Chinese regulated verse of which this poem is an excellent example has a fixed form: eight lines are divided into four couplets, with the two middle ones being parallel couplets. Each couplet is a unit of meaning; the two lines of a parallel couplet in particular bounce off against, intersect with, and supplement each other. The third couplet of Huang's poem first tackles the issue of space on a cosmic level and in vertical terms, as the girl gauges the distance between Earth and Sun by appealing to vision (whatever the eyes can see must be nearby); then, the next line returns to Earth and horizontal expanse. In both lines space is measured by human body parts—raising head, spreading hands—as was often the case in many premodern societies; but the vastness of the space being measured makes the situation poignantly ironic.

The play with Sun and Earth, the universe and the human world, as well as with the contrast between big and small, is echoed in the last couplet of the poem. The girl's faith in her sight and hands is set against the poet's futile desire to demonstrate the size of the ocean by pointing at the "Earth map" with *his* hand for her to see: futile, both because the dead moth distracts the girl and because the dimensions of a map are so diminutive that they might be more confusing than helpful.

Only twenty years before Huang wrote this poem, the Chinese minister of defense had remarked with indignation, "How could there possibly be so many countries in the world? When you think about it, there are no more than two or three. One day they call themselves England, the next day they call themselves Italy, and the next day they call themselves Sweden—all just to deceive China!" By the late nineteenth century, however, few educated Chinese would still harbor the delusion that other countries were of little importance. For them the world had expanded infinitely. The family home depicted in Huang's poem becomes an allegory of the home country, which, to the traveler who has seen the world, seems to have grown smaller. The man is changed by his journey, and to the changed man, home is both the same and not quite the same.

Each poem discussed in this essay contains an image of violence: the cooked fish, the burned moth. The survival of human society depends on violence done to nature, and the commercial exchange with which Jiang's poem commences embodies the necessary social and economic intercourse, much like the poet's travels themselves, carried out throughout the empire. The moth's death is, however, a random, futile, almost superfluous occurrence, a luxurious detail in a compact verse form with only fifty-six characters in total; it is also an image that gives the poem its power.

Evolutionary criticism attributes the universal fascination across cultures with lyric poetry to, among other things, the human mind's propensity to "play with pattern." All great poems present an intricate conclave of patterns: verbal, structural, and emotional. One of the patterns of Huang's poem is established in the image of an illuminated space that is enclosed by drawn curtains and surrounded by the dark night, an image that occurs at the beginning and end of the poem. But this is not a closed space: the outside world, in the figure of the wind, intrudes and creates a mini-scene of disruption, chaos, and death. If, as suggested by Brian Boyd, that attention is "a prime concern in any art" and "poetry makes a unique appeal to attention," attention in this poem becomes a motif because it is radically diverted in the last line on two levels: the girl's attention within the poem, the reader's without. By shifting from one visual image (a world map) to another (a dead moth), the poet juxtaposes them in an unexpected, jarring way: the large and small, global and local, have never been drawn together so dramatically and given such rich play.

In the poem, the poet finds himself caught between the intriguing silence of the wife on one side and the chattering of his little daughter on the other. While Jiang may still cherish the illusion of going home, Huang is already at home, but he no longer feels at home there—"homeless at home," as his contemporary Emily Dickinson (1830–1886) would say. His dilemma is the dilemma of China on the brink of the modern age, a dilemma he articulates most eloquently in his poetry: how to negotiate the differences between home and abroad, how to speak of, and speak to, the brave new world.

BIBLIOGRAPHY: Brian Boyd, *Why Lyrics Last: Evolution, Cognition, and Shakespeare's Sonnets* (Cambridge, MA, 2012). Huang Zunxian, *Renjing lu shi cao jianzhu* (Shanghai, 1981). Jiang Shi, *Fuyu yang shilu* (Shanghai, 2008). Liang Qichao, *Yinbing shi shihua* (Beijing, 1959). J. D. Schmidt, *Within the Human Realm: The Poetry of Huang Zunxian, 1848–1905* (Cambridge, 1994). Xiaofei Tian, *Visionary Journeys: Travel Writings from Early Medieval and Nineteenth-Century China* (Cambridge, MA, 2011).

XIAOFEI TIAN

1853

> *Quell the Bandits* is published and quickly banned by the censors of the Taiping Heavenly Kingdom.

Foreign Devils, Chinese Sorcerers, and the Politics of Literary Anachronism

Few novels from mid-nineteenth-century China can compare with *Quell the Bandits* in their impact on the politics of the time. First published in 1853, the novel was meant to be a sequel to *Water Margin*, a sixteenth-century saga about an eleventh-century rebellion against the Song dynasty. *Water Margin* chronicles 108 Robin Hood–like heroes and heroines who, based in the marshes of Liangshan, fought for their own cause of romantic fraternity in defiance of the imperial call for law and order. Although among the most popular works of fiction in early modern China, the novel was also condemned from time to time for spreading treasonous thought. *Quell the Bandits* owed much to *Water Margin*, but it sought to repudiate the "bandit ideology" of the magnum opus—its heroes and heroines rise to serve the Song court and succeed in eliminating the Liangshan rebels of *Water Margin*.

Because of its orthodox agenda, *Quell the Bandits* became a contested text during the Taiping Rebellion. When the rebellion broke out in 1850, Qing officials in Nanjing were already planning to publish *Quell the Bandits* for propaganda purposes. When Nanjing fell to the Taiping troops in 1853, these officials fled to Suzhou with the galleys of the novel and had it published there. Officials in Guangzhou soon published another edition. In 1860, the Taiping general Li Xiucheng (1823–1864) took Suzhou and ordered all copies of *Quell the Bandits* to be confiscated and its galleys destroyed. The novel was republished in 1871, and later banned again during the first decades of the People's Republic of China for being a politically incorrect national allegory.

Its tendentious conservatism aside, *Quell the Bandits* addresses a range of issues—from ideology to its disavowal, from propaganda to censorship—that became the central concerns for politically engaged writers in the twentieth century. In this way, the novel anticipates the rise of the modern Chinese political novel.

One layer of politics within *Quell the Bandits* is particularly intriguing—namely, the politics of anachronism in terms of both dynastic periodizations and conceptual paradigms. Although set in eleventh-century China, *Quell the Bandits* clearly refers to the crisis of nineteenth-century China, which culminated with the Taiping Rebellion. Contrary to the thesis of its sixteenth-century predecessor *Water Margin*, which advocates "bandit" loyalty as an alternative ideology to the imperial mandate, *Quell the Bandits* advocates unconditional loyalty to the imperial court. More intriguingly, in the aftermath of the first Opium War (1839–1842), at a time when world geography, Western scientific information, and military technologies were being introduced to China, the novel sought to mix recently acquired Western epistemology with ancient Daoist beliefs, historical saga with supernatural fantasy.

The author of *Quell the Bandits* is Yu Wanchun (1794–1849), a Confucian scholar by training who nevertheless took great interest in Daoist teachings. The novel, according to Yu, was inspired by a dream he had at thirteen of the immortal Thunderbolt General. Yu never took any office, but in his youth he assisted his father, then a local official of Guangdong, in several crackdowns on tribal rebellions. He also volunteered to serve as a strategist during the first Opium War. Thanks to his experience in Guangdong, one of the earliest gathering places of foreigners in China, Yu appeared quite open to Western innovations. His predilection for new military technology and martial arts resulted in two books on battle strategy and weaponry.

Yu's fascination with new military technology was an integral part of the ethos of the 1840s. Insofar as it echoes post–Opium War calls for reform, *Quell the Bandits* can be aligned with such enlightened, intellectual treatises as Xu Jiyu's (1795–1873) *A General Study of the World* (1848) and Wei Yuan's (1794–1857) *A Military History of the High Qing* (1842) and *Illustrated Treatise on the Maritime Nations* (1844). In particular, Wei's two works, one commemorating the military glories of the early Qing and the other introducing world geography and advanced technology, opened up new spatial and conceptual horizons, thereby facilitating the first stage of late Qing modernization. Wei's response to the challenge from the West has been crystallized into two famous dictums: "Use foreign strength to subdue foreigners; use foreigners to deal with foreigners," and "Learn from the foreigners so as to subdue the foreigners."

Unlike his peers who expressed their concerns by means of political treatise, Yu found in narrative fiction a more viable medium to engage national crises. To that end he anticipates late Qing promoters of a "Fiction Revolution," such as Yan Fu (1854–1921) and Liang Qichao (1873–1929), by fifty years. Through rewriting *Water Margin,* Yu sought to create a space where different political beliefs, timelines, and fantastic modes of narrative are brought into play. Critics have faulted *Quell the Bandits* for its blatant anachronism. Close reading reveals nevertheless that, precisely because of the radical clashes of historical causes and values, the novel creates a series of cracks through which a new sense of time, later named "modern," arose in the late Qing zeitgeist.

This strategy of anachronism is particularly evident in one specific episode of *Quell the Bandits.* In chapter 113, the Liangshan rebels suffer a major setback. As the leaders are anxiously reorganizing their troops, a foreigner by the name of Byerwhalham is recommended to them. A native of the country of Atlantic Europa, Byerwhalham is of medium height, with green eyes, blond hair, pinkish complexion, and deep features, "looking just like the foreign devils in Western paintings." This foreign devil specializes in designing and manufacturing military weapons, a skill he acquired from his father, the famous military technician Liyanili. Of Byerwhalham's new products, the most remarkable is his *se'e'ertuxi,* or "galloping thunder wagon."

Shaped like a monster, the "galloping thunder wagon" functions like a three-story mobile assault tower. On the top level of the wagon are two cannons, which can fire through the two eyes of the monster-shaped wagon. Soldiers on the middle level fight with crossbows through the mouth part of the monster / wagon, while those on the lower level fight with hooks and lances. Moreover, its wheels are all connected with an intricate spring mechanism so they can adjust to the roughest road. Were it not moved by horses, the "galloping thunder wagon" would seem to be a primitive tank. This, however, is only one of Byerwhalham's inventions; his other products include missiles, submarines, and robot lions. Thanks to this foreign devil's new weapons, the Liangshan rebels win the upper hand in subsequent battles.

But *Quell the Bandits* is not a novel merely about Western military technology; it contains other scenes in which Daoist sorcery, black magic, and divine interventions prevail. Yu, after all, believed in both Western technology and secular Daoism. The hero of the novel, Chen Xizhen, is a Daoist swordsman capable of practicing sorcery. One of the magical tools Chen owns is a "mirror of cosmos," which is able to reflect one's past and future, harmonize the forces of yin and yang, and exert the power of its incredible *qi* to quell evil. Indeed, thanks to the divinatory power of the mirror, Chen Xizhen is able eventually to capture Byerwhalham and defeat the Liangshan rebels.

The juxtaposition between Byerwhalham and Chen Xizhen sheds light on the bifurcated motivation of *Quell the Bandits*. The classical Chinese narrative tradition is not short of examples of either fantasy or the exoticism of non-Chinese cultures. What makes *Quell the Bandits* interesting is the fact that anachronism is used by Yu as a new fantastic device to foreground the dialogue between the historical memory and the interpretive power of fiction. By introducing Byerwhalham and his inventions to a simulated eleventh-century landscape, Yu is able to engage with the modern technology of warfare in a way unprecedented in Chinese fiction. Although Yu indicates a strong interest in advanced weapons in an earlier part of the novel, the idea of modernizing military technology does not become a full-fledged theme of the novel till the foreign inventor's appearance. Byerwhalham becomes a necessary agent in the changes that are to be imposed on Chinese warfare. Because of the appearance of this foreign devil, the combat between the Song troops and the Liangshan rebels enters a new stage of military technology and diplomatic tactics.

As the novel develops, to counter the threat of Byerwhalham's technology, the Song troops must come up with even more powerful weapons. And to figure out Byerwhalham's secret, what could be a better move than capturing the foreign devil? Thus, in chapter 117, the Song sorcerers set a trap and capture Byerwhalham. Much to our surprise, the capture of Byerwhalham only gives him the opportunity to pledge allegiance to Chinese civilization. Born in Macau, Byerwhalham claims to have always admired the Song, and, to prove his dedication, he divulges the esoteric text *The Classic of Technology*.

Anachronism thus appears in *Quell the Bandits* to be not a technical flaw of the novel but a conduit that facilitates the mechanism of historical awareness. As a Qing reenactment of an event of the Song, the theme of *Quell the Bandits* is one of borrowed time and plot, a rhetorical maneuver to recover something that is gone. The narrative deus ex machina proves to be part of the fantastic design of the novel; it invokes the China that was and the cosmopolitan China that might have been and merges them into one, reading the present absence into the past presence. But it is also at the level of narrative *technology* that Yu reveals his position as a storyteller trapped in the temporal device he created to arrest the past and the present.

The capture and co-optation of Byerwhalham provides an ironic twist to Wei Yuan's famous dictum "Learn from the foreigners so as to subdue the foreigners." In the context of *Quell the Bandits*, Byerwhalham is brought in not only to realize the ambitions of the Qing, but also to "update" the fictional fantasy of the Song. When the secret text of Western science, *The Classic of Technology*, is finally bestowed on the Chinese, it is said to be no more than a recapitulation of a long-lost form of Chinese knowledge. The episode offers a preferred model for Chinese acquisition of Western learning in the late Qing: it starts with an attempt at acquisition, followed by a desire for appropriation, and ends with a rationale for assimilation.

Here lies the paradox of Yu's (and his contemporaries') Occidentalism: on the one hand, the Westerner symbolizes an evil force that has to be eradicated from the civilized realm of China; on the other hand, he is treated like a benign intermediary that helps restore the lost heritage of Chinese civilization. With the capture of Byerwhalham, Wei's dictum is reversed: "Subdue the foreigners so as to learn from the foreigners." The best way to overcome the formidable power of Byerwhalham is to capture him and learn his skills firsthand. But if someone as formidable as Byerwhalham falls into Chinese hands so easily, what is so threatening about his skills and the skills of foreigners as a class? Is there any point in learning from the weak foreigner?

This is where the desire for scientific knowledge takes a big leap forward (or backward?) to the desire for fantastic power of the conventional kind. After the capture of Byerwhalham and the acquisition of the *Classic of Technology*, the storyline of *Quell the Bandits* takes us back to a world of Daoist metaphysics and black magic. The Liangshan rebels fight with the support of supernatural power, while the Song troops retaliate with recourse to magical gadgets, particularly the "mirror of cosmos."

Yet such a narrative return to conventionalism proves to be an ambivalent if not a perfunctory move. A sophisticated mid-nineteenth-century reader may have already noticed that the triumph of the Song does not point to the dynasty's reinvigoration but to further downfall, and, as Yu uses the Song as a stand-in for the Qing, drawn conclusions about the current dynasty's fate. Byerwhalham may have been subdued by the Song in *Quell the Bandits,* but as Qing history since the first Opium War revealed, more menacing technological and discursive forces were to be exerted on China by Byerwhalham's descendants. The reversion to conventional fantasy thus ends only with a painful finale. It is through navigating the narrative ambivalence that Chinese writers and readers came to terms with the intricate temporalities and conditions of modernity.

Historical hindsight offers another irony to Yu's novel. On the eve of the Boxer Rebellion (1900), it became patriotic to believe that the Boxers possessed a mysterious power that kept them "bayonet-and-bulletproof," a power that would help China win back its dignity and glory. This was a moment when Chinese conservatives willingly suspended their ingrained disbelief that Chinese magic power could win out over Western weaponry. They behaved as if they were determined to reenact the fantastic moments of *Quell the Bandits,* regardless of the fact that Yu's novel was already an anachronistic recapitulation of historical fantasy. The disastrous consequences of the Boxer Rebellion were the death knell for the Qing dynasty. When fantasy was no longer on the margins of a realistic discourse, but occupied the center of the political platform, it marked the final collapse of Qing sociopolitical and narrative discourses. Meanwhile, it helped crack open possibilities to imagine China anew.

BIBLIOGRAPHY: David Der-wei Wang, *Fin-de-siècle Splendor: Repressed Modernities of Late Qing Fiction, 1849–1911* (Stanford, CA, 1997).

DAVID DER-WEI WANG

1861

Gu Taiqing finishes *Shadows of Dream of the Red Chamber.*

Women Writers in Early Modern China

In 1861, the anthologist and poet Shen Shanbao (1808–1862) wrote a supportive preface to a novel by fellow poet Gu Chun (1799–1877), widely known by her penname Gu Taiqing. Entitled *Shadows of Dream of the Red Chamber,* Gu's novel was a sequel to the great eighteenth-century *Dream of the Red Chamber,* probably the most famous Chinese novel ever written. Gu's novel uses some plot lines and characters from the parent novel, but it is quite different. For one thing, it is much shorter (24 versus 120 chapters). And among many other differences, it projects Gu's interest in small children and music, themes that are much more muted in *Dream.*

Gu's was the first novel we can clearly identify as woman authored in all of China's long literary history, and it points the way to the twentieth century, when the novel rose in importance and when the idea of women as novelists began to take hold. In 1861, though, Gu's bold endeavor was practically unthinkable, and the taboos against it were very strong. These taboos led both Gu and Shen to use unfamiliar pennames, in Gu's case Yuncha Waishi (Cloud raft immortal), in Shen's case Xihu Sanren (Idler at West Lake). The force of taboo is also felt in the date of publication, 1877, which was sixteen years after Shen's preface was written. We do not know precisely when the novel was completed, but the publication date suggests that Gu (or her family) wanted it to come out posthumously, for 1877 was the year Gu died.

I will first review what is known about Gu, Shen, and their friendship and then report on another literary breakthrough for women writers to which this friendship gave rise: Gu's venture into the field of drama following the death of her husband.

First, who was Gu Taiqing? Gu is known primarily for her poetry. Her poems are celebrated for their simplicity of imagery and clarity of expression. Gu especially excelled at the lyric, a specialized poetic form. Her lyrics put her in the top rank of women poets of the Qing dynasty (1644–1911). She is also ranked as one of two top lyricists of Manchu origin, male or female.

Gu's family was originally from Liaoning, in what was then Manchuria, but they eventually settled in Beijing. The details of her early life are quite obscure. Questions arise over how she acquired the surname Gu, which is Chinese, not Manchu, and whether she spent some of her childhood in Hangzhou. The family's descent from E-er-tai (1680–1745), a grand secretary who was posthumously disgraced in one of the eighteenth-century emperor Qianlong's literary inquisitions, may have been a factor; another disgraced ancestor was E-chang (?–1755), who was ordered to commit suicide during the same emperor's reign. These unhappy events could account for the confusion about Gu. Her beauty and talent made her eligible for a good marriage, and giving her a Chinese surname or moving her to Hangzhou as a girl might have been strategies to combat the family's shame.

Gu's life after marriage is considerably less obscure. In 1824, she became the concubine of Manchu prince Yihui (1799–1838) after his first wife died, and was apparently very happy with him. Although he had married previously, he was so devoted to Gu that he took no other concubine. Gu had five children with Yihui, these in addition to the children he had with his first wife. The couple's shared love of poetry and painting conformed to the ideal of companionate marriage long prevalent among literary women and men. It played an important role in helping Gu to develop her talent. Both Gu and her husband enjoyed reading the novel *Dream of the Red Chamber*, among other pastimes.

With her husband's sudden death in 1838, Gu's happy life fell apart. Not only did she lose her beloved husband and literary partner; the son of Yihui's first wife, with whom she had never gotten along, also forced her out of their Beijing home. At this point she took her children to the suburbs. Because she was such a beauty, her expulsion from home fueled speculation that she had had an affair with well-known scholar Gong Zizhen (1792–1841), who, as it happened, left the capital precipitously in 1839. Sober historians have concluded that an affair never took place, but the rumor lives on. The period of banishment meant serious economic difficulties and emotional turmoil for Gu. She may have sustained herself by selling artwork and jewelry during this time. In addition, friends and certain relatives came to the rescue with much-needed gifts of food. Yihui's hostile son had no children of his own, so after his death in 1857, one of Gu's sons was adopted as his heir, and Gu was allowed to return to the family home.

As the wife and then widow of a Manchu prince, Gu was not allowed to leave the Beijing area. Somewhat before the death of her husband, she had already begun to build friendships with Chinese women from Hangzhou whose husbands were officials stationed in Beijing. Her first such encounter was in 1835, three years before Yihui died. She met Shen Shanbao two years later, in 1837, and the women immediately began exchanging paintings and poems. When Yihui died the following year, Gu was fortunate to have these new friends to help her cope with the grief and disruption, as well as with the insult of banishment from home. She also had Manchu women friends. Whether Manchu or Chinese, from Beijing or Hangzhou, these women provided Gu with solace, and they became a receptive audience for one another's poems.

Let me now introduce Shen Shanbao, on whom Grace Fong's work has been particularly outstanding. Like Gu, Shen was middle aged by 1837, the year their friendship began. Shen was no stranger to family difficulty. Her father committed suicide in 1819, when she was just a girl. Because he had educated her well, she was able to sell her paintings and poems in order to support herself and her mother. Through such activities she came to the attention of some of the leading literary women of Hangzhou, a city known for its highly developed women's culture. Shen's mother died in 1832. Five years later, she moved to Beijing to marry a widower. The marriage was arranged by her foster mother. With this change, her economic circumstances improved considerably, for her husband was a first degree holder and high official. Upon arriving in Beijing, Shen renewed contact with other writers from her old Hangzhou circle. She also maintained ties with woman friends still living in Hangzhou.

Shen's many links with Chinese women in the capital were augmented by her friendship with Manchu women, chief among whom was Gu. Shen and her friends often included Gu in their gatherings, most likely because Gu was fluent in Chinese, knew the Beijing area well, and was very sociable. It must have been crucial for Gu that, during her period of banishment from home, Shen reached out by including her in a poetry society.

Shen is best known for her collected poems and for her *Poetry Talks on Famous Women* of 1845, which describes all manner of associations between talented women of the Qing. Among many other topics that come up in its copious pages are accounts of excursions made by herself, Gu, some Hangzhou friends, and other Chinese and Manchu women to sites in and around Beijing. In this and other sources, Gu comes across as marvelously good company. Gu and Shen enjoyed twenty-five years of friendship, even though Shen was not always in Beijing and the two sometimes had to communicate by mail.

The strength of the friendship between Gu and Shen is revealed in the following passage. It was written by Gu in 1862, the year of Shen's death:

> My younger sister died in 1862, on the eleventh day of the sixth month. On the twenty-ninth day of the fifth month, I went to visit her. She suddenly asked, "How can I repay my elder sister's deep feeling?" I answered, "How can you talk about repayment when it comes to feeling between sisters? It is my wish that the two of us will be able to go on in the next life as we have in this." My sister said, "Why just the next life? I want to go on life after life as sisters." I said, "Let's take this idea as our covenant." Ten days after we parted, she left us forever. How can I not be pained!

In addition to its emotional importance, the friendship was a source of support for a broad range of literary endeavors. One sees this in the number of poems the two women exchanged and in the endorsements of one another's writings and paintings. Moreover, Shen's relationship with Gu put her at the center of Beijing's literary culture, which was an advantage when it came to assembling *Poetry Talks on Famous Women*. Likewise, Shen was a great supporter of Gu's creative output as a whole, not just her novel.

Because of the unfamiliar pennames Gu and Shen used when it came to *Shadows of Dream of the Red Chamber*, their collaboration escaped notice for over one hundred years. Drawing on some of Gu's "lost" poems (they had been preserved in Japan), a scholarly article of 1989 by Zhao Botao identified Gu and Shen as author and prefacer of Gu's sequel. One of the lost poems makes the connection clear:

> *Dream*'s illusory landscape has no basis in reality.
> Occasionally I took up my writing brush and added a few chapters.
> From her long preface, I received excessive praise.
> Frequent missives on beautiful paper demanded [that I complete
>   the project.]

The poem is followed by this note:

> I have worked intermittently on a sequel to *Dream of the Red Chamber* in several chapters. [Shen Shanbao] wrote a preface to it. She asked to see it without waiting for me to finish. She often chided me for my lazy nature and would tease me, saying, "You are almost seventy years old. If you don't finish this book quickly, I fear you will never complete it."

In fact, Gu was only sixty-two years old in 1861, the year the preface was written. Shen died the next year, but Gu had many more years to live.

Discovered still more recently, in 2006, by Huang Shizhong, are two dramas Gu wrote after the death of her husband. These are "Records of the Peach Garden" and "Prelude to Plum Flowers." The first of these is preserved in Japan, the second in China. The first has no preface; the second has a preface by Shen. In both cases Gu used Cloud Raft Immortal, the penname she would use for *Shadows,* and the preface by Shen to "Prelude to Plum Flowers" uses Idler at West Lake. Not many dramas were written by women during the Ming and Qing, so Shen's support on this other innovative project once again illustrates the literary importance of the friendship. The dating of these unpublished pieces is not certain, but they were probably both written just after the death of Yihui. If so, they preceded the novel by over two decades. If this is the case, then Shen's endorsement of Gu's drama would have been another dimension of her support for Gu during her most difficult time, and the two obscure pennames would have been the women's secret for over twenty years.

Gu's influence on Shen's poems and other output may not be quite as visible or striking as Shen's influence on Gu, but it is obvious that the two writers cherished one another personally, and we can well imagine that without each other's help the creative endeavors of both would have suffered. We can find other instances of important friendships among writing women, but the relationship between Gu and Shen was particularly vital to the literary lives of both and to the pioneering achievements of Gu.

BIBLIOGRAPHY: Grace S. Fong, *Herself an Author: Gender, Agency, and Writing in Late Imperial China* (Honolulu, 2008). Grace S. Fong, "Writing Self and Writing Lives: Shen

Shanbao's (1808–62) Gendered Auto / Biographical Practices," *Nan Nü* 2, no. 2 (2000): 259–303. Gu Chun [Taiqing], *Honglou meng ying* (Beijing, 1988 [1877]). Huang Shizhong, "Gu Taiqing de xiqu chuangzuo yu qi zaonian jingli," *Wenxue yichan* 6 (2006): 88–95. Ellen Widmer, *The Beauty and the Book: Women and Fiction in Nineteenth-Century China* (Cambridge, MA, 2006).

ELLEN WIDMER

1862 · OCTOBER 11

"Abandoned at the southern fringes of civilization"

Wang Tao Lands in Hong Kong

On October 11, 1862, Wang Tao (1828–1897) arrived in the British colony of Hong Kong. It was not a triumphant arrival. Bitter disappointment more than excitement probably best captures his mood: he did not share in the thrill of Western merchants coming to the East to find fortune and adventure, nor in the eager anticipation of Toisanese villagers transiting through the colony on their way to San Francisco, a place so famed for its riches that they called it "Gold Mountain." Wang had not even *meant* to make this voyage in the first place. He had been rushed aboard a ship bound for Hong Kong by the British consul in Shanghai, where he had taken refuge after rumors circulated about his involvement with Taiping rebels. With only a moment's notice before his abrupt departure, Wang was forced to leave behind his family—and, just as devastatingly for him, his precious books. His sense of displacement on a small island beyond the bounds of Chinese civilization, a place where commerce was valued above the literati culture he so esteemed, must have been profound indeed. Looking out over the bustling port city, Wang perhaps recalled the lines of the old poet Tao Qian (365–427), one of the most beloved poets of the classical Chinese tradition:

> I built my cottage right in the realm of men,
> yet there was no noise from wagon and horse.
> I ask you, how can that be so?—
> When mind is far, its place becomes remote.
>   (Translation by Stephen Owen)

Yet estrangement and displacement might be considered two of the most powerful driving forces of modern Chinese literary and artistic production—much as they have been powerful driving forces in the history of modern literature and art in the West. Kang Youwei (1858–1927) was an exile; Eileen Chang (1920–1995) and Bai Xianyong (1937–) were exiles; Gao Xingjian (1940–) is an exile. For Wang, his years in Hong Kong, and his later travels in Europe and Asia, offered a productive estrangement that he wrought into new forms of literary engagement, forms that ran the gamut from translation to travelogues, from fiction to journalism, and to hybrid forms of writing that defy these simple categorizations.

Wang is perhaps most renowned as a pioneering entrepreneur in modern Chinese journalism and as a reform-minded intellectual, but he was also a celebrated and prolific writer, a noteworthy translator, and an avid chronicler of life in Shanghai's courtesan quarters. A "Renaissance man" of sorts, Wang is thus central to modern Chinese political and social history, and to the history of modern Chinese literature. Wang was born near Suzhou, the ancient capital of the state of Wu located fifty miles west of Shanghai on the shores of Lake Taihu. Amid an atmosphere of literary and artistic refinement, he trained as a classical scholar, imagining a future as a scholar-official in the service of the Qing dynasty. By seventeen, he had already passed the prefectural-level civil service examinations, but he was never able to progress beyond this point. Forced to abandon this time-honored and secure route to elite status as a literatus, he set off in search of an alternate means of making a living. Wang went to Shanghai, where he took up a position as a Chinese editor at the London Missionary Society Press (all the while working on his *Record of Visits to Courtesan Houses in a Distant Corner of the Sea* [preface 1860, first print edition 1878]). Over the many years he would spend working for British and American missionaries, Wang developed a serious interest in "Western learning," and was introduced to Western science and modern journalism in addition to Christianity.

It was in the field of translation that Wang first made his mark. Beginning in 1849, he served as Walter Medhurst's (1796–1857) primary literary assistant in the translation of the Delegates' Version of the Bible, a work that Patrick Hanan called "the first Chinese translation of the Bible with a claim to literary merit." He also collaborated with missionaries to translate numerous nonreligious works, including treatises on pictorial optics, elementary mechanics, Western astronomy, and the history of Anglo-Chinese trade. Wang stayed with the Shanghai mission until 1862, when he was forced to flee to Hong Kong. Feeling himself "abandoned at the southern fringes of civilization," Wang found work in Hong Kong as James Legge's (1815–1897) assistant in his monumental translations of the Chinese classics.

Only a month before Wang began his exile, the Battle of Antietam was fought in the American Civil War. On the very day he began his exile, the Confederate Congress passed the Twenty-Slave Law, exempting any man who owned twenty or more slaves from military service. Wang had no connection with these events halfway across the globe, but a juxtaposition of his flight from Shanghai with this Confederate legislation serves as a powerful reminder that social reform and the fight for greater human liberty were being waged in both the Western and Eastern Hemispheres at this particular historical moment—though this fact was most likely downplayed by Wang's missionary friends, who were eager to emphasize the "enlightened" nature of Western civilization. Long irked by what he saw as the hypocrisy of foreigners in China, in Hong Kong Wang became increasingly concerned about the links between imperialism, racial oppression, and labor exploitation, and by 1872 he would join with his merchant friends at the Tung Wah Hospital, where he had been appointed an assistant director, to oppose the notorious "coolie trade," the traffic of Chinese laborers to mines and plantations around the world, where they often worked in inhuman conditions.

An opportunity to journey even farther beyond the "edge of civilization" came when Legge invited Wang to visit his home in Scotland in 1867. Setting out from Hong Kong, Wang encountered many new sights in Singapore, Penang, Colombo, Aden, Cairo, and Alexandria before reaching Europe. Wang arrived in the British Isles a decade ahead of the first Chinese ambassador stationed in England, and his presence in British society was very much a novelty. While in Europe, Wang enjoyed extensive attention as a silk-robed Chinese scholar and authority on "things Chinese," even delivering a lecture at Oxford University. Conversely, when he returned to Hong Kong in 1870, Wang was accorded status as an expert in Western learning, with rare firsthand knowledge of European geography and society. His experiences would serve as the basis for his famous travelogue *Random Records of My Wanderings* (1890), which was also published in an illustrated edition.

In 1874, Wang broke new ground when he helped to found the *Global Times*, a Chinese daily modeled on Western newspapers. The *Global Times* was the first modern Chinese-language newspaper entirely under Chinese ownership. The newspaper was a great success, expanding its readership beyond Hong Kong to reach subscribers in the major treaty ports in China and Taiwan, and even in Yokohama, Singapore, San Francisco, and Australia. It would serve as an important vehicle for Wang to express his ideas for reforming China.

Wang's newfound fame as a master of Western learning and influential writer brought him an invitation to visit Japan in 1879. There, he met with the Chinese diplomat Huang Zunxian (1848–1905), who may have paved the way for his return to China after over two decades of exile. Settling again in Shanghai, by 1884 Wang became a regular contributor to the *Shenbao*, one of China's earliest modern newspapers. He also published fiction and selections from his travel accounts in the widely read illustrated newspaper *Dianshizhai Pictorial*, an important vehicle for disseminating knowledge about the West, and about the new hybrid culture of treaty port Shanghai. Many of the stories that first appeared in the *Dianshizhai Pictorial* were later published in Wang's fiction collection, *Random Notes of a Recluse in Wusong* (1884–1887). Also known as the *Sequel to Strange Tales from the Liaozhai Studio*, after Pu Songling's (1640–1715) famous collection *Strange Tales from the Liaozhai Studio* (1679), this volume of classical-language tales was widely reprinted throughout the Qing and enjoyed a broad circulation, as did its sequel, *Trivial Talk on the Banks of the Wusong* (1887). Wang also became involved with John Fryer (1839–1928) in the work of the Chinese Polytechnic Institute, and for a time served as its director.

A prolific writer, Wang produced numerous works in a wide variety of genres and on diverse subject matter. In addition to the short story collections and translations mentioned previously, his most famous works include a history of the Franco-Prussian War, a brief history of France, a history of Sino-Japanese relations, treatises on Western learning, travelogues of his journeys to Europe and Japan, several profiles of Shanghai's courtesans, an *Anthology on the History of Love* (1878), poetry, and a collection of essays.

With this vast array of literary output, Wang's contribution to modern Chinese literature cannot be summed up with a simple label: Was he a "literary compradore" who translated Western scientific and religious ideas into Chinese? The "father of modern Chinese journalism"? A travel writer and author of East-West romances? The author of the definitive inside guide to Shanghai's brothels? His writings similarly defy easy pigeonholing into generic categories like travelogue, political treatise, or reportage. As Rania Huntington has demonstrated, much of Wang's literary work carved out a new "space between journalism and entertainment fiction." The pieces Wang published in the *Dianshizhai Pictorial*, for example, simultaneously served as divertissements and as vehicles to introduce readers to new ideas, current events, and information about the West. If we had to label this Renaissance man, then, perhaps we might call Wang a border-crosser who produced border-crossing texts. And thus, despite the fact that Lu Xun (1881–1936) saw Wang primarily as an old-fashioned writer of "depravity fiction" (*xiaxie xiaoshuo*)—a producer of countless classical Chinese works on the topic of courtesans and romance—Wang in fact embodies a hybridity that resonates deeply with the contemporary moment, allowing us to reclaim him in a new way for the history of modern Chinese literature.

Wang's experiences in Shanghai and Hong Kong and his travels abroad prompted him to develop a bicultural and bilingual outlook, enabling him to become both an influential interpreter of the West for the late Qing audience and a vital interpreter of the Chinese classical tradition for Victorian Westerners. Indeed, many have regarded Wang as a cultural translator par excellence. Yet, as Elizabeth Sinn argues, Wang was far more than a "transmitter" of new knowledge; rather, he helped to create and propagate a "new social and cultural paradigm" based on complex and dynamic processes of cultural transformation. Wang's own complexity can be seen in his attitude toward the West. Although he favored reform and modernization in China and was an avid proponent of Western learning as early as the 1860s, he was also critical of Western imperial aggression and cultural arrogance, and warned against the threat of foreign incursions and against outrages such as the coolie trade. Paul Cohen has called Wang an "incipient nationalist" who advocated limited Westernization combined with the promotion of Chinese national strength and dignity.

At the end of the day, the "modernness" of Wang's literary and journalistic work cannot simply be assessed in terms of "firsts" or "newness," whether in terms of subject matter, genre, or use of language. Instead of reducing modernity to the temporal concept of newness (which by force rejects the "old"), I would like instead to locate it in *place*, more specifically in the particular spaces of fringes, frontiers, borderlands, and contact zones—spaces from which Wang produced his most significant works—and in the *spatial movement* of exile and travel. Exile and travel had long been key elements of literary production in premodern China, but the radical displacement Wang experienced in traveling as far afield as he did, far beyond the "southern fringes of civilization" to the strange new world of Europe, enabled him not only to see the West through Chinese eyes, but also to see China refracted through a Western lens. It gave him a double consciousness that engendered an ambivalent and transculturated sensibility in his literary work. Through his diverse endeavors, Wang was at once a close associate of the leading Orientalists of his day and a key architect of late Qing Occidentalism. His travelogues and short fiction portrayed the West not simply as a land of progress and modern technology and industry, but also as a realm for sexual adventure and romance, as he imagined the ancient mythical "Kingdom of Women" transported to Europe. This doubleness allowed Wang to develop an outlook that was truly global.

Wang's unplanned arrival in Hong Kong in 1862 is emblematic of the contingencies that have shaped modern Chinese history, as well as of the importance of the contact zones between cultures to the productive estrangement that lies at the heart of modernity.

BIBLIOGRAPHY: Paul A. Cohen, *Between Tradition and Modernity: Wang T'ao and Reform in Late Ch'ing China* (Cambridge, MA, 1974). Sheldon H. Lu, *Chinese Modernity and Global Biopolitics: Studies in Literature and Visual Culture* (Honolulu, 2007). Elizabeth Sinn, "Fugitive in Paradise: Wang Tao and Cultural Transformation in Late Nineteenth-Century Hong Kong," *Late Imperial China* 19, no. 1 (June 1998): 56–81.

EMMA J. TENG

1872 · OCTOBER 14

China's first literary journal, the *Universal Miscellany,* is published.

Media, Literature, and Early Chinese Modernity

On the eleventh day of the ninth month of the *renshen* year during the reign of the Tongzhi Emperor—October 14, 1872—the first issue of what was to become China's first literary journal was published. Entitled *The Universal Miscellany*, the journal was printed in the International Settlement of Shanghai—the place that was to become the undisputed media capital of the Great Qing (China's name at the time). Like the other Chinese-language periodicals and newspapers at the time, the *Universal Miscellany* was part of a foreign-owned and foreign-managed company, in this case the Shenbao Newspaper Company, Shenbaoguan. The company was run by Ernest Major (1841–1908), an energetic and innovative young man from London with excellent Chinese language skills and an early insight that Chinese interest in the world, combined with the country's own heritage, could secure the commercial viability of modern print products.

The flagship of his company was the *Shenbao* newspaper. It had been started just half a year before the *Universal Miscellany*, and with the small capital stock of 1,600 *liang* (about one-tenth of the capital used to start a Chinese-language paper in Hong Kong in 1874). This means that the available equipment and staff were also minimal. Besides news, editorials, and the reprinting of the court news (the *Beijing Gazette*) and excerpts from Hong Kong Chinese papers, the paper thus invited men of letters to submit opinion articles on national affairs, as well as entertaining literary and anecdotal tidbits for publication, so as to encourage public discussion and fill its pages.

The paper soon received a flood of submissions by men of letters eager to see their work in print in this new medium. However, only a small selection of the submissions could be published. By September 1872, the paper had two and a half to three of its eight pages available for its own content, while the rest was filled with reprints (one and a half pages) and advertising. It came out six times a week with a run of about three thousand copies. In September alone, the *Shenbao* published twenty-three sets of signed poetry and pieces of literary prose, and thirty-three long pieces of news and opinion that were also often signed, all of them submitted by outsiders. The submissions retained a strong connection to the present, with "bamboo-twig" poems (*zhuzhici*) and prose pieces on the glories of the international settlement or the evils of opium addiction, as well as news pieces that ranged from debates started in earlier opinion pieces to warnings against the dangers of aphrodisiacs, or even the best way for the city to deal with beggars.

As these educated writers were the target audience of this young paper, it was wary to dampen their enthusiasm, which enhanced elite acceptance of the publication. The *Universal Miscellany* offered an additional venue for writings that were of current interest but had a less direct link to actual events, but did not reduce the number of outside contributions to the *Shenbao*. In December 1872, we find sixty-six poetry or prose pieces and forty-one opinion or news pieces from outsiders.

The programmatic preface to the first issue shows that the *Universal Miscellany* did not begin as a journal dedicated to "literature." It claims, "In its format [our journal] generally imitates the *Things Seen and Heard in China and the West* but is more encompassing." The journal referenced in the preface is a Chinese-language journal based in Beijing that was established by two Englishmen with missionary backgrounds who had since gone on to work for the Translation Office of the new Chinese Foreign Ministry. The men who established *Things Seen and Heard in China and the West* shared a commitment to China and Chinese culture, as well as critical views of many British China policies. Their title was indicative of their intentions: they were opening the world to their readers; and they were publishing "things seen and heard," namely news, introductions to science and technology, and fact-based social reportage. The *Universal Miscellany* emulated the first aspect with "universal," but was "more encompassing" with regard to the second, saying that it would include things mandated by "reason" even if not seen and heard, or suggested by the "imagination" even if not supported by reason. The form of the "miscellany" (*suoji*) implied openness to different short forms of writing, with an understanding that the pieces should be of the highest quality. The journal, which ran to fifty-eight issues over four years and had its name changed twice into synonyms, prefigured the short lifespan of many later Chinese literary journals that often suffered from the low priority accorded to them by their publishers, a certain cliquishness among their editors, and censorship.

The editorship was entrusted to Chinese men of letters, and much of the language and format corresponded to their preferences. Consequently, and in notable contrast to the practice of its Beijing contemporary and earlier periodicals by Protestant missionaries, the *Miscellany* (as well as the *Shenbao* at this stage) went by the Chinese calendar and did not insert punctuation into their texts, as this was below the cultural sophistication of their intended readership. Regardless of all the formal markers of its Chineseness, the preface of the journal went out of its way to highlight the important role of Ernest Major. It attributed a "long perspective" to him, as well as the insight that "astonishing and shocking talk as well as the broadest and most exquisitely beautiful writings" would be much more instructive than dry "classical" works; it also attributed to him the definition of the journal's purpose, which was to introduce methods of applied science, proposals for good governance, and scientific knowledge, as well as provide entertainment. In this paean, Major only appears with his studio name, but he seems to need no further introduction, a sign that the target audience of the journal and that of the *Shenbao* were largely overlapping.

The pieces published in the journal certainly tried to live up to these claims. The first issue was entertaining and instructive enough, with its articles on the nervous system; the unforeseen usefulness of the idling giant steamer *Great Eastern* in laying the first cable between the British Isles and the United States; a piece of reportage about a visit to Nagasaki that was promoted as a "model" for writing about a specific place and its people; and a spoof about a Briton who was denied welfare until he had changed his golden tooth to one made of horse bone. The issue does not contain a single piece of "literature," even when considered in the broadest sense.

This was an innovative venture, and the Shenbaoguan went on to explore possible profiles for the future of the journal. In the process, it was drawing on the experience of British journals with similarly diverse content, such as *Blackwood's Edinburgh Magazine* or the *Westminster Magazine*, while praising the stylistic models of the wonderfully concrete and entertaining parables found in the *Zhuangzi* and *Liezi*, which managed to express philosophical insights with literary flourish but without vacuous phraseology.

The selection of these very specific and concrete texts with contemporary relevance, the suggestion of taking the Nagasaki reportage as a model, the satire about an artificial tooth made of bone, and the praise of the parables from the *Zhuangzi* and *Liezi* all combine to suggest a very urban aesthetic. This aesthetic was to dominate Shenbaoguan publishing for the next twenty years, down to its famous *Dianshizhai Pictorial*. As it became increasingly attuned to the international taste for concrete and realistic writing in vogue at the time, the *Universal Miscellany* was critical of what it saw as a vacuous formalism in much traditional Chinese thinking, writing, and painting.

The second issue of the journal broadened the scope to include poetry, opera arias, and dedications in a highly literary style, as well as new subject matter including aphorisms, travelogues, and sketches of famous courtesans of the time. Most of the texts were recent, but the journal also started to print earlier unpublished writings, especially those left behind by people who had been killed during the Taiping Civil War. To explain his criteria for a piece's selection and familiarize readers with the kind of texts they themselves might submit or suggest, the editor would often attach a short comment to the end of a given piece. The increasing variety of authors included in the journal indicates that the journal was being discovered as a possible outlet for publication in the wide range of shorter genres. Writers of some status and renown started to send in manuscripts for publication, signing not as *mouke* (Mr. X) but with their names or studio names. Literary texts, on average, fill seven out of the thirty-six pages in a given issue. We also see the beginnings of a community of writers and readers with shared broad cultural interests who collectively identified themselves as "sophisticated gentlemen" (*daya junzi*). They were interested in the "world" without glorifying all that is "Western," and kept an ironic distance from grandiloquent framing of trivial content. They were a leisure class, but one that had recently gone through the trauma of a devastating civil war.

The journal's third issue gave a still more prominent place to literature. The *Shenbao* had previously published some short translations of English-language fiction, such as an excerpt from *Gulliver's Travels*, but now it set out to serialize a full-length translation, namely Edward Bulwer-Lytton's (1803–1873) inheritance novel *Night and Morning* (1841). Such a serialization also served to develop a continuous reader base, in a market where subscriptions to a periodical publication were still unknown and where readers bought each issue separately. *Night and Morning* was said to rank on a par with the great Chinese novels and joined with them a world literary genre, the novel. It was a perfect fit for the Shenbaoguan aesthetic program. The translation came with comments that used the vocabulary of Chinese literary criticism to highlight its sophisticated literary devices, such as foreshadowing, while at the same time introducing the social environment in Britain, where a girl could travel alone and a young lady could go out with a suitor without being ostracized. In this manner, *Night and Morning* was to "delight one's feelings" but also serve to "correct and improve the customs" in China by presenting alternatives without criticizing Chinese local customs. By now, the Shenbaoguan had discovered that there were unpublished or inaccessible Chinese fictional writings that suited its program. It shifted to publishing them and broke off the serialization, eventually publishing the entire translation in book form. The only other foreign work it published was the serialization of Terakado Seiken's (1796–1868) *A Record of Flourishing Edo*—a supremely concrete and satirical piece of reportage literature about 1830s Edo (now Tokyo)—in issues 24–26; it conveniently needed no translation, as it was written in classical Chinese, a prestige language in Japan before the Meiji Restoration.

With the third issue of the journal, the *Miscellany* had already developed most of the key features that would come to define it. These included descriptive poetry, such as a long series of "poems from the colleagues of the master of the Cherish the News Studio [that is, Ernest Major]"; lively biographical sketches of unusual personalities, such as male and female "martyrs" from the recent civil war and urban types, such as courtesans and a beggar; disquisitions on actual affairs, such as river floods, the quality of which were greatly enhanced by learned—mostly Chinese—references; unpublished letters from such luminaries as Zeng Guofan (1811–1872); travelogues; and a fair amount of unique literary writings that survived—sometimes only in part—from the civil war, together with commemorative introductions.

By the time the venture was discontinued without further ado in 1876, the Shenbaoguan had established itself as the premier publisher of Chinese literary and cultural heritage, as well as new works. Many of the authors who wrote for the *Miscellany* continued to contribute introductions, notes, and calligraphy to the books published by the Shenbaoguan, which set the gold standard for Chinese-language publishing for the next decades. A vast trove of manuscripts remained unpublished when the *Miscellany* ended, showing that the journal, as well as the Shenbaoguan, was a respected venue for literary production. A selection of these manuscripts was published by two of the editors. One of them, Cai Erkang (1851–1921), found new employment at the Shanghai Arsenal, where he started a new journal, the *New Records of Delicacies*. This new journal continued for another four issues the tradition and aesthetic program of both the *Miscellany* and the old *Records of Delicacies* from the Song dynasty, with its variegated collection of poetry and prose tidbits, reportage about people and customs, historical disquisitions, letters, and critiques.

This aesthetic, rather than specifically literary, program serves as the theoretical link that bound the miscellaneous pieces together and incorporated them into the overall Shenbaoguan agenda. In a critical departure from a staunch defense of a Chinese cultural authenticity, this program gently opened the door for Chinese writing to participate in the cultural and literary world fashions of the time.

BIBLIOGRAPHY: Patrick Hanan, *Chinese Fiction of the Nineteenth and Early Twentieth Centuries* (New York, 2004). Rudolf G. Wagner, "Women in Shenbaoguan Publications 1872–1890," in *Different World of Discourse: Transformations of Gender and Genre in Late Qing and Early Republican China*, ed. Nanxiu Qian, Grace S. Fong, Richard J. Smith (Leiden, Netherlands, 2008), 227–256. Catherine V. Yeh, "Recasting the Chinese Novel: Ernest Major's Shenbao Publishing House (1872–1890)," *Transcultural Studies* 1 (2015): 171–189.

RUDOLF G. WAGNER

1873 · JUNE 29

The Tongzhi Emperor receives Thomas Wade (1818–1895) and other foreign delegates in the Purple Pavilion, Beijing.

The Politics of Translation and the Romanization of Chinese into a World Language

The year is 1873 and I, Thomas F. Wade, British diplomat to China, was the initiator of this audience with the Chinese emperor. But I am allowing the Russian minister general Aleksandr G. Vlangali to lead the foreign delegation into the hall, as he was the first one I consulted about the meeting. After him comes Frederick F. Low of the United States. I follow, taking up a position at the very center of the Grand Hall. Next comes Louis de Geofroy, the French representative, and finally Jan H. Ferguson, from Holland. At the end of the line is the interpreter, who always assumes an inconspicuous and almost invisible position, although he is as important as any of us, as interpreters are in great demand on Chinese soil. We form a horizontal line in front of the young Tongzhi Emperor, helmets in hands, and bow. This is our way of showing our respect for the emperor. The Purple Pavilion is full of Chinese officials, whose chins are down to their chests and heads are almost totally covered by their formal summer hats. As I glance around, I can see their horrified faces, obviously scandalized by our lack of respect in not performing the kowtow ritual (prostration) before the young emperor. They have to prostrate themselves whenever they see the emperor. And they expect all foreign delegates to do the same because they regard all foreign states as inferior to the Chinese empire. They perceive China as the center of the world and the source of civilization, surrounded by uncivilized barbarians. Yet our failure to perform the kowtow ritual is not influenced by the emperor's age. We have had young kings in our countries too. Rather, it is the implied inferiority we object to. Diplomatic inequality has long been a major reason for the troubles and conflicts between China and the West. One of the purposes of pulling together this delegation was to demonstrate that we have the intention of fostering a peaceful and collaborative relationship in order to help China enter the modern world.

To achieve this end, I spent much time in painstaking discussion with Prince Gong, who is the prince regent and head of the Zongli yamen (Office in charge of affairs of all nations). He is thus responsible for all of China's interactions with foreign countries, including the rituals and formalities involving the reception of their delegates. Having spent the last thirty years in China, I am by far the most experienced of all the envoys, and so I volunteered to make initial contact with Prince Gong, to draft official documents, and write privately to his office.

I believe that Prince Gong has seen me as a capable mediator and cultural adviser since the signing of the Beijing Convention in 1860. By virtue of my language ability and good faith for China, I gained his trust

The Western representatives before the emperor. Credit: The National Archive of the United Kingdom. Courtesy Historical Photographs of China.

and friendship. He consulted me on the merits of setting up the Zongli yamen and its subdivision, the Tongwenguan (Interpreters' college and school of combined learning). I expounded on the urgent need to establish such an institute of learning. I told him that one of the mistakes made by our nation during the Macartney Mission (1792–1794) was that we had to rely on mercenary interpreters who had agendas different from our own. The trustworthiness of the interpreter was of paramount importance. China had to have its own interpreters; I recommended two good gentlemen, the Reverend John Burdon and the Reverend William A. P. Martin, to be teachers in the English Department of the Tongwenguan. Their main roles would be to teach English and recommend important sources of Western knowledge for translation.

I wished that China would retain its own team of interpreters with a command of various foreign languages, not merely because I am a Sinophile, nor because I began my career as an interpreter. Those factors no doubt had some influence. But more importantly, my wish had a patriotic reason. If our trade with China is to flourish, and the life and properties of British subjects in China to be safeguarded, then we must follow a mutually and internationally agreed-on practice. The problem with China is that it does not know any international practice. If China had its own interpreters, it would not have to rely on foreign interpreters, thereby reducing the chance of it resorting to other foreign powers. Maintenance of checks and balances on different powers is the first principle of international politics as we know it. Of course, there are many foreign languages. If China gets through to the foreign world and gains Western knowledge first through English, it will certainly be to our advantage.

I am no prophet in this matter. The awareness of the necessity of having a good mastery of the Chinese language and training our own interpreters came at a heavy price for our country. I myself had learned the language with sweat and tears. It is a very exotic and enigmatic language to our ears. There are so many strokes in each radical and so many components in each Chinese character. Which one indicates the sound? If we can't catch the phonetic elements in a character, how can we pronounce it? When I came to China as a lieutenant in the Opium War of 1839, I could only rely on a piecemeal phrasebook compiled for very specific missionary and mercantile purposes. During the war, the frustration hit me repeatedly. We read the map wrongly because we could not distinguish one place from another. The place-names were so similar. And amid the bloodiest battles in south China, we were misled by incorrect intelligence. My soldiers were in great fear when we marched into the inland of China without the accompaniment of interpreters.

I therefore decided to become an interpreter. I had already shown my talent and passion for learning European languages, classical and modern, while at Cambridge. However, when I wrote to the Foreign Office and War Office to seek approval for leaving the army and revealed my wish to stay as an interpreter in Hong Kong, the colony newly acquired during the first Opium War, I received only scorn and derision. Interpreting was by no means perceived as a glorious career. But I had made up my mind.

To learn Chinese more effectively, I humbly sought advice from the most renowned Sinologists and interpreters who then resided in Hong Kong. They included John Robert Morrison, Karl Gützlaff, and Robert Thom, all of whom had participated in the signing of the Nanjing

Treaty. They were actually responsible for drafting and verifying both versions of the treaty. When I told them that I wanted to learn Chinese, the first response I got was surprising and puzzling. "What Chinese is it that you want to learn, sir?" asked the first Sinologist I consulted. "There is the language of the ancient classics, and the language of more modern books, and the language of official documents, and the epistolary language, and the spoken language, of which there are numerous dialects; now, which Chinese is it that you wish to begin with?" I was totally at a loss. Ancient? Modern? Written? Spoken? Epistolary? Official? As a new learner, how could I know which was which? To make the most of my learning environment, I chose to become proficient in the local dialect, Cantonese. I started learning Cantonese by copying every entry in Morrison's dictionary *Vocabulary of the Canton Dialect.*

After five years of diligent study with on-the-job training as a court interpreter in Hong Kong, I met Thomas Taylor Meadows, a learned scholar who had once been an interpreter and by then had been promoted to consul at the treaty port of Shanghai. He generously and graciously told me that if I harbored ambitions in the Anglo-Chinese arena, I should learn Mandarin or the Pekingese dialect, which is the language spoken in the royal court and by the scholar gentry. It appeared to me that all my previous efforts had been wasted. To facilitate my own learning and save future learners the many troubles I had experienced, I decided to develop a systematic orthographic method. To begin, with the help of my native teacher, who spoke perfect Mandarin, I transliterated the Mandarin pronunciation of each Chinese character into roman letters, and set the intonation or pitch level for each romanized word. Then we cross-checked and verified each transliterated pronunciation with other Sinologists who were adept in Mandarin. In this way, an Anglophone speaker, who is used to memorizing words in a phonetic alphabet, is able to recognize Chinese words more effectively. I had the luxury of doing this because the Foreign Office had invited me to offer my views on improving the training of interpreters. This was a very agreeable arrangement, for I could not imagine wasting my time on administrative work that had nothing to do with learning the Chinese language in my early career. After a thorough discussion with students and teachers at home and in China, I drafted two proposals for improving the efficiency of learning Chinese: (1) a memorandum on respecting the study of Chinese submitted to Sir

John Bowring (1854), and (2) a memorandum to Lord Russell outlining a program for language study (1861). Both memoranda were targeted at improving learning instruments (such as glossaries, textbooks, and dictionaries) and revising the structure of the existing interpreter-training programs, which had been commissioned by the Foreign Office since 1854.

Unlike my colleagues and superiors at the Foreign Office, I do not see translation as menial work for clerks stationed in the office or at consular ports. Translators do more than merely transpose messages from one language to another. I value them as decision makers and cultural ambassadors. They make wise choices based on the robust knowledge they have gathered about Chinese culture, and their swift responses come out of their excellent language competence. They must be well informed of the nuances inherent in different phraseologies in the language, for different expressions are suited to different hierarchical positions. I am highly discriminating in selecting and training interpreters because they form an indispensable bridge between the Chinese and British governments. Selecting gentlemen between the ages of eighteen and twenty-five from the most renowned universities of the United Kingdom through a competitive examination and training them as interpreters in Chinese is a pioneering effort. We should provide them with the best training and an undisturbed learning environment before they attempt to discharge their great responsibilities in the arena of Sino-British diplomacy. I have designed three textbooks for their guidance: *Book of Experiments; Being the First of a Series of Contributions to the Study of Chinese* (1859), *A Progressive Course Designed to Assist the Student of Colloquial Chinese, as Spoken in the Capital and Metropolitan Departments* (1867), and *A Series of Papers Selected as Specimens of Documentary Chinese, Designed to Assist Students of the Language as Written by the Officials of China* (1867).

Apart from my textbooks, which focus mainly on the grammar and usage of the Chinese language in general, and specifically on the writing of official correspondence, I also require my students to broaden their knowledge of Chinese culture through a wide spectrum of reading materials. They also have to sit a qualifying examination every six months. It is necessary that they should demonstrate mastery of speaking, writing, and reading Chinese. I also require them to respond to certain contextual questions about Chinese customs and culture. My students find me harsh, eccentric, and fastidious. Probably I am. But I think this is the only way to learn such a difficult and exotic language. After they pass the examination, the students are assigned as interpreters at various consular ports and customs offices, or at the general embassy in Beijing. They are the ones who make immediate decisions and respond to all classes of Chinese people, whether officials, the scholar-gentry, or civilians. Therefore, as the Chinese secretary, I have to make sure that they are fully capable of carrying out spontaneous translation before they finish their training in my office. I may be demanding, but trailblazers are doomed to be misunderstood by others.

"British minister, Wei Toma [Wade Thomas]…British minister, Wei Toma…"

While I indulge in this memory, a very familiar voice rushes to my ears. It is the voice of Prince Gong. I look at him and refrain from prolonging my reminiscence of how I came to this audience with the Chinese emperor. Prince Gong is asking me to proceed to submit the letters of credence to the emperor. We do this one by one. The emperor does not say a word during the ceremony. Finally, Prince Gong acknowledges the royal acceptance of the letters of credence and, in typical Chinese fashion, bids our rulers good health and longevity before we leave the palace.

BIBLIOGRAPHY: James Cooley, *T. F. Wade in China: Pioneer in Global Diplomacy, 1842–1882* (Leiden, Netherlands, 1981). John King Fairbank, *Trade and Diplomacy on the China Coast: The Opening of the Treaty Ports, 1842–1854* (Cambridge, MA, 1953). Uganda Sze Pui Kwan, "The Politics of Translation and the Production of Sinology: Sir Thomas Francis Wade and the Student Interpreter Program, 1843–1870," *Bulletin of the Institute of Modern History, Academia Sinica* 82 (2013): 1–52.

UGANDA SZE PUI KWAN

1884 · MAY 8

The *Dianshizhai Pictorial* is published.

In Lithographic Journals, Text and Image Flourish on the Same Page

Chinese books have a long history of printing images and text that mutually reinforce and interact with one another, hence the phrase "A picture on the left, and historical writing on the right" (*zuo tu you shi*). This ancient tradition turned in a new direction following the arrival of Western learning at the close of the Qing dynasty. New lithographic technologies played a decisive role in this transformation. Unlike traditional xylography, or woodblock printing, lithography was performed by taking a photographic image and applying chemicals to it. Its advantages were clear: images could be reduced in size, and the printed images were much clearer reproductions of the original. Moreover, mechanical printing worked much faster than printing by hand, greatly reducing the cost of printing and resulting in low-cost, high-quality products.

Many printers demonstrated the advantages of using lithography to print books with text and images, but the most successful was the Dianshizhai Lithographic Bookstore, founded in Shanghai in 1879. The *Dianshizhai Pictorial*, which the publisher first brought out in May 1884, appeared every ten days and lasted for an impressive fifteen-year run of 524 issues, making it a deeply influential publication in Chinese media and cultural history.

With the help of lithographic technology, the *Dianshizhai Pictorial* revolutionized the style of traditional engravings and woodcuts. Whereas earlier works had favored simple compositions and spare lines, the *Pictorial* offered dense, detailed pictures. When the first issue was published, advertisements boasted that the *Pictorial*'s biggest selling points were its "lifelike drawings, fine brushwork, and beautiful scenery." The success of the *Pictorial* went beyond the high-quality images and its low price, however, as it also knew its place in the market. Unlike collections of drawings that were published for leisure readers or illustrated books that were sold for educational purposes, from the *Pictorial*'s inception, its principal manager, the English businessman Ernest Major (1841–1908), stated that the *Pictorial* also had value as "news." The outbreak of the Sino-French War (1884–1885) also generated interest in the *Pictorial* as news, as—in the words of one skeptical reader—"sensationalists drew pictures of the battles, and ordinary people bought copies to gape at and chatter over."

What Major called "news" also referred to "new, strange, and delightful events," which included current events, new knowledge, and new and odd stories. Of course, the lines between these types were often blurry. For example, in the *Dianshizhai Pictorial* from January 1898, we have "The Great Meeting of Women." The scene depicts the Conference of Chinese and Western Women, which was held at Shanghai's famed

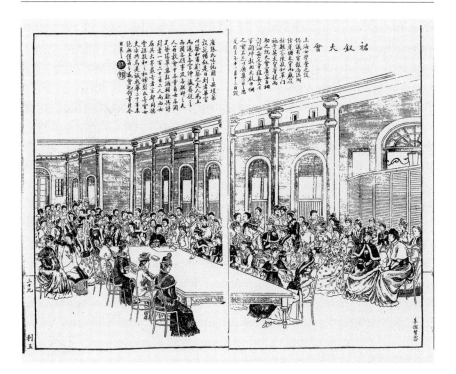

"The Great Meeting of Women."

Zhang Gardens and brought together 122 people to discuss arrangements for the first school for women to be founded and operated by Chinese people. The text at the top of the picture, which was packed with details, praised the event, calling it "a gathering that had not occurred even once in China during the past two thousand years—what good fortune to see it today!" In addition to the facts, however, this report also included titillating talk about whether the wife of a well-known pharmaceuticals magnate made an appearance.

Despite its contents being a mixed bag, we can glean from readers' subsequent recollections that the deepest impression left by the *Dianshizhai Pictorial* was its inclusion of current events and new knowledge. Consequently, its contribution to the eastward movement of Western learning cannot be understated. It would not be entirely accurate, however, to argue that Major was particularly interested in enlightening his readers. It would be closer to the truth to say that the curiosities laid out on the pages of the *Pictorial* fit perfectly with Shanghai readers' taste for the new and exciting. By including a wide range of people in its potential readership—from highly regarded officials and scholars to merchants, hawkers, and peddlers—the journal also had to become something less than highbrow, even as it found ways to innovate. The *Pictorial* even makes a cameo appearance in the late Qing fiction writer Wu Jianren's (1866–1912) famous novel *Strange Events Witnessed over the Past Twenty Years*: the main character's elder sister reads the *Pictorial* and leaves the other newspapers she has bought for her younger brother—a detail that attests to the journal's commercial success and wide distribution.

Following the successful example of the *Dianshizhai Pictorial*, nearly a hundred more pictorial magazines were launched, all of which were directed toward popular audiences. As one national crisis followed another, including the first Sino-Japanese War (1894–1895), the Hundred Days' Reform (1898), and the Boxer Rebellion (1900), voices advocating reform grew ever louder. As a result, late Qing pictorials became more focused on their social function. For example, the *Enlightenment Pictorial*, first published in June 1903, demonstrated how pictorials across the land were self-consciously pursuing a social agenda as it declared its intention to "expand and disseminate learning among the people and support reform that will strengthen the nation."

Alongside the growth of pictorial magazines during the late Qing, many literary journals also began adding new kinds of pictures and images; this development drew directly from the tradition of illustrated fiction popular during the Ming and Qing dynasties. An early example of this kind of journal is *Wondrous Shanghai*, first published by the Dianshizhai Lithographic Bookstore in February 1892, with a total run of fifteen issues. It mainly published the work of Han Bangqing (1856–1894), including short stories written in classical Chinese that were collected under the title *Sketches by Taixian* and his famous novel composed in the Wu dialect, *Lives of Shanghai Flowers*; they were all accompanied by fine illustrations. Unfortunately, it was far too difficult for one person to write, edit, and oversee the printing of a magazine on his or her own. As a result, *Wondrous Shanghai* folded in less than a year. It would be another decade before similar literary journals that combined text and image would gain a solid footing, largely due to the growing importance of ideas about enlightenment and reform.

A 1902 advertisement that appeared in the forty-first issue of the *New People's Serial* ran with the headline "China's Only Literary Journal, *New Fiction*." The ad declared that the most important characteristic of *New Fiction* was its "pictures" (*tuhua*):

> The magazine searches for portraits and pictures of heroes, famous scholars, and beauties from East and West and ancient and modern times, providing them for your enjoyment. It also includes pictures of places of great scenic beauty or historical importance. Every work of fiction also includes the finest illustrations that are made by well-known artists based on the artistic vision of the author or the translator.

It is not difficult, of course, to see the value of illustrations in magazines: including them in every issue, however, was another problem. Using pictures or illustrations that were already in circulation was a simple matter of paper and printing techniques, but it was more difficult to produce high-quality illustrations for every work of fiction. Understanding the artistic vision of a work and finding a well-known artist to make such images on a deadline was no small task. In reality, *New People's Serial* and *New Fiction*—both of which were edited by Liang Qichao (1873–1929)—along with the many other literary journals that emerged during this time, were more likely to print photographs instead of illustrations or directly reprint images of famous foreign paintings. Aside from pictorials that were devoted to illustrations, the one literary journal that worked to make illustrations for every piece it printed was *Illustrated Fiction*.

Illustrated Fiction was launched in May 1903 and was printed and published by the Commercial Press in Shanghai. From 1903 to 1906, the press published seventy-two issues of the bimonthly journal, which came to be known as one of the "big four" fiction journals of the late Qing. (The other three were *New Fiction*, *Fiction Monthly*, and *Grove of Fiction*.) Under the editorship of the famous fiction writer Li Boyuan (1867–1906), *Illustrated Fiction* worked to give readers an illustration for every chapter of every work of fiction it printed—a very difficult task to complete consistently. Unlike the pictorial magazines of Shanghai, Beijing, and Guangzhou that included images that were signed by famous

Illustrated Fiction, cover of the final issue. Credit: Library of Miscellaneous Books in Beijing (Beijing zashuguan).

artists, virtually none of the illustrations in *Illustrated Fiction* and similar literary journals bore the signatures of their makers, much in the same way that the text written for pictorial magazines often went unsigned. Here we see how publications took pride in and placed special emphasis on different aspects of their work.

As a so-called transitional era, the late Qing is best known for its intermingling of East with West and old with new. These combinations pervaded everyday life and contemporary modes of expression. Confronted with a rapidly changing world, artists were often flustered as they worked to adjust their styles to keep up with the times. Leafing through the many pictures in *Illustrated Fiction*, one sees that those pieces that depict scenes of traditional life are nearly always very good; depictions of modern life, however, seem to fall short of the mark. For instance, unlike the grand and perhaps idealized illustrations of Shanghai in Wu Youru's (1840?–1893?) *Sights and Scenes of Shenjiang* and other collections, the illustrations for Li's *Modern Times* are in fact taken from everyday scenes of contemporary Chinese life. Although the pictures in the latter may seem to contain too many trivial details, they are in fact quite natural and filled with emotion, an impressive accomplishment in its own right.

Over the thirty years that elapsed between the launch of the *Dianshizhai Pictorial* in 1884 and the gradual decline of lithographed journals following the 1911 revolution, many of the hundred-odd illustrated journals carried serializations of fiction. With the exception of Huang Shizhong's (1872–1912) novel *A Twenty-Year Dream of Splendor*, which was published in the Guangzhou-based *Current Events Pictorial*, none of these serializations were successful. Generally speaking, late Qing journals were not particularly suited to publishing long novels, instead excelling at the use of illustrations and photographs to explain the news, tell stories, and transmit new knowledge. A notable exception, the illustrations in *Illustrated Fiction* were not that impressive, but many excellent works of fiction appeared there, including Li's *Modern Times* and *Living Hell*, Liu E's (1857–1909) *Travels of Lao Can*, Wu Jianren's *Amazing Tales of a Blind Swindler*, Ouyang Juyuan's *Warming under the Sun in Winter*, and Lian Mengqing's (d. 1914) *Women's Chatter*. All these novels belong to the genre of the exposé. Liu's *Travels of Lao Can*, often hailed as the

Modern Times, chapter 17.

greatest work of late Qing fiction, depicts an itinerant doctor's quixotic encounters with cases of injustice and corruption, while Li's *Modern Times* renders a sarcastic account of a society caught in modern transformations. Because the journal folded, however, none of the serialized novels were published in complete form in *Illustrated Fiction*'s pages. Nonetheless, *Illustrated Fiction* was a crucial platform during a lively period of Chinese literary history.

As the types of publications increased and writers and illustrators grew more specialized, readers' tastes followed suit. After the 1911 revolution, fewer and fewer lithographic pictorials continued to publish fiction, and literary journals abandoned formats that required illustrations to accompany every item in the journal. With these developments, the time when pictures and text flourished together in literary publications came to an end.

XIA XIAOHONG *and* CHEN PINGYUAN
Translated by Michael Gibbs Hill

1890 · FALL

> Two failed civil service examinees trade copies of their unfinished novels on a steamship to Shanghai.

Lives of Shanghai Flowers, *Dialect Fiction, and the Genesis of Vernacular Modernity*

Han Bangqing (1856–1894) and Sun Yusheng (?–1939), both Shanghai newspapermen, met for the first time while competing in the highest-level triennial civil service examinations in Beijing. Having failed, they traveled home by steamship, passing the time by trading copies of their unfinished novels, Han's *Lives of Shanghai Flowers* and Sun's *Dreams of Shanghai Splendor,* both of which offer panoramic accounts of contemporary life in the Shanghai courtesans' quarters. One gets little sense of the significance of this moment from the basic scenario; the sight of two returning examination candidates distracting themselves from failure by exchanging their writings had been commonplace on Chinese roads and canals for more than five centuries. But hints of something new and unusual come from the ocean route and the restriction of the unfinished novels' settings to a single city (in contrast with premodern novels, which often ranged over the entirety of China). From these facts alone we realize that we are in the second half of nineteenth century, not the seventeenth or the fifteenth.

Indeed, this exchange of novels in manuscript betrays in its own slight way tectonic shifts already under way in the structure of the literate economy and in the very imagination of a national community. What was soon to follow for these novels, publication in installments, radically reconfigured the relationship between authors and readers and took the first steps toward providing an alternative sphere of literary production to replace the civil service examination system when it was abolished. At the same time, the question of whether to write in dialect, which Han and Sun hotly contested as they traded their manuscripts—one with dialogue in dialect and the other in standard vernacular—reminds us that over the course of the twentieth century, vernacular Chinese, as a modern form of writing and communication, was often anticipated, even chided into being, by predecessors in dialect form.

It is worth dwelling on what Han and Sun did not do after failing at the metropolitan testing session. By qualifying for this level of the civil service examinations, they had already substantially distinguished themselves; should they never advance further, those that reached this level could still expect comfortable careers as educators, editors of scholarly collections, bureaucratic assistants in service to magistrates or governors, or well-compensated participants in enterprises turning a profit from commodities as various as books, grain, and land. Instead, we now remember them not only as authors but also as pioneering editors and publishers in the Shanghai newspaper and magazine world, a choice of occupation that must have been as interesting in its particulars as it was low in social status and uncertain in its rewards.

In Europe, one would be hard-pressed to say that the novel and the newspaper replaced an existing structure of cultural production: through their dramatic expansion of the audience for the written word, and their unprecedented synchronization of actions taken and reported—both within the plots of complicated fictional narratives and on the pages of the newspaper—the novel and the newspaper imagined national communities in ways that were, for Europe, without comparable precedent. In the closing decades of the Qing dynasty, by contrast, we see the wholesale *abandonment* of an existing structure of literary production—the civil service examination system. The examination had involved persons and aspirations across China in regular and synchronized competition, and had thereby defined quite neatly the reach of a central administration and its ideology over the course of nearly six centuries.

Although the "new-style" schools and curricula that appeared at the turn of the twentieth century in China may seem to constitute natural replacements for the examination system abolished in 1905, the functions of that system went far beyond a narrow definition of education. The functions of the examination system ranged from the regular and regulated production of the Ming and Qing political orders to the systematic articulation of the terms on which individuals could declare their independence from, and even opposition to, those orders and the literary production on which they were grounded. The decades around 1905 are marked by energetic attempts to establish the novel as a genre worthy of public discussion in China, and periodical publication as a key mode of knowledge production and distribution, and it is in these arenas, as much as in the founding of new schools and the publication of new textbooks, that we must seek the inheritors of the examination system. Examination essays were often referred to as "contemporary prose"; this sense of connection to the present moment—whether that connection is posed positively in terms of relevance, or rather negatively as a limitation—finds an echo in newspapers and the installment fiction printed in their pages in the early twentieth century. Han and Sun stand at a crucial inflection point in this process, not from the perspective of intellectual history or ideological conflict—Kang Youwei (1858–1927) and Liang Qichao (1873–1929), among others, would be key figures in that story—but rather in a materialist cultural history of the practices and aesthetics of literary production.

The distribution of novels in Ming and Qing China had always been marked by delay and relative privacy: close friends could read novels in manuscript, waiting for the author to complete new chapters and then pass them around, but unlike poetry, essays, and letters, novels were rarely published during the author's lifetime, and filiations of influence were articulated only through sequels and continuations that appeared years or decades after the original. Well into the nineteenth century, we may say without exaggeration that the novel was one of the more private genres of Chinese writing. Han and Sun's exchange of their work in manuscript may not have been the first instance in which novels with similar topics were written simultaneously, but it was the first time that unfinished manuscripts were exchanged and subsequently published in installments, redefining the temporal relationship between authors and readers, and among authors themselves. In this way, fiction emerges to a broad readership contemporary to its author, and begins finally to challenge the conventional Chinese understanding of poetry, essays, prefaces, and letters as the primary means for timely and public constructions of one's reputation as a thinking individual. Once the novel acquired this capacity, influential genres aimed at political or cultural critique, such as the "novels of exposure" and "social novels," developed with surprising speed in the early 1900s.

Indeed, although Liang highlights European and Japanese sources of inspiration for his attempts at a political novel, if the novel had not already been established as a genre both public *and* timely by the time his *Future of New China* began to appear in installments in 1902, his own distinctive contribution, to argue that the novel could be appropriated to make explicitly political arguments about the future of the nation, would have encountered readers as yet unschooled in the reading of novels as a public practice with immediate relevance. We may borrow Miriam Hansen's (1949–2011) idea of "vernacular modernism" to better understand what is at stake here, not only at the turn of the century, but well into the 1910s and 1920s, when new generations of critique continued to depend on the very matrix of readerly practices that they reflexively condemned. From Mandarin Ducks and Butterflies romances to longer works published in installments like Zhu Shouju's (1892–1966) *Tides of Shanghai*, popular literature in the opening decades of the twentieth century continued the legacy of urban fiction like *Lives of Shanghai Flowers* and *Dreams of Shanghai Splendor*, constituting an indispensable substrate of cultural practice out of which May Fourth challenges to "tradition" could grow, and against which those challenges could in turn define themselves.

The similarity between the literary ecology of the May Fourth era and the literary ecology made possible by the examination system of the Ming and Qing, in which radical critiques of examination writing flourished, is striking. Criticism of the poor aesthetic quality, falsity, repetitiveness, and questionable morality of civil service examination essays of the sixteenth through nineteenth centuries yielded in less than a decade to criticism of the poor aesthetic quality, falsity, repetitiveness, and questionable morality of popular fiction, newspaper writing, and mass literary culture more generally. If in each case the critique failed to do justice to the variety and creativity inherent in its object, and instead responded to the diversity of the examination sphere, and, subsequently, the vernacular mediasphere, with a monotony of condemnation, we can only take that failure as a cautionary tale of the persistent limitations and dependencies of literary critique as métier.

Just over a century after *Lives of Shanghai Flowers* appeared in a volume edition in 1894, with its dialogue almost exclusively in local dialect, the noted Taiwanese director Hou Hsiao-hsien (1947–) began work on a film based on the novel. Despite the fact that few of the stars involved in the project knew Shanghai dialect, Hou insisted on using dialect as much as possible, recruiting actors and actresses who could speak in Shanghai dialect, like Rebecca Pan (1931–); encouraging others to do their best to imitate it; and, in the case of the actress Hada Michiko (1968–), resorting to dubbing. Sun would not have approved: his Shanghai novel was written in standard vernacular; he had cautioned Han against writing in a dialect "limited to one corner of China" rather than in Mandarin; and he later maintained that the popularity of *Lives of Shanghai Flowers* suffered as a result of Han's unwillingness to compromise. Shanghai dialect film has never been, and will likely never become, a substantial contributor to mainstream Chinese cultural production. But films made in another dialect, Cantonese, were for a crucial period in the second half of the twentieth century identified as the standard-bearers of Chinese film culture in Asian and global contexts, and provided both positive and negative inspiration to mainland filmmakers of the 1980s and 1990s.

Hong Kong film, a cinema often thought to be relentlessly oriented toward mass taste and the bottom line, took shape at midcentury as one element of a mediasphere dominated by newspapers and magazines, many of which depended on installment fiction to attract and keep readers. Wong Kar-wai (1958–) weaves this aspect of the colony's culture into two of his most substantial films, *In the Mood for Love* and *2046*, each of which centers on a writer of installment fiction. Unlike Shanghai installment fiction of earlier decades, Hong Kong installment fiction from the 1940s onward centered on martial arts fiction, a subject that translated smoothly onto the contemporary screen. Although scholarly attention now is focused on Hong Kong martial arts installment fiction written in Mandarin, it is telling that the earliest best-selling examples were in fact written in Cantonese. As was the case in turn-of-the-century Shanghai, dialect installment fiction in midcentury Hong Kong—quite successful in its own right—was followed by works that appropriated and reproduced its distinctive topics and tropes in Mandarin to sell even more widely.

Sun's insistence that the use of dialect places constraints on the popularity of a cultural product depends on a conception of one's audience as national: with millions of native speakers of Shanghai-area dialects and Cantonese, one can fault dialect writing and film as limited in appeal only if a broader group of all Chinese speakers, across dialects, is taken as the natural target audience. The vehemence with which Sun's argument is repeated by later critics suggests a certain unease over the relative status of cultural production in standard Mandarin vernacular vis-à-vis cultural production in dialect.

Indeed, from the end of the nineteenth century to the end of the twentieth, Chinese vernacular modernism may be understood at crucial moments to have been a modernism that began in a dialect or minor form, and crossed over to the vernacular generally identified as standard only later, whether in Shanghai novels published in installments, short fiction by the self-consciously modern and cosmopolitan neo-sensationalists, or Hong Kong film. May Fourth figures like Hu Shi (1891–1962) and Liu Fu (1891–1934) tended to frame their interest in dialect writing with reference to the politics of European languages and ideas of the folk, but they were not above acknowledging the pioneering character of a work like *Lives of Shanghai Flowers* and its potential to reinvigorate the literary language. The "root-seeking" authors of the 1980s such as Han Shaogong (1953–) struck a similar note decades later, with their rural, locally oriented narratives and their interest in "nonstandardized" culture. Han Bangqing and Sun Yusheng's 1890 conversation marks the moment at which the potential for a cultural innovation specific to dialect spheres and minor literatures was asserted; Hou's film version of Han's novel arrived in 1998 to close out the twentieth century, at a moment when Shanghai dialect encountered severe challenges on its home ground even in daily practice, and Hong Kong film looked over its shoulder at its ever-more-successful students fluent in Mandarin. Will the "post-" era (postcolonial, postsocialist, and postmodern) that is supposed to herald diversity and a movement beyond simple metanarratives of the nation turn out merely to represent a reconsolidation of cultural leadership around a linguistic center, rather than the continued diffusion of that leadership among its many peripheries?

BIBLIOGRAPHY: Alexander Des Forges, *Mediasphere Shanghai: The Aesthetics of Cultural Production* (Honolulu, 2007). John Christopher Hamm, *Paper Swordsmen: Jin Yong and the Modern Chinese Martial Arts Novel* (Honolulu, 2005). David Der-wei Wang, *Fin-de-Siècle Splendor: Repressed Modernities of Late Qing Fiction, 1848–1911* (Stanford, CA, 1997).

ALEXANDER DES FORGES

1895 · MAY 25

A fiction contest is announced in the Shanghai daily newspaper *Shenbao.*

The "New Novel" before the Rise of the New Novel

On May 25, 1895, an extraordinary notice appeared in the Shanghai daily newspaper *Shenbao*. It announced a contest for a new kind of novel (*shixin xiaoshuo*) on the subject of three evils afflicting Chinese society—opium, foot-binding, and the examination essay. Monetary prizes were promised for the best entries, and it was mentioned that some of the contestants might be offered regular employment as writers. Certain requirements were set for the entries: for example, they should describe the harm done by the three evils and also offer solutions; their argument should be thoroughly integrated into the action of the story; and their language should be clear and intelligible even to women and children. The same notice was also published in the June 1896 issue of the *Chinese Recorder*, the monthly journal of the Protestant missions, along with an introductory note in English, part of which read, "It is hoped that students, teachers and pastors connected with the various missionary establishments in China will be shown the accompanying advertisement and encouraged to take part in the competition." The notice was signed (in Chinese), "Fu Lanya, British scholar," while the note was signed, "John Fryer," and dated May 25, 1895.

Both name and date are significant. Fryer (1839–1928), the son of an English clergyman, had arrived in Shanghai in 1861. He had intended to become a missionary but was rejected by the organizations to which he applied—a scandal involving his wife is said to have been the cause. After teaching in a mission school and editing a Chinese newspaper, he was offered the post of translator with the Jiangnan Arsenal, where for the next thirty years he helped translate a large number of science and engineering texts. Although largely self-taught in the sciences, he is credited, aided by his Chinese collaborators, with introducing more Western science to China during the nineteenth century than anyone else. Besides his translation work, he also founded the first Chinese scientific journal and established the first science bookstore.

As to the significance of the date, the newspaper notice came just weeks after the signing of the Treaty of Shimonoseki, which put an end to the war between China and Japan. Public outrage over China's humiliating defeat and the harsh terms of the treaty led to unprecedented protests, particularly among the candidates gathered in Beijing for the triennial civil service examinations. (The protests foreshadowed those of Beijing students against the Treaty of Versailles in 1919—the start of the May Fourth Movement.) Amid this intellectual furor, Fryer, like others, saw the possibility of fundamental social and institutional change. In an essay he notes "the great burst of pure patriotism that the war produced in all ranks of society," and, under the heading "The Educational Outlook for 1896," he writes in the *Chinese Recorder* of January 1896,

> The educational prospect for the new year on which we have just entered is by far the most encouraging that has appeared in the whole history of foreign intercourse with China. The war with Japan, with all its disasters and sufferings, has not been without its educational lessons of immense benefit alike to the government and people of the "Middle Kingdom."

He is further encouraged by "the literary and other societies that have recently been formed," referring particularly to the Qiangxue hui (Society for the study of self-strengthening) that had recently been formed in Beijing by Kang Youwei (1858–1927) and Liang Qichao (1873–1929). He concludes the piece by affirming that "the Protestant missionary teaching and training" was essential for the reforms to succeed.

Hoping to exploit the passions of the moment, Fryer was promoting the fiction contest on his own initiative and from his own bookstore. It differs from the prize essay contests on "modern" topics that he had helped conduct for the Polytechnic Institution in Shanghai, because in this case he was not merely trying to mold opinion on the part of young intellectuals; he was trying to enlist some of those intellectuals in molding opinion among the masses. As a model of the fiction he hoped to elicit, he mentions only *Uncle Tom's Cabin*, but he may well have also had Victorian reformist fiction in mind.

Although Fryer was not a missionary himself, his career can be compared with the careers of the small minority of missionaries who devoted themselves to the cause of secular reform in China. Unlike the great majority of their peers, who spent their time in traditional evangelism, these men concluded that the best way to bring about change in China—and concurrently to spread Christian doctrine—was by influencing China's leaders through the medium of *Xixue*, or "Western learning," science in particular. Their literary work, carried out with the aid of Chinese literary assistants or "writers," brought few obvious results during the 1870s and 1880s, but became extraordinarily influential for a few years following the war with Japan. In 1887, an organization, the Society for the Diffusion of Christian and General Knowledge among the Chinese (SDK), was formed in Shanghai to further their aims. Let us briefly consider the literary work of two of the society's more influential members.

Young J. Allen (1836–1907), born and educated in Georgia, arrived in Shanghai in 1860 as a missionary of the Methodist Church, South. Due to the American Civil War, however, the mission funds were cut off and he could serve only part time. He taught in a school, edited newspapers and journals, and translated texts for the Jiangnan Arsenal. He also created the journal *The Church News*, and then, to reflect its growing proportion of secular material, changed its name in 1874 to *Global Magazine*. After leaving journalism in 1883 to accept a supervisory post with the mission, he returned to it in 1889, when the SDK revived the *Global Magazine* and invited him to be the editor. With its wide range of articles, the journal was for several years the single most powerful organ of reform in China, and Allen's own history of the war with Japan, *An Account of the Sino-Japanese War*, which included his ideas on social and institutional change, was one of the most influential publications of the time.

Timothy Richard (1845–1919) came to China in 1870 from Wales as a member of the Baptist Missionary Society. He began as an evangelist, but gradually changed his approach in an attempt to win over the Chinese leadership. The decisive change in his career came in Taiyuan in 1887. After helping to cope with a disastrous famine, he had for four years, from 1880 to 1884, put himself through an intensive course of self-study, principally in science, Buddhism, and Daoism, and for three years thereafter he gave monthly lectures to the local officials on scientific subjects. This approach appalled some of his colleagues in Shanxi, and, to avoid splitting the mission, Richard decided to leave the province. Then, before he had settled on what to do next, he received an offer, conveyed through the powerful official Li Hongzhang and others, to edit a Chinese daily newspaper in Tianjin. "The appointment," as Richard says, "was most providential." The *Times*, to which he soon added a weekly edition, supplied him with a platform from which to advocate his ideas on a multitude of subjects. After spending almost a year editing the newspaper, he was invited in 1890 to move to Shanghai and become secretary of the SDK. During the 1890s he moved increasingly beyond domestic concerns and took on the role of international statesman, producing many far-reaching—and sometimes farfetched—schemes for the future of China.

In 1891 he began translating, or rather summarizing, Edward Bellamy's (1850–1898) futuristic novel, *Looking Backward: 2000–1887* (1888), a work that was to inspire Liang Qichao's own first novel. Richard's most influential translation, however, was of Robert Mackenzie's *The 19th Century, a History*, which he began translating in 1892 with the assistance of Cai Erkang (1851–1921) and finished in 1895; the preface to the translation, expressed in vehement language, is dated the same month as that in which Fryer launched his fiction contest. Mackenzie's *History* is a popular work that, although it begins with the French Revolution and Napoleon, devotes most of its attention to Britain. It especially emphasizes the forty years of relative peace between the Battle of Waterloo and the Crimean War, and Mackenzie dwells in detail on the social, institutional, and legal reforms of that period. In his view, the Reform Bill was the necessary institutional development that made possible the elimination of many age-old inhumanities and abuses. Two triumphant chapters, labeled "The Victories of Peace," detail a long list of Victorian advances in scientific and technological invention. They describe the thorough transformation of a society by peaceful means. It was presumably the notion that a country could transform itself by laws and institutions and become modern and prosperous in a relatively short period of time that captured the imaginations of the Chinese reformers. Richard mentions happily that, whereas in the past the Chinese booksellers had refused to stock the foreigners' publications, now, in the aftermath of the war, they were only too glad to do so; indeed, they paid the foreigners the compliment of pirating their work. He estimates that a million copies of his Chinese translation of the history circulated in China.

Fryer's contest drew as many as 162 entries, which induced him to increase the number of prizes. The names of the winners were published in *Shenbao*, and the names, together with Fryer's comments, were published in *Global Magazine* and *Missionary Review*. In a note in the *Chinese Recorder* of March 1896, he remarks that at least half of the contestants were from mission schools or colleges. Although he formed a low opinion of most of the entries, some of them impressed him: "This experiment has drawn out a few stories that really are worth publishing, and it is hoped that some of them will be issued by the end of the year."

It was not to be. In June 1896, Fryer left Shanghai to take up a professorship at the University of California and rejoin his family, who had been living in Oakland since 1892, leaving the "few stories" unpublished. In fact, the contest itself was forgotten and, when scholars finally began to pay attention to it, all of the manuscripts were assumed to have been lost. It seemed that the only tangible effects of Fryer's contest, apart from his requirements and comments, were two novels directly inspired by the contest, one of which, *Delightful History of a Glorious Age*, published in December 1895, can fairly be called the first modern Chinese novel. But then came a miraculous discovery. In November 2006, most of the entries,

150 out of the original 162, were found in a cache of manuscripts in the University of California, Berkeley's East Asian Library. They have since been published, thus vastly increasing the number of Chinese novels that survive from the late nineteenth century.

Fryer's contest is noteworthy as the first attempt to induce literary intellectuals to devote themselves to the writing of novels, specifically novels that attacked social ills, for a broad reading public. His ideas had a certain influence on Liang Qichao, whose own proposals for a new novel (*xin xiaoshuo*) some seven years later had a vastly greater impact.

BIBLIOGRAPHY: Adrian A. Bennett, *Missionary Journalist in China: Young J. Allen and His Magazines, 1860–1883* (Athens, GA, 1983). Patrick Hanan, *Chinese Fiction of the Nineteenth and Early Twentieth Centuries* (New York, 2004). Timothy Richard, *Forty-Five Years in China* (New York, 1916). Zhou Xinping, ed., *Qingmo shixin xiaoshuo ji* (Shanghai, 2011).

PATRICK DEWES HANAN

1896 · APRIL 17

"Four million people wailed at once."

Qiu Fengjia and the Poetics of Tears

On April 17, 1896, Qiu Fengjia (1864–1912), Taiwan's best-known classical-style poet, then living in exile from his homeland in Guangdong Province, composed the poem "Spring Sentiments":

> To dispel my lingering spring sentiments, I force myself to look at
>   the mountains.
> The past still startles my heart, and my tears are on the verge of falling.
> Four million people wailed at once.
> Taiwan was ceded on this day last year.

William Wordsworth (1770–1850) equated "all good poetry" with the "spontaneous overflow of powerful feelings." Borrowing that definition, we must ask, What caused the overflow of feelings that we see in Qiu's poem?

Two years before Qiu wrote "Spring Sentiments," the first Sino-Japanese War had broken out. The two regional powers fought to exercise control over Korea, long considered a tribute state of China. To the surprise of many, Japan handily defeated the Qing empire. The aftermath changed how Taiwanese people viewed both China and Japan. The war was a world event, disrupting Western plans to mark out spheres of interest in East Asia, and forcing Western powers to view Japan as a formidable foe. Japan's victory marked the very beginning of the country's militaristic expansion, the effects of which the world would keenly feel in the first half of the twentieth century.

On April 17, 1895, precisely a year before Qiu wrote his poem, China signed the Treaty of Shimonoseki, which forced China to relinquish all semblance of dominion over Korea and to cede the island of Taiwan to Japan. Born into a Taiwanese Hakka family, Qiu had been a child prodigy, achieving a *xiucai* degree, the elementary degree of the civil service exam system, at the young age of fourteen. He had taken a leave of absence from government service and returned to Taiwan in order to tend to his aged father. When the news of cession reached Taiwan, Qiu acted quickly, sending several petitions "on behalf of every wailing islander" to the emperor. In these petitions, he warned the emperor that if the Treaty of Shimonoseki were not annulled, the Taiwanese would fight to the death to preserve their Chinese nationality. The emperor may have sympathized with the people, but his hands were tied—Empress Dowager Cixi (1835–1908) held the ultimate authority and the Qing government was too weak to refuse the Japanese demands. Later in the same year, when the Japanese troops arrived to take over Taiwan, they met vehement resistance from militia that Qiu had organized. Without money or ammunition, the resistance's defeat was inevitable. While fighting a desperate guerilla war, Qiu spearheaded the establishment of a nominally independent "Republic of Formosa." By declaring Taiwan a "republic" independent of China and appealing to international law, Qiu had hoped to win support from Western powers. None came to his aid.

Caught between an old empire on the verge of collapse and an imperialist power on the rise, Qiu did everything he could to save Taiwan. But he suffered from a personal crisis that mimicked the national crisis of Taiwan's abandonment. Although Qiu had vowed to perish with Taiwan, when he heard that the Japanese army had captured the vital port city of Jilong, he secretly retreated to China. Rumor had it that Qiu embezzled what remained of the soldiers' pay and provisions and ran off. When Qiu arrived in his ancestral homeland of China, the land to which he had vowed such loyalty, he himself felt out of place and became very homesick for Taiwan. The unhomeliness of his homeland, the impossibility of homecoming, and the circulating rumors of his betrayal drove him deeply into melancholy.

Seeking comfort, Qiu turned to writing lyric poems, poems notable for the prevalence of imagery revolving around tears. He found in tears the words to express his mixed feelings and to show his undying loyalty to Taiwan. His contemporaries Lin Shu (1852–1924), Liu E (1857–1909), and Wu Jianren (1866–1912) all wrote about crying for various reasons, some personal and others national, but not one of them took to heart the mutual reference between tear and language in the way that a classical-style poet like Qiu did. As Judith Nelson eloquently puts it, "Writing about crying is to describe in words what crying does without them." For Qiu, "as poetry writes itself, tears and ink become inseparable." He might not have cried ink, but he wanted us to believe that his words were written in tears.

Tears appear too frequently to count in classical-style Chinese poetry. The *Book of Songs*, the earliest collection of Chinese lyric poetry, compiled more than two millennia ago, offers lines like this: "Thinking of the beloved afar, my tears fall like rain." As tears fall, they traverse old boundaries and trace new ones. Such a hyperbolic language of tears thus provides a glimpse into the delicate overlap between a poet's selfhood and his persona. For instance, when a male Chinese poet assumes the persona of a melancholic wife pining for the long-overdue return of her husband from the military, his / her tears are as imaginary as they are real. The sincerity of tears has rarely been a subject for debate for Chinese readers. They fondly embrace such poetic tours de force; believing someone else capable of emotional duplicity indicates that one is capable of such duplicity himself or herself.

Questioning the sincerity of tears may reflect the skeptic's own untrustworthiness. Accordingly, Qiu relied on poetic tears to return the suspicious gazes of those who believed that he had betrayed Taiwan:

Abandoning Taiwan was not the original plan.
I cried to Heaven and received no mercy.

If death spares me ten years,
I am bound to return with my full strength.

And another ending he steeped in tears:

Without any grand achievement, I gave up my pursuit.
The useless assembly of talents was but my wasted effort.
In dreams I still wailed inconsolably with my petitions.
Crisscrossing were the deep traces of tears on my pillow.

He wrote the first poem in 1896, but ten years later he had still not returned to Taiwan. Qiu had betrayed his words once again.

Even if, unlike contemporaneous readers, we have no scruples about doubting Qiu's real emotions, we need not be skeptical of Qiu's sincerity; he might have expressed his true intentions. Autobiographical poems such as Qiu's are complex. Stephen Owen rightly calls Chinese poetry a "labyrinth of desire," in which one's true self and the roles one assumes mingle. This is especially true in Qiu's case because where there are tears, there are desires: the persistent desire to explain himself and the impossible desire to reclaim what was lost.

Xiaofei Tian takes this point even further. Because poetry is an ever-expanding labyrinth of both the poet's and the reader's desires, Tian argues, the writing and reading of poetry will always remain an incomplete project. Tian's insight illuminates the way to move carefully from Qiu's poetics to his politics of tears, and to consider what may have given his classical-style poems their "modern" significance.

Through the language of tears, Qiu identified with historical figures. He frequently alluded to their crying or cited their teary lines. He recontextualized bygone tears to give them a modern-day relatability, which, in turn, added historical depth to contemporary affairs. For Qiu, crying about the loss of Taiwan was crying about other past events related to death, dynastic transitions, and loyalty to the emperor. Even if in reality Taiwan's political connection to China had been severed, Qiu's tears bound the two places together again. Through the medium of tears, losing Taiwan was an event that brought the Chinese, past and present, together in wailing. In tears, as Qiu notes, "heroic spirits from various dynasties empathize with one another." Therefore whenever Qiu cried, he was not crying alone or just for himself:

> I, for the loyalists, howl again.
> East wind blows, my tears rise higher than the spring tides.

When the occasion demands, the intensity of crying escalates from a select few individual loyalists to a multitude: "Four million people wailed at once."

Simply put, to incite tears and (re)cite teary lines illustrates the exhibitive nature of language: to explain intent and to comment on current events by reflecting on what has come before. Whether or not crying was successful in helping Qiu to justify his inglorious change of heart, it became a salient feature of his poetry, one that situates him in a cultural matrix and further secures his position in the history of Chinese lyric poetry.

Notably, Qiu wrote about tears less often as he grew more accustomed to life in China, where he encountered new possibilities for writing and understanding literature and history. At the turn of the twentieth century, intellectuals sought to "rejuvenate" the old China by "revolutionizing" existing ways of writing poetry, fiction, and history. Qiu was a pillar of the "poetry revolution":

> Lately people in the poetic realm sing the tune of revolution.
> I have yet to meet a poet who reigns supreme.
> Bleed all brushes' blood in between heaven and earth.
> Battle with all the dragons in the endless sea of words.

For the poetic valiance he displayed in this poem, some considered Qiu the best of the revolutionary poets. Even though a poem like this entrenches the stereotype of revolution as bloodshed, it also casts the poet in a positive, if belligerent, light. Indeed, Qiu worked diligently to explain the fast-changing world and his shifting worldview in his later poetic works. As Jon Eugene von Kowallis points out, classical-style Chinese poetry at the time "did serve its writers and their intended readership as a vehicle to articulate a complex and sophisticated understanding of, as well as reaction to, the entry of modernity."

In the meantime, Qiu became actively involved in educational reform. It was his belief that "to strengthen China, it is necessary to cultivate its people. To cultivate people, it is necessary to establish as many schools as possible." He made trips to places as far away as Southeast Asia to meet with Chinese migrant-settlers and to raise funds. His friendship and correspondence with descendants of Chinese settlers in Southeast Asia reveals the diasporic dimension of early twentieth-century modern Chinese literature. Upon returning from his trips, Qiu established his first school of Western learning—the Lingdong Language School—in Guangdong in 1901, with the goal of modernizing the Chinese education system. He went on to establish several other Western-style schools in the remaining decade of his life.

In a poem written in 1902 to his distant cousin, who had persuaded him to retreat to China, Qiu appeared more confident than ever:

I am in the best years of my life and you too are young.
It's a pity that you hide in the ocean island.
The Asiatic continent is changing rapidly every day.
Trend of the time awaits heroes' creation.

No longer concerned about the unfounded accusations of his betrayal, Qiu now even tried to encourage his cousin to leave Taiwan to join him. He had apparently expanded the scope of both his poetic vision and his outlook on life, moving beyond the particularities of the historical loss of Taiwan. Qiu could have returned to Taiwan after a few years of exile, but he chose to take root in Chinese soil and bear the fruit of his new calling.

After a palace coup doomed the Hundred Days' Reform, a short-lived movement to overhaul the Qing government in 1898, many disillusioned reformers began to consider armed revolution. For Qiu, "It would be best if the revolution was peaceful. But if destruction and bloodshed must occur, it should not be excessive." He never threw himself into anti-Qing battles the way he had thrown himself into the battle against the Japanese. Yet he provided shelter to revolutionaries, shielding them from imprisonment and persecution. Many who took part in the 1911 Xinhai Revolution, which finally overthrew the Qing dynasty, were graduates from his schools. From pledging his life and loyalty to Qing China, to becoming a reformer-educator closely associated with revolutionaries who worked persistently to overthrow the empire, Qiu's erratic journey in life traced unlikely paths, challenging what it meant to be loyal in modern China.

On February 12, 1912, China's last emperor, Pu Yi (1906–1967), gave up his throne, marking the official end of the Qing empire. In the beginning of this new era, many had hoped that Qiu would continue to educate Chinese youths. Much to their dismay, a sudden and severe case of pneumonia claimed his life on February 25. On his deathbed, Qiu instructed, "My tomb must face south. I have not forgotten about Taiwan."

After Qiu passed away, his son collected and published his poems in 1913. Before this posthumous publication, only family and close friends had received a glimpse of his innermost thoughts. Qiu believed that his poems would "last in history for a thousand years"; and last they did. A century later, his private feelings continue to move the public. They capture the essence of what it is to be restlessly human in a restless world.

Qiu's tears may have cast him in a sentimental light, but they also illuminate certain fundamental questions about his life. Until his end, Qiu remained loyal to the belief that classical-style poetry arouses feeling and generates change. The generative force that motivated and was embodied by his poetry was the same force that gave rise to his various "revolutionary" and educational efforts. These were changes that spoke to the unsettled condition of modern times, and changes that resisted the entropic tendencies of the "modern."

BIBLIOGRAPHY: Jon Kowallis, *The Subtle Revolution: Poets of the "Old Schools" during Late Qing and Early Republican China* (Berkeley, CA, 2006). Judith Kay Nelson, *Seeing through Tears: Crying and Attachment* (New York, 2012). Stephen Owen, *Mi-Lou: Poetry and the Labyrinth of Desire* (Boston, 1989). Stephen Owen, *Remembrances: The Experience of the Past in Classical Chinese Literature* (Boston, 1986). Xiaofei Tian, *Tao Yuanming and the Manuscript Culture: The Record of a Dusty Table* (Seattle, 2005).

CHIEN-HSIN TSAI

1897

> "Countries with systems of writing are wise; those without such
> systems are not. People who are literate are wise, but the illiterate are
> not—it is the same throughout the world. Only our China has a system
> of writing, yet cannot be considered wise, even its literate population
> is not wise. Why is this? I say it is the result of the depredations of the
> classical language."

Language Reform and Its Discontents

This 1897 quote from Qiu Tingliang (1857–1943) is generally considered
to be the earliest influential statement urging that the ordinary means of
written communication be changed from the classical Chinese language
(*wenyan wen*) to the vernacular (*baihua*). Encapsulated within the title
of the essay from which it is drawn is the most important motivation
impelling the change: "On the Vernacular as the Key to Reform [*weixin*]."
The term for reform, *weixin*, is the same word used in Japanese for what
is most often referred to in English as the "Meiji Restoration," but which
should more properly be translated as the "Meiji Reform." That Qiu
uses this word a scant two years after the catastrophic Chinese defeat
at the hands of Meiji Japan in 1895 indicates the high stakes involved in
his appeal: nothing less than wholesale linguistic reform would enable
"reform," a concept that in effect serves as a stand-in for "modernity," as
the latter term had yet to enter the Chinese lexicon. Qiu's essay illustrates
his belief that extending the realm of popular mobilization for national
renewal could only be accomplished by simplifying the written language
and thereby enabling a larger body of readers to receive new ideas; his
rhetoric further indicates that the issue of language was to carry a strong
political valence thereafter. The move to language reform coincided with
the rise of the new definition of the term "*wenxue*," traditionally a general
concept signifying something like humanistic inquiry, but now with a new
meaning imported from Meiji Japan, where it was used as the translation
for the Western term "literature." Linguistic, literary, and political reform
from this point on thus become difficult to separate.

While the written vernacular had a long history in China, having
been used for hundreds of years as the primary language for fiction and
drama, as well as for numerous philosophical dialogues, the norm for

discursive writing was classical Chinese, a language for which the most unimpeachable standard was *Records of the Grand Historian (Shiji)* of Sima Qian (135?–86 BCE), composed in the first century BCE. There had over the centuries developed many subcategories of classical writing, such as *guwen* (ancient-style prose), *shiwen* (or *baguwen*, the "eight-legged essay" mandatory for the imperial civil service examination), as well as a straight expository style used in government documents, to name only a few. These various forms had incorporated much new vocabulary and many new usages over the centuries. The most prestigious form, however, was generally modeled on *guwen*, and there had been repeated academic movements through the years to ensure stylistic fidelity to old forms. In the main, these calls for the purification of writing were stated in highly moralistic terms, with stylistic precision equated with the moral soundness of the ancients and accessible primarily through immersion in the spirit of their writing. The early advocates of the vernacular continued in this didactic vein, but their focus moved from imitation of the old to the virtues of reaching a broader audience through simplification of the registers of writing.

The impetus to linguistic reform given voice by Qiu was also represented by a profusion of vernacular newspapers, published primarily in the cities located along the lower reaches of the Yangtze River. A newly dynamic notion of literature was also very much part of this general effort to create a broader audience, and since one of the principle motivations for the move to the vernacular was simplification and a wider readership, the form chosen as the principal vehicle for reaching a new audience was the novel, assumed to be popular and thus taken as the most useful vector for propagating new ideas to the people. In line with the emphasis on complete reform, it is significant that Liang Qichao (1873–1929), one of the major voices calling for the use of novels to spread the reform message, stipulated as early as 1898 that these new novels were to be based strictly on Western models. Liang believed that the Chinese fictional tradition was plagued by immorality, and therefore should be avoided.

There was, of course, a reaction from the educated elite against these calls for reform, primarily on the grounds that the classical language and the texts written in it were the repository of a cultural tradition that China needed to uphold, particularly in parlous times of aggression by Western imperialism. Significant in these calls to maintain the old language was the air of defensiveness in which they were couched, testifying to the powerful response with which the calls for reform were met. The final defense of the linguistic conservatives, however, was that the very simplicity of vernacular caused it to lack resonance and nuance, and, as the philologist Zhang Taiyan (1868–1936) put it, even when composing in the vernacular, it "lacks a sufficiency of significance, so at times it is necessary to use the classical."

Linked as they were with the push for political reform, with the latter increasingly dominant in the years after 1901, these early efforts at language reform lost momentum as the new century began, although the "new novel" called for by Liang continued to flourish for most of its first decade. Up until at least 1920, however, the discursive language of both the public sphere and private communication continued to be a sort of demotic classical, a language stripped of the elaborate allusions that had rendered some classical writing—notably that of Zhang and the pioneering translator Yan Fu (1853–1921)—quite difficult for the average reader.

It was not until late 1916 that efforts for linguistic reform would shift into high gear, with Hu Shi (1891–1962), then studying in the United States, and Chen Duxiu (1879–1942), founding editor of the reform magazine *New Youth* and newly installed as dean at Peking University, leading the charge. One of Hu's points for reform, echoing the arguments of Qiu, stated succinctly that "the common flaw of classical literature is that it cannot be negotiated by ordinary people." As set out by Hu in his "My Humble Suggestions on Literary Reform," first published in the January 1917 issue of *New Youth* and almost immediately followed by Chen's "On Literary Revolution" the next month, the force of calls to switch to the vernacular reached a new level of intensity. The reform argument by now had moved beyond just the need to expand the audience. Reformers now held that the classical language was so bound to Chinese historical usage that it was not only incapable of expressing new ideas but also made genuine personal expression impossible. The take-no-prisoners attitude that Chen brought to his advocacy of the vernacular (and of which Hu seems to have approved) is summed up in a letter Chen wrote to Hu in which he said:

> The rights and wrongs of my notion that the reform of Chinese literature should entail having the vernacular as the only authentic literature

are so clear that we should not allow room for any opposition; we should take what we advocate as absolutely correct and not allow others to correct us.

This implacability was shared by most of the young reformers who came to dominate the public sphere during and after the May Fourth Movement of the late 1910s, including the highly influential writer Lu Xun (1881–1936). Reform received official sanction in January 1920, when the Department of Education declared that, starting the following academic year, the vernacular was to be the medium of instruction in the first two grades of primary school, with its use to be expanded to higher grades in successive years.

By the time the liberal science educator and Commercial Press editor Du Yaquan (1873–1933) came to consider some of the same issues pertaining to written expression, the pressures to adopt the vernacular had developed apace, to the point of having become virtually irresistible. Du's ideas, however, did not appear until December 1919, in the final issue of the *Eastern Miscellany* that he was to edit, or, indeed, even to publish in; they in effect marked the end of an era. Perhaps because it came so relatively late in the day, there is a kind of desperation or even a sense of hopelessness in Du's attempt to resist the complete "popularization" of the Chinese language and to keep other avenues for writing open. Interestingly enough, his call for opposition to the collapse of the entirety of the spectrum of Chinese writing into one register centers on the need for more flexibility in literary language, testifying yet again to the powerful influence of the new discourse of simplification on *wenxue*. As he wrote:

> The culture of any society becomes more complex as it progresses. This is particularly true of the wide scope of our nation's literature, and it would be completely inappropriate to narrow it down by insisting on limiting it to only a single register of writing. Any form of writing possesses its own special sort of appeal...and practical writing is naturally suited to common and popular forms of writing....This practical writing is scientific, not literary. Scientific writing stresses the sense of what is being expressed, and if the sense is understood, then the words [used to express it] can be discarded or even forgotten.

> Literary language stresses the syntax and refinement of language, not the sense of what the writing expresses.

In this call for not reducing prose to one simple form that is immediately transparent, Du defines literature not by function but by form, as a type of writing in which form reigns supreme over content. That this view of literature, even at the time being put into practice in the brilliant writings of the Russian formalists, was to become anathema in Chinese letters testifies to the power of the call for absolute clarity in writing in a time of ongoing national crisis. That Du also in effect excludes all forms of discursive writing from his call for variety reveals the extent to which the reformers had already carried the day in the realm of the expression of ideas. He apparently sensed that only by retreating to a relatively narrow ground marked out by belles lettres alone would he have any chance at all of being persuasive, or of saving even a fragment of traditional means of written expression.

In this context, it should be noted that one of the most interesting things about Du's own writings while he was chief editor at the *Eastern Miscellany* in the period between 1911 and 1920 and those of other commentators in this period, such as Huang Yuanyong (1885–1915) and Zhang Shizhao (1881–1973), is their ability to write in an accessible classical Chinese, with an admirable transparency, about ideas and questions originating in the West. The clarity of their classical prose is such that it renders moot accusations that that form of writing lacks the ability for logical expression, something that even Hu Shi, almost in spite of himself, admitted when he wrote his initial proposal for prose reform in the classical idiom. Calls for linguistic diversity by Du and others, however, fell on deaf ears in an environment in which a desperate sense of a need to catch the West created sets of powerful binaries in which everything associated with the "old" was condemned.

BIBLIOGRAPHY: Chen Guoqiu, *Wenxueshi shuxie xingtai yu wenhua zhengzhi* (Beijing, 2004). Edward M. Gunn, *Rewriting Chinese: Style and Innovation in Twentieth-Century Chinese Prose* (Stanford, CA, 1991). Hu Shi, "Wushi nian lai Zhongguo wenxue," in *Hu Shi shuo wenxue bianqian* (Shanghai, 1999). Theodore Huters, "Legibility vs. the Fullness of Expression: Rethinking the Transformation of Modern Chinese Prose," *Journal of Modern Literature in Chinese* 10, no. 2 (December 2011): 80–104. Elizabeth Kaske, *The Politics of Language in Chinese Education, 1895–1919* (Leiden, Netherlands, 2008). Lydia

H. Liu, *Translingual Practice: Literature, National Culture, and Translated Modernity—China, 1900–1937* (Stanford, CA, 1995). David Der-wei Wang, *Fin-de-Siècle Splendor: Repressed Modernities of Late Qing Fiction, 1848–1911* (Stanford, CA, 1997). Yuan Jin, *Zhongguo jindai wenxue shi* (Taipei, 2010).

THEODORE HUTERS

1899

"Often, late at night, he would indulge alone, like an addict, in this secret pleasure of eating turtle flesh, quietly listening to the turtle's speech, and making a private divination in order to test out this mysterious method. He would carve a message in oracle-bones script, seeking to recreate an ancient experience." —Ng Kim Chew, "Fish Bones"

Oracle Bones, That Dangerous Supplement . . .

In the summer of 1899—or so the legend goes—Wang Yirong (1845–1900), a Qing dynasty official, purchased a concoction of "dragon bones" as a treatment for malaria. Curious, Wang inspected this mysterious ingredient of traditional Chinese medicine, only to discover, to his amazement, that the ancient bone to be ground into his potion bore written marks. These marks looked like Chinese writing, though they were unlike any known Chinese script. In a scene that connects the medical and the cultural, shortly before China would surrender to the allied forces that crushed the Boxer Rebellion, China thus (re)discovered its oldest written archive: inscriptions on tortoise plastrons and ox scapulae dating from the late Shang dynasty.

The discovery of oracle bones triggered a collecting frenzy that impelled Wang, soon followed by others, to purchase over a thousand specimens—almost as if, in the national catastrophe of the Boxer Rebellion and the impending defeat at the hands of the allied forces, the accumulation of fragments of a forgotten past served as tokens of cultural stability. After all, throughout the centuries, the act of collecting the artifacts of bygone days offered Chinese intellectuals a place within an imagined cultural continuum. We, of course, cannot know if the oracle bones actually healed Wang, or if he even ingested any after his find. What is certain, however, is that they ultimately could not "cure" Wang of the effects of national humiliation, the sickness of the Chinese nation so often evoked during China's rocky road to modernity. Not long after making his discovery, Wang would commit suicide. In the face of the impending defeat of the Qing at the hands of the allied forces, he jumped into a well, after previously attempting suicide by ingesting poison.

Intellectual infatuation with these strange bones did not cease with Wang's death, and instead this would be merely the first act in a drama about cultural continuity in the context of China's traumatic history. For instance, Liu E (1857–1909), who was present when Wang made his discovery, later acquired a collection of about five thousand oracle bone pieces, including many of Wang's own. In 1903, the same year Liu E began working on his famous novel *The Travels of Lao Can,* Liu also published a partial catalogue of the oracle bones in his possession. In the form of ink rubbings, veritable analog copies of the originals, Liu E's collection would give rise to a paper trail of catalogues, transcriptions, commentaries, and studies, and mark the beginning of a new discipline known as *jiagu*-ology, or the study of oracle bones.

Liu E's catalogue inspired a variety of other scholars, including Luo Zhenyu (1866–1940), who wrote a preface for it and went on to become one of the most eminent early voices in the field; Wang Guowei (1877–1927), who catalogued part of Liu E's collection for a subsequent owner and wrote several important works on oracle bones and Shang society; and Guo Moruo (1892–1978), whose interest in the subject originated from reading Luo's books in Japan. Oracle bones became the center of a radiating archive of artifacts, rubbings, and writings. In a time of uncertainty, change, and turmoil, they also knit Chinese intellectuals, often beyond the bounds of China proper, into a kind of imagined community, touched by the strange social and intellectual glue of these skeletal scraps and their mysterious inscriptions.

Even before the origin of these bones was traced to Anyang's Xiaotun in Henan Province in 1928, supposedly the site of the Shang capital Yin, oracle bones had already replicated themselves in textual form, reshaping the archive of Chinese culture. Oracle bones quickly became a matter of national pride: from bone pieces that locals sold for profit to coveted pieces in individual collections, they ultimately became national treasures. As objects, oracle bones straddled the old antiquarian paradigm of individual collections and the birth of modern Chinese archeology as a science with national implications. Not only did they prove that a full-fledged Chinese writing system had existed more than three thousand years ago, the bones also confirmed historical elements recorded in Sima Qian's (135?–86 BCE) *Records of the Grand Historian* by providing tangible proof that the Shang dynasty existed—until the discovery, the Shang civilization had remained less verifiable. The bones therefore bolstered Chinese cultural confidence at a time in which China's integrity and traditions were at risk.

The idea of Chinese intellectuals in the early decades of the twentieth century fiddling with yellowed bone fragments, transcribing esoteric characters, or poring over catalogues of rubbings might convey an image of immersion in the past and obliviousness to the present. To tarry with Chinese writing of millennia ago at a time of intense debates around the possible abolition, or at least reform, of the Chinese language and script might seem anachronistic. When Hu Yuzhi (1896–1986), a promoter of Esperanto to replace the Chinese written characters, fustigated stalwart supporters of the Chinese script in his essay "On Poisonous Discourse" of 1937, he called them "young and old loyalists enamored with bones." Indeed, Wang and Luo were such bone fetishists, remaining loyal to the Qing dynasty after its fall in 1911 and even after their return to China following several years of exile in Japan. And yet, research on oracle bones did not just mean an escape from the strictures and disappointments of the present into the remote and timeless glory of the Chinese past.

Wang, better known for his interest in Arthur Schopenhauer's (1788–1860) philosophy and his work on the *Dream of the Red Chamber* than for cross-referencing the genealogy of the Shang kings, and Guo, better known for his poetry inspired by Walt Whitman (1819–1892) than for his volumes on oracle bone vocabulary, were both modern thinkers. For them, oracle bones were not a topic of the past, but of the present and future. In his 1926 talk "The Past and Future of Chinese Archeology," another eminent intellectual, Liang Qichao (1873–1929), even used the charged term "revolution" to highlight the historical importance of the discovery of oracle bones. To Liang and many of his contemporaries, these missives from the remote past, forgotten for millennia, marked the modernity of the present, and its superiority vis-à-vis another past whose traditions impacted the present: "As for these [oracle bones], Confucius had not seen them, but we have; Confucius did not know about them, but we do; Confucius had it wrong, but we can set it right."

As newly discovered knowledge and a reason for national pride, oracle bones were very much part of the Chinese present. Insofar as studying oracle bones offered a different perspective on the past, and thus a different appreciation of the present, by turning China's gaze backward it actually oriented it toward the future. The year 1899 marks not so much an incisive date as a strange temporal twist. Its temporality is reversed in the forward-looking optimism of Liang's vision of China's glorious future in his unfinished 1902 novel, *The Future of New China*. In contrast to Liang's leap into the future that allows for a new perspective on the past, as textual and symbolic relics, oracle bones constituted a new way of connecting with the past that allowed a leap into the future.

The temporal warp around oracle bones in the first decades of the twentieth century echoes their purpose for the Shang, given that, as divinatory tools, they offered the possibility of transcending the limits and strictures of time itself. Holes drilled into the bone surfaces, then exposed to a heat source, caused the scapulae or plastrons to crack with a snapping sound, the voice of the turtle—the character ⼘ for divining combines the image of a crevice with the sound *puk* of cracking. These "natural" inscriptions—supplemented by carved characters to document the context and outcome of pyromancy with bones—were communications from deities and ancestors, voices conjured up from the past that allowed glimpses into the future.

Oracle bones are often treated as the essence of cultural specificity by both Chinese and non-Chinese, but their temporal logic reflects a more general tendency at large in global modernities. Even as modernity began to conceive of temporality largely in linear terms, many modern thinkers, writers, and artists remained obsessed with the contemporaneity of past and present, for instance in the guise of primitivism. In a short story by contemporary Malaysian Chinese writer Ng Kim Chew (1967–), "Inscribed Backs," the semi-ironic equation of European modernism and Chinese intellectuals' obsession with oracle bones serves as a whimsical side story. In a brothel in Singapore at the beginning of the twentieth century, a quaint Chinese intellectual (reminiscent of Wang) immersed in the project of writing a new *Dream of the Red Chamber* in oracle bone script on turtle shells inspires an English visitor to dream of creating a novel superior to *Ulysses*, tattooed onto the backs of coolie laborers. In the colonial space of Singapore evoked in Ng's story, two writers with different cultural backgrounds equally seek literary innovation through a return to archaic inscription techniques.

In an earlier short story, "Fish Bones," that opens with a series of quotes from famous scholars of *jiagu*-ology, Ng had already interrogated the symbolic charge of oracle bones for the meaning of Chinese culture in the present. The story's protagonist, a Malaysian Chinese who teaches at a Taiwanese university, enacts nightly rituals of plastromancy: he kills, cooks, and eats turtles, then uses their shells for oracle bone divination. What might seem, at first glance, a performance of identity intended to move an individual at the margins of Chinese culture closer to its imaginary center becomes an indictment of an essentialist notion of "Chineseness." Not only does the story's protagonist identify with the turtles—inspired by research on the possible southern provenance of some of the tortoise shells—that are sacrificed to, yet also bearers of, Chinese culture, his ritual also commemorates his older brother, who died in the Communist rebellion against colonial forces in British Malaya in the 1950s.

Oracle bones, then, symbolize personal and cultural loss for the protagonist, but they are also fetishized objects of desire. Trauma and sexual awakening coincide when the protagonist, as an adolescent, chances upon the skeleton of his dead brother in the jungle, surrounded by turtle shells. In the adolescent's act of masturbation, the dead exoskeleton—a relic from the site of his brother's death, as well as a token of "Chineseness" both coveted and despised—returns to life: "When he awoke, he removed the tortoise shell he had hidden in his bureau and, without thinking, placed it over his erect penis. In this way he was able to reach an unprecedented orgasm, as white semen spurted from his own swollen red 'turtle head.'"

Fuck oracle bones! Fuck "Chineseness"! Or so the story's bone maneuvers seem to tell us. And yet, as the strange *pharmakon* of Chinese modernity, as the fetishized or desecrated symbol of Sinocentrism, oracle bones will not cease to haunt Chinese culture...as a dangerous supplement.

BIBLIOGRAPHY: Chen Weizhan, *Jiaguwen lunji* (Shanghai, 2003). Gu Yinhai, *Jiaguwen: Faxian yu yanjiu* (Shanghai, 2002). Hu Yuzhi, "You du wen tan" (1937), in *Hu Yuzhi wenji* (Beijing, 1996), 3:549–555. David N. Keightley, *Sources of Shang History: The Oracle-Bone Inscriptions of Bronze Age China* (Berkeley, CA, 1978). Liang Qichao,

"Zhongguo gukaoxue zhi guoqu ji jianglai" (1926), in *Liang Qichao quanji* (Beijing, 1999), 9:4919–4925. Ng Kim Chew, "Inscribed Backs" and "Fish Bones," in *Slow Boat to China and Other Stories*, ed. and trans. Carlos Rojas (New York, 2016), 237–304 and 97–120.

ANDREA BACHNER

1900 · FEBRUARY 10

Liang Qichao stops serializing his translation of *Chance Meetings with Beautiful Women* in the *China Discussion*.

Liang Qichao's Suspended Translation and the Future of Chinese New Fiction

In October 1898, the young reformist Liang Qichao (1873–1929) was on a Japanese military vessel bound for Hiroshima when the ship's captain offered him a copy of *Chance Meetings with Beautiful Women* (1885–1897, published in eight installments), a Japanese political novel by Shiba Shirō (1852–1922) that had gained phenomenal popularity in that country roughly a decade earlier. Greatly inspired, Liang reportedly started translating it while still on board. The first installment of the translation, put together in collaboration with his fellow expatriates and entitled *Chance Meetings with Beautiful Women*, would come out only a few months later in the inaugural issue of the *China Discussion*, the Yokohama-based Chinese-language journal Liang edited in exile. The serialization continued in almost every issue, yet came to a sudden halt in the thirty-fifth issue, published on February 10, 1900.

The impressive swiftness of Liang's translation endeavor, which is by consensus the first attempt at rendering a non-Western modern novel into Chinese, should make us wonder how linguistic border crossing could possibly be quicker than physical migration, as his proficiency in Japanese must have been minimal when he left China. The language of *Chance Meetings* suggests that the transnational literary tradition created through centuries of intra–East Asian cultural communication had prepared a symbolic route for the Chinese translator. The novel is written in a particular prose style that derives from a traditional Japanese practice of reading literary Chinese according to the native pronunciation and grammar; and the influence of literary Chinese on this prose form was so thorough—in vocabulary, grammar, and rhetoric—that Liang found his existing linguistic and literary knowledge not only necessary but also almost sufficient to understand it. His natural extrapolation was that any Japanese sentence had a corresponding literary Chinese phrase upon which it was based, and all it took to read it was the recovery of that "original" phrase following a fixed set of simple rules. Eccentric as it may sound, this concept was indeed crystallized into a popularized reading manual he and his fellows compiled, conspicuously entitled *How to Read Written Japanese in Chinese* (ca. 1900).

Liang had barely escaped the Empress Dowager Cixi's (1835–1908) reactionary crackdown on the Hundred Days' Reform, the 1898 court-based reform movement spearheaded by his mentor Kang Youwei (1858–1927) in the humiliating aftermath of the first Sino-Japanese War (1894–1895). He therefore must have felt immediate sympathy with the novel's four protagonists, who identify themselves as the "loyal subjects of fallen dynasties." *Chance Meetings with Beautiful Women* is the story of heroes and heroines from Japan, China, Spain, and Ireland who meet by chance in Philadelphia and forge an alliance to fight back against the modern powers that are oppressing their societies. The Japanese hero, named Tōkai Sanshi, identifies himself with his native feudal domain of Aizu, which was ruined by the opposing Meiji government during the Boshin Civil War (1868–1869); the Chinese character, Hankei, is a loyalist of the Ming dynasty pledging to reform the country by recovering dynastic legitimacy; the Spanish heroine, Yūran, belongs to the legitimist Carlist camp; the Irish female character, Kōren, resists British colonial oppression. Into their mixed backgrounds, the narrative interweaves the embroidered biographies of historical oppositional figures as diverse as Toussaint-Louverture, Ahmed Orabi, and Fanny Parnell. Shiba's wild imagination then gives a unified identity to these heterogeneous characters, fictional and historical: cultural exemplarity. They practice refined literature and embody traditional virtue, and endeavor to turn their aesthetic and moral subjectivity into a modern political agency that can save their nations from imperialism and bring about a new world order. Faced with their enemies, however, their solidarity can only emerge at "chance meetings," engendering both suspense and a kind of utopian aspiration, which are the characteristic charms of the work.

The characters and the narrator intertextualize numerous Chinese classics in order to articulate their modern moral-political emotions in old poetic voices, as well as in terms of traditional Confucian virtues. The protagonists recite more than forty classical Chinese poems throughout the story; and, by virtue of practicing poetry in the same lyrical tradition, they forge unrelenting transnational emotional bonds. At a banquet held in the recesses of Valley Forge, the Irish heroine expresses her nationalist passion by referring to a poem by Cao Zhi, the eminent third-century poet and politician, while the Japanese and Chinese heroes recite in unison and verbatim a piece from "Nineteen Old Poems," a poetry collection featured in the great sixth-century anthology *Selection of Refined Writing,* to commemorate their serendipitous meeting. This utopian poetry gathering is initiated by Sanshi, who quotes the preface to the prominent fifth-century poet Xie Lingyun's "Imitating the Poems of the Wei Crown Prince's Gathering at Ye," a series of poems composed in the imitated voices of the celebrated poets gathered at Ye during the Jian'an era (196–220). If Xie's imitation, with its attachment to the imagined golden age of poetry some two centuries before, contributed to canonizing the tradition of classical poetry, Shiba's narrative, by imitating Xie's "Imitating," reenacts and thus retransmits that very poetic tradition, which had been cross-culturally passed on through the centuries.

With its heavy allusions to the Chinese classics and outlandish language, *Chance Meetings,* to be sure, might simply be "unreadable by modern standards," as (C. T. Hsia) argued. One has to possess certain traditional literary capital to be able to appreciate this work. But such a readership was quite sizable in late nineteenth-century Japan, and Liang himself was also part of that transnational class of learned readers. His translation elevated the register of the language even further by turning the original into fine classical-style prose, adding more allusions that echoed those used in the original, and transcribing most of the classical Chinese poems word for word. These gestures indicate that the translator expected his Chinese audience to also be part of that transnational readership. One crucial decision he made in the course of the serialization was to pull the Chinese character, Hankei, out of that pivotal scene of the poetry gathering in Valley Forge, erasing his lyrical voice and leaving his identity obscure. This reworking, while rejecting the original's idea that a loyalist of the Ming dynasty should represent the exemplary identity of the modern Chinese subject, nevertheless does not put into question the traditional cultural values the Chinese and other protagonists exemplify. Liang thus makes the pursuit of the cultural identity of the modern Chinese national hero a task for his own fiction in the succeeding years. Liang's is, therefore, a unique case of translation that took place between countries whose literary identities had been formed through a long history of tight transregional communication.

However, the flipside of their unique translational relationship is that Liang's rendition did not translate Shiba's work out of the elite readership they both belonged to. When put in a broader field of world literature, Shiba's work would still be readable only in a narrow corner of the globe despite the translation, just as its protagonists' allusive poetic communication can make sense only in the obscure depths of Valley Forge. In the novel, the heroes and heroines nevertheless strive for universal relevance, trying to translate their cultural values into a new world order without imperialist domination. As the story progresses, the protagonists are scattered around the globe, engaging in isolated battles; the Valley Forge banquet is only recalled in a nostalgic tone. It is at one of those unfavorable moments that Sanshi is persuaded, against his original ambition, to become an official for the Japanese government. Though traditional values still lie at the heart of his subjectivity, he now wants to prove their relevance by implementing them in domestic politics and strengthening the state on the world stage. The narrative then becomes linearly organized along the single itinerary of his political career; practicalities of realpolitik overshadow the suspense and aspirational imagination, making the story rather boring. As a result, the last chapters of Shiba's novel demand much patience from the reader, and probably too much so to be serialized in a journal. Liang's decision to terminate the serialization came shortly after this dramatic turning point of the original's narrative. The rationale for his decision is as unambiguous as the work's first part is aesthetically attractive and morally engaging.

The cancellation of the serialization, however, enabled Liang to take up just where Shiba had left off. For several years after this, literary projects, especially the advocacy of "new fiction," became a crucial core of the exiled Liang's sustained engagement in Chinese sociopolitical reform. His literary endeavor culminated in the 1902 launching of *New Fiction*, one of the earliest Chinese-language literary magazines. The project is epitomized by Liang's own political novel, *The Future of New China*, which he serialized in the journal between 1902 and 1903. Inspired by Edward Bellamy's *Looking Backward: 2000–1887* (1888), whose Chinese rendition by Timothy Richard first came out in 1891, the novel opens with a future scene where the imaginary Chinese state is celebrating its fiftieth anniversary and showing off its industrial and cultural prosperity to delegates from all over the world. The process of nation building is recounted as having been led by two European-educated heroes, one supporting constitutional monarchy and the other republican revolution. But the narrative invests as much in staging their rational debates over the possible courses of the country's modernization as in dramatizing their emotional bond mediated by traditional lyricism. On their return passage from Europe, the heroes express their indignation at the Russian occupation of the strategic Shanhai Pass region by alternately composing, phrase by phrase, a song lyric (*ci*) to the traditional stock tune of "Congratulating the Bridegroom" and inscribing it on a wall. Their poetic communication is later extended to another character, who inscribes right next to their piece a song lyric that matches rhyme words with theirs. There is yet another hero who is overheard chanting lines from poems by Byron to piano accompaniment. These lines are quoted in the English original first, and, right after that, rendered into Chinese so that "the Western meaning is translated with the Chinese sounds," as the author's commentary states. Not only does Byron's lamentation over the fallen ancient Greek civilization touch the heroes' heartstrings, but also the reciting voice, via the translation into the old sounds, echoes the heroes' Chinese lyricism, creating emotional solidarity among these protagonists. The narrative thus grafts the heroes' aspirations onto thick cultural roots, making those modern heroes exemplify traditional cultural values—so much so that the future nation they embody by no means replicates modernity in its contemporary manifestation. According to a publication announcement for the novel, the imagined new China was to be the leader of a new world order without racism or imperialism, and this climax was intended as a modern incarnation of the old Confucian ideal of *datong*, or the Great Community.

    The Future of New China, however, was left unfinished when the story had barely begun. Like the spine of a book, the existing five chapters bind the past and the future, painting an anachronistic picture where the lyrical tradition underlies the solidarity of the heroes to be born, and the old ideal names the society to be realized. The protagonists in this novel could indeed find their counterparts for their struggles in the assembled comrades of *Chance Meetings*, for they equally exemplify the traditional cultural values and envision the future with imaginations based thereon. If the Japanese author went on to further narrativize that utopian future by turning the hero into a state official, then Liang, precisely by not translating that latter part, could write the unfinished *Future of New China*. With its middle pages left blank, it is a lyricized articulation of a radical future that is as if excavated from old sounds and ideas, a future that will never find itself in linear temporality.

"To renovate the people of a nation, the fictional literature of that nation must first be renovated," so Liang began his celebrated inaugural editorial of *New Fiction*, entitled "On the Relationship between Fiction and the Organization of Society." The heroic solidarity in *The Future of New China* is an allegory of the new society that he hoped to create through the production of "new fiction," and an aesthetic expression of his reformist political ideals. It is then cultural exemplarity that gave identity to that imagined modern society. But if those cultural values are not something particular to a nation, but something that, de jure, can be exemplified by anyone through education and, de facto, had such "universal" relevance in premodern East Asia, then what exactly is the identity of the new society projected in Liang's novel? And what is the identity of the modern Chinese literature that he proposed and practiced? Once put in constellation with the suspended translation of the Japanese novel, Liang's discourse of "new fiction" starts to pose such haunting questions about national and cultural belonging, which would continue to reverberate in later Chinese fiction.

BIBLIOGRAPHY: Patrick Hanan, *Chinese Fiction of the Nineteenth and Early Twentieth Centuries* (New York, 2004). Liang Qichao, *Yinbing shi heji* (Beijing, 1989). *Qingyi bao*, reprint ed. (Taipei, ca. 1967). Adele Austin Rickett, ed., *Chinese Approaches to Literature from Confucius to Liang Ch'i-ch'ao* (Princeton, NJ, 1978). Shiba Shirō, *Kajin no kigū*, in *Shin nihon koten bungaku taikei Meiji hen*, vol. 17 (Tokyo, 2006).

SATORU HASHIMOTO

1900 · SUMMER AND FALL

"The Bronze Immortal pines away with teardrops, / My feelings are
stirred further by the west wind and falling leaves and cicadas."

Fallen Leaves, Grieving Cicadas, and Poetic Mourning after the Boxer Rebellion

In August 1900, the year of Gengzi in the traditional sixty-year cycle of
Chinese dating, Beijing was besieged by eight foreign powers. The court
had responded to the raging anti-Christian, anti-Western "boxer" movement, a movement that had begun in Shandong and that had spread
throughout northern China in the late 1890s, by giving in to the demands
of the movement and declaring war on the foreign powers that held
concessions within China. As the royal family prepared to flee the capital,
the Guangxu Emperor's (r. 1875–1908) concubine, Zhen Fei (1876–1900,
Consort Zhen), was found drowned in a well of the imperial palace. The
subsequent flight of the royal family, the foreign occupation of the capital,
and the ransacking and killing that took place in the city were all catastrophic
events that led to an outpouring of literature in many genres. Of these
events, the death of Zhen had a particular resonance within the scholar-
official class, and became a major source of inspiration for poems (*shi*)
and song lyrics (*ci*) from the summer of 1900 to the spring of 1901.

Joining the court in 1889, Zhen quickly became the emperor's favorite
concubine. Due to her uncompromising personality and her involvement
with the emperor's reform-minded clique, she lost favor with the conservative Empress Dowager Cixi (1835–1908). At the time of the invasion
of Beijing, both Zhen and the Guangxu Emperor were under house
arrest, and the circumstances surrounding her death will probably remain
uncertain forever. The common belief and perhaps most plausible chain of
events is that Cixi issued an order to the palace eunuchs to throw Zhen
into the well before the rest of the court fled on August 14. Others believe
that the eunuchs acted on their own. Some records even make the claim
that Zhen threw herself into the well to sacrifice herself for the nation.

In contemporary writings about this incident, the death of the royal
concubine was deeply intertwined with the national trauma and served
to crystallize a collective intellectual experience. Among those writings,
ballads in seven-character lines, entitled either "Falling Leaves" or "Gilded
Well," chronicled the emotionally charged story of Zhen's introduction

into the court, her romance with the Guangxu Emperor, her contentions with Cixi, her tragic death, and the emperor's mourning of her. Depicted as a beautiful, talented woman who endured great suffering and eventually sacrificed herself during a national crisis, Zhen was idealized as the epitome of traditional femininity and virtues, while, by way of contrast, Cixi was denigrated as a villain.

The lines quoted at the beginning of this essay are from Wen Tingshi's (1856–1904) well-known "Twelve Poems on Falling Flowers." In part because he served as a tutor to Zhen when she was young, Wen was quickly promoted by the emperor but was later dismissed from office by Cixi in 1896. His personal memories of Zhen distinguish his poems from those of other poets, who wrote about her death in general terms. Wen wrote a few poems cautiously indicating his sorrow over the death of Zhen while he himself was on the run like a frightened bird. The image of the "Bronze Immortal" refers to a bronze that was envisioned to be crying upon being moved out of the imperial palace after the collapse of the Han dynasty (206 BCE–220 CE). This was a widely used allusion in the late Qing, and in Wen's case, it represents a range of mixed emotions: his lament for the national disaster, his sorrow over Zhen's death, the emperor's absence, and his own personal fate.

In the Chinese literary tradition, romantic poetic writings were often understood as veiled political commentaries, as in the ancient trope of "the beauty and fragrant plants" used to symbolize the poet's political and spiritual pursuits. The image of a grieving woman devoted to her absent husband or lover was often taken as an articulation of the poet-minister's own loyalty to the emperor. In the nineteenth century, the deployment of this trope suffused the genre of *ci* with political and moral meaning. In the words of Yu Yue (1821–1907),

> When *ci* touches on officialdom, moral integrity, the relationships between lords and ministers, and the relationships between friends, the *ci* poet must use a limited vocabulary to convey his profound meaning and must employ images of "the beauty and fragrant plants" to communicate sadness and sentimentality, unlike the *shi* poet, who may often express himself directly.

Yu's definition of the song lyric represents a view of this genre prevalent in the second half of the nineteenth century. It is a view that considers the genre not only equal in importance to the eminent *shi*, but also capable of possessing subtle political messages and even more emotive power. Despite the promotion by the reformist intellectuals at the turn of the twentieth century of new-style poetry and "new fiction" (*xin xiaoshuo*), the traditional genre of *ci*, with its new implications, was popular with the literati class. The literati used *ci* to engage with the new reality of the weakened empire and to fulfill their moral responsibility to admonish the court. The allegorical approach to love lyrics embedded in this view of the genre and the death of a loyal consort converged at a critical historical point— namely, the summer and fall of 1900.

There are two layers of significance in using the trope "the beauty and fragrant plants" in the song lyrics written during this eventful period. On a literal level, evoking this trope in these ambiguous poems directs readers to the specific historical incidences of the death of a concubine and the flight of an emperor, at a time when poets could not directly vent their anxiety, nor speak openly about their political positions. On a figurative level, "the beauty and fragrant plants" trope works as a framework for the poets' emotions. Layers of allusions and rhetorical elements are employed to make the poems intellectually sophisticated and stylistically wrought. The female image, a composite of characters from history and a topical figure, encapsulated the profound sense of loss, sorrow, and nostalgia experienced by the Chinese intelligentsia of the time, executed in an ornamental style and with exquisite form.

Among the images used in these poems, "falling leaves and grieving cicadas" rose to a new level of popularity. The song of "Falling Leaves and Grieving Cicadas," allegedly written by Emperor Wu (156–87 BCE) of the Han to commemorate the death of his favorite concubine, became a frequently used allusion for the death of Zhen. Wang Naizhen (1861–1933) was even given the nickname "Wang of the Falling Leaves" for the popularity of his four poems, which were hand-copied and circulated in the capital. Contemporaneous anecdotes offer us some glimpses into how the poems were spread. In one instance, an official at a military camp in Fujian received letters from his friend Zhang Zhefu, accompanied by some poems on Zhen's death that were circulating in Beijing. Zhang continued to send these missives for several months. This small anecdote gives an example of how avidly these scholar-officials were sharing and reading these poems. These readers, well equipped with a shared cultural background and corresponding interpretative skills, could readily access and decode the meanings of these poems, endowing seemingly superficial laments over the death of a young lady with political meaning. The circulation of the poems following that tumultuous summer also evinces the collective cultural trauma that the intelligentsia experienced and their need to find release for their emotions. Reading, circulating, and decoding the poems served as a powerful method for consolidating these communities of scholar-officials.

The following is one such poem, a song lyric written by Zhu Zumou (1857–1931) in response to his friend's lyric to the same tune, in which the potent emotional power of love and death is used to convey political messages and allegorical meanings:

To the Melody "Sheng sheng man"

A cold cicada chirping on the broken palace steps,
A butterfly fluttering around bare branches,
Tossing weeds stir up pity in a human heart.
One departed soul,
The setting sun turns dreams into vanishing haze.

Near the fragrant moat, the old place for inscribing red leaves,
Abandoning the forbidden flowers to wither year after year.
The pressing harbinger of the cold
Again plays a dirge in the divine palace,
Carrying the tune of the grieving cicadas.

The phoenix has lost its nest forever.
And now frost descends upon the gilded well,
Cutting off lingering affections. Dancing with the swirling wind,
Only then does one know how capricious gratitude and
    resentment are.
Under an overcast sky, the waves of the Dongting Lake widen,
In the dark night, sorrow flows on the Xiang strings.
As for what trembles and falls,
Facing the open mountain, do not ask the cuckoos.

At first glance, the poem revolves around the depiction of the "falling leaves." However, the images of "broken palace steps," "forbidden flowers," and "the gilded well" contextualize the situation by indicating the death of Zhen. One story relating to the fate of women follows another; one image after another (the falling leaves, the well, the cicadas, and the goddesses) creates an allusive and elegiac mood. A mournful poetic voice is searching for the figure that has disappeared, the traces that she has left or has substituted for her body. While the sorrow that the poets experienced found an embodiment in this encrypted historical and literary image, the death of the female, distinctly written from a male perspective, was also eroticized.

While many officials fled south, some chose to stay in the occupied city of Beijing. Zhu, together with another official, Liu Fuyao (1864–?), moved into the residence of Wang Pengyun (1840–1904). The three men wrote song lyrics every night from September 19, 1900, to January 20, 1901, and together wrote 622 short song lyrics to 132 tune titles, which became the anthology *Song Lyrics of the Autumn of Gengzi*. In the spring of 1901, they continued with a dozen other friends to write the long form of song lyrics, which became *Songs of Spring Waking*. Wang, a master of the form, played a key role in organizing the frequent literary gatherings in the capital. Wang himself expressed that, in order to save himself from an "emotional suffocation" in the wake of national disaster, he had to resort to intense writing sessions. In these poems, the three men often assumed the poignant gendered persona of a woman longing for her faraway lover, or wrote from a male perspective in search of a woman gone missing from a decorative yet empty mansion. This frequent evocation of the female figure, performance of gendered voices, and fluid positioning all reflect the fragile subjectivity of the literati communities and their vulnerable psychological state. Earlier in 1900, Liang Qichao (1873–1929), the young reformist, described his vision for "young China" as a "magic flower in bud" in his influential essay "Ode to a Young China." In contrast to this magical bud, the images of falling leaves and grieving cicadas were allegories referring to the disappearing empire and culture, and to the vulnerability of a people under great pressure. While some reformist intellectuals, feeling that they had no time to waste on mourning, called for a revolution in literary writing, this group of intelligentsia in the capital mourned the death of the empire through literature in historical and metaphorical terms. The theme of Zhen resonated with a cluster of poetic and political imaginaries, and triggered an anticipatory nostalgia about the impending "fall" of a dynasty, a civilization, and history and poetry as such.

The specter of the dead female body haunts. Zhen's corpse was not lifted from the well until the spring of 1902, when she was properly buried and posthumously honored by the royal family. In the popular imagination, she has been canonized as a legendary woman who represents ideal womanhood and national sentiment. Yao Ke (1905–1991) wrote a modern play about her story, which was directed by Fei Mu (1906–1951) and debuted in Japanese-occupied Shanghai in 1941, and was later adapted into the film *Sorrows of the Forbidden City*. The character of Zhen, played by Zhou Xuan (1920–1957), a pop singer, was reinvented and given a colorful personality, full of bravery and self-sacrifice. This version of Zhen became a beloved perennial screen persona. Even today, the well is a major tourist site within the imperial palace in Beijing. The intertwined themes of the death of a beautiful woman, the fate of the nation, and the obsession with the allegorical dimension of the female in literary culture continue to linger. In 1965, the preeminent historian Chen Yinke (1890–1969), whose grandfather was a major player in late Qing politics, was confronted with the suffocating political climate of the Maoist era. Upon reading the *Draft History of the Qing,* he too penned a poem lamenting the death of Zhen, a poem containing the following couplet: "The old feeling of home and state lingering on the paper, / the residual remorse of prosperity and decline shines before the lamp."

BIBLIOGRAPHY: A Ying, ed., *Gengzi shibian wenxueji* (Beijing, 1959). Huang Jun, *Huasuirensheng'an zhiyi* (1943; reprint, Taiyuan, China, 1999). Qian Zonglian, ed., *Qingshi jishi* (Nanjing, China, 1987–1989). Shengqing Wu, *Modern Archaics: Continuity and Innovation in the Chinese Lyric Tradition, 1900–1937* (Cambridge, MA, 2013), 45–107. Wang Pengyun, Zhu Zumou, Liu Fuyao, and Song Yuren, *Gengzi qiu ci* (Shanghai, ca. 1910s; reprint, Taipei, 1972).

SHENGQING WU

1901

Black Slaves' Plea to Heaven is published.

Eliza Crosses the Ice—and an Ocean—and Uncle Tom's Cabin *Arrives in China*

Run, Eliza, run!…Run, Eliza, run!

So sang Rita Moreno, clad in luminous costume and captured on Cinemascope reels, as she played Tuptim, the slave who enraged the king of Siam with "The Small House of Uncle Thomas," a seditious staging of Harriet Beecher Stowe's (1811–1896) *Uncle Tom's Cabin.* This story-within-a-story is one of the most memorable scenes in the block-buster *The King and I* (1956), a remake of Richard Rodgers and Oscar Hammerstein's Broadway musical (1951), itself an adaptation of Margaret Landon's *Anna and the King of Siam* (1944).

Tuptim knew, as did the men who made her character, that the stories that really matter to us often arrive secondhand, thirdhand, or through even more uncertain routes, and take on new meanings with each exchange. Eliza's flight from the evil Simon Legree across a river of ice stood in for all kinds of struggles in the nineteenth and twentieth centuries, as readers from Russia, Spain, and China—especially China—found new meaning in this classic work.

How *Uncle Tom's Cabin, or, Life among the Lowly* made its way into the hands of Wei Yi (1880–1932), a man from Hangzhou who was in his twenties at the time, we can never know. He may have encountered the book in Shanghai as a student at St. John's College, a school that, until its doors were closed in 1952, trained the sons of the upper crust of Shanghai society in its English-language curriculum, including notables such as the writer Lin Yutang (1895–1976), the diplomat Wellington Koo (1887–1985), and the architect I. M. Pei (1917–).

Stowe's book had been touted by English missionaries in China such as John Fryer (1839–1928), who wrote in the *Chinese Recorder* that "the immense influence for good that a well-written story can exert over the popular mind has often been exemplified, but perhaps never more fully than in the case of *Uncle Tom's Cabin*…in awakening people against slavery." This inspiration was the basis for a fiction contest launched by Fryer in 1895. Fryer sent invitations all around Shanghai, and the *St. John's Echo,* the school's English-language newspaper, published a notice: "A Chinese story consisting of a combined description of the evils of opium smoking, foot-binding, and the literary examinations and of ways to abolish them is requested, and it may be produced by any Chinaman."

Fryer never chose a winner, but *Uncle Tom's Cabin* and the images of slavery that flowed from it eventually exerted a direct influence over the "popular mind." Wei was inspired to sit down with his much older collaborator, Lin Shu (1852–1924), and translate the book into classical Chinese. When Wei and Lin began this project, Lin had just gained unexpected notoriety for a translation of *Camille* (*La Dame aux Camélias*) that he had written with another collaborator, Wang Shouchang (1862?–1925). Lin didn't know a word of English, but wrote well in classical Chinese, a skill that proved crucial—perhaps even more valuable than Wei's command of English—in reaching readers. The book that resulted from Lin and Wei's first collaboration, *Black Slaves' Plea to Heaven*, marked the beginning of one of the most important collaborative partnerships in the history of modern Chinese literature and publishing. The other translations that Lin and Wei produced together in the early 1900s, including works by Charles Dickens, Washington Irving, and H. Rider Haggard, reached readers throughout China and influenced a generation of writers who grew up reading those translations.

Translations into Chinese from the late nineteenth and early twentieth centuries are notorious for taking liberties with their sources. The status of translations *as* translations was often in question, as rumors flew about writers hawking translations as their own original creations or, in some cases, writing new pieces and then selling them as a foreign author's latest masterpiece. When compared with these suspicious undertakings, however, Lin and Wei took a relatively straightforward approach. Although they regularly snipped and spliced and added a few choice phrases, their translations largely followed the plots of the books with which they worked.

Even so, *Black Slaves' Plea to Heaven* took Stowe's work in surprising new directions. In their prefaces to the book, Lin and Wei drew many comparisons between American slavery and the plight of Chinese laborers in the United States and elsewhere in North and South America. *Black Slaves' Plea to Heaven* also undid and even reversed much of the novel's Christian message, casting Stowe's Protestant ideals as a weak and decidedly unmodern response to the evils of slavery. Tom's martyrdom at the hands of Simon Legree was eclipsed by the heroic rise of George Harris, the mixed-race runaway slave who passes in the South as a "Spanish Gentleman," flees to Canada, makes his way to France, and then travels to Africa to help found the new nation of Liberia.

Of the many points where *Black Slaves' Plea to Heaven* strikes out in a new direction from *Uncle Tom's Cabin*, the focus on George is the most important. Although most readers know the reputation of Stowe's novel as an abolitionist classic, few are aware that she was subject to fierce criticism for her decision to end the plotline of George Harris and Eliza by sending them to Liberia. Some argued that Stowe had lent support to the American Colonization Society, which called for the removal and return of all slaves to Africa. In *Black Slaves' Plea to Heaven*, however, Liberia represents the future promise of a modern Chinese nation. When George writes of the future of Liberia, he does so in the language of "Western learning":

> I truly wish to unite [China and Africa] into a community with a shared fate, to bring together the people of Africa to form a country.... If I were to establish a state and use it to extend *international law* and *universal principle*, I would no longer need to stand by as white people slaughter my race. Only through *international law* and *universal principle* do those with a state have the power to do this.

Terms like "international law" and "universal principle" can be traced directly to contemporary discussions in China about the relations between modern nations and cultures. Such language—liberally inserted by the translators—held far greater appeal for the Chinese audience than Tom's cheek-turning martyrdom.

Readers raved. Newspapers ran essays and poems that praised the book for changing their view of the world. According to Gu Lingshi (?–1904), the book revealed to him how "people around the world are oppressed by whites—in Poland, India, Burma, Vietnam, Australia, Malaysia, and Indonesia." The book also circulated among Chinese students studying in Japan. A young Lu Xun (1881–1936), studying in Sendai, wrote in 1904 to friends in China of how the book stirred deep feelings in his heart for his nation. Chinese students in Tokyo staged a performance of the play in 1907—now recognized as the first modern spoken drama in the Chinese language.

The comparison between Chinese laborers and African slaves in *Black Slaves' Plea to Heaven* prompted the creation of another version of *Uncle Tom's Cabin* after the 1949 revolution: *Rage of the Black Slaves* (1961), a creative rewriting by Ouyang Yuqian (1889–1962) of the "original" 1907 dramatic version that had been staged in Tokyo. *Rage of the Black Slaves* played up China's new role as a leader among nonaligned nations after the Bandung Conference of 1955. In this version, George Harris and Tom join hands to fight their captors—and Tom's death makes him a martyr not of Christian forgiveness, but of the battle against oppression in the colonial and decolonizing world. Rather than a warning of the fate that might befall China, *Rage of the Black Slaves* showed how China might lead the world. One critic writing in the *People's Daily* concluded that "the Chinese people, although already liberated, will not forget the past," and could show the way forward for "the myriad struggles against national oppression that face the peoples of Asia, Africa, and Latin America."

The success of *Black Slaves' Plea to Heaven* made Stowe's novel into one of the most important works of foreign literature in China in the first half of the twentieth century—whether it appeared in Lin and Wei's woodblock edition, later reprints, versions made for the stage, or other "improved" versions. Well after Lin's death, new translations continued to circulate. How, though, could a book written in classical Chinese hold such appeal? How could a novel written in a language that has long been condemned as obscure, pedantic, and impossible to master—what Hu Shi (1891–1962) famously called "dead writing" (*si wenzi*)—find such an enthusiastic audience?

Some of the answer lies in Stowe's story—the clear lines drawn between good and evil, and the power of the metaphor of slavery itself. Both elements made Stowe's book popular in many other places around the world. But the quality of the Chinese prose, written in a prestigious "ancient-style prose" (*guwen*), also played an important role. In *Black Slaves' Plea to Heaven* and other translations, Lin and collaborators like Wei managed to render foreign fiction into elegant and, unbelievable to readers in our own times, *accessible* prose. Compared with other translations, the words produced by Lin and his collaborators were highly readable and, at times, beautifully written, enough so to let them stand on their own as literary works. By comparison, the scholar and diplomat Ma Jianzhong (1844–1900) complained that when he opened up most of the translated books that were being produced at that time, errors in content leapt off the page, and he was soon "overcome by the wretched vulgarity" of their style.

Later critics, raised on the conviction that the rise of the modern vernacular style in written Chinese was an inevitable and uniformly positive development, have almost always seen Lin's work as a dangerous last gasp of a decadent conservatism. For example, Hu's comment that Lin had "opened a new colony for ancient-style prose" paints classical Chinese as an aggressive, metastasizing force. It would be fairer to argue that Lin unlocked a new creative force in classical Chinese—even as it declined in status and utility in the face of a changing educational system and calls to reform and simplify the writing system. It helped, too, that figures like George Harris could make eloquent appeals for "new learning" and "Western learning" in the classical language—as *Black Slaves' Plea to Heaven* used the power of fiction and the authority of the foreign text to demonstrate the viability of this linguistic medium.

After the success of *Black Slaves' Plea to Heaven*, Lin and Wei began to publish the products of their collaboration with the Commercial Press in Shanghai. They turned out dozens more books for the press as it grew into China's largest publisher through its deep list of translated fiction and profitable lines of textbooks. After Wei moved on, Lin published over a hundred new translations with a host of other collaborators. The Commercial Press even recruited Lin to edit a line of textbooks— which, naturally, featured Lin's favorite samples of ancient-style prose.

Lin's experiments with translation into ancient-style prose were repeated by later writers working to establish their own name or style or to push the boundaries of the language. Readers today who crack open Lu Xun's translations of Japanese critic Kuriyagawa Hakuson (1880–1923) find jarring, knotty sentences, alien to much of "modern Chinese," that demand rereading (and more rereading) to follow the flow of the argument. This "hard translation" (*yingyi*) style practiced by Lu Xun should be seen as a continuation of the work of Lin and his collaborators, who were among the first to clear space for writers, intellectuals, and their audiences to work through the problems found in the relations between domestic prose style and information marked as foreign and new.

BIBLIOGRAPHY: Michael Gibbs Hill, *Lin Shu, Inc.: Translation and the Making of Modern Chinese Culture* (New York, 2012). Hu Shi, "Wushinian lai Zhongguo zhi wenxue," in *Hu Shi wencun* (Taipei, 1968), 2:180–261. Lin Shu and Wei Yi, *Heinu yutian lu* (1901; reprint, Beijing, 1981).

MICHAEL GIBBS HILL

1903 · SEPTEMBER

Liu E starts to serialize *The Travels of Lao Can* in the magazine *Embroidered Portrait Novel.*

Sherlock Holmes Comes to China

Starting in September 1903, Liu E's (1857–1909) novel *The Travels of Lao Can* was published in serial form in the magazine *Embroidered Portrait Novel.* Shortly after its publication, this novel became one of the most popular and influential novels of late Qing China. The eponymous protagonist, Lao Can, is a doctor by profession. The novel is about his journey through the province of Shandong, in the wake of the Boxer Rebellion. He witnesses an array of perilous scenes brought into being by foreign invasions, dynastic decline, social chaos, and legal injustice.

The author, Liu, was a renaissance man. He took an interest in Western science and attempted to promote commerce, industry, and the building of railways throughout his career. He was one of the earliest collectors of the inscribed oracle bones of the Shang period. He was an expert in flood control and a practitioner of traditional Chinese medicine. Influenced by the esoteric thought of the Taigu school, Liu's personal philosophy was a fusion of aspects of Confucianism, Buddhism, and Daoism. *The Travels of Lao Can* reflected his various interests and profound knowledge. Liu was acutely conscious of the ongoing collapse of the Qing empire and the peril it presented for China. *The Travels of Lao Can* was written as a national allegory. In the preface, Liu deplored the political situation of China: "The game of chess is finished. We are getting old. How can we not weep?" The novel was also praised by C. T. Hsia as "the earliest Chinese lyrical novel in first person" characterized by psychological inquiries and portraits of natural and human sceneries. Most intriguingly of all, it also served as the harbinger of modern Chinese detective fiction.

In the last five chapters of the first volume of the novel, Lao Can gets involved in a murder case. The suspect, Mrs. Jia Wei, is accused of poisoning thirteen of her husband's family members; worse, as was customary at the time, her father tries to bribe the judge in the hope of lessening her sentence. It just so happens that the judge presiding over this case is one known for his "incorruptible" virtue. Doubly suspicious of Jia Wei's guilt, he orders physical torture of the cruelest kind to obtain her confession. The judge's self-righteousness confirms Lao Can's view of the skewed legal system: "The incorruptible judge is more hateful than the corruptible one, because on the pretext that he disdains bribery, he gains the license to impose more unthinkable cruelty on the people."

Unable to bear the cruelty of this judge, Lao Can decides to solve the case. After examining evidence and conducting an extensive investigation, he sets up a trap to catch the criminal's accomplices and eventually arrests the murderer. For solving the murder mystery, Lao Can is lauded by Prefect Bai as a "Chinese Sherlock Holmes."

By the time Liu wrote *The Travels of Lao Can*, Sherlock Holmes stories had been translated into Chinese and had already become famous with Chinese readers. The earliest extant translation of Western detective fiction published in China was the Sherlock Holmes story "The Naval Treaty," published in the *Chinese Progress* in September 1896. Because of its popularity, three more Holmes stories were translated in quick succession. These translations were later collected and published together as *Dr. Watson and Sherlock Holmes Stories*. At that time, these stories were used in part to educate the Chinese about Western law. Late Qing reformists believed that Western scientific, legal, and law enforcement techniques and systems, as presented in detective fiction, provided viable models for educational, legal, and institutional reform. Their pedagogical purpose notwithstanding, these stories were well received by the Chinese audience. But Liu may have included Sherlock Holmes's name in his novel just to boost sales.

Before Lao Can, the "Sherlock Holmes" of traditional Chinese crime literature was a character named Judge Bao. Traceable to the Song dynasty,

Judge Bao is a semimythical folk hero: an official hailed for his impartiality, incorruptibility, wisdom, and power of divination in numerous pieces of late imperial drama and fiction. The appeal of Judge Bao began to diminish in Liu's time, when everything associated with what was seen as the fundamentally corrupt institutions of government came under suspicion. For the late Qing writers, independent and scientifically oriented detectives like Sherlock Holmes became the model protagonists for a new genre of detective fiction. Lao Can is not a judge appointed by the government and assumes no legal authority. Instead, he is merely an itinerant doctor compelled by compassion and a sense of moral responsibility to intervene. The emergence of Lao Can as a self-styled detective in modern Chinese fiction is emblematic of a sea change in the discourse of Chinese legality and investigative agency.

However, it should be noted that *The Travels of Lao Can* still inherits characteristics from traditional Chinese court-case novels. During the investigation, a Daoist hermit tells Lao Can's assistant that the victims did not really "die"; rather, they were put into a state of unconsciousness by a certain drug called "thousand days' sleep." Later in the story, Lao Can has the bodies removed from their coffins, burns an antidote named "quickening incense," and manages to bring the victims back to life. Readers familiar with Sherlock Holmes stories would certainly disapprove of an unscientific ending, but seen according to the standards of traditional court-case fiction, it is a deus ex machina charged with the magical power of poetic justice. Lao Can's method for solving the case mirrors a late Qing intellectual's endeavor to negotiate between traditional Chinese alchemic knowledge and Western forensic science.

The publication of translated Western detective fiction reached its peak between 1903 and 1909. The critic A Ying (1900–1977) estimated that detective fiction constituted almost 50 percent of the Western fiction translated in China at the time. Almost all the important translators at that time, such as Lin Shu (1852–1924), Zhou Shoujuan (1895–1968), and Zhou Zuoren (1885–1967), translated detective stories. Sherlock Holmes stories were bestsellers in China, and Chinese publishers competed with each other by claiming to have the newest or the most complete collections of the stories. Before 1949, more than ten different Chinese collections of Sherlock Holmes translations, into both the modern vernacular and classical Chinese, were published. In addition to Sherlock Holmes, the British detectives Martin Hewitt and Dick Donovan; the American detectives Nick Carter, Philo Vance, and Charlie Chan; and the French gentleman-burglar Arsène Lupin were also well known among Chinese readers of the twentieth century. Some of the narrative methods used by Chinese writers during the late Qing period—for example, the suspensive beginning of *The Strange Feud of Nine Murders* (1903) by Wu Jianren (1866–1912)—owe much to the influence of the narrative techniques and unique format of Western detective fiction.

The popularity of Western translated detective novels furthermore encouraged the writing of native Chinese detective fiction, leading to collections like *Chinese Detective Cases* (1902) by Wu and *Chinese Women Detectives* (1907) by Lü Xia (1884–1957). The most famous and popular native literary detective was a character named Huo Sang, the so-called Oriental Sherlock Holmes, created by Cheng Xiaoqing (1893–1976) during the Republican period. Cheng was born into an ordinary Suzhou family and taught himself English. It is said that he began reading Sherlock Holmes stories at the age of twelve and immediately became enamored with the character. He wrote his first Huo Sang story as an entry for an essay competition held by the newspaper *Fun Grove* in 1914. The initials of Huo Sang reveal his connection with his literary model, Sherlock Holmes—H. S., after all, is an inversion of S. H. From 1942 to 1945, Cheng published a thirty-volume collection that included all seventy-three Huo Sang stories. In addition to writing Huo Sang stories, Cheng was part of the translation team that translated the complete Sherlock Holmes stories into classical Chinese in 1916 and into the modern vernacular in 1927.

Huo Sang is an idealized modern Chinese intellectual. On one hand, he shares many similarities with his literary model Sherlock Holmes, while, on the other hand, he also represents a few traditional Chinese values. Huo Sang's assistant Bao Lang describes him as "well-learned and fully conversant with both new and traditional learning." Huo Sang belittles the wealthy class and fights for the poor. Unlike Sherlock Holmes, who is an intellectual superman with a superior air, Huo Sang is praised for his humility. In one story, Bao Lang notes, "Although [Sherlock Holmes] is a genius, he is arrogant and often looks down others. If we compare Holmes with Huo Sang, we can see the difference in manners between the Oriental and Western peoples."

The timing of the Huo Sang stories accounts for much of their popularity. They appeared shortly after the May Fourth Movement of 1919, a moment in Chinese history when science was rapidly elevated into an ideology. Cheng marketed his detective stories as "disguised textbooks for science." Cheng familiarized himself with detective techniques by undertaking massive detective fiction translation projects and took courses in criminology and criminal psychology from an American correspondence school in order to gain expertise in forensic science. In Huo Sang stories, Huo Sang can always match a suspect with a fingerprint left at the crime scene, or discover chemical traces within the body, or recognize certain facial characteristics in the suspect that correspond to a typical criminal physiognomy. Although Cheng's didacticism may discourage modern appreciation of the literary value of his stories, from 1920 to 1950, when the worship of science was fashionable in Chinese society, the didactic potential of his stories must have had a magnetic effect on his readers. Reading detective fiction was consonant with new hopes for self-improvement and national rejuvenation, and so Cheng succeeded in positioning his detective fiction at the nexus of serious literature and popular entertainment.

In the world of crime literature, Sherlock Holmes's great rivalry is with the French gentleman-burglar Arsène Lupin, created by Maurice Leblanc (1864–1941). Leblanc arranged Lupin's first meeting with Sherlock Holmes in the short story "Sherlock Holmes Arrives Too Late," published in the French magazine *Je sais tout* in 1906. As the leader of a gang of thieves in Paris, Lupin outwits police around the world. If the Holmes stories represent conventional detective fiction, the Arsène Lupin stories continue the tradition of the witty romantic hero. Lupin was first introduced into China as early as 1912. Shortly after, Sun Liaohong (1897–1958), another famous Chinese detective fiction writer, created a Chinese gentleman-thief based on Lupin called Lu Ping and arranged for him to outwit the detective Huo Sang in the first Lu Ping story, "The Wooden Puppet Play," serialized in the magazine *Detective World* in 1923.

Like Arsène Lupin in Paris, Lu Ping is also a master of disguise. Many plots of his stories rely on new devices, trends, and forms of entertainment in Republican Shanghai: sunglasses, polar bears, photography, swimming pools, museums, cinemas, and masquerade parties. But Lu Ping is not a European-style dilettante. The character was also inspired by the tradition within Chinese literature of the "chivalrous thief." These great thieves are experts in disguise, voice mimicry, and the use of drugs, and often perform extraordinary feats of martial arts. Compared to the corrupt government officials they outwit, these great thieves are considered admirable and benevolent.

In view of the corruption of the police force during the Republican era, Cheng's Huo Sang stories are part of a fantasy of legal justice. Lu Ping, who casts a more dubious image as both a burglar and a chivalric hero, seems to reflect ambivalence about justice: justice can be done only when it is undone.

The Travels of Lao Can was one of the earliest attempts of Chinese writers to incorporate the name of Sherlock Holmes into their stories and rethink the tradition of the "incorruptible judge." Ironically, almost fifty years later, the establishment of the People's Republic of China forced this famous Western detective to leave China. The new Communist regime believed that detective fiction belonged to the bourgeois ideology of capitalism: there should be no crime in socialist China. Both Cheng Xiaoqing and Sun Liaohong stopped writing their Huo Sang and Lu Ping stories after 1949. Detective fiction was replaced by anti-spy literature. Where once figures like Huo Sang and Lu Ping outsmarted corrupt government officials, now plots centered on how the Communist Party police exposed counterrevolutionary conspiracies.

BIBLIOGRAPHY: C. T. Hsia, "The Travels of Lao Ts'an: An Exploration of Its Art and Meaning," *Tsing Hua Journal of Chinese Studies*, n.s., 7, no. 2 (1969): 40–68. Tam King-fai, "The Detective Fiction of Ch'eng Hsiao-ch'ing," *Asia Major*, 3rd ser., 5, pt. I (1992): 113–132. Jeffrey C. Kinkley, *Chinese Justice, the Fiction: Law and Literature in Modern China* (Stanford, CA, 2000). Liu T'ieh-yün [Liu E], *The Travels of Lao Ts'an*, trans. Harold Shadick (New York, 1990).

WEI YAN

1904 · AUGUST 19

Kang Youwei arrives in Stockholm.

Imagining Modern Utopia by Rethinking Ancient Historiography

On the morning of the ninth day of the seventh month of the thirtieth year of the Guangxu reign (August 19, 1904), a Chinese gentleman accompanied by a young lady got off the train from Oslo at the Central Station in Stockholm. Had the Stockholm reporters known who the visitors were, they would have queued before the reception desk at the Grand Hotel, where the exiled reformer Kang Youwei (1858–1927) and his daughter Tongbi (1887?–1969) checked in.

Half a century later, when I resided in Beijing, Kang Tongbi handed me a handwritten copy of the diary that her father had kept during his two-year visit to Sweden. In 1970 I published an annotated translation of it into Swedish. Noting that the diary had not been published in China, I decided to have the original manuscript with my annotations published by the Hong Kong Commercial Press in 2007.

Kang Youwei was an inquisitive man. During his sojourn in Sweden he visited schools, universities, libraries, museums, palaces, apartments occupied by working families, concerts, nurseries, workhouses, prisons, public baths, pleasure grounds, and factories. He was received by the king and by the minister of foreign affairs. Staying first at the Grand Hotel in Stockholm and later at the equally fashionable Saltsjöbaden Hotel in the vicinity of the capital, he had ample opportunity to observe the mores of the upper classes of society.

Visiting a nursery for abandoned infants, Kang felt transported to what he had once called the Society of Great Community. In his youth he had written a work entitled *The Book of the Great Society*. A draft of the work existed in 1884, but a complete version was not published until 1935, eight years after his death. His greatly moving utopian vision of a future world state contains a number of radical ideas, which contrast with the moderate reform program he attempted to enact during his very brief time in power in 1898. For Kang, selfishness was the root of all evil. In his book he demolishes all barriers that humans have built in order to protect their own property and that of their kin. The Society of Great Community is governed by an elected parliament. All national borders have been erased. Instead, the surface of the earth is divided into numbered squares, each with a certain degree of autonomy. In order to block the creation of local pressure groups, at fixed intervals the population is moved from one square to another. As racial characteristics are determined by climatic conditions, such migrations of the population will eventually lead to a neutralization of racial distinctions. Kang considers marriage an institution that to a higher degree than all others serves to create social injustice. He therefore advocates absolute equality between the sexes. Instead of a marriage license, Kang suggests a contract, valid for one year, that may be renewed for as long as both parties so wish. State institutions, from nurseries to universities, guarantee that each child starts life with the same opportunities and is offered a proper education. The Society of Great Community obviously could not be created overnight, so Kang provides an account of society's evolution into a world state, stressing the role to be played by a union of nations, as a preparation for the world parliament.

Kang never mastered any foreign language. His knowledge of the world outside China was gained through reading Western works translated into Chinese. Nothing indicates that he had read Karl Marx before he wrote *The Book of the Great Society*, which shares a number of ideas with *The Communist Manifesto* (1848); excerpts of the *Manifesto* were translated into Chinese in 1906, and a complete translation was not published until 1920.

Common to Marx's and Kang's utopian dreams are the demand for the abolishment of private ownership, the introduction of state education, the emancipation of women, the elimination of national borders, and a concentration of all means of production in the hands of the state. But the two scholars' points of departure, motivations, and proposed methods were totally different. Marx's ideas issue from an industrialized Europe, while Kang, with his Confucian background, attacks problems from a universal angle. Marx predicts that a proletarian revolution will bring about a centralization of the means of production and thereby effectively remove the very cause for class antagonism. Kang asserts that the new society will develop gradually, and peacefully, as a consequence of public institutions eventually supplanting the family and other social units. Marx abstains from providing any moral or ethical credentials for the communist society and asserts instead that all religious, philosophical, and ideological valuations are determined by the economic status of the individual. Kang builds his utopia on the Confucian confidence that man's innate yearning for goodness makes him feel compassion for his fellow beings and for all living creatures. It is this firm belief in man's social conscience that characterizes Kang's utopian thinking. Marx considers all human suffering to be a direct result of economic exploitation. Kang, who in his youth had studied Buddhist philosophy, gives a comprehensive analysis of the various factors that cause suffering.

All utopian works contain some common features, such as the abolishment of private ownership, the introduction of state education, and sexual and economic equality between the sexes. It is therefore easy to find similarities between *The Book of the Great Society* and Edward Bellamy's (1850–1908) work *Looking Backward: 2000–1887*, published in 1888. In his work *Chinese Socialism to 1907* (1976), Martin Bernal suggests that Kang was influenced by a paraphrase of *Looking Backward*, serially published in *Global Magazine* between December 1891 and April 1892, in which the term *Datong* (great community) was used as a translation for the name of the utopia in Bellamy's work. Kang never refers to Bellamy's work. Kang's fellow reformers Tan Sitong (1865–1898) and Liang Qichao (1873–1929) are known to have read a version of the text published in book form in 1896. As Kang was acquainted with Young J. Allen (1936–1907) and Timothy Richard (1845–1919), the editors of *Global Magazine*, it is possible that he had read Bellamy's work. But what really must have inspired his utopian thinking is a short Daoist essay that found its way into *The Book of Rites*, one of the Thirteen Confucian Classics, called "Datong," which contains a wonderful description of an ideal society in the distant past.

On the third day after his arrival in Stockholm, Kang received the news that his benefactor Weng Tonghe (1830–1904) had passed away. Weng had served as tutor to the young emperors of the Tongzhi (r. 1862–1874) and Guangxu (r. 1875–1908) reigns. It was Weng who had introduced Kang to the young emperor, an introduction that would lead to his own fall from grace. In the 1890s, Kang had played a leading role in a radical reform movement that aimed at converting the autocratic empire into a constitutional monarchy. Like many intellectuals of the time, Kang realized that China's archaic sociopolitical structure and old-fashioned institutions constituted a threat to its independence. China's defeat by

Japan in 1895 had emphasized the need for radical reforms. The young emperor was willing to listen to the reform advocates. During a period of one hundred days in the summer of 1898, Kang was able to persuade the emperor to promulgate a number of minor reforms. But the Empress Dowager (1835–1908), who held the real power, managed to outwit the reformers. The reform edicts were canceled, and six of the leading members of the reform movement were executed, among them the brave Tan Sitong and Kang Guangren (1867–1898), a younger brother of Kang Youwei. Kang Youwei himself was forced to flee the country. For the next two decades Kang traveled abroad among overseas Chinese communities in order to gain support for the reform movement—and for his own luxurious living.

Attempting to win support for his reform program, in 1891 Kang published his work *On the Spurious Classics of Xin Dynasty Learning*, in which he accused a certain Liu Xin (ca. 50 BCE–23 CE) of having forged a number of ancient texts for political reasons. This strange story needs telling in some detail.

During the Western Han dynasty (206 BCE–9 CE), Liu belonged to a family that was related to the ruling house. His learned father, Liu Xiang (79–6 BCE), had been given the task of collating the canonical works of philosophy and poetry in the Imperial Library. On the basis of his father's notes, Liu Xin compiled the very first catalogue of Chinese books, which became the foundation of the important bibliographical essay in Ban Gu's (32–92 CE) authoritative *History of Former Han*. At the beginning of his career, Liu served with Wang Mang (45 BCE–23 CE) as adjutants at the Imperial Court. Wang eventually managed to usurp power. In 9 CE he ascended the throne as founder of the Xin (New) dynasty, which lasted only fourteen years. In Chinese historiography Wang's dynasty is treated as a mere interregnum. Shortly after Wang's ascent to power, Liu was appointed to the post of *guoshi*, teacher of the nation. The learned Liu took an interest in the interpretation of portents recorded in *The Spring and Autumn Annals*, a laconic chronicle of events in the feudal state of Lu covering the period 722–481 BCE, as well as in the narrative work *Zuo Commentary*, which covers roughly the same period (722–468 BCE). At some time in the early Han period, the text of the *Zuo Commentary* was rearranged and adapted as a commentary on *The Spring and Autumn Annals*. The fact that Liu's interpretations of portents were referred to in political debates at the time led to the accusation that he had manipulated and perhaps even forged the *Zuo Commentary*, to justify Wang's assumption of power.

In the Later Han period (25–219 CE), a fierce battle was waged between the adherents of the Old Text school, who believed that copies of canonical pre-Qin works written in ancient characters predating the script reform ordered by the First Emperor of Qin were authoritative, and adherents of the New Text school, who believed that canonical works written down from memory in the script current in the Han period ought to be given primacy. The controversy between the two schools was revived in the eighteenth century, mainly through the efforts of scholars of the New Text school, who asserted that the *Gongyang Commentary*, a New Text commentary on *The Spring and Autumn Annals* contained a summation of the political thought of Confucius. With the aid of that text they attempted to elucidate the cryptic formulae by which Confucius, according to the New Text school's dogma, had expressed praise and blame in *The Spring and Autumn Annals*. The ideas of the New Text scholars were developed by Kang, who presented Confucius as a political reformer and found support for his theory in the *Gongyang* school's reference to Confucius as Suwang (Uncrowned king). The assertion of the New Text scholars that the *Gongyang Commentary* describes the gradual progression of society from original disorder to perfect order supplied Kang with the arguments that he needed to bolster his reform activities. According to Kang, only the texts belonging to the New Text school were authentic and had all been authored by Confucius, while the Old Texts, including the *Zuo Commentary*, had all been forged by Liu.

The Swedish Sinologist Bernhard Karlgren (1889–1978) and the Chinese historian Qian Mu (1895–1990) each in his own way defended Liu against Kang's politically motivated accusation. In three major articles Karlgren effectively refutes Kang's claims. In "On the Authenticity and Nature of the Tso Chuan [= *Zuozhuan*]" from 1926, Karlgren shows that the work *Records of the Grand Historian* by Sima Qian (135?–86 BCE) contains a great many passages that obviously derive from the *Zuo Commentary*. In his "The Authenticity of Ancient Chinese Texts" (1929), Karlgren shows that the grammatical system of the *Zuo Commentary* exhibits certain distinctive features that uniquely characterize the text; they could not possibly have been invented by a forger. In "The Early

History of the Chou Li [= Zhouli] and Tso Chuan [= Zuozhuan] Texts" (1931), Karlgren again proves Kang utterly wrong in his assertion that not only the *Zuo Commentary* but also the *Rites of Zhou* and other canonical texts had been forged by Liu.

In his 1930 article "Chronological Record of Liu Xiang and Liu Xin, Father and Son," Qian also argues convincingly that Liu could not possibly have perpetrated the forgery of which Kang accused him. In doing so, Qian does not rely on philological criteria. Basing his argument entirely on information contained in the *History of the Former Han,* Qian poses twenty-eight commonsense questions that would have greatly embarrassed Kang had he been alive to answer them. Qian's monumental work *History of Chinese Scholarship of the Last Three Centuries* (1937) also contains one section, pages 633–709, in which the author, with great acumen and in brilliant classical prose, exposes Kang's distortion of the truth for political ends.

Within the span of five years, working independently, Karlgren and Qian had utterly demolished the credibility of Kang's politically motivated claims.

Karlgren and Qian were born and made their scholarly careers in countries separated by a vast distance. Both were born in years crucial to the development of modern China: Karlgren in 1898, the year of abortive reforms, and Qian Mu in 1895, the year of the Treaty of Shimonoseki, which ended the first Sino-Japanese War. While Karlgren was able to pursue his research in a peaceful environment, Qian's scholarly work was mostly undertaken in a country torn apart by war and internal strife. Common to both scholars were their determination to clear Liu of the charge of forgery and their insistence that politics has no part to play in scholarly research.

N. Göran D. Malmqvist

1905 · JANUARY 6

"*Wen* is the essence of the country, the beginning of national education."

Wen *and the "First History(-ies) of Chinese Literature"*

January 6, 1905 (the first of the twelfth moon of the thirtieth year of the Guangxu Emperor's reign). The semester had ended for the Superior Normal School (Youji shifan xuetang), an annex of the Imperial Peking University. After months of hard work, Lin Chuanjia (1877–1922) had finished editing his lecture notes and writing a report, which, as stated in the university regulations, had to be submitted to the academic panel chairman. He makes a remark near the end of his notes: "*Wen* [letters or literature] is the essence of the country, the beginning of national education." He reiterates the point in the preface, the part he wrote last: "Chinese literature is the foundation of our national education." This is the principle idea of *A History of Chinese Literature*, a book widely considered to be the first Chinese literary history written by a Chinese scholar.

Lin Chuanjia was born in Fujian, a large province on the coast of southern China. In his early years he attended the West Lake College, founded by Zhang Zhidong (1837–1909), governor-general of Hunan and Hubei. Attending the school that exemplified Zhang's philosophy of "Chinese learning as principle, and Western learning as application," Lin gained exposure to geography, mathematics, and other Western knowledge. He was also trained for the imperial examinations. In 1902, he was awarded the provincial-level *juren* (successful candidate) degree, but he failed to gain a more substantial qualification at the metropolitan examinations. In June 1904, following another failure at the examinations, the young Lin traveled to Beijing to take up the position of lecturer in Chinese at the Superior Normal School of the Imperial Peking University. The university was in the midst of a change at that time. Zhang's "Presented Imperial University Regulations," the last of a trio of charters that shaped educational development in the late Qing period, was granted approval by the Empress Dowager Cixi (1835–1908) a few months earlier. Lin started teaching soon after he arrived at the university. Finding the earlier sets of regulations no longer relevant and the freshly implemented one offering little practical guidance, he planned his courses according to his own understanding of the new curriculum. His lecture notes were a curious combination, if not a compromise, of a variety of factors, such as the need for defining a discipline and the objective of training practical writers. These goals seem to epitomize *wen*, a shifting and ever-changing concept in late Qing intellectuals' minds.

Wen has a wide spectrum of meaning in the Chinese tradition. It refers to the "pattern" of all forms. For example, the "pattern of heaven" (*tian wen*) means astronomy; the "pattern of earth" (*di wen*), topography; and "the pattern of humanity" (*ren wen*), culture; and it also points to written language. When used in relation to writing, *wen* has an extensive meaning, including practical writings (for example, official memoranda), writings for the purposes of entertainment and appreciation (for example, *fu* or rhymed prose), and writings that express one's inner feelings (for example, poetry). *Wen* is also understood as writings of high quality. Hence, there are expressions such as *wen-zhang* and *ci-zhang*, both referring to belles lettres. In a narrower sense, it means "prose," a term that contrasts with "verse." *Wen* thus covers notions of both practicality and impracticality (even playfulness), and it can also be perceived as the symbol of the national cultural spirit in its broader sense. Yet fiction and drama were not considered part of *wen* in the premodern time. The meaning of *wen* became even more complicated in the late Qing, a time when pressure for change and modernization was inexorable. There was great ambiguity and obscurity in Chinese intellectuals' conceptions of *wen* and *wenxue*, which most clearly manifested itself during the course of educational modernization.

The Imperial Peking University—China's first modern comprehensive university—was a product of the Hundred Days' Reform in 1898. Having gained the Guangxu Emperor's support, Kang Youwei (1858–1927) and Liang Qichao (r. 1875–1908) proceeded with their plan for reform. Liang was entrusted with the task of establishing a Western-style university, a place for nurturing talents with modern knowledge. Whereas all other reform policies were abolished that autumn when the Empress Dowager Cixi regained power, the university project survived. In 1902, the Empress Dowager ordered senior official and educator Zhang Baixi (1847–1907) to revise the country's education system. Zhang was put in charge of the Imperial Peking University until 1904, during which time he succumbed to political pressure and recommended Zhang Zhidong to be his successor. Zhang Baixi's curriculum had just been implemented when Lin entered the university. It was a curriculum that placed higher importance on Chinese literature than did the earlier curricula devised by reformist Liang, which largely treated literature as an area of general study and a subject for practicing writing skills.

Although he was a conservative statesman, Zhang Zhidong planned the Chinese literature program with a vision to bring traditional Chinese studies to the modern world, to turn the study of *wen*, or *wenxue*, from a vaguely defined concept to a discrete body of knowledge. Composed of a range of courses on classical literature, such as Literary Trends in Different Dynasties, Criticism of Prose from Ancient Scholars, and Major Writers from the Zhou and Qin Dynasties to the Present Day, as well as foreign subjects such as the literary history of the West and world history, the program was comprehensive and well structured. But the university was faced with a diversity of problems. Appropriate teaching materials were hard to find, and there was no transitional arrangement for students trained under the old system. Lin was responsible for teaching students in the second stage of the Chinese literature program. He found the students unfamiliar with subjects covered in the first stage of the new program; more specifically, they lacked knowledge in Chinese literary history. To remedy this, he prepared new teaching materials and held special classes for them. Inadvertently and unknowingly, he made himself known by later generations as the first Chinese author who wrote on literary history.

Because of its unprecedented nature, the Chinese literary history course designed by Zhang Zhidong lacked a concrete model. Since this was the case, he also specifically indicated in the regulations that instructors could prepare their own lecture notes by consulting works on Chinese literary history written by the Japanese. Lin thus drew inspiration from Japanese scholar Sasagawa Rinpū's (1870–1949) *Literary History of Shina* (1898). Lin's own book on the topic was widely acknowledged as a pioneering work of Chinese literary historiography, but many question its literary standpoint. The book is predominantly about historical changes in etymology, phonology, and prose styles (mainly prose of the ancient style and parallel prose). There are no discussions on popular fiction and drama because Lin considered the genres vulgar and lacking in literary value. The book also accords little importance to poetry because it lacks practical use. Lin's literary view is frequently criticized as conventional and pedestrian, lacking the vitality and originality one would expect from a representative treatise written in the late Qing period, a time when Chinese and foreign ideas began to fuse into many interesting and novel concepts.

Just as Lin was about to finish his notes, a scholar in Suzhou started working on another literary history, a work that would later become his chef d'oeuvre. In response to Soochow University vice-chancellor David Laurence Anderson's (1850–1911) suggestion to develop the university's own teaching materials, Huang Ren (1866–1913), a professor of literature at Soochow University, took up the work of writing a detailed description of Chinese literary history. Similar to Lin's belief that literature is the essence of a country's culture, Huang states that "preservation of literature is no different from preservation of other national essences. Literary history can inspire people's love for their country; it is thus no different from national history." But this iconoclastic literary man, who refers to himself as Moses, conceives of literature in a way that is drastically different from that of Lin. His literary view is much more "westernized." His book borrows extensively from Japanese scholar Ōta Yoshio's (1880–?) *An Introduction to Literature* (1896), which is in turn based heavily on Western literary discussions. With great fervor he introduces Chinese readers to the Western concept of defining "literature" by its affective-aesthetic value: "Beauty is the most basic element which fashions literature. Literature without beauty is like a body without a soul.... Beauty belongs to the realm of affection. Hence one can say that affection is the core substance of literature." An argument that helps delineate the boundary of "literature," Huang's emphasis on the point can be taken as another attempt to define the discipline.

Lin's handouts were published under the title *A History of Chinese Literature* in 1910. Perhaps with an aim to make it look more prestigious, a brief explanatory note was printed on the cover, above the book's title: "Lecture Notes of the Imperial Peking University." There have been numerous later editions. Huang's writings, also initially intended to be used in class, subsequently became a twenty-nine-volume treatise. A version was published in 1926, but it was not widely circulated and remained little known for decades. It had to wait until the mid-1980s, when the book finally caught the attention of literary researchers and interest in it and its author began to grow. Today, Lin is still regarded as a progenitor of Chinese literary history, but it is Huang's work that is more critically acclaimed. Huang's work, considered avant-garde in its time, has more in common with modern readers' conceptions of literature. Contrary to Lin, he not only recognizes the value of fiction and poetry, but considers these genres "literature in its purest form." In an introduction to popular Ming novels, he explains how the fiction reflects social malaises, such as inequality and injustice, that pervaded society at that time. He asserts that "literature represents freedom of speech and thought," and in line with this thinking, his literary history foregrounds the humanistic value of literature.

In 1905, Lin quit the university and became a provincial officer of various places. He focused his efforts on women's and children's education, as well as gazetteer studies. He did not write anything on literature after his brief career at the university. Later in life, he compiled a number of gazetteers on Zhejiang, Jiangsu, Anhui, and many other provinces. He died of illness at the age of forty-five, during his posting to Jilin Province as an education officer. Not a man with great literary aspirations, Lin had prepared his notes primarily for implementing Zhang Zhidong's syllabus. It was a historical coincidence that, having borrowed the title of the Japanese book he used as a reference, Lin's own book created the expectation for a thorough, systematic account of Chinese literary history. The expectation was misplaced, however, because the author never had the intention to create an account of this sort. To some extent, one might be able to use the book as a jumping-off point for reflection on Zhang's plan to uphold traditional culture by institutionalizing *wen*. Zhang's program is innovative in its own way, but aside from borrowing literary terminology from Japan, it failed to confront the issue of how *wen* is to be reconceived in the modern world.

For Huang, literature was a lifetime passion. He also wrote *Small Talk on Fiction*, compiled *A New General Encyclopedia*, published a literary magazine entitled *Fiction Forest*, and translated a variety of foreign literary works into Chinese, amid other literary activities. This multifaceted scholar died in 1913 at the age of forty-seven—the same year the Kuomintang's leading member, Song Jiaoren (1882–1913), was assassinated and Sun Yat-sen (1866–1925) fled to Japan, calling for a "Second Revolution" against provisional president Yuan Shikai (1859–1916). A strongly patriotic person, it is said that Huang was driven to mental illness by the chaotic political situation at the time. His fragile physical health further degenerated, ultimately leading to his untimely and premature death.

"*Wen* is the essence of the country, the beginning of national education." This same belief grew into two entirely different literary-historical treatises, because the authors conceived of *wen* in different ways. Lin's work, with its close association with the Imperial Peking University, represents the mainstream literati's standpoint. On the other hand, Huang worked at a university with a Western background, founded by the Methodist Episcopal Church, South. Hence, Huang had no misgivings about examining Chinese literature through the lens of Western culture. Huang was a man ahead of his time. But his perspective raises a range of questions: What is a "modernized" Chinese literature? Does it equal a "westernized" literature? What is the common ground between Chinese and Western literary cultures? What is the value and role of traditional literature in an age of modernity? These were some of the major themes that the coming May Fourth intellectuals would be forced to reckon with.

BIBLIOGRAPHY: Chen Guoqiu, *Wenxueshi shuxie xingtai yu wenhua zhengzhi* (Beijing, 2004). Chen Pingyuan, *Zuowei xueke de wenxueshi* (Beijing, 2011). Milena Doleželová-Velingerová, "Literary Historiography in Early Twentieth-Century China (1904–1928): Constructions of Cultural Memory," in *The Appropriation of Cultural Capital: China's May Fourth Project*, ed. Milena Doleželová-Velingerová and O. Král (Cambridge, MA, 2001), 123–166. Pang Maoyuan and Liu Haifeng, eds., *Zhongguo jindai jiaoyushi ziliao huibian: Gaodeng jiaoyu* (Shanghai, 1993).

KWOK KOU LEONARD CHAN

1905

Xu Nianci transforms a German tale into Chinese science fiction.

Münchhausen Travels to China

Early in the summer of 1905, the young writer Bao Tianxiao (1876–1973) showed his friend Xu Nianci (1875–1908) a story, comically entitled *An Account of Mr. Absurdity*, that Bao had adapted from a children's fairy tale by Meiji Japanese author Iwaya Sazanami (1870–1933). Intrigued by the "strange, unheard of and delightful" adventures he discovered in this text, Xu proceeded to compose his own story in classical Chinese. The science fiction text he created, which he titled *A New Account of Mr. Absurdity*, describes the travels through space and time of a curious but psychologically anguished man whose spirit becomes temporarily separated from his physical body. This novella, published in the short-lived literary journal *A Forest of Fiction* in 1905, is the result of an intricate process of literary and cultural translation of the eighteenth-century German Counter-Enlightenment text *The Marvelous Travels and Adventures of Baron Münchhausen* and presents a mode of modern writing diametrically opposed to Liang Qichao's (1873–1929) calls for realism in the vernacular, politically engaged "new prose" style. Xu's act of cultural borrowing and blending at this moment of crisis in Chinese history expands the potential of the classical literary form while also embodying novel aesthetic-philosophical ideas. His imaginative story reveals that, despite the predominant movement toward realism and modern language in literature in twentieth-century China, nonrealist texts in the classical style served as important vehicles for modern experimentation and linguistic innovation.

Xu's inventive re-creation in Chinese of originally German ideas and tropes represents one of many Chinese encounters with Western, and particularly German, cultural artifacts during the late Qing era. Xu's text came into being at a time when Chinese diplomats traveling abroad sent home travelogues that described the foreign lands and customs they had seen. Beginning in 1878, many of these diaries, composed by the first Chinese travelers overseas, such as Li Fengbao (1834–1887), Zhang Deyi (1847–1918), and Kang Youwei (1858–1927), convey a foreign world of amazing technologies, strange rituals, imposing architecture, and military might. When visiting the newly inaugurated nation of Germany, their authors wrote of inventions and progressive thought that, they believed, should be implemented in China as soon as possible. Meanwhile, Sai Jinhua (ca.1872–1936), concubine of Ambassador Hong Jun (1839–1893) but traveling to Europe as Hong's nominal wife, captured the imagination of contemporary authors and playwrights, not only on account of her beauty and adventures in Europe, but also because of her romance with General Field Marshal Alfred von Waldersee (1832–1904) during the Boxer Rebellion in 1900.

The experience of travel lies at the heart of Xu's tale and its Japanese and German textual predecessors. The original German text (itself based on humorous German source material that had traveled to England in the eighteenth century) was written by Gottfried August Bürger (1747–1794) in 1786 as a protest against the German Enlightenment. The humor in the Münchhausen tales is directly related to the jocular aesthetic of the late baroque and Friedrich von Schiller's (1759–1805) "play drive": an aesthetic impulse that allows the individual to transcend inner and outer constraints so as to attain physical and spiritual freedom. Encountering one impossible situation after another, the picaresque hero of this burlesque text travels through the world while bragging of his own powers in a self-aggrandizing way. The central figure of Münchhausen combines two opposed tendencies of the fool: the cogent narrator who deliberately tells of nonsensical acts in order to critique and unveil real absurdities, and the buffoon who inadvertently caricatures the zeitgeist. As the traveling baron recounts his outlandish escapades, both of these forms of folly merge into one, bringing about a paradoxical fusion of wisdom and foolishness, reason and capricious imagination. Assuming the mantle of a "laughing philosopher" who presents serious thoughts by means of play and says the truth through laughter, Münchhausen is an ambivalent figure who experiences potentially tragic situations while remaining grotesquely merry. By alternating between the satirical and merely humorous, Bürger infuses Münchhausen's absurd and comical exploits with themes of inner crisis that are symptomatic of the eighteenth-century Enlightenment moment.

Iwaya, like the creator of the original Münchhausen tales, recognized a profound need during the late nineteenth-century Meiji period to oppose the excessive rationality of modernity. In particular, Iwaya wrote in opposition to the body of literary works that were being created by Tsubouchi Shōyō (1859–1935) and other adherents of the *genbun itchi* (the unification of speech and writing) movement, a movement that called for rational progress in the literary arts. Rather than following the developing trend of realism in Meiji literature, Iwaya consciously and intentionally proposed a counterdiscourse that was aesthetic in nature, made creative use of Japan's rich classical literary heritage, and brought to the foreground of Meiji consciousness a vast body of traditional folk texts that played an important role in forming a newly modern Japanese sense of national identity. Iwaya's imaginative two-volume re-creation of the original Münchhausen source material, entitled *Mr. Conch* and *The Continuation of Mr. Conch*, exemplifies these literary and aesthetic priorities. The text, which Iwaya derived from the German original through direct translation, belongs to the *hon'an mono* (adapted tales of foreign origin) genre and was published in his collection *Fairy Tales of the World* in 1904. It is a *kusazōshi*, a traditional Japanese picture-book form ostensibly meant for children that absorbs and uses an array of codes, styles, and textual devices in the combination of verbal text and visual images. The two tales about Mr. Conch are narrated in a simple classical Japanese style that merges Japanese cultural elements with the German Münchhausen source material, resulting in a narrative voice that combines that of poet and child, and addresses children and a literary audience at the same time. Iwaya's artfully wrought fairy tales reveal that he uses the voice of the child in order to escape the realistically oriented exigencies of his contemporary literary-cultural moment. At the same time, along with the amalgamation of classical Japanese folk material and Western fairy tales, there occurs a fusion of traditional Japanese configurations with European symbolic references. As a result, Iwaya's tales speak of both the present and the past, address children and adults simultaneously, and reveal a mixture of classical, modern, indigenous, and foreign subject matter, literary techniques, and stylistic effects. By making aesthetic use of children's literature and picture-book conventions, Iwaya reimagines the German text and simultaneously expresses contradictions and desires within Meiji consciousness in a creative, beautiful, and playful way.

The story of Münchhausen reached China in 1905 when the prolific editor and author Bao read Iwaya's imaginative *hon'an mono* adaptation, translated it into a classical *chuanqi* (a "tale of the fantastic"), and passed it on to Xu, who decided to use it as a starting point for an entirely novel and innovative text. Like the original German tale and Iwaya's translation, Xu's story functions as an aesthetic counterdiscourse to the dominant cultural order and subverts conventional epistemological and ideological frames of reference. He also creates an effect of cognitive estrangement that is not present in any of the previous German, Japanese, or Chinese versions of the story. Xu's text is, furthermore, a philosophical-psychological inquiry and cultural critique in metaphoric terms because he uses the fantastic as a methodological instrument to disrupt and subvert the symbolic order of contemporary culture.

The text tells of Mr. Absurdity, whose body and soul are separated by a typhoon. While his body sinks down toward the center of the earth, his soul travels to Mercury and Venus. On Mercury his soul watches the transplantation of brains as a method of rejuvenation, and on Venus it discovers that rudimentary plants and animals appeared at the same time on that planet, thus refuting biologists' assertions that plants historically preceded animals. At the earth's core his body encounters a near-immortal man and watches wonderful scenes through his newly invented lens. Then, accidentally, his soul falls from outer space to merge with his body in the Mediterranean Sea. He has the good luck of being rescued by a warship heading east so that he is able to return to Shanghai. Once there he founds a university that immediately enrolls one hundred thousand students. The university only offers one course, a course on "brain electricity." In his six-day sessions, students learn how to generate and transmit electricity while sitting still and how to use, memorize, analyze, and synthesize symbolic codes. As a result, "brain electricity" becomes widely applied in everyday life and proves amazingly effective and economical.

The subject matter of the story, which portrays a superhuman voyage, futuristic technology, machines, and alien planets, is at odds with its classical Chinese linguistic form. The introduction of narratological devices properly belonging to the *huaben* (vernacular storytelling) tradition further enhances the narrative ambivalence of the text, which recalls the comically absurd, playful tone of the original Münchhausen tale and Iwaya's Japanese translation. Xu maintains the effect of incongruous duality that characterizes all adaptations of Münchhausen source material by creating a dissonance between linguistic form (classical language), tone of narration (oral storytelling mode), and subject matter (modern scientific discourse). For example, at the very beginning of the narration, Xu introduces a narrator who is placed in very particular, vivid circumstances.

Rather than being omniscient, unknown, or far removed from the events that are taking place within the story—as is usually the case in classical Chinese tales—this narrator is fictionally presented as speaking to his audience and appears to the reader to be not only a real person, but indeed a direct contemporary. Xu adapts this oral storyteller narrating persona from the vernacular genre so as to mimic the tone of the German and Japanese texts. At the same time, Xu consistently uses the first person pronoun *yu*, placing great emphasis on the self's immediate experience, sensual perception, emotions, and powers of creation. This technique, too, has a jarring effect in a classical-language text of this period.

While the original Münchhausen narrator uses the technique of (il)logical explanation to rationalize implausible events and the oral storyteller of the Japanese version incessantly addresses his audience so as to dispel doubts regarding his truthfulness, Xu connects his protagonist's travels to the necessity of achieving the transformation of the entire nation through the advancement of knowledge. The insight Mr. Absurdity acquires by means of traveling not only is significant for the field of science, but indeed serves as a reexamination of the moral thought underlying the course of China's present and future. In order to reflect the problematic situation of his own elite literati subjectivity during the late Qing moment, Xu depicts the protagonist's dramatic splitting and multiplication of consciousnesses, a journey that is characterized by the constant alternation between mobility and stagnation as well as the contrapuntal positioning of light versus darkness, wakefulness versus sleep, and crisis versus opportunity. At one point in the story, Xu plunges us directly into a fantasy of physical fragmentation:

> It is certain that you could not help but to laugh at him, the man formed from my spirit, if you saw him. In appearance, he looks like a ball, one *cun* of length in diameter [a unit for measuring length, about 3.33 centimeters], which is made of air. We can only see him clearly with a microscope that magnifies him several million times. His weight, compared with hydrogen gas, is about a hundredth of a particle of hydrogen gas. He has no eyes, no ears, no nose and no tongue, but he has better sight, a keener sense of hearing, and a keener sense of smell.... Now I have two bodies: one is formed from my spirit, and the other is formed from my original body. If I could make use of the

two bodies to research everything and invent everything, my capabilities could be double those of a one-bodied person, or even more than double!... At last the body formed from my spirit was turned into an incredible entity that emanated light.

Fantasies of dualism, such as the one we see here, link the itinerary of Mr. Absurdity's journey with a sense of crisis and the urgent endeavor to obtain and create new knowledge. Like the ancient philosopher Zhuangzi, Xu recognizes that all philosophical inquiry must originate in the riddle and metamorphosis of the self. Inspired by Zhuangzi, he describes a path of outward exploration and simultaneous inward discovery that eventually leads to Mr. Absurdity's deep desire to awaken—indeed, enlighten— the consciousness of his fellow human beings. Though he is repeatedly frustrated in these attempts to bring light to the world, his gaze becomes acutely sharpened, precisely due to his astounding escape from all the rules of reality.

Xu appropriates received tropes and techniques from previous German, Japanese, and Chinese incarnations of the original Münchhausen source material so as to make visible the deeply felt sentiments of unease, anxiety, and profound uncertainty experienced by late Qing intellectuals. By relating the subjectively felt truths hidden beneath the surface of cultural change, Xu's text remains close to human emotional reality and reveals an alternative way to create politically engaged, modern fiction— through the genre of the classical Chinese fantastic tale.

BIBLIOGRAPHY: Bao Tianxiao, *Faluo xiansheng tan* (Shanghai, 1905). G. A. Bürger, *Wunderbare Reisen und Abenteuer des Freiherrn von Münchhausen* (Dresden, 1908). Iwaya Sazanami, *Sekai otogibanashi* (Tokyo, 1904). Xu Nianci, *Xin faluo xiansheng tan* (Shanghai, 1905).

GÉRALDINE FISS

1906 · JULY 15

> "Why do I advocate the national essence? It is not because I want
> people to have faith in Confucianism, but because I want them to love
> the history of our Han nation."

Zhang Taiyan and the Revolutionary Politics of Literary Restoration

On the morning of June 26, 1906, after serving in prison for three years, Zhang Taiyan (1868–1936) was received at a prison gate in Shanghai by members of the Revolutionary Alliance, the anti-Manchu revolutionary organization founded the previous year by revolutionary students studying abroad in Tokyo. One of the most controversial figures of late Qing China, Zhang embodied the contradictions of his era. He was both a conservative yearning for national essence and a radical dedicated to revolution; both a philologist in search of the Chinese language in its quintessential form and a Buddhist scholar pondering the emptiness of all human attachments. Escorted by fellow revolutionaries, Zhang boarded a ship for Japan that evening. Their destination was Tokyo, where he would become the editor in chief of *Minbao* (The people's news), the propaganda organ of the Revolutionary Alliance.

Having witnessed the failure of the Hundred Days' Reform in 1898 and the occupation of Beijing by Western and Japanese troops following the failure of the Boxer Rebellion in 1900, Zhang abandoned his reformist position, moving instead toward a radical revolutionary ideology and advocating for the overthrow of the ethnically Manchu Qing dynasty. In an open letter to Kang Youwei (1858–1927), the leader of the Hundred Days' Reform, Zhang criticized the reformists' agenda and militated for revolution. Eventually, Zhang was jailed for his subversive writing. During his imprisonment, a revised version of his *Book of Urgency*, in which he expounded his revolutionary theories, was published in Tokyo. Both his letter to Kang and the *Book of Urgency* attracted the attention of Chinese revolutionaries in Japan, so Zhang was received with enthusiasm when he arrived in Tokyo.

Yet some of the articles Zhang wrote as the editor of *Minbao* were not nearly so well received by young revolutionaries. Zhang had diligently studied Buddhist philosophy during his time in prison, and his revolutionary theories gradually came to incorporate elements of Buddhist thought. Later, Zhang was even criticized as a propagandist of "Buddha's voice" instead of the "people's voice." Zhang's commitment to Buddhist theories is evident as early as his first speech addressing Chinese students on July 15, 1906, right after his arrival in Tokyo. In that speech, he asserts that it is necessary for revolution to "arouse religious belief so as to promote national morality." Zhang believed that Buddhism was the only suitable religion for a republic because republicanism requires a religion without deities, and only Buddhism offers enlightenment without recourse to deities.

Moreover, Zhang's immersion in classical-style discourse and language also alienated young revolutionaries. The erudite Zhang preferred to write in an obscure style. Lu Xun (1881–1936), the greatest modern Chinese writer and one of the disciples of Zhang, confessed in a commemorative essay on Zhang in 1936, "I liked his writing, but not because of his old-fashioned and difficult style of prose or his dissertations on Buddhist philosophy." Lu also commented that Zhang's writing was so difficult that he could not even punctuate the sentences—literary writings in classical Chinese were often unpunctuated, and the first task of a dedicated reader was to punctuate the text—let alone understand them. However, for Zhang, literature and religious belief were both essential for the forging of national bonds. Zhang emphasized the necessity of national essence (*guocui*), which consists of three parts: language and letters, regulations and institutions, and historical figures and their deeds.

Zhang was trained in evidential school methodology, a type of scholarship that became prominent in the Qing dynasty. The evidential school takes as its primary methodology philological work of the most meticulous kind. Zhang saw this rigorous philology as a way to restore the authentic tradition of the Han Chinese people. In his words, "Why do I advocate the national essence? It is not because I want people to have faith in Confucianism, but because I want them to love the history of our Han nation." It was therefore natural to Zhang that his scholarly preoccupations would be entwined with his commitment to revolution. For Zhang, the aim of political revolution was to restore the sovereignty of the Han people, and, along with and beyond the task of political revolution, it was also necessary to retrieve and restore the origin of the script and the diverse range of sounds of the Han language, which had been suppressed by the Manchu monarchy. As Zhang put it in his autobiography, he "promoted political restoration [of the Han] without ever abandoning scholarly commitment." In fact, while serving as the editor of *Minbao*, Zhang continually published articles on traditional learning in *National Essence Journal*. He also organized the Association for National Learning and gave lectures on such premodern texts as the *Zhuangzi*, a foundational text of Daoism from the late Warring States period that pays special attention to the issue of language, and the *Shuowen jiezi*, an etymological dictionary compiled in the Later Han dynasty (the third century CE). His followers included many young intellectuals who played significant roles later during the New Culture Movement in the 1910s and 1920s, such as Lu and his brother Zhou Zuoren (1885–1967) as well as Qian Xuantong (1887–1939) and Zhu Xizu (1879–1944).

For Zhang, the phonology and etymology represented by the *Shuowen* and the philological reading in the *Zhuangzi* were the essence of philosophy. As he wrote in a letter to the *National Essence Journal*,

> The scholarship that I have engaged in together with my peers these days regards phonology and etymology as the foundation, and philosophy of the "Hundred Schools" of the Zhou and Qin as the acme of thought, and at the same time also refers to the Buddhist canon. I consider language study the essence of scholarship, and the key to language study is phonology and etymology. Seeking truth is the goal of my scholarship, and the classics of the "Hundred Schools" of the Zhou and Qin are where the truth lies.

This notion would later structure his *Balanced Inquiries into National Heritage* (*Guogu lunheng*) in 1910, which consists of three volumes, respectively entitled *Xiaoxue* (Phonology and etymology), *Wenxue* (Literature), and *Zhuzixue* (Hundred Schools philosophy). *Wenxue* here is not merely the study of novels, poems, and other literary works. Rather, Zhang conceives of *wenxue* in terms of its literal translation and classical definition, the "study of *wen*," which entails inquiries into the style and ethics of writing on a much broader scale. According to him, because human thought is circumscribed within language, scholars and philosophers ought to begin their work with an investigation of every minute element of language. Examining the sound and shape of each letter was a necessary approach if one wished to seek the truth of humanity.

This view is reminiscent of the thought of Dai Zhen (1724–1777), the most distinguished scholar of the Qing evidential school. Dai's thought was tremendously influential for Zhang; in his first speech in Tokyo, Zhang declared that Dai was the most important philosopher in recent Chinese history, and Dai's name appears everywhere in Zhang's works. In his letter to Shi Zhongming (1693–1769) Dai wrote,

> The way (*dao*) is what the classics get at. What illuminates the *dao* is the phrases of the classics, and those phrases are made up of nothing more than the characters examined in phonology and etymology. Starting from characters, let us arrive at language, and then, starting from language, let us arrive at the spirit of the ancient sages.

Confucian classics are the written discourse that carries *dao*. In order to understand the discourse, it is necessary to study each character composing it. Therefore, Dai recognized that in order to seek the *dao*, or the substantial way of the world, one must study the language in Confucian classics.

Zhang's revolutionary impulses motivated him to cast Dai's philosophy as an expression of anti-Manchuism. Zhang argued that Dai intended to accuse the Yongzheng Emperor (r. 1723–1735) of using an arbitrary interpretation of moral criteria derived from neo-Confucianism as a pretext for oppressing his subjects. In *An Evidential Study of the Meaning of the Terms in the "Mencius,"* Dai asserts that the neo-Confucian interpretation of the concept of *li* (principle, pattern) as a moral norm that exists prior to all efforts to interpret it provided an ideological basis for social injustice. Dai sought to reinterpret *li* as the exercise of a "principle of differentiation" universally recognized as true. Zhang's anti-Manchuism was not based in racism or xenophobia, as is commonly assumed, but was instead derived from Dai's ideals of social equity. Moreover, this definition of *li* reflects Dai's knowledge of the astronomy and mathematics imported into China by Jesuits from the late sixteenth to the seventeenth centuries. Dai's syncretism and openness to Western thought were also much admired by Zhang.

Zhang was well aware of the limitations of Dai's thought, however. Zhang argued that it was limited because he only examined the Confucian classics, and not the non-Confucian philosophical classics of the pre-Qin era such as the *Zhuangzi*. Second, and most crucially, Zhang felt that Dai did not pay sufficient attention to the importance of the gap between names and things.

By way of contrast with Dai, Zhang—influenced by Buddhism—held that language ultimately cannot describe truth, but a careful examination of language reveals the unbridgeable gap between words and the world. In his "On the Five Negations," Zhang insists that the world is essentially "nothing" and that the state is also an illusion. In "On the State" he elaborates on the notion by arguing that the state is an illusion that emerges from the desire of the people to protect their own individual lives. Human existence, according to Zhang, is a false consciousness inevitably alienated from the truth. Human beings have no choice but to conform to a provisional world vision composed by language. Yet through a literary practice with the awareness of the nature of the world as nothing at its heart, society can be improved and reformed with universal ideals as the model.

Such a literary practice would emphasize simplicity, parsimony, and precision. For Zhang, written discourse itself already misleads the reader about the truth because there is inevitably a gap between an object and its name. Excessive rhetoric or exaggerating ornamentation exacerbates that problem, but so does vernacular rhetoric, which aims to mimic the spoken language and in the process adds unnecessary words.

At the same time, Zhang objects to the historical process whereby simpler or more common characters come to be used to represent words with similar sounds that used to be represented by different characters. This process reduces the number of characters available and therefore prevents people from expressing their thoughts in a precise and elegant manner. It is therefore necessary to restore old characters like those found in the *Shuowen*.

Zhang's opposition to the vernacularization of Chinese writing was not based on an antagonism toward the spoken language; on the contrary, Zhang was afraid that vernacularization would destroy the ancient diversity of sounds and accents preserved in the classical language. Zhang uses the image of "the piping of Heaven" (*tianlai*) from the chapter "Discussion on Making All Things Equal" of the *Zhuangzi* as an allegory for his vision for the Chinese language. In the original *Zhuangzi*, the "piping of heaven" refers to the vast variety of sounds made as the wind blows through each of nature's creatures and forms and is meant as an appreciation of the diversity of existence. Zhang uses this image as a metaphor for the Chinese language, enriched by its many dialects, accents, and manifestations over time.

The "piping of Heaven" was also a key image for Zhang's political philosophy. In the "piping of Heaven" he found a vision for an ideal world, in which all things are allowed to lead their own lives and have an equal right to be different—a vision that forms the core of the political philosophy expressed in his "A Discussion on the Equalization of Things." Once again, Zhang's politics are inextricably linked to his philosophy of language. Just as a universally open written discourse would allow a diversity of individual expressions, a just and equitable state would allow for a wide variety of human flourishing.

Zhang's advocacy for revolution as a way to restore the past was undoubtedly motivated in part by nationalist impulses, but it was not a mere expression of romanticism. Zhang's revolutionary ideals are strongly rooted in his profound investigations into the nature of writing, literary styles, and the ethics and politics of linguistic practice.

After the establishment of the Republic of China in 1912, Zhang was gradually sidelined from the revolutionary movement. However, his philological work inspired his followers to push for the modernization of Chinese language. The scheme of shorthands Zhang used to record phonology was eventually adapted into *zhuyin*, the first attempt at using an alphabet to represent Chinese pronunciation. Zhang's student Lu played the decisive role in the vernacularization of Chinese writing in the New Culture Movement. Although Zhang's own scholarship and thought often appeared conservative, it propelled the modernization of Chinese politics, language, literature, and philosophy, to name only a few of the fields in which Zhang's work proved influential. Making sense of this irony remains a task for contemporary scholars.

BIBLIOGRAPHY: Chen Pingyuan, *Touches of History: An Entry to "May Fourth" China* (Leiden, Netherlands, 2011). Kauko Laitinen, *Chinese Nationalism in the Late Qing Dynasty: Zhang Binglin as an Anti-Manchu Protagonist* (London, 1990). Kenji Shimada, *Pioneer of the Chinese Revolution: Zhang Binglin and Confucianism* (Stanford, CA, 1990). Viren Murthy, *The Political Philosophy of Zhang Taiyan: The Resistance of Consciousness* (Leiden, Netherlands, 2011). Wong Young-tsu, *Search for Modern Nationalism: Zhang Binglin and Revolutionary China, 1869–1936* (Hong Kong, 1989).

TSUYOSHI ISHII

1907 · JUNE 1

"Civilized drama" is born.

Global Theatrical Spectacle in Tokyo and Shanghai

On June 1, 1907, a group of Chinese students led by Li Shutong (1880–1942) staged a dramatic adaptation of Harriet Beecher Stowe's (1811–1896) *Uncle Tom's Cabin*. It was performed at the Tokyo Hongo-za Theater under the title *Black Slaves' Plea to Heaven* for an audience of 1,500 people. Receiving rave reviews in major Japanese newspapers, this performance can be understood as the birth of "civilized drama" (*wenming xi*). As a Japanese contemporary critic put it in the *Tokyo Mainichi Shinbun*, "This performance cannot be named in the same breath with our country's amateur theater…it is even far superior to those of our Shinpa stars like Takada, Fujisawa, Ii, Kawai etc." Only a few months later, in October, the performance of *Black Slaves' Plea to Heaven* was replicated in Shanghai, as an independent production at the British Lyceum Theater and directed by the Chinese drama reformer Wang Zhongsheng (1884?–1911).

At its core, the civilized drama movement was a transnational cultural phenomenon that found its roots in Japanese reformed drama in Tokyo, Japanese and Chinese reception of global theater, and indigenous Chinese efforts to modernize stage performances in Shanghai and other major Chinese cities. Civilized drama was intertwined with the global drama scene in the late nineteenth and early twentieth centuries, not only in terms of transnational adaptations and the circulation of texts but also in terms of dramatic practice. Due to its hybrid nature, however, it came under fire in the 1920s by proponents of spoken drama and was nearly relegated to the dustbin of history. The Chinese staging of *Uncle Tom's Cabin* is a perfect showcase of the hybridity and transnational character of this new drama form, but also of how foreign drama was adapted and appropriated according to local requirements and preferences.

Stowe's novel was the most widely read novel in the nineteenth century; it sold three hundred thousand copies in its first year of publication in the United States alone and has been translated into more than twenty languages. Following its success as a book, *Uncle Tom's Cabin* became even more popular in the United States by means of its manifold dramatic adaptations. For example, according to recent estimates, approximately three million people saw the adapted blackface minstrel shows between 1850 and the early 1900s.

Lin Shu (1852–1924) completed the first Chinese translation of the novel in 1901. Retitled *Black Slaves' Plea to Heaven*, it quickly became popular in China as a model for political reform novels. Even before Lin's translation, John Fryer (1839–1928) had mentioned it as an example for writers to follow when crafting submissions for his 1895 fiction contest.

The five-act drama adapted by Li and his fellows had little in common with the original novel: Uncle Tom's role was greatly reduced (as the change of title suggests), and the five acts mainly revolve around the rebellious protagonists George and Eliza and their escape. The Christian values in the novel all but disappear, and attention is focused instead on the theme of national liberation. In this process of adaptation, the dramatists probably followed Lin, who in his comments to his translation related the fate of slaves to that of Chinese coolies in the United States. They also added entirely new content—namely, an act depicting a lively celebration in a factory that allowed for the staging of music and dance. The scene incorporates the Peking opera and international folklore performed by a colorful cast of international students, including Indians, Japanese, and Koreans. The performance adopted Western-style realistic stage sets, costume, makeup, and speech, and also made use of a written script rather than an improvisational model, as was the case for many contemporary plays.

Performative hybridity, extravagance, and experimentation were typical of the civilized drama, but these qualities were not uniquely East Asian. *Black Slaves' Plea to Heaven* resembles the popular minstrel show adaptations of *Uncle Tom's Cabin*, which similarly combined elements of performance, singing, and dancing. Also, like the white immigrants in blackface who parodied racist stereotypes of African Americans in order to emphasize their superiority, Chinese actors in Tokyo highlighted their own status as "white" and "civilized" people by performing in blackface. Minstrel shows also became popular in Japan, following the unwelcome arrival of Commodore Matthew Perry's (1794–1858) fleet in 1853, and it is possible that Chinese students in Japan may have been aware of and even attended them. While this fact remains to be proven, one source does mention that male slaves in the play performed in blackface. But, of course, the students had ambitions greater than presenting a purely popular and satirically entertaining performance.

Black Slaves' Plea to Heaven was not a one-off amateur production but part of a larger program intent on reforming Chinese theater, which had long been limited to operatic styles. Li, like thousands of other students, had gone to Japan in 1905. An art student at the Tokyo School of Fine Arts and a theater aficionado, Li frequently visited Tokyo's theaters and became acquainted with their actors. He and his fellow classmates became attracted to drama after having seeing performances of Japanese "radical student theater," which emerged during the politically turbulent 1880s as a speech-based theater with heavy political undertones. This spoken-word-based model for drama was further developed by the famous actor Kawakami Otojiro (1864–1911) into the Japanese "new school" of theater, which was at its height of popularity when *Black Slaves' Plea to Heaven* was first performed in Japan. Together with his friends, Li formed the Spring Willow Society for Research on Literature and Arts—usually referred to as the Spring Willow Society—in Tokyo during late 1906. The society's full name reflects its close connection to the leading Japanese society for drama reform, the Society for Literature and Arts, headed by Tsubouchi Shoyo (1859–1953), of which Li was also a member. Sharing similar goals of reforming and modernizing traditional theater traditions by combining both old and new elements, drama activists of both groups worked closely to stage adaptations of Western and Japanese novels and dramas.

The students performed foreign plays not only based on translated texts, but also according to live performances they had seen abroad. For example, the students' production of *La Dame aux Camélias*—another hugely popular novel in Europe with numerous stage and later film adaptations—is indicative of this method. The novel, written by Alexander Dumas fils (1824–1895), was translated into Japanese as early as 1884, but it was not staged until almost a decade later. Kawakami first saw the play in France with Sarah Bernhardt (1844–1923) in the role of Marguerite in 1893. On his second tour to France, in 1901, he staged the play with his wife in Paris, only then bringing it back to be performed in Tokyo in 1903. Five years earlier, in 1898, *La Dame aux Camélias* had been translated into Chinese, again by Lin, and became another sensation in China. The students chose an adaptation of this novel for their first public performance in Tokyo, staging a minimal performance of the first act as part of a charity event in February 1907. Conducted as an informal test run, the performance was facilitated by training in acting and stage design from Japanese actors.

The students were not attracted to foreign best sellers alone; they also translated and performed lesser-known political pieces. Their next performance, *Cry of Injustice*, was an adaptation of a rather obscure play, *The Social Ladder*, by the anarchist songwriter Jule Jouy (1855–1897). The play was translated by the Chinese anarchist Li Shizheng (1881–1973), who must have seen it in Montmartre while studying in Paris.

Similar attempts at reforming and modernizing Chinese drama, transforming traditional drama by drawing inspiration from foreign models, had been undertaken in Shanghai since the late nineteenth century. In Shanghai, the Lyceum had been producing dramas since it opened in the mid-1870s; Italian, French, and English opera ensembles included Shanghai on their tours; and foreigners staged amateur theater performances in the concessions. However, contemporary sources indicate that Chinese people were rarely seen in the audiences of either the amateur or the professional shows, likely because these were regarded as foreign dramas intended specifically for foreigners. This changed dramatically with the first Chinese-language performance in the Lyceum Theater, Wang's *Black Slaves' Plea to Heaven*. While Wang's play did not seem to impress much in terms of adaptation or story line, the use of a relatively grand and modern theater for a Chinese performance—already a groundbreaking move—in addition to new lighting techniques and realistic scenery left a lasting impression on the audiences and drama groups alike.

From then on, civilized drama took shape in Shanghai. Following the return of many of the drama reformers from Tokyo to China, the movement reached its peak between 1914 and 1915 as a hybrid of reformed Japanese drama, reformed traditional Chinese drama, and European popular drama. The famous *shinpa* tragedies adapted for Chinese stages were the most popular, for their melodramatic plotting and sentimental style, and the original political impetus for drama reform gradually declined. However, given the scale of the civilized drama movement and our current level of understanding, it is difficult to make any judgment about the overall nature of it. Recent research has identified at least 120 different drama groups and over eight hundred titles of plays, of which we only know the content of or have scripts for around 340. Ninety percent of these plays have yet to be studied or analyzed.

Due to the impact of the burgeoning film industry and commercial theater, dramas took a turn toward the sentimental. The film industry was also in direct competition with drama, as many civilized drama pieces were adapted into films. Some historiographers of Chinese drama see this commercialization as the main reason for civilized drama's decline in popularity, but such judgments have to be treated with caution.

To understand why drama reform efforts were so important and also so controversial, they need to be seen in a wider and international context. In the mid- to late nineteenth century, Japanese and Chinese travelers to the West returned home with descriptions of the grand opera houses they saw in Paris, London, or Berlin. They were baffled by their grandeur, which reflected the high status accorded to drama in the West and the fact that drama was perceived as a driver of social change. Most notably, the Western opera houses were emblems of national cultural greatness. In Japan and China, by contrast, drama in all forms was seen as a vulgar, popular art form, not a respectable literary genre. In order to elevate it to the status it had achieved in the West, numerous new literary histories and treatises on the reform of drama were written, first in Japan during the 1880s and then, with slight delay, either translated or rewritten for China during the late 1890s and early 1900s.

At that time, none of today's established terms for Chinese drama— "opera," "traditional dramatic form," "spoken drama," "comedy," "tragedy," and so on—were fixed; they were in the process of being formed, mostly through translations of or theoretical treatises on Western drama. The subsequent development of drama theories for China (and Japan) sought to define a form of drama that could both be part of world theater and represent China's own national culture. However, disputes arose around the question of which form of drama was best suited to achieving this objective. By the 1920s, polarized debates reduced possibilities for a national drama to only two alternatives: Peking opera, as redefined by Qi Rushan (1877–1962) and Mei Lanfang (1894–1961), or the Westernized spoken drama promoted by May Fourth intellectuals.

When Li and his fellow students staged *Black Slaves' Plea to Heaven* in Tokyo in 1907, they did not yet use the term "civilized drama"; it was simply called "new drama." It is also unclear what exactly the term "civilized drama," in its neutral sense, meant when it was first used as a popular marketing label in the 1910s for advertising the new drama as "civilized." Some scholars relate the word "civilized" to the idea of "civilized nations," including Japan, and in this sense imply that the term simply meant "foreign drama." Others interpret it as a normative term, highlighting its educational and progressive function in "civilizing" the audience. Li made the connection between drama reform and civilization when explaining the goals of his Spring Willow Society: "The art of acting is closely related to civilization," meaning that only this new, reformed drama was able to achieve the main objectives of the modernization trajectory—to spread "civilization and enlightenment"—a project that was impeded by the vulgarity of the old drama.

Because civilized drama was a hybrid, experimental, politically engaged form of drama and a blend of traditional and modern elements, it was vulnerable to attack. Consequently, during the heated disputes and polemics about drama reform and the development of a national theater that arose in China in the 1920s and 1930s, it suffered attacks from both the conservative and the reformist camps. Civilized drama was an integrated attempt to reconcile the best of both traditional and modern drama, but by the 1930s, it had become the laughingstock of China's drama reform effort and the term was applied only in derogation, in order to stress its vulgar, dilettantish, and even pernicious nature. In this sense, it suffered the same fate as Mandarin Ducks and Butterflies fiction. It is also for this reason that this drama movement fell into obscurity, only to be rediscovered by scholars and to have its reputation restored during the 1990s.

In an ironic twist, the 1907 Tokyo performance of *Black Slaves' Plea to Heaven* is still celebrated today—2007 marked its one hundredth anniversary—but not as a form of *wenming xi*. The ideological complexity and formal hybridity of the performance appear to have been forgotten, and it is now remembered as a prototype for modern, Western-style theater in China and a seminal event in the birth of Chinese spoken drama.

BIBLIOGRAPHY: Joshua L. Goldstein, *Drama Kings: Players and Publics in the Re-creation of Peking Opera, 1870–1937* (Berkeley, CA, 2007). Jin Li, "Theater of Pathos: Sentimental

Melodramas in the New Drama Legacy," *Modern Chinese Literature and Culture* 24, no. 2 (Fall 2012): 94–128. Liu Siyuan, *Performing Hybridity in Colonial-Modern China* (New York, 2013). M. Cody Poulton, *A Beggar's Art: Scripting Modernity in Japanese Drama, 1900–1913* (Honolulu, 2010). Zhong Dafeng, Zhang Zhen, and Zhang Yingjin, "From Wenmingxi (Civilised Play) to Yingxi (Shadowplay): The Foundation of Shanghai Film Industry in the 1920s," *Asian Cinema* 9, no. 1 (Fall 1997): 46–64.

NATASCHA GENTZ

1907 · JULY 15

"Autumn wind, autumn rain, fill my heart with sorrow."

The Death of China's First Feminist

On July 15, 1907, Qiu Jin (1875–1907) was executed by beheading for plotting to overthrow the Qing empire. Pressed for a confession before her execution, she wrote the words "Autumn wind, autumn rain, fill my heart with sorrow"—the opening line of a poem that she would never finish. Her remains were dumped outside the city wall in the burial ground for unclaimed corpses. In time, she would become one of the most famous martyrs of the Republican Revolution, and her last words would be committed to memory by generations of Chinese school children.

Qiu came from a literati-official family; her choice to mark the end of her life by writing poetry was a telltale sign of her cultured upbringing. Born soon after the massive Taiping Rebellion that shook the foundation of the Qing empire, she grew up in a time of great anxiety, as well as tremendous hope: anxiety over China's dismemberment by Western powers, but hope for a new political and social order. In Chinese newspapers that had only been recently founded, Qiu was able to read daily reports on such events as Russia's incursion into northeast China, the partition of Poland, and the Philippine Revolution. Leading intellectuals made impassioned pleas for the reformation of Chinese citizenry and pointed to the lowly status of women as a major hindrance to national strength. In both cosmopolitan cities and provincial towns, new schools were being established, including schools for women. In late 1903, Qiu joined the waves of young people going to Japan to study, leaving behind her husband and two young children. In her two years abroad, she was exposed to radical political thoughts and joined revolutionary associations. After returning to China, she taught briefly at a newly opened women's school, tried her hand at running a feminist journal, and then devoted the last year of her life to planning military uprisings against the government. While Qiu was not the only woman to enter the public arena or travel abroad to study, or even to participate in revolution—many Chinese women at the time on all rungs of the social ladder answered the call to become active patriots—she did so flamboyantly, performing her role on the stage of historical transformation without apology. Her life and writing embodied the desire, adventures, and setbacks faced by modern China's "New Woman."

In many ways, Qiu's literary works reflect the cultural paradox of her time: a member of the last generation solely trained in the Chinese cultural tradition, she grew up to embrace the new and the Western. Even as she repeatedly urged her female friends to "become heroes, / And not dissipate [their] efforts in crafting fine lyrics," she herself continued to write verse, expressing her ideals and her frustrations, addressing current issues, and meditating on tradition.

In an early song lyric "To the Melody 'A River Full of Red,'" written in the days before she went to Japan, Qiu grapples with her conflicting identities. She was twenty-nine years old at the time; she had already been married for eight years and was the mother of two young children. The poem is a self-portrait, beginning with images associated with autumn, *qiu*, which happens to be the poet's own surname. The focal point of the poem is the social constraint of being born female, what Qiu calls "mere rouge and powder." Juxtaposed with this conventional femininity is the poet's true self, what she calls her *xin*—literally "heart"—a word that refers to a person's intellectual and emotional capacities, as well as her aspirations. The enormous gap between "rouge and powder" and her brave heart is what leaves her painfully isolated: "But how could they with their vulgar minds understand me?" The poem ends with a plea for a true friend, a soul mate. Unlike "they" with their "vulgar minds"— those bad readers—who cannot see past the I-as-assigned-female, a true friend would be able to recognize the poet's essence and bear witness to her heroic aspirations.

In another work, *The Stones of the Jingwei Bird*, an unfinished autobiographical fiction taking the form of a prosimetric narrative, Qiu voices sharp criticism of the practice of arranged marriage through the voice of her young protagonist: "In selecting my mate for life, why do [my parents] consider only the money and not the man? They lie to me and say it's fate, but that's absurd, accepting that women live their entire lives like beasts of burden." Such a lament had been repeated in women's quarters for hundreds of years, but Qiu's fictional imagination went further. She wanted fundamental social change that would allow a woman to live the fullest possible life, even if such change meant a long, persistent struggle. Thus, she invokes the mythic Jingwei bird, who in her former life as the daughter of the sun god was drowned in the Eastern Sea; in her incarnation as a small bird, she brings pebble by small pebble in her bill in an effort to fill the vast and hostile sea. In a leap of romantic imagination and in contrast to her own long years in an unhappy marriage, Qiu's young protagonist plots an elaborate escape before her wedding with the help of her sworn sisters. Toward the end of the narrative, we see five young women stand by the rails with linked arms on board a steamship to Japan. In front of them is not a cloistered boudoir but an oceanic vista promising great adventures, "clouds at dusk, stretching far away."

In fiction as in real life, Qiu saw her own calling as a significant actor on the stage of large historical changes. In early twentieth-century China, this larger stage was that of national salvation. Chafing at the domestic sphere then allotted to women, or even the somewhat expanded cultural arena traditionally granted to the learned woman, Qiu experimented at reinventing herself, including cross-dressing as a man. As she explained to a Japanese acquaintance, "I want to become strong like men. First I want to look like a man in appearance, and then I will become like a man in my psyche." In response to a call for volunteers to fight the Russian occupation of Manchuria, she adopted the style name Swordswoman of Mirror Lake.

Fueling her imagination were popular Western heroines whose stories were featured in the newspapers: Sophia Perovskaya (1853–1881), the Russian anarchist who participated in the assassination of Tsar Alexander II, and Madame Roland (1754–1793), a leader of a moderate faction in the French Revolution who died on the guillotine. Still, at the core of her self-invention was the traditional Chinese persona of the swordsman. According to the historian Sima Qian's (135?–86 BCE) definition, "Even though their behaviors may not follow the accepted norm, they always keep their words, their actions always bear fruit, and their promises are sincere. When others are in trouble, they do not begrudge their own lives [in trying to rescue them]." Eagerly channeling the spirit of the swordsman, Qiu wrote poems on her sword and had pictures taken of herself doing a sword dance. Here is one excerpt from her "Song of the Barbarian Sword":

> A single expanse of autumn water, so bright that a tiniest
>   hair is visible,
> Seen from afar it's hard to tell it is the gleam of a broadsword....
> When this sword is drawn from its sheath, then heaven shakes,
> And sun and moon, stars and planets quickly obscure their light.
> The ocean's waters are roused by the sound of it hitting the earth,
> And the dark winds howl when an inch of its blade is exposed.
> If you take it out, hang it on the wall, and for a time leave it unused,
> It will wail and sob night after night making the cries of an owl:
> Its heroic spirit thirsts to drink the blood of battle,
> Just as a restless heart needs a libation of wine.

Adopting the ultramasculine poetic mode known as "heroic abandon," Qiu revels in the "iron-and-blood-ism" embodied by the sword, whose lethal power is still hidden behind the deceptively calm appearance of "autumn water"—again, note the implicit reference to Qiu's own surname. In the call of national salvation, women like Qiu found a legitimizing pretext to breach the traditional gender divide that relegated women to the inner realm. The poem's most arresting image, of the unused sword wailing like an owl, gives voice to a searching and restless spirit whose vast potential is yet to be realized. As Qiu invokes the enduring mythology of ancient weaponry, she inserts herself—a mere mortal compared to steel and iron—into the rich tradition of chivalric heroism, a tradition now hitched to the grand cause of nationalism. In the end, sword and swordswoman merge into one being: heroic in ethos, dashing in physical prowess, and noble in spirit.

And yet, how could she match action with words? How could she live up to the true spirit of the swordsman and go beyond simply adopting the dashing image? Like many politically engaged scholars of her time, Qiu was troubled by these questions. In a letter to a friend, she once lamented, "There have been many men who died for the revolution...

but we have not heard of a woman yet, and that is an embarrassment for all of us women." Always striving to be the first, to leave her own significant mark as a trailblazer, Qiu's words read like a death wish. When the uprisings she organized repeatedly failed and her close comrades were brutally executed, when she knew the soldiers were coming for her, she did not escape to safety, although she had more than enough time to do so. In the end, her fight for women's equal rights came together with her nationalist activism, as she saw her own impending death as the fulfillment of a duty she had assigned herself—the duty of the vanguard, to be at the forefront in every way.

In executing Qiu and particularly in forcing the abandonment of her remains, the Qing court intended to have her go down in history as an infamous traitor. Despite the enormous risk of commemorating an executed criminal, Qiu's two sworn sisters Wu Zhiying (1868–1934) and Xu Zihua (1873–1935) retrieved her body and conducted a proper burial a few months after her death. The memorial service drew hundreds of people, many of whom did not know her personally. The occasion became a forum for public protest against the government, as would other high-profile burials in twentieth-century China, time and again. A tsunami of public mourning followed: elegies flooded the newspapers, and biographies and plays dramatized her life and its tragic end. Lu Xun (1881–1936), whose 1919 story "Medicine" took a critical slant on the spectacle of Qiu's martyrdom, famously quipped that these crowds "applauded [Qiu Jin] to death." In revolutionary circles, some young women even took on new names that meant "Emulate Qiu" or "Admire Qiu." In her death, Qiu became the icon of a new kind of womanhood. Even when her tomb was torn down by soldiers a few months later, and the chief mourners Wu and Xu found themselves on the government's wanted list, rubbings of the tomb stele and news clippings of the protest continued to circulate and draw more sympathizers to the revolutionary cause. Four years later, as the epitaph on her stele predicted, her case was overturned and the Qing empire fell. Enshrined in patriotic halls of honor on both sides of the Taiwan Strait, Qiu's official legacy is that of fearless self-sacrifice for the modern Chinese nation. Her violent death cements her status as a bona fide martyr and represents the moment when women entered modern Chinese history. In dramatic renditions and films, she is typically depicted as a flamboyant figure, dashing around on horseback while cross-dressed, performing a sword dance before a mixed audience of men and women,

heroic to the last moment, with the obligatory defiant speech and posture.
As she became more and more abstracted as a symbol of generalized
patriotism, her life story was subjected to increased editing, until, finally,
this iconoclast was thoroughly conventionalized into an icon.

BIBLIOGRAPHY: Hu Ying, *Burying Autumn: Poetry, Friendship, and Loss* (Cambridge,
MA, 2016). Lu Xun, "Medicine," in *Selected Stories of Lu Xun*, trans. Yang Hsien-yi and
Gladys Yang (Beijing, 1960), 25–33. Mary Backus Rankin, "The Emergence of Women
at the End of Ch'ing: The Case of Ch'iu Chin [Qiu Jin]," in *Women in Chinese Society*,
ed. Margery Wolf and Roxane Witke (Stanford, CA, 1975), 39–66.

HU YING

1908 · FEBRUARY

Lu Xun publishes "The Power of the Mara Poet."

1908 · NOVEMBER

Wang Guowei publishes *Remarks on Song Lyrics
about the Human Condition.*

From Mara to Nobel

In February and March 1908, an essay entitled "The Power of the Mara
Poet" appeared serially in *Henan*, an overseas Chinese student magazine
based in Tokyo. In the essay, the author, Lingfei, deplores the degenerate
condition of China and calls for a "spiritual warrior"—a poet who would
be able to "pluck people's hearts." Lingfei points to Qu Yuan (340–278
BCE), the legendary Chinese poet who supposedly wrote the major pieces
in the *Songs of the South* (*Chu ci*), as a paragon for "giving voice to what
his forebears feared to say." Still, says Lingfei, "many [of Qu Yuan's poetic
lines] were strains of rococo pathos. There was never defiance, and it is
mostly too weak to stir posterity." By contrast, Lord Byron (1788–1824),
with his recalcitrant passion and heroic deeds, personifies the true model
of the modern poet, the Mara poet.

Lingfei was the penname of Zhou Shuren (1881–1936), who was later
known as Lu Xun, the founding father of modern Chinese literature.
"Mara Poet" was one of a series of essays Lu Xun undertook to review

Chinese civilization during his formative years in Japan. Seeing China as vitiated by feudalistic traditions and ossified thought, he considered poetry, and, by extension, literature, the preferred vehicle for reviving the Chinese humanity and increasing its capacity to engage the modern world:

> For every human heart contains poetry within it, and when a poet has written a poem, it no longer belongs to him exclusively, but to others who, upon reading it, come to an emotional understanding of it in their own hearts.... [It causes] all men of feeling to look up, inspired, as though they might be gazing on some new dawn ablaze with light that has power to strengthen, ennoble, beautify and enlighten.

Lu Xun's call for a new literature to reinvigorate China resonated with many other reform-minded intellectuals of his time. Liang Qichao (1873–1929), a pioneer of late Qing political reform, argued that Chinese modernization hinged on "poetry revolution" as early as 1899. While these intellectuals were pursuing radical change for China, the way they conceptualized the link between political reform and literary re-form bespoke a poetics of contested motivations. "Literature" meant to them both an exercise in belles lettres, as prescribed by recently imported Western aesthetics, and a manifestation of the Way, as *wen* was conceived of in traditional Chinese thought, both an expression of individual sentiments and testimony to national collectivity.

In naming Byron the model "spiritual warrior" for the Chinese to emulate, Lu Xun was not the first in late Qing China to celebrate the Romantic poet. Byron had been treated as an iconic figure by enlightened Chinese intelligentsia since the turn of the twentieth century. What makes Lu Xun's engagement with Byron different is that he associates the poet with qualities drawn from a variety of intellectual sources: Max Stirner, Arthur Schopenhauer, and Friedrich Nietzsche, among others. Above all, he calls attention to the poet's "Satanic power" to transgress and demolish the status quo, thus giving his poetic vision a negative, even demonic, thrust. Lu Xun likens such a demonic power to that of Mara, the fiendish deity of the Sanskrit tradition, a figure similar to Satan.

Scholars have discussed the implications of Lu Xun's reference to Mara, who can be either a diabolical creature capable of destroying the world or a mere trickster ever ready to subvert any establishment. Still, with its exotic, mysterious origin and its capacity for total negation, Mara represents for Lu Xun the liberating force hitherto held in check by traditional literature. Insofar as poetry constituted the core of traditional Chinese literary *and* political culture, the Mara poet challenges the canonical dictum that poetry teaches one "not to stray" (*si wu xie*). Thus Lu Xun argues, if poetry is supposed to "express one's free will," "to force one not to stray [in composing poetry] is to curb one's free will. How can there be a promise of liberty under whips and halters?"

The year 1908 did not witness only the advent of the Mara poet, however. In November of that same year, the scholar Wang Guowei (1877–1927) published *Remarks on Song Lyrics and the Human Condition*. Having already written passionately about Western philosophers from Immanuel Kant to Schopenhauer, Wang sought to resuscitate in this work both the format and argument of Chinese poetics, resurrecting the framework of lyrical evocation as represented by Yan Yu (fl. thirteenth century), Wang Fuzhi (1619–1692), and Wang Shizhen (1634–1711). Nevertheless, despite his effort to recapitulate the arguments of premodern Chinese poetics, the way Wang Guowei engages with notions such as subjectivity and objectivity, idealism and realism, indicates his Western-aesthetics-informed eclecticism. At his most polemical, Wang invokes Nietzsche's dictum "The best literature is that which is written in blood" as his criterion for evaluating song lyrics.

Wang's efforts to integrate premodern Chinese poetics with Western aesthetics resulted in the formation of his own theory of a "mental vista" (*jingjie*), a state of awakening that is prompted by, but not limited to, the experience of poetic composition. This "mental vista" is subjective and aesthetically evocative, but it also resonates with the "archetypal occasion" in literature as in history. The "mental vista" registers Wang's idiosyncratic reflection on history. Having witnessed a succession of political crises in the Qing, Wang was haunted by a pessimistic outlook on Chinese civilization, such that he read *ci*—the song lyric, a unique genre of Chinese poetry known for its delicacy and exquisite imagery—as a farewell to his cherished cultural legacy.

As Wang had it, precisely because of their immersion in a most delicate form of poetry, song lyricists are more sensitive than any other poets to the threat of cultural vandalism in a time of brutal reforms and spurious modernization. The lyricist's work is unfailingly elegiac, and this quality, together with the exquisite linguistic performance of *ci*, evokes the tension between self-indulgence and self-denial—and perhaps the "modern" malaise of exhausted melancholia. Hence Wang wrote, "A song lyricist is created by heaven out of a hundred calamities."

The dialogical potential between Lu Xun's and Wang's writings makes 1908 a year of much significance for the fashioning of a modern Chinese literary subjectivity. Critics have described Lu Xun and Wang in antagonistic terms: willful volitionism versus formal aesthetics, revolutionary yearning versus cultural nostalgia. Such a contrastive reading is an oversimplification, for both Lu Xun and Wang were seeking to answer the question, each in his own way, of how a poetic consciousness can help illuminate historical circumstances. Whereas Lu Xun's Mara poet strikes with his fiendishly seductive power to provoke and destroy, Wang's melancholy song lyricist doggedly seeks a mindscape through which to reconcile poetic sentiment and historical contingency. Both Lu Xun and Wang brought Western discourse to bear on the Chinese context, and both pondered the tenability of their agendas vis-à-vis a time that appeared anything but poetic.

Of the two, Lu Xun no doubt commanded far more attention as a result of the moral urgency and polemical intensity invested in his treatise. His Mara poet would undergo multiple incarnations in the early modern period, from the romantic iconoclast of the May Fourth era to the leftist warrior of the revolutionary era. Lu Xun passed away in October 1936 and was quickly deified by Mao Zedong (1893–1976) and his propagandists; meanwhile, his Mara poet assumed, as it were, a new identity, becoming successively either a righteous Communist cadre-writer or a Maoist fanatic. It may not be an exaggeration to say that the cult of Mara-turned-Mao culminated in the Cultural Revolution, when the whole nation was bedeviled by a defiant, anarchist impulse—a poetic and political carnival of the most dangerous kind.

It would take a few more decades for us to appreciate the fact that Lu Xun was never a naive instigator of revolution, and that his Mara poet proved Janus-faced from the outset. True, Lu Xun sought to use Mara's "devilish voice" to upset traditional literature, but he was always wary of the ominous potential of the voice. Such an awareness brought him to engage not only with social and political evils but also with the "strategies of unnamable entities," the amorphous, ambient nihilism that permeates both his mind and the world beyond. That is, zeal generates not only revolutionary momentum but also an "involution-ary" thrust of entropic desire and self-reflexive discontent. With the undead, self-cannibalistic poetic subject of "The Epitaph" (1925), Lu Xun launches a polemic aimed at revealing the modern Chinese "heart of darkness":

…I tore out my heart to eat it, wanting to know the true taste. But the pain was so agonizing, how could I tell its taste?…

…When the pain subsided, I savored the heart slowly. But since by then it was stale, how could I know its true taste?…

…Answer me. Or be gone!…

Wang underwent a similar trial in deliberating the function of liter-ature and the poet's role in modern times. He ended up consumed by the melancholy of his ideal song lyricist. On June 2, 1927, Wang drowned himself in a pond of the Imperial Garden in Beijing. His brief will states, "After fifty years of living in this world, the only thing yet to happen to me is death; having been through such historical turmoil, nothing can further stain my integrity."

Wang's death has been attributed to, among other causes, domestic and psychological turbulence, his immersion in Schopenhauer's philosophy, and his eschatological vision. The most popular explanation is that the politically conservative Wang ended his life out of loyalty to the fallen Qing dynasty. However, Chen Yinke (1890–1969), Wang's friend and a renowned historian, describes his drowning as a consummation of "this spirit of independence and the freedom of thought." To take Chen's point one step further, one could argue that Wang's "freedom" and "independence" make sense not as a political belief but as a poetic pursuit, a "mental vista" of the kind he discusses in *Remarks on Song Lyrics and the Human Condition*. For at the beginning of the Chinese modern age, he had already discerned the modern as something more than the staged realization of enlightenment and revolution. Faced with the drastic incompatibilities between public and private claims, he asserted his freedom and independence negatively, in the willful act of self-annihilation.

As we reflect on the legacies of Lu Xun's and Wang's poetics in the new millennium, we again ask what we should make of modern Chinese literary subjectivity. In fact, ever since the late twentieth century, Chinese writers and readers have become less and less interested in the Lu Xun discourse of the Mara poet, to say nothing of Wang's lyrical poetics and his archetypal melancholy song lyricist. Instead, it was a different figure, Alfred Nobel (1833–1896), who emerged to command everyone's attention. The question, "When will a Chinese writer be awarded a Nobel Prize in Literature?," became a national obsession. In 2000, Gao Xingjian (1940–), a writer living in exile in France, won the prize and was immediately denounced by the Chinese government as non-Chinese. Gao's works remain censored in China to date. When Mo Yan (1955–) won the prize in 2012, it was regarded as a moment of vindication for not only Chinese literature but also China as a whole. There is something ironic, however, about the fact that this newly gained national pride was the result of a Swedish literary anointment.

Uncannier still is the fact that, as early as 1927, Lu Xun had already encountered the problem of national literature and the Nobel Prize. He was indirectly approached by the Swedish explorer Sven Anders Hedin (1865–1952), who wished to nominate him for the Nobel Prize. Lu Xun turned down the invitation and commented,

> I think there is nobody in China truly deserving of the Nobel Prize. It would be better for Sweden to ignore us. If yellow skinned people were given preferential consideration, it would encourage Chinese egotism, or could they really parallel those great foreign writers? The result would not be good at all.

Despite his sarcastic and self-deprecating tone, Lu Xun was being incisive about the unequal relationships between China and the West, as well as the cultural politics of literature as a token of exchange.

What would Lu Xun have to say about the two Chinese Nobel laureates? Or, how would his Mara have commented on Nobel? Through Mara, Lu Xun was pursuing a literature that could "pluck people's hearts" and thereby change China. In the postsocialist age, however, as China rises on the global horizon, Nobel seems to have acquired the power to pluck the Chinese heart. As modern Chinese literature arrives at a juncture where cultural critique intersects with cultural capital, we renew our exploration of the complex dynamics of literary writing, cultural heritage, and national representation.

BIBLIOGRAPHY: Kirk Denton, ed., *Modern Chinese Literary Thought* (Stanford, CA, 1996). Leo Ou-fan Lee, *Voices from the Iron House: A Study of Lu Xun* (Bloomington, IN, 1987). Julia Lovell, *The Politics of Cultural Capital: China's Quest for a Nobel Prize in Literature* (Honolulu, 2006).

DAVID DER-WEI WANG

1909 · NOVEMBER 13

Upon reflection on his poetic output, Liu Yazi writes, "The attitude of sword-play and the heart of the flute can never be chained."

A Classical Poetry Society through Revolutionary Times

On the morning of November 13, 1909, nineteen scholarly young men boarded a decorative boat and left the crowded area around the western gate of Suzhou for their first "elegant gathering" of the Southern Society. It was a late-autumn day with crisp, chilly air and colorful autumn leaves. The boat was sailing on the Shantang River, a canal channeled by the Tang poet Bai Juyi (772–846) when he governed the Suzhou area. In this energetic group, two men played key roles in organizing the gathering.

Chen Qubing (1877–1925), a social activist, was heavily involved in newspaper media and modern theater. Early in 1908, together with Xu Zihua (1873–1935), he organized a gathering to commemorate the death of the female martyr Qiu Jin (1875–1907), who was executed by the Qing government on July 15, 1907. For this, Chen himself was put on the Qing government's watch list. Owing to his connections in the Suzhou region, Chen, with the help of friends, was able to hide the planning of this gathering from the government.

Liu Yazi (1887–1958), who soon became the "soul" of the Southern Society, was an aspiring poet and activist. As a student in the heated political atmosphere in Shanghai, he researched guns and bomb making, but soon came to realize that the pen might well be his best weapon. He had arrived in Suzhou four days before the secret excursion to help prepare for the event. While there, he attended the Peking opera *The Commemorative Stone of Bloody Tears*, performed by Feng Chunhang (1888–1942). His infatuation with Feng's performance lasted for years, and he later invited Feng to join the society. The old-fashioned promotion of actors, as well as the use of the theater to spread new progressive ideas, also became popular among his coterie.

On the day of the event, the men went by boat to Tiger Hill, where they took a group photo, and then walked up to Zhang's Temple to hold the meeting proper. The partially deserted temple was full of weeds and had been built to commemorate the military official Zhang Guowei (1595–1646), who had committed suicide after his troops were defeated by the Manchus at the end of Ming dynasty. The choice of this location was meaningful. Tiger Hill was also famous for gatherings held by the Restoration Club almost three hundred years before, a group that was widely known for, among other things, anti-Qing activism. People in the Suzhou area—one of the literati cultural centers of the late imperial period—harbored memories of traumatic events and hardships suffered under the rule of the conquering Manchurians. The Southern Society, whose members were deeply rooted in China's southern culture, espoused the political position of anti-Manchurian, anti-Qing governance and cast itself in the image of the late Ming loyalists and the Restoration Club.

Like all the literati gatherings, the first meeting featured tasty dishes made of local specialties and different kinds of liquor. The men drank heavily, chatted, and played drinking games, while the formal business relating to the organization of the society was also conducted as planned. Chen Qubing, Gao Xu (1877–1925, one of the organizers who was not present), and Pang Shubo (1884–1916) were elected as editors for the society's anthologies of three major forms of classical writing (prose, poetry, and song lyrics) respectively, while Liu Yazi and Zhu Shaoping (1882–1942) would serve as secretary and treasurer. The formal regulations of the society had been drafted earlier and published in the *People's Plea Newspaper* on October 27 and would be revised many times in subsequent meetings. Liu would soon ascend to be the leader of the group and was responsible for publishing the most volumes of the *Collection of the Southern Society,* an impressive twenty-two in total over the course of a decade.

As the members drank at the banquet, an unexpected debate occurred over the preference for Tang or Song dynasty poetry. According to Japanese scholar Yoshikawa Kōjirō's (1904–1980) simplifying analogy, Tang poetry was thought to be akin to wine, while Song poetry was akin to tea. The differences in poetic taste among the members of the Southern Society also affected their views of contemporary writing, as the fashion in the late Qing was modeled after Song dynasty poetry. Liu, who favored the Tang style, had only one supporter, Zhu Xiliang (1873–1923), while many of the others, Pang in particular, gave eloquent and sharp arguments against Liu's position. Both Liu and Zhu were stutterers and not great public speakers. On the verge of being defeated, Liu suddenly burst into tears. The debate fortunately ended amicably, thanks to a concession made by Pang. Less than a decade later, however, this sharp divide in the members' views about poetic style and models escalated, and in 1917, it carried over into the *Republican Daily News,* eventually leading Liu to expel a poet named Zhu Yuanchu (1897–1921) from the society. This episode served as a catalyst for the disintegration of the society. With the overall changing political environment (the victory of the Republican Revolution and disappointment of the Republican polity), the society, founded on the eve of the revolution, lost its momentum and remained nonoperative from the late 1910s to its official dissolution in 1923.

As a literati community, the practices of the Southern Society in many ways resembled those of its premodern counterparts. It was a group for literary friendship and exhilarating contradiction, a site of meaningful or leisure activities, affinities, and rivalries. Having said that, the professionalization of the society, a set of institutional practices (organization and operation, the election of main managers, the regulations, its continuous production of publications, and so on), and the substantial involvement of newspaper media all distinguished the society from the more loosely formed literary gatherings and clubs in their traditional incarnations. Liu's individual efforts to bring the diverse members together in a variety of social settings and on a range of political occasions greatly contributed to the thriving of the society. According to scholars' estimates, from 1909 to 1923, 262 members in total participated in formal gatherings of the Southern Society, while the number of registered members went as high as 1,183, with 441 in Jiangsu Province, 227 in Zhejiang Province, and 177 in Guangdong Province. As the largest society among the mushrooming traditional and new societies and cultural clubs in modern China, the membership was distinctively marked by its hybridity in terms of profession, literary style, and gender, and its resulting volatile, unstable nature. An impressive number of the members became major Nationalist politicians (for example, Huang Xing [1874–1916] and Yu Youren [1879–1964]); a handful of members were either executed or assassinated for participating in contemporary politics (for example, Zhou Shi (1885–1911) and Song Jiaoren [1882–1913]); and many others were involved in modern journalism, education, and scholarship (for example, Yao Shizi [1891–1945], Ma Xulun [1885–1970], and Chen Wangdao [1891–1977]); the feminist movement (for example, Lü Bicheng [1883–1943]); or Buddhist practice (for example, Su Manshu [1884–1918] and Li Shutong [1880–1942]). A few subdivisions were established in 1911, among which was the Yue Society, whose membership briefly included Lu Xun (1881–1936).

Over thirteen years, the Southern Society held eighteen formal meetings, most of which were held at the Yu Garden in Shanghai. At the tenth gathering, in Shanghai in 1914, ten members took turns playing drinking games and composing couplets. The first topic they were given was ancestral history, after which they moved on to the current state of affairs, as represented by the phrase "looking south, the millet is lush" ("lush millet" being a traditional symbol of the ruined nation). Then they shifted the topic to something entirely different: "spending a spring night warmed by lotus bed-curtains," and "Luofu is charming, a graceful and gentle girl." This example illustrates that a range of topics interested society members; it also shows the permeability of emotions between loyalist feelings, romantic and erotic love, personal ambition, and political fervor. In addition to holding formal meetings, the society also frequently called for excursions, banquets, and gatherings of friends on different occasions. In the late spring of 1915, Feng Chunhang performed the opera *Feng Xiaoqing* in Hangzhou. Liu, Gao Xie (1887–1958), Yao Guang (1891–1945), and about ten other members spent more than twenty days there, watching Feng's performances, drinking, writing, and sightseeing at West Lake. They even set up a commemorative stone stele in honor of Feng's performance beside Feng Xiaoqing's tomb at West Lake, weeping over the tragic fate of this girl who died young and her modern-day theatrical reincarnation. These group activities cultivated and spread camaraderie and empathy, and helped to cement their collective identity.

While the Southern Society remained committed to classical language and traditional genres (a position that was attacked by New Cultural intellectuals in the late 1910s), it also established an iconic revolutionary image as its group identity. This image was fashioned out of the sentiments that they expressed in public forums and modern media, and was also based on the fact that many participants were members of the Revolutionary Alliance. In Chen Qubing's words, they were "using words to propel the revolution," and critiquing contemporary politics with charged emotion in newspapers and publications was characteristic of their writing. In response to Yuan Shikai's (1859–1916) attempt to restore the monarchy, Liu expressed his resentment in his poem "Lonely Anger": "daring to raise the waking eye to see the masses of corpses." As a time represented by piles of "corpses," the 1910s was a distinctively sentimental era, pervaded by a general fever of revolution, and frustration and disillusionment with politics. Modeled after the traditional literati's "playing with the sword and flute" and unrestrained, extravagant lifestyles, these literati-turned-cultural-figures publicized a range of intense emotions, including loyalism, nostalgia, despair, and anger, thereby recasting lyricism in new political terms.

This modern political practice of poetic writing was reified in the case of Wang Jingwei (1883–1944), who, in Liu's opinion, as expressed in 1936, best represented the spirit of the society. Wang had been jailed in April 1910 for his failed attempt to assassinate the prince regent, Zai Feng (1883–1951). Wang, a main contributor to the *People's News (Minbao)*, was instantly hailed as hero by the revolutionary youth and was later pardoned by the Qing government. Several lines of his poetry, such as "This head should be hung over the gate of the capital city," were extremely influential. On April 18, 1912, Wang formally joined the Southern Society as member number 260, but he never participated in any gatherings. On October 10, 1923, Wang attended the inaugural gathering of the New Southern Society, a smaller society modeled after the Southern Society. Wang's later political career as the head of the Nanjing government that collaborated with Japan in World War II has made him one of the most notorious figures in modern history. The heroic, nationalistic voice in his poems written during the early resistance to Manchurian rule was dishearteningly replaced by an elegiac and lyrical mood during his last stage of collaboration with the Japanese colonial project and its Greater East Asia Co-Prosperity Sphere. The deeply troubled emotions and craftsmanship displayed in his poetry reveal a kind of convoluted interlocking between history and lyricism, the ephemeral nature of political identities, and the perilous path of revolutionary discourse.

At another happy gathering held on October 3, 1950, the intertwined relationships between poetry and politics, as well as sentimentalism and ideology, took yet another ironic turn. After witnessing a splendid celebration of dancing and singing on National Day, Liu, urged on by Chairman Mao Zedong (1893–1976), composed a song lyric on the spot to eulogize the grand reunion of all the ethnicities in the newly established People's Republic. Liu, together with Guo Moruo (1892–1978), was among a handful poets who had the privilege of corresponding with Mao through poems, while the overall culture of poetic gatherings disappeared as a result of Mao's revolution. The changing political culture did not keep Liu from engaging in various political encounters and molding lyricism to advocate a new nation with great enthusiasm. Chairman Mao's responding poem with the same tune title, representative of revolutionary literature in its own right, cast a spell over the fate of writers and poets in the decades to come, leaving its indelible mark on China's modern literary history.

To the Melody "Washing Creek Sands"
   By Liu Yazi

Trees afire with lamps and silvery flowers light up the night,
Brothers and sisters dance merrily.
The songs ring out and the moon is full.

Without one man to lead them,
how could one hundred ethnicities join together?
What a beautiful evening and unprecedented joy!

To the Melody "Washing Creek Sands"
   By Mao Zedong, in response to Mr. Liu Yazi

A long night and difficult dawn for China,
For a hundred years, devils danced merrily.
Five hundred million people could not unite.

With one rooster's crow, the world turns to day,
Happy music spreads as far as Yutian.
Even more unprecedented is a poet's inspiration.

BIBLIOGRAPHY: Michel Hockx, *Questions of Style: Literary Societies and Literary Journals in Modern China, 1911–1937* (Leiden, Netherlands, 2003). Lin Xiangling, *Nan she wenxue zonglun* (Taipei, 2009). Liu Yazi, *Nanshe jilüe* (Shanghai, 1983). Yang Tianshi and Wang Xuezhuang, *Nan she shi changbian* (Beijing, 1995).

SHENGQING WU

1911 · APRIL 24

Lin Juemin bids farewell to his wife.

1911

Xu Zhenya invents sentimental heroism.

Revolution and Love

In the dead of night on April 24, 1911, a young man with striking features sat in a gloomy hotel room in Hong Kong writing a letter on a handkerchief. It began, "Yiying dearest, with this letter I now bid you farewell! As I write this letter, I'm still a man in the land of the living; when you read it, I'll be a ghost in the netherworld." The letter would become the most famous love letter in modern Chinese history and a perennial classic in Chinese high school textbooks.

The man in question was Lin Juemin (1887–1911), one of the eighty-six martyrs who participated in the failed Second Guangzhou Uprising, a plot hatched by the Revolutionary Alliance, a coalition of patriots led by Sun Yat-sen (1866–1925) aiming to overthrow China's last dynasty, the Qing (1644–1911). Lin had come into contact with Sun's followers while studying in Japan and became an ardent activist. In the spring of 1911, he returned to China to take part in the planned attack on the Qing governor's compound in Guangzhou. A month before the uprising, he made a brief visit to his ancestral home in Fujian to see his parents and pregnant wife before heading to Hong Kong to join his comrades. In the stillness before the storm, staring death in the face, Lin composed two letters, a short one to his father and a much longer one to his wife. The latter would be immortalized as a searing testament to the imponderable sacrifices that gave birth to Asia's first republic.

In the letter, Lin tells his wife, Chen Yiying (1891–1913), that tears have again and again stalled his brush and commingled with the ink, so profound is his love and so vast is his grief.

> I love you very much, and yet thinking of this love makes me boldly go forward in giving up my life.... Today you and I are fortunate to be both living, yet there are countless people in the world dying before their time or parting against their will. Cherishing love as we do, how can we tolerate it all?... You are fortunate to have wedded me, but how unfortunate it is for you to have been born in today's China! I am fortunate to have made you my wife, but how unfortunate am I to be living in today's China! It's no longer possible to keep a separate peace. Alas! The handkerchief is short and the feelings are long, a myriad of words choked back.... What great sorrow!

These excerpted lines should serve to convey the powerful emotions that swirl beneath the elegant classical Chinese prose that was still the standard medium of communication for the educated strata. But Lin had long turned his back on the standard career path of a classically trained Chinese male: to succeed in the civil service examination and secure a post in the imperial bureaucracy. At the age of fourteen he matriculated at the Fujian Academy, a school that offered a Western-style curriculum, and a few years later he sailed for Japan, along with numerous Chinese students flocking there to imbibe modern ideas and values. While still at the Fujian Academy, he obeyed his parents' wishes and submitted to an arranged marriage. In contrast with the unhappy experience of most May Fourth youths with arranged marriages, it seems that Lin quickly fell in love with his young bride and the two grew deeply attached to each other.

Lin's youth, courage, and depth of feeling combine to make his farewell letter irresistible to cultural mythmakers. On both sides of the Taiwan Strait, movies, television dramas, and popular songs have eulogized the marital bond that was laid at the altar of national salvation. During the centennial commemoration of the 1911 Revolution, the letter once again was used to evoke a mythic age of passion and fervor. To today's audiences, perhaps what is truly remarkable is that a man so much in love with his wife would forsake her to throw himself into the maw of a ruthless and desperately flailing regime. To his contemporaries, however, what was remarkable was rather that a man whose name was about to be forever linked to the greatest cause of his time was so strongly and avowedly attached to a woman. In Chinese this is called *ernüqing*. China's long history is full of magnificent, death-defying heroes, but few were also lauded for their *ernüqing*. For example, quite a few heroes in the fourteenth-century novel *Water Margin* become outlaws after having slain an adulterous wife or a shameless seductress. The most celebrated among them is the tiger-killer Wu Song, who stands tall and firm and disgusted before his sister-in-law's lascivious advances, and wastes little time in butchering her and taking off to join the band of blood brothers on Mount Liang. The only one of these desperadoes who demonstrates a tender side toward a woman is the brawny and blustery Li Kui, but that woman is his mother.

Indeed, the kind of heart-melting sentiment that overflows from Lin's letter has traditionally been reserved for one's parents. In the Confucian moral economy, filial piety was the most emotionally invested virtue, not romantic or conjugal love. Within the patriarchal kinship system, love for a nonkin woman was an indulgence, tolerated so long as it did not spill out of its marginalized existence—in the demimonde or as a clandestine liaison. A marriage united not two hearts, but two families to their mutual social and economic advantages. Even if love did blossom in an arranged marriage, it could scarcely speak its name lest it compete for filial devotion to parents.

Beginning in the sixteenth century, disaffected literati inaugurated a cult of *qing* (sentiment) to legitimate a horizontal mode of sentimentality. They argued that all human relationships should be modeled on the love between a man and a woman—egalitarian, reciprocal, and spontaneous—rather than on the ritualistic relationship between parents and children. In other words, filial piety and loyalty, unless heartfelt, were meaningless, even hypocritical. They wrote plays and stories to exalt sentimental attachments and companionate marriages. Tang Xianzu's (1550–1616) *Peony Pavilion*, for example, begins with a young woman falling in love with a young man all on her own and ends with their marriage receiving the blessings of her initially reluctant father. In Cao Xueqin's (1715–1763) *Dream of the Red Chamber*, however, the idea of a sentiment-based relationship proves too threatening to the patriarchal order, and the lovers are torn asunder in a matrimonial conspiracy. As late as the turn of the twentieth century, it was still difficult to reconcile horizontal love with Confucian institutions. The maudlin stories churned out by the so-called Mandarin Ducks and Butterflies writers endlessly dwell on the agony of love that has little hope of winning institutional sanction; all too often their protagonists end up committing suicide or escaping into the eremitic void.

Nonetheless, a new genre of patriotic fiction also emerged in the late Qing that seemed to point to a way out of the romantic impasse. These stories introduced a new breed of heroes who first love a woman and then die for a cause. Thenceforth the parallel worlds of *ernü* (romantic sentiments between the sexes) and *yingxiong* (hero[ism]), the warrior's derring-do and the lover's emotional plenitude, the pleasure quarters and the "rivers and lakes" of knight-errantry and outlawry, would be inextricably bound up with each other. Later schematized as "revolution plus love," the genre came to dominate literary production across the ideological spectrum well into the 1950s. The first title to achieve immense popularity was Xu Zhenya's (1889–1937) *Jade Pear Spirit*, published in 1912, merely a year after Lin's death. In this lugubrious tale told in florid parallel prose, a tutor falls in love with his pupil's widowed mother. Constrained by the codes of gender segregation and widow chastity, the two can only permit their feelings to smolder in the embers of letters, poems, and sobs. Slowly the widow wastes away and dies, and the tutor joins the Wuchang Uprising of 1911 and falls on the battleground while clasping a bundle of love letters to his bosom. The loosely autobiographical novel was an overnight sensation, reprinted some thirty times in quick succession and swiftly adapted into a silent film as well as for the stage.

While the tutor's choice may have been less gut-wrenching than that of Lin—who left behind not only a wife but also a toddler son and an unborn child—both exemplify the fundamental principle of the "revolution plus love" formula. That is, the patriotic hero is first and foremost a modern subject who has an interiority, and that interiority is structured by the grammar of horizontal, heterosexual love. If Confucianism has always demanded that one extend filial devotion to benevolence for all under heaven as a matter of duty, nationalism requires that one's love of country be a free-willed and yet impassioned commitment—precisely what defines the romantic experience. As Xie Bingying (1906–2000) puts it in her biography of Lin, "A true revolutionary is also a man of feeling." As such, the revolutionary has come a long way from the misogynist hero of traditional narratives, for he is capable of experiencing the torment of choosing between two cherished goods: love of a woman and love of country. The nationalist imperative in twentieth-century China has consistently privileged the latter, so much so that by the socialist period, dying for love was no longer ideologically or narratively viable, and the socialist fatherland was the only cause worth dying for.

After rumors of Lin's capture and execution were confirmed by the surreptitiously delivered farewell letters, the inconsolable Chen Yiying attempted to follow him in death after the fashion of the countless chaste widows whose stories populate the annals of imperial China. At the behest of Lin's parents, she desisted, but nonetheless died two years later of a broken heart. She left no testimonials behind. Indeed, the majority of "revolution plus love" stories are told from the male perspective, whereby a woman's experience of bereavement seems less poignant, less momentous by dint of passivity. But contemporary artists, more attuned to the ways in which heroism can ride roughshod over the fragile human heart, have attempted to give a voice to the silent woman. The Taiwanese female singer Chyi Yu (1958–), singing in the guise of Chen, addresses her husband's ghost thusly: "Who gave you the right to depart like this, / Turning my boundless sacrifices into / A mere written word?"

Questions like this invariably cast the moral supremacy of revolution in doubt. Can or should any political cause justify the crushing of a powerless woman's hopes for a good life? Generations of Chinese elites have thought so, alleging that the death of the nation would erase any possibility of individual happiness. Yet there were a few outlying skeptics. Eileen Chang (1920–1995), for one, has her heroine in "Love in a Fallen City" tie down her caddish suitor in domestic contentment precisely when Hong Kong falls to the invading Japanese army. Small wonder that Chang was for decades persona non grata to the Communist Party, which would rather have the Chinese simply dispose of the "love" part of the "revolution plus love" equation. This intolerance was first voiced in 1935 by Mao Dun (1896–1981), who proffered an improved formula of literature, as well as life: revolution, and then love—modestly, tamely, shorn of histrionics, and under no circumstances contesting the priority of the collective enterprise and the authority that speaks in its name. In other words, love is permissible so long as it does not become life's ultimate goal and source of meaning, or attain the kind of intensity that imbues Lin's epic heroism with a tragic pathos.

In his letter, Lin seeks solace in the prospect that others will not have to make the same painful choice in the new world he helps midwife: "Ever since you came into my life, I have wished conjugal happiness to all loving souls under heaven." A hundred years later, it is far from clear that his wish has been fulfilled. Exiled to a puritan limbo in the Mao Zedong (1893–1976) years, love has been resurrected with a vengeance in postsocialist literature and has become all the more precious as the Chinese bid a collective farewell to revolution. At the same time, it has also become ever more precarious in the relentless market-driven pursuit of happiness. Lin might be surprised to see how his sorrowful parting words have come to focus the nostalgia of a consumer age in which the absence of a shared transcendent goal has left love unable to bear the lightness of being.

BIBLIOGRAPHY: Ding Shanxi, dir., *Bixue huanghua* (Taiwan daxing dianying youxian gongsi, 1980). Haiyan Lee, *Revolution of the Heart: A Genealogy of Love in China, 1900–1950* (Stanford, CA, 2007). Jin Ge, dir., *Bainian qingshu* (Fangjin yingshi; Jinri shenghui wenhua chuanmei, 2011). Leo Ou-fan Lee, *The Romantic Generation of Modern Chinese Writers* (Cambridge, MA, 1973). Lin Juemin, "Yuqi juebie shu," 1911. Liu Jianmei, *Revolution plus Love: Literary History, Women's Bodies, and Thematic Repetition in Twentieth-Century Chinese Fiction* (Honolulu, 2003). David Der-wei Wang, *The Monster That Is History: History, Violence, and Fictional Writing in Twentieth-Century China* (Berkeley, CA, 2004). Xie Bingying, *Lin Juemin* (Taipei, 1958). Zhang Li and Jackie Chan, dirs., *Xinhai geming* (Shanghai dongfang yingshi, 2011).

HAIYAN LEE

1913

The first two parts of Kang Youwei's *The Book of the Great Society* are published.

2011 · MAY

Evans Chan's documentary *Datong: The Great Society* is released.

The Book of Datong *as a Novel of Utopia*

More than two years ago, when I first heard that Evans Chan (1961–) was shooting a film about Kang Youwei (1858–1927) and his *Book of Datong* (a term that means "unity," "commonwealth," or, as Chan titled his film, "the great society"), my initial disbelief was soon followed by anticipation, admiration, and, finally, a delightful sense of surprise. I say initial disbelief because in this day and age it seems unlikely that anyone would express an interest in Kang, much less take the man, his achievements, and his controversial book seriously. Learning about Chan's undertaking was a pleasant surprise because, coincidentally, I had just finished reading *The Book of the Great Society* and was enamored with Kang's monumental (or "crazed") vision. My anticipation stemmed from a curiosity about how Chan would choose to portray Kang in his film, and how such a portrayal might differ from the image of Kang given in the official Chinese histories of the last century. And I admired the filmmaker for his remarkable courage in choosing a topic that, thanks to its radical agenda, would most likely be challenging for the general public.

The Book of the Great Society is a work of fiction contemplating the future as well as the past. It was allegedly completed around 1901; its complete version was not published till 1935. Kang was seeking to earnestly portray his vision of a utopia. However, since all utopian concepts ultimately prove to be fabrications, Kang's work was predestined for the world of fiction. Although it will never be realized, a utopia will always stimulate people's imagination and their pursuit of an ideal world. One hundred years ago, at the transition from the Qing dynasty into the Chinese republic, and at the threshold of the twentieth century, Kang not only put forward his vision for the future of China but also delivered a comprehensive blueprint for the future of the entire world. The boldness of his imagination and the imposing scope of his treatise have created a sense of boundless wonder within readers.

Political scientists at the time may have been dismissive of *The Book of the Great Society*, ridiculing it as a fantasy. In fact, the work did not engender any change. When placed alongside the nineteenth-century works of political and social thought that originated in Europe and spread throughout the world, the book seems to have embodied a little bit of everything but offered naught. It proposes abolishing class boundaries and private property, and distrusts big government and centralized power. It advocates local autonomy yet is suspicious of anarchy, market capitalism, and liberalism. It emphasizes equal rights and civil virtue, which are yet inconsistent with democracy. Kang sought to abolish various "divisions" and overcome suffering, but the ideology of the book still falls short of a full-blown Buddhism. Occasionally the book even runs counter to the prevailing trends of the time in which it was written. In a time when European nation-states loomed over Asia, Kang paradoxically suggested the abolition of the nation-state system, and, envisioning the earth as a public domain, advocated a world without borders.

The major goal of Kang's great society, as depicted in *The Book of the Great Society*, is to abolish suffering and pursue happiness. This goal may have its origin in Buddhism, but it also is rooted in the hedonist philosophy of the West. Kang does make reference to Confucian thought, but his references seem only to serve as a pretext. Early in this book Kang describes at great length life's different modes of suffering. The poor suffer, as do the wealthy; slaves cannot escape torments, but neither can emperors; likewise, men, as well as women, have their share of pain. More concisely, to live is to suffer. These are Buddhist ideas: suffering stems from divisions, thus, it's crucial to eliminate division. What causes division? The divide between nations is the paramount division, but barriers like family, race, class, wealth distribution, and the male body and female body all create divisions within personhood, peoples, and species. Therefore, throughout the book, Kang advances methods to break down these divisions in order to achieve the great society—in his words, "abolishing the nine divisions." This task includes abolishing national boundaries to unite the world, abolishing class boundaries to equalize all people, abolishing racial boundaries to amalgamate all races, abolishing boundaries of gender to preserve (women's) independence, abolishing family boundaries to turn individuals into "the people of heaven," abolishing class boundaries and private occupations, abolishing administrative boundaries to achieve peaceful and equitable governance, abolishing boundaries between species to encourage the love of all living things, and abolishing boundaries of suffering to attain ultimate happiness.

One abolition that isn't too astounding these days—as we can see from its enactment in Communist regimes—is the abolition of private property and the collective ownership of agriculture, commerce, and industry. However, three of Kang's proposed abolitions are most interesting. First, to abolish national boundaries would mean abolishing the nation-state system, as well as all borders. The entire earth would be divided according to a grid of latitude and longitude with fifty points on each axis, creating a total of ten thousand square units, each of which makes up an administrative unit. Although a hierarchy may eventually emerge from the division between the lowest level (the autonomous units) and the highest level (the global public parliament), the lowest level is actually autonomous, and not subordinate in power to the higher levels. Second, Kang calls for abolishing racial boundaries because inequality between humans is to a large extent rooted in racial differences. He proposes achieving equality not through the advocacy of mutual respect and peaceful coexistence but through the thorough elimination of racial differences. Interracial breeding is encouraged in order to completely amalgamate all humans into one single race. Third, abolishing the boundary between the sexes reflects Kang's particularly advanced thinking. He advocates the abolition of the institution of marriage and suggests that men and women cosign a short-term contract with each other for a period of one to two years, during which time the two cohabitate. After the contract expires, if both parties so desire, they can renew the contract; otherwise, they can terminate the contract and seek other partners. As both parties are free and independent, women would be released from the bondage and suppression that they have suffered throughout the ages.

Kang even endorses homosexual relationships between men (though he does not mention lesbianism) in special circumstances. Additionally, because the post-childbirth responsibilities of childcare and child education would be relegated entirely to the public sector, women would be liberated from their role as nurturers; as a result, the traditional family relationship would come to an end. Besides proposing various institutional reforms, Kang is optimistic about advances in technology in the future world, including those in the areas of transportation, construction, information transmission, and medicine. He is so confident that a great society will be realizable in the near future that he proposes declaring 1901 as the first year of *datong*: the great society.

After reading *The Book of the Great Society* we may not necessarily agree with it, but nor should we, with historical hindsight, denigrate or praise it. On the contrary, by examining its contradictions and conflicts, or its interaction with history and the world, we can ruminate on the current global situation.

One criticism of Kang's ideology is that it's not sufficiently dialectical. For Kang, "difference" and "unity or sameness" are two states that are diametrically opposed to each other. "Difference" is the root of all evil and should be eliminated. The great society is a happy world in which all citizens are equal, but to achieve this ideal, all differences between individuals must first be removed. It's not difficult to see that there are unresolvable contradictions between civil liberties and global unification. Since a goal of the great society is to eliminate heterogeneity in order to eliminate the boundaries that cause suffering, would such an elimination harm civil rights? If the goal is to eliminate differences, whose differences, and what differences? This is a question of values and power relationships. For example, state-to-state annexation would be necessary to achieve global unification, but the annexation oftentimes would tend to be not a merger of equals but the absorption of smaller states by bigger ones.

As for Kang's abolition of racial boundaries, the situation could be even more fraught. Although he advocates racial equality, eugenics becomes the means by which he seeks to achieve this ideal. He also ranks each race, and reaches the conclusion that the white race is the best, followed by the yellow race, then the brown race, with the black race being the lowest in quality. He believes that the white and yellow races would ideally take the lead in gradually improving the human race, and that copulation between members of the black race should be minimized. If a member of the white race would selflessly offer him- or herself as a mate for someone from the inferior black race, that member should receive a "race improvement" badge of honor. Such eugenics is inherently unequal. Achieving equality via unequal means and attaining unity through the abolition of differences signal contradictions in Kang's system. From our perspective, it seems easy to speak of "seeking common ground while tolerating differences," as the old saying goes. However, we've become aware that the delicate balance between unity and difference is a key issue for humankind's coexistence.

Here's another vantage point on *datong*. The great society encompasses the idea of "the public" (and the "commonwealth"). "Public" was another keyword in *The Book of the Great Society* for Chinese intelligentsia during the late Qing and the early republic. The opposite of "public" is "private." In international relations, the state is considered to belong to the "private" domain; analogously, within the social system, the family is considered a "private" entity. All sorts of strife and upheaval stem from the "private." Therefore, another vital task for the great society is to transform the "private" into the "public"—the inverse of abolishing differences to attain unity. With a de facto elimination of the family and the private, each individual becomes a "citizen"—"a *public* person" in its literal translation—in the fullest sense of the idea. Citizens (*public* people) are brought up and educated by the public government, work in the public system, fulfill civic (*public* people's) responsibilities, and retire to the public welfare system to enjoy their later years. Such a situation may seem ideal—the establishment of public space and the fostering of public citizens. Let's put aside issues of personal desires for the moment. Should we eliminate the private domain completely for the sake of a healthy society? Shouldn't a healthy public domain be supported by an equally robust private domain? These questions, of course, can't be answered here, but as with difference and unity, the public and the private should be understood as the outside and inside of the same domain—as complementary. Kang's advocacy for eliminating one and retaining the other is another example of his emphasis on only one side of things.

The strength of *The Book of the Great Society* springs from the vastness of its scope, its remarkable spirit, and its boldness of vision, but these strengths are also its weaknesses and limitations. Its goal of "honoring the righteous cause of loving humankind" ends up denigrating the importance of individuality, putting the project at odds with respect for individuals and the tenets of human rights. However, by taking aim at the sovereignty of a nation, the rights of families, and the right of free commerce—all of which are sustained by what can be considered "private," selfish interests—the book courageously reveals the importance of public justice, public truths, and public interests. It thus opens up a path toward the development of the public domain. With the present concern for diversity and respect for differences, *The Book of the Great Society* could undoubtedly leave many modern readers dissatisfied. Nevertheless, how to combine individual freedom and rights with obligations toward, and responsibility for, the collective has always been a core issue for political science. In this regard, the reflections the book provokes are profoundly meaningful.

Humankind has repeatedly experimented with a variety of social systems, and it has paid a heavy price for those experiments. In these early years of the twenty-first century, our historical knowledge seems richer than the knowledge to which Kang had access, so we easily recognize his limitations. However, we have lost faith in, and imagination about, how human society can progress and be perfected. A work like *The Book of the Great Society*, with its grand ambitions and concerns, would be unlikely to be written today. Is it because we have become overly sophisticated and cautious? Or is it because the possibilities of human civilization seem to be diminishing? I'm afraid that this may be the greatest shock that comes from reading the book today.

The Book of the Great Society has little to offer in terms of providing a practical reference for contemporary society, but the imagination that it displays and the reflections within the reader that this imagination provokes are deep and profound. It captivates like a novel.

Kai-cheung Dung
Translated by Victor Or

1916 · AUGUST 23 · NEW YORK CITY

Hu Shi expresses his love for an American artist in vernacular poetry.

Hu Shi and His Experiments

On August 23, 1916, in an apartment overlooking the Hudson River that he sublet from Edith Clifford Williams (1885–1971), Hu Shi (1891–1962), then a graduate student at Columbia University, wrote a poem in vernacular Chinese. Williams had decamped to Ithaca, New York, to nurse her ailing father, a professor at Cornell, where Hu had attended college. This rather banal little poem—about her—turned out to be the opening salvo of a literary revolution in China:

Two yellow butterflies fly up the sky,
    One suddenly flits away, I don't know why.
The very sky looks so lonesome, that
    The one left behind no longer cares to fly.

Prior to this, Hu had composed three poems about Williams in his diary. The first, in *ci* (song lyric) form, compares himself and Williams to a pair of robins calling to each other in the trees while a *duyu* (cuckoo) beckons him home. He leaves little doubt that the *duyu*, a bird not found in America, symbolizes the semiliterate girl back in China to whom he had been betrothed since childhood. The second, also a *ci*, concludes with the line, "At this point, between you and me, how could there be room for a third?" A *shi* (classical) poem followed with this postscript: "I am a simple man. I do not know what 'love' is, but my feelings are akin to what the ancients might call 'yearning.'"

Literate Chinese men in the early twentieth century expressed themselves in a language largely frozen around the time of the Roman Empire. Moreover, they routinely marked special sentiments and occasions with verse governed by elaborate prosodic rules. They addressed *shi* poems to friends, who might respond in kind using the same rhyme scheme; *ci* poems, more intimate in tone, were often used to write about women. One might imagine Americans communicating in Latin verse or Shakespearean sonnets. The antiquarian quality of these poems underscored the writers' elite status, and placed them firmly in China's long, proud, unbroken literary tradition. A man's poetry was used to judge not only his aesthetic sensibility but also his grasp of history and literature. The ultimate honor was to have one's witty allusions quoted at social gatherings. Although vernacular novels had been around for several hundred years, and vernacular newspapers had made their appearance by the mid-nineteenth century, writing in the vernacular was considered uncouth. Thus, Hu's decision to publish "Butterflies"—a poem that used simple words and adhered to the natural rhythm of everyday speech—in the Beijing-based magazine *New Youth* was viewed as a defiant act.

This defiant gesture was not made on the spur of the moment. For two years, Hu and Zhao Yuanren (1892–1982)—whom Hu regarded as the smartest Chinese studying in America—had been discussing issues related to the Chinese language. Together they explored how speech connects with written words; how learning to read might be made easier for the common people; and, given China's multiplicity of dialects, how pronunciation might be standardized. As a result of these discussions, when Zhao and his Cornell friends launched *Science* in 1915 to popularize scientific concepts in China, they published it with Western-style punctuation marks. This was a vast improvement over traditional writing, which provided readers with, at most, the equivalent of periods.

Meanwhile, Hu became exposed to the avant-garde through Williams, an artist who moved in Alfred Stieglitz's (1864–1946) circle. Known chiefly today as Georgia O'Keefe's (1887–1986) husband, Stieglitz was an ardent and powerful promoter of modern art. Williams herself produced at least three abstract oil paintings, *1914*, *1915*, and *Two Rhythms*, the last now on permanent display at the Philadelphia Museum of Art, in what is affectionately called the "Marcel Duchamp and Friends Room." She also created, in 1916, a sculpture meant for touching, on which the critic and poet Guillaume Apollinaire (1880–1918) lectured in Paris.

Much as he tried, Hu found himself befuddled by abstract art. "It greatly pains me to think of the great disappointment which I have caused you in my failure to understand your work," he wrote Williams. In an effort to enlighten him, she arranged for him to meet the painter and art teacher Abraham Solomon Baylinson (1882–1950); she also took him to view John Quinn's (1870–1924) collection, which included works by Marcel Duchamp, Pablo Picasso, Henri Matisse, Paul Cézanne, and Constantin Brâncuşi—artists who were pushing the boundaries of what was considered art at that time. In return, Hu asked Zhao to give Williams lessons on how to use the Chinese writing (and painting) brush. This led to a lifelong friendship between Zhao and Williams. Zhao alluded to Williams in his autobiography as "a friend that Hu Shi and I shared."

Hu never developed a taste for modern paintings, but the irreverence and gleeful abandon with which the avant-garde artists worked must have made a profound impression on him. After a tour of the inaugural exhibition of the Society of Independent Artists, Hu wrote Williams, "The thing that impressed me most is, as I have said before, the spirit of experiment. Experiment is essentially individual in nature. Nowhere have I seen such a manifestation of individuality as is shown here. That is itself a sign of health and vitality."

By the summer of 1916, Hu had decided that China's classical written language was basically a dead language, since the spoken language had long evolved beyond it. He also became convinced that the vernacular was not a vulgarized version of the classical. In fact, as a means of expression, it was superior. Hu's views were contested by his friend Mei Guangdi (1890–1945), and, in July, Hu sent Mei a long doggerel poem in the vernacular to poke fun at him, incorporating such vulgarities as "temper tantrum" and "urine." This sparked a heated debate on what constitutes poetic diction, prompting another friend to ask indignantly, "If one could write poetry in the vernacular, what, then, isn't poetry?" Hu's response was that the only reason there had not been any vernacular poetry was that no one capable of writing poetry had written in the vernacular. To prove his point, he composed "Butterflies" and sent it to be published.

From then on, Hu wrote primarily in the vernacular. His famous essay in *New Youth* defending the vernacular and calling for literary reform struck a hugely responsive chord among Chinese youths. Hu became a celebrity even before he returned from the United States in 1917.

While Hu's name is now associated with the May Fourth Movement, he was not, in fact, in Beijing on May 4, 1919. He was in Shanghai to meet John Dewey (1859–1952), his doctoral adviser at Columbia, who arrived in China on an extended lecture tour. But there is no doubt that being able to write directly from their hearts and minds, without constant allusions to the past, was a crucial factor in this explosion of energy among the young, emboldening them to challenge their elders and take charge of their lives. Lu Xun (1881–1936), ten years Hu's senior, had no success as a writer until he started writing in the vernacular.

At Hu's urging, Zhao, who could have excelled in math, physics, or philosophy, all of which he had taught at leading universities, switched his field to linguistics. Zhao played an important role in the standardization of modern Mandarin—the *Putonghua* ("common speech"). He also produced the authoritative *A Concise Dictionary of Spoken Chinese* and *A Grammar of Spoken Chinese*. He set to music many vernacular poems written by their friends, including the popular "How Could I Not Think of Her" by Liu Bannong (1891–1934) and Xu Zhimo's (1897–1931) "The Sea Melody," a choral composition performed to this day.

Zhao, himself happily married, was privy to Hu's infidelities and tumultuous love life, and was ever solicitous of Hu's well-being. Harvard had awarded Hu an honorary doctorate at its tercentenary celebration in 1936—the same occasion commemorated by the tall Chinese marble stele in Harvard Yard. When Hu returned to lecture in 1943, and from 1944 to 1945, he stayed at a hotel but took his meals with the Zhao family. In 1956, at a very low point in Hu's life, Zhao secured a teaching appointment for him at the University of California, Berkeley, and tried to convince him to stay.

Hu had departed hastily from Beijing on the eve of the Communist takeover, leaving behind his papers. He was denounced in a large campaign launched in 1954 by Mao Zedong (1893–1976), who circulated a letter criticizing Hu's approach to the vernacular novel *Dream of the Red Chamber*. To prove Hu's culpability, the *People's Daily* reprinted Hu's preface to an anthology of his own works meant for students:

> My young friends, do not regard these pieces on *Dream of the Red Chamber meng* as my attempt to teach you how to read a novel.... The scientific attitude consists of a willingness to recognize facts and follow evidence wherever it may lead you—without regard to preconceived ideas or personal feelings. And the scientific method is no more than boldness in the formation of hypotheses combined with meticulous care in verification.... It is not edifying for a man to be led by the nose by Confucius or Zhu Xi, or to be led by the nose by Marx, Lenin, or Stalin.

Nine committees were organized to "rid China of the specter of Hu Shi." Hu's papers were moved, for scrutiny, from Peking University—where Hu was president when he left—to what is now the Chinese Academy of Social Sciences. This resulted in volume after volume of feigned hysterical condemnation. Hu's second son, who had refused to leave China with him, hanged himself in 1957.

We know a great deal about Hu's life because he was an indefatigable chronicler of himself and his time. His letters were treasured, and many were published by the recipients after Hu's death. People he had met only once or twice, including the writer Eileen Chang (1920–1995), wrote reminiscences of him.

Since 1978, Hu's papers in Beijing have been gradually released for publication, beginning with his official correspondence as China's ambassador to the United States during World War II, a selection of his personal letters, and his diaries from 1937 to 1944, drawing a new generation of scholars to this towering figure who, probably more than anyone else, set the agenda for intellectual discourse in China during the first half of the twentieth century. Unfortunately, his more incendiary writings were missing from the forty-four-volume *The Complete Works of Hu Shi*, published on the mainland in 2003. In 2004, Hu's scattered diaries dating back to his teens were brought together in ten fat volumes by Linking Publications in Taipei, with a preface by the eminent historian Yu Ying-shih (1930–).

Hu and his friends have proved to be endlessly fascinating to the Chinese public, much as the Bloomsbury circle continues to hold its charm for English readers. Hardly a week passes without another book or article appearing about these early modernists—so sophisticated yet so naive to our twenty-first-century eyes. In 1998, Professor Chou Chih-p'ing (1947–) of Princeton University discovered, in the archives of the Academia Sinica in Taipei, a trove of letters that Hu wrote to Williams. Chou figured she must also have written at least as many to Hu. Sure enough, he found these in Beijing, untouched all these years, being in English. The resulting book, *Hu Shi and Williams: A Fifty-Year Passion*, published simultaneously in Taipei and Beijing, was a literary sensation. These letters, more than three hundred altogether, show the remarkable extent to which Hu's political and social views were shaped by Williams. She was not fully aware of Hu's feelings in the early years, but they did become lovers briefly in the 1930s. She remained a loyal and unflinchingly honest friend, even after learning he had not been completely aboveboard with her about the other women in his life. It is not clear if the redoubtable Mrs. Hu knew the entire story, but, after joining Hu in America in the 1950s, she became very fond of Williams. The two remained in touch through gifts and translated letters long after Hu died of a heart attack in 1962 at a cocktail reception he hosted as president of the Academia Sinica in Taipei.

Experiments was the title Hu gave his 1920 poetry collection. Experimentation is, of course, consistent with his teacher John Dewey's philosophy of pragmatism. However, knowing what we now know of what was happening in Hu's life at that time, it is not farfetched to suggest that Hu's iconoclastic stance—that China should throw off the dead weight of its literary tradition and start experimenting—was inspired by the American avant-garde art movement.

BIBLIOGRAPHY: Cao Boyan, ed., *Hu Shi riji quanji* (Taipei, 2004). Chiang Yung-chen, *She wo qi shei: Hu Shi, Diyi bu: Puyu cheng bi, 1891–1917* (Beijing, 2011). Chou Chih-p'ing, *Hu Shi yu Lu Xun* (Taipei, 1988). Susan Chan Egan and Chih-p'ing Chou, *A Pragmatist and His Free Spirit: The Half-Century Romance of Hu Shi and Edith Clifford Williams* (Hong Kong, 2009). Luo Zhitian, *Zaizao wenming de changshi: Hu Shi zhuan 1891–1929* (Beijing, 2006).

SUSAN CHAN EGAN

1916 · SEPTEMBER 1

Li Dazhao interprets the "Green Spring."

Inventing Youth in Modern China

In 1916, an essay entitled "Qingchun" (Green spring, or Youth) appeared in the September issue of *New Youth*, a magazine that had begun publication under the editorship of Chen Duxiu (1879–1942) about a year before. The author, Li Dazhao (1889–1927), played an important role in the New Culture Movement and would soon become, together with Chen, a cofounder of the Chinese Communist Party. There are many explanations why Li and other enlightenment intellectuals who edited and wrote for *New Youth* could stand as the spokesmen for a new force that aimed to change China and reform its culture in the following decades. One of the most important reasons may lie in their success at clearly and vividly epitomizing their vision of the zeitgeist in a single cultural sign with a universal appeal: youth. Through an enchanting poetic discourse, Li's essay foregrounds the vitality and beauty of "green spring," the Chinese metaphor for youth, as a great force of revival, and employs it to speak of hope and the future, which are not just meaningful to an individual's growth but also yield a new historical vision for the nation's development and progress. Calling for a comprehensive youthful transformation, the author renders youth into an omnipotent sign of change that executes a symbolic power, endlessly, over an array of entities ranging from the self to family to nation to all of humanity and to the universe.

The rise of "youth" is among the most dramatic stories of modern China. Traditional Confucian teaching defined youth as filial and obedient to one's elders, and any attempt to change those power relations was seen as transgressive. Since the beginning of the twentieth century, however, a cult of youth emerged among the radical intellectuals in China, changed the hierarchy of youth and age, motivated social reforms and revolutions, and exerted a sweeping influence over modern China's intellectual outlook. During the last hundred years or so, youth, as the product of discursive practice, has functioned as a dominant trope and sustained a symbolic centrality in Chinese intellectual discourse. In a culture of modernity, youth stands for newness, the future, and change, and it gains a symbolic meaning that transcends its biological definition as the immature and vulnerable period of adolescence and makes it applicable to a wide range of reflections on a changing world. In China's twentieth century of cultural transition, the restless, elusive, and protean youth was the defining image of revolutionary potential: it comprised both the force to dismantle conventions and the vision of the ideal. From the refreshing, dynamic image of youth arise new paradigms for political, cultural, and literary imaginations.

The modern glorification of youth was first clearly presented by the late Qing reformer Liang Qichao (1873–1929) in his groundbreaking "Shaonian Zhongguo shuo" (Ode to a young China, 1900), which happened to be published in the first month of China's first lunar year in the twentieth century. With splendid metaphors and exuberant rhetoric, Liang calls for national rejuvenation, rewriting China's image as an aging empire into one of a youthful nation. He bestows upon youth, individuals as well as the nation symbolically, unbounded prospects for future development: "Beautiful is my young China, forever as youthful as Heaven! Sublime are my Chinese youths, with a future as borderless as our land."

Liang's discourse on young China registers his political wish to enable China's entry onto a global stage populated by competing young nations. By naming Young China, Liang imported to China a new nationalist ideal that would stay central to Chinese political thinking throughout the greater part of the twentieth century. It connotes not only overcoming China's frustrations in confronting the rising West, but also reshaping

China into a youthful nation on a new timetable of world history. The goal was to reinvent China, like Italy and Japan, into a strong and wealthy nation-state. In the meantime, while using "youth" to name China, Liang also elevates the significance of "young" above a mere adjective. The political symbolism he invests in youth renders it into a universal cultural sign that implies a modern vision of historical progress. The dynamism of youth not only empowers the national rejuvenation, but also motivates a new conceptualization of temporality, which is historicized as a forever renewable forward movement, or, as Li later exclaims,

> Young progressives, who are always in the middle of swirling and restless waves, should keep their spirit as resolute as a river moving forward, as steady as a mountain, firmly resisting every strong current.... This is the spirit that conquers death and revives life, this is the energy that moves mountains and builds the world. Only those who really love youth know that in the universe there is an endless youth, and only with that spirit and energy can they enjoy that youth forever.

The magazine that Chen founded in September 1915, *New Youth*, gave a collective name to a new generation of Chinese youths who answered its call to turn against tradition. What attracted these individuals to the ideal of new youth was undoubtedly its emphasis, more clearly than ever, on self-determination. The first issue of *New Youth* opens with Chen's urgent message to young readers: "I, merely, with tears, place my plea before the fresh and vital youth, in the hope that they will achieve self-awareness, and begin to struggle." Tradition was viewed as suffocating, or cannibalistic, as depicted by Lu Xun (1881–1936) in his "A Madman's Diary," and the more urgent task for Chinese youths was to liberate themselves from the deadly burden of tradition. The self-fashioning of the new youth generation gave rise to a new type of literary writing, which culminated in the rise of the modern Chinese novel. This type of writing focused on the construction of the new youth identity, with particular reference to a new historical consciousness wherein personal development and national rejuvenation are combined in one plot that unfolds as a process of writing youth into history.

Some of the most famous modern Chinese novels emphasize scenes where a young protagonist's reading *New Youth* serves as the beginning of his or her conversion to modern ideas and the pursuit of a new self. In Ye Shengtao's (1894–1988) *Ni Huanzhi* (1928), the protagonist, whose youthful idealism has been eroded by frustrations in his career and marriage, is inspired by the "new" magazine to reevaluate all his values and find a new beginning in life. In Mao Dun's (1896–1981) *Rainbow* (1930), Miss Mei feels baptized as a new woman full of self-determination after reading *New Youth*. In Ba Jin's (1904–2005) *Family* (1931), reading and discussing the articles in *New Youth* thrills the Gao brothers, and even the eldest, Juexin, who is portrayed as a conformist who submits to the power of the family heads, feels his lost youth being awakened.

At the beginning of *Ni Huanzhi*, China's first modern novel with a clear focus on the psychological development of youth, the protagonist leaves his home to explore a larger world. The journey promises a new chapter in his life. Although his boat is surrounded by darkness in the early morning, he feels as if he were being showered with beams of bright light. He is imagining all the changes that will happen: "And now the curtain goes up on a new life!" This moment, which appears in one of the earliest full-length modern novels to take account of the formative experience of China's new youth generation, is highly allegorical. Journey and dream, passion and promise, hope and future—these elements constitute the foundation of a master plot of China's modern story about youth.

Ni Huanzhi was published in 1928, nearly a decade after the glorious days of the New Culture Movement. Ni Huanzhi is portrayed as a model new youth. He dreams, struggles, triumphs, and, as the later part of the novel shows, he also doubts, compromises, eventually fails, and dies tragically. The novel is structured in a cycle of hope and disillusion, ideal and action, yearning and despair. The plot unfolds as a gradual process of the protagonist's realization of his ideals, interrupted by frustrations, failures, and fatal crisis; such a plot design would later keep reemerging in modern Chinese novels about youth's psychological development. *Ni Huanzhi* traces the entire life journey of its protagonist.

A novel like this, deeply invested in the significance of the beginning of a journey, resembles Johann Wolfgang von Goethe's (1749–1832) account of Wilhelm Meister's departure from home, Honoré de Balzac's (1799–1850) depiction of a provincial youth's pursuit of his dreams by going to Paris, and Charles Dickens's (1812–1870) great expectations for his young character's personal development. Or, to borrow the words of Lionel Trilling (1905–1975), it comes from a great line of novels that depict the development of a youth, who always "start[s] with a great demand upon life and a great wonder about its complexity and promise." Such a great line of novels is the bildungsroman, a specific type of novelistic narrative that focuses on a youth's psychological growth—the cultivating of a self, the fashioning of a personality, and the attempt to seek self-realization against the backdrop of historical movements.

As a Chinese bildungsroman, *Ni Huanzhi* presents a modern vision of personal development and social reform by narrating the life journey of a new youth who tries to change his own life, as well as his country. Ni Huanzhi is only one of the first of a series of young heroes that began to emerge in modern Chinese novels after the May Fourth Movement. Behind him stand an array of youth figures created by modern Chinese writers, including Mei Xingsu (Mao Dun's *Rainbow*), Gao Juehui (Ba Jin's *Family*), Jiang Chunzu (Lu Ling's [1923–1994] *Children of the Rich*), and Lin Daojing (Yang Mo's [1914–1995] *The Song of Youth*)—just to name a few of the most famous examples. Also, behind Ni Huanzhi's youthful figure shines the radiance of the glorious and sublime image of Young China, the central symbolic sign in modern Chinese nationalist discourse, which expresses the persistent yearning for national rejuvenation. Such was the goal of many Chinese reforms and revolutions throughout the twentieth century—from late Qing reforms to the Republican Revolution, from the May Fourth Movement to left-wing political activities, and from the Nationalist campaign to the Socialist transformation.

In a generic sense, the narrative design of the bildungsroman institutes the formalization of youth into a fully developed personality that represents certain ideals. But, as both G. W. F. Hegel (1770–1831) and György Lukács (1885–1971) have implied, such an idealized vision rarely crystallizes in the prosaic form of the modern novel. Moreover, when situated in a historical context like that of modern China's, *The Song of Youth* (1958) is a rare example of such a text that was able to fully play out its teleological rhetoric, which nevertheless betrays a Maoist political agenda in its taming of youth. In other cases, the narrative design is often imperiled by the menacing reality that dismantles idealism. As evidenced by Ba Jin's early anarchist novels, China's historical crisis undermines the narrative design originally meant to reinforce his political faith. In Ba Jin's first novel, *Destruction* (1928), for example, the protagonist's efforts to realize his ideals end in self-destruction. In Ba Jin's *Love Trilogy* (1931–1933), a moral occult enacts a melodramatic contrast of ideal and reality, and allegorizes the youth's self-perfection as "the flowering of life," which nevertheless leads to self-sacrifice that literarily ends the youth's self-development.

Sacrifice, or self-sacrifice, of youth is thus often designated as the climax of the Chinese bildungsroman. In real life, Li Dazhao met his death bravely on the execution ground in 1927. Li's martyrdom made him a national hero, a moral example, an immortal legend, and above all, an idol for Chinese youths to emulate. But Li was not the only martyr in modern China's youth history. Two decades before Li, Zou Rong (1885–1905), a young revolutionary who died in prison at the age of twenty, was immortalized as the incarnation of the revolutionary spirit, and he won an immortal title as "the god of youth" (as phrased by Sun Yat-sen [1866–1925]). Zou's contemporary revolutionary Wang Jingwei's (1883–1944) poem, composed when Wang was imprisoned after an attempted assassination of a Qing prince in 1910, contains these two famous lines: "To die on the sword, what rapture! / A fate truly worthy of a young head." Zou's martyrdom and Wang's poem show how the sacrifice of youth for revolution could heighten the sublime nature of a young death. The cultural significance attached to these deaths and the literary representations of the young martyrs, however, also laid bare a fundamental conflict in the self-development of the revolutionary youths: life versus death—the sacrifice of one's young life is a way of eternalizing youth, and youth stays "forever" at the moment of its violent termination.

BIBLIOGRAPHY: Claudia Pozzana, "Spring, Temporality, and History in Li Dazhao," in *New Asian Marxism*, ed. Tani Barlow (Durham, NC, 2002), 269–290. Vera Schwarcz, *The Chinese Enlightenment: Intellectuals and the Legacy of the May Fourth Movement of 1919* (Berkeley, CA, 1986). Mingwei Song, *Young China: National Rejuvenation and the Bildungsroman, 1900–1959* (Cambridge, MA, 2015). Lionel Trilling, "The Princess Casamassima," in *The Princess Casamassima* by Henry James (New York, 1948).

MINGWEI SONG

1918 · APRIL 2

"Save the children..."

Zhou Yucai Writes "A Madman's Diary" under the Pen Name Lu Xun

[EDITOR'S NOTE: Ha Jin's essay is a fictional account based on extensive research on Lu Xun's experience as he wrote "A Madman's Diary."]

On his way back from downtown, Zhou Yucai (1881–1936) stopped by Harmony House for an early dinner. A southerner from coastal Zhejiang, he had a low opinion of the seafood served in Beijing's restaurants, but he liked Harmony House, where meat dishes were decent and prices reasonable. Besides, it was near the ratty Shaoxing Hostel where he lived. Sometimes he'd go there at night, not to eat but to get drunk alone. Today he had a bowl of beef noodles, but without his usual—a flask of rice wine. After dinner, strolling back along the dusty street, he ran into Qian Xuantong (1887–1939), the editor in chief of *New Youth*, a literary magazine. Again Xuantong mentioned the piece Yucai had promised him, and also the deadline. Yucai had mixed feelings about soft-faced Xuantong, who only talked big, and was too lazy to write anything substantial, though the man acted like a leader in a circle of young scholars who were eager to start a literary revolution. Most often Xuantong just threw out radical ideas for others to digest or debate. Nevertheless, he and Yucai had once studied Chinese classics with the same teacher in Japan, so Yucai couldn't but take him as a friend of sorts.

"I'll write it tonight," he assured Xuantong, somewhat embarrassed by his procrastination.

"You'd better hurry. Our board was thrilled that you agreed to contribute to the May issue."

One night a month before, Xuantong had come to visit Yucai at Shaoxing Hostel and found him copying ancient tablet inscriptions. On his wobbly desk were a stack of Buddhist scriptures and a bulky album of woodcarvings. Yucai and his younger brother Zuoren (1885–1967) were known as erudite literary scholars and liberal thinkers, but, unlike his brother, who held a professorship at Peking University, Yucai was merely a clerk in the Ministry of Education.

"What's the use of copying these?" Xuantong asked, flipping through the calligraphy his friend had recently reproduced.

"No use at all," Yucai replied, dragging at a Pin Head cigarette through his ivory holder. His lean face was handsome in a stern way, complemented by a thick mustache and straight brows, but his eyes were dimmed with melancholy.

"Then why copy this old stuff?" Xuantong continued, as he took a sip of his Dragon Well tea.

"No reason at all."

"Come on, stop wasting your life like this. Write something for us."

Yucai fell silent. A few months back he had agreed to help *New Youth*, but to date he'd done nothing. He knew that the magazine hadn't published anything significant yet. Most of its editors and contributors were idle talkers like Xuantong, flaunting ideas and slogans about "a literary revolution," but few would buckle down to serious work. As a result the magazine had attracted little public attention. That coterie of "literary revolutionaries" must have felt frustrated and isolated. That must be why Xuantong had come time and again to urge him to join them.

Yucai broke the silence, saying, "What's the sense of writing? Imagine an iron room without a window, absolutely indestructible. In it many people are sleeping soundly and all of them will die of suffocation soon, but they won't feel the pain of death. Now, you shout to wake up a few light sleepers, only to make these unfortunate ones suffer the agony of the inevitable end. Do you think you're doing them a favor?"

Xuantong's eyes blazed behind his thick glasses. He said, almost in a cry, "If a few wake up, you can't say there's no hope of destroying the goddamn iron room!"

Yucai thought about it and felt Xuantong might have a point. Who is to say that the iron room is utterly unbreachable? So he agreed to join them and contribute to *New Youth*.

Actually Xuantong had spent quite a bit of time with the Zhou brothers in Japan and knew they were both devoted to promoting a new literature that might help revitalize the Chinese spirit. Yucai used to tell his compatriots that he had quit medical school because it was not his countrymen's physical illness but their mental lethargy that he wanted to cure. In other words, he aspired to become a doctor capable of treating the nation's diseased soul. Viewing literature as the best spiritual remedy, he had dropped medicine to take up the pen.

However, after quitting medical school, he did not produce any literary work. He merely studied literature. The more he studied, the more frustrated and humbled he felt. In a letter to a close friend he admitted that he'd been stunned by Fyodor Dostoyevsky (1821–1881), whose *Poor Folk* he had just read. He couldn't stop marveling how the novelist had been able to write the novel at age twenty-five. "He had such a forceful old soul," he said about Dostoyevsky.

For twelve years Yucai hadn't written a single piece of literature. The closest he'd come to literary creation was two volumes of foreign short stories, which he and his brother Zuoren had cotranslated. Most of the writers included in the anthology were from small nations oppressed by imperial powers. Deep down, he felt he had failed as a writer even before he could start. Having seen so many setbacks in the efforts to save China, he now believed that the country was doomed beyond hope. So all he wanted was a quiet, uneventful life. Through a friend's help he found a job in Beijing, which enabled him to stay away from his wife, a woman with bound feet whom his mother had made him marry. He never loved her but wouldn't divorce her, as he was reluctant to break his mother's heart; he'd left his wife back in Zhejiang so that she could care for his mother. He just sent them money every month.

Sometimes he felt trapped in this meaningless rut of life. Underneath his pallet was a knife, with which he often imagined slitting his wrist, if this torpid existence grew too unbearable.

After encountering Xuantong on the street, Yucai knew he couldn't procrastinate anymore and ought to write his piece today. He had read hundreds of short stories by foreign authors, many of which were Japanese and German translations from other languages, so he had some sense of the form. Still, he'd never written fiction before and was unsure if he could do a good job. Of all the foreign writers he had read, Nicolai Gogol (1809–1852) was the one Yucai loved the most. He had long planned to translate Gogol's masterpiece *The Dead Souls* (the translation was finished in 1935, a year before his death). He was fond of Gogol's humor, pathos, and wild spirit, which he misconstrued as Gogol's way of inspiring the Russians to fight feudalism and social injustice. He didn't know that Gogol, a Ukrainian native, had remained an outsider from the mainstream of Russian literature for many years until his play *The Government Inspector* was well received. Despite his later role as the founder of modern Russian literature, Gogol was actually a divided man in regard to his language, culture, and nationality. Except to his art, Gogol held no allegiance to anything or anybody. Yet how Yucai wished he could have the light Gogolian touches, the radiant poetic eloquence, the boisterous laughter, the mysterious aura. He knew those qualities might be beyond him, because his mind-set was too gloomy to let him laugh with gusto and tears. He didn't know how to be funny.

Lately he'd been thinking about writing a story in the convention of Gogol's "The Diary of a Madman," because in a crazed voice the narrator could speak his mind freely, and because madness might justify stark candor. The idea for this story had germinated from an incident that had been on his mind for more than a year. A cousin of his, Jiusun, had come from Shanxi Province in the fall of 1916 to seek refuge at Shaoxing Hostel, claiming that someone had been pursuing him in an attempt on his life, and that he'd made his will and other arrangements before fleeing home. No matter how Yucai tried to dissu⟨ade⟩ him, Jiusun wouldn't alter his conviction. Yucai believed that his cousin ⟨suffered fr⟩om a mental disorder, a persecution complex. Though terrified⟨…⟩ ⟨t⟩he man could be quite lucid at times, and even his ramb⟨lings had some kind of tr⟩uth. He swore that some people were thirsty fo⟨r his⟩ ⟨fl⟩esh. He etched such an impression on ⟨… that Y⟩ucai began to brood about the idea that t⟨he whole count⟩ry was man-eating. In a letter to a friend, Yucai ⟨described China⟩ as a cannibalistic country. Now, in writing his story, he w⟨ould let a⟩ deranged narrator rave about this crazy notion to decode the ⟨se⟩cret of human history, which could be boiled down to two words: eating people.

Despite the profound insight, he felt uneasy about the diary form, which might be too intimate and open to misinterpretations. Some readers might even attribute the insanity to the author. Moreover, he intended to write the story in the current vernacular, a language not used in literary fiction at that time. This meant that even the prose style could be too radical for some people. His colleagues at the Ministry of Education, especially one of his directors, might make a great fuss over the story. At any rate Yucai mustn't jeopardize his job, which was easy and paid well despite its tedium.

It struck him that he could give the story an introduction as a measure to contain the madness. He would write this foreword in the conventional literary language, in contrast to the vernacular used in the story proper; in the preamble he would emphasize that the protagonist had regained his sanity long ago and had left home for an official post. This way, despite the mad ravings, the story would appear like the man's momentary breakdown. In other words, order was already restored, there was nothing to fear, and people should treat the following pages as a pathological case. Of course, discerning readers could see the aggressive nature of the story, which dramatized cannibalism as the essence of human history and as a perennial social practice. It would be a message from a Nietzschean madman who was convinced that people, including his family members, had been plotting to butcher and eat him. Yes, let the crazed voice rant and rage with abandon so as to waken some sleeping souls.

Still, even the foreword might not be enough to protect the author, so Yucai decided to use a pen name. He picked Lu Xun, because his mother's maiden name was Lu and because Xun, meaning "quick," sounded vague as a mere adjective. He had no inkling that this simple name, unlike the others he'd chosen before, would stick. For days he'd been nagged by the thought that his story might be too derivative, too influenced by Gogol's. To counter the impression of derivativeness, he would not date the diary entries and instead would use consecutive numerals to organize them. This could make the piece resemble a genre in Chinese letters— *biji*, literary sketches. By all means he'd better make this story appear somewhat indigenous.

The writing proceeded better than he had expected. He always wrote rapidly, though he would ponder a piece for a long time before he put it on paper. As he was writing, frantically wielding his brush, he felt an upsurge of emotions—grief, despair, anger, disgust at the China that was rotten to the core—pour out. Originally he had planned to give some deadpan touches here and there, but somehow the story was getting recalcitrant, more urgent, more tragic, and frighteningly fierce. There was no way he could make it lighter. Coming to the end, he simply put: "Are there children who haven't eaten human flesh yet? Save the children…"

He was aware that such an ending echoed Gogol's penultimate sentence in "The Diary of a Madman": "Dear mother, pity your sick child!" But he couldn't help it because his story demanded a heartrending cry of an ending. *Was this plagiarism?* he wondered. Unlikely, because his "children" was in the plural. Whereas Gogol's madman pleaded with Mother Russia meekly, his protagonist didn't have a specific addressee and let out a shout.

When the waning moon glowed above a ghostly acacia in the court-yard, he laid down his brush. He had spent more than four hours on the story. *This isn't bad,* he told himself.

Then he realized that the title, "A Madman's Diary," could be a misnomer, since a diary must have dates and his way of organizing the thirteen sections with consecutive numbers was more like a device to make a dramatic line, a kind of plot. Should he hold on to this piece for a while so that he could fix the title and get everything right? That would be too much hassle, too much brushwork, so he decided to let it be. This was just fulfilling an obligation.

He lit another cigarette with the burning butt of the previous one. His forehead tight and hot, he lounged in a rattan chair while twisting his mustache with his fingertips, too exhausted to think of anything. The air smelled sweetish with a hint of apricot blossoms; spring was coming early this year. He would give Xuantong this story first thing tomorrow. He wouldn't care if his friend liked it or not. He'd just say, "I've made good on my word." He felt he wouldn't dabble in fiction again—he was already thirty-seven. His spate of masterpieces following "A Madman's Diary" was beyond his ken, nor could he sense that this was a monumental beginning.

HA JIN

1918 · SUMMER

"A confluence of sorrow and joy"

Modern Monkhood

When the poet-monk Su Manshu (1884–1918) died on May 2, 1918, in a Shanghai hospital, he was barely thirty-five. He died of a digestive disorder, allegedly, after he ate sixty pork buns at one sitting as part of a bet. Manshu insisted on fulfilling his words even when his friend, who proposed the bet, urged him to stop, and washed down all the buns with a cup of coffee.

In the same summer, Li Shutong (1880–1942) bade farewell to his friends and students and "left home" to become a Buddhist monk at Hupao Monastery in Hangzhou. Spurred by a force he was unable to explain, he received full ordination within two months after tonsure. Thenceforth he was known as Hongyi, who was to become the most revered Vinaya master of twentieth-century China. For the subsequent twenty-four years, Hongyi observed hundreds of Buddhist monastic codes, including the Precept against Untimely Eating, which forbids monks and nuns to take meals after midday under routine circumstances.

By contrast, Manshu was a glutton—when he had the means. Once, in Japan, he drank five to six pounds of frozen dessert in a single day and ended up lying still on the floor like a corpse. He reassured his housemate that he was quite alive by repeating the same feat the next day. On another occasion, he had such an irresistible craving for candy that he sold the gold filling in his denture to procure them.

Obsession and deprivation form two sides of the same coin in Manshu, who confided in his friends an "unspeakable agony" concerning his family background. Manshu was born in Yokohama in 1884. His father was a Chinese businessman from Canton and his mother, according to one theory, was the sister of his father's illegitimate Japanese concubine. When the six-year-old Manshu was sent back to China, he met with a life of hardship and disdain. This probably accounts for his seeking shelter at a monastery during early adolescence. Another clue to his predilection for Buddhism, putatively, was his first heartrending romantic experience: the engagement was broken off when the Su family suffered a decline in fortune. Seeing his first love destined for someone else, Manshu abjured the world as a pledge of fidelity to the bygone relationship.

Details of several key events in Manshu's life remain obscure, including his conversion. What matters, however, is that he consistently identified himself as a monk, even when he sent out invitation cards for sing-song girls at dinner banquets in Shanghai. In fashioning himself, Manshu alternated between a monk's robe and a Western suit. In forging a literary identity, however, there is no mistaking the deeply ingrained Buddhist sensitivities in his poems, fictions, and personal letters. The theme that is characteristically Manshu's is the bitter impossibility of romantic consummation between a monk and a lady—in fact, two ladies, each attractive in her own right and both fervently devoted to the male protagonist. This dilemma threads through *The Lonely Swan*, Manshu's best-known work with autobiographical significance. In another story, *Tale of the Crimson Silk*, he portrays a monk who passes away in meditation while wearing a piece of crimson silk—a token of affection—beneath his habit. The dead monk dissolves into dust only upon the final embrace from the lady he has loved and waited for, bequeathing her her crimson silk.

To Manshu, *qing* (feeling, love, passion) constitutes the core of his faith. In his own words, "Although I have become a monk, I seek the Way through *qing*. This explains my anguish." When love is measured not only by the intensity of feeling but moreover by the constancy of feeling, celibacy turns out to be the ultimate seal of fidelity. Besides, these "pages drenched in tears" also betray a wounded soul's inability to handle intimacy: his monk protagonists, mirroring the author in reality, hanker after yet withdraw from intimacy, opting to let one's love go in order to cherish it for eternity. In terms of existential burden, Manshu's reconfiguration of the "Passionate Monk" resonates with that of the eighteenth-century masterpiece *Dream of the Red Chamber*, furnishing a twentieth-century sequel to the age-old dialectics of desire and emptiness.

Manshu lived a short but dazzling life. He sojourned all over Asia: from Hong Kong to Java, from Siam to Ceylon, but mostly in Shanghai and Tokyo. He spent two years in Bangkok studying Sanskrit; but he seems to have much preferred the time he spent introducing Lord Byron (1788–1824) and Percy Bysshe Shelley (1792–1822) to Chinese readers. In translating (and reinventing) a portion of *Les Misérables*, he earned himself another hat as an anti-Manchu and anarchist revolutionary, joining hands with Zhang Taiyan (1868–1936) and like-minded intellectuals. Everywhere he turned, Manshu found himself in some intoxicating romantic encounter, his lovers encompassing Japanese, Spanish, and Chinese girls. All came to nothing, however, when he decided that it was time to revert to his identity of a monk. In a sense, Manshu must have undergone numerous, albeit brief, conversions. Readers who look for depth in one so characterized by youthful ardor and excess may be disappointed; but, after all, Manshu has been best appreciated for being himself. "Roughly speaking," as Yu Dafu (1896–1945) puts it, "his poetry translations are better than his own poems; his poems, better than his paintings; his paintings, better than his fictions. But above all, his romantic temperament and his demeanor and style derived therefrom are better than everything else."

When the distinguished artist Li Shutong made preparations to join the Sangha, his readiness to leave the world behind while in his prime shocked and perplexed his contemporaries. Born into a wealthy salt merchant's household in Tianjin in 1880, Li grew up accustomed to sensual and cultural refinement. At twenty, Li basked in the accolades of Shanghai's literary circle for his poetry and seal inscriptions. After his mother's death, he sailed for Japan in 1905. Among the Chinese students in Japan, if Lu Xun (1881–1936) had found in literature a road less traveled, Li chose for himself a road none had traveled. Along with his classmate Zeng Yannian (1873–1937), at the Tokyo School of Fine Arts founded by Okakura Kakuzō (1862–1913), Li became the first Chinese to study Western art in Japan. Besides oil painting, he also studied Western music and launched in Tokyo *Mini Music Magazine*, the first Chinese-language periodical of its kind. In 1906, Li and Zeng founded the first modern Chinese theater group, Spring Willow Society, the performances of which enchanted the Tokyo audience. Li's elegant debut in *La Dame aux Camélias* as the female lead Marguerite drew special acclaim. Upon returning to China in 1911, Li shouldered multiple roles: editor, illustrator, art and music teacher, and song composer. He enjoyed both worlds, the modern and the classical. The man who established China's first life-drawing studio with nude models in 1914 and adapted John P. Ordway's (1824–1880) "Dreaming of Home and Mother" into a popular Chinese song, "Farewell," also frequented poets' and seal carvers' gatherings.

Li's gifts and accomplishments, plus a decent matrimony (his principal wife bore him two sons), seem to worldly minds more than enough reason for contentment. To the man himself, however, they were not. Li's conversion, although often termed an abrupt break, was not necessarily so. The pivotal event that led to it was a three-week fast he undertook at Hupao in the winter of 1916, in the hope of alleviating his neurasthenia. From a detailed diary he kept, Li appears to have been a follower of Tenrikyō, a new religion founded by Nakayama Miki (1798–1887) in nineteenth-century Japan. Reciting the psalms and praying for oneness with the Deity, Li sought in this corporeal experiment divine healing and spiritual transformation. "Spiritual transformation" he did attain, as testified by a work of calligraphy he produced afterward bearing those exact words. For over a decade he had called himself Li Ai, *ai* meaning "grief." Toward the end of this stay at Hupao, he changed his name to Li Xin, *xin* meaning "joy." Twenty-six years later, three days before his death, Hongyi would dwell again on this character when he wrote his last words: *bei xin jiao ji,* "a confluence of sorrow and joy."

Hupao marks a seminal site in Li's spiritual peregrination. Here he saw for the first time what monastic life was like and came into intimate contact with monks. He was so moved by the experience that he returned the following winter, by which time he had already become a vegetarian and read a considerable number of Mahāyāna scriptures. On the fifteenth day of the first month in the *wuwu* year [February 25, 1918], Li took refuge in the Three Jewels at Hupao. When he returned again five months later, he changed into a black monk's robe as soon as he entered the monastery.

Hongyi set his heart on the Vinaya at the outset of his monastic career, thanks to the advice from his erudite friend Ma Yifu (1883–1967). The Vinaya refers to monastic rules, its texts constituting one of the three divisions of the Buddhist canon. Hongyi pored over different traditions of the Vinaya. From 1931 onward, he dedicated himself exclusively to the teachings of the Nanshan school, the Dharmaguptaka lineage preserved by the Tang Vinaya master Daoxuan (596–667). Hongyi more than once stated that he considered his schematic exegesis of the *Four Part Vinaya* his most important work.

Underneath his gentle mien, Hongyi's commitment to transforming himself into a living vessel of the Vinaya was awe-inspiring. He carried the ascetic through the everyday, striving for the unity of a compassionate mind and a disciplined body at all times. In the eyes of those whose paths crossed his, Buddhists and non-Buddhists alike, it was often Hongyi's understated practice that left them with an indelible lesson on the Buddhist ideal. As his student, the renowned artist Feng Zikai (1898–1975), recalled, every time before sitting down, his mentor would lightly shake the rattan chair. The reason was, Feng later learned, to let the "tiny insects" inhabiting the rattan take flight lest they be crushed to death upon one's sitting down. At thirty, Feng took refuge under Hongyi and began working on *Paintings for Protecting Life*, a series of Buddhist art advocating compassion, nonkilling, and vegetarianism. Decades later, persevering to complete the series helped sustain the artist through the Cultural Revolution.

Between Li Shutong the pioneer of modern theater and Hongyi the Vinaya maestro, there is more continuity than meets the eye. In a poem Li wrote celebrating the performance of *La Dame aux Camélias* in 1907, he thus revealed his aspirations:

> I vow to deliver the sentient beings and enable all to attain the
>   fruits of the Buddha;
> For them I shall manifest on a stage chanting the body of Dharma.

In retrospect, these lines stand remarkably prophetic. In the theatrical space of Tokyo, Li was initiated into the art of incarnating an alternative reality through human performance. He perfected it later in the Buddhist monasteries of China, where he had awakened to that alternative reality of his ultimate concern.

Throughout his life, Hongyi produced numerous works of calligraphy. Other than a handful of songs, calligraphy remained the sole form of aesthetic practice he retained after becoming a monk, rendering Buddhist messages in distinct styles as a way to spread the Dharma. It was simultaneously a way of his embodying the Dharma, when we recognize calligraphy as a performative art that fuses the power of words with the virtuosity of the calligrapher's body in brushwork. No piece illuminates this fusion of sacred text and virtuous body better than that which Hongyi wrote in his own blood on the twenty-first day of the first month in the *guiyou* year [February 15, 1933]. This seems the only occasion on which Hongyi made ink of his own blood. To the Vinaya master, the day marked his "first step" in teaching and disseminating the Vinaya, at Miaoshi Monastery in Amoy. Hongyi wrote, "Homage to Amitābha Buddha."

By all accounts, Li Shutong and Su Manshu did not develop a friendship, despite the fact that they were colleagues at the *Pacific*, a short-lived daily newspaper distributed in 1912 in Shanghai. Their divergence

notwithstanding, both artist-monks understood the extraordinary wonder of human performance. Furthermore, both cared deeply about the
place of a quintessential *bhikṣu* (a monk in the Buddhist tradition) in the
modern age, in a culture in which Buddhism has made one of its homes
for nearly two millennia. By conjuring a romantic "body of Dharma," in
reality as well as in imagination, Su Manshu recast at once the idea of a
Buddhist monk and that of love in his times. In his climactic last words,
"Love embraces all; as for impediments, there are none." In the same
crumbling world—a world of sorrow—Hongyi committed himself to a
life of discipline in quest of the profound joy of realizing the soteriological
vision of the Mahāyāna in flesh and blood. Amid a profusion of calls to
arms in twentieth-century China, the self-effacing Vinaya master commanded a quiet voice. But it continues to reverberate to this day, delivering a Buddhist awareness of enlightenment that transcends the duality
of self and other and refuses to take the mere absence of war for peace.

BIBLIOGRAPHY: Raoul Birnbaum, "Master Hongyi Looks Back: A Modern Man
Becomes a Monk in Twentieth-Century China," in *Buddhism in the Modern World:
Adaptations of an Ancient Tradition*, ed. Steven Heine and Charles S. Prebish (New
York, 2003), 75–124. Leo Ou-fan Lee, "Su Man-shu," in *The Romantic Generation of
Modern Chinese Writers* (Cambridge, MA, 1973), 58–78.

YING LEI

1919 · MAY 4

Lu Xun receives books from Japan.

The Big Misnomer:
"May Fourth Literature"

May 4, 1919, is a canonical date in modern Chinese history. On that day,
radical students from universities and colleges in Beijing took to the streets
to protest the outcome of the Paris Peace Conference, which assigned previous German concessions in China's Shandong Province to Japan, rather
than returning them to China. Students gathered in Tiananmen Square,
then marched to the legation quarter, hoping to hand a petition to the US
ambassador. Not realizing that Sunday was a day off for the embassy staff,

they did not get to see the ambassador. In their frustration, they marched on and finally converged on the residence of Cao Rulin (1877–1966), the government minister held responsible for selling out to Japan. Cao escaped the mob, but his colleague Zhang Zongxiang (1879–1962) was severely beaten up. Cao's house was burned to the ground. More demonstrations followed and spread across all major cities. A very successful boycott of Japanese goods added further pressure. Eventually the Chinese delegation in Paris refused to sign the Treaty of Versailles, and the ministers held responsible for the sellout were removed from their posts. The contested territory was restored to China following the Washington Naval Conference of 1921–1922.

The events of May–June 1919 are often seen as heralding the beginning of China's fight against imperialism and as laying the groundwork for the Communist movement.

None of these events have anything to do with literature. And yet, the concept of "May Fourth literature" is widely used in scholarship and beyond. The Chinese Wikipedia defines "May fourth literary writers" as "the writers who on May 4, 1919 overthrew the classical writing style... and promoted a vernacular writing style." However, this article is merely repeating a common misnomer. Not only did May Fourth have very little to do with literature, but also the literature referred to as "May Fourth" is in no way representative of Chinese literary output of the time. The canonization of May Fourth (literature) was a highly politicized and state-driven process, quite different from how literary canons usually come about.

The backlash against the classical language certainly did not happen all of a sudden on May 4, 1919, as the quote from the Chinese Wikipedia suggests. Vernacular writing was a crucial programmatic component of the so-called New Culture Movement, launched by professors of Peking University in the mid-1910s, well before May Fourth. The New Culture Movement aimed at tearing down the vestiges of Confucian social, moral, and cultural hierarchies. It took shape especially in the pages of the iconic magazine *New Youth*, founded in 1915 and edited at Peking University.

The iconoclasm of the professors may have inspired some of the activism of the demonstrating students. In turn, the success of those students in using the vernacular to educate the masses contributed to its acceptance as the official writing language for primary and secondary education, formalized by a government decree in 1921.

Even that has very little to do with literature. Literary texts are not solely defined by the language in which they are written. Moreover, countless texts written in the vernacular around May 4, 1919, are strangely enough not considered to be "May Fourth literature." What the label "May Fourth" refers to in the history of modern Chinese literature is an attitude toward creative writing that is largely antitraditional, at times iconoclastic, aimed at spreading new ideas and promoting new lifestyles, and generally supportive of social and political activism. Although this attitude was already in the making prior to May 4, 1919, and to some extent may have helped foster the student radicalism put on display during the anti-Japanese demonstrations, it is fair to say that the events of that day constituted a formative moment for an entire generation of Chinese intellectuals.

This makes it even stranger that the canon of "May Fourth literature" does not contain a single memorable description of the actual May Fourth demonstrations.

For Lu Xun (1881–1936), who was living in Beijing at the time, working at the Ministry of Education and writing for *New Youth*, May 4, 1919, was just another day. In his diary, he wrote, "Cloudy. Sunday rest. Xu Jixuan [1870–?] held a memorial for his father. In the morning I joined the mourners and contributed three *yuan*. In the afternoon, Sun Fuyuan [1894–1966] visited. Liu Bannong [1891–1934] visited, delivering two books to me that were sent over from Maruzen."

At the risk of overinterpretation, one might read something into the final part of the entry, when Lu Xun mentions receiving books from the Maruzen bookstore. He was a frequent customer at Maruzen while he was living in Japan from 1902 to 1909 and continued ordering books from them on a regular basis after he returned to China. It is certainly no exaggeration to say that Lu Xun's knowledge of Western society and culture was shaped to a very large extent by his readings of Japanese translations of Western books, and that very many of those were purchased from Maruzen. The innocuous diary phrase jotted down on May 4, 1919, might be seen as a gentle, almost ironic reminder that the ideologies underlying the students' anti-Japanese activism largely derived from reading Japanese books. Letters written by Lu Xun around the same time demonstrate that he was definitely paying attention to the demonstrations and boycotts. For instance, in his letter from July 4, 1919, to Qian Xuantong (1887–1939), he ironically refers to his sister-in-law, who was Japanese, as "the enemy spouse" and his nephews and nieces as "the semi-enemy children." On the other hand, there are dozens of routine references to Maruzen throughout Lu Xun's diary, so it may all be a coincidence.

What is clear, however, is that Lu Xun, too, never used the May Fourth demonstrations as a setting in any of his stories. As "dramatic" as the events of that day may have been—and many eyewitnesses have attested to the fact that they were indeed dramatic—they did not inspire writers to produce new works, or at least not the writers of "May Fourth literature."

To find fictional representations of the May Fourth demonstrations, strikes, and boycotts, we have to turn elsewhere, namely to the magazine *Xiaoshuo huabao*, which carried the English subtitle *Illustrated Novel Magazine*. This magazine first came out in January 1917 and was edited by Bao Tianxiao (1875–1973), a highly productive author, translator, editor, and journalist based in Shanghai. Bao launched his magazine with a manifesto stating that "genuine fiction is written in the vernacular" and that all contributions to the magazine must be in the vernacular. In his short introduction following the manifesto, Bao wrote that "the trajectory of the evolution of literature must be for literature in the ancient language to change and become literature in common speech." In terms of both its intention and its discourse, using modern concepts such as *wenxue* for "literature" and presenting the shift to vernacular writing as the outcome of a process of *jinhua* or "evolution," Bao's comments are highly similar to Hu Shi's (1891–1962) famous proposals for literary reform, which appeared in the *New Youth* issue of the same month. Moreover, since each issue of *New Youth* was notoriously published much later than the date stated on the cover, it is highly likely that Bao's ideas were published first. Yet Bao and his magazine have never been associated with Hu's "Literary Revolution" or the "May Fourth" tradition. Instead, Bao is generally associated with a style of writing seen as the antithesis of May Fourth literature, known as Mandarin Ducks and Butterflies.

Just as most May Fourth literature has little to do with May Fourth, most Mandarin Ducks and Butterflies writing does not feature mandarin ducks and butterflies. The term is used loosely to identify publications by a cluster of individuals from the Shanghai scene who wrote in a less Europeanized style and demonstrated a more ambivalent attitude toward tradition than

Beijing-based reformers like Hu Shi and Lu Xun. In conventional literary histories, especially those published in China, this style was the enemy that needed to be "defeated" so that the revolution in literature could be successful. This style of writing has been denigrated for so long that it is difficult, even today, to avoid an initial evaluation of such works as being somehow less "serious" or less "literary." Everything about it, including its language, use of punctuation, and refusal to adopt the vernacular in poetry, somehow works against its inclusion in the conventional canon of modern Chinese literature. Texts by people like Bao rarely feature in the canon that we teach. There are not enough English translations available to teach this style in translation, and the language of the originals is too remote from the "standard" Mandarin that is taught in our language programs to encourage teaching it in the original. Most modern Chinese literature curricula (and most anthologies of translations) either ignore this style altogether or merely pay lip service to it. Paying attention to the treatment of the May Fourth demonstrations in fiction published in a Mandarin Ducks and Butterflies magazine might be a good way to work toward a more complex understanding of Chinese literary culture of the late 1910s and early 1920s.

The June 1919 issue of the *Illustrated Novel Magazine* opens with a full-page advertisement for a book entitled *General History of National Humiliation*. The two opening stories both use the May Fourth demonstrations as their setting. The first story is by Bao himself and is entitled "Who Is to Blame?," probably a direct reference to the Russian novel of the same title by Aleksandr Herzen (1812–1870). So here we have a Mandarin Ducks and Butterflies writer writing about May Fourth and referring to a Russian realist author known for his social criticism. That is a far cry from conventional perceptions of what Mandarin Ducks and Butterflies was supposed to be.

The story is set in Suzhou at the time when the anti-Japanese protests were spreading across the country. The protagonist is a young man called Wang Guocai (a pun on *wangguo nucai* or "slave in a conquered country," a popular term used to describe the Chinese people in anti-imperialist propaganda). At the start of the story, Wang sells toys and stationery at a street stall for a Japanese company. Business is good, and when some money has been made, Wang and his wife decide to invest in some good-quality colored paper, also made by a Japanese company, and use it to decorate little boxes that his wife makes at home to earn some extra money. Then the demonstrations reach their neighborhood and the students, ironically carrying banners saying "No rioting!," smash up Wang's stall, search his home, find the paper, and then burn it, leaving Wang and his family bankrupt. Shamed by his inability to sustain his family, Wang commits suicide. The narrator ends with the rhetorical question, "Who is to blame?"

The second story is by Yao Yuanchu (1892–1954), another popular writer and editor and a kindred spirit to Bao. This story, entitled "Sacrificing Everything," is set in Shanghai. The protagonists are a Japanese-educated Chinese man who works for a Japanese bank and his young wife, who is fluent in English and helps out in the local mission school. The story starts with a description of their lifestyle, focusing on the generational difference between the young wife and her conservative mother-in-law. When the anti-Japanese demonstrations reach Shanghai, the wife enthusiastically persuades her husband to "do the right thing" and quit his job at the Japanese bank. For the sake of the nation, they give up their comfortable existence. The story has an open ending, with all three protagonists (including the mother) stating that it is correct to "sacrifice everything." It is left to the reader to imagine what might be the ultimate consequence of their decision.

Both stories contain detailed descriptions of student activities, and the illustrations also depict demonstrating students. The second story is particularly well written and features detailed descriptions of the protagonists and their interactions, reflecting contemporary social and generational differences, as well as bringing out the young couple's intimacy. Continuing the premodern fictional tradition of "complementary bipolarity" (a term coined by Andrew Plaks), but adapting it for modern magazine publication, the two texts highlight both the patriotic fervor of the demonstrations and the ugly side of violent activism and its unintended victims. With the first story ending on a question and the second having an open ending, no moral verdict is offered by either author. Readers are encouraged to make up their own minds.

Taken together, both stories represent a more complex response to the events of May Fourth than one would expect to find in literature carrying the label "Mandarin Ducks and Butterflies." More importantly, though, stories such as these encourage us to dispense with such misnomers altogether. Instead, we should read across the wealth of available publications and create new and better narratives about the stories produced during this fascinating period in modern Chinese literary history.

BIBLIOGRAPHY: Chen Pingyuan, *Touches of History: An Entry into "May Fourth" China*, trans. Michel Hockx et al. (Leiden, Netherlands, 2011). Kai-wing Chow et al., eds., *Beyond the May Fourth Paradigm: In Search of Chinese Modernity* (Lanham, MD, 2008). Milena Doleželová-Velingerová et al., eds., *The Appropriation of Cultural Capital: China's May Fourth Project* (Cambridge, MA, 2001). Michel Hockx, "What's in a Date? May Fourth in Modern Chinese Literary History," in *Paths towards Modernity: Conference to Mark the Centenary of Jaroslav Prusek*, ed. Olga Lomova (Prague, 2008), 291–306.

MICHEL HOCKX

1921 · NOVEMBER 30

A male named Taiwan is diagnosed as culturally backward and in need of a drastic remedy.

Clinical Diagnosis for Taiwan

On November 30, 1921, a twenty-seven-year-old male patient named Taiwan, who lived in Taiwan's Governor-General Office, was diagnosed as culturally backward due to prolonged and severe intellectual malnutrition. The doctor recommended a drastic remedy for the patient. The prescription included maximum doses of formal education, and significant increases in the number of kindergartens, libraries, and newspaper-reading societies in the patient's diet. It was anticipated that, if the prescription were followed closely, the patient would fully recover within two decades. The attending physician was Jiang Weishui (1891–1931), an important cultural figure and political activist of Taiwan's colonial period, and the diagnosis was Jiang's essay entitled "Clinical Diagnosis for a Patient Named Taiwan."

This highly allegorical diagnosis encapsulated Taiwanese intellectuals' profound sociopolitical concerns and their fervent ambitions for cultural enlightenment. This call for enlightenment can be said to have begun with the launching, in Tokyo, of the journal *Taiwan Youth*, a journal aimed at Taiwanese students in Japan that later made its way to Taiwan. The main group responsible for remodeling the thinking of Taiwanese people was the Taiwan Cultural Association—established on October 17, 1921, with Jiang as one of its founding members. Jiang's "Clinical Diagnosis" was published in its official journal. As opposed to the first two decades of Japanese rule (1895–1915), in which resistance manifested itself in numerous armed anticolonial struggles, in the 1920s Taiwanese intellectuals used cultural activities to vent their dissatisfaction with the colonial government. Jiang's essay illustrates this strategic change in Taiwan's anticolonial movements.

The association was the first nationwide cultural organization in colonial Taiwan. Its primary goal was to enlighten the people, but the objective was closely intertwined with its leading members' extensive sociopolitical engagements. Jiang himself serves as a good example. As early as 1912, Jiang (together with some of his classmates from the prestigious Taiwan Governor-General Office Medical School) joined the Taiwan branch of the Chinese Revolutionary Alliance to support Sun Yat-sen's (1866–1925) revolutionary movement. In 1913, Jiang planned to assassinate Yuan Shikai (1859–1916), though he never followed through on his design. In 1914, Jiang joined the short-lived Taiwan Acculturation Society, which was cofounded by Japanese liberal reformers and Taiwanese local gentry; their aim was to eliminate widespread Japanese discrimination against the Taiwanese people. Beginning in the 1920s, Jiang became even more actively involved in Taiwanese sociopolitical movements. He participated in several petition drives for Taiwanese self-governance in 1921, and was detained by the colonial government for his political activities in 1923. In such a tightly controlled political and intellectual climate, medicine was one of the few subjects in which the colonial government allowed Taiwanese access to higher education. Several key players of Taiwan's cultural and political scenes in the 1920s and 1930s, such as Lai He (1894–1943) and Wu Xinrong (1907–1967), were, like Jiang himself, doctors by training.

In order to disseminate anticolonial thinking and promote culture among a largely illiterate people, intellectuals like Jiang faced the thorny problem of finding the most effective medium for propagating their enlightenment goals. As the majority of the Taiwanese population at that time only spoke Taiwanese, neither the classical Chinese nor the Japanese language was suitable for reaching the common people in colonial Taiwan. In 1920, Chen Xin (1893–1947) had already tried to tackle the language question in the first issue of *Taiwan Youth*. In his essay "Literature and Its Mission," Chen not only stressed the social function of literature but also advocated an easy-to-understand vernacular language. Between 1920 and 1923, intellectuals wrote in different languages to express their support for writing in vernacular Mandarin Chinese—for example, classical Chinese was used by Chen, Japanese by Gan Wenfang (1901–1986), and vernacular Chinese by Huang Chaoqin (1897–1972). Through the efforts of these pioneering theorists, the use of vernacular Mandarin Chinese became increasingly prevalent. The inaugural issue of *Taiwan People's News* (1923), for instance, was written in the vernacular instead of being published bilingually (in classical Chinese and Japanese), as had been done for the earlier journals *Taiwan Youth* and *Taiwan*.

Inspired by the literary revolution on the mainland while studying at Beijing Normal College, Zhang Wojun (1902–1955) published "A Letter to the Youth of Taiwan" in April 1924 in *Taiwan People's News*. In this letter he attacked classical poetry as archaic and excessively ornate. Viewing Taiwanese literature as a branch of Chinese literature, Zhang advocated the use of vernacular Mandarin as a writing system for the Taiwanese language, which lacked a standardized writing system. After returning to Taiwan in October of that year, Zhang wrote "The Awful Literary Scene of Taiwan," in which he condemned writers of classical poetry as "tomb-watching dogs." Zhang's harsh words prompted numerous writers and critics to join the debate, which largely unfolded in *Taiwan People's News*. Among those who supported Zhang were Cai Xiaoqian (1908–1982), Lai He, Yang Yunping (1906–2000), and Chen Xungu (1891–1965). The debate surrounding old and new literature peaked in 1925, reviving occasionally in the several years that followed. By that point, many advocates of vernacular Chinese were deeply embroiled in other social movements. Consequently, when they put their theory into practice through experimental works in vernacular Chinese, their writings shared the tone and method of Jiang's "Clinical Diagnosis" in seeking to dissect social problems and express strong aspirations for reform.

One of the leading early Taiwanese writers of vernacular Mandarin was Lai, a person often hailed as "the father of Taiwanese new literature." In 1925 Lai published his first poem, "A Conscious Sacrifice," in vernacular Mandarin. In the following year, he published two other vernacular works: "Joining in the Fun" and "The Steelyard." These three works, which thoroughly condemn corrupt social practices and Japanese oppression, formed the foundation for Lai's later writing. They also illustrate the major themes of Taiwanese literature from the colonial period. Lai's "A Conscious Sacrifice" was written to express support for the farmers who were detained or imprisoned during the Erlin Incident, a conflict between local sugarcane farmers, who demanded a more reasonable price for their sugar, and the colonial authorities, who protected the interests of the Lin Benyuan Sugar Manufacturing Company. In the subtitle of this short poem, Lai addresses the farmers as his "fighting comrades." The poem exhibits profound sympathy for the exploited farmers; it salutes their struggle for their rights as "commendable and glorious." This humanitarian concern for the weak remained a central theme in Lai's oeuvre. Another recurrent theme is his portrayal of the Taiwanese people's "national character," especially as reflected in their backward social practices.

Written sarcastically with a utilitarian purpose of social reform, the story "Joining in the Fun" is a caricature of a traditional deity-worshipping fair. Through the conversations of the few nameless characters, the villagers' "face" problem—their excessive concern for keeping up appearances—is exposed. Even the destitute are pressured into donating money to make the fair more luxurious, so as to compete with the ones in the neighboring villages. While a few bystanders comment on how successful their fair may be, an elderly person recalls how the competition in precolonial Taiwan was even more exciting. At first glance, the old villager's words are a critique of the Japanese occupation; they indicate that Taiwan's social fabric was stronger when Taiwan was under local rule. Yet embedded in the story is a hierarchical distance between the insightful narrator and the ignorant crowd. Unlike the sober narrator, the crowd fails to recognize their own oppression. Like the elderly person, the masses addict themselves to their recollection of precolonial Taiwan instead of developing the necessary social consciousness to fight against colonialism.

"The Steelyard," conveying a similar message, recounts the tale of a vegetable vendor, Qin Decan (a homophonic play on "really miserable" in Taiwanese), operating under Japanese capitalist exploitation. One day, a Japanese police officer visits his stall to buy vegetables. To please the policeman, Qin underweighs the vegetables. Unfortunately, the ungrateful policeman arrests Qin for violating the rules of weights and measures. Unable to pay the bail, Qin kills the policeman and then commits suicide. The steelyard balance is supposed to signify fairness and justice. Yet in colonial Taiwan, the Japanese policemen developed their own rule of weights and measures to serve their economic interests and their aims of political control. This inequality led Lai to observe that the progress and modernity brought by Japan's colonization of Taiwan are not necessarily equal to the improvement of the living conditions of the Taiwanese population.

Concern for the laboring class, as illustrated in Lai's works, foreshadowed the increasingly leftist leaning of the Taiwan Cultural Association in 1927. Lai was involved in both the new left-wing Taiwan Cultural Association and the pro-reform Taiwanese People's Party. Under Jiang's leadership, the Taiwanese People's Party gradually moved leftward—especially through its engagement with various proletarian movements, which resulted in the withdrawal of gentry-class members such as Lin Xiantang (1881–1956) and Cai Peihuo (1889–1983). Lin and Cai established the reformist Taiwan Alliance for Local Self-government, endeavoring to use legal means to push for increased autonomy.

Although Lai did not articulate his ideological preference during the split, he felt a growing gap between the elite intellectuals and the masses. In his essay "Casual Jottings" (1930) and short story "Insults" (1931), Lai mocked himself for being useless and questioned how much the enlightenment discourse of the Taiwan Cultural Association had improved the lives of the laboring masses. Clearly, he recognized the limits of the cause of cultural enlightenment he had taken up. With the rising importance of mass movements, his sympathy for those in the lower socioeconomic strata grew. He gradually adopted a leftist stance, although his socialism remained an idealistic belief that awaited better practice. He never joined the Taiwanese Communists or partook in unionist activities, as Yang Kui (1906–1985) did.

In 1932, with the recommendation of Lai, half of Yang's "Newspaper Boy" was published in *Taiwan People's News*. Yang extended the theme of nationalistic anticolonialism in Lai's writing but shied away from provincial nationalism by placing class-consciousness above anti-imperialism. In "Newspaper Boy," international collaboration and self-help are essential for the oppressed to confront the condition of unemployment. The full story, only published two years later, depicts how a Taiwanese newspaper boy in Tokyo turns into a militant socialist and heads back to Taiwan to lead the cause against capitalist exploitation at the end.

Yang's "How the Naughty Boys Quelled the Demon" (1936) and "Model Village" (1937) satirize the thieving behavior of capitalists as well. "How the Naughty Boys Quelled the Demon" tells how a Japanese art student, Kensaku, becomes disappointed with the ugly reality of Japanese colonialism in Taiwan, and begins to considers his art lifeless if it only serves rich capitalists. Before returning to Tokyo, Kensaku leaves a painting entitled "Vanquish the Demon" for the local children, which later inspires them to devise a strategy to successfully oust the demon (in their world a local factory owner) and protect their playground. "Model Village" explores how the Japanese policy of assimilating the Taiwanese was implemented at the cost of the social well-being of local villagers. Two intellectual figures in the story challenge colonial oppression: one by fighting against Japan in China, and one by educating farmers in Taiwan. In all three stories, Yang continuously reminds us that the real demon is the exploitation of capitalist imperialism. Transnational cooperation and the popularization of literature and art are powerful weapons for the weak.

Like many Chinese intellectuals at the turn of the twentieth century who were influenced by the late Qing idea of "renovating the people" (*xinmin*) and the May Fourth discourse of cultural transformation, writers in colonial Taiwan took on the moral burden of being self-appointed agents of cultural enlightenment. Similar to Lu Xun (1881–1936), who abandoned his medical studies and pursued literature as the most effective means to cure China's spiritual ills, Jiang and Lai saw themselves as physicians when engaging with literature, aiming to identify and cure the malady of the Taiwanese society. But unlike Lu Xun, both Jiang and Lai continued to practice medicine throughout their lives. Jiang's medical practice was intimately connected with his cultural and political activities. The Daan Hospital he founded in 1916 was itself the headquarters of the Taiwan Cultural Association, and he opened a bookstore next door to the hospital in order to treat the intellectual feebleness of the Taiwanese people. The works of Jiang, Lai, and Yang paint the problem-ridden colonized society in which they were living in distinct pathological hues. Jiang's personification of colonial Taiwan as a culturally weak patient resonates with Lu Xun's appropriation of cannibalism as a metaphor for feudalistic prerevolutionary China. It is in those authors' common pursuit of a magical literary remedy for social malaise that the linkage between the Taiwanese writers and Lu Xun and his followers is most manifestly demonstrated.

From Jiang's "Clinical Diagnosis" to the debate over old and new literature instigated by Zhang, modern literature in 1920s colonial Taiwan developed into a diagnosis of, and a prescription to treat, the Taiwanese people's supposed low cultural level, of which obsolete classical genres constituted one symptom. The works of these pioneering writers underscore the intricate relationship between literature and its external sociopolitical conditions. They also helped establish anticolonial realist literature as a paradigm in Taiwanese literature. This utilitarian view, in which literature is seen as an instrument to diagnose social evils, is still valorized today in Taiwan, to the extent that any work that does not express distinct social concerns is likely to be marginalized.

BIBLIOGRAPHY: Lai He, "The Steelyard," in *The Columbia Anthology of Modern Chinese Literature*, ed. Joseph S. M. Lau and Howard Goldblatt (New York, 2007), 103–109. Zhang Wojun, "The Awful Literary Scene of Taiwan," in *Columbia Sourcebook of Literary Taiwan*, ed. Sung-sheng Yvonne Chang, Michelle Yeh, and Ming-Ju Fan (New York, 2014), 51–54.

PEI-YIN LIN

1922 · MARCH

Critical Review publishes its first article about the Harvard scholar Irving Babbitt.

Turning Babbitt into Bai Bide

In March 1922, *Critical Review* published its first article about the Harvard scholar Irving Babbitt (1865–1933). By the time the journal folded in 1933, a total of eight articles had been published about Babbitt. Among them, six were translations of Babbitt's writings, ranging from his 1921 speech at the annual meeting of the Chinese Students Association in Boston, to chapters from his *Literature and the American College* (1908) and *Democracy and Leadership* (1924). The rest were general introductions to Babbitt's new humanism, one written by Mei Guangdi (1890–1945), one of Babbitt's students at Harvard, and another (in translation) by the French writer Louis J. A. Mercier (1880–1953).

As in many cases during China's long history of cross-cultural encounters, Babbitt was given a Chinese name, Bai Bide (pure, virtuous jade).

Although Babbitt never visited China, Bai Bide was a popular cultural icon there during the 1920s and 1930s. In the early 1920s, the *Critical Review* editors presented Bai Bide as a stout supporter of classical learning when the cultural iconoclasts attacked the Confucian tradition, particularly the archaic classical language. At the height of the debate, Bai Bide was contrasted with another American scholar, Du Wei (John Dewey; 1859–1952), who actually visited China from 1919 to 1921 on the invitation of Hu Shi (1891–1962), a leader of the New Culture Movement. In the late 1920s and early 1930s, when the focus of literary debates shifted from language reform to supporting a communist revolution, Bai Bide was invoked as a critic of the politicization of literature. Again, Bai Bide's new humanism was stressed; but this time, he was presented as a literary theorist who strongly opposed turning literature into a political weapon of class struggle.

In both instances Babbitt's Chinese followers did not fully understand his views. Born in Dayton, Ohio, Babbitt was a leader of new humanism in the United States from the 1910s to the 1930s. Along with Paul Elmer More (1864–1937), Norman Foerster (1887–1972), and Stuart Pratt Sherman (1881–1926), Babbitt raised an intellectual battle against what he considered the rise of plutocracy and materialism in the United States that was coming at the expense of permanent humanistic value. In particular, he objected to changes in the curriculum of American colleges, such as the elective system, vocationalism, and the service ideal. Specializing in ancient Greek philosophy, French literature, and Buddhism, Babbitt taught at Harvard University for decades and shaped the views of many of his students. However, because of his opposition to mass society, popular democracy, and functional scientism, Babbitt spent much of his academic career on the periphery of the American cultural arena, while the country was rapidly urbanizing and industrializing.

Despite his unpopularity in his own time, Babbitt offered his American followers an alternative vision of modernity. He was critical of the modern age, symbolized by the rapid industrialization of the United States. Although not an economist or a sociologist by training, Babbitt was quick to point out the huge human tolls of this unprecedented sociopolitical disruption. Drawing on the examples of Renaissance humanists and the British tradition of liberal arts education, he argued that classical studies, philosophy, and literature must be the basis of an "education of governors" that would counter the educational trends of the industrial age. Upholding Jeffersonian "aristocratic democracy" as the model of American government, he wanted to connect the past with the present, and to give direction to what, in his opinion, were seemingly random developments.

Because Babbitt's Chinese followers knew him only as a teacher at Harvard, they did not comprehend the socioeconomic significance of his new humanism. For instance, Wu Mi (1894–1978), the chief editor of *Critical Review* and the key person who introduced Babbitt's new humanism into China, knew little about his teacher's motive in promoting Renaissance humanism and liberal arts education. As shown in his diary and autobiography, like many Chinese students of the time, Wu lived outside American society. Spending most of his time with Chinese students, he was more interested in learning about the current events in his native country than those in the United States. Consequently, his understanding of Babbitt's new humanism was based on a narrow and bookish perspective of aesthetics. He knew his teacher's scholarly writings inside and out, particularly those on Greek literature, Jean-Jacques Rousseau's (1712–1778) thought, and Buddhism. But he had no knowledge of the educational debate that consumed much of his teacher's energy, nor was he aware of the socioeconomic context of that educational debate.

Wu's limited knowledge notwithstanding, it is clear that he was attracted to Babbitt's new humanism for two reasons. One was that it offered a powerful counterargument to the cultural iconoclasm of the New Culture Movement, which attacked Confucianism as a state ideology supporting authoritarianism, patriarchy, and elitism during the imperial period (206 BCE–1911 CE). In the context of the 1920s debates over vernacularizing the Chinese written language, new humanism provided Wu with the raison d'être to link China's past with its present based on the classical language and a genteel form of poetry. Better yet, new humanism was a school of thought from an advanced industrialized country, the United States of America, which had seen both the benefits and the harms of modernization.

A case in point was Wu's creation of the persona of Bai Bide. In the editor's preface to Hu Xiansu's (1894–1968) translation of Babbitt's essay "Humanistic Education in China and in the West" (March 1922), Wu made deliberate efforts to make Bai Bide relevant to 1920s China. First, he stressed that Bai Bide, despite his inability to read Chinese, was well informed of recent developments in China. Second, he pointed out that as a leading literary critic in America, Bai Bide offered a vision of society fundamentally different from that of other Western thinkers. While other Western thinkers stressed the benefits of scientism and materialism, Bai Bide focused on the role of religion and morality in shaping an individual's spiritual life. As other Western thinkers saw modern Europe as the apex of human development, Bai Bide combined the learning of the East and the West, and the past and the present.

In addition to providing intellectual ammunition to counter cultural iconoclasm, Babbitt's new humanism was also attractive to Wu because it gave China a role in the global discourse on modernity. By the standards of his time, Babbitt was truly "transcultural" in the sense that he attempted to articulate a global culture drawn from resources in Europe, India, and China. In the *Critical Review* articles, Babbitt's globalism was constantly on display. In Wu's previously mentioned preface to Hu's translation, Wu told his readers that from Bai Bide's perspective, there was a oneness in the teachings of Plato and Aristotle in the West and those of Siddhartha Gautama and Confucius in the East. Babbitt's globalism appeared again in Wu's 1925 translation of chapter 5, "Europe and Asia," of Babbitt's *Democracy and Leadership*. In that chapter, Bai Bide compares four thinkers: Jesus of Nazareth, Siddhartha Gautama of India, Aristotle of Athens, and Confucius of China. Crossing geographical and cultural boundaries, Bai Bide first compares Jesus with Siddhartha on religious grounds, and then Aristotle with Confucius on the basis of moral philosophy. Showing the oneness in learning in all corners of the world, Bai Bide wished for all modern people to learn from the "spiritual civilizations" in Asia to counter the rapid growth of materialism in Europe and America.

Certainly, Wu's Bai Bide can be understood as a "conservative critique" of industrialization and scientism after the end of World War I. But by presenting Bai Bide as a thinker of a fast-growing industrialized country who considered Eastern philosophy a spiritual foundation of the twentieth-century world, Wu had a specific goal in mind. His Bai Bide was not merely a supporter of China's alternative modernity that included Eastern cultural elements in its modernization; he was also a critical thinker who opposed industrialization and scientism as the twin pillars of the modern world.

In 1927, two years after the publication of Wu's article on a globalized Bai Bide, Liang Shiqiu (1903–1987) presented another image of Bai

Bide. A former student of Babbitt's at Harvard, Liang debated with Lu Xun (1881–1936) about whether writers should produce revolutionary literature. On and off, the debate lasted for nine years, spanning from 1927 to 1936, overlapping to a large extent with the period that Lu Xun led the League of Left-Wing Writers (1930–1936). On one side, through rendering the writings of Soviet literary theorists into Chinese, Lu Xun argued that there is no art for art's sake. According to Lu Xun, all writings (literary or not) are expressions of class differences, and thereby an integral part of class struggle. On the other side, Liang supported art for art's sake, and argued that literature had its own intrinsic value beyond politics. In the debate, both sides focused their attention on three issues: whether literature reflected class differences, whether literature (particularly poetry) expressed human spirituality, and whether the party-state was able to control literary production by issuing literary policies. In discussing these three topics, Liang based his argument on Babbitt's new humanism. Similar to Wu, Liang turned Babbitt, the American scholar, into Bai Bide, a China specialist who offered insightful suggestions for the country's modernization.

To counter Lu Xun's argument, Liang pointed out that Lu Xun completely misunderstood Bai Bide when he criticized him for supporting art for art's sake. For Liang, the scope of Bai Bide's new humanism was much larger than his aesthetic theory. On the one hand, new humanism drew on the humanistic traditions of ancient Greece, the Renaissance, and romanticism of the nineteenth century. On the other hand, new humanism provided an alternative vision of modernity that balanced the human quest for material progress with the human yearning for moral justice and spiritual awakening. Thus, new humanism was a comprehensive system of thought that opposed the materialism, populism, scientism, and utilitarianism on which Soviet Russia was based.

Citing Bai Bide's balanced approach to modernization, Liang criticized Lu Xun for supporting revolutionary literature. For Liang, the term "revolutionary literature" was an oxymoron because all literary writings were by definition revolutionary due to their originality and creativity. Although many literary writings did not support communist revolution, that did not mean they were not revolutionary in their own right. To Liang, Lu Xun was being counterproductive by imposing a revolutionary ideology on other writers. Rather than encouraging literary creativity, Liang argued, Lu Xun actually limited writers' freedom for literary experimentation and unnecessarily confined them to the straitjacket of Marxism-Leninism. As a result, Liang contended, writers were no longer able to express the complexity of life; instead, they became the mouthpiece of the Communist Party.

Central to Liang's argument was Bai Bide's humanism. For Liang, Bai Bide's biggest contribution was his view that each individual must be treated as a unique human being with his or her dignity, character, and personality. In literature and in real life, Bai Bide looked for differences in human beings, and took seriously the complexity of the entangled human world. In contrast, Liang contended, Lu Xun supported a revolutionary literature that reduced the multitude of human beings into class labels, such as "proletariat" and "bourgeoisie." In the end, Liang concluded, this politicization of literature would not work, not only because it separated people artificially, but also because it went against human nature.

Similar to Wu's Bai Bide, Liang's Bai Bide was not Irving Babbitt. Rather, he was a constructed persona based partly on a select reading of Babbitt's writings, and partly on what Liang considered to be the new Chinese literature. Whereas in the 1920s Bai Bide opposed the vernacular movement, in the 1930s Bai Bide objected to the creation of revolutionary literature. In both cases, Bai Bide was a symbol of an alternative way to modernize Chinese language and literature that took China's past seriously.

BIBLIOGRAPHY: Irving Babbitt, *Literature and the American College* (1908; repr., Washington, DC, 1986). Irving Babbitt, *Rousseau and Romanticism* (Boston, 1919). *Critical Review* (Xue Heng) (1922–1933). Liang Shiqiu, *Pian jian ji* (Nanjing, China, 1934). Wu Mi, *Wu Mi riji*, 10 vols. (Beijing, 1998).

TZE-KI HON

1922 · SPRING

Bao Tianxiao visits Xiang Kairan.

Xiang Kairan's Monkey

Wuxia (martial arts and chivalry) fiction and film are to China what the western once was to America: tales of heroism and fantasy, set in a semimythologized past, that played a vital role in defining popular conceptions of national and cultural identity. Martial arts fiction, which now thrives on the Internet, traces the roots of its themes and material to some of the earliest classics of Chinese literature. For much of the twentieth century it maintained a vital presence in mass-market print culture: serialized in newspapers and magazines; borrowed, rented, or purchased in multivolume sets; flourishing in Hong Kong, Taiwan, and the Chinese diaspora even as it was proscribed in the People's Republic. The acknowledged father of the genre in its modern form is the Hunan native Xiang Kairan (1890–1957). His *Marvelous Gallants of the Rivers and Lakes* and *Righteous Heroes of the Modern Age,* penned under the name Pingjiang Buxiaosheng, began serialization in 1923. They are credited with launching the Republican-era craze for martial arts fiction, the closely linked vogue for martial arts film, and the successive tides of fictional and cinematic reinvention that have carried the genre into the present day. What moved Xiang to write these seminal works? It all began with a visit from the author and editor Bao Tianxiao (1875–1973) in 1922.

So at least Bao would have it. Relating the encounter in his memoirs, he doesn't specify the date, but implies that it was around the February 1922 launch of *Saturday,* one in the long list of fiction periodicals under his editorial care. For some time Bao had wanted to locate Xiang, who in 1916 had published the best-selling novel *The Unauthorized History of Sojourners in Japan,* a scandalous exposé of the life of Chinese studying abroad. Despite the novel's fame, the author's whereabouts were unknown. "Some said he'd already returned to Hunan, some that he'd gone back to Japan, but there was no consensus on the matter," writes Bao. A break came when another Hunanese litterateur, Zhang Mingfei, revealed that Xiang currently resided in Shanghai. He warned, though, that the gentleman in question was not much given to receiving visitors; and if you *do* look him up, he continued, you'd best do so late in the day, or better yet at night. "Aha!" said the savvy Bao, "an opium smoker." "Just so," laughed Zhang. The very next day found Bao making his way to a narrow alley off Xinzhalu. He found the author in the upstairs room Xiang shared with a dog, a monkey, and a mistress. Although Bao had waited until four in the afternoon to make his call, Xiang had just risen and was scarcely ready for company. "He needed to first satisfy his craving if he were to have any energy, and so without standing on ceremony I settled down across from him on the opium couch." Bao left Xiang's lodgings that night with the promise of two contributions for his latest venture, *Saturday.*

One of Xiang's contributions was the *Supplement to the Unauthorized History of Sojourners in Japan*—one of several sequels he produced to the novel that had first made his reputation. Like the original, the sequel sets out to narrate, in naturalistic detail, interlocking anecdotes that reveal the lust, venality, malice, hypocrisy, self-deception, pettiness, and sloth of the sons and daughters of China dwelling in a foreign land. Their misdeeds are, if anything, more outrageous than those of their predecessors from a decade before. As Xiang writes,

> It seems that as world civilization has progressed, the Chinese people's level of depravity has progressed along with it as well. Indeed, we need only take a look at the political and social situation within the nation over the last few years to verify the lighting speed of our compatriots' progress in depravity.

This weighing of China's social and political realities against the projected norms of global civilization places *The Unauthorized History of Sojourners in Japan* in the tradition of the great "castigatory" novels of the first decade of the century. By the 1910s, the genre, though still popular with readers, had been recast by critics as "exposé" or "black curtain" fiction. These same critics charged the genre with prurience, gossip-mongering, and even blackmail. In 1918, the Education Ministry's Committee on Popular Education called on writers to cease production of works in this vein; in the same year, "black curtain" fiction became one of the first targets of the literary polemics of the New Culture camp of literary reformers and revolutionaries. Critiques of "black curtain" fiction as antiquated in form, licentious in content, and irresponsible in attitude ignored certain points of contact between these works and the New Literature agenda—in the case of *The Unauthorized History of Sojourners in Japan*, Xiang's command of vigorous and contemporary colloquial dialogue, and the assumption that an intimate chronicle of individual misbehaviors amounts to a dragging into the light of China's sordid collective soul. The insight that the exposure is intensified by the Chinese experience in the foreign social and cultural environment of Japan mirrors a perspective reflected in some of the most canonical of New Literature / May Fourth works—Lu Xun's (1881–1936) account in the preface to *Call to Arms* of how the scales fell from his eyes in a Japanese lecture hall, or Yu Dafu's

(1896–1945) portrait in "Sinking" of an overseas student's conflation of personal and national despair. The thematic resonances between *The Unauthorized History of Sojourners in Japan* and "Sinking" are especially striking. For both Yu's protagonist and the rascals who populate the novel, sexuality is a key site for "acting out," and for identifying the transgressive self with the Chinese nation. In "Sinking" the identification plays out as humiliation. At the end of the story, after an ambiguous encounter in a resort town brothel, the protagonist gazes westward over the waves, seeking the courage to hurl himself into the abyss: "Oh China, my China, you are the cause of my death!…I wish you could become rich and strong soon!… Many, many of your children are still suffering."

Huang Wenhan would laugh. One of the central characters in the original novel, Huang is an overseas student with an avid interest in the martial arts. He shares with his peers in the novel a passion for seduction and whoring—a passion to which the "prostitute nation" of Japan gives unfettered scope. Yet while matching, if not surpassing, his fellows in the outrageousness of his behavior, Huang refuses to play any part in their spectacle of abasement and self-destruction. Early in the novel he takes a friend to visit a pair of "sisters" he favors, only to find Japanese military boots outside the door. Undaunted, he barges in on the prostitutes and their stunned but courteous guests. The Japanese officers, brazening the situation out, suggest that they and their new acquaintances share a meal. Huang racks up an enormous tab. When the Japanese present him with the bill, he seizes one of their greatcoats, announces his intention to pawn it, and strides to the door. The officers follow, and he fells one with his fist, then hails a policeman and is quickly vindicated in his expectation that, threatened with public embarrassment and professional repercussions, his foes will meekly apologize and slink off to pay the bill.

Faced with Japanese slights, real or imagined, against Chinese honor, Huang responds not with debilitating self-recrimination, but with an aggressive assertion of sexual potency and nationalistic pride. As he tells the officers,

> So you think I came here to get an education, do you? Let me tell you something, and I won't bother to be polite. When I was back in my own country, I heard it said that your honored nation's girls were the prettiest, and the easiest too. My forefathers left me an inheritance of

hundreds of thousands, and when I got tired of whoring back in China, I decided to come to your honored nation for an advanced course of study. It's precisely to do my homework that I came here today. Do you want to tell me there's something wrong with that?

It's easy to identify in this bravado a hypertrophied compensation for the very fears and lacks that bedevil Yu's suicidal character. We may glimpse as well the heroic "national character" that Lu Xun's Ah Q, grasping at memories of operatic paladins as he trundles along in his execution cart, strives so hopelessly to conjure. Xiang's exuberant Huang Wenhan tramples the line between exposure and celebration.

The second piece Xiang wrote for Bao's *Saturday* was "A Hunter's Miscellany," a series of anecdotes from his native Hunan. Like the *Supplement*, it harks back to his earlier writing; in 1916 he had published a related set of tales under the title "Turning Pale" in the journal *Elements of People's Rights*. Another "Turning Pale" appeared in *Flowers of Society* in 1924. The three pieces share a common subject matter—hunters and tigers in the wilds of Hunan—but only a minimum of material. The earlier two employ the classical language and narrative approach of traditional anecdotal (*biji*) fiction. Xiang appears in these stories as author / narrator and guarantor for the tales' provenance, relating lore he has gathered from acquaintances, as well as matters he has observed himself. The source and protagonist of the tale that begins the 1916 "Turning Pale" is a Chinese martial artist whose acquaintance Xiang made in Tokyo. Within these tales, however, the turpitude and perfidy that constitute life in *The Unauthorized History of Sojourners in Japan*'s metropolis are absent—as is, perhaps not incidentally, nearly any female presence. Hunan's mountains and jungles are the setting for raw, amoral contests of cunning, courage, and ferocity between man and beast, man and man.

The 1924 "Turning Pale" discards the classical register for a lively and chatty vernacular. Here Xiang spins tales and lore around four occasions in his youth when he himself encountered a tiger in the wild. He claims no heroic feats; he is instead frank, even comical, in his descriptions of his terror at his inadvertent encounters with the wild power of these beasts. His introductory remarks reinforce the constructed opposition of the wilds of Hunan to the modern metropolis. He ruminates on the proverb "to pale at talk of tigers," which denotes terror at the very mention of a remembered calamity. Xiang maintains that the proverb must have been minted by someone who knew tigers in their native element, for the tiger he once saw in a zoo was a sorry creature, stripped of majesty and awe. Where was this zoo and when did Xiang encounter it? In Shanghai, when he first passed through the city as a youth on his way to study in Japan. It is in the years before adulthood, in the mountain wilds, that the tiger can live in wild and terrible glory.

We can see the roots of Xiang's martial arts fiction in the physical confidence and nationalistic bravado of *The Unauthorized History of Sojourners in Japan*, Huang Wenhan, and likewise in the complementarity between the novel's dystopic urban Japan and the Hunan tales' evocation of tiger-killing heroes like those in *Water Margin*, the classic Chinese tale of gallant outlaws. But it is in Shanghai that Xiang dwelled in 1922. And Bao's visit to Xiang in the alley off Xinzhalu gave birth to modern martial arts fiction not only through the germination of material, but also through the operation of social networks and commercial imperatives. Pleased with the success of his mission, Bao showed the Hunan tales to his friend and colleague from the *Grand Magazine* days, Shen Zhifang (1882–1939). "Where did you unearth this treasure?" exclaimed Shen. Shen, the most aggressively entrepreneurial of Shanghai publishers, had recently founded the World Book Company. In a bid to challenge Great Eastern, Bao's employer, in the entertainment periodical market, he launched his flagship *Scarlet Magazine* in August 1922; among *Scarlet*'s sisters would be something new—the first Chinese periodical devoted to a specific popular fiction genre, *Detective World*. What Bao showed Shen motivated him to contract Xiang to write for his magazines. And with his famed instinct for creating new market niches, Shen commissioned Xiang to pen something novel and quite specific: "first-class romantic fiction in the sword-immortal and knight-errant vein." Pingjiang Buxiaosheng's *Marvelous Gallants* was first serialized in *Scarlet* at the end of 1922, and *Righteous Heroes* in the first issue of *Detective World* in the summer of 1923.

The habits of literary historiography and the heroic nature of martial arts fiction itself make Bao's teleological, even triumphal tale of origins appealing. One of the pleasures of Bao's account, though, is how convincingly it returns us to that rented room with its opium couch, its temperamental owner, his mistress, his dog, and his monkey. Elsewhere, Bao tells how the dog and the monkey were given to squabbling, and how Xiang joked about the "three beasts" with which he lived. And, in the forty-sixth issue of *Saturday*, Bao published an additional anecdote presumably related to him by Xiang himself:

Xiang Kairan's Monkey

Mr. Xiang Kairan kept a monkey in his household. It was a male. One day a monkey trainer came to the door. He had with him a monkey of about the same size, but female. When the two monkeys saw one another, they stroked one another's bodies and made a marvelous show of affection. Mr. Xiang had it in mind to buy the monkey as a mate for his own, but when the monkey trainer saw the situation he demanded an exorbitant price. The monkey was in fact already withered and thin. You could have bought one like it for no more than four or five gold pieces. Mr. Xiang was willing to pay ten, but the man still refused the offer. Then, as the monkey trainer made ready to leave, the two monkeys linked their hands together and would not let go. They had to force them apart. Mr. Xiang's monkey wailed in grief the whole night through.

Three beasts, but no tiger. Here in the author's garret we find neither the insistently asexual heroism of the mountains nor the ruthless sexual politics of the dystopian city, but rather, projected onto a simian doppelgänger, a pathetic drama of desire and loss. Yu Dafu's abject protagonist may in fact be closer than we had been given to think.

BIBLIOGRAPHY: Louis Cha [Jin Yong], *The Book and the Sword*, trans. Graham Earnshaw (Oxford, 2004). John Christopher Hamm, *Paper Swordsmen: Jin Yong and the Modern Chinese Martial Arts Novel* (Honolulu, 2005). Petrus Liu, *Stateless Subjects: Chinese Martial Arts Literature and Postcolonial History* (Ithaca, NY, 2011).

JOHN CHRISTOPHER HAMM

1922 · DECEMBER 2

Spring Radiance Middle School celebrates its inauguration.

New Culture and the Pedagogy of Writing

The planning began as early as 1908, showing that even during the late Qing dynasty, local gentry in Zhejiang Province were concerned about educational reform as a means for modernizing the ailing nation. By 1919, the pressure for education reform was reinforced by the national trend to create a new modern culture, and many of the teachers and writers at the center of the New Culture Movement were themselves schoolteachers, especially in Zhejiang Province. In the same year, a board of directors was consequently formed for a new private middle school. A year later, they named Jing Hengyi (1877–1938) as the new principal and selected White Horse Lake, located in Shangyu, Zhejiang, as the building site. In the summer of 1922, Spring Radiance Middle School began to recruit students, and the first class of fifty-seven pupils began matriculation on September 10, 1922. Finally, on December 2, Spring Radiance held its ceremony of "opening the school."

Jing, a native of Shangyu, had for years been an advocate of educational reforms as principal of the Zhejiang Government Normal College in the provincial capital of Hangzhou. Accompanied by the fervor of the May Fourth Movement of 1919, the progressive atmosphere he created led him to increasingly radical forms of engagement with New Culture. Jing and a group of Normal College teachers and students led an attack on traditional Confucian values. However, even under the modern, Western-style Republican government, Zhejiang Province had a tradition of celebrating Confucius and traditional morality with a sacrificial ceremony twice a year. The May Fourth Movement made intellectuals and students rethink this moral legacy, and Jing supported the student boycott of the ritual in the college. As a result, the provincial board of education demanded that Jing expel the radical student leaders immediately. Jing surprised them, however, by refusing to cooperate and instead resigning, followed by other key faculty members.

The emergence of Spring Radiance Middle School during such precarious times demonstrates the centrality of education to the New Culture Movement. Jing was named principal of the school in January 1920, about the same time he was under attack from the provincial board of education. Spring Radiance was to be a private school, funded by local gentry, with precisely the idea of liberating the educational enterprise from the government's continued cultural conservatism, represented in public schools like the Zhejiang Government Normal College. Jing turned to his former colleague Xia Mianzun (1886–1946) to assist him in assembling a faculty.

Xia Mianzun was first and foremost an educator, but he was also a creative writer. He was not alone in this regard, and invited figures with similar backgrounds to join the faculty at Spring Radiance. For instance, he extended invitations to his comrades at the Zhejiang Government Normal College, such as Chen Wangdao (1891–1977)—also a celebrated fiction writer and member of the newly formed Literary Research Association— and Li Shutong (1880–1942)—an important conduit of progressive educational ideals coming out of Japan who emphasized the role of art and music in education, as well as devout Buddhist faith with a modern sensibility. A student of Li's at the Normal College, Feng Zikai (1898–1975), was also invited to teach art and music at the school. If you look at these and other figures Xia invited to join the Spring Radiance faculty or to lecture and participate in new educational experiments—people like essayist Zhu Ziqing (1898–1948), Kantian aesthetician Zhu Guangqian (1897–1986), novelist Ye Shengtao (1894–1988), and poet and essayist Yu Pingbo (1900–1990)—it is clear that Xia paid particular attention to an individual's intellectual and cultural prominence in his selection of the faculty. But why? And why would these cultural figures come to teach in a private middle school in rural Zhejiang?

In many cases, it was due to personal connections to Xia, but in the midst of political and professional instability in China's larger cities, the opportunity to retire to a bucolic setting to play a major role in the cultivation of the next generation of Chinese intellectuals and writers must also have held some attraction. Moreover, while recruiting prominent cultural figures to serve as middle school faculty may appear superficial, it must be noted that this move exemplified the values of the New Culture Movement. In the early years of the movement, as was the case over the ensuing generation, creative writers often embraced the most progressive political stance. Their characteristic choice of literature and the arts as a mode of social engagement has its roots in the thought of late Qing reformists, like Liang Qichao (1873–1929) and Yan Fu (1853–1921), who advocated the use of literature (often specifically fiction) to modernize the nation and cultivate an informed, politically conscious citizenry that could become the foundation for democracy. The unusual move by Jing and Xia was to take the opportunity of a private school, unencumbered by the oppressive interference of the government and local conservatives, and apply the talents and political consciousness of the first generation of modern Chinese authors directly to the education of Zhejiang's children.

The story of Spring Radiance Middle School itself has a certain literary appeal: these men, at once schoolteachers and creative writers, re-created modern education in the form of a pastoral idyll away from the turmoil of history and politics. They were inspired by educational ideas coming out of Europe, the United States, and Japan that placed the student at the center of the learning process, and that reconceived the teacher's relationship to the student as an emotional one, maternal and nurturing rather than paternalistic and regimented. Their classrooms would extend out into the vegetable garden and chicken coops, making the school into a pastoral laboratory of democratic, communal living. The idealism embodied in this vision can also be seen in writer Mushanokōji Saneatsu's (1885–1976) vision of the modern, self-sufficient, and communal New Village (Atarashiki mura), actually established in Japan just a few years before. Mushanokōji's project inspired not only Xia, but also Lu Xun's (1881–1936) brother Zhou Zuoren (1885–1967). These ideals took literary form in such works as Ye's 1928 novel *Ni Huanzhi* and a fictional work cowritten by Ye and Xia in 1933 that encourages youths to proactively read and write outside school, entitled *The Heart of Writing*.

Reading and writing were truly at the heart of 1920s educational reform. What made the crossroads of literature and education special at this juncture was the awareness among contemporary authors, many or most of whom had recently been or still were schoolteachers, that the New Culture Movement, to a large extent, rejected the traditional Confucian educational curriculum and methods. Though in literary history we usually focus on artistic developments, Chinese teachers in the early twentieth century were faced with the stupendous problem of what students should now read, how they should read it, and how they should now be taught to express themselves in writing, whether or not they hoped to become literary authors. Certainly, part of the educational picture was filling in a great deal of content drawn from Western models—the natural and social sciences, the history and literature of other nations, foreign languages—but the question of the modern Chinese language, its models and canons, and the role of the traditional textual legacy, in effect the very medium through which all new modes of knowledge would be conveyed, was a more fundamental problem.

The White Horse Lake writers' solution to the problem was a practical and egalitarian writing pedagogy for their middle school students. It was "practical" in the sense that the ability to express oneself well in writing was considered essential to modern citizenship and a skill that would continually prove its usefulness in everyday life. It did not confine reading and writing to the classroom, but emphasized its integration with all facets of life, across all social strata. The teaching was "egalitarian" in that it downplayed the difference between writing by the artistically gifted and writing by everyone else; it did not celebrate genius over learning attainable by anyone, given the right circumstances. One can see here a curious mix of traditional Confucian ideas about education—in which reading and writing are placed at the center of teaching and made the student's principal mode of social engagement with society—and contrasting Western ideas of human equality and worth—the rejection of entrenched social hierarchies (including the use of education to define a social elite), the elevation of the student to the center of educational endeavors, and ideals of simple and direct expression over embellishment and artistic ingenuity.

Though we cannot observe their actual teaching, figures like Xia, Ye, and Feng exemplified these ideas in their own writing, and also wrote primers and guidebooks that clearly endeavored to help make writing a part of the everyday life of young Chinese people. One can see in their essays, such as Xia's *Random Writings from the Bungalow* (1936) and Feng's *Essays from the Fated Hall* (1931), the ideals of direct and simple expression, and the idea of only writing when you have something meaningful to say. Feng's elegant yet engaging cartoons, treasured even today, created a lyrical counterpart in visual culture to the stark, binary world of leftist woodcut art promoted by Lu Xun. Their aesthetic could be described as "utilitarian," and their essays do tend more than those of other groups to be didactic, but for them writing must also be a pleasure, as one can see from this passage from Xia's famous essay "Winter at White Horse Lake":

Listening, drawing by Feng Zikai

Listening, Drawing by Feng Zikai, 1926. Frontispiece from Jonathan Spence's *Gate of Heavenly Peace* (New York, 1982).

I used to pull my Russian hat down over my ears and work till the small hours by the light of a kerosene lamp. The wind roared down from the pine clad hills like a wild beast, frosty moonlight framed the window, hungry mice scurried squeaking over the ceiling. It was at times like these that I most keenly appreciated the poetry of desolation: all by myself, I would frequently stir the embers in the stove and prolong my vigil. Casting myself as the tiny figure we often see in landscape paintings, I gave myself up to fanciful musings.

Xia brings us into the bitter reality of the endless cold nights he experienced in a crudely built cabin by the lake, but he also finds a way to enjoy his predicament by relating himself to the literary and artistic traditions. In so doing he demonstrates how relating artistic appreciation to carefully observed personal experience, through the discipline of prose writing, can actually improve (or seem to improve) one's quality of life.

Less well known to literary historians, but even more revealing in regard to the development of this style of writing, are the many guides to reading and writing published in the early 1930s, particularly by White Horse Lake group members like Xia, Zhu Guangqian, and Zhu Ziqing. The most common type is the commentary on famous essays, in which the author will examine famous writings (including premodern ones), with particular emphasis on compositional technique, so that the student may immediately derive lessons from the masterworks that he or she can apply in his or her own writing. These short collections read very much like lecture notes from Chinese literature and composition classes, and probably are. In addition, the fiction writers among them often fictionally represented modern education in action. For instance, Ye and Xia's joint work, *The Heart of Writing*, is loosely based on the classic Italian work *Cuore: Diary of an Italian Schoolboy*. The Chinese work reflects its nineteenth-century Italian precursor and demonstrates the benefits of a student-centered education and relates learning to patriotism. Xia and Ye's work interestingly depicts teenagers instead of primary school children, however, and focuses much more intensely on the life of the mind as it is cultivated through self-guided reading and writing, and how these activities can be meaningfully integrated with modern social life.

It seems a stretch to attribute a comprehensive vision of the centrality of prose composition to modern educational ideals to a few months of teaching at a private middle school on the shores of White Horse Lake. To be sure, many of the key figures who taught there went on to teach at other experimental schools, most famously the Lida School in Shanghai. It was largely during these ensuing years, during the late 1920s and early 1930s, that the writings discussed here were published, rather than during their authors' brief sojourn at Spring Radiance itself from 1922 to 1925. Nevertheless, it is significant that these writers often harked back to that moment in time and space. It reminded them of the combination of the new educational ideas with a pastoral environment, not to mention the collegial community of teachers in their small cottages along the lakeside; it imprinted those educational ideals in their minds, and associated them, perhaps permanently, with a lifestyle of contemplative leisure and community that resonated deeply with the long tradition of Chinese prose writing.

BIBLIOGRAPHY: Geremie Barme, *An Artistic Exile: A Life of Feng Zikai (1898–1975)* (Berkeley, CA, 2002). Chen Xing, *Baima hu zuojia qun* (Hangzhou, China, 1998). Charles A. Laughlin, *The Literature of Leisure and Chinese Modernity* (Honolulu, 2008). David Pollard, *The Chinese Essay* (New York, 2000).

CHARLES A. LAUGHLIN

1924 · APRIL 12

> I am a soul that worships
> Youth, joy, and light.
> —Xu Zhimo, "Quietude"

Xu Zhimo and Chinese Romanticism

On April 12, 1924, the Nobel laureate Rabindranath Tagore (1861–1941) arrived in Shanghai, thus beginning his two-week tour of China. He had been invited to visit China by the Beijing Lecture Association, a scholarly organization founded by the intellectual Liang Qichao (1873–1929). Liang also sent his beloved student, Xu Zhimo (1897–1931), a budding poet who had returned from Britain two years earlier, to serve as interpreter and guide. The photograph of the white-haired Bengali bard, accompanied on his left side by the urbane Xu and, on the right, by the beautiful poetess Lin Huiyin (1904–1955), became one of the most iconic images in modern Chinese literature. Tagore's 1913 prose poem collection, *The Crescent Moon*, was to become the namesake of the literary society that Xu founded in the 1920s.

Arguably the most famous poet in the history of modern Chinese poetry, Xu Zhimo is known not only to academics and poetry readers but also to the general public in the Chinese-speaking world. A national figure during his lifetime, Xu started writing poetry relatively late, after he had moved from New York to London in 1920 at age twenty-three. It was his immersion in English literature and friendships with British men and women of letters that inspired him to write poetry and shaped his literary taste and style.

From his letters, in which he mentions reading the works of Virginia Woolf (1882–1941) and James Joyce (1882–1941), we know that Xu Zhimo was familiar with high modernism in the 1920s. Yet, as a result of both natural dispositions and aesthetic choices, he was most drawn to romanticism. He went on to become the most important romanticist in China. Despite a short creative career that spanned from 1920 to 1931, he changed the course of modern Chinese poetry by introducing this new aesthetic paradigm.

Xu became interested in modern poetry in 1917 when Hu Shi (1891–1962), then an overseas student in the United States, advocated reform of the stifling and decayed tradition of Chinese poetry. Instead of classical Chinese, Hu proposed a new poetry written in the modern vernacular—hence, modern Chinese poetry was also known as "vernacular poetry." Instead of the prescribed forms and prosodies of antiquity, Hu and other pioneers experimented with free verse and other forms borrowed from the West. Instead of the stock images and familiar motifs of classical Chinese poetry, Hu advanced the notion of "poetic empiricism," basing poetry on personal experience rather than literary conventions. In the poem "Dream and Poetry" he famously says, "You cannot write my poems, just as I cannot dream your dreams."

With the support of liberal intellectuals, especially those at Peking University, modern poetry flourished. However, it was also seriously flawed. The newfound freedom and the emphasis on accessibility all too often led to shallow outpourings or prosaic expressions in early modern Chinese poetry. It was in reaction to this situation that Xu, along with his friends in the Crescent Moon Society, notably Wen Yiduo (1899–1946) and Zhu Xiang (1904–1933), introduced a renewed sense of structure to modern poetry. In Xu's view, structure is essential to poetry; meaning is made manifest through the stanzaic form and sound pattern.

An excellent example of this belief is one of Xu's best-known poems. Written in 1925, "A Chance Encounter" is a poem of two stanzas, of which the first stanza reads,

> I am a lone cloud in the sky, by
> Chance reflected in your rippling heart—
>   Don't you be startled,
>   Nor should you rejoice—
> In a blink it will go out of sight.

The first stanza has a syllable pattern of 9-9-5-5-9, and the second stanza, 10-10-5-5-10. Variation within regularity defines the form of the poem. The formal parallels echo the theme of ill-fated lovers. The twain are never to meet except for a brief moment—as brief as the reflection of a floating cloud in the water or the crossing of two ships in the night. The end rhymes further enhance the affective power of the poem.

Equally notable is the language of the poem. Unlike much early modern Chinese poetry, "A Chance Encounter" is free of the traces of classical Chinese poetry and refreshingly modern in its wording and cadence. When one reads the poem out loud, it sounds natural, sincere, and pleasing to the ear. Finally, the poem deals with the perennial theme of love—specifically, fleeting love. Yet, in the nuanced feeling it conveys, it is refreshingly different from most love poems. Instead of wallowing in wistfulness or bitterness, behind the apparent indifference ("Fine if you remember / It's better to forget") is an embrace of beauty in life and a celebration of transcendence. For all of these reasons, "A Chance Encounter" has been immensely popular among readers; it has also been set to music as a pop song.

In fact, at least seventeen of Xu's poems—including "Waiting for a Cuckoo in Vain on a Moonlit Night" (1923), "In Search of a Bright Star" (1923), "Sea Melody" (1925), "Second Farewell to Cambridge" (1928), and "I Don't Know Which Way the Wind Blows" (1928)—have been made into songs. "Sea Melody" was first adapted as a song composed by the linguist Zhao Yuanren (1892–1982), then rewritten as a pop song recorded by the superstar Teresa Teng (1953–1995) in 1974. The poem consists of five sections addressing a "young girl" as "you." The girl lingers on the beach as the night falls. Rather than heeding the narrator's warning about the rising tide, she refuses to go home but, instead, bursts into song and dances wildly. At the end of the poem, the girl has disappeared, supposedly swallowed up by the sea.

"Sea Melody" may be read as an allegory. The young girl whose singing and dancing cannot be suppressed stands for the poet, while the sea that eventually consumes the girl symbolizes boundless freedom and imagination. Instead of a tragedy, the disappearance of the girl into the sea suggests an act of immersion and identification. As a romanticist, Xu espoused a poetics of multiple dimensions. He saw love as sacred and inviolable, he sang of the innocence of children and the inspiration of nature, and he never tired of pursuing spiritual freedom. Along with many other poems from his mature period, "Sea Melody" represents the pinnacle of Xu's accomplishment.

During the Sino-Japanese War (1937–1945) and the ensuing civil war between the Nationalists and the Communists, Xu's writings were understandably eclipsed by the political turbulence. After the founding of the People's Republic of China in October 1949, he became persona non grata. His work was unavailable to readers except as a target of criticism for its "petty-bourgeois decadence."

On the other side of the Taiwan Strait, however, Xu regained popularity for two reasons. First, under Nationalist rule most writers of the May Fourth era were banned, either for displaying leftist leanings or simply for staying on the mainland. Xu was one of the few pre-1949 writers who were considered "safe." His poetry and prose inspired a new generation of writers in Taiwan in the 1950s and 1960s. Xu provided an important paradigm for many poets, who imitated his poetic forms, use of rhymes, and fluent use of language. His lyrical prose, as represented by such pieces as "The Cambridge I Knew," "Chitchats at a Mountain Abode in Florence," and "Self-Dissection," was also widely read; the first piece even found its way into textbooks. His epistolary diary, addressed to his second wife, Lu Xiaoman (1903–1965), was extremely popular for its bold individualism and intensity of feeling. The first entry begins with this sentence: "Happiness is still not impossible, this is my recent discovery." And the poet goes on to say, "I hate mediocrity, ordinariness, triviality, vulgarity. I love expressions of personality."

Another reason for Xu's lasting legacy is his legendary life, as seen through the lens of his poetry and prose. His idealism, rebelliousness, and romanticism have mesmerized generations of readers. To his contemporaries, his natural charisma and endearing personality were irresistible. In "On Xu Zhimo," the renowned writer and translator Liang Shiqiu (1903–1987) recalls, "It was Zhimo who was always gay and brought joy to everyone. Sometimes he was late, and the gathering would be lackluster. The minute he showed up, it was like a whirlwind passing through or a torch lighting up everyone's heart.…He made everyone happy." In "An Elegy on Xu Zhimo," an essay written on December 3, 1931, thirteen days after a plane crash killed the poet, his close friend Hu Shi reminisced,

> Friends simply could not do without him. He was our link, glue, and yeast. In the past seven or eight years, there have been quite a few controversies and disputes on the literary scene. Many who used to be close friends stopped talking to one another. But I have never known anyone to hold a grudge against Zhimo. Nobody could resist his empathy. Nobody could sever ties with him. He had infinite love, which brought people together.…He harbored neither suspicion nor jealousy.

In addition to his charisma, Xu's dramatic love life made him well known among his contemporaries. His unsuccessful courtship of Lin Huiyin is memorialized in his early poetry, and his confession of love to Lu Xiaoman arguably became *the* model for lovestruck young men and women in China. His divorce and second marriage scandalized not only the literary scene but the entire country. According to contemporary reports, Xu invited his teacher Liang Qichao to make some congratulatory remarks at his wedding to Lu. Instead, Liang scolded Xu in front of all the guests. It is also a widely accepted view that Xu's death was indirectly caused by the financial difficulty he found himself in as he struggled to support Lu's lavish lifestyle. Regardless of what one thinks of his personal life, by all standards Xu endeavored to live by his professed ideals. In poetry as in life he was a firm believer in the divine nature of love, for which he was willing to sacrifice everything, including life itself. "In Search of a Bright Star" presents just such a heroic quest. The protagonist in the poem rides resolutely into the night on a limping, blind horse. The break of dawn witnesses both the horse and the rider lying dead in the wilderness, overcome by physical exhaustion. The poet who starts out as a pilgrim ends a martyr.

Since the late 1970s, when China reopened its door to the West, Xu has not only made a dramatic comeback but also become arguably the best-known poet in the country. During the renaissance and so-called culture fever of the 1980s, scholars and general readers rediscovered his work and were fascinated by his life. Today, Xu is as close to a household name in China as any poet may hope to be, partly as a result of *April Comes to the Human World*, an extremely popular television series based on his life story aired in 1999.

Granted, there is a price to pay for popularity. Xu's poetry and prose tend to be treated as mere illustrations of his biography rather than read for their intrinsic artistic merits. He is typically represented by a small number of poems, such as "A Chance Encounter" and "Second Farewell to Cambridge," especially the concluding lines of the latter:

> Quietly I am leaving,
>   Just as quietly I came;
> I wave goodbye with my sleeve
>   Not taking a whiff of cloud.

The beautiful imagery and melodious language of poems like this charm readers so much that they often overlook deeper meanings. Some poets in China even dismiss Xu, and by extension romanticism, as sentimental and shallow, a perception that led to a polemic on the poetry scene in the mid-2000s. Such criticism stems from a misunderstanding of both romanticism and Xu and was underscored by an evolutionist view of literary history. As pointed out earlier, Xu's affinity with romanticism is based on natural dispositions and aesthetic choices, an affinity that is both comprehensive and profound. For both romanticism and Xu, the recurring themes of spiritual communion with nature, the redemptive power of the child, and the eternal persistence of love, as well as the emphasis on creative imagination and freedom, go far beyond a superficial sense of lyricism or love.

In Xu we find not only a gifted poet but also a new paradigm for the modern poet: iconoclastic, individualistic, and innovative. In Xu we see a brilliant example of the development of modern poetry in Chinese. In Xu we reaffirm the conviction that modern poetry will have a bright future.

BIBLIOGRAPHY: Leo Ou-fan Lee, *The Romantic Generation of Modern Chinese Writers* (Cambridge, MA, 1973). Michelle Yeh, *Modern Chinese Poetry: Theory and Practice since 1917* (New Haven, CT, 1991).

MICHELLE YEH

1924 · MAY 30

"The very survival of China depends on if the Chinese people are asleep or awake." —Sun Yat-sen

Enchantment with the Voice

On May 30, 1924, while convalescing in Guangzhou, Sun Yat-sen (1866–1925) accepted an invitation from China Evening News to speak at the Leisure Time Social Club in the Nandi district. These speeches were recorded by a gramophone and later reproduced on three 78-rpm Bakelite resin records that included two lectures in Mandarin and one in Cantonese. These rare treasures are the only extant complete recordings of Sun. Today the originals are practically impossible to obtain, but thanks to digital technology it is easy to find and even download them at any number of websites. The text of the speech "Compatriots Should All Support the Three Principles of the People" was published in 1928, for the third anniversary of the approval of the Premier Memorial Edition of *The Collected Speeches of Mr. Sun Yat-sen.* This four-paragraph Mandarin transcript is subtitled "Recorded on the thirtieth day of May in the thirteenth year of the Republic, at the invitation of Shanghai's China Evening News, in Guangzhou." The shouts of "Everyone, wake up! Wake up! Wake up!" in this text were reprinted in numerous versions following this publication, though the speech's title is sometimes different. The transcript was not accurate, and these shouts are not present in the original live recording.

Oratory was of course a special gift of Sun's, as well as his primary means of espousing revolution, raising funds, and mobilizing the masses. Sun once said of himself, "When I was younger I went to America, and there I heard famous orators give speeches, each with their own distinctive style. I practiced speaking and refined my techniques, and over time I naturally became a speaker with my own individual style." Besides preparing his lectures and polishing his poise in the live setting, Sun also placed special emphasis on the daily practice of posture and intonation. It is a pity that these indispensable elements of speechcraft cannot be fully discerned through shorthand notes or complete transcripts.

The emergence of public speaking during the late Qing was certainly a consequential event. In 1899, Liang Qichao (1873–1929) sought the advice of the Japanese politician Inukai Tsuyoshi (1855–1932), who defined schools, newspapers, and oratory as "the three effective weapons of disseminating civilization." Moreover, Liang's understanding of the Chinese educational system's obstinacy led him to firmly believe that "those citizens who are less literate should make good use of public speaking." Subsequently, throughout the twentieth century in China, to effectively advance ideological enlightenment or social mobilization, regardless of whether in service of a political party, school of thought, or individual, the weapon of "oratory" was an absolute necessity.

Since its rapid rise during the late Qing, the practice of oration has had a profound impact not only on political, social, academic, and cultural activities, but also on the formal development of the Chinese essay. These "voices" written down on the page, which can include speech drafts, notes of proceedings, and edited transcripts, as well as essays that imitate speeches, represent a significant contribution to the development of the vernacular movement and the genre of essay writing. Oration in a public forum is distinct from the kind of written texts that have existed since ancient times. A speech cannot be overly bookish, nor can it be packed with quotations from others; speeches should avoid unpronounceable expressions and must use colloquial expressions whenever possible; a speech stresses a major train of thought and should exhibit exuberance and uninhibitedness. Only by possessing these features will a speech produce the desired results in a live setting.

Every benefit carries with it some drawback, and in this case the downside confronting public oratory was that speeches were hurriedly edited into essays, in order to expedite their swift dissemination. Inevitably, that crucial sense of spontaneity inherent to its live delivery is diminished. Things such as accent, intonation, gesture, cadence, and even the speaker's various uses of body language are plain to see for a live listening audience; likewise, feelings and atmosphere, so vital to the speaker, are unable to be rendered in written language. Modern history has seen many gifted political and academic orators whose brilliant speeches we can only appreciate as written texts, unable to be truly listened to and learned from.

This is not a technical impediment, but a conceptual problem. According to a great many scholars throughout history, only what is written on the page is considered authentic discourse; voices that get carried away by the wind are simply not held in serious regard. The invention of the gramophone, however, was destined to change everything. In 1877, the American Thomas Edison (1847–1931) invented the phonograph, and a mere twenty years later its successor, the gramophone, had attained global popularity. The earliest gramophones and records were imported to China around 1897 by the English company Moutrie, located on Nanjing Street in Shanghai. Leafing through the newspapers of the late Qing and early Republican eras in fact reveals many advertisements promoting the Moutrie brand. The earliest extant records of Peking opera from 1904 were manufactured abroad and marketed domestically; in 1917, the Pathé Orient Recording Company and the Great China Recording Company started producing and cutting records in Shanghai—the latter receiving substantial support from Sun, who personally christened the company with its name. In other words, by 1917 Chinese companies were able to record, manufacture, and distribute a select number of voices. Based on business considerations, along with consumer purchasing power and tastes, the content of these records was limited to Peking opera and other traditional dramatic arts, along with popular music and a certain number of educational products. Before Sun, there had never been a politician who consciously used this particular medium to disseminate his ideas.

On December 30, 1923—six months before his recording was made— Sun published a long speech he had made to the Nationalist Party in Guangzhou. In the address he stressed that "the success of the revolution depends entirely on propagandism." He elaborated, saying:

> We will make use of what history has borne out: civilization's progress around the world is for the most part the result of propagation. For example, where did Chinese culture come from? It was entirely the result of propagation. Everybody knows the most renowned person in

China is Confucius, who traveled throughout the various kingdoms. Why did he do this? To spread the lessons of the sage-kings Yao and Shun, King Yu of the Xia Dynasty, King Tang of the Shang, kings Wen and Wu of the Zhou, and the loyal minister Duke Zhou.... Today, the reason that China's old culture remains on par with the new culture of Europe and America is because of Confucius' achievement in propagation more than two thousand years ago.

In his later years, Sun came to realize that, with the exception of military affairs, nothing was more significant than propaganda to the revolutionary endeavor. While effective propaganda messaging requires more varied means than just making speeches, oratory is the paramount method for awakening the masses and mobilizing society. As he came to recognize the growing weakness of his own body, Sun decided to make use of this new technology to facilitate the dissemination of his thought.

Sun's decision was actually quite prescient; less than one year after making this recording, he died of illness in Beijing. While on one hand we may sigh at the rarity of this recording, on the other hand we cannot help but think how wonderful it would be if other esteemed figures who were as accomplished and fond of oration during that era, such as Cai Yuanpei (1868–1940), Song Jiaoren (1882–1913), Lu Xun (1881–1936), Li Dazhao (1889–1927), Tao Xingzhi (1891–1946), Wen Yiduo (1899–1946), and so on, had also left behind recorded materials. "Voice" must be differentiated from "writing," just as "listening" is not the same as "reading"; amid the turbulent storms of twentieth-century Chinese history, speeches or essays written in an oratorical style naturally deserve special recognition. Even more ideal, however, would be the preservation of these voices alongside their writings.

A rare historical echo to this case can be found in Mao Zedong's (1893–1976) speech "The Chinese People Have Stood Up." As the distillation of a century's worth of China's blood, tears, and hope, this sentence is singularly capable of arousing a sense of national pride. Most credit Mao's turn of phrase to his speech from the Tiananmen rostrum, in which he announced the establishment of the People's Republic of China on October 1, 1949; but, in fact, this is incorrect. The actual source of this quote is a speech given ten days prior on September 21, when Mao gave the opening address to the Chinese People's Political Consultative Conference

First Plenary session. This forceful, resonant line was first transcribed in the *People's Daily* on September 22, 1949, and later included in the fifth volume of *Selected Works of Mao Zedong*. If we appraise this speech as a revised essay, it is not necessarily brilliant as such. However, delivered in his thick Hunanese accent, Mao had the live audience of the time burning with righteous ire at the lines "Fellow Delegates, we are all convinced that our work will go down in the history of mankind, demonstrating that the Chinese people, comprising one quarter of humanity, have now stood up." Following more than a half century of reiteration, it is further ingrained in people's minds, to the extent that if one reads it aloud with clear and proper pronunciation, it actually loses some of its original power as a monumental declaration.

It is fascinating how these two speeches by Sun and Mao resonate with one another in terms of their substance. Both articulate how China, in the course of its long history, has risen up in the face of great adversity; the former, nevertheless, cries out with deep heartache, while the latter expresses an exultant triumph. Both employ a literary language; the former pairs "sleeping and waking," while the latter literally calls one "to rise and stand." These dynamic methods of representation, so vivid, penetrating, and rousing, are especially suited to a public address.

Twenty-five years separate Sun's plea that "the very survival of China depends on if the Chinese people are asleep or awake" and Mao's proud assertion that the "Chinese people have stood up." Preceding Sun's use of the gramophone in 1924 by another twenty-five years, however, is Liang's "Treatise on Liberty: Three Effective Weapons of Propagating Civilization." Regardless of whether the speech preserved by the gramophone is genuine, or whether the speech that was transcribed and revised into an essay is spurious, each helps us form an understanding of the kind of voice that could resonate with and stir the soul of twentieth-century China. In this sense, the question whether these speeches should be considered "literature" is in reality not terribly important.

CHEN PINGYUAN
Translated by Andy Rodekohr

1925 · JUNE 17

"When I turn to ashes, you will see me smile!"

Lu Xun and Tombstones

What I know of graveyards, I first learned in East Berlin, at the former home of Bertolt Brecht (1898–1956). He and his wife were both laid to rest there; the grave markers were two large stones, each differently shaped, both with only their names written on them.

In 1926, the flames of revolution were burning bright as the Northern Expedition reached its climax; conspiracies and the danger of violence lurked everywhere. Lu Xun (1881–1936), who had moved to southern China, had not yet been drawn into the vortex. He was living alone at Xiamen University and occasionally learned about the clamor and commotion in Guangdong through letters from his beloved. As he writes of his experience one evening, "They were still putting on a puppet show at the South Putuo Temple. The sounds of gongs rang out now and then and the night seemed to grow increasingly quiet in the spaces between them." He later published these essays—written while looking out at the jujube trees beneath his window—in a collection that also included four essays written in ancient-style prose (*guwen*) that discussed Carolus Linnaeus (1707–1778) and Friedrich Nietzsche (1844–1900).

> Although I know full well…that we cannot recover our thoughts and feelings from the past, I cannot be so ruthless in letting go. I still want to gather these dregs together and make a new little grave, both to cover them in the ground and to leave a memento.

"To cover them in the ground and to leave a memento." Lu Xun's collection *The Grave* is a past life brought together in writing, while Brecht's gravestone virtually rejects the written word. In their own way, each grave buries "a body from the past or what had been" on "a little hill."

The fates of these metaphorically and actually wordless gravestones are largely the same. At the Ming Tombs on the outskirts of Beijing, all but the tomb of the Yongle Emperor are without writing. To explain why would require a long story about politics in the court. The most famous wordless markers are the wordless stele at the top of Mount Tai and the wordless stele erected in honor of Tang-dynasty Empress Wu Zetian (624–705 CE) at the Qianling Tombs. Many stories have been told about why China's first emperor, Qin Shi Huang (260–210 BCE), would erect a wordless stele atop Mount Tai, but none can be shown to be true; Empress Wu Zetian's wordless stele follows along with this history of wordless markers, a fact that makes the arguments over the centuries about her successes and failures all the more contentious.

In fact, the tomb of Sun Yat-sen (1866–1925), which lies in the southern foothills of the Purple Mountain in Nanjing, is also a wordless monument. After Sun died, the Nationalist Party (Kuomintang) had planned to have Nationalist politicians Wang Jingwei (1883–1944) and Hu Hanmin (1879–1936) write a funereal inscription, but this idea ran into opposition. Zhang Taiyan (1868–1936), a leading intellectual who had called for the overthrow of the Qing dynasty and the establishment of the Republic of China, was then asked to write an inscription instead. Zhang's "Memorial to Master Sun," written in four-character lines, was deep and powerful: "Heaven brought our Master Sun to serve as a bell to ring out to the world; its sound was harmonious, and his words set the standards for all." When the memorial hall for Sun was completed in 1929, the Nationalist leader Chiang Kai-shek (1887–1975), who oversaw the construction of the complex, prevented Zhang's funerary inscription from being used, so that the mausoleum had a memorial stele but no inscription. Though now famous around the world, the four characters for *tian xia wei gong*—"the world belongs to all"—were added later.

Brecht's wordless headstone is neither arrogant nor humble, but something else entirely. Whether under the warm and brilliant sun or in the cold, hard rain, the window of his library looked out straight to that inevitable end point, perhaps a comment on his understanding of his existence, or a reflection of the era in which he lived. He and his second wife, Helene Weigel (1900–1971), certainly discussed their shared resting place many times. Anyone familiar with Brecht's personal life might laugh a bit at the idea of a "shared resting place," but whether they were faithful is not the same question as whether they knew one another—it was absolutely true that they shared the same interests and the same stage. Side by side, these two stones now look up to the window they once looked through. Their bodies are gone, and the desire and spirit that boiled over are now frozen in stone, facing one another.

Passing Brecht's wordless headstone, on the right we find a graveyard where Johann Gottlieb Fichte (1762–1814) and Georg Wilhelm Friedrich Hegel (1770–1831) are buried. They lie in the same row. Hegel, a critic of Fichte, is separated by one space from the target of his criticism. His short headstone tells of the latecomer's humility and unwillingness to compromise; on the stone is written only his full name and dates of birth and death, nothing more. Unlike Fichte's idea of the absolute self and recognition of the self, Hegel argued that recognition emerged from the conflict between master and slave; when the Other is left behind, there is no way to establish the identity of the self. It may be that the two gravestones imply a politics of recognition and self-recognition.

Fichte said, "I am I!"

"No, I am we!" Hegel insisted.

But is there any continuity with "we" who came after them? There probably is, because "we" name Hegel. For varying reasons, this continuous "we" is always renaming the names carved on the darkening stones. This is a refusal of the dialectic. Hegel's nearly wordless headstone seems to say, Everything will be rewritten in "my" name.

Even the most forward-thinking members of China's gentry elite, such as Liang Qichao (1873–1929), a leading reformer of the early twentieth century, would say, I am I, but I am also We. This is not the master-slave relationship, but one family made up of people who do not need conflict to recognize one another. In 1998, the magazine *Dushu* (Reading) and the Unirule Institute of Economics (Tianze jingji yanjiusuo) held a joint conference to mark the one hundredth anniversary of the Hundred Days' Reform of 1898. Much of the event focused on Liang and his teacher, Kang Youwei (1858–1927). In 1998, the participants were still able to sit and have a conversation in the same room. Nowadays, however, it is all too clear that the left and the right have parted ways like Hegel and Fichte—but they may never come back together, not even at the end of their lives.

I remember visiting Karl Marx's (1818–1883) grave in London a few years ago, where I was surprised to find that Herbert Spencer (1820–1903) was across a small road from Marx. This was a war that never ended, a standoff that began in the nineteenth century between communism and social Darwinism. I doubt that many people make a special trip to see Spencer, but his works and their many permutations are still very alive in the world, even if few know how much this is the case. According to the edition of

Spencer's work edited by the sociologist Talcott Parsons (1902–1979), "modernization" and the theories surrounding it were direct successors to Spencer's social Darwinism. The gravestone stands in silence, but each visitor who walks by harbors a different feeling rooted in the beliefs or sentiments he or she brings to this man's grave. In this sense, all that concludes one debate is a debate held by another generation. Even if the titles, terms, and phrases might change, the fundamental disagreements persist with the same passion.

We live among memorial markers of all kinds, and they define our individual positions. The grave of Liang lies in a family graveyard that is peaceful, elegant, and stately. In this secluded mountain valley, the man known as a new-style intellectual is treated as a venerable member of the gentry elite. Wife and concubine lie on either side of "the self" (*ziwo*), and sons, daughters, and grandsons all have their place and order, generation by generation. The "self" extends out through the family, accepting that it became part of a natural legacy and inheritance. This man of the Chinese "enlightenment" who was inspired by Immanuel Kant (1724–1804), Fichte, and Hegel, proved in his treatment of himself after death that he belonged to another kind of "universal particular," but was not quite able to elevate the "particular" to the level of the "universal." In the world that existed after his death, neither New Thought nor the May Fourth Movement had ever happened.

Hegel's "we" is "I," while Liang's "I" is "we." If he were to comment on the debate between Hegel and Fichte, Liang would probably say, I am we—a perfectly ordered world. The struggle between Brecht and Weigel goes on: love and betrayal, the passions of the stage, and the eventual convergence between life and performance. But in this story that goes on without limits, some things are added and some flavors change. What are they?

Night falls and a light rain slants through the sky; a hundred scenes flash before the eyes with each variation of wind and rain, night and day. While the light shines across the room, spirits gaze at me through the graveyard's endless dark. They might ask, just who is this person stooped over his desk, the one who goes reading gravestones in the daylight, sizing them up?

"When I turn to ashes, you will see me smile." These words were written on June 17, 1925. They were composed in Beijing, at Number 21, Section 3 of West Fuchengmen Road, in a room off the courtyard called the Tiger's Tail, facing two jujube trees. That year, Lu Xun was forty-four years old, engaged in a secret love affair. Even so, the prose poem he wrote, "The Epitaph," shows us something terribly cold, frozen to the marrow.

> I dreamed I was standing before the stone tablet of a tomb, reading the inscriptions on it. The tablet, made apparently of sandstone, was crumbling away and overgrown with moss. The fragments left of the inscription read:
>
> "…contracted a chill while singing and roistering; saw an abyss in heaven. In all eyes saw nothing; in hopelessness found salvation.…
>
> "There is a wandering spirit which takes the form of a serpent with poisonous fangs. Instead of biting others, it bites itself, and so it perishes.…
>
> "…Begone!…"
>
> Not until I went round to the back of the tablet did I see the solitary grave. No plants grew on it, and it was in ruins. Through a large gap I saw the corpse, disemboweled, its heart and liver gone. Yet its face bore no trace of either joy or sorrow, but had the inscrutability of smoke.
>
> Before I could turn away in doubt and dread, my eyes fell on the mutilated inscription on the back of the tablet:
>
> "…I tore out my heart to eat it, wanting to know its true taste. But the pain was so agonizing, how could I tell its taste?…
>
> "…When the pain subsided I savored the heart slowly. But since by then it was stale, how could I know its true taste?…
>
> "…Answer me. Or, begone!…"
>
> I was eager to be gone. But the corpse had sat up in the grave. Without moving its lips, it said:
>
> "When I turn to ashes, you will see me smile!"
>
> I hurried away, not daring to look back, for fear I see it coming after me.

BIBLIOGRAPHY: Lu Xun, "The Epitaph," in *Wild Grass*, trans. Yang Xianyi and Gladys Yang (Beijing, 1974), 44–45.

WANG HUI

Translated by Michael Gibbs Hill

1925 · NOVEMBER 9

"What we must say about the realism and abstraction and stylization of Mei Lanfang's art is that, exactly as in the case of classical Chinese art, we are astonished at the precision of its realistic notations and renderings, and are dazzled by the place these take in the highly stylized and removed whole that the work of art becomes."
—Stark Young, *New Republic*, 1930

Mei Lanfang, the Denishawn Dancers, and World Theater

On November 9, 1925, the critic, curator, and lecturer on Far Eastern art Benjamin March (1899–1934) was living in Beijing and made the following entry in his diary:

> This evening we went…to see the Denishawn Dancers who are on a world tour and are giving three nights to Peking audiences. It seemed to us a very good show, perhaps better because we have so little chance to see performances of this type in Peking. The greatest interest of the evening was that the great Chinese actor, Mei Lanfang, was present to watch the Denishawn Dancers. At the conclusion of their program, he appeared in a charming one act play based on a famous old Chinese legend. [It was the story] of a General and his beloved mistress who, for love of him and because his enemies demanded it, was willing to take her own life that his might be spared. The acting was exquisite, the costumes dazzling, and the gestures and singing which accompanied all Mei Lanfang did [were] delighting. Miss [Mary] Ferguson [the head of the Peking Society of Fine Arts in the 1920s] told us later that at the conclusion of the entire program the Chinese actor was photographed with Miss St. Denis and Mr. Shawn and then asked them to

tea the following afternoon. At that tea, Mei Lanfang presented Miss St. Denis, whose work he greatly admires, with the costume he wore in the play he gave the night we were there, and when she dressed in it he showed her how to walk in imitation of the Chinese woman's manner and style.

This historical encounter of China's foremost actor, Mei Lanfang (1894–1961), with Ruth St. Denis (1879–1968) and Ted Shawn (1891–1972), the founders of American modern dance, came about under trying conditions. Japan had been the first stop on the group's Oriental tour. Their performances were described as a "triumph," and they had met and seen on stage Japan's most prominent *kabuki* actors. Now St. Denis and Shawn led their Denishawn dancers to a China ravished by incessant fighting between different warlords in the north. Their trains were halted and the group had to journey by boat from their port of entry, Dalian, to Tianjin in order to get to Beijing. The group almost did not make it. In her diary, St. Denis exclaimed, "On to Peking! First we go and then we don't—now we stay and now we go! You see there is a war on in China. Hast ever heard of war in China?" When they finally made it, they found out that Mei, the main reason for their visit to Beijing, had canceled all public performances because of the fighting. Had their encounter never happened, the troupe might have returned home with the impression that China was helplessly unable to achieve even a semblance of civic order—a sentiment shared by many Chinese and foreigners at the time.

Realizing the unique opportunity offered by the arrival of the Denishawn dance troupe, however, Mei helped turn this threat of disappointment into one of the most fruitful encounters between Peking opera and modern dance. On the evening of November 9, 1925, the Denishawn group performed at Beijing's Pavilion Theater, where, as we have seen, March was in attendance. Afterward, Mei performed "Hegemon King Bids Farewell to His Concubine." Shawn later reflected on Mei's performance:

In this dance the first movement was done with an enormous circular cape, and consisted largely of postures with the cape and soft graceful movements of the hands. After the cape was removed two swords came out of the sheath, trick swords in that they appeared to be one sword at first glace, but at a certain movement in the dance suddenly became two. As the dance grew livelier the footwork became evident for the first time. The actual steps were simple and limited in variety, not exceeding a few rapid turns executed with both feet on the ground and once or twice a movement that was similar to an inhibited *Jeté tour*. Toward the end of the dance the use of the two swords became very intricate and as the swords were polished silver he achieved an effect of a network of flashing light surrounding his entire body. The power and charm, however, seem to reside mainly in his own personality, for later, when we saw other young actors attempt the same style, we realized even more the vitalizing power which Mei Lanfang possesses.

The fact that Peking opera was perceived as a form of dance was a triumph for Mei's efforts to insert dance into Peking opera. For the first time, Mei successfully brought about the unity of song, dance, and acting within this performing art form. In his highly conscious search for new sources of expression to revitalize the theater, this recasting of Peking opera rejected what Mei called the "stultified" and formulaic Peking opera tradition. On the day following the performance where Mei outlined his motivation for this change, Shawn summarized his interview with Mei:

The theatre as Mei Lanfang found it had almost died of dry rot. The drama was conventionalized to the last degree, becoming through centuries more and more divorced from real life and gradually losing its hold upon the public until its following was only from among the lower classes. Mr. Mei viewed the various foreign performances in the theaters of Shanghai and realized that the drama and dance of the American and European people were more vital, and more true to life. Very wisely, however, he did not attempt to copy foreign types of dancing, but went back into Chinese history to that period a thousand years ago when dancing was at its height. Thence by arduous study of books, pictures, manuscripts, and music, he made a recreated dance which was truly Chinese dancing at its best.

In the interview, Mei did not mention his encounter with Japan's eminent dancer Fujima Shizue (1880–1966), who in turn was the creator of a new school of dance within the *kabuki* theater tradition that left a strong and lasting impression on Mei when he first visited Japan in 1919.

"Hegemon King Bids Farewell to His Concubine," the opera Mei performed for the Denishawn group, was in fact a new work created for him by his longtime collaborator and supporter Qi Rushan (1877–1962). Based on a single scene in a fifty-act *chuanqi* (a form of opera thriving in late imperial China) entitled *The Thousand Pieces of Gold*, which dates back to the seventeenth century and tells the tragic story of the king of Chu, the farewell act (act 37) was not the centerpiece of the play, nor was Concubine Yu a chief protagonist. The new opera ends with Concubine Yu's suicide; by leaving out the succeeding story of the Hegemon King's own suicide, it transferred the central role to Concubine Yu. This momentous shift from an opera centered on the *laosheng*, or "old man" figure, to one centered on a single woman marked a pivotal and radically modern turn. With the new and innovative sword dance at its center, "Hegemon King Bids Farewell to His Concubine" quickly became one of Mei's signature pieces.

The drive to recast and rejuvenate Peking opera in China shared much with efforts to reform theater and dance elsewhere in the world. Rather than emanating from some "center," however, these diverse experiments inspired and engendered each other. The revolutionary transformation of Peking opera thus shares an impulse with the birth of modern dance. In the same manner that modern dance emerged out of a rejection of the formulaic aesthetics of ballet as it pursued a unity between nature and the beauty of the body, Mei's Peking opera was undergoing a similar process of self-criticism and rebirth in the 1920s by reengaging with the past in a search for abstract formal expressions. While Shawn was well aware that Mei's performances were as much the result of a radical recasting of the traditions of Peking opera as his own performances were a recasting of traditional ballet, in the historiography of modernism, rather than being portrayed as a modern, living art form, Peking opera is labeled a "tradition" and a "past" from which the modernity of the Denishawn group drew inspiration. In his 1929 book, *Gods Who Dance*, Shawn wrote, "Mei Lanfang is the only hope of a real renaissance of the dance art in China." With tradition as their countertext, both modern dance and Mei's unique style in fact attempted to find sources of authenticity by "returning" to the forgotten origins of dance. In Mei's case, this meant scouring fresco paintings, stone carvings, woodblock illustrations, and Buddhist temple sculptures to tap into forgotten sources of creativity from China's past, even as he and his mentor Qi were emulating the new performing and staging techniques that were being tried out on stage and screen in Europe and the United States.

The joint performance on November 9, 1925, marked one of the first direct and self-conscious artistic exchanges and collaborations between Peking opera and modern dance. Through his interaction with the Denishawn group, Mei saw that he was in sync with the modernist agenda of overcoming the calcified routines of the performing arts and creating new forms that carried the spirit of the time while drawing on resources found in the deep past and in other cultures. In a stunning example, both drew on Buddhist iconography to create hand gestures of exquisite beauty that were also endowed with spiritual meaning.

The Denishawn group wasted no time in taking up the Beijing stimulus. While still on their tour of the Far East, they went about improvising dance dramas based on Mei's signature pieces, including their formal aspects and their themes. In addition to their version of "Hegemon King Bids Farewell to His Concubine," which was now entitled "General Wu's Farewell to His Wife," these performances included "The Heavenly Maiden Showering Flowers," a play based on a scene in the Buddhist *Vimalakirti Sutra*, and "Daiyu Burying the Flowers," which is based on a scene from the novel *Dream of the Red Chamber*. When they returned to Shanghai a year later in October 1926, the group performed what was advertised as its "new Chinese and Oriental" dances.

These photographs offer us a glimpse into the inner workings of transcultural interaction and highlight the basic idea that cultures live and renew themselves by interacting with others. The images capture the process of cultural interaction with the past and with distant cultures, as well as the creative tension in generating something new out of interpreting two performing traditions through one another. May Fourth modernizers such as Hu Shi (1891–1962) insisted on characterizing Peking opera as a fossil from the feudal past. In a 1930 essay called "Mei Lanfang and the Chinese Drama," Hu wrote, "The Chinese drama is historically an arrested growth. It is not yet freed from its historical association with music, singing, dancing and acrobatic games. It has not yet succeeded in becoming a drama of natural speaking and spontaneous acting." But, in the process of transcultural exchange with modern dance, the Chinese form was radically recast. For this it drew on Chinese dance traditions

ABOVE: Ruth St. Denis in "Radha," a dance she choreographed (ca. 1906). Photograph 1926. Unpublished photograph. Courtesy of Jerome Robbins Dance Division, the New York Public Library for the Performing Arts, Astor, Lenox, and Tilden Foundations.

RIGHT: Mei Lanfang's "orchid hand gesture" photographed by Benjamin March, Beijing, 1931. Unpublished photograph. Courtesy of Freer Gallery of Art and Arthur M. Sackler Gallery Archives, Smithsonian Institution, Washington, DC.

Edith James Long, member of the Denishawn dance group, performing the silk sash dance, inspired by Mei Lanfang's "The Heavenly Maiden Showering Flowers," Shanghai (?), 1926. Unpublished photograph. Source: Denishawn collection, 1926; courtesy of Jerome Robbins Dance Division, the New York Public Library for the Performing Arts, Astor, Lenox, and Tilden Foundations.

preserved in paintings and illustrations to engage with the performance arts in Japan and the West, becoming in turn a source of inspiration for nonrealistic modernist performance styles in the West.

November 9, 1925, was not the end of this process. In 1930, Mei made a triumphant tour in the United States and the cultural avant-garde was inspired by his performances, which in this way exerted lasting influence on "Western" stage art. In 1935, Mei performed in Moscow, with the dramatist Bertolt Brecht (1898–1956), the stage director Konstantin Stanislavski (1863–1938), and the film director Sergey Eisenstein (1898–1948) (who had been alerted by Charlie Chaplin not to miss out on Mei) in the audience. Brecht's formulation of nonrealistic "alienated" acting was the direct result.

Peking opera as we know it today is the result of a concerted effort of a new generation of actors, authors, and dramatists to engage with world performing arts on both the stage and the screen in acting, dancing,

Edith James Long improvising in "Daiyu Burying the Flowers," Shanghai (?), 1926. Unpublished photograph. Source: Denishawn collection, 1926; courtesy of Jerome Robbins Dance Division, the New York Public Library for the Performing Arts, Astor, Lenox, and Tilden Foundations.

singing, and staging. In their turn, the modern performing arts that developed after the 1920s drew much inspiration from the pioneering operatic experiments of Mei and others and their engagement with earlier traditions, traditions that themselves originated from an engagement with central Asian and northern Indian performing traditions that had found their way into the Chinese empire.

BIBLIOGRAPHY: Jin Fengji, "Mei xin yuanliu yinghua guo—1924 nian Riben *Yanju xinchao* yaoqing zhuming xijujia wei Mei Lanfang quxing zuotanhui (sujigao)," *Xin wenhua shiliao* 1 (1996): 53–59. Benjamin March, "The Oriental Chronicles" (1924–1925), Benjamin March Papers, 1923–1934, Freer Gallery of Art and Arthur M. Sackler Gallery Archives, Smithsonian Institution, Washington, DC. Ted Shawn, *Gods Who Dance* (New York, 1929). "Shin bunka shiryō," *Engeki shijo*, December 1925, Chinese trans.

CATHERINE VANCE YEH

1927 · JUNE 2

Wang Guowei drowns himself.

1969 · OCTOBER 7

Chen Yinke passes away.

"This Spirit of Independence and Freedom of Thought ... Will Last for Eternity with Heaven and Earth"

On June 2, 1927, the great scholar and poet Wang Guowei (1877–1927) drowned himself at Lake Kunming on the grounds of the Imperial Summer Palace in Beijing. There was a widespread perception at the time that Wang had martyred himself for the fallen Qing dynasty, whose young deposed emperor had been Wang's student. However, Chen Yinke (1890–1969), Wang's friend and colleague at the Tsinghua Research Institute of National Learning, offered a different interpretation in his "Elegy on Wang Guowei":

Today's China is facing calamities and crises that are without precedent in its several thousand years of history. With these calamities and crises reaching ever more dire extremes, how can those whose very being represents a condensation and realization of the spirit of Chinese culture fail to identify with its fate and perish along with it? This was why Wang Guowei could not but die.

Two years later, Chen elaborated the meaning of Wang's death in a memorial stele: "He died to make manifest his will to independence and freedom.... His writings may sink into oblivion; his teachings may yet be debated. But this spirit of independence and freedom of thought...will last for eternity with heaven and earth."

Between these assertions from 1927 and 1929 is a rhetorical elision of potentially different positions. Chen seems to be saying that the essence of Chinese culture *is* "the spirit of independence and freedom of thought." This is all the more surprising because the 1927 elegy still presents Wang as abiding by the "three fundamentals" (*sangang*)—the moral authority of the ruler, the father, and the husband, although Chen takes care to emphasize their meaning as ethical ideals rather than specific instantiations. Chen thus implies that even "old-fashioned" moral precepts emphasizing authority can be embraced in a spirit of independence and freedom, especially when such ideals no longer have a legitimating context. In this sense, the simplistic division of modern Chinese intellectuals into conservatives and progressives is profoundly misleading. The retrospective gaze of cultural nostalgia can be tied to alienation, resistance, and self-conscious agency.

By the time Chen wrote about Wang's death, he was already recognized as a distinguished historian whose wide-ranging research encompassed Sanskrit, Pali, and Turkic materials; the history of Buddhism; cultural relations between China and India; and ties between China and central Asia. In the following two decades he was to write extensively on medieval Chinese political and institutional history. Chen was born in 1890 to a distinguished family of renowned poets and scholar-officials. After periods of study and research in Japan, Europe, and the United States, Chen returned to China in 1926 and became a professor at Tsinghua University. During the Sino-Japanese War, Chen ended up in southwest China. In the late 1940s, he briefly considered accepting an appointment at Oxford, in part to seek medical intervention for his failing eyesight. After the operation failed and he lost his vision altogether, he returned to China in 1949, declining opportunities to go to Taiwan or

Hong Kong. He spent the last twenty years of his life as a professor at Zhongshan University in Guangzhou.

Brilliant scholarship itself does not explain the cultural significance of Chen. What established him as a cultural icon for our time were the ways he defended the integrity of intellectual inquiry against the encroachments of political dogma, the mergence of his profession of faith as a historian with the mission to define cultural values that defy barbarism and destruction, and his embodiment of a cultural nostalgia that opens up the space for ideological resistance by redefining subjectivity and the claims of political power. All these positions are already embedded in Chen's writings about Wang, especially the summation of "independence" and "freedom," which reverberate as a refrain in Chen's writings from the last twenty years of his life. They constituted his self-definition as a scholar and as a human being.

In 1953, Chen's former student Wang Jian (1916–1966) came to Guangzhou to try to persuade him to accept an appointment as head of the newly founded Research Institute on Middle Period History in the Academy of Social Sciences in Beijing. In Chen's reply to the academy, he began by citing his memorial stele on Wang Guowei as a testament to his beliefs. He further explained that it is imperative for scholars to "pry their minds loose from the bondage of commonly accepted dictums [*sudi*]. The 'commonly accepted dictums' at the time [of Wang's suicide] referred to the Three Principles of the People"—the principles of the people's nation (*minzu*), the people's rights (*minquan*), and the people's livelihood (*minsheng*) propounded by Sun Yat-sen (1866–1925). Needless to say, the "commonly accepted dictums" in 1953 meant Communist dogma. As (obviously impossible) conditions for accepting the appointment, Chen stipulated that the institute should be permitted "not to uphold Marxism-Leninism and not to be involved in political education" and that a written dispensation affirming this should come from Mao Zedong (1893–1976) and Liu Shaoqi (1898–1969). His students were to abide by the same independence and freedom. Wang Jian had joined the Communist Party in 1950 and studied in the Marxist-Leninist Institute. Chen thus declared, "You are no longer my student." Wang was to commit suicide in 1966, one of the first victims of the Cultural Revolution.

"Independence" and "freedom" are also words Chen used to eulogize the woman writer Chen Duansheng (1751–ca. 1796) and the courtesan-poet-cum-Ming-loyalist Liu Rushi (1617–1664), the foci of his scholarly endeavor in the 1950s and 1960s. In 1953, Chen wrote a long essay on Chen Duansheng and her prosimetric narrative, *Love in Two Lives*. The heroine of *Love in Two Lives* is Meng Lijun, who is forced by intrigues against her family and her fiancé's family to take up a male disguise and to make her way in the world. She wins the highest honors in the civil service examination and becomes prime minister, eluding the efforts of her parents, her fiancé, and the emperor to expose her masquerade. The tone of the sixteen chapters tracing these events, which Chen Duansheng wrote before the age of twenty, is playful and defiant. The death of Chen's mother, her marriage, and her husband's exile put a stop to her writing. When, twelve years later, she wrote chapter 17, her husband was still in exile in Yili (Xinjiang), and by the time he was pardoned and returned in 1796, Chen had died. The mood of chapter 17 is somber and tragic: it begins with Chen's autobiographical account of her own writing and describes how the emperor finally manages to expose Meng Lijun's disguise by having her boots removed after getting her drunk. Few can forget the stark image of Meng Lijun spitting blood on the white silk cloth used for binding her feet when she realizes she has been betrayed and exposed.

It is quite likely that Chen Duansheng did not finish the book not only because of personal misfortunes but because she could not follow her own story to its logical conclusion. The pleasure and energy of the narrative for the author (and for most readers) lie in the ways Meng Lijun foils patriarchal order and imperial authority; once she is exposed, the supposedly comic reconciliation would be colored by a tragic sense of defeat, and the incongruity must have been unbearable. Chen Yinke applauds the "freedom, self-respect, that is, independence" of Chen Duansheng's thinking, evident in the ways she implicitly demolishes "the three fundamentals." Chen moved from his apology for "the three fundamentals" in 1927 to a celebration of their subversion in 1953 in part because he understood the unholy continuity between them and modern authoritarian politics. He frequently compares Marxist-Leninist orthodoxy to Confucian "thought-control" in imperial China.

In his essay "On *Love in Two Lives*," Chen Yinke patiently unravels the forgotten details of Chen Duansheng's life and times. He breaks with his earlier discursive style and introduces many of his own poems, merging his experience of wars, devastation, and repression with his reading of Chen Duansheng. He pays special attention to the autobiographical chapter 17, whose lines are echoed in his own poems and essay, which in turn acquire a distinct self-reflexive ring.

Chen brought to his *Biography of Liu Rushi*, which he wrote from 1953 to 1964, the same lyricism, self-reflexivity, fervor for rescuing a talented woman from oblivion, and interest in the disjunction between individual vision and the mores of one's times. More than the earlier work on Chen Duansheng, however, Chen's biography of Liu is colored by his empathy with the choices and dilemmas of those enduring the toll of political disorder. Chen writes not only with nostalgia for the glory and refinement of the late Ming world, but also (perhaps even more) for the symbiosis of political loss and creative energy, disempowerment and cultural authority, in the wake of the Ming collapse. The pathos of dying for or surviving a lost world no doubt spoke to his perception of the crisis of Chinese civilization during successive political movements in the 1950s and 1960s.

Chen famously describes Liu as the representative of "the independence of spirit and freedom of thought of our people." What do Wang Guowei, Chen Duansheng, and Liu Rushi have in common that they should be honored with the same epithets? In the case of Wang and Liu, one might say that they were both loyalists (of the Ming and the Qing, respectively) and in that sense stood for the right of disaffection from the current regime and the need to claim a cultural-intellectual space not governed by political authority. All three are oppositional figures that seem to bypass the dichotomy of cultural continuity and radical change. Perhaps more than Wang and Chen, Liu symbolizes the tension between center and periphery in the tradition. Learned and accomplished, she is nevertheless only a "defiant and free-spirited courtesan," a tantalizing pointer to the culture's capacity for regeneration through crossing boundaries and encompassing opposites.

The repressive forces in late imperial Chinese culture distort or suppress the "truth" or "reality" of Liu. In order to reconstruct her life and writings, Chen Yinke had to battle two and a half centuries of neglect, misunderstanding, and destruction. Many of Liu's writings are lost, and their existence or meaning can be inferred only indirectly from the works of her friends and lovers. Chen is implying that his relationship to the literary and cultural heritage of China is similarly "archaeological," as fragments are retrieved and reconstituted. But the very possibility of overcoming absence and lacunae confirms his faith in his own writings as the endeavor of cultural continuity negated by his times.

In both the essay "On *Love in Two Lives*" and the biography of Liu, Chen quoted these lines by the scholar and art connoisseur Zhang Yanyuan (815–907 CE): "Yet if I do not do that which is useless, how can I take pleasure in this life that does have a limit!" There is self-conscious irony in the epithet "useless." Only the category of "uselessness" can establish the individual's freedom to define a private realm of significance, which is in turn a response to mortality and an alienating reality. "Uselessness" may imply futility: Chen was doubtful whether his work would be published. But "uselessness" is also a proleptic reply to the possible charge that such writings about women are somehow not the appropriate crowning achievement of a great historian. By showing how Liu and Chen Duansheng became inspiring cultural ideals through their free, independent spirit and oppositional stances, Chen redefined categories of significance in history.

Chen wrote in 1952, "Where can we summon all the souls from time past?" His life and writings seem to constitute precisely one such venue for the "summoning of souls." He died on October 7, 1969, three years into the Cultural Revolution. His death was no doubt hastened by material deprivation, mental anguish, and the terror of the Red Guards' blaring broadcast right next to his apartment. It is perhaps fitting that he should be mourned as a "cultural loyalist" (Yu Ying-shih) and "the one to whom Chinese culture entrusted its fate" (Jiang Tianshu), eulogies that echo Chen's lamentation of Wang. As for the concretization of this "culture" as "independence" and "freedom," Chen already has shown us the path through tributes to the unlikely trio of Wang Guowei, Chen Duansheng, and Liu Rushi.

BIBLIOGRAPHY: Chen Yinke, *Chen Yinke ji* (Beijing, 2009). Hu Wenhui, *Chen Yinke shi jianshi* (Guangzhou, China, 2008). Li Wai-yee, "Nostalgia and Resistance: Gender and the Poetry of Chen Yinke," in *Xiang Lectures on Chinese Poetry*, vol. 7 (Montreal, 2016), 1–26. Yu Ying-shih, *Chen Yinke wannian shiwen shizheng* (Taipei, 1998).

WAI-YEE LI

1927 · JUNE 4

Lü Bicheng ascends the Swiss Alps.

The Legend of a Modern Woman Writer of Classical Verse

On June 4, 1927, while traveling in Europe for the first time, Lü Bicheng (1883–1943) proclaimed her preeminence—as a *woman* from East Asia who ascended the Alps on the Téléférique. She recorded this exhilarating experience in a song lyric using the metrical pattern for the melody "Breaching the Enemy Formation" and prefaced it with a claim for her avant-garde performance, one that tamed the awesome space and topography of the Alps in the lapidary language of the genre:

> In Europe, the Alps are highest, next is Mont Blanc, and the lower ranges are glacial mountains. Although perennially green further down, they are precipitous. Visitors must take the Téléférique suspended from a cable and sweep through the sky. I am probably the first woman from East Asia to celebrate the longevity of the mountain spirit in a song lyric.

The Primal Whole suddenly opened up
Split by wind and lightning in the dark
Implanting Heaven's Pillar aslant.
Scattered jade peaks jutting in the void look on emerald seas
In fury they would only compete with the wild waves.
Light flashes on the north and south face—
Clouds are the tidal waves
Forming their own dawn and twilight.
I find the travelers' traces
That only the flying carriage can reach.
Even if tied to the faraway red silk strand,
Its whirlwind wheels can hardly be stayed.
In this lonely corner,
Petals brighten the Jade Well peak—
An icy lotus bursts forth for the first time.

More than twenty years before, in treaty port Tianjin, then-twenty-one-year-old Lü met Ying Hua (1866–1926), founder of the progressive newspaper *Dagongbao*, on May 8, 1904. After the death of her father a few years earlier, Lü had been sent to live with her maternal uncle, an official serving in the Qing administration in nearby Tanggu. On this occasion, the young Lü had run away in anger after an argument with her uncle over her plan to visit some new schools for women in Tianjin. Lü so dazzled Ying with her literary talent and ideals for women's education that he recorded their meeting that day and copied into his diary a song lyric she had recently composed:

> To the Melody "A River Full of Red"
>
> Stirred by Feelings
>
> Dark has been our country—
> I rejoice in the ray of dawn shooting up in the distance.
> Who will sing loudly of women's rights?
> Joan of Arc.
> Eight thousand feet of snow-crested waves—grieved by a sea of evil
> I look at East Asia in the stormy tide of the twentieth century.
> If you hear mad words and weeping coming from my boudoir,
> Don't be surprised.
>
> Isolated and confined,
> Eternal as the night.
> Fettered and bound,
> With no end in sight.
> No one sees me knocking on Heaven's door—
> It's hard to pour out my angry feelings.
> Far and wide I summon the departed souls to no avail,
> There's no way to let splash the hot blood in my chest.
> Alas, a frog at the bottom of a well, my wish always denied,
> And emotions provoked in vain.

Two days later, Ying published this song lyric in the *Dagongbao*. It generated enthusiastic responses from the liberal readership and catapulted Lü to instant fame among the literary circles of the social and political elite. Ying also offered her an assistant editorship and invited her to stay at the headquarters of the newspaper while helping to raise funds for her to start the first public school for women. On June 10 of the same year, the newly radicalized Qiu Jin (1875–1907) came from Beijing to persuade Lü to join her to go abroad to study in Japan. She declined.

Lü and her sisters, along with Qiu and her close friends Wu Zhiying (1868–1934) and Xu Zihua (1873–1935), exemplify the last generation of educated women who received a classical literary training in the inner quarters of the home. The next generations, who came of age around 1919 and after, would receive their education in formal schools and universities, and learned the classical poetic genres as an academic discipline: rare would be the exceptional young women, like Shen Zufen (1909–1977) and later Ye Jiaying (1924–), who made the song lyric a part of their lifelong creative practice. Born in the waning decades of the Qing to a scholar-official family from Jingde, Anhui, the four Lü sisters were taught poetry, calligraphy, and painting as young girls by their parents. Third in birth order, Bicheng became particularly skilled in composing song lyrics, *ci*, a distinctive heterometric poetic genre. Inscribing wistful sentiment with elegant imagery, fusing nature and subjectivity, her early lyrics already exhibited an uncanny affinity to the genre's conventional aesthetic sensibilities:

To the Melody "Waves Washing Sands"

A touch of chill penetrates cloud-patterned curtains
As smoke wafts up from the precious incense.
Deep into the night I listen to rain in the little red tower:
Beautiful purples and brilliant reds—are they scattered?
I am anxious for the flowers.

Afraid to fix my gaze in the distance,
Hard to rein in thoughts of parting—
A short way from the other side of the blinds is the West Isle.
When the day comes to send off spring and bid farewell,
The flowers are anxious for me.

In comparison, Lü's song lyric "River Full of Red," with its bold display of contemporary lexicon (women's rights, Joan of Arc, East Asia) and explicit emotional articulation, is very much a product of the late Qing politicized moment and not characteristic of her overall lyric style. The lyric style she developed would seamlessly subsume her geospatial experience of modernity and Western culture in the indigenous, conventional system of lyric sentiments and signification.

During the Republican period, Lü lived a rather public life that was paradoxically concealed at the core. This may have had to do with the fact that in 1912, Yuan Shikai (1859–1916), then president of the new Chinese republic, appointed her as a secretary of the Presidential Office. She apparently resigned when Yuan began his monarchist movement shortly after. Lü also became immensely wealthy at this time, which she claimed to have been the result of her skill at doing business, although the source of her wealth remains a mystery. Innocuous incidents of her lavish modern lifestyle in Shanghai often appeared in that city's tabloid press, but Lü also maintained contact and socialized with old-style literati friends, such as Fan Zengxiang (1846–1931) and Fei Shuwei (1883–1935), as seen in her song lyrics written on those occasions.

In 1920, she realized her dream of going abroad to study. She went to New York for a year, where she attended classes at Columbia University and also took up ballroom dancing. Studio photographs taken in New York, published later in her collected works, show her sporting bobbed hair and elegant dresses, flaunting an extravagant lifestyle and cultivating the flapper image then just coming into vogue, thus making a provocative statement. At the same time, she submitted articles on American life, customs, and entertainment to the column "Free Talk" in the newspaper *Shenbao* and to a few fiction magazines edited by writers associated with the so-called Mandarin Ducks and Butterflies school. Lü deliberately circulated her dual image as a "modern girl" and "literata" back in Shanghai's burgeoning print media, announcing her unique persona.

A few years after returning to Shanghai, her desire for travel took her in 1926 on an extended tour of America and Europe, and she eventually settled down to a reclusive life in Montreux, located in the Swiss Alps on the shore of Lake Geneva. The decade in Europe, from the late 1920s to the late 1930s, marked an especially productive period. Lü wrote song lyrics and travel essays, some of which she sent back to China to be printed or serialized in newspapers and magazines. Her prolific writings culminated in the publication of two editions of her collected works in 1929. There were also three separate editions of her song lyrics, entitled *Morning Pearl Lyrics*, that were published in 1932 and 1937, all of which she mailed to friends to arrange for printing in Shanghai.

The lyric about her ride on the Téléférique up the Alps and Mont Blanc exhibits Lü's fascination with the symbolic potential of the snow-covered grandeur of these mountains. The mountainscape inspired her, as it did some women poets during the Ming and Qing, to step out of the quotidian to assume the persona of the lofty recluse—a role traditionally gendered male (thus the image of the literati-scholar with loosened hair to signify freedom in the lyric that follows). Roaming in the vast abode of the mountain spirit, sharing the snow and ice on windy heights, among clouds, stars, and the heavens, she feels cleansed and transcendent. In her travel essay about a second trip to Geneva, in June 1928—exactly one year after her first visit—she notes that she wrote the following song lyric:

To the Melody "A Fine Occasion Nears"

Climbing the Snowy Alps

Chill locks in the lofty jade mount
Sweeping past my eyes—stars that can be gathered.
With loosened hair I ascend—brushing aside the clouds,
Charging through nine layers of immortal gates.

Coming again just after a year—
It shines still with the snow of old.
I tell the mountain spirit with a clear conscience:
I have the same pure heart.

Other lyrics inscribe her lingering attachments to the world in the form of the occasional dream of her homeland, its native flora and fauna, and her lyric responses to poems and letters intermittently sent from friends back in China. She would eventually transcend the lure of the mountains, become a vegetarian and animal rights activist, and join the Buddhist sangha when the modern revival of Buddhism, led by the great masters Taixu (1890–1947) and Yinguang (1862–1940), was brought to Europe. Lü converted in 1929 and returned to Shanghai and Hong Kong to translate a sutra and propagate the dharma. She stopped writing song lyrics because, as a form of illusory attachment, they "transgress the Buddhist discipline." But her lyrical impulse returned and she found the song lyric to be "the most perfect for conveying feeling and taking hold of a state of mind or aesthetic realm." Exhausted from three years of translating the Buddhist sutra, she wrote,

> So I picked up writing song lyrics again as light amusement to nurture my faculties. But as I returned to my former addiction, I just gave myself up to the pleasure. I finished more than sixty lyrics in a hundred days. I then arranged them together with my old drafts into four chapters and copied them out without much care. From now on I will stop writing.

So she wrote in the postscript for the 1937 edition of *Morning Pearl Lyrics*. But she did not. She returned to Switzerland that year, where she remained until World War II forced her to return to Hong Kong in 1940. The last lyrics she wrote and kept form part of a small pamphlet recording omens and Buddhist signs she saw and interpreted during these years. Lü passed away peacefully in the Buddhist establishment Donglin Jueyuan in Happy Valley, Hong Kong, on the morning of January 23, 1943.

From the time the young Lü ran away from her uncle's home, to her joining the modern Buddhist movement in middle age, her will to choose and the choices she made marked a distinct strand of cultural radicalism. While Lü desired and pursued the new in multiple facets—what we now refer to as "modern" and "cosmopolitan" in her time: providing education for women, working with print media, learning English, following and helping to create fashion, and traveling around the globe—she resolutely employed the classical medium in all her prose and poetic writings throughout the many transformations in her life. In particular, she demonstrated in her consummate practice the capacity of the song lyric to inscribe a new gendered subject unlike any woman poet before or after her. In the mid- and late 1920s, ironically, she expressed her strong opposition to the use of English by Chinese government institutions, such as Customs, and, in the same breath, to the adoption of the vernacular as the national language, affirming at once the cultural and national centrality of the classical (literary) language. Although never pronounced publicly, she saw and expected others to perceive her unmarried status as a conscious choice. In Montreux, she refused a visit by her young admirer Wu Mi (1894–1978), a scholar of comparative literature and Sinologist, when he was traveling in Switzerland in 1930: he had sent her his unsolicited preface to her collection, in which he praised the melancholic beauty in her song lyrics as an effect of her loneliness resulting from never having married. Lü's literary practices and life choices remain open to reread-ing and misreading, but their alterity opens up the narrative of Chinese modernity in the twentieth century.

BIBLIOGRAPHY: Grace Fong, "Alternative Modernities, or a Classical Woman of Mod-ern China: The Challenging Trajectories of Lü Bicheng's (1883–1943) Life and Song Lyrics," *Nan Nü: Men, Women, and Gender in China* 6, no. 1 (2004): 12–59. Lü Bicheng, *Lü Bicheng ji*, ed. Fei Shuwei (Shanghai, 1929). Shengqing Wu, *Modern Archaics: Conti-nuity and Innovation in the Chinese Lyric Tradition, 1900–1937* (Cambridge, MA, 2013).

GRACE S. FONG

1927 · AUGUST 23

Sacco and Vanzetti are executed in Boston.

Ba Jin Begins to Write Anarchist Novels

In 1927, the trial of two Italian American anarchists, Nicola Sacco (1891–1927) and Bartolomeo Vanzetti (1888–1927), for an alleged robbery-murder became headline news around the world. That summer, Li Feigan (1904–2005), a young man from Sichuan who had been actively involved in the Chinese anarchist movement and had arrived in France a few months earlier, anxiously followed the news coming from Massachusetts. Li had left a Paris that was, in his eyes, "a sunless, rainy, gloomy city." As for the political cli-mate, he found all of Europe "lost in the abyss of political reaction." Indeed the 1920s saw the decline of the anarchist movement in Europe and North America. The news from China was equally bad: arrests, mass murders, and betrayals, all resulting from the recently founded Nationalist government's brutal crackdown on the labor movement. Several doyens of the Chinese anarchist movement betrayed the revolutionary cause by choosing to collaborate with Chiang Kai-shek (1887–1975) during the crackdown. To make things even worse, soon after arriving in Paris, Li's tuberculosis, with which he had been diagnosed in 1925, seriously worsened.

Following his doctor's advice, Li moved to the small town of Château-Thierry, where he became fervently obsessed with the case of Sacco and

Vanzetti. The death sentence had been pronounced six years before on flimsy circumstantial evidence, and a worldwide rescue campaign was in full swing when Li came to Europe. Moved by the high moral courage of the two defendants, Li sent letters to the rescue committee in Boston to show his support and express his admiration for Sacco and Vanzetti. Two long, warm letters came back from Vanzetti himself. In the second letter there was the sentence "Youth is the hope of mankind," which Vanzetti had uttered after viewing a picture of his young Chinese admirer. The letter set the Chinese youth's heart afire. He dreamed of the release of his two heroes and yearned for a better future for anarchism. But the hope did not last long. On August 24, 1927, news of the execution reached Château-Thierry. Li was lost in despair. After several sleepless nights, he began to jot down his inner feelings, and from his random sketches a story gradually emerged. As Li later recalled, the deaths of Sacco and Vanzetti served as the direct stimulus for *Destruction*, his first novel, which he intended to be a narrative of the life and death of an anarchist revolutionary.

After completing the novel, Li signed it with the pen name Ba Jin, which conveyed his admiration for the two greatest mentors of the international anarchist movement, Mikhail *Ba*kunin (1814–1876) and Peter Kropot*kin* (1842–1921). Li had grown up in a wealthy family in Sichuan, had rebelled against the Confucian patriarchy, and later became a devoted activist and writer in the Chinese anarchist movement. In the following decades, Ba Jin would become one of the most famous names in Chinese literature. But the pen name Ba Jin first and foremost is an emblem of his anarchist ideals. When he was a teenager, Ba Jin was deeply touched by Kropotkin's description of anarchist ethics, and he began to participate in the political activities of some local anarchist organizations. He firmly believed what Emma Goldman (1869–1940) said in a letter to him: "Anarchism is the most beautiful ideal!"

By the time Ba Jin became attracted to anarchist ideas in the 1920s, through the efforts of the first generation of Chinese anarchist revolutionaries, anarchism had become a pervasive presence in Chinese intellectual life. Before the rise of communism, anarchism served as a major source for Chinese radical thought. Even after its decline, anarchist ideas left a profound influence on Chinese intellectual thinking, with a utopian vision of an ideal society that promised to remove all authoritarian strictures and liberate individuals from any form of coercive institution. Take Shifu's (1884–1915) anarchist-inspired Conscience Society as an example. Shifu believed that an anarchist lifestyle should enable the Chinese to relinquish their habitual submission to authorities and fully develop their personalities free of the interference of institutions. He designed a set of strict moral codes and behavioral disciplines for his disciples. He required them to lead a morally clean life, as he did himself, and to strictly obey the following rules: do not eat meat, do not smoke, do not drink alcohol, do not use a sedan chair, do not marry, do not keep a family name (Shifu abandoned his family name), do not serve as an official, do not join the army or navy, and do not believe in a religion. After he died of hard work in 1915, Shifu was hailed as a moral example by the younger generation of Chinese anarchists. Shifu's influence can clearly be seen in Ba Jin's novels. For example, Gao Juehui, the protagonist of Ba Jin's most celebrated novel, *Family* (1931), like Ba Jin himself, also sympathizes with the oppressed servants and loathes sedan chairs and other forms of the exploitation of human labor.

But by the time Ba Jin was writing *Destruction*, Chinese anarchism had collapsed as a nationwide movement. Furthermore, Ba Jin might have thought that the novel would be his own dying words. In the novel, the protagonist Du Daxin's personality is marked by an absolute refusal to compromise regarding social injustice and, in a larger sense, an antagonism toward the entire reality of society in all its mundane details, which appears to his eyes as part of a conspiracy of authority. He seeks his own freedom only from within. Extremely sensitive, sentimental, and even neurotic, Du's character reminds us of demonic, nihilistic figures from nineteenth-century Russian literature, such as Fyodor Dostoyevsky's (1821–1881) "underground man" and Mikhail Artsybashev's (1878–1927) misanthropic hero Sanin. In the novel, Du's philosophy is articulated as a straightforward advocacy for hatred, which is defined as the essential force of the universe. Hatred motivates him to call for a bloody revolution to destroy the entire existing society. But meanwhile, he also believes that, as a revolutionary, he too is doomed to destruction. He composes a poem in praise of the brave death of the seventeenth-century Russian hero Stenka Razin (ca. 1630–1671) that begins with the following two lines: "For the person who first rose to rebel, he was doomed to find his own destruction."

Du, who vows to sacrifice his own life to save mankind, is driven by a death wish. In a larger context, writing performed at a historical moment that marked the demise of the anarchist movement itself signified destruction. Ba Jin, who thought he would soon die of tuberculosis, projected his own young death onto the tragic end of his protagonist's life, combining a moribund characterization with fervent idealism. Ba Jin rightly named his first novel *Destruction*. The novel evoked the symbolic "destruction" of both the revolution and his young life.

Aside from revolution, tuberculosis also plays an important part in delineating the character of Du, a tuberculosis patient, deciding the outcome of the narrative, and defining the form of Ba Jin's writing. Du's disease is not only physically fatal but also highly symbolic. In literary representations of tuberculosis, as Karatani Kōjin observes, the disease differentiates and alienates the patient from the masses. Because of its contagious nature and vicious symptoms, it transforms the patient into an individual who appears "dangerous" but also "attractive" in the eyes of others. The disease acquires an essential association with a romantic temperament, and its victims gain a superior ability to voice their inner vitality and spontaneity. The tuberculosis patients in post–May Fourth Chinese fiction marked the emergence of a new type of characterization that was often given a revolutionary significance. As seen in the works of Ding Ling (1904–1986) and Jiang Guangci (1901–1931), the tuberculosis patient is often a youth whose disease sharpens his or her sense of isolation, intensifies an inner restlessness, and, while driving him or her to the verge of decadence, also creates an ideal candidate for the romantic hero who is willed as well as destined to challenge and rebel against the established order.

The tuberculosis patient Du is undoubtedly such a romantic hero. Tuberculosis affords a palpable form to the destructive nature of his despair and agony, and dramatizes his revolutionary temperament into a psychological craze that forces him to see "destruction" as the absolute and ultimate solution to all social and personal problems. Like a prophet, who seems insane but sees more clearly the truth of the world, Du sees the entire world as moribund. The anarchist revolution he advocates is to clear humanity of its "malady." On a more profound level, the destructive "malady" that underlines Du's revolutionary temperament and actions also exhibits metaphorical symptoms in the form of the novelistic narrative of *Destruction*. For the anarchist revolutionary Ba Jin, writing fiction, as a result of his despair, is itself indicative of the demise of his revolutionary career. The form of the novel becomes a *symptom* of the chasm between cognition and action, and fictional writing, as a form to represent one's inner feelings, isolates the subjectivity and prevents it from acting out a realization of the ideal in the external world.

When Ba Jin came back to China in 1928, *Destruction* had already been serialized in the magazine *Short Story Monthly*. In the following years, when Ba Jin could no longer openly pursue his political ideals, he would write a series of anarchist novels such as *New Life* (1932) and *The Love Trilogy* (1931–1933). He would remain an anarchist in his heart until the end of his long life in 2005, or, to use his own words, he would remain a man who had faith. The strong idealistic colors of Ba Jin's novels make his style distinct from that of many of his contemporaries. His writings voice a moral mandate for the Chinese youths to pursue their ideals. When he completed *The Love Trilogy*, fiction writing became for the frustrated revolutionary Ba Jin an effectively expressive mode for spreading the moral values that he deemed indispensable for the spiritual growth of Chinese youths in a postanarchist revolutionary era. This mode can be most clearly perceived in the final volume of *The Love Trilogy*, in which the image of the young girl Li Peizhu personifies his political ideals, and in *Family*, which introduces the most popular youth idol, celebrated by many generations of Chinese readers, Gao Juehui.

Family dramatizes the conflict between the new youth generation and their patriarchs. The attack on the traditional family system is carried out through extravagant descriptions of the evildoings of the fathers, who are portrayed either as outdated guardians of Confucian morals or as hypocritical, corrupted immoralists. In *Family*, the melodramatic conflict between youths and their patriarchs is rewritten into the war between light and darkness, where the emotional capacity of youthful anger toward the family system shakes the foundation of Chinese society. The young rebel Gao Juehui is arguably more celebrated, adored, and idolized than any other youth character in modern Chinese literature. A rebellious adolescent who turns against his own family, Juehui is the archetypical hero of his time.

Through the success of *Family*, Ba Jin popularized the cult of youth, a creed closely connected to his anarchist ideals. He kept dear Vanzetti's motto, "Youth is the hope of mankind." Ba Jin held on to this belief for his entire life; he had a nearly religious faith in the innocence, rigor, and enthusiasm of youth. To borrow Ba Jin's translation of a phrase by Jean-Marie Guyau (1854–1888), a French philosopher whose ethical and aesthetic views had a substantial influence on Ba Jin's thinking, youth is "the flowering of life." This metaphor registers Ba Jin's ultimate vision of humanity. It is the foundational plot for almost all his novels about youth. "The flowering of life" is a process of the manifestation of one's vitality, not through the enlargement of the self, but, on the contrary, through the devotion, consumption, and sacrifice of the self, which serves to enrich the welfare of all humanity. Furthermore, this moral belief requires the individual's devotion to the cause to be completely voluntary—without obligation or sanction.

In *The Love Trilogy*, Ba Jin consciously foregrounds in Li Peizhu's image a literary concretization of Guyau's ethical ideal, "the flowering of life." Beautiful, energetic, and optimistic, the young girl Li Peizhu, after experiencing her moral enlightenment, appears to be a personification of Ba Jin's faith: "The vigor was growing and soon exuding from her body, wanting to be extended to others." In *Family*, youthful energies shake the foundation of Chinese society in a way that reaffirms the goal of the Chinese anarchist movement. Li Peizhu and Gao Juehui, two idealized versions of Du Daxin, revive Ba Jin's anarchist faith and deliver its core message to millions of readers, who may not know the painful passage from destruction to new life as depicted in Ba Jin's anarchist novels, but are captivated by the beauty of flowering youth.

BIBLIOGRAPHY: Chen Sihe, *Renge de fazhan: Ba Jin zhuan* (Shanghai, 1990). Arif Dirlik, *Anarchism in the Chinese Revolution* (Berkeley, CA, 1991). Olga Lang, *Pa Chin and His Writings: Chinese Youth between the Two Revolutions* (Cambridge, MA, 1967).

MINGWEI SONG

1928 · JANUARY 16

Guo Moruo writes a political poem in his diary.

Revolution and Rhine Wine

"Leafing through [the first issue of] *Cultural Critique*, I composed a poem before going to bed." Thus Guo Moruo (1892–1978) started his diary entry for January 16, 1928. He then wrote down a poem in the same entry:

> My friend, do you think the current situation is too depressing?
> This is the harbinger of the storm about to come.
> My friend, do you think the current situation is too chaotic?
> This is the eve before the new society is born.
>
> The pain of contractions has gradually reached the climax,
> The Mother's body, lying there for too long, can no longer bear it,
> We have prepared a glass of blood-red wine for celebration,
> But it must not be the wine from the banks of the Rhine.
>
> We have prepared a glass of blood-red wine for celebration.
> My friend, it is my warm blood surging in my heart.
> Let us brew a violent storm of blood in this dark night,
> In order to seize this newborn sun, this newborn universe!

Entitled "To Seize," this verse was the last of the poems Guo wrote while in hiding in Shanghai in late 1927 and early 1928. Written on a date of no apparent significance, it attests to a reversal of Guo's own fate, a moment of crisis in China's long revolution, and a turning point in modern Chinese literature.

A poet-scholar-politician of central importance to revolutionary culture in twentieth-century China, Guo made his literary debut as a lyrical poet and evolved into the founding president of the Academy of Sciences of the People's Republic. Described by the scholar David Roy as "possibly the most versatile Chinese intellectual of his day," Guo played a vital role in the invention of modern Chinese poetry and championed Western romanticism; pioneered the Marxist interpretation of Chinese ancient history and contributed to the deciphering of the oracle bone and bronze inscriptions (the most archaic Chinese writing system); redefined and politicized the genres of autobiography and historical drama; translated Johann Wolfgang von Goethe's (1749–1832) *Faust* into Chinese; and eventually became one of Mao Zedong's (1893–1976) last poetic interlocutors during the socialist period.

Controversy has long accompanied his reputation. The Chinese Communist Party (CCP) once idolized Guo as the flag bearer of China's progressive culture and the representative of "revolutionary romanticism." But many critics see him as the worst combination of a revolutionary politician and a romantic man of letters—especially considering Guo's vicissitude in aesthetic, intellectual, and political activities. The fame and infamy of the man the scholar Leo Ou-fan Lee dubbed a "left romantic" attest to one striking version of the rendezvous of revolution and romanticism in modern China.

Guo's fate in early 1928 hung in the balance precisely because he had leapt from romanticism into revolution. By the mid-1920s, Guo had already become a young icon of the New Literature Movement (initiated in 1917). In 1926, he started to get involved in revolutionary politics in Guangzhou, then the headquarters of the United Front of the Nationalist Party Kuomintang (KMT) and the CCP. During the Northern Expedition (1926–1928), Guo worked for Chiang Kai-shek (1887–1975), the KMT leader and military commander. But Guo soon betrayed his political boss by condemning Chiang's anti-Communist stance. As a result, after Chiang ended the revolutionary coalition and started a campaign of terror against the Communists, his headquarters ordered a nationwide manhunt for Guo in May 1927. In response, Guo joined the CCP and participated in the anti-Chiang Nanchang Uprising. He was lucky to survive the KMT's crackdown. Eventually he went into hiding in the International Settlement of Shanghai, and fell severely ill in late 1927. As the revolution was put to a sudden halt, his body collapsed.

However, just when it seemed the revolutionary cause had abandoned him, the muse replaced it at Guo's bedside. He later recalled:

> During my convalescence...poetic inspiration started to flow continuously. No, it was not flowing; it was more like [my existence] being invaded from outside....Whenever under the spell of poetic

inspiration, I immediately recorded it with a pencil. That grew into the book *Reconvalescence*.

Guo gave this set of poems he wrote in January 1928 an English title: *Reconvalescence* (an idiosyncratic word for convalescence; Guo probably got it from the German word *Rekonvaleszenz*). The notebook he had used for poetry then became his diary, and the poem Guo was going to write down in the entry for January 16 was to become the concluding one of *Reconvalescence*.

"To Seize" weaves together two metaphorical threads. One thread concerns the body politics of social revolution as birth pangs, while the other focuses on the image of wine as the celebration of revolution. The link between the two, of course, is the blood-wine analogy: the only revolutionary wine is our blood ("Let us brew a violent storm of blood"). Situating the reader ("my friend") on "the eve before the new society is born," and calling a revolutionary "climax" into being, this poem thus serves as a desperately prophetic gesture. Writing this piece on January 16, 1928, Guo was responding to a significant conjuncture in modern Chinese history. In his own language, *Reconvalescence* was a product of the "caesura of the revolution."

The words "depression" and "chaos," used in the poem to characterize "the current situation," not only testify on a personal level to the poet's physical and psychological status, but could also be seen as suggesting a larger context: depicting this "caesura" as a collective experience. A large number of educated youths participated in the national revolution of 1925–1927. They witnessed the twists and turns of history unfold at a dazzling pace: the military victory of the United Front, Chiang's severing of the coalition, and the nationwide massacre of the Communists. For the pro-Communist youths, a political baptism suddenly turned into a traumatic event. Calling on "my friend," Guo's poem addresses a social group of like-minded youths, and refers to their shared experience of defeat or disorientation.

Guo's writing of this poem also corresponded to the rise of "revolutionary literature" in China. Leo Ou-fan Lee notes that "when the leftist writers began to clamor for revolutionary literature, revolution was at its lowest ebb." The explosion of what was to be called the "revolutionary literature debate" dominated the cultural scene at the beginning of 1928.

As Lu Xun (1881–1936), one of the greatest modern Chinese writers, satirically observed in 1928, in the wake of the uprising, "a spate of new periodicals" suddenly mushroomed in Shanghai—the frustrated desire for revolution was relocated to the domain of literature. *Cultural Critique* was one of these new periodicals. Aiming for a "Marxist Enlightenment," the journal was founded by the newer members of the Creation Society, originally a romantic literary group cofounded by Guo in 1921. Its first issue bombarded the cultural scene with leftist neologisms, such as the transliteration of the Hegelian-Marxian concept of *aufheben* (meaning lifting or abolishing; usually translated as "superseding") as "aofuhebian." Lu Xun did not hesitate to poke fun at this translation: "I do not know why they chose this difficult transliteration, which must be harder for [proletarians] to write than the original." Such a phonetic incantation of the German concept—a linguistic putsch—bore the imprint of both the traumatic blow struck to the leftist mind and the "revolutionary literature" that served discursive "convalescence."

After reading the first issue of *Cultural Critique*, Guo wrote "To Seize." This poem has escaped the attention of most critics of Guo's work, largely because it can be easily dispensed with as a typical "political lyric," lacking artistic sophistication or poetic ambiguity. But in this unmistakable outcry for a "newborn" society, one image stands out as obscure and begs for further interpretation: the image of the wine from Rhineland, ensconced between the two references to the "blood-red wine" of celebration. Denounced by the poet, the wine from Rhineland is supposed to be a mere analogy of blood, standing in opposition to true revolutionary blood. No commentator pauses over the strange appearance of Rhine wine here. First, the most famous Rhine wines are not the color of blood—they are white wines. If Rhine wine is a poor analogy for blood, Guo's sudden mentioning of a foreign land and its white wines seems even more idiosyncratic given his emphasis on the "blood-red wine" in his heart. What did Guo mean by referring to the Rhine at a moment of China's political crisis?

The Rhine is itself an overloaded cultural-historical reference, associated with Friedrich Hölderlin's (1770–1843) poetry, the impact of the French Revolution, the young Karl Marx's (1818–1883) homeland, Richard Wagner's (1813–1883) epic opera, and so on. Guo's fleeting reference to the Rhine, in fact, embodies a more complicated intertextual rhetoric than a reader might initially assume. In early 1928, Guo was anxiously waiting for the publication of his translation of part 1 of Goethe's *Faust*. In November 1927, Guo resumed the work of translating *Faust*, a project initiated as early as 1919 when he was still a student in Japan, and abandoned after the first manuscripts were gnawed by the rats living in his apartment in 1920. Later he stated, "It was my true delight that when I lost my freedom, I was able to finish my translation." In his autobiography he also claimed that he "incorporated the experience of ten years" into the 1927 translation of part 1. Both his practice of translation and his writing of poetry marked a moment of internalization of the sociopolitical experience and a return to poetry when the revolution was at a standstill.

Guo's "wine from the banks of the Rhine" in fact comes from his translation of the German *Rheinwein*, a figure that looms large in the scene "Auerbach's Tavern in Leipzig" in Goethe's *Faust*, part 1. In his version of *Faust*, Guo translates the *Rheinwein* in this scene as *Laiyin de putao*, and uses almost the same phrase in his own "To Seize": *Laiyin hepan de putao*.

"Auerbach's Tavern in Leipzig" is a comic satire about the self-indulgent lifestyle of German academics and students. After singing comic songs about love and court politics, the students and Mephistopheles want to raise their glasses to Liberty. When Mephistopheles promises to "provide each honored guest a fine drop from my own cellar," Frosch—the personification of the freshman—makes his request:

If I am to choose, I choose Rhine wine.
Nothing can compete with what our fatherland provides.

So Mephistopheles, by way of magic, makes *Rheinwein* out of the "fire of hell." When the drinkers spill the wine, "it turns into flame." At the end of the scene, when they realize that they have been fooled by Mephistopheles, Frosch still says, "I surely thought that I drank wine" ("Mir daeuchte doch als traenk' ich Wein"). In his translation of this line, Guo specifies the wine once again as "Rhine wine" (*Laiyin de putao*).

In Goethe's satire, the Rhine wine is associated with the devil's magic and the fire of hell, and points toward the self-indulgence of German intellectuals. Guo's reference to the Rhine wine, first of all, serves as a self-criticism of China's revolutionary youths. Due to their political naivety, they were fooled by a "devil"—Chiang's KMT—and this devil's promise of revolution turned into the "fire of hell": the ensuing White Terror.

Second, it also seems to contain a mild or preemptive criticism of his comrades' obsession with the "German accent" of revolutionary theories and detachment from the *actual* revolutionary blood spilt for China. Finally, this idiosyncratic insertion of the Rhine wine into the poem is a rhetorical symptom of the political experience of caesura. Like Faust, Guo was eager to leap forward into the "joy of action and creation"—the larger world of social practice. But in 1927, he had been forced back into a literary life. Poetry was Guo's own Rhine wine, a substitute for political action. The refusal of *Rheinwein* and the call for actual revolutionary blood remained nothing more than a lyrical performance, symptomatic of the self-contradiction of an imaginary "preparation" for revolution.

The cross-reference of the Rhine wine between the domain of translation and that of lyrical poetry, therefore, could be recognized as a heavily charged allegorical figure of the revolutionary caesura. A deep mode of translation is thus discernible in this conjuncture of emerging "revolutionary literature." It involves the creative fusion of the Chinese Revolution with not only Marxist concepts but also Goethe's dramatic imagination, and ultimately means a translation of the political caesura into its historical precedents. In the diary entry of January 29, Guo wrote, "Today's China is like Europe of 1848. The February Revolution of France had a huge impact on the whole of Europe, but the revolutions in Germany, Austria, Belgium, and France all failed consecutively; the White Terror started to reign, and Marx and Engels had to go into exile." In late February, Guo boarded a ship bound for Japan, thus beginning his ten-year exile.

January 16, 1928, was only a fleeting moment in China's long revolution, but the long-neglected figure of Rhine wine serves as a snapshot of the displacement of revolutionary desire that occurred at its caesura. In it one can see a hidden mark of Guo's revolutionary romanticism: the translation of an experience of crisis into an open-ended dynamic of history.

Pu Wang

1928

> "I've never figured out what it is in me that they love: do they love my
> arrogance? Do they love my temper? Do they love my tuberculosis?"

Genealogies of Romantic Disease

The popularity of Ding Ling's (1904–1986) "Miss Sophie's Diary" was
rooted in its female protagonist's frank, first-person treatment of lust and
loneliness. Chinese literary convention at the time discouraged writing on
erotic subjects, and Ding Ling's 1928 story recording Sophie's sexual life
and search for love in Beijing titillated contemporary readers. Its popularity
also had to do with its novelty and foreignness, since Sophie's diary sounds
a lot like the 1925 Chinese translation of *Madame Bovary*. Her first diary
entry finds her cooped up in her room sleeping. She is suddenly woken by
the wind, and her head whirls with thoughts that defy her doctor's instructions prohibiting reading or thinking. In what appears to be a reference to
masturbation, she writes, "As the sunlight hit the paper window, I was
boiling my milk for the third time. I did it four times yesterday. I'm
never really sure that it suits my taste, no matter how often I do it, but
it's the only thing that releases frustration on a windy day." Sophie is a
modern, self-reflective woman, sexually liberated and living alone in the
city. She breaks from traditional social norms, but as a result often feels
lonely, melancholy, bored, and degraded: "There remained little else to
do except to sit and sulk all by myself, by the heater. The trouble was,
even sulking became routine."

Sophie's status as a modern woman is underscored by her tuberculosis.
Like many other modern tuberculars, Sophie lives in cheap apartments
and constantly engages in reflective self-pity. She fantasizes about going
out to the Western Hills, outside Beijing, where the air is fresh—and
where, incidentally, the Methodist Mission set up a tuberculosis sanatorium, managed by the Peking Union Medical College. Her diary
indicates a very intelligent and thoughtful woman, and the paradox of
debilitation and inspiration, feverish activity and frustration that comes
with consumption makes it the perfect condition to describe the semi-
liberated woman in 1920s and 1930s China, who was only partially freed
from traditional and institutionalized expectations of womanly behavior.
Sophie's story was popular in part because of her frank discussions of

sex and her ambivalent attitude toward it. She is critical of friends who "suppress the expression of their love," but she also worries that her own actions are not those of a "decent woman." She defiantly proclaims her passionate desires, yet does not feel free to indulge them. Her tuberculosis symbolizes her own suppressed desires and also her threat to social order. "I've never figured out what it is in me that they love: do they love my arrogance? Do they love my temper? Do they love my tuberculosis?"

In 1929, a health manual written in simple Chinese noted in its section on tuberculosis that "people say that 9 out of 10 people have consumption; truly, too many Chinese are dying of tuberculosis!" The perception that tuberculosis had reached epidemic levels in China's cities was probably not far from reality. From the 1920s to the 1940s, tuberculosis was by most accounts the most harmful infectious disease and leading single cause of death in China. In the 1920s, more than 850,000 people died of tuberculosis each year, and by the 1930s this annual figure increased to 1.2 million. Progressive intellectuals and Western-trained doctors, who believed tuberculosis to be particularly rampant in China in comparison to Western countries, pointed to Chinese habits and cultural practices as the primary reasons why tuberculosis was transmitted so much more effectively among its people. They came up with list after list of "the bad habits of the Chinese," citing the traditional family structure of many generations under one roof sharing brick beds, serving food with the same chopsticks used for eating, and spitting in each other's proximity as primary vectors of contagion. The Lazy Susan was even introduced to China as the "hygienic table" meant to reform family-style eating practices.

There is a stark contrast between the image of tubercular heroines dying romantic deaths in popular film and fiction of this period and the epidemic milieu in which they were created and consumed. Sophie hails from a long line of sensitive, restless women "laden with sorrow and illness" in Chinese fiction and drama, the most famous of whom was the arch-tubercular heroine from *Dream of the Red Chamber* (1791 / 1792), Lin Daiyu. It is curious that these figures of romantic agony proliferated in the fictional landscape when the real landscape was so gruesomely littered with corpses of a tuberculosis epidemic. In the early years of the twentieth century, the translation of European romantic writers into Chinese, although not at all systematic, was voracious and extensive. These writers often portrayed tuberculosis as a particularly "modern" disease—not in its etiology, but in its effects. One of these romantic, consumptive heroines was introduced to China in 1899, when Lin Shu (1852–1924) translated Alexander Dumas fils's 1848 novel *La Dame aux Camélias* into classical Chinese. From the beginning, sales of the translation were quite strong, with at least six editions published by 1906, but in the 1930s, when China's tuberculosis epidemic was at its peak, interest in this novel reached a fever pitch, with at least twelve editions of the novel published in that decade, together with the appearance of short story versions, serializations, and even a film.

The story describes the most beautiful, popular, and charming courtesan in Paris, Marguerite Gautier, and her affair with an aristocrat. He comes to love Marguerite because of her pure and seemingly virginal yearning for true love. Marguerite, to spare his reputation, leaves him and subsequently dies of consumption pining for him. The amazing popularity of Lin's translation reflected, in the words of the scholar and critic Leo Lee, "the romantic sensibilities of a whole generation gradually liberating itself from traditional values and inhibitions." Another reason for this popularity was that many contemporary French readers believed that *Camélias*, and the opera based on it, *La Traviata*, represented real events. This may have appealed to modern Chinese authors and readers who were accustomed to reading fiction as romans à clef. Either way, Marguerite provided a model of imported foreign womanhood. The significance of her particular romantic disease and wasting death, contrasting as it did with the reality of a tuberculosis epidemic that surrounded her readership, suggests that the popularity of the Chinese Marguerite was at least somewhat indebted to expectations that already had been primed by the long tradition of ailing beauties in Chinese fiction and drama.

What did not resonate with traditional beliefs in *Camélias* was often mitigated in the translation. The characterization of the protagonist as both virgin and courtesan, which is essential in the Western text, is elided in the translation, which emphasizes instead her purity and moral superiority. Marguerite's many sexual encounters with Armand are often shortened, rewritten, or removed altogether in the Chinese version; her consumption is conditioned by her desire and the inability to express it. Marguerite in China is chaster and more virtuous, and thus more like the archetypal suffering beauties from the Chinese literary tradition. While she is dying of tuberculosis, Marguerite cries, "Oh my past life! I am now paying for it twice over!" calling to mind Lin Daiyu's karmic debt, which she also pays off through a consumptive death.

For these literary characters, romantic illness was a part of their past and identity. At the end of the nineteenth century, the traditional Chinese medical term *chuanran* was adopted to translate the Western biomedical notion of "contagion." The term had previously been used to refer to three vectors of infection: direct or indirect contact with the sick, hereditary transmission, and sexual intercourse. Even under its modern biomedical refashioning, *chuanran* retained distinct traces of its earlier meaning, particularly in finding the origins of disease in the family and heredity. Some of the implications of this sort of conceptual hybridity can be found in these stories of modern women whose disease is a sign of liberation that nonetheless also ties them to traditional roles and representations. Traditional Chinese medicine discussed consumption as a disease of "taxation and depletion," usually brought on in women by excessive emotionality and longing. At its heart, consumption in premodern Chinese medicine was a disease of emotions, desire, and depletion. It could pass from mother to daughter congenitally, but it was not transmissible between people until the victim died, after which her corpse could infect someone else, likely a family member, through the passing of "corpse worms" (and hence consumption was also known as "corpse pouring" or "transmitted corpse"). The biomedical reinvention of romantic disease as tuberculosis did not displace these traditional understandings, but rather the modern conception itself became figuratively infected by its past, by its sociocultural environment, and by its literary and medical genealogies.

The Chinese Marguerite is ill more on account of her inner life—her thinking, her feeling, and her writing—than is her French counterpart, who is instead sick because of her "life of dissipation, balls and even orgies." Like the protagonist of the original novel, the Chinese Marguerite is subject to a heightened sensitivity, and her illness "continued to stir in her those feverish desires which are almost invariably a result of consumptive disorders." Tuberculosis in modern fiction is not contracted; rather, it manifests itself as a latent symptom of an inherited predisposition to desire. In Lin's translation, Marguerite writes in a letter, "I know I cannot endure—like my mother who also died because of consumption. She bequeathed to me the origin of this illness. It is the family legacy that was left to me." She, like Sophie, has escaped from her family, but not the tragedy that is her legacy. There is an inevitability to consumption in modern fiction because it was inherited as a function of "meager fate," the classic term used in Chinese literature to describe unlucky beauties. Sophie does not go to the Western Hills looking for a cure, as her European counterparts would have, seeking treatment in mountaintop sanatoriums. Rather, she accepts her meager fate, and goes to live out her few remaining days in the south.

In *Dream of the Red Chamber*, the original figure of Lin Daiyu, though supremely chaste, upsets social order because she is a willful orphan whose consumption stems from a passionate but unfulfilled attachment to the story's protagonist, leading to her death from lovesickness. Later "sequels" to the novel sought to eliminate or mollify these "traumatic antinomies" by rewriting Lin Daiyu as more domestic, more responsible, and less passionate than the original figure, but her transgressive potential contributed to her incredible popularity as a figure of fiction, film, and the popular imagination. She was even reincarnated as real women: it was a particular fashion among courtesans in the foreign settlements of Shanghai from the 1870s through the 1920s to take professional names from among the cast of characters in *Dream*, thereby suggesting something about their persona. One Lin Daiyu in particular (one of the "four famous courtesans" of the early twentieth century) was widely discussed in newspapers, guidebooks, travel essays, and fiction. These courtesan Daiyus were path-breaking figures, public women who elevated their status by claiming the roles of professional public entertainer, fashion icon, and arbiter of taste. The "real" Daiyu was, needless to say, also a threat to the social order, with her attitude, with her body, and with her popularity: "Every stinking man who talked of the courtesan quarters was saying Lin Daiyu, Lin Daiyu." The modern Daiyu was Daiyu liberated, if still afflicted.

If in the nineteenth century every languishing young woman imagined herself a Daiyu, it was no less the case for fashionable, modern young women to imagine and admire Sophie and Marguerite. But the wild popularity of these tubercular models of modern womanhood was itself a tainted inheritance for women. The figure of these consumptive characters was more contagious than the diseases that defined them, still represented in fiction as something inherited, and brought out by longing, rather than an infectious condition caused by a bacillus. For all of their modernity, the disease that defined them was not tuberculosis, but premodern consumption, a product of traditional Chinese culture. Sophie, like her disease, was infected by the transmitted corpses of romantic heroines of the past.

BIBLIOGRAPHY: Rey Chow, *Woman and Chinese Modernity: The Politics of Reading between West and East* (Minneapolis, 1991). Ding Ling, "Diary of Miss Sophia," trans. Tani Barlow, in *I Myself Am a Woman: Selected Writings of Ding Ling* (Boston, 1989), 83–103. Gail Hershatter, *Dangerous Pleasures: Prostitution and Modernity in Twentieth-Century Shanghai* (Berkeley, CA, 1997). Andrew Schonebaum, "Medicine in *The Story of the Stone*: Four Cases," in *Approaches to Teaching "The Story of the Stone,"* ed. Andrew Schonebaum and Tina Lu (New York, 2012), 164–185. K. Chimin Wong and Wu Lien-teh, *History of Chinese Medicine: Being a Chronicle of Medical Happenings in China from Ancient Times to the Present Period* (Tianjin, China, 1932).

ANDREW SCHONEBAUM

1929 · SEPTEMBER

Woman Writer is launched in Shanghai.

Gender, Commercialism, and the Literary Market

In the fall of 1929, a slick new magazine called *Woman Writer* was launched with much fanfare in Shanghai, only to fold after a single issue—a historical detail that has warranted little more than passing mention in the footnotes of modern Chinese literary scholarship. But the rise and fall of *Woman Writer* bears retelling: its story is symptomatic of complex gender dynamics at work in the early twentieth-century urban literary sphere, including the rapid commercialization of the "new woman" and ever-expanding cultural authority of female authors in the late 1920s.

Earlier in the year, the influential *Truth, Beauty, Virtue* magazine had commemorated its one-year anniversary with a special edition on "the female author." Francophile belletrist and critic Zhang Ruogu (1905–1960) was enlisted as guest editor. Articles on Sappho and Madame Récamier (1777–1849) appeared alongside contributions by Ling Shuhua (1900–1990) and Bing Xin (1900–1999), while Zhang himself prefaced an overview of Chinese women's literature with a lengthy reflection on the bluestocking phenomenon in Europe and Japan. Zhang ultimately states that the term "bluestockings" does not translate effectively into the Chinese context, but his underlying point is clear: as a newfangled specimen of *la vie moderne* itself, the contemporary woman writer demands aesthetic appreciation. What is also clear is that, for Zhang, literature itself is a decidedly masculine realm in which women function principally as inspiration: addressing the imagined authoress, he concludes the essay by noting, "Your conversation, your entertainment and companionship, your friendship, your letters, these are even more valuable and more glamorous than your handwritten manuscripts of fiction and poetry."

A quick glance at the table of contents of the artfully produced volume reveals a number of obscure names—Miss Zhijuan and Miss Jialing, authors of short stories, for instance, and playwright Miss Huishen have long been forgotten. The majority, however, were famous writers—Bing Xin, Lu Yin (1898–1934), Yuan Changying (1894–1973), Bai Wei (1894–1987), Lü Bicheng (1883–1943), and Su Xuelin (1897–1999)—most of whom apparently wrote specially commissioned pieces for the anniversary issue in the wide range of genres (poetry—both classical and modern—*xiaopin*, fiction, drama, biography, reminiscences, and criticism) that composed literature of the era. Not all the contributing authors, however, were women: Shao Xunmei (1906–1968), Zeng Pu (1872–1935), and Cui Wanqiu (1904–1990), among others, also penned biographies and critical articles for the occasion. The overt linguistic marker *nüshi* was employed to differentiate between the female and male contributors—whereas the latter are simply identified by their full names, the former are identified as women writers throughout the issue (and its accompanying publicity) though the gendered designation.

Not that the practice was novel in the Republican-era periodical press, but in the context of an issue devoted specifically to woman writers, there is an odd redundancy in this labeling. Thus Ding Ling (1904–1986), whose name is conspicuously absent from the roster of contributors, despite her newfound fame, reportedly declined the invitation for submission on the grounds that she peddled manuscripts, not the word "woman"—a prescient objection to the way in which the commercialized cultural marketplace increasingly valorized the authoress herself above the content of her writing. Ding Ling, like a good many of her contemporaries, preferred not to attach the marker *nüshi* to her name in authorized volumes of her work.

Once in print, the issue would have done little to dispel Ding Ling's misgivings. In addition to the ubiquitous female designation, the selections were accompanied by a flattering photo of the author on each title page. To the reader, the visual details on display—elegant wristwatches, eyeglasses, bobbed hairdos or permanent waves, and jaunty European-style hats, not to mention the confident poses and expressions—would have clearly signaled the exotic newness of modern *femmes savantes*. In her author photo, Chen Xuezhao (1906–1991) sports a practical bob and bangs, and a simple collared shirt, while exuding defiant self-assurance through a fixed gaze at the camera. In some cases, perhaps when a photo had not been readily available, art nouveau illustrations of feminine images by Ayao Yamana (1897–1980) and Yama Rokuro (1897–1982) are inserted. The title page of Jin Guangmei's story, for instance, features a stylized silhouette of a female nude. These editorial touches proved key selling points: the issue quickly sold a record number of copies, a publishing sensation that unequivocally established the commercial potential of "the woman writer." Moreover, it fueled a whole spate of publications marketed around the concept, among them the new magazine *Woman Writer*.

Woman Writer was the brainchild of Shao Xunmei, the wealthy Shanghai aesthete and fellow Francophile who had contributed the essay on Sappho, his literary inspiration, to the special issue. As a newcomer to the publishing business, Shao may well have seen a periodical dedicated to women writers as a lucrative venture for his recently established La Maison D'Or publishing house, and he enlisted Zhang Ruogu to serve as editor. As early as June 1929, advertisements began appearing in commercial media with announcements of its impending publication. The June 6 edition of the major Shanghai daily *Shenbao*, for instance, featured an advertisement that associated the new venture with the profitable *Truth, Beauty, Virtue* special issue by explicitly invoking the latter's record-breaking sales. The marketability of the modern woman for any number of products—whether through images aimed at selling cigarettes, pharmaceutical products, or Hollywood movies—is fully evident on the pages of *Shenbao*. The extension of the logic to the publishing industry is hardly surprising.

When the magazine eventually hit newsstands in September 1929, it proved a stunning failure, and the inaugural issue would be its last. What accounts for this reversal? Had public taste already moved on to a new literature du jour? Did this spell the (beginning of the) end of women's writing? One clue to the swift demise of *Woman Writer* may be found in *Shenbao* itself, which in late June ran a joint public statement by Su Xuelin, Yuan Changying, and Bai Wei, among others, disavowing any connection to the new magazine and its "shameless" backers, despite their earlier contributions to the *Truth, Beauty, Virtue* special issue. The ensuing boycott by established literary women resulted in decidedly meager content penned by what appears to be mostly novices and newcomers. The only writer who was to leave any kind of mark on Chinese literature was Feng Keng (1907–1931), one of the five martyrs of the League of Left-Wing Writers who would be executed in 1931. Zhang replicated his earlier editorial strategy and featured ample images alongside text. For instance, there are photos of Bing Xin as a newlywed and of the modernist painters Violet Kwan (1903–1986) and Tang Yunyu (1906–1992). But without the allure of Shanghai's famous authors, the journal failed to draw readers and folded.

The barrage of criticism directed at Zhang in the wake of the magazine's special issue may be one reason why prominent female intellectuals distanced themselves from the new venture. So hostile were reviews that Zhang eventually felt obliged to respond publicly, in the May issue of the journal, noting that reactions ranged from outrage over the explicit descriptions of love to suspicion of the commercial motives of the editors. A slight defensiveness can be detected in his response, but mostly the essay reads as a savvy ploy to seize on the controversy as a marketing opportunity. Indeed, the attention did not slow down sales, and the issue was eventually released in book form, staying in print until 1931.

So perhaps it was the reputation of the enfant terrible Shao Xunmei that put off established women authors, especially when rumors of his involvement in the elaborate Liu Wuxin hoax began to surface? The incident began as an intellectual prank in which Shao sent a (fictional) love letter under the name of a female student to cheer up his mentor, *Truth, Beauty, Virtue* editor Zeng Pu. The hoax escalated when the elderly Zeng, allegedly so taken by the young lady's literary skill, insisted on publishing "her" short story in the anniversary issue. It is not clear when the truth finally came to light, but Shao's story continued to be reprinted in literary collections into the 1930s. Contrary to the special issue's ostensible valorization—via linguistic and visual strategies—of female authorial identity, Shao's brazen literary masquerade belies a deeply condescending ambivalence toward the very premise of that project.

Above all, however, the boycott perhaps marked a protest of the blatant way in which the magazine sought to package the woman writer as part of the fetishized material landscape of Shanghai's urban modernity, including the latest fashions, imported movies, and coffee houses. Like the film starlets and socialites whose glamorous pictures permeated the tabloid press, the *femme savante* featured in the special issue is produced as an aesthetic object to be publicly admired, desired, and consumed. This visual exhibition entails a certain textual displacement: constructed as a pleasing, consumable spectacle, her physical body and appearance now compete for attention with the content of her writing. Regardless of their reasons, by the time Zhang began soliciting manuscripts for *Woman Writer*, leading literary women of day refused to lend their voices to the endeavor and in the process showed an oft-neglected facet of their cultural authority.

The demise of *Woman Writer* did not spell the end of the commercialization of women's writing. *Truth, Beauty, Virtue* had set off a flurry of publications capitalizing on the fad that would continue well into the 1930s. Thus, Shi Xisheng—an editor better known for his cookbooks—compiled a daintily packaged, ten-volume *Women Writers Mini-collection* in 1930, featuring work by writers such as Yu Hen, Hai Ou, and Wei Yuelü. However, not all advocates of women's writing in this period relied on stereotypes of femininity as a marketing device: in the ambitious series she edited highlighting different genres of women's writing, Zhang Liying opted for a neutral cover design and avoided the label *nüshi* altogether. The fact that so many experienced authors—including those who had boycotted Shao Xunmei's venture and even Ding Ling herself—were represented in the series seems to indicate that perhaps it was not the category of the *nüzuojia* they found objectionable so much as the particular ways in which it got packaged in the pursuit of profit. In fact, the literary marketplace saw a burgeoning of women's publishing. The list of works that appeared in print in 1929 alone indicates an impressive level of productivity, including the first full-length novels by Chen Xuezhao, Bai Wei, and Su Xuelin.

Cosmopolitan women of the day asserted agency in controlling their own public images—in a volume compiled in 1929, noted *ci* (lyric) poet and savvy entrepreneur Lü Bicheng, for example, conspicuously showcased photographs of herself in varied guises, from flamboyant flapper to modern educator. The result is a fascinating glimpse of a multifaceted new woman but also of Lü's own artistry in managing her identity. Other writers asserted their vision of authorship by figuring the woman writer in stories and novels. Chen Xuezhao's semiautobiographical novel *Dream of Southern Winds* (1929), for instance, features a heroine who finances her European sojourn through earnings from writing. Whereas the novel leaves it unclear if the protagonist's job as a reporter will extricate her from the domineering control of her ex-boyfriend, in real life Chen was able to support herself through her post with *Dagongbao* and other writing. The novel itself was written hastily when she returned from France to reclaim back wages from the paper (which her brothers had frozen in order to pressure her into marriage). During this stay, she published two new collections of essays, *Like a Dream* and *Remembering Paris*, in addition to the novel, while also placing work in a variety of periodicals, from highbrow literary journals to commercial venues such as *China Travel Magazine*. Once Chen put her financial affairs in order, she went back to France to complete a PhD in French literature before returning to China for good in 1935.

Public scrutiny of the commodification of the "woman writer" would persist throughout the ensuing years. For instance, in a scene from the 1935 film *New Woman*, starring Ruan Lingyu (1910–1935), a publisher greedily hatches plans to market the work of an attractive authoress by featuring her photo on the back cover; later, her suicide is turned into a media spectacle to further boost sales. As in many leftist works, the exploited new woman functions synecdochically, as both a symptom of a patriarchal culture and a potent symbol of a morally decrepit capitalist society. Women writers' representations, meanwhile, indicate that "writing women" remained a contested subject. Chen Ying (1907–1986), who had made her debut with three collections of stories in 1929, explores the particular predicament of the professional author Yushan, who contends with a literary marketplace not only in which writing increasingly circulates as a commodity, but in which her work is deemed secondary to her identity as a "female writer." The public fetishization of the female author is such that anything she writes gets (mis)interpreted as a revelation of private life. Unlike the suicidal Weiming in the film *New Woman*, the fictional author is not a hapless victim: she is presented as a knowing subject for whom the commercialism surrounding her writing is a source of irritation but hardly the stuff of existential crisis.

BIBLIOGRAPHY: Chen Ying, "Yige nüzuojia," in *Chen Ying Daibiaozuo* (Beijing, 1999), 238–245. *Nüzuojia zazhi* (Shanghai, 1929). Zhang Ruogu, "Guanyu Nüzuojia hao," *Zhenmeishan* 4, no. 1 (Shanghai, 1929). *Zhenmeishan-Nüzuojiahao* (Shanghai, 1929).

AMY DOOLING

1929

> "Some claimed that all my writings were forged."

The Author as Celebrity

When the self-described "word machine" Zhang Henshui (1895–1967) published his literary memoir in 1949, he emphasized that his motive was "to clear up the many misunderstandings people have of me." In particular, he wanted to reject the various works falsely published under his name and to respond to the false rumors about him.

At the height of his fame in the 1930s, Zhang became a favorite target of the tabloids. As the most successful writer of the Mandarin Ducks and Butterflies school of fiction—known for its middlebrow fiction and topics ranging from trashy romance to chivalric cycles—Zhang was no stranger to public intrigues, and in his later memoir, referring to himself in a combination of first and third person, he recalls how

> some claimed that all my writings were forged and written by an old scholar on my behalf. Others disagreed, asking why wouldn't the old scholar have used his own name, rather than letting Zhang Henshui take all the credit? Therefore, they speculated that the secret must lie elsewhere. Others contended that the novels were in fact mine, but were not written by me. They claimed that I had learned the foreign method of writing novels, arguing that Zhang Henshui merely dictates the works and someone else writes them out, and that there were at least three such scribes writing for me. Others theorized that it must have been a cooperative venture, with several people writing the novels together, but only my name being used—and then we split the money evenly. Finally, there were some who were convinced that

the novels were actually written by a woman, but that it would have been indelicate for her to use her own name.

Though Zhang claims to have laughed off the matter as a necessary consequence of fame ("one has to give the tabloids some material to write about"), he remained preoccupied throughout his life with the issues of authenticity, authorship, and presenting his public with the "real" Zhang Henshui.

Born Zhang Xinyuan, Zhang Henshui was the author of a massive corpus of more than a hundred works of fiction, totaling over thirty million Chinese characters. During his peak years, Zhang would often have six or seven works in serialization simultaneously and would write around five thousand characters a day, keeping track of the myriad characters and plots through a complex system of charts and outlines. He also wrote in both classical and vernacular Chinese, making use of a wide range of registers, and was comfortable with many literary forms, such as news articles, essays, film and book reviews, travelogues, and memoirs. Having started out as a prolific journalist in Beijing in 1919, Zhang later observed that by the time he embarked on writing fiction, his pen was already "slick from writing."

In 1929, Zhang began serializing his novel *Fate in Tears and Laughter* in *Xinwenbao*, which at the time was the Shanghai newspaper with the highest circulation. The novel quickly became a hot topic among the city's residents, and its popularity also marked the birth of a national literary star. By this point, Zhang was already well known in northern China, having built up a huge readership from the multiyear serializations of his novels *Unofficial History of the Old Capital* and *A Family of Distinction* in the mid-1920s. However, it was not until he was discovered by Yan Duhe (1889–1968) for *Xinwenbao*'s literary supplement "Happy Forest" that Zhang began to gain truly national acclaim. Yan notes that "from the first day *Fate in Tears and Laughter* appeared in the pages of 'Happy Forest,' it attracted the attention of large numbers of readers.... In fact, for some time now there have been many in literary circles who identify themselves as 'Tears and Laughter fans.'" Even after the serialization of *Fate* concluded, "Happy Forest" continued to run almost daily Zhang anecdotes and happenings, as well as readers' comments on the novel, side by side with large ads for the book edition of the novel.

In 1933, a tabloid reporter writing under the pen name Huayan Yigai noted that in just three years, *Fate* had been adapted for regional operas, drum songs, stage plays, radio shows, and various other performance and narrative formats. He also lists numerous spin-offs and reprints published in Xi'an, Hong Kong, Hangzhou, Wuhan, and Ningbo, as well as several pirated editions, forgeries, and adaptations from Shanghai itself. *Fate* also spawned a controversy when Mingxing and Dahua Film Studios entered into a lawsuit over exclusive rights to the story—an event that became a major news story and provided more free publicity for the novel. In contrast to contemporary culture's deep concern for intellectual property and copyright protection, the majority of writers of the May Fourth era did not take exception to these reproductions and instead viewed such processes as part of China's burgeoning cultural industry; to be imitated was a sign of one's achievement.

Following the success of *Fate*, Zhang began receiving as many as a dozen fan letters a day, particularly from women readers. At first, he would answer each letter individually, but eventually he gave up and simply wrote collective responses. At one point, some college coeds asked Zhang to publish a picture of himself in the book edition of *Fate*, and Zhang reportedly replied, "I am honored that you like reading my novels. But after you see my photograph, you won't like them anymore, so it's perhaps best I don't publish a photo." Despite this modest demurral, one of the selling points of the first book edition of *Fate* ending up being its author photo—a detail that was publicized in all its advertisements.

It is fitting that a writer later plagued by counterfeits and plagiarists began his career with a story about fakes. Serialized over six days in March 1919, the story (Zhang's first published fictional work) was called "The Real and Fake Baoyus," and describes how Jia Baoyu (a copy of the protagonist of Cao Xueqin's [1715–1763] famous eighteenth-century novel *Dream of the Red Chamber*) wakes up from a nap and finds himself surrounded by countless fake Baoyus who are all "walking his walk and talking his talk." As Baoyu walks through the garden, he is startled to also discover an array of Lin Daiyus (who is similarly a copy of Baoyu's cousin in Cao's original novel), one of whom is so realistic that Baoyu attempts to chat her up. When Baoyu sees that there is no end to this stream of imitation Baoyus and Daiyus, he exclaims, "Why do all these people, oddly sexed and oddly aged, want to copy me? Oh, Baoyu, Baoyu, this time you really have been robbed!"

Zhang's story builds on a well-established tradition of sequels and parodies of *Dream of the Red Chamber*. David Wang suggests that late Qing writers' predilection for parodying classic novels, including through sequels and rewritings, involves a play with convention and tradition that arises out of a new aesthetic of mimicry. This penchant for mimicry was aided by new technologies of mechanical reproduction, including cheaper mass printing technologies such as lithography and metallic movable type, which made possible an enormous nineteenth-century market for new editions of *Dream of the Red Chamber*, as well as a cottage industry of fanciful sequels. This practice then extended into the twentieth century, as adaptations and reimaginings of the novel were refashioned for a range of new media, including comic strips, calendar art, serial fiction in newspapers, film, and television soap operas.

A month after publishing "The Real and Fake Baoyus," Zhang published another story that was serialized over a few weeks in April and May 1919. In the latter work, "Tales of a Fiction Fan's Spirit Journey through the Underworld," the protagonist ("Fiction Fan") is summoned to the Underworld, the walls of which are plastered with advertisements for new fiction. It seems as though every title listed on the walls includes a combination of the words "flower, jade, regret, [and] tears" in bright lettering, and is accompanied by a sketch of a fashionably dressed beauty. If Fyodor Dostoyevsky's (1821–1881) vision of the devil was a world-weary French aristocrat, Zhang presents the Underworld as a modern metropolis buried in advertisements for popular fiction.

"A Fiction Fan's Spirit Journey" appeared at the height of the May Fourth Movement, but rather than merely condemning traditional fiction, the story instead reflects a concern with originality and imitation, authenticity and copyright, marketing and the marketplace, and how a contemporary writer might situate himself vis-à-vis not only great writers of traditional vernacular fiction but also the legions of foreign writers who had recently become accessible to Chinese readers through translation. In this Underworld populated by literary giants, ranging from Victor Hugo (1802–1885) and Washington Irving (1783–1859) to Jin Shengtan (1608–1661) and Luo Guanzhong (1330–1400), a fictional version of Cao Xueqin calls attention to "the question of the copyrighted reputation of *Dream of the Red Chamber*."

In his 1943 essay "A Theft of Words," Zhang expresses his distress over the manner in which his words and reputation are circulating beyond his control:

Recently, friends brought me a depressing piece of news: that while passing through Shanghai they had seen journals such as *Short Story Monthly* and *Haibao* serializing my novels. Undoubtedly this is yet another instance of my words being stolen. Since my friends did not tell me the title of these novels, I don't know whether these plagiarists have taken my old works and published them under a new title, or whether some unworthy writers have written a novel and usurped my name to get himself published. In any event, it's indisputable that this is a malicious act.

After Zhang left Shanghai following the Japanese invasion, he was often asked to write for publications operating under the collaborationist government. Though he consistently refused, several Shanghai papers began serializing his works without his permission, changing the title and printing a mimeographed version of his signature. He was therefore forced to publish newspaper notices in Chongqing, Hong Kong, and Hankou disavowing these apocryphal publications, but noted that "although I published my notices, the plagiarists continued to publish these works, and there is nothing I could do about it." He was eager to announce his refusal to cooperate with the collaborationist government, but could not prevent his name from being used without his permission. He felt, however, that if he remained silent on this matter, it would appear as though he were tacitly granting permission, and therefore declared in an article, "I cannot stash away the three characters *zhang, hen,* and *shui* in a safe deposit box, so perhaps this report won't be simply taken as an act of self-promotion?"

The length of Zhang's serializations and his close involvement with the various newspapers for which he wrote meant that many readers followed his life as though it were a novel. Unlike traditional authors, who often wrote for a close circle of patrons and friends, modern authors like Zhang typically published for a vast population of anonymous readers who nevertheless demanded a level of participation. His readers were informed of his illnesses ("Writing from My Sickbed"), of his obsession with chrysanthemums ("Buying Chrysanthemums at the Park"), and even when he simply ran out of things to write ("Xieyuedan Has Run Out of Topics for Today"). Perhaps the most intimate example of how Zhang's newspaper writings intertwined with the rhythms of his life is when he informed his readers of his young daughters' deaths, by way of apologizing for having paused the serialization of the story for a few days right before the climactic ending of the long narrative. During the six years in which *A Family of Distinction* was serialized, he writes, his eldest daughter, Wei'er, had gone from learning to speak her first words to being in her second year of school: "When I was writing this story, Wei'er would often come to my desk to ask for change to buy candy, but she would always be told: Don't bother Father; he is writing *A Family of Distinction*." Zhang notes sadly that human tragedies "are not limited to the characters in my book," as both Wei'er and his infant daughter, Kang'er, died of the flu just as he was finishing the novel that his readers held in their hands.

Zhang anticipated his own death as early as 1928, when in the afterword to *Unofficial History of the Old Capital* he notes that

> for all those who read and are pleased by my books, no matter whether I know them or not, it comforts me greatly to think of them as my friends. And long after I have passed away, when trees will be shading my grave and my body turned to dust—yet if my book is fortunate enough not to have vanished but will please future readers of a later generation—to be friends with these men and women a hundred years from now, how could that not be one of the great joys of life?

Although Zhang ultimately passed away in 1967, he has enjoyed many "afterlives," including both authorized and unauthorized adaptations of his works to screen (*Fate in Tears and Laughter* alone was filmed eleven times) and stage plays, radio shows, comic strips, *tanci* (plucking rhymes), and regional opera. There have also been a host of unofficial sequels and parodies, and the widely publicized copyright battles and ghostwriting rumors, not to mention the parallel archive of counterfeit works written under his name, including even a fake memoir.

BIBLIOGRAPHY: Perry Link, *Mandarin Ducks and Butterflies: Popular Fiction in Early Twentieth-Century Chinese Cities* (Berkeley, CA, 1981). Thomas Michael McClellan, *Zhang Henshui and Popular Chinese Fiction, 1919–1949* (New York, 2005). Zhang Henshui, *Shanghai Express: A Thirties Novel*, trans. William Lyell (Honolulu, 1997).

EILEEN CHENG-YIN CHOW

1930 · OCTOBER

I. A. Richards writes to T. S. Eliot from Beijing.

Practical Criticism in China

On October 19, 1930, I. A. Richards (1893–1979) wrote to T. S. Eliot (1888–1965) from Beijing (then called Beiping) about his work on the translation of the Chinese classic *Mencius:* "I'm now trying hard to prac-tise being on both sides of the mirror with Mencius. How successful it will be I don't know.… At the least it gives me the best exercise I have ever had in multiple definition and imagining possible meanings." Eliot had suggested that reading in a remote language was like "trying to be on both sides of the mirror at once." In Beijing in the last quarter of 1930, Richards, with the assistance of *Mencius* specialists, was testing his theory of meaning and communication to see how far he might be able to imagine "possible meanings" in a language he had not learned to read. *Mencius on the Mind: Experiments in Multiple Definition* (1932), published two years later, was the result of Richards's experiment to explore the possibility of being "on both sides of the mirror" with a foreign text.

It has yet to be recognized that *Mencius on the Mind* marked the for-mal inauguration of his critical pedagogy known as "multiple definition" or "practical criticism" in literature in China. The book is a remarkable demonstration of his analytical and interpretational agility in containing, organizing, revealing, and, through "indirectly controlled guess," imagin-ing and creating meaning. His reading of *Mencius*, though limited to a selected number of passages of special interest to him, was an extension of his most systematic method of close analysis, practical criticism, which he had introduced in 1925 while teaching literature for the English Tripos at Cambridge. Practical criticism is exemplary of Richard's notion of "mutual understanding," which held that writing and reading were formative pro-cesses wherein the writer and reader constantly shifted and modified their thinking, and in which the development of understanding would not stop until the act of writing or reading was concluded. Richards's "multiple definition" of *Mencius* brought to the fore its rich textual possibilities and semantic complexities, and demonstrated that a different approach to the "Chinese modes of meaning" would lead to the conclusion that, contrary to the prevalent view in the West, Chinese thinking was neither static nor monolithic. *Mencius* in Richards's multiple definition has acquired a richer textual life.

Mencius on the Mind is evidence of Richards's efforts to revive what might be considered the tradition of liberal humanism, which attempted not only to unify diverse systems of meaning but also to envelop historical forms of thought within the same cultural tradition. To promote and establish an understanding between Chinese traditional wisdom and Western scientific logic, one would need to have a new analytical instrument by which successful communication between China and the West could be achieved and developed. Richards's "multiple definition" presupposed the existence of cross-cultural differences, but Richards knew how to deal with these differences. What he set out to do in *Mencius on the Mind* was to offer a new approach to the understanding of meaning and to develop a new model of comparative studies that would consolidate his pedagogical regime of "multiple definition."

By 1930, Richards had already decided to withdraw from the study of literature as a subject; he was convinced that it was much more meaningful and important to devote his time to the development and constitution of Basic English as an international language. Richards's teaching at Tsinghua and his subsequent work for Basic marked a significant moment in this process of self-invention in his professional and intellectual life. Basic English was a reduced form of English, with only 850 words, including eighteen verbs. Though brutally skeletal in structure, Basic English, Richards believed, had an unlimited range of expression. He considered China's acceptance of Basic absolutely crucial for its global constitution and practice. It was his experience in teaching English literature in China that led him to design the Basic texts of Western civilization, such as the *Iliad* and *Republic*, for use in teaching. The texts Richards used in the classroom in Beijing included *Tess of the d'Urbervilles*, and what his Chinese students found most off-putting was the linguistic opacity of those literary texts. This forced him into considering once again the question that had been central to his intellectual and academic projects: On what did understanding depend? How might it be meaningfully developed? The serious linguistic difficulties that his Chinese students encountered were attributable to their lack of knowledge of Western intellectual tradition and culture. It was clear that before he could teach Western literature in English, he had to develop a program for teaching the English language, and before he could develop a program for teaching English, he had to understand the Chinese mode of articulation and signification. His *Mencius on the Mind,* cautiously subtitled *Experiments in Multiple Definition,* seemed to suggest that translation between such vastly different languages as English and Chinese had to involve not singular but multiple signs. In unraveling the semantic complexities of this Chinese text, Richards attempted to reconfirm his philosophy of reading and communication: multiple definition was the key to human understanding and communication.

This was Richards's second trip to China. During his long life, he made half a dozen trips to China over half a century, between 1927 and 1979, mostly to disseminate and promote Basic English. But it was in literary criticism, a field he had deserted, rather than in the teaching of Basic, that Richards exerted the strongest influence on several generations of Chinese critics and poets. His colleagues and students at Tsinghua University knew him to be the founding father of modern academic criticism and the man who developed and constituted practical criticism as a pedagogy that could be learned and practiced in the classroom. It had already been recognized that one of the differences between traditional critical practice and modern academic criticism was that the former relied entirely on the reader's educated taste and informed judgment, while the latter emphasized a depersonalized, objective, and analytical procedure that could be followed, studied, and reproduced. In the aftermath of the New Culture Movement, a powerful segment of the Chinese intellectual and academic community had tasked itself with the construction of a new national literature and the development of a new critical practice. For centuries, evaluation and judgment of poetry had been made on the basis of the reader's impression and experience, and how to turn conventional impressionistic criticism into a more systematic and less experiential procedure was a major challenge. Remy de Gourmont's (1858–1915) quotable pronouncement was almost a dogma in Beijing in the early twentieth century: "The whole effort of a sincere man is to erect his personal impressions into laws." Richards's multiple definition was attractive precisely because it proposed a critical method that was analytical, apparently objective, and procedurally teachable and repeatable. Ye Gongchao (1904–1981) concluded his preface to the Chinese translation of Richards's monograph *Poetry and Science* with these words: "What is urgently needed in China is not romanticism, realism or symbolism, but rather this analytical theory of literary texts."

Richards's colleagues and students at Tsinghua developed a special interest in the application of his critical theory and methodology. Zhu Ziqing (1898–1948), poet, essayist, literary scholar, and head of the Chinese Department at Tsinghua in the early 1930s, was in a good position to advocate and promote practical criticism. In an essay entitled "Examples of Multiple Meaning in Poetry" (1935), Zhu decided that it was time to leave behind the long-held view that good poetry was beyond critical analysis, that its meaning could only be grasped in its totality and its aesthetic beauty only comprehended intuitively. This traditional organic notion of poetry had long been used in defining poetic evaluation and judgment as experiential without the need for explicative and analytical support. Zhu was rather impatient with this sort of impressionistic critical practice, which characterized much of conventional criticism known as *shihua* (talks on poetry) or *cihua* (talks on *ci* [song lyrics]): "It is far from sufficient to say that a certain poem is 'good.' It is of necessity to conduct an analysis of it in order to answer the question why it is good." In arguing for a new critical orientation, Zhu quoted extensively from Richards's theory of meaning. Foregrounded in Zhu's discussion was the difference between scientific language, which required clarity and certainty in meaning, and literary language, which was emotive and thus necessarily multiple in meaning. Zhu proposed to locate a poem's meaning in its sense, feeling, tone, and intention. Four classical Chinese poems were used as textual illustrations; following the procedure of practical criticism, Zhu's reading of these poems revealed an extraordinary range of interpretational possibilities. Zhu's essay is an early application of Richards's critical methodology that gestured toward a break with traditional critical methodology.

Qian Zhongshu (1910–1998), who entered Tsinghua in 1929, made several attempts to put into practice the Richardsian method of multiple definition and close reading, including his study of the use of synesthesia in classical poetry. Qian's studies, mostly practical explications and amplifications of Richards's twin interests in the production of meaning and literary psychology, were indicative of a scholarly interest in a novel critical methodology rather than a conscious effort to indigenize it for its practice and application in China. Like his teacher Zhu, Qian did not develop a sustained critical program for appreciation and interpretation of classical poetic devices and techniques.

In the domain of poetic composition, Richards's theory of poetry contributed to the development of Chinese modernist poetry in the 1940s. Between 1946 and 1948, the poet and scholar Yuan Kejia (1921–2008) wrote a series of short essays advocating the development of a modernist poetics. In close reference to Richards's theory of language and communication, Yuan made serious efforts to further distinguish poetic language from scientific language. He argued for the importance of such poetic notions and devices as "ambiguity" and "multiple meaning" for the development of the new poetry he was committed to. The distinction between poetry and science, Yuan emphasized, would lead to the privileging of poetic language as a unique medium for creativity.

Richards's theory provided critical justification for the experimental use of poetic language in the 1940s, but a more important source of inspiration for the modernist poetic practice was Richards's student William Empson (1906–1984), who, in the footsteps of his mentor, came to China to teach English in 1937. Empson decided to leave Britain and work in the Far East after his fellowship at Cambridge was withdrawn because a contraceptive device was found in his room. Richards considered Empson his "best man" at Cambridge; he wrote to Eliot from Beijing in September 1929 expressing his indignation at Cambridge's decision to revoke the fellowship, in the hope that Eliot would help Empson find a job in London. But in the end, Richards facilitated an offer to Empson from Peking University. He was hoping that Empson would assist him in pushing forward the cause of Basic English in China. Following a stint of three years of teaching in Japan, Empson arrived in China in 1937, only to find Peking University in exile; it moved first to Changsha and then to Kunming, where together with Tsinghua and Nankai Universities it formed the famous wartime Southwestern Associated University. Empson taught there between 1937 and 1939 and exerted a massive influence on his students, among whom was the prominent modernist poet Mu Dan (1918–1977). Yuan enrolled at the University in 1941, after Empson had returned to Britain for work with the BBC. But Empson was a legendary figure. He was admired and respected not only for his poetical and critical achievement, but also because of his unwavering dedication to his work in China and his solidarity with his Chinese colleagues and students in defiance of Japanese aggression. This is perhaps where Empson differed from Richards. Richards made his fourth trip to China in 1937, but at the outbreak of the war, he departed for the United States to take up a position at Harvard. Empson would not forgive Richards for deserting China and his friends working for Basic there.

There had always been widespread reservations about Basic. Harold Acton (1904–1994), who lived in Beijing between 1932 and 1939, considered Basic an imposition on Chinese students and predicted its failure: "With their brilliant mnemonic gifts and their hereditary love of fine language, the Chinese are the last people to be seduced by this emasculate jargon." Yet Richards did not give up. In 1979, at the age of eighty-one, and against medical advice, Richards made his final trip to China. He collapsed during his visit and died shortly after he was flown back to England.

BIBLIOGRAPHY: Harold Acton, *Memoirs of an Aesthete* (London, 2008). I. A. Richards, *Mencius on the Mind: Experiments in Multiple Definition* (London, 1932). I. A. Richards, *Practical Criticism* (London, 1929). I. A. Richards, *Selected Letters of I. A. Richards* (Oxford, 1990). George Yeh [Ye Gongchao], "Cong yinxiang dao pingjie" (1934), in *Ye Gongchao piping wenjie*, ed. Chen Zishan (Zhuhai, China, 1998), 15–21. George Yeh [Ye Gongchao], preface to *Kexue yu shi*, by I. A. Richards, trans. Cao Baohua (Shanghai, 1935), 1–4. Zhu Ziqing, "Shi duoyi juli," in *Richards: Kexue yu shi*, ed. Xu Baogeng (Beijing, 2002), 95–110.

Q. S. TONG

1930 · OCTOBER 27

Tayal aborigines ambush and decapitate Japanese settlers at a school event in Musha, Taiwan.

Invitation to a Beheading

On the morning of October 27, 1930, in the village of Musha, located in central Taiwan, Tayal aborigines, Japanese and Han Chinese settlers, and provincial colonial officials and their families, altogether totaling around four hundred people, gathered in a primary school for a sports competition—a most important annual occasion in the mountain village. As the participants were about to sing the Japanese national anthem and raise the Japanese flag, three hundred or so aboriginal men, in native attire, surged onto the school ground as if from nowhere. With guns and swords, they stormed into the crowd and, in no time at all, the head of Sugano Masae, the commissioner of the Taichushu Police Bureau, was catapulted into the air. What followed was the horrific scene of a killing field. The Tayal warriors chased Japanese men, women, and children around, stabbed or shot them, and hewed off many of their heads. In the end, 134 Japanese were slain.

The Musha Incident marked one of the bloodiest uprisings in Taiwan under Japanese colonial rule (1895–1945). To quell the uprising, the Japanese government sent more than seven thousand police and armed forces, equipped with machine guns, cannons, and poison gas. The Tayal people were driven into the mountains and, after a twenty-three-day holdout, ended up either being killed or committing suicide. The final death count of the aborigine slaughter amounted to 644, more than a half of the total population of the six rebelling Tayal tribes.

How to remember and narrate the Musha Incident has been contested in Taiwanese history and literature. By the time of the incident, Taiwan had been ruled by Japan for thirty-five years, and Han Chinese resistance activities had all but disappeared. The Tayals, one of the indigenous peoples who are Austronesian by origin, nevertheless carried out what Han Chinese may have imagined but failed to see through. Since the 1950s, waves of efforts have been made to interpret the incident, in forms ranging from fiction to poetry, reportage, oral history, docudramas, music, cinema, and even cartoons. The incident found a spectacular representation in *Seediq Bale*, a movie on an epic scale that was released in 2011. None of these efforts, however, can compare to the novel *Remains of Life* (2000), by the Taiwanese novelist Wuhe (1951–), in terms of either historical pathos or polemical thrust.

Remains of Life is a peculiar work that mixes fictional narrative with ethnographical accounts, historical reflections, and personal musings. Wuhe claims that his writing derives from a two-year residential experience in Musha, where his goal was to understand not only the cause of the incident but also its consequences. In the novel, the most poignant question Wuhe raises is none other than the decapitation of the Japanese by the Tayal people. He notes how the decapitation has resulted in two types of interpretations. For the Chinese Nationalist (Kuomintang) regime, the decapitation represents a heroic Chinese retaliation for Japanese oppression. Monarudao (1882–1930), the leader of the Tayal uprising, was enshrined as a martyr by the Nationalist government in 1953 and a statue was erected in his memory in 1974. On the other hand, for the Japanese colonial power, the decapitation embodies the bitterest moment in their rule over Taiwan. While the Japanese government took severe measures to crack down on the uprising, the following years saw a substantive change in its colonial policy, from segregation and oppression to assimilation and containment.

Wuhe takes issue with both the Nationalist and colonial interpretations of the Musha Incident, regarding them as products of the same hegemonic structure. He proposes instead to examine the incident anew, by reopening the case of decapitation and witnessing its traumatic and lingering effects on the Tayal people. Through interviews with the survivors of the incident and their descendants, Wuhe comes to the conclusion that the decapitation cannot be understood as a violent form of colonial resistance, any more than it was an enactment of the time-honored aboriginal ritual of headhunting. In the words of one of the characters, "Our ancestors would have acknowledged a headhunt led by Monarudao, but they couldn't have cared less about the so-called Musha Incident."

Wuhe discerns in the Musha Incident a juncture where tribal subjectivity and colonial or national sovereignty are brought to bear on each other. He asks, In what sense do we call the Tayal aborigines Chinese? To what extent can their attack on the Japanese be interpreted as an anticolonial event? How can an aboriginal ritual of headhunting be reconciled with the colonial or national trauma of decapitation? This brings us to the most polemical point of the novel, where Wuhe calls attention to another massive decapitation, which happened five months after the Musha Incident. By then, the survivors of the six rebellious Tayal tribes had been placed in Japanese custody and held at several locations. On April 25, 1931, the surviving Tayal tribe members were attacked by warriors from the rival Toda tribe—a group that had sided with the Japanese during the first incident—and 266 Tayals were killed. Many of the dead were beheaded. Historically named the Second Musha Incident, this massacre has often been ignored or downplayed by scholars because, unlike the Musha Incident proper, it appears to be a tribal clash (though possibly instigated by the Japanese) and therefore seems lacking in immediate colonial or national relevance.

At the climax of his investigation, Wuhe suspects that the Tayal tribes fought the Japanese colonizers in the same way they fought among themselves. In both incidents, the tradition of headhunting is performed in such a way that it obfuscates the distinction between a condemnation of colonial rule and a consummation of tribal feuding. According to a senior Tayal tribal member, the Japanese could have ruled with more ease had they followed the tribal custom, treating the incident not as an anticolonial riot but as a conventional headhunt, and "reciprocating" with another headhunt, as the Toda tribe did to its rival tribe in the second incident. Wuhe presents evidence in support of his conclusion: the rival tribes who once decapitated each other have since also married each other's daughters, as if headhunts were both an exception to and part of the taxonomy of kinship systems. Claude Levi-Strauss would have welcomed the deep structure of reciprocity and revenge among these tribes.

Wuhe's defense of the Tayal people's headhunt may betray a penchant for primitivism. But he is not a romantic merely yearning for the return of the noble savage. He holds that any history predicated on a linear development, be it regressive or progressive, bespeaks reductionism. Instead, he offers a "synchronic" view of history, a view that allows him to view the bygone and ongoing events; Han Chinese, aboriginal, and non-Chinese subjectivities; and public and private concerns side by side. In his own words, "There is no history about history; truth lies only in the present that is history."

The appearance of Wuhe's novel in the new millennium is significant because it helps shed new light on the dialectic of decapitation that purportedly inaugurates modern Chinese literature. It will be recalled that in 1906 in Japan, Lu Xun (1881–1936), then a premedical school student, saw a slide show wherein a Chinese crowd idly watched as one of their compatriots was beheaded for spying against the Japanese army in the Russo-Japanese War. What ensued is by now a familiar story. Dumbfounded by this scene of decapitation, Lu Xun realized that, before saving the Chinese people's bodies, he had first to save their souls; hence, before practicing ordinary medicine, he had first to cure the spirit of China with the medicine of literature. Sixteen years after the slide incident, Lu Xun stated in his short story collection *Call to Arms*,

> The people of a weak and backward country, however strong and healthy they may be, can only serve to be made examples of, or to

witness such futile spectacles [of decapitation]....Our first task was surely to transform their spirits, and I thought at that time that literature could best meet the task of spiritual transformation.

Lu Xun was not alone in broaching the allegorical linkage between nation, literature, and decapitation. Coming to mind is Shen Congwen (1902–1988), the greatest modern Chinese writer of nativism and lyricism. As a child growing up in the Miao aboriginal area of west Hunan, Shen witnessed hundreds of decapitations that resulted from local riots, governmental crackdown, and battles among warlords. At its most appalling, he recalls how soldiers arrested innocent peasants and let them gamble their lives by participating a lottery. The winners were set free, while the losers beheaded. But unlike Lu Xun, who is both horrified by and obsessed with the spectacle of decapitation, Shen seeks to understand the multitude of ways by which Chinese struggle to carry on their lives. Instead of the corporal symbolism of rupture, he finds a complex of coexisting human motives.

Shen narrates his stories in an understated, lyrical style where a Lu Xunesque call to arms is expected. He considers writing not a task of representing the unpresentable rupture (of body and nation) but a process of weaving and unraveling the tapestry of lived and imagined experiences. In other scenes he writes about an unlucky peasant bidding farewell to his cellmates before decapitation ("Twilight"); a kid carrying the heads of his father and brother in baskets on a mountain path ("A Vignette of Guizhou"); and, more gruesomely, young soldiers playing a human-head soccer game while dogs fight over the headless bodies left on the river banks (_Autobiography of Congwen_). Throughout his works, he calls attention to the agency of writing and its power of critique and redemption. To narrate is to remember and re-member the broken past.

What does Wuhe have to offer to the decapitation dialectic of Lu Xun versus Shen Congwen? All three writers share the same kind of repulsion for social-political abuses and human cruelty. The past and the present, the barbarous and the civilized, are seen as intertwined despite the modern agenda of progress and revolution; modernity and monstrosity are but two sides of one coin. However, whereas Lu Xun abhors decapitation as that which embodies a truncated Chinese humanity, thus exposing his "obsession with China," Wuhe ponders whether the Tayals, the Japanese, and the Chinese are performing the roles of each other's predators and victims. On the other hand, whereas Shen draws the power of his writing from "imaginary nostalgia," a poetic mechanism that enables him to preempt his sense of loss by viewing the future as if it were past, Wuhe comes across as a practitioner of literary melancholia.

Above all, Wuhe appears more concerned about how to "survive China," understood as the site of trauma. His motive to rewrite the Musha Incident is not to engage with any national agenda but to contemplate the "remains of life" after the incident. For him, the ways by which the Tayal people survived the incident in the subsequent decades, by undergoing alternately coercion, humiliation, and cooptation, bring to light a history more chilling than the incident itself. Wuhe's intent is already indicated by his novel's title, *Remains of Life*. The title, writes Wuhe, is taken from the inscription of a humble "tablet for the survivors" erected by the Tayal people after the Musha Incident, as opposed to the grandiose, official one mandated for the Nationalist cause. To the Tayal people, "the governmental tablet is erected for the dead; the tribal tablet is erected for the survivors, who, upon being born, are already 'remains of life.'"

Remains of Life does not have a plot organism by conventional standards. Rather it features a parade of characters Wuhe came across during his stay in Musha. These characters' stories constitute a constellation of voices, which may or may not be relevant to the incident. For Wuhe, to juxtapose these voices has become the only viable way to recapitulate the fractured circumstances of the Tayal people since the incident. The result is an array of genres, taken at random, from reportage to ethnography, sketch, anecdote, interview, hearsay, fantasy, and interior monologue, among others, that relate the abject life of the Tayal people. These genres, rendered as if they were remnants from various sources, form a peculiar aesthetics of what precisely constitutes the "remains of life."

The Musha Incident represents a point of *no* return for the Tayal people. After the two bloody "headhunt" battles, they have been thrown into a state of prolonged disgrace and disorientation. As a Han Chinese, Wuhe is sensitive to his unwarranted ethnic and linguistic stance in writing *Remains of Life*. He nevertheless considers such a shaky position as a point of departure to reflect on the precarious circumstances of aborigines' lives and the untenability of mending their history. Today, the Tayal people and other Taiwanese aborigines, totaling no more than half a million, still suffer from far lower economic and political status than Han Chinese. Euphemized as the "indigenous inhabitants" of Taiwan, they have been treated at best as symbolic tokens whenever the slogan of nativism is invoked. At a time when Taiwanese nativists, who are mostly descendants of Han Chinese immigrants by origin, are claiming their supreme legitimacy on the island, a novel such as *Remains of Life* reminds us of the haunting specter of the Tayal decapitation.

BIBLIOGRAPHY: Leo Ching, *Becoming "Japanese": Colonial Taiwan and the Politics of Identity Formation* (Berkeley, CA, 2000). David Der-wei Wang, *The Monster That Is History: History, Violence and Fictional Writing in 20th Century China* (Berkeley, CA, 2004). Wuhe, *Yusheng* (Taipei, 2000).

DAVID DER-WEI WANG

1931 · FEBRUARY 7

Five young leftist writers are executed by the Nationalist Party.

The Chinese League of Left-Wing Writers, 1930–1936

On February 7, 1931, twenty-three men and women, all members of the Chinese Communist Party (CCP), were executed in secret in Shanghai by the Nationalist (Kuomintang, hereafter KMT) regime for their antigovernment activities. Among them were five writers: Li Weisen (1903–1931), Hu Yepin (1904–1931), Rou Shi (1901–1931), Yin Fu (1909–1931), and Feng Keng (1907–1931), all active members of a literary organization known as the Chinese League of Left-Wing Writers (Left League). In Communist literary history, they have been remembered as the "Five Martyrs of the Left League."

The execution of five young and promising writers aroused deep sympathy. The oldest one, Rou Shi, was twenty-nine. He was very close to Lu Xun (1881–1936), who considered him an outstanding talent. The youngest one, Yin Fu, twenty-one years old when he was executed, had already published a collection of poetry. Feng was a female writer—one should remember that China in the early 1930s had only a handful of renowned female writers. Thus when the news was ultimately made known to the public, loud uproars and protestations broke out not only in China but also abroad. Left-wing literary magazines in the United States, such as

New Masses and *New Republic*, published articles condemning the massacre, and the International Union of Revolutionary Writers, whose members included such famous writers as Alexander Fadeev (1901–1956), Henri Barbusse (1873–1935), and Upton Sinclair (1878–1968), issued a statement severely criticizing the KMT's persecution of writers.

The KMT had indeed been brutal in their suppression of the leftist literary movement. Strict censorship was imposed, and publishers and magazines were raided and closed down for propagating antigovernment ideas. In September 1930 the Left League was banned and orders to arrest its members were issued. However, the five martyrs were arrested and executed not because they were leftist writers but because they were directly involved in the activities of the Communist Party. It is now known that they were arrested together with other CCP members at a secret party meeting held on January 17, 1931, to settle issues of intraparty strife. There is strong evidence that their enemies within the party tipped off the authorities about the meeting. The five martyrs were in fact victims of CCP power struggles.

The Left League had been a strong combating force against the KMT on the literary front. Inaugurated on March 2, 1930, in Shanghai, it quickly attracted a large membership and grew into an organization of over four hundred members, with branches in Tokyo, Beijing, Tianjin, Guangzhou, Nanjing, Jinan, Wuhan, and Baoding. It represented the first attempt of the CCP to gain control of the literary world, as the league was set up on orders issued from the highest level of the party. Badly hit by the violent purge by the Nationalists, who staged a coup d'état from a united front in 1927, the Communists were eager to unite the writers under their banner in order to put up a better fight. They were successful in securing the support of the giant of modern Chinese literature, Lu Xun, who became disillusioned with the KMT after witnessing the arrests and killings of the coup. Although he was never a CCP member, his support was important to the Communist cause because he had great influence on young people. With the exception of several established writers, most of the league members were under thirty years old and many were in their teens when they joined the league. Only a handful of them had produced some literary works worthy of attention. With such a membership, the Left League could hardly live up to its name as an organization of "writers." But the young members were courageous and strong fighters in the struggle against the authorities, and in this way, they very well served the political purposes of the CCP.

The Left League had set a distinctive political agenda for itself from the beginning. In the program adopted at its inaugural meeting, the leading cadres of the league declared categorically that they were "to stand on the battle front of the struggle for proletarian liberation." They would devote themselves "to the bloody 'victory or death' struggle" against "all the reactionary forces that oppose the proletariat." Literature was seldom mentioned; politics was clearly the focus. To the members of the Left League, art and literature were adopted only as tools for the war of liberation of the proletariat and humankind. In other documents, they explicitly urged people to support the Jiangxi Soviet rule led by the CCP.

The Left League did not fight on paper only. There were calls for its members to go to the factories and villages to organize people for struggles. They staged mass demonstrations, which they regarded as part of the military insurrection of the party. To avoid arrests, they adopted shock tactics. In what was known as a "flying meeting," they would gather a group, quickly distribute pamphlets, shout some slogans, and, upon the arrival of the police, disperse immediately. They also secretly put up posters criticizing the authorities. Although it is impossible to know how effective these activities actually were, many league members were very positive about them and joined them most enthusiastically.

Nevertheless, although they tried to avoid directly confronting the police, many members were arrested and put in jail for these demonstrations and other political activities. This alarmed the moderates within the organization, especially when league members were ordered to drop their pens and participate in actual fighting. Within the organization, a group of people, mainly the established writers like Lu Xun and Mao Dun (1896–1981), deliberately ignored these instructions and concentrated their efforts on the literary front. Because of their contributions, the Left League was able to make advancements in promoting the left-wing literary movement.

Left League members published many literary journals and magazines, and some of them made great impact. The *Dipper*, launched in September 1931 at the instruction of the Propaganda Department of the CCP, is generally regarded as one of the most influential literary magazines of the 1930s. Ding Ling (1904–1986), the well-known female writer, was chosen as the editor because she was able to enlist nonleague writers. Works by writers like Bing Xin (1900–1999), Ling Shuhua (1900–1990), and Xu Zhimo (1897–1931), who had been previously attacked by leftist critics as bourgeois, were published. The editors of the *Dipper* were also keen to bring in new writers. Some who subsequently became famous writers, such as Ai Qing (1910–1996), had their first works published in the *Dipper*. Seminars were organized for readers to meet the writers, and these seminars proved to be good opportunities to recruit new members into the ranks of the league. Apart from the *Dipper*, at least four official organs were launched within the first six months of the founding of the Left League, although they were all soon suppressed by the authorities.

Members of the Left League actively promoted popular literature to enhance their influence among the largely uneducated common people. While they agreed that literary works should be written for the masses, they could not reach a consensus on a central issue: Should the artistic value of literature be sacrificed? Some held the view that in a time of crisis, "one would need black bread, not fine biscuits"—meaning that it was more important for a work to be politically correct than artistically polished. Others warned that bad literature that didn't appeal to the masses wouldn't do them any good. They also argued over who should write popular literature. Some believed that popular literature should be written by professional writers for the consumption of the masses, while others thought that popular literature should be produced by the masses themselves. League members published many articles on these issues but never came to a consensus. They had to wait for about a decade, until Mao Zedong (1893–1976) gave the definitive answer in the famous *Talks at the Yan'an Forum on Literature and Art* in 1942: writers would go among the masses to learn how to write for the workers, peasants, and soldiers.

Apart from these debates among fellow members on literary issues important to their cause, the Left League also actively engaged itself in polemics against the literary groups supported by the authorities. With strong support from the regime, the pro-government writers initiated the so-called Nationalist literary movement in June 1930. Many of its advocates were closely linked with the government, and some even worked in the Shanghai municipal police department. They attacked the left-wing writers for creating an abnormal, morbid literary scene. The Left League took the challenge of the Nationalist movement very seriously. All the heavyweights wrote articles to criticize the Nationalists, whose works, both theoretical and creative, were mercilessly torn into pieces.

With all these achievements, the Left League has been hailed by literary historians of the People's Republic as a great success. There is truth to this claim, but the success was certainly not unqualified. Without a doubt, the literary arena of the 1930s was largely dominated by the left-wing writers. On the one hand, they promoted leftist literature, urging the creation of literature for the proletariat. On the other hand, they attacked and eliminated the influence of literary works and literary thought that they found disagreeable. It was also true that they had united a great number of writers under their banner. Even the KMT came to believe that a major reason for the loss of China to the Communists in 1949 was the latter's control of the literary world. The KMT had been unequivocally dominant in matters military and political, but the pen was, ultimately, mightier than the sword.

However, the united front of the Left League was actually not as united as scholars in the People's Republic have claimed. From the very beginning, the unity of the Left rested on an unstable and fragile base. There were two centers of gravity within the organization: Lu Xun and the CCP leadership. Lu Xun attracted many young people to the cause, and was unambiguously supportive of the leftist literary movement. But because of his age, he was often exempted from many activities. He seldom attended meetings, let alone demonstrations, and was often sidelined or even alienated as a result. More importantly, as Lu Xun was not a CCP member, he would often decline to follow party policies and instructions. On the other hand, the leading cadres of the party group within the league were in charge of the Left League. Harmony between these two centers of power depended largely on how the party members communicated and worked with Lu Xun, and if Lu Xun was convinced of the party's policy. In the early years of the Left League, Lu Xun was given great respect and prominence, because the secretary of the party group was Feng Xuefeng (1903–1976), a close disciple of Lu Xun. Qu Qiubai (1899–1935), the de facto leader of the leftist literary movement in Shanghai, was also a very good friend of Lu Xun. Unfortunately, both Feng and Qu left Shanghai, in December 1933 and January 1934, respectively. The young and inexperienced Zhou Yang (1908–1989) became the secretary of the league's party group, and he was never able to win the confidence of Lu Xun. The bridge between the two leaderships of the league was completely shattered. By the time the Left League was dissolved in late 1935, Zhou and Lu Xun were engaged in a polemic, and the leftist camp was bitterly divided. It was not until the death of Lu Xun in 1936 and the outbreak of the second Sino-Japanese War in 1937 that the leftist writers truly united around the cause. Tragically, however, after the establishment of the People's Republic of China, all the leading league members were purged at one time or another, their deeds and writings from the Left League period used as evidence of antiparty crimes. As for the five writers executed by the KMT in 1931, their premature death might have been, ironically and sadly, a blessing. They would never know about the fearsome power struggle within the party or the eventual breakdown of the Left League. Their reputations unsullied, they have always been remembered as martyrs sacrificing their lives to fight for the lofty cause of proletarian revolution.

BIBLIOGRAPHY: Merle Goldman, *China's Intellectuals: Advise and Dissent* (Cambridge, MA, 1981). T. A. Hsia, *The Gate of Darkness: Studies on the Leftist Literary Movement in China* (Seattle, 1968). Leo Ou-fan Lee, ed., *Lu Xun and His Legacy* (Berkeley, CA, 1985). Paul G. Pickowicz, *Marxist Literary Thought in China: The Influence of Ch'u Ch'iu-pai* (Berkeley, CA, 1981). Wong Wang-chi, *Politics and Literature in Shanghai: The Chinese League of Left-Wing Writers, 1930–36* (Manchester, UK, 1991).

LAWRENCE WANG-CHI WONG

1932

Hei Ying publishes his first short story.

Hei Ying's "Pagan Love Song"

Midway through "Daughter of Empire," the Shanghai modernist writer Hei Ying's (1915–1992) 1932 debut story, three English words float up out of the sea of surrounding Chinese like a tropical archipelago. Yasuko, a Japanese woman who has fallen into a life of prostitution in an unnamed Southeast Asian city, embraces a young Chinese man in the wake of love-making, and dreams of a world in which the boundaries of nationality and the enmities of an incipient war no longer separate them from their homes and from one another: "What a pity that we are so far apart, even as our bodies are pressed together. Not for us the happiness of taking up a guitar to play a romantic song, on a beach fringed with moonlit palms, to sing a 'Pagan Love Song.'" What can we make of this reference to a long-forgotten popular song? What does it tell us about the world within the story, and about the world of its author? Might listening in on this melody, embedded like a fossil in this story, tell us something new about Chinese writing in a world in which modernism and a new globally circulating mass culture had come to be tightly intertwined?

Chinese modernism is usually seen as a Shanghai-centric phenomenon. Yet the world from which it emerged extended far beyond the Shanghai Bund. Hei Ying himself arrived by steamship in that city as an eighteen-year-old traveler from the distant island of Sumatra, just months before "Daughter of Empire" was published in the *Shenbao Monthly*. The publication launched him into a short-lived and prolific career. Hei Ying may have heard "Pagan Love Song" at a screening of *The Pagan*, a 1929 Metro-Goldwyn-Mayer production, either in his hometown of Medan or at one of the second-run cinemas he frequented in Shanghai. *The Pagan*, filmed in a lush, pictorialist style in the Paumotu islands, portrayed an exotic romance between a half-caste plantation owner and a beauty in the South Seas. Hei Ying would certainly have heard one of the plethora of different recordings of the song made in the wake of the film's success. Shanghai—a major port along the Pacific steamship circuit that stretched from the West Coast of the US mainland across to the Hawaiian Islands and Japan, and fanned out across the European colonial entrepôts and Chinese settlements of Southeast Asia—was awash with Hollywood films and the Jazz Age sounds of Tin Pan Alley.

This same marine circuit also became the medium for the circulation of a new Chinese textual culture throughout the Chinese diaspora. Even before he had arrived on the Bund, Hei Ying had grown up with Mandarin Chinese–language primers and had been initiated into a wider literary world by way of the influential modernist journal *Xiandai* (or *Les Contemporains*). Born Zhang Youjun in Medan in 1915 to a Hakka family of limited means, Hei Ying's pen name ("Black Baby") was a cipher, signaling pride in his precocious talent, a sometimes painful sense of his Malay provenance and outsider status in the Chinese metropole, and his passion for the jazzy cadences and Hawaiian lilt of the global hit parade of the early 1930s. Dark child of the archipelago of Dutch empire, Hei

Ying engaged with his own displacement in an unrelentingly restless world of migration and cultural miscegenation through his fiction. The formal experiments and musical cadences of his writing can help us map his movements and chart the complex material and media circuits out of which Chinese modernism emerged.

Referred to by one critic as China's "Yokomitsu Riichi # 4," Hei Ying's work was frankly derivative of more famous neo-sensationist authors like Mu Shiying (1912–1940) and Liu Na'ou (1905–1940), who had in turn modeled themselves after the Japanese modernists. Hei Ying's years as a man about town were brought to a sudden halt by the advent of hostilities with Japan in 1937. While Liu (scion of a wealthy Taiwanese family) and Mu (a bourgeois Shanghainese) took up editorial posts at the same Japan-friendly newspaper, only to be targeted as collaborators and fall victim to assassination by Nationalist agents, Hei Ying was driven by a longing to rally overseas Chinese to the national cause. He returned to Indonesia to take up the editorship of the local Chinese newspaper, only to spend four punishing years as a prisoner in a Japanese concentration camp in Java. And, in the wake of the revolution in 1949, he returned to a "home" he had never before seen, settling in the cold climes of Beijing, and pledged himself to work toward the construction of a new nation as a newspaper reporter. Home, it turned out, was for Hei Ying a necessary fiction: a story that may well have saved his life.

Let's return to the song he mentions in his debut. There are many different versions, but perhaps the most haunting is sung by Annette Hanshaw (1901–1985), backed by Frank Ferera's (1885–1951) Hawaiian Trio, and was released in 1929 on the Harmony label. The song, set to a deceptively simple waltz, conjures up an evanescent tropical soundscape from out of the sweeping glissando slides and second-order harmonics of Ferera's steel guitar. Notes flutter in the air like fireflies by the beach, flicker for a moment, and then fade. Ferera was a descendant of a nineteenth-century wave of Portuguese-speaking migrants to Honolulu from the north Atlantic island of Madeira, laborers who had brought to their new island home the diminutive four-string guitar that came to be known in Hawai'i as the ukulele. Ferera and his band were the talk of the 1915 Panama-Pacific International Exposition in San Francisco, helping to ignite a craze for

Hawaiian sounds in the continental United States that lasted throughout the 1920s, transforming the sound of American vernacular song. Hawaiian performers and records also journeyed east, on the steamship lines stretching from Honolulu to the seaports of Yokohama and Kobe, putting a tropical stamp on Japanese *kayokyoku* pop. From Japan, it was a short step to the rest of East Asia, as well as to southerly ports of call such as Singapore, Penang, and Jakarta. Javanese *kroncong,* the earliest and most important popular genre of modern Indonesia—to which Hei Ying would certainly have been exposed throughout his childhood in Medan—is built around the sound of an ensemble of strummed ukuleles. By the early 1930s, just as Hei Ying enrolled in Shanghai's Jinan University, the ukulele had become a fashionably exotic accessory for stylish urbanites, and steel guitars were as much a part of the sonic signature of the new "modern songs" of the Chinese Jazz Age being produced in Shanghai's Pathe-EMI studios as the saxophone.

Hei Ying, who became an avid filmgoer and habitué of taxi-dance halls upon his arrival, was captivated by these musical worlds. His prolific writings for the popular press in these years, which included short stories, South Seas travelogues, and reviews of the latest films, habitually name-drop Hollywood songs, from Jeannette MacDonald's (1903–1965) 1930 smash "Only a Rose" (from the 1930 Technicolor talkie *The Vagabond King*) to Dick Powell (1904–1963) and Ruby Keeler's (1909–1993) famous "Shadow Waltz" duet from Busby Berkeley's (1895–1976) *Gold-Diggers of 1933.*

Many of his readers also would have seen *The Pagan,* and known the tunes for "Pagan Love Song" or "Shadow Waltz." And thus a simple allusion in the text would make the experience of reading vividly synesthetic, as aural images bloomed from the printed page, infusing the surrounding text with their sonority.

Hei Ying's prose also strives for such modish effects. Along with Mu and Liu, Hei Ying constantly calls our attention to, and in the process defamiliarizes, the act of seeing, and of writing about what we see. Eyes (*yanjing*) become eyeballs (*yanzhuzi*); adjectives are consistently prefaced not by run-of-the-mill intensifiers such as "very" (*hen*) or "quite" (*po*) but by the newly fashionable "strangely" (*guai*). Exclamation points and English words like "ukulele" repeatedly poke through the surface of the text, serving as visual and metrical syncopations. Hei Ying often offers up imagistic tableaux that aspire to a gritty photographic materiality:

The water in the stream was turbid and yellow, it had rained in the past few days, and the current was fast, floating plantain fronds, floating banana peels, floating garbage piles. Without so much as rowing, floating downstream, floating with the garbage, floating with the banana peels, floating with the plantain fronds, floating...

The verbal repetition is deliberately incantatory. Elsewhere, recurring refrains (like "Black girl, I love you!" in his "South Seas Love Song") string together whole stories, mimicking the strophic structures of recorded popular song.

Nor did Hei Ying abandon the old-fashioned semantic functions of allusion. The evocation of "Pagan Love Song" is complex and moving. In a story that keeps his characters' minds and motivations largely opaque to readers, it is the song itself that is an affective flare—lighting up, if only for a moment, their inner worlds. The English lyrics also stand as a nearly perfect cipher of the story:

Native hills are calling
To them we belong
And we'll cheer each other
With the pagan love song.

Exiled from their respective "native hills," our protagonists in Hei Ying's story will ultimately be alienated from one another's affections as well, precisely by virtue of a nationality to which neither seems to fully "belong." Yasuko, we learn, has been spurned by a previous Chinese lover, and fallen from her position in polite Japanese society as a result of her transgression. Yet the young Chinese man, adrift in a strange city, and initially torn between erotic desire and his disgust for Yasuko's Japaneseness, learns to see her as something more than a "daughter of empire," not so much a victimizer as a fellow victim, someone to comfort and in whom to take comfort, if only for a moment.

Written in the wake of the Japanese annexation of Manchuria in 1931, the story thus complicates questions of national identity and community in ways that are entirely uncharacteristic of the literature of "national salvation" that would accompany the widening of the Sino-Japanese War. Hei Ying's protagonist, who not incidentally communicates with Yasuko in English and Malay, is a son of empire, and of the maritime networks linking the South Seas not only to China and Japan, but to the imperial West as well. And thus the presence of "Pagan Love Song" speaks, with a Hawaiian inflection, not only to Hei Ying's own tropical otherness, but also to the complex material and cultural circuits by which his identity was circumscribed.

A striking number of Hei Ying's writings, both fictional and essayistic, take place aboard steamships plying the waterways between Sumatra, Singapore, and Shanghai. In "The Sinking Ship," a 1933 ensemble piece in which the fractured lives of a motley crew of young Chinese lovers, foreign colonials, and sailors collide, before meeting a common, and predictably watery, fate, the thrumming of the engines belowdecks—sonic allegory of a modern mobility powered by soulless machines—is likened by one character to "Jazz! Stormy, powerful, transfixing the hearts of all [who hear it]." In a personal reflection published in *Shenbao* and entitled "On the Indian Ocean," Hei Ying speaks of his own fate as he approaches an unknown and "ancient" motherland aboard a mail steamer:

> How could an overseas Chinese born and raised in a colony have had any political consciousness? The people in power there are quite clever, and they know how to ensure that we understand nothing at all...that I was able to leave at all was a miracle akin to the sun rising on the ocean's floor.

In the end, of course, Hei Ying, his patriotic hopes fired by the revolution, chose to leave the tropics behind forever. In 1951, having migrated to the mainland along with his family, he began a long and successful career as a reporter and literary editor for the *Guangming Daily* in Beijing. Yet, as with many other patriotic returnees, this act of high commitment to the national cause became a terrible liability in the tumult of the Cultural Revolution, during which any foreign ties were suspect. Having been confined for four years to a Japanese prison cell, Hei Ying returned to the motherland, only to be sent twenty years later to the Hebei countryside for hard labor and reeducation. Fortunately, the persecution he suffered was relatively light, and he was left physically unharmed. His collection of music dating back to his years in Shanghai and Sumatra, however, did not survive. In the days just before the Red Guards came to ransack his home, he and his family shattered his records as a precautionary measure.

Two decades after Hei Ying's death from natural causes in Beijing in 1992, a deeply disturbing documentary directed by a young American named Joshua Oppenheimer (1974–) pried open the painful historical memory of the mass killings of nearly five hundred thousand civilians in the Indonesia of the mid-1960s. Many of the victims of this political violence, ostensibly massacred on account of their Communist sympathies, were ethnically Chinese. *The Act of Killing* follows two unrepentant gangsters, Anwar Congo and Adi Zulkadry, as they unselfconsciously reminisce, and eventually reenact, their transformation from small-time ticket scalpers at the local cinema to leaders of a paramilitary death squad responsible for the deaths of thousands of Chinese. The impunity with which these paramilitaries murdered their victims, the film suggests, is rooted in a long history of ethnic conflict, and the ongoing disenfranchisement of the local Chinese population. As early as 1932, Hei Ying himself complained, without elaborating, of the "misery" and "oppression" of being Chinese in the Dutch East Indies. The city in which Congo carried out his program of ethnic cleansing was Hei Ying's hometown, Medan. Had Hei Ying not come full circle, following the dictates of his heart and of fate to return to his "native hills" and help construct a nation to which even he might belong, he would almost certainly have died at Congo's hands.

ANDREW F. JONES

1934 · JANUARY 1
1986 · MARCH 20

Shen Congwen and Mo Yan publish new novellas.

Roots of Peace and War, Beauty and Decay, Are Sought in China's Good Earth

Two remarkable novellas, modest in proportions but startling to the avant-gardes of their eras, greeted the springs of 1934 and 1986. *Border Town*, the 1934 opus, is the abiding masterpiece of Shen Congwen (1902–1988). *Red Sorghum*, which a year after its 1986 publication became chapter 1 of a full-length novel, was quickly hailed as the signature work of Mo Yan (1955–). To some readers it remains so, thanks in part to the celebrated 1987 film adaptation by Zhang Yimou (1951–), his breakout work as a director and the first post–Mao Zedong (1893–1976) movie to turn experimental Chinese fiction into a domestic box office hit.

Shen was a thirty-one-year-old ex-soldier author when he published *Border Town*. His earlier works had shocked readers with tales of executions and bloody "bandit pacifications" he witnessed in China's vast rural Unknown, circa 1918–1923. Mo Yan, likewise thirty-one in 1986, wore the People's Liberation Army uniform in peacetime. The army had trained him as a writer, as Shen's warlord superior had made Shen his librarian, then funded his departure for higher education in Beijing in 1923 or 1924. The novellas of 1934 and 1986 contest the "realities" of their day with seemingly opposite kinds of nostalgic idealism. Shen's work imagines peace during a time of war; Mo Yan's conjures up a past war to awaken contemporaries lulled by peace. Both works upend the morals and myths their authors imbibed as young soldiers. These novellas mark defining moments for their authors and for global images of China and Chinese literature.

Border Town and *Red Sorghum* enjoy no particular genetic connection. A decade and a half of further war and civil war and three subsequent decades of Maoist strictures separate the works. Effectively banned for decades, *Border Town* came before a new generation of Chinese readers after 1980, but when Mo Yan joined the post-Mao avant-garde in 1984, he preferred foreign to previous Chinese literary modernists, save Lu Xun (1881–1936). Common themes discovered by readers of *Border Town* and *Red Sorghum* bespeak, if not literary history repeating itself, the persistence of the Chinese people's modern longing to redefine their national identity, find beauty amid war and cultural upheaval, and contemplate newly discovered gaps of gender and generation.

Also common to the two novellas is an attempt to make sense of the urban-rural gap, although it is addressed less directly than the writers' countrified origins and reputations might suggest. The border town, with its early Republican-era boatmen, soldiers, and wharf-side demimonde, draws life from the rivers, not the fields; its heroes are an old ferryman and his granddaughter. They enjoy a dreamy seclusion undisturbed by landlords, capitalists, marauding armies, imperialists, and crusading students. The anonymous narrator of *Red Sorghum* likewise makes grandparents—his own, in 1939, when they were young and fighting Japanese invaders—the heroes of the book. This occasionally ecstatic narrator's magical ability to see history through the eyes of forebears he never met initially lent the fiction and the film "experimental" éclat. He admits that Granddad in his prime was a ruthless highwayman. In later chapters, Granddad betrays Chinese troops of every cause and color, and even Grandma. Further, the narrator at the end of the novel observes "species decline" in the human and sorghum stock *since* those grisly pre-revolutionary times. The film version elevates Granddad from bandit chieftain to natural-born leader, but still he is not a peasant.

Border Town and *Red Sorghum* seem earthbound mostly by the light of China's century-old (but only century-old) search for an essence more particularly Chinese than the ancient and universal Way (Dao). Critics in the 1980s named *Border Town* a prewar progenitor of a recently rede-fined subgenre called *xiangtu* literature (regional or earthbound literature, without Mao's "poor peasant" worldview). Critics in 1986 likewise fitted *Red Sorghum* into a just-invented category of "root-searching literature," in which experimentalists ameliorated their own xenophilia by addressing bedrock, regional Chinese cultural phenomena outside foreign modernity. The leisurely paced *Border Town* and even the more agitated, nonlinearly plotted *Red Sorghum* pause to gaze at nature: the eternal and cyclical Way that stuns the eye and *can* be named.

West Hunan and Shandong's Gaomi County, Shen's and Mo Yan's respective homelands and the partly fictionalized locales of their rural works, have acquired literary fame far beyond their geographical dimen-sions. The striking semiarid landscapes and "Northwest Wind" songs of *Red Sorghum*, the film, however, suggest Shaanxi, Zhang Yimou's homeland. Eastern Shandong, northern Shaanxi, even west Hunan—particularly west Hunan, inhabited by exotic "aboriginal" Miao (Hmong) folk—any Chi-nese region was special enough to represent the new Chinese nation when the hinterlands, not the politically contested capital, became the central kingdom of the heartland and the heart. *Border Town* and *Red Sorghum* (novella, novel, and film) met national audiences halfway by toning down local dialect and generalizing regional customs.

Like their twentieth-century colleagues, the demobilized Shen and the maturing Mo Yan felt that "serious" literature must promote *world* progress, literary revolution, and modernism. That meant debunking what they saw, respectively, as the pseudo-universal classicism of Confucianism and the pseudo proletarian internationalism of Maoism. Like Lu Xun, they traced China's misfortunes to China's own ideological wrong turns, not simply imperialism.

The two writers ultimately won global kudos acknowledging their transnational aspirations and achievements. According to Göran Malmqvist, Shen would have won the 1988 Nobel Prize for Literature had he not died earlier that year. The award would have insulted "China" (the regime), for Shen ceased creative writing after 1949. Mo Yan did win the Nobel Prize in 2012. Political criticism fell on him from outside China, for he fit comfortably into the Communist literary establishment. Some of his works had been banned, but Mo Yan was a satirist, not a dissident. And to nationalistic critics in China and the diaspora, any artist who made eye candy out of China's "old society" could be charged with self-Orientalizing or rebranding China in ways it did not need. (*Border Town*, too, was panned by certain 1930s critics as "unneeded"—unhelpful to China.) Shen and Mo Yan, moreover, danced in linguistic chains; they created astonishing new literary languages from contemporary vernaculars, including Mao-era figures of speech in Mo Yan's case, ignoring or jettisoning the tropes of China's ancient language and literature. That led to invidious comparisons with more formally educated writers.

Both writers belonged to the Chinese "avant-garde mainstream" of their time. Shen was anxious to *épater le bourgeois* and the Confucian *gentilhomme*. Mo Yan, in the late 1980s, aimed to *épater le cadre*, particularly the entrenched local tyrants. But *Border Town* and *Red Sorghum* were also contrarian. *Border Town*'s pastoral images ignore the critical realism and romantic activism that 1930s Chinese critics required of fiction. Shen wanted his writings to build a "little Greek temple." Likewise, *Red Sorghum* sidesteps the paradoxes and non sequiturs of elite 1980s Chinese experimentalism. Mo Yan preferred the baroque detail of magical realism and used it in *Red Sorghum* to adorn, of all things, military heroism. Nature in *Red Sorghum* is pantheistic and affective, as in Shen's late works. Mo Yan finds beauty within violence and decay, again as in certain works by Shen. Both authors leaven tragedy with humor, even poke fun at the folk in their novellas. That went against the tide of both their eras.

Mo Yan's expansion of *Red Sorghum* into an epic novel of linked episodes paved the way for a 1990s movement of full-length highbrow novels that rewrote all twentieth-century Chinese history. Mo Yan, Yu Hua (1960–), Su Tong (1963–), Li Rui (1950–), Zhang Wei (1955–), and others who had witnessed the Cultural Revolution created a new historical novel depicting a Chinese past of endless life-and-death, "Darwinian" struggles. In the early twentieth century, serious fiction had itself competed for survival against chivalric and romantic bestsellers, a popular fiction that in the 1990s also enjoyed a second life, post-Mao. Post–*Red Sorghum* highbrow historical novels survived that new competition and the censors, and even gained a mass readership.

Border Town appeared during a previous transition from shorter to longer fiction among the 1930s avant-garde. During the war, Shen began writing his own epic tale of west Hunanese and national history, *Long River*. He never finished it, however, due to censorship and personal malaise. His postwar literary legacy rested largely with his students, but most of them, too, fell silent after 1949, as Maoist epics extolling past peasant armed struggles replaced experimental works.

Whence the heightened concern with rural China in the 1930s and 1980s, when peasants, culture, and power appeared city bound? The 1980s were a time of rural decollectivization and cultural renewal, accompanied by nostalgia for China's prerevolutionary past. The 1920s and 1930s were the era when earthbound China was first "discovered" as a social realm of its own. Reformist and Marxist ideologies, rural reconstruction movements, and China's first social surveys played a part. Model villages attracted, besides revolutionaries, literary humanists (Shen's colleagues Zhou Zuoren [1885–1967] and Xu Zhimo [1897–1931]), practical reformers (James Y. C. Yen [1893–1990]), and even Confucian modernizers (Liang Shuming [1893–1999]). But in image making at home and abroad, fiction and film held sway. In America, Pearl Buck's (1892–1973) *The Good Earth* was the best-selling novel of both 1931 and 1932. Chinese translations of it were numerous by 1934, though the film did not appear until 1937. The author's first husband, John Lossing Buck (1890–1975), was a noted agricultural economist in China; her parents, China missionaries, represented another force creating images of China for Western audiences—typically of China as a needy nation requiring spiritual and material reformation from abroad. *The Good Earth*'s Chinese heroes are the salt of the earth: hardworking, mostly sympathetic, and practical rather than constitutionally "feudal." But in China it seemed outrageous for an ethnic outsider to gain such authority to speak for China—"backward" China.

Border Town, popular in China and by 1936 already available in English, must have struck many domestic readers as an "authentically Chinese" intervention in a long-standing contest to shape China's global image. Meanwhile, Chinese writers to the left of Shen saw *Border Town*'s vision of a harmonious inland kingdom as a too-clever riposte to their view of a China torn by class and gender oppression. *Border Town*'s innocent maiden hero, Cuicui, gets to pick her own mate in a serenading contest. Unlike Buck's Olan and numerous downtrodden women characters created by China's progressive writers, Cuicui is filial and yet free.

In 1938, Buck won the Nobel Prize in Literature; no Chinese was so favored until 2000, when the award went to Gao Xingjian (1940–). Still, China's 1980s avant-garde chose Nobel laureates (not including Buck!) for their stylistic models. Mo Yan favored William Faulkner (1897–1962) and Gabriel García Márquez (1927–2014). His cohort also admired *Lord of the Flies*, William Golding's (1911–1993) fable about human ignorance and conflict.

The specter of armed conflict loomed over the 1930s. Some Chinese critics condemned the idyllic *Border Town* as a fairy tale, a Daoist utopia (though, perforce, a counter-Confucian utopia) that overlooked realities Shen himself had seen while in the service. On the other hand, *Red Sorghum*, which appeared in more optimistic times, makes patriotic war beautiful—literally. But gallantry comes from the "wrong" kind of people. Their bravery is vengeful and inflated, often selfish instead of patriotic. The old Maoist narrative of a China saved by righteous peasants is thereby unmasked as fairy tale. Mo Yan's later novel, *Big Breasts and Wide Hips* (1996), has even clearer antiwar overtones. Mo Yan's works continue China's century-old quasi-Darwinian view of life as struggle, but revise it from a less nationalistic perspective. Shen, for his part, became a pacifist in the 1940s.

Both novellas climax with the death of a grandparent. In the fearful and anxious 1930s, Shen closed *Border Town* by letting his ferryman die in his sleep during a flood. That passing suggests a chance for renewal. *Red Sorghum*, conceived in a time of real hope and rejuvenation, kills off Grandma in a hail of bullets—foretelling, ironically, a future of fading national vitality.

Border Town and *Red Sorghum* depict communities in which love and personal commitment bridge modern kinds of interpersonal alienation, even despite impenetrable, fated misunderstandings (in the former work) and violence and betrayals from primal instincts (in the latter work). Successive generations of Chinese readers have appreciated *Border Town* and *Red Sorghum* as word pictures of the regions, the professions, and the Chinese nation they depict. But the novellas' staying power lies in their transcendence of boundaries of place, people, and era.

Shen and Mo Yan were unusual, particularly in their respective eras, for engaging their readers in a search for "roots" not just of individual or collective identity, but of more abstract human connectedness, beauty, and goodness. The novellas seek the springs of heroism and creativity, whether in courtship or battle. Shen and Mo Yan used village China to challenge their nation's old and new identity myths. They created vivid personal and transcendental alternative myths, even as the old rural way of life was vanishing from the Chinese earth.

BIBLIOGRAPHY: Janice Leung, "Meet Göran Malmqvist, Nobel Prize Member and Champion of Chinese Literature," *South China Morning Post*, April 18, 2014. Mo Yan, *Hong gaoliang* (the novella), *Renmin wenxue* 1986, no. 3 (March 20, 1986): 6–38. Mo Yan, *Hong gaoliang jiazu* (the full novel) (Taipei, 1988). Mo Yan, *Red Sorghum*, trans. Howard Goldblatt (New York, 1993). Shen Congwen, *Bian cheng* (*Border Town*), *Guowen zhoubao* 11, nos. 1–2, 4, 10–16 (January 1–April 23, 1934). Shen Congwen, *Border Town*, trans. Jeffrey C. Kinkley (New York, 2009). Zhang Yimou, dir., *Hong gaoliang* (the film) (Xi'an, China, 1987).

JEFFREY C. KINKLEY

1934 · OCTOBER–1936 · OCTOBER

"We shared joy and suffering."

Recollections of Women Soldiers on the Long March

The well-documented Long March is essential for understanding many aspects of the Chinese peasantry, the young Chinese Communist Party, and the Red Army leadership, but until quite recently it was an entirely male story. Within the past few decades there has been increasing interest in the women who made that journey.

In 1934, the Communist Party, which had been outlawed by Chiang Kai-shek's (1887–1975) Nationalist government, was being starved out of its base in Jiangxi Province. Encircled by Nationalist troops and without adequate food or medicine, the top leaders decided to move north and west to combine the Jiangxi forces with elements of the Red Army in Hunan and Sichuan Provinces. The First Front Army, of about eighty-six thousand men, left stealthily to avoid the Nationalist troops encircling them, thus beginning what came to be known as the six-thousand-mile Long March. This army included the top leadership of the Communist Party and about thirty-five women. Fighting battles and under constant bombardment, they moved west and south before turning north near the western border of Yunnan Province. The Second Front Army, of about twenty thousand troops, including about twenty women, left Hunan Province, following the same route a year later. The Fourth Front Army, with more than eighty thousand troops, including at least two thousand women soldiers and possibly as many as eight thousand, were in Sichuan Province. The three strands of the Red Army converged in Gansu Province in 1936.

Between 1986 and 1989, I had the privilege of interviewing twenty-three Long March women veterans from seven provinces who served in three strands of the Red Army. Their responses were wonderfully rich in detail on many subjects, especially health. The women cared for wounded soldiers; some traveled with the convalescent corps in the First Front Army; several worked in field hospitals; three were pregnant and gave birth during the Long March; another began the journey with her month-old baby; many assisted at childbirth. The women themselves suffered variously from dysentery, typhus, malaria, and food poisoning; they all stopped menstruating; they all experienced the effects of marching at altitudes in excess of twelve thousand feet while suffering from malnutrition and dehydration. The men soldiers thought the women had the harder time, but the women did not think of themselves as victims: they assumed they were merely doing their jobs.

The First Front Army required the young female soldiers on the work team to have a health exam just prior to leaving the base area. These strong young women had previously demonstrated their ability to recruit soldiers and gather grain for the Red Army. Deng Liujin (1911–2003) remembered that shortly before the First Front Army left on the Long March in October 1934, the director of the Organization Department came to tell us that we women would be sent to the front. We were very, very happy at the thought we would go to the front as real soldiers! But there were three conditions for going to the front: you can walk [long distances]; you are in good health; you can carry 15 jin [16.5 pounds]. And there was another condition: we had to have a medical check-up, difficult for us because we'd never had this experience. We said we'd rather not. He [the director] said, "If you don't, you can't go to the front." We struggled and finally said, "OK!" They took our blood pressure, listened to our hearts, checked our ears and noses.

Wang Quanyuan (1913–2009) described the health exam in more detail, underscoring the army's need for soldiers with strong reflexes, good lungs, no night blindness, and good hearing. She added:

The doctors were men. There were female doctors, but the one who examined us was a man. Did they check for pregnancy? If your body has a baby in it? No! None of the twelve of us had that [were pregnant]. The doctor would never ask if we were pregnant. We were chosen after the Central Government discussed it.

Besides those women assigned to the work team, others accompanied the First Front Army troops on the Long March because they were married or engaged to men in the top leadership. They traveled with the convalescent unit and were not required to have the health exam, although several of them were pregnant and some had serious health issues. Deng Yingchao (1904–1992), Zhou Enlai's (1898–1976) wife, was carried on a stretcher most of the Long March because she had an active case of pulmonary tuberculosis. He Zizhen (1909–1984), Mao Zedong's (1893–1976) wife, was already pregnant at the outset, as were Liao Siguang (1911–2004), wife of the head of security, Kai Feng (Deng Fa, 1906–1955), and Yang Houzhen (1908–1977), wife of Luo Binghui (1897–1946). She had bound feet.

Xie Xiaomei (1913–2006), also in the women's work team, was still in a hospital with her new baby until just before the army left on the march. Her leaders asked her to place the baby with a local family because no children would be allowed to travel with the First Front Army.

Women in the Second and Fourth Front Armies, where discipline was less strict, were able to bring their babies on the Long March, and to keep those born along the way. Chen Zongying (1902–2003) and Jian Xianfo (1916–), two of the Second Front women interviewees, gave birth in the Sichuan grasslands, after climbing glacial mountains in their third trimester.

Jian Xianren (1909–2004), wife of He Long (1896–1969), general of the Second Front Army, was unable to find a family to care for her newborn. She brought their baby daughter on the Long March, an arduous ordeal since she herself was ill. She dragged herself and her baby along as the army moved and fought across Hunan Province and marched into Guizhou and Yunnan, where the army briefly stopped to rest.

> I went to the medicine shop and got little pills for blood deficiency to build up the yin and decrease the yang. I recovered my health and got a smallpox vaccination for my daughter. My baby was quite pretty. I thought it would be terrible if she were pock-marked when she grew up.

Chen Zongying, the wife of Ren Bishi (1904–1950), political commissar of the Second Front Army, delivered her seventh child in Sichuan shortly after climbing glacial mountains. The other interviewee from the Second Front Army who gave birth in the grasslands was Jian Xianfo, a general's wife. Her sister, Jian Xianren, said, "We knew . . . the delivery could be very difficult, but she was quite strong. We aren't laboring women, but on the march we had quite a lot of exercise." Jian Xianfo explained,

> I didn't feel well and didn't understand why. While we were walking, my stomach hurt. My waters broke but I didn't realize it. I kept on walking in a stupor from morning until three or four in the afternoon, when my sister caught up with me, carrying her baby. When she realized that things were not normal, she persuaded me to go to a dirt fortification. We made a pile of our bundles. I couldn't lie down on the ground, so I sat on the bundles, put them under my back. My husband supported my back and my sister cut the cord. After the baby was born, there was a violent storm. We had a small tent and [tried to cover] ourselves but everything got wet. I had the

baby in my arms—he was very healthy. The following day we started off again as usual.

Her sister, who had already given birth to two children, helped deliver the baby. They were in an area with no clean water, so she simply cut the umbilicus and wrapped up the baby without bathing him. She said, "We named him Baosheng, meaning 'born in a fort,'" and added that they left the day after her sister gave birth. Jian Xianfo was carried on a stretcher for the next three days.

The women in the First Front did not mention husbands being in attendance and only wives of top leaders had doctors at delivery. However, no matter how high their husband's position, First Front Army women all left their babies where they were born, whether or not there was anyone around to care for them.

Qian Xijun (1905–1990), who was married to Mao Zedong's brother, Mao Zeming (1896–1943), reported that Liao Siguang's baby was left at the foot of a hill, with no civilians around. When Mao Zedong's wife, He Zizhen, gave birth to her third child not long after, her sister-in-law reported that they found an old, blind woman to take in the newborn. When the army reached Sichuan, Zeng Yu was the next First Front woman to give birth. The army was in a Tibetan minority area and the civilians had all hidden in the mountains when the soldiers came. Deng Liujin said:

> I was with Zeng Yu when she was in labor. Liu Caixia and I were on either side of her, pulling her up the mountain. We reached the top [and then] started down, but her pains were so strong that she couldn't go on. She had the baby that night.
>
> … [Only] the two of us, who knew nothing about this, helped her pull the baby out. Three days later we all left. What could we do? We just put the baby on a pile of grass in someone's house. Zeng Yu was still bleeding. Maybe the conditions were better for the other three because they were senior leaders' wives. All the babies were left behind in local homes. There are no traces of these babies left.

The women, along with the men soldiers, also suffered from lice, common colds, dysentery, malaria, tuberculosis, typhoid, malnutrition, accidental poisoning, swollen and desiccated feet, and wounds.

Deng Liujin told a poignant story of suffering from an attack of dysentery so severe that she could not keep up with the troops. All of the women were terrified of falling behind to be captured and killed by the Nationalists, but Wei Xiuying (1910–2005) stayed with Deng, helping her along until they caught up with their units. Deng said Wei insisted, "If we die, we die together."

> She carried all of our things, and we went on with our walking sticks. Because I had one bout of diarrhea after another, I could only move on very slowly. I had no medicine. When it got dark, we just rested under a tree, back to back. I kept telling her, go on alone and catch up with the others. We suffered together, really sharing joys and sorrows.

Those who fell ill in the Fourth Front Army were put in the field hospital, where the patients were trained during convalescence to help the shorthanded medical staff. When Li Yanfa joined the Fourth Front Army at thirteen, she was assigned to the propaganda team until she became ill with typhus. When she recovered, she was not permitted to leave the hospital. She worked as a nurse, putting mercurochrome or sulfa on wounds, changing dressings, sterilizing bandages, and giving injections.

He Manqiu (1919–2014) of the Fourth Front Army was unique in receiving formal medical training on the Long March. When she became ill with malaria, she was sent to the army hospital, where she quickly recovered after taking "only 3 grams of quinine." When she saw the extent of the need for educated medical practitioners, she decided to stay with the hospital and train as a nurse. As she explained, "The nursing schools at that time didn't really teach nursing: we had just a couple of classes each day and spent the rest of the time caring for the injured soldiers." She was especially concerned about women patients, as the Fourth Front Army had as many as eight thousand women soldiers. Most of the doctors she worked with had been captured from the Nationalist Army, but none had been trained in gynecology. "Whatever the problem might be, the doctors would just say they had *ganxuelao*, a form of tubercular disease found in women, which was characterized by menostasis, low fever and general debility."

When the Fourth Front Army settled in northwestern Sichuan, the medical school that had moved from Jiangxi with the First Front Army opened a class, and He Manqiu was among the few who passed the entrance exam, attended classes, and graduated.

When the Long March was over, Li Jianzhen (1906–1992) reported that she had no health problems as a result of the yearlong trek, but that she was very thin. Others also said that they had no adverse medical condition they could attribute to the march.

The march under fire and often at night, without adequate food and shelter, was just a part of the long fight before the Communists came to power in 1949. Although the interviewees said they did not consider the Long March a separate or heroic part of their revolutionary life until they heard the men describe it that way, they did have sharp memories of the challenges to their health that they experienced that year. The strength and pleasure they derived from "sharing joys and sorrows" with their female comrades is a theme common to stories about health in all the interviews.

BIBLIOGRAPHY: Benjamin Yang, *From Revolution to Politics: Chinese Communists on the Long March* (Boulder, CO, 1990). Helen P. Young, *Choosing Revolution: Chinese Women Soldiers on the Long March* (Champaign, IL, 2001).

HELEN PRAEGER YOUNG

1935 · MARCH 8

"Gossip is a fearful thing."

On Language, Literature, and the Silent Screen

That one of the pivotal moments in Chinese silent cinema was memorialized by an idiom whose nearest English equivalent is "people will talk" might seem something of a paradox. As the closing line of a suicide letter attributed to the 1930s silent film star Ruan Lingyu (1910–1935), "gossip is a fearful thing" served as a ghostly epitaph—perhaps even a sort of intertitle—to her mysterious death on International Women's Day, 1935. The handwritten line would be reproduced in newspapers, inscribed on banners at her funeral, and circulated and contested for months, years, and decades ahead. "Gossip is a fearful thing" long had carried intimations of danger or lament for the person defamed. The charged phrase was already deeply embedded in Chinese culture, from *The Book of Songs* to *The Palace of Everlasting Life*, the famed Qing opera of seduction and loss. But what would these words now mean in an era of modern media, when motion pictures, the emergent periodical press, serialized novels, vernacular fiction, teahouse storytelling, new-style operas, and spoken drama all jostled for attention? Who, in turn, would "speak" for Chinese silent pictures? What would they say? What stories would they tell?

The first motion pictures in China were virtually wordless and fragmentary, at once exotic and accessible. Patrons at a Shanghai teahouse in 1897 marveled at the succession of imported images, according to one breathless contemporary observer,

> lovely blonde Western women dancing…two men wrestling…a woman, entirely naked, bathing in a tub…a magician….The switching on and off of these shows symbolizes our own lives, like a dream or an illusion, which may vanish like a soap bubble.

Running just a few minutes, these "living moving pictures" or "electric shadowplays" emanated as technological wonders, conjuring up extraordinary tableaux and micronarratives, often embellished by live interpreters, music, descriptive playbills, and posters. Brief selections could summon whole worlds, as when photographers at Fengtai studio in Beijing's entertainment quarter experimented with filmmaking in 1905 by having the Empress Dowager's (1835–1908) favorite martial opera star, Tan Xinpei (1847–1917), perform short scenes from the historical epic *Romance of the Three Kingdoms* for the camera.

Ever since the earliest days of film production in China, cross-fertilization among literature, theater, and cinema prompted adaptations of a vast range of works, whether traditional or new, indigenously sourced or translated, particularly after 1921, when extended narrative films became possible in China. Pu Songling's (1640–1715) Qing dynasty collection *Strange Tales from the Liaozhai Studio* inspired at least three feature-length productions during the mid-1920s. Major movie studios Minxin, Mingxing, Tianyi, and others filmed established favorites from fiction and drama, such as *Mulan Joins the Army* and *The Romance of the Western Chamber*, along with recent serial novels like *Marvelous Gallants of the Rivers and Lakes* by Xiang Kairan (1890–1957), which was revamped for the screen as an eighteen-episode martial-arts extravaganza entitled *Burning of the Red Lotus Temple* that ran from 1928 through 1931, with multiple sequels and remakes thereafter.

The art of mixing verbal and visual language in silent cinema seized the imaginations of some of China's best-selling writers. Bao Tianxiao (1875–1973), who had been seeing movies in Shanghai since the 1910s, notably admired economy in intertitles, observing that "in film, as in stage drama, subtle suggestion works far better, and often no talking at all can greatly surpass talk." Talented actors, he wrote, could "'hear' with their eyebrows, 'speak' with their eyes, and perform with their gestures." Even so, Bao thought explanatory intertitles were indispensable to Chinese film at that time. He would eventually craft scenarios and intertitles for at least a dozen films by Mingxing and other studios.

Targeting a primarily urban audience that included avid readers, China's leading movie companies publicized their collaborations with popular authors and promoted the international quality of their productions. Mingxing ads for the 1926 two-part hit *Orchid in the Ravine* celebrated its origins in "Mr. Bao Tianxiao's most satisfying novel" and as "the most acclaimed new-style play" adapted for stage by dramatist Zheng Zhengqiu (1889–1935) a dozen years earlier. In the company's magazine, Bao described for readers the cosmopolitan roots of this family drama, derived from a Japanese novel that itself was a translation from English. The same year, Mingxing also released Bao's rendition of Leo Tolstoy's (1828–1910) *Resurrection*, similarly transposed to a Chinese setting. Filming homegrown best sellers could be contentious: for the coveted adaptation rights to *Fate in Tears and Laughter* by another famed Mandarin Ducks and Butterflies writer, Zhang Henshui (1895–1967), there were fierce disputes, erupting in bomb threats—but Mingxing pressed on, paying off competitors and making headlines with the extraordinary salary paid to its star, Butterfly Woo (Hu Die, 1908–1989).

Silent film actresses from China and abroad commanded public attention in 1920s and 1930s media as the most visible manifestations of a fashionable new social type—the "modern girl" or "new woman." Their images were omnipresent: on covers of fan magazines, in newspaper movie supplements, and in advertisements for consumer goods. These women attained such fame that Bao, who routinely went on set to observe the action and devise dialogue for their "cherry lips," compared them, tongue in cheek, to grand masters of the past: "Just as in the olden days we composed 'eight-legged essays' for the civil service examinations that 'gave voice to the sages,' today we 'give voice' to the female movie stars."

Writers would also craft fiction with plots revolving around silent cinema. Ding Ling (1904–1986) launched her career with the 1927 short story "Mengke," about a young woman who pursues acting in Shanghai—just as the author had once tried to do. Though Ding Ling had little success as an actress, she imagined for her protagonist what stardom might bring. Two years later, Zhang Henshui would pen a novel with a similar plotline, *Two Stars on the Silver Screen*, which was soon picked up by Lianhua, one of Shanghai's three major studios of the 1930s, modified into a screenplay by Zhu Shilin (1899–1967), and rendered as a partial-sound film with music tracks and elegant bilingual intertitles in Chinese and English.

As represented by Ding Ling and Zhang, the young starlet in the glamorous, high-stakes world of movie acting inevitably finds herself exploited and degraded—a holdover from former times, when entertainers were relegated to the margins of polite society. Could she ever overcome this fate and achieve a voice and authority of her own? Some actresses tried. Ai Xia (1912–1934), who performed in both silent and sound films, seemed a prototypical "modern woman," scripting and starring in *A Woman of Modern Times* (1933). On screen, she played out a liberating finale for her character in which she discards her romantic dreams and leaves "the cage of love." Yet, in real life, just a year later, Ai Xia took another path and committed suicide.

"To restore speech to this China that has been silent for centuries is not an easy matter," asserted Lu Xun (1881–1936) in 1927. He was addressing the challenges of literary reform, but he could just as well have been invoking the imminent transition from silent to sound cinema: the links between Chinese language, literature, and film would prove to be conspicuous stress points for directors, scriptwriters, and studios deep into the 1930s. Just as May Fourth advocates of vernacular language cast classical writing as "dead" and could argue that a single spoken dialect might help revitalize China, some filmmakers and critics saw the talkies as a more lifelike alternative to the medium they now called "soundless film." Others, like "neo- sensationist" writers Liu Na'ou (1905–1940) and Mu Shiying (1912–1940), championed the use of visual over verbal language in cinema. Yet many continued to rely on intertitles for exposition and dialogue, sometimes with added sound effects or music tracks, which prompted innovations and eccentricities. Defenders of classical language and silent cinema rightly noted their transregional comprehensibility and cultural distinction—one reason why so many feature films remained silent in China longer than in America, through at least 1937. Moreover, while writers could bring a revolutionary voice to literature with a pen or a typewriter, doing the same in film production and exhibition was much harder with the enormous cost of new sound technology and training.

China's "late silents" and partial-sound features would be more steeped in words than ever, as if struggling to speak out, pushing the boundaries of the medium to their limits. A case in point: the 1933 Mingxing film *Spring Silkworms*, based on the recent novella by Mao Dun (1896–1981)—itself foregrounded in the credits as a book cover opening onto the action. In adapting this story about the struggling countryside to film, Mao Dun's fellow vanguard members of the new left-wing arts movement, dramatist Xia Yan (1900–1995) and director Cheng Bugao (1898–1966), were intent on bringing a political edge to cinema. Negotiating increasing censorship, Cheng deployed a documentary style that earned *Spring Silkworms* recognition as China's first realist film, and experimented with creative textual and sound enhancements to emphasize the socioeconomic message: inserts showing legal contracts and signage, intertitles with expressively skewed or scaled fonts, and animated screen graphics of the Chinese character for "money."

At the artistic culmination of this trend, writers and the print media became focal points in *The New Woman*, produced just a year later by Lianhua. The protagonist, mesmerizingly embodied by Ruan Lingyu, is an aspiring novelist and music teacher named Wei Ming, who discovers that publishers and journalists are less interested in her art than in marketing her attractive image and personal life. Her book's ominous title, *The Tomb of Love*, evokes the melodramatic genre of tragic romance fiction so commercially popular in the 1920s. *The New Woman* eventually intimates such a backstory for Wei Ming—college love affair, elopement, pregnancy, abandonment—through flashbacks that resemble silent films from a prior era. The "tomb of love" recalls the "cage of love" in Ai Xia's earlier film, though for Wei Ming there is no escape except suicide, an ending that paralleled the demise of Ai Xia herself. Yet in *The New Woman*, there is another writer who offers a vision—and a voice—akin to the assertive one Ai Xia had projected for her protagonist in *A Woman of Modern Times*. Wei Ming's friend Li Aying composes lyrics promoting women's liberation and national salvation, which are collectively sung as an original vocal track for this intertitled film.

With its careful attention to writing and images, *The New Woman* appeared to literalize an equation its scriptwriter, Sun Shiyi (1904–1966), had earlier articulated: "Unexposed film is the paper, the camera is a pen, the actor's gestures are the calligraphy, and the director's approach to filming and editing are the grammar. Only when these things are combined artistically and technologically, to address the audience's visual perception directly, can they become a film story." Furnishing a grammar for Ruan's calligraphic performance, *The New Woman*'s director, Cai Chusheng (1906–1968), subtly deployed a wide range of textual and visual devices, most dramatically at the film's conclusion, when Wei Ming's life hangs in the balance. Gossip-filled headlines—displayed in bold inserts—awaken Wei Ming's anger. She declares, "I want revenge!" then struggles to rise and cries out, "Save me!" "I want to live!"—the Chinese characters inscribed on the image, superimposed over her mouth, and trembling as they expand to fill the frame.

When Ruan's own suicide, only weeks after *The New Woman*'s premiere, appeared to reenact the fate of Wei Ming—replete with tabloid gossip and news coverage nationwide and overseas—the resulting spectacle lodged a durable impression on writers and filmmakers. Even as the published letters themselves were viewed with some suspicion, and theories about "who killed the New Woman?" proliferated, "gossip is a fearful thing" endured. Just two months later, Lu Xun famously invoked the phrase for a scathing indictment of the press:

> Since Ruan Lingyu physically appeared on the silver screen, she was recognizable to all and thus more prone to becoming fodder for journalists intent on sensationalism to expand their market.... If we first imagine ourselves in her position, well, we'd probably realize Ruan Lingyu's belief that "gossip is a fearful thing" was true, and that others' belief that her suicide was linked to the press, was also true.

"Gossip is a fearful thing," in a sense, summed up the lingering challenges of language itself during China's era of silent and partial-sound cinema—and, with an unexpected turn, framed a vocabulary for filmmakers, artists, and writers probing their own complicated lives along the borders of public and private experience. More than half a century later, Hong Kong director Stanley Kwan (1957–) would dissect and rework this critical period of Chinese filmmaking in his 1992 masterpiece, *Center Stage*, refining the losses, elisions, and silences of history into the elusive biography of Ruan. The writer Ba Jin (1904–2005), having lived through the Cultural Revolution, would finally recycle the phrase "gossip is a fearful thing" as a sly mnemonic for the pernicious political rumors and social inequalities afflicting women and men, past into present:

> Back in the 1930s, when I survived only through my own individual struggle and the care of my friends, an artistically talented, successful female movie star committed suicide because "gossip is a fearful thing." But today, when individual struggle is widely criticized, why is there still so much "gossip"? And why has "gossip" once again become so "fearful"?

BIBLIOGRAPHY: Kristine Harris, *"Two Stars on the Silver Screen:* The Metafilm as Chinese Modern," in *History in Images: Pictures and Public Space in Modern China*, ed. Christian Henriot and Wen-hsin Yeh (Berkeley, CA, 2012), 191–244. Law Kar and Frank Bren, "Full Text of the Account of an Early Film Show in Qi Garden Published in *Youxi Bao* on September 5, 1897," in *Hong Kong Cinema: A Cross-Cultural View*, ed. Law Kar and Frank Bren (Lanham, MD, 2004), 313–314. Lu Xun, *Silent China: Selected Writings of Lu Xun*, ed. and trans. Gladys Yang (Oxford, 1973).

KRISTINE HARRIS

1935 · JUNE 18

"Superfluous words"

The Execution of Qu Qiubai

In late February 1935, former Chinese Communist Party leader Qu Qiubai (1899–1935) was captured by the Nationalist Army in southern Fujian and imprisoned. He had been attempting to reach Shanghai after departing from the Jiangxi Soviet, which the Communists had abandoned the previous autumn in the face of Chiang Kai-shek's (1887–1975) "encirclement" onslaught. Qu was able to keep his identity a secret for the first months of his incarceration, but its eventual revelation gave the Nationalists a potentially significant propaganda victory against the insurgent Red Army. For two months they pressed Qu, one of the most prominent Communists of his day, to renounce the cause. Qu was steadfast in his refusals. His eloquent and convincing defense of his communist principles, learned fifteen years before in Moscow and honed in the heady, intense political and literary debates of Shanghai, even reportedly persuaded at least one of his captors to join the Communists. His fate sealed, on the morning of June 18, Qu was led from the prison to a nearby park, where he had a drink, smoked a cigarette, and sang "The Internationale" before being shot.

Qu's literary legacy, however, complicates this story of political martyrdom. It was his passion for and talent in literary criticism that led him to take up the revolutionary cause, and he became the first in China to develop a sophisticated Marxist approach to literature. Yet it was also the cultivation of a literati persona, rooted in the lyrical sensibilities of traditional China, that would haunt Qu's final days. As a captive of Nationalist forces, Qu composed his final long essay, *Superfluous Words*. Written over the course of five days in May, just days before the orders for his execution were received, this remarkable and confounding document—alternately memoir, confession, and self-analysis—not only deepens our historical understanding of Chinese Communist Party (CCP) history, but also reveals a literary paradox at the heart of the revolutionary agenda. The affirmation of superfluousness that Qu articulates in *Superfluous Words* came after almost two decades of attempts to overcome this very sense of historical uselessness. Far from a sudden realization of fecklessness before an untimely death, the notion of the superfluous was for Qu a recurring motif throughout his life—a source of lyrical inspiration, an object of literary inquiry, and a target of political critique. For all his efforts to avoid a superfluous fate, however, at the end Qu found himself the very embodiment of the term, literally left behind and excluded from the narrative of revolutionary history.

Like many intellectuals of his generation, Qu was raised in a traditional gentry family in the midst of a steep decline. His education focused primarily on the Confucian classics, but was later invigorated through an enthusiastic interest in Buddhism. More concerned with transcending worldly affairs than with joining the emerging current of political activism,

Qu traveled to Beijing in 1916 to study traditional Chinese philosophy. Instead, he enrolled in the National Institute of Russian, enticed by the absence of tuition fees and the offer of a modest stipend. In *Superfluous Words* Qu admitted that he had no idea Russia was experiencing a revolution at that time, much less any inkling of the significance of Russian literature. Nevertheless, Qu's literary interests and linguistic talents soon intersected with the trends of cultural and social rebellion that roiled Beijing those years.

Though he continued to study Buddhism in his spare time, even for a time advocating national salvation through the practice of Bodhisatt-vahood, it was his knowledge of Russian, gleaned from intensive readings of authors such as Leo Tolstoy (1828–1910), Aleksandr Pushkin (1799–1837), and Nikolai Gogol (1809–1852), that pushed his thinking to become more politically conscious and helped him forge contacts with revolutionary-minded intellectuals. When the May Fourth Movement erupted across campuses in Beijing in 1919, Qu led the institute's delegation in the protests. The thrilling experience of mass action and participation in national affairs gave his literary studies a vigorous urgency. Like many of his May Fourth compatriots, Qu came to believe that literary revolution held the key to national rejuvenation. At the same time, Qu's research into Russian literature, which he saw as a model of realism that Chinese writers could emulate, introduced him to his literary doppelgänger: the superfluous man.

Qu's transition from aspiring literatus to political radical produced a "fragile dual personality," the very conundrum that afflicts many of the superfluous characters that populate the nineteenth-century Russian novels that fascinated Qu during his political awakening. The superfluous character expresses a yearning to belong to the nation and the historical moment, to overcome cynical social constraints like class, and to achieve an organic reunion with "the people." Though talented, the superfluous man's personal weakness and social alienation prevent fulfillment of his desire for cultural and political change. In his study of Russian literature, Qu took these failures to heart and used them to motivate his own political and literary undertakings. Acutely aware of the limits of an intellectual in an era of mass politics, Qu deployed superfluousness as a rhetorical bludgeon to attack China's "Europeanized" May Fourth intellectuals, who clung to their elitist conceits instead of merging with the masses. Qu acknowledges in *Superfluous Words*, however, that he was never successful at realigning his own viewpoint to that of the proletariat and had to suppress his own dreams of giving up politics to devote more time to reading. The tension between these contradictory personae—the leftist revolutionary on one hand, and the high-minded literary scholar on the other—constituted for Qu a dialectical confrontation that intensified his historical consciousness. Rather than characterize Qu's superfluousness simply as an incongruous lyrical moment in the course of epic history, we need to account for the simultaneity and reciprocity that exist between these sensibilities. *Superfluous Words* speaks not to a totalizing notion of history or self, but instead privileges the fragmented, disparate, and surplus possibilities that cannot be absorbed into the whole.

In 1920, with the goal of finding lessons for China's social transformation in the newly established Soviet Union, Qu set out for Moscow as a correspondent for Beijing's *Morning Post*. Though he was full of romantic hope and ambition, his two-year stay in Moscow was fraught with poverty, hunger, and loneliness, as well as bouts of tuberculosis, which tormented him throughout his life. Qu nonetheless dutifully carried on in his quest to locate the spiritual sources of Russia's revolution, which he describes in his collections *Journey to the Land of Hunger* (1922) and *History of the Heart in the Red Capital* (1924). These works are notable for their personal, melancholic tone as Qu discovers himself "enrolled in the vanguard of the world cultural movement"; the triumph of the proletarian masses, on the other hand, is nearly entirely absent. Nevertheless, Qu's serious investigation of Marxist texts in Russian while in Moscow helped solidify his political convictions and sharpened his theoretical acumen.

Returning to China in early 1923, Qu set out to devote his energy to systematizing Marxist literary thought, but his political involvement gradually overwhelmed his literary endeavors. His return happened at the urging of CCP leader Chen Duxiu (1879–1942), for whom Qu had served as an interpreter at the Comintern Congress in Moscow the previous November. He worked tirelessly in his new political role; in addition to editing several journals, he taught courses on Marxism and literary theory at Shanghai University. In *Superfluous Words*, Qu attributes his swift rise in the CCP to a "historical misunderstanding," claiming his true identity as that of a "dilettantish 'literatus'" and likening political work to "a nightmare." Qu's stint as leader of the CCP came during a chaotic period in the party's development, following the breakdown of the alliance with the Nationalists in 1927 and Chiang Kai-shek's bloody extermination campaigns. Trying to seize the advantage in the opening throes of a civil war, CCP policy under Qu swung from a united front to armed insurrection. Subsequent uprisings in Nanchang, Hunan, and Guangzhou ended in devastating defeats for the Communists. After just one catastrophic year, Qu was removed from his leadership position in 1928, accused of following the dangerous political line of "blind adventurism." In *Superfluous Words*, Qu claims that the end of his stint as party leader came as something of a relief and that a "common man of letters" like himself has no place in politics. "If this isn't a 'historical misunderstanding,'" he asks, "then what is it?"

Qu's return to the cultural arena following this frustrating tenure as party leader and a further fractious period as CCP representative in Moscow in 1929–1930 was marked by a passionate reengagement with literature, and in particular with the question of the role of the intellectual writer in revolutionary times. As leader of the League of Left-Wing Writers in Shanghai in the early 1930s, Qu argued forcefully for the vanguard position of aesthetics in revolution. The polemical essays he issued in those years were primarily addressed to his comrades in the league, mostly former May Fourth–era intellectuals like himself. The most formidable obstacle to the "massification" of art and literature, Qu argues, are those so-called "revolutionary writers" who "stand outside the masses" and, rather than modify their own ways of thinking, use their social status to admonish the proletariat. Qu's prescription for a "people's literary revolution" instead requires making direct contact with the masses of rural peasantry by adopting their language and aesthetic forms, fostering their own writing abilities, and living among them. His trenchant rhetoric foreshadows Mao Zedong's (1893–1976) injunctions made a decade later at Yan'an in both style and substance; he was no longer identifying foreign models for emulation (the Russian masters disappeared from his writings), but offering solutions anchored in the countryside, solutions meant to rectify the kind of ideological aberrations he later confessed to committing in *Superfluous Words*. The key to any progress on the cultural front, according to Qu, was resolving this problem of distance between urban intellectuals and the rural peasantry by establishing a new, grassroots revolutionary language capable of serving as a common vernacular between them. Qu, along with Soviet colleagues, developed the Latinxua Sin Wenz romanization system of Chinese, which was intended to not only facilitate literacy in the countryside but eventually supplant character-based Chinese script altogether.

Qu's role in the league forced him into hiding in Shanghai on several occasions; often he received shelter from his closest friend, Lu Xun (1881–1936). In early 1934, he was dispatched to the Jiangxi Soviet to serve as commissar of education. Leaving behind his wife and friends in Shanghai, Qu reported to Ruijin, where he put his theories on proletarian revolutionary literature and language reform into practice, setting up schools, training teachers, and organizing cultural activities, particularly in theater. Although the next year Qu would confess that in fact there was no "common language" between himself and the rural masses, his contributions were considered exemplary. The workload and rustic setting took a toll on his worsening health, however, and when the decision to abandon the Soviet was made that autumn, Qu stayed behind.

The retreat of the Red Army from the Jiangxi Soviet was the initial stage of what would later become known as the Long March, the mythic "manifesto" of the Chinese Communist Party. Qu, left out of the momentous movement of history, turns once again to the superfluous man. "Now that I have been completely relieved of my armaments and pulled from the ranks," he writes in the preface, "all that remains is myself." In this final moment of futility, Qu embraces a repressed lyrical mode of expression: "In my heart I have an irrepressible urge and need to speak the words of my inner being, to thoroughly reveal the truth deep in my heart." Standing outside history in this way, Qu affirmatively identifies as a *wenren*, a classical term for a "literatus" from China's traditional past. The *wenren* figure, "truly a character of utter uselessness" in Qu's estimation, is a far cry from the politically and socially awakened intellectual, much less a revolutionary. Rather than realizing communion with the masses, the literatus is left behind, a remnant of an irretrievable past.

Qu's reputation since his execution, like that of many Communist Party leaders, has fluctuated according to the political needs of the time. Criticized and removed from power during his life, Qu was eulogized as a martyr after the Communist triumph of 1949 and even had his remains transferred to Babaoshan Revolutionary Cemetery in Beijing in time for the twentieth anniversary of his death. Qu's posthumous veneration, however, was conditional; emphasis was placed on his contributions to cultural work in developing Marxist literary thought and the work of language reform, while *Superfluous Words* was disavowed altogether. Thought to be altered, or even forged, by his Nationalist captors for propaganda purposes, Qu's authorship of *Superfluous Words* was not acknowledged, ironically, until the outbreak of the Cultural Revolution, when it was used to vilify Qu's "traitorousness" and imprison the family that had survived him. While the legitimacy of the text is no longer in question, its ruptured historical path suggests a continuing unease with the "superfluous" words that capture such historical disquiet.

BIBLIOGRAPHY: Jamie Greenbaum, *Qu Qiubai: Superfluous Words* (Canberra, 2006). Tsi-an Hsia, "Chü Ch'iu-po: The Making and Destruction of a Tenderhearted Communist," in *The Gates of Darkness: Studies on the Leftist Literary Movement in China* (Seattle, 1968), 3–54. Paul G. Pickowicz, *Marxist Literary Thought in China: The Influence of Chü Ch'iu-pai* (Berkeley, CA, 1981). Ellen Widmer, "Qu Qiubai and Russian Literature," in *Modern Chinese Literature in the May Fourth Era*, Merle Goldman (Cambridge, MA, 1977), 103–125.

ANDY RODEKOHR

1935 · JULY 28 AND AUGUST 1

Zhang Leping invents his Sanmao comic strip and the Nationalist regime announces the year as "Children's Year."

The Child and the Future of China in the Legend of Sanmao

The famous cartoon figure Sanmao (Three Hairs) was created by the cartoonist Zhang Leping (1910–1992), who dedicated most of his work to the theme of orphans. The Sanmao comic strip was first published in installments beginning on July 28, 1935, in the Shanghai paper *Little Morning Daily*, during the Children's Year promoted by the Nationalist regime. When Sanmao first made his debut, Zhang represented him as a "naughty and innocent little boy from an ordinary Shanghai family," without many pronounced political characteristics. During the war years of 1937–1945, however, Zhang stopped working on Sanmao, but he picked up the theme again and, in 1946 and 1947, created the two comic strips *Sanmao Joins the Army* and *The Orphan Sanmao on the Streets*, respectively. By this time, Sanmao had been transformed into a boy from the countryside who became a homeless orphan on the streets of Shanghai. In 1949, *The Orphan* was adapted into a film with two endings. One ending places the homeless Sanmao back on the streets; the other has Sanmao celebrating the liberation of Shanghai and the whole nation. These two endings preface the ambiguous fate of Sanmao in the 1950s: Is Sanmao a dark and uneasy symbol of an old China, or the hope for a new China? This entry will document the multiple transformations of Sanmo and the implications for understanding the cultural history of modern China.

The story of Sanmao is one of the major pictorial narratives about the fashioning of modern Chinese subjectivity. The birth of this cartoon figure is underlain by a "discovery of the child" as a "figure" of modernity since the late Qing. As part of a "literature of mankind," the child was created as a new, modern subject. This process was tied to the broader promotion of previously underprivileged groups, such as women and peasants, which was part of the ongoing development of modern Chinese literature. As a recurring site for expressing concerns about the reform of national culture in modern China, the child was configured or reconfigured into several different literary and political beings, from the "little hero" during the late Qing, to "little readers" (Bing Xin [1900–1999]) and "little savages" (Zhou Zuoren [1885–1967]) in the 1920s, to "little teachers" (Tao Xingzhi [1891–1946]) during the war period, to young pioneers in the 1950s. But, as demonstrated by Lu Xun's (1881–1936) famous outcry, "Save the children…," the child as a new subject in modern Chinese culture manifests itself in a highly paradoxical manner. While the child is often considered the agent of renewal in modern China and tenaciously associated with the national culture, whom can we rely on to save them if the adults are already corrupted as Lu Xun has claimed? Also, the child could be construed as a subversive power that challenges the political, social, and cultural order on which the nation is constructed. Xia Yan (1900–1995) wrote, "The issue of Sanmao is both social and political." It is in this conjunction that the graphic illustration of Sanmao became a much-contested representation of Chinese modernity.

To begin, as can be seen in the strip "Overcorrection," taken from the 1935 series, the early Sanmao is not an orphan but appears to be

Zhang Leping, "Overcorrection." Source: Originally published in 1935. Reproduced in Ding Yanzhao and Yu Zhi, eds., *Shanghai Memory: The Thirties under Zhang Leping's Brush* (Shanghai: Cishu chubanshe, 2005), 22. I am indebted to Zhang Leping's family for allowing me to use the four images in this essay.

from an urban middle-class family, which could also be confirmed in his apparel and the various objects in his surroundings (such as a refrigerator). Despite the occasional allusion to the Japanese invasion of China in 1936, the early series was generally light-hearted and Sanmao was usually just a cute and innocent boy from a bourgeois family. The revitalized Sanmo that appeared after the war, however, took on entirely different characteristics. In the final strip of *Sanmao Joins the Army*, the whole space is occupied by the letter *V*, which could be understood as the first letter of the word "victory." However, the whole meaning of the cartoon turns out to be much more politically ambiguous and depressing. On the bottom is Sanmao with a confused expression, the arms of the *V* forming two roads, one of which leads to the backward countryside and the other reaching toward postwar Shanghai, with spider webs on tall buildings

Zhang Leping, the final strip of *Sanmao Joins the Army*. Source: *Shenbao*, October 4, 1947, 12.

indicating the dilapidated postwar condition of the city. What is very striking is that the V is made visible by way of a visual field constituted of graves. Surrounded by the dense tombs, little Sanmao seems grotesque: Both roads are built on death, so which way should Sanmao go? What choice should he make? Zhang poses a very important social and political question. If we connect this with his later work, *The Orphan Sanmao on the Streets* (1947), we can infer that Zhang's answer for Sanmao was to go to Shanghai and to become a homeless boy.

In *The Orphan*, Sanmao starts out as a poor orphan in the countryside and arrives in Shanghai in the hope of making his fortune—a dream that is swiftly crushed. A strip entitled "The Disillusionment of Beautiful Dreams" tracks his attempts to make a living in the big city; the exploitation of child labor is represented as an essential part of the consumer society in Shanghai. He helps to push a rickshaw, picks up cigarette ends on the street, and also works as an apprentice to a printer and as a servant to a rich family; pervading all is a sense that this abject being cannot fit into any corner of the consumer city, not even the dustbin. Sanmao's tiny body is always pushed to a corner by the crowds of the city and his face is often distorted because of the fear, anger, or sadness he encounters, which also makes him funny in a mode of excess. The Sanmao figure conjoins grotesque and abject together and, being ugly and aberrant according to conventional culture, he contests the frequent use of healthy and beautiful children as the embodiment of a new China's future.

An ambiguous contrast in the cartoon is between Sanmao and other children. A very typical example is a strip entitled "All Are Children." In the picture, the setting is a public space in the city. The half-naked Sanmao and his master are performing, surrounded by a crowd of parents and their children. Sanmao is held high in the air by only one hand of the barnstormer and his thin limbs are tied by ropes, contorting him into a ball. Probably because of this bodily torture, as well as fear, he is crying, with big tears flying into the sky. In contrast to Sanmao's pain, the audience's faces are full of excitement and surprise. Most of the audience members are children the same age as Sanmao, but they are dressed very well and have modern toys and food in their hands. In other words, Sanmao, to a certain degree, is also a toy for these children and entertains these future masters of the nation using his young and tortured body.

A slogan on a pole nearby reads "Celebrate Children's Day," while behind the pole stands another poor boy with a long face who is holding a basket of food to sell. He leers at Sanmao, which may show his dissatisfaction with the performance, since it is drawing most people's attention away from his product. At the pictorial level, this boy is almost invisible and alienated, just as he is ignored by society. Also bizarre is the contrast between these two groups of children in terms of number. In the drawing, most of the children are well clothed and well fed, from middle-class bourgeois families, and only Sanmao and the other poor boy are excluded from the group.

If, therefore, most children are happy and well bred, what can Sanmao and the other poor boy tell us? That their miserable condition is only an unfortunate accident? Or that they represent the social reality of Chinese children of the time? Another important issue is the question of which group of children represents the future of the nation. Using Lu Xun's term, the children in the audience can be defined as cold onlookers, or, maybe much worse, they are enjoying the spectacle. What will happen if they become the masters of future China? Conversely, if Sanmao embodies

同是儿童

Zhang Leping, "All Are Children." Source: *Dagong Daily,* unspecified date in 1948. Reproduced in *The Orphan Sanmao on the Streets* (Shanghai: Shaonian ertong chubanshe, 2006), 155.

the future national subject, that is also not necessarily positive. He is far from perfect or revolutionary. This drawing puts the homeless Sanmao, an almost invisible and impoverished boy, and his young bourgeois audience all in quite problematic positions.

In 1949, the Shanghai-based and left-leaning Kunlun Film Company adapted the 1948 cartoon series into a film. Produced at the crucial historical moment when the control of the Nationalist Party was about to give way to the Chinese Communist Party–led government, *The Orphan Sanmao on the Streets,* scripted by Yang Hansheng (1902–1993), was one of the first few films shown after the Communists came to power. The ending of this film deserves more attention. It originally concluded with Sanmao leaving the rich family and returning to the cold and windy street, a conclusion that runs parallel to Zhang's cartoon version. In the cartoon, the final strip is a single picture with the caption "A Big Uproar" and depicts a small Sanmao trapped at a crowded crossroad. After the liberation of Shanghai in 1949, however, the film appended a coda

Zhang Leping and Xu Changming, "Welcome the New Year." Source: The cover image of the journal *Little Red Soldier* (Shanghai), no. 240, January 1978.

set in liberated Shanghai, where Sanmao is seen happily joining the celebratory parade with other homeless children, a sharp contrast to the ambiguous endings of the cartoon and original film versions. It certainly prefigures the new style of orphan narrative that would develop after 1949.

Following liberation, the creation of a new, young generation included two processes: one was to remold the "old" representations of children; the other was to establish a new model going forward. In the 1950s, Zhang finished a few new series of Sanmao cartoons, including *Sanmao's Indictment, Stories of Sanmao's Liberation, The Present and the Past of Sanmao,* and *Sanmao Celebrates Liberation.* And in the period of the Cultural Revolution, Sanmao also became a little red soldier (see "Welcome the New Year"). In these series, Sanmao changes into the healthy and plump boy of the new China, rather than the lonely and bony homeless child of prerevolution Shanghai.

Just as one of the endings of the 1949 film puts Sanmao back on the street, the transformation was not a smooth one, and there were debates about Sanmao's image. Some argued that Sanmao was a homeless child and a member of the *Lumpenproletariat*, and therefore was not worthy of being drawn. Others claimed that Sanmao was too angular, which was only proper for representing the children of the old society. In addition, the three hairs on his head also implied malnourishment, so if Zhang continued to paint Sanmao, he was urged to add more hair to create a healthier image. Others made harsh comments about Sanmao's age. In their view, it was against the laws of nature for Zhang to still depict Sanmao as a boy, considering that Zhang had created the character more than ten years earlier. All these different opinions frustrated Zhang and made him question how he should deal with Sanmao.

In May 1950, the Committee of Shanghai Cartoon Artists organized a symposium for Zhang to discuss his cartoons of Sanmao. Eventually they came to the conclusion that Sanmao should not change his characteristics, because he had left a deep impression on his readers. The age of Sanmao should also remain constant, around ten years old. But they also emphasized that Sanmao should be represented as a boy of the new China, and should show the happiness of the children of the new China. So, in his later manifestations, Sanmao participates in various revolutionary activities in Shanghai. He exemplifies the idealized fresh image of children in the new society.

Through the example of the Sanmao figure, this always incomplete being, I suggest that each figuration of the child not only condenses particular material-semiotic practices, but also brings a particular version of Chinese modernity into being. The different figurations of the child embody Chinese intellectuals' and thinkers' desire for transformative changes in different periods. In other words, Sanmao is needed to remain forever as a child, just as China's quest for modernity is always a work in progress, never truly completed or "matured."

Zhang's Sanmao series thus provides us with the historical evolution of the meanings of the child's body in modern China. Together with the transformation of the protagonist from a naughty boy in a middle-class family into a little soldier in the Nationalist army, then a homeless child on the street, and finally a healthy and happy child in the new Communist China, Sanmao gradually acquired different political significances. This figure was always in a process of becoming rather than being a closed, individual body. Moreover, its continuing transformation epitomizes the multiplicity and instability of the trope of the child in representations of Chinese modernity, while at the same time capturing the different ideological orientations during these periods.

BIBLIOGRAPHY: Mary Ann Farquhar, *Children's Literature in China: From Lu Xun to Mao Zedong* (Armonk, NY, 1999). Andrew F. Jones, "The Child as History in Republican China: A Discourse on Development," *positions: east asia cultures critique* 10, no. 3 (Winter 2002): 695–727. Xu Lanjun and Andrew F. Jones, eds., *Ertong de faxian: Xiandai Zhongguo wenxue ji wenhua zhong de ertong wenti* (Beijing, 2011).

LANJUN XU

1935 · DECEMBER 21

"Spoken drama of, for, and by the peasants"

Crossing the River *and Ding County Experimental Theater*

On the cold evening of December 21, 1935, over two thousand villagers from East Buluogang and neighboring villages in Ding County, Hebei, gathered for a night at the theater. Even before the first line of dialogue had been delivered, several novel aspects signaled that it was to be an evening of distinction. First, the play to be staged was not the traditional *da yangge* (great rice-sprout opera) but a three-act modern drama, *Guodu* (Crossing the river; hereafter *Crossing*), written by Xiong Foxi (1900–1965). Second, the cast did not come from a standard traveling company but consisted of two kinds of amateurs—local villagers from East Buluogang and their teachers in the Theater Division of the Mass Education Movement (MEM). Finally, the performance space was not the usual temporary stage surrounded by crowds, but an open-air theater that had been renovated by the East Buluogang villagers themselves. Because of these innovations, the audience awaited *Crossing*'s debut with eager anticipation.

Perhaps even more excited than the local villagers and the cast were the VIP spectators, prominent critics from Beijing (which was temporarily renamed Beiping during the 1930s and 1940s) and Nanjing invited to witness the event, who were noticeably enthralled by the spectacle of peasants performing modern drama. By the mid-1930s, spoken drama had won significant audiences in urban China, but when it came to the peasantry, it had been much less successful in striking a responsive chord. Despite the plethora of discursive appeals for spoken drama to "go to the people" and the efforts of dramatists to write for and about the peasantry, the results were largely disappointing. Peasants viewed spoken drama with suspicion, considering it to be foreign and, because of its psychological explorations and depictions of modern love, even morally corrupt. Thus, for both the VIP critics and their urban readers, peasants' participation in *Crossing*, as both performers and audience, seemed unprecedented.

In such a state of heightened expectation, *Crossing*'s opening was particularly striking. While singing the "Song of Crossing the River," an adaption of a popular local tune, peasant performers who played bridge builders charged through the audience, "hauling rocks and lumber … pushing carts, or shouldering baskets," and then climbed on the stage, where they unloaded their construction materials around the scaffolding that constituted the main set design. Audience members, who were not assigned specific seats, sat in a lower auditorium area that was connected to the stage by steps. In between the audience and the stage were male and female peasants acting the roles of ferry crossers and onlookers, wandering and chatting as the local villagers would likely do in their everyday lives. Watching their fellow villagers sing, dress, and act in such a realistic manner made it easy for the audience to identify with *Crossing*'s theatrical reality.

Of course, much of *Crossing*'s success can be attributed to the play's content, which centers on a struggle between upright villagers and a hooligan ferry owner surnamed Hu. Zhang Guoben, an intellectual who has just returned to his hometown, organizes a group of oppressed young peasants to build a bridge across the local river. The benefits that such a bridge would bring the community, however, threaten the status of the ferry owner, who enjoys a monopoly over river crossings. Hu's attempts to sabotage the project are eventually revealed, and he is arrested by a policeman sent down by the government. The play ends with Hu being collectively judged by both the performers and audience.

Critics praised *Crossing* as "a mixed-blood child" that skillfully combined Western theatrical perceptions with the local flavor of Ding County peasant life. They also took note of the social functions of the performance, viewing the theater as a public space that transformed and accommodated a still-forming rural public. In this manner, their reviews contextualized *Crossing*'s relevance to the twin projects of drama popularization and rural reconstruction then taking place in China. "Dingxianism," as Edgar Snow (1905–1972) called it, became an unlikely factor in China's cultural and political development over the following decades.

Ding County's transformation from a rural community (located 128 miles south of Beijing) to the home of China's first "experimental theater" stemmed from the combined efforts of the Mi family, local gentry who had promoted village reconstruction since the early 1900s, and James Yen (Yan Yangchu, 1890–1990), who cofounded MEM in 1923. Yen envisioned MEM to be a fourfold project, comprising the study of literature and art, economy, hygiene, and citizenship, that would cure "the four root evils"—ignorance, poverty, disease, and civic disintegration—Yen diagnosed as causing China's "rural crisis." When the Mi family invited MEM to come to Zhai Village in Ding County in 1926, Yen was given the perfect laboratory to pursue his dream of bringing "modernity" to rural society and turning China's peasants into "new citizens."

Soon after arriving in Ding County, MEM established a Department of Literature and Visual Education, which conducted several surveys and investigations regarding the popular performance forms of *da yangge* and *dagu* (big drum). Qu Junong (1901–1976) and Sun Fuyuan (1894–1966), the department's directors, quickly noted that the rural theater relied heavily on thematic motifs with strong local characteristics. Furthermore, they saw that the local peasants not only enjoyed watching these performances, but also sometimes were inspired to imitate them. Grasping the medium's potential for social transformation, MEM decided to reform and employ local theater techniques in pursuit of "modernization." Yen chose Xiong Foxi to lead this effort.

Xiong was a leading voice in China's National Drama Movement (1925–1926), the purpose of which he saw as "drama of, for, and by all Chinese." By the early 1930s, Xiong had already directed several plays and published frequent reviews and translations of drama in the periodical *Beijing Morning*. However, these plays, written and directed in Beijing, enjoyed popularity only among a small circle of urban intellectual youths. Xiong was not able to make dramas "of, for, and by" the Chinese masses—the peasantry, which constituted more than 80 percent of China's population—until 1932, when Yen asked him to head MEM's newly formed Theater Division.

The first spoken drama Xiong staged in Ding County was *Trumpet* (1929), a play he had written several years prior that addressed the relationship between a performer (that is, an outsider) and a rural community. Performed two nights in a row in early 1932 in MEM's Demonstration Theater (a remodeled examination hall), *Trumpet*'s rural setting, "natural acting," and humorous dialogue won it a full house and a favorable response from its audience. *Trumpet*'s success ensured that Xiong would continue to write and stage spoken dramas that took peasants' everyday lives as their subject.

In order to do so effectively, Xiong adjusted his writing style. First, he conducted social surveys and investigations to learn how the rural community worked and lived. His efforts at uncovering the rural mind-set paid off, and from 1932 to 1937, he wrote several plays, including *A Strong Son with Hoe* (1932), *Butcher* (1933), and, most famously, *Crossing*, that enjoyed great popularity among rural audiences. Second, Xiong realized that plays with down-to-earth peasant themes left little room for the psychological nuances, plot subtlety, and themes of modern love that were popular in urban theaters. Accordingly, Xiong chose to highlight dynamic and "masculine" actions. For example, when writing *Crossing*, Xiong chose not to include a romantic subplot, fearing that it would weaken the "group dynamics" from which the "major power" of the play derived.

Soon after *Trumpet*'s debut, which was performed by the staff of the Theater Division, Ding County peasants began acting under Xiong's direction; at the same time, the Theater Division received frequent requests from villagers to expand their fast-growing repertoire. During 1933 and 1934, thirteen villages, under the supervision of MEM, formed spoken drama troupes that recruited both men and women to perform plays in their own villages and tour in others. In this manner, "spoken drama of, for, and by the peasants" also became produced "by" the peasants.

While excited by the natural talent and enthusiasm of the villagers, Xiong was not willing to completely surrender artistic quality to peasant hands. Instead, he aimed to guide his performers through the entire process of theater making (including the rehearsal system, directorship, and technical design). The Theater Division's supervision took the form of rehearsal workshops that were usually held every night for two to three months before the performance. In these workshops, peasant performers studied the plot and sentiments of the play; practiced cold readings; made props; and expanded their technical skills. Xiong and the Theater Division were thus able to promote MEM's goal of modernization while also guaranteeing the quality of their works.

Equally crucial for the Theater Division's success was to find the appropriate space for its performances. When MEM first arrived in Ding County, the Mi family suggested that Yen use the examination hall as a headquarters for conducting literacy classes and making print and visual materials for the rural masses. Then, when Xiong staged *Trumpet* in this newly christened "Demonstration Theater" in 1932, the imperial-cum-Republican education center was further transformed into a public space accommodating both performances and public assemblies. The architectural structure (walled boundaries, grand examination room, and open-air court) provided an innovative performance space that the makeshift stages common to the rest of rural China could not match.

Aware of the advantages that a fixed performance space could offer, such as a clear "center" that would hold the audience's attention and a more intimate sense of community between performers and spectators, in late 1932 the Theater Division proposed organizing the peasants of neighboring villages to build their own modern theaters. Nearly two years after the initial proposal, East Buluogang was chosen out of thirty villages to be one of two such "experimental fields" (the other being West Jianyang). Once East Buluogang was selected, around fifty local peasant-performers, working under the supervision of the Theater Division, began a sustained regimen of construction and rehearsals, building their new theater by day and training for their performances at night. After nearly a year of such efforts, East Buluogang's open-air theater was ready for use, just in time for *Crossing*'s debut.

Contrary to the accounts of *Crossing*'s VIP spectators, the play's local success was not entirely unprecedented. The fact that the majority of spoken dramas staged in Ding County during the 1930s had either an all-peasant cast or a mixed cast of peasants and teachers greatly enhanced the genre's local popularity. Watching their friends and acquaintances essentially play themselves on stage, peasant audiences gradually became accustomed to the theatrical power of spoken drama, a power that blurred the lines between theatrical representation and reality. In this manner, the audience was transformed from being a mere crowd of neighbors and fellow villagers into a rural public with a shared life, identity, and sentiments.

Furthermore, given that in the mid-1930s, spoken drama troupes in cosmopolitan cities like Shanghai were still struggling to find designated spaces for performances, the fact that rural communities in Ding County had theaters built for and by peasants was quite remarkable. One of the reasons why MEM's theater experiments attracted such media attention was that intellectuals viewed peasant-directed theater construction not only as a means of offering modern theater to the rural masses, but also as part of the process of turning them into new citizens. In other words, the cooperative labor required for such construction would contribute to forging the communal identification that would be further cultivated among peasants by performing and watching spoken dramas. Ding County's still-forming rural public was thus built on both sentiments and materials; and the communal identification was at once imagined and materialized.

These political overtones made "Dingxianism" an enticing model for dramatists and social reformers of all political persuasions. When the war broke out in 1937, leading figures of the Theater Division (including Xiong, Chen Zhice [1894–1954] and Yang Cunbin [1911–1989]) applied the "Ding County model" to their respective drama movements in the greater Chongqing area. Likewise, the mass theater movement in Yan'an shared commonalities with the Ding County experience. One can easily read in Mao Zedong's (1893–1976) *Talks at the Yan'an Forum on Literature and Art* an affiliation with Xiong's call for drama "of, for, and by" the peasants. Finally, MEM's theater experiences found echoes in the rural amateur drama troupes and mass campaigns of the 1950s and early 1960s.

Thanks in part to the attention given to MEM's theater experiments within China's 1930s mediasphere, *Crossing* and other spoken dramas staged in Ding County developed into a mass cultural movement. By contextualizing the successful 1935 production of *Crossing*, one finds that the popularity of spoken drama among Ding County peasants was far from accidental. Instead, MEM's Theater Division made necessary adjustments to its language and performative modes to create a new form of modern theater that negotiated with local realities, enlisted and disciplined the rural masses' participation, and strengthened the entertaining and didactic functions assigned to theater. Indeed, from today's vantage point, much of the development of Chinese drama in the middle of the twentieth century can be traced back to the actions of Ding County teachers and peasants during those prescient days and nights between 1932 and 1937.

BIBLIOGRAPHY: Li Jinghan, ed., *Ding Xian shehui gaikuang diaocha* (Beijing, 1933). Liu Siyuan, "'A Mixed-Blooded Child, Neither Western Nor Eastern': Sinicization of Western-Style Theatre in Rural China in the 1930s," *Asian Theatre Journal* 25, no. 2 (2008): 272–297. Kathryn Alexia Merkel-Hess McDonald, "A New People: Rural Modernity in Republican China," PhD diss., University of California, Irvine, 2009. National Association of Mass Education Movements, ed., *Guodu yanchu teji* (Beijing, 1936). Sun Huizhu, "The Peasants' Theatre Experiment in Ding Xian County (1932–1937)," PhD diss., New York University, 1990. Xiong Foxi, *Xiju dazhonghua zhi shiyan* (Nanjing, China, 1947). Zhang Yu, "Visual and Theatrical Constructs of a Modern Life in the Countryside: James Yen, Xiong Foxi, and the Rural Reconstruction Movement in Ding Country (1920s–1930s)," *Modern Chinese Literature and Culture* 25, no. 1 (Spring 2013): 47–95.

MAN HE

1936 · MAY 21

"To reveal the entire face of China during one day"

One Day in China

In modern times there have been many projects that have endeavored to collectively document a date or a moment in history, but few have been as successful and influential as *One Day in China*. This thick, richly illustrated volume was edited in 1936 by a committee led by Mao Dun (Shen Yanbing, 1896–1981), and published only months after issuing the call for contributions. The first project of this type was perhaps *One Day in the World* (*Den mira*), initiated about a year before in the Soviet Union by an aging Maksim Gorky (1868–1936). Such projects try to bring the greatest possible variety of voices together to display a cross section of humanity and history at a certain point in time. The Soviet project was typically global in scope, but in its execution ended up being primarily a scrapbook of newspaper items published around the world on September 27, 1935. It also was published later than the Chinese project, and after Gorky's death.

Spin-offs of *One Day in China* were numerous over the ensuing two decades, but stayed within a national or regional scope: writers were mobilized to contribute to collections such as *One Day in Shanghai* (1938) and *One Day in Central Hebei* (1940). In June 2014, Beijing's Penghao Theater staged a collaborative avant-garde play inspired by *One Day in China* in Beijing under the direction of Japanese director Sato Makoto (1943–), using the same date of May 21 to commemorate Mao Dun's 1936 book. The "one day" idea seems to have limitless appeal across generations.

An interesting feature of this impulse to capture a global moment, especially in the early years of Gorky and Mao Dun, is the revolutionary perspective that inspires it, and the belief that the collective voice of the masses can authenticate that perspective. Contributors to *One Day in China* were instructed to capture their experience of May 21, 1936, in a written essay of no more than two thousand words, a piece of artwork, a handbill, or a leaflet. Most contributions were in written form. In his editorial commentary, Mao Dun writes:

> We required that the essay had to deal with an event that occurred on May twenty-first. Next, this event had to have social significance or at least reflect the living conditions of a certain segment of society....
>
> We drew most heavily on the essays written by those who had never before written for publication (that is, the non-professional writers). This is because their essays conformed most closely to our criteria, and they are the reason why the material in this book is unmonotonous and lays bare the many faces of life on one day in China.

Leftist literature in the 1930s worldwide already tended toward writing realistically to the point of documentary accuracy. The emergence of "reportage literature" at the time, whose supposed veracity imbued it with literary value, is the clearest evidence of this trend. There was a related impulse toward a panoramic comprehensiveness in perspective. After Mao Dun's first fictional works appeared in the late 1920s, although he considered himself a decidedly leftist and revolutionary writer, he was attacked by leftist critics for representing only a narrow sliver of the social horizon (namely progressive-minded, youthful intellectuals from relatively privileged backgrounds) in his works. Mao Dun defended himself against this at the time, pointing out that a writer can only write

about the world with which he is familiar. But in fact, his later writings—
such as *Spring Silkworms* (1933), a story trilogy about a peasant family in
southern China—demonstrate a shift toward broader representation of
different sectors of society, from peasants all the way up to industrialists,
politicians, and financiers. Thus, while Mao Dun's unique fictional idiom
was preserved, he seems to have been influenced to change his fictional
world in response to these critiques.

Mao Dun was one of the most important Chinese novelists of the
twentieth century. His own evolving fictional approach also showed a
tendency toward the documentary. In his largest novel, *Midnight* (1933),
he adopted the methods of reportage writers, such as entering into factories and slums and interviewing members of the lower classes to gather
authentic information about working conditions, to add a greater sense
of realism to the novel. From this we can see the connection between
realist fiction and the panoramic perspective of the *One Day* project: to
accurately represent contemporary history, realistic writing privileges
the voices and words of real people, especially when they represent
communities outside the author's personal experience. Thus, a project
that documented the lives of hundreds of different kinds of people in
their own words, across boundaries of class, profession, age, gender, and
region, promised to deliver an unprecedented genuineness of historical
experience that fiction, with its often limited focus on individuals or small
social groupings, could not attain. Mao Dun was probably not thinking
of abandoning fiction in favor of collective documentary projects (his
subsequent career developments do not bear this out), but at the same
time there is a tendency in his writing leading up to 1936 that made a
project like *One Day in China* practically inevitable, if only as a singular
experiment.

Authenticity in itself, though, was not enough. This project was not
to be an unadulterated transmission of an unlimited variety of voices; the
large editorial committee (eleven members, including writers, historians,
educators, and journalists) had before them a large job. Mao Dun's committee received over three thousand submissions, of which only a small
fraction were adopted for the collection. While we cannot help but be
impressed by the sheer number of contributions collected in such a short
time, the editors' need to create a "cross section" of Chinese experience
that fit their own perspective and sense of China's reality guaranteed a

distinctive slant in the content of the final product. We do not and perhaps cannot know what was excluded from the collection, but it seems
safe to assume that some of it, if not most of it, is material that did not
adequately emphasize tensions among social classes, the threat of war
against Japan, and the threat of every other kind of military, economic, and
political oppression confronting China at that time.

Mao Dun goes on to write that the book, with its prevalence of nonprofessional writers, proves that the prospects for Chinese literature in
the future are bright:

> Truly, here there is everything: the dissipation and indulgence of the
> rich, the writing masses on the edge of starvation, the patriots devot-
> ing their lives to the people's revolution, the backward and insensate
> classes, the rampant religious superstitions, the degeneracy of the
> public servants, the overbearing swagger of the local bullies and evil
> gentry, the oppression of women, the hesitance of the petty bour-
> geoisie and intellectuals, the bitter pain and enduring spirit of the
> martyrs. Truly! From the main streets and back alleys of cities, from
> the tall buildings and thatched huts, from the deserted little market-
> places of small towns, from the broken-down walls and dilapidated
> houses of farming villages, from schools, from the sleeping quarters
> of the unemployed, from the army barracks, from the prisons, from
> the companies and the government offices, from the factories, from
> the markets, from the small shops, from the old families governed by
> strict family rules—from every single corner of China there have arisen
> anguished and strong calls to arms, grief-stricken utterances, bitter
> cursing, tearful smiles, restrained but boiling passions, the sleeptalking
> of those leading lives without a sense of purpose, the charlatanism of
> religious converts, the sardonic laughter of heartless ones! This is the
> spectacular orchestra heard on one day in today's China, but it is not
> confined only to this one day!

The rhetoric Mao Dun employs in this closing paragraph to his editorial commentary resembles the rhetoric used in articles published in the
previous years promoting reportage literature: the value of the writing
lay in the rich social diversity it represents, and he also makes it clear
that the book has a clear political posture. To this social diversity of

reportage literature, the *One Day in China* project adds a broad, geographical expanse. This publication was unique in its time for including writers from almost all parts of China (in fact, this is one of the editorial principles that determined the final 469 contributions) in one volume, and for giving preference to previously unpublished voices. In fact, the entries were organized geographically, so that making one's way through the book is a virtual journey around the entire nation.

Across the political spectrum, the short prose essay had by the mid-1930s become the chosen mode of written expression. From the reportage pieces of the proletarian literature movement to the familiar essays promoted by Zhou Zuoren (1885–1967) and Lin Yutang (1895–1976), most people writing anything at all at the time were making their point in no more than two or three thousand Chinese characters. In this sense, *One Day in China* was also a product of its time, as it defined the standard entry as an essay of two thousand words or fewer. In practice, at least among the pieces in the final product, these entries were overwhelmingly narrative in form. Most people recorded their observations and experiences on May 21 in the form of a short story, using techniques of characterization, description, and a surprising amount of irony: it is as if even untrained writers already were in the habit of viewing their experiences in symbolic terms, and were commonly skeptical of government pronouncements and slogans. Other entries consisted of letters written to or by the contributors, which usually included strong messages of political conviction and the depiction of human suffering and abuse, as well as leaflets or handbills provided by the contributor with a paragraph or two of explanation.

The China that emerges from *One Day* is a China in crisis, in which the republican government is not able to govern with fairness and humanity, nor able to manage military tensions with warlords and Communists, much less fend off the threat of Japanese invasion. Businessmen, missionaries, and Western or Westernized educators and other professionals are frequently drawn negatively as oppressors of a hapless and skeptical public, and the rare positive character is almost always shown to be powerless and marginal. Just as the entire collection is geographically organized, a vast number of the entries are vivid portraits of populous social spaces, such as teahouses, temple fairs, prisons, hospitals, schools, and crowded courts and government offices.

The ideological homogeneity that predictably resulted from the editorial process is balanced by a refreshing diversity of voices: peevish, outraged, selfish and vain, humorous, pathetic, and sometimes even surprising. For example, it is difficult to gauge the tone of this court clerk from Jiangsu discussing his day's work:

> Besides beautiful women, what interests us is the most gruesome and bizarre news. An incident of this sort was the next to come up: A twelve-year-old girl had been raped by a man over thirty. The girl's mother, who came to start a lawsuit, was shaking, shedding tears, and saying that her daughter was about to take her last gasp. This news certainly gave us no small amount of excitement. I immediately rushed out to tell another worker. Soon the clearinghouse was full of people, hustling and bustling, and laughter was rising as high as the heavens.

At other times, a writer can convey surprisingly nuanced views of gender, modernity, and morality in a few short lines, as in this passage from a man in Guiyang who has taken a coworker, Miss Chen, to see the film *The New Woman*:

> In Guiyang, a semicivilized place, I'm not sure whether an unmarried couple going to see a movie together is a topic for gossip. But I know that Chen herself has progressive ideas. By "progressive," I don't mean she has reached the stage where she has romances that create contradictions of the kind that women have in the big city. I mean she has strong willpower, and she is able to use a silence which seems almost like passivity in resisting the old notions of proper conduct. Because of her silence, people who shouldn't be backward but still are do not quite reject her.

Even more progressive is a woman visiting the Soviet Union, who writes to her journalist friend:

> The appetite for food and sex is human nature. Every woman here has a job (with a few exceptions, of course). Every woman has the freedom to choose her own loving companion. Thus, the most important problems in life are solved. Especially, the most important problem

for women, child-rearing, has been solved because day-care centers are everywhere.

Though this vast mosaic of voices resonates clearly with the left-wing, social realist vision of Chinese society espoused by its editors, the astonishing diversity of the voices themselves makes *One Day in China* extraordinary in modern Chinese literature and a unique artifact of the global culture and history of the 1930s.

BIBLIOGRAPHY: Charles A. Laughlin, *Chinese Reportage: The Aesthetics of Historical Experience* (Durham, NC, 2002). Charles A. Laughlin, "Mao Dun," in *Chinese Fiction Writers, 1900–1949*, ed. Thomas Moran, *Dictionary of Literary Biography*, vol. 328 (Detroit, 2007), 164–177. Mao Dun, ed., *One Day in China: May 21, 1936*, trans. and ed. Sherman Cochran, Andrew C. K. Hsieh, and Janis Cochran (New Haven, CT, 1983). Mao Dun, "On Reading *Ni Huanzhi*," trans. Yu-shih Chen, in *Modern Chinese Literary Thought*, ed. Kirk A. Denton (Stanford, CA, 1996), 289–306.

CHARLES A. LAUGHLIN

1936 · OCTOBER

Roar, China! is on display.

Resonances of a Visual Image in the Early Twentieth Century

One of the most evocative images displayed at the Second National Traveling Woodcut Exhibition, which opened in Shanghai on October 2, 1936, was a black-and-white woodcut by Li Hua (1907–1995). Measuring twenty by fifteen centimeters, the print depicts a naked man, blindfolded and tightly bound to a stake, screaming with his mouth wide open while he tries to reach for a dagger on the ground next to him. His large hands are taut and sinewy, and his body is muscular and animated with the exertions of his desperate struggle. Yet he is no mere object for a dispassionate viewer, as his voice is irrepressibly projected toward us and demands a response. The print is entitled *Roar, China!* and has since been widely regarded as a masterpiece in modern Chinese art, not only for demonstrating the expressive capacity of a woodblock print, but also for effectively articulating a national psyche.

Roar, China! by Li Hua

For the group of young Chinese artists that in the early 1930s took to the modern-style woodcut as an avant-garde art form, depicting the human voice was an enduring fascination, as well as a conceptual commitment. This fascination reveals a deep indebtedness to the German expressionists, for whom the black-and-white woodcut had been an emblematic medium. At the traveling exhibition of 1936, at least ten artists presented more than a dozen prints seeking to render visible the reverberations of an outcry, individual and collective.

Yet *Roar, China!* resonated far beyond the field of visual arts in the mid-1930s. The title Li chose for his work paid direct tribute to a much broader cultural movement that was literary in origin and international in impact. It came from an experimental play, initially written by the Soviet futurist poet and playwright Sergei Tret'iakov (1892–1937) and produced at the Meyerhold Theater in Moscow in 1926. In the following years, this agitational drama about a community on the Yangtze River confronting British imperialists was staged in Berlin, Frankfurt, Tokyo, New York, and eventually Manchester, England. The Broadway production in late 1930 logged over seventy performances, with unprecedented participation of Asian American actors and Chinatown residents. Coinciding with the onset of the Great Depression, *Roar, China!* was one of the first global blockbusters of the modern age, its appeal stemming from a vision of transnational political activism and solidarity against imperialist power driven by capitalism. This revolutionary vision would find a passionate echo in Langston Hughes (1902–1967) in 1937, when the African American poet joined the anti-Fascist forces in the Spanish Civil War and wrote, in Madrid, a rousing poem under the title "Roar, China!"

From its inception, the play *Roar, China!* caused great excitement among the Chinese. It was first introduced in 1928, when Tian Han (1898–1968), a charismatic playwright, commented on a production by the Tsukiji Little Theater in Tokyo the year before. (Some Chinese students studying in Moscow had seen the 1926 Meyerhold production.) By 1930, two translations had appeared in Shanghai, all based on the Japanese script and performance. In reviewing one of them, Tian highlighted the concept of collective identity emphasized in the play, and observed, "A China that is as unglued and desolate as a desert needs just such an 'art of outcry'!"

The first production of Tret'iakov's play in China took place in Guangzhou during the summer of 1930, with support from the governing Nationalist Party. It was a sensational success, in part thanks to the large cast, who engaged the audience directly and brought to life the idea of a "people's theater." In 1933, a coalition of theater groups overcame many technical difficulties and brought *Roar, China!* to Shanghai. The cast for this well-received production was also sizable and included local longshoremen as extras. The commentary following the performance focused on the urgent need to represent China as a self-determining nation and to give the Chinese a collective voice in the fight against an expansionist Japan. Though the play had previously attracted mostly left-leaning writers and critics, its message of unity and resistance now drew broad support in a time of national emergency. Within two years, the Liangyou Press published a full translation, along with photographs of the Shanghai performance and its set designs, making it a handy reference for future productions elsewhere. Some seventeen theatrical troupes across China undertook to put on the play in the 1930s, but only a few succeeded. During the Pacific War of 1941–1945, the play, adapted to voice an anti-Western Pan-Asianism, was staged in Japanese-occupied Shanghai and Beiping (Beijing). In October 1943, it was performed in Japanese in Taiwan, colonized by Japan in 1895.

Throughout the 1930s, "Roar, China!" was a familiar expression and rallying cry for resistance against imperialism. In December 1931, for instance, the inaugural issue of a publication launched by the League of Left-Wing Writers in Shanghai adopted "Roar, China!" as the title of its lead editorial. "Now is the time for us to unite and issue a collective outcry," proclaimed the editors while referring to the recent Japanese takeover of Manchuria. In May 1933, the influential mainstream literary journal *Les Contemporaines* published a series of woodblock prints, including *To the Front!*, made by Hu Yichuan (1910–2000), in direct response to the aerial bombing of Shanghai by the Japanese in 1932. Presenting a man passionately calling his countrymen to action, the print foregrounded the reach of the human voice and struck a keynote for the rising woodcut movement.

Most notable was the film *Youth in a Troubled Time*, released in 1935 as part of a general mobilization against Japanese aggression. Its theme song, "March of the Volunteer Army," would instantly catch on and serve as a collective call to arms in the upcoming Sino-Japanese War from 1937 to 1945. Two lines in the song were particularly resonant: "The Chinese nation now faces the gravest danger. / Everyone is forced to make a final outcry." The lyrics were penned by Tian Han and the music composed by Nie Er (1912–1935), who insisted on including nonprofessional singers in recording the soundtrack in an effort to achieve vox populi. Less than two decades later, "March of the Volunteer Army" would be designated as the national anthem of the People's Republic.

When Li Hua's print was exhibited in 1936, therefore, it had many thematic and intermedial resonances and addressed the contemporary viewer on many levels. Yet an even deeper historical echo became unmistakable when Lu Xun (1881–1936) came to see the Second National Traveling Woodcut Exhibition. The prominent writer's support of the modern-style woodcut since the late 1920s is an integral part of the history of this art form in modern China. When he visited the exhibition, Lu Xun must have felt exceedingly gratified by the evident success of an art movement that he had spared no efforts promoting and defending. There is no direct record of him commenting on Li's print, but he knew the artist and had been in close correspondence.

In viewing *Roar, China!*, Lu Xun would have seen an extraordinary, if uncanny, reference to a moment that he had once witnessed, a fateful event that he later described as the cause for his decision to pursue literature as a calling. This is the famous lantern-slide incident, in which the young Lu Xun, a medical student in Japan, obliged to watch images from the ongoing Russo-Japanese War of 1905, was shocked one day when he saw in a photograph a crowd of Chinese standing passively around one of their own. The man in the middle, accused of spying for the Russians and all tied up, was to be beheaded by a Japanese officer as a warning. The gruesome image that Lu Xun was subjected to in a Japanese classroom traumatized him deeply; it suddenly exposed a complex web of looking and being looked at that was at once petrifying and destabilizing. The spectacle was also haunting aurally, because the execution was witnessed in a deathly silence: no anguished or defiant scream was let out or made audible.

The desire to cry out and to disturb a suffocating silence would turn into an existential imperative for Lu Xun. In an essay on the potency of romantic poetry that he wrote soon after giving up medical studies to devote himself to literature, Lu Xun put forward "the voice of one's heart" as both the goal and effect of great literature. Equating silence or the lack of a voice to death and national decline, he longed for "a genuine voice" that would lift the spirit and renew the nation. Voice in this case is both a metaphor for self-consciousness and a sensory experience to be achieved or performed; it is a transformative force that must first come from within oneself.

Lu Xun's call for a magnificent and stirring voice in 1907 was part of the extensive reformist discourse that was gaining force in China at the turn of the twentieth century. A central and enduring metaphor for this enlightenment agenda was to "awaken China," a process through which a new citizenry with a modern national consciousness was to be called forth. To achieve this general awakening, many writers and polemicists resorted to journalism, poetry, fiction, drama, historiography, and even oral storytelling as effective means, indeed as necessary technologies, of mass education. As a result, writings from this period, literary or expository, were often replete with terms such as "awakening," "self-awareness," and "crying out."

In 1918, Lu Xun, now based in Beijing, gave voice, through an innovative short story called "A Madman's Diary," to a radical antitraditionalism that had been an implicit part of the enlightenment agenda but was gaining momentum in the nascent New Culture Movement. The madman, who famously decries the Confucian moral code as a disguise for cannibalism, is a lone hero who is courageous enough to speak out and urge fellow villagers to change, but whose relentless skepticism also entails profound despair. A few years later, when Lu Xun named his first collection of short stories *Call to Arms* (1923), he presented to a younger generation the "awakening" project as a complex and sobering challenge. It was in this context that he related the lantern-slide incident. He also pondered the ethical implications of crying out in an indestructible iron house only to alert some light sleepers inside and let them die an agonizing and hopeless death. He decided, however, his voice still mattered. "I sometimes issue a few battle cries of my own," he wrote, "to encourage those fighters still galloping on in loneliness, so that they do not lose heart."

The ardent outcry from Lu Xun's madman was far from an isolated affair. Exuberant modern-style poems that Guo Moruo (1892–1978) composed while studying in Japan in the late 1910s, for instance, bespoke a loud, uninhibited, and cosmopolitan self. "I run, / I roar, / I burn. / I burn like a fire! / I roar like the ocean! / I run like electricity!" declared the poet in the ecstatic voice of a celestial hound. In 1921, Guo published his first poetry collection, *Goddesses*, in Shanghai and inspired many, especially young, readers with the expressive possibilities of free verse.

By the mid-1920s, as a new political culture began to emerge in the wake of the anti-imperialist May Thirtieth Movement of 1925, both Lu Xun and Guo would address the impact of a collective voice. It was during this time that "awakening China" evolved from cultural transformation into a political program and campaign. Mass mobilization became a systematic operation, making ready use of newer technologies such as the gramophone, radio broadcasting, and film. A "silent China," Lu Xun remarked in 1927, should acquire a living voice and become sonorous. He called on the young to speak their heart using modern expressions, for an inarticulate, because woefully archaic, nation could claim no presence in the world. Within a year, Guo, now a committed Communist, urged young people to take action, to respond to and relay, like a gramophone, the thunderous battle cry of the laboring masses that had risen and arrived.

The question of who might speak as the subject of a roaring China and why it must cry out was raised poignantly, rather than answered, in the woodcut by Li Hua. This open-ended question would continue generating different responses, while *Roar, China!* as a visual image allows us to recognize and ponder the complexity of a multimedial, international, modern "art of outcry."

BIBLIOGRAPHY: Kun-liang Chiu, "Theatre's Performance, Circulation and Political Struggle: Focusing on the History of the Performance of *Roar China!* in East Asia," *Xiju yanjiu*, no. 7 (January 2011): 107–150. John Fitzgerald, *Awakening China: Politics, Culture, and Class in the Nationalist Revolution* (Stanford, CA, 1996). Xiaobing Tang, *Origins of the Chinese Avant-Garde: The Modern Woodcut Movement* (Berkeley, CA, 2008).

XIAOBING TANG

1936 · OCTOBER 19

Zhou Shuren dies.

Lu Xun and the Afterlife of Texts

The death of Lu Xun (1881–1936), an accomplished scholar, writer, translator, and cultural critic and one of the most prominent literary figures of his time, was commemorated with pomp and ceremony. To accommodate the crowds, the viewing of the body was held over three days. By some estimates, over ten thousand mourners lined the streets to watch the procession of his coffin from the funeral parlor to the grave site. Mourners bore wreaths, eulogies written on white banners, and portraits of the literary giant; some sang songs of mourning. Among the pallbearers and those who delivered oratories at the funeral were leading figures of the day, such as the writer Ba Jin (1904–2005), the reformist educator Cai Yuanpei (1868–1940), and Song Qingling (1893–1981), the widow of Sun Yat-sen (1866–1925). Draped over Lu Xun's coffin was a white banner bearing the words "soul of the nation." After his death, he was quickly canonized by the Chinese Communist Party. In a commemorative speech delivered in 1937, Mao Zedong (1893–1976) referred to him as "the sage of modern China."

Such public displays of mourning and posthumous exaltation went explicitly against Lu Xun's stated wishes. In a makeshift will written in the twilight of his life, he requested that he be forgotten after death. This was not a mere self-deprecatory move. By the time he emerged as one of the leading figures of the League of Left-Wing Writers during the 1930s, he was well aware of his own literary stature and used it to promote the leftist cause. In his lifetime, he made concerted efforts to order and preserve his writings, leaving voluminous published works for posterity. Why, then, this expressed wish to be forgotten after his death?

Lu Xun was acutely aware that after the death of the subject, texts representing the dead may take on lives of their own, as posthumous accounts can no longer be challenged by the deceased subject. Indeed, his writings self-consciously deal with the ethics of narration and the limits of representation, as he pondered over the following questions: Who has the authority or "sanction" to narrate? Can a text truly represent a subject, or does it, in the end, just betray it?

His concerns over the limits of representation and doubts over the ability of texts to speak for the subjects they claim to represent are amply illustrated in his two vernacular short story collections, *Call to Arms* (1923) and *Hesitation* (1926). Lu's experimental short stories often draw attention to the ethics of narration by scrutinizing the narrator's motives for telling a tale. The narrators are often unsympathetic and unreliable (for example, in "A Madman's Diary," "New Year's Sacrifice," "Regret for the Past," and "The True Story of Ah Q"), offering highly subjective accounts of events in order to present more flattering images of themselves or to relay a more colorful tale; these accounts wreak a particular kind of violence on their subjects, preserving images that distort and possibly even negate their identity. Some of Lu Xun's stories ("My Old Home,"

"The Village Opera") show how the distortions of narrative may be linked not only to subjective interpretations, a powerful human need for self-justification, or attraction to dramatic tales; in the case of renarrating the past, the fallibility and unreliable nature of memories also play a contributing role.

As Lu Xun once commented, he "dissected" himself no less mercilessly than he did others. Not surprisingly, one of the hallmarks of his writing is his self-consciousness of his own limitations as a writer and of the narratives he created. Many of his essays and the prefaces to his written collections convey a sense of uncertainty and ambivalence toward the endeavor of writing. His autobiographical and biographical essays likewise express skepticism over his own writings' ability to capture an accurate view of the past and the lives of the once living. Yet, as the volumes of writings he left behind attest, Lu Xun was an inveterate collector of memories. He painted colorful vignettes of his childhood and young adulthood in his memoir, *Morning Flowers Plucked at Dusk* (1928), and fastidiously chronicled the lives and events of his time in his essays. For even as he draws attention to the unreliability of memories and the limits of textual representations, his writings also contain an urgent, almost desperate plea: for the need to bear testimony to loss and the imperative of commemoration.

Lu Xun's enduring sense of loss is in part manifested in his preoccupation with death. Themes and images of death and loss recur with some frequency in his vernacular short story collections and in his last creative endeavor, *Old Tales Retold* (1936), which consists of rewrites of old myths and legends; his confrontation with death in literal and allegorical terms—be it the deaths of others, his own mortality, or as symbol of a bygone era—was registered as well in the dark and macabre tone of his essays, most notably, in his radically experimental essay collection, *Wild Grass* (1927). While often referred to as prose poems, the volume is composed of an eclectic mix of short anecdotes and creative essays, as well as a poem and a play. Some of the pieces are among his most abstruse, yet also most brilliant, creative writings.

In *Wild Grass*, images and themes of death and decay are frequently tied to regeneration. Indeed, behind Lu Xun's seeming obsession with death lies a preoccupation with the ephemeral nature of life itself and an urgent desire to capture some of its essence in writing. His refusal to mourn—that is, his insistence on keeping the past and the deceased alive in his writings—was a reflection of his conviction to be true to the memory of loss. To be sure, his form of remembrance was often accompanied by a lingering nostalgia for the past and a sense of resignation to the fact that traces of the events he recorded and images of the lives he eulogized were, even as he wrote, on the verge of vanishing. This enduring sense of loss, however, may have made his need to pay written homage to the past and present all the more pressing.

Behind the competing impulses of remembrance and forgetting in Lu Xun's writings lies the notion of radical hope—a persistent faith that, in spite of his doubts over the reliability and efficacy of writing, his written works might somehow capture specters of the past and the spirit of the once living. Lu Xun harbored the hope that in the hands of a discerning reader, his works, like the texts of the literary precursors that inspired his own, would allow glimmers of the past to flicker alive, to serve as instructive lessons and sources of inspiration that would guide readers as they struggled with similar issues in their own time.

Lu Xun largely gave up his creative writing endeavors in 1926. The form of the *zawen*, the short polemical essay, became the primary venue through which he captured snapshots of the lives and events of his time in the last decade of his life. It was also a vehicle through which he defended his name and explained his motivations for writing. In an essay entitled "How the True Story of Ah Q Came About," Lu Xun speculated on and facetiously mocked the wide range of possible ways in which he might be remembered after death—be it as a scholar, pioneer in thought, or warrior, or as bureaucrat, literary bandit, or obstinate old man. In spite of appearances, Lu Xun was, in fact, quite self-conscious of the public image he cultivated and preoccupied with the legacy he would leave behind. In his lifetime, he remained guarded against "misrepresentations" of his character, which he attempted to correct through his own self-representations. He publicly refused titles such as "revolutionary," "warrior," and "mentor," which admirers were quick to bestow on him; cognizant of the immortal afterlife of words and images, he vigorously defended himself against assaults by his adversaries. In many of his *zawen*, Lu Xun deftly combined his knowledge of Chinese and foreign texts, command of classical and vernacular idioms, and biting sarcasm to craft rebuttals that cut down his rivals. His foes were far outmatched in wit, rhetoric, and delivery, and rarely escaped unscathed; the humiliation many of his adversaries suffered in defeat continues to be displayed in the republication of many of their venomous exchanges.

Indeed, Lu Xun seemed to thrive on such hostilities, even near death. In the essay "Death," written a few months before his own demise, he concocted the following scenario: If someone were to ask his opinion of the European deathbed ritual of forgiving and seeking forgiveness from one's enemies, how would he respond? His answer was that his enemies should go on hating him, since he would not forgive a single one of them either. Declaring enmity for his foes in perpetuity was not a mere reflection of the obstinate character and unforgiving nature of an aging Lu Xun. Conciliatory gestures, such as making peace with one's enemies in the face of death, were forms of false consolation that Lu Xun derided and resisted all his life. He remained no different on his deathbed. But perhaps, too, he knew all too well that the literary battles he engaged in during his lifetime would assume a life of their own after his death.

Lu Xun's name has since been invoked and appropriated to lend support to various political views and causes he would not have endorsed. Titles such as "the soul of the nation" and "sage of modern China" are ones he surely would have repudiated. Read in this light, Lu Xun's public request to be forgotten and his private efforts to publicize his writings might be interpreted as a mode of "self-preservation"—to preempt the last word on his life and character from going to others, in particular, his adversaries, of which he had many, and to let his own texts speak for themselves. From his writings emerge a picture of a complex thinker, writer, and cultural critic who held an ambivalent relationship to the act of writing—at once wary of its dangers and limitations in presenting a distorted picture of the past and the once living, and also attracted to its power and potential in capturing the essence of its subjects and granting them a textual afterlife.

BIBLIOGRAPHY: Marston Anderson, *The Limits of Realism: Chinese Fiction in the Revolutionary Period* (Berkeley, CA, 1990). Eileen J. Cheng, *Literary Remains: Death, Trauma, and Lu Xun's Refusal to Mourn* (Honolulu, 2013). Theodore Huters, "Blossoms in the Snow: Lu Xun and the Dilemma of Modern Chinese Literature," *Modern China* 10, no. 1 (1984): 49–77. Jonathan Lear, *Radical Hope: Ethics in the Face of Cultural Devastation* (Cambridge, MA, 2006). Leo Ou-Fan Lee, *Lu Xun and His Legacy* (Berkeley, CA, 1985).

EILEEN J. CHENG

1937 · FEBRUARY 2

Sunrise premiers in Shanghai.

Cao Yu and His Drama

Staring at a bottle of sleeping pills—preparing to swallow them—Chen
Bailu murmurs her last words:

> The sun is risen, and the darkness is left behind.
> But the sun is not for us, for we shall be asleep.

Thus concluded the February 2, 1937, premiere of *Sunrise* in Shanghai.
Rapturous applause during the curtain call served as evidence to all that
Cao Yu (1910–1996), the then-twenty-seven-year-old playwright, had
created another masterpiece of modern Chinese theater. Building on
the success of his maiden work, *Thunderstorm*, Cao Yu had now firmly
established his values and voice in the theater world—the titles of both
symbolize his suppressed anger, his bitter denunciation of the Chinese
family and society, and his eagerness for "the ray of sunlight" to reach
everyone's life.

Thunderstorm was written in 1933, when Cao Yu was a final-year student in the Department of Western Literature at Tsinghua University in
Beijing. At the university he fell in love with its library, especially the play
scripts (mostly in English) he found there of Greek tragedies, William
Shakespeare (1564–1616), Henrik Ibsen (1828–1906), Eugene O'Neill
(1888–1953), Anton Chekhov (1860–1904), and others. "I loved reading
plays and often read a play many times." This new hobby made him see
more clearly the differences between Western drama and the Chinese
traditional song-dance theater that had fascinated him since he was a
child. As his fascination grew, he decided to write plays, only plays.

During his summer vacation in 1933, after completing his thesis
"On Ibsen," Cao Yu resolved to write *Thunderstorm*, a story and characters
that he had conceived over the past five years, based on the people surrounding him. "To me, *Thunderstorm* was the lure. The sentiment that
came along with thunderstorms formed my imagination, which I found
difficult to describe, about the mysteries of the universe. *Thunderstorm*
can be regarded as the remains of the primitiveness in me." Centering on

two families, the Zhous and the Lus, *Thunderstorm* exposes the oppressive realities of contemporary society. This four-act play raises issues of family hierarchies, adultery, incest, and labor unrest, and its themes reflect the spirit of iconoclasm prevalent during the 1920s and 1930s, particularly the liberation of the individual from the patriarchal family. The story's various relationships—masters and servants, parents and children, stepmother and stepson—not only reveal love and hatred, but embody an exploration of fate, while the drama's tragic ending, partly inspired by Greek tragedy, is also a meditation on this theme.

Upon its publication in 1934 and first professional performance in 1935, *Thunderstorm* attracted the attention of readers, performers, and audiences across China. As performances of the play were staged in several cities, Cao Yu started working on his second play, *Sunrise*. If the protagonist is the cause of the stifling atmosphere in Cao Yu's maiden work—the sunlight is literally shut out by the master of the Zhou family—the second play, in contrast, places the image of the sun in the center. As indicated previously, the heroine kills herself just before the sun is about to rise: the lines she chants prior to her suicide assert that the sun does not belong to her or to other unfortunate people who have been cast off by society.

Cao Yu wrote in the style of "spoken drama" (*huaju*), a term that distinguishes it from traditional musical theater by emphasizing the importance of verbal texts. Spoken drama was still relatively new in China during the 1930s and was closely associated with young radical intellectuals at the turn of the twentieth century, who advocated the adoption of Western knowledge as a means to eradicate the decadence and backwardness of China's society. In 1907 a group of young Chinese students studying in Japan were inspired by European-influenced modern Japanese theater in Tokyo. They decided to organize their first performance of this new theater there. A few weeks later, the new-style theater also appeared in Shanghai. Responding to the demands of the time, modern theater was promoted as embodying the spirit of a changing society.

Despite modern drama pioneers' efforts, new theater struggled to compete with the long-established indigenous operatic genres and the increasingly popular film industry. Cao Yu's success in aiding this nascent, nonindigenous Western drama style to develop in both form and audience reception during the mid-1930s is widely acknowledged. His first two plays earned him the reputation as the foremost figure in the development of a modern Chinese drama. By reacting critically and creatively to the foreignness of the imported culture, Cao Yu and other dramatists enabled spoken drama to develop deep roots in the Chinese soil.

Sunrise is an exemplar of Cao Yu's work because of its innovative concept of theater, its intervention with topical subjects, and its portrait of the "structure of feeling" at the time.

In contrast to *Thunderstorm*'s observance of the classical "three unities" within the confines of two families, *Sunrise* adopts an open structure to display a broad spectrum of contemporary characters in 1930s China. Such diversity includes a banker, government official, university graduate, wealthy widower, gangster, and gigolo, together with exploited clerks, workers, servants, and prostitutes. Parallel plot developments revolve around Chen Bailu, a student-turned-courtesan who lives in a luxury hotel supported by a wealthy banker. Chen attempts to rescue Shrimp (a teenage countryside girl) from being sold into the sex trade, but ultimately fails; the girl dies a wretched death in a brothel. This storyline skillfully links the so-called crème of society with a group of the lowest of the low, focusing on the distinct individual tragedies suffered by three women: Bailu, Shrimp, and Cuixi (a middle-aged prostitute). During a crisis in the financial markets, a bank clerk's gamble for an opportunistic promotion does not pan out, while another clerk takes his own life after he has been ruthlessly sacked. Finally, even the wealthy banker suffers an absolute bankruptcy, and Chen Bailu is left with no hope in her future. Despairing over her "new self," referring to her life as a courtesan, while at the same time reluctant to return to her "old self," an impoverished university student, Chen Bailu sees no alternative but to kill herself.

The postscript, written by Cao Yu in response to *Dagongbao*'s "Collective Reviews," expresses how much the playwright was inspired by Chekhov. Describing his feelings after reading *Three Sisters*, Cao Yu refers to the characters as "live human beings with souls," and notes that "in this great play there are no exaggerated bits at all." Calling himself an "unqualified apprentice to the great master," Cao Yu explains how he wanted to create a group of characters as convincing as those in Chekhov's plays: "Everyone is equally important.... There is no 'main action' in the play." A further source of inspiration was pointillism, the late impressionist style of painting, as Cao Yu relates:

Sunrise is a painting composed by such dots. If *Sunrise* has a little bit of vividness, as people have commented, and if it presents some real aspects of society, this is because of those colored dots representing characters like prostitutes, servants, and many others living in this hell. They are also the elements that create the truthfulness of the play.

What made Cao Yu decide to present these characters to his audiences? The answer can be found, most likely, in his personal life. He was born into an upper-class family, yet even in his childhood he was fascinated, often bitterly, by the multifaceted nature of human beings, as he witnessed how people assumed different stances toward his parents when their financial fortunes suffered a dramatic change. Faced with the dark side of humanity, the young Cao Yu could hardly control his emotions: "Being burnt by unfair and bloody events, one after another, I could not control my rage any more.... During these sleepless nights, I behaved like a trapped animal, pacing its cage." In such unbearably difficult days, Cao Yu smashed many objects that he had cherished, including the small china horse and Buddha given to him by his stepmother. He howled as the broken china pieces cut deeply into his fingers. "Blood, drop by drop, oozed out cathartically." He was thirsty to find answers to help him deal with "this pitch-dark universe" that pressed down and stifled him. He then "desired for a ray of sunlight."

Cao Yu began to read the Bible, the *Laozi* (The Book of the Way), and other works from which he wished to be enlightened to the right way of life. However, he discovered that human beings did not follow the path opened by those great masters. As part of his statement of intent for writing *Sunrise*, Cao Yu selected eight quotations from the previously mentioned works. Two lines from the *Laozi* exemplify the central concept that binds the diverse strands of life in *Sunrise*:

The people who have not enough are despoiled
For tribute to the rich and surfeited.

These words are also a key for later readers and audiences to open the door to this poetic play and its various characters.

Sunrise prominently depicts the plight of "despoiled" people who are struggling for their living, as the audience follows the poor country girl

Shrimp's inexorable descent from the luxury hotel (in act 1) to a lowly brothel (in act 3), where she encounters Cuixi, a warm-hearted prostitute in her forties. With respect to Cuixi, Cao Yu remarked:

> What really touched me is that she, like a dog, is so loyal to the elderly and young ones in her family, and her tender concern, expressed unconsciously, for those who are more helpless than herself. . . . In order to support the whole family, she has to offer her own body and lives on insensitively.

Cao Yu compared the dismal existences of Cuixi and the young Shrimp:

> The young one committed suicide (please read the newspapers—we can always find such reports); the other, like most of them, has to live on. . . . We should never forget this group of people. They live in the darkest corner of society that "despoils those who have not enough for tribute to the rich and surfeited." They are the people who need the sun most.

This "darkest corner" referred to by the playwright is presented in act 3 of the play. In order to portray such characters and their environments truthfully, Cao Yu—then a young man in his twenties—went to visit the red-light district. On one cold winter night, he was badly beaten when his interest in these people aroused suspicion that he might be a spy for the police.

Thus, Cao Yu considered the play's third act to be "the heart of *Sunrise*"; it also proved to be its most controversial. For example, in *Dagongbao*'s "Collective Reviews," Harold R. Shadick (1902–1993), the then-head of the Department of Western Languages at Yenching University, rates *Sunrise* as the "most powerful play in modern Chinese drama," which can "stand shoulder to shoulder with masterpieces by Ibsen and Galsworthy"; nevertheless, he argues that act 3 causes problems for the play's structure, and refers to the act as merely an "interlude." Ouyang Yuqian (1889–1962), the theater director, even cut this act from *Sunrise*'s premiere in Shanghai.

In terms of style and approach to writing, *Sunrise* is very different from *Thunderstorm*. For Cao Yu, the impetus to write both plays issued from an "emotional surge." He felt that *Thunderstorm* was too "melodramatic," however, because it elaborated complicated relationships among eight characters from two families, where familial relationships (for example, father and son) are intertwined with commercial ones (for example, employer and employee). Cao Yu resolved to develop a different dramatic approach when he started composing *Sunrise*. Drawing inspiration from Chekhov and impressionist art, he created a mosaic of everyday life. This wide range of portrayals of real people on the stage conveyed his full-hearted sympathy for those people still living in the dark: "Like tiny and thin blades of grass in the field after winter, they wanted the sun, the sun of spring days."

Over the next ten years, Cao Yu's playwriting flourished despite the disruption of war. He never ceased to express how people suffered from the unbearable darkness in their lives and their longing for the brightness of the sun. In *The Wilderness* (1937), a rebellious young woman and her fugitive lover, dreaming of a "far, far away" world, escape in pitch-black night to seek a bright place "covered with gold." *Beijing Man* (1941) portrays the decline of a once-prominent scholar-official family and their poignant interrelationships, while fiercely critiquing the suffocating tensions and hypocrisy of that dark era of humanity. His powerful explorations of human complexity reflect a profound understanding of the agonies suffered by China's population, as a consequence of the nation's recurrent transformations over the past century.

The pains of such transformations have been sharp, and even today readers and audiences still desperately echo the need for sunlight. This explains why Cao Yu's centenary commemoration in 2010, which included performances, exhibitions, film screenings, and lectures, drew great attention from people in China, Hong Kong, Macao, Japan, Europe, and North America.

BIBLIOGRAPHY: Cao Yu, *Cao Yu quanji* (Shijiazhuang, China, 1996). Tian Benxiang and Hu Shuhe, eds., *Cao Yu yanjiu ziliao* (Beijing, 1991). "Xiju Gongzuoshe shouci gongyan *Richu*," *Shenbao*, February 2, 1937, 4.

LI RURU *and* DAVID JIANG

1937 · SPRING

"A house in the wilderness"

A Chinese Poet's Wartime Dream

Ai Qing (1910–1996) awakens from a premonitory dream:

> We are crowded into a large house,
> a house in the wilderness.

Women suckle infants. An old man jerks his head spasmodically. Then a sound from without, like the crescendo of an approaching train. "Airplanes, airplanes," calls a frightened voice from the corner. Faces press against the window. Black wings are passing over the house, blotting out a leaden sky. What to do? Everyone out! Old and young, the lame hauled piggyback, they issue from the door into a dead, scorched land colored in hues of mud and blood. The land was not like this in the past, Ai Qing (1910–1996) remembers. He once had lain in the scent of flowers, among colors of red, green, yellow, and violet. But now the sky presses down as more airplanes hum overhead. The crowd shuffles along a road. Why this road? Does it lead to a peaceful place? Who can point the way? The sky drops lower. More planes. The poet looks back to see a geyser of earth, bricks rocketing up and arching down. The house collapses. In the wilderness the trees and grass have perished, but the people still live...

Ai Qing named his poem simply "A Dream." By the summer of 1937, the dream was real. Fighting with the Japanese broke out near Beijing on July 7. By August enemy planes were bombing Shanghai, and brutal street fighting consumed the city. Rivers of refugees fled their homes on China's eastern seaboard as Japan's mechanized armies moved inland on campaigns of premeditated terror calculated to shock the Chinese into surrender. Cities and town were bombed, invaded. Those who chose to stay home risked being shot, bayoneted, tortured, or raped. Tens of millions took to the roads and riverways: some for days, others for months, many for years. Cut off from the familiar, sustaining local networks of community and family, and facing unknown danger and hardship, the terrain of China was, for its refugees, wilderness.

Ai Qing left Shanghai, too. But in a way he had been a refugee for many years already, rootless by choice. Born in 1910 to a well-off family in a mountain village near the county capital of Jinhua, Zhejiang Province, as soon as he was of age Ai Qing set out from his ancestral home to study at the city of Hangzhou's West Lake National School of Fine Arts. There the modernist painter Lin Fengmian (1900–1991) urged him to go to Paris to study art. Grudgingly, his father, a prosperous shopkeeper and landowner, dug up one thousand Mexican silver dollars from under the floorboards and handed the fortune to his eldest son, the family's hope. The return on his investment was nil. Coming back to China in 1932, Ai Qing avoided home, making his way alongside the progressive-minded youths who, like him, were drawn to the literary and artistic communities abuzz in the modern metropolis of Shanghai. Before the year was out, however, he had landed in jail. Swept up in a raid on an Esperanto class by the Nationalist government's secret police, he was sentenced to six years' imprisonment on charges of subversion. Painting was no longer an option, so he wrote poetry in his cell and asked his lawyer and his friends to smuggle out manuscripts and publish them in Shanghai's avant-garde literary journals.

Ai Qing's poems from before the onset of war in 1937 are redolent with romantic loss and urban exotica. Like many of his peers also back from European sojourns, he liked to pepper his verse with foreign words in alphabetic script: crème, Chagall, orange, melancholic, radio, Pompeii, adieu. China's modern poetry was barely two decades old in the 1930s, and the country's dynastic order had fallen around the same time the poets in Ai Qing's cohort were born. So poems that, for instance, called Paris a lewd seductress, or told Apollinaire that the Shanghai police had locked you up for owning a copy of *Alcools*, were just as much public badges of cosmopolitan authenticity as pokes in the eye of the old cultural and political order. The best known poem written during his prison years, well known even today, is "Dayanhe, My Wet Nurse," a long and lachrymose paean to the peasant woman who breast-fed the child Ai Qing, and who becomes, through the pathos of the poem, the poet's symbolic mother.

By projecting the image of sensitive cosmopolite and surrogate son of the oppressed, Ai Qing's early poems won him some renown among Shanghai's small but contentious literary bohemia of the interwar years. But no literary persona was complete without a change of name. In prison, as the story goes, he found intolerable the match between his original family name, Jiang, and that of Jiang Jieshi, aka Chiang Kai-shek (1887–1975), head of the reactionary regime that had incarcerated him. By literally crossing out the lower component of the character *jiang* 蔣, he formed the new surname Ai 艾, symbolically cutting ties with his kin and effacing his accidental association with the ruling powers.

Ai Qing wrote "A Dream" well over a year after being released from jail. The poem retains a touch of the symbolist, surreal style of his earlier work. After all, as Ai Qing insists in a footnote, the poem is an exact written record of his nocturnal vision. Yet there was something new here: for the first time Ai Qing placed the "I" of a poem within the destiny of a collective. "A Dream" describes a mass exodus, a forced expulsion from home into the wilderness. It also depicts a move from interior to exterior, a symbolic renascence of sorts, and one that shows the poet's partiality to myth. If the situation in "A Dream" seems biblical, it probably should. In his early career, Ai Qing was partial to rewriting New Testament stories in verse. While in prison he had produced the long narrative poem "Death of a Man from Nazareth," which concludes with the crucifixion of Jesus on the barren hill Golgotha. The parallels with "A Dream" ought not to be missed; like the persecuted Jesus, the people and the poet in "A Dream" are forsaken, left with no road back and no clear way forward.

The time was ripe for mythmaking during the first years of the war. The Japanese invasion visited chaos and uncertainty on everyday life, as we know from the many personal narratives of these years. But the war also lifted into stark relief the fear of the Chinese nation being destroyed, and its people reduced to "nationless slaves." Ai Qing and many other writers were thus obliged to wed their art to the wartime cause, with poetry now devised to blend art and propaganda. Doing anything less was traitorous; you will search in vain for a Chinese Wilfred Owen (1893–1918) bitterly exposing the "old lie" of patriotism. Instead, war's disorder had to disclose a higher purpose lying somewhere above and beyond the intolerable present. For Ai Qing in particular this meant taking on the role of prophet in the wilderness. He became, in short, a maker of myth for a Chinese national idea, an idea still new and unsettled, but in that very inchoateness holding out the promise of a brighter place in the future. Ai Qing's poetry of this period favored metaphors of renewal and transcendence: spring, dawn, resurrection, the sun. War itself was welcome. It came as a Great Flood that would wash away the old, decayed society still holding China back from a new day. An admirer of Walt Whitman (1819–1892) and Vladimir Mayakovsky (1893–1930), Ai Qing knew how to unleash a torrent of apocalyptic verse:

> Sorrow not—
> Let war carry off the old China
> Let cannon-fire obliterate China's rot
> . . . .
>
> Show no mercy as we send off
> a China packed with
> opium fiends
> smugglers, hoodlums
> warlords
> bureaucrats
> traitors
> spies

What would remain after the purge was an exalted unity of land and people. Among the most ambitious early wartime poems he wrote on this theme is "Toward the Sun," published during the effervescent though short-lived mobilization of culture and politics in the tri-cities of Wuhan, the Republic of China's de facto wartime capital during 1938. Through nine separately titled subsections—starting with "I Arise" and ending on "I Go to the Sun"—the poem breathlessly narrates Ai Qing's poetic persona shedding a gloomy past and striding into a new day. "Toward the Sun" begins at dawn with the poet awakening in the forest like a weary, wounded beast. He emerges into a sunlit land of glad and active multitudes: old and young, men and women, soldiers, laborers, volunteers all "driven by the same desire." The sun rises in the sky, brightens to the color of blood, and prompts the poet to thoughts of "Equality, Liberty, and Fraternity," Democracy, "The Marseillaise," "The Internationale," "Washington, Lenin, Sun Yat-sen…the names of all those who have delivered humanity from suffering." The poem concludes in an ecstasy of redemption as the transcendent sun consumes the poet himself:

> The sun overhead
> with unsurpassed radiance
> scorches my flesh

the thrill of its heat
lifts my hoarse voice
to sing:
    "now is my breast
    rent by fiery hands
    my decayed soul
    cast away on the riverbank..."
All that I see, all that I hear
fills me with a relief and passion I've never felt before
for a shining moment, in which I could die....

Ai Qing excelled at expressing the rapture of nation, a talent that eventually earned him the nickname "people's poet." In "The North," inspired by his first experience with the dry, barren landscape of the Yellow River basin during the winter of 1938, he ties his emotions to China's geographic myth of origin.

I love this tragic land,
    this ancient land
————The land
    that has nurtured
    the world's most long-suffering
    most ancient race
    whom I love.

Ironically, the "people's poet" Ai Qing dealt most comfortably with people when he could represent them in broad categorical abstractions: the multitudes of happy, hard-working citizens in "Toward the Sun," or the trunk of a national family tree as described in "The North." Poetic confrontations with actual people, the ones forced to survive in the wartime wilderness, compelled a different kind of tableau. Published in edgy, avant-garde journals of the early war years, such poems of encounter resemble monochrome photographs from disaster zones. They are motionless, detached, and troubled, especially so when the people pictured return the poet's gaze, like the north country refugees in "Beggars," who

stare at you
with stubborn eyes

to see what you are eating
or watch how you pick your teeth with your fingernail.

"Beggars" has no glowing finale, only the image of starving, homeless mendicants, arms extended for copper coins they never receive.

Ai Qing could strike many tones in his poems, but he is rarely ironic. A disquieting gap appears when we compare his poems on the living, like the two quoted previously, with his poems on the dead. There the salvational, inspirational endings that go missing in poems like "Beggars" find their place next to victims of atrocity depicted in macabre still-life scenes. Put bluntly, corpses bring closure. "Human Skin," dated July 1938, just three months after "Toward the Sun," is Ai Qing's most grisly poem of this period, and perhaps of his entire oeuvre. The poet sees hung on a tree a tattered human skin, crawling with flies, above "a putrefying, stinking mound / of mingled blood, flesh, and mud":

> …it is a skin
> peeled from the body of a Chinese woman
> poor woman!
> Cannon-fire destroyed her home
> her children, her kin
> everything that held her life together.

Here Ai Qing has crossed paths with a solitary victim, one whom we might well imagine among the mass of refugees fleeing beside him in the exodus of his prewar dream. For this woman the war is over, and there is no symbolism—only mutilated remains abandoned to rot slowly into the earth. Ai Qing concludes this grim vision by describing how the wind "wafts the stench of decay / far, far off in every direction." But the poem is not over, and he launches into the final stanza:

> People of China,
> today you must
> make this skin
> into a banner,
> waving
> waving

bright in your memory forever.
May it rouse you
to remember always
that this is Chinese soil.

Like many other writers and artists, Ai Qing's wartime search for China's future eventually brought him, in 1941, to Mao Zedong's (1893–1976) Communist base in Yan'an. From there he rose through the ranks of Beijing's literary elite in the post-1949 "New China," only to fall from favor in 1957, one among thousands of intellectuals purged during the Anti-Rightist Movement. After more than two decades of internal exile in China's northern regions of Heilongjiang and Xinjiang, he was rehabilitated by the party in 1979, and returned to public life in China's literary establishment. Ai Qing died in 1996.

BIBLIOGRAPHY: Ai Qing, *Ai Qing quan ji* (Shijiazhuang, China, 1991). Ai Qing and Eugene Chen Eoyang, *Selected Poems of Ai Qing* (Bloomington, IN, 1982). R. Keith Schoppa, *In a Sea of Bitterness: Refugees during the Sino-Japanese War* (Cambridge, MA, 2011).

JOHN A. CRESPI

1937 · NOVEMBER 18

William Empson begins teaching at the Temporary University in Hunan.

1938 · FEBRUARY 28

W. H. Auden and Christopher Isherwood arrive in Guangzhou from Hong Kong.

William Empson, W. H. Auden, and Modernist Poetry in Wartime China

On November 18, 1937, William Empson (1906–1984) began teaching at Peking University, which, together with Tsinghua and Nankai, had just formed the wartime Temporary University in Changsha, Hunan. The

Faculty of Arts was located in the Nanyue Mountains, about seventy miles from the city. Empson was thirty-one years old, not much older than his students, unmarried and energetic; deep in the interior of China, he devoted his time to writing, teaching, and conversation, typically over whisky or *baijiu* (Chinese liquor). It was a time of war. Students and teachers lived and worked like soldiers. Nanyue was a "holy mountain," one of the sacred Daoist sites, but it was terribly isolated. In the absence of an academic library, syllabus texts had to be delivered through memory. The first text to read for Empson's course on Shakespeare was *Othello*. Empson recalled the text from memory, wrote down on the blackboard long passages from the play, read them out, and explained the difficult parts; in the English poetry class, for the first few weeks, some of the early English poetic texts were entirely reproduced from memory. "Autumn on Nan-Yüeh," the longest of Empson's poems, was a poetic account of life and work at the Temporary University:

> The abandoned libraries entomb
> What all the lectures still go through,
> And men get curiously non-plussed
> Searching the memory for a clue.
> The proper Pegasi to groom
> Are those your mind is willing to.
> Let textual variants be discussed;
> We teach a poem as it grew.

Those were exciting and happy days. Many of Empson's students remember fondly how he typed out syllabus texts for distribution in the classes. The course on modern poetry he later offered in Yunnan would be a major influence on his students, some of whom were to become prominent poets, scholars, and translators, including Mu Dan (1918–1977), one of the most innovative poets in the vanguard of modernist poetry in the 1940s.

It was a period of extraordinary intellectual fecundity and productivity, despite, or rather because of, the difficult circumstances under which teaching was conducted. Empson and his Chinese colleagues were engaged in the writing of some of their signature works. He began *The Structure of Complex Words*; Feng Youlan (1895–1990) completed *Neo-Confucianism*;

Jin Yuelin (1895–1984) finished *On the Dao;* Tang Yongtong (1893–1964) drafted the first part of his *History of Chinese Buddhism;* Wen Yiduo (1899–1946) continued his work on *The Book of Songs* and *The Songs of the South;* and Qian Mu (1895–1990) began the groundwork for his *Outline of National History.* Students and faculty members alike developed a communal sense of belonging and a collective understanding of their role as "an intellectual and civil leadership"; from now on, Empson "would always think of the mountain as his ideal of the academic community."

The Temporary University stayed in Changsha for just one semester, from November 1937 to February 1938; it was then relocated to Kunming, Yunnan, where it was renamed the Southwestern Associated University. It was there that Empson began to teach modern English poetry. This was a significant moment in the history of modern Chinese poetry. Empson was well known among students as a distinguished poet and literary critic. He did not teach his own poetic work, but a modernist English poet teaching modern English poetry in wartime China surely was a literary event. His very presence at the University was a source of inspiration to the young aspiring poets. An unintended effect of the course was that many of his students would reach the conclusion that modernist poetry was superior to the romantic poetry that they had loved; some even refused to attend lectures on Walter Scott (1771–1832). T. S. Eliot (1888–1965) and W. H. Auden (1907–1973) were their new poetic gods. It's certainly an oversimplification to consider Anglo-American modernism as necessarily antiromantic, but it was a shared belief among the young student-poets at the University that they must move beyond the emotional spontaneity and sentimentalism of Xu Zhimo (1896–1931), the Chinese romantic poet par excellence. Empson's teaching would be remembered and spoken about among several generations of students; his course on modern poetry was considered the single most important source of inspiration for the development of a new poetic taste at the University and in modern Chinese poetry as a whole.

Empson's students admired Auden, whose popularity among them was in no small part attributable to his visit to China and his expressed solidarity with Chinese people in the War of Resistance against Japan. Auden and Christopher Isherwood (1904–1986) arrived in Guangzhou from Hong Kong on February 28, 1938, about the time Empson left Nanyue with the Temporary University. Commissioned by Faber and

Faber of London and Random House of New York to write about the
war as part of the global effort to contain and defeat fascism, they spent
about four months in China. In Hankou, the wartime capital of China,
they met with Madame Chiang Kai-shek (1897–2003), whom they found
pretentious but vivacious and charming, and some of the literary figures
in Hankou at the time: Tian Han (1898–1968), Hong Shen (1894–1955),
and Mu Mutian (1900–1971). *A Journey to a War*, Isherwood's narrative
of their trip, includes one of Auden's best war poems, "In Time of War,"
a sequence of twenty-seven sonnets and a poetic coda, in which Auden
reflects on humanity's tragic fall into irrationality, the most compelling
evidence of which is its willingness to wage war against itself. For Auden,
China's War of Resistance is of global significance, as we live "now in a
world that has no localized events."

Empson considered Auden one of the very few poetic geniuses in
his generation. He reviewed Auden's work as early as 1931, and they met
briefly in Hong Kong in 1937, before Auden traveled to Guangzhou. In his
modern poetry class, Empson taught Auden's "Spain" (1937). Auden had
intended to drive an ambulance for the Republic in the Spanish Civil War;
for students at the Associated University, he stood as a living example
of poetic heroism and exerted a profound influence on, for example, Mu
Dan. Mu Dan's "Peasant Soldier" (1945) brings to mind Auden's sonnet
XVIII in "In Time of War," entitled "Far from the heart of culture he was
used," which reflects on the nonbeing of a nameless peasant solider who
has "vanished" into the earth. Auden's musings on the discontinuities of
human history in "Spain" resonate in Mu Dan's "Hungry China," part
III (1947), which considers China's present a negation of its own past,
with no promise of a better future:

> Yesterday all the past, pastoral
> Like eloquent spring water, flowing into
> A significant tomorrow; but to-day hunger
> . . . .
> Yesterday peace of holiday; but to-day hunger.

These lines echo Auden's "Spain" (1937):

> Yesterday all the past....
> . . . .

Yesterday the installation of dynamos and turbines,
The construction of railways in the colonial desert;
Yesterday the classic lecture
On the origin of Mankind. But to-day the struggle.

In 1942, Mu Dan joined the Chinese Expeditionary Force as an interpreter to fight the Japanese in the mountainous terrain between Burma
and Yunnan. The expedition was a catastrophic failure. Half of the
expeditionary troops, nearly fifty thousand men, perished in the treacherous Burmese jungles. His "The Demon of the Forest" (1945) records
heart-wrenching grief, pain, and despair, in response to the unbelievable
brutalities of war he witnessed and experienced. Poetry for Mu Dan
was an act of life, as it was for Auden and his teacher Empson: "We
teach a poem as it grew." The poetic sublime in Mu Dan is best understood in relation to this sense of modern heroism that must be tested
in action. The war had a devastating effect on Mu Dan, from which he
would never fully recover. Shortly after the War of Resistance, China
was plunged into another war, the civil war between the Nationalists
and the Communists. It was impossible to continue writing poetry
in the same way; not yet thirty years old, Mu Dan found his poetic
energy consumed in "the fire of destruction" ("My Thirtieth Birthday,"
1947). In 1948, he left for the United States to do graduate studies at
the University of Chicago.

That the Associated University was the wartime center of poetic experimentation had much to do with the fact that it was a modern Western-style
university, combining three of the best universities in China at the time.
Many of its faculty members were Western educated. Though tucked away
in a remote corner, the University was nevertheless intellectually cosmopolitan. Empson described the time there as the "last of great days of the
effort of China to digest the achievement of Europe, when a well-educated
Chinese was about the best-educated man anywhere in the world." His Chinese "colleagues habitually talked to each other in a jumble of three or four
languages, without affectation, merely for convenience," and "the standard
of the students was very high." A constellation of poets were assembled
there. Among its senior faculty members were Wen Yiduo and Zhu Ziqing
(1898–1948), who had made their names for their new poetry in vernacular
Chinese during the 1920s. Also on staff were well-known avant-garde poets
Feng Zhi (1905–1993), whom Lu Xun (1881–1936) considered to be "the

most distinguished lyric poet in China," and Bian Zhilin (1910–2000), who had returned from a trip to Yan'an in 1938. Other writers of note included Shen Congwen (1902–1988) and Li Guangtian (1906–1968). However, it was the student-poets, including Mu Dan, Du Yunxie (1915–2002), Zheng Min (1920–), and Yuan Kejia (1921–2008), who were more self-consciously innovative in creating a new poetic style, although the full significance of their work would not be recognized until nearly half a century later, in the early 1980s, when they and other poets of the wartime generation were grouped together and named the Nine Leaves Poets.

The designation of "Nine Leaves" was retrospectively bestowed, following the publication of *Poetry of Nine Leaves* (1981), edited by Yuan Kejia (1921–2008). The anthology included four Associated University poets: Mu Dan, Du Yunxie, Yuan Kejia, and Zheng Min; the other members of the group were Xin Di (1912–2004), Chen Jingrong (1917–1989), Hang Yuehe (1917–1995), Tang Qi (1920–1990), and Tang Shi (1920–2005). This self-classification as "Nine Leaves" is not without controversy, not least because it tends to be exclusionary, but it did allow them to establish a collective poetic identity. Although deeply concerned with the fate of the country during the 1940s, the Nine Leaves Poets were inclined to record the individual's response to the conditions of life, rather than directly or explicitly depict social reality. They were distinguished from other poets by being willing to emulate Anglo-American modernist poetry, with its emphasis on depersonalization and the objectification of emotion. The publication of Yuan's anthology also had an unintended effect on the emerging poets of the early 1980s, who sought to rid themselves of the thoroughly politicized literary practice adopted and constituted during the Cultural Revolution. The Nine Leaves Poets offered a model of poetic modernism and contributed to the carving out of a liberatory space of poetic experimentation in the post-Mao era. Not unrelated to this belated recognition and revival of literary modernism is the adoption of modernist narrative techniques, especially stream of consciousness. Yuan played a leading role in disseminating and promoting Western, especially Anglo-American, modernist literature that he first studied at the Associated University in the early 1940s.

In January 1939, Empson took war leave from the Associated University to work at the BBC amid Britain's war against Nazi Germany. Shortly after the war, he returned to Beijing to resume teaching at Peking University in 1947. "Chinese Ballad" (1952) was the last poetic work he completed in Beijing. It was an English translation of a fragment from the long narrative poem *Wang Gui and Li Xiangxiang,* composed by the revolutionary poet Li Ji (1922–1980). The beautiful ballad is a celebration of love between Wang Gui, a Red Army soldier going to the front line, and his peasant lover, Xiangxiang (Hsiang-Hsiang):

> Now he has seen the girl Hsiang-Hsiang,
> Now back to the guerrilla band;
> And she goes with him down the vale
> And pauses at the strand.
> The mud is yellow, deep, and thick,
> And their feet stick, where the stream turns.
> "Make me two models out of this,
> That clutches as it yearns.
> "Make one of me and one of you, And both shall be alive.
> ·
>
> "So your flesh shall be part of mine
> And part of mine be yours.
> Brother and sister we shall be
> Whose unity endures.
> "…Come back to me,
> Come back, in a few days."

Empson left China in the summer of 1952 to take up a chair professorship at the University of Sheffield; his inaugural lecture was entitled "Teaching English in the Far East."

BIBLIOGRAPHY: W. H. Auden, *Selected Poems,* ed. Edward Mendelson (New York, 1979). W. H. Auden and Christopher Isherwood, *Journey to a War* (London, 1973). William Empson, *Complete Poems,* ed. with introduction and notes by John Haffenden (London, 2000). William Empson, "Teaching English in the Far East," *London Review of Books* 17 (August 1989): 17–19. Mu Dan, *Mu Dan shi quanji* (Beijing, 1996). Wang Zuoliang, "Huai Empson," *Waiguo wenxue,* no. 1 (1980): 2. Michelle Yeh, ed. and trans., *Anthology of Modern Chinese Poetry* (New Haven, CT, 1992). Yuan Kejia, *Bange shiji de jiaoyin* (Beijing, 1994).

Q. S. TONG

1939 · OCTOBER 15

Ah Long completes the first full-length novel about the events
in Nanjing during the Japanese invasion.

The Lost Novel of the Nanjing Massacre

Today the Nanjing Massacre (1937–1938) not only looms as one of the truly
horrific events in twentieth-century military history, but also has taken
on a highly symbolic identity. The collective memories of the massacre
are often intertwined with complex feelings of loss, victimization, martyrdom, and nationalism, sentiments that continue to cast a dark shadow
over contemporary Sino-Japanese relations. Over time, a rich body of
Chinese-language materials has been published about the massacre:
a massive seventy-two-volume compendium of historical documents,
dozens of monographs, biographies of witnesses, oversize photo books,
diaries of survivors and soldiers, translations of foreign accounts, and
numerous collections of poetry, short stories, and novels. The event has
also been the inspiration behind countless documentary films; several
television miniseries, most notably *Scarlet Rose* (2007); and some of the
biggest-budget Chinese feature films ever produced, such as Lu Chuan's
(1971–) *The City of Life and Death* (2009) and Zhang Yimou's (1951–)
The Flowers of War (2011).

The Nanjing Massacre has become such an emblematic, even iconic,
site for modern Chinese national memory that many may find it hard
to imagine a time when the event was largely absent from popular discourse—no novels, no films, and certainly no museum. In fact, it was not
until the mid-1980s that the memory of the Nanjing Massacre, fueled
in large part by shifting Sino-Japanese relations and the ugly shadow of
Japanese revisionist denial, reemerged from the footnotes of history to
take its place in a series of publications, television documentaries, and
feature films. During the preceding decades, there was one lone voice that
had attempted to preserve the memory of the Nanjing Massacre through
fiction. This is the story of that silenced voice.

On October 15, 1939, just a few months shy of the massacre's second anniversary, Ah Long (1907–1967) completed the first full-length
novel about the events in Nanjing during the Japanese invasion. Born as
Chen Shoumei in 1907, Ah Long was best known as a poet and for his

groundbreaking works of reportage literature. He also had a long association with the writer and literary theorist Hu Feng (1902–1985) and his
July School (the group of writers associated with *July* magazine, edited
by Hu during the second Sino-Japanese War). Having served as a soldier
and been wounded in battle, Ah Long drew on his own experiences as
well as published accounts of the massacre to write the work, originally
titled *Nanjing,* while recovering from an eye injury in Xi'an. Although the
novel was written in just two months (from August to October 1939), it
quickly gained recognition when the manuscript was awarded the Chinese
National Arts and Literature Anti-Japanese Committee's prize for best
novel. The novel must have been circulated to the jury in manuscript form,
because it was still not officially published. The novel no doubt attracted
the attention of the jury due to its explosive and timely subject matter,
which took on the Japanese atrocities in Nanjing and offered detailed
depictions of battles imbued with poetic language and frequent use of
onomatopoeia. While this early acclaim seemed to indicate a promising
future for the novel and its young author, that was not to be. *Nanjing*
would not be published until 1987—almost fifty years after it was written
and a full twenty years after the author's death.

The reasons for the novel's suppression were complex: the chaos of
the postwar years and the ensuing Chinese Civil War, the author's own
alternately strained relationships with both the Chinese Communist
Party and the Nationalist Party (Kuomintang), and a new Cold War
power structure in which the Nationalists—not the Japanese—would
become the Communists' chief rivals. These were certainly all factors that
led to the novel's suppression and exile from the pages of official literary history. When the novel was first completed and awarded its prize,
the Nationalist regime's New Life Movement championed by Chiang
Kai-shek (1887–1975) was in full swing. Coming out of the New Life
Movement, which is often characterized as having a mixture of Christian ethics and fascist discipline, was a move toward a "national defense
literature," inspiring stories that captured lofty patriotic sentiments and
fearless struggles against the enemy and embodied a strong vision of a
nation destined to rise victorious. From this perspective, the novel *Nanjing*
was a work out of step with the times.

Straddling fiction and reportage, *Nanjing* stands out for its unique use
of language, including rich descriptive accounts of warfare, onomatopoeia,

and poetic metaphor. In some ways, it is more of a prequel to the massacre, focusing on the events leading up to December 13, 1937, than an actual, direct representation of the massacre itself. But most startling for many readers must have been the novel's portrayal of Chinese characters. As a poet most deeply inspired by the writings of Lu Xun (1881–1936), Ah Long had a penchant for criticism, satire, and black humor. Moreover, many of his writings seem to offer a naked censure when it comes to various aspects of the Chinese national character. Given the subject matter, *Nanjing* could have been well positioned to fulfill the needs of "national defense literature" and further rally citizens around the principles of the New Life Movement; however, the actual novel was much more indebted to the concerns of the May Fourth Movement and Lu Xun's tradition of examining the dark side of the Chinese soul.

Ah Long undertakes this through his repeated descriptions of the self-brutalizing, or, in the words of Lu Xun, "cannibalistic," tendencies of the Chinese people on the eve of the Japanese invasion of Nanjing and the ensuing massacre. Much attention is paid to the Nationalists' "Scorched-Earth Policy," which was intended to destroy useful goods and property in order to prevent these resources from falling into enemy hands. In Ah Long's novel, the focus is not on the contribution of this policy to the war effort, but on the plight of the everyday men and women whose lives are decimated by the policy when their property is forcibly confiscated and destroyed by Chinese soldiers. In one passage, where a widow is forced by soldiers to leave her home behind, she pleads,

> Let the Japanese come! Let them come! Let us die at the hands of the Japanese!...You have driven everyone away and there are no customers left to buy my sweet potatoes; now you want to burn my house down and force us to leave. You're not even leaving us a way out! We'll have died by your hands before the Japs even get here!

Such passages clearly demonstrate Ah Long's strategy of presenting the Nationalists not as noble fighters resisting the Japanese, but as terrorizing their own people on the eve of the massacre.

As the novel unfolds, this type of cannibalistic vision of the Chinese people becomes increasingly powerful. In one scene, Ah Long describes an elderly grandmother frantically trying to find shelter during a Japanese air raid. First she must contend with an abusive Chinese soldier who screams at her and threatens to hit her with the butt of his rifle, but the true horror comes later. The grandmother decides to throw her bag of personal effects into a shallow well and come back for it after the air raid, but accidently throws her bundled grandchild into the well instead. Such examples abound throughout the novel and in some sense become even more unforgettable than any portrayal of violence committed by the Japanese. This Lu Xun–like writing is nowhere more sharp and ironic than in the case of the character Zhong Yulong. Described as a feminine Buddhist vegetarian with a weak stomach when it comes to violence, Zhong features in an extended plotline that begins with him witnessing an airstrike victim. The casualty moans for help, but Zhong is unable to provide assistance due to his aversion to blood. Ah Long then takes his metaphor of Chinese cannibalism to a new level when he describes the aftermath:

> Something soft flew into Zhong Yulong's mouth, lodging itself in his throat, almost choking him…bright, bright red and seeping with juice. He took a closer look—it was a piece of meat!…He began to vomit.…He let out a terrible scream;…I, I—I never—killed—a single—a single ant, not even an ant!…but today I ate, ate, ate human flesh!

Besides the perceived political problems that publishers under the Nationalist regime may have anticipated given the book's radical treatment of its subject matter, there were of course the practical problems involved with many publishing activities during the time of fighting, chaos, and massive migration and relocation that marked the Sino-Japanese War of 1937–1945, and was then extended by the Chinese Civil War until 1949. Just a few years after the establishment of the People's Republic of China, the novel's author faced a new challenge that would further doom *Nanjing*. When his close associate Hu Feng, who criticized Mao Zedong's (1893–1976) theories on realism in art and literature, was purged by the Chinese Communist Party in the early 1950s, Ah Long also became a target. The ensuing national campaign against the so-called Hu Feng counterrevolutionary clique resulted in mass criticism, public scorn, and later imprisonment for Ah Long. Ah Long eventually died on March 15, 1967, after almost twelve years of incarceration.

In 1955, Yang Chunying, former student of Ah Long, wrote,

> This cunning and sinister executioner known as Ah Long, worried that the youth might not fall into his trappings, twisted the creative experience of famous writers in order to deceive his students. Even more malicious is the way he explained the maxim of "write more" as held by Lu Xun and Mao Dun as "write more about everyday life."

Four years later, Fang Ji (1919–1998) wrote,

> My instincts told me that something smelled funny [about Ah Long's writings]: I could sense that not only did he not reference Chairman Mao's *Talks at the Yan'an Forum on Literature and Art*, he never mentioned literary works from publicly acknowledged liberated areas, and when it came to his own works he used an unfamiliar language to write something that appeared correct but was actually very, very wrong.

These quotes are taken from just two examples of the public censure and mass criticism of Ah Long published in the 1950s and represent but a small sampling of the nationwide attack on the writer and his comrades. Those critical essays that appeared in newspapers and magazines fueled nationwide attacks, in which millions of Chinese were mobilized to participate. For many years, those were the types of writing that represented the "cunning and sinister executioner" Ah Long—not his poetry, not his path-breaking work in reportage literature, not his robust body of work on literary theory, and certainly not his remarkable novel *Nanjing*, which was never mentioned in any of the published attacks on him. Sadly, Ah Long's brutal characterization of his compatriots in *Nanjing* was more prophetic than he could ever have imagined.

By the time the novel was finally published in December 1987, it was retitled as *Nanjing Bloody Sacrifice*, and subjected to "necessary revisions" (the extent to which these editorial changes may have altered Ah Long's original vision is unknown) in order to appear alongside a new wave of novels and films produced as part of a state-sponsored movement to commemorate the fiftieth anniversary of the massacre. This period marked a new level of cultural engagement with the Nanjing Massacre, signaling new forms of political appropriation of historical memory. In the 1990s and 2000s, the Nanjing Massacre took on renewed meaning in a global context thanks to a new series of English-language books on Nanjing, from Iris Chang's (1968–2004) breakthrough nonfiction best seller and uncovered diaries by Minnie Vautrin (1886–1941), John Rabe (1882–1950), and others, to novels by Ha Jin (1956–), Mo Hayder (1962–), R. C. Binstock (1958–), and Shouhua Qi (1957–). At the same time, a new flock of Chinese writers like Ye Zhaoyan (1957–) and Yan Geling (1958–) began to tackle this page of history through Chinese-language fiction. China's leading filmmakers also adapted the tragedy into a series of multiplex-ready blockbusters, and the massacre even graced primetime television as a serial action spy thriller. But between these new memorials and commemorations, a never-ending flow of literary and visual reworkings, and an ever-growing body of unearthed historical documents that continue to be published each year, it is up to us to remember the once lost literary voice of Ah Long. As the politics of Nanjing Massacre commemoration become increasingly embedded in the machinery of state-sponsored memory, literary works about the events of 1937 appear ever more formulaic, predictable, and propagandistic. With most post-1987 Nanjing Massacre novels and films highlighting a series of people, places, and events that have become compulsory components for representation—the foreign witnesses, the International Safety Zone, tropes of "proof" to refute Japanese denial, emphasis on the death toll of three hundred thousand, and numerous graphic depictions of beheadings, rapes, mass burials, and all of the other acts of violence the massacre has become known for—Ah Long's novel *Nanjing* is important not only for being the first Chinese novel written soon after the actual events depicted, but also for the author's unique, at times idiosyncratic, strategy of representation. Fueled by an idealistic May Fourth spirit, real battle experience, and the rich, imaginative language of a poet, Ah Long created a portrait of the 1937 Nanjing Massacre completely unlike any other account written since. And while Ah Long's novel has been reprinted several times since its "rehabilitation" in 1987, after decades of being forgotten, *Nanjing* is still a lesser-known work in the larger cannon of modern Chinese fiction.

BIBLIOGRAPHY: Ah Long, *Nanjing xueji* (Beijing, 1987). Michael Berry, *A History of Pain: Trauma in Modern Chinese Literature and Film* (New York, 2008). Ken Sekine, "A Verbose Silence in 1939 Chongqing: Why Ah Long's *Nanjing* Could Not

Be Published," Modern Chinese Literature and Culture Resource Center, Ohio State University, 2004, http://u.osu.edu/mclc/online-series/sekine/.

Michael Berry

1940 · SEPTEMBER 3

Liu Na'ou is gunned down at a restaurant in Shanghai.

The Poetics and Politics of Neo-Sensationism

On September 3, 1940, Liu Na'ou (1905–1940)—the Taiwan-born and Japan-educated leader of the Shanghai neo-sensationist school of modernism—was gunned down at a restaurant by an unknown party. He was there to attend a lunch celebrating his succession to the directorship of *National Subjects Daily* following Mu Shiying (1912–1940), a fellow neo-sensationist writer and filmmaker. A little more than two months before, Mu had likewise been assassinated on the job.

National Subjects Daily was a news agency run by Wang Jingwei's (1883–1944) government in Nanjing, a puppet regime collaborating with the Japanese. No one knew if these two murders were connected or instigated by the same agency. Some thought the Japanese, suspecting that he was a double agent for the Chinese Nationalist Party, were responsible for Liu's death; others believed the party had him killed for collaborating with the Japanese. Shi Zhecun (1905–2003), another neo-sensationist writer, even claimed that the killer was sent by Du Yuesheng's (1888–1951) gang as a consequence of outstanding gambling debts. There were sufficient reasons for these speculations. Before his murder, Liu had served as the director of the Screen Playwrights and Film Directors Committee of the Central Film Studio, run by Wang's puppet regime. In that capacity he made an anti-Japanese movie, *Secret Code*, in 1937. He also made movies for several leftist companies, such as *Everlasting Smile* in 1936 (starring the famous actress Hu Die [1908–1989]), *First Love* in 1936, and *Daughter of the Earth* in 1937, adapted from Pearl Buck's (1892–1973) novel *Mother*. In 1939, he was hired to manage the China Film Studio, a group established by the Cultural Bureau under Japan's Asia Development Board. With such extensive involvement in the complex of semicolonial politics, Liu was walking on thin ice. He was ultimately a victim of his own recklessness.

Born into a landlord's household in colonial Taiwan, Liu first attended the Presbyterian School of Tainan and transferred to the high school division of Aoyama College in Tokyo in 1920. He graduated with honors from the English Department of the Advanced Learning Division of the same college in the spring of 1926. Shortly thereafter, he arrived in Shanghai and entered the special French program at L'Université L'Aurore, where he met Dai Wangshu (1905–1950), Shi Zhecun, and Du Heng (1907–1965). Together with Liu, these young talents would go on to make a name for the neo-sensationist school, which is now famous for its modernist penchant amid the rightist and leftist mainstream realism promoted by literary circles in Shanghai at the time.

Like many of his contemporaries in China, Liu began his literary career with a few mediocre stories written in the proletarian vein, while the bookstore he established in 1929 with his own funds was a rendezvous for leftist intellectuals before being eventually shut down by the Nationalists. Tired of the proletarian emphasis on content at the expense of form, he switched to modernism almost immediately. Lou Shiyi (1905–2001), a literary critic and Liu's contemporary, criticized the modernist stories Liu's coterie produced, perceptively pointing out in 1931 that Liu's group merely "transported Neo-Sensationism to Shanghai from Japan." In fact, before that moment Liu and his coterie had never called themselves the neo-sensationist school. In April 1934, however, the cartoonist Guo Jianying (1907–1979), acting as editor in chief of *The Women's Pictorial*, acknowledged the label: "Mr. Hei Ying [1915–1992] is a newcomer to the modern Chinese neo-sensationist school." By that time, the *Pictorial* had become the mouthpiece of Liu's coterie, combining photographs, cartoons, and "palm-of-the-hand stories," which are a form of ministory originally made famous by the Japanese neo-sensationist writer Kawabata Yasunari (1899–1972) that focus on the dazzling image of the modern girl.

The Japanese did not invent the palm-of-the-hand story. They learned it from Paul Morand (1888–1976), the French modernist writer. In French it is called a "conte," and it always has a dandyish male narrator—the author's doppelgänger—ogling an alluring modern girl, who is sexually free and capricious and enjoys torturing her suitors. But Liu's diary from 1927 discloses that descriptions of the modern girl reveal in fact the dandy's own mindset. How he looks at his wife reveals Liu's basic attitudes toward women. She was one year older than Liu and was his first cousin, their mothers being sisters. They were married in 1922, when Liu was only seventeen years old. From the outset, he was dissatisfied with the marriage. This was partly because it was an arranged marriage, a "feudal remnant" blighting his modern sensibilities, and partly because the two were incompatible in education and personality. Like most women of her time, she was educated at home by private tutors. In the diary, he complains about her letters written in poor Japanese. In April 1927, he returned home from Shanghai for his grandmother's funeral. In one diary entry he takes his wife as a representative of "woman," or even femme fatale, in general, while disclosing a deep-seated male chauvinism and misogyny on his part. When she lures him into sex, he calls her a "vampire" who saps man's energy and blood, a reference to Charles Baudelaire's (1821–1867) poem "Le Vampire," included in *The Flowers of Evil*. For Liu, "woman," incapable of true feelings or love, wants nothing but sex, and her libido more often than not is the cause of man's downfall. In the vocabulary of the dandy, man is the emblem of intellect and ruler of the spiritual, while woman serves as a symbol of sex and carnal pleasures. To Liu, "woman" has only two functions, both of which are tied to her body: to bear children and to make love.

On the one hand, the dandy is an incorrigible misogynist, mistrusting the modern girl for her intellectual inferiority and infidelity. On the other, he adores her bodily form and adornments as the quintessence of modernity. In the diary, we can see that Liu is constantly strolling the streets and back alleys of Shanghai, moving from one café or dance hall to another, looking for images of women that would satisfy his taste. Like Baudelaire's poem "To a Passer-By," these women are passers-by, or chance encounters in a café or a brothel, unknown to him, but all of them reveal the same quality: an intensity of desire that draws out their beholders' passions more than their own. For him, these women are specimens of what Baudelaire calls in the poem a "fugitive beauty." The French word *la modernité*, the emblem of Baudelairean aestheticism, appears twice in Liu's diary, both in connection with prostitutes. Once in a brothel, looking at a young prostitute who awaits his patronage, he sighs, "Ah, my hungry heart! Ah, the translucent eyes that I can hardly devour, the face of *Modernité!*" Under the entry for November 27, 1927, the French word is used again to describe an unknown prostitute's eyes: "I chose her because of the look of *modernité* in her eyes." Under the dandy's gaze, an insignificant brothel girl is instantly transformed into a symbol of modernity.

In Shanghai, Liu indeed led the life of a dandy. He was amply provided for by his mother, his father having died when he was twelve years old. He established two bookstores consecutively in Shanghai, and published journals and books with his own means. In the early 1930s, he even began investing in real estate in Shanghai. He built a block of houses where his family lived after moving from Taiwan, lent two units to Dai Wangshu and Mu Shiying, and rented many of the remaining units to Japanese tenants. In addition, he bought nearly a whole block in a business area. It is said that after his death, his mother and wife got into a serious dispute over the estates he had acquired in Shanghai.

Liu and his literary friends worked and played together, running Liu's bookstore by day and frequenting dance halls and brothels by night. In the dance halls, Liu was always marveled at when he tangoed; people would stop dancing, spread out, and leave room for him to perform. Nicknamed "the Dancing King," he regularly practiced dance steps with his friends, and to perfect his skill, he studied dance manuals such as *Apprenons à danser* (Let's learn to dance), *Danses modernes* (Modern dance steps), and *Dancing Do's and Don'ts*. He was on close terms with his relatives and friends from Taiwan, frequently entertaining and letting them stay in his apartment. Guests included his younger brother, who was studying in Tokyo when he came to visit, schoolmates from the Presbyterian School of Tainan, and the renowned advocate of the vernacular literature movement in Taiwan, Huang Chaoqin (1897–1972).

Around that time Huang was looking for employment in Shanghai— in 1928, he would go on to work for the Overseas Chinese Bureau of the Ministry of Foreign Affairs of the Nationalist government. When Liu met with Huang, the usual activities they engaged in were conversing, eating in restaurants, frequenting dance halls, and playing mahjong.

In Shanghai at the time, amid the day-to-day threat of civil war and foreign invasions, the carpe diem mentality seemed pervasive. Despite his dandyish lifestyle, Liu was serious about his literary career. In addition to writing short stories and establishing literary journals, he published a volume of translations of Japanese proletarian and neo-sensationist stories in 1928. The authors he translated include Hayashi Husao (1881–1963), Nakagawa Yoichi (1897–1982), Yokomitsu Riichi (1898–1947), and Kataoka Teppei (1894–1944). In 1930, he rendered into Chinese the Russian Marxist critic Vladmir Friche's (1870–1929) book *The Sociology of Art*

(1926) from a Japanese translation. Following these accomplishments, he changed trajectories and became the first serious film theorist in China. In contrast to leftist film theory, for Liu the success of a movie depends not on the content, but on the way the subject matter is handled and adapted in the movie. In other words, it is the form and autonomy of art that matter. In 1932, via French reading, he wrote an article entitled "On Cinematic Art," analyzing the techniques of montage and kino-eye developed by Russian directors Vsevolod Pudovkine (1893–1953) and Dziga Vertov (1896–1954). In 1933, he established a film magazine called *Modern Screen*, and published in it a series of articles on movie techniques, such as the rhythm, angle, and position of the camera.

Modern Screen soon became host to a series of debates, known as the "Hard Films and Soft Films" debate, which most notably included the leftist film critic Tang Na (1914–1988). The debate was triggered by Liu's friend from Taiwan, Huang Jiamo (1919–2004), who complained in an article that the leftist "revolutionary movies" had "hardened" the soft celluloid of the film and that such meaningless sloganeering and didacticism drove away audiences that once thronged to the theaters. He emphasized the entertainment function of the movie by saying, "Movies are the ice-cream for the eye, and the sofa for the soul." Liu and his coterie's modernist stance, which valorized the autonomy of art and implemented their literary aesthetic in the form of dandyism, and their entertainment theory about film were poles apart from the politicized aesthetics of proletarian literature. A controversy of this nature was inevitable.

Although he was born in colonial Taiwan, Liu became famous in Shanghai and then was assassinated there, and he was not reestablished in Taiwan as a literary man until more than half a century later. In the summer of 1997, when his family entrusted his 1927 diary to me, they were still uncertain whether it was "safe" or appropriate to have its content meet the public eye. Ten years after the lifting of martial law, his second daughter was still uneasy when talking about his murder. It had been a subject of taboo since her family's return to Taiwan shortly after the violent event. Then only a child of seven, she keenly felt the shock and horror that would persist for decades to come, both surrounding the postwar retrocession of Taiwan to the Nationalist government and throughout the White Terror from the 1950s to the 1970s. In the summer of 1997, she vaguely remembered her mother's description of her father having been active in Shanghai's literary circle and film industry during the 1930s, but she would not know until the publication of his five-volume *Complete Works* in 2001 his stature and significance as a literary man.

BIBLIOGRAPHY: Liu Na'ou, *Diary*, ed. and trans. Peng Hsiao-yen and Huang Yingzhe, in *Complete Works of Liu Na'ou*, vol. 1, ed. Kang Laixin and Xu Zhenzhen (Tainan, Taiwan, 2001). Peng Hsiao-yen, "A Dandy, Traveler, and Woman Watcher: Liu Na'ou from Taiwan," in *Dandyism and Transcultural Modernity: The Dandy, the Flâneur, and the Translator in 1930s Shanghai, Tokyo, and Paris* (London, 2010), 22–58.

PENG HSIAO-YEN

1940 · DECEMBER 19

Fei Mu's *Confucius* premiers at the Jincheng Theatre in Shanghai.

Between Chineseness and Modernity: The Film Art of Fei Mu

On December 19, 1940, the renowned filmmaker Fei Mu's (1906–1951) *Confucius* premiered at the Jincheng Theatre in Shanghai. After a brief release of a recut version in 1948, the film disappeared from sight. Long thought lost, a nitrate negative of this significant work was rediscovered more than half a century later in Hong Kong, the place the film was originally conceived.

It all began with the fall of Shanghai on November 11, 1937. From that day until December 8, 1941, when the Pacific War erupted, the foreign concessions of the city came to be known as the "orphan island," an urban enclave left untouched by the Japanese occupying forces. During this murky period of history, the political and cultural landscape took on a new complexion in the concessions. Like many Chinese at the time, Fei took temporary refuge in Hong Kong—from 1938 to 1939—after the fall of Shanghai. It was there that he made his stage directorial debut with *The Ladies' Apartment*. This is significant for two reasons: first, Fei would go on to abandon filmmaking for the stage during the period of Japanese occupation, from 1941 to 1945, when the Shanghai film industry was monopolized by the Japanese-controlled China United Company; second, his films *Confucius* (1940) and *Spring in a Small Town* (1948) manifested a strong stylistic influence from the stage, including both traditional opera and modern theater.

It was also in the British colony that Fei met old friends, such as businessman Jin Xinming and actor Zhang Yi (1909–1983). Both would participate in the film project *Confucius*, the former contributing generously as producer and the latter cast as one of the master's favorite disciples, Zi Lu (452–480 BCE). Fei may have met Tang Huaiqiu (1898–1954) in Hong Kong as well. Tang, who would play the leading role of Confucius, was also in Hong Kong giving performances with his theater troupe at the Queen's Theatre. According to Jin's recollection, Jin formed Ming Hwa Motion Picture on September 18, 1939, the anniversary of the Mukden Incident, a day of national humiliation for the Chinese. For the debut work of their venture, Fei suggested, "Either we make films on subjects others aren't taking on, or we don't make films at all. Don't make ones that only entertain and make money. Let's make a film on Confucius, the great educator in ancient China." By that time, the situation in Shanghai had stabilized, the film industry there had revived following the initial setback of occupation, and the people's nerves were being eased with a flood of mediocre productions, especially costume dramas.

At the end of 1939, Fei returned to the orphan island and he began shooting *Confucius* in early 1940, originally planning to wrap up filming in March. In the end, however, it took him an entire year to complete, with the final bill coming in at more than five times the film's initial budget. Although the filmmaker had always been known for his slow delivery of films, that it took almost a year suggests that he must have encountered multiple obstacles, some of a technical nature, but certainly also more substantial ones. The end of the 1940s saw world politics take a turn for the worse, with the situation in China especially bleak. He could very well have been locked in a paralyzing creative impasse. The circumstances remind one of *The Magnificent Country*, a film project Fei initiated after the war ended in 1945. It is the story of two brothers, allegedly based on the third United Front formed between the Nationalists and Communists to negotiate a coalition government and rebuild a unified country after victory against the Japanese. Contrary to the hopes and expectations of the Chinese people, the end of the Sino-Japanese War was followed not by peace, but by another war, the Chinese Civil War. For almost three years, Fei revised his script in light of the ever-changing political situation; the film was never finished.

Fei was above all an artist. If the heavy and obscure biographical film *Confucius* still somehow manages to strike a chord in our hearts today, it is undoubtedly due to the strength of its artistic sensitivity, a sensitivity born of the tragedies and sorrows of the Sino-Japanese War but one that also inspires reflection on our present-day situations. Here I would like to highlight two scenes that have attained an almost iconic significance in Chinese cinema since the film's rediscovery.

Scene one. Unable to convince the viceroy of Lu to dedicate his rule to the well-being of his people, Confucius decides to resign from his post as chancellor of Lu to travel throughout the land to spread the Doctrine of the Virtuous. Before relating his decision to his disciples, he spends the night pacing his room in solitude. The room is sparsely furnished, featuring only a low wooden table in front of a large rectangular window, a window with neither frame nor lattice. The foliage outside, though not particularly heavy, is suggestive of life and hope. Gazing out the window with his back to the audience, the mind of the master seems to be wandering far into the unpredictable future. There is a serene beauty in the abstractness and spirituality of this scene.

Scene two. Confucius's most cherished disciple, Yan Hui (512–481 BCE), dies at the young age of thirty-two. Emerging from Yan's room, the grieving master walks over to a window. Beams of daylight sneak in through the door, underlining a contrast between the somberness of the interior and the brightness of the exterior. Following a close-up of Yan, the camera captures a devastated Confucius from outside the house, framed in a stylized way by a square-shaped window. "Heaven is killing me! Heaven is killing me!" he moans in agony and despair. A few shriveled branches stretch across the screen, their shadows falling on the external wall of the shabby hut. Following a fifteen-year journey, the seventy-year-old master encounters the deepest sorrow of his life, after which he returns to Lu with only his grandson by his side. This scene is certainly one of the most desolate moments of China's national cinema, a far cry from the maddening chaos of contemporary Chinese history.

As in traditional Chinese painting, in which empty space plays a significant role in the visual representation of nature, Fei leaves much room for imagination in the two scenes; at the same time, his framing and lighting manifest a certain resemblance to the spatial concepts of Western modern art. In retrospect, we could arguably trace the roots of *Confucius* all the way back to one of Fei's earlier works, *Bloodshed on Wolf Mountain*, made in 1936. The film had received rave reviews from left-wing critics, who saw it as an exemplary work of "national defense cinema." While left-wing intellectuals of the 1930s generally propagated realism in art, *Bloodshed on Wolf Mountain* is stylistically minimalist, reducing the anti-Japanese story to almost allegorical abstractness. With its very stylized visual flair and use of music, the film bears a striking affinity in aesthetic sensitivity to *Confucius*.

At this point, it would help to draw attention to the ideological atmosphere of the 1930s and 1940s. While many left-wing intellectuals hoped that Fei would "use his film [*Confucius*] as a pointed and satirical commentary to critique the fundamentals of Confucian teachings, to highlight the disparity between the time of Confucius and ours, and to show that Confucianism is no longer valid in China nowadays," Nationalist leaders had been conveniently blending Confucianism into their own ideology, rendering it a tool of state machinery. But Fei stood firmly by his own line of thought. In "Confucius and His Times," published in a promotional brochure for *Confucius*, Fei quoted extensively from Hu Shi's (1891–1962) *Outline of the History of Chinese Philosophy*. Coincidentally, Hu's article "How China Fights a Long War" appeared in the *Shenbao* on January 5, 1941, shortly after the initial release of *Confucius*. Discussing the historical consciousness of the Chinese nation, Hu traced its origin back to "living under one empire, one administration, one law, one literary tradition, one education system and one historical culture for more than 2,100 years." While Hu referred to the persistence of China's ancient and long-lasting "historical culture," Fei portrayed Confucius as a failure in the real world but one whose spirit nevertheless refuses to succumb. In the grim reality of the time, Chinese intellectuals such as Hu and Fei sought spiritual strength in the nation's long-standing historical and cultural traditions.

Only two Fei-directed films from the 1941–1948 period have survived: *Spring in a Small Town* (1948) and *A Wedding in the Dream* (1948), a Peking opera film. *Spring* is Fei's most accomplished work and an undeniable masterpiece. Over the past three decades, it has been hailed as one of the most important works in Chinese cinema. *Spring in a Small Town* is a simple story of the relationship between a husband, a wife, and the wife's former lover. It is told mostly from the perspective of the wife, in the form of a mesmerizing voiceover by the charismatic actress Wei Wei (1922–). The monologue, oscillating between past and present, reality and fantasy, manifests a modernity comparable to Alain Resnais's (1922–2014) landmark film *Hiroshima mon amour* (1964), though Fei's film was made sixteen years before it.

There are only five characters in the film—the husband, the wife, the lover, the husband's teenage sister, and a servant. Apart from a brief reference to war early in the film, the story is set in a kind of void, totally disconnected from the real world, similar in a way to the allegorical setting of *Bloodshed on Wolf Mountain*. Seen today, *Spring in a Small Town* is surprisingly unconventional, in spite of its close affinity to traditional Chinese aesthetics and ethics.

The characters live in separate quarters in a half-ruined old-style residence, where each door opens onto each individual's own private universe, curiously reminding us of the separate lodges inside the lush landscaped garden where Jia Baoyu and his beautiful cousins reside in the eighteenth-century novel *Dream of the Red Chamber*. Fei aptly transforms living space into psychological space, in much the same way that Cao Xueqin (1715–1763) grounds his characters in their colorful residential space. Their bedroom destroyed in the war, the husband and wife now live in adjacent parlors. The husband resides in a room filled with old books that smells of incense and herbal medicine, but he spends much of his time drowning himself in bitter nostalgia amid the ruins of the garden. The wife's room is gloomy and lifeless, so much so that she has to seek refuge in her sister-in-law's room during the daytime. The sister-in-law's room, situated on the other side of the garden, seems to be the only place in the house graced by sunshine. Whereas the windows of the other rooms are tightly closed, those of this cheerful space open out to an inviting spring landscape. The unexpected visitor, former lover of the wife and childhood friend of the husband, stays in a study in an almost deserted part of the house. It is discreet and laden with hidden desires, a little fan-shaped window subtly revealing the lovers' game of seduction and the glass-paned door acting as a last line of defense against longings that transgress social norms.

Fei's film is an exquisite piece of work that explores the eternal theme of love and marriage. But viewed in a broader context, it also expresses the reflections of an intellectual and artist caught in the vicissitudes of contemporary Chinese history. While traditional Chinese literati customarily responded to their times through poetry, Fei did so through his films. In *Confucius*, he tried to reconcile his frustrations in the face of the gruesome realities of the Sino-Japanese War, attempting to seek self-assurance in the strength of China's long-standing history. In *Spring in a Small Town*, he responded to the ideological dilemmas of his times by choosing to fall back on the remnants of traditional culture while remaining sensitive and open to the possibilities of the outside world, much like the married couple who eventually stay within the confines of the half-fallen town wall at the end of the film, watching their youthful sister and humble servant walk their friend / lover toward an unknown future.

Since his first ventures in film directing during the early 1930s, Fei had been very conscious of the uniqueness of film language, and his writings about his early films expressed an urge to dissociate film from "civilized drama" and develop a new visual form. *Bloodshed on Wolf Mountain*, with its idiosyncratic compositions and dynamic montage, could be considered the culmination of this early period. In the following year, he experimented with the collision between stage and film art, avant-garde in the expressionistic *Nightmares in Spring Chamber* (1937) and traditional in the adaptation of the Peking opera *Murder in the Oratory* (1937). With *Confucius*, Fei aptly integrated the art of mise-en-scène with an episodic narrative. While he had taken great pains in the filming of *Confucius*, *Spring in a Small Town* was delivered smoothly within three months. Fei breathed poetry into every frame, with the grace of Chinese operatic stage art and overtones of traditional literary works, rendering it the most sensuous film in Chinese cinema. Viewed as ideologically "unprogressive" and even "decadent," the work was dismissed by pre-1949 left-wing critics and post-1949 film historians alike, and it faded into obscurity in a historical abyss until the early 1980s, when it was unearthed by film circles in Hong Kong. When post-1949 filmmakers and critics were ardently discussing the notion of national style in Chinese cinema in the 1950s and 1960s, they failed to recognize that Chineseness is not necessarily at odds with modernity. With his subtle psychological depth and lyrical filmic language, Fei Mu demonstrated a vision that was far ahead of its time.

WONG AIN-LING

1940–1942

Zhou Libo runs a lecture series entitled "Selected Readings of Literary Masters in Western Literature" in the Lu Xun Academy.

Chinese Revolution and Western Literature

In December 1939, after a long journey in a savage blizzard, Zhou Libo (1908–1979) arrived in the wartime Communist capital of Yan'an. A novelist and critic, Zhou was appointed the director of the translation department and teacher of literature in the Lu Xun Academy. A little over thirty, Zhou had been known to the residents of Yan'an as a translator of Russian literature. Having been involved in street rallies against the Nationalist government and served time in jail for his activism, Zhou was reputed to be a leader in protest movements in Shanghai. His pen name Libo stemmed from the English word "liberation," and was intended to signal his devotion to the cause of national liberation, as well as that of the working class.

From 1940 to 1942, Zhou ran a lecture series entitled "Selected Readings of Literary Masters in Western Literature" in the Lu Xun Academy. On the reading list were novels by Russian socialist writers Maksim Gorky (1868–1936) and Alexander Fadeyev (1901–1956), as well as works by writers who had lived under the czar, such as Aleksandr Pushkin (1799–1837), Mikhail Lermontov (1814–1841), Nikolai Gogol (1809–1852), and Leo Tolstoy (1828–1910). The selected European masters included Johann Wolfgang von Goethe (1749–1832), Honoré de Balzac (1799–1850), Stendhal (1783–1842), Guy de Maupassant (1850–1893), and Prosper Mérimée (1803–1870). Written on coarse paper that was precious in Yan'an, Zhou's lecture notes were crammed with Chinese characters and English words, leaving no blank space. Although books in Yan'an were rare commodities, Zhou referred constantly to English and Chinese texts, frequently citing long passages from memory. Zhou's lectures were a magnet for students and staff from the departments of drama, music, and arts. Seated on the ground in front of cave dwellings, the audience was captivated by Zhou's expressive and articulate delivery and explanations, taking notes and responding to his occasional questions. Explosions from bombing raids nearby were frequently heard, but the lectures would continue uninterrupted. The participants of the seminar recalled that it was a rare pleasure to hear Zhou speak.

The Japanese intrusion into North China on July 7, 1937, marked the beginning of the War of Resistance against Japan. As anti-imperialist, patriotic sentiment swept through the nation, Yan'an quickly became the center for the resistance movement. A large number of idealistic urban young men and women flocked to Yan'an, and Zhou was among them. These intellectuals, artists, and students came and found a new home in Yan'an, hoping to participate in war efforts and to turn over a new leaf in their life and career. Educated in cosmopolitan cultural centers, fluent in foreign languages, and talented in arts and letters, they enforced the military resistance with their culture and spirit. Dubbed "cultural workers," they set up theaters, formed study associations and societies, published journals and magazines, and built schools. The Anti-Japanese Military and Political University, established in Yan'an in 1937, was the base area's comprehensive institution for higher education, and the Lu Xun Academy was its humanities and arts division. In the mission statement Zhou Yang (1908–1989), the vice president of the academy, declared that the academy was to play a role in the nation's anti-imperialist and independence movement. Upholding critical thinking as a guiding principle, Zhou urged students not to turn a blind eye to the dark side of the emergent society. Instead, revolutionary artists should criticize and correct social problems, strive to be independent in their thinking, and reserve the right to critique. Edgar Snow (1905–1972), the American journalist, wrote about how the education in Yan'an fostered a spirit of internationalism. Rank-and-file soldiers tried to keep abreast of the news and developments of the Spanish Civil War and its relevance to antifascist struggles elsewhere. Peasants knew rudimentary facts about the Italian conquest of Abyssinia and the German-Italian invasion of Spain.

The Lu Xun Academy constituted what David Apter (1924–2010) and Tony Saich (1953–) have called a discourse community, a public arena in a dramatic setting. In this space soldiers and intellectuals pored over texts, interpreted their experiences, and expressed themselves in ways that forged ideological bonds. A method known as *qifa* (illumination) evolved out of this environment. This method departs from the traditional lecture format, with its rote memorization and simple questions and answers. The *qifa* approach is a method of investigation that moves from induction to deduction. The investigator proceeds from the near to the far, from the concrete to the abstract, from part to whole.

Zhou Libo's lecture notes, published in 1984 in book form, illustrate his style of teaching the Western masters. He approached a literary work not only by looking at the author's biographical background but, more importantly, by examining the work's social and historical circumstances. Biography was embedded in the social and historical dynamics of the author's nation. Due to the lack of reference books, Zhou resorted to citing remarks and observations by literary masters to illuminate the text, making productive connections between texts, writers, and critical works. He frequently cited Chinese writers as well, notably Lu Xun (1881–1936), and invoked elegant, poetic passages from the literary classics. His generalizations and conclusions arose from a sustained hermeneutic immersion in the texts. Bringing Western literature to revolutionary China, Zhou's lectures belonged to the revolutionary cultural program for training writers and artists. His class greatly contributed to the Chinese revolutionary understanding of Western writers as creative agents and as national writers seeking political liberation and independence.

Although ideas of "human nature," "individualism," and "love" in Western fiction were to be criticized later by the authorities as bourgeois, Zhou in his lectures blended humanistic discourse into the revolutionary theory of art. He identified two aspects of the novel as a medium for modern political change. Raising the key questions of the apprehension of life and its representation in the novel, Zhou initially focused on romantic individualism. He then went on to discuss the novel's role in propelling historical change and popular democracy.

Discovering human nature in the works of Stendhal, Balzac, and Tolstoy, Zhou illustrated the broad scope of the romantic individual's structure of feeling. Love escalates into a revolutionary passion; the intensely romantic imagination of these writers and their characters led them to take the whole-hearted, even quixotic plunge into revolutionary movements. Beginning with a biographical sketch, Zhou showed how Stendhal was deeply involved in the Napoleonic War and worldwide political and social upheavals throughout Europe. While he deemed romantic love for women as his primary passion and listed the names of six women he had loved on his epitaph, Stendhal portrayed love broadly, as a risky yet challenging experience, consonant with the tumults of historical times. As his love shifted to passion, passion became an aesthetic of power, empowering revolutionary men and women. Far from a private, heterosexual love based on personal attraction, love in Stendhal's work was a widening expanse of emotion and sympathy, a sublime passion. Love is fulfilled only by giving others happiness; it is intimate, kind, and altruistic.

In Zhou's reading of European and Russian novelists, the novel's aesthetic power thrives on the tension between utopian imagination and historical realism. This view foreshadowed the then still tentative notion of socialist realism. The new novel scrutinized reality under the light of future visions, investing realism with romanticism. In Stendhal, Balzac, Tolstoy, and others, Zhou discovered a theory of fiction that places social man in natural history. Wedded to mutating social manners and customs, protagonists in the realistic novel are social products of their specific time and place. In this vein the novelist excels at depicting the layouts of a city in its multiple complexities, with a density of details. This realistic side is supplemented with legendary and romantic projections. While enamored of exaggeration and fantasy, Stendhal wove the exciting and extraordinary into realistic narrative. Blending melodramatic motifs such as passion, jealousy, power, women, sex, and murder into realistic depiction, he turned his work into a crucible for the clash of fiction and reality.

More significant than romantic individualism and melodrama is Zhou's reading of European fiction as historical novels. Deeply indebted to Walter Scott's (1771–1832) Waverly novels, Stendhal's work moved away from the fantastic and romantic toward a historical, epic expanse, signaling a unity between making art and making history. Linking Stendhal to a keen sense of historical change in Balzac's fiction, Zhou defined the latter as a triumph of realism. Balzac's novels reflected the tendentious stance of French writers toward the historical transformations from 1816 to 1848 in the wake of the French Revolution. This turbulent era witnessed the inevitable decay of the autocratic ancien regimé under the pressure of the new bourgeois class. A staunch conservative, Balzac was nevertheless quick to see the social upheavals that swept away old strata. Fantasy and reality, imagination and epic were rolled together in his novels, which mixed poetry and vernacular, drama and characterization.

China's revolutionary art honors the idea that art should be a harbinger of revolutionary change and a catalyst for a new reality. Zhou's view of fiction and history resonated with fellow Communist intellectual György Lukács's (1885–1971) theory of the historical novel. Lukács defined the historical novel in terms of its transformative potential and epic scope.

An example of this new genre, Scott's novels, indebted to the German nationalist discourse and the legacy of the French Revolution, captured an emergent sense of national as well as world history. German nationalism delved into primary folk culture and made Germans aware of their nation as a process of self-making and becoming. National art and culture reasserted national identity and contributed to the nation's rebirth. The French Revolution, on the other hand, made history a mass experience. The upsurge of mass movements among European nations in the nineteenth century conveyed the experience of history to broad masses. This new world-historical consciousness, coupled with the acute awareness of constant social transformations, departed from the traditional romantic notion that sees historical communities in an organic, long lineage and as embedded in time-honored tradition, customs, and language. A nostalgic throwback to that frozen landscape, the old historical novel is mere costume history, mired like museum pieces in exotic curiosities and oddities. In contrast, the revolutionary historical novel portrays the epochal transformations of history in the depths of lives of men and women, and depicts how social changes affect everyday life, economy, and mentality. The popular character of the new historical novel is premised on the belief that the people could be a driving force in changing social institutions and in propelling historical progress.

In Zhou Libo's teaching, national literature proffers images of a people. But the Communist movement also seeks to go beyond national boundaries to attain international solidarity. Communist cultural ideology holds that peoples with shared experience of victimhood and subordination can forge alliances and that artworks for the people should promote a sense of ideological solidarity among working classes of different nations. Although works by Tolstoy depict the Russian peasantry, to Zhou they project a sense of an international community of the peasantry. Similarly, in nineteenth-century European literature, a people or nation rebelling against the ancient or foreign regime resonates with a peer people striving for the same goal. So the internationalist impulse, enriched with Western humanist as well as third-world culture, goes together with national independence. Internationalism does not strive to overcome national culture with an uprooted transnational outlook. Within a national territory, a national people constitutes the nation. Domestically, the oppressed, liberty-seeking people as the revolutionary class make a genuine nation, forming a broad populist identity and claiming national sovereignty. Internationally, peoples of disadvantaged classes in the South, in their common cause, are genuine internationalists. If a certain class in a nation served as lackeys of the imperialists, it did not deserve to be considered genuinely national, for it failed to represent the will of the people. This class-based notion of world peoplehood projects a spirit of third-world internationalism, which combines far-reaching international bonds with historically endowed national-cultural identity.

BIBLIOGRAPHY: David Apter and Tony Saich, *Revolutionary Discourse in Mao's Republic* (Cambridge, MA, 1994). He Zhiqiang et al., eds., *Lu yi shihua* (Xi'an, China, 1991). David Holm, *Art and Ideology in Revolutionary China* (New York, 1991). Huang Ke'an, *Yan'an wenxue yanjiu* (Beijing, 2009). Joseph Levenson, *Revolution and Cosmopolitanism* (Berkeley, CA, 1971). Georg Lukács, *The Historical Novel* (Lincoln, NE, 1983). Edgar Snow, *Red Star over China* (New York, 1944). Ban Wang, ed., *Words and Their Stories: Essays on the Language of the Chinese Revolution* (Leiden, Netherlands, 2011). Zhou Libo, *Zhou Libo luyi jianggao* (Shanghai, 1984).

BAN WANG

1941 · DECEMBER 25

"She would never be the same again[,] she thought."

Eileen Chang in Hong Kong

In a recently discovered autobiographical novel in English, *The Book of Change*, Eileen Chang (1920–1995) writes,

> The next minute she was struck in the face by an illumination that lit her up from tip to toe in the small portico painted cream color with bulbous columns. It took her a moment to realize it was the searchlight from across the bay. It remained fixed on her as she stood petrified, enshrined.... In the darkness she half laughed soundlessly, her body still saturated with light. She would never be the same again[,] she thought.

The time was late 1941 and the place was Hong Kong, where Chang had enrolled at the University of Hong Kong. That magical moment, recollected with Chang's evocative lyricism half a century later, is like a moment of Joycean epiphany that prefigures her writing career. The searchlights were in reality ominous signals of the impending Japanese invasion and seizure of Hong Kong, which finally occurred at Christmastime, 1941. Two years later Chang indeed found herself in the limelight of Shanghai's literary scene; she was the "talk of town" in her own beloved city. A new literary star was born.

What if Chang had not gone to Hong Kong but stayed in Shanghai? Would she have pursued a different career? Probably not, for the seeds of creativity were already sown in her Shanghai childhood. Her Hong Kong experience is crucial because it marks a turning point in her life at which a new "extra-traditional" dimension was added to her writing. Without her Hong Kong experience, she would not have been able to produce one of her two most memorable novellas, *Love in a Fallen City*, in its current narrative form. Nor would she have been able to evoke the kind of psychological and moral intensity of her essay "From the Ashes"—certainly one of the finest achievements in the essay genre in the history of modern Chinese literature. Even if Chang had not produced any other work, these two pieces alone would ensure her place in the modern Chinese literary canon.

In fiction as in real life, it can safely be said that Chang's three years in Hong Kong (from summer 1939 to summer 1942) marked her transition from adolescence to maturity. Instantly seasoned by her direct witnessing of what she calls "the brutality of war and gratuitousness of any human attachments," she was already a changed person before she returned to her hometown, Shanghai. It was perhaps with a sense of the return of the "prodigal daughter" that she eagerly dedicated her first crop of stories, some of which were set in Hong Kong, to her beloved hometown readers. Her sojourn in the British colony had apparently unleashed a torrent of creativity. In the first two years after her return (1943–1944), she produced at least a dozen short stories and an equal number of essays. In 1944, her first collection of short stories was published and sold out in four days, and later in the same year she published an essay collection, which was likewise a best seller. As David Wang has observed, "Such a bemused look at the contingencies of history and human fate was to become a constant theme of Chang's writings. To that end, Hong Kong takes on a metaphysical dimension as a city where changeability and normalcy, individual desire and societal fate, interact with each other in a mercurial way."

Chang's first pair of stories (entitled "Incense Burners I" and "Incense Burners II"), both set in Hong Kong, evoke an outlandish landscape unlike anything she had previously written about Shanghai, for they are populated with an assortment of English colonials, Sino-Portuguese mixed-bloods, and Indians. On the surface, the depiction of scenery and setting has all the exotic elements of a South Seas romance. In the first story, Hong Kong is represented as a high-class whorehouse in a white mansion on top of a hill covered with exotic wild flowers—an alluring setting for the depiction of the willing seduction and corruption of the young heroine, an ingenue from Shanghai. In the second story, the sexually repressed Victorian heroine on the island colony suffers a trauma on her wedding night. Had they first been written in English—as was Chang's later practice as an exile in America—these stories could have been mistaken for works by W. Somerset Maugham (1874–1965). Still, if one compares these two works with Maugham's novel *The Painted Veil*, a story of adultery and redemption set in Hong Kong and an fictive southern Chinese town, Chang's Hong Kong stories contain more authenticity and emotional truth than does Maugham's rather condescending portrait of British colonials and Chinese people.

Chang's unfinished novel *Links in a Chain* is another case in point. Set in the Hong Kong of an earlier era, it describes the checkered life of a low-class Chinese woman with her four successive lovers / husbands— one Indian, two Chinese, and one English—with whom she bears five children. The work offers a rare glimpse of Hong Kong's lower-class residents, whose activities center on the densely populated hub of Indian and Chinese merchants, fish vendors, and servants in the Western District (Saiwan) and the western part of Central. One can chart the heroine Nixi's footsteps across the narrow, stone-paved streets lined with shops and crowded pedestrians who wear black (since "the poor people always wore black short shorts and pants; their color is black"). One such shop is a silk fabric shop run by a prosperous Indian who first buys the fourteen-year-old Nixi as his concubine. The Chinese herb medicine shop, to which the heroine next moves, is located on Caine Road in Central, with a branch office on King's Road. Later on in the novel, Nixi invites a group of nuns to the distant village of Yuen Long on the Kowloon side to visit its temple festival. Although Chang openly acknowledges that in the novel she has intentionally presented a Hong Kong that the Shanghainese would like to imagine—that is, with a dose of Orientalist (and self-Orientalizing) exotica—it could not have sprung entirely from her imagination.

As a university student Chang lived in the university's May Hall, a dormitory for female students. The University of Hong Kong campus—which provides a key setting for her story "Jasmine Tea" and her essay "From the Ashes," as well as the site of the searchlight incident in *The Book of Change*—is located in the midlevel Pokefulum area overlooking the Chinese commercial district, whereas the high-ranking colonial officials and their families lived in the lavishly decorated mansions on the Peak. The young Chang, as a scholarship student majoring in English literature in a colonial university, enjoyed a privileged status that distanced her from the majority of the native Chinese population who lived downhill. Perhaps her occasional forays into the Chinese side of town did not give her a good impression, since the language she used daily was English, and not the local dialect of Cantonese. Her teachers were English; her classmates were mostly from rich upper-class families in Hong Kong, India, Malaya, and Singapore. (One of them, a mixed-blood Chinese Ceylon woman named Fatima Muheeden, or Yan Ying (1920–1997), became her close lifelong friend; she later designed the front cover of the second enlarged edition of *Romances* and is frequently mentioned in her essays.) Still, despite her alienation, her sheltered life as a student of an elite colonial institution had given her some comfort and stability, which was abruptly cut short by war and Japanese invasion.

As noted previously, Chang's recollection of this direct encounter with the terror and atrocity of war helped inspire her essay "From the Ashes," which vividly describes how her classmates were totally unprepared for the war—one classmate still worried about what to wear for dinner; another went to town to watch a cartoon movie—until Japanese bombs and gunfire landed at their feet. In the middle of the essay, Chang evokes the extraordinary scene of an empty trolley car standing forlornly in a deserted street. Suddenly time seems to stand still, as if frozen in a cinematic montage sequence. "Outside the streetcar, a ray of pale sunshine; inside, also sunshine—only the streetcar itself, a scene of primitive barrenness." This is surely another moment of epiphany that serves to turn a young girl into an adult. Its cold surrealism offers a pointed contrast to the author's warm evocation of the sound of the Shanghai streetcars in another contemporary essay, "Pleasures of Apartment Living," in which

Chang claims that she can never fall asleep without hearing the sound of streetcars pulling into the depot late at night, "chattering like a bunch of children."

The other landmark in Chang's Hong Kong stories is the Repulse Bay Hotel, which was situated on the south shore of Hong Kong Island but is now no longer standing. On its old site is a modern deluxe apartment high-rise with a veranda restaurant whose nostalgic décor of hanging fans and colonial-style furniture recalls a scene from Chang's novella, *Love in a Fallen City*.

The narrative in this famous story is divided into two halves: the first half takes place in Shanghai, where Bai Liusu, a divorced Shanghai woman, is imprisoned in a traditional household where she first meets Fan Liuyuan, a Chinese playboy from England. Liuyuan invites her to visit him in Hong Kong. With this change of scenery, the story takes a new course. Suddenly a new world opens in which the old rules are bent and Liusu is forced to play the role of a gay divorcée, as if in a screwball Hollywood comedy or musical, and hence in every way an equal match for her philandering suitor. The Repulse Bay Hotel offers a perfect venue for romantic dallying and trysts. In this change of scenery, she finds herself liberated, able to find her own identity and define her own destiny for the first time in her life. Clearly it takes an outlandish place like Hong Kong to turn a petty tragedy into comedy. Had Liuyuan and Liusu remained in Shanghai, their romance would never have a chance to bloom. At the end of the story, the narrator wryly comments that it takes a big war and the deaths of thousands to give the heroine's life a happy ending. Indeed it takes an unusual combination of time (a war) and place (Hong Kong) to turn the ordinary into the extraordinary, history into romance.

As Chang recalls, it was during the University of Hong Kong's summer break in 1941 when, on one of her visits to her mother at the Repulse Bay Hotel, she first heard of the story about a couple, both of whom belonged to her mother's circle of mahjong friends, who fell for each other and lived together after the woman seduced the man over her mother's shoulders at the mahjong table. From this small item of gossip and hearsay Chang crafted a masterful romance.

One might ask, What were these people from Shanghai doing in a place like Hong Kong to begin with? Simply escaping from war in

Shanghai? In 1941, Shanghai was not yet occupied by the Japanese; the concessions remained untouched as an autonomous "orphan island" until 1943. And what was Chang's own mother doing in Hong Kong, aside from the excuse of keeping her daughter company? The young Chang did not visit her often, and most visits were fraught with tension. With the publication of *The Book of Change* and *Little Reunion*, the mother-daughter relationship was brought into the open, amplified with more details to complicate the picture. In earlier works, Chang treats her mother almost as her role model—a modern woman who gave her the Western name Eileen that also provided the basis for her Chinese name, an independent-minded mother who was always at loggerheads with Chang's traditional father and eventually divorced him. If the young Chang owed nearly everything to her mother as opposed to her tyranni- cal father in Shanghai, then in Hong Kong the tables were turned. Her later novels reveal the mother's character to have been "harsh, willful, promiscuous," an "ever-wandering" woman who took British paramours in exchange for protection and financial support. She even gambled away her daughter's scholarship money at the mahjong table. Her high-society lifestyle was a veil of hypocrisy and decadence. Her daughter, looking back across a time span of half a century, now wanted to "collect [her] own debt" by returning fictionally to the time and place in which she ceased to adore her mother.

In short, Chang's Hong Kong stories present a mixed picture of glam- our and decadence, romantic appeal and mental depravity. This island colony held a distorted mirror to Chang's vision of the tradition-bound Chinese world of Shanghai; it became a metaphor of the "other" to her Shanghai-rooted self. Later in her life, when she was forced to leave Communist-controlled Shanghai in 1952, she had no other recourse but to go to Hong Kong first, and it was from this temporary base that she tried to launch a new writing career that brought her to America. It was Hong Kong, accordingly, that made all of her subsequent literary production possible.

BIBLIOGRAPHY: Eileen Chang, *The Book of Change* (Hong Kong, 2009). Kam Louie, ed., *Eileen Chang: Romancing Languages, Cultures and Genres* (Hong Kong, 2012). Leo Ou-fan Lee, *Shanghai Modern: The Flowering of a New Urban Culture in China, 1930–1945* (Cambridge, MA, 1999), ch. 8.

LEO OU-FAN LEE

1942 · JANUARY 22

Xiao Hung dies in occupied Hong Kong.

2014 · FALL

The Golden Era, Ann Hui's biopic of Xiao Hong, is released.

In War She Writes

On January 22, 1942, five weeks after Hong Kong fell to the empire of Japan, Xiao Hong (1911–1942, real name Zhang Naiying), whose displacement began with the Japanese invasion of her Manchurian hometown in 1931, died in a hospital. Another war refugee, Eileen Chang (1920–1995), had come to Hong Kong to continue her education but found her studies interrupted again and was reluctantly serving as, as she described herself, "the world's most heartless nurse" at a temporary medical station. Arguably the two most talented of all modern Chinese writers, these women never met, but their simultaneous sojourns in Hong Kong nonetheless drove them both to produce some of the best works of modern Chinese literature.

During her last year in Hong Kong, for example, Xiao Hong finished her most critically acclaimed writing, including the autobiographical *Tales of Hulan River.* The novel is a lyrical recollection of her childhood in a remote rural village in Northeast China, a place where modernity was beyond all imagination. In 1943, a year after Xiao Hong's death, Chang returned to Shanghai and published most of her best fiction, beginning with *Love in a Fallen City,* in which the struggle of her diasporic hero and heroine to break free from the stifling oppression of social norms is set against the backdrop of Hong Kong's fall to the Japanese.

More than seven decades after their concurrent visits to Hong Kong, the two authors have finally been "joined together" by the internationally acclaimed Hong Kong filmmaker Ann Hui (1947–). Hui is a product of war herself—born to a Manchurian father and Japanese mother—and is known for tackling diverse themes in her work, including themes of cultural displacement. In 1984, Hui adapted Chang's *Love in a Fallen City,* and in 2014, she released *The Golden Era,* a biopic that follows Xiao Hong as she wanders across China during the turbulent Sino-Japanese War.

Both films prominently feature scenes in wartime Hong Kong. For *Love in a Fallen City*, for example, Hui rebuilt and preserved the Repulse Bay Hotel's verandah, where Chang's characters finally fall for each other. In *The Golden Era*, Hui reimagines the love triangle between Xiao Hong, Duanmu Hongliang (1912–1996), and the young Luo Binji (1917–1994), and juxtaposes the romance with Xiao Hong's deteriorating health and the Japanese bombing. Watching the end of *Love in a Fallen City*, we might wonder if Hui imagined Xiao Hong in the same scene, among the corpses and wounded bodies that littered a Hong Kong in ruins. Had she foreseen that, thirty years later, she would shoot *The Golden Era* and again re-create the war-torn Hong Kong where Chang's heroine found love and Xiao Hong died and was buried?

Bearing in mind Hui's reputation as an art film director specializing in literary adaptation, we might wonder why she would choose to portray Xiao Hong's life rather than her works. Xiao Hong's deceptively lyrical writing style, which leads readers to ponder the author's private life, likely led Hui to adopt an inventive, pseudo-documentary style for *The Golden Era*. Interweaving the writer's literary career with her romantic adventures and China's loss of Manchuria to Japan, *The Golden Era* has spurred new interest in Xiao Hong's life, a life that, despite the modern, ostensibly pro-female-liberation "new woman" ideology of her era, had been obscured for over half a century.

Born to a minor landowning family in a remote village in Hulan, a suburb of Harbin, the capital of Heilongjiang Province, Xiao Hong, like a typical May Fourth "new woman," fled an arranged marriage at age eighteen to seek freedom and self-fulfillment. Not long after running away, Xiao Hong surprisingly reunited with her former fiancé, whose hand she had once refused, but soon found herself abandoned at a hotel in Harbin. Pregnant and penniless, she reached out to a local newspaper for help and was rescued by Xiao Jun (1907–1988, real name Liu Honglin), a young leftist journalist. The two Xiaos lived and wrote together, publishing a joint collection, *Arduous Journey*, in 1933 before fleeing Japanese-ruled Harbin for Qingdao in Shandong Province. They eventually made their way to Shanghai and met Lu Xun (1881–1936) in 1934, who helped them to publish three books: Xiao Jun's *Village in August*; Xiao Hong's first novel, *The Field of Life and Death*, which provides probably the earliest sketch of fatalistic peasant life in Northeast China; and their joint collection of autobiographical essays, *Market Street*. These publications made them overnight sensations among leftist literary circles.

The full-scale outbreak of the Sino-Japanese War in 1937 extended their journey of displacement across half of China, from Shanghai to Wuhan, from Chongqing to Xi'an. The couple's intense relationship, Xiao Jun's affairs with other women, and their ideological split (Xiao Hong, despite her leftist literary inclinations, largely avoided politics, while Xiao Jun joined the Red Army in 1938) compelled Xiao Hong to end their romance. While still pregnant with Xiao Jun's child, she fell in love with and married another writer from Manchuria, Duanmu Hongliang, putting herself once again into an awkward situation. Fleeing both the disapproval of their fellow leftists and the war that had caught up with her again, Xiao Hong and Duanmu left for Hong Kong, where she published two more novels, *Ma Bole* and her acclaimed final work, *Tales of Hulang River*.

Japan began bombing Hong Kong on December 7, 1941. At that time, Xiao Hong was hospitalized for lung disease and other complications. Duanmu unwisely entrusted her to the budding writer and smitten fan Luo Binji while he sought shelter, and Xiao Hong, according to Luo, began to fall for him. At age thirty-one, Xiao Hong died a little more than a month after Hong Kong fell to Japan, having lived a life full enough for a woman twice her age: two children who died soon after birth, and several lovers, including her unlikely deathbed romance with Luo.

Though there is no shortage of biographical writing about Xiao Hong, her romantic adventures have received little attention, probably because they are not in keeping with her image as a writer of anti-Japanese literature and a refugee of the Japanese invasion. She became a subject of overseas interest in the 1970s when the prominent translator Howard Goldblatt (1939–), then a graduate student at the University of Indiana, rediscovered and championed her work. Goldblatt's work sparked renewed interest in her work in Sinophone communities, leading to her inclusion in school textbooks and some theatrical adaptations of her work. In these contexts, her work was often framed within patriotic narratives of resistance. Beijing-based theater director Tian Qinxin's (1968–) award-winning 1999 stage adaptation of *The Field of Life and Death*, for instance, emphasized her fight against Japan, foregrounding the actually largely insignificant wartime background of the novel.

Despite the attention she received from anthologists and dramatists, Xiao Hong was largely ignored by filmmakers until Huo Jianqi's (1958–) *Falling Flowers* was released in 2013. Funded by Xiao Hong's hometown, *Falling Flowers* is melodramatic and indulgent, and unwisely biased, siding with Xiao Jun and Luo while demonizing Duanmu. Hui's *The Golden Era*, by way of contrast, is aimed at facilitating different understandings of the idiosyncratic writer from the 1930s.

Filming in the context of China's renewed twenty-first-century interest in the early Republican era (1911–1949), Hui painstakingly avoided romanticizing the tumultuous epoch Xiao Hong inhabited: characters from Xiao Hong's leftist literary circles speak directly to the camera about what they know or do not know about her, with most of the lines drawn from their literary works, letters, and historical documents. In one scene, Hui presents two versions of the same event. In the first iteration, a character recounts Xiao Jun's claim that he heroically accepted Xiao Hong's decision to break up with him and take Duanmu's hand. Immediately afterward, we see Duanmu reminiscing late in life about how Xiao Jung had confronted him, thrown a tantrum, and only reluctantly accepted Xiao Hong's decision. Hinting that Xiao Hong's version of the incident differed from both Xiao Jun's and Duanmu's, the film provokes questions about memory and reality, literature and history. Hui also presents several scenes about the physical and mental toll of hunger on the impoverished writing couple, derived from the essay collection *Market Street*, rendering the film a lyricized reality, or a fictional documentary, about Xiao Hong. This style recalls the deceptively innocent tone that permeates Xiao Hong's work, making it a tribute to her literary achievement.

In his foreword to *The Field of Life and Death*, Lu Xun praised Xiao Hong, commenting that the novel "may look like nothing but a brief sketch whose narration of events and scenic descriptions are superior to its characterization" but that "the northerner's tenacious will to survive and resistance in the face of death nonetheless forcefully permeates the pages." His endorsement, together with her unusually compassionate portrayal of peasants in the remote northeastern corner of China, then under occupation by the Japanese, made Xiao Hong into the patriotic emblem of the "northeastern writer." When Xiao Hong later found temporary asylum in Hong Kong's Repulse Bay, she again wrote about the unchanging villages of rural Manchuria in *Tales of Hulan River*, a book some critics at the time unsurprisingly disregarded as nostalgic. It is set, after all, in the small town of Hulan, where "people led their lives, looking neither ahead nor behind; that which was in their past was forgotten, while they held out no great hope for the future. They simply passed their days in their stolid fashion, uncomplainingly accepting the lot handed down to them by their ancestors." But in this autobiographic novel, the stories told by the young girl who serves as Xiao Hong's narrator—stories of ordinary events like town festivities, and ordinary townspeople including the narrator's beloved grandfather, a child bride, a bean-flour sifter, and a miller suffering from a harelip—cumulatively reveal the complexity of the society. A passage from chapter 1, in which Xiao Hong describes a quagmire in the middle of the main road of Hulan, exemplifies her writing style:

> How many carts and horses are extricated from this quagmire every year may never be known. But, you ask, does anyone ever think of solving the problem by filling it in with dirt? No, not a single one....
>
> In all, this quagmire brings two benefits to the residents of the rear. The first is that the drowned chickens and ducks always produce a lot of excitement....
>
> The second is in relation to the matter of pork. Were there no quagmire, how could they have their infected pork? Naturally, they might still eat it, but how are they to explain it away? If they simply admit they are eating infected pork, it will be too unsanitary for words, but with the presence of the quagmire, the problem is solved: infected pork becomes the meat of drowned pigs....

Chapter 5 of *Tales* is about a child bride who is "diagnosed" as possessed by an evil spirit. Her "cure" involves being cleansed with scalding hot water. The villagers' routine violence is presented without judgment, drawing the reader into the intimate logic of village life and inviting, rather than proclaiming, criticism of her subjects.

> Originally, the child bride had fought having her clothing taken off out of a sense of modesty, but she'd been stripped on the order of her mother-in-law. Now here she was, oblivious to everything, with no feelings at all, and her mother-in-law was worried about how she looked.

The sorceress beat some tattoos on her drum, as the attendant said something to her, and the onlookers cast glances back and forth. None could say how this episode would end, whether the child bride would be dead or alive; but whatever the outcome, they knew they had not wasted their time in coming. They had seen some eye-opening incidents, and they were a little wiser in the ways of the world—that alone made it all worthwhile.

If Xiao Hong's lyrical realism demands that her readers take multiple perspectives of the world she wrote about, Hui's *The Golden Era* seems to follow this same strategy. Juxtaposing historical anecdotes, literary documents, and vivid imagery, Hui challenges what viewers know and do not know about her legendary subject, making the film a rare companion to the literary achievements of Xiao Hong herself. By using this strategy, Hui follows in the footsteps of Xiao Hong and Chang, writers who rejected the simplistic patriotic narratives of their male counterparts; writers who were able to see how the chaos of war could paradoxically lead to liberation, and how the eternally oppressed peasants could be agents of oppression themselves within their own community. Perhaps it was a story that only Hui—a woman in a male-dominated industry, born to two people brought together by war—could tell.

BIBLIOGRAPHY: Ann Hui, dir., *The Golden Era* (Stella Mega Film, 2014). Ann Hui, dir., *Love in a Fallen City* (Shaw Brothers, 2002). Huo Jianqi, dir., *Falling Flowers* (Talent International Film, 2013). Xiao Hong, *The Field of Life and Death & Tales of Hulan River*, trans. Howard Goldblatt (Boston, 2002). Xiao Hong, *Xiao Hong: Novels* (Beijing, 2014).

KATHERINE HUI-LING CHOU

1942 · MARCH 16

Lü Heruo's family burns his diaries.

Taiwan's Genius Lü Heruo

As one of the most skillful and sophisticated of the prewar nativist writers in colonial Taiwan (1895–1945), Lü Heruo's short life (1914–1951) is punctuated with many firsts. While still an elementary school teacher in

Hsinchu, at the tender age of twenty-three, Lü published his first short story, "The Ox Cart," in a prestigious Japanese journal (*Bungaku hyōron*, 1935; it was later translated into Chinese by the Marxist writer Hu Feng [1902–1985]). It was the first piece of Taiwanese fiction to be introduced into mainland China during the colonial period. Lü was also the first and only Taiwanese writer to have a single-volume short story collection published in the prewar period (1944), as well as the first of a few writers who successfully switched their creative language from Japanese to Chinese in the postwar era. Having enjoyed a colorful career as a singer and stage performer in Japan, he later became a newspaper reporter and a founding member and actor in the theater group Kōsei engeki kenkyūkai (1943). Lü participated energetically in every aspect of cultural life in the colony, and his multifaceted talent and unwavering dedication to art won him the endearing descriptor "premier genius of Taiwan." His postwar involvement in the Taiwanese Communist Party and, finally, his mysterious and premature death at the age of thirty-eight all contributed to making Lü a legendary figure in modern Taiwanese literary history.

Born into a landed gentry family in Taichung in 1914, Lü received a modern, Western-style education. After graduating from Taichung Normal College in 1931, he taught music at an elementary school in Hsinchu and started writing fiction. In 1939, he left for Japan to study voice with the famed opera singer Nagasaka Yoshiko (1891–1970), and later became a chorus member of the Tōhō Musical Theater (1940–1942). Lü's unusual sojourn into music may not have been his most successful endeavor, but his contact with the most important figure in modern Japanese music, Yamada Kōsaku (1886–1965), and Yamada's theories on national music paved the way for Lü's later engagement in activities especially related to music and drama. Returning to Taiwan, he joined the like-minded writer Zhang Wenhuan's (1909–1978) editorial team at the journal *Taiwan Literature* and published many of his short stories in that journal.

No writer was better at illuminating the conflicts between art and politics, the private and the public, modernity and tradition, than Lü. A teacher and musician by training, and a showman by profession, Lü lived in a tumultuous time that exacted a high personal price. Angst and disillusionment, as well as a hesitation between the embrace of romantic idealism and the harsh economic and social reality, lace his deceptively gentle and pastoral lyricism. Lü's fiction surpasses the works of both

Yang Kui (1906–1985), the leading socialist writer in Taiwan, and Lü's editorial partner Zhang, who was a chronicler of Taiwanese manners and morals. Whereas Yang's passion for social causes sometimes shrilly overwhelms his narrative and Zhang is overly reliant on sentimentalism, Lü's stories demonstrate a perfect balance. With measured dignity he negotiated between the quiet drama of the interior life and the tension of the harsh public world.

Lü's first short story, "The Ox Cart," drew the attention of metropolitan literary circles in the metropole, Tokyo. It relates the experience of an ox cart driver who has suffered fierce competition from motorized carts ever since the opening of a modern highway to his village. His dream of owning a modest piece of arable land is crushed by the loss of work, compounded by the hyperinflation brought on by modernization. He is no longer able to provide for his family; his wife is forced to turn to prostitution. The story ends with the humiliated protagonist further punished with a hefty fine for driving his ox cart on the newly paved road. In order to pay the two *yuan* fine, the protagonist steals two geese and is caught by the police.

Even though Lü came from a humble rural background and "The Ox Cart" echoes Yang's socialist inclinations, Lü's subsequent writings in fact avoid this kind of overt protest and opt for a more understated style. Yet, the story set the tenor for Lü's subsequent writings, which show a sympathetic concern toward the little people and their daily struggles. To a certain degree, all native writers of the colonial period, whether the nationalists who stressed Taiwan's cultural ties to China, the nativists who advocated a distinctive Taiwanese identity, or the imperial subject writers (*kōmin sakka*) who sought to assimilate into Japanese civilization, confronted this issue of how to navigate between their native Chinese or Taiwanese cultural heritage and the vision of modernity promoted by the Japanese colonial establishment. The issue was further complicated by the generational shifts in language use, as seen in the debates on "native literature" (*xiangtu wenxue*); the writers of Lü's generation had gradually shifted to writing in Japanese. Unlike the stories written by the imperial subject writers, contemporaries of Lü who shrilly advocated total assimilation to take full advantage of colonial modernity, Lü's narratives tend to be nuanced and ambivalent, frequently invoking an acute sense of loss. Lü was as cosmopolitan as any of these writers, yet as a writer his gaze was always set on the here and now. His stories deal mostly with native issues and feature few Japanese characters or Japan-related events, even though the presence of the colonial regime always lurks beneath the surface.

Lü's most productive period began in 1942 after his return from Japan. His prewar writings deal with three major themes: family conflicts over new ideas; women in the new society; and the frustrated melancholia of youthful intellectuals. "Fortune, Children and Longevity" (1942), "Geomancy" (1942), "A Happy Family" (1943), and "Pomegranate" (1943) belong to the first category. They deal with old-fashioned domestic issues complicated by factors such as marriage, kinship relationships, and economic worries within the feudalistic familial institution. These stories reveal the conflicts arising from the discrepancy between new and old values. Lü's narrators stay as objective as possible, resolutely refusing to take sides, and the stories' endings remain open and ambivalent, allowing the reader to grasp the many contradictions in their value system. Lü injects gentle humanity into all of his characters, who range from stubborn old patriarchs and filial sons to struggling peasants, impulsive men who commit violent crimes after being bullied by the rich and powerful, and devoted prostitutes, but he saves his deepest sympathy for women who want to break away from the old ways. He has a soft spot for young girls who were married off early to the husband's household as half future wife and half free laborer, a traditional Taiwanese arrangement known as *xifuzai*. "Moonlight Night" (1942) and "Strange Tale of Marriage" (1935) belong to the category that focuses on women and their plight, squeezed between patriarchal and colonial expectations.

Lü's strongest work includes his more lyrical pieces, such as a brief encounter between a Japanese drifter and a Taiwanese boy in "Magnolia" (1943) or the endless anxiety and melancholy that awaits the young protagonist in "Clear Autumn" (1944). Both evoke a deep and universal emotional dimension without parallel in the works of other writers of that era.

Born two decades into Japanese colonial rule, Lü was typical of the generation that was educated in a colonial education system that emphasized the supremacy of the Japanese language over one's native tongue. Today, unfortunately, the average Taiwanese must read Lü's works in Chinese translation, since the majority of his works were written and published in Japanese. This is one of the reasons that this body of refined literary gems remained untouched by readers and scholars alike until the mid-1990s, after the lifting of martial law, when the study of the colonial period began to gain academic legitimacy. Many writers could not navigate the language shift from Japanese to Chinese during the immediate postwar era and fell silent. Lü, however, trained himself to write in Mandarin Chinese and became one of the handful of writers who were able to make this linguistic transition successfully. He published several short stories in Chinese (such as "Winter Night" [1947], written two weeks before the February 28 Incident), which take sarcastic jabs at the Japanese occupation, the newly inaugurated Nationalist rule, and the people trying to profit from that chaotic time.

Lü's postwar treatment of the colonial condition is understandably more direct and overtly critical than his writings during the colonial period. His command of the Chinese language in these short stories does not compare to his mature works in Japanese, but his distinctive style—detached, thoughtful observations and a finely honed, though somewhat dark, sense of humor—is still evident in these postcolonial stories. Yet, as time went on, Lü's passion for politics took him further and further away from creative writing.

On February 27, 1947, agents of the Nationalist government and policemen got into a skirmish with an old female vender while trying to suppress unauthorized cigarette sales. In the process of confiscating her cigarettes and money, they shot and wounded her and another bystander. Outrage over this incident, which many felt reflected the overly harsh treatment of civilians by the Nationalist government, built up until a riot broke out. The next day, February 28, some Taipei residents went on strike, closing their shops and marching to the Tobacco Monopoly Bureau to protest and petition the bureau chief. Guards opened fire on the marchers, killing and wounding many citizens. The news quickly spread across the island and brought forth even more protests. One year and four months after the Kuomintang (KMT) took over Taiwan, simmering dissatisfaction on the part of the islanders had finally boiled over, triggering this unfortunate incident. The mutual distrust deepened as a contingent of the Nationalist army arrived in Taipei on March 8 to forcibly put down the civil disturbance. On March 10, the whole island of Taiwan was put under martial law.

In the ensuing purge, the Nationalist army killed an estimated eighteen to twenty-eight thousand people, wiping out a large portion of the elite class of intellectuals; those who were not executed en masse were forced to go underground.

After the February 28 Incident, Lü joined the Chinese Communist Party and became the editor of their underground paper, *Guangmingbao*. In 1949, he also accepted a post teaching music at a girls' high school and gave a personal recital at Sun Yat-sen Hall. That same year the newly arrived Nationalist government-in-exile led by Chiang Kai-shek (1887–1975) intensified its crackdown on Communist Party members in Taiwan. In August, the founder of *Guangmingbao*, who was the principal of Keelung Middle School and also a Communist Party member, was arrested. When KMT agents came looking for Lü, he was forced to flee to the hills on the outskirts of Taipei, where he attempted to set up a shortwave radio base. In 1951, he was declared dead. His widow recalls that he was planning to escape to Okinawa. To this day, the mystery surrounding Lü's death has not been resolved, but accounts suggest he was bitten by a poisonous snake and buried privately by family members.

The White Terror snatched many native sons of Taiwan who could have been a formidable force in rebuilding the island nation. Lü was known for keeping a meticulous diary, in which he jotted down personal thoughts about the writing process and his family life. Upon his death, his family, fearing that the diary would be a political liability, burned all but one of the journals—the journal covering the years 1942–1944. The sensitive postwar political climate prevented any scholarly study of his works. The 1991 publication of a selection of his works in *Works of Lü Heruo*, as part of a series on Taiwanese writers, followed by the 1995 single-volume collection of all his writings, *The Complete Works of Lü Heruo*, were the first steps in restoring his place in Taiwanese literary history. Despite his doubts concerning traditional society, Lü was also ambivalent about modernity. He chose not to confront colonialism directly in his writings—that would have been a perilous and perhaps fruitless task, given the level of censorship and social control that prevailed at the time—but insisted that he "wanted to write fiction that reflects the life of the Taiwanese without exaggeration, [something] with Taiwanese characteristics." To this day, one cannot help but lament the lost opportunity and wonder if, had this dynamic and multifaceted talent lived, he would have rewritten the history of Taiwanese literature.

BIBLIOGRAPHY: Chen Fangming, *Zuoyi Taiwan: Zhimindi wenxue yundongshi lun* (Taipei, 1998). Chen Yingzhen, *Lü Heruo yanjiu: Taiwan diyi caizi* (Taipei, 1997). Lü Heruo, *Lü Heruo ji,* ed. Zhang Henghao (Taipei, 1991). Lü Heruo, *Lü Heruo xiaoshuo quanji,* trans. Lin Ahijie (Taipei, 1995). Shi Shu, *Rijushidai Taiwan xiaoshuo shuan* (Taipei, 1999). Yang Kui, *Yang Kui ji,* ed. Zhang Henghao (Taipei, 1991). Ye Shitao, *Taiwan wenxue shigang* (Kaohsiung, Taiwan, 1987). Ye Shitao, "Qingqiu: Weizhuang de huangminhua ouge," *Taiwan wenyi* 77 (1982): 21–26.

FAYE YUAN KLEEMAN

1942 · MAY 2–MAY 23

Literature and art must glorify "the labor and struggle of the people."

The Cultural and Political Significance of Mao Zedong's Talks at the Yan'an Forum on Literature and Art

On May 2, 1942, the Central Propaganda Department of the Chinese Communist Party convened over one hundred artists and writers to participate in a forum held at the party headquarters at Yangjialing in Yan'an. In the introduction to the report that became *Talks at the Yan'an Forum on Literature and Art,* Mao Zedong (1893–1976) emphasizes that literature and art must "become a constituent part of the whole revolutionary machine," must "take the Party's position," and must sing the praises of "the people's army, and the people's party."

When the second session of the Forum was held on May 16, the famous writer Xiao Jun (1907–1988) was the first to speak. In his remarks, he declared that writers must have "freedom" and must be "independent." When Lu Xun (1881–1936) was in Guangzhou, Xiao Jun pointed out, he did not accept the direction of any organization or any party and, what's more, insisted that he would never write an article eulogizing or singing anyone's praises. At that point, Hu Qiaomu (1912–1992), who was acting as Mao's secretary, rose to refute Xiao Jun, saying:

> Literature and art must follow the direction of an organization. That Lu Xun did not accept the leadership of the organization at that time was no honor, but instead a failing. In the final analysis, it is a question of whether the party should or should not, can or cannot, lead art.

Years later, Hu would recall that Mao was very pleased by his speech and made a point of inviting him to dinner after the meeting in order to "congratulate him on opening the struggle."

Zhu De (1886–1976), the commander in chief of the Eighth Route Army, made a speech at the final session of the Forum on May 23. Refuting Xiao Jun once again, Zhu said that one must not be afraid to discuss "transforming" one's ideological position: "Not only is there transformation, but there's also surrender. I'm an old soldier, and yet I have surrendered to the Communist Party." When Zhu invited Mao to make the concluding remarks, the first thing Mao said was, "Commander Zhu has spoken very well; he has already given us our conclusion."

In this way, Zhu's speech, an episode triggered by Xiao Jun's critical remarks throughout the course of the Forum, acquired a unique symbolic significance. Zhu's remarks elucidated the fundamental spirit behind the Communist Party's convening of the forum and Mao's opening remarks: the key to realizing the party's absolute leadership over literature and art, to making literature and art into "the Party's literature and art," was the reform and surrender of the intellectuals.

On May 16, as discussions at the Forum were under way, the official newspaper of the Central Committee of the Communist Party, *Liberation Daily*, pointedly quoted a passage by Vladimir Lenin (1870–1924), in which he discusses the "antagonistic relationship" between the intellectuals and the proletariat. This antagonism, according to Lenin, is not rooted in economic interests, but is rather an expression of an "antagonism that exists in their sentiments and in their mindset." In his *Talks*, Mao again brings up the idea that "the petty-bourgeois intellectuals" must allow for "their demeanor to be remade by the party and society," and sternly issues a warning: "The proletariat cannot yield to you. If it were to yield to you, it would be yielding to the large landowners and the big bourgeoisie, and in so doing, it would run the risk of destroying the Party and destroying the nation."

Mao's severe criticism of the intellectuals was grounded in the complex circumstances of the internal struggles within the party. Before the 1942 Yan'an Rectification Movement, the massive two-year party purge during which the Yan'an Forum took place, the person in charge of literature and art was Zhang Wentian (1900–1976), who at that time was general secretary of the party, as well as chief of the Propaganda

Department. Zhang promoted a lenient policy toward intellectuals and a relatively relaxed line on literature and art. Zhang argued that party leadership "should think highly of culture workers" and "must strive to avoid interfering in or limiting their writing. We should, in point of fact, guarantee their complete freedom to write.... [We should] advocate for a vivid, lively, democratic style of writing characterized by freedom of thought, freedom to investigate, and freedom to argue." Because of this stance, the writing circles in Yan'an had emerged as a relatively independent society. The resulting forest of publications left an indelible impression on many old residents of Yan'an. In his *Talks,* Mao chiefly sought to change what had been seen as the "chaos" of "an inundation of liberalism" and establish and strengthen the party's system of unified leadership. The core of this policy was compelling intellectuals to completely and thoroughly surrender and pledge allegiance to the party, and, in so doing, effect a grand unification of politics, ideology, and culture. The goal of the Yan'an Rectification Movement was to establish Mao's absolute leadership. To surrender to the party, in truth, meant pledging allegiance to the representative of the party—that is, Mao himself. Behind this policy was the ideal on which Mao founded the nation: achieving a unity between politics and faith by placing political, spiritual, and moral authority in the hands of one man. He took seriously literature's ability to educate and enlighten. He wanted to create a "Mao Zedong age" of literature and art that would use his thought to remake and purify hundreds of millions of Chinese souls.

In this way, in the Mao era, which started precisely at this point, to surrender or not to surrender became a choice that intellectuals had to make, and it was this choice that decided their fate. In Yan'an, the first to announce their surrender were the famous leftist writer Ding Ling (1904–1986) and the poet He Qifang (1912–1977). Ding Ling even went so far as to say, "I must hand over my armor. My volumes upon volumes of writing must be seen as a heap of nothing. I must do away with my self-regard and my pride." Those who refused to yield, like Xiao Jun and Wang Shiwei (1906–1947), were subjected to intense criticism. Wang, who had been a Communist since the 1920s but had been vociferous and personal in his criticism of Mao, was expelled from the party the year after the Forum and imprisoned. In 1947, when the Nationalists temporarily drove the Communists from Yan'an, Wang was summarily executed in the midst of the Communist retreat. Mao dispatched He to the Nationalist Party–controlled areas on the pretext of having him spread the message of the *Talks*. In reality, it was to urge surrender. Guo Moruo (1892–1978) and Mao Dun (1896–1981), both of whom understood the Communist government deeply, promptly rushed to write supportive responses. The bookish Hu Feng (1902–1985), on the other hand, was oblivious to the tenor of the party's message, and published Shu Wu's (1922–2009) *On Subjectivity*, which put forth an interpretation of the *Talks* that differed from that of Mao Zedong. Due to activities like this, Hu was considered a bad seed during the 1950s, one that needed to be driven out of the party and from Communist society.

What is an undeniable fact is that many intellectuals, particularly leftist intellectuals, embraced and obeyed the Chinese Communist Party, Mao, and his *Talks* not simply because they were timid and overcautious, or because they wished to hitch themselves to its power and influence, but because they themselves saw its ideological logic. Chinese leftist intellectuals were nationalists before they were anything else, with the ideal of establishing an independent, unified, powerful, democratic, free, modern nation-state. Their first visions of modernization emerged during the May Fourth Movement and came primarily from Western Enlightenment ideology. When they embraced Marxism and became leftist intellectuals, however, their positions—critical of capitalism and particularly opposed to Western imperialist aggression—became opposed to the vision of Western modernization that they had once embraced. The distinguishing feature of the new ideology and culture of the Chinese Communist Party and Mao, which included the *Talks*, was the construction of a new, anti-Western model of modern Chinese government, economy, and culture—a model according to which the party would construct a unified, independent, strong, and modern nation-state. The aim was to maintain the independence of the Chinese race as it underwent modernization, thereby simultaneously realizing the two great and often contradictory goals of twentieth-century Chinese politics. It was precisely because of this aim that party ideology seemed to appeal to leftist intellectuals, whose paradoxical positions left them bewildered and mired in contradictions.

As a politician who deeply understood China and its intellectuals, Mao grasped this point completely, advocating from the start the proposition that "Marxism must comport with our nation's particular circumstances, and can only be realized through a defined national form." And the *Talks* was mainly seen as a Sinification of Marxism, a self-conscious attempt to find a path of Marxist cultural development with Chinese characteristics. This Sinified Marxist Mao Zedong Thought satisfied the dual demands of leftist intellectuals for Marxism and nationalism. In the end, leftist intellectuals chose to obey Mao and Mao Zedong Thought for important ideological reasons. For this reason, even Hu and Shu Wu, who held dissenting views, never fundamentally opposed the *Talks*.

Seen objectively, even if it were only an expression of a radical leftist ideological trend, Mao's *Talks* still would have its historical rationale and unique value. For example, starting from the fundamental truth that China's population is overwhelmingly composed of peasants, Mao advocates that literature and art should serve the worker, farmer, and soldier; he takes popularization seriously; and he emphasizes using folk forms that would please the eyes and ears of China's common people. These points were readily embraced by those leftist intellectuals who had a flesh-and-blood connection to the lowest strata of the people. Later, literary creations appeared under the guidance of the *Talks* that not only realized party ideology, but were also innovative with regard to artistic form. It was no coincidence that these works—such as He Jingzhi (1924–) et al.'s *White Haired Girl* (a new opera that drew on elements of regional theater), Li Ji's (1922–1980) *Wang Gui and Li Xiangxiang* (a new poem modeled after folk ballads), and Zhao Shuli's (1906–1970) "Xiao Erhei's Marriage" and "Rhymes of Li Youcai" (short story and novella modeled on traditional storytelling)—also became popular among the common people, particularly peasants.

The problem was that the *Talks* was never simply a way of thinking about art and literature in the abstract, but from the start was party ideology. After the founding of the People's Republic, it became the national ideology and the national policy on literature and art. When united with the power of the nation, the policy's absolutism and exclusivity, combined with the submission and obedience it compelled, inevitably evolved into a dictatorship over thought and culture. A document that spoke so often of returning literature to the people was used to deprive that same population of their ability to express themselves through literature; a document aimed at uniting intellectuals and the party irrevocably placed a wedge between the two groups. Pushed to an extreme, the *Talks* achieved the opposite of the rationale it was originally intended to serve. In this irony, there is a profound historical lesson.

BIBLIOGRAPHY: Ai Ke'en, *Yan'an wenyi yundong jisheng* (Beijing, 1987). Ding Ling, "Guanyu lichang wenti wojian," in *Ding Ling quanji*, vol. 7 (Shijiazhuang, China, 2001), 65–70. Hu Qiaomu, *Hu Qiaomu huiyi Mao Zedong* (Beijing, 1994). "Liening Sidalin deng lun dang de jilü yu dang de minzhu," *Jiefang ribao*, May 16, 1942. Luo Fu [Zhang Wentian], "Kangzhan yilai zhonghuaminzu de xin wenhua yundong yu jinhou renwu," *Jiefang ribao*, April 1, 1940. Mao Zedong, "Zhongguo Gongchandang zai minzu zhan-zheng zhong de diwei" (October 1939), in *Mao Zedong xuanji*, single-volume edition (Beijing, 1966), 507–534.

QIAN LIQUN

Translated by Dylan Suher

1943 · APRIL

Zhao Shuli's "Little Blackie Gets Married" is published.

The Genesis of Peasant Revolutionary Literature

In 1943, a little-known Chinese peasant named Zhao Shuli (1906–1970) shot to national fame after publication of his short story entitled "Little Blackie Gets Married." The story deals with a couple of rural youths in pursuit of love despite the feudal interferences of superstition and arranged marriage. Written in simple, colloquial, and beautiful language, coupled with lively village characters, the story was an immediate success and was quickly adapted for the stage. Productions of the story by local theaters were immensely popular with illiterate peasants. Sales of the story reached a high of forty thousand copies, a record that surpassed that of even the revolutionary and iconic writer Lu Xun (1881–1936), whose work was reprinted annually on revolutionary bases.

The rise of Zhao, perhaps the most famous modern Chinese peas-ant writer, signaled the successful expansion of modern Chinese litera-ture from being a strictly urban endeavor to including rural and nonelite voices. Zhao taught revolutionary writers how to use "old bottles to contain new wine," namely to educate peasant readers about revolutionary ideas by packaging them in older and more familiar local mediums. His literary achievement was eventually recognized by the Chinese Communist Party

(CCP), and in the 1950s he was awarded the highest literary honor and called a master of the Chinese language, placing him in the company of Guo Moruo (1892–1978), Mao Dun (1896–1981), Lao She (1899–1966), and Ba Jin (1904–2005).

However, the acceptance of Zhao's new writing was not without controversy, particularly among Marxist intellectuals whose elitist training in classic and Western learning refused to recognize the value of Zhao's reinvention of rural cultures. They deliberately expressed their disapproval by publishing Zhao's books on low-quality paper, which struck a sharp contrast to the fine materials they used when reprinting the works of Lu Xun.

This discrimination was by no means a personal episode, but rather reflected the ongoing battles taking place on the national literary stage since the late Qing dynasty over the nature of modern Chinese writing. Respective emphasis on the aesthetic and functional natures of literature, also understood as a debate over high and low literature, alternated to shape the course of literary development in the various periods since the turn of the twentieth century, and the unresolved tension between the two directions continued to stimulate efforts to define the identity of modern Chinese literature well into the revolutionary era.

When the CCP started to shift their revolutionary bases to the countryside during the late 1920s, they were put in a position to imagine a new literary project specifically catering to the masses. This "people's literature" was essentially pro-peasant literature used to fulfill the urgent political purposes of the party. It was in this political context that the reputation of writers like Zhao began to take shape, as it was Zhao and his contemporaries who were able to attract peasant readers by adapting new ideas into old artistic forms.

Zhao's background is unique. Born in 1906 into a poor peasant family in Northern China, his artistic talent was cultivated by daily contact with local forms of art. At an early age, he had mastered local musical instruments, opera, herbal medicine, and fortune telling. In 1927, he joined the CCP. In order to extol his newly found faith, he changed the character for his family name from the "Li" for virtue to the "Li" for truth, reason, and principle. However, his Marxist conversion did not channel him into urban cultural spaces, as was the normal course of social promotion for youths at the time. On the contrary, his major activities were still largely confined to the countryside, which explained why he never felt an intellectual belonging to the mainstream metropolitan cultures.

One phenomenal feature of modern Chinese literature is that its driving engines were two, not one. The metropolitan space can mobilize the best human and institutional resources and become a spatial origin for new modern culture—the entire body of May Fourth Chinese enlightenment literature is deeply imprinted with this urban character. But the Communist movement, especially after the beginning of the Anti-Japanese War (as the Second Sino-Japanese War is sometimes called) in 1937, made a concerted effort to open up the rural space of northwestern China and introduced the new ideological forces of social and literary revolution.

Led by the CCP, rural cultural space was subject to constant reforms and reinstitutionalizations, so that it soon became another productive fountain of modern Chinese literature for the next half century. Rural writers, readers, topics, and styles all served as the main point of reference for Mao Zedong (1893–1976) when he proposed his famous theory of the "new democratic culture," which is defined as "definitively democratic, popular and scientific and carrying the essence of Chinese cultural sophistication and elegance." To build up this new democratic culture, Mao needed the twin engines of urban and rural production to be working closely together. In this context, the Communist Revolution can be best understood not as halting the first engine of urban literary production, but as firing up the second. Zhao's work thus served as a timely harbinger of this new direction.

Zhao's rise to fame in 1943, therefore, must be understood as the result of these specific historical conditions. In fact, his early works received almost no critical attention, much less praise. Zhao's first two short stories, "Regret" and "Story of a White Horse," were written in 1929 while he was being held in Nationalist (Kuomintang) custody, but left little impression. His style continued to mature into the 1930s with the further publication of a handful of short stories, plays, and novels, but his rustic style kept him out of step with the urban tastes of the time. The sudden about-face of Zhao's literary fortunes can thus be attributed to the CCP's cultural movement, which simultaneously promoted authors like Zhao and created a new, peasant-based readership to welcome his works. These historical circumstances were a necessary precondition for his nationwide popularity.

In light of this history, Zhao's emergence on the national stage and his writing's popularity can be said to reflect the unidirectional thrust of the dual-engine literary system in the People's Republic. On the one hand, Zhao was familiar with Chinese enlightenment literature, himself a deep reader of Lu Xun and a fan of Russian writer Anton Chekhov (1860–1904). His indebtedness to enlightenment literature cannot be overstated, and it is no coincidence that "Little Blackie Gets Married" reflects the tenets of enlightenment literature more than revolutionary dicta. As suggested by the title, the story focuses on the marriage of Little Blackie. The idea of "free marriage" in the novel, however, is borrowed subject matter from earlier enlightenment literature; it is merely that the typical urban backdrop has been exchanged for the countryside. For all its enlightenment influence, "Little Blackie Gets Married" departs from the tradition in significant ways. For instance, the story identifies three major factors as detrimental to the dignity of new human life: superstition, female eroticism, and official corruption. The latter two of these scourges are largely absent in enlightenment-period literature, and yet the love of the young rural couple seems extremely short on romantic feelings or any intimate bodily contact. Another significant divergence is the problem-solving method of the story. Indeed, it is necessary for the Communist administrative power to intervene, but its violence can only be directed toward corrupt bureaucrats; for the old-minded peasants, the revolutionary authority is only allowed to function as a moral council on the matter of rural affairs. In this sense, enlightenment values proceed in the countryside not as abstract truth-ideas and universal principles, but as recuperative values that had been lost as a result of the oppressive forces of feudalism and capitalism.

On the other hand, however, Zhao's thought was immersed in the timely spirit of rural populism. He was a person who clearly recognized the backward status of the rural economy and culture, but still refused the tendency to devalue it in favor of the theory of urbanization. He looked forward to a great revolution that would drive away all the reactionary forces from rural lands, and truly believed that this could only be achieved by the peasants themselves. In this view, developing peasants' productivity, originality, and revolutionary will was crucial to the goal of their liberation, closely echoing Mao's political ideals. Zhao's cooperation with Mao and the Communist Party has its roots in their common vision of a rural populism.

Mao's intellectual politics are clearly linked to this populist platform. In his *Talks at the Yan'an Forum on Literature and Art*, Mao remarks, "In the final analysis, the workers and peasants are the cleanest people, though their hands are soiled and their feet are smeared with cow-dung, they are actually cleaner than the bourgeois and petty-bourgeois intellectuals." The result of this populist proclamation would be the call for urban intellectuals to go to the countryside to study the peasants' language, to learn their purity of purpose, and to work for their development. Zhao's extraordinary familiarity with peasants' language, needs, habits, and mentality, as well as his extreme comfort associating with them, made him the ideal candidate to represent the CCP model of unification.

In 1947, the concept known as the "Zhao Shuli direction" began the iconization of Zhao. Zhao represented the direction other Chinese communist writers should follow. What was the essence of this direction? Despite various interpretations, it can be put simply as a writing position where the double consciousness of a writer writing for the peasant other is overcome. A careful investigation into his literary forms proves the successful unification of the double consciousness. Taking the example of "Little Blackie Gets Married," its outstanding aesthetic features include the application of local dramatic plot devices, detailed and relatable character portrayal, and the careful production of a dramatic climax. In all his works, Zhao intently abandons modernist techniques such as psychoanalysis, objectification of the environment, monologue, and even the role of a major hero, which are essential to the modernist nature of a novel.

After this short story, Zhao continued to keep his creative energy for almost ten years. His other most famous works are "Rhymes of Li Youcai" and "Changes of Li Village." In addition to fiction writing, he also created essays, plays, and biographies of model workers.

Zhao's major literary contribution after the founding of the People's Republic was *Three Mile Bay* (1953), the first novel to recount the "rural cooperation" movement. However, the rapid changes in the political atmosphere during the 1950s soon reversed the fate of Zhao's literary career, and radical Chinese Marxists with a different vision of "people's literature" began to criticize his work. Zhao was ultimately accused of lacking a grand historical narrative for rural transformation, writing dull and slow-paced stories, and neglecting to include heroism in his characterizations. At the turn of the 1960s, Chinese readers had developed a taste for new genres, among which the most significant were the heroic tale, the bildungsroman, and the epic rural novel.

Even Zhao was not always able to steer himself in the "direction" presumed by his grand title. His writing was eventually labeled as reflecting a different kind of "double consciousness": peasant artist and national writer. His eclipse in literary circles was indeed a personal tragedy but, more importantly, it reflected the vacillation of the party's policies concerning the countryside—between populism and urbanization—and the irresolvable conflict of interest between the state and the peasant classes. One of Zhao's last stories touches on the theme of betrayal among the rural youths who cannot resist the lure of the urban. Zhao became deeply depressed and began to doubt if his works were still read and appreciated by contemporary peasants. He died a painful death during the Cultural Revolution in 1970.

The end of the Cultural Revolution and the demise of Mao's revolutionary ideals ushered in a new era of modern Chinese history and literature. The literary discourse began to break free from the yoke of socialist ideology and produce new literary movements. Few of these, however, were inspired by the values upheld by Zhao and his contemporaries. Literature was no longer regarded as an instrument for transforming the people, and was instead relocated to an autonomous sphere of artistic activities with independent value. Though interest in the "peasant question" is still discernible in contemporary Chinese writings, the terms of their representation have undergone a significant change. In this sense, Zhao does not have a real successor.

Although Zhao's literature is still revered in contemporary China by leftist critics, the closest semblance to a literary legacy is to be found in the burgeoning genre of migrant workers' literature. The ethos of this writing and of Zhao's oeuvre are perhaps best captured in his 1945 debate with a young revolutionary poet, who argued, "Art is higher than life and peasants are backwards classes, so art should not learn from them." Zhao responded by saying, "The masses are backwards indeed, but they are the majority. Without the support of the majority, there would have not been a great victory in the Anti-Japanese War; also, without them, there would have not been great art and literature."

BIBLIOGRAPHY: Yi-Tsi Mei Feuerwerker, *Ideology, Power, Text: Self-Representation and the Peasant "Other" in Modern Chinese Literature* (Stanford, CA, 1998). Zhao Shuli, *Zhao Shuli Quanji*, 5 vols. (Taiyuan, China, 1999).

HUI JIANG

1944 · NOVEMBER 14

Mei Niang's novel *Crabs* is honored with the Greater East Asia Literary Award at the Third Greater East Asian Writers' Congress in Tokyo.

The North Has Mei Niang

On November 14, 1944, the career of twenty-four-year-old writer Mei Niang (1920–2013) was marked by an event that cast a fateful shadow over her life. On that day, at the Third Greater East Asian Writers' Congress, a trans-Asian literary association operated under Japanese auspices, her novel *Crabs* was honored with the Greater East Asia Literary Award. For that distinction, and a cash prize reputedly worth 20,000 yen, Mei Niang traveled from Beijing (then named Beiping) to Nanjing, a city traumatized by the Japanese military. It was a signal honor for the young writer, bestowed with terrible timing in a location haunted by the horrors of Japanese atrocities. Within months of her celebration, Japan's empire was swept from China, leaving in its wake a deeply divided people. In the following decades, those who had achieved success during the Japanese occupation and remained in China, including Mei Niang, saw their lives torn apart as the Communist Revolution expelled foreign imperialists and turned the Chinese on each other. As a young adult, under Japanese dominion, Mei Niang forged a career criticizing patriarchy and socio-economic decline. For that, she was persecuted for three decades. But Mei Niang survived, and in 1997 she was officially recognized as one of modern China's one hundred most important writers.

Mei Niang, the most popular pen name of Sun Jiarui, was born in Vladivostok on December 24, 1920, and grew up in a wealthy household in Changchun. Her mother, a concubine, was hounded to suicide by her father's wife, leaving the girl to be raised by a cold step-mother and doting father; Sun's chosen pen name, Mei Niang, is a homonym for "motherless." From childhood, she aspired to a career in writing, hoping to emulate authors who had a formative influence on her, including Bing Xin (1900–1999), Lord Byron (1788–1824), and Maksim Gorky (1868–1936). Following the Japanese invasion in 1931, her father, a wealthy industrialist, rejected offers of high-ranking positions and moved his family south of the Great Wall. Economic pressures soon forced their return to Changchun. Back home in the newly formed Manchukuo, Mei Niang resumed middle school.

The year 1936 was momentous for Mei Niang. At the age of sixteen, her first volume of short stories, *A Young Lady's Collection*, was published. Shortly thereafter, Mei Niang's father died and she was sent to Japan to study. There, she fell in love with Chinese student Liu Longguang (1916–1949), who worked at Tokyo's Chinese-language bookstore, where they enjoyed access to literature that was difficult to acquire at home. In 1938, Mei Niang returned to Changchun (then renamed Xinjing [New capital]) and Liu followed in 1939, whereupon they lived together in defiance of her family's attempt to arrange her marriage. Mei Niang busied herself with work at the capital's Japanese-owned, Chinese-language newspaper, *Great Unity Herald*, and helped establish the Literary Collective, a group of writers who sought to "describe" and "expose" the realities of local life. Their dark writings violated literary regulations, but with the support of progressive Japanese intellectuals who shared similar artistic inclinations, they published several of the most important books of the occupation, including Mei Niang's second volume of collected works.

In the summer of 1939, Mei Niang wrote *Clam*, the first of a series of stories (including her award-winning *Crabs*) that critique local life and the status of women; it was published in serial form in the *Chinese Osaka Daily*, a biweekly Japanese-owned, Chinese-language journal that was distributed across the Japanese Empire. *Clam* is the story of an ill-fated young Chinese couple in Manchukuo whose relationship is devastated by contemporary mores and gossip. The female protagonist, Meili, works in an office and is critical of her job and her education, arguing their inadequacy for achieving real independence. Further, she argues with colleagues about serving tea to the Japanese bosses, stressing her repulsion with such subservience. Meili also rejects the idea of an arranged marriage, asserting that she would rather be independent and working in the sex industry. Defending premarital sex with her boyfriend as natural, she questions why women need to be virgins on their wedding night when men do not. A central tenet of *Clam* is that women must become conscious of patriarchal subjugation—and fight to overcome it. This story sets the tone for much of Mei Niang's literary legacy.

On June 24, 1940, Mei Niang's second volume of fiction, *The Second Generation*, was published. Hailed by critics, it is composed of eleven short stories highlighting social instability, poverty, and drug use. *The Second Generation* was credited by writer Liang Shanding (1914–1996) with introducing "liberalism" to Manchukuo's literary world. Living in the capital and publishing frequently, Mei Niang's reputation continued to grow. At the end of 1940, Liu accepted a position as a reporter, and then editor, with the *Chinese Osaka Daily*, and the couple moved to Japan. Mei Niang busied herself with writing, improving her Japanese language skills, and translating Japanese works, most notably those by Kume Masao (1891–1952), into Chinese. In 1942, they returned to China and settled in Beijing, where her husband was a founding member of the North China Writers' Association and she continued her writing and editorial work at *Woman Magazine*.

In 1941, Mei Niang began work on two of her most famous works of fiction, "Fish" and *Crabs*. In "Fish," the protagonist, Fen, decries her unhappy relationships and attacks the patriarchal subjugation of women. Fen asserts that her education instilled in her an unquenchable thirst for spiritual liberation. Her quest for true love drives her away from her parents, her husband, and her lover when she decides to leave them all. Mei Niang's sympathetic portrayal of the pregnant Fen violates nearly every caveat of the officially promoted ideal of "good wife, wise mother," especially when Fen declares that she would rather be a prostitute than continue her affair with her husband's cousin, whom she discovers is already married. The ranking Japanese scholar of Chinese literature, Yoshikawa Kōjirō (1904–1980), condemned "Fish" as among the "most degenerate pieces" he had ever read. Similarly, Iizuka Akira (1907–1989) dismissed Mei Niang's work as "a feminist statement overladen with eroticism." For all of their criticism, "Fish," the title story of the author's third volume of collected writings, proved popular with readers—it was republished eight times within half a year and earned second prize from the Second Greater East Asia Writers' Congress in 1943.

Crabs first appeared in 1941, as a serial in the *Chinese Osaka Daily*. It was later published in toto as the title work of Mei Niang's fourth volume of collected writings in 1944. It is the story of two young Chinese women, Cui and Ling, from a wealthy family in Changchun. Their lives are negatively impacted by the Japanese occupation, as the Chinese are unable to endure Japanese rule, which proves more heavy-handed than the previous warlord reign or Russian dominance. The Japanese workplace is incomprehensible to the Chinese, who have no respect for the regimented environment involving long hours of work dictated by schedules and none of the friendly exchanges of gifts that are so commonplace in Chinese culture. Socioeconomic decline is linked with an immoral inflation of the importance of money at the expense of personal relationships. This wreaks havoc among the Chinese and, ultimately, devalues women even more, leaving Cui a "money tree" to be sold off to the highest bidder. At the end of the story, the more privileged daughter of the family, Ling, is inspired by a setting sun to abandon her family and seek her freedom elsewhere. Mei Niang's choice of a setting sun, rather than the Japanese Empire's symbol of the rising sun, has been interpreted by critics as indifference to, or a rejection of, contemporary pro-Japan propaganda. It is this story of Chinese socioeconomic decline under Japanese rule, the patriarchal subjugation of women, and the immorality of a money-obsessed society that won Mei her greatest acclaim.

The stories *Clam*, "Fish," and *Crabs* each provide a woman-centered critique of contemporary Japanese male-dominated Manchukuo society. They focus on Chinese female protagonists who actively seek to improve their circumstances. In each of the stories, the Japanese remain at arm's length. Their presence is explicit in both *Clam* and *Crabs*, but contemporary censorship regulations expressly forbade direct criticism of Japan and its subjects. Restrictions also extended to dark portraits of society, denigration of ideals of "good wives, wise mothers," and depictions of poverty, but these dominated Mei Niang's work, which attracted readers in Manchukuo, Japan, and the Republic of China. Her writings found sympathetic audiences across East Asia, as did those of other women writers, including the Manchurian expatriate Xiao Hong (1911–1942) and, in Japanese-occupied Shanghai, Zhang Ailing (1920–1995; aka Eileen Chang), whose name was reportedly linked with Mei Niang's in a catchphrase that resulted from a bookstore competition in 1942 to name the most popular contemporary Chinese woman writer: "The south has Eileen Chang, the north has Mei Niang."

Mei Niang was the most celebrated woman writer from Manchukuo, but she was not alone. Other writers who flourished in Manchukuo (many with the encouragement of Mei Niang) included Dan Di (1916–1995), Lan Ling (1918–2003), Wu Ying (1915–1961), Yang Xu (1918–2005), and Zhu Ti (1923–2012). These writers, like Mei Niang, criticized the patriarchal subjugation of women and socioeconomic decline. They were educated in Manchukuo and used the opportunities afforded them to engage in social criticism. All worked in addition to their writing careers. Their careers as outspoken social critics must have influenced their workplace activities in ways still not fully understood. During the final two years of Japanese rule, most of them experienced persecution that Mei Niang eluded, as she then lived in Beijing. Despite considerable focus, Manchukuo officials had a difficult time controlling the content of popular literature. Literary production was structured by regulations, official organizations, and censors. However, as state resources were stretched thin, especially from the start of the War of Resistance against Japan in 1937, irregular enforcement ensued. To complicate matters, local Japanese writers often tended toward social realism in their works, implicitly legitimizing their Chinese counterparts. Government workers and officials could disregard critical literature in the belief that it was an appropriate form of cultural expression, perhaps hoping that a unique Manchukuo culture would divorce the region's Chinese majority from the Republic of China. Male Chinese writers might have been intimidated, jailed, or executed, but their female counterparts appear to have been freer to violate the weighty regulatory framework. Local writers Li Zhengzhong (1920–) and Zhu Ti subsequently argued that the misogyny of Manchukuo officials blinded them to the political nature of women's writings, and contributed to the creation of a unique body of antipatriarchal social criticism in a militarized colonial context.

Following the collapse of Manchukuo in 1945, Mei Niang and Liu moved briefly to Changchun, then to Shanghai and Taiwan. In 1949, the couple decided to return to the mainland to participate in national reconstruction. En route, Liu died when the ship he was traveling on sank. Mei Niang arrived in Beijing with their two daughters and pregnant with their son. In short order, her wartime career was turned on her. In 1952, she was criticized for "degenerate bourgeois ideas." In 1955, she was persecuted for being a suspected spy for Japan and in 1957 she was condemned as a rightist. Her persecution reached its climax during the Cultural Revolution, when she was labeled a traitor to the nation. The rest of the Maoist era passed in a succession of imprisonment and hard labor, during which two of her children died. In 1978, the blanket condemnation of Manchukuo writers was overturned, and Mei was able to return to her surviving daughter, Qing, and writing. In the mid-1980s, her wartime writings began to be republished. In 1997, nearly two decades after her persecution ended, Mei Niang's portrait was placed in the National Museum of Chinese Literature. To the very end of her life, she continued to write with a spirit that remained indomitable. Mei Niang passed away on May 7, 2013.

When Mei Niang was fêted in Nanjing on that fateful day in November 1944, the young writer could never have known that she had reached the pinnacle of her career. The award briefly enhanced her stature, yet that high profile under Japanese dominion resulted in decades of hardship and pain. In her most famous works, Mei Niang criticized the subjugating patriarchal norms and institutions of Chinese life under Japanese rule and was punished for it with decades of unbearable persecution. Ironically, Mei Niang was freer to pursue her personal and professional aspirations under Japanese military rule than under a Maoist regime ostensibly dedicated to the liberation of the Chinese people. Mei Niang's life and writings testify to the complex and contradictory forces that convulsed twentieth-century China and twice lifted her to the forefront of China's twentieth-century literary world.

BIBLIOGRAPHY: Hou Jianfei, ed., *Mei Niang jinzuo ji shujian* (Beijing, 2005). Norman Smith, "'Only Women Can Change This World into Heaven': Mei Niang, Male Chauvinist Society, and the Japanese Cultural Agenda in North China, 1939–1941," *Modern Asian Studies* 40, no. 1 (February 2006): 81–107. Norman Smith, *Resisting Manchukuo: Chinese Women Writers and the Japanese Occupation* (Vancouver, BC, 2007). Zhao Hui, "Lingwai yi bu 'Bailian zhi ge,'" trans. Kishi Yoko, in *Kang Ri zhanzheng shiqi lunxian qu shiliao yu yanjiu*, ed. Zhang Quan (Nanchang, China, 2007), 190–201.

NORMAN SMITH

1945 · AUGUST 1

Bian Zhilin and Wang Li collaborate in Kunming.

Ideologies of Sound in Chinese Modernist Poetry

Beginning around August 1, 1945, at the National Southwestern Associated University in Kunming, the poet Bian Zhilin (1910–2000) helped the linguist Wang Li (1900–1986) write a book chapter on the rhythms of contemporary Chinese poetry. This encounter both represented and encouraged a change in Chinese poetics from the prospective to the descriptive—it marked the end of a period in which poets invented new poetic music and the beginning of a period in which commentators attempted to analyze and understand what that poetic music meant. In the early 1940s, Bian had been encouraged to leave Sichuan University on account of his overt support for the Communists; Wang had arrived earlier from Guangxi University in Nanning, near his hometown. Both men were fleeing the Japanese advance that was sweeping through North and Central China. Southwestern Associated University was an amalgamation of three premiere schools in the north that had been seized by the Japanese, located far from the front in the heart of Yunnan Province. There, scholars from these universities formed a politically, geographically, and intellectually diverse group, all trying to continue their intellectual pursuits as the bombs of the Japanese air force rained down around them.

When he arrived in Kunming, Bian was a poet in transition. Primarily known for his complex, richly sonic symbolist verse, he had been deeply affected by a trip to the Communist base at Yan'an and had recently begun publishing poems intended to support their cause. In the 1930s, he had written poetry that shared the broad motivations of the May Fourth Movement, poetry that sought out new sonic patterns in order to enrich and structure the new Chinese vernacular that had recently become the nation's common written and spoken language. By 1940, he was applying his experience with the music of poetry to write conceptually simple verse intended for soldiers and workers, exemplified by his 1940 collection *Letters of Comfort*. Over the same period, Wang was fast becoming one of the finest academic linguists of his generation. Having earned a doctorate at the University of Paris in 1932, by the early 1940s he was studying and publishing on Chinese linguistics and phonology, doing his own part to understand and systematize *baihua*, as the vernacular is known. These lifelong projects came together, briefly, when Wang decided to feature Bian in a book chapter on the rhythms of contemporary verse, a chapter that he called "Vernacular and Europeanized Poetry."

Although the two had much in common, they also had many differences: while Bian was well learned in English and French literature, by 1945 his experience abroad was limited to a brief stay in Japan. During his studies in China, he had been inspired by writers who were at the heart of New Poetry, especially Wen Yiduo (1899–1946) and Xu Zhimo (1897–1931). Members of the Crescent Moon Society, Wen and Xu tried to fight against the increasing dominance of free verse in China's new poetry. Their challenge was to supply metrical forms that were different from the classical poetic forms that their politics—as well as the new language in which they were writing—required them to replace. One of their tools was the adaptation and translation of foreign poetry for contemporary Chinese purposes, at both a practical and a conceptual level. Practically, by 1940 Bian had translated poems by Paul Verlaine (1844–1896), Paul Valéry (1871–1945), W. B. Yeats (1865–1939), and T. S. Eliot (1888–1965); conceptually, he attempted to construct some of his poetry according to Wen's idea of the *dun* or beat. A *dun* is a rhythmic unit based on a semantic unit. An invention of the twentieth century, it mixes traditions from classical Chinese poetry, which is syllabic or syllable counting, with opportunities insinuated by more accentual foreign verse. Usually, a *dun* is a single word, especially the kind of two-syllable or three-syllable word that was common in the new Chinese vernacular. How a *dun* actually sounded, in practice, was worked out not in theory but in poems, and each artist's interpretation and use of this new metrical building block was slightly different. The point, after all, was not to reproduce foreign systems but to produce new Chinese systems.

By contrast, when Wang sat down with Bian to discuss new poetics, he had undergone five years of intensive training in Paris, and he used Western conventions of linguistics and prosody as fundamental structuring devices. His *Study of Chinese Regulated Poetry*, in which the section featuring Bian appears, is written in a numbered, lettered outline format that greatly resembles the preferred formats of scholars like the Swiss linguist Ferdinand de Saussure (1857–1913). The effect is to produce a profusion of analytical categories, each featuring a few examples as a scientific-style demonstration of their utility. The structure also makes the implicit claim to describe or contain the vast majority of all possible works: the book's four chapters on classical poetry cover all of the major generic traditions of lyric poetry. When tonal patterns are listed for different kinds of verse, every tonal pattern for which examples exist is listed, even those that are quite rare. What the structure does not feature is a sense of the permeability of conceptual and categorical borders. Bian's poems, whether or not they were composed in *dun*, often feature syllabically fixed line lengths. They therefore visually and sonically resemble earlier forms. Wang remarks on this, but he does it while reproducing examples in the chapter entitled "Vernacular and Europeanized Poetry": the Europeanized quality of these works is identified as their defining and locating factor, and their traditional Chineseness is considered an ancillary quality.

The influence of Wang's conversations with Bian on Wang's writing is significant. Wang's chapter is dominated by Bian's verse, as well as that of Feng Zhi (1905–1993), another exile to Southwestern Associated University who was interested in European poetic forms. Non-Chinese literature provided the chapter's touchstone. In the section on initial identical rhyme, Wang gives an example from Alfred Noyes (1880–1958), then one from Rabindranath Tagore (1861–1941), then finishes with an excerpt of Bian's "The Round Treasure Box." The logic is clear: the practice begins in Europe as represented by Noyes, undergoes a European-Asian transition through Tagore, and ends with Bian, who was in fact a reader of both Noyes and Tagore. The differences between the poems—for example, the Noyes example is not an identical rhyme, and its rhyme connects multiple individual sentences, whereas the Tagore and Bian poems use identical rhyme to list parallel clauses in the same sentence—are not emphasized. Wang tells a story whose shape we might recognize from etymology or evolutionary biology: Where does this word, this beast, come from? What is its ultimate progenitor? In nearly every case, the answer for Wang is *Xiyang*: the West, particularly the English and French traditions with which he was most familiar.

Perhaps it is for this reason that Wang transforms Bian's preferred metrical terminology. Rather than speak in terms of the Chinese-specific beat or *dun*, Wang prefers to talk about the foot, which he translates literally as *yinbu* or "sound step." This paradoxically produces Western verse as both the origin and the goal of new Chinese poetry. At the end of the section on the metrical foot, after two Bian poems that are presented as exceptions to foot rhythms, Wang concludes, "Overall, in terms of the foot, it seems that Europeanized poets have not yet reached a level of true excellence. Future poets may want to improve upon this." Of course, Bian was not composing in metrical feet to begin with. Wang's commentary, however, indicates the deepest part of the gulf between Bian's practice and Wang's theorizing: the form of Bian's poetry is resolutely inventive, possessing characteristics that come not from English and French practice but from the conceptual and linguistic space he bridged by adapting foreign poetics for his own use. In this respect, Bian's poetry was deeply connected to the revolutionary and transformative ardor of the May Fourth Movement, albeit with respect to metrics and poetics rather than societies and governments. His poem "White Shell," which Wang prints as an example of a poem "not limited by identical feet, but only by identical rhythms," is in fact a poem in which each line is made up of three beats, where punctuation is used to reinforce the boundaries of the beats. It also has an idiosyncratic *ababccxdxd* rhyme scheme, as well as the seven-character line length of classical regulated verse. The poem is not the end of a long Western poetic tradition but is the invention of a new rhythm. Wang understood Bian's materials, but not what he made of them.

As the 1940s progressed, the practice of prosody across China increasingly resembled Wang's analytical, putatively objective method, with its interest in measurable and identifiable poetic categories, the origins of technique, and the importance of poetic forms as representative of the essence of national identity. Bian's practices, which were inventive, transnational, and often driven by aesthetics, fell by the wayside. By the end of the 1940s, he stopped writing poetry entirely, and at no point did his creative output ever again approach what it had been in the 1930s. Instead, Bian was drawn into a long debate over what impact his prosodic choices had on the politics of his poetry. Mao Zedong's (1893–1976) 1942 *Talks at the Yan'an Forum on Literature and Art* instructed artists to imitate the (mostly rural) masses, whose poetic practices still sat at the intersection of music, recitation, and traditional five-character and seven-character forms. The consensus decision of leftist poets was that they should write ideologically communist poems in the form of traditional folksongs; this left little room for Bian to create new styles. In the polemics supporting new folk songs, they were seen to represent not just party ideology but Chinese national character. Bian was forced to defend his choices to adapt Western forms, and Wang's analysis was used as evidence that his poetry written in the 1930s was essentially, rather than tangentially, Europeanized. Bian evaded the most dangerous effects of the Mao period through a combination of heartfelt loyalty to Communism and a willingness to repudiate his early work. After the 1950s, when it was possible, he translated and taught foreign literature, becoming a scholar of Western literature much in the way Wang had. Although Wang was caught up substantially in the suffering of the Cultural Revolution, his work remained influential and important. His *Study of Chinese Regulated Poetry* was even reprinted in 1962, albeit with the section featuring Bian excised on the grounds that it was unnecessary to speak so much about foreign literature.

In 1945, though, the two men sat together and discussed poetry collaboratively, without any specific political intent. In many ways, Bian's focus on artistic technique, his creativity, and his willingness to borrow from distant traditions were consistent with earlier Chinese practices. Wang's more radical approach, more thoroughly influenced by foreign ideologies and practices, better matched the Chinese national attitude toward poetry; after all, this was a period in which Russian-style communism became nativized as a Chinese national undertaking, and one in which China was under mortal threat from highly nationalist Japan. Mao began writing and publicizing poems in classical meters, poets abandoned the study and imitation of Bian's type of poetry, and the future possibilities of his work were closed off. As the 1950s progressed, even Bian began to defend his 1930s work not as invention but as the reflection of essential structures in Chinese language and culture. Contrary to Wang's and Bian's expectations in the 1940s, Wang's chapter on new verse forms was not the first of many, but signaled the end of a nascent tradition.

BIBLIOGRAPHY: Bian Zhilin, *Bian Zhilin wenji* (Hefei, China, 2002). Bian Zhilin, "Tan shige de gelü wenti," *Wenxue pinglun* 2 (1959): 79–83. Lloyd Haft, *Pien Chih-Lin* (Dordrecht, Netherlands, 1983). Jiang Ruoshui, *Zhongxi shixue de jiaorong* (Taipei, 2009). Lucas Klein, "Foreign Echoes and Discerning the Soil: Dual Translation, Historiography, and World Literature in Chinese Poetry," PhD diss., Yale University, 2010. Wang Li, *Hanyu shilü xue* (Shanghai, 1962, complete ed. reissued 1979).

NICK ADMUSSEN

1945 · AUGUST 29

Chinese merchant Zhao Lian disappears in Sumatra, Indonesia.

The Enigma of Yu Dafu and Nanyang Literature

On the evening of August 29, 1945, a fifty-year-old ethnic Chinese named Zhao Lian left home with an Indonesian-speaking man of unknown ethnicity and was never seen again. Before his disappearance, Zhao had held a meeting at his home for friends from the Southern Sumatra Overseas Chinese Plantation Company, where they discussed future plans for the overseas Chinese in Southeast Asia following the August 15 surrender of the Japanese.

The disappearance of Zhao was major news to the Nanyang Chinese community—the Mandarin Chinese term for Chinese living in Southeast Asia—and intellectuals in China. This was because Zhao was actually the fake identity adopted by May Fourth writer Yu Dafu (1896–1945), which he had used to protect himself while living in exile in Indonesia during the Japanese occupation of the region.

In August 1946, the Allied forces in Medan, Sumatra, reported that Yu was murdered by the Japanese military police. Years later, after the Japanese archives were made public, the assumption that Yu was executed in a political cleanup by the Japanese military was affirmed. When Japanese scholar Suzuki Masao (1939–) published his research in 1969, however, this conjecture concerning Yu's fate was subject to a subtle alteration. Suzuki interviewed more than one hundred Japanese, including ten soldiers who were friends with Yu, and concluded that Yu's execution was performed by a small group of Japanese military police stationed in Bukit Tinggi whose intention was to cover up evidence about their involvement in the war; it was not a direct order from the higher authorities.

Yu was one of the harbingers of modern Chinese literature and a contemporary of prominent figures such as Lu Xun (1881–1936) and Guo Moruo (1892–1978). His short-story collection, *Sinking*, has been regarded as the first of its kind to emerge during the May Fourth period. The collection showcases Yu's penchant for romanticism and psychoanalytical narrative structure. While realist writers like Lu Xun focused on the promotion of a national spirit and character, and Guo celebrated the coming of a new and modern nation, Yu invested in the exploration of the modern Chinese psyche, especially the psychological struggle of young intellectuals at the crossroads of tradition and modernity. This collection also served as the inaugural work of a new genre, namely psychoanalytical fiction, which became one of Yu's primary contributions to modern Chinese literary aesthetics. In addition to fiction, Yu also wrote essays and literary criticism that rigorously censured Chinese customs and traditions.

Despite the fact that Yu repeatedly lamented his lack of political involvement, his writings served as an inspiration for those involved in orchestrating China's modern transformation at the turn of the twentieth century. Through the lens of a literary scholar, Yu observed and critically examined political happenings in his essays, especially during the period between the 1920s and the 1940s, when politics and social change directly impacted literary and cultural production in China.

In December 1938, Yu received a telegram from Hu Zhaoxiang (1901–1975) inviting him to work in Singapore as the new editor for *Sinchew Daily*. He arrived in Singapore on December 28 and immediately took over editorial responsibility for *Sinchew Daily*'s morning edition literary supplement, *Morning Star*, its weekly, *Arts and Literature*, and its evening edition's literary supplement, *Stars*.

During the three years, two months, and eight days Yu was in Singapore, he became one of the most influential literary figures in the region. Besides having literary exchanges with established local and mainland writers, Yu invested a significant amount of time supporting and helping young, aspiring writers in Malaya.

At the beginning of World War II, Yu assisted the British Information Bureau in disseminating antiwar messages in his capacity as the editor of *Overseas Chinese Weekly*. He was also appointed the chair of the Wartime Cultural Working Group. When the Pacific War broke out on December 8, 1941, the local Chinese formed the Singapore Overseas Chinese War Resistance Support Force. Yu was nominated as the acting committee chair for the department of arts and culture. He was also the chair of the Intellectuals' Anti-Japanese Association. Due to his active participation in anti-Japanese activities, however, he was soon forced to flee to Dutch-occupied Sumatra on February 4, 1942, when Japanese troops began their occupation of Singapore.

In May, Yu arrived at Pajakumbuh, a small town in Sumatra. He changed his name to Zhao Lian and opened the Zhaoyi Distillery. The distillery was a refuge for anti-Japanese literary exiles like himself. While managing the distillery, Yu also acted as a translator for the Japanese military police. This was a task he could not reject for fear of retribution from the Japanese. He was able to eventually resign by bribing a doctor to write a note claiming he was suffering from tuberculosis. Nevertheless, he still worked upon request whenever the Japanese needed a translator. According to Hu Yuzhi's (1896–1986) account, Yu saved many Chinese and locals from being tortured or killed by the Japanese military police.

In Southeast Asia, Yu mainly published essays in newspapers and journals, with topics ranging from antiwar propaganda to literary criticism, and even to debates on Nanyang literature. As for creative writing, he wrote only a dozen poems under the catchall title *Miscellaneous Poems Written in Exile*. Even though Yu's writings while in Southeast Asia did not receive the level of praise garnered by his earlier works, his involvement in the war effort in the region made him a patriot in the eyes of mainland and overseas Chinese alike. Consequently, his disappearance became a point of fascination for many literary scholars, especially those in Southeast Asia, who creatively ventured their conjectures about his fate.

Among this group of curious scholars is the contemporary Sinophone Malaysian writer and literary critic Ng Kim Chew (1967–). Ng has written three short stories surrounding the fate of Yu: "The Disappearance of M" (1990), "Death in the South" (1992), and "Supplement" (1998). The search for a literary master of Sinophone Malaysian literature in "The Disappearance of M" indirectly resurrects Yu, the idealized and unattainable target of their search. Yet, the allusion remains ambiguous. Regardless of whether "M" refers to Yu or a literary master to come, Sinophone Malaysian literature's present lack of a foundational or canonical text prevents the coherent articulation of a literary identity and genealogy. In "Death in the South," Yu returns in the form of posthumous writing fragments that are uncovered by a Sinophone Indonesian first-person narrator who is skeptical of the official account of Yu's disappearance and death. Taking Yu's "Sinking" as an alternate title, "Supplement" follows a Taiwanese television producer on a journey to uncover the truth about Yu's disappearance, with the help of a Japanese scholar who specializes in Yu's work. The "truth" turns out to be debatable and subjective. From highlighting Sinophone Malaysian literature's lack of a literary paragon and canon to rewriting the story of

Yu's disappearance, Ng's stories highlight the need to (re)examine the genealogy of Nanyang literature.

Nanyang literature's roots can be traced back to 1919. Its appearance is, to a large extent, an epiphenomenon of China's May Fourth Movement. Literature produced in the Nanyang community was often regarded as an extension of Chinese literature, because many overseas Chinese still saw the mainland as the origin of their cultural belonging. Because of Yu's involvement in developing Nanyang literary history and politics, he is seen as an iconic figure who pits the presumption of an inherent cultural affinity between Nanyang and modern Chinese literatures against the literary genealogy of the former. The divergent genealogies of the familial and the familiar are frequently played out in the projection of Yu's imagined influence on Nanyang literature. This has the dual effect of staging the difficulty of seeking a linear literary genealogy while at the same time constructing new literary relations through a literary imaginary that disavows specific historical connections.

The physical loss of Yu, the most prominent May Fourth writer to sojourn in Southeast Asia, simultaneously symbolizes the loss of Nanyang literature's link to the homeland and its literary legacy—a legacy the former desires to be recognized as part of, however tenuous their link. Recognizing this problematic obsession with a Sinocentric literary tradition, Ng invented a fictional fate for Yu in "Supplement" (Yu survived and was forced to assimilate to Islam by marriage) in order to propose a different history for Nanyang literature. This fate allows Nanyang literary history to create its own voice and mature beyond its nostalgic yearning for the specter of May Fourth splendor.

I think it is important to return to Yu's presence in Southeast Asia after much obsession with his disappearance. Yu fell right into the middle of a debate on the status of Nanyang literature when he first arrived in Singapore. Shortly after he arrived, Yu published an essay entitled "A Few Questions" on January 21, 1939. This essay was written as a response to questions raised by a group of writers from Penang. When asked how Nanyang writers should regard literary and cultural influences from China, and whether the local literary circle should wholeheartedly inherit the issues at stake in modern Chinese literature, Yu claimed that since Nanyang writers write using the Chinese script, it was natural to adopt topics of interest in China, such as those involving antiwar themes. This focus on the Chinese script as a cultural signifier for a unified Chinese identity upset the local writers; to them, the uniqueness of Nanyang literature was its local characteristics, not a wholesale inheritance of Chinese cultural tradition. When asked how Nanyang writers should promote local characteristics, Yu maintained that because Nanyang Chinese write with Nanyang as the backdrop, their writings always already included elements of local flair—*Nanyang secai* (South Sea color).

Yu's remarks immediately embroiled him in a series of passionate debates with Nanyang writers. To many, Yu had failed to see the significance and embedded sarcasm in their first question concerning literary inheritance: the question implied that Nanyang literature lacks originality, and hence, Yu's advice was sought. Assuming that Nanyang literature is an extension of modern Chinese literature, Yu glossed over this major concern of the Nanyang writers. As for the second question, concerning the promotion of a local aesthetics, though Yu acknowledged the significance of *Nanyang secai*, to him, local characteristics were mere stylistic decorations to topics and themes often inherited from Chinese literature. Furthermore, instead of seeing the promotion of *Nanyang secai* as an important step toward building the Nanyang literary tradition, Yu naively suggested that in order for Nanyang literature to promote itself as an independent literary tradition, it needed the birth of a literary genius.

It is necessary to keep in mind that Yu had just arrived in Singapore and felt compelled to respond to the questions from the group of Penang writers. His lack of understanding concerning Nanyang literature and its characteristics was inevitable. Instead, his willingness to engage in debates with local writers exemplified his interest in contributing to Nanyang literature and helping to groom a young generation of local writers. In a constructive turn, the debate triggered by Yu's essay indirectly contributed to the consolidation of Nanyang literary history: first, it forced Nanyang writers and artists to defend, embrace, and advocate for *Nanyang secai* as the defining trait of their literary tradition; second, it placed Yu directly in contact with the concerns of local writers, facilitating his eventual role as editor of *Sinchew Daily* and mentor to young local writers. I believe this represents an important contribution to the birth of Nanyang literature as a Sinophone expression, although it is too often overshadowed by the literary obsession with Yu's disappearance.

BIBLIOGRAPHY: Jing Tsu, *Sound and Script in Chinese Diaspora* (Cambridge, MA, 2010). Ng Kim Chew, *You dao zhi dao*, ed. David Der-wei Wang (Taipei, 2001). Yoonwah Wong, "Yu Dafu in Exile," in *Essays on Chinese Literature: A Comparative Approach* (Singapore, 1988), 11–27.

E. K. TAN

1946 · JULY 15

Zhou Zuoren makes his defense against charges of collaboration with the enemy in the Capital High Court in Nanjing.

On Literature and Collaboration

On July 15, 1946, Zhou Zuoren (1885–1967) stood up in the Capital High Court in Nanjing to make his defense against charges of collaboration with the enemy. Zhou had been a leading intellectual figure since the May Fourth Movement and the foremost practitioner of the literary essay, and his failure to join the inland relocation of Peking University after the fall of Beiping (Beijing) in July 1937 had attracted widespread condemnation. For those who wanted him in unoccupied China, there had been much at stake: Zhou was the younger brother of Lu Xun (1881–1936), symbol of the progressive left; moreover, his high standing among Japanese intellectuals meant his departure would deliver a strong message. But Zhou remained in Beijing.

The charges against him were that, in August 1939, he had accepted a professorship and become head of the Literature Department at Peking University before going on, in January 1941, to become education minister in the North China government installed by the Japanese. He was accused of having "enslaved education to serve the Japanese" by serving in a university that had become a puppet organization. The trial had started a month earlier, and detailed evidence was presented to the effect that Zhou had used his positions to benefit Chinese property and citizens. He had protected and even increased library holdings, he had kept the curricula as close to preoccupation ones as possible, he had maintained the teaching of English, he had thwarted attempts to propagandize youth organizations, and he had shielded teachers working for the underground.

He used his positions throughout to exercise passive resistance against the enemy.

Zhou began his defense with a brief summary of events: When North China fell, he was one of four professors who did not leave because of age or, in his case, dependents. Shortly afterward, they were instructed by the university chancellor, Jiang Menglin (1886–1964), to protect university property, and Zhou had managed to prevent the biology faculty building from being taken over. Initially, when Beiping fell, Zhou had thought to support himself by writing and began teaching at Yenching University. However, he was soon the target of a failed assassination attempt at his home on New Year's Day 1939. The attempt succeeded in making Zhou feel he could no longer teach at Yenching and caused him to accept a post at Peking University Library, which he hoped would enable him to avoid any further attention. Urged by Peking University president Tang Erhe (1878–1940), Zhou eventually overcame his misgivings about becoming a bureaucrat and accepted the professorship and head of department posts in August 1939. He made it his maxim that "though the school was collaborationist, the students were not collaborators; although politics were collaborationist, education should not be made to collaborate."

Zhou's belief in the necessity of education and his valorization of the individual and the use of individual judgment and action are hallmarks of his earliest thinking. His intellectual life took off in 1906, when, aged twenty-one, he won a scholarship to study in Japan. Zhou then joined Lu Xun in Tokyo, where he took part in his brother's literary projects, learned English and Greek, and developed a lifelong interest in anthropology. He returned to China with his Japanese wife in 1911. In 1917, encouraged by Lu Xun, he joined the faculty at Peking University. Under the innovative, enlightened chancellorship of Cai Yuanpei (1868–1940), Peking University became the center of intellectual ferment over China's future that culminated in the May Fourth New Literature and Culture Movement. Zhou's article "A Literature of Mankind" pushed him to the intellectual forefront. In it, Zhou argues that humanity is one and that each individual is a part of it. This basic relationship is something that has always existed, for "as soon as men were born in the world, humaneness was born," although Europe had only been aware of it since the Renaissance, and in China "the problem of man has never been solved, let alone of women and children." Literature should foster this ideal by advocating the new scientific view of man as an evolved creature, whose body and spirit should be seen in harmony, not conflict. The touchstone for literature was whether it promoted an individualistic humanism or an inhuman view of life. The scientific view of man, as embraced by Zhou, included Havelock Ellis's (1859–1939) ideas of human sexuality as a natural component of human dignity and acceptance of women's sexual rights, hence women's equality. In another article on how to solve "the woman question," he stresses the importance of a basic education in general knowledge for men and women of all backgrounds.

Zhou's views on the relationship between the individual and a wider humanity brought him very close to the Japanese writer Mushanokōji Saneatsu (1885–1976), the leader of the humanist, antiwar Shirakaba school, and Zhou visited the utopian New Village community set up by Mushanokōji in May 1919. Zhou's articles about this experience inspired the young Mao Zedong (1893–1976), then working as a library assistant at Peking University, to call on Zhou to discuss ideas, but Hu Shi (1891–1962) and Lu Xun disapproved of what seemed to them an impractical idealism. Zhou wrestled with the problem of how an individual should find his or her own direction, ultimately deciding that there is not just one road to follow in the realm of thought. In 1922 he wrote "In My Own Garden," calling for society to allow people to respect their own individuality, as by doing so, they would repay their debt to society. Growing flowers, which had no practical purpose, should be valued as much as growing fruit and vegetables. To refuse this principle and force people to conform to social expectations would be "as unreasonable as enforcing loyalty to a ruler in the name of Confucian prescribed relationships," he said, referring to the hierarchical pairings (ruler-subject, father-son, husband-wife, elder brother–younger brother, and friend-friend) that had been codified during the Han dynasty to structure society. That same year, his conviction that human integrity was profoundly threatened by any attempt to impose a particular viewpoint in the name of whatever good led him to oppose the newly formed Antireligion Federation. Freedom of belief, within the limits of the law, was written into the constitution, and he did not want to see intellectuals interfering with it, for fear that freedom of thought or speech might be banned in the future. He announced his commitment to the form of the essay, a form that shared something of fiction and poetry, and in which, most importantly, a writer could strive to express ideas with genuine simplicity and clarity.

In his subsequent writings, Zhou developed a poetics of locality and material culture: the writer should be unafraid to write about anything he or she liked, confident that one's perceptions, inevitably informed by place and environment, could manifest the intrinsic value of human life. As a writer conveyed the particular values, customs, and artifacts of a setting, he or she would also be conveying part of their individuality. Zhou also promoted the idea that a writer should strive to express his or her critical judgment, based on genuine efforts to arrive at intellectual and moral understanding. To do so, he drew on the traditional aesthetic categories of "flavor" (*quwei*) and "clarity of understanding" (*bense*) that had been immensely important in sixteenth- and seventeenth-century philosophical and aesthetic discussions. Zhou identified in particular with the broad-minded Confucianism of the iconoclast Li Zhi (1527–1602). In 1932, lecturing on the origins of the New Literature Movement, Zhou argued that self-expression and a modern type of individualism had emerged in the late Ming, but had then been repressed during the Qing dynasty, leading to the May Fourth reaction against intolerant neo-Confucian orthodoxy. Zhou believed that New Literature had been transformed by modern, Western scientific views of man, but that the fundamental tenor of the modern essay remained Confucian and Daoist, and that this was to be welcomed, as these philosophies, in their original form, focus on the material world of human feelings and the natural order of things.

When the Japanese set up the North China government, their local ideological collaborator, Miao Bin (1899–1946), launched a massive propaganda campaign to criticize the Nationalists (Kuomintang). Now the time had come to wash the "Western rubbish" out of China, and in this endeavor Japan would lead and guide China, which had forgotten its Confucian heritage, to an East Asian cultural renaissance. One of Zhou's most important actions during the war was to write a series of essays that forcefully rejected this line of thinking. The core of Confucian doctrine is epitomized in the *Analects* as the recognition of the innate positive impulses of human nature, which, articulated as the principles of devotion to duty (*zhong*) and empathy (*shu*), result in benevolence. These principles are exemplified by the altruism and good government of the legendary kings Yu and Ji, who understood that benevolence and survival were linked. This commonsense, practical approach to life was understood by every Chinese, from the sages to the lowliest illiterate, but anyone who tried to develop the principles into a fanatical belief system would be rewarded by chaos. Zhou's articles were the most outspoken rebuttal of Japanese propaganda within the occupied areas, and in August 1943 he was denounced at a literary conference in Japan as a reactionary old writer, an obstacle to the Greater East Asia project who ought to be swept away.

Zhou was initially sentenced to fourteen years' imprisonment for serving in a puppet organization, later reduced to ten years on appeal. The court acknowledged that he had done many positive things and his wartime writings, particularly "The Problem of China's Thought," were laudable, but maintained nonetheless that it confused people to see him working for the collaborationist government, so he was still guilty as charged. In January 1949, Communist troops took Nanjing, and Zhou and other inmates were released from prison. He later moved back to his home in Beijing and spent his remaining years translating Greek classics and writing about Lu Xun, before dying in captivity during the Cultural Revolution in May 1967. To the general reader, however, like many other writers active before 1949, he may as well have been dead. It was only in the post-Mao period that it became possible to begin to reconsider Zhou and his work. Yet, although his literary achievements are recognized, the issue of collaboration still confounds assessments of him.

The majority of scholars see his failure to leave occupied China and participation in the collaborationist government as indicative of selfishness and weakness of character. There is, as of yet, no attempt to "suspend judgment over who is guilty for having worked with the Japanese until after we have seen them at work," as Timothy Brook requests in his study of wartime China, nor an attempt to understand the complexities of a treacherous, changing environment. (Zhou's defense lawyer noted the atmosphere of fear after the war that led "avoiders of misfortune and beaters of dogs in water" to bray that Zhou was a traitor, while others stayed silent.) In 1987, documents published in the journal *Historical Materials on New Literature* revealed that underground resistance agents had asked him to take the education minister post, as otherwise the odious Miao Bin would get the job. The Communist Party agent involved had denied directing the move, but this information cast a new light on Zhou's activities. Also published was a letter Zhou wrote to Zhou Enlai in July 1949, as the Chinese Civil War ushered in the epic changes of the new era. He had been immensely heartened, Zhou said, to hear of how the

Communist government was handling women's issues and the question of peasant livelihood, as well as reports about the high degree of discipline among Communist troops; now, perhaps some of the hopes for change that had been entertained since the 1911 revolution would be realized. He had always opposed the Confucian prescribed relationships and felt that the ruler-subject relationship in China was modeled on the man-woman relationship, making it particularly pernicious. While citizens had a moral obligation to the nation and people, to see this relationship only in terms of the chaste womanhood of Confucian propriety was outmoded. In his case, he accepted the education minister post in order to mitigate, as far as he could, Japanese interference and oppression. He felt that this was the right thing to do, although fleeing to unoccupied China and teaching there for a few years would have been much easier. "If people say I've offended Confucian propriety I can accept that, but if they say I've offended the people of the nation, I don't believe it to be true," he wrote.

Of course, the complexities concerning the issue of collaboration have never been acknowledged by either the Communists or Nationalists, both Leninist parties. Since the turn of this century, memories of the Anti-Japanese War (as the Chinese sometimes call the second Sino-Japanese War) have been remobilized and shaped anew by the complex demands of present-day domestic and international politics. It may be some time before the issue of collaboration can be reexamined in China. When it is, Zhou Zuoren's example of critical independence and his courageous resistance, even as it won him the ritual condemnation of his fellow countrymen, may well prove illuminating.

BIBLIOGRAPHY: Timothy Brook, *Collaboration: Japanese Agents and Local Elites in Wartime China* (Cambridge, MA, 2005). Susan Daruvala, *Zhou Zuoren and an Alternative Chinese Response to Modernity* (Cambridge, MA, 2000). Edward Gunn, *Uncertain Muse: Chinese Literature in Shanghai and Peking, 1937–1945* (New York, 1980). Lu Yan, *Re-understanding Japan* (Honolulu, 2004).

SUSAN DARUVALA

1947 · FEBRUARY 28

"Formosa Killings Are Put at 10,000." —*New York Times*

On Memory and Trauma: From the 228 Incident to the White Terror

The February 28 Incident, also known as the 228 Incident or the 228 Massacre, was a gruesome tragedy that erupted in Taiwan in 1947. In a March 29, 1947, article entitled "Formosa Killings Are Put at 10,000," the *New York Times* reported the incident and its aftermath in graphic detail:

> Troops from the mainland arrived there March 7 and indulged in three days of indiscriminate killing and looting. For a time everyone seen on the streets was shot at, homes were broken into, and occupants killed. In the poorer sections the streets were said to have been littered with the dead. There were instances of beheadings and mutilations of bodies, and women were raped, the American said.

Two months later, the May 24, 1947, edition of the *Nation* confirmed the extent of the massacre: "More than a thousand unarmed Taiwanese in the Taipei-Keelung area alone were massacred....Bodies floated thick in Keelung Harbor and in the river which flows by Taipei."

Today, most people believe that the 228 Incident was triggered by a dispute between a Taiwanese female cigarette vendor called Lin Jiangmai and a Nationalist (KMT) government agent on February 27, 1947. But by all accounts, the 228 Incident was an inevitable tragedy that sprang from Taiwanese discontent with the Chinese Nationalist government. Initially, the Taiwanese people, who had been under Japanese rule from 1895 to 1945, were overjoyed at the Allies' victory in World War II. They truly welcomed Chinese Nationalist rule. But the Nationalist authorities were corrupt and repressive. Favoritism was rampant, as most governmental positions were reserved for mainlanders rather than local Taiwanese. The joy that the Taiwanese had experienced at the beginning of Nationalist rule gradually led to anger and despair. It came as no surprise that a mere dispute about the sale of tobacco would quickly escalate into a full-scale confrontation between the Taiwanese and the mainlanders on that fateful day in February 1947.

My family, as an example, were among the first mainlanders to go to Taiwan, leaving China in the spring of 1946, when I was only two. At the time, Chiang Kai-shek's (1887–1975) KMT still ruled China. World War II had ended only a year before: a year of victory for the Chinese after eight brutal years of war with Japan. Immediately after the war ended, however, inflation and civil war began to plague China. Taiwan suddenly became a new land of opportunity. Many mainlanders went to Taiwan to assume new positions in government. Because my mother originally came from Taiwan, immigration was even more desirable for us.

No one could have foreseen that, in the following year, the February 28 Incident would suddenly erupt in Taiwan. My family was caught in the storm tides of that event. At the time, we lived by Keelung Harbor, where, as the *Nation* wrote, "bodies floated thick." My father served as the chief of the General Affairs Section at the Keelung Harbor Bureau. At the time, the KMT military automatically executed any Taiwanese they met who could not speak Mandarin. My family grew extremely anxious, as my Taiwanese mother was not fluent in Mandarin. On March 8, the day the KMT troops came ashore, my father was trapped in the Harbor Bureau building amid the forest of guns and the rain of bullets, unable to return home. As evening fell, my mother began to prepare for an emergency. She moved aside the planks under the tatami mats, bent over and crawled down to the concrete substrate, cleared away the mud and sand, and then spread a thick cotton quilt on the ground. At the sound of a gunshot or any clamor in the alley, my mother would hurriedly lift up the floorboards and take my younger brother and me under the floor. I was three years old. Subsequently, throughout my childhood and adolescence, I often relived that terrifying scene in my mind.

A more traumatic experience was to follow three years later. One day in January 1950, when I was not quite six years old, the head of the Secret Police, Gu Zhengwen, came to our house to arrest my father. Based on my father's later recollection, throughout the long night he endured rapid interrogation under intense lamplight. Finally, just before dawn, he was pushed into a pitch-dark prison cell. A month after his arrest, he was suddenly released. By that time our household belongings had all been confiscated, and we were forced to move into another dwelling. A guard was appointed to keep watch on the house all day and night.

As for my father, the head of the Secret Police took him to every city in Taiwan, pressuring him to reveal where certain friends and relatives were hiding. Many decades later, I learned that Gu had hoped to discover the whereabouts of my uncle Chen Benjiang (1915–1967), a leftist leader. But my father refused to cooperate and, on May 5, he was arrested again. He remained in a martial law observation cell for a long time. He had received no sentence; he was only given a prisoner number. In the middle of the night, he often heard certain numbers or certain names shouted out, one after another, after which he saw the guards pushing young people out of the prison to be executed by firing squad. Most of them were outstanding Taiwanese youths. Almost all of them were students at National Taiwan University.

Not long after the Korean War broke out on June 25, my father was finally sentenced to ten years of imprisonment. He spent most of his sentence at the military prison in Xindian, Taipei. For two of those years, he was sent to the Green Island Concentration Camp to do forced labor. During that ten-year period, my mother worked as a sewing teacher in southern Taiwan to support her three children. In January 1960, a full decade after his first arrest, my father was finally released from prison. Still, our troubles were not over. No one dared to hire a former political prisoner, and my father remained unemployed until a courageous high school principal took a chance and appointed him as an English teacher. It was not until years later that I learned we had been the victims of the aftermath of the 228 Incident. We were survivors of the so-called White Terror.

In the summer of 1977, I went to visit Gu, confronted him directly, and asked why he imprisoned my father. He admitted that my father had been innocent, but said that my father had lost his temper and defied Gu, and therefore had to be punished. Gu also said that cases like that of my father were numerous; many young and promising intellectuals had all been imprisoned under similar circumstances.

In the history of Taiwan, the era of the White Terror is generally understood to be the decade following the withdrawal of Chiang's Nationalist government from mainland China to Taiwan in mid-December 1949, although technically the terror lasted throughout the entire period of martial law from May 19, 1949, to July 15, 1987. During the height of the White Terror era, the Nationalist government implemented a policy of "better to kill ten thousand by mistake than to set one free by oversight." As a result, many innocent civilians, along with political dissidents, became victims of ferocious purges and persecutions. It has been estimated that during the first decade of the White Terror, at least eight thousand Taiwanese and mainlanders were either imprisoned or executed. It was during this time, in 1949, that the late Harvard anthropologist Kwang-chih Chang (1931–2001), then only seventeen years old, was arrested and put in prison. Professor Chia-ying Yeh (1924–), a renowned scholar of Chinese poetry, was also incarcerated during the 1950s, while her husband was also sentenced to several years in prison.

These and other stories of persecution, suffering, and injustice did not come to light for decades because the White Terror was a taboo subject in Taiwan. Under martial law, the Nationalist government silenced the victims and prevented their families from speaking out. It was not until the mid-1990s, almost three decades after I had immigrated to the United States, that I came to know that my uncle Chen, whom Gu had pursued so relentlessly during the White Terror, had attempted to organize armed resistance against the Nationalist government in the village of Luku, an attempt that resulted in the brutal collective punishment of the village in the Luku Incident during the early 1950s. Several years later, after further excavation, I discovered that Chen had formed a deep friendship with the great novelist Lü Heruo (1914–1951), one of the leading writers of postwar Taiwan. Like many Taiwanese, Lü shared in the euphoria over the restoration of Chinese rule on the island after fifty years of Japanese occupation. His patriotic hopes were soon shattered by the February 28 Incident, which prompted him to join in the underground resistance activities. He eventually went to the Luku mountains to join Chen and the other leftists, and died there in 1951 from a snake bite. Coming to light only much later, Lü's and Chen's leftist activities provide great insight into the truth of their times. Most importantly, one learns that the number of leftists in Taiwan dramatically increased after the 228 Incident. Before the incident, only about seventy people had joined their leftist group. After the incident, however, membership rose to nine hundred. These facts were not known to the public until after martial law was lifted in 1987. Writers such as Lan Bozhou (1960–) and Chen Fangming (1947–) were finally allowed to publish works on the leftists that commemorated the innocent victims of the 228 Incident and the White Terror.

Indeed, political censorship led to this belatedness of remembering. The particularly painful fact remains that the people of that generation were doomed to silence, and that cycle of voicelessness continued for some time. During the ten years of my father's imprisonment, I, too, learned to silence myself, never allowing myself to speak about my father's arrest unless there was no alternative. In such extraordinary times, even young children had to learn to control their own tongues.

Like many others, I endured the pain of losing my native language. Having been born in Beijing, I spoke the Beijing dialect of Mandarin growing up. After we moved to Taiwan in 1946, I continued to speak with my father's Beijing accent. Following my father's arrest in January 1950, shortly after arriving in southern Taiwan, the base of many Taiwanese-dialect-speaking people, I lost all memory of my Beijing accent. For the next year, I spoke only Taiwanese. Later in school I had to relearn Mandarin, but this time the Mandarin I learned from my teacher was a Taiwanese-accented Mandarin. In the everyday atmosphere under the KMT administration at the time, Taiwanese or Taiwanese-accented Mandarin was considered vulgar and culturally backward. In school the humiliating experiences occasioned by my Taiwanese accent cast a frightening, dark shadow. Similar to the experiences related by writers such as Zhong Zhaozheng (1925–), I became afraid of my own voice and confused about my cultural identity. After immigrating to the United States in 1968, I started to speak English all the time, finally doing away with my former linguistic worries. My exile into the foreign world of English ironically healed that childhood trauma.

Similar experiences and parallel cases continue to surface, as my generation continues to recover from the last generation's experience. A sixty-nine-year-old woman called Lin Mingzhu gave an impassioned eyewitness report in a March 6, 2006, article in the *World Journal.* She was none other than the daughter of Lin Jiangmai, the Taiwanese cigarette vendor whose confrontation with a government agent, many believe, instigated the 228 Incident. On that fateful day of February 27, 1947, Lin Mingzhu (then a ten-year-old girl) was with her mother at her tobacco stand by the Yanping North Road in Taipei. In the article, Lin crucially disputes the long-held view that the flashpoint of the 228 Incident was the abuse of a Taiwanese woman by a mainland officer. It was instead, she explained, the problem of language barriers that had led to the uncontrollable chaos afterward.

According to her recollection, the KMT officer, who approached them with smiles instead of ill intent, was apparently trying to buy a cigarette from her mother. When he asked for the price of the cigarette, neither Lin Mingzhu nor her mother could understand what he was saying because they only knew Taiwanese and Japanese, not Mandarin. When they turned to the people in the streets for assistance, the crowd suddenly gathered to confront the officer, thinking that he was trying to harass the Taiwanese woman and her daughter.

It is difficult for people to explain the complexity of the 228 Incident and the White Terror, when even language itself can be confusing. Under such circumstances, how does one bear witness with responsibility and accountability? That indeed has been the greatest challenge for writers and intellectuals alike who continue to grapple with Taiwan's literary and political history. As for myself, for all these years, I have been trying to find the right voice, a voice once lost to me, to remember that which resisted remembrance.

BIBLIOGRAPHY: Kang-i Sun Chang, *Journey through the White Terror: A Daughter's Memoir*, 2nd ed. (Taipei, 2013). Tillman Dardin, "Formosa Killings Are Put at 10,000," *New York Times*, March 29, 1947. Peggy Durdin, "Terror in Taiwan," *Nation*, May 24, 1947. Lai Tse-Han, Ramon H. Myers, and Wei Wou, *A Tragic Beginning: The Taiwan Uprising of February 28, 1947* (Stanford, CA, 1991). Denny Roy, *Taiwan: A Political History* (Ithaca, NY, 2004).

KANG-I SUN CHANG

1947

Socrates visits Beijing.

The Socratic Tradition in Modern China

In November 1947, a dialogue appeared in a Beijing-based literary journal announcing the Beijing arrival of a special guest—Socrates. Yes, *that* Socrates, the Athenian philosopher, the teacher of Plato, with his snub nose and wide mouth. Professor Zhu and Mr. Lin, the other participants in the dialogue, like us readers, cannot believe their eyes upon recognizing Socrates on a Beijing street by those eccentric facial features. Yet the guest not only claims to be Socrates himself, but also acts like Socrates.

Invited to a gathering, he gets lost on the way, just as he does in Plato's *Symposium*. Even more convincingly, he shows an unrivaled drinking capacity. Plato records that Socrates is a great wine drinker and no one ever sees him drunk. Who could fake such an ability?

This must be Socrates himself. In the turbulence of the Chinese Civil War, he comes to Beijing. Not bothering to inform anyone of his arrival, he lodges in a small apartment as a tourist and talks to people on the street, as he used to do in the Athens marketplace. But undoubtedly he is waiting for China's serious minds, and Professor Zhu and Mr. Lin—two of those intellectuals perplexed by the ongoing catastrophe—cannot afford to let Socrates go. They immediately engage him in conversation about the intellectual problems aggravated during the wartime. This conversation becomes the dialogue "Socrates in China: the National Character of China and the Weakness of Chinese Culture." The recorder is Zhu Guangqian (1897–1986), an established aesthetician and professor of literature at Peking University, who presents himself in the discourse as one Professor Zhu.

One of the people who happened to read the dialogue was a thoughtful writer named Wang Yuntong. At the end of 1947, with everyone busy with Christmas, who would think of Socrates, alone in the old capital? Worried, Wang invites Socrates to dinner. Wang Yuntong was the pen name of Shen Congwen (1902–1988), a great novelist of modern China. After the end of the second Sino-Japanese War, Shen returned from China's hinterland only to find a vulgarized Beijing, its old beauty disappearing from urban scenes, as well as from human hearts. Alarmed by this situation, he consults with Socrates. Then, in the essay "Socrates Discusses What Beijing Needs," Shen recapitulates Socrates's proposal for a new Beijing, a proposal that highlights the reformation of colleges, libraries, and the Palace Museum, as well as the importance of aesthetic education, especially for young people. This project is essentially a praise of beauty that echoes the *Symposium*. As readers will recall, at that drinking party (in Greek, *symposium* literally means "drinking together") Socrates and a group of Athenian elites gather to spend a festival evening paying homage to Eros, the Greek god of love, who, as Socrates contends, leads people to the ideal of beauty.

Thus, at a critical moment in China's history, Socrates was summoned to join the discussion of China and her future. Both Socrates and his Chinese interlocutors had come a long way to reach these imaginary encounters. The two Socratic essays, inspired by Plato's *Symposium*, marked the climax of Socrates's journey to China since the late Qing period. In those early years Socrates first appeared as a vague figure. He was Suo-ha-da-di-shi in an 1882 religious book, Suo-ge-di in an 1892 history book, Suo-ge-la-dì when young Lu Xun (1881–1936) mentioned his tragic death in a 1907 essay, and at some time in the 1910s became Su-ge-la-dǐ, as Chinese people commonly know him now. In introductory booklets and essays that featured Western learning, he deservedly secured a portion of the discussion, ranging in length from a paragraph to a chapter. From there, he entered salons and the imagination, becoming a household name in China.

The 1920s witnessed the honor of Socrates in China. He occupied center stage for both the advocates and opponents of the New Culture Movement at a time when their debates rattled the country's intellectual and literary scenes. Responding to a solicitation by *Jingbao* (a major newspaper of the day) for reading lists for Chinese youths, Dr. Hu Shi (1891–1962), a prominent advocate of the New Culture Movement, nominated *Apology*, *Phaedo*, and *Crito*, Plato's trilogy about Socrates's trial and death, as one of his ten major recommendations. Meanwhile, a coterie of cultural conservatives, aiming to rectify what they saw at the rootlessness of the cultural reforms then in vogue, paid even greater tribute to Socrates. In printing Socrates's image beside that of Confucius on the head page of the first issue of their journal *Critical Review*, they made a statement about the tremendous importance of Socrates and endorsed his teachings as being able to play a positive role in making a modern culture for China. It was also a junior member of the *Critical Review* circle, Guo Binhe (1900–1987), who first made a complete translation of the *Symposium* for Chinese readers in 1925. His beautiful rendition in classical Chinese dresses up Eros as solemnly as a Chinese deity, a presentation that might not have quite satisfied Socrates. But Guo's translation, welcomed even by conservative minds, remained the only serviceable version through the 1940s, when Zhu and Shen wrote their essays. Especially for Shen, who did not know any foreign languages, Guo's translation was influential.

For Zhu, the advent of Socrates was a moment rewarding his diligence and erudition. Zhu had immersed himself in Greek literature and arts throughout his life, eventually becoming confident enough to bring Socrates to his home and converse with him in person. However, preoccupied as he was with the intellectuals' position in a brutal time, the aesthetician takes on a practical topic rather than his usual aesthetic concerns. He inquires into the reaction of Chinese intellectuals to the challenges imposed by the historical circumstances. Amid the war's turmoil, this topic is not only an objective observation of what intellectuals do, but also an ethical inquiry into whether they are obligated to prioritize their responsibility as intellectuals over their well-being—their safety, even—as ordinary people.

We must acknowledge that the summoning of Socrates in the late 1940s, when bewilderment about the future of both China and her intelligentsia permeated the country's intellectual life, could not be more appropriate. In 399 BCE Athens, the trial and execution of Socrates revealed the symbiotic relationship between politics and philosophy. Socrates is never far away from Athenian political reality, and reality is the stage on which he displays his power as an individual, the individual power that makes him a philosopher. The *sophia* that a Socratic philosopher loves designates a desire to become divinely righteous and just. This is an unbent critical conscientiousness toward one's society that stands opposed to worldly, conventional wisdom in political affairs. When Socrates criticizes the Chinese, pointing to their lack of spontaneity in free thinking, Professor Zhu is silent. Here spontaneity is the antonym of conformity. His silence in the face of Socrates's query betrays his uneasiness and the powerlessness of words to resolve the problem. He knows too well that Socrates's gloomy vision has to be disproved in real life.

Notwithstanding his doubts, in his next Beijing conversation, Socrates warmly encourages his interlocutor to confront the brutality and vulgarity of the time. A self-educated writer from an isolated countryside region, Shen barely knew anything about faraway ancient Greece. In fact, he used to sneer at those urbanites who "talk about Greece and Rome to kill a long day"—a category that would certainly include Zhu. Yet a decade before the dialogue took place, Shen dreamed of building a little temple of Hellenism so as to worship the humanity he often tried to portray in his writings. This nativist writer, the self-positioned provincial man, is rather open-minded, displaying the cosmopolitan understanding of humanist tradition that would later lead him to find support in the teachings of Socrates.

Socrates, despite being a pagan, joined Shen at his house on Christmas Eve, out of a shared belief in solemn and divine beauty, and its manifestations in earthly existence. While Socrates initiates the seeking of the

Ideal from the appreciation of a beautiful body, Shen finds solemnity and divinity in seasonal harvests, in the instincts of insects, and, most importantly, in those common people, possessed with integrity, who fulfill their duty in their humble lives. It is this reverence for such a divine humanity that gives his fiction a unique charm. In Shen's fiction, which typically features his hometown, those common men and women fall in love, and meet their destiny. In both fortunes and misfortunes, they respect the gods and follow their fates like their ancient ancestors. Their justice and sincerity are in sharp contrast to the pervasive arrogance and philistinism that often masqueraded as modernity in Shen's era.

To cure the atrocities of the time, Socrates prescribes instilling a desire for beauty through aesthetic education. Such an aesthetic education would revive the hearts that dried out long ago—the origin, in Shen's opinion, of many of China's social and political problems. Socrates urges Shen to keep his dream of the little temple alive precisely in war-torn Beijing, so as to restore the solemnity and divinity of humanity. Like Zhu, Shen points to the responsibility of an intellectual to confront historical atrocity, while aesthetic education and cultural inheritance are their shared belief and reliance. However, in an age when war and revolution were relied on to resolve national crisis and to deliver a promised golden future, their voices, which sought inspiration from prior human experience, were doomed to be neglected.

In modern China, Socrates was by no means the only Greek who garnered attention. From the mythological figure Prometheus to the Spartan king Leonidas, from Sappho in the Archaic period to Lucian in the Roman Empire, modern China was so crowded with Greeks that Mao Zedong (1893–1976), in the isolated Communist base of Yan'an, was provoked to satirize those Westernized intellectuals who "mention Greece whenever they utter a word." Yet Socrates stood out among his compatriots; at this turning point of history, he contributed to the characterization of the modern Chinese intellectual tradition.

Only one year after Socrates's fictional visit, the balance between the warring parties was obviously tipping in favor of the Communists. Camped outside the besieged Beijing, Mao wrote an address to the nation on the occasion of the approaching New Year, 1949. Ironically, in this address, he mentions the Greeks again. He advises not to take pity on the enemy, invoking a fable by Aesop about a farmhand who is killed by a snake he has spared out of pity. For Mao and his followers, such serpents included so-called bourgeois writers inside Beijing. After May 1948, both Zhu and Shen were subject to harsh criticism by Communist propagandists. This campaign was part of the ideological preparation for the Communist takeover; its aim was to defang the bourgeois intellectuals before initiating them into the revolution. In other words, in exchange for their membership in the new society, the regime was imposing compliance—the social compliance Socrates gave his life to oppose. We thus perceive the shadow of his death over his Chinese interlocutors.

In November 1949, Zhu published a self-criticism denouncing his former scholarship in the *People's Daily*, the mouthpiece of the Chinese Communist Party. This marked his conversion into a Marxist aesthetician. Afterward, Zhu remained a professor at Peking University. But, like many of his friends, he was always targeted for humiliation during the post-1949 political campaigns, while in translations and lectures, he never forgot Socrates. Zhu's forced ideological conversion only created his fractured relationship with both the Communists and Socrates. In the end, he was left stranded under the burden of history.

As for Shen, the stinging critiques he received triggered a serious nervous breakdown, culminating in an attempted suicide in spring 1949. It was then arranged for him to serve as a curator in the National Museum of History. Shen never again published fiction after 1949. In the opinion of many, this was a dire ending to the career of modern China's best nativist novelist. However, although Shen did have a chance to leave the museum, he chose to stay and eventually became a groundbreaking scholar of ancient Chinese material culture. For Shen, the clothes and utensils from ancient China retained the memories of the people who created and used them in their humble lives. In his meticulous studies, he paid his ultimate respect to ancient craftsmen, preserving his dignity and fulfilling the duty he saw himself as having as a human being.

In hindsight, we again recall Plato's *Symposium*, the text that so inspired these Chinese intellectuals. The symposium took place historically in 416 BCE, immediately before the collapse of Athenian power in the Peloponnesian War. However, it was forty years later, in the dim postwar days after Socrates and his symposiasts were all dead, when Plato composed the *Symposium* to recapture a lost brilliant moment. Similarly, the two Chinese Socratic dialogues held at the end of the old era now manifest to us the doomed efforts of one generation to sustain its belief in human-ism in the face of political cataclysm. After all the historical drama, Zhu's words about the heroes in the Athenian tragedies linger: what compels us about tragedy "is not disaster, but resistance to the disaster."

BIBLIOGRAPHY: Shen Congwen, "Socrates Discusses What Beiping Needs," in *The Complete Works of Shen Congwen*, vol. 14 (Taiyuan, China, 2002). Zhu Guangqian, "Socrates in China: The National Character of China and the Weakness of Chinese Culture," in *The Complete Works of Zhu Guangqian*, vol. 9 (Hefei, China, 1993).

JINGLING CHEN

1948 · OCTOBER
2014 · FEBRUARY

Where is Nana Hsu?

The Life of a Chinese Literature Textbook

When Nana Hsu (Xu Gesheng) sat down to take her first Chinese lit-erature (*guowen*) exam in the fall of 1948, the guns of the Chinese Civil War were rattling the nation. Schools across the country were in turmoil, and students from embattled Beijing and Tianjin streamed south into Shanghai as refugees. As the war settled into the south, the National-ist (Kuomintang) authorities even sent students to the remote island of Taiwan to continue their studies. It was a chaotic time for everyone, including teachers and students. Perhaps even for the chic Nana Hsu.

In August of 2011, I was finishing up a stint at the Shanghai Library, where I was collecting materials related to middle school Chinese liter-ature textbooks. I had been searching through an old wooden card cata-log looking for items that did not make it into the digital catalog. There I found a card for a 1947 reprint of a 1936 textbook published by Zhong-zheng shuju in Shanghai. I suspected that it would not reveal anything that I did not already know, but went to the circulation desk to order it anyway. They said that the volume was in an off-site storage facility and probably would not be delivered before I was scheduled to leave. Still I placed the request. The afternoon before I was to leave Shanghai, I went by the circulation desk, and, lo and behold, there was the volume: the third in a six-volume set. I glanced at the clock—just a few hours left.

When I opened the tattered and brittle volume, out fell a sheet of lined paper with precise handwriting on both sides: a student's exam from, I calculated, the fall of 1948, probably in mid-October. In the upper right-hand corner was written the name Xu Gesheng, and then, in roman letters, "S. M. II. B / No. 48." That would be Saint Mary's High School, sophomore class, section B, student number 48. Ms. Nana Hsu, as I have come to know her, received a very respectable 87 for her efforts. I had myself a small treasure. And there was more.

The volume I had in hand was like many others in its conservative nature, emphasizing the classical literary texts that are still often considered the "national literature." Yet, unlike most textbooks held in libraries and archives, this one had passed through the hands of a student, and her hands had been busy throughout the volume. Not only were there extensive interlinear and marginal notes related to the readings, Nana also was an incessant doodler. When her mind drifted away from the droning voice of her *guowen* teacher, it entered other worlds of language and fantasy: worlds that revolved around her adolescence, modern Shanghai, and the materiality of writing.

In the spring of 2012, I was on leave, spending every day at the National Library in Taiwan, plowing through dry and turgid materials related to *guowen* textbooks and educational policies of the early twentieth century. In a moment of desperation, I happened on the idea of instrumentalizing Nana's textbook to breathe imaginative life into my research. I did a sweep of the Internet to see if Xu Gesheng showed up. Finding no likely suspects, I went on to my creative solution of inventing fictional lives for her. It took me the rest of the semester to bring the study to a close. Seventy-five pages long, it was neither an article nor a book. I began to call it my "novella."

Nana Hsu, as she called herself in English, was a bright but somewhat distracted sixteen-year-old girl making her way through adolescence and the routines of her sophomore year at Saint Mary's High School. Saint Mary's was an elite Episcopal girls' school established in 1881, which by then had moved to 16-5 Bresnan Road in the western suburbs of the city, just beyond the old International Settlement. Saint Mary's was definitely not accepting refugee students. Its most famous graduate, the writer Eileen Chang (1920–1995), had returned to Shanghai in 1941 and was then a celebrity in the Shanghai literary scene. Chang's most productive years were 1943–1945, just when Nana was entering her teens, and Nana grew up devouring the elegant urbane fiction of Chang and her compatriots. Young and pretty, Nana was looking forward to a new, exciting life—and so was China. We do not know, however, how those two young lives—one personal, one national—played out together. The question is, where did Nana go for her last year of middle school? Did she graduate Saint Mary's and go on to a life in new China? Or did she flee to Taiwan with two million other Nationalist refugees, to live a life parallel to but separated from China? That would have made a world of difference for this young schoolgirl: her elite Christian education would have been a burden in one place and a blessing in the other.

As a woman in her twenties living in the People's Republic of China (PRC), Nana would have run into the gristmill of the Anti-Rightist Movement and the Great Leap Forward of the 1950s and early 1960s. I imagine her emerging from that turmoil, a young mother with an eight-year-old daughter, when the Cultural Revolution would send them down to a bitter life in Qinghai Province, the far hinterlands of western China. There, amid the poverty and persecution they faced in their adopted village, her daughter's education would fall entirely to Nana (there were neither public schools nor textbooks), and Nana would draw on what she had learned at Saint Mary's. Her daughter would become part of that lost generation created by the radical politics of the Cultural Revolution, but she would have been educated in a conservative version of *guowen* pedagogy. They would return to Shanghai in the 1980s ill equipped to deal with the new economic realities. At the turn of the century, as the ideological winds of the PRC turned sharply nostalgic, *guowen* textbooks from the 1930s were reissued in facsimile editions for supplementary and self-study. The literary learning of Nana and her daughter would be, like colonial Shanghai, back in vogue.

If, instead, Nana had gone to Taiwan, she would have been enfolded into the relatively comfortable existence of the exiled elite in Taipei. In this alternate life, her family could have taken up residence in a large Japanese house, such as Number 27, Lane 17, Yongkang Street, near National Taiwan Normal University, where Nana would matriculate in 1951. In the 1960s, this young mother would go on to teach *guowen* at the elite middle school, First Girl's High of Taipei (Beiyinü), working with a curriculum that looked quite familiar—conservative, elitist, and peppered with Nationalist ideology. Her daughter would inherit that mantle of privilege but also be drawn into the local conditions of Taiwan, her birthplace. The *guowen* textbooks would not adjust to those local conditions, however, remaining mired in Nationalist ideology, forever gazing back to the mainland. The Taiwanization of textbooks would come only with the lifting of martial law in the late 1980s, when the Ministry of Education would lose its monopoly on textbook production, and a variety of new *guowen* textbooks would emerge. Authors long banned and associated with communist ideology, such as Lu Xun (1881–1936), would again be read in middle school.

If she were still alive when I wrote this in 2012, Nana would have been in her eighties, perhaps living in peaceful retirement just down the street from the National Library where I pored over her textbook. I deeply hoped so, but I did not actually want to know. If I did, I could not have written the lives that I have imagined for her.

Nana's textbook can be viewed as an emblem within the debate surrounding the Chinese nation (*guo*) and its literature (*wen*) throughout most of the twentieth century—the first *guowen* textbook and national curriculum standards both date from 1904. The textbook Nana used stood on the conservative side of that debate, arguing that Chinese literature was primarily from before the twentieth century—three thousand years of texts necessarily overshadowed thirty. This volume begins with selections from the "Airs" of the *Book of Songs* and concludes with poems and prose of the Tang dynasty. The authors and texts are mostly familiar: for example, Sima Qian's (135?–86 BCE) biography of Qu Yuan (340–278 BCE), Tao Yuanming's (365–427 CE) "Returning to Dwell in Gardens and Fields," and Yuan Zhen's (779–831 CE) memorial (*ming*) to Du Fu (712–770 CE). Yet, in Nana's textbook we also sense a resistance to that conservatism in the dissonance between the classical texts and her marginal notes. That resistance was, of course, carried out in another form as well in the larger national arena, specifically the challenge posed by the leftist curriculum and pedagogy of the 1940s, which rejected the classical materials as irrelevant to the modern condition. Despite the often-claimed victory of the vernacular literary movement, a strongly conservative tendency remained in many layers and locations of Chinese society, identifying the national literature as that of the pre-twentieth-century past, particularly Tang poetry. The imagined trajectories of Nana's doubled life embody that debate.

On April 12, 2013, I received an e-mail from Chen Yao, the East Asian librarian at the University of Minnesota; its subject line certainly caught my attention: "Found Your Nana." Chen Yao had discovered that in March 2013, months after I had blithely finished my Nana narratives, someone posted an old document on his blog. This was a confession written by a young man, Di Lujia, during the counterrevolutionary purge of 1955. He was trying to explain his relationship with the family of Wang Yunwu (1888–1979), publisher and former Nationalist minister of finance, and a war criminal in the eyes of the PRC authorities. Di had a complicated, and ultimately damning, connection to the Wang family through their son, Wang Xueyi, a middle school friend and later college roommate. The two had met in wartime Chongqing, and the Wang family took Di under its influential and protective wing. When they moved back to Shanghai, Di became even closer to the Wangs. He describes that relationship in no uncertain bourgeois terms:

> In June of 1946, after the demobilization of Jiaotong University [back to Shanghai], I would sometimes go over to his [Wang Xueyi's] house on Saturday to spend leisure time. His home was at 688 Haiwei Street, and there I came to know his female cousins [on his mother's side], Xu Gexin, Xu Gefei, and Xu Gesheng. Their home was in Hong Kong, so they were all living in Wang Xueyi's house. Later they asked me to tutor Xu Gexin. From then on, I went to their home every Saturday to hold tutoring sessions, after which we would chat, sometimes listen to music, or ask his sister to play the piano, to which we would all sing. Later I also tutored Xu Gefei and Xu Gesheng.

Thus, in 2013, Xu Gesheng, my Nana Hsu, emerged from my fantasy lives to occupy a specific historical position. She was the niece of Wang Yunwu, through his famous marriage to the Xu sisters of Hong Kong—Xu Baolian in 1910, and Xu Baopan in 1917. Their brother was Nana's father. Thus, the Wang Yunwu whose name appears in elegant cursive several times on page 236 of Nana's textbook is a familial reference to her uncle, not to the minister of finance; and the address that she writes so clearly on page 105, Number 28, 2nd Floor, Baolei Street, Hong Kong, was probably her family's home.

Di's confession contained further information on our now very real Nana:

> At the beginning of 1951, Xu Gesheng returned to Beijing to enter college.... After that, I learned from Xu Gesheng that in 1951 Wang Xueyi's sister and Xu Gexin both went to the United States to study. The last time I saw Xu Gesheng was in the summer of 1953, when she was studying in the Department of Public Health of Beijing Medical College.

So much for Nana's privileged life in Taiwan. She had returned to the maw of Mao's China.

Early in the morning on February 28, 2014, the day before I was to give my first public presentation on the textbook and my imagined lives of Nana, I received this e-mail:

> Professor Zhou [Allen],
>
> Thank you for this very odd discovery. I am flabbergasted by it, just flabbergasted. Yes, I am indeed that student who only got an 87 while she doodled away in her *guowen* textbook, and I am the youngest of the three sisters....
>
> Best, Xu Gesheng

Nana now not only has a position in the history of modern China, she also has a contemporary voice.

JOSEPH R. ALLEN

1949 · MARCH 28

Shen Congwen attempts suicide and is consequently institutionalized.

Shen Congwen's Journey: From Asylum to Museum

On March 28, 1949, Shen Congwen (1902–1988) tried to commit suicide in his Peking University dormitory. Shortly afterward, Shen was committed to a mental asylum for treatment. With this abrupt termination of his renowned literary career, he chose to work in the National Museum of History in Beijing. When Shen rejected the invitation to go to Taiwan and decided to remain in Beijing, he was not unaware that something like this might happen. He wrote to a novice writer in 1948:

> For these past twenty or thirty years my writing has been based on contemplation [*si*]. Now, however, one has to see everything from the perspective of conviction [*xin*]. I might not be able to accomplish such a transformation. Before long, even if I were not forced to, I would eventually stop writing. This is the fate of certain people of our generation.

With the imminent victory of the Chinese Communist Revolution, the conversion from individuality to a collective mind set, from reflective thinking to conformity, confronted Chinese intellectuals with great urgency. Like many of his contemporaries who failed to assimilate in response to the Communist mandate, Shen experienced poignant changes in both his career and his personal life.

By late 1948, Shen had felt increasing political pressure from the Left and a bitter sense of alienation from his friends and even family. Guo Moruo (1892–1978), the leading leftist writer and theorist, denounced Shen as a pornographic, "peach-pink" writer who had been an active reactionary. Progressive students at Peking University, where Shen held a teaching position, copied Guo's article on massive wall posters and petitioned the university to fire Shen. Shen suffered serious nervous breakdowns before his attempted suicide. At the asylum, he was completely enveloped in hallucinations, delusions, and fear. He later described his mental state in a letter to his once-close friend Ding Ling (1904–1986), who was at the time the vice president of the National Association of Literature and Arts and the chief editor of *Literary Gazette:* "Those dreadful impressions, painful feelings, and the consequent bouts of humiliation, horror, and utter delirium brought on by hypnotherapy—they have become a permanent burden of my life." The phantasms of paranoia and Shen's persecution complex best testify to the mechanisms of social exclusion and confinement at work in the mental asylum, as well as the ideological restraints of Communist society.

When the inaugural All-China Congress of Literary and Art Representatives took place in July 1949, Shen, the veteran modern Chinese writer, was not invited. In 1953, he was informed by the Kaiming Press that all extant copies of his works, along with the corresponding printing plates, had been destroyed. Meanwhile, his writings were censored in Taiwan, along with the bulk of May Fourth literature. Eradicated from the official Chinese literary histories, Shen would devote the next forty years of his life to art and archeological research. His greatest contribution to the field was his magnum opus, *Studies on Traditional Chinese Costumes*, which was first drafted in 1964 and went through multiple revisions before coming out in 1981 in Hong Kong.

Sent to the Northern China Revolutionary University in 1950, Shen tried painstakingly to study party policies and accomplish "thought reform." His efforts were emblematic of the broad determination of liberal intellectuals at the time, who were seized by the urge to transform themselves in order to serve the new nation. His friend Feng Zhi (1905–1993), for instance, successfully disavowed his Rainer Maria Rilke–inspired self-reflective poetry and forced his lyrical finesse into the mold of propagandist political hymns. In spite of his desire to write again, Shen's unpublished, post-1949 fictional writings can barely match up to his previous literary artistry and were unable to meet the demands of new socialist literature. In an unsent letter to an anonymous journalist in 1951, Shen wrote of his thoughts about literature for the new era: "Nowadays, anything [short stories] equipped with political consciousness seems to work. Actually, literature doesn't work that way. Something else is needed: feelings [*qing*] and fine ways of configuration and expression."

"Literature with feelings" (*qing*) was accordingly considered as an antithesis to literature with a practical function (*zhiyong*), the kind of literature written by the orthodox Socialist writers Zhao Shuli (1906–1970), Li Zhun (1928–2000), and Zhou Libo (1908–1979). Revisiting the Chinese literary tradition, Shen viewed works such as *Legends of the States* and *Records of the Grand Historian* as exemplars of "literature with feelings": "They became the only vehicles to connect past and present, self and other. Hence, they created historical continuity and enabled feelings to be revivified across different times and spaces." Literature, like other forms of art, exists to abstract feelings, make impressions visible, and configure them into distinctive shapes, a process that Shen later called "abstract lyricism" (*chouxiang de shuqing*).

Such artistic contemplations can be traced back to the 1940s, when Shen, then a refugee in Kunming in the southwest of China, struggled strenuously, even to the point of mental derangement, to create a new form of literature different from his earlier, realistic nativist writings: "I'm crazy for the abstract. I saw an utterly complete form of life, which is present in the abstract, but vanishes in the face of facts." Shen experimented with innovative styles so as to reach beyond the constraints of language. Literature, to be sure, is a significant way to represent beauty and therefore to convey life and feelings; however, since beauty is abstract and contingent, Shen maintained that it is "better captured in painting than literature, in mathematics than painting; better still, in music." Precariously balanced between the abstract and the material, the ephemeral and the constant, the illusory and the apparent, Shen sought an ideal expressive form in vain. His arduous aesthetic explorations drove him to the edge of a nervous breakdown. In 1949, at the asylum, he reflected that his aesthetic crisis in wartime Kunming inflicted severe psychological damage.

Shen's aesthetic vision and his faith in the sustained power of literature and art to articulate beauty and humanity would be continued and further developed across the 1949 transition in related fields: art and archeology. His shift originated in his lifelong passion for art and antiques. In the early 1920s, Shen worked as a secretary for Chen Quzhen (1883–1952), a reformist warlord in west Hunan. His main responsibilities were to catalogue Chen's collection of old books, paintings, porcelain, and other antiques, an experience that Shen later identified as his history education. In these artifacts, he saw fragments of cultural memory and crystallizations of beauty, history, and humanity. History is therefore composed of "a slice of color, a bundle of threads, a slab of bronze or a pile of earth and an arrangement of words, merging with the life of the artist," and art is essential to the construction and revival of human civilization. Viewed in this vein, his post-1949 undertaking constitutes a continuation of his exploration of art, humanity, and history. When the second conference of Chinese Literature and Art Workers took place in 1953, Shen participated as a member of the sector of fine arts.

Friends and family could hardly understand his decision to work at the National Museum of History. Like the mental asylum, the museum has been considered yet another modern institution of enclosure, a place where old, useless objects were stored. Shen, however, found in the museum a sanctuary of true human history and historical manifestations.

For all the trials he endured after 1949, he managed to complete a broad range of writings on silk, textile designs, Tang and Song mirrors, Ming brocades, jade, porcelain, lacquerware, and other types of artwork. His major work, *Studies on Traditional Chinese Costumes*, which constructs a distinctive history of Chinese sartorial civilization, best represents his creative vision—one that blends literary imagination and archaeological evidence, material culture and historical consciousness.

Shen began his research on ancient Chinese textiles, which had been overlooked as trivial artifacts, shortly after he joined the museum. He scrutinized hundreds and thousands of textile objects in the collections of the Palace Museum in the Forbidden City, provincial museums, and archeological excavations. He proposed, to no avail, to establish a national textile museum. In 1963, Shen was commissioned by the Ministry of Culture, following the request of Zhou Enlai (1898–1976), the prime minister, to compile a book on Chinese clothing and textiles to give as a diplomatic gift to foreign dignitaries. The first draft of two hundred thousand words and two hundred illustrations was completed over a short span of five months. However, before reaching the book production process, Shen was asked to revise the book substantially: its structure and classification of illustrations needed to be rearranged on the basis of class identity rather than individuality. During the Cultural Revolution, the manuscript was confiscated as a reactionary "poisonous weed" that honored "emperors and generals" and "scholars and beauties" of the imperial past. In 1969, after undergoing many rounds of inspection, thought struggle, home raids, and forced labor, Shen was asked by the special investigation team in his work unit to pick up some of his confiscated materials, which, much to his surprise, included the manuscript of the costume study. When he was sent down to a cadre school in Hubei Province for reeducation the following year, this large pile of handwritten pages and sketches was in his meager luggage. In spite of the grueling conditions and his declining health, Shen managed to continue working on his costume manuscript until after the end of the Cultural Revolution, when he finally received permission for its publication.

With the flamboyance of past fashions discarded as obsolete, poisonous weeds, Socialist China was dominated by navy blue or gray Mao suits. In an era of collectivity and uniformity, Shen's study of fashion, a study that foregrounded diversity in texture, color, pattern, and style, provided a different vision of history and culture. Exploring daily scenes, social events, or moments related to topics as diverse as patterns of embroidery, buttons and sleeves, hairstyles, jewelry and accessories, dishes, furniture, means of transportation, and water supplies, Shen's *Study on Traditional Chinese Costumes* used cultural artifacts as a means of rethinking history. In his view, fashion and clothing come to define the parameters of human existence throughout history. He saw history not as a teleological narrative from oppression to revolution, but as a lineage of moments and fragments that surpasses the instantaneous veneer of realpolitik and illuminates beauty and humanity—a "history with feelings." Shen saw in the artistic fragments a way to write a "history with feelings" that did not line up perfectly with the dominant discourse of a history of feats (*shigong*), in which history unfolded in a planned manner.

Reflecting on Sima Qian's (135?–86 BCE) *Records of the Grand Historian*, his inspiration, Shen noted that *Records* seeks not simply to make sense of the past, but to contemplate the historical and intellectual horizon. It displays an artistic engagement with the past; it opens up history to humanity and the present to new cultural possibilities. Great works like *Records* have the capacity to transmit feeling to and communicate with future generations. They are a product of their times, but go beyond the immediate reality to reach the future. Their notion of history is therefore future-centric. The same can be said of Shen's own post-1949 art historical work: his engagement with the cultural objects of the past had a future-centric look at the present time, when the entire nation was caught in the fanaticism of socialist modernization. His practice of lyrical archeology opens up the socialist present to broader cultural possibilities.

Shen's costume study needs also to be considered as a piece of literature. In the preface, he wrote, "There might still be correspondences between this work and the literary creation of the first half of my life in terms of approaches and viewpoints." His approach, to entwine vignettes of scenes surrounding a piece of clothing or furniture, surely is reminiscent of his 1930s writings, which feature a constellation of sketches of local customs, landscapes, family stories, anecdotes, and legends. Moreover, by excavating moments of feelings that were woven in the pattern of a garment, crystallized in the design of a jade hairpin, documented in a passage of a historical text, or evoked in a line of poetry, Shen's cultural historical work reinforced his vision of art and literature as a form of lyrical expression. As he spelled out in an unfinished 1961 essay entitled "Abstract Lyricism," a work of literature and art exists to "express feelings" (*shuqing*) and to give a shape to transient and vulnerable human lives. In the capacity for lyrical excavation and evocation, Shen sees the value and meaning of literature and art. Such a distinctive vision not only goes beyond the strictures of socialist literature but also broadens the narrowly defined paradigm of May Fourth literature. In 1988, Shen was nominated for the Nobel Prize for Literature. According to Göran Malmqvist of the Swedish Academy, he was in line to win it, had he not passed away that year. From asylum to museum, from fiction writing to art and archeological research, against all adversity, Shen Congwen created an artistic vision that greatly contributes to Chinese as well as world literature.

BIBLIOGRAPHY: Jeffrey C. Kinkley, *The Odyssey of Shen Congwen* (Stanford, CA, 1987). Shen Congwen, *Shen Congwen quanji* (Taiyuan, China, 2002). David Der-wei Wang, *The Lyrical in Epic Time: Modern Chinese Intellectuals and Artists through the 1949 Crisis* (New York, 2015). Xiaojue Wang, *Modernity with a Cold War Face: Reimagining the Nation in Chinese Literature across the 1949 Divide* (Cambridge, MA, 2013). Zhang Xinying, *Shen Congwen de houbansheng, 1948–1988* (Guilin, China, 2014).

                                                            XIAOJUE WANG

1949

"Time Has Begun"

1958

"Seize Every Second!"

A New Time Consciousness: The Great Leap Forward

When the People's Republic of China (PRC) ushered in its first National Day on October 1, 1949, time emerged as a key to the definition of the new Communist state. "Time Has Begun," a famous poem by Hu Feng (1902–1985) published in the *People's Daily* to commemorate this historic event, captured the very essence of the new time scheme. In passages like "transcending eternity in an instant" and "transcending infinity in a moment," the time of the present was about not merely the boundless potential of the new nation, but also China's *longue durée*. More importantly, it was one of countless revolutions underpinning Chinese history.

Time, like the spirit of Chinese society, had decayed and reached a point of emptiness, only to begin anew on what Hu memorialized as that "very day," and at that "sacred moment." Apart from the beginning of this new chapter in history, a temporal revolution had in fact been created even earlier, through the institution of a single, nationally unified "Beijing time," in place of the five time zones previously instituted by the Nationalist Party. One by one, each province that was "liberated" by the Communist forces began to adopt Beijing time in order to be synchronized with the primary national time zone, setting in motion one of the fundamental transformations in the social conception of time. Within just months after the founding of the PRC, various parts of the country—with the notable exceptions of Xinjiang and Tibet—all adopted Beijing time as their unified time standard.

With the establishment of Communist China, time became palpably alive. In contrast to the static crowd that held its breath in deferential anticipation, time was "surging ahead," "leaping onto its rightful stand" before the nation. Time and the nation had been reinvigorated with a youthful dynamism. In an effort to consolidate the significance of time, and as if to seal his own literary reflection *in* time, Hu added a time stamp to his work, marking the poem's birth and its subsequent revision. His careful documentation of the dates, hours, and minutes reflects an unusual sensitivity to temporal precision. While his intention was to historicize his poem, his record arguably became a precursor to yet another change in Chinese time consciousness during the 1950s, when the Communists unveiled their development agenda.

Amid the early jubilance, the country also faced daunting economic challenges: China's large and rapidly growing population was faced with high unemployment rates, which was further exacerbated by the government's emphasis on capital-intensive industries. The Great Leap Forward campaign that began in 1957 thus aimed to provide an immediate solution to these issues. It inaugurated a shift toward labor-intensive industries and, in particular, the development of heavy industries like steel, iron, chemicals, and machinery, alongside other sectors such as agriculture and light industries. More critically, the focus was on achieving a rapid rate of "simultaneous development" across all sectors.

By early 1958, as the campaign intensified, time became a form of narrative. What emerged was a more specific perception of time, one that demanded a detailed account of every minute and second. This highly regulated notion of time also began to reshape people's consciousness and the way they experienced everyday life, particularly in the newly industrializing cities and towns. The national, collective narrative "to seize every second" and "to calculate time by the minute and second" became synonymous with the production campaign. In an ode to the steel furnaces published in the *People's Daily* on August 26, 1958, Gu Zhengrong, the deputy manager of Anshan Steel and Iron Company, exults:

> To tabulate the steel and iron production requires the
>   denomination of 100 million and 10 thousand tons,
> To calculate the time we need the minutes and the seconds,
> We are the giants of steel and iron,
> We will answer the call of our duties only when we know what we
> ought to do.

In addition to Gu's poem, two additional proclamations echoing this new system of valuing every minute and second likewise found their way into the *People's Daily*. The first was a celebratory announcement made just after the National Day of the PRC in 1958. The announcement tells how the steel production at Capital Steel Company in Beijing achieved a remarkable victory on September 29, attaining a daily production of 1,016.5 tons, or 6.48 times the average daily production, during the previous month. To accomplish this unprecedented production record, the workers had been called on to "toil for molten steel with their sweat, [and to] calculate the time by the minute and second." The second proclamation was a more contemplative open letter to the press, published in 1959, at the height of the production campaign to "seize every second!" Reflecting on the use of time during this period, Wang Wentao observed that people were already optimizing even the smallest fraction of it. His focus, however, was on the significance of each second, and how to "seize" and "fight" for every usable minute in order to maximize one's work potential.

As the Communist Party shifted gears from post–civil war reconstruction to a new phase of rapid—albeit brief—economic growth and development that emerged from new technological learning and advances, this transition also altered the mode of production and its social relations. Throughout the country, the population was reorganized into self-sufficient people's communes in order to enhance productivity and efficiency in agriculture and industry. The slogan of "more, faster, better, and cheaper" became the definitive ethos of the Great Leap Forward. Moreover, the drive to achieve the ambitious production targets set out by the central government thus etched a minute-and-second-based time consciousness deep within the labor force. In essence, the campaign invoked a new narrative of time, mobilizing the nation and its people to "read" history through a different lens.

The eminent writer Yi Ding (1906–1996), also publishing in the *People's Daily*, expressed his opinions about the importance of time at the dawn of the new, socialist industrial era. In "A Communist's Conception of Time," he comments that

> the Great Leap Forward in industrial and agricultural production, achieved at the time of writing in 1958, was the victory of 600 million people in optimizing time under the leadership of the party.... Every communist member ought to live with passion and value time, rather than wasting it. Valuing time is not merely about being punctual, but being able to seize every available moment; not just being able to seize every available moment, but being able to optimize it, to rationally allocate time and fully utilize it. This is precisely what we mean when we speak of the need to compete with time, and to be ahead of it.

This production frenzy was derived from the strategy of mass mobilization and collectivization as argued by Mao Zedong (1893–1976) and his faction within the Chinese Communist Party, as opposed to the more technocratic approach put forward by his opponents, such as Zhou Enlai (1898–1976), Liu Shaoqi (1898–1969), and Deng Xiaoping (1904–1997). A key point of contention between the two groups was the rate of change in the agricultural sector, and for Mao and his supporters, speed was of the essence. To instill the desired urgency of each second and minute required the provision of easy access to means of telling time; it demanded the broad circulation of working clocks and watches to the people in both urban and rural circumstances, in order to enable them to tell the time at any given second. While the manufacturing of clocks and watches was centered in Shanghai and Guangzhou before the Communist era, the country embarked on a mission to manufacture its own watches domestically in the post-1949 period, giving rise to other clock and watch production centers such as those in Beijing, Yantai, Chongqing, and Tianjin.

Deemed one of the four daily necessities of the time, clocks and watches were in popular demand. As the demand for timekeeping devices grew, clock and watch repair services began to emerge and expand. Two months after the Great Leap Forward movement was launched, the Beijing No. 1 Clock and Watch Repair Cooperative, for example, advertised their services in the typical *dazibao*, or big-character poster, stating that the cooperative would send its members to the *hutongs* (lanes and alleys) every Friday between 12:00 and 1:30 p.m. to collect and repair clocks and watches, servicing up to twenty-six different kinds of timepieces. As observed by local residents, this was a "new phenomenon of the Great Leap Forward." Such repair services were not unique to Beijing and were in fact extended to other cities, like Wuhan, as well as some rural townships and villages. These initiatives were very well received and, in retrospect, integral to the development of a stronger time consciousness.

In addition to cultivating a greater awareness of time, the PRC injected new values into the idea of time and constructed the image of the people as timekeepers, especially during the Great Leap Forward. The new time was political: people and workers were not enslaved to their employers but were new masters of their country and new rulers of their own time. Possessing a clock or watch was thus the ultimate symbol of these revolutionary social and temporal relations. Wu Yan (1918–2010), a renowned translator of foreign literature and writer during the 1950s and 1960s, confessed in his essay "Time Composition" that, like many others after the liberation, he also bought himself a Shanghai-brand watch to "experience the dynamic pulse of life in the factories, and through the process, got acquainted with many forward-looking individuals who constantly strove ahead of their times."

Toward the end of 1959, however, Mao's Great Leap Forward began to flounder and time began to slow down. Within the party, certain members began to criticize Mao's development strategy, culminating in Peng Dehuai's (1898–1974) "Letter of Opinion" denouncing the commune system and collapse of national planning. Although Peng was removed from the key positions he held, his criticisms marked a watershed moment; shortly thereafter, the shortcomings of the Great Leap Forward were acknowledged rather candidly by an official communiqué. Mao himself came to accept the inevitability of dismantling this movement, and as he withdrew from the day-to-day running of the party and his role as the head of state, more moderate policies were implemented in a futile bid to improve the people's living conditions.

Despite the unwinding of the campaign and its catastrophic outcomes, the themes of time discipline and temporal consciousness persisted in both literary and political contemplations. The relationship with time was further developed in another of Wu's essays published in 1961, entitled "The Clock," where he recounts three stories about clocks that were shared with him by an anonymous protagonist. Through the recollections and personal experiences of the protagonist—later revealed to be a model employee, he is deemed by his production team as a progressive worker—Wu essentially reconstructs the changing relationship between the people and clocks, as well as the general public's comprehension of time.

Jiao Zuyao's (1935–) short story entitled "Time," which was published in *Harvest* magazine in 1965, sought to reflect the working people's attitudes toward labor and time through the conflict between a father and his son. Ji Yangchun, a young mine worker, depends on his stainless steel watch to determine his work hours, arriving for work and knocking off punctually after eight hours on the dot. His father, Ji Aishui, however, is of the belief that time is not only the element that is recorded by the hands of the watch or clock, but is in and of itself a "grand communist revolutionary endeavor." Unlike his son, he is motivated by his sense of responsibility toward the revolutionary cause, preferring to arrive earlier for work and stay on later than required.

Equally emphatic about the importance of time was mathematician Hua Luogeng (1910–1985), who contributed a short piece, "Time and Tide Wait for No Man," to the *People's Daily* in 1964. Hua's message for readers was to seize each passing moment and fully utilize time at work and beyond. He argued that,

> for a revolutionist, his or her entire life belonged to the party and the people. Thus, whether at work or during one's spare time, the revolutionist would try to effectively utilize every minute and second for

the revolutionary enterprise. Even when left to work independently, he or she should still seize each minute and second with verve and dedication to work on behalf of the people.

In both Jiao's and Hua's contemplations, there is a clear distinction between time that is seen as a productive measure and time understood as a quality imbued with the values and spirit of the revolutionary cause. Every minute and second mattered for production output, but this emphasis on mechanical time often translated into the lengthening of the work-day, separate from a more intense mobilization of labor. The real value of time was derived from one's passionate dedication to the radical enterprise, such that workers were supposed to disregard their physical toils and the exhausting passage of time for the greater good of the People's Republic. Hence, while much of the discourse was couched in mere temporal units, reiterating the move for accelerated production, the concept of time was arguably much more than that; it was undoubtedly a rallying call for a fun-damental restructuring of human consciousness and social relations that lay at the heart of the Communist Revolution and the Great Leap Forward.

BIBLIOGRAPHY: Maurice Meisner, *Mao's China and After: A History of the People's Republic* (New York, 1999). Wang Wentao, "Yi miaozhong ye bu fangguo," *Renmin ribao*, July 26, 1959. Yi Ding, "Gongchan zhuyi zhe de shijian guannian," *Renmin ribao*, June 23, 1958.

HAR YE KAN

1951 · SEPTEMBER

Wang Yao publishes *A Draft History of New Chinese Literature.*

1952 · SEPTEMBER

Literary Gazette criticizes Wang Yao's history of new literature.

The Genesis of Literary History in New China

In September 1952, *Literary Gazette* reported on a forum attended by eighteen high-profile literary critics and writers that was jointly organized by the State Bureau of Publications and the *People's Daily* on August 30,

1952. The forum's purpose was to evaluate volume 1 of *A Draft History of New Chinese Literature*, written by Wang Yao (1914–1989) and published by Kaiming Bookstore in September 1951. Wang was a young scholar whose specialty was medieval Chinese literature but who taught two classes on modern Chinese literature at Tsinghua University from 1948 to 1949. Both the *People's Daily* and *Literary Gazette* were top Chinese Communist Party (CCP) propaganda organs, and the unusual media attention lavished on Wang's book testifies to its significance as the first history of modern Chinese literature to appear in the People's Republic of China (PRC) after the subject was newly instituted as a required course for Chinese majors.

Contrary to Wang's expectation, his book was severely criticized. Among other things, he was censured for neglecting the proletarian leadership of the new literary movement and giving a symmetrical treatment to "revolutionary writers" and "reactionary writers." His "purely objective" approach was labeled as "bourgeois" or "petty-bourgeois," and he was accused of committing serious ideological errors because he did not pursue class analysis and quoted extensively from "counterrevolutionary" writers. A politically sensitive scholar, Wang responded quickly to the criticism. He immediately asked the bookstore to stop selling his volume 1 and submitted an article of self-criticism to *Literary Gazette*, confessing to his "bourgeois" ideas of arts as manifest in his consistent privileging of art over politics. While completing his second volume, Wang spent time revising the first, and in August 1953 his revised volume 1 was published together with volume 2 by the New Literature and Arts Press.

Three areas were conspicuously revised in Wang's first volume. First, "proletarian literature" now assumed the leadership position within "new democratic literature," and Lu Xun (1881–1936) was seen to have been compelled by Communist guidance to follow the direction sanctioned by Mao Zedong's (1893–1976) theory of literature and arts. Second, in lieu of the United Front, which explained the coexistence of "progressive" and "regressive" writers during the War of Resistance against Japan from 1937 to 1945, class struggle became the dominant trope and writers were assigned to their respective class designations. For example, Xu Zhimo (1897–1931), a flamboyant poet, was no longer linked to the desires of "city dwellers" but to "right-wing bourgeois thought." Third, realism was upheld as the preferred style for new literature, and other literary schools (for example, symbolism and modernism) were refuted as regressive or even reactionary, hence representing countercurrents to revolutionary literature.

Why was Wang so eager to accept criticism and revise his history within one year? Why did he go outside his specialty and volunteer to write a history of modern Chinese literature in the first place? To answer these questions, we need to revisit the Republican era, when classical literature dominated the institution of literary scholarship and modern literature was rarely taught at school. During the 1920s–1930s, famous scholars like Hu Shi (1891–1962) and Zhou Zuoren (1885–1967) published books on Chinese literary history, but new literature represented only a small part of their longer historical investigation. From the 1930s onward, new literature attracted the exclusive attention of historians like Wang Zhefu and Li Helin (1904–1988), yet in general the historiography of new literature remained experimental prior to 1949. The urgency to fill this gap in scholarship in an underdeveloped field must have excited Wang Yao, but he also had his ideological motivations. When he started as an undergraduate at Tsinghua in 1934, Wang became an activist and was reportedly arrested twice. He joined the CCP in 1935, although his membership was discontinued in 1937 due to the war. In 1936 he served as the editor of *Tsinghua Weekly* and published numerous essays on social issues, earning him the nicknames "Little Zhou Yang" and "Little Hu Feng"—Zhou Yang (1908–1989) and Hu Feng (1902–1985) were two famous left-wing literary theorists at the time. Given his youthful profile as an aspiring left-wing theorist, it was no surprise that Wang accepted the task of teaching modern Chinese literature upon his Tsinghua students' request and dedicated himself to writing a new literary history that would legitimate the CCP's new cultural policy.

Wang's enthusiastic embrace of the new cultural policy paid off and he was duly rewarded: he was invited to participate in a group project sponsored by the Ministry of Education in 1951, at the age of thirty-seven. Together with senior critics and writers Cai Yi (1906–1992), Li Helin, and Lao She (1899–1966), he was in charge of drafting the pedagogical outline on new literature, which Wang likened to a constitution for teachers nationwide. Published in July 1951, the outline contains Li's acknowledgment of Wang's contribution, including his draft references consisting of works by Mao, as well as those by Zhou Yang, Hu Feng, and Feng Xuefeng (1903–1976). Wang was apparently a rising star in the early

1950s, but his scholarly training owed much to his Tsinghua mentors, in particular Zhu Ziqing (1898–1948), who began teaching new literature as early as 1929. It was under Zhu's supervision, from 1943 to 1946, that Wang completed his graduate training and became a reputable scholar of classical Chinese literature.

When *Literary Gazette* published its criticism in September 1952, Wang had been transferred from Tsinghua to Peking University in a nationwide restructuring of higher education. The 1952 criticism might be read as a symptom that invites a threefold diagnosis. First, it sent an unmistakable signal to scholars nationwide that, from then on, politics took precedent over scholarship, and there would be no room for negotiation between individuals and the CCP. Second, it foreshadowed the periodic crackdowns on intellectuals to come and marked the increasing frequency with which precarious policy changes would take place in the PRC. Third, precisely because of such uncertainties involving party politics and cultural policies, the vulnerability of scholars became all the more obvious.

Despite his earnest efforts to toe the party line, Wang's history was criticized again in the October 15, 1955, issue of *Literary Gazette* because his second volume acknowledged Hu Feng's contribution. By this time, Hu and his associates had been labeled an antiparty clique; a turn in fortune that the July School (the group of writers associated with *July* magazine, edited by Hu during the second Sino-Japanese War) were unable to foresee. In a repeat of what happened in 1952, Wang quickly published another piece of self-criticism in the October 30, 1955, issue of *Literary Gazette*. Unable to presage the large-scope Anti-Rightist Movement to come in 1957, however, his praise of "revolutionary" writers and critics like Ding Ling (1904–1986) and Feng Xuefeng in his history became politically incorrect, as they were classified as "bourgeois rightists" and banished from literary history. It was under such unpredictable conditions that Wang's history, which had gone through five printings, was removed from circulation in 1955—the year in which a Japanese edition appeared in Japan—and did not receive approval for republication in the PRC until 1982.

During the early 1980s, literary historiography returned to the PRC in a "new era" of depoliticization in which "rewriting literary history" became a top priority and Wang's symmetrical treatment was rediscovered and held as a standard. Wang's history had appeared at a time when the new regime urgently needed a textbook on the newly instituted subject of modern Chinese literary history and was still in the early stages of formulating its cultural policy. Consequently, this brief transitional moment gave Wang a rare opportunity to synthesize the previous scholarship on literary historiography and to develop a compromised approach that would hopefully satisfy CCP expectations while acknowledging literary achievements from a large number of writers (close to one hundred) of varied ideological and artistic persuasions. In this respect, Wang was doubly fortunate. Sure enough, Wang Yao improved Wang Zhefu's 1933 methodology of combining theoretical discussion, historical account, and detailed analysis of individual writers, and adopted Li Helin's 1939 scheme of periodization in terms of monumental sociopolitical events, highlighting the ideological "nature" of modern Chinese literature. Like his mentor Zhu Ziqing, Wang organized his discussion of writers in terms of literary genres and devoted chapters in each period to poetry, fiction, and drama, as well as nonfiction prose (*sanwen*) and reportage. Moreover, similar to Hu Shi, who in 1922 had instituted an evolutionary paradigm wherein "new literature," understood as "living literature," would inevitably replace "dead" or "half-dead" classical literature, Wang charted a linear development toward a certain telos. In this scheme, however, modern Chinese literature was shown to "progress" toward the ends legitimized by Mao's 1942 *Talks at the Yan'an Forum on Literature and Art*, namely, literature's coming to serve party politics and appeal to the masses.

In comparison, literary historians after Wang were less fortunate because they operated under increasingly tightened ideological control. Having learned from Wang's experience, Ding Yi's (1913–1954) 1955 history clearly labels writers as "revolutionary," "progressive," and "bourgeois." A year later, this three-way demarcation, which was also found in Wang's history, was narrowed down to two opposing camps, the "enemy's" and "ours" in Liu Shousong's (1912–1969) 1956 history, which devotes three chapters to redefining Lu Xun as "a great Communist" writer, even though Lu Xun had never formally joined the CCP. Tragically, despite the fact that Liu's two-volume history would come to replace Wang's as the primary textbook adopted in the PRC from the mid-1950s onward, Liu could not escape political persecution during the Cultural Revolution and committed double suicide with his wife in 1969. Although his tragedy harks back to a long tradition of political persecution in Chinese history, Liu's case demonstrates once more that the CCP would not tolerate any deviation from its rigid—albeit periodically modified—view of history.

Wang was "fortunate" as he had survived several rounds of criticism, in part thanks to his resilience in submitting timely self-criticism—a peculiar type of writing that all Chinese intellectuals mastered during the 1950s–1970s. Upon closer scrutiny, Wang's willingness to admit his mistakes retrospectively and his tactful recourse to political jargon in his self-criticisms proved more than merely a self-defense—decades later it could serve as evidence of heavy-handed ideological manipulation in scholarship. As he wrote in his 1958 self-criticism (collected in an appendix to the 1972 Hong Kong edition of his history), "When analyzing a literary work, I often first paid attention to whether its characterization is strong, its structure complete, or its style unique, rather than first examining its theme and educational significance." Wang apologized for "separating politics and art" and taking the latter to be the primary criterion, thus siding himself with the "bourgeois position" in diametric contrast to Mao's insistence on politics as the primary criterion for literature. Among other mistakes, Wang acknowledged his serious flaw of objectivism, which had resulted in a muddy entanglement of the mainstream, tributaries, and countercurrents in his literary history. Precisely because of such self-criticism, future readers know that Wang was forced to surrender.

It would take more than twenty years before scholars in the PRC were allowed to revisit the issues Wang had raised in his history and his self-criticism, and to explore the alternative space outside the rigid demarcation of politics and art, socialism and capitalism, revolution and counterrevolution. Back in the 1950s, Wang was compelled to write articles denouncing Hu Feng and Feng Xuefeng, but he remained a major target of criticism by his Peking University students, whose articles—first collected in a volume published by the People's Literature Press in 1958 and then recollected in the 1972 Hong Kong edition—used almost the same political jargon as he did, and who represented a new generation of intellectuals eager to denounce their predecessors and embrace the latest party directives.

A look at the most frequently used phrases in Wang's history reveals the dilemma of PRC intellectuals during the 1950s–1970s. In Wang's delineation, many modern Chinese writers followed a trajectory from "discontent" to "rebellious" or "resistant," and then to "progressive" or "revolutionary" in their ideological reorientation. The following logic is seen to prevail in Wang's narration: "revolution" equals "reality," and "non-revolution" means not only "unreal" and "nonprogressive" but also "inappropriate" and "immoral." The dilemma for PRC intellectuals, however, was that they wanted to join the revolution and help the CCP write its revolutionary history, but they simply could not keep up with constant policy changes and were unable to predict political fallouts that would implicate them in the future.

The 1952 *Literary Gazette* criticism of Wang is just one example of such a dilemma. Wang's original ambition was to become a first-rank scholar in classical Chinese literature, but in 1952 he was aware of the difficulty of becoming "an everlasting first-rank scholar" if he switched to modern Chinese literature. Nonetheless, precisely because of his symmetrical treatment and his artistic sensibility, his history is treasured as a groundbreaking contribution, and he is credited as a founder of the new discipline of modern Chinese literature.

BIBLIOGRAPHY: Li Helin et al., *Zhongguo xin wenxue shi yanjiu* (Beijing, 1951). Liu Shousong, *Zhongguo xin wenxue shi chugao*, vols. 1–2 (1956; repr., Beijing, 1979). Wang Yao, *Zhongguo xin wenxue shi gao* (vol. 1, 1951, vol. 2, 1953; repr., Hong Kong, 1972). Yingjin Zhang, "The Institutionalization of Modern Literary History in China, 1922–1980," *Modern China* 20, no. 3 (July 1994): 347–377. "Zhongguo xin wenxue shi gao (shangce) zuotanhui jilu," *Wenyibao* 20 (1952): 24–30.

YINGJIN ZHANG

1952 · MARCH 18

> The *People's Daily* announces award of the Stalin Prize to Ding Ling and Zhou Libo.

Transnational Socialist Literature in China

On March 18, 1952, the *People's Daily* announced proudly that two Chinese writers, Ding Ling (1904–1986) and Zhou Libo (1908–1979), had been awarded the Stalin Prize. In her acceptance speech, Ding Ling highlighted the significance of the award not just for herself, but for Chinese literature as a whole: "I am just a small and insignificant person, and my work accounts for very little.... This honor belongs to all Chinese writers, belongs to the Chinese people." Set up in 1939 to honor outstanding achievements in the Soviet sciences and arts, the Stalin Prize had been internationalized in the late 1940s, becoming the equivalent of the Nobel Prize in the socialist world, the highest award for writers and artists. The annual selection process not only identified excellence in recent works, but also served to consecrate new creative forms—most notably those associated with socialist realism—and popularize them throughout the Socialist bloc. The recognition of Ding Ling and Zhou was an affirmation of the two writers, and also confirmed that China's emerging socialist literature had successfully appropriated the literary norms defined in Moscow and had thus become part of a socialist world literature.

Ding Ling and Zhou were at the forefront of a wave of socialist cosmopolitanism that united readers and writers from Berlin to Beijing, from Hanoi to Warsaw, and from Bucharest to Pyongyang. Their prize-winning books, Zhou's *Hurricane* (1948) and Ding Ling's *The Sun Shines over the Sanggan River* (1948), were the most prominent Chinese land reform novels. They fictionalized—in near-real time, as land reform was only just unfolding in large swaths of the countryside—the struggle of China's peasants to rid themselves, under the leadership of the Communist Party, of millennia-old forms of oppression and exploitation. Suffused with earthy idioms and anchored deep in the microcosm of the Chinese village, it is paradoxical that an ostensibly localized branch of modern Chinese literature turned out to be the most transnational.

The books' appeal to the judges in Moscow was derived in part from the authors' adherence to the prescriptive standards of socialist realism. Enshrined by the 1934 Congress of Soviet Writers as the official mode of literary creation and spreading across the socialist world in the late 1940s, socialist realism created a common language, a shared repertoire of themes, narrative modes, formulas of characterization, and poetics. These facilitated literary exchanges and communication across the bloc. Works such as *The Sun Shines over the Sanggan River* and *Hurricane* bear the hallmarks of transculturation: the process of adaptation and transcription through which creative texts are imported into a native idiom. This kinship is by no means accidental. Zhou, for instance, had learned the writer's craft as a translator, rendering into Chinese Mikhail Sholokhov's (1905–1984) acclaimed *Virgin Soil Upturned*, which describes the process of collectivization in a Cossack village. Later generations accused Zhou of plagiarism, pointing out the numerous correspondences between Sholokhov's novel and Zhou's book. Such criticism misses the point: transplanting foreign forms and experiences and fusing them with local context was exactly the logic driving the formation of a pan-socialist new literature that would transcend national boundaries and appeal to audiences all across the socialist world. The efforts of Zhou and Ding paid off: in the early and mid-1950s, *The Sun Shines over the Sanggan River* was translated into at least nine different languages, while Zhou's novel saw editions in eight languages of the socialist nations of Eastern Europe and East Asia. When Ding Ling collected her Stalin Prize in Moscow, she learned from her hosts that her novel had sold five hundred thousand copies in the Soviet Union, probably more than it had in China itself at this point. The prize further affirmed her status as a transnational author.

If Chinese novels were becoming best sellers in the Soviet Union, the reverse was also true. Throughout the 1950s, Chinese publishing houses produced a flood of translations of Soviet literature: the classics of socialist realism, new Soviet fiction of the "thaw" era after Joseph Stalin's (1879–1953) death, Soviet adventure novels and science fiction, and Soviet children's literature all found an eager audience in the People's Republic of China (PRC). A 1955 catalogue lists more than 1,500 editions of Soviet novels, poetry, plays, and short stories published in the first five years of the PRC, with print runs of up to a million copies. A perennial best seller in China, the appeal of Nikolai Ostrovskii's (1904–1936) *How the Steel Was Tempered* for Chinese readers has far outlasted its popularity in Russia. *Steel* captured the imagination of Chinese readers like no other Soviet novel and became not just one of the most beloved novels in Socialist China, but the prime template for fiction writing in the PRC.

How the Steel Was Tempered appealed to Chinese readers with a plot that celebrates heroism and fuses the excitement of wartime adventure with calibrated doses of romance. The novel's protagonist, Pavel Korchagin (Bao'er in the Chinese version), grows up in an impoverished workers' family in Ukraine. After being expelled from school, he becomes an apprentice first in the locomotive plant where his brother works, and then in a power station. After the October Revolution, Pavel joins the

Red Army's cavalry and the Communist Youth League, taking up the fight against interventionist foreign troops, which ends in the final victory of the Bolsheviks. Pavel pays a heavy price, losing an eye in battle, but sacrifice is what it takes to become a model fighter, standing up in defense of the Socialist republic and the party. Yet even more trials lie ahead. Pavel is demobilized and takes up the post of a Youth League secretary, shifting his energies to the front of production and socialist construction. The novel's second part sees Pavel fighting against waste and corruption, sabotage and bureaucracy. He leads the efforts to ensure the city's supply of firewood in the bitterly cold winter, but falls ill with pneumonia resulting from overwork. Riddled with multiple health problems and convalescing in a sanatorium in the Crimea, Pavel considers suicide, but ultimately rejects it. Instead, he writes an autobiographical novel, thus moving on to yet another battlefront. No one, he concludes, is useless in the fight for the revolution; everyone can dedicate his life to this grandest of goals.

The unabashed glorification of the revolution and the propagation of heroism and ideological purity appealed to *Steel*'s Communist promoters. As the title suggests, the novel exemplifies the forging of a revolutionary hero, the growth of a hot-blooded but naive youth into a seasoned fighter with a mature ideological consciousness. The book's readers, however, in China and elsewhere, connected with Pavel in many other ways as well. The wartime episodes of the novel's first part, featuring Pavel on horseback, fighting evil and avenging the suffering and oppressed, are not only composed in captivating prose; they also take up the moralistic language of traditional adventure and martial arts fiction of the kind popular in Republican China. Pavel's romantic encounters, in turn, echo those in other Chinese genres, from the May Fourth narratives of "revolution plus love" to sentimental Mandarin Ducks and Butterflies novels. In fact, many Chinese readers in the 1950s and 1960s, a time of moralistic puritanism, were drawn to *Steel* precisely for its depiction of love and passion. The discourse of desire in *Steel* is of course embedded in the novel's larger ideological framework. Pavel feels strongly attracted to Rita, a fellow cadre at the Youth League, but is unwilling to reduce the pace of his work for the pursuit of private happiness. They meet again years later, when Rita is married and has a daughter. Yet it is Pavel's first love, Tonia, who represented the greatest attraction for many Chinese readers (although they would admit so only decades later). Tonia is the daughter of a local bureaucrat, a girl from a petit bourgeois milieu with all the qualities of a middle-class woman. Needless to say, Pavel separates from Tonia when the latter demands that he give up his revolutionary ambitions. The passionate kisses and embraces before Pavel leaves to join the Red Army—nowhere to be found in Chinese socialist fiction—added greatly to the novel's allure.

How the Steel Was Tempered was originally serialized starting in 1932; the first Russian book edition was published in 1936. It was translated into English by Alec Brown (1900–1962), appearing in 1937 under the title *The Making of a Hero*. The book's Chinese translator, Mei Yi (1913–2003), used this English edition, though his translation was checked against the Russian original in the early 1950s and carefully revised. Other Chinese translations have appeared since the 1990s, but Mei Yi's rendering has remained a favorite with Chinese readers. Appreciated for its fluency and vivid prose, it remains in print in the twenty-first century. Mei Yi's translation was first published in 1942 and saw several editions in different Communist Party base areas even before the founding of the PRC. After 1949, Ostrovskii's novel became the most widely read Soviet book in China, with hundreds of thousands of copies distributed in the 1950s and 1960s. The book's popularity was further helped by a screen adaption, a 1942 film directed by Mark Donskoi (1901–1981) that was widely shown in the PRC. *Steel* reached even more readers in abridged popular editions for young readers and for use in literacy classes. In contrast to many other Soviet novels circulating in China in the 1950s, *Steel* retained its popularity even after the Cultural Revolution. In 1999, a China Central Television crew headed for Ukraine to shoot a twenty-part television drama based on Ostrovskii's novel—to the disbelief of many locals, with whom *Steel* had long since fallen out of favor. Needless to say, the television drama was a success in China, and Pavel, Tonia, and Rita remain household names in the PRC.

How the Steel Was Tempered inspired numerous Chinese novels in the 1940s and 1950s, informing not just war-themed fiction and novels depicting the struggles to establish Socialism but also providing a formula of the hero's coming of age that Chinese writers avidly emulated. Pavel's trajectory, the progressive taming of youthful enthusiasm and the growth of the ideologically conscious fighter, has echoes in heroes from

Zhou Dayong, the protagonist of Du Pengcheng's (1921–1991) *Defend Yan'an* to Lin Daojing, the heroine in Yang Mo's (1914–1995) *The Song of Youth*. Yet translated Soviet fiction offered inspiration for Chinese writers across a much wider range of literary registers. The locomotive plant and the power station, symbols of industrial modernity and progress that feature prominently in the early chapters of Ostrovskii's novel, became the backdrop of the first two novels by Cao Ming (1913–2002), China's pioneering writer of industrial fiction. Du's *Defend Yan'an*, in turn, takes cues from the military life portrayed and the glory of the battlefield celebrated in Soviet fiction. New settings and symbols required the rise of a new aesthetics—from the whistle of locomotives and the humming of diesel engines to the rattling machine guns onto which both Soviet and Chinese fictional heroes hurled themselves, sacrificing their lives for the Motherland and the revolution.

Chinese writers were not alone in their appropriation of the new literary language—plot structures, hero worship, symbolism, and aesthetics. As a prototype of socialist realism, Ostrovskii's novel was translated and read all across the socialist world, in East Asia and Eastern Europe, where it was joined by translations of books such as Zhou Libo's *Hurricane* and Ding Ling's *The Sun Shines over the Sanggan River*, the two Chinese Stalin prize winners. Other laureates from Eastern Europe, adhering to the very same patterns of narrative, characterization, and poetics, were in turn translated into Chinese. All of these texts, read next to each other, emphasized the common concerns and the shared culture emerging across the socialist world. The new Chinese socialist literature was not an isolated effort, but was understood by readers and writers alike as part of a much larger development. China in the 1950s had become a part of a new world literature.

BIBLIOGRAPHY: Mark Gamsa, *The Reading of Russian Literature in China: A Moral Example and Manual of Practice* (New York, 2010). Donghui He, "Coming of Age in the Brave New World: The Changing Reception of the Soviet Novel, *How the Steel Was Tempered*, in the People's Republic of China," in *China Learns from the Soviet Union, 1949–Present*, ed. Thomas P. Bernstein and Hua-yu Li (Lanham, MD, 2010), 393–420. Nicolai Volland, "Inventing a Proletarian Fiction for China: The Stalin Prize, Cultural Diplomacy, and the Creation of a Pan-Socialist Identity," in *Dynamics of the Cold War in Asia: Ideology, Identity, and Culture*, ed. Tuong Vu and Wasana Wongsurawat (New York, 2009), 93–112. Nicolai Volland, *Socialist Cosmopolitanism: The Chinese Literary Universe, 1945–1965* (New York, 2017). Rudolf G. Wagner, "Life as a

Quote from a Foreign Book: Love, Pavel, and Rita," in *Das andere China: Festschrift für Wolfgang Bauer zum 65. Geburtstag,* ed. Helwig Schmidt-Glintzer (Wiesbaden, Germany, 1995), 463–476.

NICOLAI VOLLAND

1952 · JULY

Eileen Chang leaves China for good.

A Provocation to Literary History

On a certain day in July 1952, Eileen Chang (1920–1995) crossed the border between mainland China and Hong Kong and stepped into a new life of exile that would take her farther and farther away from Shanghai. Shanghai was the city that had defined and inspired her literary produc-tivity in the previous decade. Chang had spent most of her childhood and adolescent years in Shanghai. She was best known for the ten short stories later published in her first and only collection of short stories, *Romances* (1944). These stories were initially serialized in Shanghai liter-ary magazines *Lilacs* and *Panorama* between 1943 and 1944. Depicting complex romantic entanglements and intricate familial relationships in an urban setting, they made Chang a rising star in the Chinese-language literary circles in the tumultuous period of the second Sino-Japanese War (1937–1945).

Chang's decision to leave China shortly after the founding of the People's Republic of China was inevitably a symbolic gesture that con-veyed her unease with the dominant political culture of the new Com-munist state. Although this decision was a personal one, the ramifications of her departure far exceeded the scope of the individual. It indexed a significant shift and an important threshold in modern Chinese literary history. Around 1949, modern Chinese literary history, yet to be fully integrated into a singular and unified national story, further splintered into multiple and competing histories. Its fragmented landscape reflected the different ideologies and positions that were adopted by the various political regimes in the post–World War II era. After this period, one cannot speak of modern Chinese literary history without evoking an acute awareness of the borders of the nation-state that separate those inside from the outside. To place an influential writer like Chang, who crossed those territorial borders in the early 1950s, in that divided history and geography presents a great challenge.

A little more than ten years later, Chang recalled this fateful moment in her English essay "A Return to the Frontier." She remembered particularly well a young People's Liberation Army soldier patrolling the border: "Beside us stood the Communist sentry, a round-cheeked north country boy in rumpled baggy uniform. After an hour in the hot sun, the young soldier muttered angrily, speaking for the first time 'These people! Keep you out here in this heat. Go stand in the shade.'" This country boy—sharply contrasted with the Hong Kong policeman standing nearby—"a lean tall Cantonese with monstrous dark glasses, look[ing] cool and arrogant"—touched Chang deeply, making her feel "the warmth of race wash[ing] over me for the last time." This controlled identification with the People's Liberation Army soldier, although not enough of an identification to turn Chang back, spelled out the ambivalence of the soon-to-be-diasporic subject facing a momentous personal and historical transition that would eventually make her into one of the most enigmatic and controversial figures in the Chinese worlds for the rest of the twentieth century.

Chang's departure from China corresponded to and foreshadowed a radical shift in the reception history of this writer. By way of contrast with her image as an up-and-coming literary star widely recognized for her talent in producing popular romantic stories in the Japanese colonized Shanghai in the 1940s, Chang disappeared completely from the official literary history of mainland China from the 1950s to the 1980s. In the meantime, her stories from the 1940s acquired a steady fan base in Taiwan, Hong Kong, and other overseas communities, thanks largely to the American-based literary critic C. T. Hsia (1921–2013), who promoted her works in his seminal study *A History of Modern Chinese Fiction.* If Chang's displacement from the so-called center of China proper is but a symptomatic manifestation of the politics of the Cold War, her landslide comeback to almost all Chinese-speaking communities in the 1990s signified a form of recovery from Cold War trauma. More importantly, it signified a new alliance among Chinese worlds, worlds that had been reconfigured in response to globalization. Chang was, in a way, a writer of all times and no time. As a literary witness to the political and social histories of the Chinese worlds, rife with trials and tribulations, she makes us reflect metacritically on the very concept of history, of which literary history is a specific form. Does the uneven reception history of Chang's works also map out the randomness and irrationality of history? What does Chang, who belongs to everywhere and nowhere, tell us about the collective modern experience of the Chinese worlds?

If Chang herself had anything to say about how histories are made, she would tell us, as she did in one story after the other in the 1940s, that history is a fatalistic march toward destruction. In the preface to the second edition of the short story collection *Romances*, she observed with some melancholy that

> our age plunges forward and is already well on its way to collapse, while a bigger catastrophe looms. The day will come when our culture, whether interpreted as vanity or as sublimation, will all be in the past. If "desolate" is so common a word in my vocabulary, it is because [desolation] has always haunted my thoughts.

These statements are certainly not meant to be read as a footnote to a nihilistic worldview. Nor should Chang be held exempt from this so-called self-destructive history, in which she played a commemorated, if tragic, role. If we read these statements together with her stories in *Romances*, they clearly convey Chang's overall understanding of modernity as violence and trauma. This dark worldview struck a chord with the collective Chinese experience in the twentieth century, but was rejected by most canonical social and literary histories of Chang's times. A misfit in this light, Chang voiced her protest by writing an alternative view of Chinese modernity and literary history that was at odds with the official May Fourth account of this experience.

Chang's stories examine the everydayness of violence and trauma, as it is played out in the psychology of ordinary people on a scale unaccounted for in canonical histories. Focusing largely on displaced and disempowered individuals, especially women, Chang situates her characters in complex love affairs and intricate familial relationships, often set against the backdrop of China's transition from tradition to modernity or the devastation of the second Sino-Japanese War. Though romantic relations often occupy the center of these tales, the stories themselves do not fit the mold of romance or sentimental fiction in the Western sense. In Chang's eyes, they were realist depictions of "ordinary people who can serve more accurately than heroes as a measure of the times" ("Writing of One's Own"). Admittedly, the realism that Chang claimed for herself differs significantly from the canonical realism upheld and practiced by mostly leftist Chinese writers in the 1930s and 1940s. Chang did not view these exploited characters as members of the proletarian class. She also did not subscribe to the political ideals of revolution or nationalism that drove most leftist realist experiments. From the outset, Chang expressed her empathy with the "ordinary people" by drawing from a different source of inspiration: the popular fiction of the Mandarin Ducks and Butterflies school and the classical tradition of Chinese vernacular fiction as represented by the classic eighteenth-century novel *Dream of the Red Chamber*. Her emulation of traditional-style fiction led some to criticize her for not engaging overtly with major political themes and social issues. The literary establishment in China received Chang's early works with ambivalence, though her attentiveness to formal technique and language received much praise.

In actuality, Chang was far from apolitical. Her writings exhibit an acute sensitivity toward issues of ethics and power, as they manifest in both subtle interpersonal relations and national and historical crises. In "The Golden Cangue," for instance, she focuses on uncovering the mode of oppression in domestic power struggles in an aristocratic family. The female protagonist, Cao Qiqiao, who first appears before us as an innocent young bride who married into the family, gradually hardens into an embittered widow and abusive mother, as her former victimhood reproduces itself as sadistic agency. While exposing the injustice inflicted on the "ordinary people," Chang never loses sight of the fact that victims are equally capable of violence and cruelty. Thus, although she sometimes offers happy endings like a popular novelist, her nuanced explorations of the darkness and desires of the human psyche generally set her works apart from most market-driven popular literature.

Chang is an outlier of modern Chinese literary history in yet another sense. She was bilingual and wrote in both Chinese and English. Her earliest works were a number of essays that she wrote in English for the newspaper *Shanghai Times* and the magazine *XXth Century* in the early

1940s. Even though these essays were written with an eye to Anglophone readers who knew little about Chinese culture and customs, Chang's unique insights into Chinese culture and cross-cultural communication were evident in a number of them. While her short stories were, in contrast, written entirely in Chinese, they still exhibit similar distinct bicultural sensibilities. In the romantic stories such as "Ashes of Incense" and "Red Rose, White Rose," for instance, Chang is particularly attentive to the power imbalance in East-West intercultural exchange and adept at describing the subtle and complex feelings that underlay interracial relations in colonial cities.

After a brief two-year sojourn in Hong Kong, Chang's bilingual writings took a turn when she immigrated to the United States. Eager to attract an audience beyond the Chinese worlds at the time of the Cold War, she collaborated with the United States Information Agency, whose mission was to enhance American influence in the global context through cultural exchange and propaganda. This collaboration produced the Chinese translation of Ralph Waldo Emerson's (1803–1882) essays and Ernest Hemingway's (1899–1961) novel *The Old Man and the Sea*, as well as two English-language novels with some explicit anticommunist passages: *The Rice-Sprout Song* and *Naked Earth*. These two English novels implicate her, somewhat unfavorably, in the geopolitics of Cold War history, but they also continue to demonstrate her consistency in giving voice to the sufferings of ordinary people. Chang's knack for details in the everyday allowed her to paint richly textured pictures of Chinese life, which somehow exceeded both the geopolitical conditioning of the Chinese writer during the Cold War and the Orientalist abstractions of things Chinese.

After immigrating to the United States, Chang also rewrote some of her earlier Chinese works in English. In spite of her excellent command of English, most of her efforts to reach out to English readers beyond China ended in partial success or total failure. Chang chose to live a life of obscurity and voluntary exile in the several decades before her death in 1995. Yet her posthumously published works in Chinese and English, namely *Xiao tuanyuan* (Little reunion), *The Fall of the Pagoda*, and *The Book of Change*, show that she remained preoccupied with the thematics of Chinese life and worlds of a time gone by. Just like in her early stories, her imagination was fueled much more readily by the haunting of the past than the promise of the future.

Although the popularity of her works among English-language readers cannot match the influence her stories exerted in the Chinese-language worlds, it would be simplistic to think of her writings in the United States as utterly valueless in the context of her overall oeuvre. A frustrated immigrant writer trapped in an abyss of cultural and linguistic differences, Chang was nevertheless also in the vanguard when it came to experimentation with bilingual and bicultural writing. Chang's writings as a whole question the linguistic purity underlying most nationalistic understandings of "Chineseness" and Chinese literary history. Her bilingual writings offer a glimpse into a neglected dimension of modern Chinese literary history, consisting of literary works written in nonstandard Chinese or not written in Chinese at all, by bicultural, diasporic, immigrant, and non-Chinese writers, written and circulated in locales beyond China proper. Chang's works anticipate this unruly and global cartography of Chinese literature, and thus continue to be relevant to us today.

BIBLIOGRAPHY: Han Banqing, *The Sing-Song Girls of Shanghai*, trans. Eileen Chang (New York, 2007). Eileen Chang, *The Book of Change* (Hong Kong, 2010). Eileen Chang, *The Fall of the Pagoda* (Hong Kong, 2010). Eileen Chang, *The Rice-Sprout Song* (New York, 1954). Eileen Chang, *Rouge of the North* (London, 1967). Zhang Ailing, *Chi di zhi lian* (Hong Kong, 1954; later published as *Naked Earth* [New York, 2015]). Zhang Ailing, *Chuanqi* (Shanghai, 1944). Zhang Ailing, *Hong lou meng yan* (Taipei, 1976). Zhang Ailing, *Liu yan* (Shanghai, 1944). Zhang Ailing, *Xiao tuanyuan* (Beijing, 2009).

SHUANG SHEN

1952 · OCTOBER 14

"Patent Approved: Lin Yutang's Chinese Typewriter Goes Global"

Salvaging Chinese Script and Designing the Mingkwai Typewriter

In April 1946, Lin Yutang (1895–1976) filed an application with the US Patent Office in New York for his invention, a Chinese typewriter. Unlike other previous attempts, this one promised to be truly revolutionary. Its keyboard carried not merely the customary twenty-six letters of the Latin alphabet, but sixty-four fragments derived from Chinese characters, capable of generating ninety thousand characters in print. The idea alone took Lin years to develop. It cost him several failures and an important friendship with Pearl S. Buck (1892–1973) and her husband, Richard Walsh (1886–1960), who had invited him to come to the United States to write as China's voice in America. Contrary to his success as a writer, the typewriter venture left Lin with a $120,000 (equal to $1.4 million in 2014) debt, but it was well worth it. The Mingkwai—"clear and quick"— typewriter ushered the Chinese script into the then-cutting-edge era of teletype, radio typewriters, and Linotype machines. More than that, it catapulted the Chinese language to the world stage, landing it in the midst of Cold War military research, cryptography and machine translation, and China's own language wars.

Not even Lin could have expected his obsession to have such an eventful afterlife. The most renowned bilingual Anglophone Chinese author of fiction and essays of the first half of the twentieth century, Lin harbored a long-standing passion for the Chinese language. Apart from considerations of how a given Chinese character might have sounded at different times and places, or what the best way to transcribe and categorize might be, Lin was set on transforming the Chinese written script into a modern science and technology. This was consonant with the writing reforms of the late nineteenth century. Western missionaries led the way by introducing new systems of transcription as a means to quickly learn Chinese and spread the gospel in a heathen tongue. These precedents were followed by the efforts of native Chinese to remedy the high rate of illiteracy by devising easier, sound-based writing systems. In the name of radical scientific objectivity, some of these early Chinese reformers proposed to do away with the use of Chinese characters altogether.

By Lin's time, the difficulty of the Chinese written language was seen as an impediment to modernization in general. As the tide of nationalism rose, however, abolishing the Chinese script was out of the question. Attention turned instead to how to improve and salvage the existing system, which had been time consuming to learn and even harder to master. Under the growing pressure to absorb massive volumes of foreign knowledge through translation, to update China's traditional canon of learning, and to secure the nation's advantage in international relations, the Chinese language was ill equipped to meet the demands of the modern era. As leading intellectual and reformer Hu Shi (1891–1962) once commented, the problem of the Chinese script was the challenge of all challenges. Hu also acknowledged that it was not the kind of work that high-minded intellectuals wished to undertake, owing to its technical tedium and laboriousness, but nevertheless insisted that it was a vital and indispensable endeavor. Basic tasks such as reorganizing and revamping the heritage of "national learning" (*guoxue*), let alone looking up a character in a dictionary with ease, depended on this gateway technology. What could be done with the Chinese script therefore had massive implications for the flow and control of information and commerce, which in turn translated into the protection of national ownership over an increasingly vital infrastructure.

Lin, along with others, put his mind to the challenge. While the Mingkwai typewriter was a discrete outcome, its conceptual roots go deeper. Before Lin made his writer's fame with his trademark humor and elegant style in China and America during the 1930s, he was embroiled in China's own fraught process of national language standardization. Along with the famous linguists Zhao Yuanren (1892–1982) and Qian Xuan-tong (1887–1939), he was a vociferous defender of National Language Romanization (Gwoyeu Romatzyh), an alphabetic system derived from the northern-based official Mandarin dialect. Their main rival was Qu Qiubai's (1899–1935) Soviet-inspired Latinization system of regional dialects (Latinxua Sin Wenz). Lin continued his research into traditional phonology and dialectology, seeking inspiration in China's rich philological past, as well as modern Western linguistic science. He obtained a PhD in historical phonology from the University of Leipzig in 1923, with a dissertation on traditional Chinese phonology. He was critical of what he learned. Objecting to the indiscriminate import of available models of easy English spelling, he did not embrace transplanted remedies. When I. A. Richards (1893–1979) tried to break into China's pedagogical market with his and C. K. Ogden's (1889–1957) *Basic English* during the first half of the 1930s, the system's paltry 850-word vocabulary struck Lin as insufficient and colonial in its mission. He believed, instead, in China's own path to romanization and simplified usage.

Beginning in the 1910s, Lin began to develop important views on the material medium of the Chinese script. Two short essays in 1917 and 1918 on the problems of traditional Chinese lexicography first broached the subject of how to classify, arrange, and retrieve Chinese characters according to empirical and predictable laws. His views inaugurated the race for the optimal "character retrieval method," a bottom-up movement that raged from the 1920s through the 1940s and attracted hundreds of proposals and schemes from participants at all strata of society. At the same time, China was undergoing one of its most politically tumultuous and divisive periods, yet somehow the movement grew into a unifying national pastime. Factory workers, librarians, officials, amateurs, linguists, and hacks jumped in with enthusiasm, if only to distract themselves from the bleak reality of the present; the country had barely recovered from the end of dynastic rule, was suffering the growing pains of a young nation, and was already torn between a civil war and the Japanese occupation that began during the Pacific portion of World War II. Some schemes were more credible than others, but Lin maintained his lead as the first mover. While others continued to copy and improve on his original proposal, he turned his attention back to the Chinese typewriter. His original proposal of parsing and retrieving Chinese characters according to new definitions of character components, rather than relying on whole characters or traditional radicals, was an unprecedented breakthrough. It was also the cornerstone for the development of the Mingkwai typewriter's operating keyboard—yet more hard times lay ahead.

Between the time Lin filed the patent application and the time it was approved in October 1952, he launched numerous campaigns and interviews to showcase his innovation. His daughter and later biographer, Lin Taiyi (1926–2003), was with him for the publicity photos and live demonstrations. She was the typist, while Lin, posed to look relaxed, stood over her with a pipe in hand. What happened in 1947, however, nearly shattered all confidence. That summer, Remington Typewriter Company in Manhattan expressed an interest in seeing Lin's prototype, having failed to produce a Chinese phonetic script keyboard in 1921. Lin carefully wrapped his typewriter and hurried out one afternoon in the pouring rain for the interview. In front of ten of Remington's top executives in the conference room, Lin explained the principles behind the machine and its significance. He then cued his daughter to begin the demonstration. Lin Taiyi, she later recalled, turned on the machine. Under everyone's watchful eyes, she pressed a key. But the typewriter did nothing. She pressed a second key, and still no response. The meeting room was dead silent. No pin dropped, but the sounds of the keystrokes grew feeble as doubts rose. Whispers were heard around the long conference table. Lin himself then tried typing on the machine, only to confirm his utter failure and embarrassment.

The typewriter malfunctioned due to a fixable mechanical error. Setbacks, indeed, were wholly unexceptional in the history of Chinese typewriting. Even when perfectly functional, one idea would soon be outdone by another. American Presbyterian missionary Devello Zelotos Sheffield's (1841–1913) 1897 Chinese Type-writer was the first and the most cumbersome. Resembling a cross between a gramophone and a modern-day disc jockey's turntable, it was a workout to operate. Subsequent Chinese typewriters were made by Chinese abroad, as well as in China. Zhou Houkun (ca. 1889–?) and Shu Zhendong, successively hired by the Chinese print industry's major player, Commercial Press in Shanghai, were once household names. Under the aegis of the press and building on Zhou's prototype, Shu's typewriter was displayed at the Sesquicentennial International Exposition, a world fair, in Philadelphia in 1926 and won a modest award. Without such powerful backing, other inventors looked to gain an edge via alternative means. Notoriously, amateur inventors such as Yu Bingqi came under scrutiny for pirating a Japanese typewriter. He was later doubly persecuted for being a Japanese collaborator, however, by virtue of his piracy. These native examples were not cited in Lin's patent application. He drew from, instead, the precedents set by those Chinese who, like him, had significant exposure to the mechanics of Western typewriter building and philological principles. These included government foreign attaché Pan Francis Shah, a student attending Columbia University named Heuen Chi (Qi Xuan), and Chinese teletype inventor Kao Chung-chin (Gao Zhongqin)—one of Lin's closest competitors.

Lin kept up the publicity campaigns while the patent was pending and subsequently ran out of money. In a desperate appeal in early spring 1947, Lin contacted Pearl S. Buck and her husband, the owner of the publishing company that printed Lin's English-language works, and professed that he needed just a little monetary help to see the project through. Buck promptly responded with regrets, a refusal that left Lin in dire straits and created a noticeable rift in their long friendship. In 1951, Lin officially sold the copyright to the Mergenthaler Linotype Company for $25,000.

Due to high overhead costs, the Mingkwai typewriter never went into mass production. Its commercial failure, however, marked the beginning of an unexpected afterlife. Around the same time, the United States Air Force inaugurated a research project to investigate the possibility of machine-automated translation, an endeavor that would last into the 1970s. Though the target language was primarily Russian during the Cold War, the air force's interest in natural language processing, especially those with complex semantic units and syntax, led them to the Chinese language. After multiple inquiries, they concluded that they needed Lin's indexical keyboard as a prototype for further research. They then handed the project over to the International Business Machines Corporation (IBM).

In collaboration with Sinologists at various American universities, the IBM Research Center pursued the project with vigor, beginning in 1960. In summer 1963, IBM unveiled its own "Sinowriter" in an issue of *Scientific American*, citing concurrent research in Russian-English machine translation. A team of researchers, under the directorship of Gilbert W. King, had developed a system for photographic storage and optical information retrieval that would greatly enhance the speed and memory capacity of machines for storing and retrieving characters. Essentially, they had a way to augment processing power but lacked the proper keyboard to fully utilize it. Missing was a Chinese keyboard that people could learn relatively quickly and without necessarily knowing the Chinese language. Importantly, Lin's promise for the Mingkwai typewriter was that anyone could pick it up on the spot. It involved a three-step process. First, the operator, who need not know how to read Chinese at all, locates the top and bottom of a given print sample of a character. Second, he or she finds the corresponding keys on the keyboard and presses both keys down simultaneously. At this point, based on Lin's ingenious statistical analyses from his previous work with character classification schemes, a range of no more than five to eight qualified characters will appear in a visual indicator window near the top of the typewriter. Characters in this visual window, or "magic viewer," are exposed type fonts from the internal cylinder that have been put into proper alignment based on a match between the first two keys. Once the desired character has been visually selected from the listed choices, the typist then strikes one of eight additional keys—numbered one through eight—that corresponds to the number assigned to the chosen character. In a similar layout, present-day Chinese language software is programmed to guess the character you want, as you type in the input, by predicting a list of possible candidates in a horizontal display window. Anyone who has even dabbled in the language would see the unmistakable legacy of Lin's original visual selection device.

Lin's character retrieval scheme provided a crucial access point for the Chinese language to connect with the outside world. It entered the world stage through the back door. Such is the anonymity that any idea ahead of its time can expect to suffer. The notion of abandoning the old systems of radical classification continues to have immense implications for the current digital age. It gave rise to a new conceptualization of the structural logic of the Chinese script, where each part played the role, as it were, of a letter in an alphabet. The Chinese script can thus be taken apart and reassembled as the finite, basic units of a codable and decodable language, in addition to having made its debut on a computer screen.

The Chinese retrieval system was the success of alphabetization without the alphabet, romanization without Rome. In the end, it realized the twin imperatives of modernity, defined at the beginning of the twentieth century as having both "Mr. Science" and "Mr. Democracy." Lin's typewriter was a sober, scientific take on the culturally laden symbol that is the Chinese language. It was a machine for every man and woman—beyond the circle of native users. Compared to China's efforts to romanize Mandarin via Pinyin and other phonetic systems, the reconceptualization of the logographic structure was the truly revolutionary linguistic reform. In the end, you can take the Chinese script out of the alphabet, but you can't take the alphabet out of Chinese.

JING TSU

LATE 1953

Lao She, famous American author, purportedly dies.

Lao She and America

Sometime in late 1953, Pearl S. Buck (1892–1973) became very worried about her good friend, the Chinese novelist Lao She (1899–1966). Buck and her husband, Richard Walsh (1896–1960), had served as sponsors for Lao She when he visited the United States in 1945, on the invitation of the State Department. The three had met in Shanghai in the mid-1930s; Buck had read *Rickshaw Boy*, which she admired, and Lao She had read *The Good Earth*, which he admired in turn. With the establishment of the People's Republic of China in late 1949, Lao She had decided to return home. Buck disliked communism and socialism. She urged Lao She to stay in America—she was confident that the US government would grant him citizenship if he wanted it. Buck worried about the safety of creative writers within the new Chinese Communist state. Lao She laughed off her concerns. He looked forward to returning, and felt sure that he would occupy a position of importance under Mao Zedong's (1893–1976) regime. At first, Lao She's letters from China to his old American friends were encouraging. Things were good. Conditions in the country were safe and inviting. The people were happy. But, as relations between the United States and China began to deteriorate, his letters became sparse. By 1953, all communication from Lao She had ceased. Buck grew very worried indeed. In a letter to her friend Ida Pruitt (1888–1985), Lao She's former collaborator, Buck suggested that there could only be one explanation: Lao She was dead. The state had killed him.

In four short years, Lao She had become an American literary celebrity. He had become famous in America before he had even stepped foot in the country. In the early 1940s, Buck helped to commission a translation of his major realist novel, *Luotuo Xiangzi* (Camel Xiangzi). *Luotuo Xiangzi*, originally published in 1937, was a popular and critical success in China and remains a classic of Chinese realist fiction. The book was translated by Evan King (1906–1968), a former US State Department official, given the English title *Rickshaw Boy*, and published by Reynal and Hitchcock in 1945. It became an unlikely best seller. The American public was hungry for all things Chinese in the early 1940s as a result of the war, which found the two nations allies, and Lao She's friend, Lin Yutang (1895–1976), had paved the way for the reception of *Rickshaw Boy* with a series of best-selling English-language American novels such as *A Moment in Peking* (1939). With the end of the war in sight, the US government was eager to shore up relations with the Chinese, and sought to invite a popular Chinese author to serve as a "guest of the state." They queried Buck and John Fairbank (1907–1991), who would later become an eminent Harvard historian. Both Buck and Fairbank recommended their mutual friend, Lao She, and the recent popularity of *Rickshaw Boy* made the government's decision all the more easy. An invite was extended.

Despite increasingly identifying with the leftist camp in Chinese politics, Lao She immediately accepted. Diplomatic relations between the United States and the Chinese Communists were still somewhat cordial in 1945, yet his easy acquiescence is still surprising. Why was he so eager to come to America? One doubts that many of his other left-wing colleagues, such as Mao Dun (1896–1981), would have so quickly accepted this invitation or even accepted it at all. Lao She's letter of application to the State Department's exchange of persons program reveals an unexpected fondness for America. "America is a great country," he writes. "It has a proud and venerable tradition of democracy.... While still a fledging modern state, China could learn much from this tradition," Lao She concludes. None of these phrases come off as contrived or fake. There is a deep earnestness to his prose. If the US state officials who read this essay were convinced of Lao She's admiration of American democracy, it is because the person who wrote such statements truly believed in them. His application buzzes with enthusiasm.

Within ten months, Lao She was living in New York City. He was set up to work with Pruitt, the distinguished author and Sinologist, to cotranslate his novel *Four Generations under One Roof* into English, but the work quickly became much more than simple translation. Pruitt and Lao She would sit in a room together; Lao She would read out loud a sentence from his original manuscript in Chinese; Pruitt, who spoke fluent Chinese, would jot down the substance of that sentence in English on paper; Lao She would look at the sentence and make corrections to Pruitt's English, often significantly altering her language. This process would go on for hours. Days and nights were heavy with work and flashes of inspiration. Their collaboration—a throwback to "team translations" between Chinese and

Western writers during the late Qing—was no mere mechanical rendering of Chinese into English. Meaning was created, new ideas projected, and the original text became altered through this process. Somewhere within their endless give and take of *this is what I mean, no this is what I mean, let me try to find the right word, ah yes, this is what I mean, yes this,* a new work of literature was produced. The end product was called *The Yellow Storm,* a translation of *Four Generations under One Roof* by the Chinese author Lao She, with the help of Ida Pruitt. But it was much more. It was an act of collaboration.

The translated novel was a commercial success. The publisher was eager for a follow-up. Lao She had begun work on a new novel, *The Drum Singers,* and he thought that once again he could work with Pruitt to render the text in English. Yet their relationship had begun to sour. Lao She began to complain to Buck that Pruitt was starting to take too aggressive a hand in their cotranslation. She had some essentializing ideas about "China"—what we might today call "Orientalism." In one moving letter to his editor, Lao She describes his desire to write a novel that somehow conveyed a vision of the world as "the coolie sees it," in the language of the "coolie" himself. He wanted to appropriate and transform the Orientalist notion of Chinese suffering, the very idea of "the coolie" itself. Pruitt, a missionary's daughter, was in love with "old Beijing." The two couldn't see eye to eye anymore. As for Pruitt, she felt that she deserved more credit for her contribution. Indeed, she informed the publisher that she wanted top billing on the next novel she translated with Lao She because what she did was "much more than just translation." Pruitt imagined herself as a creative artist in her own right. She did not want to play second fiddle to Lao She. She saw herself as Lao She's equal.

The partnership was dissolved. However, Lao She still held high hopes for the American literary scene. He had grown intrigued by the idea of "American democracy" in the 1930s, and he saw in American literature the wellspring of that idealist tradition. With the help of his friend Agnes Smedley (1892–1950), the left-wing journalist and novelist, he garnered an invitation to spend a few months at the Yaddo Writer's Colony in upstate New York. The first month was pleasant: mornings were resplendent with sunshine and quiet time for writing, while the afternoons and evenings were robust with delicious meals and exciting conversation with fellow writers. But his time at Yaddo was quickly spoiled. It was the dawn of the

Red Scare in America, and Robert Lowell (1917–1977), the eminent US poet and, later, Cold Warrior, decided to lay siege to the leftist writers at Yaddo, whom he branded anti-American "Communists." Smedley became his main target. In Lowell's view, Smedley's writings contaminated literature with politics. Ever the high modernist, Lowell espoused a purist view of art in which works of literature embody instances of individual genius independent from politics or social context. The irony, of course, is that Lowell was quite happy to use this ideology as a political weapon to discredit the rising popularity of Soviet theories of literature. In any case, Smedley had to go. Lowell called in the CIA to spy on leftist writers at Yaddo such as Smedley; her friend Lao She was caught in the cross fire. In perhaps the most surreal moment in Lao She's time in the United States, an unnamed CIA agent wrote a brief report on meeting him. The agent identifies Lao She as "Mr. Shoe," a Chinese author of some distinction.

The newly formed People's Republic of China warmly invited Lao She to come back to China in late 1949, and he accepted. Always the cultural activist, he felt that the new Chinese state held great promise, particularly for the revival of Chinese culture, and quickly began writing again in Chinese. A number of essays and stories in accord with the typical spirit of Chinese literature at the time were published in the early 1950s, and Lao She joined the swelling chorus of leftist writers who criticized the United States as an imperial, capitalist nation, but he still, for the time being, maintained his contacts with the United States. Publicly, he castigated the US literary scene; privately he wrote warm, personal letters to Buck and Walsh. He even continued to accept royalties from *The Yellow Storm*, which, as he told Buck, helped to finance the refurbishing of his Beijing home. Perhaps Lao She was simply playing the role expected of him in China. But there is too much earnestness in his anti-American writings from this period, and there is too much sincerity in his letters to his American friends. Perhaps he was just torn.

Ties back to America soon became unsustainable in the political climate within China, and Lao She suspended all contact with Buck and others by the mid-1950s. The Americans assumed the worst. Yet during the next decade, Lao She lived quite well in China and experienced significant literary success. Did he miss his friends across the Pacific? We don't know. He never again mentions those friends or his time in America in letters or in any other form of writing. The past seemed expunged from memory; it never existed. But we know that Lao She was and remained torn. His writings from this period are saturated with an ambivalence about the new Chinese political regime, and he spent significant time in Hong Kong after the Communist revolution, returning only after a request from Zhou Enlai.

Tragedy eventually caught up with Lao She in the mid-1960s. At the very onset of the Cultural Revolution, the esteemed author became a target of the state, and was subjected to severe persecution. In August 1966, he purportedly threw himself into a lake in Beijing, where he subsequently drowned. Lao She, the famous Chinese author, had suffered an ignominious end—not unlike his double, Lao She, the famous American author. Both had been murdered by the Maoist state.

What were his last thoughts? What memories raced through his mind before the water filled his lungs and his consciousness faded forever? Did he think about his time in America? Did he feel any fondness for that time abroad? Did he have any regrets for leaving? Our conjectures over his final thoughts double as an intriguing counterfactual history. If Lao She had stayed in America and become an American citizen, he would have likely remained an important American author. Perhaps he would have joined or even led (he was inclined to leadership) the emerging Asian American political and literary movement in the 1960s and 1970s. We might today remember him in the same breath as such important Asian American writers as Maxine Hong Kingston or Frank Chin. The counterfactual possibilities are tantalizing, all the more so because Lao She's death in China was needless. He could have stayed in America, but he deliberately decided to leave. Lao She had come to deplore America. That much we know. If we remember his time in America and ponder the counterfactual possibilities, we should always remember the tragedy of his decision: between an unhappy life in America and a tragic death in China. The rest of the story sinks to the bottom of the lake.

BIBLIOGRAPHY: C. T. Hsia, *A History of Modern Chinese Fiction* (Bloomington, IN, 1999). Lau Shaw [Lao She], *Rickshaw Boy*, trans. Evan King (New York, 1945). David Der-wei Wang, *Fictional Realism in 20th Century China: Mao Dun, Lao She, Sheng Congwen* (New York, 1992).

RICHARD JEAN SO

1954 · SEPTEMBER 25–NOVEMBER 2

Married to a Heavenly Immortal is performed with great success
at the East China Theater Festival.

The Emergence of Regional Opera on the National Stage

From late September to early November 1954, Shanghai hosted the East
China Theater Festival. At this event, the Huangmei opera *Married to
a Heavenly Immortal*, one of the plays submitted by Anhui Province,
obtained a string of first prizes, and it was soon decided that the play was
to be turned into a movie. That movie (directed by Shi Hui [1915–1957],
who was to commit suicide in 1957 as a victim of the Anti-Rightist Movement) was released in early 1956 and became by far the biggest box office
hit of the 1950s: by the end of 1958, the movie had been seen by more than
140 million spectators, many of whom had watched it multiple times. It
also enjoyed considerable popularity outside the People's Republic of
China, and even stimulated filmmakers in Hong Kong and elsewhere to
produce a large number of musicals, known as Huangmei tune movies.
During the Cultural Revolution, *Married to a Heavenly Immortal* was
condemned as "a poisonous weed," but when it was released again in the
early 1980s, it drew huge crowds as before, and some of the arias from
the movie have remained popular to this very day. The life story of the
play's leading lady, Yan Fengying (1930–1968), who was hounded to death
during the Cultural Revolution, has been adapted into novels, television
biopics, and even its own Huangmei opera.

Nothing predicted the immense success of *Married to a Heavenly
Immortal*. Few people outside the Anqing region were even aware of the
existence of Huangmei opera before 1949, and the few attempts to perform
Huangmei opera in Shanghai before that date had not met with success.
Moreover, the story of *Married to a Heavenly Immortal* was based on the
legend of the filial son Dong Yong. Every Chinese with only a smatter-
ing of literacy would know that story, as Dong Yong was featured in the
Twenty-Four Exemplars of Filial Piety, a primer that was widely used in
late imperial times and beyond. Those who did not know the story from
that source would know it from retellings in popular songs and ballads,
from adaptations for the stage, or from paintings on temple walls. But filial
piety, the foundational virtue of Confucian society, was seen by modern

Chinese reformers and revolutionaries as the root of China's backwardness: it demanded, they said, an unquestioning obedience of the younger generation to their elders. Filial piety was decried as the backbone of the traditional family system that prohibited young men and women from following their hearts in choosing a mate. As romantic love came to replace filial piety as a foundational value in the early decades of the twentieth century, "free love" (the freedom to choose one's own marriage partner) became the ideal for all progressive young people, and novels such as Ba Jin's (1904–2005) *Family*, which described the multiple evils of the traditional family system, became hugely successful. Whereas some other traditional stories, such as the legend of the White Snake and the romance of Liang Shanbo and Zhu Yingtai, two stories of transgressive passion, could easily be adapted to serve the modernizing and nation-building project, the legend of the filial son Dong Yong was a very unlikely choice for such an adaptation indeed.

The development of the legend of Dong Yong can be followed for a period of two millennia. The Dong Yong of legend may perhaps derive from a certain Dong Yong who, in the earliest years of the Eastern Han dynasty (25–220 CE), regained a noble rank that his father earlier had lost by means of his conspicuous display of immoral behavior. By the second century, Dong Yong was renowned for the filial piety he displayed toward his father during the latter's life, but in the succeeding centuries it was his filial piety following his father's death that ensured his fame: in order to provide his father with a proper funeral, it was said, Dong Yong had sold himself into servitude for three years as a bonded laborer. The *Twenty-Four Examplars of Filial Piety* provides the following account of this act and its divine reward:

> Dong Yong of the Han was so poor that when his father died he sold himself into servitude and buried him with borrowed money. When he set out to repay his debt through labor, he met a woman on the road. She offered to become his wife, and together they arrived at his master's house. The latter ordered her to weave three hundred bolts of double-threaded silk, and then they could go back. She completed the task in just one month. When on the way back home they arrived at the spot where they had met in the shade of a scholar tree, she said goodbye to Yong and disappeared.

To bury his father he needed to borrow money;
Out on the road he ran into an immortal beauty.
Weaving silk she paid off his debt to his master:
His filial piety managed to move heaven above!

While this would remain the canonical version of the story, later versions of the legend soon turned the "immortal beauty" into the Weaving Maiden. But that became problematical when still later versions made her into Dong Yong's wife and the mother of his son, because the Weaving Maiden was well known for her love for Buffalo Boy, so the "immortal beauty" is also often identified as Seventh Sister, a younger sister of Weaving Maiden.

As long as the legend circulated in narrative form, it could be told from a purely male perspective. From such a perspective, the "immortal beauty" could be treated as an object: a gift from the Jade Emperor to reward a filial son. Once the legend was adapted for the stage, however, the conventions of *chuanqi* plays of the Ming and Qing, as a form of opera, required that the male and female protagonists be given equal opportunity to declare their mutual love in song. From that moment onward, the legend of Dong Yong and Weaving Maiden became a tale of true but thwarted love, because she is forced to leave the man she has learned to love at the end of the one hundred days the Jade Emperor has set for their time together. No full text of a Ming dynasty play on Dong Yong and Weaving Maiden has come down to us, but the preserved scenes show that the playwrights greatly elaborated the comical scene of their first meeting—Weaving Maiden, sent down to earth, forces herself on an unwilling Dong Yong—and the pathetic scene of the final parting, in which she doesn't know how to break the news to her happy lover. The play was a popular item in the repertoire of many varieties of local theater. In many of these plays, the landlord who gives Dong Yong the loan marries his daughter to Dong Yong upon Seventh Sister's departure for heaven, and comic relief is provided by his son, who unsuccessfully tries to seduce Seventh Sister.

This story of the love of Dong Yong and Weaving Maiden was also popular with the mostly rural audiences of Huangmei opera in the early decades of the twentieth century. During the first half of the twentieth century, Huangmei opera had barely started to emerge from an earlier phase in which its repertoire mostly consisted of short skits, often quite sexually explicit, on the affairs of young country lasses and farmhands. But even while Huangmei opera developed into a more mature drama genre and started to appeal to an urban audience in Anqing, its music remained quite simple, and the accompanying instruments were mostly limited to drums and clappers.

Following the establishment of the People's Republic of China, the situation quickly changed. Distrusting the pre-1949 world of the commercial theater and its patrons, and emboldened by its experiences in reforming both Peking opera and local skits during its Yan'an years, the new government initiated a theater reform movement that envisioned a reform of content, people, and organization: plays that were condemned as feudal, unpatriotic, or obscene were banned; actors and actresses were subjected to thought reform; and theater owners and impresarios were replaced by state-owned and collective theater companies, each with its own party committee. Local authorities were encouraged to emphasize the development of local forms of theater and to meet the need for a new repertoire by revising popular items in the old repertoire in such a way that they would meet the ideological needs of the new era. To showcase these revised plays, national and regional theater festivals were organized, starting with a national theater festival in the fall of 1952 in Beijing. Huangmei opera was not included in this event, but owing to the positive reception of certain revised Huangmei opera skits (and single scenes of larger plays) in Shanghai, the Anhui provincial authorities decided to establish an Anhui Provincial Huangmei Opera Company, headquartered in Hefei. Despite protests from Anqing, the best actors and actresses were assigned to this company; directors were brought in to enhance the quality of acting, while composers were mobilized to develop Huangmei opera music. When a date had been set for the East China Regional Theater Festival, the provincial authorities decided that one of the submissions from Anhui would be *Married to a Heavenly Immortal*. A new version of the play, based on a collectively revised script written down by Lu Hongfei (1924–2007), had been performed in Anqing in the fall of 1953 to considerable success. Throughout the summer of 1954, script, music, acting, and scenery were further improved and revised. The role of Dong Yong was entrusted to the experienced actor Wang Shaofang (1920–1986), while the role of Seventh Sister was played by the young actress Yan Fengying. Their superb performance and the melodious nature of Huangmei opera music mesmerized audiences, and would continue to do so for many years.

In order to make *Married to a Heavenly Immortal* acceptable in the new political climate, Lu Hongfei and all others who had a hand in the revision of the play made drastic changes to the story and the characterization. Dong Yong, who had been a down-on-his-luck student in the traditional version, had been turned into a handsome and honest peasant, whose sufferings derive not from his own decisions but from the structure of society—his filial piety is barely mentioned. The central character of the play is now Seventh Sister, who does not descend to earth because she is ordered to do so by her father, the Jade Emperor, but secretly escapes from heaven (which she experiences as a prison) because she has fallen in love with Dong Yong—she will only return to heaven after a hundred days on earth because the heavenly authorities threaten to pulverize her husband. The landlord who provided the loan to Dong Yong is not a kind benefactor anymore, but a rapacious representative of his class who tries by every means to exploit the couple—fortunately, he is outwitted by Seventh Sister at every turn. The landlord's daughter is dropped from the play, and his son is reduced to a foolish sidekick because the salacious humor in his attempts to seduce Seventh Sister were anathema to the new political pundits. The many scenes in the traditional play following Seventh Sister's return to heaven (Dong Yong's return to his benefactor, his presentation of the brocades woven by Seventh Sister to the emperor, his appointment to high office, Seventh Sister's delivery of their son, and his marriage to the landlord's daughter) were all removed. In short, *Married to a Heavenly Immortal* was rewritten into yet another play about the doomed struggle for free love of young men and women in traditional society, but this time without the heavy use of ideological jargon and almost without any explicit moralizing. The high point of the play now was the opening of the final scene, when Dong Yong and Seventh Sister, having served out their term, are on their way to Dong Yong's cottage and are looking forward to a life of shared labor and love, inspiring them to give voice in a duet to their high hopes for the future. But this happy mood soon turns to high pathos when Seventh Sister (during a temporary absence from stage by Dong Yong) is ordered to immediately return to heaven by an angry father who has discovered her absence.

When the play was adapted for film, the direction was entrusted to Shi Hui, one of the most gifted actors and directors of the 1940s. From the outset, Shi was determined not to produce a documentary. While broadly adhering to the outline of the play and departing in many details from the script prepared by Sang Hu (1916–2004), he produced a "fairy-tale feature film with music and dance." Shi made good use of special effects to stress the fairy-tale elements and enhanced the melodious nature of Huangmei opera music by doing away with the drum. While the political message might have been crystal clear to Lu Hongfei, Sang Hu, and Shi, that message, which was implicit, may well have escaped the majority of the audience, who will have enjoyed the movie first of all as a tragic love story. The success of the movie turned Wang Shaofang and Yan Fengying into national stars overnight, and made Huangmei opera one of the most popular forms of regional opera throughout China.

BIBLIOGRAPHY: Wilt L. Idema, *Filial Piety and Its Divine Rewards: The Legend of Dong Yong and Weaving Maiden, with Related Texts* (Indianapolis, IN, 2009). Wilt L. Idema, *The Metamorphosis of "Tianxian pei": Local Opera under the Revolution (1949–1956)* (Hong Kong, 2015). Wilt L. Idema, "Old Tales for New Times: Some Comments on the Cultural Translation of China's Four Great Folktales in the Twentieth Century," *Taiwan Journal of East Asian Studies* 9, no. 1 (2012): 25–46. Paola Iovene, "Chinese Opera on Stage and Screen: A Short Introduction," *Opera Quarterly* 26, nos. 2–3 (2010): 181–199.

WILT L. IDEMA

1955 · MAY

"Primitive power of the people" and "subjective fighting spirit"

Lu Ling, Hu Feng, and Literary Persecution

In the main lobby of the Modern Literature Museum in Beijing is a large, two-part mural in the form of a collage of famous fictional characters from works of modern Chinese literature. To the right are images of "sufferers"—those like Lu Xun's (1881–1936) Kong Yiji, who is beaten down by life—and to the left are images of "resisters"—such as Lu Xun's Madman, who defies social norms. Proposed in the 1980s but not opened until 2001, the museum is the product of the post–Mao Zedong

(1893–1976) liberalization, and many of the writers it glorifies, with the notable exception of Lu Xun, were attacked during the political campaigns that punctuated the Mao era. One of the characters in the "resisters" mural is Guo Su'e, the protagonist of *Hungry Guo Su'e*, a 1943 novel by Lu Ling (1923–1994), one of the targets of the 1955 anti–Hu Feng campaign.

In the mural, Su'e appears half-naked, one of her breasts exposed— the very picture of suffering and sexuality. As Lu Ling himself described her in a letter to his mentor Hu Feng (1902–1985), she

> is not a woman who is crushed by the old society. What I have intended to search for … is the primitive power of the people, the positive liberation of the individual … I am only trying to disturb with all my might in order to "revolt" against life.

With her primitive vitality and desire, Su'e embodies a larger hunger for radical social transformation, what Hu would call the "subjective fighting spirit," a political ethos at the core of the Republican-era leftist literary tradition. Why, then, did Su'e's creator, along with Hu and scores of his other associates, become the target of a major Communist cultural purge in 1955, just six years after the 1949 revolution?

The names of Lu Ling and Hu Feng are inextricably intertwined—the latter a leftist literary theorist and poet and the former his most celebrated literary protégé. In the 1930s, Hu had developed close ties with Lu Xun when the latter was the head of the League of Left-Wing Writers. After Lu Xun's death and the dissolution of the league in 1936, Hu ventured out on his own with the publication of the independent literary journals *July* (1937–1941) and *Hope* (1945–1946) and book series and publishing houses also using the July and Hope names. These literary enterprises attracted the attention of young writers and readers from around the country. Lu Ling was one of these writers. From the late 1930s through the 1940s, his fiction was published, almost exclusively, in Hu-run journals and book series.

Although he has sometimes been depicted as such, Hu was no anti-Communist dissident. He was deeply influenced by Marxist and Soviet literary theory and had joined the Communist Party while studying abroad in Japan in the 1930s. He was a devoted Socialist who embraced the new regime in 1949, a devotion he expressed fervidly in a long narrative poem, "Time Has Begun." But his literary thought—for instance, his belief in the centrality of the writer's subjectivity to the creative process and the notion that fiction should depict the "wounds of spiritual servitude"—was subject to accusations of "idealism" because it appeared to position both the writer and fictional characters outside the materialist realm. Although in their critical writings both Hu and Lu Ling describe subjectivity as intertwined with material-historical forces—a basic precept of Marxist thought—they favored realism and psychological fiction that was dark and despairing and that drew attention to the effect of social oppression on individual minds. To the postrevolutionary cultural bureaucracy, Hu's ideas thus seemed to challenge the party on the absolute primacy of political ideology not only to literary creation but also to the larger arena of social transformation.

After the revolution, Hu was unhappy with the literary state of affairs and not shy about openly expressing his discontent. His bold defiance of party control over literary matters culminated in a long report—often referred to as his "memorial"—submitted in 1954 to the Chinese Communist Party (CCP) Central Committee in which he repeated long-held views about the importance of the writer's subjectivity to the creative process and his distaste for literature dictated by doctrinaire political ideology. Hu also audaciously proposed the idea that literary journals should have editorial independence from the party. Lu Ling was closely involved in helping Hu write the report.

The report was the final straw. In the spring of 1955, as part of a larger effort to bring intellectuals into the ideological fold, the party launched a huge campaign against Hu and some eighty other writers alleged to be part of his "clique." Using a pseudonym, Mao himself initiated the attacks in an editorial, writing, "The Hu Feng elements are counterrevolutionaries who put on a disguise to hide their true features," and, "We must never permit bourgeois idealism and thought such as Hu Feng's, which stands in opposition to the people and to the Party, to get away from us under the cover of [being merely regarded as a] 'petty bourgeois viewpoint.' Instead, we ought to criticize and repudiate them thoroughly." In May and June 1955, the *People's Daily* published in installment letters exchanged among members of the Hu group in order to show "the masses" the "double-dealing tactics" of these "counterrevolutionaries." The die was cast, and with this damning indictment, Hu and the "core" of his group were arrested, interrogated, and imprisoned.

The media campaign against Hu exposed the group's nefarious sectarian deeds—opposing the ideas on culture in Mao's canonical *Talks at the Yan'an Forum on Literature and Art*, conniving to establish independent journals and form secret literary networks, and committing subterfuge with the Nationalists, for instance—and the bourgeois, individualist values conveyed in their works. The campaign was part of the larger ideological effort, in the general uncertainty of the early postrevolutionary years, to draw distinct lines between us and them, Socialist and counterrevolutionary, and set the political parameters for new forms of community in a Socialist society.

One of the particular foci of the attack on Hu was the concept of "subjective fighting spirit," a literary concept that Lu Ling's writing was seen to best embody. Lu Ling was generally seen as "one of Hu Feng's big generals." During the 1955 campaign, his Republican-era fictional characters were described in highly moralistic terms as "full of a kind of primitive wildness, an extreme madness, the spasmodic and base feelings of life's desires." Guo Su'e was typical of these characters.

Context changes everything. In the 1940s, critics generally praised *Hungry Guo Su'e* for its bold depiction of raw animalism—both sexuality and violence—and its dissection of human psychology. The novel tells the story of a poor woman named Guo Su'e who is forced by her unfortunate circumstances to marry an opium addict twice her age. She recoils, and in reaction has an affair with a young miner. When the affair is discovered, Su'e is captured, tortured by branding, and raped by the old man's henchman. The henchman's ejaculant oozing from "beneath her belly," Su'e is left to die alone, forsaken but still hungry. Su'e's lover flees town, but another male admirer attempts to fight the local powers that be on her behalf—to no avail. Although tragic and despairing, the story hints at the role of the people in initiating, if not realizing, social change.

Hungry Guo Su'e would appear to be a classic leftist text that depicts the powerful desires of the oppressed classes to overthrow their masters and destroy "feudal" social values. In the context of Maoist China, however, these desires were seen as narrowly "self-initiated," a political buzzword meaning that they were not tamed by the CCP and channeled for party-defined revolutionary purposes. In a postrevolutionary society, this kind of primitive power of individuals is potentially dangerous; it must be harnessed not for subversive change but for building socialism—collective agriculture and massive public works projects. In socialist realist litera-ture, which the new regime raised as the literary ideal, the CCP is never far from the scene; it instigates and orchestrates all action. Rather than a well of desires, the people are, as Mao put it, a "blank sheet" on which "the freshest and most beautiful characters can be written; the freshest and most beautiful pictures can be painted." The problem with concepts like "primitive power of the people" and "subjective fighting spirit" is that they seemed to place social transformation in the hands of the people, not the party. Hu's ideas on subjectivism also posed a threat to Mao's hegemony in theoretical matters and undermined the notion that his thought was the sole fount of revolutionary action.

Children of the Rich (1944–1946), another of Lu Ling's well-known works, is a novel of a very different sort. Like Ba Jin's (1904–2005) *Family*, the novel focuses on three brothers representing three generations of intellectuals: Jiang Weizu, a traditional literatus; Jiang Shaozu, a May Fourth–style enlightenment intellectual; and the youngest, Jiang Chunzu. Part 2 of this massive novel is a bildungsroman that traces the psycho-logical development of Chunzu, who comes across as a kind of Nietz-schean superman striving heroically to reject all forms of truth imposed from outside the self. Whereas for one reader of the novel in the 1940s, Chunzu's "painful process of self-alienation, his disdain for vulgar phi-listinism, his honesty and persistent unwillingness to yield to the forces of evil" had an enlightening effect that "made us dare... to seek a new spiritual liberation," for another, writing in the heat of the 1955 campaign, Chunzu is "an extreme individualist, fanatically worshipping himself." Chunzu was, such critics asserted, the "true hero of the author's heart." In the preface to the 1948 edition of the novel, Lu Ling described his protagonist as "tragic" and "noble" because of his distrust of doctrine and scorn for petty ambitions. Lu Ling shared Hu's disdain for doctrinaire ideology, and one can see how, in the postrevolutionary context, this would be taken as politically subversive.

Although the Communists had previously engaged in campaigns targeting writers and intellectuals—the Yan'an Rectification of the mid-1940s is the most obvious example—the anti-Hu campaign of 1955 was one of the largest and nastiest to date. The state corralled all the mass media at its disposal to attack Lu Ling and the other core members of Hu's "counterrevolutionary" clique. Literary critics, writers, intellectuals, and cartoonists were pressured into taking public stances against Hu. The philosopher Shu Wu (1922–2009), who had been close to Lu Ling and Hu in the 1940s, gave up the letters (inadvertently, he claims) exchanged between members of the group that served as evidence of the clique's "anti-Party, counterrevolutionary" activities and attitudes. Ba Jin, who would in his post-Mao collection *Random Thoughts* come to rue his actions, wrote a piece denouncing Hu. Wang Ruowang (1918–2001), who would himself be a target in the Anti-Rightist Campaign and go on to become a dissident in exile in the 1990s, contributed an entire book called *The Demise of Hu Feng's Black Gang*. The poet Zang Kejia (1905–2004) attempted to rile up his readers' hatred for Hu with a poem entitled "Why Can't You Hate Your Enemy?," which reads,

> Hu Feng hates us to our marrow
> But your hatred has no edge to it
> Hu Feng's hatred for us is like hard liquor
> But your hatred is like grape wine.

Hundreds, perhaps thousands, of articles written by writers, intellectuals, and cultural bureaucrats appeared in the state media denouncing Hu and his followers. The system set up by the Communists turned intellectuals against each other—to not comply to the pressure to join in the chorus of attacks would mean, at best, a career slide and, at worst, punishment. Literary campaigns were an important tool used by the state to compel writers to toe the party line, conform to political and ideological norms, and propagate party policy. Targeted writers such as Hu and Lu Ling served as negative examples for other writers, causing them to internalize censorship demands and to think long and hard about the potential consequences of dissent.

The case of the anti-Hu campaign defies the post-Mao state myth that the 1950s was some sort of golden age of socialism untouched by the excesses of radical Maoism. As a memory, the campaign continues to haunt the present, in particular the children of Hu's associates, who have mostly died by now. Hu's own children have been instrumental in writing biographical accounts and republishing their father's work—a form of filial commemoration and an attempt to address the charges against him. The Shanghai filmmaker Peng Xiaolian (1953–), daughter of Hu's associate Peng Boshan (1910–1968), who was beaten to death by Red Guards in 1968, made a moving film (in collaboration with Louisa Wei) about the anti-Hu campaign called *Storm under the Sun* (2007). As Peng Xiaolian puts it in a published preface to the film, "The Hu Feng group completed their last poems for us with their lives: simple, pure, and reaching the highest state of poetry." After they were arrested in 1955, Hu and Lu Ling were incarcerated, on and off, for the next twenty years. In prison, they displayed the very subjective fighting spirit embodied in their literary works, defying their captors and denying any guilt. Only in the post-Mao liberalization were their names rehabilitated and their works republished, but it was too late: Hu and Lu Ling emerged from their years of incarceration psychologically damaged and mere shells of their formers selves.

The suffering yet passion-filled figure of Guo Su'e in the mural in the Museum of Modern Literature in Beijing ironically calls to mind the suffering and stubborn resistance of her creator, Lu Ling, and his mentor, Hu Feng. Even as it buys into hackneyed literary narratives—the division of literary characters into "sufferers" and "resisters" hinges on a larger historical narrative of humiliating victimization and heroic resistance and finds no room for the more nuanced and complex characters of, for instance, Eileen Chang's (1920–1995) fiction—the museum mural is haunted by the specters of writers like Hu and Lu Ling who suffered so much for their faith in the literary depiction of human suffering.

BIBLIOGRAPHY: Kirk A. Denton, *The Problematic of Self in Modern Chinese Literature: Hu Feng and Lu Ling* (Stanford, CA, 1998). Peng Xiaolian and Louisa Wei, dirs., *Storm under the Sun* (Blue Queen Cultural Communications, 2007). Louisa Wei, ed., *Storm under the Sun: Introductions, Script, and Reviews* (Hong Kong, 2009). Mei Zhi, *F: Hu Feng's Prison Years*, trans. Gregor Benton (London, 2012).

KIRK A. DENTON

1955

Poetry Blossoms is founded.

Hong Kong Modernism and I

In "Lament for Ying," Qu Yuan (340–278 BCE) wrote,

> Unjust, Imperial Heaven's way:
> How the commons were shocked and tried!
> People scattered, separated, lost.
> Middle of spring: eastward exodus began.
> Away, hometown! Toward distant lands!
>
> . . . .
>
> Heart netted and knotted: no way to undo.
> Thought all tangled: no release.

This was the story of Qu Yuan in the third century BCE. This is also my story and that of my fellow poets in 1949. Ours is a massive exodus from the mainland to Hong Kong, Taiwan, Europe, and America. The internecine war between the Nationalists (Kuomintang) and the Communists created a divide overnight that brutally separated parents and children, husbands and wives, siblings and friends. The Iron Curtain terminated all traffic and communications between the mainland, on the one hand, and Hong Kong and Taiwan on the other. While Hong Kong and Taiwan faced the same situation, the modernist writings that emerged have different morphologies. Hong Kong poets underwent a radicalized crisis of cultural identity under the British colonial government, whereas their Taiwanese counterparts wrestled with Nationalist suppression (which was later called the "White Terror"). Both groups found language strategies from Euro-American modernism modified by classical and contemporary Chinese poetry.

One night in 1949 I was uprooted and found myself in the British colony of Hong Kong, where "white" Chinese oppressed "yellow" Chinese, where

> we can only envy or stroll around mansions:
> rising piano notes, signs of "PRIVATE: NO TRESPASSING,"
> "FIERCE DOGS INSIDE," "NO LOITERING."

To a twelve-year-old country boy, this sister city of London, Paris, New York, or Chicago was a culture shock. The social isolation, outright coldness, criminal activities, and poverty-induced restlessness around me drove me toward a quest for some kind of raison d'être in an imaginative flight. Thus a budding poet was born.

It was a divine accident that I met Wucius Wong (1936–) in a student gathering sponsored by *Chinese Student Weekly*. Wong was my Virgil, who led me to the paradise of poetry even though he later abandoned poetry almost completely. I was hardly a writer then; yet, through his warm persuasion I took the first steps. Further encouragement came from his close friend Quanan Shum (1935–), the "Prince" among student writers whose "Fragments of a Naked Soul" in *Sing Tao Daily News* had captured the hearts of many readers. All educated in bilingual English high schools, the three of us—jestingly labeled the "Three Musketeers of Hong Kong" by the poet Ya Xian (1932–) in Taiwan—launched a short-lived but important magazine called *Poetry Blossoms* in 1955.

I left Hong Kong later that year and entered the Department of Foreign Languages and Literature at the National Taiwan University. I joined the *Epoch* Poetry Society and the group of writers of *Modern Literature* in my department to resurrect a Chinese culture, which, I hoped, would help rejuvenate the quickly vanishing Chineseness. I believed that the world should appreciate not just Chineseness but that which gave Chinese writers the strength to resist power and to create a counterdiscourse to hegemony as revealed in classical Chinese poetry and poetics.

During the next six years or so, traveling between the two islands, I helped Shum and Wong in Hong Kong to establish the Modern Literature and Art Association, which sponsored two magazines, *Cape of Good Hope* and *New Trends*, and held international art salons that featured and promoted local artists such as Wong, Lui Shou-kwan (1919–1975), and Zhang Yi (1936–), as well as modernist painters from the Fifth Moon and Dongfang groups in Taiwan. We also supported *New Trends of Literature and Arts*, founded by Ma Lang (1933–), who had been an acclaimed poet in 1940s Shanghai. I published poems, translations, and essays in this and other journals. In Taiwan I published in *Literary Review* (edited by our teacher and mentor, Professor T. A. Hsia [1916–1965]), *Epoch*, and *Modern Literature*.

The 1949 national divide known as the Great Rupture caused complex psychical displacements, with a profound impact on the writers in Hong Kong. Before the Iron Curtain came down, cultural identity was hardly a concern because, although Hong Kong was a colony, movement to and from the mainland was open and free. After the Great Rupture, however, the colonial education system adopted strategies to suppress Chinese national consciousness, enforce economic and cultural dependency on Britain, and create a climate that desensitized the historical consciousness, sense of community, and cultural identity of the colonized. The desensitization process took the form of allurement and pacification with the offer of monetary gain. By reifying and commodifying traditional and new cultural activities, the government hoped that any residual interventionist impulse would be wiped out and that all serious literature and art would be replaced by consumerist literature, soft-porn sensationalism, superficial lyricism, and pandering tabloids. Among the modernist poets, Shum and Wong were the most vocal critics.

It was against this background that Hong Kong poets reached out for the expressive tropes of Western modernist poetry that had developed since Charles Baudelaire (1821–1867), while at the same time drawing on classical Chinese poetry to inscribe the angst and tattered sensibility caused by the historical rupture.

During the *Poetry Blossoms* days in the mid-1950s, we perused works by hundreds of foreign poets to select examples for translation. We resurrected important Chinese poets from the 1930s and 1940s who were marginalized after 1949 by both the Nationalists and the Communists. We critiqued the current poetry scene. All along, we felt strongly about invigorating aesthetic elements; we believed that the saving grace of the Chinese people was to create good poetry. To build our brand of modernist poetry as a counterdiscourse, we looked to the West for models, including Baudelaire, Stéphane Mallarmé, Arthur Rimbaud, Paul Verlaine, Rainer Maria Rilke, Paul Valéry, Arthur Symons, Ernest Dowson, early W. B. Yeats, T. S. Eliot, W. H. Auden, D. H. Lawrence, Dylan Thomas, Allen Ginsberg, Gregory Corso, Federico García Lorca, Guillaume Apollinaire, André Bréton, Paul Eluard, Jules Supervielle, Saint-John Perse, Henri Michaux, René Char, Octavio Paz, Jorge Luis Borges, Jorge Guillen, and so on. I introduced some of the surrealist poets to Taiwan through the essays of my friend Wallace Fowlie (1908–1998).

In 1954–1955 I came across a Chinese book entitled *New Literary and Art Movement in Fin-de-Siècle England*, written by Xiao Shijun. The book highlights the works of Arthur Symons (1865–1945) and his cohort influenced by Walter Pater (1839–1894), in particular by the conclusion to his *Studies in the Renaissance*. I was particularly taken by his comment on a sentence from Victor Hugo (1802–1885): "We are all under sentence of death but with a sort of indefinite reprieve—*les hommes sont tous condamnés à mort avec des sursis indéfinis*: we have an interval, and then our place knows no more." The passage resonates so closely with the condition we were forced into. Pater argues that modern thought cultivates the "relative" spirit in place of the "absolute." Nothing is, or can be, rightly known except relatively and under conditions "so that every hour in his life is unique, changed altogether by a stray word, or glance, or touch. It is the truth of these relations that experience gives us, not the truth of eternal outlines [logos, God] ascertained once for all, but a world of gradations." In the conclusion to his *Renaissance*, Pater says to be successful in life is

> to maintain the ecstasy, to dwell in every intense moment ... in expanding that interval, in getting as many pulsations as possible into the given time.... Not the fruit of experience, but experience itself, is the end. A counted number of pulses only is given to us of a variegated, dramatic life.... To burn always with this hard, gem-like flame, to maintain this ecstasy, is success in life.

This we must do.

My meditation started with the refinement and tightening of the Chinese vernacular (*baihua*) as a medium for poetry by poets of the 1930s and 1940s. To refine *baihua*, however, one should not begin by reverting to the classical Chinese language, but instead by reappropriating it through a process of tensional modifications. I tried to reduce discursiveness to a minimum and use pregnant images or image clusters as leitmotifs in a sequence in which they play out the pulses and impulses from a not fully narrated drama of existential and historical predicament. This describes the architectonic structure of my "Fugue" (1958–1959), which is symphonic in form. The images in the poem present abbreviated, highly suggestive events, captured in a transformed *baihua* with a distinctive classical

Chinese ring. The various montage layouts evoke the devastation of war both ancient and recent, both historical and mythical, in creative tension with the West. The poem contains three sections like three symphonic movements, and ends with an incomplete quest and persistent questioning. The choice of musical tropes was inspired by the fact that music, as a medium, is not built up by *meaning-discharging* units but instead by the modulations of tone and timbre, both spatially and temporally, both diachronic (melodic) and synchronic (chordal), to emulate the morphology of feeling. Like "Fugue," "Crossing" contains five moments, or viewpoints, of the exodus of epic dimensions, each a lyric focusing on a pregnant moment that interweaves with those in the other four sections into a tapestry of the destinies of my fellow countrymen in exile.

What the Hong Kong modernists created was a continuously evolving pattern of dialogues between and within traditions, a chance for readers from both the East and the West to witness the morphology of cross-fertilization, to rethink poetry in a larger context, and to achieve a dynamic fusion of imaginative horizons. In contrast to postwar Taiwan, where the modernist poets created a counterdiscourse to the repressive orthodoxy of the ruling party, in Hong Kong we tried to achieve the same effect by maintaining the poem as an aesthetic object par excellence— unsullied, as it were, by the so-called objective realism with its historical and ideological limitations. We wanted to create a poetry of aesthetic objectivity, a true-to-self poetry, through a pure self-awareness of language as a holistic carrier of culture. We aimed to keep alive a truly new realism, a supra-realism that depicted the undisfigured Moment in all its tremblings.

WAI-LIM YIP

1956

"My Lifelong Worship of Violet"

Zhou Shoujuan's Romance à la Mandarin Ducks and Butterflies

In 1956, the sixty-one-year-old Zhou Shoujuan (1895–1968) wrote an essay entitled "My Lifelong Worship of Violet" describing his endless longing for his first lover, a woman named Violet:

> Violet and I, frankly speaking, had an affair, which has affected me so deeply that I haven't been able to get over it even after forty years. Her Western name was Violet, so I named my magazines *Violet Petal* and *The Violet....* My house in Suzhou was called the "Violet Villa" and my room the "Violet Studio."... Almost all of my writings— essays, fiction, poetry—were imprinted with the figure of violet.

Beginning in the early 1950s, the Communist Party launched a series of antiliberal movements in the worlds of literature and art, and Zhou himself was criticized as a leading writer of Mandarin Ducks and Butterflies romance, a genre of popular fiction mostly on sentimental love that catered to the middlebrow tastes of urbanites in the Republican era. Yet even under the pressures of those movements, Zhou wrote nostalgically, as extravagantly as ever, and seemed to embrace his somewhat naive passion, thereby asserting his "old" stance. If we start from here and trace the violets that appeared at the very beginning of Zhou's literary career, almost a century ago, like a kind of archeological excavation for what David Der-wei Wang terms the "repressed modernity" of Zhou's work, we will find a unique myth in the context of modern Chinese literature. Driven by unrequited love, Zhou intricately wove the figure of Violet as his mysterious lover into his fiction and nonfiction narratives. Especially throughout the 1920s, in the magazines *Violet Petals* and *The Violet*, Zhou, a group of his fellow writers, and his readers developed his sad romance into a dynamic discourse around the ideas of flowers, beauty, the "New Woman" of modern China, and magazines as a literary commodity. This discourse was conducted across private and public realms, and engaged with tradition and modernity, politics and aesthetics, functioning as a sentimental education for urbanites in the Republican era.

Zhou was born to a poor family in Shanghai. As a native of Suzhou, the slightly effeminate Zhou was fortunately influenced by the local tradition. Seventeenth-century Suzhou was a center of literati culture, characterized by the celebration of flowers, beauty, the art of gardening, and the deployment of refined taste in daily life. It was in middle school that Zhou first encountered the violet flower, in a botany class taught by an Englishwoman. With this inspiration, images of violets appeared in his earliest fiction, published in 1911, identifying the flower with pretty women and romantic liaisons.

Just as he described it in his essay, Zhou fell in love with a girl whose Western name was Violet, after seeing her perform on stage at her girls' school. Then, as if possessed, Zhou waited every morning at the gate of her school in order to get a glimpse of her. Violet, seemingly indifferent to him, began to mockingly refer to him as Mr. Eyebrowless when talking with her friends. Zhou had caught a strange illness years earlier and as a result his hair and eyebrows had fallen out. After some hesitation, the girl replied to his letters, but her parents opposed their relationship because of Zhou's lower social standing, and, not long after, Violet was forced to marry a rich man.

Zhou seems to have never recovered from this loss; his sad love stories about his unrequited love frequently appeared in *Saturday*, a best-selling fiction magazine at the time, and his literary renown grew. Zhou was a genius of self-fashioning. A sketch drawn by his friend shows him at twenty, handsome and delicate, wearing a Western suit with a bowtie and a flower above the upper pocket, and a particularly fashionable pair of glasses. Zhou won many female admirers; some went so far as to keep his photo in their wallet.

In a plethora of love stories, Zhou interwove variant representations of violets with the theme of lost love, literary conventions, classical poetics, and new techniques borrowed from Western literature. In "A Diary of a Heart-Broken Girl" (1914), a girl stores her boyfriend's letters with fragrant violets. The sentimental plots of Zhou's short stories were combined with narrative modes of irony, fantasy, allegory, or the grotesque, articulating urban mentalities in spaces of daily life. In the story "A Pair of Gloves Knitted by His Lover" (1925), a man is haunted by a ten-year-old memory of lost love. He keeps a pair of gloves, the only gift from the girl, yet, although the gloves are invaluable to him, he forgets them time and again: in a cosmetics shop, in a bookstore, or on a rickshaw. At the end of the story, he descends from a trolley, only to realize he forgot the gloves on the trolley car. When he runs to catch up, he is hit by a car. Dying in a hospital, in a delirium, he still asks for the gloves.

In 1920, as editor of *Free Talk* of *Shenbao*, a major newspaper in Shanghai, Zhou did even more to promote the image of the violet. He created a column called "Violet Petals," through which he sent intimate messages to his secret lover. The next year, in the revived magazine *Saturday*, Zhou's bosom friend Yuan Hanyun (1889–1931) published a piece entitled "A Diary of Miss Violet." The fictional Miss Violet is pretty, educated, and modern, fond of watching Hollywood movies, playing violin, and making sketches in the suburbs of Shanghai. She is engaged to a literary talent, a thinly veiled representation of Zhou. In spite of her free spirit, she is a model of domesticity, and wants to be a perfect housewife after marriage. This piece not only promoted the violet motif, but also promoted the magazine in which Yuan skillfully knit into the diary passages chosen from the texts recently published in *Saturday*.

Surprisingly, the invented Miss Violet evoked popular fantasies, and after Zhou launched a new fiction magazine, *The Half Moon*, Miss Violet became a literary commodity. Zhou's friends made new stories about Miss Violet, and Zhou received responses from readers who identified her with the magazine, as well as their own lovers. Zhou carefully lent out the symbol of the violet to his partners, who often ambiguously spread gossip about his secret amour for the titillation of the public. For example, Zhou Shoumei, wife of the notable historiographer Zheng Yimei (1895–1992), wrote a short note claiming that she saw Miss Violet on a boulevard and was amazed at her extraordinary beauty: "I was told that recently she has been close to the novelist Zhou Shoujuan. For those who are interested in their affair, it is not difficult to find them somewhere together in the city." This salacious note, however, was followed by Zhou Shoujuan's comment in parenthesis: "The Miss Violet Zhou was referring to was the cover girl of the coming issue of *Half Moon*. Please don't misunderstand." As the games went on, the tragedy of Zhou's unrequited love was almost obscured.

Zhou and his friends continued to build the legend of the violet in his popular magazine *The Violet*, first published in 1925. For Zhou and his colleagues, the violet, this literary and cultural chimera of a beautiful women, a flower, and love, was present everywhere. In the fictional "violet world" of Zhou's group, the violet appears as the goddess of love in Greek mythology, was a symbol of love in William Shakespeare's plays, and was used by Napoleon Bonaparte as a badge for his supporters in the Hundred Days. *The Violet* was a vehicle for the cultural agenda of mixing the "new" with the "old": representing modern urban life through Chinese poetic lyricism.

One of the most fascinating interpretations of Miss Violet, Zhang Chunfan's (?–1935) *Violet Knights Errant* (1929–1930), a novel serialized in *The Violet* in the late 1920s, took a liberal stand for Republican constitutional politics. The story is set in the late Qing (the early twentieth century). A group of female warriors wearing badges of violet, evidently inspired by the legend of Napoleon, join the revolutionaries led by Sun Yat-sen (1866–1925) against the Manchu regime. These female warriors, however, disapprove of Sun's militant actions, and instead insist on a "nonviolent" revolution. They fly over hills and rivers to rescue soldiers in peril; though armed with an advanced type of pistol, they never kill people, as the rubble bullets the pistols fire are harmless. Significantly, though it imitated the combination of romance and politics typical of "revolution plus love" fiction, it departed from the leftist models aiming at revolution by class struggle. Moreover, it maintained a critical distance from violent party politics at a time when the Nationalist Party was trying to tighten its rule after unifying the whole country during the Northern Expedition of 1926–1928.

The literati tradition of flowers, beauty, and love, represented by *The Violet* seems to have fallen into decline in the late 1920s, not only due to the pressure of national crisis but also due to literary tastes, which were changing rapidly in favor of avant-garde modernism and leftist politics. Despite the decline of the literary romance with violets, Zhou's true romance with his Violet did not end. In 1944 he published *A Confession of Love* in the restored *Violet* magazine, exposing their three-decade-long passion. This love confession, a gem in modern Chinese literature, consists of one hundred classical *ci* (song lyric) poems, full of ecstasy and sorrow, longing and regret, each with annotations in vernacular language. Zhou reminisced,

It was six years later, after she married and I had a family. We should have buried the past and got rid of our pain forever. But our pain was so deep that it penetrated the marrow. Sharing the same fate, we had to find a way to console each other.... Nevertheless, as we became more intimate, we sank into deeper despair because of our incurable regret.

This unusual romance offers us a glimpse of how the Western idea of marriage was received in modern China. During the first year of her marriage she remained a virgin, staying loyal to Zhou, her true lover in her heart. When she heard he was engaged, she lost her hope. She only told him that she had tried to remain true in 1927, ten years after they were reunited. Of all the details about their illicit relationship, the accounts of how they carefully avoided public attention elicit the most sympathy from us. While they met in public places such as dancing halls, movie theaters, or public parks, she was often chaperoned by her mother. Once, while sitting in Zhou's new automobile, she covered her face with a handkerchief so as to avoid being seen by her acquaintances. Realizing that they had to accept the status quo, Violet promised Zhou that, although she was already married, she would be his "fiancée" for a lifetime. She sent him a golden ring engraved with the word "love" in English, and Zhou put it on his ring finger as a token of their "spiritual marriage." Yet, at the same time, he felt guilty toward his wife, to whom he wrote a poem of apology: "My heart is divided into two rooms, one for you, the other for her."

Violet—whose real name, unknown to the public until 1981, was Zhou Yinping—was intelligent, reserved, and independent. In the mid-1930s she went to Nanjing and got divorced; during the second Sino-Japanese War she lived as a bank clerk in Chongqing, the provisional capital of the Republic of China during the war. When Zhou declared his intention to publish *A Confession of Love*, his friends worried that it was not appropriate to celebrate a personal love affair at a time when the whole nation had devoted itself to a war of resistance. Someone asked Zhou, "Are you afraid of 'public criticism'?" He answered, "All I know is that love is the most supreme undertaking in the world. I never care about 'public criticism'!" Despite his praise of love, a feeling of desperation pervaded the *Confession*, and his strong hope for her return home was expressed as part of a collective wish for a quick end to the war.

When the war ended in 1945, Yinping returned to Shanghai. It happened that Zhou's wife died the following year, and there was a chance for them to consummate their love, but for some reason Yinping did not accept Zhou's proposal. Shortly afterward Zhou got remarried to another woman.

After returning to Shanghai, Yinping worked for a steamship company. After 1949, persuaded by her son, she went to Beijing and married Zhuang Xiquan (1888–1988), a member of the Standing Committee of the People's Congress. They survived the Cultural Revolution, and Yinping lived into her eighties. Nevertheless, Zhou Shoujuan was not as lucky as Yinping. Despite his loyalty to the Communist regime, driven by the constant persecution of the Cultural Revolution, he committed suicide by jumping into a well in 1968.

BIBLIOGRAPHY: Chen Jianhua, "Zhou Shoujuan's Love Story and Mandarin Ducks and Butterflies Literature," in *The Columbia Companion to Modern East Asian Literature*, ed. Joshua S. Mostow et al. (New York, 2003), 355–363. Perry E. Link Jr., *Mandarin Ducks and Butterflies: Popular Fiction in Early Twentieth-Century Chinese Cities* (Berkeley, CA, 1981).

JIANHUA CHEN

1956

Taiwanese writer Wu Zhuoliu's *Orphan of Asia* is published in Chinese.

1983 · SEPTEMBER 20

Pop singer Lo Ta-yu releases his song "Orphan of Asia."

Orphans of Asia

The Taiwanese singer-songwriter Lo Ta-yu (1954–) released his second album, *Masters of the Future*, on September 20, 1983. The common theme that unites songs on the album is undoubtedly the notion of "growing up." Among them, "Orphan of Asia" stands out. Today, even more so than during the three previous decades, it is a Taiwanese favorite:

The orphan of Asia is crying in the wind
His yellow face stained with red dirt
His black eyes bespeak his white fear
The west wind sings a sad song in the east

The orphan of Asia is crying in the wind
Nobody cares to play fair with you
Everybody tries to take your favorite toy
Tell me why you are crying my dear boy

How many try to answer the unanswerable question
How many sigh at night in helpless dejection
How many wipe away their tears without a word
Dear mother, can you please explain this rejection

Lo employs the orphan as a metaphor for Taiwan's increasingly difficult position vis-à-vis Cold War politics since the late 1960s. Historical twists and political dramas set the undertone for the lyrics. The tripartite relation between China, Taiwan, and the United States seemed calm on the surface, but tensions quickly escalated after Richard Nixon (1913–1994) took office in 1969. Nixon sent Henry Kissinger (1923–) on a secret mission to the People's Republic of China (PRC), with the hope of normalizing relations between the two countries. The constant and imminent threat from the Soviet Union brought the PRC and the United States closer together.

Nixon's new foreign policy surprised and hurt the Chinese Communist Party's arch-nemesis Chiang Kai-shek (1887–1975), who had been a faithful ally to the United States since the 1940s. As Nixon later commented, "It had not been easy for me to take a position that would be so disappointing to our old friend and loyal ally.... In this case, however, I felt that the national security interests of the United States lay in developing our relations with the P.R.C." In the end, Chiang's Taiwan lost the support of his allies regarding the issue of Chinese representation in the United Nations, and the Republic of China (ROC) left the family of nations and was replaced by a newly empowered PRC.

When Lo released his song in 1983, Taiwan was still under martial law—a policy implemented by Chiang in 1947. The record company was concerned that the Nationalist (Kuomintang) state censor might dislike the word "orphan," as it also conjured images of Chiang's inglorious exit from the family of nations. They decided to add a subtitle to "Orphan of Asia": "Red Nightmare—to the Refugees in Indochina." On the one hand, the subtitle recalls the Khmer Rouge or Red Khmer—radical supporters of the Communist Party of Kampuchea in Cambodia. On the other hand, it cleverly gives the song a philanthropic tone that echoes the Indochinese Migration and Refugee Assistance Act, signed by President Gerald Ford (1913–2006) after the Vietnam War. For whichever reason, the song successfully evaded censorship. By way of association, "Orphan of Asia" alerted the audience to the unstable political conditions in Indochina that involved native and foreign powers alike.

After the Vietnam War, the PRC and the United States established official diplomatic relations. As the Joint Communiqué on the Establishment of Diplomatic Relations between the United States of America and the People's Republic of China, dated January 1, 1979, recognized the PRC as the sole legal government of China, it rendered Chiang's Taiwan a renegade state. To minimize hard feelings, the communiqué stressed that "the people of the United States will maintain cultural, commercial, and other unofficial relations with the people of Taiwan," echoing Nixon's rhetoric. Even so, this subsequent remedial measure could not effectively alleviate the sense of abandonment felt by Taiwan. To this day, Taiwan has yet to be readmitted to the United Nations.

Lo's "Orphan of Asia" has other inspirations and archetypes. In 1949, when Chiang ordered a large-scale migration to Taiwan, he accidentally left behind a battalion of soldiers in southwestern China. These soldiers had gone beyond the borders on a mission to Indochina and did not retreat in time. They became accidental immigrants and were forced to settle in a foreign land. Their descendants scattered throughout Indochina and became Indochinese refugees. The Taiwanese writer Bo Yang's (1920–2008) reportage novel, *The Alien Realm*, recounts the lost battalion's undying loyalty with heart-wrenching detail, exposing the frailty of life and the absurdity of warfare. The orphan-soldiers fought hard battles for themselves and for China, but in the end they couldn't realize their homecoming dream. Director Chu Yen-ping (1950–) released an impactful film adaptation of the novel in 1990 entitled *A Home Too Far*, which became the best-selling Taiwan film of the year. Incidentally, Chu chose Lo's "Orphan of Asia" to be the theme song. But that was not the only instance of cross-media borrowing. Lo, in fact, adopted his song title from *Orphan of Asia*, a novel by Wu Zhuoliu (1900–1976).

Wu Zhuoliu wrote *Orphan of Asia* in colonial Taiwan between 1943 and 1945. He originally named the novel after the protagonist, Hu Zhiming, and published it under that title in 1946. When the novel was reprinted in 1956, however, he changed the title to *Orphan of Asia* and the protagonist became Hu Taiming. The name change is significant because "Hu Zhiming" is the Mandarin pronunciation of Ho Chi Min (1890–1969), the Vietnamese Communist leader. Given that the Vietnam War had only just begun, Wu took measures to avoid unintended association. Whether or not this part of history inspired Lo Ta-yu's subtitle, "Red Nightmare—to the Refugees in Indochina," remains a speculation. Hindsight nevertheless helps illuminate that so-called national history is always already international by virtue of several countries' political engagement.

For five decades, from 1895 to 1945, Japan ruled Taiwan. After defeating China in 1895, Japan annexed Taiwan. In 1945, Japan returned Taiwan to China, but the new China was no longer the Qing China that had first ceded it. The Nationalist Party had overthrown the Qing dynasty in 1912 and established the first republic in Asia, the Republic of China, and in turn became the new owner of Taiwan.

The political handover in 1945 confirmed the Nationalists' inheritance of all of the Qing's possessions per the 1943 Cairo Declaration and the 1945 Potsdam Declaration. Though in accordance with international law, the Nationalists' claim over Taiwan, made on the basis of the Qing's administration, remains contentious, constantly giving rise to heated debates over Taiwan's (de facto, not de jure) independence from China. All US presidents after Nixon followed his path and maintained relations with the PRC, not the ROC. As the 1979 joint communiqué clearly states, "The Government of the United States of America acknowledges the Chinese position that there is but one China and Taiwan is part of China." Throughout the years, one thing remains unchanged: no government—not that of the Qing, the United States, Great Britain, the Nationalists, or the Communists—ever asked what the people of Taiwan wanted before meeting to determine the island's political status in the world. Indeed, not only was Taiwan orphaned, it had been through several adoptions.

By definition, an orphan is a child whose parents have prematurely passed away. Strictly speaking, Hu Taiming has a family. The "orphan of Asia" is someone whom both the ancestral homeland and the colonial government have disowned. Wu relies on the idea of the orphan as a metaphor to capture the predicament of Hu Taiming, and, by extension, all Taiwanese, as caught between Japanese colonialism and Chinese nationalism. Hu Taiming suffers from a strong feeling of displacement wherever he sojourns. In colonial Taiwan, the Japanese consider him everything but a Japanese citizen. His diligence and kindness at best beget some preferential treatment, but he is still regularly subject to outright discrimination and even false accusations of misconduct. When he studies abroad in Japan, his Chinese classmates consider him Japanese, a sycophant, or a traitor. Wu once commented, "I was like an orphan who reveres the parents he never knew, yearning for the warm embrace of a family which alone could provide what he was searching for in life. It was almost instinctive." However, as Wu also points out, this instinctive feeling—coming from an imaginary nostalgia—changed as soon as he arrived in China. Likewise, Wu's protagonist's identification with China undergoes the same change. He must continue his travels and search for home.

Born in colonial Taiwan, Hu Taiming is either insufficiently Chinese or insufficiently Japanese. What is at stake is the "nature versus culture" impasse. While the Japanese base their prejudice on consanguinity—assuming an innate and inseparable connection between the Taiwanese and the Chinese people—the protagonist's Chinese classmates subscribe to the prevalent belief that one's loyalty should be to his or her birthplace. Both positions ignore the fact that identity corresponds to and changes with a range of factors, such as ethnicity, language, place of residence, politics, and religion. The thorny questions of identity and identity politics, which give rise to the sense of alienation and abandonment that drives the protagonist to the brink of insanity, would continue to haunt Taiwan for generations to come.

If all we see is the protagonist's status as a victim, however, we will have missed Wu's point. Hu Taiming's mishaps shape rather than shatter his life. Wu's "orphan" is not so much a frail human being as he is an emotional realization, a sense of abandonment that originates from a series of historical factors and takes on further layers through several migrations.

The circuitous journeys he makes from Taiwan to Japan and China correspond to the convoluted path of identity formation in (post)colonial Taiwan. Wu characterizes an orphan as a migrant who takes great risks to press on in life. Without embarking on his journey for a place called home, Hu might never have felt estranged and dispossessed. One leaves, only to realize that there's no place like home. Meanwhile, without leaving home, he may have missed the opportunity for self-realization. Rather than saying that the meaning of home does not remain static, *Orphan of Asia* makes an even stronger point: home acquires its multiple meanings through these different vectors of migration.

We may add Wu's Hu Taiming to the gallery of memorable literary orphans—Anne of Green Gables, David Copperfield, Huckleberry Finn, Jane Eyre, and Oliver Twist—whose life experiences encapsulate the despairs and hopes of particular historical places and periods. Wu's orphan-cum-metaphor carries additional weight as national allegory, alerting readers to the nation's (parent) neglect of its subjects (children). Meanwhile, while the figure of the orphan reflects a romantic emphasis on a child's expected vulnerability, Hu Taiming also casts light on himself as a pioneer who eventually rises above circumstantial victimization. Rather than indulging in endless self-pity, he joins the military to fight against the Japanese in southwest China. Did Wu's orphan become the "lost battalion" in Bo Yang's *The Alien Realm* and Chu Yen-ping's *A Home Too Far*? We can only speculate. And such speculation helps trace how the metaphor of the orphan comes full circle, traversing the boundaries of music, history, literature, cinema, and politics.

Orphan of Asia presents and predicts the liminal status of Taiwanese people during the colonial period and thereafter. People in the former colonies of the United Kingdom and France, such as Hong Kong, India, and Algeria, were also subject to similar trials of political inequality and social injustice. There are, however, obvious differences between Taiwan and the former European colonies. For instance, Taiwan, unlike Algeria and India, is yet to be recognized as an independent country in the name of the Republic of China. Taiwan, with the self-interested help of the United States, used to play a crucial role in the anti-Communist coalition in East Asia; that is, until US-Soviet tensions began to escalate. At that point, the United States sought the support of the PRC and Taiwan's marginalization began. To date, Taiwan's international status remains ambiguous. The "orphan of Asia" thus remains an apt metaphor through which to rethink many issues. For instance, how do romanticized notions of kinship, for better or worse, continue to structure and reflect a sense of personal and national identity? Precisely because one is always born, as it were, into a nation-family, how do fictional and filmic reconfigurations of the "orphan" reflect more broadly on the state of international politics? Who are the parents of Asia and the world? Who and what bestows the power of care that defines, as well as exploits, Taiwan's precariousness? What does the future hold for Taiwan?

To believe is one thing, and to act without asking questions is another. These are very difficult but not "unanswerable" questions, despite what the singer-songwriter Lo Ta-yu says in his lyrics. Raising them is the first step to finding answers.

BIBLIOGRAPHY: Zhuoliu Wu, *The Fig Tree: Memoirs of a Taiwanese Patriot, 1900–1947* (Dortmund, Germany, 1994). Zhuoliu Wu, *Orphan of Asia: A Novel* (New York, 2008). Bo Yang, *The Alien Realm* (London, 1996).

CHIEN-HSIN TSAI

1957 · JUNE 7

Iasyr Shivaza arrives in Beijing.

Sino-Muslims and China's Latin New Script:
A Reunion between Diaspora and Nationalism

In 1957, Iasyr Shivaza (1906–1988) sang before an audience of Chinese Communist cadres and writers in Beijing. It was his first—and only—visit to China. At this point in the Cold War, the relationship between the Soviet Union and the People's Republic of China was at its warmest. Mutual exchange of "friendship commissions" offered tutelage and solidarity in the name of socialism. The circle widened to include other sites of struggle against Western imperialism in the Global South—Latin America, Africa, Southeast Asia, the Caribbean. Shivaza, a lone voice from a forgotten corner of Sinophone diaspora, had traveled far from Soviet Central Asia. He was a second-generation Dunganese poet and writer, a descendant of the Chinese Muslims who fled across the border from northwestern China to Czarist Russia, after a series of failed uprisings, in the last quarter of the nineteenth century. Coming from Kyrgyzstan via Xinjiang, Shivaza was no stranger to some of those in the audience.

The year before, he was part of a group of Kyrgyz writers who welcomed a delegation of sixteen writers from China. It was the first Sino-Soviet friendship mission in Frunze (now named Bishkek), the capital of the Kirghiz Soviet Socialist Republic. Shivaza found only one Chinese delegate with whom he could converse in Russian: Ge Baoquan (1913–2000), writer and translator of Aleksandr Pushkin (1799–1837) and Maksim Gorky (1868–1936). Their dialectal differences were too great to communicate without the aid of Russian. Ge's Chinese was the Shanghai dialect of the Yangtze River delta of eastern China, while Shivaza's Dunganese had its roots in the spoken dialects of two northwestern provinces in China, Shaanxi and Gansu. At that time, Shivaza was already quite familiar with the works of Lu Xun (1881–1936), Xiao San (1896–1983), Ba Jin (1904–2005), and Zhao Shuli (1906–1970). He himself had translated some of Ba Jin's short stories into Dunganese from Russian. As much as he admired the Chinese revolutionary writers, though, he was even more intimately impacted by the works of Kyrgyz, Kazakh, Uzbek, and Uyghur writers and poets. With them he shared the same land and breathed the same language.

The event in Frunze led to a reciprocal invitation to Beijing. The itinerary itself allegorized the journey from a place between worlds to the heart of the Chinese cultural center. Shivaza began his tour by attending a meeting of writers of the Xinjiang-Uyghur Autonomous Region. Then the national poet of the Kirghiz Soviet Socialist Republic, Shivaza was one of seven representatives from the Soviet Union, a delegation that included representatives from Uzbekistan, Kazakhstan, Turkmenistan, and Tajikistan. During the fifteen-day meeting, Shivaza read a poem before the audience entitled "For the Poet Qu Yuan," an ode to the third-century BCE poet and political exile whose loyalty to his ruler is retold in *The Songs of the South*. Though it was delivered in Dunganese, no translator was deemed necessary. To their own amazement, the Chinese listeners recognized the regional inflections in Shivaza's speech. At the end of the Beijing conference, Shivaza was left with the reminder that "the Chinese, though friends, are aliens and quite different from Dungans."

This feeling of familiarity and separation betrays an entangled history of diaspora that, until now, has been little known.

The northern Sinitic dialects of Shaanxi and Gansu were spoken by peasants who were illiterate. These oral traditions never acquired the written form of the Chinese script. They traveled with the Muslim exodus, before the time of modern literacy campaigns. Over a century and a half, Dunganese absorbed lexical elements from Russian, Persian, and the Turkic tongues of Central Asia, especially in present-day Kazakhstan, Kyrgyzstan, and Uzbekistan. It was continuously reformed under the language policies of Vladimir Lenin (1870–1924) and Joseph Stalin's (1879–1953) Soviet Union—first written in Arabic as a language of religious instruction, then formally in Cyrillic, then in Latin letters, and eventually in Cyrillic again. A Sino-Tibetan minority language in the region, it is a true "double minority," having survived between two modern national histories.

Having charted an unlikely path of survival, Dunganese challenges even our most capacious imagination for marginalized voices. Yet, during one of the most pivotal periods of Chinese language reform, it could not have played a more central role in the mainstream of modern Chinese history. Before the latinization phase for Dunganese got under way, a young Iasyr Shivaza, together with his classmates at the Tartar Institute in Tashkent Yu. Yanshansin and H. Makeev, worked on creating the first Dunganese alphabet. Although they had initially based the alphabet on the Arabic script that they had learned from reading the Koran in Muslim classroom instruction, they eventually drafted a Latin scheme in 1927. When the different Turkic nationalities in Soviet Central Asia began to adopt the Latin-based New Turkic Alphabet, the Dungans followed their example. But it soon became clear that it would not suit the linguistic requirements of spoken Dunganese, which preserved the dialectal tones and lexica of northwestern Chinese. Though the latinized alphabet was adopted by the Dungans in 1928–1929, by spring 1930 the process was halted until further official review. Meanwhile, the research for China's Latin New Script (Latinxua Sin Wenz) movement, a mass project to devise an easy, purely phonetic script that can be used for any dialect, gathered momentum in Moscow.

Qu Qiubai (1899–1935, adapted Russian name as Strakhov), an important writer and figure in the Chinese Communist Party, collaborated with

Soviet experts. He began to work out a concrete latinization scheme at the end of 1928. Earlier, in February 1928, a group at the Communist University of the Toilers of the East in Moscow had begun to study whether Chinese could be latinized. By then, attempts to help the Chinese laborers in Vladivostok and Khabarovsk to acquire literacy in the Chinese language had failed, partly due to the manipulations of the Soviet government. At the Institute for Scientific Research on China of the Communist Academy in Moscow, Qu worked with Sinologists and linguists V. S. Kolokolov (1896–1979) and A. G. Shprintsin (1907–1974), along with Wu Yuzhang (Burenin, 1878–1966), Xiao San (Emi Siao), and other members of the Chinese Communist Party. Kolokolov helped Qu devise the Chinese Latin alphabet and transcription system. Qu gave an internal report on a draft of the Chinese latinization scheme in early 1929 to a small audience of specialists and Chinese students. The pamphlet, *A Draft of China's Latin-Style Letters,* appeared under Qu's adapted Russian name.

Up until May of that year, the proposed alphabet was primarily tested on the hundreds of Chinese students who were studying in Moscow at the time. A larger conference was then held toward the end of May. For the most part, it was Sinologists who were invited to have a broad discussion about the proposal. Additional support came when, in April 1930, the project leaders made contact with the Commissariat of Education, the Council of Nationalities of the USSR Central Executive Committee, and the Down-with-Illiteracy Society. The new alliance led to further collaboration with A. A. Dragunov (1900–1955) of the Institute of Oriental Studies of the USSR Academy of Sciences in Leningrad. Dragunov had also been conducting research on Chinese latinization and made a presentation in Moscow in May 1930, before an audience that included many of the latinization campaigners for the New Turkic Alphabet in the Soviet East. In principle, they supported Qu and Kolokolov's scheme. It was decided that Qu, Kolokolov, and Dragunov would work together on the final draft of the proposal. *China's Latin New Script* was published in 1930. The title on the cover appeared in three scripts: latinized Chinese, Chinese characters, and Russian.

Admittedly, Qu was less trained as a linguist than his Soviet and Chinese colleagues. But his ideological perspective offered a trenchant critique of the national language that captured the general tenor of the debate in China. How Chinese was to be romanized was not merely a question of convenience. Whether China was better off going with the Communist or the Nationalist vision also divided the conversation. When the Nationalists proposed a return to the use of literary Chinese during the conservative swing represented by the New Life Movement in 1934, language politics was catapulted to the forefront of the culture wars. The battle over language standardization was not a Chinese problem, Qu underscores in the pamphlet, but emblematic of the fate of all national languages. The national interest to extend and consolidate its sphere of influence at home as well as abroad inevitably steered the debate.

When Qu submitted the first draft of the scheme, Dunganese and Latin New Script inched ever closer together. Dragunov became the nodal point, along with colleague B. A. Vasiliev, who published on Dungans and their literature in the early 1930s. After working with Qu on Latin New Script, Dragunov began to write about the Dungans and the peculiarities of their language. He eventually became the chairman of the Committee of Experts for the Creation of a New Dungan Alphabet in 1952, when Dunganese made its belated transition to the Cyrillic script.

Shivaza continued to be involved in the subsequent proposals for Dunganese and served on this committee. Not only did the latinization of Dunganese and China's New Script share the same sources in the Soviet language campaigns, but the latinization of Dunganese was a crucial precedent for Latin New Script, directly intercepting as it did the fate of modern China's sounds and scripts. This collaboration has been all but forgotten in modern Chinese literary history. By the time Shivaza arrived in Beijing, he was received as a guest from afar. Shivaza's living testimony to modern China's twisted linguistic fate was too distant from his Chinese counterparts, even though it was at the very core of the regional speech and literary movements they rushed to champion.

In Beijing, Shivaza met Lao She (1899–1966), Mao Dun (1896–1981), Guo Moruo (1892–1978), Xiao San, Zhou Enlai (1898–1976), and pioneering scholars of Chinese Muslim history like Bai Shouyi (1909–2000) and Ma Jian (1906–1978). He had met Lao She and others the year before at a conference. A photograph of Shivaza with Lao She and Yan Wenjing (1915–2005) in Urumqi shows the excitement of a young Kirghiz minority writer standing next to the renowned Lao She, who was himself not ethnically Han but Manchu. Lao She was at the time deeply involved in promoting local culture and speech in the writing of literature, especially for China's ethnic minorities or "brother nationalities." His trip to Xinjiang was one of a number of appearances he made in promotion of the socialist brotherhood between China and the Third World from the early Communist period up through the Cultural Revolution. Yet he made no mention of Shivaza. The ceremonial aspect of meeting and greeting fellow writers on this occasion, we know from his diary, left him exhausted. He could barely remember the names of the writers he greeted.

While Lao She and Shivaza's encounter was a missed opportunity, Shivaza had an emotional reunion with Qu's close collaborator in the Latin New Script project, the poet Xiao San. Shivaza had met Xiao almost twenty years earlier in the summer of 1938, when Xiao was welcomed by the Union of the Kirghiz Writers in Frunze. Xiao celebrated Shivaza as a great Dunganese poet and dedicated a poem to him in the spirit of socialist brotherhood:

> You and I had known each other for thousands of years,
> Together we once sang the same song.
> But you were forced to leave your home country.
> It's your good fortune that you found a wholly new ancestral land.
> But you and we are still singing that same song.
> I believe that the two households will merge as one,
> And many families will unite into a large family.
> Perhaps here, perhaps there, you and I will see each other again.
> We will sit down around the same table,
> And together let our voices soar in singing that song!

It is an ironic reflection on modern Chinese literature that Dunganese was not recognized as one of its dialogic counterparts. While leftist Chinese writers were heavily invested in developing the cultural arts and languages of the masses, no one seemed to recognize Dunganese's extraordinary preservation of regional and ethnic speech against the odds of history. Dunganese's expressivity of the mother tongue in script embodied the very form they sought. Lao She, in many ways, missed what was right in front of him. The historical possibility of Dunganese was unthinkable in the Chinese context. The kind of dialectal or local color that Lao She promoted took standard Chinese as the reference point for inscribing ethnic identities. Ethnicities had their places in the Chinese nation, insofar as they submitted to its monolithic history. Dunganese, on the other hand, was both a language and a diasporic history that was out of place. It is thought provoking not only as an early example of writing Chinese in different scripts. It also poses a fundamental challenge for rethinking the foundation of literacy for the writing of modern Chinese literature.

BIBLIOGRAPHY: John DeFrancis, *In the Footsteps of Genghis Khan* (Honolulu, 1993). Svetlana Rimsky-Korsakoff Dyer, *Iasyr Shivaza: The Life and Works of a Soviet Dungan Poet* (Frankfurt am Main, Germany, 1991). A. G. Shprintsin, "From the History of the New Chinese Alphabet," in *The Countries and Peoples of the East: Selected Articles*, ed. D. A. Olderogge (editor-in-chief), V. Maretin, and B. A. Valskaya; trans. from the Russian by I. A. Gavrilov and P. F. Kostyuk (Moscow, 1974), 329–338. Jing Tsu, "Romanization without Rome: China's Latin New Script and Soviet Central Asia," in *Asia Inside Out: Connected Places*, ed. Eric Tagliacozzo, Helen F. Siu, and Peter C. Perdue (Cambridge, MA, 2015), 321–353.

JING TSU

1958 · JUNE 20

The World Peace Council commemorates Guan Hanqing.

A Monumental Model for Future Perfect Theater

Set during the late thirteenth century, when China was ruled by the Mongol Yuan dynasty, the spoken drama play *Guan Hanqing* opens on a small street just outside the Dadu (contemporary Beijing) city walls. There, the character Guan Hanqing—based on the historical playwright of the same name (ca. 1244–ca. 1300)—and local residents bear witness to the unjust execution of a chaste and filial young woman named Xiaolan. In response to this experience, Guan resolves to write a play condemning the corrupt political system that would sentence such virtue to death. The play that results is none other than the historical Guan Hanqing's most famous work, *Injustice to Dou E*. When he pitches the idea to his close compatriot, the actress and courtesan Zhu Lianxiu, she responds with a line that would be quoted in nearly every review of Tian Han's (1898–1968) play: "If you dare to write it, I will dare to perform it!" Perform it she does, turning the play-within-a-play into a truly daring deed by staging it for none other than the mother of the Mongol prime minister. The old dowager loves the play, but the performance runs afoul of one Deputy Prime Minister Akham, who is less than pleased by its thinly veiled jabs at the ruling system of which he is a part. He commands Guan and Zhu to amend the script and stage the revised version for him; when they refuse to change even a word, Akham sentences them to execution and orders the eyes of Zhu's disciple, Sai Lianxiu, gouged out. After a moving scene in jail, during which Guan and Zhu pledge undying commitment to justice and to one another, a lucky confluence of events results in the commutation of their death sentences, and the two heroes depart to exile in Hangzhou.

Composed in honor of the historical Guan Hanqing's seven hundredth anniversary in June 1958, this play by leading People's Republic of China (PRC) dramatist Tian Han stages a key moment in Chinese theater history and recasts the creative process of the play's eponymous playwright as an act of resistance. The audience for this commemoration, however, extended far beyond the national public. On the international front, Guan had been designated a "giant of world culture" by the World Peace Council, a largely Socialist organization that feted historical figures from its member countries with public celebrations, performances, and publication of their works. The privilege of holding opening ceremonies for Guan's commemoration therefore went to Moscow, where a program on June 20, 1958, featured musical and dance pieces, as well as a scene from Guan's *Injustice to Dou E* performed by actors of the Stanislavski and Nemirovich-Danchenko Moscow Academic Music Theatre. Back in China, the attention of the World Peace Council helped to revive domestic interest in Guan, and the year surrounding his anniversary saw numerous scholarly articles on Guan, several collections of his poetry and drama, and films made of contemporary opera adaptations of his plays. On the day that the Beijing People's Art Theater premiered *Guan Hanqing* at the Capital Theater—June 28, 1958—an exhibit on the playwright also opened in the Building of the Gate of Divine Might in the Forbidden City and Guan-related festivities took place in major cities throughout the country.

For the theater community, the play carried particular significance in that it marked Tian's return to writing spoken drama after a hiatus of more than a decade. One of the founding fathers of "modern" Chinese theater,

Tian was educated in Japan and an early proponent of Chinese spoken drama. He formed a major dramatic society, the Southern Nation Society, in the 1920s, took an active role in left-wing drama during the 1930s, and went on to become a prominent member of the cultural bureaucracy of the Chinese Communist Party. In addition to penning numerous spoken dramas, Tian was one of the architects of opera reform in the early 1950s and composed several pieces for Peking opera, such as a revolutionary adaptation of *The Legend of the White Snake*. He also spearheaded efforts to collect and publish historical materials from Chinese spoken drama in commemoration of the genre's fiftieth anniversary in 1957.

Tian's grounding in both the spoken drama and the traditional opera worlds made him an ideal candidate to compose a play in the former genre on a historical figure from the latter. The hybridity of *Guan Hanqing*, cemented by a few well-placed arias, nods to the importance of both "traditional" operatic forms and "modern" spoken drama during the first seventeen years of the PRC. On the one hand, local and regional operatic forms remained popular with audiences composed of the "workers, peasants, and soldiers" who formed the backbone of the new Chinese society. At the same time, however, the (socialist) realism offered by spoken drama seemed particularly well suited to the party's mandate that art accurately reflect the lives of those workers, peasants, and soldiers, and that it serve a political purpose. The government therefore actively promoted the growth of spoken drama by founding professional People's Art Theaters in major cities, encouraging the spread of spoken drama to the factories and countryside, and hosting festivals of new works in Beijing. This state sponsorship was largely successful, and the most iconic spoken drama productions of the 1950s, such as the Beijing People's Art Theater stagings of Cao Yu's (1910–1996) *Thunderstorm* (1954) and Lao She's (1899–1966) *Teahouse* (1958), would cement certain plays' status as modern classics. *Guan Hanqing* did not meet such a happy fate— the play was labeled a "poisonous weed" during the Cultural Revolution and its author persecuted—but the success of its premiere attests to a once-warm reception for the author's dual attempts to frame Chinese theater history within spoken drama and to embed spoken drama in that historical narrative.

Tying the writing and staging of Chinese theater history to commemorative moments, such as the seven hundredth anniversary of Guan, moreover played into practices of celebration and spectacle that were central to political life in the young PRC. Official state holidays like National Day and May Day were heralded with parades, mass performances, and public decorations, especially in the capital of Beijing. The ephemerality of these living commemorations was balanced by the more permanent construction of edifices such as the Monument to the People's Heroes in Tiananmen Square (completed in 1958) and the Ten Great Buildings of central Beijing (1959). In the composition of *Guan Hanqing*, Tian perhaps borrowed from the monumental impulse that drove political memorialization to establish the importance of a particular moment in theater history. That is to say, like a physical monument, *Guan Hanqing* celebrates a particular historical event—the moment at which Chinese drama proper is said to have matured—and pays homage to a foundational figure of the theater. Moreover, this gesture was sanctioned by the participation of the World Peace Council and state-sponsored arts organizations like the Beijing People's Art Theater.

Indeed, until this moment, the legacy of Guan was hardly secure. While his extant works were often cited in theater histories, the general paucity of biographical materials left the playwright himself an enigma. And it was precisely the lack of concrete historical data that allowed Tian to appropriate Guan as a historical precedent for using the theater to resist oppression. In order to make *Injustice to Dou E* into a playwright's response to systemic social injustice, Tian blurs history with a fictional narrative aligned with 1950s ideology. In particular, *Guan Hanqing* casts its main characters as clear heroes with ideologically correct social consciences. This technique, broadly speaking, conforms to the tenets of socialist realist literature and PRC propaganda plays. The social organization within *Guan Hanqing*, for example, emphasizes a clear hierarchy of heroic characters. Guan and Zhu Lianxiu emerge as the main protagonists by courageously using their art as a weapon against oppression and corruption. Guan, in particular, exhibits the most important characteristic of the model artist and model member of society: a commitment to responding to the needs of the people. However, the main heroes are also surrounded by a circle of positive supporting characters, thereby positioning collaborative creativity as central to the success of socially minded theater. Guan only dares to write *Injustice to Dou E* after Zhu encourages him and promises to perform it (scene 2), the play is perfected through suggestions from other actors and musicians (scene 5), and his imprisonment ultimately comes about when he refuses to allow his acting troupe to be punished for refusing to change the lines and lyrics that he wrote (scene 7). Guan may be the most prominent hero in the play, but his work could not be accomplished without his companions.

Already thus blurring the lines between history and fiction in order to update the life story of a historical figure to fit contemporary ideology, Tian pushed even further to blur the boundaries between Guan's various roles as doctor, playwright, actor, and audience within the play. In the play, Guan is a well-respected doctor, yet he also works closely with the theater community and is revealed to occasionally tread the boards himself. Guan also begins the play as audience to the execution of Xiaolan, and the general theatricality of that opening scene, which emphasizes the show-trial nature of Xiaolan's execution, signals from the outset that the characters in the world of the play are both spectators of a corrupt justice system and spectacles at its mercy.

Beyond the theater walls, this blurring of roles may have resonated with the audiences both for performances of *Guan Hanqing* in particular and for commemoratory events more generally. At the very time that Tian wrote the play, hundreds of thousands of workers, peasants, and soldiers were finding themselves transformed from audience members into actors as they joined work unit and village cultural troupes. The widespread promotion of amateur cultural production and the amateurization of professions like writing, music, and theater can be traced to the cultural policy proceeding from Mao Zedong's (1893–1976) *Talks at the Yan'an Forum on Literature and the Arts* in 1942. But it was during the 1950s that amateur theater came to permeate Chinese society to a greater degree than ever before. The beginning of the Great Leap Forward in 1958 was a period of especially intense focus on mass production of literature and the arts, with theater as one area of particularly high activity. Even Tian himself wrote a manifesto calling for a Great Leap in the theater that would require the participation of the masses and cooperation between professionals and amateurs.

Thus, in staging a point of origin for Chinese theater, *Guan Hanqing* also provided a history of relevance to all of its audience members. In fact, in the context of the sustained growth of amateur theater, the increased participation of nonprofessionals in theater activity, and the importance of the didactic link between professionals and nonprofessionals, *Guan Hanqing* may have been meant as a model for theater troupes from which any actor, professional or amateur, could learn and draw inspiration. The fact that the values embodied through Guan and his cohort are not theater-specific values but rather general socialist-revolutionary values adds another twist. The play may be not only a how-to guide for aspiring actor-audiences but also a more general metaphor for social interaction. That is to say, if an everyman can be an actor, then, to some extent, plays about actors might also be plays about every man. Heroic behavior encourages the common man to be heroic, and the model cooperation of the theater troupe suggests the proper behavior for all manner of collectives.

It is, moreover, a model that is inherently theatrical. *Guan Hanqing* is a play about a playwright keenly aware of his social and artistic agency. It is this awareness of the theatricality of the self and of one's own social role, as well as its more obvious use of the play-within-a-play construct, that brings *Guan Hanqing* close to Lionel Abel's seminal definition of the metaplay. Abel defines metatheater as theater that involves characters aware of their own theatricality and that reflects a world that is already theatricalized. Metatheatricality is therefore descriptive and self-reflective. *Guan Hanqing* echoes this, but if we read the play as having a didactic, "how-to" function, it becomes as much a projection for the *future* as a comment on the past. Far from a realistic reflection of existing social relationships, it models—and preemptively commemorates—a future perfect world in which professionals and amateurs, actors and masses, are one, and in which daily life is theatrical.

BIBLIOGRAPHY: Lionel Abel, *Tragedy and Metatheatre* (New York, 2003). Chang-tai Hung, *Mao's New World: Political Culture in the Early People's Republic* (Berkeley, CA, 2011). Liang Luo, *The Avant-Garde and the Popular in Modern China: Tian Han and the Intersection of Performance and Politics* (Ann Arbor, MI, 2014). Colin Mackerras, *The Chinese Theater in Modern Times, from 1840 to the Present Day* (Amherst, MA, 1975). Tian Han, *Guan Hanqing*, trans. Amy Dooling, in *The Columbia Anthology of Modern Chinese Drama*, ed. Xiaomei Chen (New York, 2010), 385–460. Rudolf Wagner, *The Chinese Historical Drama: Four Studies* (Berkeley, CA, 1990).

TARRYN LI-MIN CHUN

1958

"Six billion people in the divine land are all Yaos and Shuns."

Mao Zedong Publishes Nineteen Poems *and Launches the New Folk Song Movement*

"I read in the *People's Daily* of June 30 that Yujiang County had terminated the 'blood-sucking parasite.' This filled my mind with so many thoughts that I spent a sleepless night. As a balmy breeze is blowing and the morning sun shines on the window, I gaze at the southern sky and take up my brush with delight."

This is the preface, composed by Mao Zedong (1893–1976) on July 1, 1958, to his two poems written in a classical verse form upon learning of the eradication of the parasitic disease known as schistosomiasis in Jiangxi. Mao was not a poet. In premodern China, writing poetry was what one did among many other things in life; it had become an essential form of cultural capital in late imperial times, but it was not what defined who one was as it does in modern times. Mao was a Communist revolutionary and the chairman of the People's Republic of China, and he happened to also write poetry—he was not a poet in the modern sense of the word, even though his poems, all in classical forms, are so popular that few Chinese today have not heard them or cannot recite a few lines from them. The question, however, remains: Why is this fact—that Mao was a writer of classical-style poetry—important, if it is important at all, for China's modern history and literature?

While there is no simple answer to this question, some other happenings in China that same year offer some tantalizing clues. The year 1958 was when truth and desire were not distinguished from each other, when delusions and lies were lived out on such a grand scale that they entrapped the entire nation in their intricate web. On August 25, the *Anhui Daily* printed a picture of a young girl sitting atop wheat stalks in a wheat field, indicating that the wheat stalks were growing so thickly that they could hold up a person's weight. The girl was from Fanchang, Anhui, a county on the southeastern bank of the Yangtze River. Just two days earlier, inspired by Macheng, a Hubei county that had announced the miraculous production of 36,900 catties of wheat in one *mu* (about 0.16 acres), Fanchang claimed to have produced 43,075 catties (roughly

47,300 pounds) of wheat in one *mu*. Even in a year when astronomical production figures filled headlines, the news appearing in the *People's Daily* caused such a stir that Guo Moruo (1892–1978), the cultural luminary of the People's Republic, was moved to write a poem to celebrate the event. The poem, composed in the classical form of a seven-syllable-line quatrain, ends with the couplet, "Fanchang truly deserves its name—'thriving and prosperous'; / it comes right on the heels of Macheng." The poem was printed in the *People's Daily* on September 2, 1958. As if goaded by the poem, Macheng proclaimed the new record figure of 52,000 catties per *mu* two days later, and Guo followed up with another poem. In the essay published alongside the new poem, Guo laments, "The speed of our pen cannot catch up with the speed of [grain] production."

This story provides an allegory of the key events of 1958. This was the year of the Great Leap Forward, during which the Chinese Communist Party, led by Mao, launched its socioeconomic campaign to vastly accelerate the nation's industrial and agricultural production. Across China numerous small blast furnaces were set up to produce steel, and regions competed to declare the largest grain production per *mu* ever. At the same time, there was another "great leap forward" under way, in the form of words and rhymes: it was the movement of producing poems—referred to as "folk songs"—in mass quantity, from urban to rural areas throughout the country. Barely one hundred miles to the north of Fanchang was a town called Sijixiang, which had 267 production teams and 267 "poetry writing units." In the summer of 1958, the town residents reportedly produced over two hundred thousand poems. A popular slogan summarizes the agrarian and literary escalation: "Reap a double harvest in production and poetry." Poems were written on posters, blackboards, walls, and wooden or bamboo plaques. They could be found from factories to villages, from city streets to farming fields. They were printed in newspapers and magazines or as collections. They also appeared as oral performances, improvised in countless public poetry competitions.

If Guo underestimated the speed of the pen, he made up for it by editing, together with another powerful cultural figure, Zhou Yang (1908–1989), a volume entitled *Red Flag Ballads*, which includes three hundred poems—all anonymous—from the 1958 poetry movement. The book is divided into four sections: "Odes to the Party," "Songs of the Agricultural Great Leap Forward," "Songs of the Industrial Great Leap Forward," and

"Songs of Defending the Motherland." The selections aspire to represent various Chinese provinces and as many non-Han ethnic peoples as possible, with each poem's place of origin given at the end of the poem. Typical of the poems produced in 1958, these are usually short and isometric, rhyming *aaba*; the preferred line length is seven syllables, with each syllable represented by a single Chinese character. Such formal features strongly evoke a certain kind of classical Chinese poetry. Interestingly, with a few exceptions, only poems attributed to the ethnic peoples are in the "free verse" that characterizes modern Chinese vernacular poetry, indicating that they have been translated from a non-Han language.

The volume, on one hand, epitomizes the socialist modern: the poems are strewn with fashionable neologisms and contemporary political lingo such as "People's Commune," "general line [of the party]," and "electric welding." On the other hand, it is eerily old fashioned: in many ways it is a socialist transformation of *The Book of Songs*, China's earliest poetry collection, which took shape from the eleventh through the seventh century BCE. Supposedly edited by Confucius himself, *The Book of Songs* was studied by every student throughout imperial China. It contains just over three hundred Zhou dynasty ritual hymns and ballads divided into four sections: the "Airs" or the "Airs of the Domains," grouped into fifteen regions that represent many of the feudal domains of the early Zhou monarchy; the "Odes," subdivided into "Great Odes" and "Lesser Odes"; and the "Hymns." The number of poems and the number of sections of the collection form a neat parallel with *Red Flag Ballads*. To further drive the lesson home, the editors of *Red Flag Ballads* explicitly point out the volume's correspondence to *The Book of Songs*: in their preface they call the poems "the new 'Airs of the Domains' of the new socialist age," compared to which, however, "even the Three Hundred Poems [a traditional reference to *The Book of Songs*] are outshone." The preface effectively places the editors in the position of Confucius.

Throughout the preface the editors cite from tradition to demonstrate the present's superiority to the cultural past, though the comparison only serves to highlight the deep ties to tradition. But the editors also quote the canonical statement about poetry from the *Book of Documents*, another Confucian classic, in a positive light: "The Poem articulates what is on the mind intently; song makes language lasting." This statement about the nature of poetry, which shows how *The Book of Songs* was understood in premodern China, is clearly meant to be the framework of interpretation for *Red Flag Ballads.*

Not all Chinese poetry was understood in the same way as *The Book of Songs* , but *The Book of Songs* had a profound influence on the way later poetry—and literature in general—was understood. Poetry was never just an art, but had a central position in Confucian political theory. It was considered the direct expression of an individual in a particular historical situation, the direct outcome of social and historical circumstances. The poems of the "Airs" section were supposed to have been popular songs sung by the common folk. When the people are happy, they sing to express their joy; when the people are distressed about the condition of the age, they sing to express their distress and to criticize. Since every song that becomes popular is a symptom of something, if the king gets to hear the distressed songs and is wise, he reforms the government. One legend about the origin of the "Airs" is that the Zhou kings sent officials to villages to collect songs in order to learn the people's concerns. In 1984, Chen Kaige (1952–) directed his famous movie, *Yellow Earth*, which opens with a Communist soldier walking the barren plateau of northern Shaanxi and collecting local songs. Shaanxi is known as the birthplace of the Communist Revolution; it was also the old Zhou heartland. The immense cultural resonance of this seemingly strange gesture on the part of a Communist soldier—collecting folk songs—was not lost on the Chinese audience.

The Chinese term used for the "Airs" is *feng*, whose root meaning is "wind," the wind that blows on plants and makes them bend—the wind that "sways." By way of a metaphor, it refers to influence: "a program of moral education" implicit in the poems of *The Book of Songs*, as well as in the structure given to the collection by its legendary editor, Confucius. Although most of the "Airs" are about a world gone wrong, they were believed to be composed by good people in bad times, and so reading them would give a reader immediate, emotional access to the goodness in the past and transform the reader. Reading *The Book of Songs* is thus a moral education that makes a person good; collectively, this education can change culture and society. The impact of the traditional interpretation of *The Book of Songs* could still be seen in the twentieth century: in Mao's decision to launch a *"cultural* revolution," in his intense concern with literature and art, and in his fascination with poetry in particular.

The Cultural Revolution (1966–1976), one of the most traumatic events in all Chinese history, is already incipient in *Red Flag Ballads*. In contrast to the "Airs," all poems in *Red Flag Ballads* are joyful: there is not a single word of discontent. It is supposed to be symptomatic of a grand age, testifying to the moral perfection not only of the composers but also of the times. With the people so happy, there is no need for the government to reform its ways, and the moral education implicit in this volume is directed at a different target altogether. In the words of the editors, *Red Flag Ballads* is intended to enlighten "our writers and poets"—known as the scholar elite in the past and intelligentsia in the present, for "the new folk songs will produce a greater and greater influence on the development of modern poetry." Mao was intent on transformation: transforming the common folk into self-conscious, progressive proletariats, and the intellectuals into humbled members of laboring masses. Ironically, he chose to start with "teaching through poetry"—the ancient Confucian method of bringing about social change.

Mao's own poetry is also most certainly intended as *feng*, a wind and influence from above to transform those below, like the breeze and the sun in the preface to his schistosomiasis poems. It was probably no coincidence that September 1958 witnessed the publication of a collection of nineteen of Mao's poems in English translation by Beijing's Foreign Language Press. The number nineteen, like the number three hundred, has a special significance because of the canonical group of poems traditionally referred to as the "Nineteen Old Poems," which, along with *The Book of Songs*, stands at the fountainhead of classical Chinese poetry.

In *Red Flag Ballads*, a poem from Fanchang, Anhui, and a poem from Macheng, Hubei, are placed next to each other (they are conspicuously absent from the edition printed in 1979, after the end of the Mao era). While the Macheng poem is about harvesting, the Fanchang poem sings of plowing, as well as praising the power of singing. And yet, the term used in the Fanchang poem, *"rammer's* chant" (italics mine), is at odds with the image of plowing, revealing an embarrassing level of ignorance of the alleged "peasant author(s)" and of the editors. But this is something that only the intellectuals, imagining pure simplicity and sincerity in their romanticized "folk," would care about; the folk themselves were happily gathering wheat stalks into one field to create astronomical production figures.

Mao's schistosomiasis poem number 2 states, "Six billion people in the divine land are all Yaos and Shuns." Yao and Shun are legendary sage emperors in antiquity. Mao seemed blissfully unaware of the irony (and the impossibility) of using the very discourse he wished to eliminate to accomplish the elimination. In other words, in trying to change the past, he reproduced it. He certainly could not have foreseen that it would take capitalism, the Internet, and flourishing social media to finally transform China.

BIBLIOGRAPHY: Guo Moruo and Zhou Yang, ed., *Hongqi geyao* (Beijing, 1958; rev. ed., 1979). Mao Zedong, *Nineteen Poems* (Beijing, 1958). Stephen Owen, *Readings in Chinese Literary Thought* (Cambridge, MA, 1992). Tianying, *1958 nian Zhongguo min'ge yundong* (Shanghai, 1959; repr., 1978).

XIAOFEI TIAN

1959 · FEBRUARY 28

Make changes, make changes with no hesitation!"

On The Song of Youth *and Literary Bowdlerization*

At the end of February 1959, Yang Mo (1914–1995) attended a conference at Beijing Film Studio to discuss how to adapt her novel *The Song of Youth* (1958) into a movie for the tenth anniversary of the founding of the People's Republic of China. At the conference she met Guo Kai, a worker at Beijing Electron Tube Factory, who had just published a harsh critique of her novel in the magazine *China Youth*, and learned from Guo that he had been repeatedly urged to write his article as a spokesperson for workers. Sensing Guo was telling the truth but unable to figure out who might be behind him, Yang grew worried and wrote down, "Make changes, make changes with no hesitation!" in her diary on February 28. She then spent the next three months revising her novel to correct the mistakes Guo had pointed out, namely, petit bourgeois self-expression, an inattention to workers and peasants and to revolutionary intellectuals' integration with workers and peasants, and a failure to describe the processes of thought reform, especially in the heroine Lin Daojing's mind.

In fact, Guo was not the first person to find fault with *The Song of Youth* from a class standpoint. In January 1956, Ouyang Fanhai (1912–1970), a veteran literary critic asked by China Youth Publishing House to review Yang's manuscript, wrote a lengthy report detailing the manuscript's deficiencies in its analysis and criticism of the heroine's petit bourgeois mentality. Effectively shelved because of Ouyang's negative assessment, the manuscript would have to wait for the Hundred Flowers Campaign for its second chance.

The revisions Yang had to make to her novel reveal the risks a writer faced in Socialist China. After the Communist takeover in 1949, literary activities in China came increasingly under government control. Under the general direction of the party, the Chinese Writers' Association, the only public ladder of success for writers, recruited, guided, and monitored writers throughout the country, as Perry Link points out. Mao Zedong's (1893–1976) 1942 *Talks at the Yan'an Forum on Literature and Art* became the sacred guidelines for writers, forcibly implemented by Communist ideologues. Brought in the spirit of Mao's *Talks*, Guo's charges against Yang could not be easily brushed aside. That Guo appeared to have political backing from above only made Yang's situation even more fraught with potential danger. The control of literature, though heavy handed, was not standardized and left room for party leaders' overt and covert interventions. Mao, for example, intruded into the field of literature in 1955 and set the tone for the persecution of the Hu Feng (1902–1985) group with editorial comments he wrote anonymously for the party newspaper, the *People's Daily*. Faced with ideological pressure and potential political danger, Yang had no choice but to give in.

To placate her critics, Yang trimmed Lin Daojing's sentimentality and added eight chapters in an expanded version of *The Song of Youth* that came out in 1960. In the eight chapters, Lin's mentor Jiang Hua instructs her to join a group of poor peasants in their revolutionary struggle against oppression and exploitation. Ironically, getting close to the peasants only makes Lin realize her own political otherness, a result of her birth into the exploitative class, and her own inferiority in political consciousness. Kept in the dark by her peasant leader, she can only watch from a distance and imagine how the peasants snatch a harvest from a landlord.

The differences between the two versions of Yang's novel bore out the irreconcilable contradictions in the party's stand on intellectuals. To obtain their cooperation in socialist construction, the party needed to make intellectuals believe that they could be transformed and could put their expertise to full use in the new society. The thought reform campaign of the early 1950s, as Eddy U notes, was built on the assumption that intellectuals, no matter how careerist or antirevolutionary they had been, could turn over a new leaf through diligent study and reflection. Accordingly, Yang fleshed out the educability of most of the intellectual characters, including senior professors, in the earlier version of her novel, finished in April 1955. On the other hand, the party also remained highly suspicious of intellectuals because of their impure class origins. Since intellectuals could not change their class origins, thought reform became a rather Sisyphean task. As illustrated by the added chapters, Lin Daojing, with her inextricable connection to the exploitative class highlighted by the author, can never truly join the ranks of the working class, no matter how energetically she works for the revolution.

The triumph of anti-intellectualism, however, was not complete. In the second version, three intellectuals—Lu Jiachuan, Jiang Hua and Lin Hong—still remain Lin Daojing's mentors on her revolutionary journey, despite their non-working-class origins. The peasants, for all their political consciousness and revolutionary potential, still need to be awakened, organized, and directed by Jiang Hua in their struggle against the landlord. Even the climax of the novel, the December 9, 1935, student rally in Beiping (Beijing), is still portrayed as an event arising from the educated and the enlightened, an event essentially unrelated to the suffering of the working class.

The durability of Yang's belief in the enlightening role of the revolutionary intellectual was made possible not so much by personal courage as by the ambivalent attitude toward intellectuals in Marxism. While acknowledging intellectuals' weaknesses, such as their individualism, their lack of "revolutionary steadfastness," and their incapacity to submit to political discipline, both Karl Marx (1818–1883) and Vladimir Lenin (1870–1924) believed the theory of socialism would arise among the revolutionary socialist intelligentsia, who then would guide the working class toward socialist revolution. Left to its own devices, the working class would only be capable of developing at most a "trade-union consciousness." Besides, the personal histories of both the founders of Marxism and the vast majority of Communist leaders in China, including Mao himself, would prove to Yang that a nonproletarian origin was not necessarily an insurmountable obstacle for the revolutionary intellectual in the process of self-transformation.

As the only classic in the canon of Chinese socialist fiction that features an intellectual as its main character, *The Song of Youth* shows how the ambiguities in Marxism and in the party's stand on intellectuals both facilitated and constrained Yang's writing. While taking advantage of the party's positive views of intellectuals, Yang also tried to hold on to a modicum of life experience and self-identity in her novel, especially in the earlier version. Cast in the form of a bildungsroman that contains certain autobiographical elements, this version demonstrates the function of the self in striving for knowledge of the world and in making one's own choices in life. As a work that offers a textbook case of romantic sublimation, as Ban Wang argues in light of Lin's growth from a May Fourth youth to a Communist, it also manages to keep its realist elements, including the complexities of Lin's mind, from being completely erased.

Belief in the revolutionary intellectual remained an article of faith for Yang for the rest of her writing career. In *Dawn Is About to Break in the East* (1980), a novel written under the influence of the Cultural Revolution, the hero, an educated revolutionary knight-errant, always seeks guidance from an intellectual mentor at times of difficulty. In *The Song of Beauty* (1986), remodeled from *Dawn Is About to Break in the East*, the heroine, a young doctor and Lin Daojing look-alike, contributes to the revolution with her medical know-how and political reliability. Clearly this image echoes the party's new respect for scientific knowledge and trust in intellectuals in the drive toward the Four Modernizations, launched in the era of reforms. More significantly, in *The Song of Heroes* (1990), the last novel in her career, Yang goes to a considerable length to glorify Lu Jiachuan and Lin Daojing for their courageous opposition to a campaign against imagined Trotskyites in the revolutionary ranks. As she praises Lu and Lin for their intellectual independence and criticizes Jiang Hua for his blind faith in the party's infallibility, Yang tries cautiously to reclaim modern intellectuals' central values, such as personal autonomy and the use of critical reason. At the same time she also calls attention to Lin's need for love, a need Lin's husband, Jiang Hua, fails to satisfy because he is too busy with his work for the party. The comeback of love connects *The Song of Heroes* to what Haiyan Lee calls the social imaginary of the self in modern China, an imaginary that heralds the rise of the private, the personal, and the everyday. Emotional richness, once condemned as a symptom of petit bourgeois mentality, is rehabilitated as a corrective for blind submission to the party.

Always trying to stay in the party's good graces, Yang was rewarded with social status and material privileges after the first version of *The Song of Youth* made her a renowned writer. However, her career was also marked by precariousness. She could not afford to stray from Marxism. While the ambiguities in the official ideology provided some room for her negotiation for self-expression, she was not exempt from attacks launched by critics who resorted to the same official ideology. Moreover, the desire to follow the party at all times compelled her to make continual adjustments to her works, in accordance with the latest shift in official policies. As a result, change became an important characteristic of her fiction, as could be seen in the different emphases in her portrayals of intellectuals. Worse still, her efforts to keep pace with policy changes resulted in inconsistencies in her fiction over time. In short, she had to pay a price as she tried to "serve politics" for the moment.

BIBLIOGRAPHY: Haiyan Lee, *Revolution of the Heart: A Genealogy of Love in China, 1900–1950* (Stanford, CA, 2007). Perry Link, *The Uses of Literature: Life in the Socialist Chinese Literary System* (Princeton, NJ, 2000). Eddy U, "The Making of Chinese Intellectuals: Representations and Organization in the Thought Reform Campaign," *The China Quarterly* 192 (2007): 971–989. Ban Wang, "Revolutionary Realism and Revolutionary Romanticism: *The Song of Youth*," in *Columbia Companion to Modern East Asian Literature*, ed. Joshua Mostow (New York, 2003), 470–475. Yang Mo, *The Song of Youth*, trans. Nan Ying (Peking, 1964).

YUNZHONG SHU

1960 · OCTOBER

An underground Chinese Malaysian war novel is published.

Hunger *and the Chinese Malaysian Leftist Narrative*

In 1960, a handwritten and mimeographed Chinese-language novel of limited circulation was published in Penang, a city in Kedah Province, not far from the current Malaysia-Thailand border. In 2008, twenty years after its author's passing and fifty years after Malaya's declaration of independence, the book received its first official printing in Kuala Lumpur, the Malaysian capital city. Beginning in the early nineteenth century and lasting until the end of World War II, the Malay Peninsula and the island of Singapore were variously under British control, and the area was called British Malaya. In 1957, the peninsula became an independent state called the Federation of Malaya, and then, in 1963, joined with Singapore and two other states to become Malaysia (although Singapore would become independent again only two years later). The novel's reappearance in Malaysia had far-reaching repercussions across the Sinophone world, particularly among the ideological left, as it caused Chinese Malaysians to recall and confront a nearly forgotten yet bitter past. Written by a member of the Malayan Communist Party (MCP) who published under the pseudonym Jin Zhimang (1912–1988), the novel *Hunger* sheds light on the diverging realities of the global socialist movement during the mid-twentieth century and highlights the power of spiritual sustenance to overcome even the harshest of physical trials.

Jin Zhimang (given name Chen Shuying) and his wife arrived in Singapore in 1937, after deciding to leave Shanghai in protest of their parents' objection to their marriage. As an active leftist in Shanghai, Jin was already predisposed to consider agitating for revolution overseas, and his family's resistance provided the necessary motivation for him to take his beliefs abroad. Upon his arrival, Jin was met with the news of the Marco Polo Bridge Incident (July 7–9), a battle between the Republic of China's National Revolutionary Army and the Imperial Japanese Army that occurred outside Beijing, and consequently decided to actively promote the anti-Japanese movement among the Malayan Chinese community. During the early period of his life in Malaya, he and his wife lived in Tualang, a small coastal town in the state of Perak, where they taught at the Tong Han

Chinese primary school. There, the dramatist and MCP member Wu Tian (1912–1989) encouraged Jin to engage in creative writing, a moment that marked the beginning of his literary career. When the Japanese occupied Malaya during World War II, Jin joined the underground Anti-Japanese League and put his newfound literary skills to work on its behalf.

Jin's decision to immigrate to Malaya is representative of a larger trend of Chinese literati's "southern migration," which began during the early twentieth century and continued into the mid-1960s. According to one study conducted by Guo Huifen, more than 159 authors either traveled to or settled in Southeast Asia between 1919 and 1949, and even greater numbers migrated south after the victory of the Chinese Communist Party (CCP) and the establishment of the People's Republic of China (PRC). In the case of Malay(si)a, this trend manifested itself as an ever-growing overseas Chinese population that was confronted with an unwelcoming cultural atmosphere and series of oppressive political policies, first implemented by the British colonial government and later expanded by the independent Malayan Federation. Despite an increasingly antagonistic political atmosphere, however, this group of diasporic Chinese intellectuals played a crucial role in promoting Chinese education and developing the local publishing industry. Significantly, as part of this process, they fostered the development of Chinese-language literature in Malaysia (including Singapore, before 1965, when Singapore revolted and gained independence from Malaysia), and many of them left indelible traces on the Chinese literary tradition, particularly left-wing writers from the prewar period.

As a member of this pioneering group of Chinese intellectuals living in diaspora, Jin's distinct contribution to the Malaysian literary scene not only reflects his dedication to leftist values, but is also prescient of literary debates to come. After the Japanese surrender and withdrawal from Malaya in 1945, Jin left his small-town job and moved to Kuala Lumpur. He first worked as the editor for *Friends in Arms*, a publication of the Anti-Japanese Veteran Comrades Society, and later as editor of *New Winds*, the literary supplement to the MCP-organized newspaper *The People's Voice*. It was in this capacity that Jin was also drawn into several ideological conflicts with members of the CCP-affiliated literati in Malaya, most notably in regard to the question whether Chinese-language literature should be localized. This literary event, known as the "debate over the uniqueness of Chinese Malayan literature," even gained the attention of writers such as Guo Moruo (1892–1978) and Xia Yan (1890–1957), who were far away in Hong Kong at the time—a testament to the high stakes invested in the outcome of the debate.

In these debates, Jin expressed the view that creative writing should pay close attention to the "present time and place" of Malay(si)a, a view that solidified his place in Chinese literary history. He argued that literature lacking such a focus would otherwise be unsuitable to call "Chinese Malayan literature" and could only be properly named "expatriate literature." This opinion contradicted the views of the majority of Chinese literati who had also migrated south and were loyal to their homeland, in turn establishing a tacit bright line that distinguished the political agenda of the CCP in Malaya from that of the MCP. For the CCP, questions of national allegiance and betrayal lurked just below the surface of such literary ruminations; for the MCP, an agenda of Malayan independence from the British colonial presence permeated such remarks, without any regard for one's loyalty to a supposed Chinese homeland. As a revolutionary Communist devoted to the ideal of socialist internationalism, it is not surprising that Jin was ready and willing to lay down his roots beyond China. At the same time, however, the PRC's unique path for realizing the socialist dream was ideologically irreconcilable with Jin's internationalist vision. Considered in a broader historical political context, this literary debate can therefore be understood as a microcosm of the deteriorating Sino-Soviet relationship.

At the same time that Jin was engaging in these literary debates, he was also actively involved in the anti-British movement organized by the MCP. The movement's ultimate goal was the establishment of a "Malayan People's Democratic Republic," to be achieved by the twin processes of expelling the British and fostering a Malayan national consciousness among the overseas Chinese in Malaya. On June 20, 1948, however, the British colonial government declared a state of emergency in response to Communist agitation in Malaya, and the twelve-year guerrilla war known as the Malayan Emergency—or the Anti-British National Liberation War, depending on one's affiliation—was set in motion. Jin immediately decided to join the MCP forces and took up position in the jungles in Temerloh, Pahang, located near the current Malaysia-Thailand border.

His sojourn in the jungle would last thirteen years, ending only when the MCP sent him to the PRC in 1961.

Jin's experience in the jungle would also serve as the foundation for his war novel, *Hunger*. The novel takes place following the implementation of the 1950 Briggs Plan—a British strategy whereby overseas Chinese in Malaya were forcibly relocated into "New Villages" in order to monitor the Chinese population and limit the sending of supplies to MCP insurgents—and is based on an incident that occurred in April 1952, when British marines were photographed holding the decapitated heads of two MCP insurgents. It tells the story of a group of fifteen MCP guerrillas—a group of men, women, and children—who lose contact with the main force, are cut off from the supply chain, and flee into the jungle; it is not difficult to imagine the struggles they face. After enduring the hunger and hardship of the Malayan jungle, as well as surviving the defection and sacrifice of several comrades-in-arms, only five members of the original party remain.

With a skilled, simple, and straightforward style—reminiscent of early period Soviet revolutionary literature, such as Alexander Alexandrovich Fadeyev's (1901–1956) *The Rout*, once extoled and translated by Lu Xun (1881–1936)—Jin brings together two seemingly unrelated subjects, namely, revolution and hunger. Author and literary critic Ng Kim Chew (1967–) notes that given Malaya's dense forests and fertile soils, the extreme famine *Hunger* depicts exceeds the conditions of reality, and that the lost band's physical poverty consequently takes on symbolic and allegorical dimensions. Moreover, the novel's visceral presentation of the guerrillas' struggles with exile, starvation, and death is at odds with the general leftist literary model of "Big, Tall, and Perfect," in turn augmenting the symbolic power of Jin's leftist ideological commitment to provide spiritual sustenance for the starving faithful. The merciful release of death vindicates the soldiers' revolutionary zeal, while at the same time conveying the necessary regret and remorse over abandoning the world they hoped to change. *Hunger*'s ambivalent presentation of spiritual catharsis at the cost of physical annihilation captures the zeitgeist among leftists at the time, encapsulating their fervent desire for revolution in Malaya and their coming to terms with its price.

What Jin's *Hunger* does not consider, however, are the alternative actors that could achieve Malayan independence. In 1955, Tunku Abdul Rahman

(1903–1990), the chief minister of the government of the Federation of Malaya, initiated the Baling Talks—a joint meeting between the British, the Malayan elected officials, and representatives of the MCP—as a means of diffusing rising tensions. While the talks ultimately failed, the symbolic gesture of peace provided Tunku and his supporters with the necessary political capital to pressure the British to accelerate the independence process, which culminated in the Federation of Malaya gaining independence two years later, in 1957. After independence, the MCP lost its primary bargaining chip as the anti-imperial and anticolonial party, and subsequently became the new government's target of pursuit. In 1963, on the premise of preventing the expansion of communism into Southeast Asia, Tunku united the four regional political entities—Singapore, Sarawak, North Borneo, and the Federation of Malaya—to form a new federal government over the territory they would call Malaysia. It is widely believed that the British and Americans orchestrated this process, and it is therefore not surprising that the MCP refused to recognize the new government—a predictable yet unavoidable result of Cold War–era politics.

It was also at this juncture that the overseas Chinese members of the MCP were faced with a unique challenge: As ethnic minorities in a foreign country who promoted staunch internationalist socialist values, what happens next? Should the goal be to clarify their position on the revolution and fight for a place for Chinese people in Malaysia, or perhaps to overthrow the newly established political authority (dominated by ethnic Malays)? Or should they try to link up with the international proletariat? For Jin, the MCP's decision to send him to the PRC simplified this potential crisis of intentionality. For many others, however, détente was over a decade away, and Malaysia's increasingly hostile domestic policies, aimed at controlling the overseas Chinese population, would continue to test their revolutionary resolve.

As a means of remembering and re-membering the historical narrative of the international socialist movement, *Hunger* gives new life to a lost generation of dedicated Marxist revolutionaries in Malaya. Considering once more the novel's allegorical potential, the title of the novel appears to speak for itself—it represents a boundless yearning that can never be fully satisfied, one to rectify the fundamental physical impoverishment and psychological deficiency of one's existence. But this is perhaps Jin's greatest contribution, as *Hunger* provides an inexhaustible reserve of spiritual sustenance in the face of an existential crisis, enabling one's convictions to justify one's existence. It is in this way that Jin's soldiers are able to understand their death as an eternal homecoming, at the same time that they are forced to come to terms with the limitations of their corporeal existence. Despite Jin's unwavering apology for leftist values, David Der-wei Wang also observes something transcendental his work: "Jin Zhimang makes the details of realism speak, yet, whether intentionally or not, his most realistic moments reveal the absurd undertones of war and revolution—without regard to the left or the right."

In 1989, after decades of struggle, the MCP was finally dissolved. Jin did not live to see the party's dissolution, however, and passed away in 1988 in the PRC, where he had remained since his assignment there in 1961. As the few remaining guerrilla soldiers left the jungle for good, the memory of a generation of Malay(si)an revolutionaries was slowly forgotten in the forward march of History—until, that is, the pangs of *Hunger* reminded the world once more of their righteous sacrifice.

BIBLIOGRAPHY: Chong Fah Hing, *Ji'e de wenxueshi jushou: Jin Zhimang yu zuoyi mahua* (Hong Kong, 2007). Jin Zhimang, *Ji'e* (Kuala Lumpur, 2008). Ng Kim Chew, *Zuihou de zhanyi: Lun Jin Zhimang de Ji'e* (Kuala Lumpur, 2010). David Der-wei Wang, *Zhanzheng xushi yu xushi zhanzheng: Yan'an, Jin Men, ji qi yiwai* (Beijing, 2015).

CHONG FAH HING *and* KYLE SHERNUK

1962 · JUNE

Ru Zhijuan's story "The Lost Night" is published in *Shanghai Literature.*

Three Ironic Moments in My Mother Ru Zhijuan's Literary Career

My mother's (Ru Zhijuan, 1925–1998) writing career peaked precisely when my father's (Wang Xiaoping, 1919–2003) was in decline—which, you could say, was the first of her three ironies. This was during the late 1950s and early 1960s, at the apex of the establishment of socialism in China. Against the backdrop of the global Cold War, as mainland China's autonomy became inevitable and a brand-new set of worker-peasant political rights demanded a spiritual value in accordance with their original intention, literature came to offer a way of reconstructing culture, incorporating ideology, and achieving communist ideals. Authors like my parents who joined the revolution—and in the process were exposed to a body of Chinese-style communist theory that would change their lives—could not but have a radical attitude toward society, to the point that they willingly accepted their mission, hoping to channel their individual efforts into those of the collective and work to advance the goals that they had sworn to achieve.

The odd thing, however, was that two people with such similar backgrounds and aspirations could end up following such different paths. Father had been working for one of the army's theatrical troupes, but he was sacked during the Anti-Rightist Movement in the late 1950s. To this day, I am still not entirely clear on the precise reason why he was fired. It was presented as a personnel issue, but also seemed to be related to his status as a returned overseas Chinese (he was originally from Singapore). At the same time, his dismissal also seemed to have something to do with his personality. Whatever the reason, he was kicked out of the army and made an ordinary civilian, as a result of which our family's standard of living fell precipitously.

Mother would often say that, to prevent our family from going down the drain, it had been necessary to "apply the brakes and focus on her children"—these children being my sister and me. I later heard Mother explain that because of Father's pay cut, they had to remove me and my sister from our expensive preschool. This didn't bother us, however, and it could be said that leaving the preschool was the first time we were able to experience the trials and tribulations of the real world. This is what it meant to experience childhood after Mother had applied the brakes. At the same time, Mother also wanted to demonstrate that her and Father's spirits truly belonged to the collective, and therefore she began to write even more prolifically.

However, literary composition is a unique form of labor and, unlike material production, it is shaped not only by collective need but also by individual experience, emotion, and understanding. Given that Mother—based on her experience, circumstances, personality, and temperament—was deemed to be a petit bourgeois intellectual, her writing therefore had to address the tricky question of the relationship between the individual and the collective. This impasse ultimately yielded something that was more than a mere sensibility but less than a comprehensive worldview—so perhaps we should simply call it a state of mind. Furthermore, I thought Father's situation inevitably complicated Mother's relationship to the collective, leaving her at the margins of history with no alternative but to rely on her own resources. As a result, in her war-themed writings, she used detailed descriptions of characters and settings to write works that were even praised by the minister of culture, Mao Dun (1896–1981).

Even today, decades later, Mother's short story "Lilies" is still included in Chinese middle school textbooks, and her name, Ru Zhijuan, is familiar to all lovers of literature. More importantly, she was encouraged to develop her own style. However, it was precisely her act of settling down to write that aroused the most suspicion and came to be referred to critically as focusing on "household affairs" and "family bonds." This was the second irony of her career. In the 1980s, as China's new literature began to emerge, Mother used these critiques as inspiration for two new works, which she titled "Household Affairs" and "Family Bonds." She did this both to help rehabilitate herself and also to help rectify these phrases. Even during that period, when private emotion was tightly regulated, Mother and others of her generation continued to display a unique form of expression—one that was not limited to accidental words or phrases, but rather characterized entire works.

To this day, I still remember the evening when Mother first told us the story about a girl called Yebao who ran away from her orphanage. We asked what happened to her, but Mother said she didn't know. At this point, my sister began to cry, and although I didn't, I nevertheless felt a deep sense of unease. This story of Yebao is recounted in my mother's work "The Lost Night," but I first heard it around the time I started school, when my sister was in second or third grade. I remember that at the time Father had not yet moved to Shanghai to join us. Later, when looking through my mother's records, I noticed that "The Lost Night" was published in the journal *Shanghai Literature* in June 1962, which was about a year after she first told us the Yebao story—meaning that what she was telling us must have been an embryonic form of the eventual narrative.

Her story "Lilies" had been published in March 1958, and at that point Mother entered a period in which her writing career proceeded rather smoothly. Her writing peaked between 1960 and 1962, with works such as "The Towering White Poplar," "The Peaceful Maternity Hospital," and "Ah Shu." In fact, in the first half of 1962 alone, she published the sequel to "Ah Shu," which was entitled "The Second Step," as well as

"The Lost Night" and "Give Me a Gun." For other authors, this rate of publication might not have been very extraordinary, but Mother typically wrote rather slowly. Furthermore, in the 1960s there were very few literary journals to which one could submit one's work, and both the manuscript review and the censorship process were much stricter than they are today. Moreover, the time from submission of the manuscript to publication was also much longer. As a result, the amount of literature available for consumption was extremely limited. Thus, Mother's productivity during this period could actually be seen as quite good.

I attempted to return to that period and have a young girl named Yebao float to the surface. Twenty years later—after our generation had emerged on the literary stage in the 1980s—Mother published another version of this story in her novel *She Came up along That Road*, this time explicitly presenting it as a quasi-autobiographical narrative. After her death, I found the manuscript of the second half of *She Came up along That Road*, which I edited and released as a three-thousand-character-long novel. This expanded version of the story described Yebao's entire experience in the orphanage, and was significantly longer and more detailed than what had appeared in "The Lost Night." The characters were also more clearly developed and, most importantly, the author's identity was clearly affirmed. In Mother's writing, however, the individual was invariably occluded.

By 1962, the nationwide famine had subsided. Father's name, Wang Xiaoping, was not particularly well known, though he published a number of influential works during the 1930s under pen names such as Xiaoping, Xiaoke, Yang Sao, Wang Ge, Pu Ke, and Ye Bing. He then left Nanjing to join Shanghai's People's Theatre Academy, and welcomed the opportunity to return to normal family life, particularly to his former career as a theater director. Come to think of it, his rightist dunce cap had already been removed, but he would need to wait another twenty years for a historical correction before he could be completely reformed.

Around that time, Mother's writing also seemed to loosen up a bit. In "The Lost Night," she used class consciousness to explain the immorality of the old society, though Yebao's specific situation was informed by a stark contradiction between the emptiness of religion and secular life. Poverty is poverty, but the mortal world always finds a way to make people advance. This mortal world was symbolized by the clay doll—or what people called a "big lucky baby"—that Yebao was carrying when she fled her foreign-run orphanage. In retrospect, the title "The Lost Night" seemed to evoke an era's waning splendor, even as it avoided collective topics that might elicit praise or condemnation and instead focused on private life.

It appears that not long after finishing the relatively relaxed semiautobiographical "The Lost Night," mother's writing tensed up again. For instance, in 1962 she published "Lightning Kicks Song Fuyu," which is not so much a work of fiction as it is a character sketch of a commune's model workers. The following year, she was "experiencing life" in a rural area outside the city. The phrase "experiencing life" suggests that this so-called life has inherent boundaries, such that it doesn't necessarily include *all* people and things but rather only those that are recognized by politics. That year, Mother's productivity was very limited, and she only finished one short story, "Backward-Looking Soldier," about an elite peasant with selfish desires. Critics who had warmly received Mother's previous work greeted this one more coldly. She then stopped writing for more than a decade, and it was not until 1977 that she finally published another short story, "Leaving the Mountains." As literature began to enter a new era, the public zeitgeist opened up a space of individual expression, even as individual expression began to enter the public zeitgeist. It was precisely at that time that Mother, who was known as a sentimentalist who prized household affairs and family bonds, began to reveal a rare sharpness. Her "Story of an Editing Mistake" used black humor to satirize the misunderstood People's Republic from that misunderstood historical period—and this marked the third irony of her career.

WANG ANYI

Translated by Carlos Rojas

1962–1963

C. T. Hsia and Jaroslav Průšek debate the nature of modern Chinese literature in *T'oung-Pao*.

The Legacies of Jaroslav Průšek and C. T. Hsia

I have been assigned to write this essay because I might be the only student of modern Chinese literature who can proudly claim that both Professors Jaroslav Průšek (1906–1980) and C. T. Hsia

(1921–2013)—the two acknowledged founders of the discipline in the West—were my mentors. This entry is meant to be as much an assessment of their legacy to the field as a personal tribute to their scholarship. I also have had the privilege of editing a volume of Průšek's papers on modern Chinese literature that included their famous exchange of views on the "proper" study of modern Chinese literature, a volume entitled, according to his own wishes, *The Lyrical and the Epic* (1980). These two review articles—Průšek's review of Hsia's *A History of Modern Chinese Fiction* (1961) and Hsia's rebuttal—can be regarded as the methodological groundwork of the discipline. To trace the legacies of these two founding giants, one must first put them in their proper context.

Let me begin with a few words of personal reminiscence about the late professor Průšek. I first met him when he came to Harvard in 1967 as a visiting professor in modern Chinese literature for one academic year. I was then a graduate student in modern Chinese intellectual history with an avowed interest in literature, so I eagerly took his two courses. I still recall that, at one of his first lectures, he introduced his *Studien zur modernen Chinesischen Literatur* (Studies of modern Chinese literature; 1964). Průšek wrote a long introduction for the volume, which was also my first exposure to his scholarship. In it he laid out a grand narrative of the revolutionary nature of China's "modern democratic literature," its relation to "old literature," some of its new writers, and some characteristics of this new literary creation, such as its basic tendency toward realism. At the risk of sounding immodest, I must say that I was initially not too impressed. Průšek's views seemed to follow the general ideological contour of the standard works of literary history by Chinese scholars at that time, with the exception of a few insights such as his high estimation of Lu Xun's (1881–1936) prose poetry collection *Wild Grass*, which he regarded as an artistic "miracle" and placed on the same pedestal as modern French poetry from Charles Baudelaire (1821–1867) to Stéphane Mallarmé (1842–1898). When I later read his other articles, my impression changed. I began to realize that the best of them, such as "Subjectivism and Individualism in Modern Chinese Literature" (1957), "A Confrontation of Traditional Oriental Literature with Modern European Literature in the Context of the Chinese

Literary Revolution" (1964), and, above all, "Lu Hsün's 'Huai Chiu': A Precursor of Modern Chinese Literature" (1969)—all included in my edited volume of his papers, *The Lyrical and the Epic*—are all concerned with the complex relationship between modern and classical Chinese literature. This is obviously due to his research in the field of traditional vernacular literature.

It must also be borne in mind that at the time I attended Průšek's lectures, the only major work in English on the history of modern Chinese literature was Hsia's *A History of Modern Chinese Fiction*. Obviously Hsia wrote the book for an American readership unacquainted with modern Chinese writers. Consequently, he incorporated copious translations throughout the book from the major texts he introduced. On an academic level, the book has the evident hallmarks of a comparatist steeped in the Anglo-American tradition of New Criticism, for Hsia's alma mater Yale was then an acknowledged bastion of this prevalent methodology. Adopting the pose of a literary historian, Hsia revealed himself as a trained literary critic. One even detects a certain discrepancy between its historical chapters and its analyses of the works of different writers. The author's anticommunist political bias is evident in the former and not in the latter. Thus, as is well known by now, Hsia, through his critical acumen, spotted the high artistic merits of the stories of Eileen Chang (1920–1995), whom he regarded as modern China's finest writer, as well as those by Qian Zhongshu (1910–1998), Shi Tuo (1910–1988), and Shen Congwen (1902–1988). Half a century later, Chang has continued to soar and become a legend. The immortality Hsia sought to grant her was already guaranteed as a result of this single book. Whether one agrees with his political stance or not, it is the author's critical judgment, based on his comparative insight, that shines through its rather perfunctory summaries of the literary-historical background, a factor Průšek considered crucial to the understanding of modern Chinese literature. The two approaches cannot be more dissimilar. Indeed they are diametrically opposed to each other. That these two giants should be engaged in a deadly scholarly debate was a foregone conclusion.

At the time of Průšek's Harvard lectures, the European journal of Sinology *Te Eur Pao* had only recently, in 1962, published his lengthy review of Hsia's book entitled "Basic Problems of the History of Modern

Chinese Literature and C. T. Hsia, *A History of Modern Chinese Fiction*."
Hsia's "On the 'Scientific' Study of Modern Chinese Literature—a Reply
to Professor Průšek" followed a year later. In his lectures at Harvard, he
did not specifically mention his debate with Hsia, but we students were
all discussing it behind his back, and some dared to take sides. However, I found myself drawn to both positions. Indeed, I considered it my
great fortune to have studied with both Průšek and Hsia (the latter via
his brother T. A. Hsia). We should also bear in mind that, despite the
polemical vehemence of the exchange, the two men remained cordial
when they met in person.

The basic differences between their approaches are self-evident.
Průšek in his review faults Hsia for being politically biased and failing
to grasp the "objective truth," as would befit the "scientific endeavor"
of every "scholar or scientist." In the section called "Confrontation of
Methods," he gives detailed analysis of Lu Xun's stories as a counter-
point to Hsia's view and cites a battery of European, including Russian,
scholarly works on Lu Xun to prove his point. At the end of the review,
Průšek chooses to contrast the views of the Hsia brothers by praising
T. A. Hsia and quoting the latter's more judicious verdict on Lu Xun,
that his "early stories and essays seem to me to have spoken best for the
conscience of China during a period of agonizing transition." To use the
views of C. T. Hsia's beloved brother to find fault with him with must
have been a scathing blow. To add insult to injury, Průšek also quotes a
sentence from T. A. Hsia, whom he considers a "Taiwan critic," to verify
the moral truth of his own position:

> It is easy now to laugh at the naiveté and wishful thinking of the
> leftist writers and their unobservant distortion of social reality, but
> having surfeited myself with a steady diet of vaporous writings, I do
> sometimes miss the hardness, the fiery concern with social justice that
> we find in the best works of the Leftist school.

T. A. Hsia's "vaporous writings" referred to the steady diet of government-
sponsored or government-sanctioned works of cliché-ridden anticommunist fiction in Taiwan in the 1950s, which represented an ironic contrast
with the hard-edged realism of leftist writers in the 1930s such as Zhang
Tianyi (1868–1936) and Wu Zuxiang (1908–1994).

Whether by chance or by recognition, C. T. Hsia himself later coined a vivid phrase (and used it in conversations, though not in print) to refer to the best specimens of this literature whose politics he nevertheless detested: he called them "hardcore, rock-bottom" humanism. Indeed, he developed a grudging respect for such works (he later added the fiction of Xiao Hong [1911–1942] and Duanmu Hongliang [1912–1996], in addition to those mentioned previously) precisely because, as he told me several times, the harsh and hard-edged world of poverty and suffering depicted in this fiction is so different from and utterly alien to the bourgeois sensibilities of the present-day reader of the cities. In his famous essay "Obsession with China" (added as a special appendix to the paperback edition of his *History*), he developed a more subtle thesis: this hallmark of modern Chinese fiction—an obsessive concern with the plight of its own people—can be a double-edged sword that tends to cut out all comparisons to foreign literatures and serves to make this literature rather provincial.

C. T. Hsia's 1963 rebuttal is pointedly titled "On the 'Scientific' Study of Modern Chinese Literature," and takes issue directly with his opponent's "scientific" methodology. For Hsia, Průšek's method is an example of "intentional fallacy," a yardstick prevalent in New Criticism: a fallacy that confuses the intention of the author with the content of the text. Thus he states, "The intention of the author is not to be erected as a standard for judging the success of a work of literary art." In Hsia's view, Průšek's "intentionalist approach" inevitably carries his own bias: namely, that "literature is but the handmaiden of history" (specifically Chinese revolutionary history). Consequently, Průšek's approach ignores the literary texts' own value and significance as works of art. Again, it can be said in Průšek's defense that in fact he did not entirely neglect a work's artistic value. His high praise of Lu Xun's *Wild Grass* is a case in point. In my view, however, as a modern scholar, Průšek's dilemma lies rather in his high esteem of the best of traditional Chinese literature—both popular vernacular fiction and the elite writings of poetry and prose. Indeed, the "lyrical" impulse is to be found only in the elite literature that, in its modern transformation, led to a "confrontation" with the equally lyrical modern elements in European literature. This argument, sketched only briefly at the end of his article, gives us a rare glimpse of a comparative intention, but Průšek, unlike Hsia, chose not to pursue this intention very far.

A student of comparative literature can find an echo of this view in the work of the Princeton comparatist Ralph Freedman, who, in his book *The Lyrical Novel* (1963)—exactly concurrent with the time of the Průšek-Hsia debate—argues along a similar line using the fictional works of three major European modern writers: Hermann Hesse (1877–1962), Andre Gide (1869–1951), and Virginia Woolf (1882–1941). Freedman defines the lyrical novel as a new mode of the modern novel in which the technique of poetry tends to penetrate the old realistic mode, thereby replacing its narrative structure with a poetic mood and poetic imagery. It seems to be a more sophisticated adumbration of Průšek's point about the dialectic of the "lyrical" and the "epic": if the former tends to focus on the subjective feelings of the writer and on an artistic evocation of mood, color, and imagery, the latter portrays an objective panorama of life and society. For Průšek, Yu Dafu (1896–1945) and Lu Xun are the two prime representatives of this new lyrical tradition, whereas Mao Dun's (1896–1981) novels are examples of the modern "epic." Of course, Průšek sidesteps the issue of generic form; or, more precisely, he sidesteps the issue (first raised by György Lukács [1885–1971]) of whether the nineteenth-century world of the realistic novel, with its new mode of temporality, can encompass the epic form.

If Hsia's criticism owes a debt to a host of Anglo-American New Critics, where lie the origins of Průšek's theoretical leanings? I would say that they can be found no farther than his hometown, Prague. In his Harvard lectures he referred more than once to the theory of the "Prague school"—to its central notion that there is a structural coherence in the "fiction world" based on its employment of "literary language." One can in fact trace a lineage from the Prague school of linguistic structuralism to the American school of New Criticism. This unintentional coincidence would put Hsia and Průšek in the same theoretical bed as "strange bedfellows." Yet Průšek chose not to apply the Prague school method. It remained for his disciple Milena Doleželová to introduce its application to the field of modern Chinese literature in North America at several conferences in the 1970s. As for his vaguely formulated "lyrical" and "epic" modes, none other than Hsia's successor at Columbia University, David Wang, has seen fit to resurrect them by turning them into a more nuanced but also dynamic formulation by extending Průšek's argument: If the epic mode is more fitting for a revolutionary era, what then is the meaning of the lyrical in the epical revolutionary vortex? This quest has led Wang to give lectures and write books on the meaning of what he calls "lyrical history" (*youqing de lishi*).

Rereading the polemical exchange between Průšek and Hsia more than half a century after that momentous event, I can only agree with Marian Galik (1933–), one of Průšek's disciples from Bratislava, that in this debate "there was no winner and loser"; rather, it has encouraged younger generations of scholars to plow the field further and explore newer methodologies. We should all be grateful to these two giants of the field. They have both achieved scholarly immortality. May their spirits rest in peace.

BIBLIOGRAPHY: Milena DoležELová-Velingerová, ed., *Jaroslav Průšek (1906–2006) Remembered by Friends* (Prague, 2006). Marián Gálik, *Jieke he Siluofake hanxue yanjiu* (Beijing, 2009). C. T. Hsia, *A History of Modern Chinese Fiction* (New Haven, CT, 1961; 1st paperback ed., 1971; 3rd ed., with an introduction by David Der-wei Wang, Bloomington, IN, 1999). Leo Ou-fan Lee, "Guangming yu hei'an zhi men: Wo dui Xiashi xiongdi de jingyi he ganji," *Dangdai zuojia pinglun* 1 (2007): 10–19. Jaroslav Průšek, *The Lyrical and the Epic: Studies of Modern Chinese Literature*, ed. Leo Ou-fan Lee (Bloomington, IN, 1980). David Der-wei Wang, *The Lyrical in Epic Time: Modern Chinese Intellectuals and Artists through the 1949 Crisis* (New York, 2015).

LEO OU-FAN LEE

1963 · MARCH 17

Fu Lei: "Intellectually I'm purely Chinese, but emotionally and instinctively I'm very much like a westerner."

Fu Lei and Fou Ts'ong: Cultural Cosmopolitanism and Its Price

On the morning of September 9, 1966, not long after the onset of the Cultural Revolution, Fu Lei (1908–1966) penned his will, and then he and his wife, Zhu Meifu (1913–1966), hung themselves. In a coldly objective manner, he detailed how their belongings should be handled, and very briefly denied their "crimes" against their country and people. As the most famous translator-cum-literatus of the time, Fu knew the worth of his words.

Among the countless intellectuals purged in this chaotic movement, Fu represented a somewhat special case. He could have survived, but apparently he chose not to. The solemn poise Fu demonstrated at his last moment showed that his suicide was less forced than decided on out of free will. There was a self-conscious magnanimity in him about the inevitability of his destiny, which made his death Socratic. His death was not just a personal tragedy but also an intensified symbol of the cultural-political conflict in twentieth-century China.

Like many Shanghai cosmopolitan intellectuals in the first half of the century, Fu was steeped in the aesthetic and moral values of various traditions, but firmly anchored himself in Chinese culture. His interpretations shed a typically Chinese light on European texts, paintings, and music; enrich the expression of both cultures; and unveil their surprising parallels. As Fu describes, "Intellectually I'm purely Chinese, but emotionally and instinctively I'm very much like a westerner." With the help of his cultural cosmopolitanism, he found home not in any geographical location but in the many cultures with which he identified. When he was uprooted from this home, he fought at the cost of his life.

Born in 1908 in Shanghai, Fu was sensitive, lonely, and aloof from early on. After a rebellious and politically active period at the Jesuit-founded Collège Saint Ignace, he traveled to France in 1928 to study art theory and French literature at the Université de Paris; however, he returned to China in 1931 without receiving a degree. On this journey he was accompanied by the French Sinologist and musicologist Louis Laloy (1874–1944), author of *Mirror of China*. This journey marked the end of Fu's formal education.

Today his most influential work remains the Chinese rendition of Romain Rolland's (1866–1944) Beethoven-inspired *Jean-Christophe*, a work now almost forgotten in its native land. This is a striking example of world literature that gains rather than loses in translation. But in his typical meticulous manner, Fu reworked the entire book a few years later, managing to improve the already brilliant first version. He also translated fifteen of Honoré de Balzac's (1799–1850) novels, and works by Voltaire

(1694–1778) and Prosper Mérimée (1803–1870). His art of translation combined scholarly precision with literary sensitivity. Borrowing a metaphor from traditional Chinese painting, he stated that his philosophy was to translate the "spirit" rather than the "appearance" of the original. Fu often had a deeply personal connection with the works he translated. The translations of Rolland's *Jean-Christophe* and *Beethoven*, for example, were products of youthful passion. The translation of Hippolyte Taine's (1828–1893) monumental *Philosophy of Art*, on the other hand, provided a consolation for the aging and isolated scholar threatened by political perversity. Fu's deep emotional investment explains why so many readers have found his translations deeply spiritual and touching. Today, Fu is still remembered mainly as one of the greatest translators of modern China.

However, his reputation as a translator overshadows his versatile career as a critic of literature, art, and music, and as a curator. Fu fashioned himself as a "critic of art." Indeed, for him, translating literary texts was only part of a much broader transculturation project. A nonexhaustive list of his activities shows not only the diversity of his interests but also a cosmopolitan vision that endeavored to bring Western and Chinese cultures into dialogue while retaining an acute awareness of their subtle differences.

He published widely on French and English writers, as well as on literary history and theory. He translated Rolland's *Tolstoy* and corresponded with the author. He befriended the French comparatist René Étiemble (1909–2002), who would send his latest books to Fu and later would attend Fu's pianist son Fou Ts'ong's (Fu Cong, 1934–) recitals in Paris. He was also an active member of the circle of Shanghai cultural elites that included Qian Zhongshu (1910–1998), Yang Jiang (1911–2016), Ke Ling (1909–2000), and Stephen C. Soong (Song Qi, 1919–1996), a close friend of Eileen Chang (1920–1995) who would become the executor of her literary estate. One highlight of Fu's literary career is an insightful essay on Chang's fiction—so insightful that it prompted the usually haughty fiction writer to publish a serious response. Chang was to reconsider Fu's criticism and at least partially agree with it three decades later.

In the field of art history, he prepared twenty lectures for his art history course at Shanghai Art College, covering artists from the Renaissance, the baroque period, classicism, and romanticism all the way to the Barbizon school. Despite his love for Western culture, however, Fu's most important contribution to this field is surprisingly his consistent advocacy of the traditionally inclined landscape painter Huang Binhong (1865–1955). When Huang was already seventy-four, Fu curated his first-ever solo exhibition, at a time when the now-canonized painter was still much neglected.

Fu's aesthetic sensitivity is even more emphatically expressed in his music criticism, a "translation" that goes beyond the ordinary linguistic rendition of something written in a foreign language. He translated Rolland's *Beethoven*, published concert reviews, and wrote biographical notes and criticism on Ludwig van Beethoven (1770–1827), Wolfgang Amadeus Mozart (1756–1791), Frédéric Chopin (1810–1849), and Claude Debussy (1862–1918). He spent much effort tutoring his son Fou, who won third prize and the Special Mazurka Prize at the 1955 Chopin Competition in Poland. However, Fu was denounced during the 1958 Anti-Rightist Movement for his criticism of the government. This "crime" threatened both the father and the son, forcing Fou to permanently leave China and settle in the United Kingdom. In a 1980 interview, Fou described his situation at that time as follows: "All signs told me that I stood no chance, and I was especially scared because in this case it wasn't only myself but also my father."

Fou made a sensational debut in London, and soon established himself as a first-class musician, counting Yehudi Menuhin (1916–1999) and Hermann Hesse (1877–1962) as his admirers. From 1954 till Fu's death in 1966, the father wrote nearly two hundred letters to his son, containing extensive comments on art and literature. These letters were no dry sermons, but were instead the sole vehicle for intimate confessions of a father and a person of integrity at a time of universal hypocrisy and extreme political pressure. The two were each other's soul mates, finding consolation in the values they both cherished. Fu reminded his son that he should first and foremost be a human being in the best sense of the word; to be an artist came second, to be a musician came third, and to be a pianist came last. In a letter to his younger son Fu Min, Fu Lei quoted Fou as saying that his ideal personality was to be "at the same time passionate and serene, profound and simple, affectionate and proud, subtle and straightforward." Indeed, this is the most precise description of Fu Lei. These letters were published posthumously as *Fu Lei's Family Letters*, and they have had a deep influence on rehabilitating the values shattered by the Cultural Revolution.

A touching testimony to the friendship between father and son is preserved in the sixty-thousand-word manuscript of the chapter on Greek sculpture in Taine's *Philosophy of Art* that Fu copied in exquisite calligraphy for the London-based Fou. The latter wrote,

> After reading Taine, I am more convinced of my opinion that [George Frideric] Handel's works, especially his oratorios, are the closest to the Hellenistic spirit in music. He had a natural sense of bliss, majestic poetry, simplicity, and was never vulgar; his expression was straightforward, proud and magnificent, attaining an ecstasy and impersonality almost on a physical level.

Fu Lei replied, "I already anticipated your excitement upon reading this chapter. A time like that [of the Hellenistic era] is completely gone, just like one's naïve and lovely childhood, or our Pre-Qin [before 221 BCE], Jin, and Six Dynasties [220–589 CE] eras."

Deeply hurt by the Anti-Rightist Movement in 1958, Fu embarked on a translation of Taine as an act of silent resistance. Because he was denounced, this work that cost him so much effort could not be published under his name, and Fu preferred to withdraw it rather than publish it using a pseudonym.

In a 1965 letter, Fu commented,

> For so many years, I have often told Mom that the more I study Western culture, the more I feel the beauty of Chinese culture; it resonates much more strongly with my temperament. The moment I fell in love with Chinese painting was when I was in my early twenties, studying Western painting in the Louvre.

No wonder Fu eventually found the full realization of his ideal in Huang Binhong. For Fu, Huang represented the creative essence of Chinese painting because he declared the expressive power of the calligraphic line as its central tenet, rather than mimesis. This in turn enabled Fu to put Chinese art in dialogue with the antimimetic, nonfigurative, and two-dimensional nature of the European modernist movement. Fu's description of Western art was accurate and scholarly, but his judgments, Chinese.

Fou interprets European classical music in the same vein. As an act of anthologizing, he selects his repertoire with a Chinese taste. The fact that he champions Handel (1685–1759) over Johann Sebastian Bach (1685–1750) and Mozart over Beethoven, and that he counts Domenico Scarlatti (1685–1757), Franz Peter Schubert (1797–1828), Chopin, and Debussy as his favorites, may seem off the mainstream for Western audiences, but his choices make perfect sense if one considers his Chinese taste—one that emphasizes a humane, subtle, and lyrical sensibility over religiosity, abstraction, and transcendence. Even within the oeuvre of Beethoven, he always favors the lyrical repertoire. These judgments, having a profound cultural resonance, come naturally from his temperament more than from his education. Fu and Fou realized the same cultural vision. The only difference is that what for the father was a conversion is for the son something innate.

For both of them, there were consistent aesthetic principles determining why certain works of art were preferred to others. For Fu, Huang's seemingly traditional brushwork was more avant-garde in its suggestive abstraction than the pseudomodernist or half-classicist, half-proletarian styles of other contemporary Chinese artists. For Fou, Chopin had an infallible sense of taste that his admirer Sergei Rachmaninoff managed to approach only with a kitschy imitation. What these judgments share in common is the importance of taste—not in Immanuel Kant's (1724–1804) sense, but in accordance with the value system established in classical Chinese poetics regarding the depth and integrity of emotion, as well as the economy of expression. It is necessary to add that this system applies not only to the judgment of art but also to persons; both Fu and Fou loved *A New Account of the Tales of the World,* the fifth-century collection of anecdotes of self-styled literati and intellectuals. However, nothing is more distant from both father and son than cultural chauvinism. Quite the contrary, one finds in them a cosmopolitanism that fully recognizes and appreciates the values of different traditions. Their own tastes, deeply rooted in Chinese culture, only serve to enrich the expression of foreign cultures.

Today Fu is remembered mainly as a translator; this reputation has prevented people from recognizing the full range of his cosmopolitan vision. Apart from the fact that his translations have been immensely influential, there is another reason why he is known as a translator: his career was eclectic but fragmentary, and presented a mode of intellectual engagement that is difficult to define. Staying away from the establishment and choosing not to become any kind of professional, he retained the aura of a mandarin connoisseur. He was independent and unyielding in the self-fashioning of his life and career. But he nonetheless managed to exercise an influence too important to be ignored.

Fu's death was not simply the result of being critical of the government; nor was it accidental. It was the result of a clash that challenged the cultural values shared by him and his cosmopolitan contemporaries like Qian Zhongshu and Eileen Chang. But Fu had such a firm conviction about his values that he was ready to give up cosmopolitanism for indigenous adherence. On the other hand, Fou has chosen to cling to cosmopolitanism at the price of being an expatriate. To borrow Walter Benjamin's (1892–1940) words, this was a time of rivalry between fascist aestheticization of politics and communist politicization of art. Fu could not be tolerated by either paradigm, and he chose suicide to assert his integrity. In comparison, the still-difficult survival of their many contemporaries through the turmoil of the time seems almost a cynical compromise.

BIBLIOGRAPHY: Chen Guangchen, "Fu Lei and Fou Ts'ong: The Art of Hermeneutics," *Poetry, Calligraphy, Painting* 5 (2011): 45–50. Fu Lei, *Fu Lei on Art* (Nanjing, China, 2010). Fu Lei, *Fu Lei's Family Letters* (Nanjing, China, 2010). Lek Hor Tan, "Fou Ts'ong: Taking Chopin to China," *Index on Censorship* 9, no. 1 (February 1980): 47–48. Claire Roberts, *Friendship in Art: Fu Lei and Huang Binhong* (Hong Kong, 2010).

GUANGCHEN CHEN

1964

The East Is Red—or is it?

The "Red Pageant" and China's First Atomic Bomb

The legend goes that in 1943, during the War of Resistance against Japan, Li Youyuan (1903–1955), a peasant folk singer from Shaanxi Province, adapted a rustic local love tune into an early version of what is now known as "The East Is Red" in order to express his gratitude toward the Chinese Communist Party (CCP) headed by Mao Zedong (1893–1976). His nephew, Li Yuanzhen, popularized the song at local gatherings, and composers in Yan'an, then headquarters of the CCP, added three verses. The lyrics begin:

> The East is red
> The sun has risen
> Mao Zedong has appeared in China
> He is devoted to the people's welfare
> He-er-hai-yo
> He is the people's great savior.

After its 1944 publication in *Liberation Daily* in Yan'an, the song spread far and wide in CCP-controlled areas. Further polished with the professional touch of musicians and composers, "The East Is Red" became one of the most popular chorus songs after the founding of the People's Republic of China (PRC) and replaced the conventional collective singing of "The Internationale," for example, at the opening ceremony of the First Congress of the Literary and Artistic Workers in Beijing in 1950.

In the ensuing years of dwindling freedom of expression, "The East Is Red" was a constant refrain at mass gatherings and public performances, culminating in its role as the theme song to the 1964 revolutionary music-and-dance epic, also entitled *The East Is Red*. The epic begins with a prologue in which seventy graceful dancers in long, blue silk dresses wave silk sunflowers in time to "The East Is Red" toward a red sun projected onto the stage backdrop. With elegance and tenderness, these "sunflowers" walk toward the radiant sun rising from the ocean, symbolizing the guiding leadership of the CCP over the masses. The effect of the song, the beauty of the choreography, and spectacle of the mise-en-scène reinforces the "red sun" allegory of Mao as the indispensable leader of the Chinese masses.

Premiered on the occasion of the fifteenth anniversary of the founding of the PRC, this grand revolutionary epic narrated the glorious history of the CCP, from its birth in 1921 to its victory during the civil war against the Nationalists in 1949. Drawing from the rich aesthetic heritage of China's traditional, folkloric, popular, leftist, and socialist cultures, *The East Is Red* was a "living textbook" of party history that would have long-lasting effects on contemporary Chinese performance culture. On October 10, 1964, Premier Zhou Enlai (1898–1976) announced the successful explosion of China's first atomic bomb when he received the cast of *The East*

Is Red in the Great Hall of the People in Tiananmen Square. On this extended stage of political theater, Zhou simultaneously celebrated China's rise as a nuclear power in the Cold War era and the grandeur of China's artistic achievement, which had created a "red pageant" with over three thousand cast members in a brief period of three months, from script to premiere.

The premiere of *The East Is Red* can be seen as the real beginning of the Cultural Revolution because of its critical role in popularizing Maoist "red songs and dances." After the film adaptation of the epic further popularized its theme song in the remote, rural areas of China, the song was also played to accompany Mao's appearances in Tiananmen Square, where he received, on eight separate occasions, a total of eleven million Red Guards. The song became a central component of political gatherings and public mass performances, and a recording was even played by China's first space satellite, launched in 1970. By the time of the Cultural Revolution (1966–1976), when Tian Han (1898–1968), the writer of the lyrics of the national anthem, was being persecuted as a counterrevolutionary, "The East Is Red" had become a de facto anthem.

In the wake of the Cultural Revolution, the song fell out of favor, but it regained popularity from the late 1980s onward, and it continues to be featured in annual concerts celebrating the birth of the party, the army, and the nation, and even in the amateur performances of retirees and ordinary citizens for whom the song gives voice to nostalgia for a bygone Maoist society of equality, fairness, and idealism.

Whereas for some the song evokes the Maoist past and expresses discontent with a postsocialist regime plagued with corruption and exploitation of the poor, scholars and theater artists have attempted to restore the song to its original roots in rural folk culture. A 2002 folk opera entitled *Song of the Sun*, for example, explored the original meaning of the folk songs that became "The East Is Red." The plot is set in the 1930s, when Li Youyuan creates the original tune of "The East Is Red," whose lyrics tell of the daily life of ordinary peasants. A few years later, Li rescues a girl from being offered as a sacrifice to heaven in a ritual by locals praying for an auspicious spring; he marries her and is inspired to create new lyrics—a love song for his bride. In 1941, Li composes a third version of the song that expresses his longing for his pregnant wife while he is away at war fighting against the Japanese invaders. Communist doctors save his wife's life after a difficult birth and also heal an eye injury he has sustained during the war. Upon regaining his eyesight, Li is inspired by the sight of the sun rising from the east, and yet another version of "The East Is Red" bursts from him:

> The East is red
> Rises the sun
> China gave birth to a Mao Zedong
> He seeks happiness for the people
> He is their great savior.

Song of the Sun celebrates "the new life" in 1942 in Yan'an, when "revolution was making great strides with its own marching songs"; at the same time, however, it also challenges the one-dimensional interpretation of the song as pure CCP propaganda and emphasizes the fact that the CCP can only win people's support when it truly serves their interests—an indirect critique of party corruption in contemporary times.

The legend of "The East Is Red" continues to point to a multifaceted propaganda that reflects changing party ideology and a critique of the party's abnegation of its own ideological roots. This explains why Li Youyuan has appeared as a character in other postsocialist performances—for example, the television serial *The East Is Red 1949* (2009)—as a reminder of the CCP's rural roots and its initial promise to bring happiness to ordinary people, and as a pointed critique against corruption and privilege within the party. The story takes place on March 23, 1948, when Mao and his comrades crossed the Yellow River to launch the last round of military campaigns against the Nationalists in the civil war. As they bid farewell to the rural people of Shaanxi, they hear a local peasant singing the folk song "The East Is Red." In response to Ren Bishi's (1904–1950) statement that "in the song, the people have regarded us as their 'great savior who fights for their survival,'" Mao, deeply moved, replies, "We should fight for their happiness, not just survival," a reminder to himself and others never to forget the support of the people. As a shrewd right-hand man who eagerly agrees with him on everything, Zhou Enlai echoes Mao's words: "The chairman is correct: this lyric should be changed into 'he fights for the people's happiness.'" Whereas the folk opera *The Song of the Sun* reconstructs the song's creation story, this television drama highlights how the "great leaders" first received the song as a timely warning against betraying the people's trust.

This critique of a disappointing CCP is underlined in *The East Is Red 1949* with the appearance of a humane and intelligent Chiang Kai-shek (1887–1975)—archenemy of the Chinese people—who is shown to possess wisdom and insight into the cause of his loss to the Communists. "I did not lose to the CCP; I lost because of a corrupt KMT," Chiang declares. Upon hearing the news of Mao entering Zhongnanhai on the eve of his own retreat to Taiwan, Chiang predicts that Mao will "repeat the mistakes of our own KMT" and believes that he will return to the mainland in the not-too-distant future. The scene that follows—of Mao and his colleagues gleefully waving to the cheering crowds in Tiananmen Square—highlights the promising beginning of the PRC, while leaving room for audiences to remember the blunders Mao is yet to make. The rising strains of the majestic song "The East Is Red" accentuate Mao's earlier pledge to his people before entering Beijing, while also foreshadowing the song's extreme popularity during the Cultural Revolution.

Just as the history of the song has been reinvented, the eponymous revolutionary music-and-dance epic has been transformed into various productions with different ideological messages. The 1984 premiere of *The Song of the Chinese Revolution,* a so-called sister epic of *The East Is Red,* received a lukewarm response despite an all-star cast and state support equal to that of its predecessor. Staged in conjunction with the "great parade" of 1984, when the new "great leader" Deng Xiaoping (1904–1997) first saluted the masses in Tiananmen Square in celebration of the thirty-fifth anniversary of the founding of the PRC, *The Song of the Chinese Revolution* reproduced, for the first time in theater or film, the 1949 founding ceremony of the PRC. In this scene, Mao appears on the Tiananmen rostrum with four leaders of various democratic parties: Song Qingling (1893–1981), Li Jishen (1885–1959), Zhang Lan (1872–1955), and Shen Junru (1875–1963), all elected as vice presidents of the Central People's Government. Together they signify the promise of political consultation to establish a free and democratic China, a dream dashed in the ensuing political campaigns against dissident voices both within and outside the CCP. The scene celebrating the Seventh Congress of the CCP, convened in Yan'an in 1945, presents another gathering of powerful characters: Mao, Zhu De (1886–1976), Liu Shaoqi (1898–1969), Zhou Enlai, and Ren Bishi, who were elected during the congress as "five great secretaries." Even though the congress is known for its resolution to acknowledge

Mao "as the unquestionable leader" of the CCP, *The Song of the Chinese Revolution* opted instead to give credit to the *collective* leadership of the Central Committee. The grand finale hailing the hoped-for future of "a new era," ushered in by the initial success of economic reforms, confirmed Deng as a greater trailblazer than Mao: whereas Mao brought Chinese people "liberation," Deng brought them happiness.

If *The East Is Red* features the predominant theme of carrying out Mao's call to prevent Socialist China from regressing into a "Western capitalist society," *The Song of the Chinese Revolution* celebrates, by contrast, a peaceful evolution from Maoist socialism to Dengist capitalism, the very ideology *The East Is Red* had fought against. *The Song of the Chinese Revolution* presents a seemingly coherent history of the development from socialism to capitalism, while still claiming to uphold the spirit of the "red classic"; it does so by juxtaposing contradictory narratives and transforming them into spectacles to present "a common ground," and by erasing contradictions in political discourses. Unlike *The East Is Red*, which eulogizes the brilliant sun of Mao Zedong Thought, *The Song of the Chinese Revolution* starts with a spectacular scene celebrating the motherland in the Deng reform era, the morning sun shining over a universe "blooming with life and vitality." It also ends with the glorious image of Deng projected on the backdrop and set off against a magnificent red sun, an image clearly recalling the earlier epic, though without the familiar sound track of "The East Is Red" and without the Maoist ideology it once represented.

Twenty-five years later, in 2009, when a group of producers brainstormed about a new epic drama to celebrate the sixtieth anniversary of the PRC, they emphasized the "most earth-shaking and colorful" thirty years of success in the reform era. In contrast to the earlier works, which were concerned with how China could catch up with the rest of the world, the resulting *The Road to Revival* benefited from the vantage point of a proud and prosperous China in the post–Beijing Olympics era. While acknowledging the monumental precedent of *The East Is Red*, the producers wanted to create a new kind of epic that younger generations would revere. Bathed in rich, brilliant colors, this third epic offers a grand celebration of the great achievements that resulted from the transition to capitalism "with Chinese socialist characteristics." In place of tales of great leaders, *The Road to Revival* focuses on the power of the people and their spirit of self-sacrifice that facilitated the creation of an illustrious civilization. When the red sun finally appears in the lyrics of a chorus in the grand finale, it rejoices over "the brand-new path toward national revival," during which the "heroic Chinese sons and daughters" "stand firmly" in the Eastern part of the world. The sun now represents hope, happiness, the people's power, and national pride, and the color red remains merely a familiar trope that faintly recalls a distant socialist experience and its core values and practices.

Rather than credit their success to Mao's thoughts on literature and art, as seen in the reception of the first two epics, critics now applauded the brilliant mind of director Zhang Jigang (1958–), who achieved the enviable status of having produced one of the most difficult revolutionary epics in a nonrevolutionary time, with passion, talent, determination, and efficiency. Originally from a small town in Shanxi, Zhang grew up with the kind of rustic folk culture depicted in the original song "The East Is Red"; having codirected the opening ceremony of the Beijing Olympics in 2008, however, Zhang offered the perfect combination of a socialist heritage with an expertise in the global market of capitalist art needed for this kind of production. With the admiration of Zhang finally displacing the cult of Mao, *The Road to Revival* itself embodied, through a unique artistic form with a cast of 3,200 performers, "a complete restoration to capitalism."

One cannot help but reflect on Mao's insights in perceiving Chinese artists and writers as deadly enemies of the proletariat and on his determination to initiate the Cultural Revolution to purge unhealthy ideological tendencies. The power and danger of the performing arts, and their potential to both reinforce and challenge the status quo (as seen in the 2002 folk opera and 2009 television drama), find their best manifestations in the revolutionary stories of the three "red classic" epics and of the song "The East Is Red," the inspiration for them all. The story narrated here shows that propaganda with "Chinese characteristics" has manipulated folk and popular culture, historical narratives, ideological orientations, and nationalistic sentiments, and embodies multiple, shifting, and complex identities in the formation of performance culture in contemporary China.

XIAOMEI CHEN

1965 · JULY 14

Lin Zhao writes to the *People's Daily* in blood.

Red Prison Files

In May 1957, in response to Mao Zedong's (1893–1976) call for pluralistic expression in the Hundred Flowers Campaign, Peking University students posted criticisms of the party on the university walls and demanded more democracy on campus. Among those students was a journalism student named Lin Zhao (1932–1968). Speaking in front of fellow students, she once announced her name as "Lin 林, 'double tree thirty-six' (36 = 2 × 18, written as 十八, superimposed as 木 or tree) and Zhao 昭, 'the day 日 the sword 刀 is over the mouth 口.'"

In 1968, before she reached the age of thirty-six, Lin Zhao was taken from a prison hospital bed and executed as a "counterrevolutionary"— her last act as a martyr for free speech. With half a million Chinese intellectuals, Lin Zhao was labeled a "rightist" by the end of 1957, yet unlike most others, she refused to submit to "thought reform" and instead began writing dissident poetry to circulate among her friends. While utopian images of the Great Leap Forward led to and concealed ensuing catastrophes, Lin Zhao joined with a small group of like-minded friends to print an underground journal to expose the famine in the countryside. Unsurprisingly, the authorities seized all mimeographed copies and arrested everyone involved.

While imprisoned in Shanghai from 1960 to 1968, Lin Zhao wrote volumes of diaries, essays, letters, and poetry, documenting her life in prison and reflecting on the trajectory of the Communist Revolution. A 1964 poem commemorates the execution of her maternal uncle by the Nationalists in the White Terror of 1927:

> April 12—a date buried in dust
> Who remembers the blood from 37 years ago?
> The posterity of the deceased performs sacrificial rites,
> Brimful with blood and tears
> My uncle—your niece in the red prison weeps for you!
> I know you—in the melody of *The Internationale*,
> I learned it from my mother, who learned it from you.

If only you knew, the millions of compatriots for whom you gave
    your life
Are to this day but fettered prisoners and hungry slaves.

Entitled "Family Sacrifice" and written in blood, this poem poignantly
melds personal history with national history, telling the tale of an elder
generation of idealistic revolutionaries that sacrificed themselves in support of a revolution that later devoured its children. Born five years after
her uncle's martyrdom, Lin Zhao grew up enchanted by his legend as
recounted by her mother, also an underground Chinese Communist
Party member. As a high school student, Lin Zhao cofounded a club for
progressive youths and was blacklisted by the Nationalists for her leftist
activism. In the late 1940s and early 1950s, she embraced the communist
dream of a better, more egalitarian society. She called Mao "Father" in her
letters and renounced her biological father, a former Nationalist official
condemned as a "historical counterrevolutionary" after 1949. It wasn't
until Lin Zhao turned into an opponent of the regime that she reconciled
with her father, who committed suicide shortly after her arrest.

On July 14, 1965, Lin Zhao began composing a long letter to the editorial board of the *People's Daily*:

> On this famous date, the sublime and ardent humanist passion of
> which continues to strike a chord in the heart of every freedom lover,
> I—your strange reader—am beginning to write you another letter.
> If the memory of this tortured, frail, and ailing body has not entirely
> lost its accuracy, then this must be the anniversary of the beginning
> of the French Revolution.... Of course, I am not writing to you Sirs
> to discuss history.... Where I am is not a study, not to speak of the
> fact that for all its vastness China can no longer accommodate a quiet
> desk, nor tolerate a righteous intellectual!... This strange reader...
> already wrote two letters to you... in blood because I had been illegally
> deprived of pen and paper.

Recalling the storming of the Bastille, the letter's opening paragraphs
direct the reader's attention to the special time, location, and medium of
its composition, to the physical and mental condition of its author. This is
not merely a literary performance composed of floating signifiers in a cozy

environment. Instead, each word is bound up in the physical, social, and political reality giving rise to its production and inhibiting its transmission. This *is* a letter, after all, but can it break free of its own monologue? Lin Zhao believed in Lu Xun's (1881–1936) dictum that "truth written in blood" cannot be concealed by "lies written in ink," but she also believed, more cynically, that her body of writing would automatically be transmitted through the "arteries of the police state" right into the "heart" of the regime, if only to be used as evidence of her "guilt" or "insanity." Thus she was keen to keep a copy of her writings in her dossier, knowing that her family and friends often destroyed her writings in order not to further implicate her or themselves. Moreover, she considered every interrogation an opportunity to coauthor her dossier, which she hoped would be passed on to posterity.

Written over five months, the letter would go on for approximately 150,000 characters. Lin Zhao calligraphed the main text in ink, yet spoke of copying over or reproducing from memory what she had written in blood earlier. She also "stamped" the manuscript all over with her own signature in blood, authenticity markers that ironically compounded the illegibility of later black-and-white copies. Mixing various genres, this work of graphomania is at once a letter to the editor, a critical remonstrance, a political treatise, a memoir, a diary, a confession, a testament, and a compendium of poetry. Her feverish style is meandering yet mesmerizing; lucid kernels of impassioned thought are entangled in implausible accounts and incoherent rants that may invite cold, clinical readings as symptoms of delusion or paranoia. Her text addresses the party newspaper and its readers, Mao and the Communist leadership, prison wardens and court judges, family and friends, God and heaven, the dead and those yet to be born.

Lin Zhao knew well that the true pathos of her prison writings derived less from their content than from their medium: blood. The practice had premodern precedents in imperial memorials and suicide poems, as well as the copying of sutras by Buddhist devotees. In her last visitations, Lin Zhao wore a white handkerchief over her head inscribed with the word *yuan* (injustice) in blood, self-consciously referencing *Injustice to Dou E*, a Yuan dynasty (1271–1368) drama by Guan Hanqing (ca. 1224–ca. 1300) in which the blood of an unjustly beheaded heroine spurts up to stain a strip of white gauze hanging overhead. In her writings, Lin Zhao invoked the revolutionary poet and heroine Qiu Jin (1875–1907), as well as Communist martyrs whose blood, she lamented, was shed in vain. Christ was a further source of inspiration, as Lin Zhao had gone to a missionary middle school and converted to Christianity in prison. Beyond all influences, however, Lin Zhao's blood writing presented her own unique, original response to the Communist Revolution itself. As if anticipating the skepticism of her future readers, she wrote:

> Is this not blood? Insidiously exploiting our innocence, childishness, righteousness; exploiting our good and simple hearts; inflaming and harnessing our impassioned spirit. When we became more mature, felt alarmed at the absurdity and cruelty of reality, and began demanding our democratic rights, we came to suffer unprecedented persecution, abuse, and repression. Isn't this blood?

Blood writing was an indictment, not only of literal bloodshed, but also of the physical and symbolic exploitation of the young. Mao famously said that the Chinese people are like "a blank sheet of paper free from any mark," on which "the freshest and most beautiful characters can be written; the most beautiful pictures can be painted." Writing in blood, Lin Zhao responds to Mao, as it were: You write and paint your utopian visions with human flesh and blood, aestheticizing politics and anesthetized to its human costs. During the Great Famine (1958–1961), Lin Zhao's poetry in blood envisioned a violent uprising by "hungry slaves" against Communist dictatorship, but in prison she asked: Is revolution the best way to achieve freedom, equality, and human rights? She wrote in her 1965 letter:

> True, we do not stint sacrifice and do not even flinch from bloodshed, but can [a free life] be established from a pool of blood with a bloodbath? All along the Chinese have shed not too little but too much blood. In the stormy state of the world in the 1960s, even on the profound medieval ruins of China, is there a possibility for political struggle to take on a more civilized form and not resort to bloodshed?

The prison archives absorbed these writings, and on April 29, 1968, Lin Zhao was executed. Two days later, a policeman knocked on her mother's door to collect five cents for the bullet, an obscene fact later publicized in a 1981 *People's Daily* article indicting the Gang of Four, though it remains unclear to this day who had ordered her death sentence. At this point, many victims of the Cultural Revolution were being officially rehabilitated. The relatively relaxed political climate made it possible for a public security officer to smuggle out to her sister a few of Lin Zhao's manuscripts, among them the long letter to the *People's Daily*. Soon afterward, the sister immigrated to the United States, taking the manuscripts with her.

In the 1980s and 1990s, Lin Zhao's surviving friends and family members published memorial articles about her, later edited into a volume entitled *Lin Zhao, No Longer in Oblivion*. Her legend and fragments of her writing came to be known among many university students and intellectuals, but the most powerful resurrection of her memory came with a 2004 documentary film, *In Search of Lin Zhao's Soul*. The filmmaker, Hu Jie (1958–), worked as a cameraman for Xinhua News Agency when he first heard about Lin Zhao through a friend in 1999. Delving ever deeper into her story, at the cost of his job, he began tracking down many of Lin Zhao's former friends and relatives, some of whom overcame their distrust and fear to talk about her on camera and to revisit with him the known sites of her life. Some shared with him photographs, documents, and artifacts associated with Lin Zhao, such as a tiny boat she made in prison from a cellophane candy wrapper. Hu even tracked down the box containing her ashes and found a lock of her hair wrapped in Cultural Revolution–era newspapers. He also found a former prison inmate who used to deliver meals to Lin Zhao in her last days and used his description to create a composite drawing of her, as would a forensic artist.

But Hu wanted above all to have Lin Zhao tell her own story. In time, he located a black-and-white photocopy of Lin Zhao's 1965 letter, which her sister had left with a cousin in China before her departure to the United States. For the film, Hu applied a digital special effect to give the text a reddish-black color against a yellowish background, while his voiceover guides the viewer in deciphering the handwriting. It is thus within this audiovisual frame that most of Lin Zhao's latter-day audiences would "read" her words. Hu traveled with rough cuts of the film to various Chinese university campuses and listened to audience opinions, making revisions and additions. Like a missionary, he gave out video compact discs of the documentary and allowed, even encouraged, his friends to duplicate them and pass them on. The documentary spread even more rapidly via the Internet, as numerous viewers uploaded and downloaded it faster than censors could take it down. Netizens posted about Lin Zhao in tens of thousands of blogs, and created fan sites as well as poetic, fictional, and musical tributes. Every year around the anniversary of her death, many go to sweep her grave in Suzhou—so many that a few local elderlies made a living selling them incense and flowers. Surveillance cameras later appeared at the site to monitor and intimidate visitors.

Albeit in fragmented quotations, the replication of Lin Zhao's prison writings in old and new media at once enhanced and diminished the aura of the originals. After refusing Hu's many requests to interview her, Lin Zhao's sister condemned the film as illegal and in violation of her copyrights, a perplexing attitude many attributed to the depth of her trauma. Instead of publishing Lin Zhao's prison writings, she donated the original manuscripts in her possession to Stanford's Hoover Archives in 2009. They are now accessible only in digital format onsite, and those who wish to read the manuscripts are only permitted to hand-copy quotations. These stipulations create a sacred, forbidding aura surrounding her oeuvre, a synecdoche for myriad case files compiled in a period of unprecedented graphomania among intellectuals and ordinary people pressed or exhorted to write confessions and denunciations. Such "dossier literature" is not defined by form, genre, or even literary merit, but rather by its brush with state power, whose censors were the first and sometimes only readers with a complete overview of a file's heterogeneous contents. Words in the Mao era had graphic power to judge, sentence, and kill. It was not only "the day the sword was over the mouth," but also the day the pen was a sword. Might this have been a reason for Lin Zhao's sister to dictate that faithful readers pay pilgrimage to the file and bodily reenact the act of writing? After all, words written in blood are not merely signs, but relics.

JIE LI

1966 · OCTOBER 10

Literary Quarterly is founded in Taiwan.

Modernism versus Nativism in 1960s Taiwan

"Yin Xueyan never seemed to age," Bai Xianyong (1937–) wrote in a short story. "Everyone who saw Baimei could tell that she must have been very beautiful once," Huang Chunming (1935–) wrote in his own story two years later. Between 1965 and 1967 these two defining short works of modern Chinese fiction from Taiwan were written, works that epitomized the contrasting aesthetics and cultural backgrounds of literary culture in Taiwan during the 1960s and 1970s. Yet the two stories share certain traits, such as textual sophistication, the challenge a male author faces as he delves into the female psyche, the theme of relations between the sexes, and the issue of prostitution and the "comfort" trade, as well as particular cultural resonances such as the Chinese view on fate, destiny, and patriarchy. Bai Xianyong's "The Eternal Snow Beauty," which would become the opening piece in his highly acclaimed *Residents of Taipei*, was first published individually in 1965 and quickly followed by five other stories within twenty-four months, all of which would be included in that classic volume. Huang Chunming's "Flowers in the Rainy Night" was one of three of his most important stories, all published in 1967. The mid-1960s window represented a peak of literary fecundity in Taiwan, with Bai and Huang among the best writers. The stories are mirrors of each other in certain ways: Bai's is urban, interior, obsessed with the uprooted class of former mainlanders adjusting to life in Taipei; Huang's is immersed in the countryside, both seaside and farmland, featuring the native Taiwanese who have inhabited the island for hundreds of years. Bai is typically interested in the trials of the formerly wealthy and powerful, while Huang relates the struggles of the very poor. Both authors exhibit insight into the human psyche, deeply empathize with their characters, and spin wonderful yarns.

Bai's story of the enigmatic femme fatale Yin Xueyan (translated as "Snow Beauty") sets the tone for his collection of dislocated misfits from a bygone era. The palatial physical interior of Yin's parlor for night activities provides a sheer contrast to the utter denial of information regarding Yin's psychological interior. Some readers have criticized Yin's emotional inaccessibility, but it serves important purposes. The hollowness of the psychological core is a trope of modernism in the work of such notables as T. S. Eliot (1888–1965). Bai casts his protagonist as an enigma to underscore the vacuity of midcentury Chinese subjectivity, when older values had not fully dissipated but newer ones remained untested, were considered foreign, and were often treated with a mixture of disdain and envy. Yin's mystery functions to entice her patrons, who desire to escape their present reality, if only through a temporary diversion.

The "ageless" Yin acts as an illusion for her patrons of the stoppage of history itself. The contrast with her clients, who are all in decline or on the precipice of demise, is a stark reminder that time passes in its own relentless manner. Yin whispers in the ear of her guests, helps them recover from their losses, reassures them that next time their fortunes will improve. Bai constructs an elaborate inner world of wealth and comfort in central Taipei, depicting an intimate salon of magnificent appointments designed to remind one of the past, as well as reinforce a sense of affluence and privilege. His distinctive lyricism is the perfect medium through which to convey the rarefied world of refined culture from China's prewar times. This group, ironically labeled "residents," is part of a lost generation of early modern Chinese industrialists, tycoons, and scholars, whose hopes for China were dashed by the world war and by civil war between the Nationalists and Communists. Yin's home is a protected realm that shields her customers from the vagaries of reality in contemporary Taipei. For them, Taipei is a geographic emblem of their defeated lives on the mainland. For these "residents," it is a vestige of their past glory.

A succession of male characters are supposedly ruined by their association with the eternal Yin Xueyan. Her irresistibility is only matched by her notorious reputation for emanating misfortune. She is likened to the sort of vixen that appears in traditional Chinese folklore. A litany of ill-fated men succumb to her charms, beginning with Wang Guisheng in Shanghai, a speculator executed for manipulating currency markets. It continues with Director Hong, whom she marries but divorces when he goes bankrupt. In Taipei, Yin's parlor becomes a place of homecoming for the stranded mainlanders. When Mr. Wu, an elderly patron, brings his nephew Xu Zhuangtu along for a night of mahjong, the story relates Xu's collapse. Xu is in the prime of his life, a successful cement factory manager. He has always been a responsible boss, faithful husband, and doting father. But with Yin's "special treatment," he becomes obsessed with her. He explodes in front of his wife and children at home. His wife, at a loss, seeks the counsel of Granny Wu, a character reminiscent of the smooth-talking matchmakers common in early Chinese fiction. Granny Wu suggests that Yin is a demon who puts curses on her clients. The downfall of Mr. Xu is inevitable, but the surprise comes when Yin shows up for his funeral. Dressed in white, the color of death, she causes a commotion as she pays her final obeisance. There is no telling for sure whether she is merely branded a femme fatale or whether she is indeed evil. But to underscore the inexorable march of time, the party carries on without Xu that very evening, with Mr. Wu having his best luck ever at the mahjong table. The story is a lyrical rendition of the tragic denouement that mainlanders suffered after being displaced to Taiwan.

Huang's "Flowers in the Rainy Night" contrasts with Bai's story in terms of characters and setting. Whereas Bai's story exhaustively depicts the comfortable interior of Yin's home, Huang's story is set almost completely outdoors, in rural Taiwan. "Flowers," literally entitled "Sea Gazing Days" in the original, takes place on the rugged east coast of Taiwan, where fishing dominates and prostitution to service the fishermen has flourished for decades. The descriptions are infused with the smells of the seashore. The story features a prostitute named Baimei and the disheartening story of her sale to another family because her own family is too poor to raise her. Huang is especially adept at weaving together action that takes place in the present with flashbacks to previous moments in the characters' lives. Baimei was born in southern Taiwan to a poor farming family in the mountains and then sold to an abusive adoptive family that in turn sold her into prostitution. Baimei kindles a relationship with a younger woman named Yingying who also ends up in the brothel, far too young to be a prostitute. She later encounters Yingying on a train, now married and with a baby. The reunion ignites in Baimei the desire to become a mother herself. She vows to do so when she has met a man she feels is fit to be the biological father of her offspring.

Huang's hallmark is his touching, individualistic portraits of simple characters, often but not exclusively women. He describes the scene in the story where Baimei becomes pregnant by a young and unwitting fisherman in tender detail, devoid of anything lurid. One of the complexities of the story is Baimei's effort to rid herself of her identity as a prostitute, combined with the aspiration to find emancipation in the birth of a son, which she does by painstakingly saving her money and plotting her conception by this naive patron. She views the change in status from prostitute to mother as one that gives her a new self-worth. After the liaison with the young fisherman, she returns to her birth home, where she learns of the grave condition of her brother, whose leg is afflicted with an advanced case of gangrene. She pays for the necessary amputation. She reconciles with her mother and helps devise a solution to the drop in price for sweet potatoes in the wake of a bumper crop. The story ends with her return to the seacoast with her newborn son, whispering to him a fictional version of his father, whom she casts as a hero lost at sea.

Huang fashions an intricate tale of someone victimized by feudalistic social values that entrap women who seek liberation, in part by subscribing to the conventional reproductive logic that values sons over daughters. The story is free of the hard ideological edge common in May Fourth–era works, but nevertheless engages similar issues of sexual exploitation and the critique of patriarchy. Its unresolved ambiguities enhance the verisimilitude for which Huang is so well known and mark it as an advancement over the more tendentious examples of social realism from the first half of the twentieth century.

In these two stories, Bai and Huang highlight female characters on the margins of society. How they negotiate that marginality leads to different predicaments, but each story is concerned with the vulnerability of its respective heroine. Yin Xueyan shifts the attention to her clientele and thus allays any ostensible suspicion that she is vulnerable. She is perceived as a vixen by some and a provider of emotional refuge by others. Baimei finds solace in motherhood. The former is an urbane denizen of the city, first Shanghai and then Taipei. She would be totally out of place in rural Taiwan. The latter is the product of Taiwan's rugged eastern countryside. She must move around Taiwan from time to time for economic reasons, but she is not at home in the metropolis. The distinguishing characteristic of Bai's short fiction is its painterly quality. It functions almost like narrative poetry. Exquisite description of the scenery, the attire of his characters, and the food they eat is paramount in his work. For Huang, the presentation of natural scenery has an effortless flow, but equally crucial are dialogue and character development. His stories often contain several layers of flashbacks.

It would be a misapprehension to consider Bai and Huang as radically opposed to one another, though their upbringings are admittedly fundamentally different. Bai was raised as the scion of a high-ranking Kuomintang military family, born in mainland China before coming to Taiwan. Huang grew up penniless in the northeastern town of Luodong, Taiwan. His mother died when he was young and, as the oldest, he carried a large portion of the responsibility for caring for his siblings. He had difficulties in school and did not graduate from a prestigious university. Bai, on the other hand, was a graduate of the leading university on the island, National Taiwan University. He was part of a wave of new authors who sought to redefine what was important in literature: careful textual craftsmanship, economy over verbosity, and an unobtrusive authorial voice. Under the tutelage of T. A. Hsia, a professor at Taiwan University, he and his classmates founded the seminal journal *Modern Literature*, which promised to revolutionize literary writing in Chinese by making excellence in writing the most important criterion.

Huang received mentorship from Lin Haiyin (1918–2001), a public intellectual with some government ties. She nurtured several Taiwanese authors, including Huang. After publishing some of his stories in the *United Daily News*, Huang was able to develop camaraderie with Chen Yingzhen (1937–2016), Wang Zhenhe (1940–1990), and Yu Tiancong (1935–). Together they founded their own journal a few years after *Modern Literature* called *Literary Quarterly*. The journal featured the writing of Taiwanese authors. The emphasis on textual merit was unmistakably manifest in their works. Like their "modernist" counterparts, these writers, subsequently branded "nativists" in the literary debate on nativism in the 1970s, also privileged the text. Their works were known for their craft, economy, and beauty. They often highlighted marginal social characters, as did modernists such as Bai Xianyong. The primary difference lay in their contrasting backgrounds and life stories. Huang was accustomed to hearing and speaking the Taiwanese language at home and among friends. The sights, sounds, and smells of his youth were those of the farmer and fisherman. He did not gravitate toward Taipei until he was nearly thirty years old. The modernists were more familiar with the social milieu of the recent migrants from mainland China. These authors more vividly reflected the notion of diaspora in their fiction. Their work is frequently situated in the city. In both cases, though, the exemplars of modernism and nativism in Taiwan during the 1960s and 1970s generated an impressive body of tightly woven compositions. These texts crystallized an age and are beloved by many as some of the best specimens of Chinese literature from their era.

BIBLIOGRAPHY: Bai Xianyong [Pai Hsien-yung], "The Eternal Snow Beauty," in *Taipei People* (Hong Kong, 2000), 1–36. Huang Chunming [Huang Ch'un-ming], "A Flower in the Rainy Night," in *Chinese Stories from Taiwan: 1960–1970*, ed. Joseph S. M. Lau (New York, 1976), 195–242. Christopher Lupke, "Huang Chunming," in *Dictionary of Literary Biography: Chinese Fiction Writers, 1950–2000*, ed. Thomas Moran and Ye Xu (Columbia, SC, 2013), 100–110. Steven Riep, "Bai Xianyong," in *Dictionary of Literary Biography: Chinese Fiction Writers, 1950–2000*, ed. Thomas Moran and Ye Xu (Columbia, SC, 2013), 3–17.

CHRISTOPHER LUPKE

1967 · APRIL 1

"The inner-party struggle has never been so frivolous."

The Specter of Liu Shaoqi

On May 17, 1980, the Great Hall of the People in Beijing was packed to capacity for a memorial service that came eleven years too late. More than ten thousand people attended the ceremony, and millions watched the event's live broadcast on television. Dominating the stage was a giant black-and-white photographic portrait of the former state president, Liu Shaoqi (1898–1969). The photograph, roughly 3 meters high and 2.3 meters wide, framed the face of a gray-haired Liu in the frontal head shot of an official portrait. Stripped of all positions and Communist Party membership, Liu had died in 1969 after suffering torture and solitary confinement. Now, with softened face and probing eyes, he looked on quietly from a black-and-white image that had not been seen in public for thirteen years.

Exclusion from the media was one of the immediate punishments for a fallen leader. Photographs of Liu were systematically cleansed from Chinese media and public spaces after his downfall in 1967. His official portraits, once ceremoniously hung next to those of Mao Zedong (1893–1976), were taken down and destroyed. Films with positive images of Liu were recalled and banned from further exhibition. Those that were too important to recall and ban, such as the popular newsreels documenting Mao's inspections of the Red Guards, went through painstaking reediting so that Liu's images were completely purged before the next printing.

Why is a photographic image so frightening? A multivalent relic from the past, a photograph has metonymic power: it refers beyond itself to multiple historical processes that give rise to the photographed moment. An imprint of a person's gesture and physiognomy, a photograph communicates personhood and humanity, and offers its subject some scope for self-representation. To purge a photographic image, then, amounts to an act of violence. It confiscates the possibility of self-representation, modifies the historical narratives to which the image testified, and annihilates the humanity of the subject. While Liu's photographic images were destroyed, cartoon images of him and his wife, Wang Guangmei (1921–2006), proliferated. In a Kafkaesque story of metamorphosis, Liu and Wang woke up to find themselves transforming, in public eyes, into monsters with the sharp noses and slouching backs typical of the "capitalist" class. Unable to assert their human dignity with their frail bodies, the unfortunate couple were dragged out, ridiculed, and tortured until their backs became truly slouched, and they looked more like ghosts than humans.

It was, however, not true that all positive photographic images of Liu had been confiscated. One marked exception was a 1963 documentary film entitled _Chairman Liu Shaoqi Visits Indonesia_, which actually enjoyed a rerun in 1967 and 1968, though with an added denunciatory soundtrack and a new title, _Traitor Liu Visits Indonesia_. After the Sino-Soviet split, the Chinese state had sought to build relationships with political elites in non-Communist Third World countries through the new tactic of "wife diplomacy." _Chairman Liu Shaoqi Visits Indonesia_ followed Liu and Wang on a state visit to Indonesia, filming them as they were entertained by the Indonesian ruling class in lavish palaces and on excursions. Upon its first release, the film created a national sensation with its glamorous portrayal of the People's Republic of China's unprecedented "first lady" Wang Guangmei, whose elegant appearance in a stylish Chinese _cheongsam_ (a body-hugging one-piece dress) became a new model of femininity for young women at the time. Yet with the 1965 coup in Indonesia and the subsequent massacre of millions of Indonesian Chinese and Communists, and with Liu exposed in 1967 as the "biggest capitalist roader" (a person who demonstrates a marked tendency to bow to pressure from bourgeois forces) in the party, the images of Liu and Wang's carefree mingling with Indonesian political elites became, anachronistically, solid evidence for their traitorous dealings with murderous capitalists. On April 10, 1967, at a three-thousand-strong mass rally at Tsinghua University in Beijing, Wang was forced to put on the *cheongsam* and the hat she had worn in Indonesia, as well as a chain of ping-pong balls meant as a parody of her necklace. Two Red Guards held her arms and forced her to bow to the spectators below, and in this humiliating reenactment Wang was again photographed and filmed. Meanwhile, the Central Cultural Revolution Committee ordered a large number of reedited film copies to be made and sent to local "revolutionary committees," commanding the latter to organize mass rallies around screenings of the film.

If the cleansing of the photographic image testifies to its testimonial and humanizing power, then in this case, its reappropriation points to images' malleability to sway mass passions from love to hatred. The added soundtrack aimed to offer a "lesson in seeing," instructing viewers to find hidden traces of criminal intention and class betrayal in minute details such as Liu's facial expression and Wang's necklace, and guiding viewers to experience the thrill of detective work, the pleasure of iconoclasm, and a strange sense of certainty that everything truly fit together in a conspiracy that had predictably failed. The purge of Liu and his conspirators was the largest purge during the Cultural Revolution, involving the persecution of tens of thousands of Liu's alleged followers nationwide. Mass rallies against Liu and his "conspirators" took place all over the country, and it's hard to know to what extent screening this film at the rallies indeed managed to transform voyeuristic pleasure into sadistic abuse. In some cases, film projectionists had to undertake the tedious task of scratching Xs on Liu's and Wang's faces on the negative in order for the viewers to overlook the human images and see the couple as the ghosts they were supposed to be.

If images had fueled the mass politics of the Cultural Revolution, they also played a role in the struggle for history afterward. Images of Liu and Wang began to return to public view upon Liu's rehabilitation. Two documentary films commemorating Liu were released in 1980. *Long Live the Memory of Comrade Liu Shaoqi* (forty minutes, 1980) documented Liu's memorial service at the Great Hall of the People. *Comrade Shaoqi, the People Remember You* (eighty minutes, 1980) was a biopic composed of archival images from Liu's revolutionary career. Both were screened widely in China, and many viewers published essays and poems to celebrate the return of Liu's image as a "victory of History." However, this return was carefully controlled. Images of Liu during the Cultural Revolution, for example, were kept strictly away from public view. Rehabilitation, as a whole, had been conceived as an instrument to appease public grievances, bring capable people back to productive life, and reassert the legitimacy of the Chinese Communist Party. Therefore, while the Deng Xiaoping leadership was ready to clear Liu's name and bring Liu back into the pantheon of Chinese Communist Party leaders, a proper investigation of what led to Liu's persecution, particularly the role of Mao, was out of the question.

The state's wish to quickly close the chapter of the Cultural Revolution was reflected in its framing of Liu's rehabilitation as a belated state funeral. Funerary rituals had been used in premodern and modern China to create unity among mourners and domesticate grief through prescribed behavior. By 1980, cinema representations of state funerals in the People's Republic of China had established a highly conventionalized form borrowed from Soviet practices and precedents in Republican China. The documentary film on Liu's memorial service, *Long Live the Memory of Comrade Liu Shaoqi*, mostly followed these conventions, yet included two exceptional scenes that resisted the closure the state had sought to achieve. In one scene, the camera followed Wang as she visited Kaifeng, where Liu had died. Framing Wang in close-up, the camera accompanied Wang as she wept bitterly in the small room where Liu had spent his last days. In the other scene, as the grieving family scattered Liu's ashes into the ocean according to his last wishes, the camera boldly framed the ashes in a close-up, as they were scooped up and held in the palms of his wife and children, before being blown away by the wind into the ocean. Ashes had never been shown in funeral films. Zhou Enlai's ashes had been scattered as well, yet Zhou's funeral film ended with a ten-minute-long sequence composed of live film footage of the deceased premier, as if he had suddenly come back to life. In Liu's funeral film, however, there was decidedly no resurrection. The camera lingered on Liu's ashes, confronting the viewer with the finality and senselessness of his death. Shot with a handheld camera, these two trembling scenes were intimate, spontaneous, and devastating, standing out from the stable composition and solemn authority of the rest of the film. Later in the decade, these two images would return, again and again, to call for the reexamination of the past.

Theodor Adorno observes that a true "working through of the past" must involve serious inquiries into the "objective conditions" that produced the past. The past can only be overcome when its causes in the present are also overcome; otherwise the spell of the past will remain, and history will repeat itself. While rehabilitation in the early 1980s closed the chapter of the Cultural Revolution as far as the state was concerned, the lack of fundamental change in how political and social life was organized, and the lack of thorough historical reflection on the causes of the Cultural Revolution, became a source of concern and anxiety. In the mid-1980s, the writer Ba Jin (1904–2005) warned that cultural revolution might happen again: "Some people say, happening again? That's impossible. I want to ask, 'Why is it impossible?'" As Ba Jin saw it, "It's not true that there is no soil or climate today to breed a second Cultural Revolution; on the contrary, it seems that all conditions are ready for it.... After all, there are many people who could profit from it." The writer Su Xiaokang (1949–) recalled a surge of hysteria just before 1988, twelve years—or a complete zodiac cycle—since 1976, when Mao had passed away and the Cultural Revolution had come to an end. As 1988 approached, Su wrote, rumors began to spread that another round of disasters was to hit China, and people rushed to the stores to purchase firecrackers to fend off evil spirits.

In 1988, the images of Liu's ashes, like specters from the past, appeared in two documentary films. Made to commemorate Liu's ninetieth birthday, *Fortunately History Is Written by the People: Fragments from Liu Shaoqi's Life* included, at the end of the film, images of Liu's ashes being scattered at sea. As Liu's son held out the ashes to the ocean wind, an urgent narrative voice commented, "We must reflect upon history. We must ask how we can stop such tragedies from happening again." The film's own answer to the call of historical reflection was a visual chronology of Liu's downfall composed of newsreel footage that had not been seen in public after the Cultural Revolution: Mao inspecting the Red Guards, mass rallies condemning Wang and Liu, and the Twelfth Plenum of the Eighth Party Congress, which expelled Liu from the party. Documentary's evidential value had been highlighted earlier in the decade, during the trials of the Gang of Four. The courtrooms of the trials were equipped with projectors and an audio record player, and archivists lauded the ability of audiovisual materials to retain stubborn traces from the past: it was documentary clips that substantiated the involvement of the worker rebel and Gang of Four member Wang Hongwen (1935–1992) in violent factional fighting in Shanghai, and audio recordings that registered the extent of torture in interrogations during the Cultural Revolution. Refraining from easy conclusions on causality and responsibility, this film testified to Mao's involvement in Liu's purge—Mao was present at the party plenum and chaired the vote that decided Liu's expulsion—and urged a better understanding of the dynamics of both elite and mass politics during the period. *River Elegy*, a six-part television documentary series that sparked explosive discussions nationwide, also reused images of Liu's ashes in its fifth episode, "Mindful of Potential Perils." Placing Liu's tragedy in a much longer history of recurring despotism and violence, *River Elegy* called for a nationwide soul searching to understand the mechanisms underlying the disasters that repeatedly haunted Chinese society.

In April 1967, after reading Qi Benyu's (1931–2016) infamous attack on him in the guise of a film review in the *People's Daily*, Liu gravely commented to his family, "The inner-party struggle has never been so frivolous." Mass mediated images—photography, cinema, political cartoons, and posters—were among the mechanisms that generated this "frivolous" politics, replacing real politics with stardom and villainy, and turning revolution into tragedy and farce. The struggle to come to terms with this period would therefore include a struggle to understand its image politics, as well as to regain ownership of images that had disappeared from public view. The lessons and legacies of the Cultural Revolution remain heatedly debated in China today. The spectralization of Liu when he was alive, and the stubborn return of his specters through cinematic replay long after his death, forces us to contemplate the deep connections between mass mediated image and mass politics.

BIBLIOGRAPHY: Theodor W. Adorno, *Can One Live after Auschwitz? A Philosophical Reader*, trans. Rolf Tiedemann (Palo Alto, CA, 2003). Ba Jin, "Wenge bowuguan," in *Wuti Ji: Suixiang lu*, vol. 5 (Beijing, 1986), 121–124. Lowell Dittmer, *Liu Shaoqi and the Chinese Cultural Revolution* (New York, 1998). Harold Hinton, ed., *The People's Republic of China, 1949–1979: A Documentary Survey*, vol. 3, *The Cultural Revolution, Part 1* (Wilmington, DE, 1980). Qi Benyu, "Aiguo zhuyi haishi maiguo zhuyi: Ping fandong yingpian 'qinggong mishi,'" *People's Daily*, April 1, 1967, 1.

YING QIAN

1967 · MAY 29

"Successors must carry forward the cause of our martyrs / Here I raise the red lantern, let its light shine far."

The Red Lantern:
Model Plays and Model Revolutionaries

Successors must carry forward the cause of our martyrs
Here I raise the red lantern, let its light shine far.
Dad!
My father is as steadfast as the pine,
A Communist who fears nothing under the sun.
Following in your footsteps I will never waver,
The red lantern we hold high, and it shines
On my father fighting those wild beasts.
Generation after generation we shall fight on,
Never leaving the field until all the wolves are killed.

So sings Li Tiemei in *The Red Lantern* after being told of her family's mission for the Communist Party, in defiance of the Japanese occupying forces. She pledges allegiance to communist ideology, assures her listeners of its smooth transmission to the younger generation, and—perhaps most importantly—demonstrates that she knows how to distinguish right from wrong. She has what it takes to be a true revolutionary. She embodies the Chinese people rising against imperial aggression and class oppression. She is the paragon of Mao Zedong Thought and action. She is the model for all who will rally to the cause of the Cultural Revolution and the point of reference for all who will look back in the post-Maoist period with longing for an era of fervor and devotion.

In 1966, *The Red Lantern* was declared a "model play" (*yangban xi*), one of the eight paragons of new stage performance, including five "modern revolutionary operas," two ballets, and a symphony. In the early 1960s, the Chinese Communist Party (CCP) presented models for each and every activity. The revolutionary workers, peasants, and soldiers were encouraged to learn from the model industries in Daqing, the model farm collective in Dazhai, the model soldier Lei Feng (1940–1962), and the model troops of the Good Eighth Company.

Each work unit around the country named its own model workers. Such exemplars were chosen for their efficiency, as well as ideological rectitude. The model plays, too, were supposedly tailored for the enjoyment, as well as edification, of the audience. Like Li Tiemei, who undergoes maturation and initiation, the viewers learned how to carry out revolutionary work.

The model plays assumed a pattern of imitation: what is good for the stage is good for everyday life. Audiences were required to learn from the dramatic characters, and the onstage drama became part of daily life. The plays were viewed time and again, performed at every working unit, and sung among friends. The audiences soon internalized the operatic tones and dramatic gestures, repeating them offstage and imagining themselves as heroic figures.

The Red Lantern foregrounds revolutionary heroism. The plot focuses on Li Yuhe, a railway switchman and member of the Communist underground in Manchuria during the late 1930s. Li receives a telegraph codebook to hand over to the guerrilla Chinese forces. He is betrayed by a fellow underground member who becomes a Japanese informer. Li and his mother are executed, while his daughter, Tiemei, escapes and joins the mountain guerillas, completing for Li the task of delivering the codebook. Li is portrayed as larger than life—in fact, the original cast was changed so that the character would be played by the tall and sturdy Qian Haoliang (1934–). Li towers over the others, and he sings more arias than the other dramatis personae. In the process of the opera's revision, all allusions to Li's fallibility were brushed away—in Qian's words, "to make this heroic image more prominent, more ideal, and more sublime." It is always clear, to both audience and onstage characters, who the heroes and villains are, and who is the most heroic of them all.

The careful crafting of the model plays was sponsored by Jiang Qing (1914–1991), Mao Zedong's (1893–1976) wife and the self-appointed patron of the modernization of Chinese opera. Jiang Qing saw *The Red Lantern* in a Shanghai opera version in 1963 and immediately promoted its revision and honing according to her aesthetic standards and ideological goals. The play was approved by Mao in June 1964 and designated as one of four exemplary "revolutionary modern operas" a month later. *The Red Lantern* was the first to be called a "model" when in March 1965 the *Liberation Daily* stated that *The Red Lantern* was "a prominent model of revolutionizing Peking opera." When eight pieces were endorsed as model plays by the *People's Daily* in December 1966 and proclaimed as Jiang Qing's "model plot," Jiang Qing proceeded to oversee their detailed revision. In an article entitled "Summary of the Forum on the Work in Literature and Art in the Armed Forces with Which Lin Biao Entrusted Jiang Qing"—known as "The February Summary"—the *People's Daily* states, "It is necessary to ... repeatedly undergo the test of practice over a long period, so that a work may become better and better and achieve the unity of revolutionary political content and the best possible artistic form.... Otherwise, no good models can be created." Jiang Qing continued to introduce changes to tunes, dresses, makeup, and other details until *The Red Lantern* was filmed in 1972. In personally supervising each stage of the play's creation, Jiang Qing refashioned the process of cultural production in the People's Republic of China.

In parallel with the rise of the model plays, the politics of performance in the People's Republic also changed drastically. In 1966, the Cultural Revolution began, characterized by Mao's personality cult and the persecution of his political enemies. The streets filled with new spectacles: "loyalty dances," public destruction of cultural relics, and violent struggle sessions against designated "counterrevolutionaries." Onstage messages were tightly controlled. Theaters showing Western-style spoken drama—about ninety existed in China at the time—came under attack as Konstantin Stanislavski's (1863–1938) acting method, the foundation of Soviet onstage socialist realism, was denounced as bourgeois. Traditional operas, which featured emperors, generals, literati, and beauties and few working people, were condemned as feudal relics and "poisonous weeds," and were replaced by modern revolutionary opera. Very few films were screened in public, with the exception of film versions of the model plays.

Jiang Qing's interest in modernizing Chinese opera and making it into a revolutionary tool seems to have been genuine, but the reform of stage arts also gave her a chance, for the first time since marrying Mao in 1938, to be involved in state affairs. By making the model plays into the flag bearers of the Cultural Revolution, Jiang Qing could leverage her role as patron of the stage arts to gain control over propaganda organization. The CCP propaganda apparatus consequently grew even stronger during the Cultural Revolution, and the model plays brought together literary and political concerns in terms of concrete, institutional power.

Jiang Qing's rise as a political decision maker may be dated to the
Forum on the Work in Literature and Art in the Armed Forces, which
took place in Shanghai on February 2–20, 1966. On May 29, 1967, after
several revisions—probably an indication of top-level struggles about
cultural policy—the *People's Daily* published the February Summary.
Once published by the *People's Daily*, the mouthpiece of the CCP, the
summary made Jiang Qing's position on modern opera into official
policy. The document fashioned the model plays as a tool of class
struggle:

> Literary and art workers engaged in revolutionizing Peking opera
> have launched a heroic and tenacious offensive against the literature
> and art of the feudal class, the bourgeoisie, and the modern revision-
> ists.... Peking operas with contemporary revolutionary themes like
> *The Red Lantern* ... are pioneering efforts that will exert a profound
> and far-reaching influence on the Socialist Cultural Revolution.

The ideological underpinning of the model plays, as expounded in the
February Summary, was taken as a license for invigorating those seen as
revolutionaries, as well as persecuting anyone dubbed as counterrevolutionary: "We must ... break the monopoly of literary and artistic criticism
by a few so-called critics.... We must place the weapon of literary and
artistic criticism in the hands of the masses of workers, peasants, and
soldiers and integrate professional critics with critics from among the
masses." The control over art production and criticism was translated
into a call for an institutional makeover: "Reeducate the cadres in charge
of the work of literature and art and reorganize the ranks of writers
and artists." By May 1967, when the summary was published, the target of such attacks against "revisionists" and "counterrevolutionaries,"
though unnamed, was in no doubt. Shortly after the forum met in
1966, Mao had used the Cultural Revolution to purge the CCP of the
more pragmatic faction led by Liu Shaoqi (1898–1969), who was deposed
from his position as party deputy chairman in July of that year. It is in
this fashion that the model plays provided a convenient foundation for
political maneuvers.

    The persecution of counterrevolutionaries is also central to the plot
of *The Red Lantern*. Li Yuhe and Tiemei bravely face the Japanese

occupying forces, but equally important, they ferret out conspirators from within. Li Yuhe is handed over to the Japanese by the turncoat Wang Lianju. A 1970 interpretation makes explicit the connection to intraparty conflict: "Li Yuhe's ... indignant condemnation of the traitor Wang Lianju continues to criticize Liu Shaoqi's sinister revisionism today." Tiemei takes over and uses passwords and agreed-on gestures—culminating in raising the symbolically laden red lantern—to distinguish friend from foe. Her talent stands out against the incompetence of the Japanese and their collaborators in detecting false signals, for example, when Li's mother uses a different lantern, and when Tiemei escapes after exchanging coats with her neighbor.

It is emblematic of the play's message that Tiemei's mission is to safely hand over a codebook. The missive is not a meaningful text in itself, but rather an interpretive tool that will allow the revolutionary forces, and them alone, to decipher future communications. The codebook motif resonates with Mao's and Jiang Qing's concern over determining the correct revolutionary ideology, while at the same time delegitimizing alternative centers of power. The plot indicates the importance if not supremacy of the propaganda apparatus.

This totalitarian semiotics—keeping all interpretive authority in the hands of the propaganda leaders—largely disappeared after the Maoist era. The CCP has kept a tight grip over the stage arts through censorship, but the propaganda authorities can replicate neither the monopoly over cultural production nor the charisma of earlier modes of control. By the twenty-first century, model units are a thing of the past. The paradigmatic model, the soldier Lei Feng, has been at the center of repeated government-led attempts to resuscitate revolutionary enthusiasm, and the online *Communist Party of China Encyclopedia* displays the entry "Lei Feng Spirit Lives On." Yet such attempts have been quickly rebuffed: one of Lei's iconic photographs, in which he is standing in Tiananmen and supposedly identifying with the state, was shown to be retouched to erase a bag in his hand. Was Lei simply going shopping? The texts and images of the Cultural Revolution are often viewed with detachment and spoofed.

The party propaganda looks back with nostalgia and can no longer produce contemporary heroes. The reliance on the past stands in contrast with the February Summary, which explicitly requires art to not

only portray dead heroes and stresses, "In fact, there are many more living heroes than dead ones." Since the 1990s, however, the public mostly
looks up to media idols, social celebrities, and financial tycoons. As the
cultural critic Wang Xiaoming (1955–) notes, the model for admiration
and emulation since the 1990s has been the "successful person," whose
riches and leisure are portrayed by the media in an idealized manner. In
the post-Mao era revolutionary fervor has been supplanted by a growing
faith in neoliberalism and the belief that "to get rich is glorious." And yet,
as in Jiang Qing's days, the models for emulation must rely on the media
to uphold their image.

BIBLIOGRAPHY: Yomi Braester, "The Purloined Lantern: Maoist Semiotics and Public
Discourse in Early PRC Film and Drama," in *Witness against History: Literature, Film
and Public Discourse in Twentieth-Century China* (Stanford, CA, 2003), 106–127. Lois
Wheeler Snow, *China on Stage: An American Actress in the People's Republic* (New
York, 1972). Wang Xiaoming, *Banzhanglian de shenhua* (Guangdong, China, 2000).

YOMI BRAESTER

1967

"Where there are human beings, there will be power struggles."

Jin Yong Publishes The Smiling, Proud Wanderer *in* Ming Pao

On May 6, 1967, massive riots broke out on the streets of Hong Kong,
leading to an event dubbed the "Great Proletarian Cultural Revolution of
Hong Kong." Starting with a labor dispute in a factory in San Po Kong,
confrontations between the police and picketing workers quickly escalated
into a violent crisis. After the arrest of several workers, pro-Communist
leftists formed the Hong Kong and Kowloon Committee for Anti–Hong
Kong British Persecution Struggle. Carrying Mao Zedong's (1893–1976)
little red book, protesters demanded labor rights, equality, the end of
British imperialism, and social justice. These large-scale demonstrations
against British colonial rule and in support of the Cultural Revolution
on the mainland met with brutal government crackdowns. The leftists

then switched to guerrilla tactics and planted bombs around the city. On August 24, Lam Bun (1929–1967), a famous radio commentator who had sharply criticized the leftists, was burned alive on his way to work. The leftists were then ready to move on to the next target on their black list: Jin Yong (1924–), the most celebrated martial arts (*wuxia*) novelist in modern Chinese literature. How did a fiction writer become entangled in these riots? How did the Cultural Revolution and the Hong Kong riots of 1967 shape Jin Yong's writing and, in turn, the contours of modern Chinese literature?

In 1967, Jin Yong started writing his thirteenth martial arts novel, *The Smiling, Proud Wanderer*, which was serialized in *Ming Pao* over the next two years. Executed with vigorous imagination and stylistic brilliance, the novel is not only one of the finest works in the genre, but also a deeply moving reflection on the emotional landscape of the Cultural Revolution. Although the 1967 Hong Kong leftist riots threatened Jin Yong's life, they did not turn him into a staunch anti-Communist writer. Instead, Jin Yong wrote a novel that explores the ways in which political labels— such as leftist, conservative, Communist, and anti-Communist—divide our world into normative values and fossilized beliefs, often with violent consequences.

Also known in English as Louis Cha, Jin Yong is the best-selling living writer of Chinese literature. A newly baptized subfield of academic studies, "Jinology," has emerged around the study of his works. In 1994, an authoritative new history of modern Chinese literature written by a group of scholars at Beijing universities ranked Jin Yong as modern China's fourth-greatest author (after Lu Xun [1881–1936], Shen Congwen [1902–1988], and Ba Jin [1904–2005]). The canonization of Jin Yong, or the "Jin Yong phenomenon," as critics are now calling it, signifies a change in the conditions of literary evaluation. Prior to the 1990s, both Jin Yong and the martial arts genre as a whole were largely considered middlebrow fiction that posed a threat to impressionable young minds. In fact, martial arts fiction was banned in both Communist China and Taiwan under martial law for decades, due to a widespread belief that "traditionalist" works such as martial arts fiction and Mandarin Ducks and Butterflies fiction (romance novels) were somehow responsible for China's backward economic, military, and social situation.

In 1959, Jin Yong founded the newspaper *Ming Pao*. The perception of Jin Yong as an enemy of socialism issued largely from the debates between *Ming Pao* and the pro-Communist leftist newspaper *Dagongbao*. In 1962, Jin Yong published a series of essays criticizing the response of the People's Republic of China to the crisis of refugees from the regime fleeing to Hong Kong, which, he argued, reflected an increasingly rigid dogmatism within the Communist Party that detached it further and further from the reality and livelihood of the masses. On October 16, 1964, China successfully detonated its first nuclear bomb, an event its foreign minister, Chen Yi (1901–1972), described as the pride and glory of all Third World countries in their common struggles against the Soviet Union and the United States. A few days later, Jin Yong published an essay condemning China's entry into the global arms race. He maintained that by choosing atomic bombs (*hezi*) over pants (*kuzi*), Mao's brand of socialism had shifted its aims from a sustainable livelihood for its citizens to militant nationalism. In response, *Dagongbao* described Jin Yong and his newspaper as an "anti-Communist, anti-Chinese, unpatriotic propaganda machine that worships England and America."

Between 1955 and 1967, Jin Yong wrote twelve martial arts novels, including the famous Condor Trilogy (1957–1959, 1959–1961, 1961), *Flying Fox of Snowy Mountain* (1959), and *Book and Sword* (1955–1956). Jin Yong's works before 1967 are fictionalized historical novels set in specific dynasties, containing an encyclopedic display of cultural lore drawn from Chinese historiography, medicine, astrology, mathematics, and botany about those periods. The characters are either real historical figures or fictional personalities he created to provide an alternative interpretation or etiology of well-known historical events. By contrast, *The Smiling, Proud Wanderer* of 1967 has no specified time frame, which gives the novel an explicitly allegorical, even fable-like, feel that draws attention to the connections between the text and the immediate context of the Cultural Revolution. The story recounts the intrigues, betrayals, secret deals, and battles between an alliance formed by the five orthodox martial schools and their dreaded common enemy, the Sun-Moon Sect, to which they give an unpleasant name: the Demon Cult. Linghu Chong, the novel's protagonist, and other disciples of the orthodox schools are prohibited from fraternizing with members of the Demon Cult, which is a clear allegory for the Chinese Communist Party. The name of its leader,

Dongfang Bubai (Asia the Invincible), is a reference to Mao Zedong, whose name means "he who brings prosperity to the East." Dongfang Bubai's actions in the book replicate the most destructive aspects of the Cultural Revolution. He forces young children—think Red Guards—to denounce their parents' political mistakes in public. The same children will then cheerfully explain to the world the physical and spiritual benefits of "studying and reciting the teachings of our holy master" every day, as if they were carrying a copy of Mao's little red book instead of a martial arts manual.

But *The Smiling, Proud Wanderer* is not an anti-Communist novel. Linghu Chong falls in love with the daughter of the ousted leader of the Demon Cult and begins to recognize that its members are, despite their factional differences, simply human. And after the young couple deposes Dongfang Bubai and restores the old master to power, he simply becomes another dictator just like Dongfang Bubai. Violence begets violence, and power corrupts even the best of us. Linghu Chong then is pursued by the leader of the orthodox alliance, Zuo Lengchan (whose name means "the zen [philosophy] of Cold [War] leftist [politics]"), who sees Linghu Chong as all that stands in the way of "unifying all of China under one rule"—his own. Ultimately, Linghu Chong is betrayed by his own teacher, who had raised him as his son ("Where there are human beings, there will be power struggles," the teacher said). We learn, then, that both the Demon Cult and its critics have dark sides. The object of the novel's critique is neither communism nor Americanism, but dogmatism: the slavish following of inflexible political beliefs. Rather than treating Jin Yong as a leftist or a conservative, it is perhaps more accurate to call him a humanist deeply immersed and invested in China's cultural tradition, something he believes the proponents of the Cultural Revolution— and their critics—have distorted, destroyed, or else forgotten in their ceaseless power struggles and search for modernity. Linghu Chong is a tragic hero in this sense. He recognizes that the spectrum of human values and actions cannot be reduced to a Manichaean good and evil, but is himself unable, at the end of the day, to transcend fossilized ideological binaries.

Manichaeism is the telling metaphor here. The idea that the world can be divided into absolute good and evil, and the various historical religions based on binary principles such as Manichaeism and Zoroastrianism, fascinated Jin Yong and provided rich resources for his craft. In his 1961 novel *Heavenly Sword, Dragon-Slaying Saber,* Jin Yong uses Manichaeism as the actual name for an underground society of martial heroes. Set in the final years of Mongol rule in China, the novel is similarly concerned with the internecine struggles between an alliance of orthodox schools and a menacing opponent, the Religion of Light. Like the Sun-Moon Sect, the Religion of Light is also referred to as the Demon Cult by its enemies. However, the members of the Demon Cult turn out to be the heroes who lead the Han Chinese to throw off the yoke of Mongol rule. Jin Yong's construction of the story reveals the influence of a theory put forth by the Chinese historian Wu Han (1909–1969) in the 1940s. According to the theory, the leader of the rebellion against the Mongols, Zhu Yuanzhang (1328–1398), chose the name Ming (light) for his new dynasty to acknowledge the assistance of the Manichees. As Jin Yong's novel correctly explains, the Religion of Light is what Manichaeism was called in medieval China, but Jin Yong's representation contains a confused tangle of knowledge about Persia, Arabs, Nestorianism, Zoroastrianism, and other fragmentary ideas associated with the Middle East. For example, the Manichees are said to be fire worshippers like Zoroastrians, while in fact they worshipped symbols of the sun and the moon, but not fire. The novel discusses the "strange ways" of the Manichees, including nude burial for deceased members, vegetarianism, and a lineage of virgin female rulers. According to the novel, the word *mani* was changed into the similar-sounding *mo,* the Chinese word for demon, during the Tang dynasty. In this instance, Jin Yong's characteristic blending of fact and fiction adds much flavor to the story.

It is safe to assume that the Sun-Moon Sect in the 1967 novel is a code name for the Religion of Light as well, for the Chinese character of *ming* is in fact an ideogram made up of the pictograms for "sun" and "moon." *Ming* is also clearly an emotionally evocative character for Jin Yong, who once explained that he named his newspaper *Ming pao* to emphasize its objective, nonpartisan character and his belief in political transparency. But does the representation of the Demon Cult, or the Communist Party, as the Religion of Light and the Sun-Moon Sect embody such values? The Demon Cult occupies an ambivalent place in Jin Yong's social commentary. In the 1961 novel, it is unambiguously the victim of a witch hunt, persecuted by self-appointed guardians of tradition and morality. In the 1967 novel, the Demon Cult itself becomes an oppressive and violent doctrine. The difference in Jin Yong's thinking is discernible in the constructions of the two protagonists. Both characters are eventually invited to join the Demon Cult, but while the protagonist of the earlier novel readily accepts, Linghu Chong rejects the offer and makes an even more radical choice: he becomes the head of a convent of Buddhist nuns, to the outrage and consternation of his peers. In crossing the gender line, Linghu Chong challenges a different kind of ideological divide. If the earlier novel challenges social conventions by vindicating evil characters as falsely demonized heroes, its strategy is still predicated on a binary opposition. The latter, more sophisticated novel dispenses with the language of good and evil altogether.

Although *The Smiling, Proud Wanderer* was born of the Cultural Revolution and the 1967 crisis, it is a rich novel that highlights the possibility, and necessity, of crossing and unlearning all kinds of boundaries. These boundaries are not always political ones. Tsui Hark's (1950–) film adaptations of the novel, *Swordsman* (1990), *Swordsman II: Asia the Invincible* (1992), and *Swordsman III: East Is Red* (1993), foreground the novel's gender-bending elements. In the novel, Dongfang Bubai castrates himself according to the instructions of a martial manual in order to attain superhuman powers. The second film in the series focuses on this episode but casts the luminously beautiful Hong Kong actress Brigitte Ching-Hsia Lin (1954–) as Dongfang Bubai, and Lin's brilliant performance humanizes the character. One could read the story of Dongfang Bubai's self-castration as the author's attempt to portray him as an ambitious politician ruined by his own dogmatic beliefs, but Tsui's films and other adaptions of the novel in the postwar era indicate that other readings are possible. The reception history of the popular novel indicates an openness that has perhaps exceeded the author's intentions, as if provoked by the moment of 1967, when Jin Yong's social canvas broadened considerably to engage questions of sexual difference, as well as multiculturalism. With Jin Yong's rising fame, these literary experiments on the Chinese periphery entailed nothing less than an unanticipated cultural revolution of their own.

BIBLIOGRAPHY: Daisaku Ikeda and Jin Yong, *Tanqiu yige canlan de shiji* (Taipei, 1998). John Christopher Hamm, *Paper Swordsmen: Jin Yong and the Modern Chinese Martial*

Arts Novel (Honolulu, 2005). Ann Huss and Jianmei Liu, eds., *The Jin Yong Phenomenon: Chinese Martial Arts Fiction and Modern Chinese Literary History* (Amherst, MA, 2007). Kwai-Yeung Cheung, *Jin Yong yu bao ye* (Hong Kong, 2000). Samuel Lieu, "Fact or Fiction: Ming-chiao (Manichaeism) in Jin Yong's I-t'ien t'u-lung chi," in *Jin Yong xiaoshuo yu ershi shiji Zhongguo wenxue guoji xueshu yantaohui lunwen ji*, ed. Lijun Lin (Hong Kong, 2000), 43–66. Petrus Liu, *Stateless Subjects: Chinese Martial Arts Literature and Postcolonial History* (Ithaca, NY, 2011).

PETRUS LIU

1970

> I think to myself, "This is really miserable;
> For what reason does the blue sky today
> Imprison me, this humble person, in a wooden building?"
> Without a trace of news, it is truly hard to bear.

The Angel Island Poems: Chinese Verse in the Modern Diaspora

One day in 1970 (no one seems to remember exactly which one), California State Parks ranger Alexander Weiss noticed Chinese writing on the walls of the detention building of the former Bureau of Immigration Station on Angel Island. This island sits not too distant from its more (in)famous neighbor, Alcatraz, in the middle of San Francisco Bay. Ranger Weiss was on a routine patrol of the facility, which had at last been slated by the Parks Administration for demolition, when he noticed the written and carved Chinese characters filling the walls. In an act of deep historical wisdom and cultural foresight, Weiss contacted his professor, Dr. George Araki of San Francisco State University, and told him of his discovery. Himself inspired by the spirit of Asian panethnic solidarity that had taken shape through the rise of the Asian American movement in the Bay Area at the time, Araki went with his Japanese American colleague, Mak Takahashi, back to Angel Island to photograph the barracks walls. The writing turned out to be dozens upon dozens of poems, which had been inscribed into the walls of the detention building by anonymous Chinese detainees held at the station.

This discovery, in turn, sparked the interest of the local Asian American, and especially Chinese American, communities, who undertook a broad effort to save the station. The ensuing campaign included lobbying to preserve the facility based on its historical significance for Asians, and especially Chinese, in the United States. In 1976, the California State Legislature appropriated $250,000 for the preservation of the detention building. Now, the entire Angel Island facility is a historical monument that commemorates the experiences and contributions of Chinese immigrants to the United States. In 1980, a collection of some 150 poems from the walls was compiled, translated, and published by early champions of Chinese American literature Him Mark Lai (1925–2009), Genny Lim (1946–), and Judy Yung (1946–).

These foundational achievements have, in their own turn, spawned a variety of preservation and recovery projects that are ongoing still today. As a result, the number of documented poems composed at this site continues to grow. Accordingly, the Angel Island poems stand out as a developing body of Chinese poetry written during the early decades of the twentieth century. Indeed, since its initial (re)discovery in 1970, this dynamic archive of Chinese vernacular literary production has achieved a level of visibility that was unimagined and almost certainly unwanted by those who created it. Many detainees were seeking entry to the United States under false identities as "paper sons." And, much like their questionably documented authors, the Angel Island poems have challenged official protocols of recognition, along with violating numerous conventions of cultural, and particularly literary, decorum. Yet precisely by doing so, they have helped to expand the dimensions of several interrelated cultural formations, particularly the sanctioned literary histories and canons. For in conveying through classical poetic forms the experiences of an anonymous group of largely uneducated Cantonese-speaking rural migrants from Guangdong Province in southern China, the Angel Island poems offer a diasporic, nonelite model for thinking about the shifting features, meanings, and functions of "Chinese literature" under the conditions of global modernity. More specifically, this vernacular body of poems expands the geographical, dialectal, and class boundaries of "modern Chinese literature" as a cultural and critical category. And, by doing so, they have served as one of the beginning points for the emergent formation that has variously been referred to as "overseas Chinese" or Sinophone literature.

In its heyday, the Angel Island Immigration Station was a bustling, if not necessarily exciting, place. From 1910 to 1940, the station and its staff processed nearly two million individuals from all different races, parts of the world, and social classes who sought to enter or exit the United States via the West Coast. In particular, the station served as the point of entry for nearly 175,000 Chinese who gained admittance to the United States during that span under the terms of formal exclusion. This federal immigration policy had officially begun with the passage of the Chinese Exclusion Act in 1882, and it remained continuously in place through periodic extensions and modifications until its repeal in 1943. To this day, it remains the only example of a particular group being singled out by the US government for exclusion based on ethnic or national identity. Motivated at least as much by wartime strategy against Japan during World War II as by any commitment to ideals of racial equality or justice, the repeal of Chinese exclusion fundamentally changed the legal and ideological environment surrounding Chinese immigration in the United States. And, in doing so, it rendered facilities like the Angel Island station largely obsolete, since it was no longer necessary to detain arrivals from China in order to determine their status.

As one of the earliest feats of expressly literary cultural production by people of Chinese descent in the United States, the Angel Island poems have up to this point gained renown primarily as an important milestone in the ongoing attempt to establish a canon of Asian American literature that can boast the authority of historical depth. In discussing this group of poems, however, scholars of Asian America have valued them mainly as sociological documents and for the pathos they express. As a result, scholars have tended to overlook the most distinctive features of these works precisely as verse written in Chinese. Comparably, due to the humble origins and abundant aesthetic limitations of these poems, scholars of modern Chinese literature have up to now almost entirely ignored these works of early twentieth-century written poetic production, which in general exhibit what might best be called a strained adherence to classical Chinese rules of verse composition. In producing these poems, the detainees employed a variety of canonical forms, including both five- and seven-character verse forms from the medieval period and four-character patterns based on works as old as *The Book of Songs*. Though some individual poems exhibit a measure of skill and training, the vast majority suffer from numerous technical flaws of rhyme and tone distribution. Still, produced within a very different set of material and cultural conditions than the contemporaneous achievements of acknowledged Chinese modernist masters like Chen Duxiu (1879–1942), Xu Zhimo (1897–1931), Lu Xun (1881–1936), Ding Ling (1904–1986), and Hu Shi (1891–1962), the Angel Island poems underscore that not all Chinese subjects who responded to the forces of global modernity in literary terms did so from a socially authoritative position of class or educational privilege.

The rural villagers who composed the poems at Angel Island during their efforts to migrate to the United States were responding in their own ways to the same unsettling forces of global economic and sociopolitical modernity that confronted their more elite counterparts. Their choice of classical poetic forms, which in other circles were considered sorely outmoded, in part reflects their relatively low levels of education and cultural exposure. It seems unlikely that the Angel Island poets enjoyed any knowledge of the various literary innovations promulgated by different movements in Beijing and Shanghai. Nevertheless, precisely because these older poetic forms still enjoyed considerable prestige at the time, based on the historical legacy of their importance in the imperial examination system, their use by the Angel Island poets might best be understood as a formally or generically strategic attempt to maintain a proud sense of "Chinese" cultural identity within a decidedly hostile, yet in many ways still economically attractive, environment, in which such an identity was systematically devalued.

> Many days on Island without freedom;
> Living in loneliness and desperation, tossed in with prisoners;
> Grievances filling my belly; I rely on poetry to express them.

Thematically, the Angel Island poems take up different aspects of the immigration experience, from the difficulties of the sea voyage to the emotional toll and indignities of internment. So one detainee laments:

> I have awakened to laws of gain and loss because my country is
>   weak;
> Understood rules of decay and growth since I sought after wealth.
> In idle moments, I have another sort of wild, mad thought:
> That I have gained consent of the western barbarians to land in
>   America.

Some voice sharp indictments against the hypocrisy and injustice of American immigration and foreign policy:

> I utterly despise the barbarians; they do not respect justice,
> Constantly passing harsh laws to show off their heroism.
> Cruel and insulting to overseas Chinese, they back out of treaties.

Tonally, individual poems range from despair and nostalgia for the conditions of life as they existed before emigration, to resigned acceptance of the author's currently diminished fortunes, to anxiety and indignant outrage against the affronts suffered by detainees. In fact, a strong hortatory strain runs throughout the body of the Angel Island poems, as many individual writers had in mind both fellow and future detainees as their main audience.

> For certain, my Compatriots, do not despair!
> Only, we must remember the hardship of the wooden building.
> On that day after we have united the masses and lifted our nation,
> Then we can pay back in kind to America!

This expressly social quality in turn reveals a vitally performative dimension to these poems, one registered in the material conditions of their production. Here, their inscription on the walls of the detention building connects them with the time-honored Chinese literati tradition of poems written on walls, a practice that gained legitimacy and prestige from as far back as the Tang dynasty. Moreover, the expressly nationalist sentiments marking so many of these poems demonstrate the capacity (or perhaps function) of nationalism itself to serve as a primarily defensive strategy for shoring up the terms of a cultural identity in response to systematic discrimination and naked displays of power that have their roots in world-scale political and economic asymmetries.

In addition to a tremendous range of quality, in relation to traditional measures of poetic achievement in Chinese, the Angel Island poems also exhibit a variety of problems in the more basic arena of character usage. In many instances, incorrect characters were mistakenly used in place of ones with the same, or similar, pronunciation, though with different radical components to indicate an entirely different semantic meaning.

Comparable mistakes in English would be the use of "there" in place of "their" or "wait" for "weight." Whereas the many violations of classical rules for rhyme and tone distribution constitute mistakes of a fairly high order, these errors reflect a more basic limitation, demonstrating an incomplete grasp on the part of their authors of written Chinese and its complexities. However, the various linguistic and grammatical irregularities offer more than just evidence about the lack of education among the Angel Island detainees. They also suggest a substantially oral (or, perhaps more accurately, an aural) dimension to the process of composition. And in doing so, the Angel Island poems at once attest to and illustrate the importance of verse as a cultural and social practice in providing a means for even relatively uneducated people of Chinese descent in the United States to assert a counterpoetics of Chinese difference, in response to their confrontations with the discursive and bureaucratic regimes of American racial discrimination, including the machinery of Chinese exclusion.

Accordingly, the Angel Island poems embody a kind of populism different from that pursued in the canonical works of Chinese modernism, which famously promoted and employed spoken vernacular as the basis for literary language. Thus, they indicate the need to broaden the parameters for Chinese literary study of this period. Composed in Chinese, but on avowedly American soil, by migrants held in legal detention, the Angel Island poems were produced and continue to occupy a liminal political and cultural space. Crucially, this space exists both at the margins of and at odds with the dominant regimes of monolingual national identity, which elide linguistic diversity under the homogenizing idealization of a unified territory. In both their resonances with and stark differences from the established canon of modern Chinese literature, the Angel Island poems testify to the importance of literature in general and poetry in particular as a means for negotiating the forces of global modernity no less for the Cantonese-speaking transnational migrant commoner than for the cultural elite:

> From now on, I am leaving far from this building.
> All of my fellow villagers are rejoicing with me.
> No matter that everything inside is Western style.
> Even were it made of jade, it has become a cage.

BIBLIOGRAPHY: Him Mark Lai, Genny Lim, and Judy Yung, eds., *Island: Poetry and History of Chinese Immigrants on Angel Island, 1910–1940* (Seattle, 1991). Erika Lee, *At America's Gates: Chinese Immigration during the Exclusion Era, 1882–1943* (Chapel Hill, NC, 2003). Erika Lee and Judy Yung, *Angel Island: Immigrant Gateway to America* (New York, 2010). Steven G. Yao, *Foreign Accents: Chinese American Verse from Exclusion to Postethnicity* (New York, 2010).

STEVEN YAO

1972 · 1947

> "The ship, relying upon human ingenuity, loaded with human tumult,
> and invested with human hope, proceeded on its boisterous course,
> each moment returning a small square of humanity-corrupted water
> to the unfeeling, unending, unbounded ocean."

In Search of Qian Zhongshu

By the time of his death in 1998, Qian Zhongshu (1910–1998) had become universally acknowledged throughout the Chinese-speaking world as the leading man of letters of his age, a distinction rendered all but indisputable by a grounding in European arts and letters as thorough as his extraordinary knowledge of the Chinese literary tradition. He lived through a time that was particularly difficult for people of his background and education, choosing to stay in China after 1949 in spite of various attractive offers abroad, and in spite, also, of some evidence that he had a good idea of the hardships ahead when he made his choice. His wife, Yang Jiang (1910–2016), had an almost equally illustrious career extending over more than sixty years, first as a playwright, then as a translator, and finally as the author of an extraordinary corpus of fictional and autobiographical works, including the landmark works *Baptism* and *We Three*.

Qian's father was a professor and scholar of Chinese literature, and the young Qian received an impeccable Chinese education at home, then went to study foreign literature at Tsinghua University in 1929. Qian and Yang departed for Oxford in 1935, where he received the BLitt degree in 1937. The couple returned in 1938 to a China that had already been at war for a year. In the years between 1938 and 1941, Qian went twice to teach in the Chinese interior, but was trapped in Shanghai in December 1941 by the outbreak of the Pacific War. In the years after 1945, he held a variety of teaching posts in Shanghai, eventually returning to Tsinghua in 1949 as a professor in the Foreign Languages Department. In 1952, he was one of the founding members of the Institute of Chinese Literature at the new Chinese Academy of Social Sciences, where he remained for the rest of his career.

I first encountered Qian's fictional masterpiece, *Fortress Besieged* (first published in 1947), in September 1972, when I was visiting Hong Kong just after having completed my MA degree. One afternoon I was randomly walking along Queen's Road East in Wanchai. I can't remember why I was there, but I do remember clearly the surprise I felt upon encountering a bookstore in what I thought of as an unlikely place for any sort of cultural activity. Not expecting to find anything of note, I wandered in, if only because in those unhappy days there were not many serious bookstores in Hong Kong, with most of those being branches of the major publishers in China, such as Sanlian, Zhonghua, and the Commercial Press, which in those Cultural Revolution days carried little beyond the works of Mao Zedong (1893–1976), the novels of Hao Ran (1932–2008), and collections of Lu Xun's (1881–1936) work. I quickly discovered that this Bowen Book Company, small as it was, had shelves covered with interesting books, particularly reprints of works of literature and literary criticism. I struck up a conversation with the proprietor, Wong Bingyan, who soon revealed himself to be extraordinarily well versed in modern Chinese literature and literary history.

Mr. Wong asked me if I knew about a book that he reached for on one of his shelves, a copy of Qian's masterpiece, in this case of the third Shanghai printing by the Chenguang Press, dated March 1949. The novel presents a mordant tale of a young man's journey through central China in the early years of the war with Japan, in which the foibles of the urban elites are played off against the urgent crises China was up against in those times. The book had been, after its initial printing in 1947, as Qian said at the time with a characteristic lack of false modesty, a "best seller." This third printing, however, was issued just a few weeks before the entry of the People's Liberation Army into Shanghai, and a work as focused as it was on the educated and moneyed classes of pre-1949 Shanghai suddenly found itself in a hostile environment, in which the less said about it, the better. (Wang Yao's *A Draft History of New Chinese Literature*, for instance, completed in 1952 in response to the new government's demand to set up a modern literary canon congenial to its needs, doesn't even mention Qian's work.) Most of the 1949 printing thus eventually found its way to Hong Kong, and could be found in bookstores there well into the 1970s, Qian by then as obscure there as he was everywhere else.

Mr. Wong entreated me to read the book, which I did, and by the time I had reached the third page, I knew I was dealing with something unlike anything I had encountered before. I was delighted by Qian's sharp satires of the bourgeois Shanghai of the late 1930s, but particularly impressed by the agonizing contrast between the frivolity of the human players and the seriousness of the events that were in the process of engulfing them. The quotation at the beginning of this essay encapsulates the mordant view of the human condition that saturates the novel. It was only upon reaching the second half of the work, however, with its accounts of Fang Hongjian's arrival at Sanlü University in the interior, his departure back to the coast, his marriage to Sun Roujia, his return to the "orphan island" that Shanghai had become in the late 1930s, and the eventual dissolution of the marriage in the coldness of an isolated and wintry city that the work's full power revealed itself. Reading the account of the sudden fight between Fang and Sun that precipitated the split, and Fang's subsequent lonely wandering on the city's unforgiving streets, moved me as nothing in my reading of Chinese literature ever had before.

The novel's highly conspicuous mode of narration, in which the author flamboyantly plays with language and seems always at pains to demonstrate his erudition, is not something with any real precedent in Chinese narrative. Satire of social pretension, however, has been a staple of Chinese fiction since the mid-eighteenth century, reaching a crescendo in the waning years of the Qing dynasty between 1900 and 1910. One of the interesting technical features of the work is the frequent virtual fusion of the narratorial voice and that of Fang the focalizer. The conflation of voice lulls the reader into an easy identification of Fang and the narrator, even as it imparts a sense of the durability of the playfulness that characterizes both voices. Both the reader and Fang are, however, rudely awakened as the novel draws to a close when we are suddenly confronted with the fact that Fang's apparently random progress through China will be brought to an unhappy end: reader and Fang alike are presented with the sudden and frightening realization that his ill-considered acts have actually been creating their own consequences the whole time. All the casual encounters that Fang had handled with so little concern now come back to matter, something Fang realizes only when it is too late to do anything about it. In other words, the narrator turns out to have been the voice of a notably hard fate all along, and Fang's inclination to go along for the ride, combined with a complete incapacity to imagine what the future holds in store, renders him a suitably pathetic emblem of his epoch by the time the novel draws to its harsh conclusion. This irony of knowledge gained always too late, if gained at all, is something that *Fortress Besieged* shares with a number of the novels of the late Qing, as well as much work of the 1920s and 1930s, such as Lu Xun's "The True Story of Ah Q" and many of the stories and novels of Shi Tuo (1910–1988).

When, by 1974, I had decided to write a dissertation on Qian's fiction, I immediately ran up against a real problem: hardly anyone I knew had heard of him, and what little there was written about him was dated, contradictory, and of doubtful value. Those who did know of him, more-over, regarded him primarily as the incredibly erudite scholar who had produced that landmark of literary criticism, *On the Art of Poetry* (or, to put it more accurately, the "landmark modern colloquy on poetry"). In those days of the mid-1970s, China was still virtually closed to Americans, and cultural activity was strictly limited. Of Qian, no one seemed to know anything at all, even whether he was still alive. In fact, after hearing a rumor of Qian's death, C. T. Hsia (1921–2013) wrote a long eulogy to Qian that he published in Taipei's *China Times* in early 1976. During the time when I was actually writing my dissertation in 1976–1977, then, I wrote as if about someone I would never have the chance to meet, as remote to me as any historical figure long departed from the scene. With the death of Mao in September 1976, Chinese academic life gradually put itself back together, and by 1978 it became evident that Qian was still very much alive.

Once I completed it, I was also faced with the need to transform my dissertation, which had had an almost exclusive focus on Qian's creative prose and fiction, into a book, which would be obliged to cover all aspects of his intellectual production. This meant coming to grips with *On the Art of Poetry*, something I had steered away from earlier, telling myself that my field was modern literature and that Qian's poetic commentaries were something else altogether. While his extraordinary erudition was evident to me from reading the novel, the full extent of his learning was still a closed book to me, out of my ignorance of many of the figures and issues he discussed so brilliantly in *On the Art of Poetry*. All the time I had that was not devoted to teaching in 1978 and 1979 was, therefore, given over to reading that work, and coming to grips with his interpretations of traditional Chinese poetry and poetics, composed in the most elegant classical style. This was more often than not a painful struggle between me, Qian's learning, and all the reference books I could muster, working from a poor Taiwan reprint of the 1948 Kaiming Book Company edition of the work, barely punctuated in the best late Qing style. As the struggle proceeded, however, a new world of aesthetics and an austere but richly rewarding means of understanding it opened before me; the essays on Li He (790–817), Yuan Mei (1716–1797), and Han Yu (768–824) in particular gave me impressions of these three figures, and of their vital importance, that would have been impossible to gain anywhere else.

Finally, in the spring of 1979, Qian visited the United States with a delegation from the newly established Chinese Academy of Social Sciences on a tour that included calls at both Berkeley and Stanford. I duly went down to Palo Alto in May 1979 to meet with Qian, and I was given an hour to interview him alone. I used part of the time to clear up matters of fact, part to ask about various opinions I had developed about his work, and part simply to wonder at the great man's wit and erudition. I had begun my research as a strictly academic venture, basing it primarily on written texts. The chance to talk with the ultimate authority on Qian's life and work, however, obviously required a shift to another mode of inquiry, which brought with it as many problems as it solved.

Being confronted with the man himself after I had already completed my thinking and writing about him and his work, more than anything else, kindled a vast sense of inadequacy. The quality and quantity of his learning and judgment were staggering, and I could only ask myself how I could dare to try to take the measure of the man and his work. Qian did his best to put me at ease, but each instance in which I brought up an assumption about his work that he demonstrated not to be true could only serve to increase my doubts. For instance, owing to the similarity in tone between *Fortress Besieged* and the novels of such interwar British authors as Evelyn Waugh (1903–1966) and Aldous Huxley (1894–1963), I assumed that he had read these writers while studying at Oxford. He assured me that he had not, concentrating instead on reading through Marcel Proust (1871–1922). Of course, Proust had been all the rage among British writers at the time, so the tone of *Fortress Besieged* still might have had something to do with his residence in that particular English milieu, but the direct influence I had taken for granted now seemed unlikely.

A few years later, with the making of *Brideshead Revisited* into a television series, Waugh became hugely celebrated in the United States, at a time when *Fortress Besieged* had already appeared in English translation. The gap in understanding between China, even modern China, and the West was at no time more evident than at that point. Reading Waugh, Kingsley Amis (1922–1995), Huxley, and the like against *Fortress Besieged*, it seemed plain to me that Qian's novel was superior to anything they had written, having all their wit, but also a power of high seriousness where they often ended up floundering in sentimentality. The translation of Qian's novel, however, soon ended up on the remainder tables, and, even though subsequently reprinted, has yet to find much of an audience. It is easy to blame this unhappy fact on the conclusion that the virtuoso wordplay renders *Fortress Besieged* untranslatable—and I have to confess that I was never satisfied with my own limited efforts at casting the text into English—but the miserable fate of the translation must stand at least to a certain extent as a mockery of pretensions on the part of American letters to true cosmopolitanism.

BIBLIOGRAPHY: Edward M. Gunn, *Unwelcome Muse: Chinese Literature in Shanghai and Peking, 1937–1945* (New York, 1980). C. T. Hsia, *A History of Modern Chinese Fiction* (New Haven, CT, 1971). Theodore Huters, *Qian Zhongshu* (Boston, 1982). Qian Zhongshu, *Fortress Besieged*, trans. Jeanne Kelly and Nathan K. Mao (New York, 2004).

THEODORE HUTERS

1972–1973 · 2000

"Days of the past appear as if behind dust-laden glass: visible,
yet never reachable."

A Subtle Encounter:
Tête-bêche *and* In the Mood for Love

A man leaves his editorial office at around five o'clock. He gets on a bus to
Central, a place where he often has dinner. A woman is waiting at another
bus stop only a few blocks away. The bus stops in front of her and the man
gives her a wave. She smiles, boards the bus, and proceeds toward him.

This is a scene not from a film but rather from the daily routine of
Mr. and Mrs. Liu Yichang during the 1970s. The old couple likes to share
this memory with researchers. Liu Yichang (1919–) is regarded as one of
the most important contributors to the formation of Hong Kong literary
modernism during the 1950s and 1960s. The quotidian scene described
here—of a city bus bringing together a man and a woman—echoes the
opening scene from the novel *Tête-bêche*. The novel was serialized from
1972 to 1973, precisely the time when the Lius' daily ritual was taking place.
The rapid urbanization of Hong Kong during the 1970s inspired Liu to
depict a new sensitivity emerging in human relationships at the time. The
first cross-harbor tunnel in Hong Kong was launched in August 1972, just
a few months before *Tête-bêche* was published. Instead of crossing the
harbor on the slow yet relaxing ferry, people could use the cross-harbor
bus, which further enabled the mobility of Hong Kong residents and
shortened the psychological distance between people, without necessarily
deepening the bonds between them. *Tête-bêche* could be read as an aimless trip in the city, in which the characters experience an unsuccessful
relationship; yet Liu's literary experiment planted the seed that twenty-
eight years later would give rise to a hallmark film of Hong Kong cinema.

At the turn of the twenty-first century, the award-winning Hong Kong
director Wong Kar-wai (1958–) debuted his film *In the Mood for Love*
(2000). The film is widely regarded as a milestone in Hong Kong film
history and earned Tony Leung (1962–) the award for best actor at that
year's Cannes Film Festival for his portrayal of Mr. Chow. On the day
In the Mood for Love premiered in Hong Kong, Liu was in the theater

waiting silently for the film to start. When the lights dimmed, however, the film opened with a quotation from his own *Tête-bêche*, and would go on to feature two more long quotations from the novel, all appearing as intertitles. The film concludes with Liu's poetic rumination, "Days of the past appear as if behind dust-laden glass: visible, yet never reachable." Furthermore, the director acknowledged Liu by presenting the author's name at the end of the film. *In the Mood for Love* is not a straightforward adaptation of *Tête-bêche*. To the contrary, they have completely different plots and characters and are set in different time periods. The allure of the relationship, however, lies in the subtle and even secret liaison between the two texts.

In the same year, Wong published an art book entitled *Tête-bêche: A Wong Kar Wai Project* (2000), which includes the English translation of *Tête-bêche* and a short interview with Liu. In the preface, Wong gives hints to his fans on the source of his inspiration. The term *tête-bêche*, as Wong writes, could refer to the intersection of time: the intersection between a 1970 novel and a 2000 film. More specifically, *tête-bêche* is a philatelic term, referring to a pair of stamps in which one is an upside-down version of the other. Liu himself is a professional stamp collector, and in 1972 he bought a *tête-bêche* pair of Qing dynasty stamps from an auction in London. This curious pair of stamps inspired him to write a novel that revolved around the encounter of two characters that "meet" without ever knowing each other. There are two versions of the story of *Tête-bêche*. The long version was first serialized in the *Sing Tao Evening Post* from November 18, 1972, to March 12, 1973, and the shorter version was published in 1975 in the literary magazine *Four Seasons*.

Liu is a modernist writer who strives for purity of form; his other famous novel, *The Drunkard* (1963), is a stream-of-consciousness effort that is considered a pioneering achievement in postwar Sinophone literature. *Tête-bêche* does not have a plot in the conventional sense of the word. Instead, the literary form bears the meaning of the story. The encounter of the two main characters, Chunyu Bai and Ah Xing, is never developed into a relationship. As suggested in the beginning of the novel, the story is situated during the 1970s after the cross-harbor tunnel has been opened. Chunyu Bai is a middle-aged man who fled to Hong Kong from Shanghai twenty years earlier. He dwells on his past at the expense of participating in the reality of Hong Kong. Ah Xing, a girl born and raised in Hong Kong, dreams about a future beyond her means. Though living in the same city, the two characters walk along parallel and inverse temporal trajectories—paths leading to the past and the future, respectively—yet both are unwilling to confront the reality of the present. In order to convey the unrelated fates of the two characters from a single locale, Liu employs an alternating narrative structure, wherein odd- and even-numbered chapters tell the story of Chunyu Bai and Ah Xing, respectively. They go to the same places and encounter the same people, but their own paths never cross. They are both flaneurs in the same city without knowing each other. It is the coincidental structure that brings us to the subtlety of the novel's filmic adaptation, *In the Mood for Love*.

Some critics argue that the opening scene of the film, in which Mrs. Chan and Mr. Chow are both looking for new homes, echoes the structure of *Tête-bêche*. Mrs. Chan and Mr. Chow do not know each other, yet both are searching for new homes and eventually become neighbors. The mise-en-scène also subtly echoes the alternating narrative structure of *Tête-bêche*. The noodle stall is a good example. Shot mainly in slow motion, the mood of the scene is carefully adorned with emotional music and vivid colors. Because both Mr. Chow and Mrs. Chan frequently dine alone in the noodle stall, they sometimes cross paths in the narrow stairway nearby, Mrs. Chan coming up while Mr. Chow is going down. The intimacy of embarrassment in the urban space is utterly romantic. Moreover, a feeling of loneliness common to urban dwellers permeates the whole scene.

The affection between Mrs. Chan and Mr. Chow can be understood as a reflection of their respective spouses' love affairs—it never exists in any real sense, but springs into imaginative existence through role playing. The two finally part ways, as they ultimately decide that they could not bear to be unfaithful. At the end of the film, Mr. Chow and Mrs. Chan cross paths again, but the encounter is edited in such a way that their previous emotional attachment is restrained. There is a medium shot that shows Mr. Chow standing in his old flat and gazing toward Mrs. Chan. Tony Leung's subtle expression suggests that Mr. Chow can see Mrs. Chan. He then stops in front of her door, but ultimately decides not to knock. The camera then turns to Mrs. Chan inside the flat preparing to go out with her son. The camera cuts back to the hallway outside, but Mr. Chow has already departed. The two characters never appear in the same shot, but the editing suggests their subtle encounter. For Wong, this scene is not about Mr. Chow's nostalgia for a former love, but rather about the painful and tender ways by which love endures.

The subtle relationship between *Tête-bêche* and *In the Mood for Love* can also be found in the psychological narration. *Tête-bêche* uses a third-person narrative, which focuses on the characters' stream of consciousness and attempts to bring out the characters' sense of detachment. Chunyu Bai and Ah Xing are both "silent" characters, insomuch as they do not communicate through dialogue. This silence can also be found in *In the Mood for Love*. Sentimental voiceover is a trademark of Wong's films, as seen in *Days of Being Wild* (1990), *Chungking Express* (1994), and *Ashes of Time* (1994). Surprisingly, *In the Mood for Love* has no voiceover at all. Mr. Chow and Mrs. Chan are highly suppressed characters in traditional families who express their love by putting on masks. The film's lack of voiceover helps reinforce the suppression of the characters living in early 1960s Hong Kong.

Tête-bêche and *In the Mood for Love* reflect markedly different sensibilities, with *Tête-bêche* appearing cool and sober while *In the Mood for Love* appears moody and sensational. The former is a modernist novel, while the latter could be seen as an art film in the commercial industry, or what David Bordwell has called the "avant-pop cinema." Made in the post-1997 era, *In the Mood for Love* is a reinterpretation of the old Hong Kong before the leftist riot of 1967. The majority of the events in the film occur during the first half of the 1960s, when the social and political atmosphere was comparatively calm. Viewers have also criticized Mrs. Chan's apparel for being too lavish for an ordinary clerk, but as a commercial consideration this seems wholly acceptable, and even normal. From an artistic point of view, we should not approach *In the Mood for Love* as a strictly realist depiction of 1960s Hong Kong. The exaggerated patterns and colors of the dresses and décor, and the peculiar camera angles that focus on the lower half of the human body, all suggest a subjective point of view.

Tête-bêche was written when Hong Kong was entering a period of rapid growth. By depicting two characters that shy away from the present of the 1970s, *Tête-bêche* aims to lead readers to critically engage with that very moment. It seems to indicate that reality is something still able to be grasped, if only we are willing. In contrast, *In the Mood for Love* presents a desolate picture in vibrant colors. Across Wong's oeuvre, critics tend to look for allegorical potential. It is in this vein that I offer the following interpretation: *In the Mood for Love* can be understood as a nostalgic reminiscence of a beautiful past, at a time when Hong Kong was presented with a boundless future in the post-1997 era. Ironically, this beautiful past appears as if behind dust-laden glass—visible, yet never reachable.

BIBLIOGRAPHY: David Bordwell, *Planet Hong Kong: Popular Cinema and the Art of Entertainment* (Cambridge, MA, 2000). Leung Ping Kwan, Tam Kwok Kan, Wong King Fai, and Wong Shuk Han, eds., *Liu Yichang yu Xianggang xiandai zhuyi* (Hong Kong, 2010). Leung Ping Kwan, Wong Shuk Han, Yuki Shan, and Matthew Cheng, eds., *Xianggang wenxue yu dianying* (Hong Kong, 2012). Wong Kar-wai, ed., *Tête-bêche: A Wong Kar Wai Project* (Hong Kong, 2000).

MARY SHUK-HAN WONG

1973 · JULY 20

Bruce Lee is found dead.

The Mysterious Death of Bruce Lee, Chinese Nationalism, and Cinematic Legacy

On July 20, 1973, Bruce Lee (1940–1973) died in mysterious, if not suspicious, circumstances in the bedroom of a lover in Hong Kong. Lee had based himself in the British colony (as it was then) and had worked there as an actor since 1971. He had had a meteoric rise as a martial arts star and had been a marvel on the screen for only two years and just four movies before his death, which came as a shock to his millions of fans. His death was akin to James Dean's (1931–1955) death some eighteen years earlier, or perhaps Princess Diana's (1961–1997) death in more recent times. Forty years since Lee's death, it is a worthwhile exercise to reassess Lee's legacy. What kind of a cultural phenomenon was he? Was he a martial artist or just an actor who relied on natural, instinctive feelings? What is his legacy from the standpoint of cinematic and literary culture?

Like Dean and Diana, Lee received universal admiration in life and immortality in death, his memory frequently rekindled by Chinese and non-Chinese alike. At the time of his death, his fame had already spread worldwide following his starring roles in *The Big Boss* (1971), *Fist of Fury* (1972), *The Way of the Dragon* (1972), and *Enter the Dragon* (1973). He had legions of African and Asian fans, not to mention Western ones. Lee's appeal is truly global, and he was (and still is) the only Chinese star to be so widely venerated. But it was probably his Asian and African fan following that was the foundation of his stardom at its height. In his book *Everybody Was Kung Fu Fighting* (2001), Vijay Prashad offers an encomium to Lee; he analyzes his international appeal, particularly to Africans and Asians in the Third World (and among Asian immigrants and blacks in the United States), racial groups that had long suffered from slavery, racism, and imperialist oppression. M. T. Kato's (1961–) book *From Kung Fu to Hip Hop* (2007) also offers an encomium to Lee, discussing him and his films from a political standpoint. Kato puts Lee in sociohistorical context and assesses his status as a revolutionary cultural icon: struggling, in his movies, against Japanese imperialism, and then against neo-imperialism.

Prashad and Kato value Lee for his political and revolutionary significance, a significance that has not lost relevance even today. Lee's heroic-revolutionary status transcends the cultural moment of the 1970s. However, scholars like Prashad and Kato may actually have underestimated the current of nationalism that is clearly a factor in Lee's popularity. Lee certainly pandered to nationalistic feelings in his films, and it would be pertinent to reassess the nationalism of Lee's films and to ponder the issue of whether his perceived revolutionary status overrides his nationalism. Kung fu itself was always routinely described as "Chinese kung fu"; for Lee himself, kung fu was part of a narrative of Chinese personal pride and selfhood if not of a struggle to revive the Chinese nation. He was very conscious, therefore, of his Chinese identity. This is borne out by his films. *Fist of Fury* is his most nationalistic movie, touching on the humiliation of Chinese by the Japanese and other foreigners. One of its most memorable scenes has Lee kicking and breaking the infamous "No Dogs and Chinese Allowed" sign in a Shanghai park. The movie is pervaded throughout with anti-Japanese sentiment such that it remains quite potent today, given the China-Japan tensions over disputed islands in the East China Sea. If we say that Lee is still politically relevant today, then his influence may still drive Chinese nationalism in the present time, and this would undoubtedly be a part of his legacy. *Enter the Dragon*, a Hong Kong–Hollywood coproduction, is his most internationalist film. But even here Lee was very consciously Chinese in his performance: going into action dressed in a traditional Chinese silk suit and essentially playing a Chinese kung fu variant of James Bond. As a result, his millions of Chinese fans saw Lee as the archetype of a Chinese kung fu artist.

In *Enter the Dragon*, Lee was keen to disseminate the art of kung fu to the world as a Chinese art form (even if he used non-Chinese implements such as nunchakus), and although he might have wished to emphasize the global practice of kung fu, Lee comes across as a uniquely Chinese practitioner. Compared with his Western counterparts in the film (the characters played by John Saxon [1935–] and Jim Kelly [1946–2013]), Lee adopts a far more stoic persona. The more he is set off from the Western characters, the more he stands out as exceptional and exclusive in his application of kung fu. *Enter the Dragon* also contains a key moment early in the film where Lee's character is asked by a Shaolin master to explain the art of kung fu and his motivation for fighting. The scene, and its philosophical undertone, is fleeting, and tangential to the bare-knuckle realities of the action and excitement that kung fu was meant to represent according to the Hollywood coproducers; it was in fact cut from the international release but has since been restored in DVD and Blu-ray editions. Unfortunately, *Enter the Dragon* never really lives up to that brief moment of philosophical repose.

Although his films remain popular and available, and are the main embodiments of his martial art and his reputation as an actor, they are probably not an adequate basis for defining Lee's philosophy. Kato's frequent use of the adjective "kinetic" to describe Lee's films and his performances suggests that the films themselves might just be too kinetic for their own good, even, as they are often criticized for being, cartoonish and kitschy. Lee's films are also typical genre movies in the commercial Chinese cinema; they display an essentialism of good and evil that is an inherent quality of the kung fu form. Though Lee had a philosophical streak, he comes across only very rarely as a kung fu philosopher in his films, and it is probably just as problematic to regard him as a philosopher as it is to view him as a nationalist.

Lee's vision of kung fu lies in the way he embodies the martial art of the "intercepting fist" (Jeet Kune Do), which was his own special method of kung fu, and the art of Wing Chun, which was imparted to him by his master Ip Man (1893–1972). In a sense, his body was his method, and the movies, by virtue of their audiovisual as well as visceral nature, amplified his body methodology many times over, making him beautiful to look at and to listen to. His aesthetic athleticism has not been surpassed by Jackie Chan (1954–), Jet Li (1963–), Donnie Yen (1963–), or any of the current martial arts stars. Lee became known for his idiosyncratic style and moves, his catcalls and gesticulations; his philosophy of kung fu, by contrast, is not as accentuated and is therefore often misunderstood and inadequately theorized.

Lee left behind more than just films. Some of his writings have been published posthumously—such as *The Tao of Gung Fu* (1997) and *The Tao of Jeet Kune Do* (1975). In *The Tao of Gung Fu*, Lee defines kung fu as "the *Way* to the object—be it the Way to health promotion, to spiritual cultivation, or to the Way of self-defense" (emphasis Lee's). "Kung fu" itself means "training and discipline," and, as such, the term "kung fu" can be applied to any situation. It is best known, however, as a term in martial arts, where training and discipline are so critical. With intense training and discipline, kung fu could point one toward the Way (or *dao*). However, kung fu is often mistaken for pure technique. "All techniques," Lee wrote, "become the 'one' without opposites, infinite and unceasing, and all movements were stripped to their essential purpose, without any wasted and unnecessary motions." The transformation into the universal "one" was influenced by the philosophies of Daoism, Chan (Zen), and the *Book of Changes*. Lee saw kung fu as an instrument and at the same time as a kind of spirituality. It could serve as a means through which to achieve the *dao*, the central notion of Daoism, the very *dao* that Lee interpreted as "the Way to the object." Here kung fu represents the vessel by which the body and the *dao* could become one, achieving a concord or union of physicality and spirituality. When Lee formed his own production company, he named it Concord, and he used a *taiji* symbol, commonly known in the West as a "yin-yang" symbol, symbolizing that very concord of materiality and spirituality.

In his short life, Lee undoubtedly achieved the *dao* through kung fu or the martial arts if *dao* is understood as the Way to superstardom, or if it is understood as the Way to perfection, reaching the acme of practice in one's career and life-forming experience. We will never know how Lee would have developed had he lived to make more kung fu movies on his own terms, perhaps even in Hollywood for the big studios. He might have infused them with more philosophy and his image might be quite different from that of the revolutionary figure characterized by Prashad and Kato, based as it is on the handful of films that he made in Hong Kong. Lee is remembered today primarily as a martial artist par excellence. As a martial artist, then, did Lee achieve health, spiritual cultivation, or self-defense according to the tenets of his *Tao of Gung Fu*? It might be instructive to return to that fateful day of July 20, 1973. His death itself suggests that his kung fu training was incomplete, as he failed to protect himself and maintain his health. Officially, it was a death by misadventure. An intense personality, Lee might well have exhausted himself in his training, therefore adversely affecting his health, or else a lapse of discipline might have broken down his defenses. After all, he was found dead in the bedroom of an actress who later admitted that they were lovers. Abstinence is part of one's training in the martial arts, and a lapse into sexual indiscretion would be a major behavioral infraction (as illustrated, for example, in a scene in *The Big Boss* where Lee as the hero is seduced by a Bangkok prostitute, and this finally causes him some embarrassment). And as for spiritual cultivation, was Lee spiritually fulfilled? Alas, we shall never know.

Lee's legacy, then, may be a mixed one if we take into account the circumstances of his demise, which make him more human and vulnerable, less of a super kung fu being than he is often seen as. There may be a dark side of his character that has yet to be exposed. As the film scholar Chris Berry has pointed out, Lee's films hint at homophobia and xenophobia, which may or may not be part of Lee's character. All these suggest a more complex legacy for Lee than simply unparalleled genius in the practice of kung fu. Yet, his practice of martial arts and its blending of the Chinese philosophy of universal oneness suggest that Lee was on the right philosophical track. He made kung fu truly universal. Lee was an independent spirit and an idiosyncratic martial artist whose style evolved out of a refusal to adhere to any style. His universality obscures the fact that his legacy might be one in which the individual's training and discipline (the real meaning of "kung fu") is crucial in determining how the union of body and spirituality may be achieved. There have been many Bruce Lee imitators, but only one Bruce Lee.

BIBLIOGRAPHY: Chris Berry, "Stellar Transit: Bruce Lee's Body or Chinese Masculinity in a Transnational Frame," in *Embodied Modernities: Corporeality, Representation, and Chinese Cultures*, ed. Fran Martin and Larissa Heinrich (Honolulu, 2006), 218–234. M. T. Kato, *From Kung Fu to Hip Hop: Globalization, Revolution and Popular Culture* (Albany, NY, 2007). Bruce Lee, *The Tao of Gung Fu* (Boston, 1997). Vijay Prashad, *Everybody Was Kung Fu Fighting: Afro-Asian Connections and the Myth of Cultural Purity* (Boston, 2001).

STEPHEN TEO

1974 · JUNE

Yang Mu writes "Manuscript in a Bottle" in a fishing village in Rockport, Washington.

Yang Mu Negotiates between Classicism and Modernism

On a June day in 1974, a man in his early thirties, aimlessly driving along the Pacific coast, decided to stop at a fishing village in Rockport, Washington. He took a walk on the beach and sat down to watch the rising tide. Missing his hometown, Hualien, on the other side of the Pacific Ocean, he said to himself, "Hualien has many earthquakes and typhoons, but what exactly is a tidal wave?" He stayed at the beach until nightfall, when it became too windy and cold to remain. He returned to the inn and wrote the poem "Manuscript in a Bottle." At the end of the poem, the poet imagines himself stepping into the ocean:

> … when I set my foot in the water
> a minuscule addition in weight causes the level to rise
> and wet the shore even farther on the other side
> and as I walk on, if I submerge myself
> seven feet to the west off this lonely shore
> will Hualien, my Hualien in June
> start a rumor of a tidal wave?

The composition of "Manuscript in a Bottle" marks not only a critical juncture in Yang Mu's (1940–) career as a poet but also a turning point in the history of modern poetry in Taiwan. Born Ching-hsien Wang, Yang

Mu graduated from Tunghai University with a BA in English literature. After his mandatory military service, he left for the University of Iowa in 1964 at Paul Engle's (1908–1991) invitation to attend the International Writing Program. He stayed on to complete an MFA in creative writing in 1966 and proceeded to pursue a PhD in comparative literature at the University of California at Berkeley. Since 1970 he has held appointments as a professor in the United States, Hong Kong, and Taiwan. His successful academic career aside, Yang Mu is considered by many to be the greatest poet in the Sinophone world today.

At the age of sixteen Yang Mu began publishing poems. Writing under the penname Ye Shan in the 1950s and 1960s, he was among the youngest poets of the first postwar generation in Taiwan. In the bleak, conservative, and repressive atmosphere at the time, a coterie of young poets and poetesses formed a close-knit community under the tutelage of such senior poets as Ji Xian (1913–2013) and Qin Zihao (1912–1963). Veering away from a mainstream literature dominated at the time by traditional lyricism and anticommunist ideology, they took a deep interest in the avant-garde movements in Europe and America, particularly surrealism and high modernism. They also drew inspiration from romanticism, and not only from the English romanticists, but also from Xu Zhimo (1897–1931), the Chinese romanticist par excellence. Finally, the Chinese lyrical tradition, of both elite and folk origins, was a legacy that helped shape their language and sensibility. These three strands converged into a robust modernist movement in postwar Taiwan, creating a golden age in twentieth-century Chinese poetry. Ye Shan embodied the movement at its best: surrealism in his charged images and enigmatic numbers; a profound affinity with John Keats (1795–1821), his reverence of beauty, and his contemplations on time; an exquisite phrasing derived from classical Chinese poetry. All three elements converged into a uniquely powerful poetry.

By the time Ye Shan left Taiwan for the United States in 1964, the modernist movement in Taiwan had begun to wane. In the early 1970s, Taiwan suffered a series of setbacks in the international arena, most notably the loss of its seat in the United Nations and the severing of diplomatic ties with the United States and Japan. No longer regarded as the legitimate representative of China, Taiwan faced an identity crisis. This crisis surfaced on the literary scene when some poets and literary critics castigated modern poetry for being excessively Western, solipsistic, and oblivious to local reality. The so-called modern poetry debate erupted in 1972, and Ye Shan became one of the first targets for his ornate language and precious sensibility. Other poets under attack included Yu Guangzhong (1928–) and Zhou Mengdie (1921–2014).

What the critics ignored, wittingly or unwittingly, was that since the late 1960s Ye Shan had been undergoing a dramatic transformation. At UC Berkeley he studied classical Chinese poetry under Shih-hsiang Chen (1921–1971), who, while an undergraduate student at Peking University in the early 1930s, cotranslated the first English anthology of modern Chinese poetry with his teacher Harold Acton (1904–1994). Under Chen, Ye Shan focused on the twin fountainheads of Chinese poetry, *The Book of Songs* and *The Songs of the South*. His dissertation on the former was later published as *The Bell and the Drum: "Shih Ching" and Formulaic Poetry in an Oral Tradition*, the first full-length study of the Confucian classic in English. As a major in comparative literature, he also studied Old English, ancient Greek, and German literatures.

It is no surprise, then, that it was during this time that Ye Shan the poet developed in a new direction. "Jizi of Yanling Hangs Up His Sword" (1969) retells the story of a historical figure from the Spring and Autumn period (770–476 BCE) in order to lament the degradation of the Confucian spirit. "King Wu's Night Encampment: A Suite" (1969) critiques the military expeditions of the Zhou king in the eleventh century BCE. "A Sequel to Han Yu's Seven-Character Ancient-Style Poem 'Mountain Rock,'" written the same year, relates the Tang poet's ambivalence toward politics and his longing for self-fulfillment through art. These poems teem with historical and literary allusions. However, rather than belonging to the traditional genre of poetic commentary on history, they are deconstructive and ironic. In 1972, Ye Shan changed his pen name to Yang Mu.

Historically speaking, Yang Mu's appropriations of the Chinese tradition provided a new paradigm for poets in Taiwan seeking to reject modernism and turn toward Chinese heritage. Moreover, his representations and embrace of Taiwan predated the Nativist Literature Movement in 1977. Besides "Manuscript in a Bottle," cited at the beginning of this chapter, "Kaohsiung, 1973" critiques the government policy of the free-trade zone, where local women provided cheap labor for foreign-owned factories. Written in 1975, "Fort Zeelandia"—the Dutch name for Tainan,

the oldest city on the island—problematizes the dominance of the colonizers. Through Yang Mu's eyes we see the majestic mountains and the
Pacific Ocean in Hualien, we contemplate the multifarious history of the
island, we share his indignation at injustice and his delight in the natural
curiosity of children, and we see Taiwan paralleled to Ireland, especially
the Ireland of William Butler Yeats (1865–1939).

In the 1980s, a nativist consciousness gained momentum and eventually became mainstream in Taiwan. Yang Mu wrote "Someone Asks
Me a Question about Righteousness and Justice" in 1984 at the height
of the democracy movement. The poem takes a moving probe into the
historical tension, as a result of the Nationalist Party's discriminatory
policy, between the Hokkien (or Taiwanese) people and the postrevolu-
tion émigrés from the mainland. However, Yang Mu is neither a realist
nor a nativist poet and refuses to subscribe to a mainstream ideology. He
remains, above all, a lyrical poet who engages with reality through the
mediation of a finely crafted language.

Since his teens, Yang Mu has been a firm believer in the Keatsian
aphorism "Beauty is truth, truth beauty." Poetry is worth lifelong pursuit
because it is true and eternal; as expressed in Yang Mu's words,

> I believe in the quest and attainment of art
> and music, I place them in
> specific Time and Space, one by one
> They burn and diffuse through eternity. ("Rabbit," 1997)

Like Yeats in "Sailing to Byzantium," Yang Mu is acutely aware of the
tension between physical decay and spiritual transcendence, between
human mortality and the immortality of art. Remembering a little girl
who tries to catch a butterfly so she can put it between the pages of a
book, the poet looks to the future:

> By then we'll both be old—
> without our dry, colorful clothes, we will have only an awakened
>   soul
> in the embrace of a book, close to words
> living in the sympathy and wisdom that we seek. ("Tree in the
>   College," 1983)

Music, with its organic structure and its intrinsically abstract and thus amoral nature, is not only a major motif in Yang Mu's work but also integral to his poetics. In the suite of four poems dedicated to Federico García Lorca (1898–1936) entitled "The Forbidden Game" (1976), musical images contrast the permanence of art with the impermanence of love:

> Try to remember
> the great concern in Granada
> try to remember your language and pain
> green winds and green horses, your
> language and happiness—your occasional happiness.

Yang Mu's poetic vision may be summed up with these words from his preface to the 1995 collection: poetry is that which "passes through time—traversing its dimness, uncertainty, and fragmentation—gathers and stitches together all the transient moods and reticences—to make it last, lasting in an ever-renewed structure."

From 1960 to 2014, Yang Mu published fifteen volumes of original poetry, the bulk of which is collected in four tomes. Deep engagement with world literature and culture has given his work a versatility and profundity that is unparalleled among Chinese poets in the modern period. He has created a language that is uniquely his own, a language that is dense, reticent, lyrical, and fully charged. His diction runs the gamut from the colloquial to the archaic; the poet speaks of his effort to "resuscitate words that have been forgotten." His syntax is supple and surprising line by line; the resultant ambiguity adds to the richness of the poems. His imagery is precise and original, complex and engrossing. His use of sound is natural and convincing: even when the words don't make sense, the music does. His tone ranges from playfulness to passion to despair:

> Angel, if you cannot, with your glorious, sacred heart,
> understand this brocade of words to be tears and blood
> then I beg for mercy ("To an Angel," 1993)

Equally important is Yang Mu's reinvention of the dramatic monologue, a device that has become a staple feature of his poetry since the late 1960s. The poet has created a wide range of personae, both historical and fictional. They come from both Chinese and Western sources: Virgil (70–20 BCE), Dante (1265–1321), and Christopher Marlowe (1564–1593), as well as Zheng Xuan (127–200) and Du Fu (712–770). Fictional characters such as Lin Chong from *Water Margin*, Miao Yu from *Dream of the Red Chamber*, and the Chechen resistance fighter in *The Lost Ring* also come alive under Yang Mu's pen with their disillusionment and heroism, inner struggles and triumphs. "Lama Reincarnated" (1987) is based on the life story of "Boy Lama" Tenzin Ösel Hita (1985–), a five-year-old boy born in Spain who was selected as the reincarnation of Lama Thubten Yeshe (1935–1984). In the poem, he calls out to the Tibetan monks searching the wide world for the Lama's reincarnation:

> Come, come, come to Andalusia
> Come find me, come find me in faraway Granada
> Let us sing and praise eternal Granada
> Let us sing a new song about old Andalusia

With the rhymes and repetitions, the poem presents a mesmerizing chant, evoking hope and peace.

Yang Mu's dramatic monologues may owe their inspiration to such Anglo-American modernists as Robert Browning (1812–1889) and T. S. Eliot (1888–1965). He is a master of the narrative and the dramatic mode, but at the same time, he emphasizes the lyrical that underlies all poetry. As he has written, "Lyric poetry is the first step of poetry and the ultimate end of poetry" ("Literature and Reason"). His work expands on it and demonstrates new possibilities.

For more than half a century, Yang Mu has been a formative force in Taiwan and increasingly influential in the Chinese-speaking world. He has mentored many young poets and has been a role model for several generations. His reverence for art and emphasis on cultural knowledge both Chinese and Western have led some to call him the founder of the "Academic School" of poets, a title he gladly accepts. Clearly, the depth and breadth of Yang Mu's poetry and poetic vision defies any and all labels. In addition to being a world-class poet, Yang Mu is a master of the personal essay; a scholar of classical Chinese poetry and comparative literature; a prolific translator of William Shakespeare (1564–1616) and Yeats, among others; and an astute editor of both Tang poetry and modern

Chinese poetry and prose. Yang Mu now lives in Hualien, where he holds an endowed chair at the National Hwa Dong University. Indeed, he has become the giant "tidal wave" that he imagined in "Manuscript in a Bottle"!

BIBLIOGRAPHY: Lisa Lai-ming Wong, *Rays of the Searching Sun: The Transcultural Poetics of Yang Mu* (Brussels, 2009). Michelle Yeh and Lawrence R. Smith, trans., *No Trace of the Gardener: Poems of Yang Mu* (New Haven, CT, 1998).

MICHELLE YEH

1976 · APRIL 4

> "I don't believe the sky is blue."

Poems from Underground

On April 4, 1976, the police swept Tiananmen Square of chrysanthemum wreaths, banners, placards, and people honoring Premier Zhou Enlai (1898–1976), who had died January 8 of that year. It was Qingming Festival, or grave-sweeping day, but while they swept away a number of poems, they did not sweep away the new blossoms of Chinese poetry. In fact, they may have created the conditions for its popularity.

Mourners were not happy to see the tributes they had left their fallen leader on Sunday removed by Monday. Three decades later, the poet Bei Dao (1949–) remembers what he learned when he got home from work:

> That afternoon an angry crowd not only attacked the Great Hall of the People, but also overturned vehicles and burned the headquarters building of the workers in the square. That night news of the suppression circulated via non-official channels; it was said that batons had been used to kill numerous people, and the square had run with blood.

The historian Jonathan Spence (1936–) writes that a reported 388, labeled "bad elements carrying out disruption and disturbances and engaging in counter-revolutionary sabotage," were arrested and either put on "people's trial" at Peking University or sent to prison camps for "reform through labor." The event is significant historically as a spontaneous popular outcry against what would later be called the Gang of Four and the governmental policies of the Cultural Revolution (1966–1976), and for how the Politburo attempted to blame the event on Deng Xiaoping (1904–1997). It plays a role in literary history, too, for its relationship with a poem by an electrician in his twenties who would eventually become known to the world as Bei Dao.

To understand the relationship between the 1976 Tiananmen "incident" and Bei Dao's "The Answer," one must first understand that the 1976 event—in what it meant, and where it came from—was already an act of literature, from its sound to its curious symbolism. Pronounced in Chinese, the date April 4 (*si si*) sounds like "to die, to die." Also, while many of the poems left in Zhou's honor took the opportunity to criticize the Cultural Revolution's policy makers, did anyone really know what the premier thought or said, or had he only been cast as a bulwark against Mao Zedong (1893–1976), Jiang Qing (1914–1991), and her supporters? As Richard Curt Kraus (1944–) asks, "Was he the great moderator, who kept Mao's enthusiasms under some control? Or was he the great opportunist, a sycophant to Mao who protected some underlings while sacrificing others when useful?" Better to say that Zhou was a signifier detached, as literary language must be, from the reality of its referent.

This is not to denigrate the sincerity of people's mourning for Zhou; when we cry over fictional figures in literature, our tears are real. But there is a literariness to how people would have understood Zhou's opposition to the leaders of the Cultural Revolution, involving even the radical Anti–Lin Biao Anti-Confucius Campaign, which since 1974 had been admonishing everyone to reconsider recent and ancient history. On a guided tour through China with a cadre of French radical intellectuals, for instance, Roland Barthes (1915–1980) found pleasure both in the campaign's textuality—he writes down (incorrectly) its Chinese characters—and in its phonics—he refers to it by its jingling romanization "Pi-Lin Pi-Kong." But he did not understand that it was what historians such as Roderick MacFarquhar (1930–) and Michael Schoenhals (1953–) have described as "ultimately an allegorical vehicle for an attack on Zhou Enlai." (Barthes even wonders, "Role of Zhou Enlai in the campaign?") Astute readers of the name in its fuller form, "Criticize Lin Biao, Criticize Confucius and the Duke of Zhou," would have been able to figure out the way a duke admired by Confucius would signify an official, whom some considered Confucian, via a pun on their common surname. *The Book of Songs* sings,

> Broken were our axes
> And chipped our hatchets
> But since the Duke of Zhou came to the east
> Throughout the kingdoms all is well.
> He has shown compassion to us people,
> He has greatly helped us. (Arthur Waley, trans.)

In the early 1970s, though, both the possibilities of noblesse oblige and of literary interpretation were curtailed.

"They have to be taken *literally*," Barthes copied into his journal. "They are not interpretable." It is unclear to which slogans on which posters Barthes is referring, but the statement appears right after his handwritten transcription of "Anti–Lin Biao Anti-Confucius" in Chinese. Yet if such a directive was impossible to follow when it came to understanding the slogans and events of the day, it is a fine example of the era's official policy toward language and literature. Not only must "the thoughts and feelings of our writers and artists," as Mao put it, "be fused with those of the masses of workers, peasants and soldiers," but the fusion must produce literature that is clear, direct, and as close to being literal as possible. Consider the proscription by He Jingzhi (1924–), one of the few poets to publish during the Cultural Revolution:

> We shall
> Open our diaries
> To write down boldly—
> The truth of Mao Tse-tung's thought
>
> Write: the sky
> Will never fall!
> Write: the earth
> Will never be destroyed! (1965, Hsin-sheng C. Kao, trans.)

Or this poem, written by one of the twentieth century's more renowned poets, Ai Qing (1910–1996), in 1978, two years after the Cultural Revolution ended:

Red fire,
Red blood,
Red the wild lilies,
Red the azalea blooms, a red flood,
Red the pomegranate in May,
Red is the sun at the birth of day.

But most beautiful of them all,
    the red flags on forward march! (Hsu Kai-yu, trans.)

against Bei Dao's "The Answer":

Debasement is the password of the base,
Nobility is the epitaph of the noble.
See how the gilded sky is covered
With the drifting twisted shadows of the dead.
    (Bonnie McDougall, trans.)

Bei Dao's poetry was different even from the poems left in honor of
Zhou:

Waking, our Premier would rejoice;
His loyal heirs are battling the demons. (Xiao Lan, trans.)

Bei Dao was in Tiananmen Square on April 4, 1976, but he did not
write "The Answer" to be left on the Memorial to the Martyrs of the
Revolution in honor of Zhou. Though the earliest drafts of the poem
were from 1972, its publication in 1978 dated it April 1976; its lines

I came into this world
. . . .
To proclaim before the judgment
The voice that has been judged

place it between the violence of April 5 and the "people's trials." More
importantly, a new poetry was defined in the defiance of this prejudged
voice:

I don't believe the sky is blue;
I don't believe in thunder's echoes;
I don't believe that dreams are false;
I don't believe that death has no revenge.

Most of these statements of apostasy indicate a kind of humanism that, if familiar to North American readers today, would have been understood as philosophically dangerous to Chinese readers in the 1970s. But what about "I don't believe the sky is blue"? Today the sky over Beijing is not blue, which makes Bei Dao's line as inadvertently prophetic as Federico García Lorca's (1898–1936) "assassinated by the sky." But the danger in 1976 of not believing the sky was blue would have been its promotion of a strange literariness, because the line cannot be taken literally—because it is only, and always, interpretable. If the sky is not blue, the Sun might not be Red.

Not that Bei Dao's poetics were without precedent. His poetry reflects his visits with underground poets amongst the "educated youth" who had been "sent down" to Baiyangdian, Hebei, to learn socialism from the peasants (similar underground poetry movements were taking place near Shanghai and in Guiyang, Guizhou). These young men and women wrote a poetry that counteracted the Cultural Revolution's "inflation of language" and opened up a new interpretive space for familiar iconography. From Mang Ke's (1950–) "Sky" (1973):

The sun rises
The sky—a blood-soaked shield (Jonathan Stalling and Yibing
    Huang, trans.)

and the beginning of Duo Duo's (1951–) "Night" (1973):

On a night full of symbols
The moon is like an invalid's pallid face (Gregory Lee, trans.)

This is a poetry in part inspired by foreign literatures, whether from the "yellow books" of contemporary Western literature translated for "internal circulation" among party cadres, or indirectly from the work of more cosmopolitan poets who had come of age in the 1930s and 1940s before turning to the safer work of literary translation in the 1950s. Duo Duo would point out the contrast between the domestic and international poetic environments: "While we sang each day: 'Chairman Mao is like the sun', Baudelaire said: 'The sun is like a poet.'" Bei Dao would later explain that he wrote poetry in the "translation style" of this reshaped Chinese.

The "I—do—not—believe" of Bei Dao's "The Answer" also answers "Believe in the Future" (1968) by Shi Zhi (1948–), the first poet to write lyrical pieces of personal expression during the Cultural Revolution, from rural Shanxi, where he had been sent down:

> As spider webs mercilessly seal off my stovetop
> As smoldering cinders sigh over the sorrows of poverty
> I still stubbornly spread out the hopeless cinders
> And write with finely powdered snow: believe in the future
>   (Jonathan Stalling, trans.)

and Bei Dao's opening lines echo the opening lines to Shi Zhi's "Destiny" (1967):

> A good reputation is a banknote that can never be broken
> A bad reputation is a chain from which one cannot break free
>   (Jonathan Stalling, trans.)

Several decades and a language away, what is disappointingly banal about Bei Dao's and Shi Zhi's lines may undermine what was evocative and arresting in their imagery. Chinese readers at the time, though, found these poems startlingly fresh. We can appreciate this historically, but, familiar with poetry's present-day marginalization, we may be surprised at the breadth of its readership. When between 1978 and 1980 Bei Dao and Mang Ke published *Today*, the first unofficial literary journal in the People's Republic of China—covering their bicycle plates as they rode to tack the issues up to a briefly tolerated area of public dissent known as the "Democracy Wall" and distribute stacks of issues to official organs and bureau buildings—it achieved unprecedented popularity: in a year-and-a-half run of nine bimonthly issues and seven series titles, *Today* distributed almost twenty thousand copies to readers in Beijing and throughout China. They also held "discussion meetings," which Bei Dao called "the largest salons Beijing ever saw," and public poetry readings, with the first attracting "only five hundred people" because of the rain, and the second over a thousand. China is a populous country, but why was this poetry so popular?

In addition to the work of Bei Dao, Mang Ke, Duo Duo, and Shi Zhi, *Today* also published the socialist alienation poetry of Shu Ting (1952–), from Fujian, one of the few women in the group:

> We come down from the factory assembly lines
> And join the assembly line going home
> Overhead
> An assembly line of stars trails across the sky
>   (1980, Eva Hung, trans.)

along with the mythopoetics of Yang Lian (1955–), who had begun writing classical-style verse:

> Let this mute stone
> Attest my birth
> Let this song
> Resound
> In the troubled mist
> Searching for my eyes (1980, John Minford with Seán Golden, trans.)

and the childlike genius of Gu Cheng (1956–1993), whose "A Generation" he supposedly wrote at the age of sixteen:

> The dark night gave me dark eyes
> But I use them to search for light (translation mine)

Because *Today* was published unofficially, and posted on the Democracy Wall, poetry attained an association with opposition to the government—an association it retains today (in contrast with fiction, for instance, which tends to publish in official venues). Predictably, the establishment dismissed it, calling it *menglong*, which is often translated as "misty" but which has none of the word's connotations of sentimentality or vagueness in English, and so should rather be "obscure." ("If you cannot understand, your son or grandson will understand some day," Bei Dao has said.) Because so many of their influences were foreign, critics both within China and without have asked, "Is this Chinese literature?" But after the Cultural Revolution's smashing of the "four olds"—customs, culture, habits, and ideas—a "Chinese" literature defined according to the past would have a hard road to walk. Nevertheless, it is worth noting that its popularity is related to the rebirth of a traditional holiday: the Qingming Festival of 1976.

More importantly, the "obscure" poetry gained popularity because it resonated with a readership trained to interpret current events as they would with literature, even as they were starved for literature in the writing available from official channels.

BIBLIOGRAPHY: Bei Dao and Li Tuo, eds., *The Seventies: Recollecting a Forgotten Time in China*, English edition ed. Theodore Huters (Hong Kong, 2012). Richard Curt Kraus, *The Cultural Revolution: A Very Short Introduction* (New York, 2011). Roderick MacFarquhar and Michael Schoenhals, *Mao's Last Revolution* (Cambridge, MA, 2006). Song Yongyi, "A Glance at the Underground Reading Movement during the Cultural Revolution," *Journal of Contemporary China* 16, no. 51 (2007): 325–333. Jonathan D. Spence, *The Search for Modern China* (New York, 1991). Maghiel van Crevel, *Language Shattered: Contemporary Chinese Poetry and Duoduo* (Leiden, Netherlands, 1996). Eliot Weinberger, "China Is Here," in *Outside Stories* (New York, 1992), 126–132.

LUCAS KLEIN

1976

> "Why do I roam to distant lands? Because of the olive tree in
> my dreams."

A Modern Taiwanese Innocents Abroad

On May 1, 1976, the Taiwanese writer Chen Ping (1943–1991)—born Chen Maoping, but better known by her nom de plume and alter ego Sanmao, literally "three locks of hair"—published her first book, *Sahara Stories*, a compilation of twelve stories that had already been circulating for over a year in the literary supplements of Taiwan's major newspapers based on her experiences living in Western Sahara. This autobiographical work, the first of more than twenty such books she was to eventually publish, became an overnight sensation in the Sinosphere, was reprinted three times in the first six weeks, and went on to be reprinted more than thirty times. In this book and continuing throughout the rest of her career, Sanmao fashioned herself as the female incarnation of the vagabond orphan Sanmao created by cartoonist Zhang Leping (1910–1992) in 1936, whose adventures living on the streets of Shanghai starkly reflected the misery of that period. She went on to participate in the prosperous urbanization of Taiwan, document the rapid globalization of the Sinosphere that occurred between the 1940s and the 1990s, and witness the decolonization of Western Sahara.

Born in the provisional capital of Chongqing in 1943, Sanmao and her family migrated throughout China during the chaotic civil war before finally settling in Taipei in 1948. Growing up in a middle-class family, she became a maverick at an early age. She adopted the English name Echo from the mythological Greek nymph, which intimated her own narcissistic personality and presaged the later tragic loss of her husband. Her father, an attorney, later recalled incidents from her eccentric childhood and adolescence including playing with mud in a graveyard, dispassionately watching goats being slaughtered, ignoring warnings about the danger of being submerged in a large urn, and deceiving a young cadet about her true age in order to initiate a love affair. Unsuited to the standard secondary education system, Sanmao eventually withdrew during her second year of junior high school after her math teacher humiliated her by painting two zeroes around her eyes to represent her poor grades. This incident foreshadowed her overly sensitive and self-abased character as an adult, as well as her pervasive sense of insecurity and fear of intimacy—sentiments that were common among her generation, growing up under oppressive martial law in Taiwan.

Wisely employing her time after leaving school, Sanmao focused on cultivating her interests in painting, music, and literature. She became conversant in the Chinese literary classics, and at the age of nineteen published her debut essay, "Confusion"—the story of a young girl's hallucinations after viewing the 1948 Hollywood film *Portrait of Jennie*—in the periodical *Modern Literature*. The protagonist consciously denies identifying with the tragic female phantom in the film, but at the same time cannot resist her disturbing tune: "Where I come from nobody knows and where I am going everything goes. Where the wind blows, where the sea flows, nobody knows. And where I am going nobody knows." These lyrics profoundly influenced Sanmao's life as she also subconsciously fathomed the question of her own origin and destination and as she prepared to make her own unique contributions, from the perspective of a stranger in a strange, distant land, to the modern Chinese lyricism then thriving in postwar Taiwan's literary community.

Sanmao soon shifted her aspirations toward study overseas. Following a failed love affair that led her to abandon the study of philosophy at the Chinese Culture University in Taipei, she moved to Madrid in 1967 to study Spanish. Her penchant for seeking adventure, excitement, and escapism after suffering failure was recurrent throughout her life. Subsequently, she studied and worked in Germany and the United States, then traveled throughout Europe before returning to teach in Taiwan in 1971. Romantically involved with several foreigners during her time abroad, she describes her experiences of cultural displacement in vivid detail: "I spoke Japanese in Spain, English in Germany, Chinese in the U.S. and German in Taiwan." Sanmao became engaged to a German who died of a heart attack on the eve of their wedding. Devastated, she returned to Spain in 1972 and agreed to marry José María Quero y Ruiz (1951–1979), who had pursued her during her earlier residence there. In 1973 the couple moved to El Aaiún in the Spanish colony of Western Sahara, where they were married and lived off his income as a diver. Sanmao was fascinated by the exotic landscape and the customs of the local Sahrawi people of this region, but also became bored living as a housewife isolated in the harsh desert environment, which inspired her to write about her everyday experiences there as a "peripheral observer." Her first story from this period, "Restaurant in the Desert," humorously depicts a sly, resourceful housewife dwelling in the desert, comforting her simple-minded foreign husband and his colleagues with homemade Chinese cuisine. Published in Taiwan's *United Daily News*, the story presented her Sinophone audience with a confident and able Chinese female thriving in an alien environment. Impressed by her domestic wisdom, readers were drawn to the consistently sentimental, innocent, curious, and sympathetic first-person narrator. Sanmao later followed her husband to the Canary Islands after Spain's withdrawal from Western Sahara, at which time this piece was included in her first collection, *Sahara Stories*, which secured her literary reputation. In her later collections *Scarecrow Notes,* *Weeping Camel,* and *Soft Night,* she continued to romanticize the exotic African people and landscapes while enchanting her audience with her vagabond lifestyle.

The success of these books resulted from Sanmao's translucent and engaging style, exotic plotlines, and ability to fully capture the broad spectrum of her experience of colonial life during the 1970s. Concerned about appealing to all ages and classes, she bridged the gap between popular fiction and highbrow literature, entertaining with sentimental tales while educating readers about the outside world, enriching not only her audience but also herself in the process. The journalist Gui Wenya (1949–) reconciled the discrepancy between the overwhelming self-preoccupation in her early essays and the mature, compassionate attitude toward others in *Sahara Stories* as follows: "Only those who can comprehend the principles of things, life and death, joy and anger, can completely comprehend life." Cognizant of her audience's lack of familiarity with the places she depicted, Sanmao presented a romanticized version of harsh desert life that enchanted her readers and enabled them to imagine a utopian "peach blossom spring" hidden in that desolate environment. In this sense her stories about the desert appear to be an altruistic transformation, but they are also a continuation and displacement of the lyricism and self-dramatization found in her early writings. Her romantic style was so engaging that it managed to overshadow her representation of the dangers and pitfalls of colonialism.

Many of Sanmao's travel stories about Africa depicted the histrionic and innocuous misunderstandings between different cultures interpreted through a Chinese lens. At the same time she exhibited sympathy toward the poverty and emotional suffering of the Sahrawi people, especially women, in a manner reminiscent of Mark Twain (1835–1910) minus the satire. In comparison with other modern Sinophone travel literature, for example the *Silent Traveller* series by Chiang Yee (1903–1977), Sanmao's narrator is less of an observer and more central to the plot. Skillfully designing narratives to delight and entertain her audience, she based her stories on Spanish colonialist practices, making use of her status as an Oriental female with a Spanish husband, situating herself at the impasse between two conflicting political systems. In her previous stories about studying abroad, Sanmao was seen as a sensitive and victimized overseas student traumatized by being stereotyped and discriminated against for being an Oriental in developed countries. Now being protected and empowered by Spanish colonial hegemony, she intimated an imagined Taiwanese superiority vis-à-vis underdeveloped Africa and was unconcerned about the possibility of misrepresentation. As Miriam Lang and Anna-Stiina Antola have suggested, Sanmao keenly anticipated Taiwan's complicated status in global colonial discourse while playing along with her Sinophone audience's expectations of anticolonialist and nationalist sentiments, combined with her ethnic pride, while balancing her political thrusts with humanitarian concerns over colonial life and the suffering of the exotic people she observed.

After surviving wars and struggles, it was a tragic accident that brought Sanmao's halcyon days to an abrupt end. Mirroring the tragedy that befell her namesake Echo, who lost her lover, Narcissus, Sanmao lost her husband, José, to a diving accident on September 30, 1979, less than a week before the Mid-Autumn Festival, when Chinese families traditionally reunite. The formerly optimistic and independent writer never recovered from this loss and memorialized her deep mourning and melancholia in works such as *How Many Flowers Have Fallen in My Dream?* and *Offering You a Horse.* In 1980 she began translating Spanish and English literature into Chinese, including most of Agatha Christie's (1890–1976) works. She traveled to South America, taught literature and creative writing, gave lectures throughout Taiwan, and continued to publish further collections of short stories. She also composed lyrics for popular songs and authored the screenplay for the big-budget movie *Red Dust,* which centered on a controversial romance between a female writer and a traitor in Shanghai during the anti-Japanese war, a story that was based on Eileen Chang's (1920–1995) life.

Yet these diversions could neither dispel Sanmao's depression nor relieve her grief, and instead they merely exhausted her. In her final travelogue, *Crossing Myriads of Rivers and Mountains,* she takes great pains to depict the experience of visiting the wilderness of South America but appears to have lost the exaggerated, radiant liveliness of her former collections. Disenchanted with previously exciting foreign lands, she restrains the emotions that once captured the exotic spectacles of Africa and attempts instead to empathize with the tenacious lives of overseas Taiwanese. At this juncture she gazed back toward her own roots and returned to mainland China in 1989 for the first time in four decades, where she finally met Sanmao cartoonist Zhang Leping in Shanghai, visited the film crew of the movie *Red Dust* in Beijing, and met the famous folk music composer and ethnomusicologist Wang Luobin (1913–1996) in Xinjiang Province.

Even before Sanmao's visit, mainland readers had already begun to admire her bohemian writings as early as 1983, when the periodical *Literary Garden* published her story "The West Wind Does Not Recognize Complexion," which depicts foreigners bullying and exploiting the virtuous heroine during her studies abroad. The story's being co-opted as ideological propaganda was implicit in its mainland dissemination, as it vividly depicted the Chinese, eager but wary of reentering the global stage; pondered the preconceptions and prejudices they would face in unfamiliar contexts; reassured their anxieties about their ethnic pride; questioned conventional racial stereotypes; and acted as a defensive mechanism against "capitalist erosion." The later introduction of her other writings, however, quickly submerged this one-dimensional interpretation and unwittingly created an enigmatic, romantic, and individualist image for her. The mainland's younger generation—facing a barren cultural atmosphere, suffering from a communication breakdown with their cultural legacy, and harboring a rebellious desire to make a clean break from the past after the disastrous Cultural Revolution—discovered an alternative, romantic, vagabond lifestyle and an imaginary escapist utopia in Sanmao's stories and worshipped her as a cultural icon. This also intensified the overwhelming outpouring of grief when news of her sudden demise spread through the Sinophone world.

On the morning of January 4, 1991, Sanmao was found dead in the bathroom of her Taipei hospital room, apparently having committed suicide. There was widespread speculation over the cause of her death: some hypotheses included a response to failing health, although her doctors had told her she was healthy; the effects of sleeping pills; depression over her screenplay for *Red Dust* being snubbed at the Golden Horse Film Festival; and an obsession to seek the spirit of her deceased husband. Rumors also circulated that she was murdered because of her criticism of the Kuomintang. Her untimely death served only to mystify her readers even further, a reflection of the politically and culturally intricate nature of the Sinosphere.

Even though Sanmao was not a political opportunist, her writings do present a dangerous appeal, as they powerfully represent the romantic imagination of a vagabond and mobilize the emotions of her multitude of readers. A unique star in the constellation of modern Chinese literature, she became the incarnation of the comic book orphan, epitomized the cross-straits political breakdown after 1949, nurtured the romantic and sentimental dreams of Chinese-speaking youths, and synthesized the Chinese experience of postcolonialism, globalization, and diaspora. The distant land she portrays in her famous song "Olive Tree"—"Why do I roam to distant lands? Because of the olive tree in my dreams"—is forever an imaginary hometown to those hearts moved by her work, tenderly offering refuge from tumultuous modern society.

BIBLIOGRAPHY: Anna-Stiina Antola, "Foreign Characters in San Mao's Short Stories," paper presented at the Nordic Conference on Chinese Studies, Helsinki, June 2005. Miriam Lang, "San Mao Makes History," *East Asian History* 19 (2000): 145–180. Miriam Lang, "Taiwanese Romance: San Mao and Qiong Yao," in *The Columbia Companion to Modern East Asian Literature*, ed. Joshua S. Mostow (New York, 2003), 515–519.

CLINT CAPEHART

1978 · SEPTEMBER 18

> "In 1974 the traitor Jiang Qing reached out her black hand to me, and I was used by the Gang of Four."

Confessions of a State Writer: The Novelist Hao Ran Offers a Self-Criticism

Between September 15 and 21, 1978, the Federation of Chinese Writers and Artists assembled at the Workers' Gymnasium in Beijing. The gathering marked the restoration of an institution dissolved at the beginning of the Cultural Revolution, a restoration made possible by the death of Communist Party chairman Mao Zedong (1893–1976); the arrest of his widow, Jiang Qing (1914–1991) and her three closest associates (the Gang of Four); and the gradual rehabilitation of previously condemned officials, writers, artists, and performers. On September 18, the novelist Liang Jinguang (1932–2008), better known by his pen name Hao Ran, was invited to speak. Hao Ran's literary career had flourished over the previous decade while many in his audience had suffered beatings, incarceration, humiliation, and ostracism, either for works published earlier and considered out of line with the radicalism of the age, or for their connections with institutions and leaders swept aside in the revolutionary zeal of the mid-1960s. In a period of national catharsis, the mood was one of grief for comrades victimized and time lost, and anger at those responsible. A recurring cliché held that during the Cultural Revolution decade there had been only "eight model operas and one author," and Hao Ran, as the "one author" in question, was the object of considerable resentment.

Hao Ran spoke for an hour, and later included a reconstructed version of his self-criticism in an "oral autobiography." The speech, entitled "Lessons I Have Learned," occupies most of the chapter on his activities in the Cultural Revolution. Since much of the recent criticism had concerned his support for Jiang Qing, he focuses on that relationship. The two met, he reports, only four times, on no occasion with fewer than seven people in the room. The first meeting was in 1974, as the first generation of Communist Party leaders neared death and a battle for succession was under way. Hao Ran claims to have known little of Jiang Qing other than that she was Mao's wife and a member of the leadership in her own right. Thus he was flattered by her professed admiration of his work and persuaded to be of service, though he did plead to be spared any official position, a move that would be his salvation after the fall of the Gang of Four.

Jiang Qing had a commission for Hao Ran, one for which, as a chronicler of the lives of the peasants of the North China Plain, he was seriously ill suited. He was to join a delegation to the contested Xisha (Paracel) Islands in the South China Sea, and on his return write in celebration of the youthful members of the militia protecting China's interests from the other nations claiming sovereignty over the islands. His novel *Sons and Daughters of the Xisha* was, as demanded, swiftly executed and presented to Minister of Culture Yu Huiyong (1925–1977), a close ally of Jiang Qing. On Yu's instructions, he added a short passage appearing to attribute victory in a skirmish on the islands to Jiang Qing's inspirational leadership, rather than Mao's, an addition later seen a crime of lèse-majesté on the part of Jiang Qing.

For his final novel of the Cultural Revolution, *Hundred Flower Valley*, Hao Ran returned to a village setting but wrote a story designed to accord with the campaign then orchestrated by Jiang Qing's faction, the struggle against "capitalist roaders." In the novel, a radical young female party member leads the opposition to an older male manager; such plots were subsequently seen as allegories for Jiang Qing's rivalry with more prudent economic planners.

In these works written between 1974 and 1976 and in talks he gave on his own writing and the cultural scene in the mid-1970s, Hao Ran confesses in his speech, he spread the poison of the Gang of Four and brought harm to the cause of the Communist Party. Hao Ran presents himself as a naive loyalist led astray, duped by Jiang Qing ("In 1974 the traitor Jiang Qing reached out her black hand to me, and I was used by the Gang of Four"). According to Hao Ran, he was saved from further ideological error by her downfall; he expresses his gratitude and loyalty toward the new leadership of the party. Hao Ran acknowledges the criticism of him in the press, recalls the encouragement and support of his peasant readership, and asks his audience for their assistance and instruction. Evasive and self-serving as this confession may have been, it proved successful: he was subsequently assigned the highest rank in the state cultural hierarchy, and was able to continue writing without further official reproach. This he did for a further two decades, dramatizing the changes to rural life in the brave new world of economic reform, in the final stage of the longest literary career in the history of the People's Republic to date.

Hao Ran published over a hundred books over the course of that career: reports, essays, memoirs, and stories for children, as well as novels and collections of short fiction. Almost all of his creative work was about peasant life, and most of it was set in his native Hebei Province. He began writing in the mid-1950s, at a time when the Communist Party was keen to sponsor young writers of peasant and proletarian origins to complement those urban and cosmopolitan writers who had created much of the leftist literature of the 1930s and 1940s. Like the state writers of the Soviet Union, this new generation of authors would be responsible for showcasing the achievements of socialism in the settings they knew best, which would thereby strengthen their readers' resolve to work toward the goals set by the state. The particular task of those writing about village life was to depict "new peasants," who had first been given land following the Communist victory, and were then led toward mutual aid and cooperative farming as a means to survival and sufficiency.

Hao Ran's credentials as a peasant author were impeccable. His was an archetypal story of a peasant rescued from poverty by the Communist Party who then dedicated himself to the party's cause. The son of landless peasants born in 1932 in a landlord's manure shed, he received only three and a half years of schooling. In 1945, he came in contact with the Communist military, and joined the Communist Party in his sixteenth year. He wrote bulletins and short skits for the army, and after Communist victory and the establishment of the People's Republic, he worked as a reporter for the Hebei provincial daily and a journal for Soviet readers. His first published short story appeared in 1956, and several volumes of short fiction followed in quick succession, establishing him as a leading author of rural fiction. His early stories were charming and persuasive celebrations of village life in the new Socialist China: tales of achievement; character sketches of exemplary peasants, including many young women; and love stories. Hao Ran's fictional world is a place of optimism and shared endeavor; conflicts are between conservative and progressive thinking, and they are resolved in favor of the latter through the lessons of experience. It was an image of the countryside not quite as it was—the famines that devastated the countryside in the early 1960s are nowhere to be found in the fiction of Hao Ran and his peers—but as a loyal writer felt it should be, and would be, if only the Communist Party policies were embraced by his readers.

Hao Ran later asserted that while he had received official support and encouragement, he had initially received little political instruction, and had not studied Mao's essays on the arts before starting to write. Later, however, he was to demonstrate amenability to changes in policy, a quality essential for an artist wishing to retain patronage in a Socialist system. In 1962, Mao returned from a period of relative inactivity and found himself at odds with what he perceived as the complacency of those who were managing the state. Mao's new slogan was "Never Forget Class Struggle," and it had an effect throughout society; for artists, it meant a requirement to show conflict between members of the favored classes (peasants and proletarians) and malignant remnants of the landlords and business owners dispossessed in the early years of the People's Republic. Moving away from his vignettes of social harmony, Hao Ran wrote his three-volume novel *Bright Sunny Skies* in order to dramatize this new view of reality, in which the successes of collective farming were threatened with sabotage by the enemies of socialism. The village party secretary at the center of the novel, a character modeled on a friend of the author, leads his neighbors through the harvest season, which leaves him too busy for romance with an ideal peasant girl (our hero is a widower). He maintains his focus on agricultural production even as his son is abducted and killed. At the end of the novel, the class enemies are exposed and arrested, and a bountiful harvest is secured.

The ruthless infighting within the leadership during the mid-1960s led to social disruption and the persecution of establishment figures, including many leading writers and artists, among them village writers who had been slower to adapt to political change or otherwise offended those who emerged as the cultural vanguard. After a five-year hiatus in fiction publishing, Hao Ran, alone among nationally recognized authors, returned in 1972, this time with an epic novel set against the agricultural collectivization of the early 1950s, and created in line with a new view of that history. In *The Golden Road*, the defining struggle is not between classes, but between opposing development strategies, or "lines," within the party. Mao's collectivization policy, which Hao Ran had always portrayed in a positive light, is the "golden road" of the title. The opposing line is a policy encouraging enrichment of individual families over collectivization, and is here condemned as undermining socialism; proponents of the enrichment strategy are seen to align themselves with the selfish interests of former landlords, wealthy peasants, merchants, and counterrevolutionaries. The author's considerable story-telling skills create a powerful narrative for this revised history, set in a village that stands as a microcosm for the nation. The novel was celebrated at the time, and derided thereafter, for its towering hero, the village party secretary Gao Daquan, whose name means "Lofty, Large, and [by homophony] Complete" (the two characters of his given name mean literally "Large Spring [of water]"). Like the theme of historic "line struggle," the depiction of a single preeminent heroic character in every work of art was a Cultural Revolution requirement, a principle derived from the revision under Jiang Qing of operas into model works. No character in Mao-era fiction is as lofty, large, and complete as Gao Daquan, a prodigious worker and a self-sacrificing and inspirational leader, whose support of Mao's collectivization initiatives is both instinctive and reasoned; yet the author insisted, even as his hero was dismissed as a fantasy, that he had met real-life peasant leaders of the same caliber. The novel and its central figure remained the author's favorite among his creations long after collectivization was abandoned by the Communist Party in the early 1980s.

How is a state author like Hao Ran, who adapted his political orientation on three occasions (in 1962, 1972, and 1978) to the changing priorities of the nation's leadership, to be judged? Was he just a party hack, changing with the prevailing wind to secure his privileged position and the comforts it brought him? Or was he, as he claimed, a creative artist loyal (perhaps to a fault) to a ruling party he believed in, providing the pleasurable and instructive fiction his readers needed? If he had not written in the early 1970s, he later reasoned, who else was there to do so? His speech of September 18, 1978, and the tone of contrition in which it was delivered, must have struck a chord with his audience in the Workers' Gymnasium. Certainly they were in a more magnanimous mood than the audiences many of them had encountered when they were themselves called to account in earlier mass gatherings. No slogans were shouted, and Hao Ran was able to leave the stadium unscathed in time to attend the wedding celebration of his elder son.

BIBLIOGRAPHY: Evgeny Dobrenko, *The Making of the State Writer: Social and Aesthetic Origins of Soviet Literary Culture*, trans. Jesse M. Savage (Stanford, CA, 2001). Hao Ran, *Jinguang dadao* (Beijing, vol. 1, 1972; vol. 2, 1972; four-volume complete edition, 1994). Hao Ran, *Wode rensheng: Hao Ran koushu zizhuan* (Beijing, 2000). Hao Ran, *Xisha ernü*, 2 vols. (Beijing, 1974). Hao Ran, *Yanyangtian* (Beijing, vol. 1, 1964; vols. 2 and 3, 1966; repr., 1974). W. H. F. Jenner, "Class Struggle in the Countryside: A Novelist's View," *Modern Chinese Studies* 1, no. 2 (1967): 191–206. Richard King, *Milestones on a Golden Road: Writing for Chinese Socialism, 1945–1980* (Vancouver, BC, 2013). Sun Dayou and Liang Chunshui, eds., *Hao Ran yanjiu zhuanji* (Tianjin, China, 1999). Zhang Dexiang, "'Shenhua' yu 'shishi'—wo kan *Jinguang dadao*," *Qingnian wenyijia* 2 (1995): 10–15, 61–64.

RICHARD KING

1978 · OCTOBER 3

> "Son, you'd better remember this from now on. First and foremost,
> you are God's son; secondly, you are China's son. And, yes, you are
> my son." —Chen Yanxing

Chen Yingzhen on the White Terror in Taiwan

On October 3, 1978, Taiwan's Intelligence Office sent the secret police
to arrest Chen Yingzhen (1937–2016), charging him with engaging in
subversive and pro-Communist activities. This was not the first time
Chen was taken to custody. A Marxist and existential humanist born
into a Christian family, Chen was among the most prominent novelists
and outspoken persons concerning Cold War politics in Taiwan. He had
been a political prisoner from 1968 to 1975, spending seven dark years on
Flame (now renamed "Green") Island. Chen wrote about this event as a
case of belief and betrayal, themes that often inform the critical thrust of
his fiction in regard to intellectual life in contemporary Taiwan. Instead
of focusing on his own trauma and memory, Chen refracts the experience
through his father's emotional response: how the old man wept and collapsed upon seeing his son return home. Chen is particularly indebted to
his father Chen Yanxing (?–1996), whose words on God and fatherland—
such as in the epigraph of this essay—serve as his most cherished "three
principles" in life: filial piety, nationalism, and the Holy Spirit.

These ardent yet romantic convictions are held together by Chen's
belief in Cultural China, which is itself sustained by several levels of
irony. First, Chen escaped the further political persecution of the Marxists in Taiwan under the auspices of the US government, which he held
responsible for launching the global Cold War. Second, he continued to
be a rebellious figure in the erstwhile anti-Communist mecca, Taiwan,
while remaining critical of the regime and nostalgic for his imaginary
homeland on the other side of the strait. Third, Chen relocated to China
in 2006, yet remains a Marxist idealist who refuses to come to terms
with a Communist China turned protocapitalist, where the state leaders
advocate the "Chinese Dream" in the hope of imitating and overtaking
the United States. Fourth, before his passing in November 2016, Chen
had been in a coma and receiving treatment in Beijing for years, much
like his character Old Zhao, who appears in the last novella of his trilogy

about the White Terror—both are incapacitated and unable to engage with contemporary Chinese affairs, despite a lifetime dedicated to being their most honest critics.

Chen began his literary career in 1959, when he wrote a short story called "Noodle Stand," published in *Pen Ensemble*. Since then, Chen has published numerous short stories, novels, and critical essays. In 1988, the initial collection of his writings amounted to fifteen volumes. Chen's works appeal not only to critics like Jeffrey Kinkley, who hails him as "Taiwan's greatest author," but to a number of mainland Chinese New Left critics, such as Qian Liqun and Wang Molin, who tend to interpret Chen's protest literature in the same vein as Lu Xun's (1881–1936) critical realism. However, such insightful comments are often generated by the oversight of local particularisms and historical contexts, for Chen also draws on the Japanese socialist (as well as modernist) tradition, Christian humanism, and existentialist thought. The influence of these schools of thought manifests itself most clearly in Chen's White Terror trilogy.

Chen was born into a Hakka community in Chunan and later moved with his parents to Yingge, another Hakka county in northern Taiwan. In his memoirs, Chen discusses the historical circumstances that caused him to develop a complicated and contradictory understanding of modern Taiwanese history, notably marked by the departure of the Japanese colonial regime and the arrival of the replacement Nationalist (Kuomintang, KMT) government. In the name of upholding martial law and the anti-Communist campaign, the KMT received military, material, and diplomatic support from the US government. Using his pen name, Xu Nanchun, Chen writes, "Tormented by surreal and compelling dreams that are inundated with Red flags—a stark contrast to the fear and despair produced by the regime in power—he creates a series of fictional characters that entertain ambiguous and idealistic visions, but often see themselves misled and ultimately self-deconstruct." To many of his readers, Chen is best known for his pro-Communist (or leftist) discourse, in which he often expresses romanticized and essentialist notions of a "Cultural China" or "Greater China."

Similar to writers Chen Ruoxi (1938–) and Bai Xianyong (1937–), Chen Yingzhen considers himself a Chinese intellectual in diaspora who longs to return to his "imaginary homeland," despite being a Taiwanese native and highly sympathetic to the island's transregional economic exploitation, social oppression, and political co-optation. His three short works on the White Terror in Taiwan during the 1950s, "Bell Flowers" (1983), "Mountain Path" (1983), and *Zhao Nandong* (1987), mourn the banality and brutality of the KMT colonial administration in its dealings with Taiwanese citizens and fault American McCarthyism for backing the widespread political persecutions on the island.

In his White Terror trilogy, Chen provides three accounts: the gruesome tale of an elementary school teacher who hid in an mountain enclave during the anti-Communist purge; a woman's recollections of what happened during the White Terror; and a description of the final days of a moribund political prisoner. Through the innocent eyes of two fifth-grade schoolchildren, "Bell Flowers" reveals the incompatibility of contemporary politics with its citizenry, as the rural and naive schoolboys cannot understand why their teacher suddenly disappears and mainland Chinese officers are taking over the county. The teacher's name later appears on a list of known victims of anti-Communist cleansing. The failure on the part of the children to comprehend the atrocity highlights the irrationality and absurdity of the regime's actions, as it causes trauma and suffering to even the most peripheral and innocent members of society.

"Mountain Path," in contrast, is narrated from the perspective of the protagonist, Cai Qianhui, and recounts the devastating effects of the Cold War, including the death of her beloved older brother, friends, and relatives, as well as the deteriorating promise of freedom in the public sphere. Cai's account relates various historical moments, from the economic miracle in Taiwan to the hard-working people's willful erasure of the political and collective memory of state violence against intellectuals during the 1950s and 1960s. Again, Chen's novel suggests that quite a few young intellectuals and patriots were either executed or imprisoned during the 1950s, despite their dedication to the local social reform. In the form of a posthumous letter, Cai confesses that she has completely forgotten about what happened to her brother and friends:

> Within the last thirty years, my family and relatives have been busy with weddings, banquets, and all sorts of merry making, as if those who used to be close to them had never existed or been incarcerated and tortured on a desolate island. Because of such amnesia, we made

money and established our businesses, we greatly improved our livelihood... we moved to Taipei seven years ago and have since enjoyed
comfortable, leisurely lives in the city.

It is this internalized impulse to avoid politics and repress the memory of
those history makers who struggled to set Taiwan free from an authoritarian regime that led the Taiwanese people to turn their attention to the
single goal of economic prosperity.

The final work in the trilogy concerns the family of a political prisoner,
Zhao Nandong. Unlike his father and older brother, Zhao Nandong has
not the slightest interest in understanding his parents' experiences during
the White Terror. He chooses instead to live a decadent and debauched
life. As Father Zhao (or Old Zhao) lies dying in the hospital, only his
friends and confidants can still recall the pain and torture of their time
in prison.

Chen once remarked that

the KMT regime has never been sincere in reforming or re-educating
political suspects. For more than thirty years, no political prisoner was
ever released on the grounds that he or she had confessed and behaved
well. The authorities designed numerous re-education programs, but
even they don't have any faith in them.

The policy is to "punish" rather than to discipline or reform the accused.
Chen also holds the US government responsible for supporting the
KMT's repressive practices. Although Chen once benefited from US intervention in clearing his name, his fictional characters continue to express
the staunch conviction that the United States launched the political purges
to wipe out the labor party in Japan and then the Socialist (often wrongly
categorized as Communist) activists in Taiwan, in order to dominate the
free world unopposed. In a similar vein, the elaborate debate that occurs
in *Zhao Nandong* at the outbreak of the Korean War (1950–1953) suggests
that the Taiwanese are naive to place trust in the United States and their
promise to protect global human rights. Throughout the novella, Father
Zhao remains hopeful that the US government will take the necessary
steps across the Taiwan Strait and serve as a shield against Communist
aggression; after all, "the US is pro-democracy and very likely to monitor,

or even cut down, the unjust and severe political persecution in Taiwan." Cai Chungyi, one of the smarter and more informed inmates, disagrees. He knows what happened to Japan's left-wing intellectuals immediately following US occupation: "General MacArthur's headquarters in Tokyo initiated something wholly unexpected: he launched a political purge to arrest union leaders and socialists, thereby severely undercutting the power of the labor party." Old Zhao refuses to believe this, however, and ultimately has his hopes dashed. He has no alternative except to seek solace in the choral fantasia that Zhang Ximin, another inmate and also a composer, put together during their dark days together. In the end, Old Zhao dies having not seen the light of the day, as his failing heart puts him in a coma.

In this way, the three stories intersect each other and are ultimately punctuated by the dying old man's failing heartbeat. Why should Chen Yingzhen title his final novella after the younger son, who seems oblivious to Taiwan's history and the suffering of his compatriots? By doing so, does Chen imply that Taiwan's younger generation not only has no memory of February 28 (1947) and of the consequences of the civil war in China, but also is indifferent to history?

Of interest is the fact that even though Chen did benefit from US intervention on October 3 and 4, 1978, he refuses to believe that the American government acted sincerely to help the Taiwanese people during the Cold War. This is a stance that Cai Qianhui, the narrator in "Mountain Path," reinforces in her posthumous letter, where she links Taiwan's economic miracle to the people's attempts to forget historical trauma and their efforts to render the island an offshore industrial wasteland, so that American companies like RCA, IBM, and Apple could thrive. The expressivity of his characters, such as the symbolic father (Old Zhao) and mother (Cai Qianhui), are so overwhelming that they powerfully stand in for Chen's own lived experience. His experience with the KMT regime in Taiwan positions him to look on the United States as complicit with their authoritarian and tyrannical policies. Consequently, he embraces the notion of a "Cultural China," and in 1997 even congratulated Hong Kong for its timely return to the People's Republic of China; it was only fifteen years later that he realized Hong Kong residents have no say in electing their own officials or chief executive of their Special Administrative Unit. However, his life ultimately concludes by imitating art: in an uncanny parallel to Old Zhao, Chen has been in a coma since his return to the fatherland and subsequently hailed as China's last Marxist.

BIBLIOGRAPHY: Chen Yingzhen, *Fuqin: Chen Yingzhen sanwen ji*, vol. 1, 1976–2004 (Taipei, 2004). Chen Yingzhen, *Lindanghua: Chen Yingzhen xiaoshuo ji*, vol. 5, 1983–1994 (Taipei, 2001). Jeffrey C. Kinkley, "From Oppression to Dependency: Two Stages in the Fiction of Chen Yingzhen," *Modern China* 16, no. 3 (1990): 243–268.

PING-HUI LIAO

1979 · NOVEMBER 9

"Incurring somebody's opposition"

Liu Binyan and the Price of Relevance

Fall 1979 was an exhilarating time for writers in mainland China. They were emerging from the straitjacket of the Mao Zedong (1893–1976) years, and excitement was in the air. They felt a special energy and—if not quite freedom—at least a sense that there was suddenly much more room to explore. A year earlier Deng Xiaoping (1904–1997), the new man at the political top, had urged them to "look forward" and to "liberate thought." A sort of informal competition ensued to see who could be best at "breaking into [previously] forbidden zones."

Yet shadows remained. Deng's advice to writers also included the phrase "harbor no residual fears," but many writers could remember the fearful Anti-Rightist Movement of 1957, which had come a few months after Mao had urged intellectuals to speak out. Many who did so were then attacked, ostracized, or banished to the countryside, and in some cases driven to divorce, insanity, or suicide. Mao's lieutenant in that great purge had been this same man, Deng Xiaoping, which meant that Deng's current counsel to "harbor no fears" could almost seem a gentle reminder that a reasonable person might want to harbor some. As if to underscore the point, in mid-October 1979, the Deng regime sentenced Wei Jingsheng, an electrician who a few months earlier had "liberated his thought" sufficiently to issue a public call for democracy, to fifteen years in prison.

In broad outline, if not in particulars, the message to writers was clear. Go with the political flow, make the standard denunciations (of the Maoist Gang of Four and their policies), and observe the standard "upholds" (of the socialist system, the Communist Party, and so on). Feel free, while swimming in the mainstream, to be emotional, or even to fulminate—just be sure your spittle flies in prescribed directions. But don't step out of line. In particular, *don't offend certain people.*

Liu Binyan (1925–2005), a seasoned journalist, victim of the 1957 Anti-Rightist Movement, and in 1979 a special correspondent for the *People's Daily*, chose to flout the message about not offending people. In September 1979, he published a long piece of literary reportage entitled *People or Monsters?*, about a major corruption case in Bin County in his native Heilongjiang Province. A report on the case had already appeared in the *People's Daily* five months earlier, and Wang Shouxin (1927?–1980), the main culprit, had been detained and was awaiting trial. Later she would be executed, and her case held up as an example. The government seemed on top of everything. But Liu set out to find something deeper. He traveled to Bin County, did extensive interviews, and wrote a detailed account not just of how one big boss had been corrupt but how a whole system of corruption had evolved and included many people—*some of them still in power.* He noted that all of the corrupt actors were Communist Party members and dared to ask, "What does this tell us?"

He analyzed the mechanics of corruption in a way that showed Bin County to be no exception, but broadly representative. In the days and weeks after *People or Monsters?* appeared, readers from all across China wrote letters to Liu and his editors praising him for pinpointing *our* problems, *right here.* The experience was a repeat for Liu. In 1956, before his two-decade banishment, he had had similar responses to a piece called "At the Bridge Worksite," which exposed corruption, and to a 1957 piece called "The Inside News at This Newspaper," about censorial pressures on journalists.

Not every letter about *People or Monsters?* supported Liu. He got letters from irate officials who took his revelations as personal accusations. These letters came from several provinces, including places Liu had never written about, and carried warnings that he should never even try, with threats attached. The letter writers seemed oddly unaware that their energetic cries of "I'm innocent!" could be seen as signs of concealed guilt. Wags on the popular grapevine called this "self-assigned seating."

Against this background, Liu delivered a major speech in Beijing on November 9, 1979, to a congress of the All-China Association of Literature and Art Workers. This huge group had not convened since 1960, which was a very different time. Mao had died in 1976, and the 1979 meeting now seemed historic. Delegates were especially looking forward to Liu's address. When it came, they repeatedly interrupted him with applause, not least for these lines: "I have awoken to a hard fact: in today's China, if one speaks or writes and *does not* incur somebody's opposition, one might as well not have spoken or written at all. One has no alternative. The only alternative is to cower in a corner and fall silent." Here Liu was not advocating contrariness for its own sake. He was advising his fellow writers to tell the truth as they saw it and just let the effects be what they will be. People might love you or hate you, but that was beside the point. The point was that if you tell only certain truths, only the approved or "safe" ones, you will always be doing something that many others are doing. You will make no difference beyond footnotes or embellishments. Actually making a difference almost requires that you be willing to irritate someone. Indeed you can often gauge whether you have written something worthwhile by seeing whether anyone objects. By the same logic, you needn't feel bad if attacks arrive; sometimes they are your best evidence that you said something that needed to be said.

In 1985, for the first and only time, the Chinese government allowed writers to freely elect the officers of the state-sponsored Chinese Writers Association. In nationwide balloting, the senior writer Ba Jin (1904–2005) won the most votes and became president, while Liu got the second-highest number and became vice president. The voting reflected the high value that Chinese writers were putting on "truth telling." Ba was famous for his fiction from the 1930s and 1940s, but in the late 1970s he had also published a collection of essays called *Random Thoughts* in which he made several pleas to "tell the truth" and for a "spirit of repentance." In one essay he apologizes to his fellow writer Hu Feng (1902–1985), whom he had denounced in a political campaign two decades earlier. In another he calls for a museum of the Cultural Revolution—to help ensure that the horrors would not recur. But a careful review of Ba's timing in these matters shows that he lacked Liu's readiness to "incur somebody's opposition." He called for a museum only after state leaders had labeled the Cultural Revolution "ten years of catastrophe"; he apologized to Hu only after the state had officially "exonerated" Hu. As state-sponsored attacks on his fellow writers continued during 1980s—during the 1987 campaign against "bourgeois liberalism," for example, that targeted Liu and drove him into exile—Ba Jin remained silent.

Liu, meanwhile, showed that he was ready to cross not just the Chinese government but anyone, including his own admirers, if that was where truth telling led. In 1985, at the height of his popularity, he published a piece of reportage called *The Second Kind of Loyalty*. It traces the lives of two people who survived Mao's prisons even as they clung to the socialist ideals that they saw Mao and his regime as violating. Liu's notion of a "second kind" of loyalty quickly drew opposition from two very different sides. The party-state had no use for the idea. One kind of loyalty—loyalty to us—is quite fine, thank you. We don't need another kind. From the opposite end, liberal intellectuals expressed annoyance that Liu would call for loyalty of any kind—"second" or not—to an ideology that had brought China so much pain. In Liu's own mind, the point had not been to pick a fight with either side. Liu had always been intrigued by the notion of "socialism with a human face" that had emerged from the popular uprising in Prague in 1968, and the question that animated *The Second Kind of Loyalty* was, "Is humane socialism possible?" If raising it had drawn criticism, this was only evidence—once again—that the question itself was worthwhile.

I got to know Liu very well during his years of exile from 1988 until his death in 2005. On one of his last visits to my home, I offered him Chinese tea, as I usually did. He took a sip and said, "You're a Sinologist, Perry. You speak Chinese and you act Chinese—how come I have never tasted really good Chinese tea at your house?" The comment did not "incur my opposition"; I already knew and revered this man, and was not surprised. But it did show me how his philosophy applied all the way to the minutiae of daily life. Even here, he told a truth that could make a difference.

He asked me once about the academic study of literature, because he had tried to read some scholarly criticism and was baffled. "I read articles about modern Chinese literature and have no idea what the author is trying to say. I can't even understand the articles that are about me." I explained to him a bit about Western "theory," in which the point is to begin with some of the latest fashions and catchwords from the elite reaches of academe and then show how they apply to texts that one selects—including, sometimes, texts from China. "Isn't that imperialism?" he asked. His voice was kind. He was always kind. As I paused to think of an answer, he filled the void with his own. "The main difference between that and imperialism is that at least the imperialists said things you could disagree with. These academics write down sentences that no one really understands, so no one can disagree. They have figured out that nonsense has something in common with truth—you can't disprove either." I include this paragraph so that readers of this book, who may include practitioners of irrefutable academese, can get a firsthand feel, as I did when he commented on my tea, for his unsparing honesty.

Liu suffered from colon cancer for most of 2005 and died on December 5 of that year in a New Jersey hospital. His saintly wife, Zhu Hong (1929–2015), was with him, and their son Dahong and daughter Xiaoyan traveled from China for the memorial service and cremation. Hundreds of people, mostly Chinese living in America, and some who traveled from as far away as Europe and Australia, packed the largest lecture hall at Princeton University for the memorial.

In China, though, news of Liu's passing was blocked. Beginning in 1987, when he was labeled a "bourgeois liberal" and expelled from the Communist Party, state media had been barred from mentioning his name and references to him had been removed from textbooks. A writer who in 1985 had been one of the most famous in China by 2005 was almost entirely unknown to young Chinese.

Yet Liu's power to plant fear in the minds of party officials lived on. Even his ashes inherited some of it. Before he died, he had expressed a wish that his ashes go back to China for burial. His family wanted to honor that wish, but could they? They worried that the ashes of this fierce critic of China's regime might be viewed as "destabilizing" and be confiscated at the border. Under tight secrecy, the family did get Liu's ashes back to China and did get them buried in a graveyard outside Beijing. Then they asked the cemetery staff if they could erect a tombstone bearing these words:

> Here lies a Chinese person who did some things that were right for a person to do, and said some things that were right for a person to say.

Liu himself had chosen the words. The cemetery staff agreed. A few days later, though, the stone carver approached the family in person to apologize that those particular words could not go onto the stone. The "superiors" had said no. They said that nothing but Liu's name and dates of birth and death could appear. They gave no explanation, but apparently the prospect of a bit of truth, carved in stone, had frightened someone. The family, after deliberating, decided to withdraw its request for the inscription, bide its time, and hope for a day when the stone might appear as it should. Until then it could remain blank. On one level, it was an inadequate monument to Liu. On another, though, that wordless stone might have been the best imaginable echo of the truth that Liu had uttered on November 9, 1979: "In today's China, if one speaks or writes and *does not* incur somebody's opposition, one might as well not have spoken or written at all."

BIBLIOGRAPHY: Michael S. Duke, *Blooming and Contending: Chinese Literature in the Post-Mao Era* (Bloomington, IN, 1985). Perry Link, *The Uses of Literature: Life in the Socialist Chinese Literary System* (Princeton, NJ, 2000). Liu Binyan, *China's Crisis, China's Hope*, trans. Howard Goldblatt (Cambridge, MA, 1990). Liu Binyan, *A Higher Kind of Loyalty: A Memoir by China's Foremost Journalist* (New York, 1990). Liu Binyan, *Two Kinds of Truth: Stories and Reportage from China*, ed. Perry Link (Bloomington, IN, 2006). Liu Binyan with Ruan Ming and Xu Gang, *Tell the World: What Happened in China and Why* (New York, 1989).

PERRY LINK

1980 · JUNE 7

Bizarre natural phenomena hover over Xi'an.

1996 · APRIL, ON AN UNSPECIFIED DAY

A mysterious Taiwanese woman in the guise of a Japanese tourist arrives in Taipei.

A Tale of Two Cities

On February 21, 1993, Jia Pingwa (1952–) put down his pen after finishing the final touches on what would become one of post-Socialist China's most monumental novels, *Decayed Capital*. This is a tale driven by the haunting of the past amid an economic reform unprecedented in the long history of this old civilization. On November 1, 1997, across the Taiwan Strait in the city of Taipei, Chu T'ien-hsin (1958–) put forth her best work in her long writing career, *Old Capital*, a story that interweaves the haunting of the (island of Taiwan's colonial) past and the nation-state's democratic transformation in the context of the onslaught of global capitalism.

Jia and Chu have thus come together through their shared lamentation of the unshakable past—the dead haunting the living, ruins clinging on to memories of time, and demolition sites marking (mocking?) the erasure of what once was. Emerging from these two novels is a tale of two cities, Xi'an and Taipei, which imparts to us a new urban experience: uncanny encounters with the past in every unlikely corner of two urban spaces, one threatened with no memory and the other burdened with too much memory, but both faced with constant demolition and reconstruction.

Here is our tale of two cities.

Xi'an

In the year 1980, at high noon on the seventh day of the sixth month of the lunar calendar, an unexplainable natural phenomenon took place in this ancient capital of China, Xi'an: out of the blue skies four suns appeared. One by one, people on the streets began to realize that their shadows were no longer attached to them, and they started to scramble in all directions. This eerie occurrence lasted for about half an hour and then everything gradually returned to normal.

The Chinese have long believed that an unusual natural phenomenon is a foreshadowing—a prophetic sign of sorts—of something monumental that would soon befall the human world: if not the collapse of a civilization, a kingdom, or a dynasty, then the rise of a new power, or a new ruler, or the arrival of a savior. In his story of the decadent, morally corrupt everyday life of the residents of Xi'an, Jia has thus captured the rapid decay of Xi'an's rich culture as it gives way to post-Socialist China's new pursuits.

The novel's protagonist Zhuang Zhidie, Xi'an's leading writer, commands an unsurpassed cultural prestige in Xi'an, which in turn wins him the sexual favors of women, from married women to virgins—favors he has no qualms about enjoying. The excessive descriptions of sexual acts in the novel have earned *Decayed Capital* a place as one of the most scandalous Chinese-language novels in recent memory. The novel has been compared to *The Plum in the Golden Vase*, the archetypal erotic novel in premodern China. Against the backdrop of China's drastic changes, the sexually overindulged Zhuang Zhidie seems to emit the stench of the decay of his society's spiritual structure.

Aside from his sexual excess, Zhuang Zhidie has an unusual fondness for mournful songs. He finds in such music emotional abandon, retrospection, and the feelings of fear and of eternal entrapment. He also enjoys climbing up to the city's historic walls for a moment of solitude. On one such day he leaves the house in search of peace and quiet and climbs up the city wall. He comes to a bend, and sees a man. Thinking he might find a like-minded fellow city dweller, Zhuang Zhidie moves closer—only to find this person obliviously engaged in masturbation. Upon overcoming his initial disgust and embarrassment, Zhuang Zhidie has an uncanny moment: he wonders if that man is in actuality a reflection of his own image in a pool of muddy water among the wild grass. His reverie is disrupted by a hoarse call from an old scrap man: "Any scrap for collecting? Any scrap for collecting?"

The glorious moments of Xi'an serving as the capital of the Han and the Tang dynasties have faded into the long continuum of history. What remain, as "scraps" of time, are the follies, the quandaries, and the imaginary nostalgia found in the mundane everyday life of this ancient city's contemporary residents. True to its title, *Decayed Capital* captures precisely the fin-de-siècle moment the new post-Socialist China faces.

Hidden underneath China's transformation into a global economic powerhouse is a moral vacuum created by the bankruptcy of Maoist socialism-communism and the subsequent struggle to reconcile the fiction of the Chinese Communist utopia with the reality of a deteriorating socialist structure in everyday life. Materialism without a spiritual anchor breeds decadence, and when the 1989 Tiananmen Incident destroyed all hopes of political transparency and democracy, this decadence further compounded the pervasive spiritual crisis. Published in the aftermath of the Tiananmen Incident, *Decayed Capital*'s brazen erotic themes and language scandalized the nation and brought post-Tiananmen Chinese decadence to new heights.

Xi'an, also known as Chang'an in the Tang dynasty, declined rapidly as soon as its dynastic heyday ended. Does Jia intend a political allegory in his portrayal of a decaying and demoralized Xi'an in the context of contemporary China's economic supremacy? Is this novel a prophecy of what post-Socialist China is to become? The timing of this novel's publication being so close to the Tiananmen Incident inevitably twists the novel's otherwise straightforward political allegory or prophecy into a zigzag. The Tiananmen democracy movement was a revival of youthful revolutionary zeal reminiscent of the Cultural Revolution, albeit with a completely opposed agenda. The democracy movement's bitter end and the subsequent disillusionment among Chinese intellectuals thus present the 1989 Tiananmen Incident as an elegy to the end of the revolutionary spirit and the optimism for any substantive reform. *Decayed Capital* thus is an elegy to a historical moment that could have set post-Socialist China on a different ideological path; the novel is also an elegy to a political era that had promised so much and yet failed so spectacularly to deliver.

Taipei

On a cool April day in 1996, an airplane from Tokyo touches down at Taiwan Taoyuan International Airport. Among the passengers disembarking is an unremarkable middle-aged woman who, although a native of the city of Taipei, will later be mistaken for a Japanese tourist. As soon as our nameless heroine accepts this misrecognition and decides to return to her home city as a foreigner, everything begins to take on a different look. A Japanese tourist map of colonial Taipei, which she finds in her bag, inspires her to revisit the city just as it existed half a century earlier. The map lays out Taipei the way it was designed by the Japanese during the colonial period (1895–1945), with its streets, government buildings, and other landmarks appearing under their original names. Our heroine's recent memories of Kyoto, the city from which she had just returned a few hours ago, accompany her as she roams around Taipei, guided by the map. A beloved city, Kyoto is for her an eternal city where the history of a place is never disrupted and the memory of an individual is never severed from the place. Taipei, on the other hand, is a place where not only concrete records of history such as monuments and historical buildings are constantly in danger of demolition, but private memories of the individual are also relentlessly threatened by the possibility of total erasure.

In this bustling city, our wandering heroine—shall we indulge ourselves for just a moment and imagine her as an end-of-the-century, female, Asian version of Leopold Bloom—feels alienated by the incessant construction and reconstruction of streets and buildings; once-familiar sights are now entirely lost to her. It is no wonder that, in her imaginary rediscovery of the old city through the lens of the colonial map on which Taipei is drawn as a replica of Kyoto, she is relieved to recognize that Taipei once occupied a similar geographical significance as Kyoto did in Japan, and Taipei thus could easily be a replica, or doppelgänger, of Kyoto.

As our heroine walks on, she checks off every name on the map when she visits the corresponding contemporary site. The original colonial map creates a paradoxical alliance between the island's colonial past and the increasingly alienating present-day Taipei. The Taiwan Bank, built in 1903 and designed by Nomura Ichirō (1868–1942) in the Mansard style, is, in the opinion of our wandering heroine, a perfect double for a Tiffany store. Seimonjō, the Japanese red-light district indicated on the map, is deemed by her a decayed district filled with filth and desperation. The Red Chamber Theater, designed by Kondō Sūrō and built in 1908, assumes a supernatural flair that evokes the classical Chinese utopian fable of the Peach Blossom Spring. The whole lost colonial city, for our heroine, was the embodiment of such a paradise.

This idealization of the past against the vision of the present day as dystopia is particularly brought out by the symbolism of the Peach Blossom Spring, but not without a disturbing twist. This fifth-century fable of an ethereal utopian community where humans live in perfect harmony with nature has become a literary archetype for Chinese writers who seek to imagine an impossible ideal existence in an otherwise chaotic world. Will our heroine find her Peach Blossom Spring in present-day Taipei? Her wandering in the city reaches an abrupt end when she loses her map. As she wanders into an obscure section of the city, she finds men and women sitting under trees or on broken chairs in complete idleness, with Peking opera playing in the background. The Peach Blossom Spring that she searches for is darkly reflected in this modern-day cityscape: helicopters circle in the sky, perhaps looking for floating dead bodies in the river ... across the river on the other bank high-pitched funeral music plays faintly...grass is burning somewhere...near the highway are tall gray walls blocking the way like prison walls, so clean there is not even a single stroke of graffiti on them. Where is this place?

In our heroine's mind, the historicity that Kyoto represents is authentic, and the previous colonial connection between Japan and Taiwan provides for her a reference with which to retrace the old colonial city of Taipei. A fragment of Taiwan's history can only be found in the map of the colonizer. The marks of Japanese culture can still be vividly seen in Taiwan's culture today; these colonial imprints are clues with which one can retrace the island's (partial) history and a source to the (several) roots of Taiwan's cultural heritage. Both the Nationalist government and native Taiwanese politicians often obliterate history in the name of progress and hasten the destruction of Taipei's natural environment. Kawabata Yasunari's (1899–1972) Kyoto, a fictionalized Japanese city, ironically becomes the origin of the author's nostalgia, as well as the symbol of history.

As a second-generation Chinese mainlander in Taiwan, Chu must reconsider her place in Taiwan's newly democratized cultural and social environment. With *Old Capital* she establishes not what the Taiwanese individual's cultural identity should be, but what it no longer can be—through the colonial map and the pastiche of Kawabata's novel, she points out the dispersal of Taiwan's history, her memory, and the place from which the two originated. Chu recognizes that though Taiwan's culture is based on Chinese culture, it also has absorbed a tremendous amount of Japanese and Western (mainly American) cultural influences—the result of both colonialism and capitalism. But this recognition alone is not sufficient for defining cultural identity, because identity must also be situated within history. *Old Capital* thus captures the silhouette of history and a shadowy outline of memory. It betrays its author's contempt for contemporary Taipei, and yet in this contempt it evinces a distinct feeling of nostalgia for the past (and better) Taipei.

Two texts, two cities, one tale—Chu and Jia, each in a distinct style, voice, and perspective, have told the common story of our time. We can look straight ahead as we move toward a richer and finer material life, but the specter of the past will always lure us and pull us back, compelling us to turn our gaze backward, even if only for a partial glance. Whether we suffer from "not enough history," like the colonial city Taipei, or are burdened with "too much history," like the ancient capital Xi'an, both Chu and Jia, with their respective novels, turn our attention to the particular discourse of history the individual is bequeathed. When forces of globalization have changed our way of looking at oneself and of relating to one another, and have promoted the tendency to privilege space over time, speed over slowness, and movement over stillness, our tale of two cities points out our likely blindness to amnesia and our penchant for historical fetishism.

BIBLIOGRAPHY: Lingchei Letty Chen, *Writing Chinese: Reshaping Chinese Cultural Identity* (New York, 2006). Yiyan Wang, *Narrating China: Jia Pingwa and His Fictional World* (New York, 2006).

LINGCHEI LETTY CHEN

1981 · OCTOBER 13

Liang Shiqiu publishes his culinary essay "Craving."

Food, Diaspora, and Nostalgia

On October 13, 1981, Liang Shiqiu (1903–1987), a Beijing native, Taipei resident, distinguished writer and scholar, and sophisticated gourmet, published an essay, "Craving," in Taipei's *Literary Supplement* in the *United Daily*, in which he wrote, "Perhaps we Chinese, in particular, have a greater craving for good food." In Taiwan in the 1970s and 1980s, Tang Lusun (1908–1985), ethnically Manchu and descended from the elite Bannerman class of the Qing dynasty (1644–1912), born in Beijing and living in Taipei after 1946, established himself as an amateur author but prolific master of culinary writing, famously calling himself "a man who craves fine food," or "Mr. Gluttonous." In "Craving," Liang argues that "a person tends to feel the strongest craving for a particular food at a time when it is not available.... It is human nature to maintain a nostalgic longing for the distinctive culinary flavor of one's hometown."

Around 1949, with the Chinese Communist Party's takeover of mainland China and the Nationalist Party's retreat to Taiwan, millions of people were uprooted from their hometowns and forced to migrate. Liang and Tang were part of that diasporic movement. More precisely, they belonged to a community of native Beijing writers who were relocated to Taiwan after the 1949 division, and they projected poignant aesthetic and political aspirations onto their reminiscences about a lost hometown. Also part of this group were Qi Rushan (1877–1962), Bai Tiezheng (1904–1976), Xia Yuanyu (1909–1995), Ding Bingsui (1916–1980), and Guo Licheng (1915–1996), just to name a few. Their nostalgia for their hometown, Beijing, loomed large in the 1970s and 1980s. Their body and mind were hungry for hometown dishes; they attempted to satiate their homesickness by writing about food. Through Liang's and Tang's passionate recollections of the variety of culinary life in Beijing, food is rendered as both nutrition for the body and an art of life, and, more importantly, as a tangible embodiment of nostalgic sentiments. Culinary writing paved foodways for an imaginary return to an inaccessible hometown besieged by Cold War ideology. In this way, Liang and Tang make their lost geographical and spiritual hometown reappear in their "republic of letters" and the gourmet world.

As early as the 1920s, Liang was already a representative figure in the prominent literary school of the Crescent Moon Society, known for its adoption of European salon culture, especially the English afternoon tea gathering, as well as for its conscious and continuous dialogue with Chinese literati tradition. For the literary minds of the Crescent Moon Society, the ways of tasting food and drinking tea or coffee represented not only a particular lifestyle but also a loosely defined "lyrical philosophy" found in the writings of English- and American-trained Chinese authors and scholars—Xu Zhimo (1897–1931), Hu Shi (1891–1962), Chen Xiying (1896–1970), Lin Huiyin (1904–1955), Wen Yiduo (1899–1946), and Ye Gongchao (1904–1981), among others. Liang was one of the most prolific of these writers.

Particularly active from 1940 to 1949, Liang composed thirty-four essays while living in Chongqing and Beijing for *Weekly Review* and other newspapers. These essays formed the first volume of *From a Cottager's Sketchbook*, published after he had left the mainland and resettled in Taiwan. For the next four decades, Liang continued to produce little prose pieces, which first appeared in newspapers and periodicals and were subsequently collected and reissued under the same title: thirty-two essays in *From a Cottager's Sketchbook*, volume 2 (1973), thirty-seven in volume 3 (1982), and forty in volume 4 (1986). Moreover, in the 1970s and 1980s, he wrote a substantial number of essays on Chinese food and Chinese ways of eating and drinking, which were collected in the widely circulated anthology *On Culinary Art* (1985), and showcased his humanist illustrations of Chinese culinary aesthetics. Liang compiled a sensational list of food items, everyday eateries, and decent restaurants that were quintessentially Chinese, a list colored by a "keen sense of humor" and a sustained mood of nostalgia. In *On Culinary Art* and *From a Cottager's Sketchbook*, food sustains the body and the mind of the diasporic Beijing native when there seems to be no hope of returning home. The writer's unquenchable nostalgia for his hometown is channeled into his lavish descriptions and verbal exhibitions of New Year's offerings, local rituals of ancestral worship, and distinctive family gatherings, as well as into his long list of fine foods and beverages and the idiosyncratic ways of consuming them.

In his *On Culinary Art*, in order to satisfy his starving stomach and his longing for a bygone age and a lost home, Liang describes in an amusing and seductive way fifty-seven quotidian Beijing dishes and drinks, A closer look at his choices is intriguing: Beijing's *suanmeitang* (a black, sweet-and-sour drink), a favorite for people of all walks of life, including the eponymous rickshaw-pulling protagonist of Beijing writer Lao She's (1899–1966) novel *Camel Xiangzi; tang hulu*, made of sweet red hawthorns, a sweet "unafraid of the dust of 'New Times'" according to the poetic imagination of Lin Huiyin, one of the most talented women writers of modern China and Liang's fellow member of the Crescent Moon Society in the 1930s; and the versatile chestnut, which reminds Liang of the lovely chestnut tree in his Beijing house. Liang cites Hu Jinquan's (1932–1997) famous proposal about *douzhi'er*, a typical Beijing breakfast drink made from fermented soybeans—"One who can not enjoy *douzhi'er* should not be regarded as a true Beijinger"—and attempts to depict and define diversified regions and local identities according to Chinese people's habits of eating and drinking. In a compelling way, Liang blends food knowledge and cultural memory in his depictions of Beijing culinary culture written in Taiwan.

It is worth noting that Liang's long list of foods and beverages mainly covers snack food and street dishes, popular food for the masses mostly related to quotidian life. In contrast, Tang's provocative depiction of

Beijing foods not only pays more attention to the genealogy of cuisine and customs of eating and drinking but also focuses on the gourmet culture of the imperial court and palaces, the grand aristocratic families, and the upscale restaurants. After all, Tang's distinguished background as a Manchu Bannerman, with ties to the former imperial clan, greatly shaped his appetites and cultivated his tastes.

Tang's sophisticated introductions to elite culinary practices, written primarily to entertain himself in his diasporic life, also entertained overseas Chinese-language readers in the 1970s and 1980s. In recent years, Tang's work has also been published in the People's Republic of China. As a result, readers from mainland China and the global Chinese community can also enjoy his writings. In his twelve-volume anthology on Chinese lifestyles, 70 percent of the essays focus on culinary art, and Tang dedicated the largest portion of his work to Beijing cuisine. Tang conveys his nostalgia for his hometown in essays with unparalleled erudition and nostalgia, collected in books such as *Tang Lusun on Culinary Art, Feeling for Hometown, Chinese Culinary Art, Stories about Chinese Culinary Art,* and *Sour, Sweet, Bitter, Spicy, and Salty.* In a sophisticated and exquisite style, Tang recalls hometown items and culinary practice in encyclopedic essays such as "Beijing Snack Foods Unavailable in Taiwan," "Milk Snacks in My Hometown," "Eating in Beijing" (parts 1 and 2), "Unique Foods in Beijing" (parts 1 and 2), "Desserts in Beijing," "Breakfast in Beijing," and "Secrets of Beijing Restaurants," among many others. The most elegantly written essays are dedicated to depictions of refined gourmet dishes in imperial courts, gardens, and palaces: "Imperial Drinking and Eating," "Qing Dynasty Palace Food and the Full Manchu-Han Banquet," and "Delicacies from Land and Sea." In these essays, Tang shares with his readers the carefully guarded secrets of imperial cuisine. With mythical ingredients and secret recipes, such writings stir up readers' curiosity and nostalgia toward a collapsed empire and enable them to take an imaginary journey back to the ancient capital. Of particular note is his use of Beijing idiom. He never intended to discard his Beijing accent in his writings. Rather, his distinctive Beijing dialect, tone, style, manner, and taste occupy a unique position in the Sinophone literary world in the 1970s and 1980s. Tang's collection and recollection of authentic Beijing food and beverage are warm to touch, delicious to taste, pure to drink, and subtle on the palate.

In modern Chinese literature, an array of writers have dealt with the poetics and politics of the metabolic and metaphysical desire for food. Examples that come readily to mind are Lu Xun's (1881–1936) allegory of cannibalism at the inception of modern Chinese literature and Eileen Chang's (1920–1995) hunger aesthetics in her novel *The Rice-Sprout Song*. In the short story "Lust, Caution," Chang quotes an English saying that "the way to a man's heart is through his stomach" to explain the difference between men and women. In Liang's and Tang's culinary writings, food serves as both the evidence of material existence and a cultural trope. Both of them retained their strong appetite for local Beijing cuisine. As authentic Beijing foods were not easy to obtain in Taipei at the time, these diasporic writers sought to satisfy their yearning and longing for home through exquisite writings about food, its flavor, and its aftertaste.

Liang's and Tang's repetitive and obsessive writings on Chinese cuisine, and Beijing food in particular, reveal a poignant relationship between the gastronomic and the political. Their nostalgic sentiments aim not only at the flavor and taste of the lost hometown cuisine but also at a mode of life and culture that disappeared with the end of a historical epoch defined by political antagonism between the Communist and the Nationalist regimes, and with the changes wrought by Chinese modernization. In Taiwan in the 1970s and 1980s, when Liang and Tang wrote those essays, the hope of recovering the mainland was becoming ever dimmer. With the blossoming of Taiwanese nativist literature, the image of a new homeland emerged, and for mainland immigrants, the island might well have become their new native soil. At such a turning point, recollecting their Beijing experiences through writing its food culture, mainland émigré writers Liang and Tang registered not only nostalgia for their native city but also anxiety about the shifting notion of China and Chinese tradition. When the concepts of China and Chinese cultural authenticity were being seriously contested, what could be more bitter and untimely than recollecting and mourning the culinary and cultural authenticity of a lost "homeland"?

In these collections of essays about food and gastronomic practices, readers can start from and end at any piece, and the major theme remains the same: nostalgic passion and longing fueled by a ceaseless flow of Chinese gourmet food. By repeating various stories of eating and drinking, Liang and Tang describe an intriguing relationship between necessity and extravagance in their diasporic life: on the one hand, their culinary writings depict a rich and vivid Chinese food culture of ancient wisdom and secret recipes; on the other hand, that literary luxury is informed and reinforced by a strong sense of loss, which points not only to the lost hometown and old Beijing customs and tastes but also to the awareness of the impossibility of returning to the spiritual home of Chinese culture. Therefore, the more they write about food, the more appetite they have for it; the more words the reader consumes, the more unquenchable the desire for a bygone history and a vanished hometown.

Liang's and Tang's culinary essays recollect and remap Beijing and Chinese gourmet dishes in terms of emotional affiliation and spatial rearrangements, and make the disappeared reappear in the kingdom of the gourmand and the "republic of letters." The culinary aesthetics of their short essays about food and diet, taste and aftertaste, serve as a symptomatic remedy for homesickness and an imaginary satisfaction of their everlasting hunger and craving for home.

BIBLIOGRAPHY: Liang Shiqiu, *From a Cottager's Sketchbook*, vols. 1 and 2, trans. Ta-tsun Chen (Hong Kong, 2005, 2006). Liao Ping-hui, *Chi de houxiandai* (Taipei, 2004). Weijie Song, "Emotional Topography, Food Memory, and Bittersweet Aftertaste: Liang Shiqiu and the Lingering Flavor of Home," *Journal of Oriental Studies* 45, nos. 1/2 (December 2012): 89–105. Tang Lusun, *Tang Lusun tanchi* (Guilin, China, 2007). David Der-wei Wang, "Beijing menghua lu," in *Ruci fanhua* (Shanghai, 2006), 41–53. Sau-ling Cynthia Wong, *Reading Asian American Literature: From Necessity to Extravagance* (Princeton, NJ, 1993). Gang Yue, *The Mouth That Begs: Hunger, Cannibalism, and the Politics of Eating in Modern China* (Durham, NC, 1999).

WEIJIE SONG

1983 · JANUARY 17

"I am Human."

Discursive Heat: Humanism in 1980s China

On January 17, 1983, an article entitled "In Defense of Humanism" appeared in the influential Shanghai daily *Wenhuibao*, causing a hubbub among avid readers of intellectual prose in the early years of "reform and opening up." It has since become one among a handful of articles frequently cited as representative of Chinese critical thinking of that period. Its author, Wang Ruoshui (1926–2002), was then deputy chief editor of the Communist Party's premier newspaper, the *People's Daily*. A committed Marxist, Wang first attracted public notice in 1979 for arguing that Mao Zedong's (1893–1976) Cultural Revolution was a form of "socialist alienation." Wang identified three aspects of this alienation—cognitive, economic, and political—and traced each to Mao's absolute rule from 1949 to 1976. "In Defense of Humanism," which Wang completed in the summer of 1982, was a passionate call for an end to socialist alienation. He presented humanism as essential for China's recovery from a "total dictatorship." Socialism, Wang argued, must rid itself of the "cruel struggles" mandated under Mao and become henceforth synonymous with humanism.

For Wang, humanism meant, among other things, "mutual respect, mutual loving care and mutual help." He began the article with an adaptation of the *Communist Manifesto*'s opening statement, changing it to read, "A specter is haunting the Chinese intellectual world—the specter of humanism." The article's conclusion remains frequently quoted by mainland social critics as a catchcry for political reform:

A specter haunts this vast land of China—
"Who are you?"
"I am Human."

In 1983, Wang was far from alone in criticizing Mao and his thought. In the party leadership's portentously entitled and much anticipated "Resolution on Certain Questions in the History of Our Party" released in June 1981, the once-exalted chairman was posthumously cut back to distinctly human proportions. The document declared Mao to have been, in word and deed, 70 percent correct and 30 percent wrong. Freed from Maoist orthodoxy by state sanction, party and nonaffiliated intellectuals alike now flexed their minds on the question of "what is to be done," and contending views flourished as they had not since 1949. In their discussions, humanism, which Mao had hitherto disparaged as a bourgeois conceit, acquired a brand new authority.

"Humanism fever" became the first of many "fevers" (*re*) that would characterize the 1980s. There were the general fevers of "culture," "knowledge," and "intellectualism"; thematic ones like "alienation fever," "methodologies fever," and "root-searching fever"; and fevers centered on particular authors and works such as "the fever over *One Hundred Years of Solitude*" (Gabriel García Márquez's [1927–2014] work had struck a powerful chord among mainland readers), "Weber fever," "Sartre fever," "Nietzsche fever," and "Freud fever." For reasons of space, this account of the 1980s is confined to the fever over "humanism." But "humanism" is also the best overarching rubric under which to subsume the multifarious spectrum of "fevers" that seized intellectual China in that decade.

The term *re* now refers to fads and trends, but in the early 1980s, it carried a lingering connotation of enthusiasm (*re qing*), a much-lauded emotion in Chinese revolutionary discourse. Under Mao, enthusiasm meant the ardor needed to wage class war. When the first post-Maoist humanists denounced that ardor as a form of state-induced derangement, it was not the emotion per se that they rejected but its misdirection to serve an oppressive state. They sought above all to raise consciousness of the ills that had beset society under Maoist politics. As their publications multiplied in tandem with rising demand, their optimism about the transformative powers of language grew. A large majority of intellectuals found the idea of invoking a "specter of humanism" desirable. Like Wang, they were increasingly convinced that, if more and more people could be drawn to declare, "I am human," the cold and inhumane world that repressive rule and dogma had forged would be dispelled.

In this self-assigned, collectively embarked on mission of post-Mao intellectuals to return life and warmth to the People's Republic, writers were especially prominent. A mountain of realist works explored existential ills and alienation from self, family, and society under Maoist rule. Dai Houying's (1938–1996) 1980 novel *Oh Humanity* was an early prime example of this genre. Dai wrote in the novel's postscript that she sought to "give voice to the concept of humanity" precisely because she had previously been duped into denying it. Party theorists promptly accused the author and her work of distorting reality. As the attacks intensified, *Oh Humanity* gained domestic notoriety along with international interest. It became a centerpiece of the broader discourse on humanism and one of China's most talked-about books of the 1980s.

Humanism signified intellectual optimism about life after the Cultural Revolution. It grew out of the power vacuum opened up by Mao's death in September 1976. Hua Guofeng (1921–2008), who succeeded Mao as the new chairman (subsequent leaders would avoid using this title), was fearful of being undermined by Mao's widow, Jiang Qing (1914–1991), and her "extreme leftist" allies—the so-called Gang of Four—and consequently moved quickly to arrest them in October 1976. A two-year contest for control of the party and national politics then ensued between Mao loyalists led by Hua and supporters of Deng Xiaoping's (1904–1997) far more sweeping reform agenda. Both sides were mindful of the enormous destruction that Mao's "permanent revolution" had wrought on China's economy and society. After three decades of Communist Party rule, China remained poor and government institutions were in disarray. The rival factions agreed that economic reform was the government's most urgent task but differed on questions of approach and scope. Deng's triumph over Hua in 1978 enabled market mechanisms to be introduced more rapidly and widely than the rival Hua camp would have allowed. The new Deng-led leadership declared the arrival of a "new era" and introduced a greatly modified ideology: one that made extensive but eclectic use of Mao's words to focus on "modernization." Whereas Mao had insisted on "class struggle" in the 1960s and 1970s, his successors now invoked his earlier dictum from the 1940s to "seek truth from facts" as the requisite attitude for a rapidly modernizing China.

"Socialist alienation" and "socialist humanism" were keywords in the new conceptual vocabulary that grew out of this state-led process of distancing mainland public culture from Maoist doctrine. The process itself, officially named the Movement to Liberate Thinking, was described by the historian Xu Jilin (1957–) in 2000 as something of "a Lutheran-style rebellion within the orthodox Marxist-Leninist world" of party culture. The rebellion, confined as it was to rhetoric, was curtailed from the outset by nervous state censors who clamped down on anything that gave them pause. By late 1983, Wang, despite his party credentials and voluble support from the eminent cultural commissar Zhou Yang (1908–1989), had become a casualty of the leadership's mounting unease. He was dismissed from his post at the *People's Daily* as part of the "anti–spiritual pollution" campaign launched that year. In the 1940s and 1950s, Wang's patron Zhou had been instrumental in establishing Mao Zedong Thought as state orthodoxy. In the late 1960s, despite his loyalty to Mao, he fell victim to the Cultural Revolution. Zhou's 1980s defense of humanism hence carried a poignant charge: he now disavowed the doctrine he had zealously propagated for the better part of his career.

In the 1980s, censorship and harassment notwithstanding, an independent or *minjian* (nonofficial) discourse flourished as the economic reforms widened. It began with privately circulated underground writings but was increasingly brought into the light of publishing with the backing of progressive senior party officials. The *guakao* (leaning) arrangement was a game-changing innovation of 1980s Chinese intellectual life: whereas publishing was entirely state controlled in the Maoist period, the emergent post-Maoist market economy allowed nonofficial publishing ventures to be openly pursued under the sponsorship and supervision of a friendly state agency or institution serving as the *guakao* unit. In the mid- to late 1980s, this *guakao*-facilitated intellectual marketplace hosted a wide spectrum of views. Three group enterprises—the publishing ventures *Toward the Future* and *Culture: China and the West*, and the independently funded Academy of Chinese Culture—became particularly prominent. Several key contributors to these three enterprises have since become leading public figures in the Chinese-speaking world.

Disquisitions on alienation and humanism were complemented by an abundance of translated works, literary and academic, firing imaginations and stimulating the production of new fiction, experimental poetry, critically engaged research, and reflective essays on major life questions. Literary depictions of rural and urban society and everyday experience now drew on cosmopolitan insights into existential dread and institutionalized oppression. Writers like Jean-Paul Sartre, George Orwell, Milan Kundera, and Franz Kafka found particular favor in China. In fiction and poetry, the exploration of China's ancient past and regional cultures grew fashionable, eventually becoming what was known as the "root-searching" movement. These works, such as *Red Sorghum* (authored by the 2012 winner of the Nobel Prize in Literature, Mo Yan [1955–]), suggested an entire way of life developed out of continuing human attempts to master and tame a thoroughly primeval nature, even as nature inevitably compels people to fit their lives around it. In scholarship, calls abounded for a thorough reinvestigation of the Chinese intellectual tradition. The writings of the then-Beijing-based philosopher Li Zehou (1930–) fueled debates about the causes of and remedies for China's cultural and economic stagnation. In particular, Li's thesis of "Western learning as foundational, Chinese learning as functional" (*Xi ti*

Zhong yong, a neat inversion of the "self-strengthening" motto of nineteenth-century Confucian reformers, *Zhong ti Xi yong*) caused a stir.

Li argued that modernization, as a universal developmental process based in Western science and technology, required a specific mode of being or "subjectivity" (a signature concept of the 1980s) to succeed in China: a subjectivity in which Marxist theory and Confucian ethical thinking would be productively integrated. In effect Li affirmed human potential (as the potential to develop an autonomous and specifically Chinese subjectivity) against state indoctrination. His ideas inspired a raft of publications on the importance of "cultural subjectivity" (in the sense of an informed understanding of the positive and negative effects of different forces at work in the mainland cultural environment) of which the literary scholar Liu Zaifu (1941–) was the initiator and chief exponent. Li's ideas also accorded, initially, with the party leadership's articulation of market reform under one-party rule as a matter of "building socialism with Chinese characteristics." When Deng Xiaoping first used this phrase in September 1982, his description of the process as one of "integrating the universal truth of Marxism with the concrete realities of China" fitted Li's *Xi ti Zhong yong* like a glove. But with tightened state control following the purge of the student-led democracy movement on June 4, 1989, Li's works were banned on the grounds that they encouraged "bourgeois liberalism." He left China in 1992.

By 1986, "culture fever" had become the term of choice for the burgeoning intellectual discourse and related forms of cultural production (spanning the spectrum from art exhibitions to literature, to film and television, and to conferences focused on "modernization" and short courses on Confucianism and other aspects of traditional Chinese thought) that had developed alongside China's economic reforms. In academic circles, "culture fever" was hailed as a "New Enlightenment" movement. Academics and graduate students sharing the thrill of discovering the human condition anew soon generated an ever-expanding critical vocabulary, drawn from hitherto inaccessible works and as much from Western as from Chinese sources, ancient and contemporary, with discussions focused on how humanistic thinking would set things right in China. In particular, the idea of democracy as a fundamental human need and right took root and grew. As economic reform progressed, the status quo of one-party rule was vigorously, albeit obliquely, debated. There were those who defended it as a benevolent "New Authoritarianism," arguing that strong leadership was required to deliver a viable constitutional democracy along with economic prosperity. There were others who supported a transition to one or another form of Western-style democracy, in the name of "New Enlightenment."

The discursive heat generated by these contentious voices in the late 1980s, coupled with an inherited Chinese intellectual disposition to style oneself as "worrying" on the nation's behalf, provided the initial energy for the student protests that would erupt and swell in the spring and summer of 1989. At any rate, by decade's end, the critical tenor of "culture fever" had grown far more insistent than Wang Ruoshui's plaintive defense of humanism in 1983. The intricacies of "culture fever" and its links to the 1989 democracy movement in Tiananmen have spawned thousands of articles, books, commentaries, and dissertations in different languages, not only because "culture fever" has become an important part of recent intellectual history but because a humane, free society, the shining prospect of which guided the passions of the "culture fever" intellectuals, remains elusive. Those passions have weakened and turned instead into nostalgia for the 1980s, which has been a notable feature of recent Chinese intellectual discourse. The "specter of humanism" that Wang invoked lingers on, not least in the form of online buzzwords such as "speak human language," which since 2012 has been widely used to disparage the language of China's one-party state as "inhuman."

BIBLIOGRAPHY: Geremie Barmé and John Minford, eds., *Seeds of Fire: Chinese Voices of Conscience* (Northumberland, UK, 1989). Chen Fong-ching and Jin Guantao, *From Youthful Manuscripts to River Elegy: The Chinese Popular Cultural Movement and Political Transformation, 1979–1989* (Hong Kong, 1997). Jing Wang, *High Culture Fever: Politics, Aesthetics and Ideology in Deng's China* (Berkeley, CA, 1996). Xu Jilin, "The Fate of an Enlightenment: Twenty Years in the Chinese Intellectual Sphere (1978–98)," trans. Geremie Barmé and Gloria Davies, in *Chinese Intellectuals between State and Market*, ed. Gu Xin and Merle Goldman (London, 2004), 183–203.

GLORIA DAVIES

1983 · SPRING

Dondrup Gyel's "Waterfall of Youth" is published.

The Advent of Modern Tibetan Free-Verse Poetry in the Tibetan Language

In 1983, the Tibetan literary magazine *Light Rain*, based in Xining, the capital of Qinghai Province, published a poem that spanned seven printed pages. The cascading lines of each stanza, likely inspired by Vladimir Mayakovsky's (1893–1930) staircase technique, were linked to an equally metaphorical title: "Waterfall of Youth" ("Lang tsho'i rbab chu"). The significance of this poem and the life of its author, Dondrup Gyel (1953–1985), reverberate in literary and general intellectual discourse among Tibetans in China even today. The writer, who died prematurely in 1985, has become iconic—his visage is enshrined in traditional *thangka*-like portraits where he is portrayed alone or alongside another intellectual pioneer, Gendun Chophel (1903–1951). As the first officially published instance of Tibetan free verse in the People's Republic of China, "Waterfall of Youth" was an early watershed for modern Tibetan literature.

This vernacular turn in Tibetan writing is so recent that critics have barely agreed on a set of terms for discussing the movement. Despite eight centuries of Tibetan belles-lettres (*snyan-ngag*), the Tibetan word most commonly used for "literature"—*rtsom-rig*—was coined only in the 1950s by translators seeking to render the term "literature" as it is used in the works of Karl Marx (1818–1883), Vladimir Lenin (1870–1924), and Mao Zedong (1893–1976). It is a calque translation of the Chinese *wenxue*, a term that had existed for a couple thousand years and by the early twentieth century was adopted to refer to an independent discipline that reflects on the distinct cultural and aesthetics aspects of national identity.

"Waterfall of Youth" possesses several Whitmanesque qualities: a cataloguing technique that lists objects in an effort to call the reader into the immediate narratorial present; an emphasis on landscape and environmental beauty; repetition that creates an incantatory rhythm; and the punctuation of a line with a string of ellipses at the end. The similarity raises questions about the inspiration for this famous poem. Contemporaries have suggested that the poet was primarily inspired by the writings of his Chinese counterparts.

Indeed, Dondrup Gyel wrote "Waterfall of Youth" (1983) while at the Central Nationalities Institute in Beijing from 1979 to 1984, when free verse was already becoming popular among the larger Chinese reading public. Chinese poets had been publishing modern, free-verse "obscure poetry" (*menglongshi*) since the late 1970s. At the same time, Dondrup Gyel was well versed in Tibetan classical poetry, folk literature, the life and writings of the fifth Dalai Lama (1617–1682), and even the Old Tibetan manuscripts of Dunhuang. Such training was uncommon for his generation of writers. Dondrup Gyel was among the lucky few to achieve literacy in Tibetan during the tumultuous years of the Cultural Revolution. After graduating from only middle school in 1969, he was hired by the Qinghai Radio Broadcasting Station to serve as a translator and a newscaster for the Qinghai Tibetan News program. In 1979, he went to Beijing for graduate studies in Tibetan literature at the Central Nationalities Institute, where he studied under the esteemed scholar Dungkar Lozang Trinlé (1927–1997), whose contributions to Tibetan literature include a widely used textbook on *kāvya* poetic theory, Indic-derived conventions that had informed a vast share of Tibetan writing since the fourteenth century. Upon obtaining his master's degree in 1981, Dondrup Gyel was hired to teach a select group of students with advanced skills in Tibetan. It was then that he wrote his groundbreaking poem. Shortly after the publication of "Waterfall of Youth," Dondrup Gyel returned to Qinghai Province, where he began to teach at the Normal College in Gonghe. Two years later, on November 30, 1985, he committed suicide in his home. While the note he left behind calls on Tibetans to defend their cultural heritage, scholars familiar with his situation suggest that professional and personal difficulties contributed to his unfortunate choice.

During his abbreviated lifetime, Dondrup Gyel also wrote fifteen or so short stories—another still relatively unexplored genre in Tibetan in those early years. It was his first free-verse poem (*rang mos snyan ngag*), however, that has become a cornerstone of modern Tibetan literature. Writing under the pseudonym Rang-grol (literally, "Self-Liberated"), Dondrup Gyel both extols and exhorts Tibetan compatriots of his generation:

> Listen!
> The sound of the flowing water is clear, soothing to the ear.
> The song of youth is the song of the gods,

The melody of Brahma,
The voice of Sarasvatī,
The sound of the cuckoo.......

Kye!—No ordinary waterfall of nature, this has
A majestic and splendid appearance
Fearless heart,
Uncowering mettle,
Hale and hardy body,
Beautiful and resplendent ornaments,
Soft and pleasant refrain.......

This—
Is the waterfall of youth of the young people of Tibet,
Land of Snows.

This—
Is the innovative courage of the young Tibetans
of the 1980s.
It is the stance of struggle,
The song of youth.

As the some thirty-odd stanzas continue, they form a fervent appeal to revitalize traditional Tibetan scholarship, which had a several-hundred-year legacy and was organized around the "five major sciences" (arts and technology, medicine, logic, grammar, and Buddhism) and the "five minor sciences" (astrology, poetics, prosody, synonymy, and drama).

Do you hear me—Waterfall?
Do you hear these questions of the young people of Tibet,
the Land of Snows?
What to do if the great horse of Poetry is suffering from
thirst?
What to do if the elephant of Prosody is tormented by
heat?
What to do if the lion of Synonymy is afflicted with pride?
What to do if the boy of Dramaturgy is left orphaned?

Who will care for the Astrology of our fathers if left arcane?
How will the young man Science be welcomed if taken as
    groom?
Who will be husband if the young woman Technology is
    welcomed as bride?

So be it—Waterfall,
    These answers which derive from your pure and pleasing croon
        —are held in our minds like drawings carved in stone.

Truly,
    Yesteryear with its glorious shining sun is no substitute for
        today;
    And how can yesterday with its salt-water quench the thirst of
        today?
        If the corpse of history, which is hard to locate,
        Is bereft of the life-force appropriate for the times,
            The pulse of development will never beat,
            And the heart and blood of the avant-garde will never
                flow,
            Much less the march of progress.

The final lines of the poem are the most strident and evoke a zeal that
echoes that of Deng Xiaoping's (1904–1997) Four Modernizations campaign, which in preceding years had promoted Chinese industry, agriculture, military modernization, and science and technology.

Look—
    These troops standing in formation are the
    new generation of Tibet.

Listen—
    This song of steady beat is the step of the
    youth of Tibet.
        The great road of light,
        The tremendous task,
        The life of happiness,
        The song of struggle,

Will never fade for the youth of the waterfall; and
The waterfall of youth, for this reason, is even less likely to wane.

This is—
The waterfall of youth intoned in the throats of the
young generation of Tibet.

This is—
The waterfall of youth cascading in the minds of the
youth of Tibet.

While Dondrup Gyel has been called the "James Dean of modern Tibet," he was not an iconoclast. Dondrup Gyel was deeply rooted in classical Tibetan scholarship. In his master's thesis on *mgur*—a song form that can be traced back to the Tibetan imperial period—he renders the classical Tibetan version of the Ramayana into the vernacular. In the poem "Waterfall of Youth," he supports the revitalization of tradition and declines to follow the Cultural Revolution path of ousting the "Olds." His heartfelt appeal was written in the wake of the Cultural Revolution, and proposed a path for recovery after the "bitterness of winter."

Even in the more lenient period of the 1980s, however, free-verse writing among Tibetan writers did not immediately flourish. Free-verse poems began to appear only in 1986, and they did not become a regular fixture in literary magazines until about 1990. Many of the earliest experiments were directly inspired by Dondrup Gyel's trailblazing poem rather than by Chinese poetry. Several works mimic Dondrup Gyel's piece so closely in both form and theme that they would be considered plagiarism by Western standards.

Today, the Tibetan literary scene has diversified. In 1983, only a few publishing outlets were available to writers. Since then, more than a hundred official and private Tibetan-language journals have been founded. The Internet and the use of mobile devices have created new opportunities for literary expression and criticism. Tibetan authors currently engage a much wider range of styles and genres, from historical fiction and reportage to magical realism and contemporary folktales. A small corps of accomplished writers have also turned to film. Pema Tseden (1969–) (who also is known by the Chinese name Wanma Caidan) and Chenaktsang Dorjé Tsering (1963–) (aka Jangbu), for example, who were in their teens when Dondrup Gyel published his poem, are now internationally recognized filmmakers. Though Tibetan-language novels published in China number only in the dozens, the writings of the most published novelist, Tsering Dondrup (1961–), are worth mentioning, as well as a fascinating autobiographical work by Naktsang Nulo (1949–) that offers a rare glimpse of Tibetan nomadic life and political change in the 1950s.

In retrospect, "Waterfall of Youth" might be considered a somewhat awkward combination of Chinese Communist-style rhetoric and the manifesto overtones of an idealistic and nationalistic youth. The poem reveals an ambivalence toward the past, which is both "glorious" and pejoratively "salty." Dondrup Gyel's use of the em dash for emphasis is inconsistent and often meaningless, as if he were trying the technique on for size. Yet his poem struck a deep chord with young Tibetan readers and made him into a literary hero. Few Sinophone writers enjoy such stature among Tibetan readers. One exception is Yidam Tsering (1933–2004; also known by the Chinese name Yidan Cairang), who developed a technique that one Western scholar calls the "Tibetanization" of the Chinese language, such that deep comprehension of his poetry requires oral fluency in Tibetan, and whose works abound with references to Tibetan history and culture. Other authors who write in Chinese, such as Tashi Dawa (1959–) and Alai (1959–), have earned literary acclaim in China and abroad, but their work has been criticized by critics and authors who write predominantly in Tibetan.

As the contours of a "Tibetan literature" continue to be negotiated, its future is constrained by the reality of a small readership. The Tibetan population totals about six million, and literacy rates are among the lowest in the People's Republic of China. Economic incentives to publish Tibetan-language material other than school textbooks and religious texts are therefore minimal. The situation is further exacerbated by the vicissitudes of language policies and local politics. Nevertheless, Tibetan publishing activity remains quite vibrant, thanks to large state-sponsored projects, an increasing share of private funding, and the very low cost of publishing online and via mobile text services.

The debate over free verse waned in the 1990s, as the form achieved a certain standing. The relative merit of "obscure poetry" (*go dka' ba'i snyan ngag*) and other questions, however, remain contested. Among those who argue for the right to unfettered literary forms and content are the self-dubbed "Third Generation" writers, a coterie of iconoclastic thirty-something poets, short-story authors, and essayists that emerged at the start of the new millennium. Their stance, however, is not embraced by all in a Tibetan literary scene that largely remains on the margins of both Chinese modernity and global literary discourse. For a Tibetan writer to follow the lead of Western writers, theorists, and the Chinese avant-garde is to risk the criticism of certain literary peers who argue for the urgency of Tibetan literature's own survival. Disturbed by the proliferation of Tibetan free verse, for instance, senior teachers have insisted that the adherence to classical *kāvya* conventions better preserves "the unique characteristics of the Tibetan nationality" in poetry. Other Tibetan literary critics argue for achieving a greater "authenticity" through the resurrection of pre-Buddhist literature. A more radical proposal is embodied in the Third Generation call to eschew traditional Tibetan, Western, and Chinese literary models altogether.

BIBLIOGRAPHY: Pema Bhum, "The Life of Dhondup Gyal: A Shooting Star That Cleaved the Night Sky and Vanished," *Lungta* 9 (1995): 17–29. Lauran R. Hartley and Patricia Schiaffini-Vedani, eds., *Modern Tibetan Literature and Social Change* (Durham, NC, 2008). Lama Jabb, *Oral and Literary Continuities in Modern Tibetan Literature: The Inescapable Nation* (Lanham, MD, 2015). Jangbu, *The Nine-Eyed Agate: Poems and Stories*, trans. Heather Stoddard (Lanham, MD, 2010). Naktsang Nulo, *My Tibetan Childhood: When Ice Shattered Stone* (Durham, NC, 2014). Rang-grol [Dondrup Gyel], "Lang tsho'i rbab chu," *Sbrang char* 2 (1983): 56–61.

LAURAN R. HARTLEY

1984 · JULY 21–30

"Moon Seal" is serialized in the literary supplement of the *China Times*.

Literary Representation of the White Terror and Rupture in Mid-Twentieth-Century Taiwan

From July 21 to July 30, 1984, *Moon Seal*, an elegant, artistically sophisticated novella set against the backdrop of the White Terror in mid-twentieth-century Taiwan, was serialized in the literary supplement of the *China Times*, Taiwan's leading mainstream newspaper. Its author, Guo Songfen (1938–2005), a Taiwanese writer based in New York, had been blacklisted by the island-country's Nationalist ruling regime since 1971. That the publication of *Moon Seal* in Taiwan did not wreak political havoc is likely due to the fact that, by then, three years prior to the lifting of martial law, government surveillance had appreciably relaxed. Another explanation is that, compared to the robust opposition to the reigning party that was fueled by an ascending separatist-inclined Taiwanese nationalism, left-leaning intellectuals like Guo and Chen Yingzhen (1937–2016), who held a comparably favorable stance toward China, posed a much lesser threat.

Guo emerged as a charismatic leader of the Protect Diaoyutai (also known as the Senkaku Islands) movement (1970–1972; hereafter Bao-diao) while a PhD student in comparative literature at the University of California, Berkeley. Baodiao was launched by patriotic overseas Chinese students on North American campuses, in protest against the US government's decision to hand over Diaoyutai to Japan and the Nationalists' weak response to the issue. Guo, along with other Taiwanese students, shifted his allegiance to Taiwan's Cold War adversary, the Communist-ruled People's Republic of China (PRC). His academic career thus irrevocably disrupted, Guo joined the PRC's translation team at the United Nations in 1972. While a monthlong trip to mainland China in 1974 triggered doubts about China's socialist experiments, for ten years Guo passionately dedicated himself to reading Western Marxism, penning long critical essays on the Sartre-Camus debate and publishing them in *Dousou*, a Hong Kong–based radical magazine. Overextending himself to the point of falling gravely ill, in the early 1980s Guo finally switched paths again, this time pursuing an illustrious literary career marked by continual, if sparse, publication of highly refined works of fiction until his passing in 2005.

Guo's return to literature after a decade of infatuation with politics had momentous consequences not only for Guo and his wife, Lee Yu (1944–2014), but also for the literary historiography of contemporary Taiwan. (Guo's lifelong soul mate, Lee was a fine writer in her own right, as well as an art historian, whose suicide in 2014 is widely attributed to unalleviated grief over the loss of her husband ten years earlier.) Guo's aesthetic orientation intersected with multiple artistic positions in the literary field of postwar Taiwan in distinctive ways, at once backtracking to and anticipating dominant cultural trends and shifting sociopolitical dynamics. *Moon Seal*, indisputably Guo's magnum opus, announced his belated debut as a full-blooded modernist and powerfully heralded major localist themes that would later assume preeminent status in Taiwan's cultural production. As a whole, Guo's fiction compels us to rethink the literary landscape of Taiwan during that period.

Guo's pedigree as a modernist is impeccable. As early as 1961, as a senior in the Department of Foreign Languages and Literature at National Taiwan University, Guo wrote an essay introducing Jean-Paul Sartre (1905–1980) and existentialism in the magazine founded by his classmate Bai Xianyong (1937–), *Modern Literature*. He also contributed to *Literary Star* and *Theatre*, key harbingers of the modernist trend, while teaching English poetry at his alma mater before going abroad in 1966. In subsequent years he received a liberal humanist literary education in graduate programs at the University of California—first at Santa Barbara, and then Berkeley. As a fiction writer, Guo is known for his low productivity, which is attributed to his extravagant investment in revealing the darker recesses of the human psyche through singularly poetic language. A specific remark Guo made in two published interviews from 2004 drives home the deeply entrenched affinity between Guo and such hardcore modernists as Wang Wenxing (1939–), Li Yongping (1947–), and Wuhe (1951–). There, Guo suggested that a reencounter with the French classic *Madame Bovary* in the early 1980s, a text he had regarded as decadent and unworthy in his younger days, had worked a miracle in steering him back to literature as a lifetime vocation. The Flaubertian notion of *les mots justes* may be considered the supreme vision animating and sustaining the extraordinary aesthetic enterprises of contemporary Taiwan's "latter-day modernists."

In the 1970s, however, Guo set out on a path that diverged from most other modernists of his generation. The leftist turn of Baodiao activists from Taiwan was inseparable from a projection of their nationalist zeal onto the PRC, which, in turn, was closely connected to their rebellion against Taiwan's Nationalist-sponsored culture in the early days of the Cold War. Their anti-Nationalist and socialist tendencies resonated with the island nation's nativist literary movement. At that time, the nativists vehemently attacked Taiwan's modernist literature as inauthentic, symptomatic of cultural imperialism from the liberal West. As a matter of fact, there existed pivotal ties between the overseas Baodiao activists and Taiwan's nativist trend. Tang Wenbiao (1936–1985), a Hong Kong–born visiting mathematics professor in Taiwan from 1972 to 1973, whose critical essays in *Chung-wai Literary Monthly* posited socialistic ideals that were clarion calls for the nativist trend, turns out to have been a close friend and Baodiao compatriot of Guo's at Berkeley.

By the late 1970s and early 1980s, news of China's catastrophic Cultural Revolution had become known to the world. Both Chen and Guo went through a moment of introspection with regard to their prior commitment to leftist ideology, as attested by two eloquently written stories, "Mountain Path" (1983) and *Moon Seal*, respectively.

Chen's "Mountain Path" opens with a hospital scene in which the heroine, Cai Qianhui, passes away without a medically diagnosable cause. The real reason, the author insinuates, was a total loss of the will to live, resulting from deep remorse, self-blame, and utter despair. Thirty-some years earlier, to help the family of Li Guokun, a White Terror martyr, Qianhui resolutely plunged into the miserable life and hard labor of Guokun's poverty-stricken, mining-district family. Dedicating herself to raising Guokun's younger brother, she unwittingly succumbed to the indoctrinated mainstream values of martial-law Taiwan until, one day, her fiancé's return from imprisonment awakened her. Living with the family of Guokun's brother, now a successful accountant in 1980s Taipei, she found herself surrounded by the creature comforts of an affluent capitalist society. Did she not, along with the rest of society, in effect betray the leftist ideals of those who vanished in the 1950s, in the prime of their youth? What's more, the "bright socialist future" they had all envisioned proved to be an illusion, attested to by the failed socialist experiments in mainland China that were reported in the newspaper.

Guo's *Moon Seal* was published a year after "Mountain Path" and, though they share a mood of despondency, the two stories reveal very different resolutions to their authors' crises of faith. Qianhui's death symbolizes the unacceptability—to her and likely also to Chen—of the inadvertent betrayal of cherished leftist values. *Moon Seal* is also a story of betrayal, yet its author apparently casts the worth of ideological commitment in a more equivocal light. Wenhui, a young Taiwanese wife, informs the local police of her husband Tiemin's illegal possession of a box of banned books, thus unwittingly implicating him as an underground

Communist. Wenhui's motives are banal—a moment earlier her husband had left home with Sister Yang, a gorgeous Chinese woman and the Communist ringleader. The two had shared a tung oil umbrella, the scent of which still lingered in the house. The punishment Wenhui receives for her reflexive act of vengeance, however, is disproportionately harsh— Tiemin is arrested the next day and executed shortly afterward. If Wenhui represents the political apathy that Chen condemns in "Mountain Path," she is also undoubtedly intended to engender our sympathy. Like a Greek tragic hero, Wenhui is duped by the Fates, her tragic flaw a petty jealousy. Moreover, previously, amid the postwar turmoil that culminated in the February 28 Incident, Wenhui had barely snatched from death her husband, whose tuberculosis had worsened right after their wedding. Their marriage had never been consummated, as she had insisted they abstain from sex until his full recovery. Consequently, she is also doomed to childlessness after losing Tiemin to the White Terror.

If Chen was still striving to salvage his leftist faith, Guo was evidently troubled by the clash between two regimes of truth, those informing, respectively, progressive political action and the innocuous aspirations of ordinary, disengaged men and, especially, women. The conspicuous absence in *Moon Seal* of such leftist motifs as class exploitation, suffering masses, or utopian dreams of a bright socialist future is coupled with the characteristically "liberal" ideal of a political public sphere. The main thrust of the political message of *Moon Seal*, therefore, harks back to the Baodiao movement, which indicted state violence and advocated civil disobedience. In the meantime, however, one cannot but sense a tempered pessimism that echoes an earlier story by Guo, "Autumn Rain" (1967), in which he laments the futility of liberal endeavors under a repressive regime, specifically marking the failure of his mentor-hero Yin Haiguang (1919–1969), a well-known intellectual dissident in 1960s Taiwan.

The comparison between Guo and Chen also foregrounds the polarization of "cultural China" vis-à-vis "indigenous Taiwan," a movement that had just begun to pick up momentum in the 1980s. In contrast to Chen's staunch advocacy of Chinese nationalism, Guo excelled at, and heralded, artistically representing the mid-twentieth-century political upheavals that later culminated in Hou Hsiao-hsien's (1947–) *A City of Sadness* (1989). Drawing from his childhood memories of the old-town district

Dadaocheng and the life experiences of his father's generation—Guo's father, Guo Xuehu (1908–2010), was a renowned artist from the colonial period—Guo's stories from 1982 to 1987 are populated by browbeaten, uncommunicative fathers who are ambivalent survivors of the February 28 Incident and psychologically troubled sons who are melancholic dreamers exiling themselves from claustrophobic Taiwan to the New Continent.

A tour de force treatment of the historical rupture in mid-twentieth-century Taiwan appears toward the end of *Moon Seal*. As Wenhui is still in a state of shock over Tiemin's execution, the new mainlander police chief pays a visit, showering her with praise for her noble and patriotic *dayi mie qin*, "sacrifice of loved ones for a greater cause." Wenhui's mother, who does not understand Mandarin, offers him tea, while politely ignoring the fact that he has been pacing the tatami without taking off his boots. The scene signals a total breakdown in cultural communication: the mainlander policeman's ignorance of the etiquette of middle-class Taiwanese resonates ironically with Wenhui's deficient understanding of the "rule of the game" in the new political era. They are all part of the same, larger tragedy.

Guo suffered from a serious bout of depression between 1988 and 1989. In the early to mid-1990s, he became deeply infatuated with *This Life, This World* (1959), a collection of essays by the erudite and ostentatiously self-aggrandizing former husband of Eileen Chang (1920–1995), Hu Lancheng (1906–1981). Hu's brief sojourn in Taiwan during the late 1970s made him an enormously revered, key inspiration for several baby-boom-generation writers, notably Chu T'ien-wen and Chu T'ien-hsin. Traces of Hu's fanciful renditions of imaginary Chinese landscapes and his idiosyncratic fetishization of "Chinese women" are discernible in Guo's final two works of fiction, "Tonight, Stars Are Bright" (1997) and "Nine Fallen Flowers" (2005). Featuring historical figures of Republican China, plotlines in these two stories are fairly obscure and fragmentary. Figuring prominently instead is Guo's enchanting linguistic texture, melding classical Chinese lyricism with modernistic intensity, as well as an enigmatic narrative agent that traverses easily between the interior and exterior.

Guo's deeply ingrained fascination with emblems of cultural China was presaged in the novella *Moon Seal*: while attending a party at a friend's house, Wenhui finds herself instantly captivated by the hallowed aura of an old plum bonsai, a gift to the host from some Chinese mainlanders, among them Sister Yang, whose irresistible attractiveness is explicitly attributed to her embodiment of "Chineseness." The mesmerizing ambience conjured up by the exquisitely poetic, sensuously affective images of "China" found in Guo's last two stories, however, are further removed from the referential world. They are more properly viewed as masterful explorations of the potential of the Chinese language as an artistic medium. This particular aestheticizing strategy is strongly reminiscent of *Retribution: The Jiling Chronicles* (1986) by Li Yongping, a baby-boom-generation modernist. Hailing from a liminal space and temporally out of sync with trends in Taiwan's literary field, Guo presents us with such a first-rate literary corpus that we are compelled to think deeper and harder about the intricacy and connectedness of literary genealogy.

BIBLIOGRAPHY: Sung-sheng Yvonne Chang, *Literary Culture in Taiwan: Martial Law to Market Law* (New York, 2004). Sung-sheng Yvonne Chang, *Modernism and the Nativist Resistance: Contemporary Chinese Fiction from Taiwan* (Durham, NC, 1993). Jian Yiming, "Guo Songfen fangtan," appendix, in *Jinghun* (Taipei, 2012), 175–243. Wuhe, "Bu weishui weihe er xie: zai Niuyue fangtan Guo Songfen," transcribed by Lee Yu, *INK Literary Monthly* 23 (July 2005): 36–54.

SUNG-SHENG YVONNE CHANG

1985 · APRIL

> "Literature has its roots, and those literary roots should be planted
> deep within the earth of traditional folk culture. For if those roots lack
> depth, the leaves will find it difficult to flourish." —Han Shaogong,
> "The Roots of Literature"

Searching for Roots in Literature and Film

In the April 1985 issue of the prominent Chinese literary journal *The Writer*, thirty-two-year-old Han Shaogong (1953–) published an essay entitled "The Roots of Literature," urging writers to look to "local culture" in an attempt to reembrace and reconnect with cultural folk traditions that had been drowned out in the maelstrom of political movements and socialist ideology during the previous three decades.

The phrase "searching for roots" was coined by cultural critic and scholar Li Tuo (1939–) in an essay published in early 1984, more than a year before Han's proclamation. Whether Li and Han started a movement or instead merely articulated a cultural zeitgeist already in the air, once theorized and defined, the Searching for Roots Movement took on new power and went on to become one of the defining cultural movements of 1980s China. While the movement was interpreted differently by many of its proponents, what binds the roots writers together was a shared dedication to the project of rethinking China's cultural heritage as the nation tried to emerge from the shadow of the Cultural Revolution and enter a new age of economic openness and market reform.

But what was it about the roots movement that penetrated so deeply? Although on the surface the roots writers referenced Chu culture— a historical period that gave rise to early Chinese philosophical thought— and looked deep into China's long cultural, ethical, religious, and folk traditions, the term "roots" can also be understood on other levels. The movement was in part a reaction to the Cultural Revolution and, more broadly, the cultural policies instituted under the Chinese Communist Party (CCP) in line with Mao Zedong's (1893–1976) 1942 Yan'an Forum on Art and Literature. Mao's policies offered a literary and artistic model meant to serve workers, peasants, and soldiers, established guidelines for ideologically "correct" and "incorrect" art, and set the stage for the socialist realist literature that would dominate the literary scene of the People's Republic of China from 1949 to 1978. Han's move toward tradition was not rooted in superficial sentimentality and nostalgia, but instead was heavily influenced by Western modernism and Latin American magical realism, which had a great impact on the Chinese cultural scene in the 1980s. His essay quickly came to be referred to as the "Searching for Roots Literature Proclamation," in recognition of its far-reaching impact.

Works emerging from the roots movement were radical in terms of not only their content but also their form. Therefore, the movement was not just about a philosophical inquiry into the relationship between culture and history in contemporary China; it was also a revolution against a literary form dominated for several decades by socialist realist models. While the immediate forerunners of the roots movement, the scar movement and the reflection movement, were also sparked by the nightmare of the Cultural Revolution, in formal terms both of those schools were much more clearly tied to more conservative Maoist literary models. Moreover, whereas scar and reflection literature were closely bound to depictions of the Cultural Revolution, roots literature used the Cultural Revolution as a springboard to explore deeper questions, experiment with new literary forms, and in some cases rejuvenate the Chinese language itself.

Even as Han and others wrote about what it meant to "search for roots," they simultaneously emerged as the representative figures of the movement on account of their fiction. Following the trajectory of his earlier stories like "Homecoming?" and "The Blue Bottlecap," for instance, Han's first fictional work published after his proclamation was the novella *Ba Ba Ba*, in which village idiot Bing Zai is the sole survivor of a mass suicide in Chickenhead Village. The novella highlighted an eerie primitivism in its depiction of a village closed off to the outside world and steeped in ignorance and brutality. Although *Ba Ba Ba* was set during the Cultural Revolution, Han tried to downplay the historical backdrop in order to highlight the fact that this story could take place at any time and in any place, pointing to a more sweeping criticism of the Chinese national character.

One of the most influential works of the roots movement, meanwhile, was Ah Cheng's (1949–) Three Kings trilogy, composed of *The King of Chess*, *The King of the Children*, and *The King of Trees*. All three novels are set in Yunnan Province during the Cultural Revolution, where Ah Cheng spent several of his formative years as a sent-down youth. *The King of Chess*, for instance, portrays an educated youth who is a bona fide "chess nerd," and, amid the political absurdity of the Cultural Revolution, the story climaxes with the protagonist's public blind match with a venerable chess master. *The King of Trees* could be described as an early work of Chinese eco-fiction, as it reveals the catastrophic environmental impact of many of the ill-designed political policies of the Cultural Revolution. And then there is *The King of the Children*, where another educated youth unexpectedly gets assigned to teach children at a rural school, but just as he gets a new insight into the lives of the kids and begins to make some positive changes, he is abruptly removed from his position. Of course, lurking behind the teacher's dismissal is a much larger indictment leveled against Chinese society at large for the ways in which creativity and critical thinking are stifled by an absurdist educational system—a level of absurdity matched only by that of the political system from which it arose.

On April 12, 1985—the same month Han published his roots manifesto—Chen Kaige's (1952–) debut film, *Yellow Earth*, premiered at the Hong Kong International Film Festival. The premiere would come to be remembered as a major cultural event marking a new page in Chinese film history. Unlike other films from the period, *Yellow Earth*'s dialogue and plot are not reliant on the literary and dramatic conventions that had dominated other Chinese films of the era, and instead the work features a rich palette of visual language, film aesthetics, and innovative cinematic techniques. The film's use of unusually high and low horizon lines, "empty shots" of the mountains and valleys, and aesthetic elements derived from traditional Chinese painting were all cinematic breakthroughs. Moreover, behind many of these aesthetic innovations were nuanced layers of symbolism, making *Yellow Earth* an important film in terms of opening up the ideological underpinnings of Chinese cinema.

Although superficially *Yellow Earth* might appear to resemble countless official post-1949 films (the protagonist is an Eighth Route Army soldier, the story portrays the CCP's mission to preserve traditional folk culture, and so forth), at its heart it contains an ambiguous moral tone and a critical spirit. The soldier Gu Qing is indeed engaged in the collection of traditional folk melodies, but the process of cultural preservation is also predicated on its destruction—Gu's job is not only to collect the songs, but also to transform the lyrics into a propaganda tool of the CCP. And though Gu is a soldier working for the CCP, he no longer resembles the Socialist heroes of yesteryear. Instead of a look of heroic determinism and a gaze to an idealized future, Gu's expression belies a tortured struggle. While Gu may indeed dream of liberating all of China, in the end he is unable to save even a single child bride from an arranged marriage. Although this certainly undermines China's post-1949 idealization of the "soldier hero," on another level *Yellow Earth* also challenges the one-dimensional, black-and-white portrayal of characters that had previously dominated literary and cinematic works thanks to the influence of Mao's 1942 Yan'an Forum. Instead, Chen offers a form of characterization that is imbued with a rich humanism and much closer to a realistic moral tone.

During the early stage of his career immediately following *Yellow Earth*, Chen continued this exploration with films like *The King of the Children* (1987), which was based on Ah Cheng's aforementioned novella while also relying heavily on cinematic language and a rich palette of symbolism.

The King of the Children expanded on the avant-garde tone of *Yellow Earth*. In his adaptation, Chen takes a story that unfolds in the original novella like a Greek tragedy and gives it a realist tone with nondramatic acting and authentic set design, yet punctuates the film with powerful, almost abstract images of desolate landscapes, barren trees, and dancing silhouettes. The film perplexed many audiences but stands as a testament to the probing and uncompromisingly experimental stance of Chen during this stage of his career. A few years later, *Life on a String* (1991), an obtuse and philosophical film about a blind musician and his young disciple traversing a dreamlike landscape, took Chen's exploration of China's cultural roots to its most extreme destination.

While the collective that graduated from the Beijing Film Academy in 1982 has traditionally been identified as the Fifth Generation, a bold group of filmmakers fueled by a searching, rebellious spirit who used innovative new cinematic techniques to reflect on Chinese history and culture, I would argue that many of the early works of this group were in fact ideologically and artistically driven by the same vision behind the roots movement in literature. In particular, the roots movement and the Fifth Generation unfolded almost simultaneously, from the early 1980s to the early 1990s. Many of the landmark early Fifth Generation films were adapted from roots literary works, while others shared similar concerns about and criticisms of the Chinese cultural tradition. There was also a large degree of cross-pollination between the core figures in each movement, with Ah Cheng, for instance, working as a screenwriter on several Fifth Generation films and Chen publishing his own autobiography that could be read as part of the roots movement. Both movements, moreover, experimented with literary and cinematic form in such a way as to challenge previous notions of what was deemed ideologically and aesthetically correct. All of the major figures in each camp were of roughly the same generation and most had served as educated youths during the Cultural Revolution, an experience that directly influenced their major works. Finally, both movements were decisively shaped by a simultaneous renegotiation with traditional Chinese culture *alongside* the profound impact of newly imported Western literary and cinematic theories and works.

Although the cinematic and literary seeds sown in April 1985 continued to germinate and sprout new life well into the 1990s, today much has changed. While some of the major roots writers like Mo Yan (1955–)

and Han continue to write and have even joined the pantheon of officially endorsed writers, others like Ah Cheng have largely withdrawn
from the literary scene. So, too, have many leading members of the Fifth
Generation long turned their backs on the experimental films of their
youth, like *Yellow Earth* and *The King of the Children,* in favor of more
commercial fare. But the biggest change seems to be in society at large:
as Chinese society continues to focus on money and material comforts,
the act of reflecting, criticizing, and interrogating the nation's cultural
and historical roots has seemingly become passé and even dangerous.
The idealistic youths of the 1980s who fervently debated *The King of
Chess* and *Yellow Earth* on college campuses throughout China have been
replaced with practical-minded youths who study economics and cram
for TOEFL exams. But once upon a time in China, there was a group of
artists who dared to break artistic molds, search for their cultural roots,
and challenge the limits of the imagination.

BIBLIOGRAPHY: Ah Cheng, *The King of Trees: Three Novellas,* trans. Bonnie S. McDou-
gall (New York, 2010). Chen Kaige and Tony Rayns, *King of the Children and the New
Chinese Cinema* (London, 1989). Han Shaogong, *Homecoming? And Other Stories,* trans.
Martha Cheung (New York, 1995). Bonnie S. McDougall, *The Yellow Earth: A Film by
Chen Kaige* (Hong Kong, 1992).

MICHAEL BERRY

1986

> "A date is mad: it is never what it is, what it says it is, always more or
> less than what it is. What it is, is either what it is or what it is not."
> —Jacques Derrida, "Shibboleth"

The Writer and the Mad(wo)man

How does one date madness? How may one meet madness head on,
while also assigning it a date? Does insanity have a beginning or end? How
does one circumscribe, in conceptual as well as temporal terms, something
that by definition exceeds the measures and paradigms of the "normal"?
The new wave of writing that emerged after the Cultural Revolution,
particularly the experimental writing in the short decade before 1989,

liked nothing better than to challenge the very idea of the normal, to mock and disrupt the very notion of sanity. After ten years of maddened crowds and individuals pushed beyond the bounds of civility, literature started to write back with a vengeance. Aided by the availability of Western literary models—from modernism to postmodernism, by the likes of Franz Kafka, Samuel Beckett, and Jorge Luis Borges—the literature of that short decade exulted in abject topics and crass corporeality, while madmen and madwomen infested Chinese narrative like a plague: from the satirical, such as the gamboling fools in Xu Xiaohe's (1956–)1986 short story "The Madhouse Director and His Inmates," to the tragic, such as the heroine of Su Tong's (1963–) 1989 novella *Wives and Concubines*, whom the horrors of a polygamous household force into insanity.

None of these various madmen, however, captures the links between history and madness more poignantly than that of Yu Hua's (1960–) short story "1986." Published and set in 1986, Yu's story features a madman who inflicts archaic punishments, such as branding, castration, and flaying, on his own body as bystanders watch in horror. Driven into insanity by the persecution of the Cultural Revolution, the protagonist acts out the subject of his former research, the history of execution techniques, on his own body, thus disrupting the everyday lives of people eager to forget the atrocities of recent history. The text's title dates the story to ten years after the end of the Cultural Revolution, thus also echoing the ten-year duration of the Cultural Revolution itself. But the apparent delay of ten years effectively shows that temporal distance does not erase past traumas. The madman relives the bygone brutality and forces the traumatic past to erupt in the present, belying, through the appearance of ancient corporeal punishments, any reassuring notion of historical progress. In fact, the cruelties of the past—both ancient and recent—cannot be laid to rest, but haunt the present and continue to darken the future.

The attempts in the 1980s to reach beyond the bounds of reality or normalcy through literature were not without precedent. In fact many 1980s texts were themselves revenants of earlier works. The textual insanity of the 1980s is double, since it invokes the textual madness rife in the earlier literature of the May Fourth generation. In "A Madman's Diary," for instance, Lu Xun (1881–1936) marks the breakthrough of a new mode of literary expression by pitting two textual types against each other. The first section of the story, a short text in classical Chinese, frames the rest of the story as the diary entries of a madman that consist of free-floating jottings in a vernacular style, the first example of a new literary Chinese in the making. Lu Xun's textual frame assigns the madman of the title a precise medical diagnosis—paranoiac schizophrenia—and hence his diary entries become material for a medical case study. But Lu Xun's famous madman is also identified as a *kuangren*—a term that connotes an inspired, clairvoyant voice that cries out against stifling cultural and societal norms. Where others might see the ravings of a madman who thinks that all who surround him are cannibals, we are invited to read in an allegorical manner. Namely, it is possible to take the protagonist's delusions as truth: China is a man-eating society, mired in self-destructive beliefs and traditions. What makes such a reading possible is precisely the text's invitation to reject the modern, clinical definition of mental illness offered at the beginning and to read according to a view of inspired madness influenced by Friedrich Nietzsche's (1844–1900) revaluation of values that counters the scientific frenzy to diagnose, catalogue, and contain that Michel Foucault (1926–1984) describes in his *History of Madness*.

Another short story, "Notes of a Mad Person" (1922) by female writer Bing Xin (1900–1999), constitutes an uncanny companion piece to Lu Xun's short story. Like Lu Xun's madman, the mad person in Bing Xin's story, which makes frequent nods to Indian mythology as a reminder of a supposed transcendent pan-Asian knowledge, stands for creative inspiration. And yet, Bing Xin's mad(wo)man oscillates between creative activities that are traditionally framed as masculine (literary endeavors) and feminine (darning shoes), spinning tales and perceiving reality as an intricate network of crazily tangled strings. In contrast to the double textuality of Lu Xun, Bing Xin's first-person narrator, who professes to write as a remedy against madness—to write "so as not to become"—exposes his or her madness through the spinning of an insane text, replete with strange metamorphoses, phantasmic binaries, and temporal incongruities.

The depictions of madness in Chinese literary texts from both the May Fourth period and the 1980s invite allegorical readings. The uncanny figure of the madman or madwoman becomes a cipher for the horrors of history, an individual robbed of sanity embodying a disturbed and disturbing time. However, Chinese literary madwomen and madmen of both eras are not confined to their diegetic and allegorical attics and closets, but rather they present challenges to social normalcy and literary conventions.

These mad(wo)men not only freely roam their textual worlds, but also threaten to push a literary text to the edge of sanity. No longer are they neatly framed by textual normalcy, marked as mad exceptions in an otherwise normal textual universe that is coherent and amenable to understanding. Instead, their perspectives also tint the reader's perception of a textual world or even plunge the text itself into insanity, presenting fictional universes that resist coherent readings and defy references to some recognizable reality or intelligible order. Here, not only do texts feature madmen or madwomen, madness also transforms (into) literature, or rather literature shows that its powers to defy reality have always placed it in close vicinity to madness.

The tendency to interweave insanity and literary style distinguishes not only Bing Xin's disorienting and disturbing short story but also the work of Can Xue (1953–), a contemporary author active since the 1980s. The textual universes Can Xue constructs resist any coherent reading, and her protagonists—not unlike Lu Xun's madman—are often paranoid or prone to compulsive behavior. For instance, the protagonist of "Hut on the Mountain" (1985), the text that catapulted Can Xue onto the literary scene, does not recognize herself in the mirror. She externalizes part of her suppressed inner life in the form of a person locked into the little hut on the mountain of the title—a hut that, as we learn at the very end of the story, does not even exist. In Can Xue's stories, there is no "normal" textual space left for a reader to gauge, define, and thus contain madness, as her 1986 story "What Happened to Me in That World" illustrates. The text oscillates between a hostile, absurd world in which the female first-person narrator is threatened and persecuted and a fantastic space of sublime, chthonic beauty marked by floating icebergs. The reader, confined to a single perspective, finds herself imprisoned as in a textual cage, shuttling back and forth between two different realms that are equally alienating. Even the two disturbing spaces that the story depicts—readable as part of the protagonist's psychic life as it swings from paranoia to delusion—start to lose their contours, as the demonstrative pronouns *this* and *that* constantly change their point of reference, instead of fixing "this world" as the realm of persecution, and "that world" as the escape fantasy of the ice world. Through the perspectival prism of the narrator's disorienting inner world, the categories of reality and fantasy, of experienced and imagined worlds, of creation and determination, begin to blur. If the barriers between the "real" and the fictional world, between creating and creation, performance and copy, cannot be sustained any longer, this also means that the distinctions between outside and inside, between reality and a subject's interiority, and between perception, interiority, and fiction must be reassessed. Much as the referential function of language turns out to be a perspectival illusion, literature escapes from its traditional rules, expectations, and uses.

This also means that even though literary madness invites allegorical reading, it also contests and threatens such textual domestication. Literary insanity is not confined to a specific time or purpose, but rather it subverts clear boundaries—of time and context, of inner and outer experience, and of literature and representation. It appears frequently as a thematic and stylistic revenant where historical trauma and aesthetic crisis coalesce; as a vehicle for contestation, rupture, and innovation, for a radical redefinition of the bounds and definitions of (real and literary) normalcy. In fact, apart from the resonance between two key moments of Chinese literature, the 1980s and the generation of May Fourth, madness also plays an important role in texts from other Sinophone contexts, from the perturbed protagonist of the Taiwanese novelist Bai Xianyong's (1937–) "Death in Chicago" (1964), to the raving, murderous female protagonist in "The Butcher's Wife" (1983) by the Taiwanese writer Li Ang (1952–), to the schizophrenic main character in *Mulberry and Peach* (1976) by the Sinophone writer Nieh Hua-ling (1925–). If madness makes us question the very tenets of reality, as Shoshana Felman argues in *Writing and Madness*, namely, what it means to "know" or what it means to make sense (rather than no(n)sense), then literature and madness share a similar essence. In other words, the literary is not only a vehicle for describing madness, but becomes a medium for and of madness. By the same token, textual insanity thematizes and questions the power of the literary. Between the May Fourth and the 1980s, between the People's Republic of China and other Sinophone contexts, between sense and nonsense, reality and literature, male and female—from text to text, the writer dallies with (becoming) a mad(wo)man as literature dates madness and insanity untethers literature.

BIBLIOGRAPHY: Can Xue, *Congwei miaoshuguo de mengjing* (Beijing, 2004). Can Xue, "Hut on the Mountain" and "The Things That Happened to Me in That World," in

Dialogues in Paradise, trans. Ronald R. Janssen and Jian Zhang (Evanston, IL, 1989), 46–53, 86–93. Jacques Derrida, "Shibboleth: For Paul Celan," in *Sovereignties in Question: The Poetics of Paul Celan*, ed. Thomas Dutoit and Outi Pasanen (New York, 2005), 1–64. Lu Xun, "Kuangren riji," in *Lu Xun xiaoshuo quanji* (Taipei, 2011), 15–23. Ban Wang, *The Sublime Figure of History: Aesthetics and Politics in Twentieth-Century China* (Stanford, CA, 1997). Yang Xiaobin, *The Chinese Postmodern: Trauma and Irony in Chinese Avant-Garde Fiction* (Ann Arbor, MI, 2002). Yu Hua, "1986," in *The Past and the Punishments: Eight Stories*, trans. Andrew F. Jones (Honolulu, 1996), 132–180. Yu Hua, "Yijiubaliu nian," in *Xianshi yizhong: Yu Hua zuopin xilie* (Shanghai, 2004), 118–167.

ANDREA BACHNER

1987 · SEPTEMBER

Issue 5 of *Harvest* is published.

The Birth of China's Literary Avant-Garde

In the autumn of 1987, I received my copy of issue 5 of the literary journal *Harvest*. I opened it and saw my name, together with some unfamiliar ones. Although each issue of *Harvest* typically brought together a collection of famous authors, this one instead introduced a group of relatively unknown figures whose writing style must have struck readers as very alien. This issue was published during a crucial period when literary journals were trying to boost their subscription rates for the following year, but while other journals were publishing new works by famous authors, *Harvest* instead featured works by a group of virtually unknown writers.

This issue of *Harvest* later came to be known as the avant-garde literature issue. Editors of other literary journals remarked in private that *Harvest* was making mischief—referring both to the works' narrative form and the political risk they were taking. *Harvest* continued making mischief by publishing another special issue on avant-garde literature in issue 6 of 1987, as well as issues 5 and 6 of 1988. Works by Ma Yuan (1953–), Su Tong (1963–), Ge Fei (1964–), Ye Zhaoyan (1957–), Sun Ganlu (1957–), Hong Feng (1957–), me, and others were featured.

At the time, Ge Fei was teaching at East China Normal University, and *Harvest* would always put us up in a guesthouse at his university when we came to Shanghai to submit our manuscripts. Su Tong and I were probably the ones who stayed there most often. During the day, we would take the bus to the *Harvest* editorial office. Editors Li Xiaolin (1945–) and Xiao Yuanmin (1954–) were both women, in addition to being our seniors, and so it was not very appropriate for them to hang out with us. Cheng Yongxin (1958–, the executive chief editor of *Harvest*), however, was a bachelor, and he would take us out to all of the little restaurants around the *Harvest* editorial office. Wang Xiaoming (1955–, a professor of modern and contemporary Chinese literature at East China Normal University) frequently came to the editorial office for business and would see Ge Fei, Su Tong, and me sitting there chatting. He would always tell others that we treated *Harvest* as though it were our own home. At night, Cheng would come back to the guesthouse and chat with us until late into the night. When we got hungry, we would go out in search of food. Given that the university's outer gates were locked at eleven o'clock each night, though, we would have to climb the iron gate to get out and then climb it again to get back in. At first we did this very awkwardly, but soon we became quite nimble.

Because *Harvest* had such a high stature in China's literary scene, anything it published would inevitably attract wide attention. In this respect, the journal was comparable to the *New Yorker*. However, while the *New Yorker* only publishes works by established literary darlings, *Harvest* instead featured works by avant-garde authors who at the time were but literary foundlings. Many years later, when people asked me why I published more than three-quarters of my works in *Harvest*, I would explain that it was because at a time when all the other literary journals were locking me out, *Harvest* had invited me in.

The reason other journals offered for rejecting my submissions was that what I was writing was not real literature. Needless to say, they also claimed that what Su Tong and Ge Fei were writing was not literature either. At the time, Chinese literature had only just begun to emerge from the shadows of the Cultural Revolution, and authors usually displayed their courage primarily through their choice of topics, as opposed to narrative form. We *Harvest* authors, however, were not satisfied with the uniformity of the narrative structure found in literary works at the time. We therefore began seeking a more diverse array of narrative forms and struggled diligently in our writing to find different forms of narrative progression. As a result, many journals decided we were being politically incorrect and not heeding the Communist Party, some going so far to claim that we were not writing literature but rather merely playing with it.

Harvest didn't heed the party either, and believed we were in fact writing literature. The journal recognized that a crucial period of narrative transformation was approaching, and therefore leapt at the opportunity to publish these four special issues. *Zhongshan, Huacheng, Beijing Literature,* and a handful of other literary journals also sensed this impending transformation but didn't pursue it with the same enthusiasm, instead only publishing the occasional avant-garde work. Why is this? The answer is very simple: they didn't have Ba Jin (1904–2005).

Chinese literature in the 1980s suffered many setbacks. The Anti-Spiritual Pollution Campaign and the Oppose Bourgeois Liberalization Campaign caused the newly expanded literary environment to become as tense as though it were under martial law. Avant-garde literature is a product of bourgeois liberalization, and several other journals came under severe criticism from the authorities after publishing some avant-garde stories. They asked abjectly, Why is it that *Harvest* can publish this sort of literature while we can't? They received the comical response, "*Harvest* is a target of the united front."

Ba Jin enjoyed high prestige and nearly universal respect, and none of the bureaucrats who were in charge of overseeing ideological issues dared to challenge him. When Ba Jin was appointed editor in chief of *Harvest,* the official censors turned a blind eye to the journal, and in this way it became a target of the united front that had to be won over through persuasion. Ba Jin's longevity ensured that *Harvest* would long remain a unique case, thereby permitting those of us who published with the journal to have plenty of time to mature.

Even with Ba Jin at the helm, however, the road trod by *Harvest* was filled with thorns. The two special issues on avant-garde literature that *Harvest* published in 1987 infuriated the authorities, and when the journal published two more special issues the following year, the authorities vowed to replace its entire editorial board. Although at the time Ba Jin's daughter Li Xiaolin was technically only an associate editor, in reality she was the one in charge. The authorities, accordingly, did not attempt to take away her title, but rather sought to strip her of her authority and replace her with someone they trusted. The justification they offered was that she was not a party member, while at that time the people in charge of literary journals were all party members. The authorities' attempts to restructure the journal's editorial board lasted from late 1988 until March 1989, but in the end nothing came of their efforts and Li retained control. Later, I asked her why this was, and she said that it was partly because the authorities were worried about how her father might react, and partly because the journal was supported by a number of other famous authors, such as Ru Zhijuan (1925–1998), Wang Xiyan (1914–1999), and Ke Ling (1909–2000).

When Li escaped danger, so did *Harvest* and the body of avant-garde literature it supported. There was also another factor that helped to improve the conditions for avant-garde literature, namely, that it was widely believed that avant-garde literature was not real literature and that its authors were merely a group of people playing with literature, ephemeral as a night-blooming cactus. As a result, the authorities stopped trying to suppress it, on the assumption that it would soon perish of its own accord.

Naturally, we were all amused by the sudden popularity of the viewpoint that avant-garde literature was not real literature. After all, what *is* literature? We felt narrative structure should be open, indeterminate, and never fixed. Our reading habits helped inform our understanding of what literature was. After enduring the Cultural Revolution, when there were virtually no books, we suddenly found ourselves surrounded by veritable swarms of literary works, including both classical and modern Chinese works. Nineteenth- and twentieth-century Western classics arrived in China simultaneously and, blinded by this splendor of riches, we began reading voraciously. We avant-garde authors were scattered throughout China and initially didn't know each other. Independently of one another, however, we all started reading Western literary works— for the simple reason that, compared with classical and modern Chinese works, there were significantly more Western novels and they featured a much wider range of narrative forms.

We read works by Leo Tolstoy, Franz Kafka, and many others. We read with little regard for literary history, and had no interest in understanding the era and background of the works' authors. Instead, we just read works for their own sake, and in this way were exposed to all sorts of different narrative forms. When we ourselves started writing, accordingly, we knew that it was possible to write using virtually any narrative structure. The literary establishment, however, found it difficult to accept our modernist tendencies. They felt that the critical realism found in the works of nineteenth-century authors such as Tolstoy and Honoré de Balzac was part of its own literary tradition, while Kafka, Marcel Proust, James Joyce, William Faulkner, and Gabriel García Márquez, together with symbolism, expressionism, and absurdism, were all regarded as foreign. We found this attitude to be rather odd, since were not Tolstoy and Balzac themselves also foreigners?

Literary sensibilities at that time resembled that iron gate at the entrance of East China Normal—when we *Harvest* authors were hungry, the fact that the gate was closed would not prevent us from going out to find food. Climbing the gate was against the rules, and in much the same way our writing violated the consensus of the literary establishment. Today, twenty years later, East China Normal no longer locks its gates at night, and you can now enter and leave at any time. Not only Tolstoy and Balzac, but also Kafka, Proust, Joyce, García Márquez, and others, have similarly become part of our collective literary tradition.

Yu Hua
Translated by Carlos Rojas

1987 · DECEMBER 24

"When a man leaves his so-called motherland, there is a kind of distance, and when he writes, he can be detached and calm."

Gao Xingjian's Pursuit of Freedom in the Spirit of Zhuangzi

Throughout his life, Gao Xingjian (1940–) has been frequently on the run. In 1983, after his play *Bus Stop* was banned, he was diagnosed with lung cancer. He made a quick decision to flee Beijing, the political center, for the remote forest regions of Sichuan Province. After a spell in Sichuan, he then roamed along the Yangtze River—a journey that inspired his famous novel *Soul Mountain* (1990). In 1987 he traveled to Germany as a visiting artist and later decided not to return to China; he eventually settled in Paris, where he has since made his home. His flight made his 2000 Nobel Prize in Literature controversial in mainland China, where most of his works remain banned.

As the first Chinese Nobel Prize winner in literature, Gao occupies a singular position in the history of Chinese modernist drama. In the 1980s, when most Chinese people still had no clue what Western absurdist drama was, he had already published *A Preliminary Discussion of the Art of Modern Fiction* (1981). This pioneering theoretical book introduced Western modernism to China and helped Chinese writers to transcend realism, the dominant mode of fiction at the time. During this same period, Gao initiated the birth of avant-garde theater in China. As a playwright, he has left an innovative legacy of experimental dramas such as *Alarm Signal* (1982), *Bus Stop* (1983), *Wild Man* (1985), and *The Other Shore* (1986). Although he could have stayed in China enjoying a prestigious life as one of the elite, he chose a life of self-exile, settling in Paris, an action that can be described as a form of self-salvation. Composed in self-exile, his writing has transgressed the geopolitical boundary of nation-state. Through his unique mode of diasporic expression, Gao maintains distance from the political center, searches for inner space and freedom, and advocates a set of universal values for mankind.

When Gao won the Nobel Prize, the award provoked a protracted debate in China about the politics of the Nobel Prize, as well as Gao's diasporic writing. Those who denigrated Gao's writing complained that the award of the prize was politically motivated by anti-Communist sentiments and criticized his decision to run away from his home country. His French citizenship allowed the Chinese government to deny that he was the first Chinese writer to win the Nobel Prize. Regardless of his citizenship, however, Gao won the Nobel Prize through his Chinese writing, which perfectly combined Western modernist narratology and traditional Chinese philosophy. By defining writing as an escape, a challenge to the ruling ideological paradigm of the moment as well as the material conditions of one's environment, Gao proclaims that only through escape can he find his true self, as well as the real meaning of literature. The action of fleeing or self-exile, both political protest and aesthetic adventure, has therefore become one of the central themes in Gao's writing.

He has defined his own writings as "cold literature," a "literature that entails fleeing in order to exist. It is literature that refuses to be strangled by society in its quest for spiritual salvation. If a race cannot accommodate this sort of non-utilitarian literature it is not merely a misfortune for the writer but a tragedy for that race." In *Soul Mountain*, the protagonist escapes from the political center to peripheral cultures and the primeval forest. In his play *Flee* (1990), the middle-aged protagonist wants to abscond from revolution, as well as from the hell of the self, which leaves a shadow on his heart:

> Being alive means being always on the run. We are running away either from political persecution or from other people, and we also run away from ourselves. Once we are awakened, we will find that is exactly the self that we cannot run away from. Such is the tragedy of modern man.

In Gao's famous play *August Snow* (1997), the Sixth Patriarch of Zen Buddhism Huineng runs away from various kinds of authorities, refusing to be the savior of the world or the idol of others, and instead advocating "self-salvation" with which to pursue the "total freedom" that comes from one's heart.

First written in 1982 in China and then completed in 1989 in Paris, *Soul Mountain* can be read as a record of a flight, as well as a story of searching for the meaning of life. In other words, the escape itself is for the purpose of spiritual searching. Creatively written, the novel restages the narrator's experience of the world. Instead of characters, Gao only gives us personal pronouns to indicate who is speaking; instead of an externally driven plot, we have the protagonist's psychological rhythm. Even though Gao is well known for his assimilation of Western modernist techniques of writing, in this novel he seriously delves into the origins of nonmainstream Chinese cultures that have been marginalized by the dominant Confucian culture, such as the reclusive culture of Chinese intellectuals, the ecological culture of Daoism, the wisdom-seeking culture of Zen Buddhism, and the lost folk culture. The similarities between these four cultures lie in their unorthodoxy, their rejection of tyranny and promotion of individual freedom, their emphasis on the individual life, and their opposition to mainstream cultural concepts. In short, the core of these four subcultures is the individual spiritual liberation advocated by Zhuangzi (ca. 369–286 BCE), whose wisdom has been preserved in *Zhuangzi*. As one of the most influential works of early Chinese thought, *Zhuangzi* embodies the ancient Daoist wit that continues to have an enormous impact on a wide variety of contemporary Chinese writers, including Gao.

Like the writers of the "root-searching literature" that emerged in the 1980s, Gao's central concern in *Soul Mountain* is nature: not only the outer nature of mountains, rivers, and trees, but also the inner cosmos of the human psyche. The ecological themes that appeared as early as the 1980s in his play *Wild Man* continue to pervade the text of *Soul Mountain*. Gao makes use of his protagonist's journey through the primeval forest to vehemently criticize the ravaging of nature by modern man. Facing a forest deeply wounded by human beings, the protagonist feels furious, but has no way to stop the trend toward "development" in contemporary China or to change the greedy nature of human beings. He therefore realizes there is no way to save the world.

Soul Mountain contains eighty-one chapters, similar to the eighty-one tribulations of the sixteenth-century novel *Journey to the West*, alternatively known to Western readers as *Monkey*. *Journey to the West* can also be read as a journey of interior dialogue, and the pilgrims making the journey are searching exactly for a "soul mountain": the holy site of India's Vulture Peak. What is meant by a "soul mountain"? Does the protagonist eventually find it? This is the vital theme of the novel: "soul mountain" can be interpreted to mean a mountain of the Buddha, or a mountain of freedom, of the unrestrained. The novel ends with the image of a frog's twinkling eyes—an ending without any answer, because the author wants readers to come to the answer by themselves.

Gao's interpretation of freedom stems from his understanding of and commitment to Zhuangzi and Zen Buddhism, both of which hold that only through returning to original human nature and freeing oneself from the fetters of the external world can one regain vast freedom and comfort. This concept also influences the complex interweaving of Gao's literary concepts. As he has written, "The freedom of writing is not given by God, nor can it be bought; instead, it derives from your inner necessity.... It is better to say freedom is in your heart than to say the Buddha is in your heart. Whether to use it or not is totally up to you." The truth of *Soul Mountain* is to open the gate of the heart, inviting the Buddha as well as freedom to come out. In the spirit of Zhuangzi, *Soul Mountain* calls for an awakening that transcends all the obstacles set by mundane value systems.

By identifying with Zhuangzi's philosophy of absolute spiritual freedom, Gao diverges significantly from the theme of participating in society and saving the country established by Lu Xun (1881–1936) and other mainstream Chinese writers. During the twentieth century, Chinese writers were frequently called on to play the role of savior of the nation or to take on serious historical or political responsibilities. Yet Gao comes to question the concept of the national hero. In *August Snow*, Gao tells the story of Huineng, the Sixth Patriarch of Zen Buddhism, who entirely liberates himself from fame, power, and everyday problems and therefore obtains vast freedom. This drama corresponds to the spirit presented in *Zhuangzi*'s "Easy and Free Wandering" chapter, but is rooted in the sense of "an ordinary mind." Similarly, by accepting Huineng's notion of "an ordinary mind," Gao is no longer concerned with fulfilling any social responsibility or becoming the ideal person, but seeks the spiritual path leading to eternal freedom. Therefore his notion of what it means to be a writer is quite different from that of Lu Xun, who encourages Chinese writers to plunge into national affairs. For Gao, only by forsaking the utopian idea of changing or saving the world can a writer rediscover real freedom.

Although Gao is best known for being the first Chinese writer to create absurdist drama and investigate modernism within China, he has proven to the world that he is a multidimensional writer and artist: he is not only a successful novelist, but also a successful dramatist, drama director, film director, painter, critic, and poet. It is not surprising that Gao's writings still cannot be openly published in mainland China, even if what he insists on is solely aesthetic in nature. What distinguishes Gao from the others is his political as well as aesthetic understanding of escape, with which he has fully gained the freedom to write, to innovate, and to produce. As he has said, "I believe that even if politics and society are touched upon in literary creation, it is better to 'flee' than to 'participate' because this would deflect social pressures from oneself and also cleanse one spiritually." Compared to other Chinese writers such as Mo Yan (1955–), who dwells on local culture and nativist spirit, Gao represents a trend of inner reflection and inner searching typical of highly educated intellectuals who have been influenced by Western existentialism, Zhuangzi's philosophy, and Zen Buddhism. His gestures of flight, self-exile, and traveling—all part of diasporic writing—allow him to embrace the universal values of humanity.

Since freedom is perhaps the most important keyword for understanding Gao and his oeuvre, his case propels us to ponder the relationship between freedom and literature. What is freedom and how can one obtain it? During the twentieth century, modern Chinese intellectuals had a hard time accepting and understanding Zhuangzi's spirit of individual freedom, and their different attitudes toward his work reflect the winding spiritual journey of modern Chinese intellectuals. During the May Fourth Movement, Lu Xun rejected Zhuangzi because he considered national salvation more important and more urgent than personal freedom. Guo Moruo (1892–1978) eulogized and embraced Zhuangzi in the most romantic and enthusiastic way in his early literary career, but after he accepted Marxism, he made an about-face and began to vehemently criticize and denigrate Zhuangzi. His changing attitudes toward Zhuangzi perfectly encapsulated how the inner space of freedom was gradually invaded and devoured by external political power in modern China. Other Chinese intellectuals such as Zhou Zuoren (1885–1967), Lin Yutang (1895–1976), and Fei Ming (1901–1967) were fond of the dream of Zhuangzi, but such a dream could barely survive in the face of national crisis. During the revolutionary period in the 1960s, Zhuangzi was put into "the court of politics." His thought was made the target of a large-scale campaign by radical leftists, who sought to portray him as the irreconcilable class enemy of the mainstream ideology—Marxism. Only after the 1980s did we see the return of Zhuangzi in the novels of Wang Zengqi (1920–1997), Han Shaogong (1953–), Ah Cheng (1949–), and Yan Lianke (1958–). Yet it is Gao Xingjian who has brought Zhuangzi's spirit of absolute liberation and freedom to the highest level by writing the novel *Soul Mountain*.

Modern Chinese writers praise, satirize, criticize, or denigrate Zhuangzi, but only Gao clearly affirms Zhuangzi's spirit of individual freedom and liberation. In doing so, Gao insinuates that the "soul mountain" is not external, but internal. Only through inner awakening can one find Soul Mountain. That is to say, freedom is not bestowed by others, but is self-given. Freedom hides in everyone's heart and only by relying on oneself can it be discovered. Gao's triumph represents the most compelling example of the interplay between literature and freedom at the end of the twentieth century. It is the triumph of a modern Zhuangzi.

BIBLIOGRAPHY: Gao Xingjian, *Cold Literature: Selected Works by Gao Xingjian*, trans. Gilbert C. F. Fong and Mabel Lee (Hong Kong, 2005). Gao Xingjian, *Meiyou zhuyi* (Taipei, 2001). Gao Xingjian, *Soul Mountain*, trans. Mabel Lee (Sydney, 2000).

LIU JIANMEI

1988 · JULY 1

Two young scholars launch a new column in *Shanghai Literary Forum.*

"Rewriting Literary History" in the New Era of Liberated Thought

In July 1988, Wang Xiaoming (1955–) and I began to coedit a new column, which appeared in the fourth issue of the theoretical journal *Shanghai Literary Forum* under the title "Rewriting Literary History." At that time, Xiaoming and I had just begun our teaching careers as lecturers in Shanghai, at East China Normal University and Fudan University, respectively. We had both published literary review articles, and our new approaches to literary studies began to attract attention. The motivation for editing a special column on "rewriting literary history" was to contest the Communist Party–dominated opinions that had prevailed in literary histories published previously in the People's Republic of China (PRC) and to engage more academically in literary criticism. Like many of our peers studying literature at that time, we thought that literary history should be more objective, more diverse, and less biased.

Xiaoming and I belong to a generation of Chinese scholars who entered colleges and universities after the Cultural Revolution and faced a profound change in the nature of academic work in the PRC. The "thought liberation" campaign that the Communist authorities launched in the late 1970s to liquidate the extreme leftist currents within the party had gradually extended its influence over many academic fields in the humanities and social sciences. Thought liberation particularly resonated with Chinese writers who lived through the Cultural Revolution, and afterward created a "new era" in contemporary Chinese literature. Correspondingly, literary critics and scholars were confronted with the tasks of bypassing the government's political interventions in literary studies in order to seek new, independent intellectual positions in academic work. The column "Rewriting Literary History" came about precisely in this cultural climate.

As guest editors, Xiaoming and I explained the goal of the column in an editorial preface: "We have opened this column with the hope that it will stimulate and energize literary criticism, and will challenge those conventional, seemingly conclusive opinions on literary history. Through doing so, we hope to reignite people's passions for reflecting on what happened yesterday, so as to serve today." Here, "today" refers to the efforts to embrace thought liberation and critically reevaluate those ideas and conclusions found in the leftist literary histories dictated by the government.

"Rewriting Literary History" opened with two articles criticizing Zhao Shuli (1906–1970) and Liu Qing (1916–1978), two famous PRC writers. The opinions presented in the column challenged the orthodox discourses on these writers and modern Chinese literature in general by arguing against the exclusive emphasis on the political when interpreting literary works. Zhao used to be regarded as a representative Maoist writer, and Liu Qing's reputation was largely based on a novel that depicted Mao Zedong's (1893–1976) agricultural cooperation movement. Both writers were persecuted to death during the Cultural Revolution, after which their names were rehabilitated in the orthodox narrative of literary history. Their works were considered landmarks of post-1949 Chinese literature. However, the two articles that opened the column "Rewriting Literary History" questioned precisely the politicization in the fiction works of these two writers, pointing to the fact that their writings mainly served politics with their manifestation of political formulas and concepts.

Later, criticism of other important authors, such as Ding Ling (1904–1986), Guo Xiaochuan (1919–1976), and He Qifang (1912–1977), as well as a critical reevaluation of the PRC literary canon directed at works like Mao Dun's (1896–1981) *Midnight* and Yang Mo's (1914–1995) *The Song of Youth*, appeared in the column. These writers all had long-standing reputations as major voices of the official literary establishment of the PRC. The criticism of these left-wing or Communist writers expressed in the column was fairly mild, but because it appeared in the name of "rewriting literary history," controversy followed and strong responses were heard.

"Literary history" was closely related to the state ideology in China, particularly during the second half of the twentieth century. The efforts to rewrite literary history, particularly those efforts that led to negative opinions of established authors and literary works, elicited strong reactions in academic circles. Leftists saw these efforts as unwelcome gestures of bourgeois liberalization. What came after was the rapid popularization of the discourse of "rewriting," which was not limited to "rewriting literary history" in a modern context but also quickly spread to studies in classical Chinese literature, art history, and other related fields, where similar pleas for "rewriting" were voiced. The column "Rewriting Literary History" ran from the fourth issue of 1988 to the sixth issue of 1989 in *Shanghai Literary Forum*. It became a "phenomenon" that attracted attention from the entirety of Chinese academia in the last two years of the 1980s.

The modern Chinese tradition of writing literary history began with two publications bearing the same title, *The Literary History of China*, authored by Lin Chuanjia (1877–1922) in 1904 and Huang Ren (1866–1913) in 1905, respectively. From then on, the writing of literary history has been closely connected to the notions of recognizing or building China as a modern nation-state. After 1949, the Communist regime further strengthened this connection by strictly controlling the practice of writing literary histories, particularly histories of modern Chinese literature. On the one hand, modern Chinese literary history was prioritized as an academic subfield, which elevated it to the same status as classical Chinese literature and theories of literature and art, and a large number of teaching faculty and researchers were assigned to work in this new field. On the other hand, the writing of modern Chinese literary history was strictly regulated, according to the guiding principle of making it a part of the narrative of the "new democratic" revolutionary history as defined by Mao in the orthodox discourse on the Communist-led modern Chinese revolution.

As a result, a large group of excellent writers, including Shen Congwen (1902–1988), Eileen Chang (1920–1995), Zhou Zuoren (1885–1967), and Lin Yutang (1895–1976), who did not adhere to the Communist revolutionary line, did not occupy even a minor place in the literary histories of modern China compiled under government control from 1949 to the 1980s. In the meantime, overly high praise was given to a small number of literary works produced prior to the 1949 change of regime in Communist-occupied liberated areas, where Mao's *Talks at the Yan'an Forum on Literature and Art* (1942) prominently dictated the direction of literature. Furthermore, the content and opinions of the literary histories shaped by such partisan prejudices were still constantly changing, due to the numerous political campaigns launched by the Communist Party after 1949, in which a great number of intellectuals, including many left-wing writers, were purged. Therefore, the literary history of modern China was continuously being revised to serve political needs. Those writers who had once been held in high esteem—established left-wing literary theorist Hu Feng (1902–1985), the revolutionary feminist Ding Ling, the Communist literary critic Feng Xuefeng (1903–1976), and the revolutionary poet Ai Qing (1910–1996)—would completely disappear from or become targets for denigration in literary histories as soon as they were purged in political movements. After China entered the reform era in the late 1970s, this kind of government-dictated standard narrative of literary history became increasingly unacceptable for the new generation of scholars, such as Xiaoming and me, who had received completely different training in literary studies.

The revival of the field came out of the ruins of the Cultural Revolution. During the Cultural Revolution, nearly all modern Chinese literary works were labeled counterrevolutionary. Modern Chinese literary studies became dysfunctional as a field. The reconstruction of the field relied in the first place on a group of older scholars who survived the Cultural Revolution. These scholars included Wang Yao (1914–1989), a Peking University professor who wrote the first history of Chinese new literature after 1949; Tang Tao (1913–1992), a member of the Institute of Literature in the Chinese Academy of Social Sciences and a senior Lu Xun (1881–1936) expert; Li Helin (1904–1988), who taught at Beijing Normal University and served as the first director of the Lu Xun Museum; Jia Zhifang (1916–2008), a writer of the left-wing July School and a professor of Fudan University; and Qian Gurong (1919–), a literary theorist teaching at East China Normal University. These veteran scholars had all suffered from political persecution before and during the Cultural Revolution. After returning to their teaching and research positions, they consciously carried out the tasks of reviving and remapping the field of modern Chinese literary studies and passing on the heritage of the May Fourth "New Culture," particularly the "fighting spirit" of Lu Xun, who was considered forever uncompromised and always ready to battle conservatism. The major accomplishment of this older generation of scholars was to train a good number of students in universities and research institutes. Nearly all the young scholars emerging in modern Chinese literary studies and actively reviving the field during the 1980s were former disciples of these veteran scholars. They kept their serious engagement with knowledge and scholarship alive and attempted to do away with the political interventions and ideological constraints imposed on the field.

In May 1985, Qian Liqun (1939–), Chen Pingyuan (1954–), and Huang Ziping (1949–), three scholars of Peking University, presented the new concept of "the twentieth-century Chinese literature" at the junior scholar forum hosted by the Chinese Association of Modern Chinese Literature at the Wanshou Temple location of the National Museum of Modern Chinese Literature. At the same forum, I presented the idea of studying Chinese "New Literature" as a total, continuous tradition, which, like the concept of "twentieth-century Chinese literature," aimed to break down the barriers between the three subfields of modern Chinese literature: "early modern" (1840–1919) Chinese literature, "modern" (1919–1949) Chinese literature, and "contemporary" literature. The distinction between these three eras was based on the Communist narrative of Chinese revolutionary history. The efforts of those young scholars to recognize modern Chinese literature as a coherent and continuous movement, with an aim to bring the field back to normal academic and scientific practices, dissolved the ideological and political significance of the periodization based on political narrative.

During the 1980s, young scholars began with case studies of individual writers and managed to thoroughly reevaluate and restore some important Republican-era authors who were either completely overlooked or critiqued according to Communist ideology in previous literary histories. Even more provocative and refreshing research appeared in the study of Lu Xun, which liberated the spiritual heritage of the great mentor from his ossified image in Communist propaganda. In the meantime, under the sponsorship of the Institute of Literature of the Academy of Social Sciences, a nationwide collaboration among university and college professors teaching modern Chinese literature resulted in the publication of two major series of research materials: *The Collection of Materials in Modern Chinese Literature* and *The Research Materials in Contemporary Chinese Literature*. Each series included dozens of volumes that systematically covered the biographies, bibliographies, and related criticism of nearly a hundred writers. These publications enabled the rewriting of literary history to be deeply grounded in historical materials, and the individual case studies eventually led to the remapping of the entire field of modern Chinese literature. What lent force to this new trend was the influence of overseas scholars. C. T. Hsia's (1921–2013) *A History of Modern Chinese Fiction*, Leo Ou-fan Lee's (1942–) *The Romantic Generation of Modern Chinese Writers*, and Edward Gunn's (1946–) *Unwelcome Muse* in particular helped the young scholars in China become interested in writers excluded by orthodox PRC literary scholarship, such as Eileen Chang and Qian Zhongshu (1910–1998).

By 1988, when the column "Rewriting Literary History" was launched, the field of modern Chinese literary studies had already made great advances in terms of material collection, theoretical experimentation, and the research team. The column met the demand for the development and reinvention of the field, a reinvention that required the further liberation of thought, a greater stress on scientific methods in scholarship, and a concerted effort to fight back against the intervention and constraints imposed by the political system.

After the Tiananmen Incident in June 1989, "Rewriting Literary History" received attacks from extreme leftists, who attempted to categorize the column as "bourgeois liberalism." But the authorities never released any official opinion on this controversy. The editorial work of the *Shanghai Literary Forum* was not interfered with directly. The last issue of the journal that featured the column, published in the winter of 1989, was entirely devoted to "Rewriting Literary History." Xiaoming and I published a long dialogue to refute the attacks of the leftists and announce the end of the column.

In the 1990s, the party-dominated literary history textbooks gradually lost market share, and more and more serious scholars pursued studies in modern Chinese literature. Approximately a decade later, a number of new studies in literary history emerged and testified to the lasting verve of scholarly efforts to "rewrite literary history." For examples, the emphasis on interpreting classical Chinese literature through the lens of humanism and the new concepts of the *minjian* (nonofficial) and "invisible writing" have all opened up new space for literary history.

In 1993–1994, Xiaoming and I were involved in the debate over the "humanist spirit" on the eve of China's rapid marketization. Once again, we, together with other scholars of our generation, took a stand against the prevailing trends within Chinese society, and defended literature not only against political interventions, but also against a sweeping commercialization, which has changed China since the 1990s. The effort to "rewrite literary history," still a lively part of China's intellectual life, has continued.

BIBLIOGRAPHY: Dai Yan, *Wenxueshi de quanli* (Beijing, 2002). Yang Qingxiang, *"Chongxie" de xiandu: Chongxie wenxueshi de xiangxiang he shijian* (Beijing, 2011).

CHEN SIHE
Translated by Mingwei Song

1989 · MARCH 26

We love for poets to kill themselves.

Anything Chinese about This Suicide?

The freight train near Shanhaiguan was going slow. Haizi (1964–1989) threw himself under the wheels from the side. His head and heart remained whole, but his body was cut in two at the abdomen. His glasses weren't even scratched. The train crew never realized what had happened.

Thus died Haizi in March 1989 at age twenty-five, in the words of his fellow poet and posthumous editor Luo Yihe (1961–1989). His suicide would make him a god. Luo died less than two months later after collapsing in Tiananmen Square in the heyday of the protest movement, a few weeks before the tanks rolled in on June 4. He didn't take his own life, but his death has been made to look like suicide, in the popular imagination and in scholarship, as an expression of loyalty to Haizi, and another sinister moment in that fated year to link to the massacre—martyrs of poetry as an omen of national-cultural tragedy.

A spree of lesser-known suicides in poetry circles followed. One was Fang Xiang (1962–1990), who took poison in 1990. He was reported to have traveled to Haizi's hometown in Anhui Province to perform memorial rites in his honor before ending his own life. The next high-profile poet suicide came in 1991, when Ge Mai (1976–1991) drowned himself in a sewage ditch near Peking University. Another came in 1993, when Gu Cheng (1956–1993) hanged himself after murdering his wife, Xie Ye (1958–1993), near their home on Waiheke Island in New Zealand.

Within a few years, a major publisher successively brought out the complete works of Gu Cheng, Haizi, Luo Yihe, and Ge Mai in four big, black volumes. Especially for the latter three, who had published little while alive, these tomes / tombs embody the fascination we feel for suicide—always, but especially if the self-killer is an artist, and dies a young and violent death.

Going back through China's long twentieth century, we see Wen Jie (1923–1971) inhaling gas in 1971, Yang Hua (1906–1936) hanging himself in 1936, Zhu Xiang (1904–1933) jumping off a ship into the Yangtze in 1933, and Wang Guowei (1877–1927) going under in a pond in the Imperial Gardens of Beijing in 1927. Further back in time—in lore, if not myth—we see Tang dynasty great Li Bai (701–762), whose "madness" aligns him with the allure of the modern poet suicide, compensating for the fact that his death by drowning in 762 was really a drunken accident. We also see Qu Yuan (340–278 BCE), legendary ancestor to tragically dying Chinese poets through the ages, whose self-killed body sank to the bottom of the river Luo well over two thousand years ago.

Suicide

Suicide has been around forever, and not just for the poets. Since Émile Durkheim (1858–1917), it has been on the menu in sociology, anthropology, psychology, philosophy, medicine, law, religious studies, history, and the study of literature and art. It is also a favorite topic in popular media. Naturally so, since suicide is as existential as it gets. Ending one's life, and leaving the Order of Things in both biological and social terms, is a transgression so fundamental that it *cannot be ignored*. Paradoxically, as a turning-away if not an ultimate gesture of rejection, suicide forces those who live on to respond, to speak to one who has gone irreversibly silent and deaf, to reach out to one who has let go. The response almost invariably includes the question of why, as an utterance of personal despair or of professional reflection, be it by a psychiatrist or a music critic. Even if the question is not asked, it is usually answered, whether we know what we're talking about or not.

Like other topics that are arguably beyond comprehension, we have managed to categorize suicides nonetheless. From a sociological viewpoint, Durkheim speaks of egoistic, altruistic, and anomic suicides. The respective causes are insufficient integration in society, complete absorption by a group or a cause, and bewilderment after overwhelming, radical change in one's social position. If we contextualize these categories today, they still make sense. Clinical psychologist Thomas Joiner sees the danger zone in feelings of ineffectiveness and being a burden to others, a sense of isolation, and the acquired ability to hurt oneself and to endure pain. For pain, think of prostitutes, soldiers, and athletes. But perhaps of poets too, on account of their extreme, sometimes maniacal, exertion for their art.

The state of mind and body preceding the act of suicide is incommunicable in language. As such, discussing actual, completed suicide—always someone else's—is the domestication in words of the unspeakable, and there is something obscene about it. But we do it all the time, from emotional accounts of loved ones dying by their own hand to polite conversation on strangers perishing under political repression in faraway places.

Poets

We know that poets—and painters, and rock stars—are especially prone to taking their own lives, and we find their suicides especially interesting. We find them glorious and glamorous, at the same time as tragic. In fact, we love for poets to kill themselves. We highlight the agency in their stories, not the helplessness. The image of suicide as the poem to end all poems is a case in point, as attractive as it is questionable.

Our love of self-killing poets bears no relation to how well we have read their poetry. (Outside the halls of academe, that other "death of the author" has gone unnoticed.) It is to do with our fascination for the poet as one whose genius has enabled a previous transgression, from our pedestrian realities into a realm that is enchanted and Other. Like all art, this process mobilizes *and* violates distinctions of the public and the private, so each one of us can privately own the public poet. By burning the bridges back to our world, the suicide reaffirms the poet's genius. Hence, the reflex to scan their poetry after the event for predictions of their death, as an extreme instance of the process of communicating *and* short-circuiting communication that lies at the heart of much modern poetry.

On September 21, 2006, Jeroen Mettes (1978–2006), whose relentless critique of the Dutch poetry scene was shaking texts and authors to the core, and whose posthumous *N30+* is a shocking masterpiece, left a final blog post before he stopped speaking and listening forever. It was empty.

China

Is there anything Chinese about poet suicides in or from modern China, beyond the language in which they wrote? Might Chinese poets be especially inclined to die from the Self ($\approx$ egoistic), or to die for a Cause ($\approx$ altruistic)? Might dying by one's own hand be more glorious and glamorous for a poet in or from China than elsewhere, or less so? And might the violence and upheaval of China's modern times move us to expand the category of the anomic suicide to include deaths triggered by disintegration of the social and epistemological fabric at large, such as when an empire collapses, or a society turns on itself in mass psychosis?

The legacy of romanticism has made modern poethood the stuff of proud singularity and tragic heroism, maladjustment, alienation, and exile in every sense of the word, not to mention suicide. In late Qing and early Republican China, romanticism fell on fertile ground, feeding into multiple reinventions of poethood throughout the twentieth century and beyond. These emerge against a background in which the towering status of the poet in imperial China looms large—even if poethood was then not a profession, or a social category, in itself. Rather, writing poetry came with membership of a literate elite whose privilege it was to dedicate their lives to the issue of ultimate concern: governing the state. When the imperial order crumbled, Chinese poethood entered an identity crisis that has become the habitat of the moderns, without stopping them from writing beautiful poetry.

Early in the twentieth century, during the New Culture Movement, reformist, often foreign-educated intellectuals attacked the Chinese cultural tradition, including classical poetry. At the same time, they remained obsessed with that tradition. As such, modern Chinese poets tasked themselves with fundamentally rethinking and "modernizing" Chinese poetry, while grappling with the loss of the status the poet had traditionally enjoyed, and negotiating a complex, uneasy relationship with foreign literatures. This balancing act has continued to the present day, in various historical settings. From the mid-1920s onward, as a result of political conflict and war, the literary scene was thoroughly politicized. In midcentury, this culminated in censorial, suffocating Maoist prescriptions for literature and art that reduced them to tools in the service of politics. Initially, individual poets could still enjoy exceptional fame, as long as their poetics fit the bill, but the Cultural Revolution (1966–1976) razed personal status for any poet but Mao Zedong (1893–1976) himself to the ground.

*Under*ground, a new generation of poets turned away from Maoist aesthetics, and found inspiration in clandestinely circulated foreign literature in translation. From the 1980s onward, their "avant-garde" poetry has flourished and outshone "orthodox," state-sanctioned modern poetry, certainly outside China's borders. At the same time, it continues to suffer from political repression, now coupled with marginalization by the forces of commercialization and popular culture. Throughout all this, the avant-garde has seen the emergence of a "cult" of poetry, and of poethood. Its religious overtones, penchant for the grandiose, and infighting suggest subtle complicity with Maoist aesthetics, and distant kinship with the New Culture Movement. The cult facilitates a favorable view of the poet's suicide. This enables the portrayal of Zhu Xiang as having "died for poetry," against all the evidence. It lends credibility to the story of Fang Xiang performing memorial rites for Haizi and then killing himself. It makes martyrdom for poetry seem a self-evident thing. And so on.

To be sure, the cult has not gone uncontested, and its harshest critics—poets themselves—ridicule the poet suicide. Like the cult's proponents, its detractors are near-exclusively male, which has held for aggressively vocal activists on the modern mainland Chinese poetry scene. It also holds for all the well-known Chinese poet suicides to date.

Yes and No

Does all this help in reflecting on the Chineseness of poet suicides in modern China?

Yes, it helps, if we indulge in speculation on the unspeakable, and accept that even then, the picture remains incomplete. Let's look at four of the poets encountered previously, whose motives may have been the most mutually distinct.

1927. For Wang Guowei, the sheer scope and depth of the crisis of meaning he experienced when his China seemed to fall apart offers a credible explanation of his decision to drown himself. So, let's call this a modern Chinese suicide of the anomic kind, and charge it to social upheaval. But was it the *poet* Wang Guowei who drowned himself—or the intellectual caught between the millstones of cultures in conflict, or the Qing dynasty loyalist?

1971. The subjective and the political offer helpful perspectives for categorizing motives, and reflection on Wen Jie's (1923–1971) ordeal requires both. And yet, would he have killed himself if he had not suffered the cruelties of Maoist China at its maddest? So, another modern Chinese suicide chalked up to social upheaval. But again, was it the *poet* Wen Jie who gassed himself? Or the human being with limits to his tolerance for torture?

1989. Haizi's life, his death, and his apotheosis were locally rooted in the cult of poetry. So, a modern Chinese suicide that was at once egoistic and altruistic, with Self and Cause—poetry!—difficult if not impossible to disentangle. And even though he suffered from illness in the months prior to his death, yes, it was the *poet* Haizi who threw himself under a freight train.

1993. "Dee-de-lee-dee." This is the title of an (in)famous, nonsensical poem by Gu Cheng, typical of the disintegrative turn his art took in his later years. Of the four deaths here subjected to speculation, his was most clearly linked to the linguistic meltdown that some modern poetry wants to trigger, without quite crossing the line into incomprehensibility, arbitrariness, and insanity. So, no, there is nothing Chinese about this suicide, which comes under the egoistic kind. And if we say yes, it was the *poet* Gu Cheng who hanged himself, this does not blind us to his mood disorders—or to the unimaginable impact of murdering someone he could not live without.

And no, of course it doesn't help.

BIBLIOGRAPHY: Alfred Alvarez, *The Savage God: A Study of Suicide* (London, 1971). Maghiel van Crevel, *Chinese Poetry in Times of Mind, Mayhem and Money* (Leiden, Netherlands, 2008). David Der-wei Wang, *The Monster That Is History: History, Violence, and Fictional Writing in Twentieth-Century China* (Berkeley, CA, 2004). Michelle Yeh, "The 'Cult of Poetry' in Contemporary China," *Journal of Asian Studies* 55, no. 1 (1996): 51–80.

MAGHIEL VAN CREVEL

1989 · MAY 19

"Nothing to My Name"

The Song That Rocked Tiananmen Square

Cui Jian (1961–) wrote "Nothing to My Name" to perform at a nonprofit concert held at Beijing's Workers Stadium on May 9, 1986, in celebration of the International Year of Peace. More than a hundred young Chinese singers were invited to perform the theme song of the concert, "Let the World Be Full of Love," and some would also have the chance to present their own songs during the rest of the program. Cui, then twenty-five years old and not as well known as some of his contemporaries, could not have anticipated how the audience would respond to his new song, a simple piece revolving around only a few chords.

In retrospect, the well-intended optimism of "Let the World Be Full of Love" was never fully convincing to the listening public, even though the song was replayed endlessly subsequent to its premier. In contrast, "Nothing to My Name" went on to become one of the most influential songs in China, loved by rockers and karaoke singers alike. Although rock music has been considered suspect and sometimes has been suppressed by the government, "Nothing to My Name" has never been banned in China, and even the official *People's Daily* has acknowledged it as one of the great songs of the recent era. Since its first broadcast, the song has accumulated meaning and significance, transforming from the love song that Cui initially intended into a hymn of individual freedom in defiance of the authorities in the post–Mao Zedong (1893–1976) era. Cui has already secured his position as the founder and godfather of Chinese rock music, yet, although he has gone through several stages of evolution as a musician and artist, "Nothing to My Name" still overshadows all his other creative undertakings.

Before "Nothing to My Name" made history, the Chinese general public had had virtually no exposure to the sound and feel of rock 'n' roll. For decades revolutionary songs and model plays, with their theatrical gestures and politically charged heroism, had constructed a soundscape that was both ubiquitous and stifling. With the exception of a few Russian folk-influenced songs such as "Moscow Nights" and "Katyusha," people rarely heard anything expressing individual sentiments and values. In the early 1980s, Taiwanese and Hong Kong pop music, themselves highly derivative of Western and Japanese pop music, began to emerge as alternatives to state-sponsored music for radio listeners and the much-envied owners of stereo systems. These songs were typically characterized by light, catchy rhythms, saccharine lyrics, and easy-listening melodies. In that musical environment, "Nothing to My Name," with its intense and explosive energy, was something entirely new, and it expressed the shock, painful self-doubt, and sense of loss shared by many people in the aftermath of the Cultural Revolution.

"I used to ask you again and again / when you will go with me?" With the sound of those first two lines, the audience at Workers Stadium shouted and burst into applause. Then Cui sang the next famous lines: "But you always laughed at me / Because I had nothing to my name." The song continued with a complaint about an unnamed lover's contempt for the speaker's poverty—his lack of both material means and political connections. The audience would easily recognize the allusion to the anthem "The Internationale": the standard translation of "Nous ne sommes rien" at the end of the first verse is "yi wu suo you" (nothing to my name).

The rest of the song expresses the speaker's resolution to hold the reluctant lover's trembling hand so that they might walk away together, but it is unclear whether the lover agrees and in what direction they are headed. This inconclusive ending also left the audience wondering what the song should mean to them. They might ask themselves whether the common people in a socialist society should possess nothing for themselves and contribute selflessly to the future communist utopia, which then would reward the whole of humanity. This grand empty promise was shattered by Cui's powerful repetitions of the word "nothing" in the song.

"Nothing to My Name" resonated socially and emotionally with Chinese listeners of different ages and backgrounds, from disillusioned former Red Guards to young college students, and from middle-aged factory workers to the "educated youths" who returned to the cities from rural China and tried to start a new life. When Cui performed the song at the home of Ah Cheng (1949–) in 1986, the famous "educated youth" writer and his friends were so taken by it that they asked him to sing more. As Ah Cheng said, Cui's songs are "like Tang dynasty poetry in that they have an original power and simplicity, and are easy to sing along to." "Nothing to My Name" also quickly became a standard number for guitar players to cover, although it was not necessarily recognized as rock music. At the time, the song was often identified as a masterpiece of the "Northwest style," a style that combines powerful vocals with folk influences from the northwestern region of China.

In the late 1980s, the Taiwanese music producer Landy Chang (1962–) shrewdly recommended that Cui stop using the term "rock 'n' roll" to describe his music and instead adopt the more descriptive name "knife songs," taking a cue from Cui's own song "Like a Knife." Chang suggested that in so doing, Cui could highlight the most important characteristics of his music: cool, sharp, and to the point. In the end, Cui did not take Chang's advice. His music falls unmistakably into the category of rock, but it took him and other Chinese rockers several more years to establish rock 'n' roll as musical genre in the eyes of music critics and their growing fan base. But "knife" is still a valid metaphor for both his attitude and his sound. As Cui proudly claimed during a concert in 2006, "As we said twenty years ago, if Western rock music was like a flood, then Chinese rock was like a knife. Back then we were faced with an even harder soil than now, but our rights were like a knife firmly thrust into this land."

Although most cultural commentators, music critics, and cognoscenti today agree that Cui was the first Chinese rock star, the infiltration of rock into Red China actually started much earlier and had already influenced several generations before Cui's. Along with modernist literature, rock 'n' roll was openly criticized in Communist propaganda as decadent, poisonous, and rotten to the core, an epitome of the moribund capitalist culture of the West. As early as the late 1950s, critiques of Elvis Presley (1935–1977) appeared in Chinese newspapers and magazines. His music was branded "both shameless and pointless," but the music itself was not made unavailable to Chinese listeners. Over the years, rock music gradually transcended the Iron Curtain. In the 1960s and 1970s, rock 'n' roll was emblematic of a dangerously enticing undercurrent of youthful rebellion; it was, however, only accessible to elites and those in the cultural vanguard.

The magnetism of rock's raucous sounds and heavy beats first inspired curiosity from people close to the center of power. A case in point is Lin Liguo (1945–1971), the ambitious son of veteran army commander and vice chairman of the Chinese Communist Party Lin Biao (1907–1971). A graduate of Peking University turned high-ranking official in the air force, Lin Liguo was an avid fan of Western rock bands, including the Beatles. Much of his short life is shrouded in mystery and guesswork, since his father's coup against Mao ended in the demise of Lin Liguo and his entire family in 1971. Lin's love of rock music and his guitar playing, however, remained legendary in the 1970s among the young Beijing elite.

Rock and other Western popular music genres also managed to reach some forward-looking members of the "educated youth," urban youths sent to the countryside during the Cultural Revolution, through shortwave radio. As Ah Cheng recalls, he and his friends were fascinated by "enemy radio stations" in the 1970s. Ah Cheng particularly liked to listen to the BBC, not because he wanted to learn English, but because it broadcast live concerts. When he first listened to Teresa Teng (1953–1995), a Taiwanese pop star, he became desperate to gain access to more of her music. Upon hearing the news of Mao's death and the downfall of the Gang of Four in 1976, he and his friends went swimming in the nude and partied with girls in the wilderness; songs played on a guitar were an indelible part of his memory of the end of the Cultural Revolution. As China entered the post-Mao era, it was only a matter of time before someone would introduce rock music to a wider audience in China.

Cui was born into a musical family. His father was a professional trumpeter in the air force band and his mother was a dancer. Both were ethnically Korean. Cui began to study the trumpet at the age of fourteen and became a professional musician in the Beijing Philharmonic

Orchestra in 1981—a "cultural worker" and a cog in the socialist cultural industry. In the early 1980s, foreign tourists and international students introduced waves of new music from the West to young Chinese musicians. Cui quickly explored a wide range of rock, pop, and country music, and felt compelled to pick up a guitar and write his own songs. In 1984, he released an album of pop songs entitled *The Return of the Prodigal Son*. Though the songs easily surpassed the standard of the time, the album failed to exert much influence on the contemporary music scene and has been largely forgotten even among his fans. Cui's strength as a musician lay elsewhere: in the alchemy that seamlessly blended Western influences with Chinese folk styles and instruments. For instance, one of his earliest rock songs, "It's Not That I Don't Get It," is an uplifting combination of reggae and a vocal delivery that resembles both rap and the traditional form of rhythmic Chinese storytelling known as "bamboo talk."

Yet it is Cui's extraordinary talent as a lyricist that makes his songs so attractive to young listeners. Avoiding age-old clichés and sugarcoated sentimentality, his lyrics flow with verve and ingenuity. In 1996, the lyrics to "Nothing to My Name" and "The Space Here" were included in *Classics of a Hundred Years of Literature*, an anthology published by Peking University Press. The editor, Xie Mian (1932–), is a preeminent poetry critic and a professor of Chinese literature at Peking University. The anthologization of Cui's song lyrics as literary masterpieces established him as a poet and a major cultural voice in the long tradition of Chinese poetry. Cui's canonization was reaffirmed by the novelist Wang Shuo (1958–), who gave him the epithet "contemporary China's greatest troubadour."

Cui's song "Go beyond That Day" is a good example of his power as a poet so sensitive to the realities in China that his work can sometimes seem prophetic. The song was written in 1997 to commemorate the transfer of sovereignty over Hong Kong from the United Kingdom back to China. The lyrics dramatize the relationship between the singer and Hong Kong as being akin to that of a brother and his lost sister, whom he has never met. The brother is confused that his mother (metaphorically representing the Chinese government) never told him about his sister, but then suddenly announces that she is coming home. He fires a torrent of questions at his mother: "Will she really respect you? Will she really admire me? If you're really angry, will she fear you like I do? If we're close for a few years then start to fight, will we love each other then? If you two decide to part, who should I go with?" The rhetorical devices at work here are simple, but they serve as a deep representation of a Chinese artist's fear and insecurity, and the way those emotions are bound up with the nation's politicized history and unpredictable future.

Today, Cui is still one of the most active musicians in China. A national and international icon, he sang "Wild Horses" with Mick Jagger (1943–) as a special guest at the Rolling Stones' concert in Shanghai in 2006. He has been awarded many prizes, including international honors. Most recently he won the Italian Tenco Prize in 2013, whose past recipients include such luminaries as Elvis Costello (1954–), Patti Smith (1946–), and Joni Mitchell (1943–).

Aside from Cui's first foray into the mainstream in 1986, his most memorable moment as a performer may well be his free live show in Tiananmen Square on May 19, 1989, when nearly a million people gathered to demonstrate their yearning for democracy, social justice, and freedom. By then the demonstration had lasted more than a month and the public mood was becoming increasingly tense. Few in the square, however, could have foreseen that the demonstration would culminate in a bloody military crackdown ordered by the government on June 4. The incident marks the last mass movement with a revolutionary fervor in twentieth-century Chinese history, but it has since remained a forbidden subject in China. May 19, 1989, thus becomes a date for anticipatory nostalgia. As Cui sang "Nothing to My Name" in support of the movement, a multitude of voices joined him like a maelstrom of hope for a better future. Today, Cui still continues his musical explorations, though that future has not yet arrived.

BIBLIOGRAPHY: Ah Cheng, "Ting ditai," in *Qishi niandai*, ed. Bei Dao and Li Tuo (Beijing, 2009). Ah Cheng, *Weinisi riji* (Beijing, 1997). Jonathan Campbell, *Red Rock: The Long, Strange March of Chinese Rock and Roll* (Hong Kong, 2011). Sheng Zhimin, dir., *Night of an Era* [documentary] (2009).

AO WANG

1989 · SEPTEMBER 8

A City of Sadness wins the Golden Lion Award and the prize for best picture in the competition section of the Forty-Sixth Venice Film Festival.

Trauma and Cinematic Lyricism

A City of Sadness (1989), the first installment of Hou Hsiao-hsien's (1947–) Taiwan trilogy (followed by *The Puppetmaster* in 1993 and *Good Men, Good Women* in 1995), was the first Chinese-language picture to win a major international film award. The film depicts the February 28 Incident in 1947 Taiwan—a brutal attack on civilians and an atrocity inflicted on leftist dissidents—the boiling point in the strained relations between the people of Taiwan and the Nationalist government following Japan's return of the island to China at the end of World War II.

Hou's achievement was monumental, as a leading European film body affirmed not only the significance of his own creation but also the creative energy of the Taiwan New Cinema and literature. Drawing on the literary resources of Taiwanese authors Chu T'ien-wen (1956–) and Lan Bozhou (1960–), Hou's *A City of Sadness* incorporates fiction and reportage into a cinematic rendering of Taiwan's scarred past. And "monumental" is hardly an overstatement in describing Hou's milestone, given that it was the first Chinese-language film honored at Venice and also a brilliant collaboration between a filmmaker and his literary muses. In reconstructing a notorious trauma in modern Taiwanese history, Hou's film conveys a literary dimension thanks to Chu and Lan. Lan's *Song of the Covered Wagon* provided the epic structure of the film, while Chu's screenplay contributed a lyrical stroke to the narrative, and the resulting collaboration between the three yielded an exquisite synergy of cinema, fiction, and reportage. The film's compelling depiction of history and memory is rendered through the interstices of biography and fiction, and the interplay of voice and image. It is the concerted delivery of a cinematic lyricism created by Hou, Chu, and Lan that enabled a lost "history" to be made, and then remade, in late twentieth-century Taiwan.

A City of Sadness centers on a local Taiwan family, the Lins, who, like most people on the island, anticipate better times after the war. The family has four brothers, and each copes differently with the postwar situation.

The central focus, meanwhile, is on the youngest son, Lin Wen-ching, who is deaf and mute and supports himself by operating a photo studio. Wen-ching and his circle believe socialism is the answer to Taiwan's postcolonial predicament. Wen-ching is arrested after the February 28 Incident but soon released. His best friend, Hinoe, decides to continue the struggle against the Nationalist Party (Kuomintang, or KMT) by joining the leftist guerrillas. Wen-ching supports the cause from behind the scenes, along with his wife, Hinomi, sister of Hinoe. Hinomi keeps a diary that includes a record of the February 28 Incident and the terror clutching the island. Hinoe's guerrilla commune is then raided by soldiers and Wen-ching is arrested again. Wen-ching's fellow prisoners are taken out and shot. The film ends with what is left of the deeply scarred Lin family, living through the wounds by struggling to maintain the mundane basis of their lives.

Restrictions on representing politically sensitive topics in Taiwan meant that depictions of the February 28 Incident had, up to that point, been completely suppressed. Audiences therefore flocked to see *A City of Sadness*, a film promising to violate a taboo in local history. Before the release of the film, Taiwanese who were interested in knowing this material had limited choices. One source was George H. Kerr's (1911–1992) *Formosa Betrayed* (1965), an eyewitness account that was banned in Taiwan. Another was far more informal but compelling—to consult close family members who were at the scene. For instance, my mother, a bystander during the uprising in February 1947, contradicted my high school history lesson, which represented the incident as a mild dispute between Chinese soldiers and local Taiwanese. She showed me a scar on her left leg, the result of stray gunfire, and shared her eyewitness account of the summary executions performed at the train station. When I told her about *A City of Sadness*, she was excited to learn that finally a feature film on this subject would be released and, perhaps, would exorcize a variety of demons.

Many viewers who shared similar sentiments about their scarred past anticipated seeing the film as a historical representation, if not a true recollection, of their generation's collective trauma. But most viewers were frustrated, including film critics and intellectuals, who proceeded to attack the film and the filmmakers for not using the suppressed history to make a clear indictment of the KMT. Critics quibbled over Hou's choice to render the film an elegy for the ill-fated historical past ("a city of sadness") instead of a hagiography of heroes and victims, those who sacrificed themselves for the cause of Taiwan's democratic future.

Why was there such an anguished reaction to the film that took Taiwan onto the world stage? Is *A City of Sadness* a historical film? Yes. There is no doubt about this, judging by its period setting and its subject matter. Is it an epic? This is uncertain, as it is not an epic narrative that focuses on the lives of people who changed history. Displacing the grand narrative concerning the sacrificial story of local heroes, Hou chooses to use a feminine voice and other textual resources, such as writing and photography, to historicize the February 28 Incident. In so doing, he draws from Lan Bozhou's reportage to ground his cinematic visualization of history. In other words, the film offers at least two textual accounts of history—one a macro account, a collective history of Taiwan and China; another one a micro account, a personal record of things past and present. These are not disparate accounts, and instead they intertwine and mutually accentuate one another: the macro account outlines the shape of the story, whereas the personal instills the past with a subjective autobiographical tone, resurrecting the past from its decay. The intersection of the collective and the personal is where we find the other, perhaps the most compelling part of *A City of Sadness*'s monumentality.

In "Thirteen Questions on *A City of Sadness*," the preface to the published screenplay of *A City of Sadness*, Chu T'ien-wen writes about the film's lyrical narration and how that may have caused the public's suspicion of the film. She argues that the core of Chinese literature resides in poetry and its lyrical mode, in comparison to the epic narrative style common in Western literature. Main differences between the lyrical and the epic include the following: first, the lyrical in Chinese literature does not privilege conflicts and therefore lacks the epic's drive to resolution; second, in Chinese poetry, nature is conceived as a transcendental being, without personality, and thus needs no reproach. Embodying precisely these lyrical cornerstones, the historical narrative of *A City of Sadness* chooses reflection over dramatization and forgiveness over confrontation. In many of the key moments of the film—the outbreak of the February 28 Incident, the execution of Wen-ching's friends, the capture of Hinoe, and the eventual arrest of Wen-ching—we see little excitement. Rather, Hou uses Hinomi's diary, her letters, and Wen-ching's photographs to relate the events of the incident and subsequent government crackdown on leftists, which destroyed many families in Taiwan. Through lyrical narration, *A City of Sadness* exceeds the bounds of a historical film and becomes a polyvalent text with a strong literary anchor.

Hou's foray into the mode of lyrical narration was inspired by Chu, his longtime scriptwriter. In many ways, Chu's contribution to Hou's oeuvre exceeds her writing credit. Chu has been Hou's closest collaborator since the 1980s, and to date they have worked together on fifteen pictures. It is no exaggeration to say Hou's authorship is indebted to his muse, Chu. An award-winning fiction writer in Taiwan, her noted works (including "Fin-de-Siècle Splendor" [1990] and *Notes of a Desolate Man* [1995]) offer a symbiosis of history, providence, and psychosis in complex interplays of time and space. When Hou faced a creative predicament in making his first autobiographical picture, *The Boys from Fengkuei* (1983), Chu offered him Shen Congwen's (1902–1988) autobiography. In reading Shen's depiction of his childhood life in the provinces of west Hunan, Hou found a new approach to rendering memory, and history. Taking stock of Shen's lyrical voice, which filters memory via a cosmic view of compassion and acceptance, Hou began to develop a cinematic lyricism tailored to the unique history of Taiwan.

Chu has inspired Hou to stage remembrances of the past by the careful filtering of emotional excess via Chinese lyricism. By embracing lyricism, Hou turns trauma into ambivalence toward brutality, or even resignation. With *The Boys from Fengkuei* and his biopic *A Time to Live, a Time to Die* (1984), Hou began to explore, with Chu's input, varieties of cinematic lyricism. He started to focus on a prolonged temporal duration in wide-shot compositions where dramatic actions are reduced to a minimum, inviting viewers to ponder events beyond the frame, and screen. The experiment with lyricism culminated in *A City of Sadness*. Photographs taken by Wen-ching, correspondences between Wen-ching and his comrades, and diary entries read aloud by Hinomi are all used as lyrical devices to forge a cosmic view of compassion and forbearance. These elements work as techniques of subjective poetics, a means of plunging the exteriority of cinematography into mental states and moods.

Aside from cinematic lyricism, and in order to anchor his depiction of Taiwan's past, Hou sought out biographies to sustain his engagement with the Chinese lyrical tradition. Here, Hou draws on the work of Lan Bozhou, a reportage writer specializing in Taiwan's dark past during the 1950s. Lan's *Song of the Covered Wagon* incorporates interviews, archival documents, and memories into his portrait of a Taiwanese couple, Zhong Haodong and Jiang Biyu, in their lifelong struggle against colonialism and authoritarianism. Zhong and Jiang grew up in Japanese-occupied Taiwan. Having strong anticolonial views, they went to South China to join the war effort against Japan. After the war, Zhong pledged allegiance to socialism, hoping to liberate Taiwan from yet another authoritarian government. He was arrested, imprisoned, and then executed in 1950 for his refusal to renounce socialism. Jiang was also arrested but was acquitted for not having been directly involved in the subversion of the government.

"Song of the Covered Wagon" is a popular Japanese ballad from the 1930s, and it is also a song favored by Zhong and Jiang. The song conveys an unbearable separation, carried in the clip-clop of a covered wagon taking the beloved one away for good. Hence, Lan titled his book of the revolutionary couple after the song to commemorate their extraordinary deeds. Lan's manuscript was completed in 1988 and published in 1991. While preparing the script for *A City of Sadness*, Hou and Chu adapted Lan's story to set the stage for the principal characters and their calamity. A direct allusion to Lan's book can be found in the decision to feature "Song of the Covered Wagon" as the prison song in the film, when detained activists bid farewell to their comrades who are soon to be executed. Furthermore, Hou relies on and borrows from the record of Zhong's sacrifice for his delineation of the February 28 Incident, including the guerrilla war against the KMT and the subsequent scenes in the prison. Jiang, too, is the prototype for Hinomi. Before marrying Zhong and following him to China, Jiang was a nurse who admired Zhong's courage and devotion to the liberation of Taiwan. Hou therefore casts Hinomi as a nurse before she marries Wen-ching. Like Jiang, who is devoted to her husband and the revolutionary cause, Hinomi supports the underground Socialist movement against the Nationalist Party. After Zhong's execution, Jiang is left alone to raise her family. This too is mirrored in Hinomi's life after Wen-ching's arrest. In the last scene of the film, Hinomi writes to a family member reporting her husband's detainment, and her son's first tooth. Here Hou and Chu transform Jiang's devastation into a reticence toward death and separation by inserting Hinomi's calm voice in the soundtrack, as if she has overcome her grief and is ready to face the worst possible outcome. Here we see a poignant deployment of lyricism in counteracting the monstrosity of history.

In the Hou-Chu duo, we see a powerful connection between literature and film in Taiwanese cinema. This lyrical, literary imprint renders *A City of Sadness* a unique entry in Taiwan's cultural heritage of the twentieth century. The cinematic lyricism Hou crafted in *A City of Sadness* would continue to thrive in his later works, sustaining Hou's high reputation and tenure in world cinema. And the story of Zhong and Jiang continues in Hou's *Good Men, Good Women*, a sequel to *A City of Sadness* and the third picture in Hou's Taiwan trilogy.

A City of Sadness commemorates the sacrifice of Taiwanese civilians and their courage in the face of terror inflicted by authoritarian rule. This, rather than validation by a European jury, is the film's brilliance: it gave form to an event that for decades was invisible and unspeakable to a whole generation. It is a monumental vision presented through memory, reportage, and lyrical transposition.

BIBLIOGRAPHY: Markus Abe-Nornes and Emilie Yueh-yu Yeh, *Staging Memories: Hou Hsiao-hsien's "A City of Sadness"* (Ann Arbor, MI, 2015). Lan Bozhou, *Huangmache zhi ge*, expanded ed. (Taipei, 2004). Wu Nianzhen and Chu T'ien-wen, "Xu," in *Beijing chengshi* (Taipei, 1989), 1–31. Emilie Yueh-yu Yeh and Darrell William Davis, "Trisecting Taiwan Cinema with Hou Hsiao-hsien," in *A Treasure Island: Taiwan Film Directors* (New York, 2005), 133–176.

EMILIE YUEH-YU YEH

1990

Yearnings debuts in the People's Republic of China.

1991

The Golden Age wins Taiwan's Unitas Fiction Award.

From the Margins to the Mainstream: A Tale of Two Wangs

During the 1990s, writers Wang Shuo (1958–) and Wang Xiaobo (1952–1997) represented opposing poles of contemporary culture in the People's Republic of China (PRC). In November 1990, Wang Shuo proudly debuted his television series *Yearnings*, a melodramatic recounting of the tribulations of the Cultural Revolution. An instant success around the country, *Yearnings* placed Wang and his works at the heart of Chinese popular culture. The following year, Wang Xiaobo's novella *The Golden Age*, which would not be released on the mainland until 1994, won Taiwan's Thirteenth Annual Unitas Literary Award for Medium-Length Fiction, making him the first ever writer from mainland China to win the prize. The story's publication in China's Taiwanese periphery both literally and metaphorically reflects Wang's marginalized position in the PRC. The two men's careers represent distinct trajectories out of the exclusively state-controlled culture industry of the Maoist era: while Wang Xiaobo maintained his independence from the system, Wang Shuo helped to revolutionize the mainstream.

Like many in their generation, the two Wangs were deeply influenced by their experiences during the Cultural Revolution (1966–1976). In 1968, at the age of sixteen, Wang Xiaobo arrived in rural Yunnan as a member of Beijing's *zhiqing*, the "educated youth." At the height of the Cultural Revolution and faced with a society increasingly paralyzed by violent clashes between youth factions, Mao Zedong (1893–1976) and other leaders of the Communist Party made the decision to send some sixteen million urban teenagers to labor on farms in the distant countryside. For some, going to the countryside was a voluntary experience that represented the highest commitment to and faith in the Maoist world order. But for the vast majority of the so-called sent-down youth, it was a nightmarish exile. Many were beaten and abused by their resentful peasant hosts, the very people from whom they were supposed to learn the lessons of socialism firsthand. While some only remained in the countryside for a few months, others did not return to their homes for over a decade.

The time Wang Xiaobo spent in Yunnan profoundly shook his faith in Chinese society. In what became one of his most venerated essays, "The Silent Majority," Wang recalls how he began to view his interactions with the locals as a kind of performance: "How the local people viewed us, besides noting that we dressed a little better and had whiter skin, is a complete mystery to me. I believe they thought of us as people standing onstage, and felt they had to speak to us in stage language." Convinced by his experience as a sent-down youth that he "could not trust those who belonged to the societies of speech," Wang chose to remain "silent" for nearly twenty years, refusing to participate in political debates or publish his prose or fiction.

While Wang Xiaobo was banished to the southwest, his fellow Beijinger, Wang Shuo, was just young enough to avoid being sent down. The young Wang relished the Cultural Revolution as an opportunity to defy the hypocritical Maoist authority figures who surrounded him, particularly his father, who had served as a policeman for the Nationalist government before becoming a Communist political instructor. Wang ran wild in the streets of Beijing with a gang of his fellow youths, and was arrested twice before he reached the age of eighteen.

Following the end of the Cultural Revolution, Wang Shuo's lawless, aimless companions grew up to become the great social specter that haunted China during the 1980s—the *liumang*. The word *liumang* encompasses a wide range of social delinquency; one list proposed by the scholar John Minford includes the "rapist, whore, black-marketeer, unemployed youth, alienated intellectual, frustrated artist or poet." Wang himself undertook a variety of occupations, ranging from the unsavory to the outright illegal: working as a salesman for a pharmaceutical company, serving as a bagman, and smuggling. When Wang began writing in the early 1980s, he saw it as yet another hustle. He based his choice of subject for his breakout 1984 hit, *The Stewardess*, on market considerations: "Writing something about a girl was a good trick." The considerably talented Wang made a name for himself by telling stories of *liumang*—and their slightly more innocuous brethren, the *pizi*, "hooligan" or "punk"—in their own language, in such works as *Surfacing from the Sea*, *Masters of Mischief*, and *Playing for Thrills*. By selling what his critics demonized as *"pizi* literature," Wang was successful enough to become something even more threatening to the socialist order than a *liumang*—a *getihu*, or self-employed worker.

As Wang Shuo's books flew off the shelves, Wang Xiaobo, still troubled by his experience during the Cultural Revolution, kept his writing to himself. On party orders, Wang returned to Beijing in 1973 to become a factory worker. He later passed the first college entrance exams held following the Cultural Revolution, and in 1982 became a professor of accounting at Renmin University. When his wife, the now renowned sexologist Li Yinhe (1952–), went to study abroad in the United States in 1984, Wang followed her, and the couple remained there for four years. All the while, Wang continued to write about his various life experiences, although he still did not dare to share them with the public.

Following the death of his father—a logician by training, he expressly forbade his children from engaging in the humanities because he knew the political risks associated with it—and no longer willing to suppress his talent, Wang finally decided to break his silence. In 1991, he published what would become his representative work, *The Golden Age*, a sexually charged, carnivalesque story that reveals and revels in the unreliability of speech for a sent-down youth in Yunnan during the Cultural Revolution. Narrated by protagonist Wang Er in retrospect from the early 1990s, the novella tells the story of his evolving relationship with Chen Qingyang, who is sent down from Shanghai. Chen and Wang find themselves consistently at odds with the arbitrary goals and regulations of the collective and are eventually arrested. When forced to confess their "crimes," the most egregious turns out to be having fallen in love.

Although Chen and Wang avoid consummating their relationship at first, they are ultimately shunned by the commune as a sexually depraved, bourgeois couple. Consequently, they decide to engage in the behaviors of which they have been accused and learn to revel in the abuse they receive for playing their reactionary roles so well. As it turns out, it is precisely the party's drive to discipline improper socialist subjects that enables the protagonists to freely engage in their private pleasures. Owing to the novella's irreverent treatment of socialist values and ideological dogma, Wang was originally forced to publish *The Golden Age* outside the PRC, and the story's later domestic release was only made possible due to his relationships with members of the publishing industry. Despite its tumultuous road to publication, *The Golden Age* won Wang many supporters overseas, and his work presaged the focus on individualism and individual desire that would come to dominate many of the cultural discussions during the 1990s in the PRC.

The year before *The Golden Age* won accolades abroad, Wang Shuo produced a very different account of the impact of the Cultural Revolution on the individual: the television drama *Yearnings*. Wang initially saw television writing as a way to get his name in the papers and drum up free publicity for his novels. In collaboration with a team of writers for the Beijing Television Arts Center, Wang, in his typically cynical and irreverent *pizi* fashion, applied a simple set of crowd-pleasing heuristics ("Raise up the good and punish the bad"; "Those of humble origins are the smartest, the high and mighty are the most foolish") to create a program sure to corner the market. The result was a soap opera centering on the relationships between the working-class Lius and the intelligentsia Wangs as they suffered through the Cultural Revolution and the culture shock of the early reform era. In the aftermath of the Tiananmen Square Incident, this simple morality tale met the needs of a traumatized and politically exhausted nation that wished for nothing more than the promise made by the show's treacly theme song, that "good people will lead peaceful lives." *Yearnings* was such a massive (and ideologically correct) hit when it debuted in 1990 that the *liumang* writer earned the public praise of a sitting member of the Politburo, Li Ruihuan (1934–).

In part owing to the mainstream success of *Yearnings*, Wang was able to turn the entire publishing system of the PRC on its head. During the Maoist era, writers were compensated through manuscript fees set at a pitifully low rate, which forced them to make ends meet through sinecures in the state cultural bureaucracy. Wang, who had always hated the staid bureaucrats and hack writers supported by the system, was determined to break it. When it came time to release a collection of his complete works in 1992, he hired a professional literary agent and negotiated a contract that awarded him royalties—two firsts for mainland China.

For Wang, financial independence also meant creative independence. As he put it in an interview for *Shanghai Literature*, "In the past I wrote fiction because I had to make a living. Now you can really say it's a loving relationship: I write fiction for myself." Indeed, even as he found mainstream success, Wang continued to create works of high literary merit, such as the 1991 novella *Ferocious Animals*. *Ferocious Animals* is a semiautobiographical account of a teenager named Fang Yan and a gang of kids who cut school and roam a semideserted Beijing one summer during the final years of the Cultural Revolution. The novella combines sentimental lyricism and disturbing bouts of violence, the thrill of youthful liberation and the abuse of the resulting power. It ends in a meaningful comment on the historiography of the Cultural Revolution, as the narrator, an adult Fang Yan, begins to question the reliability of his own memory—just as the deeds of the adolescent Fang Yan become unforgivably reprehensible.

As Wang Shuo became a household name in the PRC, Wang Xiaobo continued building his reputation outside its borders. After much persuasion by his wife, Wang Xiaobo agreed to adapt his novella *Gentle like Water* into what would become the international film-festival sensation *East Palace, West Palace*. The novella is a fictional abstraction based on a series of sociological surveys conducted by Wang and his wife that were later published under the title *Their World: Perspectives from the Male Homosexual Community in China*, the first study of its kind to be published in the PRC. The story takes place in a Beijing public park known for its *particular* clientele, and relates the experience of one such individual's arrest by a policeman and subsequent interrogation. What begins as a public official's attempt to correct a socially deviant member of society, however, turns out to reveal that official's own desire to transgress against public morals; knowing full well that the woman kneeling before him is in fact a biological man, the policeman receives fellatio in a state-owned police box. Consequently, the line between perversion and pleasure is proven to be ambiguous, if not mutually reinforcing. When the film was selected for the 1997 Cannes Film Festival's Un Certain Regard series, Wang Xiaobo and the film's director, Zhang Yuan (1963–), rocketed to art-house fame.

Over the course of the 1990s, Wang Xiaobo transformed from a member of the "silent majority" into an outspoken public intellectual. In his capacity as a writer, Wang took it as his personal mission to confront the despotism of the Chinese Communist Party and advocate for the freedom to pursue individual desires in Chinese society. On November 4, 1997, however, that mission was tragically cut short when Wang died suddenly of a heart attack. In a piece written to memorialize her husband, Li Yinhe styles Wang a "Romantic Knight"—an honorable man who resolutely defended the people's right to justice and equality in a world that refused to recognize his value. These same qualities have helped to foster a cult following for Wang's work among the PRC's disempowered and downtrodden. A champion for those on the margins of Chinese culture, Wang Xiaobo was and remains a voice for the voiceless.

Wang Shuo, on the other hand, lived on to struggle with his own success. Occupied with a nearly endless conglomeration of media enterprises, Wang rarely published after 1992. In 1996, the state finally had enough of Wang's antisocial irreverence and temporarily banned his works. By the time Wang returned to print in 1999, he had transformed into an embittered cultural critic. In his 2000 essay collection *The Ignorant Fear Nothing*, Wang rails against a mass culture landscape in which "the tastes [of the masses] are the sole yardstick by which a work's success or failure is measured." Ironically, however, no one man is more responsible for this state of affairs than Wang himself; his name, along with that of his protégé, Feng Xiaogang (1958–), is now synonymous with mass-market entertainment. Wang Xiaobo's tragic and untimely death—at the height of his talent, and before he had a chance to become compromised by the system—transformed him into a revered cultural icon. Wang Shuo, meanwhile, has lived on to see himself become what he had always hated: the establishment.

BIBLIOGRAPHY: Geremie R. Barmé, *In the Red: On Contemporary Chinese Culture* (New York, 1999). Michael Berry, "Wang Xiaobo's Golden Age of the Cultural Revolution," in *A History of Pain: Trauma in Modern Chinese Literature and Film* (New York, 2008), 261–267. Lu Xiaowei, dir., *Kewang* (1990–1991). John Minford, "Picking up the Pieces," *Far Eastern Economic Review*, August 8, 1985, 30. Wang Xiaobo, *Wang in Love and Bondage: Three Novellas*, trans. Hongling Zhang and Jason Sommer (Albany, NY, 2007).

KYLE SHERNUK *and* DYLAN SUHER

1994 · JULY 30

Friends in a dorm room play a Dadaist word game.

Meng Jinghui and Avant-Garde Chinese Theater

Escaping the heat of midsummer on July 30, 1994, Meng Jinghui (1964–), a recent graduate of the master's program in directing at the Central Academy of Drama, joined his fellow alumnus Wang Xiaoli, along with composer-lyricist Huang Jingang (1970–) and academy library professor Shi Hang (1971–), in Shi's relatively cool cement room in the faculty dormitory. Lounging on the upper and lower bunk beds and cracking watermelon seeds between their teeth, the quartet tossed around an idea for a new play, an idea that Meng had thought up while trying to impress an attractive coed in the student dorm. The premise: What if every line of a play began with the phrase "I love…"? And what if this play had no plot, no characters, no story? What form would this "antiplay" take? What effect would it have on audiences? This kernel of an idea prompted the four pals to play a Dadaist word game that led to the most pathbreaking mainland Chinese theater production of 1994 (and arguably of the 1990s), *I Love XXX*.

Meng, Wang, Huang, and Shi fleshed out this idea with the aid of a book they had borrowed from the library: a Chinese translation of Clifton Daniels's (1912–2000) panoramic history *Chronicle of the 20th Century* (1987). The illustrated almanac presented history not in the typical socialist frame to which they were accustomed, but as a chronicle of notable political events juxtaposed with noteworthy daily happenings in the lives of individuals, as represented by the *New York Times* headlines from the first day of 1900 to the last day of 1986. Shi scribbled notes as the four friends took turns completing the phrase "I love…" with the names of significant people who died at the dawn of the twentieth century:

> I love the beautiful new century that began in 1900, the beautiful
>   new century that began in 1900
> I love that those great masters died, all those great masters died,
>   each and every one of those great masters died at the beginning
>   of the beautiful new century in 1900
> I love that German philosopher Friedrich Nietzsche died

I love that French writer Emile Zola died
I love that Russian playwright Anton Chekhov died
I love that Czech composer Antonin Dvorak died
I love that American authors Mark Twain, O. Henry, and Jack
    London died
I love that Russian literary giant Leo Tolstoy died
I love that Russian socialist theorist Vladimir Plekhanov died
I love that French painter Paul Gauguin died
I love that Norwegian composer Edvard Grieg died
I love that Norwegian playwright Henrik Ibsen died
I love that French sculptor Auguste Rodin died
I love that German bacteriologist Robert Koch died
I love that French science fiction writer Jules Verne died
I love that those great masters died, all those great masters died,
    each and every one of those great masters died, and that those
    stars were born, all those stars were born, each and every one of
    those stars was born
I love that this is an age when great masters die and stars are born

Shi, Meng, Huang, and Wang then listed important historical events
spanning the globe, events that are presented both affirmatively and
negatively in the play. This antihistorical gesture echoes the subversive
nature of the antiplay itself and its invitation to both recall and reimagine
modern history:

I love that all this happened
I love that all this never happened
I love that those absurd realities didn't happen…
I love that World War I didn't happen
I love that World War II didn't happen
I love that World War III didn't happen
I love that World War X didn't happen
I love that the assassination of the Archduke didn't happen
I love that abuse of prisoners of war didn't happen
I love that Haley's Comet blazing towards earth didn't happen
I love that ten million people dying of war and twenty million
    people dying of influenza didn't happen…

I love that the obscene rock 'n' roll singer Presley becoming US
   Army Private 53310761 didn't happen
I love that on his way back to Beijing the famous love poet Xu
   Zhimo being lost in a plane crash, being lost in a train crash,
   being lost on the operating table, and "Saying Goodbye to
   Cambridge Again" didn't happen

In addition to those of Xu Zhimo (1897–1931), the play *I Love XXX* integrates the lives and works of many traditional, modern, and contemporary Chinese writers, poets, and artists into its litany, along with Sinophone and international literary texts and cultural motifs. The resulting pastiche contextualizes Chinese literary production and domestic political culture in a pan-Chinese and global context. Ancient poetry is mentioned alongside the contemporary craze for English-language learning, and the names of iconic historical Beijing landmarks follow pop music hits of the 1970s–1980s:

I love *Three Hundred Tang Dynasty Poems*
I love *Four Hundred Song Dynasty Poems*
I love *Five Hundred Yuan Dynasty Poems*
I love *One Thousand and One Nights*
I love *Eight Thousand Miles of Clouds and Moon*
I love *One Hundred Thousand Whys*
I love Xu Guozhang's *English Book One*
I love moral, intellectual, physical education
I love math, physics, chemistry
I love male classmates, female classmates
I love substitute teachers and classroom monitors…
I love morning exercise
I love young love
I love sideburns
I love bell-bottoms
I love Sanyo tape recorders
I love Teresa Teng's "Fine Wine and Coffee," "When Will You
   Return?"
I love midterm exams, final exams, school entrance exams, college
   entrance exams

I love applications, transcripts, permission slips
I love Beijing's Chang'an Avenue
I love Beijing's Tiananmen Square

There are more than six hundred utterances of "I love" in the play, with the line "I love Beijing's Tiananmen Square" being among the most powerful. Though it appears only once in the written script, the line was repeated consecutively more than twenty times onstage in the December 1994 and May 1995 performances. This declaration mixes patriotic nostalgia with subversive commemoration, as it conjures both the revolutionary song that every Chinese citizen knows and the tragic controversial events of five years prior, when the prodemocracy movement in the enormous public square was violently suppressed on June 4, 1989.

If the political content did not push the boundaries enough, the erotic recitation of body parts in a section echoing Walt Whitman's (1819–1892) poem "I Sing the Body Electric" challenged mores and invited censorship. Indeed, the play was halted due to Meng's failure to procure a mandatory performance permit. Three months later, Meng was reprimanded after bringing the production to the Tiny Alice Festival in Tokyo without securing permission from his official work unit, the Central Experimental Theatre. Part of Meng's charm and appeal is his ability to take aesthetic and political risks in his work and his posture as a playful "badass." He was writing his MA thesis on Vsevolod Meyerhold (1874–1940) at the Central Academy of Drama during the June Fourth demonstrations, and began adapting classic Western experimental works such as Harold Pinter's (1930–2008) *The Dumb Waiter* and Samuel Beckett's (1906–1989) *Waiting for Godot*. Two years after his graduation, when he was assigned to the Central Experimental Theatre, he mounted a production of Jean Genet's (1910–1986) *The Balcony*. Meng acknowledges movements like Dadaism as a major influence, along with legendary global avant-garde theater directors and theorists like Meyerhold, Jerzy Grotowski (1933–1999), Bertolt Brecht (1898–1956), and Richard Foreman (1937–). In China, where he has attained similarly canonical status, his distinct aesthetic (and works by other directors who imitate it) is referred to as "Meng-style theater." His rehearsal techniques emphasize a playful atmosphere and collective improvisational techniques, much in keeping with the themes of collectivization that are prominent in *I Love XXX*. This staged "manifesto" was created by Meng, the other three playwrights, and the cast of actors in the same spirit as the material in the script: by mining their memories of their own childhood, during China's Cultural Revolution. The play functions as a theatricalized historical archive marked by emotional nostalgia for youth and the camaraderie of socialist education. The language is replete with grammatical confusions, double meanings, and satire and marked by the ambiguity that characterizes this generation's relationship to its lived history.

For the past twenty-five years, Meng has been the most prominent avant-garde theater director in China, but his work should be considered in the context of Chinese and Sinophone artists of the past century. Meng was inspired not only by foreign muses, but also by early twentieth-century pioneers of avant-garde theater in China. His immediate predecessors, including playwright Gao Xingjian (1940–) and director Lin Zhaohua (1936–) of the Beijing People's Art Theatre—China's premiere theater company, known for its locally grown "Beijing-flavor" plays—were part of the post–Cultural Revolution flowering of experimental theater in the mid-1980s. While Meng regularly disparages the repertoire of plays staged at the Beijing People's Art Theatre, he admires and respects Lin's productions, which include domestic plays like Jin Yun's (1938–) *Uncle Doggie's Nirvana,* adaptations of William Shakespeare's (1564–1616) *Hamlet* and *Richard III,* Johann Wolfgang von Goethe's (1749–1832) *Faust,* and a 1988 Anton Chekhov–Beckett mash-up entitled *Three Sisters Waiting for Godot.*

Meng was also aware of practitioners in Taiwan such as Lai Sheng-chuan (1954–), founder of the Performance Workshop. Like Meng, Lai is a director who makes use of improvisational collaborative work with actors in his creative process. His landmark 1986 production, *Secret Love in Peach Blossom Land,* is credited with nurturing new audiences for the modern theater. Revivals and new stagings of the play continue to proliferate (in both Chinese and English versions), most recently at the Oregon Shakespeare Festival in 2015. Lai has lived and worked in Taiwan, the United States, and mainland China, lending a distinct intercultural dimension to his more than twenty plays.

Hong Kong's Zuni Icosahedron, founded by Danny Yung (1943–) in 1982, has also influenced the development of avant-garde theater in mainland China. Meng collaborated with Yung for three projects between 1996 and 2000, all experimental adaptations of classics (*One Hundred Years of Solitude*, *Journey to the West*, and *King Lear*) featuring Zuni's hallmarks: use of digital media, reinterpretation of tradition, and social consciousness. Following in Meng's wake are younger directors like Beijing-based Wang Chong (1982–). Wang is adept at procuring international sources of funding and increasingly resourceful in finding ways to exhibit his works abroad. He deconstructs classic plays from the Western and Chinese canons alike (refashioning Ibsen in *Ghosts 2.0* and Lao She [1899–1966] in *Teahouse 2.0*), and has staged edgy plays like Eve Ensler's (1953–) *The Vagina Monologues*.

Meng and the critical discourse that surrounds him and others of the new avant-garde reflect China's postsocialist condition, a condition in which artists and critics seek to reconcile the political, the progressive, and the popular. With productions like *Rhinoceros in Love* (1999, written by his wife, Liao Yimei [1971–]) and *Two Dogs' Opinions on Life* (cocreated in 2007 with actors Chen Minghao and Liu Xiaoye)—both of which are still being staged and have been performed more than 1,500 times each for more than one million spectators—Meng has ignited heated debates about the commercial mainstream versus the avant-garde fringe in Chinese theater. His brand of "pop avant-garde," as Rossella Ferrari has dubbed it, became the prevailing artistic trend and audience preference in late twentieth- and early twenty-first-century Chinese theater. In a return to his earlier, more socially conscious, exploratory aesthetic, Meng restaged *I Love XXX* in 2013, almost two decades after its premiere. The newer, younger cast did not personally experience the socialist collective reality the play embodies, but are the inheritors of its legacy. Meng typifies a generation for whom the Cultural Revolution and June Fourth were significant turning points, yet his theater resonates strongly with the subsequent generation that did not personally experience these events and remains largely ignorant of them. The ideal—but also dilemma—of collectivity resonates in Meng's work in both its form and its content. Plays like *I Love XXX* create nostalgia, critique, and desire, reflecting the attempts of the twenty-first-century generation of artists and audiences to recapture Maoist revolutionary ideals and deploy them for a capitalist, postsocialist future.

BIBLIOGRAPHY: Claire Conceison, "China's Experimental Mainstream: The Badass Theatre of Meng Jinghui," *TDR / The Drama Review* 58, no. 1 (Spring 2014): 64–88. He

Donghui, "Cultural Critique and Avant-Garde Theatre in Post-Socialist China: Meng Jinghui's 'I Love Therefore I Am,'" *China Information* 29, no. 1 (2015): 60–88. Rossella Ferrari, *Pop Goes the Avant-Garde: Experimental Theatre in Contemporary China* (London, 2012). Meng Jinghui, Huang Jingang, Wang Xiaoli, and Shi Hang, "I Love XXX," trans. Claire Conceison, in Meng Jinghui, *I Love XXX and Other Plays*, ed. Claire Conceison (London, 2016) [includes video DVD with excerpts from the 2013 production].

CLAIRE CONCEISON

1995 · MAY 8

"The Moon Represents My Heart"

The Death of Teresa Teng

Near the conclusion of director Peter Chan Ho-sun's (1962–) 1996 film *Comrades: Almost a Love Story*, two former lovers each wander the streets of New York City, both alone and despondent over the news of pop singer Teresa Teng's (1953–1995) death. When Li Qiao (played impeccably by Maggie Cheung [1964–]) pauses in front of an electronics store window to mournfully watch the news reports of Teng's passing, she is joined by Li Xiaojun (Leon Lai [1966–]), her erstwhile partner in romance and various entrepreneurial schemes in Hong Kong. Now, following years of separation, heartbreak, and loss, they meet again in a foreign country, reunited by the sudden news of Teng's early death. Qiao turns to face Xiaojun as the strains of one of Teng's greatest hits, "Sweet as Honey" (the title of which also serves as the Chinese title of the film), swell in the background, and her look of surprise suggests disbelief, as if Xiaojun is a memory brought to life through Teng's music. Their exchange of gazes gradually solidifies the reality of the other, and their speechless smiles as the scene ends ensure the sort of impossibly fated ending only available to us in movies and pop songs.

Teng's role in the film, which nearly swept the 1997 Hong Kong Film Awards, does more than serve as a convenient plot device or saccharine soundtrack. Rather, Teng's melodic presence demonstrates the remarkable and profound effects that popular music and mass-mediated stardom can manifest in the lived, sentimental experiences of history. Her delicate voice, ubiquitous throughout the world's Chinese-speaking communities for more than two decades, speaks not to the national sorrow, historical monumentality, and cultural anxiety that dominated the discourse of Chinese artistic production throughout the twentieth century. She sings instead, and almost exclusively, of matters of the heart: love and loss, romance and yearning. It was in this mode of poignant pathos that Teng transcended the prevailing ideological obstacles that fractured China and forged a kind of sentimental unity: as the saying goes, "Wherever there are Chinese people, you can hear Teresa Teng's songs."

Pop music occupies a misty, overdetermined position in our narratives of history. Theodor Adorno (1903–1969) set the tone for decades of derision of pop as superficial, deceitful, and essentially disposable when he famously declared it to be "a perpetual bus man's holiday" for the deluded masses. More recently, however, scholarship has found in popular music sociological and even political value, although less on its own terms and more on the occasions it intersects with broader social movements. Existing outside the spectrum formed by these two poles (pop either as ideological machinations of the "culture industry" or as another illustration of historical and social change), however, is the unresolved possibility of what the case of Teng exemplifies in the wake of her untimely death. As a star, she reflects the changing understanding of what it meant to be Chinese in the 1970s and 1980s, but as a voice, she is also actively articulating, constructing, and shaping that very experience. Though Teng's historical significance as a (cross-)cultural icon has long been recognized, the emotional import of her songs remains under-studied, despite the "structure of feeling" she intoned for an entire generation of listeners in Asia and the continued outpouring of sentimental testimony from her countless fans across the globe. How we account for this dimension of lyrical possibility in our approach to modern China, encapsulated here by Teng, necessarily refocuses our inquiry away from the overarching, grand narratives of history and onto individual experiences and sentimental resonances.

Perhaps Teng's most fondly remembered hit, and still a karaoke favorite, is "The Moon Represents My Heart." Like many of the most cherished songs, its lyrics are striking for their utter sappiness:

You ask me how deep is my love for you?
How strong is my love for you?

My feelings are true
My love is also true
The moon represents my heart

Teng's delivery captivates through its innocent charm: just above a gossa-
mer whisper, her voice achieves pure sweetness, without ever crossing into
cloying mawkishness. The song was part of an astounding string of hits
Teng released in the late 1970s and early 1980s, but it especially struck a
chord in mainland China. Teng was among the first recording artists from
Hong Kong or Taiwan to reach an audience in the mainland, a passage
aided in no small part by the increased availability of modern electronics
under Deng Xiaoping's (1904–1997) "open-door" economic policies. Tran-
sistor radios and boom boxes allowed listeners on the mainland to hear
broadcasts from Taiwan and Hong Kong, or to play bootlegged cassettes
of pop music in their private homes, opening a new realm of personal
enjoyment. This newly discovered realm of personal sentiment and private ownership was totally disconnected from the collective aspirations
disseminated through state propaganda media during the revolutionary
era. After decades of blaring, collective anthems in praise of the red sun
of Mao Zedong (1893–1976), there suddenly appeared Teng's soft voice
singing to "you" about "my" love. Even the stark declaration of "representation" is stripped of its political connotations and reanimated with lyrical
intent. The impact of such sentimental force was so thoroughgoing that
people soon began to remark that although the daytime was still the sonic
domain of the "Old Deng," or Deng Xiaoping, the night belonged to the
"Little Deng"—Teresa Teng.

Teng was born in Taiwan to parents who had fled to the island in
1949 as the Communists took control of the mainland. She first gained
notoriety as a teenager in the mid-1960s for her renditions of folk
and operatic tunes, especially of the Huangmei tune variety popular
among Chinese émigrés in Hong Kong and Taiwan due to its strong
nostalgic association with unrequited love. At the same time, she was
pioneering an emerging, mass-mediated youth market. On her first
series of records in the late 1960s (she recorded twenty albums for
Taiwan's Cosmos Record Company between the ages of fourteen and
eighteen), she effortlessly alternates between upbeat rhythmic numbers
backed by saxophone, guitar, and drums and traditional folk ballads

with classical Chinese instrumentation. Her voice, even while modulating between styles, remains remarkably constant and unifying; the poppy tracks hint at Asian acculturation, while the traditional songs are softened around the edges and incorporate a sense of Western harmony. Already tinged with a knowing expressiveness beyond her years, Teng's light, spirited voice of her teenage years captured simultaneously the eloquence of Chinese traditional performance and the new, Western mode of popular, youthful ebullience. Her ability to evoke longing both for something lost to history and for a sophisticated modernity of the present parallels the struggle for identity that characterized Taiwan after 1949, as the island ostensibly claimed legitimacy as "China," yet was increasingly being defined through its geopolitical relationships in the global capitalist system.

As she achieved fame throughout East and Southeast Asia in the 1970s and 1980s, Teng continually traded on a pervasive sense of nostalgia. Several of her biggest hits and most fondly remembered songs are updated renditions of the "modern songs," or, as they are pejoratively referred to, "yellow music," made popular in 1930s and 1940s Shanghai by singers such as Zhou Xuan (1920–1957) and Bai Guang (1921–1999). They evoked the bygone sounds of the hybrid, colonial modernity of Shanghai and generated an antecedent for Teng's own transnational cultural sensibility. The emotional tenderness that imbues her singing voice is, however, unable to be wholly attributed to either its Chinese or its Western influences. Teng's trademark style is perhaps most gleaned from *enka*, the modern Japanese ballad style whose popularity was embedded in the local music of former Japanese colonies in East and Southeast Asia, including Taiwan. Just as Teng's adaptation of "modern songs" indicates a nostalgic connection with Shanghai cosmopolitanism of the colonial era, Teng's absorption of *enka* may be seen as a marker of her personal negotiation with her Taiwanese upbringing. Both of these cultural appropriations complicate the very notion of placing her in a single ethnic, cultural, or political framework.

Remarkable for its simplicity and sincerity, her soft, whispery intonation connects with her listeners' innermost, heartfelt sentiments and is absorbed into their emotional consciousness. Her music is easy in the truest sense: pleasant to the ear, never intrusive or challenging. Her biggest hits are archetypes of commercial, soft pop: melodious and romantic, but always with a hint of authentic melancholy in the maudlin phrasing and gentle vibrato of her voice. The lyrics, enunciated with clear confidence and in standard, unaccented Mandarin (or Cantonese, Japanese, Hokkien, or English), never ventured into the realm of social commentary; her domain was love and romance, and Teng ruled with a benevolent, feminine grace.

This ability to negotiate her identity as a singer and act out multiple cultural attributes allowed her not only to thwart political constraints, but also to become the most popular singer in every region of East and Southeast Asia. Her marketing savvy (she signed a recording deal in 1973 with Polydor Japan, the largest and most widely distributed label in Asia) and carefully constructed public image fueled her global fame and set a template for later cross-cultural, multilingual figures like Faye Wong (1969–) and Jay Chou (1979–). Although she avoided overtly political statements and personal scandal by design, her fame inevitably carried a degree of political consequence. Most notably, she was widely criticized in the Taiwanese media in 1979 after being caught using a forged Indonesian passport to travel to Japan, which was seen as a kind of national betrayal: the severing of official diplomatic relations between Japan and Taiwan seven years earlier had made travel for citizens of the Republic of China difficult. Teng was able to redeem herself in her homeland the next year by appearing in a television special, "Teresa at the Forefront," in which she performed for Nationalist Army troops on the island of Quemoy, a frequent Cold War flashpoint only a mile from the mainland. Not long after, on the other side of the strait, her songs were officially condemned by the Beijing government as examples of "decadent music" and "spiritual pollution." Despite these complications, Teng always seemed to rise above the political realm through her musical focus on love and sentiment, conveyed by the honeyed sounds of soft pop.

Examinations of how Teng was able to forge a transnational Chinese identity can take us only so far in explaining her significance to the millions of fans that she touched. Throughout the twentieth century, and in particular during the years when Teng's fame was at its peak, Chinese identity was being actively determined by historical and political forces that mobilized culture to foster collective belonging. Certainly, Teng was not immune to these forces. Yet, the way her voice was able to sound out an identity based on sentiment, not politics, completely transformed how her listeners defined themselves. For all of its shallow clichés and maudlin melodies, pop music, perhaps more than any other form of cultural product, produces a sense of ourselves as emotional beings. Teng's most significant legacy is not what she means to "China" or Chinese culture, but the effect she has on "you" and "me"—possessed by each of us and built into the structure of our own sentimental self.

Teng died suddenly of a severe asthma attack while vacationing with her boyfriend in the northern Thai resort town of Chiang Mai. Though her popularity was already in decline from its peaks of the previous decade, her passing was experienced as a collective loss, with tributes, television specials, an elaborate funeral service fit for a head of state, and even the circulation of dark conspiracy theories on the circumstances of her demise. Yet the loss resonated most deeply at the personal level of feeling and memory. The sense of nostalgia created with Teng's passing not only conjures bittersweet memories of romances of the past, but also creates an uncanny sense of anticipation: a destiny of reunion, no matter the travails and ruptures of history.

Nearly two decades after her death, Teng's honeyed lilt and charming smile are still captivating fans by way of a wider variety of media and technology than ever. At a concert in September 2013, she was spectacularly resurrected for a duet with superstar Jay Chou. As Chou finished the first chorus of Teng's classic "What Do You Have to Say?" words appeared on screens flanking the stage: "I have a fantasy that if I could transcend time and space, I'd go back thirty years to sing a duet with her." As he solemnly welcomed Teng, the audience audibly gasped as a three-dimensional hologram of Teng's youthful figure, wearing a white cheongsam with red flower trim, appeared on stage and began singing the next verse. The ease with which Teng's image and sound are adapted to new, innovative media portends further reanimations, while the song selection testifies to the continuing inspiration she provides for today's Chinese pop: the digital Teng joined Chou on two of his own recent hits before disappearing from the stage in a shimmering swirl. In her absence as much as in her virtual presence, Teng's embodiment of the heartache of loss, the sweetness of remembrance, and yearning for reunion has only grown stronger.

BIBLIOGRAPHY: Rey Chow, "By Way of Mass Commodities: Love in *Comrades, Almost a Love Story*," in *Sentimental Fabulations, Contemporary Chinese Films: Attachment in the Age of Global Visibility* (New York, 2007), 105–120. Ping Lu, *He ri jun zai lai—da mingxing zhi si?* (Hong Kong, 2009). Shi Yonggang and Zhao Jun, *Deng Lijun quanzhuan* (Hong Kong, 2005).

ANDY RODEKOHR

1995 · JUNE 25

> Twenty-six-year-old writer Qiu Miaojin stabs herself in the heart in her Paris apartment.

Formal Experiments in Qiu Miaojin's "Lesbian I Ching"

[AUTHOR'S NOTE TO THE READER: Please read the following text fragments, which appear as paragraphs, in any order you wish. In the spirit of Qiu Miaojin's (1969–1995) *Last Words from Montmartre*, whose chapters can be read in any order, the order of paragraphs in this essay is arbitrary; I printed each segment on an index card and then shuffled the deck.]

The book opens unassumingly, but closes in a maelstrom of densely woven thematic motifs and literary references that have been gathering momentum from the beginning. We have followed the author-narrator down the rabbit hole.

Last Words from Montmartre, a memoir-like novel, consists of a series of loosely connected, epistolary "chapters" that form what is essentially the author's extended suicide note. Its mood is stark and mostly cheerless, and its style—alternately obscure and colloquial—runs the gamut from memoir to manifesto. The novel obsesses over the demise of a relationship between two women, and ends with the narrator's reaffirmation of her commitment to kill herself, a commitment that Qiu honored: late in the summer of 1995, the twenty-six-year-old author stabbed herself in the heart in her Paris apartment, leaving the manuscript behind with instructions to publish it.

Qiu is in many ways Taiwan's (beloved) native son. Her work exposes the uncomfortable tension between public and private expressions of sexual identity during the 1990s. It embodies a side of Taiwanese cultural identity that resists sanitization—the side that misbehaves and counters larger idealist narratives of Taiwanese democracy or Western-style liberalism. As Liu Jen-peng and Ding Naifei note:

> That there is no obvious public violence against [gay people] in Taiwan … does not imply that they are therefore any less oppressed. Here, the force of homophobia may not be expressed by spitting in your face, but rather in *conscientiously protecting the faces of other people*, in order to maintain a complete and perfect formal totality.

An epigraph in *Last Words from Montmartre* urges readers to peruse the chapters in any order: "If this book should be published," she wrote, "readers can begin anywhere. The only connection between the chapters is the time frame in which they were written." The Taiwanese novelist Luo Yijun (1967–) characterized *Last Words from Montmartre* as "the lesbian Bible" of the past two decades. But owing to the innovative, nonlinear structure of the novel—the injunction to open it randomly and read from any page—I would argue that it's more of a lesbian *I Ching* (*yijing*), or *Book of Changes*, the esoteric Chinese classic about the Way of yin and yang.

Even readers from highly divergent backgrounds can appreciate the familiar architecture of a coming-of-age story, told from the inside out, that deals with issues of sexual awakening, alienation, loss, and love.

Qiu's writing protects the faces of no one; formal totalities are exploded. In *Last Words from Montmartre*, we see the fulfillment and maturation of a number of themes brought out in her earlier novel *Notes of a Crocodile*. Of particular note is her attempt at mingling writing and desire, where the confusion of love and writing represents a sort of apotheosis of the art of literature; a kind of intertextual and intergenerational dialogue that brings many cultures, writers, languages, and genders into conversation with each other. In this sense, *Last Words from Montmartre* is Qiu's most mature contribution to global modernist literary conversations.

As the novel progresses, the analogic language grows denser, and individual "letters" or "chapters" begin to bleed into each other in a chronological way. In spite of the author's instructions to read the chapters in any order, we nonetheless detect the emergence of discrete micro-narratives that build on, and expand outward from, each other.

In 2003, the scholar Tze-lan Deborah Sang observed that "Qiu Miao-jin...had an exceptional talent. Her voice is assertive, intellectual, witty, lyrical, and intimate. Several years after her death, her works continue to command a huge following...in Taiwan." A decade later, Chinese readers in Hong Kong, Singapore, Malaysia, and worldwide knew her work, and in 2012, the first official editions of her novels were published in mainland China. If the world of contemporary Chinese literature is too often divided by region, dialect, nation, and tradition, Qiu's work has somehow transcended these divisions to become part of an emerging canon of *global* Chinese literature.

Qiu, had she lived, would have been almost exactly my age. I think about that when I read her work, marking inevitable comparisons between the structural and conceptual timelines of our lives. We had followed each other around the globe: We had certainly been to the same lesbian club in Taipei in the early 1990s. We had friends in common, two degrees of separation. Qiu and I, studying French, overlapped in Paris. Had we watched Theo Angelopoulos (1935–2012) in the same theater at Odéon, been to the same Act Up rally at Notre Dame, had we felt alienated on the sidelines at the lesbian nightclub Privilège?

Wang Dan (1969–), the prominent mainland Chinese Tiananmen dissident and Harvard PhD, comments that Qiu's *Last Words* is

> deeply, soulfully moving in its excruciating revelation of the author's innermost self, which is after all what makes the magic of literature. For too many authors the psychology behind writing is to deliberately craft something of interest to the reader, to use plot and word structure to create a fictitious love so that the product is a kind of literary labor of love.... We can get a great deal of reading pleasure from this kind of work, but can we be moved by it?... Life is full of problems, one of which is: When you are in dire straits—weak, distraught, about to crack—you don't want anyone to see you. But at the same time you want someone to share it with. At times like this, often only writing will do. Though it's not face-to-face, only through writing can one have the kind of heart-to-heart exchange needed to get through the tough times. And this is why I'm moved by Qiu Miaojin's writing. I felt a secret intimacy [with her] from the first page.

An icon of gay subcultures whose first novel, *Notes of a Crocodile*, arguably provided the vocabulary for a whole generation of Taiwanese lesbians, Qiu nonetheless also earned mainstream literary respect as a modernist and formal innovator, winning prestigious national awards.

> Xu, I'm an artist, and what I really want is to excel in my art.... My goal is to experience the depths of life, to understand people and how they live, and to express this through my art. All my other accomplishments mean nothing to me. If I can only create a masterpiece that achieves the goal I've fixed my inward gaze on during my creative journey, will my life not have been wasted.

From 1993 to 1995, Qiu studied clinical psychology and feminism at the Université de Paris VIII. It was in Paris that she killed herself. She left behind a unique experimental novel in epistolary form, arguably her most complex work, called *Last Words from Montmartre*.

Qiu is Taiwan's best-known lesbian author, but is also widely considered a literary national treasure. As the cultural studies scholar and Taiwanese literature expert Fran Martin has written of Qiu's work, "Qiu's unique literary style—mingling cerebral, experimental language use, psychological realism, biting social critique through allegory, and a surrealist effect deriving from the use of arrestingly unusual metaphors—is strongly influenced by both European and Japanese literary and cinematic modernisms." Stylistically, her use of psychoanalytic lyricism and her deliberate engagement with modernist and postmodernist masters such as Andre Gide, Jean Genet, Kobo Abe, Yukio Mishima, Haruki Murakami, Andrei Tarkovsky, and Derek Jarman take her works beyond the boundaries of Taiwan and of Sinophone literature and into a more global dialogue.

Reading through her last work, I (and many of her readers) can identify with the youthful earnestness of the twentysomething Qiu: not only in our shared coming-of-age within the queer literary confessional zeitgeist of the mid-1990s (a last gasp of a certain kind of homesickness narrative before the Internet buried the tradition once and for all?) but in her expatriatism, her solemn attachment to the ideals of higher art and love, and her paradoxical ability to inhabit a spectrum of genders and identities across multiple platforms, cultural, linguistic, and otherwise.

At dusk I watched Laurence twirl her hair in the Seine as she does when she's saying something exciting, her bangs smoothed to the side. Whether in the water or on land, she punctuates herself with a comma. Her skin was tan, an even, light coffee-brown, lighter and silkier than the chestnut color of her hair. Amid the glossy dark green trees of spring, the extravagantly bewitching dance of the leaves on both shores, illuminated by the glow of Parisian culture, Laurence was like a fish leaping gracefully toward a million shimmering leaves, swimming against the current toward the light.... When she dives into the water to swim she reveals the impossible curve of her ass and the river water runs and runs off her back.... I want to touch the curve with both hands; I want to suck the curve with my lips; I want to use the scorching heat between my legs to melt to the curve of her spine, no matter who she is.... Swimming the backstroke, the shape of her breasts silently break the water and I think she must be turned on, the tips of her nipples catching the light, the muscles of her abdomen expanding and contracting along with her breath, the rippling wind like the sound of fish shuttling, weaving back and forth, as if weaving the water with the beautiful contours of Laurence.

Last Words from Montmartre tells the story of the demise of a relationship, and ultimately the unraveling of the narrator, in a voice that veers from self-deprecation to hubris, from compulsive repetition to sublime reflection, from reticence to vulnerability. It is both the author's suicide note and her great masterwork and labor of love. The book consists primarily of a series of letters—presented like chapters—from the narrator in Paris to her lover in Taipei and to family and friends in Taiwan and Tokyo. It "opens" with the death of a beloved pet rabbit and closes with a portentous expression of the narrator's resolve to kill herself. In between, we follow Qiu's narrator along the streets of Montmartre; into descriptions of affairs with both men and women, French and Taiwanese; into rhapsodic musings on cinematic masterpieces; and into wrenching and clear-eyed outlines of what it means to exist not only between cultures but, to a certain extent, between and among genders. More *Confessions of a Mask* or *No Longer Human* than *Well of Loneliness*, the novel marks Qiu as one of the finest experimentalist and modernist writers of our generation in any language.

I practically bounced with joy all the way home [from the lecture by Hélène Cixous]. It must have been almost eight when I exited the Simplon Métro stop on the number 4 line and walked along rue Joseph Dijon. In the middle of Montmartre, in front of the Mairie, the church bells rang out from the Église Jules Joffrin, reverberating through my body and soul…. I grabbed the professor's novel from my backpack, reread the inscription, and realized that the "message" she'd been waiting for me to "send" to her was the exact one I had written, as if possessed by a spirit, transcribing "I love you" in Chinese…. "Message" was a key word that she often talked about in her lectures as well as used as *une métaphore*. What did this minor *transport* signify for my life?

Qiu's work is the nexus of multiple ongoing dialogues with the living and the dead: Osamu Dazai (1909–1948) and Mishima and Genet, but also Taiwanese authors Luo Yijun and Lai Xiangyin (1969–) and Sinophone readers everywhere who dialogue about and with her work (angrily, lovingly) online. Her work lends itself to this second life in new social media because it resists having a beginning, a middle, and an end.

Almost twenty years after the author's death, lively debates still exist about whether *Last Words* should be remembered as the consummate romantic statement or the consummate artistic sacrifice—or whether it's too dense to read at all.

BIBLIOGRAPHY: Larissa Heinrich, "Begin Anywhere: Transgender and Transgenre Desire in Qiu Miaojin's Testament from Montmartre," in *Transgender China: Histories and Cultures*, ed. Howard Chiang (New York, 2012), 161–181. Liu Jen-peng and Ding Naifei, "Reticent Poetics, Queer Politics," *Inter-Asia Cultural Studies* 6, no. 1 (2005): 30–55. Fran Martin, *Situating Sexualities: Queer Representation in Taiwanese Fiction, Film, and Public Culture* (Hong Kong, 2003). Fran Martin and Larissa Heinrich, eds., *Embodied Modernities: Corporeality, Representation, and Chinese Cultures* (Honolulu, 2006). Qiu Miaojin, *Last Words from Montmartre*, trans. and with an afterword by Ari Larissa Heinrich (New York, 2014). Tze-lan Deborah Sang, *The Emerging Lesbian: Female Same-Sex Desire in Modern China* (Chicago, 2003). Wang Dan, "Shengming yu aiqing de jizhi: Zaidu Mengmate yishu," *INK Literary Monthly*, no. 22 (June 2005).

ARI LARISSA HEINRICH

1997 · MAY 1

> "What does the 'world atlas' mean to the Tau? A chain of islands in Oceania."

Modern China as Seen from an Island Perspective

The publication of Syaman Rapongan's (1957–) essay collection *Cold Sea, Deep Passion* in May 1997 introduced a significant new islanding and archipelagic perspective into contemporary Sinophone literature. Rapongan, a writer from the Tau ethnic group—a group indigenous to Orchid Island (Pongso no Tau in the Tau language, literally "island of real people"), an island located twenty-five miles southeast of Taiwan— spent his school years in Taiwan, returning to Orchid Island in the 1980s to participate in the indigenous protest against the government's storage of nuclear waste on his home island. Upon his return, he dropped his Chinese name, Shih Nu-lai, and, following the traditional Tau naming system, adopted the name Syaman Rapongan—"the father of Rapongan," his firstborn son. Since 1997, he has published a series of works based on his own seafaring experiences, as well as those of his fellow islanders, including *Black Wings* (1999), *The Memories of the Waves* (2002), *The Sailor's Face* (2007), *The Old Seaman* (2009), *Eyes of the Sky* (2012), *The Drifting Dream on the Big Ocean* (2014), and *The Death of Anomin* (2015). These narratives are not only vehicles through which Rapongan can come to terms with his own "oceanic" identity as an islander, but, as selections of his work have been translated into English, French, Japanese, Spanish, and German, these books also serve as a way for Rapongan to join a global conscientious effort to challenge continental ways of seeing the world.

To contextualize Rapongan's work, it is necessary to touch briefly on the (dis)connection between China and Taiwan. In 1949, with the mainland all but lost to the Communists, Chiang Kai-shek (1887–1975) took his followers, numbering approximately 1.5 million, across the Taiwan Strait to settle in Taiwan. Ever since then, cultural nostalgia for the mainland has permeated the lived experience of the island: the streets of Taipei and other cities were renamed Luoyang, Chang'an, Kaifeng, and so on, after mainland Chinese cities, turning the island topography into a history of Chinese diaspora. This painful departure from the mainland, the trauma of separation that makes their old home uninhabitable but their stay on the island always provisional, is epitomized in the often cited lines of poet Yu Guangzhong (1928–):

> At present
> Nostalgia becomes a shallow strait
> Me on this side
> Mainland on the other.

The pathos for a lost mainland lingers on today. On the sixtieth anniversary of Nationalist exile in 2009, the writer and scholar Ch'i Pang-yuan (1924–) published *River of Big Currents*, a memoir that bears witness to the turbulent era of 1949. The story begins with the Liao River, or River of Big Currents, which flows through her hometown in Liaoning, a province located beyond the Great Wall, and it ends with the Yakou Sea (Sea of Dumbness and Silence) in Hengchuen in southern Taiwan. The condition of displacement in which she has existed from a very young age strikes her belatedly in her eighties, and suddenly assumes inexpressible poignancy. Part of her story became the central narrative for the 2015 documentary *The Rocking Sky*, which offers unique female perspectives on the history of modern China. For the Chinese forty-niners, the rift separating them from the mainland constitutes an inescapable sadness, a memory that runs in the blood and can never be removed.

But by 1997, a new cultural discourse had emerged that confronted this continental and Nationalist legacy of loss and diaspora, a discourse that constructed a distinct Taiwanese nativist identity that took the ocean and the island as its center. The advocates for this discourse are Han people who emigrated from the mainland before 1949, some as early as the 1660s, when the Ming loyalist general Koxinga (1624–1662) expelled the Dutch from the island. As an ethnic group that has lived in Taiwan for almost four hundred years, the pre-1949 Han Taiwanese are eager to sever the umbilical cord to China, particularly in the face of the hegemony of the mainland, and go native. Han Taiwanese writers such as Liao Hungqi and Dong Nian (1950–) have contributed enthusiastically to this discourse, but the work of Rapongan was hailed as essential for defining and exemplifying the new cultural paradigm of a distinct Taiwaneseness. As a Tau, Rapongan's ethnic identity was indisputably independent from the Asian continent, and his work therefore strengthened the cause of

Taiwanese nativism. The late Taiwanese critic Yeh Shih-tao (1925–2008) put it straightforwardly, writing that "the future of Taiwanese literature will be shouldered by indigenous authors." The indigenous people on the Taiwanese margins were appropriated in an effort to establish a distinct body of national literature and, in this way, to construct a narrative of a native Taiwanese national identity

Rapongan has not endorsed such a discourse, however; quite the contrary, his work transcends national boundaries to embrace a spacious world of oceanic belonging. Rapongan recuperates a tribal island tradition, created and reinvented to name the indigenous self and to mediate between colonial conquest and indigenous history. Rapongan's work is inspiring for the way it recontextualizes the national divide of modern China through its distinctive island perspective and serves as a portal to an ocean world that has been obscured by the dominant continent-based discourse. Rapongan calls for a transnational and transindigenous solidarity between seafaring people. Coincidentally, his home of Pongso no Tau has served an important role for forging such connections in the past. In 1936, for instance, the English zoologist and seafaring ethnographer James Hornell (1865–1949), in an article for the *Monthly Record of Anthropological Science*, pointed out the convergent development in boat construction and design between the Tau and the peoples of northern Europe.

Rapongan substitutes a rich ocean culture for systems of colonial and national demarcation. The Tau feed on flying fish, and Tau rituals and calendars center on their movement. In *Black Wings*, Rapongan uses the lines of mobility and escape configured by the flying fish to question the territorial sovereignty of modern nation-states:

What does the "world atlas" mean to the Tau? A chain of islands in Oceania. The islanders share common ideals, and savor the freedom of the sea. On their own sea and the sea of other neighboring islands, they pursue their unspoken and unspeakable passion for the ocean, or, perhaps, they pursue the words passed down from their ancestors. The dense schools of flying fish dye patches of the wide and vast ocean black. Each school consists of three or four hundred fish, swimming about fifty or sixty meters apart. They stretch unbroken for one nautical mile, looking like a mighty military force going into battle. They follow the ancient course of the Kuroshiro current, gradually heading toward the sea north of Batan in the Philippines.

Indifferent to the dichotomy of Chineseness versus Taiwaneseness, the poet reaches out for "a sea of islands" interconnected with one another, and Pongso no Tau becomes part of the interconnected heritage of Oceania. Living close to the pathway of the Kuroshiro current and nurtured by the richness of the Pacific ecosystem, the Tau had thrived for decades by making use of their traditional ecological knowledge. This existence was disrupted when the Chinese Nationalist government moved to Taiwan in 1949 and placed four labor camps, ten farms for the resettlement of veterans, and a garrison's commanding headquarters on Orchid Island over the course of the 1950s. But the traditional knowledge of the Tau, as preserved in their songs, myths, and stories, has managed to sustain this vigorous ocean culture. The Tau people's egalitarian system of resource distribution and environmental governance provides an excellent model for ecological sustainability. The tribal people alternate seasonally between migratory fishing and fishing off the local coral reefs so as to conserve the ocean and maintain the biodiversity of the surrounding waters. The cultivation of taro grown in wet fields with irrigation channels is supplemented by the rotating cultivation of dry taro, yam, and millet. The Tau cultivate woods and plant trees (*mi mowamowa*), leaving the cultivated lands to their offspring as an invaluable inheritance. They harvest forest timber in the interior mountains for the building of the assembled boats and traditional houses. They select and rank the wood and use their adroit skills of boat building (*mi tatala*) to produce both decorative (*mivatek*) and nondecorative boats, streamlined carriers of traditional beauty, the design of which incorporates a profound knowledge of the waves and bespeaks a symbolic order that binds together the individual Tau and their clans, that creates a bond between the Tau, the fish, and the ocean. The Tau maintain a set of ceremonies, rituals, and prayers based on the myths of the sea creatures. They practice a unique method of reckoning time that is based on the rhythm of the moon and waves. The customary regulations of everyday life observed by the Tau provide a very different model for ecological conservation from that of the continent-based Han.

In his work, Rapongan demonstrates his extensive knowledge of the stars, the ocean, and the many species of the Pacific, as well as the physical skills of fishing, canoeing, boat building, and celestial navigation. In *Cold Sea, Deep Passion* he calls into being a Pacific perception of place and space not only via an evocative sensibility for the ocean but also through a quest for the ancestral words passed down as bodily codes, as a memory in the blood. He opens up the large world of "the planet as ocean" or "ocean planet" by delineating a rich vocabulary of planetary consciousness, at one point, for example, recounting all the different species of wood used in boat building:

> Father (which is what "Syaman" means) of my grandchildren, this tree is *apnorwa*, and that one is *isis*. That tree is *pangohen*.... They are all excellent timber for building boats. This *apnorwa* has been waiting for you for more than a decade; it's the timber best suited to join together both sides of the hull. This kind of timber rots the most slowly. This tree is a *syayi*, and it's the one we will cut down today for the keel.

His indigenized Sinophone writing opens up possibilities for tribal voices not circumscribed by "Chineseness." The richly hybridized dialogues between the indigenous and the mainstream groups are subversive. Situated between two worlds, he violates cultural boundaries and the boundaries of Chinese writing. He effects a(n) (un)conscious subversion and remaking of the language, culture, and history by supplementing that language, culture, and history with an extensive indigenous vocabulary, tribal expressions, and multiple voices. It is significant to note that in the Tau language, the word for "placenta" and "womb" is also the word for "land" and "sea." Rapongan himself represents an interface between land and sea. Conflating his indigenous body with his sea or island body, he pronounces in Tau, "Nu yabu o pongso yam, ala abu ku u" (If it were not for the island / ocean, I would not exist).

The Pacific Islanders have contributed to the world with their navigating techniques and the canoe, which has sailed across the ocean for eight thousand years, well before Westerners arrived in the Pacific. The canoe is called by many names: in Maori, it is *waka moana*; in Fiji, it is called *camakau*; in the Marshall Islands, it is named *waan aelon kein* or *walap*; in Tonga, it becomes *tongiaki* or *kalia*; in Samoa, *taumalua* or *alia*; in the Cook Islands, *vaka taurua*; in Kiribati, *baurua*; in Pongso no Tau, *mi tatala.* With these well-crafted boats and with sophisticated maritime technology, the Pacific Islanders settled roughly two-thirds of the globe's southern oceanic hemisphere. The indigenous subject acts to interpret and reconstruct Oceania as transborder indigenous belonging. Though Rapongan received a Han education for a long and formative period, he returns to an oceanic perception of transnational island community. The ocean is re-worlded through the poet's countervision and counter-memory. Navigating a course that is not overdetermined by the trajectories of colonialism and modern nation-states, Rapongan turns the "cross" (of Yu Guangzhong's "shallow strait") into the "crisscross" of transpacific mobility and interconnection. The reciprocal relationship of the indigenous and the migrant offers an alter / native model of reckoning with space, place, and time to reenvision "modern China" from an island perspective—an island that is neither confined nor isolated but invokes a powerful planetary consciousness.

BIBLIOGRAPHY: John Balcom and Yingtish Balcom, eds., *Indigenous Writers of Taiwan* (New York, 2005). Chen Fang-ming, ed., *The Anthology of Taiwan Indigenous Literature* (Taipei, 2015). Chen Fang-ming, ed, *Chronicle of Significant Events for Taiwan Indigenous Literature, 1951–2014*, trans. Shuhwa Wu and Ying-jou Chen (Taipei, 2015). Hsinya Huang, "Sinophone Indigenous Literature of Taiwan: History and Tradition," in *Sinophone Studies: A Critical Reader,* ed. Shu-mei Shih, Chien-hsin Tsai, and Brian Bernards (New York, 2013), 242–254. Basuya Poiconu, *The Literary History of Taiwanese Indigenous Peoples* (Taipei, 2012).

HSINYA HUANG

1997 · MAY 3

Bai Xianyong attends the closing-night performance of the English stage adaptation of his novel *Crystal Boys* at Harvard University.

"The First Modern Asian Gay Novel"

The cover of the English translation of Bai Xianyong's (1937–) *Crystal Boys* is striking. A shirtless Asian youth, tanned, with jeans slightly unbuttoned, stares out at the viewer. The title, in purple, looms above. It is not a literal translation of the Chinese title, more accurately rendered as *Outcasts,* but instead a more alluring title provided by the translator, Howard Goldblatt

(1939–). In the bottom left corner appear the words "The first modern Asian gay novel," a subtitle added by the publisher, Gay Sunshine Press. Though not exactly false advertisement—the novel does tell the stories of a group of gay youths in Taiwan—that subtitle reduces Bai's nuanced novel to a single note. A novel with homosexual characters is not necessarily a "gay novel." The descriptor "Asian" only locates the novel somewhere on a continent, when the novel is specifically set in Taiwan—an island that is on the very edge of the continent, just as the group within the novel are on the fringes of society—and written by an author who had been, and is still, living in the United States.

My own interpretations of *Crystal Boys* have shifted with the passage of time and experience. From my initial private reading of the novel in 1992 to my public staging of it as director of the Harvard University production in 1997, and from my first time meeting Bai in the United States in 1993 to speaking about *Crystal Boys* in Taiwan as Bai's invited guest in 2003, my participation in the international scholarly discourse surrounding the novel has gone through different phases. What I once viewed as a primarily "gay" novel, I now view as a uniquely "Taiwanese" one.

That is not to say that a reader largely ignorant of Taiwan cannot enjoy *Crystal Boys*. I certainly did. So, too, did many in the audience of the Harvard production; one American gay couple drove more than 150 miles to see it. Nor is the novel's gay content insignificant. Years before the rise of more activist-oriented queer literature in Taiwan, *Crystal Boys* revealed a clandestine gay culture centered on the cruising grounds around the lotus pond in Taipei's New Park. Bai makes a relative newcomer to the park into his protagonist and first-person narrator: the amiable A-qing, a high school senior kicked out of school and home after being "caught in an immoral act" with a school staff member. A-qing serves as the reader's tour guide to the "kingdom" he himself has only recently discovered in New Park: "There are no days in our kingdom, only nights. As soon as the sun comes up, our kingdom goes into hiding, for it is an unlawful nation; we have no government and no constitution, we are neither recognized nor respected by anyone, our citizenry is little more than rabble." The collection of characters within that citizenry proves to be far warmer and more endearing than that foreboding introduction to the kingdom may suggest. For gay readers, clandestine or otherwise, longing to connect with others like them, *Crystal Boys* can be a welcome read. Winston Leyland's (1940–) Gay Sunshine Press, founded with a core belief that gayness exists in all cultures, publishes works with gay themes from various parts of the world. The ability of *Crystal Boys* to draw a certain readership not otherwise interested in Chinese literature supports this core belief.

For those who *are* interested in Chinese literature, the work that established Bai's reputation was his 1971 collection of short stories given the broad title *People of Taipei*, but specifically focused on Taipei's "mainlanders," those who fled to Taiwan in the late 1940s when Chiang Kai-shek's (1887–1975) Nationalist government lost the Chinese mainland to Mao Zedong's (1893–1976) Communists. Bai's mainlanders come from various walks of life: high-ranking generals and their ladies, humble soldiers and servants, Shanghai courtesans and taxi dancers, a noodle shop owner from Bai's own hometown of Guilin, and even an aging homosexual silent film star whose tale prefigures *Crystal Boys*. Bai titled the English version, which he himself translated with Patia Yasin, after the story "Wandering in the Garden, Waking from a Dream," a flashback-laden tale set at a dinner party of high-ranking Shanghai exiles. The stated goal of those elites is reconquering the mainland, but they are in fact more intent on using nostalgia for the past as an antidote for the disappointments of the present. These people of Taipei reflect one aspect of Bai's own life. The son of eminent mainlander general Bai Chongxi (1893–1966), Bai Xianyong was born in Guilin in 1937 and retreated with his family first to Hong Kong in 1948 and then to Taiwan in 1952. One can imagine that the kind of ennui-ridden Kuomintang ladies who soothe their sadness at the party in "Wandering in the Garden, Waking from a Dream" were frequent visitors to the Bai home.

Or were they? Bai's writing can easily be misread as autobiographical. *Crystal Boys* is a case in point. His 1977 serialization of *Crystal Boys* was viewed as a "coming out" of sorts—not a small scandal in the conservative atmosphere of Taiwan society at the time—yet Bai is not A-qing, nor any other specific character in his own novel. He made that point explicitly to me the first time we met, and I believe him. *Crystal Boys* is an ensemble-based novel, and within the cloistered world of New Park, each of the many different subgroups who have come to inhabit the island of Taiwan is represented. A-qing is the son of a rank-and-file mainlander, one of the soldiers brought to Taiwan during the retreat from the mainland.

The "Dragon Prince" Wang Kuilong is a mainlander of a higher class, the son of a high Kuomintang official. His legendary lover, the "Phoenix Boy" A-feng, is an "aboriginal," a descendant of the Austronesians who first settled in Taiwan around eight thousand years ago. A-qing's roommate, Little Jade, is a "native" Taiwanese, not native in the American sense of the word, but a descendant of settlers from Fujian Province on the mainland who began coming to Taiwan in the seventeenth century. *Crystal Boys* is intimately linked to Taiwan's uniqueness within the Chinese world. Grandpa Guo, the elderly photographer who immortalizes young arrivals to New Park in his photo album entitled "Birds of Youth," sends new arrival A-qing off into the gay world by linking him to Taiwan: "Go on, A-qing, now it's your turn to fly. It's in your blood. All you wild youngsters who've grown up on this island have that strain of wildness in your blood, just like the typhoons and earthquakes that are part of this island." As a descendant of mainlander exiles determined to prove themselves the true heirs to Chinese culture, Bai was bold to state that the children raised on the island of Taiwan—*all* of them—carry specifically Taiwanese qualities. As much as "Wandering in the Garden, Waking from a Dream" is about ignoring one's Taiwaneseness, *Crystal Boys* is about accepting it.

It is in this moment, when gayness and Taiwaneseness become metaphors for one another, that the essence of *Crystal Boys* emerges. Initially, the shame of homosexuality, reflected in the novel's literal title of *Outcasts*, parallels the shame of the loss of the mainland. The Kuomintang authorities may have tried to recreate the mainland on Taiwan by naming the cities' streets after places on the mainland, and by maintaining a government with "elected" representatives of every province in China for over forty years, but at the end of it all, Taiwan will not be reconquering the mainland. As much as a gay son's family may try to pressure him to get married, have children, and lead a normal Confucian life, in the end, the gay son will not become straight. The gay hustlers of New Park, wandering around the lotus pond each night, are as aimless as the Kuomintang generals and soldiers of their own "unlawful nation." As the nations that recognize Taiwan's sovereignty dwindle to a handful of Caribbean islands and small African countries, A-qing's assertion that "we are neither recognized nor respected by anyone" applies as much to the leaders of Taiwan as to A-qing and the other wandering hustlers. The Confucian catastrophes befalling both groups are, to an extent, eased toward the novel's end, when A-qing briefly serves as final caregiver to the elderly Papa Fu Chongshan, and as potential mentor to Luo Ping, New Park's most recent young arrival. These poignant scenes, despite their brief glimmers of hope, only reinforce *Crystal Boys'* realization that both the father and the fatherland will always be disappointed.

What is remarkable about *Crystal Boys* is how the metaphor stands the test of time. Two decades after the novel's initial publication, local attitudes toward gayness and Taiwaneseness had both changed, leaving the metaphor revised but intact. By 1997, when I staged the Harvard production and then went to Taiwan for the first time, increased gay pride paralleled increased pride in Taiwan's unique culture. The final months of that year were a watershed for both halves of the revised metaphor. On November 29, the then-opposition Democratic Progressive Party gave the ruling Kuomintang its first major defeat at the polls; the Democratic Progressive Party won twelve out of twenty-three seats in the November 29 elections for city mayors and county magistrates, while the Kuomintang hung on to only eight. Two days later, on December 1, World AIDS Day was formally observed in Taiwan for the first time. Held on a rainy night at a park on Heping Road, the event featured a speech by a "Professor Ma." Friends in Taiwan would explain to me, and I suppose it could be true, that this man was Ma Ying-jeou (1950–), known for his support of gay rights when support was not yet politically correct in Taiwan; what none of us knew at the time was that he would someday be elected mayor and then president. That an aspiring Kuomintang politician, of the Wang Kuilong class, could step forth and support this event is testament to both Ma's own modernity and a changing ethos in Taiwan. Taiwan's first AIDS walk, the debut of the first of Taiwan's glossy gay and lesbian magazines, and the first weekly drag shows were other examples of the cultural shift happening in that same year. The Taiwanese language became more prevalent in schools, and celebrations of a distinctive Taiwanese culture became more widespread. Just as gay men were no longer ashamed to be gay, the Taiwanese were no longer ashamed to be Taiwanese.

My own experience of Taiwan will always be inextricably linked to *Crystal Boys.* When I first lived in Taiwan, I was drawn to an apartment on Jinzhou Street. The address seemed strangely familiar. After some time living on what was a rather odd street for a foreigner's residence, I realized it was the same street where A-qing and Little Jade lived with Jade's cousin Moon Beauty. In 2003, when Taiwan's National Central Library held a conference celebrating *Crystal Boys*, Bai himself invited me to speak on a panel with two other adaptors of his novel: film director Yu Kanping (1950–) and television miniseries cocreator Cao Ruiyuan (1961–). In my presentation, I spoke of the many streets in Taipei that felt familiar to me because they had appeared in *Crystal Boys*. For me, Nanjing East Road will always be linked to the aging mansion of Wang Kuilong, and Longjiang Street will always house the childhood home of A-qing. One place-name—the most important one of all in *Crystal Boys*—was no longer on the map. By the time I reached Taiwan, New Park had already been renamed 228 Peace Memorial Park. The long-awaited honoring of the victims of the February 28 Incident, in which Nationalist troops shot down many native Taiwanese, simultaneously erased a bit of the history of the men who had flocked to New Park for years to fulfill their longing to be with others like them. Just a bit, though. Whatever the real history of New Park and its denizens may be, Bai's *Crystal Boys* will always remain the definitive ethnography of these universally gay, yet specifically Taiwanese, birds of youth.

BIBLIOGRAPHY: "Election Aftermath," *Free China Review* 48, no. 1 (1998): 1. Fran Martin, trans., *Angelwings: Contemporary Queer Fiction from Taiwan* (Honolulu, 2003). Pai Hsieng-yung [Bai Xianyong], *Crystal Boys*, trans. Howard Goldblatt (San Francisco, 1995). Pai Hsieng-yung, *Wandering in the Garden, Waking from a Dream: Tales of Taipei Characters*, trans. Pai Hsien-yung and Patia Yasin, ed. George Kao (Bloomington, IN, 1982).

JOHN B. WEINSTEIN

1997

> "In the beginning, there was plenty of light, when the hotel was first opened." —Wong Bik Wan, *Doomsday Hotel*

Hong Kong's Literary Retrocession in Three Fantastical Novels

The most dramatic recent event in Hong Kong has been its retrocession to China in July 1997. Colloquially known as the handover, the event is described in three novels: anticipated by default in Lillian Lee's (1959–) *Rouge* (1984), first published in the year that the United Kingdom agreed to cede its control over Hong Kong; apprehensively forecast in Kai-cheung Dung's (1967–) *Atlas*, written and published in the year of retrocession; and retrospectively displaced in Wong Bik Wan's (1961–) *Doomsday Hotel*, published fourteen years after it. None of these novels explicitly mentions the retrocession but each can be read as expressing concern for Hong Kong's identity and survival. In their language (Mandarin with some Cantonese) and narrative style, the three works range from conventional to experimental; it is their common theme that suggests Hong Kong's complexity.

The best known of the trio is *Rouge*, if only because of its film adaptation by the same name released in 1988. In Lee's Hong Kong, the population is entirely Chinese, living for the present, fearful of the future, and haunted by the past. The British colonial superstructure has disappeared from both present and past; the expatriate communities do not intrude. The author creates three imaginary Hong Kongs: a past that ignores the imposition of colonial rule, an early 1980s present invented from within by the city's own compulsions, and a future in which the giant to the north plays no apparent role.

The main narrative has two layers: one is set in an everyday urban geography of newspaper offices, beauty contests, and electronic secret codes for telecommunication. The central lovers are bored with life and with each other. It is only when a ghost from fifty years earlier invades their lives, bringing with her a tale of passion, suicide, betrayal, and sacrifice, that they awake to the excitements of jealousy, eroticism, and tenderness they had let drift away. This darker narrative, the ghost's story, is set amid Hong Kong's old brothels, opium and gambling dens, and the fantasy world of Cantonese opera.

By the time she wrote *Rouge*, Lee was an experienced writer whose works were popular best sellers. As in her other novels, Lee constructs the stories, characters, and descriptions in *Rouge* in a conversational style that makes an effective contrast with its supernatural and romantic tone. The contrast becomes more problematic, however, in the story's fantastic denial of outside political and economic rule.

It has been claimed that *Rouge* is the first Hong Kong novel to find inspiration and color in its own recent history. However, China is hardly present, and neither is British colonial rule nor the foreign institutions that, along with wealthy native companies, control Hong Kong's financial life. To re-create Hong Kong in the 1930s and the 1980s without these elements not only ignores the colonialism and economic imperialism that, in inverse ratios, dominated Hong Kong during these two periods; it also ignores a newly powerful China across its borders, whose intention of reoccupying the city evokes increasingly nervous speculation beginning in the early 1980s.

Since the history of Hong Kong has always been treated as subordinate to the colonial or national discourse, any account of Hong Kong's past and present as either a colony or a special district cannot but fail to tell Hong Kong's story in its own terms. Instead, in Lee's version, the fantasy of a 1930s romance is doubled in her fantasy of a self-contained society. Whether or not Lee consciously created a negative narrative space in her novel is not important: readers then and now can still appreciate the ironies of multiple fantasies.

The full title of Dung's novel, *Atlas: The Archaeology of an Imaginary City*, acknowledges the element of fantasy in its depiction of 1990s Hong Kong, in which an archeologist from the distant future shuffles through maps, blueprints, and policy statements to excavate fragments of a lost city. Yet these documents are limited; they draw also on local Chinese legends and early colonial tales; and although they include relics from the 1990s, there appears to be no trace of colonial administrators (with one exception), businesspeople, or other foreign interests after the 1950s. An intimidating "other" is occasionally glimpsed in the narrative, however, appearing as an unnamed northern power.

Where Lee indulges in nostalgia for a romantic past and denial about its present and future existence, Dung is for the most part detached and rational about the disappearance of the Hong Kong in which he grew up and which he is about to lose forever: a sense of personal loss appears only in occasional lyrical passages. In the preface, Dung notes that *Atlas* was written and published in 1997, the year the colony of Hong Kong was returned by its British rulers to the People's Republic of China to become a special administrative region. The perspective is set in an unknown future time but with a retrospective, archaeological orientation, inquiring into the origin and long-lost past of the city. The city is supposed to have vanished, and efforts are made by scholars to re-create its history through imaginative readings of maps and documents unearthed only recently. The city is literally rebuilt by relics and fragments, casting a shadow on the question of reality and authenticity and in turn making way for the introduction of fiction into the process of history making.

Dung's narrator pieces together the remnants of a city whose native inhabitants were ruled by outsiders and whose own history was forgotten; a city conquered by an alien invader who reduced it to a prison camp; a city whose population was artificially swollen by floods of refugees from the country that was about to repossess it; a city where wealth and privilege coexisted with the poverty and squalor of much of its native population and its frequently impoverished and corrupt neighbors to the north.

Dung invented his own precisely executed style for *Atlas*, creating a sometimes inextricable mix of history and fiction, philosophical reflection and bureaucratic planning, maps and poetry, and legends that are both cartographic devices and societal myths. While Lee's chief concern is with the destinies of her characters, Dung's novel, by contrast, has no overarching narrative, only episodes in which romance and passion make brief appearances but where no character, apart from the unnamed narrator from the future, persists from chapter to chapter.

The most recent of the three novels, Wong's *Doomsday Hotel*, retreats to a colonial past, but it is not Hong Kong's past. The novel is set in Macao, which might represent to Hong Kong readers a substitute view of colonialism (Hong Kong being the "grown-up" version to other former colonials). As a fantasy of colonial life, it may be less disturbing to Hong Kong readers because of its displacement to Macao; it is nevertheless ominous in its portrait of a community in decline.

Doomsday Hotel was written and published on the eve of the fifteenth anniversary of the retrocession and the third restricted election of Hong Kong's chief executive. Its idiosyncratic and occasionally impenetrable style is appropriate to its bizarre colonial identity. The ostensible subject is a loose history of a famous Macao hotel, the Bela Vista, favorite of generations of visitors from Hong Kong, the mainland, and abroad. In the words of Philippe Pons, a French journalist,

> More than a hotel, the Bela Vista was one of those romantic places seemingly untouched by time. Before... 1992 it was a charming and quaint old establishment: an incarnation of the spirit of Macao, a kind of metaphor for this city. Built on a height in colonial style with large verandas, its two stories dominated the Praia Grande.... Far from the war, Macao had a bohemian, ephemeral existence.... The staff seemed as aged as the building and under as little pressure as the water coming out of the bathroom taps.... [It had] the serene charm of those old ladies who have experienced much and do not deny their age.... The old Bela Vista, dusty, where the curtains in the large rooms moved in the breeze and where the poorly fitted windows let in strong gusts and rain in the typhoon season, nonetheless haunted the memories of those who had stayed there. The Bela Vista was Macao. With the definitive closure of the hotel, another page has been torn out of the history of the city.

In Wong's novel, the Doomsday Hotel is a microcosm of a colonial society, in which the Portuguese-descended Macanese, only fitfully aware of the majority Cantonese population, are doomed to extinction in the modern world, while their replacement rulers lack their sense of history, tradition, and love of life.

Wong's characters drift in and out: they are born, love, suffer, die, and are replaced by others similarly afflicted. There are lapses of several paragraphs (sometimes pages) after they first appear before they are identified by surname, occupation, and their relationship to other characters. Events are rarely associated with specified causes or outcomes; long descriptive passages serve no overt purpose. Passion, betrayal, and violence repeatedly occur among the characters, but usually without sustained narrative justification; just as often the characters muse on life's mysteries. Titles of European musical compositions punctuate the narrative; paintings, fountains, and sculptures appear and disappear. Only dedicated readers might succeed in tracing the storylines between the book's two indistinctly marked sections: the history of the hotel between 1936 and 1941, and that of the first-person narrator, whose family runs the hotel from 1941 to 1956. Wong's narrative may read like a spontaneous outflow, but there are indications of measured control. Although nothing appears particularly new or inventive, her narrative strategy of displacement is both unusual and appealing.

Not all fiction related to 1997 seeks recourse in a realm of fantasy. Wong, for instance, has also written more directly about reactions to the pending retrocession on the part of British expatriates and Chinese families in Hong Kong, including those who migrated in the 1980s but returned in the 1990s. Originally published in 1994, her short story "Lost City" was considered too provocative for republication on the mainland. Similarly, John Lanchester's (1962–) award-winning *Fragrant Harbour* (2002) combines stories from the author's personal experiences of life in colonial and postcolonial Hong Kong with additional passages on Chinese migration to Australia in the 1990s and repatriation after 1997.

Against such mimetic works on Hong Kong's dilemmas, the three novels described here form a curious trilogy. What remains distinctive about them is their conviction that a specific identity exists in the peculiar phenomenon that is Hong Kong and in their resort to fantasy: whether taking shape through romance, nostalgia, or distance in time or place, fantastic narrative seems an appropriate mode for expressing this identity.

If China has experienced constant turmoil from the turn of the nineteenth century to the turn of the twenty-first century, change and turmoil have also been constant in the smaller compass of Hong Kong, reflecting but not necessarily reproducing movements and countermovements on the mainland, while undergoing its own trauma in the passage from village to city, from imperial periphery to colonial outpost, and from foreign rule to at best a mixture of local and mainland governance.

At the start of this period, low literacy prevailed while local culture flourished. An early example of a globally positioned society, Hong Kong gradually transformed itself into a modern cosmopolitan center of cultural diversity, set against the mainland's monocultural and backward-looking society. From 1911 on, China was no longer a colonized country, although it retained its colonizing predilection and occupied areas populated by non-Han people and cultures. In contrast, Hong Kong's response to world currents has been vigorous and inventive; its respect for tradition profound yet also sporadic and often satiric; and its neglect by the rest of the world more a matter of global politics than its merits as a sophisticated literary culture. By 2013, tensions between China and Hong Kong had only increased: the relentless polls on Hong Kong and Chinese identities that showed a stubborn resistance to the greater power; the unprecedentedly hostile reception accorded the new chief executive both before and after he was sworn in; and the locals' profound resentment toward mainland visitors to Hong Kong are among the issues that have stirred debate on Hong Kong's identity. Fantasy in fiction is generally its own reward; in the context of postcolonial and modern Chinese writing, it may offer a different kind of hermeneutics.

BIBLIOGRAPHY: Dung Kai-cheung, *Atlas: The Archaeology of an Imaginary City*, trans. Dung Kai-cheung, Anders Hansson, and Bonnie S. McDougall (New York, 2012). Dung Kai-cheung, *Ditu ji: Yige xiangxiang de chengshi de kaoguxue* (Taipei, 1997). Lee Bik-Wah [Lillian Lee], *Yanzhi kou* (Hong Kong, 2003). Bonnie S. McDougall, "Diversity as Value: Marginality, Post-colonialism and Identity in Modern Chinese Literature," in *Belief, History and the Individual in Modern Chinese Literary Culture*, ed. Artur K. Wardega (Newcastle upon Tyne, UK, 2009), 137–165. Wong Bik Wan, *Mori jiudian*, includes English translation as *Doomsday Hotel* by M. Klin (Hong Kong, 2011).

BONNIE S. MCDOUGALL

1997

> "Can't you speak, Ah! What ethnicity are you? Chinese, no?"
> —Tsai Ming-liang, *I Don't Want to Sleep Alone*

Representing the Sinophone, Truly: On Tsai Ming-liang's I Don't Want to Sleep Alone

In the third scene of Tsai Ming-liang's (1957–) *I Don't Want to Sleep Alone*, a film set in the Malaysian capital of Kuala Lumpur in the aftermath of the 1997 Asian financial crisis, a homeless man—one of two central characters played by Lee Kang-sheng (1968–)—is accosted by a group of local Malays who demand money from him as payment for some magic lottery numbers given by a street magician. There is clearly a language problem. The homeless man cannot understand their requests in Malay and does not respond. In utter frustration, the extortionists, who initially think he is Chinese, guess at his ethnicity by repeating to him that they want money in different languages: first by saying "money, money, money," then "baht, baht," and finally "peso," all currencies of nearby Southeast Asian countries. When this does not work, they do him grievous bodily harm. If they had tried *renminbi*, the currency of the People's Republic of China (PRC), or a dialect version of *qian*, the general Mandarin term for "money," or even *lui*, a Malaysian Hokkien and Cantonese pronunciation of *duit*, a Malay word for "money" that is derived from the name of a copper Dutch coin, they might have had more success. Although the homeless man's ethnicity is never specified, it is strongly suggested that he is a recent illegal Chinese migrant. He doesn't understand Malay, and we learn later that he does not have an identity card or passport, or even know how to tie a sarong.

The scene's significance is threefold. First, the image of a Chinese person without money is jarringly at odds with representations of the overseas Chinese as material men identified with commerce and as the personification of capital. This representation is common to two different and sometimes conflicting concepts of Chineseness: the official discourse of various colonial powers in Southeast Asia, which constructed "Chinese" subjects as *homo oeconomicus* through the colonial census because of their important role as middlemen in the colonial economy, and the discourse of *huaqiao* (a Chinese term sometimes used to refer to the overseas Chinese) nationalism, a broad appeal to the Chinese in Southeast Asia (the region known to the Chinese as Nanyang) in an effort to tap their financial resources, knowledge capacities, and economic skills for Nationalist causes. The latter discourse develops out of the attempts of the late Qing state, literati social reformers, and Republican revolutionaries to mobilize the overseas Chinese in order to strengthen the existing nation or build a new one. The Republican effort is epitomized by the famous characterization of the overseas Chinese as "the mother of the revolution" attributed to Sun Yat-sen (1866–1925).

Second, the violence against the homeless man is an ironic comment on the social position of Southeast Asian Chinese in the age of the PRC's ascendancy on the world stage as an economic superpower. For the PRC, 1997 was both the year of the return of Hong Kong, an event that symbolized the redress of China's humiliating victimization at the hands of

Western imperialism from the first Opium War to the first half of the twentieth century, and of the Asian financial crisis. The ensuing economic hardship in Southeast Asian countries had tragic social consequences, including a rise in anti-Chinese sentiment. In Indonesia, this erupted in the mass violence of the May 1998 anti-Chinese riots, in which atrocities such as the rape of ethnic Chinese women occurred. Such anti-Chinese feeling is rooted in images of overseas Chinese as economic oppressors of native Southeast Asians. These images, which are radically different from the self-characterization of Chinese as victims of Western imperialism, are deeply sedimented in the social consciousness of Southeast Asian countries.

In their "divide and rule" policy, the colonial authorities encouraged the stigmatization of overseas Chinese as aliens who exploit the indigenous population for material gain. However, this image of the Chinese as economic oppressors also intersected with the historical tradition of Middle Kingdom chauvinism in relation to its peripheries. The reformer Liang Qichao (1873–1929) declared that "in the hundred or more countries in the Southern seas, the majority of the population are descendants of the Yellow Emperor. Whether from a geographical or historical perspective, they are the natural colonies of our race." In the earlier stages of Deng Xiaoping's (1904–1997) economic modernization program, the PRC state deployed a revised version of the *huaqiao* paradigm to pull in foreign capital and entrepreneurial know-how from the overseas Chinese, thereby redefining the overseas Chinese as long-distance economic patriots of sorts. Within the context of anti-Chinese sentiment in Southeast Asia, this market-impelled re-Sinicization unfortunately revived images of ethnic Chinese as politically disloyal profiteers. Indeed, the contemporary emergence of the PRC as a source of transnational capital flows to other countries and the new waves of emigration from the PRC have renewed fears of Chinese as unscrupulous competitors and the agents of economic exploitation in Southeast Asia.

Third, the film's provocative focus on the daily lives of Malaysian Chinese and their relations to other ethnicities touches on a central issue in the recent academic debate on Sinophone literary studies: the oppressiveness of Chinese literary tradition and contemporary Chinese literary language in relation to the experiences of the Sinophone world. Ng Kim Chew (1967–), the brilliant Malaysian Chinese writer and literary critic, has noted that the conventional modern Chinese written language, which is based on Mandarin, fails to depict the sounds of Malaysian Hokkien, Cantonese, Teochew, and other dialects, and argued that existing Chinese literary genres cannot capture the reality of Southeast Asian societies because they do not fully engage with the social environment of those societies. Ng's social, cultural, and educational background is similar to Tsai's. Born ten years apart, both are Malaysian Chinese, received their university education in Taiwan, and have made Taiwan their home and base for artistic production. Although Tsai's earlier films are not explicitly concerned with issues of Chineseness, *I Don't Want to Sleep Alone* addresses the hierarchical relations between various Sinitic languages and cultures.

The asymmetrical socioeconomic power relations of the Malaysian Chinese to other ethnicities are part of the film's mise-en-scène. As Tsai observes, the financial crisis had tragic consequences for the many migrant workers who came to Malaysia to work in construction projects that had to be abandoned: "They'd been lured by the economic boom of the mid-1990s and they'd lost everything—including their dreams—in the economic crash.… The workers found themselves unemployed overnight and many went into hiding, becoming illegal laborers." The existing Chinese community regards these workers with suspicion. A Mandarin radio news report in the film blames illegal construction workers for starting plantation fires. At the same time, the construction firms that directly exploit migrant labor are predominantly owned by ethnic Chinese. When the homeless man is given shelter in an act of generous hospitality by a construction worker named Rawang, his fellow workers, who live in the same squalid lodgings, comment on the importance of keeping the guest's presence a secret from their landlady, who is explicitly ethnicized as Chinese: "We can't let the Chinese landlady know. We will be in trouble if she knows."

The film, however, disrupts the neat antithesis between Chinese and non-Chinese ethnicities by dramatizing the harsh exploitation of Chinese labor through the figure of a Chinese coffee shop waitress played by Chen Shiang-chyi (1969–). In addition to being a waitress, the character also cares for her petit bourgeois Chinese employer's invalid son, also played by Lee Kang-sheng, who is comatose and on life support. She lives in the cramped attic of the shop and the boss and her son live on the floor below.

The hierarchical relation is cogently evoked in a long take of the shop windows that shows the sharp spatial and symbolic divisions between the two floors: her boss sits at her dressing table in her brightly lit room performing evening skincare activities while the waitress moves around in the dark attic.

The film suggests that ethnic and social divisions can be transcended through humble quotidian gestures of care and affection that have no selfish financial motivation and that cut across ethnic boundaries. These gestures create a domain of being-with-others that temporarily shields its participants from the pressures of global capital flows and their impact on the politics of Chinese ethnicity. Rawang nurses the homeless man back to health despite insurmountable obstacles to verbal communication. His caring gestures stand in stark contrast to the waitress's brusque treatment of the invalid's body. The waitress, however, finds respite from her daily servitude by seeking erotic love in the homeless man's arms. Like the other migrant workers in the film, the three central characters derive whimsical pleasure from the small activities of making a habitat for themselves in a cityscape polluted by haze from forest fires from neighboring Indonesia. They decorate their lodgings with posters of vibrant hues, erect a makeshift Hindu shrine, and drag home discarded mattresses to be used for bedding.

Even when these relations are in danger of being sundered, as when Rawang, in a fit of jealous rage at the homeless man's sexual involvement with the waitress, attempts to cut the homeless man's throat with the jagged lid of a can, Tsai neatly resolves the tensions in a highly contrived, aestheticized set piece that closes the film. The three characters are shown in affectionate embrace in a beautiful, magical space that is quarantined from the outside world. They lie atop a mattress floating on a pool of water in the basement of an abandoned, partially constructed building. That such a magical space can be found amid the ruination and detritus of capitalist globalization is a minor miracle. However, the fact that this space is devoid of ethnic tensions is a utopian disavowal of the earlier scene where the homeless man is beaten. Although the homeless man's invalid doppelgänger is Malaysian Chinese, the viewer cannot definitively identify him as Chinese because we never hear him speak. By keeping verbal dialogue to a minimum, the film strips its main characters of ties to a language community, the conventional marker of ethnic identity, thereby enabling them to withdraw from and transcend the political tensions of ethnicity and labor migration. The earlier scene, however, indicates that ethnicization is inevitable. The very undecidability of the homeless man's ethnicity leads the Malay thugs to mark and fix him as Chinese in order to make sense of his behavior. This gesture is unavoidable in multiethnic Southeast Asian societies.

The socioeconomic power relations in the everyday lives of Malaysian Chinese portrayed in Tsai's film do not map neatly onto the hierarchies that Sinophone literary studies seek to contest. Sinophone literary studies seek to address the oppressiveness of Chinese literary history, the determination of the rightful inheritors and upholders of this literary cultural heritage, and which subjects and experiences are excluded because they are not sufficiently Chinese. For example, the heterogeneity of Malaysian Chinese dialects and non-Chinese languages in a multiethnic society cannot be adequately expressed in the Sinitic script of Chinese literature and its genres. Part of the brilliance of Tsai's film is that it points to the class-based structure of these literary debates. By focusing on the active expression of Sinophone languages in literary writing, these debates naturally privilege literary culture. The problem, however, is that the predominant culture of Malaysian and other overseas Chinese societies is not literary and, indeed, may not even involve an active use of Chinese writing.

What is striking about Tsai's film is that we never see any of the Chinese characters writing or even reading books or newspapers. Indeed, there is a complete absence of Chinese dialogue in interactions between the boss, the waitress, and the homeless man. The sparseness of dialogue, a hallmark of Tsai's films, has an added significance here. It suggests a largely passive audiovisual relation to Chinese languages and culture. We only know that the film portrays Malaysian Chinese because of the pervasive presence of Chinese radio as a medium for circulating Chinese popular culture: Cantonese and Mandarin news and informational programs, Cantonese opera, and Li Xianglan's (1920–2014) Mandarin songs. In *Sleeping on Dark Waters*, a companion DVD to the film, Tsai observes that as a child, he listened to Cantonese operas on the radio with his grandfather and was also fond of Mandarin popular music, especially Li's "If Only," which remains his favorite song today.

The film's emphasis on the passive reception of the products of the global Sinophone information and culture industry and the heteroglossia of Indian- and Malay-language popular culture suggests that the most appropriate representation of Sinophone Malaysian experiences is not literature and its written script but instead the audiovisual textuality of popular song and film. These textual forms would circumvent Sinophone literature's problem of confronting what Ng diagnoses as "a vernacular script that appears dull, impoverished, and strained, as well as dialects that are difficult to tame in this script (not to mention the languages of other ethnic groups)." What is crucial to the making of the lifeworld of the Malaysian Chinese is not the relation to cultural China, its authorized literary tradition, and its museumized cultural heritage but the relation to the constellation of various localized forms of Chineseness through global flows of popular Sinophone culture. This can only be adequately portrayed by audiovisual mimetic representation.

BIBLIOGRAPHY: Lim Song-Hwee, *Tsai Ming-liang and a Cinema of Slowness* (Honolulu, 2014). Zakir Hossain Raju, "Filmic Imaginations of the Malaysian Chinese: 'Mahua Cinema' as a Transnational Chinese Cinema," *Journal of Chinese Cinemas* 2, no. 1 (2008): 67–79. Shu-mei Shih, Chien-hsin Tsai, and Brian Bernards, eds., *Sinophone Studies: A Critical Reader* (New York, 2013). Tsai Ming-liang, dir., *I Don't Want to Sleep Alone* (2006). Tsai Ming-liang, dir., *What Time Is It There?* (2001).

PHENG CHEAH

1998 · MARCH 22

Chu Hsi-ning passes away.

The Silversmith of Fiction

The summer after my father passed away (March 22, 1998), the director of the planned National Museum of Taiwan Literature contacted our family with the hope that we might donate my father's remaining manuscripts to the museum.

The family members all tacitly agreed to the request. Besides giving the director what he wanted, we were also thinking about the place where the museum is located—the former offices of the Japanese colonial administration and then the Nationalist (Kuomintang, KMT) government in Tainan—the first place my father set foot on the island when he followed the KMT army to Taiwan in 1949, the place where his marriage was notarized.... And just like that, the manuscripts were donated to the museum—a most fitting way to remember him.

Sixteen years later, the museum, which has now sponsored countless exhibitions about individual writers, presents to the public "The Silversmith of Fiction: A Donated Exhibit on Chu Hsi-ning." The special exhibition was prepared with great care and serves as a proper introduction to this important writer who has been, intentionally or not, forgotten and overlooked by Taiwan.

We had, however, withheld from the donations his most authentic and suggestive three-volume work, *A Diary of Babes*, which truly represents his intentions as a writer—as his daughters, we could not help but feel a little guilty.

A Diary of Babes is written in the voices of his three daughters, each born two years apart. Through the innocent eyes of his children, it attempts to understand anew both family matters and the great affairs of the world. It even contains those private thoughts he kept buried deep in his heart and was only willing to confide to his daughters, whose lips he knew were sealed tight.

The diary opens in the voice of his first child, Chu T'ien-wen. There is a newspaper clipping stuck to the title page. It reads:

> Casting off family relations: having already reached the legally mandated age for marriage, and after entreating her parents several times to no effect, Liu Huimei now claims the freedom of marriage. Seeking a lifetime of happiness, she has legally emancipated herself from her family and established herself independently. From the day this announcement appears in the newspaper, she is no longer subject to interference from the law.

This was two years after the 228 Incident of February 1947. After governing Taiwan for fifty years, the Japanese withdrew from the island following their defeat in World War II. The 228 Incident marked the suppression of a conflict between the Nationalists, who took control of the island from the Japanese, and the native people of Taiwan. Both parties were equally unfamiliar with each other, and the Taiwanese feared and were hostile toward the majority of people from other provinces who had moved to Taiwan following the defeat of the Nationalists on the mainland in 1949, especially members of the military. It was under these circumstances that the daughter of a doctor from a small town exchanged letters with my father for a year, met him in person four times, and then decided to run away with him; it was the only available means by which they could pursue their freedom and happiness as a couple.

During the Japanese invasion of China, my father was a middle school student wandering back and forth between Jiangsu and Anhui Provinces. He was diligently preparing to take the entrance exam for Tsinghua University's engineering program. He hoped that after the war he could dedicate himself to the Yangtze River Water Conversation Project, a Nationalist policy devised in imitation of the Tennessee Valley Authority Act. One day, a building that resembled today's mammoth luxury shopping malls was erected in the Xinjiekou neighborhood of Nanjing, where my father was staying with his elder sister's family. Walking by it, he could only think about how incredibly small people had become. He then made up his mind to respond to General Sun Li-jen's (1900–1990) call and join a youth volunteer military unit. Just like so many other ardent youths of the time, he set aside his pen and joined in the war effort.

Also during this period of his life, there was a photo album; a dip pen had been used to draw a cross, holly and ivy, and a small angel in white paint. Below it was written, "Our little Ah-Gu, today we present you to God. 'God himself will provide the lamb for the burnt-offering, my son!' (Genesis, 30) Dedicated to you by your father on Christmas, 1956. Congratulations to you on your four months of life." [Chu T'ien-wen was born on August 24, 1956. —Trans.]

My father wrote this? I thought that was the letter that Pierre wrote to his and Natasha's child in *War and Peace*.

My father's paternal grandfather was heavily influenced by the Germans who occupied Shandong, and consequently became a preacher. After her baptism, my mother became the thirty-ninth Christian in the Chu family. Given this background, it is not difficult to understand why my father would take the Boxer Rebellion, the Shandong-based reaction against Western missionaries, as the starting point of his *A Record of the Hua Taiping Lineage*, in which he attempts to deal with both the profound impact of Christianity on modern China and the Sinicization of Christianity. It is a work that consumed eighteen years of his life and remains unfinished.

For the last ten years of my father's time preaching at a local church, complaints were filed by fundamentalist Christians that eventually led to his expulsion—the same fate my grandfather suffered before him. When my grandfather was expelled, he took his wife and two sons from Shandong and moved to Suqian in Jiangsu. My father simply went to the Baptist church one street over, where he preached until he retired.

The diary, written from the perspective of an infant T'ien-wen, states, "Later, Mom and *Dada* (my father seemed to like me to call him this, since that was what he called his own father) discussed the names they had originally chosen for me: You-ning (for a boy) and You-lang (for a girl), based on each of their pen names."

So, what was my mother's pen name back then? We asked my father once when we were older. He said it was Liu Lang, or "Wanderer." Their dream at the time was to one day go to the vast grasslands of Northwest China and cultivate the virgin soil. They also thought about one day organizing a magazine with Uncle Caihua (Duan Caihua, 1933–2015), which they wanted to call *Pioneers*.

There was a paragraph in my father's handwriting:

> At dusk, Mom carried me while she strolled with *Dada* around the small railway platform next to the sugar refinery. It was a beautiful autumn evening, but what is beauty really? One of the neighbors' children is even younger than me, perhaps less than one month old. Strapped to his mother's back—she is cutting the green grass while carrying a heavy load on the pole that lies across her shoulders—he tilts his pitiful, tiny head and is fast asleep. Ah, I am so happy! But how can I share my happiness with this little friend?

Without a doubt, my father was a typical humanist of his age, completely enamored by the enlightenment spirit (though not the leftist ideas) of the May Fourth Movement and the 1930s. He was not at all like those people who stayed on the mainland and were forced to become leftist writers. The reason is probably very simple: his two older brothers were both killed by the Communist Party. He did not trust the Communist Party, nor their illegitimate definition and depiction of the Left. Take, for example, his works produced during his "Molten Iron" phase, one of his most spirited and critical creative periods. Literary history has designated this group of works—a group that includes the short stories "Daybreak," "Suokemen Village," and "Molten Iron"—as works of "nostalgia for the homeland." One certainly does not see the recollections that typically characterize this style, wherein writers far from home aestheticize their hometowns, legends abound, and the people are always good. As for my father's works, there is not one that fails to evoke in readers a sense of awesome tragedy. Adopting a dark and ominous tone, they depict a heartless world and its inhabitants. This was probably the most powerful ideological critique the contemporary authorities could tolerate. Moreover, the wise and intelligent characters that appear in the stories always possess an enlightenment-style "progressive" consciousness. Even such uneducated characters as the uncle from "On the Mule Cart"—a man who refines worldly wisdom out of everyday life—possess sharp insights and even a degree of craftiness. What is important is knowing right and wrong, and truth and falsehood, not the inexhaustible nature of moral leniency.

My father greatly admired and spoke of Eileen Chang (1920–1995) throughout his life. But the fiction writer Liu Da-jen (1939–) is right: my father's fiction, especially the works of his "Molten Iron" phase, is far more reminiscent of Lu Xun (1881–1936).

A Diary of Babes also reveals the early growing pains of *A Record of the Hua Taiping Lineage:*

> *Dada* took a break and the two of us, father and daughter, had a sleeping competition. When we woke up, *Dada* helped change my diaper while telling me what was troubling him. He told me that the family affairs of the Chu household truly represent the course of Chinese history during the last hundred years—my great-great-grandfather's highly renowned and influential household, its financial decline, my grandfather's single-handedly reestablishing the family fortunes, the family's later ruin during the invasion of the Japanese warlords, and again due to the Communist Party's national betrayal.... *Dada* can't be blamed for getting lost in his thoughts, struggling day and night to figure out how to go about writing his long work, *Changing Tides.*

Midway through the writing process, *Changing Tides* was renamed *A Fallen Nation, a Fallen City*, only to be renamed once more *A Record of the Hua Taiping Lineage*. Once he started writing, his writing table and the walls were all plastered with the chronological tables of our family and all its members—we are larger in size than the Rong and Ning clans of *Dream of the Red Chamber!* Eileen Chang once said, "In my opinion, 'Molten Iron'—this kind of story so rich in local flavor and national characteristics unfamiliar to most people, such as the brave deeds of the Warring States Period—is everything that I and my compatriots have lost and let slip away."

My father wrote such formidable works, yet they all issued from a place of peace. Bent over the table below the desk lamp was a head of gray hair; several decades passed this way, each and every day the same.

In his last few years, my father moved downstairs to write his manuscripts. In the beginning it was for the convenience of answering the telephone and coping with the many people who would come by the house—the mailman, the rice deliveryman, the repairman. It was also to help his elementary-school-age granddaughter, Mengmeng. He would help her record Pingju operas and pick her up after school; they would watch plays and eat dim sum together. Gradually, a corner of the sofa in the living room became their nest. My father would sit cross-legged on the couch and write, his manuscript clipped to a hard acrylic sheet and the armrest serving as his desk. People would come and people would go, cats and dogs would run amuck, but nothing bothered him as he sat there peacefully writing. That nest in the corner of the living room became Colonel Aureliano Buendía's silver workshop.

My father began writing *A Record of the Hua Taiping Lineage* in 1980. In ten years, he revised the manuscript seven times and restarted it eight times. When the manuscript was just about to break the thirty-thousand-character milestone, it was completely devoured by termites. After this, he embarked on his ninth effort, and that is the manuscript now on display at the National Museum of Taiwan Literature. He was just like Colonel Aureliano Buendía, who ceased to sell those small silver goldfish but would still make two new ones every day, and, when he reached twenty-five, melt them down and start again.

The first chapter of the manuscript is called "Making a Vow." It starts with a five-year-old child and his silver-belled winter cowl and ends with the insertion of a personal afterthought, in which he describes how he selected the ninth day of the ninth lunar month of the ninth year of the project to begin anew: "The ninth time will be the last, and here I say a prayer to God: stretch the rules a little for me, beyond the span of my life, let me borrow another ten years, so that I can finally finish this work on our family traditions."

My father was born in 1926 and his zodiac symbol is the tiger. His granddaughter Mengmeng was younger than him by precisely a sexagenary cycle; they are the two tigers of the Chu family. It was once said, "Tigers do not live past the age of 65." When he passed away, though, my father was already seventy-two. One day, Gabriel García Márquez (1927–2014) appeared to be weeping as he was coming upstairs. His wife saw him and asked, "Did the Colonel die?" On that day, there were seventeen goldfish in the tin bucket in the workshop.

CHU T'IEN-HSIN
Translated by Kyle Shernuk

1999 · FEBRUARY

Hsia Yü buys a computer.

The Poet in the Machine: Hsia Yü's Analog Poetry Enters the Digital Age

It's easy to take for granted that the content of a work of art is influenced by the tools at the artist's disposal, that "the medium is the message." But what are the larger implications of digital technology and the Internet for poetic production? Conceptual artist Kenneth Goldsmith (1961–) has suggested that, with the rise of the Internet, writing has reached a juncture not unlike the challenge posed to painting by photography. Not only do digital technologies provide powerful tools for copying, editing, repurposing, and manipulating text, the Internet creates entirely new modes of distribution and platforms for reception, which further challenge the meaning of writing and the role of the writer. Above all else, the Internet is a repository of vast amounts of written text, in the midst of which even the most beautiful poem is just a drop in the ocean. How can the poet respond to this ongoing evolution in the technologies of reading and writing?

The question is all the more pertinent to a writer such as female Taiwanese poet Hsia Yü (1956–), whose work thematized technologies of reproduction and dissemination long before personal computers or the Internet made those processes effortless and instantaneous. As in conceptual art, the way Hsia Yü's poems are created is frequently more important than the meaning of the words. Her collections are three-dimensional pieces of design with careful attention paid to paper stock, physical dimensions, typeface, and typesetting, such that the poems contained inside always lose something in transcription or reproduction. She makes a point of subtly improving each collection whenever it is reprinted, gesturing at uniqueness even in an immanently reproductive medium. Her works frequently bear the traces of her own imperfect handiwork, or sometimes even that of the reader, who may be called on to tear open the uncut pages of the collection (*Salsa*, 1999), or contribute to its cover design by scratching off colored paint (*Sixty Poems*, 2011). Further, her experimental writing techniques—her deployment of collage and procedural writing, her playful appropriation of nonliterary language, and her penchant for concrete poetic forms—seem to drift away from the poet's lyrical self-expression and toward mechanical regurgitation or reproduction (not writing but typing, as Truman Capote [1924–1984] said of Jack Kerouac [1922–1969]). She has even said that she prefers copies to originals. Yet, even as her interest in technologies of mechanical reproduction is an attack against familiar notions of authorship and originality, her obsession with the imperfect copy is an effort to reintroduce randomness, humanity, and subjectivity back into art.

In her second poetry collection, 1991's *Ventriloquy*, Hsia Yü began experimenting with cut-ups and collage, techniques associated with avant-garde artistic movements of the early twentieth century. For one poem entitled "Séance III," she cut a page of printed characters into pieces and reassembled them into original, unreadable characters of her own invention. In another, she borrows Wang Bi's (226–249) third-century commentary on the *Book of Changes* ("Once one gets the images, one forgets the words") and replaces every instance of the word "image" (*xiang*) with an actual image, a simple black-and-white icon denoting an animal or object (cat, turtle, snake, dinosaur, alligator, crab, penguin, whale, chick, ladybug, flower, pineapple, and so on). In a final touch of sarcasm, Hsia

Yü titles the poem "The Missing Image"—or "The Missing Elephant," since *xiang* can mean both "image" and "elephant" in Chinese, an ambiguity that highlights the unreliability of the written word.

Yet, collage for Hsia Yü is not just a game, but also a response to the contradictions of personal identity. She recounts how, while living in Provence in 1995, confronting the inevitability of autumn as the indolent Mediterranean summer gradually waned, she was suddenly overcome by dissatisfaction—dissatisfaction with her poetry, with her life, with herself.

> Because it was autumn I discovered that my discomfort with pretty much all the poems I had written came from my inability to write them any other way. I thought maybe I wasn't the person writing these words right now either. If you just put two letters you mailed at the same time into the wrong envelopes, all karmic cause-and-effect would be slightly off and you would never know whose reincarnation you were.

Scramble the past just a little and you inherit an unrecognizable present.

One early morning, after a sleepless night, Hsia Yü's gaze fell on a copy of *Ventriloquy*, which had been printed in a rather large physical format, thirty-seven by forty-two centimeters. Feeling that it "took up too much space," Hsia Yü fell on it with scissors, slicing her poems into individual characters 1.5 centimeters square, piling them up like a thicket of tangled branches. For four days straight, she rearranged the dissected characters into new poems, held in place by a ring-bound scrapbook. Before she knew it, she had finished thirty new poems, stitched from the severed limbs of her previous book, bloated and tedious as it seemed to her now. The new poems became her third collection, *Friction Indescribable*. The book was a monster of Frankenstein, but at least it was alive.

Starting over. Trying again. Hsia Yü has no time for anything finished, fixed. Her poem "Letting Physical Objects Move on Their Own" includes the lines

> Each time I seriously think:
> "Next time will count so much more than this time"
>
> This is how I came to define
> the time after next time

I had better prepare for next time they barge out
to say loudly:
"That doesn't count."

Next time always counts more than this time. The time after next time
counts even more. "That still doesn't count," the poem concludes. "Even
that 'doesn't count' doesn't count."

Friction Indescribable takes the failure to reproduce accurately as its
beginning and end. It is a "rewrite" of *Ventriloquy* that preserves nothing substantial of the original; it is a two-dimensional photocopy of a
three-dimensional collage, replicating the handmade collage's uneven
arrangement while failing to reproduce its texture ("friction"), its existence
in space. The irony of *Friction Indescribable* is that, far from destroying
Ventriloquy, it actually fixes that collection more firmly in place, subverting Hsia Yü's rewriting instinct. "*Ventriloquy* can't be revised, because
every word in *Friction Indescribable* has its source. I couldn't even change
the font, or else *Friction* can't stand on its own, or it could stand but it
would become a different book, a different thing." To alter the original
after the copy has been made, she says, would be "to go back to the past
and rewrite the future." But wasn't Hsia Yü's original intention to turn
one set of poems into another, precisely to rewrite the future, the present?
Has Hsia Yü's preference for copies progressed to such an extent that the
original now depends on the copy for its life—that the copy demands
faithfulness from the original, rather than the other way around?

It happens that, as Hsia Yü was developing her poetic art along the
lines of a handicraft, her country was playing an important role in the
production and dissemination of digital technologies, namely semicon-
ductors, the building blocks of the personal computer—technologies that
enable lossless reproduction, where the kinds of traces Hsia Yü loved to
leave in her works do not naturally occur. As the semiconductor industry grew in Taiwan, as personal computers and eventually the Internet
penetrated markets around the world, how would Hsia Yü respond to a
computerized medium characterized by, in Charles Bernstein's (1950–)
words, "invariance [and] accuracy"? Hsia Yü's subsequent collection, *Salsa*,
arose out of fragments amassed in a notebook over seven or eight years,
which the poet revised "until each fragment found its best place—some
fragments wandered off and got lost and eventually became another

poem." This time, instead of photocopying the resulting collage-poems, she copied them out by hand in "very dark, very dark" black ink. In January 1999, she finished the collection's forty-six poems in Paris; in February, she returned to Taipei with a floppy disk containing all the poems, typed out by a friend. Hsia Yü, it turns out, couldn't really type. However, she soon bought a computer and began to edit the poems again herself, this time digitally. She describes this revising process as "one key at a time, but quite off-key." Slowly, tentatively, the analog poet entered the digital age.

During the eight years between *Salsa* and Hsia Yü's next collection, *Pink Noise*, technologies from digital cameras to MP3 audio to e-books drastically changed how images, music, and literature were consumed. Hsia Yü's fans had endured those years of silence in great anticipation, but *Pink Noise* left them at best baffled, at worst annoyed—reactions they were, by now, expressing in blogs and online discussion forums. With *Pink Noise*, the poet who achieved cult literary stardom through her avant-garde impulses finally outdid herself, publishing a volume of what she herself labeled "pseudo-poetry" or "non-poetry." The book was printed entirely on transparent celluloid, so that the words appeared as an impenetrable jumble (the promised "noise") and could only be read by inserting a blank piece of paper behind each page, leading one Internet commentator to label the book "anti-reading." The text of the collection consisted of thirty-three poems printed first in English, left justified and in black ink, and then on the following page in Chinese translation, right justified and in pink ink. Nor were the poems any more approachable than the material form of the book: for one thing, the English poems in *Pink Noise* were translated into Chinese not by a human being, but by a computer program called Sherlock, which, needless to say, made countless grammatical, lexicographic, and idiomatic errors, some of them quite hilarious (more noise). For another thing, the English originals were not written by Hsia Yü either, but cut and pasted from texts she found on the Internet—texts that were in most cases not literary, and in some cases semiliterate. Alongside snatches of Philip Larkin (1922–1985) and Walt Whitman (1819–1892) were advertisements for lesbian porn and discussion threads on Japanese sex toys; even lines from Karl Marx (1818–1883) and a bit of Kurt Cobain's (1967–1994) suicide note make appearances. The first edition sold out quickly, but the response was lukewarm. Another blogger paraphrased Hsia Yü's gesture: "My love, I've made my poetry collection transparent! (And water-proof, moisture-proof, and insect-proof, three-in-one)." Transparent, perhaps, but also impossibly opaque; not only waterproof, but reader-proof.

Hsia Yü had seemingly embraced digital technology with great gusto: *Pink Noise* was created entirely inside the computer, its process automated to the greatest extent possible. At the same time, as a collage made from a found text, *Pink Noise* is a rewrite of Hsia Yü's previous rewrite, *Friction Indescribable*, which had highlighted the imperfections of the handmade copy. As a result, Hsia Yü's interaction with the computer is nothing like the ideal of "invariance and accuracy": it is clear that she approached Sherlock in the hope not that it would produce accurate translations of her source texts in Chinese, but rather that it might produce something more or less. She was not disappointed. "When he (my mechanical poet) is right," she says, "he's righter than right, and when he messes up, he's as wrong as could possibly be." Sherlock's imperfections produce something resembling intelligence, even personality. Hsia Yü refers to Sherlock in increasingly personal terms, first as "mechanical poet" and soon as "mechanical lover." Hsia Yü has found the poet in the machine.

Even the idea of printing on transparency had occurred to Hsia Yü while she was deciding on a form for *Friction Indescribable*, but she ultimately used drawing paper for that project "because of Cézanne (in the end perhaps I saw myself as an oil painter)." For *Pink Noise*, Hsia Yü no longer identifies with a creative genius such as an oil painter, but with a model closer to Marjorie Perloff's (1931–) "unoriginal genius," which Kenneth Goldsmith explains as such: "While traditional notions of writing are primarily focused on 'originality' and 'creativity,' the digital environment fosters new skill sets that include 'manipulation' and 'management' of the heaps of already existent and ever-increasing language." When Hsia Yü was asked in an interview what exactly her role in creating *Pink Noise* was, given that she had composed neither the originals nor the translations, she replied, "I found the poetry, I found the form." Using ready-made material attacks the notion of author as creative genius, but it also raises her to the level of organizer. By automating and outsourcing her processes, Hsia Yü promoted herself to management.

At first blush, Hsia Yü's follow-up collection to *Pink Noise* seems already to show her weariness with the unlimited editing made possible by digital technology: the cover of 2011's *Sixty Poems* is covered in the same material as a scratch-off lottery ticket, so whatever design the reader engraves onto her copy is the one she is stuck with, no do-overs allowed. The Internet, however, intervenes again: a group on the photo-sharing site Flickr solicits readers to submit pictures of their designs, and 194 have been collected as of this writing. The creative possibilities continue to multiply.

BIBLIOGRAPHY: Kenneth Goldsmith, *Uncreative Writing: Managing Language in the Digital Age* (New York, 2011). Hsia Yü, *Fusion Kitsch: Poems from the Chinese of Hsia Yü*, trans. Steve Bradbury (Brookline, MA, 2001). Michelle Yeh, "Toward a Poetics of Noise: From Hu Shi to Hsia Yü," *Chinese Literature: Essays Articles Reviews* 30 (December 2008): 167–178.

BRIAN SKERRATT

1999 · MARCH 28

"Just write about this!"

Sixteen-Year-Old Han Han Roughs Up the Literary Scene

"Just write about this!" said the editor of the youth journal *Mengya* to Han Han (1982–) as he tossed a crumpled piece of paper into a glass of water. The sixteen-year-old Han was one of China's "problem" students. He earned bad grades and only managed to get into high school because he was good at sports. He was, in other words, a stereotypical loser—one of the kids who did not fit into the Chinese educational system. But what this good-for-nothing student wrote during the next hour amazed the jury of the first-ever National New Concept Competition. In his essay, "Seeing Ourselves in a Cup," he used the crumpled paper ball dissolving in a glass of water as a metaphor for the Chinese people dissolving in Chinese society. He quoted Latin, classical Chinese literature, and modern authors like Lu Xun (1881–1936) and Qian Zhongshu (1910–1998). How could this social misfit have written such a sophisticated, mature, and philosophical essay? This question started a lively Internet debate now known as the Han Han Phenomenon.

It was raining in Shanghai on that Sunday, March 28, 1999, when Han went to the Pine City Hotel to pick up his first-place prize. Although

Han began publishing in 1997, when he was still in junior high, it was this award and the discussion it provoked that provided his ticket to stardom. It was on this day that the former high school loser became a literary star.

At that time, Han was already writing several pieces of literature. His most ambitious project, the novel *Three Gates of Honor* (2000), was strongly influenced by Qian Zhongshu's novel *Fortress Besieged*, but set in contemporary times and written from a student's perspective and partly autobiographical, like all of his novels so far. Since the public was anxious to learn about the background of the award-winning essay, and this novel provided it, the novel therefore became a best seller. It quickly sold over two million copies and became China's most popular novel from the previous two decades. Millions of school-age kids identified with it and adults enjoyed the nostalgic memories it evoked. The title, *Three Gates of Honor*, refers both to three historically important gates in ancient China and to the modern school gate, lecture building entrance door, and classroom door. It is a postmodern satire on education and authority. In it, even before the protagonist (Yuxiang) goes to school, his father asks him to memorize characters and read both classical and modern Chinese books, but only those published before 1949, and it is precisely this sort of training in literature that helped explain Han's success with his first essay. Han uses proverbs from classical Chinese and makes them literally come true, in turn creating the plot twists and absurdities of his early novels. He possesses a sharp wit and his sense of humor often makes use of word plays, idioms, and colloquialisms, which makes his novels, especially his early ones, difficult to translate. His blogs, however, and the newer novel *1988: I Want to Talk with the World* are available in English, and he is widely known as a blogger, both in China and throughout the world.

In contemporary China, there has been a trend toward favoring younger authors. For example, Jiang Fangzhou (1989–) published her first essay collection at the age of nine. But Han is not just another young author. With the royalties from his novels, he started a career as a racecar driver, and winning competitions on the national level brought him additional fame and celebrity. Demonstrating a social-critical conscience, he uses his fame to help shape public opinion during television appearances and in interviews. His sarcastic comments on contemporary politics have already achieved a cult status.

As such a cultural and political celebrity, Han took advantage of the booming Internet culture and, in 2006, started to write the blog *Two*

Cold—*So Warm*, which is hosted on China's biggest blog portal, sina
.com. He has not written an extraordinarily large number of entries, but
most of his entries are short essays. His blog soon became the portal's
most popular site, drawing millions of followers. When Han opened an
account on Weibo by typing "Hello," he instantly got 750,000 followers. Two years later, in 2008, his novel *His Land* was published serially
on the leading online literature platform, qidian.com, becoming a best
seller electronically before being published as a physical book (which also
became a best seller). His book *Three Gates of Honor* was turned into a
television series, his novel *1988: I Want to Talk with the World* into a road
movie. He acts in his own music videos, and has edited an issue of the
literary journal *Party*. Han is a new type of Renaissance man, transcending genre borders by publishing the same story in different media forms.

Han uses his blog to address various facets of social injustice. In 2010,
after the imprisoned dissident Liu Xiaobo (1955–) won the Nobel Peace
Prize, Han published a pair of quotation marks, an equivalent to the
empty chair in Oslo, and drew 1.5 million hits. Han writes about censorship and the suppressed freedom of expression, land eviction, corrupt
party cadres, poisonous factories, and those who lost out on China's
economic rise. In one entry, he questions the term "one-party system" on
the grounds that if there is only one party, it cannot be a "system" at all.
In 2010, he argued that cadre Han Feng, who kept a diary on his abuse
of power (including accepting bribes and keeping mistresses), was actually a good cadre, because his abuse of power was relatively small in
comparison to cadres in general. Han Han started a poll and found that
97 percent of respondents agreed with him. He also reports about little
incidents, such as the time when he left his cell phone in a taxi during a
visit to Taiwan. The taxi driver brought the cell phone back, something
that would probably not have happened in mainland China. Han asked
if traditional Chinese moral values like these had survived only in Taiwan. He comments on things that are widely discussed in society, like
the case of a two-year-old girl, Yueyue, who was hit by a car and then left
bleeding on the ground to die even as eighteen passersby ignored her, to
which he remarked, "Indifference and selfishness have become a part of
the Chinese national character." His blog entry "Let Some People Start
Having Elections First" refers to Deng Xiaoping's (1904–1997) famous
slogan during the 1980s reform and opening policy, "Let some people get
rich first." Han's version refers to the villagers of Wukan, who organized

their own elections after protesting against illegal seizure of their land. In his blog entry "Three Talks" (a reference to Deng's ideological theory), he attacks the limits of Chinese reform and speaks of democracy and freedom. He expresses his disgust with the educational system, bribery, and corruption and openly mocks them. He writes with depth and conviction.

In 2010, *Time* magazine named Han the second most influential person in the world. China has a time-honored tradition of viewing intellectuals as the critical conscience of society, and in the twenty-first century celebrities and artists have been taking over this role and becoming opinion leaders. Experts and laymen join in debates online and the masses are more involved, though the discussion topics have become more short-lived.

Han represents youth culture in the postsocialist age. In the eyes of some of China's youths, the government lost its legitimacy when it shot its own people during the Tiananmen Incident in 1989. It is only tolerated as long as it goes the capitalist way and offers the vision of an Americanized China. The young opinion leaders in the 1920s were students and intellectuals, absorbing Western education and knowledge to overthrow the establishment of traditional Chinese culture. Youths in the 1940s had a burning desire to improve China through a utopian ideology, and it remained enthusiastic until the nation's hidden true face, the "real existing socialism" became obvious in the mid-1950s. In the 1960s, the youth was mobilized to continue the Communist Revolution, throwing the country into chaos instead. During the 1980s, following Deng's reform and opening policy, there emerged a more mature generation of youths with considerable knowledge about the outside world. However, the crackdown on the democracy movement in 1989 marked a turning point, as young people turned away from politics and concentrated on their education, study abroad, career, and business opportunities instead. Han is one of the few critical opinion leaders who has yet to be persecuted.

Like Franz Kafka (1883–1924), Nikolai Gogol (1809–1852), and Lu Xun, Han typically takes a fictional element and places it in a realistic environment. In *His Land*, for instance, the pollution in a local lake makes the crabs grow big. Instead of stopping the pollution, the locals make these monstrous crabs a best-selling export. When the corrupt cadres profiting from this fraud joyfully jump into the lake, however, they die—because a fisherman is illegally using electricity to shock the fish. In another scene, during a song contest, the party choir and the choir of the business people are described as almost unbeatable. So when the protagonist Zuo Xiaolong wants to build his own choir, "the only choir member finally registering is a dependent, mute child."

Although Han Han became famous through a casting competition, and his restaurant chain, named after his 2013 short story collection *Nice Meeting You*, bases its success on his fame, he is not a commercial product. He simply represents a new generation of authors that is using all media channels to offer its literary messages to the masses. His message is refreshingly critical, with a good sense of sarcastic humor and playful creativity.

BIBLIOGRAPHY: Han Han, *1988: Wo xiang he zhe ge shijie tantan* (Beijing, 2010); translated by Howard Goldblatt as *1988: I Want to Talk with the World* (Seattle, 2015). Han Han, *San chong men* (Beijing, 2000); translated by Guan Jian and Sylvie Schneiter as *Les Trois Portes* (Paris, 2004). Han Han, *Ta de guo* (Shenyang, 2009). Han Han, *This Generation: Dispatches from China's Most Popular Star (and Race Car Driver)* (New York, 2012).

MARTIN WOESLER

2002 · OCTOBER 25

> If the West Lake is drained of its water
> And rivers and ponds are dried up,
> If Thunder Peak Pagoda crumbles,
> Only then can the White Snake again roam the earth.
> —From "Lady White Forever Imprisoned beneath Thunder Peak
>   Pagoda," 1624

Resurrecting a Postlapsarian Pagoda in a Postrevolutionary World

The Buddhist monk Fa Hai says the quote at the beginning of this essay in one of China's most popular legends, "The Legend of the White Snake," as he traps an errant snake spirit and her coconspirator, the Green Snake, beneath Thunder Peak Pagoda, a famous landmark on the shores of Hangzhou's West Lake. To Fa Hai, the White Snake's imprisonment is just punishment for her grave sins: transgression of the human-animal spirit boundary, deception and seduction, and an attack on a religious institution. This fictional incantation, as recorded in *Stories to Caution the World*, a 1624 collection of short stories by the writer Feng Menglong (1574–1645), is meant to serve as a promise of eternal imprisonment beneath an indestructible edifice, but ironically foretells historical fact: the pagoda would collapse on September 24, 1924. Its fall made a powerful impression on early twentieth-century iconoclasts as a metaphor for the eagerly awaited crumbling of oppressive institutions—many would have been happy to see both the pagoda and its associated superstitions fully disintegrate. Yet, despite its physical instability, the pagoda has held fast in popular imagination, and in the late 1990s the local Hangzhou government decided to restore the pagoda to its rightful place as one of the Ten Scenic Vistas of West Lake. When their "authentic" reconstruction of Thunder Peak Pagoda opened in 2002, it contained both the ruins of the former pagoda—encased in plexiglass and viewable to visitors—and a set of exquisitely carved reliefs depicting the White Snake story. No longer a symbol of China's dark past, the new pagoda safely ensconces the old in a slick design that claims to blend tradition with the latest architectural technologies, draws revenue from entrance tickets, and mirrors postrevolutionary China's embrace of its (reimagined) national history.

Just as the original pagoda is now impossible to separate from its reconstruction, it is difficult to disentangle the original White Snake tale from its many retellings. The common premise of popular versions involves a white snake spirit transforming into a beautiful woman, Lady White, in order to roam the human realm. She meets a man, Xu Xian, on the banks of West Lake; they court, wed, and live happily until the day Lady White accidentally reveals her true form and frightens her husband to death. She successfully restores him to life, only to find their happiness threatened by another plot twist: a vengeful monk, Fa Hai, convinces Xu Xian to leave his snake-wife and enter his monastery. An epic water battle between snake and monk ensues, drowning both temple and innocent bystanders in the swells. When Fa Hai ultimately triumphs, Lady White is justly sentenced to eternal imprisonment. In some versions, a second part then recounts the story of Lady White's son, Xu Mengjiao, who embarks on a quest to atone for his mother's sins and secure her release.

May Fourth intellectuals of the early twentieth century, while hardly children of the White Snake, became as devoted to tearing down oppressive structures and releasing their prisoners as Xu Mengjiao. In literature, drama, and journalism, pagodas became concrete symbols of confinement by Confucian mores, patriarchal hierarchy, and rigid class structure, and their destruction functioned as a powerful allegory for an end to traditional social order. When the real pagoda actually fell, iconoclasts—such as Lu Xun (1881–1936), who wrote a famous essay on the event, "On the Collapse of the Thunder Peak Pagoda"—felt vindicated. Other authors—such as the female playwright Bai Wei (1894–1987) in *Breaking Out of Ghost Pagoda* (1928) and Eileen Chang (1920–1995) in *The Fall of the Pagoda* (1950)—would continue to use pagodas as images of decay and ultimately inescapable social prisons. The fall of the pagoda, supposedly caused by local villagers picking away stones they believed to have magical properties from its base, also anticipated the more violent and purposeful destruction of monuments and artifacts representing the "four olds" during the Cultural Revolution by Red Guard mobs.

As writers wrestled with the meaning of the pagoda's fall and reformers struggled to build new institutions on the ruins of the old empire, the White Snake story itself, as if it were actually liberated, began to shift and move between storytelling media. Both the edifice and its legend became aligned with certain key epochal shifts central to China's modernization: the emergence and proliferation of new technologies like radio and film, the spread of revolutionary romanticism, and the ever-increasing ease of international travel. Film in particular contributed to the transformation of the story of White Snake, allowing her to move more easily across geographic and cultural borders. The first White Snake film premiered in 1926 and played primarily to a domestic market, but only a few decades later, the Japanese company Toei Animation would give the White Snake a chance to travel across the Pacific via Japan. In 1958, when Toei made the White Snake into its first-ever full-color anime feature film, they were targeting a US-based audience raised on Disney. The film effectively shed any dark associations with the transgressive and the demonic by adding a cohort of cavorting magical animal pals to accompany the White Snake. The legend became approachable, even cute—palatable fodder for audiences worldwide.

The White Snake underwent an equally radical transformation when she came to play the role of righteous romantic heroine on the mid-twentieth-century Peking opera stage. Part of the dramatic canon since at least the eighteenth century, the *Legend of the White Snake* (1954) became a modern, revolutionary opera thanks to Tian Han (1898–1968), a play-wright and the lyricist of China's rousing national anthem, "March of the Volunteers." Tian's *White Snake* begins with the two snake women already in human form, almost encouraging audience members to forget that the characters have supernatural origins. The play unfolds like a Hollywood romantic comedy: love at first sight hastens Lady White and Xu Xian into a happy marriage, and when Fa Hai enters the picture, he is recast as a malicious villain. In Tian's telling, the Buddhist monastic system that Fa Hai represents is a corrupt institution, and the play ends not with the capture of the White Snake, but with vengeance. Years after Lady White's imprisonment, Little Green returns with an army of creatures to free her mistress from her unjust fate, and revolt against the system carries the day. It took Tian nearly thirteen years of rewriting to purge the story of its "feudal" superstitious elements and develop an adaptation consistent with the socialist values of New China; when his final version took the stage in 1954, it gave audiences a White Snake who fought with zeal for her right to free choice in love—a perfect storm of revolutionary fervor, righteous suffering, and romantic passion. No longer a cautionary tale or allegory of the demise of the old social system, Tian's *White Snake* offered a heroine befitting a generation of romantic revolutionaries.

Echoes and imitations of Tian's now-canonical Peking opera text can still be found across all genres of the performing arts in China. Yet, at the same time, iterations of the White Snake story proliferated with each passing generation and successive waves of transnational cultural trans-mission. A popular television show from Taiwan with an international cast—*The New Legend of Madame White* (1992)—and a campy Hong Kong film adaptation of a pop novella—*Green Snake* (1993)—brought the White Snake to the fore of "pan-Asian" cultural production. In *Green Snake*, the focus shifts to Lady White's companion, Little Green, which somehow licenses the fabrication of a love triangle between Lady White, Little Green, and Xu Xian, as well as the inclusion of a hot springs bath-ing scene featuring the two snake women frolicking suggestively. But where the *Green Snake* film exploits this lesbian love scene to titillate the audience, more radical rewrites such as Taiwanese playwright Tian Qiyuan's (1964–1996) *White Water* (1993) and mainland writer Yan Geling's (1958–) novella *White Snake* (1999) have appropriated the story for more weighty explorations of sexuality and gender. With an all-male cast, Tian's *White Water* applies the White Snake's erasure of boundaries between human and animal to contemporary gender roles, and focuses its attention on the fundamental question of what constitutes love, loyalty, and jealousy in human relations. Homosexual attraction also features in Yan's novella, which is provocatively set during the Cultural Revolution. In it, a cross-dressing young woman in the guise of an official interrogator seduces a ballet dancer who once played the part of the White Snake. The theme of deception is mirrored by the story's narrative structure, which slips back and forth between "official account" and "untold story," exposing the shape-shifting nature of Cultural Revolution history and memory. In embodying these new forms of boundary crossing, the once-shackled White Snake comes to actively give voice to suppressed people and repressed memories.

Thus released and transformed by new writers, new media, and new geographic possibilities, by the turn of the twentieth century the White Snake came to fully embody her transgressive potential. The reconstruction of the Thunder Peak Pagoda at precisely this moment—in careful replication of its earlier architecture and with accompanying artistic representations of a family-friendly version of the White Snake story—thus seems staid, conservative, and out of touch with what the legend has come to be. Given that the project was sanctioned and sponsored by the local government, such containment of a white-washed White Snake could even be read as an attempt to reassert control over a legend gone wild and reestablish an official version legitimized by location and monumentality. However, the new pagoda is not unequivocally tied to the White Snake story; the legend is a presence and a draw for visitors, but not the main attraction. Tourists may be more impressed by the spectacular view of West Lake offered by the pagoda's upper levels or the valuable religious relics on display, which were unearthed in excavations preceding the new pagoda's construction. The artifacts have toured to museums outside Hangzhou, and beautifully produced, glossy art books for sale at the gift shop allow visitors to purchase and take home a reminder of the site's historical and archaeological value. Some newspaper articles reporting on the construction of the new pagoda, including one with the unsubtle title "The Thunder Peak Pagoda Does Not Equal Xu Xian plus Lady White," attempted to fully dissociate the new structure from the old legend. If the fall of the pagoda in 1924 released Lady White to travel and transform, its rebuilding in 2002 may have paradoxically freed the site to be repositioned in relation to the story and have its historical and cultural significance rewritten.

Escape, ruin, containment. Collapse, rubble, rebuilding. In the neoliberal, post-Socialist China of 2002, the liberated pagoda and its version of the White Snake once again function as a metaphor, but this time it is an uneasy coexistence of new and old paralleling the ambivalence toward history that has replaced hyperbolic revolutionary rhetoric. Publications marking the opening of the new pagoda referred to the project as fulfillment of the "desire of the people" to see a beloved landmark restored, while the bilingual Chinese-English signage and proud restoration of the Ten Scenic Vistas of West Lake anticipated international visitors and later application for UNESCO World Heritage Site status (granted to the West Lake Cultural Landscape in 2011). Today, the site still acknowledges only the most orthodox of literary and historical narratives, but sexy new versions of the White Snake legend continue to appear. The Ming Hwa Yuan Taiwanese opera troupe's White Snake Spectacular, featuring rock concert–style simulcast projection, has been performed annually since 2004 for outdoor audiences occasionally topping one hundred thousand. Productions like Jet Li's (1963–) 2011 film *The Sorcerer and the White Snake* or the 2013 stage production of *Green Snake* by the acclaimed Beijing director Tian Qinxin (1968–), continue to create a new breed of fans and West Lake pilgrims. Thus, whereas the fall of the Thunder Peak Pagoda in 1924 resonated strongly with the destructive, revolutionary energy that drove China's early modernization, the resurrected pagoda is too layered with associations and too full of artifacts couched in discourses of commercial tourism and heritage preservation to give it any single, clear meaning in the contemporary world. It stands again on the banks of West Lake, a perfect postmodern metaphor for a postrevolutionary world.

BIBLIOGRAPHY: Donald Chang and William Packard, trans., "The White Snake," in *The Red Pear Garden: The Great Dramas of Revolutionary China*, ed. John D. Mitchell (Boston, 1973), 49–120. Wilt L. Idema, trans., *The White Snake and Her Son: A Translation of The Precious Scroll of Thunder Peak with Related Texts* (Indianapolis, 2009). Lu Xun, "On the Collapse of the Leifeng Pagoda," trans. Gladys and Xinyi Yang, in *Selected Works of Lu Xun* (Beijing, 1957), 2:82–85. Eugene Y. Wang, "Tope and Topos: The Leifeng Pagoda and the Discourse of the Demonic," in *Writing and Materiality in*

China: *Essays in Honor of Patrick Hanan,* ed. Judith T. Zeitlin and Lydia H. Liu, with Ellen Widmer (Cambridge, MA, 2003), 488–552. Geling Yan, *The White Snake and Other Stories* (San Francisco, 1999).

Tarryn Li-Min Chun

2004 · APRIL

> "Wolves truly are class enemies. We must resolutely and thoroughly
> wipe wolves off the face of the earth." —Jiang Rong, *Wolf Totem*

Wolf Totem *and Nature Writing*

Jiang Rong's (1946–; born Lü Jiamin) *Wolf Totem* (2004) was an instant sensation in China, with tens of thousands of copies sold in the weeks following its release and millions more since. The novel has also been a great success abroad, with translations to date into some two dozen languages. *Wolf Totem* is based on Jiang Rong's experiences in Inner Mongolia between 1967 and 1978, or the Cultural Revolution and its immediate aftermath. The novel follows Chen Zhen, a young Beijing intellectual who is sent to Inner Mongolia as part of a production team and becomes enthralled with the region. He witnesses an influx of Han Chinese (China's most populous ethnic group) into the Inner Mongolian grasslands, which transforms the space from one of nomadic herding to one of grain cropping and wolf-extermination campaigns. Decades later, when Chen Zhen returns to the region, much of the grassland has become desert.

Wolf Totem is a critique of the Cultural Revolution, Chinese nationalism, and the destruction of ethnic minorities, as well as of environmental degradation. The novel portrays the hatred of wolves as having penetrated the Han Chinese psyche so deeply that nothing can convince them to halt the mass slaughter of these animals; most Han Chinese in the novel believe that wolves are a destructive, evil force that must be exterminated as swiftly as possible. For instance, the narrator cites a Red Guard leader who claims, "Wolves truly are class enemies. Reactionaries around the world are all wildly ambitious wolves. . . . We need to organize the masses to hunt them down and apply the proletarian dictatorship against them. We must resolutely and thoroughly wipe wolves off the face of the earth." Here the Red Guard is recycling conventional Chinese convictions concerning wolves: while the dragon is the symbol of Chinese civilization, the wolf has generally been associated with vice and greed. The term "class enemy" refers primarily to so-called reactionary elements, particularly technocrats, within the Chinese Communist Party; when the Red Guard speaks of "reactionaries," he means those with elitist, antiegalitarian attitudes who prioritize education and other bourgeois practices over reliance on the sheer energy of the people, and by so doing increase the gap between rich and poor.

As the Red Guard's comments suggest, reactionaries and class enemies were heavily persecuted during the Cultural Revolution. Interesting here is how the Red Guard mixes metaphors and species: just as "wolves" are "class enemies," so too are "reactionaries" wolves, and "wildly ambitious" ones at that. Not all Han Chinese in Inner Mongolia were convinced that wolves were real enemies of the people, and many individuals sent to rural China did not yield to the rhetoric of the Red Guards. In fact, *Wolf Totem's* protagonist Chen Zhen admires wolves, much like the author himself, and studies their "wolf virtue"—survival based on cunningness, ruthlessness, and violence. Even though most Chinese in the novel perceive the wolf as emblematizing vice and greed, so too is this animal regarded as a virtuous one whose survival, often in the harshest circumstances, depends on its ability to attack other creatures, including people. Nevertheless, many who were sent down to the countryside believed that wolves needed to be destroyed. The novel's Han Chinese criticize the Mongols for their "primitive" methods and ways of thinking, stressing that China and the world have entered the atomic age, an age in which satellites circle the earth and animals such as wolves are no longer needed. But the novel also stresses that for all China's scientific advances, problems as basic as how to feed its burgeoning population are becoming more acute. The bitter irony underlying the novel's great popularity is that "wolf virtue" was brought to bear on the virtue of China's market-driven, post-socialist "virtue." *Wolf Totem* is both a nostalgic recollection of the hardships of life in Inner Mongolia during the Cultural Revolution and an unlikely fable of the laws of China's socialist and capitalist jungles.

Although Chinese tend to read *Wolf Totem* as a story about the Cultural Revolution, audiences abroad have focused more on the environmental resonances of the novel. The editor of the Japanese translation of *Wolf Totem*, for instance, calls attention to its ecological significance, commenting that "at a time when nature is being destroyed, the number of species is decreasing, and the human spirit and character are day by day getting weaker and becoming ever more corrupt, modern readers are truly lucky to be able to read a long, epic novel like this that describes wolves." We are fortunate that novels such as *Wolf Totem* have been received so enthusiastically, yet it is important to see Jiang Rong's text not as an isolated phenomenon, but instead as part of an increasingly powerful trajectory of Chinese-language literature in both China and Taiwan that engages with environmental concerns.

Wolf Totem arrived on the heels of growing environmental consciousness in China. Chinese leaders in the 1980s no longer spoke as explicitly of a war on nature as they had during the Cultural Revolution, and they in fact issued propaganda posters urging people to "green the motherland," "plant trees and make green," and "cherish greening and treasure old and famous trees." But believing ecological protection to be incompatible with economic growth, the Chinese ultimately launched even greater attacks on their landscapes during the 1980s and 1990s. In the past two decades, the Chinese government has announced numerous environmental laws, regulations, and policies that, where implemented, have enjoyed at least limited success. To be sure, efforts to curb environmental degradation are often ignored in favor of economic growth or, in some cases, simple survival. On the other hand, Chinese are becoming less tolerant of living under such conditions and are growing increasingly demonstrative over the industrial poisoning of both themselves and their ecosystems.

Environmental degradation has been a part of Chinese literature from its beginnings—everything from *The Book of Songs* (sixth century BCE), China's first poetry anthology, which contains verses on clearing away grasses and trees and replacing less desirable flora with grains, to Zhang Yingchang's (1790–1874) edited volume *Qing Bell of Poesy* (1869), which includes poems such as Wang Taiyue's (1722–1785) "Chant of the Copper Hills" on the difficulties of miners confronted by deforestation and increasingly scarce mineral reserves. These and other similar texts laid the foundation for twentieth-century Chinese creative negotiations with local, national, and eventually regional and global environmental degradation. Prose and illustrations by Feng Zikai (1898–1975), one of early twentieth-century China's most inspiring essayists and painters, are vivid testimonies not only to thriving ecosystems but also to natural and manmade disasters. Just as significant is Shen Congwen's (1902–1988) acclaimed novel *Long River* (1943), which best represents the pathos of this leading nativist writer regarding the environmental and cultural decline of his hometown region as a result of the advent of modernization. Also noteworthy is Chen Jingrong's (1917–1989) poem "City Scene at Dusk" (1946), which begins, "The noises of the city have drowned dusk"; urban clamor is strong enough to drown an entire segment of the day.

But it was not really until the late 1980s that the health of the environment became a sustained concern in Chinese literature; at this time writers and critics began speaking more earnestly of environmental literature and green literature, and then ecological literature. The degree to which a text needs to engage with environmental matters in order for a Chinese critic to consider it "environmental literature," "green literature," or "ecological literature" varies. More significant is the diversity of Chinese texts that talk about damaged ecosystems, addressing such problems as soil and air pollution, deforestation, desertification, water shortages, flooding, species extinction, and global warming.

A key example of 1980s Chinese environmental fiction is Ah Cheng's (1949–) novella *The King of Trees* (1985), which discusses devastation to China's ecosystems during the Cultural Revolution. Published the same year, Shen Rong's (1936–) *A Dying River* focuses more on environmental protection, celebrating efforts to control the pollution of Mata Lake in Shandong Province. Also noteworthy from the 1980s are writings such as the Nobel laureate Gao Xingjian's (1940–) drama *Wild Man* (1985) and novel *Soul Mountain* (1989). While the characters in *Wild Man* condemn habitat loss and species eradication and speak as well of the paradoxes of nature conservation, the narrator of *Soul Mountain* incorporates a thorough ornithological and botanical taxonomy of China's natural realm and comments throughout the novel on the ecological problems that plague his country and the planet more generally.

Concerned with ecological degradation and hoping to develop the genre of environmental literature in China, in January 1991 Chinese writers founded the Society of Environmental Literature; this group was established nearly two years before the Association for the Study of Literature and Environment, the United States' premier ecocritical organization. The following year Chinese launched *Green Leaves*, the nation's first journal devoted to environmental literature, which in five years published more than one thousand environmental texts and continues to flourish today. In the inaugural issue, the organizers of *Green Leaves* speak of their admiration for Rachel Carson (1907–1964) and the impact of her *Silent Spring* (1962) on the American environmental movement. Not surprisingly, it was also at this time that Chinese began publishing anthologies of "green" literature, making more accessible writings they deemed to be of urgent national and planetary significance.

The twenty-first century has so far proven fertile for Chinese literature concerning human damage to ecosystems. One of the new millennium's first such novels was Jia Pingwa's (1952–) *Remembering Wolves* (2000). This text features Gao Ziming, a journalist and environmentalist who, together with two hunters, sets out to document Central China's fifteen remaining wolves but ultimately ends up killing them. Also noteworthy are Guo Xuebo's (1948–) *Wolf Child in the Desert* (2001) and *Wolf Child* (2006). Far from being deceived by official rhetoric on "greening" environments, Chinese authors have actively engaged with the increasing destruction of the nation's landscapes.

Taiwan has been another active site of writing on environmental degradation. The retreat of the Chinese Nationalists (Kuomintang) from the mainland to Taiwan in 1949, four years after decolonization, increased the island's population by several million. This growth, combined with rapid industrialization and economic development under a military dictatorship that smothered opposition and harshly punished dissenters, led to unchecked exploitation of the island's ecosystems and unprecedented pollution of its land, water, and skies.

Taiwan's antipollution protests and nature conservation movement date to the early 1980s, but damage to the island's landscapes was addressed in earnest only after martial law was lifted in July 1987. Taiwanese writers have participated actively in the island's environmental movements since their beginnings, joining campaigns to rescue endangered species and spaces, modifying industrial development projects, and limiting human behaviors harmful to ecosystems. In addition, since the 1980s they have published a robust array of environmental poetry, fiction, and nonfiction. Much of Taiwan's environmental nonfiction has scientific roots: travel and historical reports that emphasize Taiwan's diverse ecologies, ecological essays, compositions that objectively address environmental problems, and what commonly is referred to in Taiwan as "nature writing." Definitions of the latter vary, but Liu Kexiang (1957–), Taiwan's preeminent nature writer, is careful to distinguish between this genre and conventional landscape literature, emphasizing that the language of nature writing is replete with elements of natural science and informative descriptions, and that authors often engage in considerable fieldwork, focusing on specific ecosystems.

A more recent presence in Taiwanese environmental literature and also the recipient of numerous awards is the artist and activist Wu Mingyi (1971–), who has spoken of consciously developing a new kind of nature writing. Wu made his mark with two essay collections on butterflies— *The Book of Lost Butterflies* (2000) and *The Dao of Butterflies* (2003). He theorizes environmental literature in *Liberating Nature through Writing: Explorations in Modern Taiwanese Nature Writing* (2011). Most striking, however, is his recent apocalyptic novel *The Man with Compound Eyes* (2011), which centers on a young Pacific Islander who rides an island of trash to Taiwan, where he finds that people are more concerned with developing the coast than with cleaning it up.

East Asian creative writing has been addressing ecodegradation for millennia and with particular urgency since the 1960s, but it was arguably not until the publication and translation of Jiang Rong's *Wolf Totem* in 2004 that literature from this region engaging with environmental trauma gained a worldwide following. Interest in such texts is likely only to increase as damage to nature becomes ever more severe around the globe.

BIBLIOGRAPHY: Ah Cheng, "The King of Trees," in *The King of Trees*, trans. Bonnie S. McDougall (New York, 2010), 1–56. Hsin-Huang Michael Hsiao, "Environmental Movements in Taiwan," in *Asia's Environmental Movements: Comparative Perspectives*, ed. Yok-shiu F. Lee and Alvin Y. So (Armonk, NY, 1999), 31–54. Jiang Rong, *Wolf Totem*, trans. Howard Goldblatt (New York, 2008). Karen L. Thornber, *Ecoambiguity: Environmental Crises and East Asian Literatures* (Ann Arbor, MI, 2012).

KAREN L. THORNBER

2006 · SEPTEMBER 30

Poetry goes naked.

Chinese Verse Going Viral:
"Removing the Shackles of Poetry"

If modern Chinese poetry has often been motivated by the desire to strip away the conventions that accompanied China's classical poetry tradition, then September 30, 2006, is a date that will forever be synonymous with the most stripped-down and unconventional kind of poetry yet created: the totally naked kind. That evening, a group of poets convened for a poetry recitation event entitled "Supporting Zhao Lihua, Defending Modern Chinese Poetry." At first glance, the recital seemed no different from the hundreds of poetry events that take place weekly throughout the country. The audience was small, and its modest surroundings, a café tucked within the Disanji Bookshop in the northwest of Beijing, seemed likely to destine the event to future obscurity. That might have been the case, were it not for two things. First, the poet Su Feishu (1973–) decided to up the ante by reciting his poem "This Is All There Is" stark naked. Assisted by his girlfriend, Su removed the sixteen layers of clothing he had donned for the occasion before taking to the stage. Ironically, despite having explained his performance as symbolic of his desire to "remove the shackles of poetry," Su ended up in handcuffs himself as he was led away by police and held in custody on charges of obscene behavior.

Second, Su's performance, which later became known as the "naked recital" or "naked show," was designed as an exhibition of public resistance toward criticisms of modern Chinese poetry that had recently been circulating widely on the Internet and in the news media. On September 11, a netizen using the web ID "Redchuanbo" had posted a series of poems by the poet Zhao Lihua (1964–) on an overseas Internet forum under the heading "The most sweat-inducing poems in history!" The netizen explained, "While searching for a name online, I inadvertently came across a great poet and read some of her great works. On the verge of fainting, I managed to conserve enough energy to write this post, after which I will return to thinking of the yellow earth." The netizen gave a brief rundown of Zhao's biography, noting that she had published her poetry in national journals, served as a judge for a number of literary awards, and won prizes for her own poetry. One of the twelve poems included in the post was entitled "Alone in Tennessee," and reads as follows:

> Without a shadow of a doubt
> my pancakes
> are the best
> in the entire world.

The netizen concluded the post with an original poem of her or his own:

> It turns out
> poetry
> can also
> be written
> like this
> !!!!!!!!

Redchuanbo's post proved to be a portentous event in the history of modern Chinese poetry, and an unexpected consequence of poetry's encounter with the web. Within hours, it was forwarded to Internet forums in mainland China, including Tsinghua University's SMTH (*shuimu tsinghua*) (literally, Water is clear, with trees in floresence) forum, whereupon it started to go viral and reappeared on sites throughout the Internet. In a pun on Zhao's name, her colloquial style of writing was labeled "pear blossom form" and Zhao was heralded as the "Lotus of the poetry arena," an analogy to one of China's Internet celebrities, Sister Lotus, notorious for her "S-shaped curves" and attempts to belly-dance her way into one of China's top graduate degree programs. Hundreds of thousands of netizens joined in what had by now turned into a large-scale spoofing event, with many producing their own pear blossom poems and expressing horror that *this* was what had become of China's illustrious poetry tradition. One spoof poem reads,

> If
> the return key on your keyboard
> works particularly well
> then

feel free to join us
if you
happen to also stutter
or suffer from chronic constipation
then
before long
you'll become
a poet above all others.

On the one hand, these developments were very much a product of the contemporary era, when texts circulate through digital media technologies beyond their authors' control and netizens are active producers of culture as often as they are passive consumers, and when "even" poets have grown savvy to the free publicity that the media provides when you provide them with a scandal to report on. On the other hand, the story of naked poetry is one that cannot be told without looking back at the history of modern Chinese poetry, and in particular at its roots in the "poetry world revolution" of the late Qing dynasty and New Literature Movement of the May Fourth era in the early twentieth century.

In recent decades, the early twentieth-century goal of writing poetry in vernacular Chinese so that it might appeal to more of the population and participate in the process of nation building seems to have been taken to its natural conclusion in the hands of certain writers: poems have been written in increasingly colloquial language about ever more relatable concerns, whether they be regarding school life (demonstrated by Sichuan's Macho Men poets in the mid-1980s), sex (demonstrated by the Lower Body group in the early 2000s), or shit (a common theme within the School of Rubbish, part of the Internet's Low Poetry movement). Chinese netizens' collective reaction upon discovering the current state of poetry writing suggests that they had retained their own standards for poetry, despite widespread assumptions of the genre's marginalization within contemporary society. Poetry, they implied, should not only be worthy of China's reputation as a "nation of poetry," but should do something to complicate the process of communication. Boasting about one's culinary skills or sexual prowess in short, broken-up lines is not enough: poetry is supposed to be difficult, to make its readers think, and to strive for some kind of illusive beauty lacking in everyday speech.

In other words, opening up poetry to a wider audience by adopting the modern vernacular language is all very well, but it shouldn't be *too* open, otherwise—horror!—anyone can call themselves a poet!

Ironically, it is not the vernacular language but the Internet that has truly popularized modern Chinese poetry in the vernacular, which began as an elite form among intellectuals and reflected their revolutionary ideology at the beginning of the modern era. Contrary to the claims of these revolutionaries and to popular perception, traditional poetry is not essentially an elite form, despite being used by the elite. Indeed, in pre-modern China anyone could call themselves a poet, so long as he or she could write in the prescribed poetic forms, the most standard of which was a quatrain with four five-syllable or seven-syllable lines, usually with an *aaba* rhyme scheme. One may call such a verse a good or bad poem, but, as the modern Chinese writer Fei Ming (1901–1967) famously stated, "You cannot claim that it is not a 'poem,'" at least not in quite the same way that a reader might do to a modern vernacular poem that fails to measure up to her or his standard of what poetry "is." Classical poetry could be erudite and densely allusive, but it could also be so simple and direct in diction that even an illiterate person or someone with the most basic education could understand it. That a poem should by definition resist understanding and easy interpretations is itself a modern notion.

Modern Chinese poetry in the vernacular started out as a negative movement, in the sense that it defined itself as anticlassical, and it is for this reason that this "new poetry," also known as "free verse" (in a slightly different sense from the Western poetic term *vers libre*), can be written in any form except the classical forms. Beginning in the 1990s, however, poets have increasingly stressed "everydayness" in poetic topics and diction, and increasingly demonstrated a desire to strip the divine halo from poetry and return it to the "yellow earth." There is in particular a common sense of revulsion against the values of "high culture," a complex entity that comprises the official discourse of the Chinese state, the traditional belief in the moral power of the scholar elite, and the romantic sentimentality and theatricality surrounding the view of vernacular poetry in much of twentieth-century China. Poetry groups such as the Lower Body and School of Rubbish carry the sense of negation inherent in the birth of modern vernacular poetry to an extreme. Such a renewal of the May Fourth intellectuals' vision coincides with something new and unexpected, namely, the media revolution that has taken the world by storm.

The World Wide Web, instead of being just a newer, fancier venue for the production and consumption of poetry than print media, plays a crucial role in the dramatic development of modern Chinese poetry. First, it has forcefully brought into the open something that had been going on but remained largely invisible to the casual observer: not only is the engagement with poetry quite widespread in this "nation of poetry," but there is also an intense fascination with the continued practice of traditional poetic forms. Tianya.com, China's top forum website, which claims to represent the country's largest online community, has one forum devoted to modern-style poetry and one to classical-style poetry. As of March 18, 2013, the former had 371,708 original posts and 2,271,021 replies, while the latter had 294,559 posts and 2,470,774 replies. Another *tianya* forum, called "Elegant Seating for Parallel Couplets," had 217,911 posts and 3,026,281 replies, and the parallel couplet is of course the key component of "regulated verse" in classical Chinese poetry.

Second, the Internet has recreated "poetry societies"—literary communities that can be traced to the twelfth century—but with a twist: if conventional poetry societies have largely remained a local phenomenon, the online communities are a national and global one. Last but not least is the emergence of the voices of the "common folk"—that is to say, people who are not necessarily scholars or professional literary critics but nevertheless have much to say about poetry and find in the Internet a public venue to express their opinions and be heard. Admittedly, many of these people are likely urban white collars (although by the end of 2012 the number of Chinese netizens in rural areas had exceeded 156 million, 27.6 percent of the total netizen population), but this still represents a significant change from the days when print media were the main venue for poetry criticism and were largely under the control of academia and other state-sponsored cultural institutions. Contemporary poetry no longer belongs to an enclosed, self-perpetuating elite circle, and literary establishments are fast losing their former authority in the eyes of the public. Capitalism and technology, with their democratizing power, are undermining the old cultural elite like never before.

Herein, however, lies the irony. While vernacular poets may desire to "go naked," turning away from high culture, the common folk want their poetry to be covered up. The antielite values are always advocated by members of the elite, but the folk to whom they yearn to return tend to be much more conservative. For everyday fare and a dose of yellow earth, the folk have classical-style poetry for consumption. Vernacular poetry, on the other hand, is implicitly entrusted with the task of "marching toward the world"—it is, after all, the official form designated for participating in international competitions, represented by such literary awards as the Nobel Prize. No classical-style poet aspires to be China's poet laureate, despite the state's promotion of classical literature in recent years to boost national pride. Classical-style poetry seems fated to be the new local poetry in the global market of literature. Vernacular poetry must bear the weight of representing China, yet "rubbish" and the "lower body" are not quite what the Chinese folk think should be the new literary face of the "nation of poetry." But poets in China, like everywhere else in the world, do not always do what the folk think they ought to be doing. Besides, they understand that in order to put on new clothes, you have to strip first.

BIBLIOGRAPHY: Michel Hockx, *Internet Literature in China* (New York, 2015). Heather Inwood, *Verse Going Viral: China's New Media Scenes* (Seattle, 2014). Christopher Lupke, ed., *New Perspectives on Contemporary Chinese Poetry* (New York, 2008). Stephen Owen, "Stepping Forward and Back: Issues and Possibilities for 'World' Poetry," in "Toward World Literature: A Special Centennial Issue," *Modern Philology* 100, no. 4 (2003): 532–548. Xiaofei Tian, "Muffled Dialect Spoken by Green Fruit: An Alternative History of Modern Chinese Poetry," *Modern Chinese Literature and Culture* 21, no. 1 (2009): 1–45. Maghiel Van Crevel, *Chinese Poetry in Times of Mind, Mayhem and Money* (Leiden, Netherlands, 2008).

HEATHER INWOOD *and* XIAOFEI TIAN

2007

Han writer Li Juan recounts her barriers to communication in Kazakh Xinjiang.

Suddenly Coming into My Own

When I was little, my family opened a small shop in the city, but business wasn't particularly good. The population in the county town didn't amount to much, and the streets were silent and deserted. Besides a tree-shaded path, a retaining wall, and two or three big factory gates, the main avenue my family lived on was essentially barren; the smaller shops aren't even worth mentioning. It seemed like even if our store were open for a hundred years, it would never be graced with the presence of a customer. But, if you pushed open that silent door and strode inside, you'd always find the entire room filled with people—everyone would be drinking.

Our store had a tall counter topped by thick wooden planks. Leaning against the bar, one next to the other, the patrons would all boast loudly with one another as they held their glass or bottle of alcohol. In the very middle of the room was a square table with four tall stools on each side; there were always people surrounding it. The table would be covered with empty alcohol bottles and peanut shells. This was my earliest encounter with the Kazakh people.

Little me was always curious. I could never understand exactly what it was that people in this Podunk town could talk about from morning until night, from today until tomorrow, from this month until the next; what could they talk about that could pass the whole winter (in a place where winter can last up to half a year!)? Life was so monotonous. When they talked, their tone was calm and their voices deep, just quietly talking, talking. Heated discussions were rare; there was never anything to get worked up about.

In a more distant era, this land was boundless and the signs of human life even scarcer. Communication was probably like this even then—patient like this, tenaciously passing along information, spreading life and civilization.

At that time, I didn't understand a single word of Kazakh. Despite coming into contact with it every day, it still felt entirely distant and removed, like being faced with a castle that sits high on a sheer cliff.

Now at least I can speak a little Kazakh, or at least enough to maintain a basic exchange. But I'm still faced with that unreachable castle, struggling to advance even one step at a time.

Kazipa has his own friends. Simaghul has his own friends. Auntie Jahipbay also naturally has her own friends, like Jaziman's mother, Shariphan. The two of them will even exchange pictures with each other and whatnot. Whenever I want to take everyone's picture, they quickly scurry to stand next to each other.

Whenever the two of them have a free moment, they get together to spin and weave, braid rope, boil soap, or sew and mend. The handiwork is never ending, and neither is their conversation—talking and talking, they carry on that way until the work is finished, only then saying their goodbyes and parting ways. After returning home and taking stock, however, once again they find themselves with nothing to do, so they grab another piece of work to be done and walk straight back to each other, sit down, and carry on chatting.

I have no idea what they're talking about, what could be so fascinating! Round and round the spindle would go with lightening speed, their voices never fluctuating in tone. It is only when someone mentioned Shugila that their hands finally stopped working and, suddenly worked up, had a lively discussion. Then they turned to look at me and said, "Li Juan! Shugila cried again yesterday! He took his horse and rode into the county town today!"

I asked, "What was he crying about?"

"That one time someone called Aynur's house looking for her; she cried too! She also went to the county town after that."

"Then what about this time?"

Auntie Shariphan reiterated the point, saying, "Last time she cried at the banquet! She even drank alcohol!"

It felt like we were talking at each other, missing each other's point, but I also wasn't so curious as to inquire further, so I just sat there silently.

But the two of them then turned to look at me and diligently gave voice to a litany of opinions. The various details and twists and turns of their conversation soon wrapped me in darkness. Shugila is alone, her body yearning. Auntie Jahipbay and Auntie Shariphan are also alone; they can only speculate and comment from afar. The most alone of all, though, is me—I'm unable to understand anything.

I remember the time when I had just become a part of Auntie Jahipbay's world of household life. In the spring grazing pastures of Jihrat one evening, she sent me to go check and see if the camels were on the large hill to the south or not.

I ran down to the mountain and made a sweep, then ran back and made my report, panting all the while: "The camels are gone! There are only 'mountain goats'!"

At that time though, I didn't know how to say "mountain goats" in Kazakh, so I just used Mandarin to say it, and she didn't understand.

I wrung my brains out trying to explain, "It's… that white thing! Like a sheep, with pointy things on its head, and a long…"

Auntie Jahipbay was even more confused.

Once I became flustered, I started using my hands to rub my chin, gesturing like I was rubbing a beard: "You know, this thing, it has one of these! It looks like this, it's really long!"

She suddenly had an epiphany, gave a great laugh, and ran off.

That evening at dinner, when everyone was gathered together, she told this story five times—at the very least. Ever since then, whenever I'm sent to herd the goats, everyone will rush over to me and start rubbing their chins, saying "Li Juan, go quickly! The white ones, with the long things!" This is obviously just a joke. But with time these kinds of jokes only increased, and there was something not quite right about it. What was I doing here?

For every square kilometer, there wasn't even an average of one person: this is the reason I don't always have to feel lonely. It's the opposite situation, when there are lots of people, that causes the loneliness to set in. It's when I'm among the throngs of people at the local singing gatherings that the loneliness becomes almost unbearable.

In the camp situated at the base of Stony Hill in Dongkor, it is extremely tranquil, but tranquility cannot conceal loneliness. The radio was broadcasting *Aken Aytis*—a traditional Kazakh style of singing competition—the man was singing aggressively, the woman gravely and earnestly. Kazipa clicked his tongue in admiration and sighed, "It's really good! Li Juan, this woman is really good!" I had trouble identifying what about her exactly was "good"; I had even more trouble finding an opening into his emotional and intellectual world at all.

Whenever there is free time, I always go on long walks by myself, but I'm never able to get where I want to go. I can only mount some great height and look for it in the vast distance.

Every time I set off on an adventure, I yearn for some unknown place and march relentlessly toward it. My heart, though, is always concerned with the journey home. Even after I've been gone a long time, though, I return and find that everything has remained the same. The goats still gather around the camp and eat grass; Simaghul and Kaderbek are still silently reclining in the pasture. Halfway up the slope, three horses in reins bearing empty saddles stand silently in a row together. On the grass by the creek, Auntie Jahipbay and Kazipa are milking the livestock. I watch for a bit, then look behind me to see that Simaghul and Kaderbek have sat up and are engaged in a heated discussion, neither willing to yield to the other.

I stand atop the highest point on the hill, looking this way, then that. The sky begins to darken. That is the loneliest time.

One time I left on a long journey, and since they didn't have a phone, no one knew exactly on what date I was supposed to return. So Simaghul had to ride his horse to the asphalt road the cars used and look for me every day. Eventually, we did finally run into each other. But he only had one horse, and it had to carry not only me but also my two bags. In the end, he let me ride the horse while he walked alongside. We passed through a great forest, a river valley densely packed with white birch trees, and expansive shrubbery that sat on the height of a slope. We walked for more than two hours, and only then did we finally make it back to Dongkor.

Although I was riding the horse, I couldn't manage to keep up with Simaghul's walking pace. Each time we started up an incline, he would quickly disappear into a height of flowering shrubs. I don't know why, but no matter how I whipped the horse, it completely disregarded me. Instead, it just casually ambled along while grazing on roadside grasses. The forest was never ending, and it seemed like we would never fully round the bend of the winding path ahead of us. It looked like we had already gotten separated from Simaghul…. When I arrived at the flowering shrubbery on top of the slope, the little path still extended endlessly into the distance. The back of Simaghul's red jacket flickered there on the horizon for just a second then disappeared.

The entire journey was a game of pursuit, and the little path that seemed to vanish and appear at will gradually became more clearly defined. Just when I thought that it was certainly going to take me somewhere, I rounded a bend and had to continue walking down an increasingly fuzzy path that eventually faded into nothingness. My horse and I emerged onto a shoal; below us water went gurgling by. Not far in front of us a black-backed marmot scurried past. Skittering back and forth, it turned and looked at me.

I once again gradually descended into another valley bereft of sunlight, and the further along I went, the narrower it became. It was just then that Simaghul suddenly jumped out from behind a rock and charged at me with a huge grin on his face. I quickly reigned in the horse and asked him where we were. He laughed and said, "Just ahead is pretty water."

I didn't know what "pretty water" was, but I followed him all the same. My horse, however, suddenly decided it was finished taking orders, and, after fussing about a good while, was still unwilling to leave the original path. All I could do was dismount, lead my horse on foot, and follow him into the distance. Beside my feet a narrow rivulet was flowing, and I could hear the rushing of water up ahead. The sound continued to grow. I rounded a huge stone and—a waterfall! There was a waterfall ahead!

Simaghul gazed proudly at me and smiled as he stood beside the flowing waters. He led me from the main path to make a detour here, and, as expected, I was pleasantly rewarded for my faith in him. I could feel his overwhelming happiness and friendship. He was actually the lonely one.

Back in Dongkor at our northern camp, a goat came limping back nearly crippled late one night. Everyone saw it and sighed. Two hours later, its hind legs could no longer support its weight. Dragging itself along the ground, it struggled to use its forelegs to crawl along. The next day when the herd was sent out to graze, only it remained behind. Convulsing, it lay moaning next to the stream and soon died. What before was a heart-wrenching scene later ended in a sense of relief. It was as if death was the only appropriate homecoming; its suffering had finally come to an end. Simaghul removed its pelt and buried the corpse. At the same time, the other goats were off merrily grazing in the distant pasture. In this rich and fertile summer pasture, what does my modicum of loneliness amount to anyway?

Li Juan
Translated by Kyle Shernuk
Kazakh transliterated by Guldana Salimjan

2008

"In every human heart is a stretch of land ... in every human heart is a dream." —Li Yongping, preface, *The End of the River*

Writer-Wanderer Li Yongping and Chinese Malaysian Literature

Beginning in the latter half of the twentieth century, some of the most sophisticated and compelling Chinese-language writing has come from what may seem like a surprising source: Malaysia. Malaysians of Chinese descent compose roughly a quarter of the country's multilingual, multiethnic population. Despite governmental policies marginalizing expressions of Chinese culture since Malaysia's independence in 1957, Chinese Malaysian authors have created a vibrant literary archive, in which they explore themes that reflect their distinct cultural origins while attempting to forge a new relationship to the Chinese language and literary tradition. This literature highlights the intricacy of its authors' identities through a dual identification with their Malaysian and imaginary Chinese homelands. Further complicating matters, much of what is generally still considered "Chinese Malaysian literature" flows from the pens of Malaysia-born, Taiwan-based authors; Li Yongping (1947–) is representative of this group. Yet, Li is also a quintessential diasporic Chinese author—in this essay's epigraph taken from Li's *The End of the River*, the quoted song lyric composed by popular Taiwanese writer Sanmao (1943–1991) encapsulates the ethos of his work. He has meditated more deeply on his heritage than most in similar circumstances and taken advantage, aesthetically, of his extraterritorialized position vis-à-vis the Chinese literary tradition in particularly innovative ways. Li's profound inquiries into morality, diaspora, exile, identity, settler colonialism in Borneo, and ethnic and international relations represent a significant contribution to modern Chinese literature and could only have come from someone of his background and literary imagination.

Chinese Malaysian literature owes much of its development to the region's newspapers and schools. Writings in modern Chinese appeared in the literary supplements of Chinese newspapers in colonial Malaya as early as 1919, the pages of which featured writings by both local and well-known mainland Chinese authors. China's political turmoil during the 1920s and 1930s compelled many intellectuals to sojourn in Southeast Asia, where they served as newspaper editors or teachers in Chinese schools; Yu Dafu (1896–1945), who went to Singapore in 1939 to become a newspaper editor and later disappeared in Sumatra in 1945, is the most famous example. Today's Malaysian Chinese newspapers support local literary talent by publishing their works in their literary supplements; *Sinchew Daily*, one of the largest Chinese newspapers in Malaysia, also offers the Floral Trail literary prize—the goal is to nurture local authors, link them with authors elsewhere, and advance Chinese literature globally. Another crucial component in the development of Chinese Malaysian literature is the availability and advancement of Chinese-language education, which has existed in the region since the late eighteenth century. While Chinese education is a point of controversy in postcolonial Malaysia, with Chinese schools often depending on community funds to sustain themselves, its availability remains important for cultivating new generations of writers.

Li was born in 1947 in Kuching, Sarawak, located in northwest Borneo, when Sarawak was still a British crown colony. He attended Chinese elementary and middle schools and a British high school. Reflecting on his boyhood reading experiences, it becomes clear that early exposure to traditional Chinese literature, and the Chinese writing system, fostered Li's lifelong fascination with China. In a 1992 interview, Li admits to an infatuation with the Chinese script while recalling his experience reading *Dream of the Red Chamber* as a five- or six-year-old child. He describes how his quick mastery of Chinese characters gave rise to an intense longing for China. Li's now-infamous "China complex," prominent in works like *Retribution: The Jiling Chronicles* (1986) and *Haidongqing: A Fable of Taipei* (1992), likely originates with this childhood encounter with the traditional Chinese literary canon.

Sarawak joined the independent Federation of Malaysia in 1963. Li left Borneo in 1967 to pursue a university education in Taiwan, thus joining the waves of young Malaysians of Chinese descent hoping to visit the China of their dreams but willing to accept Taiwan as a substitute. This route's popularity increased after postelection ethnic riots on May 13, 1969, led Malaysia's government to adopt policies favoring Malays and restricting educational and professional opportunities for Chinese Malaysians. Li graduated from National Taiwan University in 1971, and later earned MA and PhD degrees in comparative literature from, respectively, the State University of New York at Albany, and Washington University in Saint Louis. He became a citizen of the Republic of China in 1987. In addition to his creative writing, he has worked as a teacher and magazine editor, and translated into Chinese books by writers like Harold Bloom, Paul Auster, and V. S. Naipaul.

Li's multiple homes and homelands—Borneo, Taiwan, and his spiritual home in the Chinese literary tradition—appear implicitly and explicitly across his short stories and novels, reinforcing the identity of "wanderer" or "roamer" that Li has recently embraced. In his early short stories, Li confronts the ethnic tension and violence that beleaguered his hometown and family. In "A Dayak Woman" (1968), the third son of a Chinese family in Sarawak marries an aboriginal woman. When the family patriarch arrives from China, he regards the new daughter-in-law with disdain, but over time it is her husband who mistreats her so terribly that she dies prematurely. The story is told in the first person by a younger family member recalling mostly past events. Harking back to Lu Xun (1881–1936), the narratorial style poignantly conveys the narrator's earlier complicity with his family's derogatory behavior toward the Dayak woman—along with his ineffectual regret. That the narrator is called Ah Ping by the Li family invites an autobiographical reading.

The stories collected in Li's *Retribution: The Jiling Chronicles* (1986), a Taiwanese modernist classic that established Li's literary reputation, at once evoke Kuching, Southeast Asia, and China. In *Retribution*'s opening story, "In Great Blessings Lane," the lovely young wife of a coffin maker is raped by a local thug and then hangs herself, prompting her husband to kill the rapist's wife and mistress in revenge. The other stories introduce additional characters and perspectives as these and other events are recounted and recalled, weaving a multiyear history of the city of Jiling. The language used to chronicle the various events is adapted from that found in traditional Chinese novels, and Li has described exerting "painstaking" efforts in this regard. Along with the stories' cultural references, this creates the impression that Jiling is a traditional mainland Chinese village. Consequently, the collection seems to embody Li's pursuit of his spiritual home within China's literary tradition, or even a nostalgic yearning for an abstract China that can only be written into existence. Other references—to sun, heat, and humidity—bring to mind Borneo's tropical climate. In this respect, *Retribution* anticipates later developments, as the uniqueness of the Southeast Asian environment becomes an exotic signifier helping to market Chinese Malaysian literature in 1990s Taiwan. While Jiling's ultimate geographical referent remains artfully obscure, less disputable is that, with this collection, Li successfully claimed his place in the Chinese literary heartland.

In his later works, Li pairs movement with narration to confront themes of diaspora, identity, colonialism, postcolonialism, and relations between Borneo, Taiwan, Japan, China, the Netherlands, and Britain. In a collection of quasi-autobiographical short stories called *The Snow Falls in Clouds* (2002, 2013), Li reminisces about growing up in Borneo and then moving to and living in Taipei, as Li himself did, through a first-person narrator named Li Yongping. The confessional stories emerge through conversation with a young girl named Zhu Ling, who becomes confidante and muse to Li as they wander through Taipei at night. In "Look Homeward," Li divulges to Zhu Ling his tale of befriending, then betraying a group of women in Kuching who had been brought to Borneo from Taiwan during World War II to serve as "comfort women" for Japanese soldiers. Li summons Zhu Ling again in his fictionalized memoir, *The End of the River.* Fifteen-year-old Yong experiences his first summer away from home when, in 1962, his father sends him to West Kalimantan to visit the plantation of a Dutch woman named Christina Van Loon, also a former comfort woman. Christina and Yong join an expedition of international travelers up the Kapuas River to Batu Tipan, the Dayaks' holy mountain. Though Yong grew up in Kuching, the expedition exposes him to cultures and peoples that share his home island but of which he previously knew very little; the adolescent Yong also encounters strange, dark sides to himself and others. In *The End of the River,* Zhu Ling helps Li recount an uncanny journey into "the heart of darkness" that transpires physically and emotionally.

In *The Snow Falls in Clouds,* a style adorned with classical allusions highlights noteworthy aspects of Li's personal trajectory. In one story, Li recalls crowding with his middle school classmates in front of the school's bulletin boards to read the local Chinese newspapers. The teachers posted newspapers to acquaint students with world events, but students instead clamored for the Taiwan and Hong Kong novels serialized in the literary supplements: romances by Qiong Yao (1938–) and martial arts novels by Jin Yong (1924–). (Li defied gender stereotypes and joined the girls in preferring Qiong Yao over Jin Yong). Li suggests that his decision to pursue university education in Taiwan stemmed from his love for Qiong Yao's fiction: he wanted to visit Taipei to explore the lanes and alleys so richly described in Qiong Yao's popular novel *Boat*.

While Li might be unique in thus characterizing his decision, many Chinese Malaysians have gone to Taiwan for university, and many of those with literary inclinations went on to launch careers and stay—finding more publishing opportunities than in Malaysia, and often receiving prestigious literary awards. Sarawak-born Taiwan author Chang Kuei-hsing (1956–), for example, vivifies the Borneo rainforest, its history, and its peoples, especially in his novels written since the 1990s. Taiwan author-scholar Ng Kim Chew (1967–), born in Johor, Peninsular Malaysia, satirizes Malaysian history and politics in his clever metafiction. Renowned filmmaker Tsai Ming-liang (1957–) was also born in Kuching, attended university in Taiwan, and went on to establish his career there. Other critically acclaimed Chinese Malaysian writers who studied in Taiwan include Chen Dawei (1969–), Pan Yutong (1937–), Shang Wanyun (1952–1995), Wen Rui'an (1954–), Wong Yoon Wah (1941–), and Zhong Yiwen (1969–). Some have remained in Taiwan and others have either moved elsewhere or returned to Malaysia.

However, Li Tianbao (1969–), who finds inspiration in early twentieth-century Shanghai popular fiction, and Li Zishu (1971–), whose writings tackle Malaysian history, among other themes such as gender and sexuality, exemplify those acclaimed Chinese Malaysian authors who did not study in Taiwan and have remained mostly in Malaysia, though they publish in Taiwan and Li Zishu recently lived in England and China. Tensions exist between the Chinese Malaysian literary scenes in Malaysia and Taiwan. While Chinese Malaysian literature allows "Malaysia" to inhabit Taiwanese literature as an exotic foreign landscape, Chinese Malaysian writers and critics in Malaysia often accuse their Taiwanese counterparts of mischaracterizing contemporary Malaysia. Meanwhile, when Chinese Malaysians first started going to Taiwan (mainly during the 1960s and 1970s), studying abroad in the People's Republic of China was not an option. Now, Malaysians can visit and study in China and increasing numbers of Chinese Malaysian authors live there; this change in circumstances allows the People's Republic to join Taiwan, Hong Kong,

Singapore, other Southeast Asian nations, and the world in helping to shape a contemporary Chinese Malaysian consciousness.

While Chinese Malaysian literature has developed in dialogue with the literary traditions of China and Taiwan, these connections also generate controversy in the Chinese Malaysian sphere. Chinese Malaysian literary history thus reveals the struggles for validation and anxieties over real and perceived hierarchies that preoccupy diasporic authors and that accompany the global advancement of modern Chinese literature. Chinese Malaysian writers have long striven to achieve recognition for an autonomous Chinese Malaysian literature acknowledged as equal rather than subordinate to Chinese literatures produced in China and Taiwan; in Chinese Malaysian literary circles, debates over China's and Taiwan's influence on Chinese Malaysian literature and movements to cultivate a more authentically localized Chinese Malaysian literature have frequently recurred. Chinese Malaysian writers also vie for domestic recognition: within Malaysia, having not being written in the national language of Malay, Chinese Malaysian literature cannot be considered national literature, its producers denied access to apparatuses of state support available to Malay writers.

Still, Li Yongping and his fellow Chinese Malaysian writers have invented aesthetic strategies that permit them to exploit the political and cultural marginalization they grew up with; their diasporic positioning, moreover, enables them to offer cultural insights, stemming from histories of migration, colonialism, imperialism, and postcolonial development, that are particularly relevant for our globalized era. Their writing also yields a wealth of literary pleasure. When readers accept the invitation to explore the literary homelands Li writes into existence—to traverse the "stretches of land" he creates from the dreams, and memories, in his heart—they emerge the richer for having done so.

BIBLIOGRAPHY: Alison M. Groppe, *Sinophone Malaysian Literature: Not Made in China* (Amherst, NY, 2013). Li Yongping, *Retribution: The Jiling Chronicles*, trans. Howard Goldblatt and Sylvia Li-chun Lin (New York, 2003). Jing Tsu, *Sound and Script in Chinese Diaspora* (Cambridge, MA, 2010). David Der-wei Wang, "Imaginary Nostalgia: Shen Congwen, Song Zelai, Mo Yan and Li Yongping," in *From May Fourth to June Fourth: Fiction and Film in Twentieth-Century China*, ed. David Der-wei Wang and Ellen Widmer (Cambridge, MA, 1993), 107–133.

ALISON M. GROPPE

2008–2009

"One Born a Dragon"

Chinese Media Fans Express Patriotism through Parody of Japanese Web Comic

These lines are excerpted from dialogue in "One Born a Dragon," a mainland Chinese fan comic released on January 1, 2009:

> "You carry heaven's will, as you have and must continue to for millennia and generations to come. Your life will last as long as this world."
> "You were born a dragon. Though they might crush your fangs and tear off your scales; be you blinded or de-clawed; should you fall weakened in shallow waters, a dragon is ever a dragon!"
> "What is your wish?" "That while I have life, I may behold your majesty rule all under heaven."

The comic is the eponymous capstone piece in a printed fanzine conceived, amid the high spirits following the Beijing Summer Olympics and the reflective solemnity of Sichuan earthquake relief efforts, by young artists working in China's burgeoning ACG (animation, comics, and games) industry. Drawing its characters and concepts from a Japanese web-comic series notorious for its controversial treatment of world history, *One Born a Dragon* elicited mixed reactions from ACG fan communities even while in production. After its release, these lines in particular were the subject of intense discussions regarding the nature of media fandom, national identity, and patriotism.

The story "One Born a Dragon" tells parallels China's emergence from the political angst of the 1990s to embrace a twenty-first-century narrative of national revival and pride. The quoted lines are spoken by a *qilin*, a fantastic beast from Chinese mythology, to a young man, Wang Yao, a character from the Japanese manga who is meant to personify the Chinese nation. At the start of the manga, Wang's battered, nearly lifeless body appears on a dirt road tracked with his blood. When the *qilin* appears, he hopes it is a sign that he is finally to "return" to rest. As Wang recounts the "betrayal" and "loss" he has suffered, his weary visage is set against a dark background of sinisterly poised characters personifying the United

States, France, England, and Japan. This is an unsubtle reference to the "century of humiliation," a period of foreign invasion and exploitation China suffered beginning with the first Opium War. It is a trope that both mainstream media and public education have employed since the 1980s to invoke and instill Chinese nationalist sentiment.

Rather than grant him respite, however, the *qilin* reminds Wang that he has inherited the ancient mandate ("heaven's will") to lead and that the dignity of his nature will bear him through his present pain and humiliation ("a dragon is ever a dragon"). Hearing this, Wang sits up with a half smile, as if recognizing truth in the *qilin*'s words, and asks, "What is your wish?" The last panel of the comic is a double-page spread of the *qilin* and Wang, a majestic dragon and a king, now seated in full court attire on a celestial throne. In the lower right-hand corner, the *qilin*'s response reads, "That while I have life, I may behold your majesty rule all under heaven." As much as these lines recall costume drama clichés, the way they draw on the power of China's long history and tradition, particularly discourses of sovereignty in ancient China, lends a sense of pathos and righteousness to its recent rise to global strength. They represent a shift from the indignity that colors late twentieth-century nationalism toward the image of a forward-looking nation that is resilient, forgiving, and self-assured of its place in the world.

This twenty-first-century national creation myth may resonate with the official discourses of nationalism in contemporary China, but it is actually a product of ACG subculture, a story told by and for Chinese ACG fans. Media fan culture, which took shape independently in Japan and in North America in the 1970s, has become an open and unruly space of transcultural interaction. Fan creativity cross-fertilizes across textual sensibilities and geopolitical borders, paying little mind to modern aesthetic theory or industry checkpoints. It tugs at the loose ends of a source text, chasing the intense responses the text elicits, and draws on whatever resources are available—be it production technologies, cultural knowledge, linguistic capacity, personal experience and skills, or distribution platforms—to convey to others the expressive potential of the source's various elements. The resulting music video, fiction, cosplay (role-playing a character in costume), artwork, fanzine, comic, animation, edit, translation, caption, essay, or manifesto is labor dedicated solely to the fandom, where self-selecting participants with similar interests gather.

Since fans play in the gray areas shunned by defenders of both copyright and institutional standards of artistic merit, fan production is usually excluded from the economies of established culture. The motivation that feeds fan creativity is varied and contradictory, but in its own articulation, fandom is, simply put, love.

The operations of fan production are not entirely a new phenomenon in China. The late Qing proliferation of unauthorized "sequels" and "side stories" to Ming-Qing vernacular novels are not only examples of derivative fiction; they also display the same enthusiasm for genre experimentation and speculative "what if" scenarios as their counterparts contributing to the online publishing boom of the more recent "fin de siècle." Just as simultaneous interpreters loosely translated and improvised film content during the exhibition of films in early twentieth-century China, making use of various performance elements such as voice, commentary, and localization, so fan-generated anime translations often creatively interpret a source text, drawing on local color and pidgin fan language in dubs, while using graphic elements and translator's notes in subtitling. These supratextual elements, which facilitate in-group humor and build community intimacy, all speak to the collaborative and interactive nature of fan production as a cultural practice.

Media fan culture in contemporary China is heavily influenced by developments in media content industries in postwar Japan. Japanese animation (anime) and comics (manga) officially entered China with the 1980 CCTV (Central China Television) broadcast of *Astro Boy*. Although Sino-Japanese relations have grown hostile in the decades since, Japanese media content has continued to make its way into China through both official licensing and broadcast and the unofficial channels of pirated VCDs (video CDs, a film storage medium popular in Asia), black-market publications, and, more recently, file sharing on the Internet. For those growing up in the 1980s and 1990s in China, Taiwan, and Hong Kong, anime and manga likely formed a significant part of their shared cultural memories. The power of such memories can be seen in the heavy use of Japanese pop slang and references to themes and characters from Japanese content properties in popular media produced in these locales. In China, soundtrack music plagiarized from anime can often be heard in a wide range of domestic television programming.

Since the mid-1990s, fan communities in Chinese contexts have grown more widespread and organized. This period saw the emergence of the first large-scale comic markets, conventions where fanzines and fan-created goods can be sold and distributed, as well as the active circulation of ACG content and news in the form of printed magazines. These early publications functioned partly as fanzines where fans could share creative work and criticism and partly as news magazines that reported on popular series, genres, and trends. They drew inspiration and knowledge from established Japanese ACG industry publications, often compiling and translating their content, such as "best of" ranking lists. Along with the spread of ACG fan interaction on social media and Internet platforms, a variety of new printed magazines have emerged in the 2000s to address the growing specificity and diversity of fan interests. In this way, Chinese fans have been able to remain current with the latest trends and titles released in Japan.

The manga series that *One Born a Dragon* parodies is called *Axis Powers Hetalia* (2006–present). The four-panel gag comic started attracting international fans around 2008 with the online streaming of its anime adaptation. It appealed to audiences with its premise of personifying nations as young men and boys (plus a few women and girls) and casting of historical events as opportunities to stage quaint, sometimes sexually suggestive, interactions between them. Although the first season recounts the history of the world wars, *Hetalia* sidesteps the violent realities of wartime conflict and foregrounds, instead, the endearing incompetence of its character-nations. "Make pasta, not war!," the tagline of the anime series' North American DVD release, celebrates the pacifism of the series' protagonist, Italy, who spends the whole of World War II manufacturing white flags. The chorus to the anime's ending theme chimes "draw a circle; that's the earth" while the nations march in line to take their place around a globe. In a manner that recalls Disney's "small world" vision of globalization, this image conflates world diversity with accessible character design. Politics of difference are reduced to a clash between cutesy stereotypes that can be easily spread across multimedia merchandise, intensifying and encouraging fetishistic fan consumption.

Starting in 2009, there was a boom in *Hetalia* fan works in ACG comic market conventions held in Japan, China, Hong Kong, and Taiwan. As one of the works released during this time, *One Born a Dragon* managed to achieve exceptional circulation, selling out in conventions in all three Chinese-speaking territories and going through several print runs during its first four months of distribution. Secondhand copies of the fanzine have been listed on Chinese online auction sites such as Taobao for as much as RMB 2,000 (a little over US$300).

In some ways, the popularity of *One Born a Dragon* speaks to the ways in which the shifting landscape of national pride was aligning with shifting attitudes and strategies employed in Chinese youth culture industries. By 2005, domestically produced comics and animation in China had started to attract a viable market. While rooted in Japanese anime and manga style, local artists strove for a distinctly "Chinese" approach to ACG storytelling by drawing on Chinese source texts, aesthetics, and techniques. Today, in the context of Chinese ACG industry and culture, the term "nationally produced" not only denotes that the works are made in China; it is also a nationalistic rebranding of Chinese ACG content that rejects earlier notions of it as mere knock-off versions of Japanese "originals." Many of the contributors to *One Born a Dragon* are some of the first big-name fan artists to enjoy commercial success in the domestic ACG industry. The magazines in which their works have appeared likewise grew from a popular ACG fan news magazine that had been rebranded to publish "nationally produced" comics exclusively.

As a work helmed by artists self-consciously engaged in the production of "nationally produced" comics, there are many ways in which *One Born a Dragon* can be read as a reappropriation (or even repatriation) of Wang Yao, rather than a straightforward fan parody of *Hetalia*. Illustrations in the fanzine integrate elements of manga-style cute and digital fantasy art with Chinese ink-brush painting and martial arts aesthetics. The cover of the fanzine features an image of Wang striking a kung fu pose midflight. His left hand clasps one end of a scroll, which trails behind him and across the spine to the back cover, where his right hand is shown holding an inked brush. The design of this cover suggests the fanzine itself is a scroll that has been filled with stories told in the reclaimed voice of China's youths.

While using local strategies to bypass Wang's problematic origins, *One Born a Dragon* nonetheless reproduces *Hetalia*'s fetishistic tendencies by centering Wang and his desirability as a character designed for fan consumption. Neither the comics nor the illustrations in the fanzine reference any material realities of China; instead, they configure Wang in a broad mix of tropes that evoke Chineseness via a multimedia matrix of yearning and recognition. "One Born a Dragon" appropriates Chinese cultural heritage, official patriotic discourse, and costume drama aesthetics to dramatize the dignity of an immortal youth. Other works in the fanzine variously depict Wang as an indomitable triad boss; a flirtatious beautiful boy character (*bishōnen*); a wounded soldier; the first emperor, Qin Shi Huang (260–210 BCE); a young urbanite; a caretaker of pandas; and a gentle older brother to other Asian nation-characters. In the end, *One Born a Dragon*, rather than expressing love for China, constructs a self-affirming pastiche of Chinese national identity through love of Wang.

As fan participation brings beloved characters closer to the lives of contemporary Chinese youths, it also pulls Chinese youths closer to first-world cultures of late capitalism and cosmopolitan consumption. The final image in "One Born a Dragon," that of a reinstated Wang accompanied by the text "rule all under heaven," hints at the hypocrisy and dangers, already evident in *Hetalia*, of participating in those cultures. These include the Disneyfication of world diversity, as well as complacency toward the very violence and imperialist greed that undergirded China's "century of humiliation." As Chinese official discourse shifts toward the "Chinese Dream" of mobilizing individual desires in pursuit of national and global prestige, the contradictory nature of patriotic yearnings remains unresolved.

BIBLIOGRAPHY: Sandra Annett, *Anime Fan Communities: Transcultural Flows and Frictions* (London, 2014). Toshio Miyake, "Doing Occidentalism in Contemporary Japan: Nation Anthropomorphism and Sexualized Parody in *Axis Powers Hetalia*," in "Transnational Boys' Love Fan Studies," ed. Kazumi Nagaike and Katsuhiko Suganuma, special issue, *Transformative Works and Cultures* 12 (2013), http://journal.transformativeworks .org/index.php/twc/article/view/436/392. David Der-wei Wang, *Fin-de-Siècle Splendor: Repressed Modernities of Late Qing Fiction, 1849–1911* (Stanford, CA, 1997). Kinnia Yau Shuk-ting, "Meanings of the Imagined Friends: Good Japanese in Chinese War Films," in *Imagining Japan in Post-war East Asia: Identity Politics, Schooling, and Popular Culture*, ed. Paul Morris, Naoko Shimazu, and Edward Vickers (London, 2013), 68–84.

CASEY LEE

2010 · JANUARY 10

> "She didn't have the look of a dancing girl, but if she was an actress, he couldn't put a name to the face. She had, in a past life, been an actress; and here she was, still playing a part, but in a drama too secret to make her famous." —Eileen Chang, *Lust, Caution*

Ang Lee's Adaptation, Pretense, Transmutation

Describing Wang Chia-chih, the heroine of her novella *Lust, Caution*, Eileen Chang (1920–1995) projects onto a nearby stranger how Wang might appear. To the stranger she looks vaguely famous, though not an A-list figure, and in this way the "actress" of the first and second sentences changes shape. As a secret performer, Wang more closely resembles a chameleon, changing colors in order to blend in, evade detection, and survive. This indicates her adaptability, survival instinct, and perhaps even a degree of opportunism. Still another nuance of this metaphor is facility, or worldliness: the ability to pass in language, customs, or repertoire. This is especially useful for spies and explorers, such as T. E. Lawrence (1888–1935) and Richard Burton (1925–1984), and the director Ang Lee similarly has a remarkable ability to move between different genres, subjects, and styles. In January 2010, Lee earned his scuba diving certification in Belize, a necessary undertaking to prepare for filming his upcoming movie, *Life of Pi*. The local paper trumpeted this headline: "Oscar-Winning Director Ang Lee Gets SCUBA Certified in SP [San Pedro]!"

The image of Lee, certified scuba diver, is fascinating because here he appears as out of place as a Chinese lady with bound feet skiing in the Swiss alps (as did Chang's worldly mother, according to Julia Lovell). Lee's reputation—tasteful and somewhat bookish, yet popular—is related to his bent toward literary adaptation. His evident sincerity and devotion to his craft are upheld in contrast to many crass Hollywood directors. In all his projects, Lee is invariably prepared and in control. He seems utterly modest, in contrast to a trickster like Orson Welles (1915–1985), Billy Wilder (1906–2002), or Quentin Tarantino (1963–). The trickster is a fitting role for a director-magician, especially in Hollywood. But then, so is the chameleon, able to play games with a nimble wit. Yet the chameleon image is underwritten by what is in the films, which is to say dramas of impersonation. It is not his jack-of-all-trades versatility that

Director Ang Lee took his scuba diving certification course with White Sands dive instructor Samuel Lin in Belize, January 2010. Courtesy of Earth's Ocean Foundation. Photographer: Charlie Croughwell.

makes Lee a chameleon, but his narratives of intimate performativity and fear of being exposed. Careful, consistent role-playing is thus tied to mutability, and constant mutability yields precarious forms of constancy. This dialectic of transformation and mutability is a recurrent theme in Lee's films, and also reflects the relationship between his cinematic adaptations and their literary sources.

Animal magnetism—a private compulsion, locked in a struggle with socially acceptable norms—is common in Lee's films, including *Lust, Caution* (2007), *Brokeback Mountain* (2005), *Hulk* (2003), *The Wedding Banquet* (1993), and even *The Ice Storm* (1997). These works explore secret lives, of spies, or cowboys, scientists, or bourgeoisie, whose inner passions—should they break out—augur violent reprisals. There is the "killer lesson" in *Life of Pi*, when the protagonist as a young boy is forced by his zookeeper father to watch a tiger slaughtering a live goat. Father's harsh lesson is meant to ensure Pi never again approaches the beast. Similarly, in *Brokeback Mountain*, Ennis Del Mar is haunted by the sight, displayed by his father, of the outing and grisly execution of a gay man. Given his own sexual drives, Ennis keeps this nightmare in mind—and in the closet—for the rest of his life. These are cautionary scenes, prohibitions of the most chilling sort.

Animal-to-theological transitions are typical of Lee. This involves transformation or passage from state to state, from page to screen, like in Eadweard Muybridge's (1830–1904) famous photographic study of a horse, where a series of tripwires attached to cameras confirmed that a galloping horse really does lift all four legs off the ground, though this is impossible to see with the naked eye. Another sort of passage or conversion can be found in the rabbit-duck illusion, where the image shifts according to observers' mental orientation, such that it appears as either a rabbit or a duck, but never both at the same time. Another version is the drawing of a young girl, who switches to an ugly witch with a sudden change in perspective. Similarly, in *Lust, Caution*, Wang Chia-chih's perceptions shift when she finds herself outside the jewelry shop in Shanghai. When she shouts "Run!" Wang has just given the fateful signal to Mr. Yee, and in the process gives herself away as a lure in the assassination plot. It is as though she has thrown a switch: "Pedestrians and vehicles flowed on by, as if separated from her by a wall of glass, and no more accessible than the elegant mannequins in the window of the Green House Ladies' Clothing Emporium—you could look, but you couldn't touch." In the novel, the traffic is described as gliding along, "imperviously serene," as if in a different dimension from the one she occupies. In the film, however, we must infer this from the visual image, as the camera pans along shop windows and reveals mannequins and a stuffed leopard alongside an opulent fur. Inside, there is an indistinct couple, apparently on a date. It seems Wang is being compared to the mannequins in the window, which is exactly what she has become in the spy ring. We see either the figure (Wang) or the ground (mannequin), but never both at once.

Speaking about the process of adapting writing into images, Paul Theroux (1941–) also flips a switch when he uses theological terms for this transmutation:

I [the novelist] had dreamed it all. But they had to tangibalize it, as Father Divine used to say. You have to agree with God: in the beginning was the Word, and the Word was made Flesh. It is not always an easy transition, but that is cinematic transubstantiation, the making of movies out of novels.

Making the word flesh is what Lee did with *Lust, Caution*, a flesh that literally bares the devices of seduction and conquest. He and his team tangibalized Chang but also cannibalized her, exposing to all the pleasures (and fears) of physical yielding. Yielding assumes a proposition, which in turn intends a movement, turn, or passage from aloof to enamored.

Here, there is an ethics or theology of "shedding" (for example, snake, beetle, or butterfly) and conversion. Passing, in this usage, suggests an audience or interlocutor, someone who sees and judges a turn of behavior. There is a conversion, or transformation, that brings adjustment—jettisoning the old and assuming the new. It is a theology of forgiveness, trust, adaptation, and amelioration, with viewers who recognize and accept the postconversion status. In discussing *Crouching Tiger, Hidden Dragon*, Lee remarked that Yuen Wo Ping's (1945–) choreography changes martial arts into performing arts. On the other hand, there is also the opposite, as when Lee describes how he develops an unconscious yen for tyranny when in the director's chair, moving from the mild personality of Lee the writer and stay-home dad to the imperious perfectionist that he is on the set.

Lust, Caution flaunts its own dissembling, revealing masquerade and performance as cruel, even exploitative "acts." Viewers are shown what appears to be real sex, and although it recalls hard-core pornography, the picture nevertheless ensures that it will be perceived as real, not playacting. Lee has observed that Chang "understood play-acting and mimicry as something by nature cruel and brutal: animals, like her characters, use camouflage to evade their enemies and lure their prey." In her novella, Chang herself wrote, "And now he possessed her utterly, primitively—as a hunter does his quarry, a tiger his kill. Alive, her body belonged to him; dead, she was his ghost." Lee treasures the animal magnetism, mentioning the "ghost following the tiger," meaning a spirit that shadows the beast and helps lure other prey.

In the trace of killings past, there is the pagan notion that to devour is power, lending the eater the flesh, heart, and mind of the kill. This is totemism, primal stand-ins that become and channel another person, tribe, or holy spirit. Recall the Christian Eucharist, where bread is not just symbol, it *is* body, wine *is* blood. *Lust, Caution* opens with a close-up of a German shepherd, a watchdog checking for intruders, or impersonators. Instinct, stalking, and implacable predatory traits are blended with the methodical crafts of surveillance, trap setting, interrogation, and "slow, reasoned torture." Producer and cowriter James Schamus goes further, noting that Mr. Yee (the mark) wants Wang Chia-chih (the lure) not in spite of his suspicion that she's a spy, but rather "it is precisely *because* he suspects her that he desires her.... And so lust and caution are, in Chang's work, functions of each other, not because we desire what is dangerous, but because our love is, no matter how earnest, an *act*, and therefore always an object of suspicion."

In *Life of Pi, Lust, Caution*, and *Crouching Tiger, Hidden Dragon*, one finds a cannibalistic urge to eat or be eaten. Undercover, Pi, Wang, and Jen are bait, at risk of being "taken" or swallowed up by the mark or his inner circle, and possibly devoured. Like undercover police thrillers, the role-playing is lethal because the role can rise up and overwhelm its player. The cop must convince his criminal mates he is as tough, amoral, and depraved as they are. But does the cop's assumed depravity touch him and shape his character beneath? What are the effects of sustained, convincing impersonations? When does the pretense take over? Must the mole believe in order to make surrounding compatriots believe? Or is it just technique, tricks of behavior, dress, and speech? In all these films, the character must pass for something, such as an animal trainer, available *tai-tai* (missus), reputable daughter, or a disciple of *wuxia* (martial arts). The game is to *pass muster*, be accepted, taken for a credible member of a team. With exposure comes nasty consequences, so it is crucial to inhabit, to become, not only play the part.

Lee's work has its way with the writing, as all films do, choosing and magnifying details that expose the tale's deepest meanings. Describing the cinematic adaptation of his book *The Mosquito Coast*, Theroux asked, "Isn't the whole point about a good movie that it takes liberties?" We may say that Lee's cinema exemplifies its literary sources through a series of betrayals, guiding viewers' attention to elements that may or may not be there. *Crouching Tiger, Hidden Dragon*, for instance, revives martial arts fiction on the global screen by salvaging forgotten works from the past. Wang Dulu's (1909–1977) multivolume fiction is not read much today, unlike more standard sources for martial arts pictures such as Jin Yong (1924–) and Gu Lung (1938–1985). Moreover, Lee effects a betrayal of the original work's scale: Wang Dulu's sprawling *wuxia* saga from the 1930s is distilled to psychodrama, female intrigues, and even *Kammerspielen* (pausing on intimate suspicions, denials, and hesitation). The adaptation also introduces sacrifice as a way to domesticate Jen's power, departing from the May Fourth ethos of free love, hidden in the heart of the Wang Dulu story. Instead of restaging free love in the martial art setting, Lee uses Wang's story to unveil the centrality of teaching in his film. Central to Jen's character are learning, correction, and the havoc aroused by the power of knowledge, and awareness of it.

Lee's treatment of literary texts prompts us to see adaptation as the act of resurrecting a new work from literary remains, which evokes the image of a predator medium, hyena-cinema stalking and picking off literary prey. But this would be wrong, because literature has a stature that movies can never usurp. Alexander Sokurov (1951–), the acclaimed Russian director, has said that despite his work as a filmmaker, he is nevertheless a child of literature, which for him is the most important art form, while cinema is at best three or four steps away. There cannot be anything in cinema that literature has not already done, and this, he says, is something cinema can never forgive.

The relationship between literature and cinema, accordingly, is not so much that of a chameleon, but rather that of a shapeshifter. If the chameleon changes appearance based on environment, shapeshifters change bodily substance as well as appearance, and can therefore help us understand the artistic process—like the mutation of a written story into moving image, or a demure actress disappearing into her role. Mild-mannered Bruce Banner mutates into the terrifying Hulk, just as a cerebral film director becomes a certified scuba diver. *Brokeback Mountain* has become an opera with a new libretto by Annie Proulx, who provides a soaring viewpoint for Ennis Del Mar:

> We look down on them hawks.
> We look down on them pine trees.
> We're like eagles, Jack.

BIBLIOGRAPHY: Eileen Chang, *Lust, Caution*, with afterword by Ang Lee and special essay by James Schamus (New York, 2007). Emilie Yueh-Yu Yeh and Darrell William Davis, *Taiwan Film Directors: A Treasure Island* (New York, 2005).

DARRELL WILLIAM DAVIS

2011 · JUNE 26

"Thou art translated."

Encountering Shakespeare's Plays in the Sinophone World

On June 26, 2011, during a three-day visit to Britain, China's premier Wen Jiabao (1942–) visited the birthplace of William Shakespeare (1564–1616). The event drew much media attention. He alluded to his boyhood love of Shakespeare in his speech to British prime minister David Cameron (1966–). Wen's state visit was planned with the goal of projecting China's newly acquired soft power, but international economic relations and political capital were also at stake, as well as tourism revenue. British culture secretary Jeremy Hunt (1966–) was blunt: "I am hoping that a billion Chinese might see some pictures on their TV of their premier coming and visiting the birthplace of Shakespeare" and flock to Britain in droves. Art is political.

Numerous Chinese and Sinophone performances of Shakespeare have already been staged in Britain since the 1980s, and the Royal Shakespeare Company toured Loveday Ingram's *Merchant of Venice* to Beijing and Shanghai in 2002. The cultural capital of Shakespeare is evoked in tandem with Chinese modernity. As in other areas of the arts, the involvement of nation-states helped to reconfigure the relationships between Chinese, Sinophone, British, and global localities.

Along with a number of Japanese and Western canonical poets and writers, Shakespeare and his works have played a significant role in the development of Chinese and Sinophone cultures in mainland China, Hong Kong, and Taiwan. The encounters between "Shakespeare" as a cultural institution and the values represented by the icon of "China" have enriched Chinese-language traditions, as well as global Shakespearean performance history.

The transmission of Renaissance culture in China began with the arrival of the first Jesuit missionaries in 1582, followed by the Dominicans and Franciscans in the 1630s. Illustrated British travel narratives record the experience of British emissaries, including those attached to the mission of Lord George Macartney (1737–1806), attending theatrical productions in Tianjin and Beijing during the reign of the Qianlong Emperor (r. 1736–1795). One of the emissaries' diary entries briefly comments on the similarity between an unnamed Chinese play and Shakespeare's *Richard III*. With the decline of the Qing empire in the nineteenth century, Chinese interest in Western modes of thinking and political systems intensified. Both Shakespeare and China were "translated"—to use the word to mean "transformed" or "metamorphosed," as Peter Quince does in *A Midsummer Night's Dream*—in the late nineteenth century, under the influence of clashing ideologies of modernization and the revalidation of traditional Chinese values. Shakespeare's name was first mentioned in passing in 1839 in a compendium of world cultures translated by Lin Zexu (1785–1850), a key figure in the first Opium War. By the time Chinese translations became available and substantive critical engagements with Shakespeare were initiated, there was already over half a century of reception history in which Shakespeare was frequently evoked to support or suppress specific agendas.

There are several recurrent themes in Chinese-language adaptations of Shakespeare. Chinese directors and translators have largely preferred to view Shakespeare's plays, in their original forms and settings, as works of art with universal appeal, rather than attempting to localize the characters, storyline, and setting for the domestic audience. This strategy has produced plays performed "straight," with visual and textual citations of what were perceived to be authoritative classical performances (such as Laurence Olivier's [1907–1989] versions). Early performances in Shanghai tended to follow this pattern, such as *Woman Lawyer*, the first Chinese-language performance of Shakespeare, adapted by Bao Tianxiao (1875–1973) from *The Merchant of Venice* and performed by students from Shanghai Eastern Girls' High School. If the play seems foreign, according to advocates of this approach, that only guarantees its aesthetics have been preserved in a way that benefits the audience.

A second strategy is to localize the plot and setting of a play, assimilate Shakespeare into local worldviews, and fold Shakespeare into local performance genres. An example is Huang Zuolin's (1906–1994) *The Story of Bloody Hands* (1986), a *kunqu* opera adaptation of *Macbeth*. The complex idioms of Chinese opera forms were increasingly seen by performers and their sponsors not as an obstacle but as an asset in creating international demand for traditional theater forms.

The third strategy involves pastiche, dramaturgical collage, and extensive, deconstructive rewritings. It sometimes changes the genre of a play by accessing dormant themes that have been marginalized by centuries of Anglocentric criticism and performance traditions. The emergence of parody is a sign that Shakespeare's global afterlife has reached a new stage. The stories have become so familiar to the "cross-border" audiences that the plays can be used as a platform for artistic exploration of new genres. For instance, in writing a play of spoken drama (as post-1907 Western-influenced spoken drama theater is known within China) called *Shamuleite*, or *Shamlet* (1992), Lee Kuo-hsiu (1955–2013), one of the most innovative Taiwanese playwrights and directors to emerge in the 1980s, turned high tragedy, or what was known to Renaissance readers as "tragic history," into comic parody. He suggests in the program that *Shamlet* is a revenge comedy that "has nothing to do with *Hamlet* but something to do with Shakespeare."

This strategy has been used to counter stereotypical constructions of local and foreign cultures. It has also been used by artists seeking to build their brand for intercultural theater works in international markets: Wu Hsing-kuo (1953–), for example, inserts his own life story into his Buddhist-inflected solo Peking opera *Lear Is Here* (2000). Playing ten characters from Shakespeare's tragedy, Wu takes the play's themes of domestic conflict, construction of selves and others, and notions of duty to family and duty to the state and mingles them with his autobiography. One of the most powerful scenes is "Lear in the Storm." At center stage stands a dispirited King Lear, who has just taken off his Peking opera headdress and armor costume in full view of a packed audience. Following his powerful presentation of the scene of the mad Lear in the storm and on-stage costume change, the actor—now dressed as if he were backstage—interrogates himself and the eyeless headdress while touching his own eyes, a somber moment that that evokes Gloucester's blinding and the undirected gaze of the viewer in a play about sight and truth. "Who am I?" Lear asks in Shakespeare's play, "Doth any here know me? This is not Lear. / Doth Lear walk thus? speak thus? Where are his eyes?" Here, the performer is self-conscious of the ways in which his own eyes become Lear's eyes. These two pairs of eyes represent the necessary split many performers experience on stage, a process of making null the performer's own identity so that he or she becomes the part being performed. Wu's adaptation of Shakespeare enriches our understanding of acting in traditional Chinese theater.

These three strategies coexist throughout the history of Chinese and Sinophone Shakespeares. As in almost all instances of transnational borrowing, a select, locally resonant group of "privileged" plays has held continuous sway in the Chinese-speaking world. *The Merchant of Venice* is the first Shakespearean play known to be staged, and it continues to fascinate Chinese audiences today. In the midst of the early twentieth-century "New Women's Movement," Portia ("the female lawyer") took center stage as a symbol of the debate about the admittance of women into the legal profession and higher education. The play has also been parodied on stage. A travesty by Francis Talfourd (1828–1862) entitled *Shylock; or, The Merchant of Venice Preserved* was staged in Hong Kong in 1867 for British expatriates. The Hong Kong Amateur Dramatic Club revived the production in 1871, as the mercantile-themed play proved relevant to the social milieu of a trade colony. In time, Mandarin-language performances began to dominate the stage, and today the play remains a staple of high school and college curricula and is often chosen for the graduation spoken drama productions of Chinese and Taiwanese universities.

In terms of performance style, Shakespeare has figured prominently in the shaping of contemporary Chinese theater, where the genres of traditional Chinese opera and performing arts (stylized theater, often including operatic elements, with more than 360 regional variations) and spoken drama coexist. The earliest documented Shakespeare in traditional Chinese opera, *Killing the Elder Brother and Snatching the Sister-in-Law*, was based on *Hamlet* and performed in Sichuan opera style. In 1925, the Custom Renewal Society (a progressive organization founded in 1912 to promote social reform through new *qinqiang* operas) staged *A Pound of Flesh* in the *qinqiang* opera style in Shaanxi Province in northern China. Although performances of Shakespeare in different genres of Chinese opera have existed since the early twentieth century, the 1980s were a turning point. Shakespeare became more regularly performed in different opera styles in China, Taiwan, Hong Kong, and elsewhere, and entered the collective cultural memory of Chinese opera performers and audiences. The revived interest in Chinese-opera Shakespeare was encouraged by increased exchanges among performers based in mainland China and in the Chinese diaspora.

Beyond Chinese opera, Sinophone performances of Shakespeare frequently highlight linguistic differences. Languages serve as markers of ethnic differences in *Yumei and Tianlai*, a bilingual Taiwanese-Mandarin *Romeo and Juliet* staged at the Shakespeare in Taipei festival in May 2003. The Montagues and the Capulets are each assigned a different language, complicating the experience of artists in the Chinese diaspora and the play's capacity to serve as a national allegory. Key scenes from *Romeo and Juliet* were staged in two plays-within-a-play in Ning Caishen's (1975–) *Romeo and Zhu Yingtai*, directed by He Nian (1980–) and produced by the Shanghai Dramatic Arts Center (May 2008), in which French, Japanese, English, and Mandarin Chinese were spoken. In what Ning called "a tragedy told in comic manners," the star-crossed lovers traverse 1937 Shanghai and present-day New York in search of new personal and cultural identities.

The presence of Shakespeare at theater festivals in Taiwan in the 1980s and 1990s took a different form from mainland China's postrevolutionary Shakespeare boom, which was initiated by state-endorsed and government-sponsored Shakespeare festivals in 1986 and 1994. The month-long Shakespeare in Taipei festival in 2003, for instance, focused more on providing a platform for artistically innovative and commercially viable experimental works. As a multilingual society (Mandarin, Taiwanese, Hakka, and aboriginal languages), Taiwan has produced a significant number of mainstream performances entirely in a dialect, in a mixture of Mandarin and a local dialect, or in English. Some of these works reflect Taiwan's multiply determined history, while others question that history and the much-contested "Chineseness" of the island's identity. These tendencies provide interesting contrasts to the ways in which mainland Chinese artists imagine China. By the same token, while mainland China is certainly multilingual, it is Taiwan and Hong Kong that have established strong traditions of Shakespeare performances in one or more dialects. The linguistic diversity of Taiwan and Hong Kong theaters fosters distinctive views of "Shakespeare" and what counts as "Chinese."

With strong dual traditions of English and Cantonese Shakespearean performances in spoken drama and Cantonese opera, Hong Kong theater reflects the tension between southern Chinese culture and the British legacy. After Hong Kong was ceded to Britain for 150 years in the 1842 Treaty of Tianjin, "Englishness" was given significant cultural weight throughout the social structure. Under the British government, theater was supported and encouraged as "a wholesome diversion from the tedium of military life." English literature was established as a subject of study in

Hong Kong's school system, and in 1882 students began studying Shakespeare for exams, initiating a form of colonial "domination by consent." Shakespearean drama became part of the repertoire of the Hong Kong Amateur Dramatic Club, a theater society active in the 1860s and 1870s. Since the 1980s, as the "handover" of Hong Kong after 1997 became an increasingly pressing topic, a considerable amount of energy has been directed not toward the postcolonial question but toward Hong Kong's global status and its Chinese heritage, as evidenced by the productions of the Hong Kong Repertory Theatre (founded in 1977), the largest professional theater in Hong Kong, and performances by students of the Hong Kong Academy for Performing Arts and other universities.

Despite the association of Shakespeare and Englishness, Shakespeare was not resisted as an image of colonization. Political changes have hardly affected him. Some contemporary Hong Kong scholars are surprised to find that "local experimentations with Shakespeare in post-modernist and Chinese styles have continued to flourish [in Hong Kong]." This continued prominence, they argue, shows that "Shakespeare has transcended his British heritage and become part of the Hong Kong Chinese tradition." While partly true, this view blurs the historical conditions surrounding early performances. One crucial reason why Shakespeare seems to transcend his British heritage is that Britain never colonized Hong Kong the way it did India. This special historical condition—an indirect colonial structure that Mao Zedong (1893–1976) later called "semicolonialism"—informed Hong Kong's performance culture in the late nineteenth and early twentieth centuries. If the practitioners of the new theater were resisting anything, it was the Chinese past. The same is true of other treaty ports, such as Shanghai, that were home to a host of European concessions but had no overarching colonial institution.

The uses of Shakespeare's plays in spoken drama and Chinese opera are informed by a paradigm shift from seeking authenticity to foregrounding artistic subjectivity. Shakespearean themes and characterization have enriched, challenged, and changed Chinese-language theaters and genres. Chinese and Sinophone Shakespeares have become strangers at home.

BIBLIOGRAPHY: Alexa Huang, "'It Is the East': Shakespearean Tragedies in East Asia," in *The Oxford Handbook to Shakespearean Tragedy*, ed. Michael Neill and David Schalkwyk (Oxford, 2016). Alexa Huang, "Thou Art Translated! How Shakespeare Went Viral," *Conversation*, April 23, 2015, https://theconversation.com/thou-art-translated

-how-shakespeare-went-viral-40044. Alexa Huang and Peter Donaldson, eds., *MIT Global Shakespeares,* open-access digital video archive, http://globalshakespeares.org. Alexa Huang and Elizabeth Rivlin, eds., *Shakespeare and the Ethics of Appropriation* (New York, 2014).

ALEXA HUANG

2012

Mo Yan wins the Nobel Prize in Literature.

"Length, density, and difficulty: these are the hallmarks of a novel,
and it is in these qualities that the dignity of the great art form resides."

Defending the Dignity of the Novel

[Excerpted from the postscript to the Chinese edition of Mo Yan's 2006 novel *Life and Death Are Wearing Me Out*]

When I say length, naturally I mean the literal length of the novel. If a novel is less than two hundred thousand characters long, it lacks the gravitas it ought to have. A novel that doesn't reach that length is just like the character Tang Long from *Outlaws of the Marsh.* Although he too is brave and powerful, although he too is quick and fierce, in the end, because he is small of build, he could only have become king of the mountain fortress with great difficulty. Of course, I know that there are many short novels that are more powerful and are of greater value than certain overstuffed longer novels, and I know that there are many short novels that have already become classics, but even in those exquisite short works that are as beautiful as the surging waves and dramatic bends of the Yangtze River, there is something missing. A novel should be long; if it's not long, how can it be a novel? To write a full-length novel is certainly not an easy task. We are accustomed to hearing calls to make long novels shorter, but I, on the other hand, want to issue the following call: novels ought to be longer.

If one insists on the importance of length for the novel, it's very easy to find ready-made counterexamples of writers who did not write long novels: Lu Xun, Shen Congwen, Eileen Chang, Wang Zengqi, Chekhov, Borges. I of course do not deny that the above-mentioned are important, outstanding writers, but they are not in the same class as Leo Tolstoy, Dostoyevsky, Thomas Mann, Joyce, or Proust. Their writings do not have the vast, complex narrative structure, the dramatic bends and surging waves, that one finds in the brilliant masterworks of the latter category of writers. I think this fact is indisputable.

I believe that the key to whether or not a writer writes, and moreover is able to write, a good novel is whether or not he can tap into "the heart of the novelist." Great melancholy, great compassion, great ambition; a great spirit, like that of a heavenly steed soaring across the skies; and a great openness, a mind as clear as a sheet of freshly fallen snow—that is what the heart of the novelist contains.

I don't need to expand on great melancholy, great ambition, great spirit, or great openness, but I'd like to say a few words about great compassion. Compassion is not simply "whosoever shall smite thee on thy right cheek, turn to him the other also." Compassion is not simply grace under fire or remaining kind in the face of adversity. Compassion is not fainting when you see blood, or yelling loudly, "I'm going to faint," when you see blood, and it's certainly not prevaricating about that which is evil and vile. The Bible is a classic of compassion, but there is no shortage of scenes filled with graphic carnage. Buddhism is a philosophy of great compassion, but Buddhism has a hell with awful punishments that make your hair stand on end. Any compassion that covers up the iniquities and ugliness of the human race is no different from hypocrisy. The novel *Plum in the Golden Vase* has an awful reputation, but discerning critics say that it is a book of compassion. This compassion is a Chinese-style compassion. This is a compassion built on the foundation of Chinese religion and philosophy, and not a compassion built on Western religion and philosophy.

A novel is a great art form that includes the myriad things of the world: lambs and little birds, lions and crocodiles. You cannot say that just because a lion eats a lamb or a crocodile swallows a bird, it is not compassionate. A world with nothing but lambs and little birds in it is not a world, and fiction with nothing but good people in it is not fiction. Even lambs must eat grass, even little birds must eat bugs and worms, and even good people have evil thoughts. If you stand at a higher vantage point and look down, both good people and bad people are people to be pitied. To only sympathize with good people is petty compassion. Great compassion means not only sympathizing with good people, but also sympathizing with bad people.

To only describe the scars other people gave you, and not describe the scars you gave other people, is not compassion. In fact, it could even be called shamelessness. Only exposing the evil within the hearts of others, and not baring the evil within your own heart, is not compassion. This too could be called shamelessness. One can be truly compassionate only by facing up to the evil of mankind, only by recognizing one's own ugliness, only by describing the pitiful fates brought about by the weaknesses that mankind cannot overcome and by the pathological dispositions of select individuals. Only an examination of such depth and power that it can be called an interrogation of the soul—only that is great compassion.

When I talk about the density of a novel, I mean the density of events, the density of characters, and the density of thought. I mean tides of thought that rush up and crash like the waves of the ocean and sweep along events and characters. I mean shockwaves of thought that arrive with the force of a landslide, such that one cannot take it all in at once. A dense novel is not the kind of novel that can say everything clearly in just a few sentences.

A density of events of course does not mean a simple enumeration, a day-to-day chronicle of events. Hemingway's "theory of the iceberg" is applicable here.

When I say a density of thought, I mean a life-and-death struggle between many different kinds of thought. If a piece of fiction only has so-called correct thought, only has that which is good and praiseworthy, or if it only has a simple, formulaic opposition between good and evil, the value of that piece of fiction is suspect. Those pieces of fiction that signify progress can very well be written by a writer with a reactionary mind-set, and those pieces of fiction that possess philosophical insights are most likely not written by philosophers. A good novel should be a heteroglossia. It should allow for many different understandings, and in many cases those understandings should run counter to the writer's personal convictions. There should be a hazy middle ground between good and evil, beauty and ugliness, love and hate, and that middle ground is precisely the vast universe in which the writer can exercise his brilliance.

Or, to put it another way, a novel with density is a novel that can be misread by generation after generation of readers. This misreading is of course a reading that is directly counter to that which the author personally intended. The enchanting power of literature lies in the fact that it can be misread. A piece of fiction in which the personal convictions of the writer match up perfectly with the feelings of the reader after reading can become a best seller, but not a great novel.

When I talk about the difficulty of a novel, I mean its artistic originality. What is original is always alien. It always requires the reader to rack his or her brain. Reading an original work will always cause more pain and hardship than reading one of those slick novels that is light as a feather. The difficulty of the novel can be further understood in terms of the difficulty of the novel's structure, the difficulty of its language, and the difficulty of its thought.

A novel's structure can of course be simple and straightforward. That is the customary way of writing for those classic writers of critical realism [that is, the socialist realist style of writing prescribed by the People's Republic of China during the Maoist period —Trans.]. This way of writing is also quite economical. Structure is never just simple form; sometimes structure is also content. A novel's structure is an important constituent element of a novel's art. It is a demonstration of a writer's bountiful imagination. A good structure can bring out the significance of the story, or it can complicate the significance of the story. A good structure can transcend the story, or it can deconstruct the story. I have said several times in the past few years, "Structure is politics." If you want to understand what I mean when I say, "Structure is politics," please read my novels *The Republic of Wine* and *The Garlic Ballads*.

When I talk about the difficulty of a novel's language, this is of course to say, the use of language that is distinctly individual and defamiliarized. But this defamiliarized language should be a kind of language that has been essentially domesticated by the writer, not dialect and regionalisms used to purposely manufacture difficulties for the reader. Naturally, dialect and regionalisms are a linguistic goldmine, but if the writer only uses these expressions within dialogue, with the aim of realizing the individuality of each character's speech through these expressions, he has misunderstood their proper use. Only by incorporating dialect and regionalisms into the narrative language of the novel will the use of such expressions truly contribute to the language.

A novel's length, density, and difficulty together create its stately ambience. The great novel rejects petty gimmicks and happy accidents. It is clumsy and magnanimous. The good comes along with the bad. It is not maudlin, nor is it overly clever. There is no need for it to pander or to act up to get attention.

   A novel cannot sacrifice the dignity it ought to possess for the sake of catering to these inflammatory times. A novel cannot for the sake of accommodating certain readers curtail its length, decrease its density, or lower its difficulty. I'll make it as long as it needs to be, as dense as it needs to be, and as difficult as it needs to be; if you're willing to read it, you can read it, and if you don't want to read it, don't read it. Even if that only leaves one reader for my novel, that's the way that I will write.

Mo Yan
Translated by Dylan Suher

2012

Zhang Chengzhi republishes *History of the Soul.*

2014

Alai's *Zhandui* receives no votes for the Lu Xun Prize.

Minority Heritage in the Age of Multiculturalism

The problem of the ethnic minority in the People's Republic of China (PRC) is fundamentally an issue of representation. Even the category of the "ethnic minority" itself cannot be taken for granted: Is an individual's ethnic status decided unilaterally via self-identification, in conversation with or by one's community, or in top-down fashion by his or her national governing body? Each option carries specific implications that affect a person's notions of self, understanding of his or her cultural heritage, and ensuing political rights. In today's China, the Chinese Communist Party (CCP) rose to power on the promise of being able to better represent "the people." In practice, however, this has resulted in a wide range of policy prescriptions, from striving for full assimilation of minority groups into mainstream culture, to promoting minority languages and cultures as legitimate alternatives to majority cultural mores. As a long-standing point of contention in the PRC, literature has regularly served as an outlet for exploring possible permutations of the minority politics of the status quo, as well as a means of extoling or decrying those politics wholesale. This essay will look at two examples of such literary responses: Hui Muslim writer Zhang Chengzhi's (1948–) 2012 republication of his 1991 best-selling novel, *History of the Soul*, and Rgyalrong Tibetan writer Alai's (1959–) 2014 award-winning nonfiction work, *Zhandui*. These two texts are responses to hegemonic state narratives about ethnic minorities in the PRC, and reflect the political quagmire that surrounds the "representation" of minorities as part of the PRC's current platform of multiculturalism.

Since the founding of the PRC in 1949, the CCP has made several attempts to formally document the extent of China's ethnic diversity. The many field surveys and censuses conducted in the country's more heterogeneous western provinces, such as Sichuan and Yunnan, ultimately yielded results that were robust beyond expectations and, consequently, politically inexpedient. After realizing the inadequacy of the previously preferred Soviet model for establishing nationhood, or *natsia*—interpreted as the equivalent of the Chinese *minzu* (translated as either ethnic minority or nation) and evaluated on a scale of a population's distance from achieving capitalist modes of production—their efforts to schematize the nation's ethnic populations ultimately resulted in the creation of fifty-six officially recognized (and sometimes invented) ethnic groups. Of that number, fifty-five are considered minority ethnic groups and are constitutionally guaranteed representation in the National People's Congress and relevant provincial and prefectural governments, and in some cases are awarded autonomous regions that allow for the primary use of local languages and customs. In China today, although ethnic minority groups collectively compose less than 10 percent of the total Chinese population and are far outnumbered by the single remaining Han ethnic group, they still compose a compelling force at approximately 123 million individuals.

What appears as a comprehensive attempt to provide representation for the entire population, however, has not gone uncontested. In an attempt to organize the chaotic reality of China's diversity, the CCP made the decision to not recognize groups that failed to claim a certain threshold number of members, and instead consolidated them into larger populations that they considered to be ethnically related or similar in custom. This has led to people such as the Mosuo, who are classified as part of the Naxi ethnic group, to protest this system of categorization due to its homogenizing effect and disregard for actual circumstances. Even among the larger, more cohesive ethnic categories in the PRC, such as the Hui (ethnically Han, Chinese-speaking Muslims) and Tibetans, this impulse for uniformity across wide swathes of the population has caused many minority individuals to struggle to identify with the artificially constructed political identities created on their behalf.

It is precisely the CCP's failure to adequately represent minority traditions, combined with the ideological vacuum of the post–Mao Zedong (1893–1976) 1980s, that inspired Zhang Chengzhi to search for a legacy of his own. Born in 1948 in Beijing, Zhang came of age during the Great Proletarian Cultural Revolution. It was Zhang and his schoolmates who coined the phrase "Red Guard," helping to inaugurate the mass mobilization of students in the name of revolution. Following Mao's death in 1976 and the loss of his ideological idol, Zhang experienced a period of self-doubt, and consequently became a leading figure of the Root-Seeking Movement in the 1980s—a group devoted to rediscovering and excavating the lost remains of traditional (Han) Chinese culture. Yet Zhang was not Han—his family was Hui, with roots in the Jahriyya sect of Islam, a Chinese order of Sufi Islam founded in the 1760s—and by the end of the decade, he felt compelled to search for his own origins and cultural legacy, and represent his own experience as a member of an officially recognized but in practice marginalized minority. The result was his novel, *History of the Soul*.

Published as a response to the Han-centric nature of the Root-Seeking Movement, *History of the Soul* recounts the development of the Jahriyya sect of Islam in northwest China over the course of nearly two hundred years, as well as the group's oppression by the Chinese. Despite its polemical position, the novel still debuted to rave reviews. Its reception can be understood as a result of two diverging social trends. On the one hand, it met the demand of the Han ethnic majority for something that demonstrated a historically significant cultural tradition, which captivated them with its enchanting prose and compelling narrative of unbroken faith. On the other, it served as a guide for members of the Jahriyya sect in particular, and the Hui more generally, who continued to feel ignored or lost in the spiritual vacuum left by the eclipse of Maoism. Whatever the reason, the novel's success is undeniable: in 1994, it was the second-most popular novel in the PRC.

Despite his success, Zhang was troubled by the many distortions of his intent and ultimately decided to revise and republish the novel. His concerns stemmed from a number of sources, ranging from the exoticizing tendencies among his Han readers to Hui Muslims' own misapprehension of Zhang's intentions. Determined to get it right, he spent nearly twenty years studying the real-world history behind his fictional world and an additional three to four years revising the manuscript, only completing his revisions in 2010. When the time came to find a publisher, however, none were willing to accept the manuscript; the story had become too politically sensitive.

Unable to feel properly represented inside China, Zhang was forced to look elsewhere. He decided to privately publish a commemorative edition of *History* and donate the proceeds to those he feels are his true compatriots, the Palestinian refugees. Zhang's increasing notoriety for his polemical politics has made him a de facto representative for the Hui in China, but his unorthodox positions reveal both the distance between himself and the image of the "model Hui minority," and the personal sacrifices a minority individual would have to make if he or she desired to be assimilated into Chinese culture. Zhang has maintained a strong affinity for Palestine since his youth—the loud speakers during the Cultural Revolution would daily reiterate their support for Palestine and all victims of imperialist aggressors—and felt his suffering as a discriminated and ignored class in the PRC resonated strongly with their struggle. Collecting donations from among the Muslim community in China, he raised more than US$100,000, which he delivered in person to Palestinian refugee camps in Jerash and Irbid, Jordan. Philanthropy aside, he felt he had a moral obligation to help his compatriots from the "Arabic world of West

Asia," a place far from the PRC where he finally found some semblance of roots and a sense of true belonging.

Whereas Zhang found himself better represented beyond China's borders, Rgyalrong Tibetan writer Alai discovered his roots inside China's historical archives. Born in 1959 in Ma'erkang prefecture of Sichuan Province in southwest China, Alai is the son of a Hui Muslim father and a Rgyalrong Tibetan mother. Alai's first language is a dialect of Rgyalrong called *situ*, and he only acquired Mandarin at great effort. After the Cultural Revolution, he began to write poetry and establish himself as a man of letters. During the late 1980s, much like Zhang, Alai craved a cultural heritage he could relate to and embarked on his own root-seeking mission. Taking nearly a decade to complete, the resulting novel, *Red Poppies*, tells the story of the rise and decline of a chieftain clan in the Rgyalrong territory in the lead-up to the founding of the PRC. The novel went on to win the fifth Mao Dun Prize for Literature in 2000, catapulting Alai to national fame and making him the begrudging face of Tibetans in the PRC.

Since winning the award, Alai has been frequently called on to represent the Tibetan Chinese community in the PRC—a responsibility that he tirelessly and vocally rejects. In interviews with the author, even the slightest insinuation of such a weighty burden often triggers what is now a well-rehearsed lesson on the diversity contained within the seemingly uniform ethnic group known as "Tibetans," as well as his carefully delimited purview of expertise, namely, his own experience. Although he shies away from explicitly political statements, his personal politics are clearly at odds with national policies. For instance, he openly admits to being ignorant of life and customs in Lhasa—the capital city of the Tibetan Autonomous Region in the PRC—and of life in Amdo, another culturally Tibetan region of historical importance. Even the situation in his own home region of Kham, he argues, contains diversity beyond his own experience, and so he rejects any claims that he might be able to speak even on "Kham's" behalf. His refusal exposes the artificial nature of both geographical boundaries and political identities in modern China, and forces politicians and his readers alike to reconsider the multicultural model that has privileged efficacy over specificity as the guiding principle for ethnic policy in recent decades.

With this desire for precision and accuracy in mind, Alai set out to write his own "history of the soul," a work that established the historical roots of the people from his home region and their relationship with the Chinese. This time, rather than writing another work of fiction—like his prize-winning novel *Red Poppies*—he opted for a nonfictional style that incorporated the results from his intense archival research. In 2014, Alai finally published *Zhandui*—the Qing-dynasty administrative name for a Tibetan-majority region in what is now western Sichuan and also a Tibetan expression for an "iron knot" or "sore"—which critics praised as proof that nonfiction literature could be engaging and have mainstream appeal in China. The novel was entered into competition for the Lu Xun Prize for Documentary Literature that year. Given his status as the chairman of the Sichuan Writers' Association—a government-administered organization that supports literary production—and having previously won the Mao Dun Prize, the novel was advanced to the final round as a matter of course. When the final ballots were counted, however, the book failed to receive even a single vote—the source of no small controversy.

While the ensuing response from Alai and remarks by the award's committee focused on questions of genre, specifically the difference between nonfiction and documentary literature, both parties' silence regarding the book's content is equally discussion worthy. Alai himself raised the question that gestures to the broader politics surrounding their debate about genre: If his novel was not "documentary" enough from the outset, why allow it through to the finals in the first place? Coming two short years after Zhang's novel was rejected for republication in an ever-intensifying system of political oversight, one must wonder if Alai's *Zhandui* did not fall subject to a similar fate. The strong historical grounding underlying the work may have been viewed as too polemical by the authorities, as it could provide a basis for contesting national narratives about the peaceful coexistence of fifty-six discrete and finite Chinese ethnic groups. Moreover, awarding the book a prize of such prestige would have further encouraged its discussion in public forums, causing people to reflect more critically on the state of affairs for ethnic minorities in China. In the end, the fate of *Zhandui* remains open to speculation, but the lingering tension between Alai and the award's committee hints at what was left unspoken.

Perhaps to their chagrin, Zhang and Alai can still be said to represent their respective minority groups in the PRC, but not because they approximate an ideal type. In both cases, they were surrounded by Han

Chinese cultural and historical narratives that either overlooked or exoticized them. Consequently, they were forced to embark on a search for their own roots, both within and without China. Zhang has on several occasions decried his association with China and prefers to emphasize his cultural-religious heritage from abroad, while Alai has chosen to confront the Chinese legacy in the Rgyalrong region and attempts to excavate local histories from the homogenizing force of national myth. Although they make use of diverging approaches to reconcile their individual ethnic identities, their shared anxiety points to a growing dilemma in modern China, namely, the limits of the multicultural platform to adequately reflect and represent its diverse populations. In this way, we might understand both Zhang and Alai as able to represent not only their own ethnic groups, but also the shared desire of members from all ethnic minority groups in the PRC for recognition on a meaningful and personal level.

BIBLIOGRAPHY: Alai, *Red Poppies* (Boston, 2002). Alai, *Zhandui* (Chengdu, China, 2014). Thomas Mullaney, *Coming to Terms with the Nation: Ethnic Classification in Modern China* (Berkeley, CA, 2011). Zhang Chengzhi, *The Black Steed* (Beijing, 1990). Zhang Chengzhi, *Xinling shi* (Guangzhou, China, 1991).

KYLE SHERNUK

2013 · JANUARY 5

Hong Kong poet Leung Ping-kwan (Ye Si) dies.

Ye Si and Lyricism

On Saturday, January 5, 2013, after coping with lung cancer for over three years, the author Leung Ping-kwan (pen name Ye Si; 1949–2013) died. It is difficult not to think of this as the untimely passing of a remarkable writer whose contributions to postwar Chinese-language literature have yet to be fully understood.

In a writing career that spanned several decades, from the 1960s to the early 2010s, Leung produced volumes of poetry, essays, short stories, novels, and newspaper columns, as well as literary, film, and cultural criticism. As is evident in his experiments with different genres and in his moves between artistic creativity and scholarly study, Leung was greatly versatile. He also collaborated with photographers, visual artists, musicians, choreographers, translators, and academics in various multimedia projects. Leung's work is an excellent example of how intellectual work is not necessarily divorced from the rest of society but, on the contrary, is intimately connected with it; and, instead of declaring that connection in purely theoretical formulations, he demonstrated time and again the rich possibilities of partnership that lie between the two realms.

A recurrent theme of Leung's writings—one that only a few readers have discussed to date—is his investment in the literary and artistic mode he refers to as *shuqing*. Although a common translation of this term is "lyrical" or "lyricism," what Leung means by it clearly exceeds this translation. As a tribute to his work, I would like to offer some observations about the connotations and implications of this, his beloved mode.

Leung has a distinctive manner of depicting the quotidian aspects of the world around him. Be the subject matter an exhibit, a performance, a landscape, an encounter with people, utensils, the elements, or a repast, Leung not only describes but also attempts to discover the singularities of each entity and phenomenon he chances on. His pursuit of things is, as he tells us in the essay "Notes on Thing Poems," traceable to the Chinese poetic genre known as *yongwushi* (thing poem). While classical in lineage, this curiosity about the material world is combined here with the imagination of an erudite reader who has also studied modern poets from Rainer Maria Rilke, Ezra Pound, and T. S. Eliot to W. H. Auden and Pablo Neruda; modern fiction writers such as Virginia Woolf, Shen Congwen, Fei Ming, and Wang Zengqi; and contemporary literary critics such as Jaroslav Průšek, Ralph Freedman, and Paul de Man. No discussion of Leung's work would be complete without mention of the considerable influence exerted on him by cinema. A film enthusiast and well acquainted with various national cinemas throughout the twentieth century, Leung makes fascinating uses of the cinematographic sense of capture and montage to produce novel spatial connections and contractions in his poems and narratives.

The first notable feature of Leung's writing is thus a strong sense of a formal aesthetics. If poetry specializes in reflections through time (as mediated by language), cinematography's visualizing techniques, such as zooming, close-ups, long takes, and the like, enable experiments with space. When Leung writes about things as surprising as the patterns on a leaf, the face of a bitter melon, the color of seaweed, or the flavors of a pomegranate, his pen is also a camera lens, an instrument for revealing an endless series of what the German Jewish critic Walter Benjamin (1892–1940) in his discussion of photography and film calls the optical unconscious. As well as purely formal innovations, however, Leung insists on the significance of emotion, which he describes in a technical-sensorial vocabulary composed of terms such as "symbolism," "atmosphere," "tone," "condensation," "ellipsis," "skipping," and "lightness of touch." Leung considers these practices essential to the production of undramatic, indirect, and understated effects. What he seeks to articulate by the category of *shuqing* is, in sum, the combination of a poetic and cinematographic formalism, on the one hand, and, on the other, a type of emotion-cum-practice of (self-)restraint and (self-)discipline. Contrary to a more popularized, romantic sense of free expression, *shuqing* for Leung is a style of reflexivity, an inward vision in which the self as such has become objectified through composition and blended into the world.

How does this lyrical mode, to which Leung repeatedly refers in his discussions of fiction and film, materialize in his own writing, a writing that is so closely associated with Hong Kong, where literary and cultural production has always led a marginal existence? How does Leung negotiate between his fondness for *shuqing* and what seem to be the crude, because overdetermined, geopolitical factors shaping Hong Kong—the history of British colonialism, Orientalism, commercialism, overcrowding and scarcity of resources, fraught and often tense relations with China, and so forth? Whereas for some authors lyricism would mean immersion in a subjective universe, isolated from and impenetrable to the rest of society, Leung's pursuit of *shuqing* is decidedly different.

During an interview, when discussing the lack of official support for writers in Hong Kong, Leung raises this hypothesis: "Should things improve someday, enough to produce a professional writer, who can live within his own circle, enjoy beneficial terms, ignore practical issues, write in a vacuum and receive praise for it, and have no need to face hardships— would work written under such conditions be better?" His response: "I doubt it." This ability to see another side, to doubt a facile solution to even an oppressive situation—one that afflicted his entire career—gives Leung's work its admirably resilient quality. Even as he speaks against the systemic indifference to writers in Hong Kong, he understands that writing is not something that will automatically improve simply by being officially sponsored. Leung's own work may be the best case in point of how strong writing is about creating spaces where no space and no nurturance exist.

The attractive sense of stillness in his poems, then, stems less from a poetic consciousness's aloofness than from an engagement with unexpected shades and dimensions of the most negligible of objects. What seems like stillness is really the poetic consciousness's way of stepping aside to allow the other's world to emerge. Such stepping aside brings about the movement Leung calls *you*, a journeying through that is not only physical but also mental and spiritual. Whereas others may associate lyricism with fleeting sensations, Leung's *shuqing* is rather about lingering: instead of fetishizing the phenomenon of disappearance, his poetic consciousness sticks around patiently to allow objects and scenes the opportunity to speak for themselves. This is why in Leung's lyricism the poetic voice is seldom solitary. More typically, Leung invents dialogues among different imagined voices: not only clogs, furniture, buildings, streets, statues, piers, birds, trees, ghosts, and mountain goblins but even the obnoxious real estate developer, a leading culprit of Hong Kong's deteriorating environmental conditions, has a voice and a place in his universe.

Not surprisingly, we find in many poems the interesting insertion of the second person, *ni*, a "you" with whom the poet conducts an imaginary conversation. With this simple address, a poem becomes the setting for a relationship unfolding between the poet and his object. The point is that there is always a position, a perspective, and an angle on the world other than our own. As Leung puts it in the poem on a flame tree ("Royal Poinciana"): "You don't want me to see you in a fixed way" and "I don't want you to see me in a fixed way." Insofar as this relationship with the other is the key to Leung's lyrical mode, the frequent appearance of the conjunctions *he* and *yu* (and) in his titles is something of a signature: *Island and Mainland, Thunderclap and Cicada Chirping, Book and City, Postcolonial Food and Love, String and Sound,* and *Fly Heads and Bird Claws,* to name just a few. Even when it is not explicitly invoked, the "and" is often implied through Leung's attention to questions of marginality, exile, diaspora, and postcoloniality, which he approaches in ways that are at once sensorially and linguistically concrete, giving to migrants and transient phenomena an innovative set of spatial accommodations. In the repeated gesture of making room for the other, what begins as an aesthetic experiment—the proliferation of spaces through unusual visual perspectives—becomes a democratic ethos, the capaciousness of which is best summed up in the term Leung often uses in relation to *shuqing: kuanrong,* commonly translated as "tolerance."

Leung's relationship to Hong Kong should, ultimately, be understood in terms of this mutuality between his aesthetics and ethos. Encapsulated not only in the form of photographic images but also in its incessant demolitions and reconstructions, its mobile and intractable class distinctions, its relentless shifts, and its ubiquitous commodities, the city in its exasperating impossibility also inspires, paradoxically, an enduring feeling of tenderness and attachment that can only be called love. The grasp of this dialectical bond between the urban and the lyrical distinguishes Leung's work from that of some of his fellow Chinese-language writers, for whom lyricism often remains a vehicle of transcendent yearnings, reserved for the nation, the people, revolution, and comparably heroic topics. Insofar as intellectuals in mainland China, as elsewhere, are increasingly confronted in the global era with the material consequences of rapid urbanization, they may, in due course, come to recognize the prescience of Leung's thoroughly immanent visions.

In Leung's hands, senses, things, and relationships are brought into play in such ways as to become a gathering, both in the sense of an artistic collection and in the sense of a community in formation. How to gather all possible senses, things, people, and their stories, and pass them on to future generations? Among the many memorable images from Leung's work, one seems an eminently apt symbol of the challenge of such a transmission. Interweaving Leung's favorite themes of historical rootedness, chance, metamorphosis, hybridization, and involuntary cohabitation, the image is that of a weird-looking, big banyan tree found on a street in Hong Kong. Imagining a gathering of storytellers and listeners across the generations, Leung addresses his readers in such a way as to guide them, ever so gently, toward his deepest concern: How to write? In his words,

> Perhaps our reality itself is absurd and disjointed! I look up: what we find is a weird-looking, big banyan tree. Weird, not only because it is lush with (aerial) roots and leaves but also because its branches and

trunks are all entangled with the brick wall, and still bearing faint traces of a door frame, as though we could open a door right there and go live inside. Turns out that the tree used to grow next to the house. When the Japanese came, the inhabitants fled; unobstructed, the tree grew liberally, crushing and leveling the house. The tree swallowed the house, ending up as this thing that looked like a tree and yet is not a tree, that looked like a house and yet is not a house. As we sit under this tree listening to stories, past customs of storytelling are changing. If the stories are fictional, those listening will notice that their own circumstances, too, are unstable....

As we stand under this big tree, how do we begin to tell our stories?...

Under these circumstances, the realism that is usually considered the mainstream of modern Chinese fiction seems rather limited, as it cannot fully articulate the complex relations between our feelings and thoughts and the world outside. We can only supplement it with other methods. For my part, I greatly cherish the experiments with the lyrical novel, Chinese and Western.

BIBLIOGRAPHY: Chen Huiying, "Shuqing xiaoshuo yu shiyan (jiexuan)," in *Ye Si zuopin pinglun ji*, ed. Chen Suyi (Hong Kong, 2011), 149–156. Rey Chow, "Things, Common / Places, Passages of the Port City," in *Ethics after Idealism* (Bloomington, IN, 1998), 168–188. Douglas Kerr, "Leung Ping-Kwan's *Amblings*," *Cha: An Asian Literary Journal* 15 (November 2012). Leung Ping-kwan, *Amblings*, trans. Kit Kelen et al. (Macao, 2010). Leung Ping-kwan, *City at the End of Time*, ed. and intro. Esther M. K. Cheung, trans. Gordon T. Osing and Leung Ping-kwan (Hong Kong, 2012). Leung Ping-kwan, *Fly Heads and Bird Claws*, trans. Brian Holton and John Minford, ed. Christopher Mattison (Hong Kong, 2013). Leung Ping-kwan, *Islands and Continents*, ed. John Minford with Brian Holton and Agnes Hung-chong Chan (Hong Kong, 2007). Leung Ping-kwan, *Travelling with a Bitter Melon*, ed. Martha P. Y. Cheung (Hong Kong, 2002). Ye Hui, "'Yu' de 'zhongjian shixue,'" *Wenxue pinglun* 14 (June 2011): 13–18. Zheng zhengheng, "Ye Si: Zai renjian xiezuo," *Ming Pao Daily*, January 11, 2013, D6.

REY CHOW

2013 · MAY 12, 7:30 P.M.

Poets from four Chinese ethnic minority groups gather in Chengdu to read poems written in their "mother tongues."

Lightning Strikes Twice: "Mother Tongue" Minority Poetry

An unusual poetry event happened in Chengdu, capital of Sichuan Province, at 7:30 p.m. on May 12, 2013: poets from four Chinese ethnic minority groups gathered in an upscale downtown mall to read poems written in their "mother tongues." The event was staged in the Sisyphus Bookshop, a trendy bookseller that caters to the cultivated tastes of upward-bound, forward-looking, globally and environmentally aware young urbanites. Placed among the bookshelves filled with literature both domestic and foreign, and with titles addressing subjects ranging from investment portfolio management to love-life advice, were rows of chairs facing a large screen displaying the title of the day's event. Bold block letters spelled the word *MIND*, the title of a well-tailored new journal on contemporary art and literature founded by a group of twentysomething young women with foreign pedigrees, having graduated from universities in Leeds, Nottingham, and Paris. The vision of the editors is to diversify and enrich contemporary cultural life, a mission that includes raising awareness of writing and art produced by ethnic minority writers and artists. The theme of the evening's reading was "Verses and Islands," the verses being the poems written and performed in the native languages of the poets, and the islands being the individual voices of ethnic minority poets reading in languages that are mutually unintelligible. By juxtaposing these texts in oral performance, the organizers hoped, gaps of language and culture between the audience and poets could be bridged by poetic feeling.

How ethnicity is configured in contemporary China is linked to the birth of China as a Western-style republic in the early twentieth century and especially to policies introduced since the establishment of the People's Republic of China in 1949. In the early 1950s, official government recognition of distinct ethnic minority groups was institutionalized, a policy that imitated the earlier nationality policy of the Soviet Union. Today there are officially fifty-five ethnic minority groups, making up about 9 percent of the population. The majority of China's population is registered as members of the Han ethnic group, an ethnonym for the people most outsiders typically think of as Chinese that dates back to the ancient Han dynasty (206 BCE–220 CE). Most people classified as ethnic minorities live in the borderlands of China's north, west, and southwest. The largest groups are the Zhuang, Yi, Zang (Tibetan), Miao (Hmong), Mongol, Hui (a Muslim group), and Manchus, each of which number in the millions, but there are dozens of smaller groups, like the Hezhe, Evenki, Salar, Qiang, and Molao. Like the Han, all of these ethnic groups have rich oral traditions of folk song and narrative, though many of these traditions are in decline. Several groups, such as the Uyghur, Tibetans, and Mongols, have traditions of writing based on Middle Eastern and Indic traditions. Truly native writing systems include Chinese written characters (China's main writing system), the ancient Yi script, a women's secret script from a small area in rural Hunan, and less developed writing systems used by ritualists and diviners in a few minority groups in southwest China such as the Naxi and Shui. Since the 1950s Roman scripts have been developed for most of the minority languages, though despite efforts to popularize them, few are in daily use due to the economic and cultural pressure to use Standard Chinese as a common means of interaction in China. Indeed, most ethnic authors today write their creative works in Standard Chinese, which gains them national audiences and, in a few cases, like the Tibetan novelist Alai (1959–), international recognition. A major hub of ethnic writing today is Chengdu, a dynamic economic and intellectual urban center that has attracted significant ethnic minority populations from adjacent upland areas in the southwest.

As China began to open up its economy in the 1980s, Chengdu became home to the Not-Not Poetry Movement, a new wave of young avant-garde poets who helped revitalize the Chinese literary scene after the disastrous Cultural Revolution (1966–1976). The city continues to be a regional powerhouse of contemporary Chinese poetry today. The Not-Not Movement consists almost entirely of ethnic Han poets. One exception is Jimu Langge (1963–). Although the majority of Jimu's poems are about life in mainstream society, some of his work touches on his own ethnic culture, the Yi. The Yi ethnic group numbers about eight million, and most of its members live high in the mountains of southern Sichuan and Yunnan, following until very recently a highly traditional lifestyle based on herding and farming. In the dynamic era of the 1980s, Jimu was among the first of his ethnicity to gain national recognition as a poet. Another Yi voice to awaken in that era was that of Jidi Majia (1961–), whose lyrical Chinese language poems often use images of traditional clothing, dance, and music to communicate a sense of unique Yi identity. His work has offered inspiration and creative strategies for many Yi poets and poets of other ethnicities in the southwest. Now a high official in western Qinghai Province, Jidi has in recent years used his position to host massive multiethnic poetry readings, drawing regional Chinese and international participants, on the magnificent shores of Lake Qinghai. Other ethnic poets writing in Chinese include Miao poet He Shaozhu (also associated with the Not-Not Poetry Movement), Bai poet and painter Liyuan Xiaodi (1964–), and the female poets Bamo Qubumo (1964–) and Lu Juan (1982–), all from Sichuan. Poets of the Wa ethnic group, who live near the border of Myanmar in Yunnan Province, include Burao Yilu ([1981–] whose prose and poetry often touch on women's issues) and Nie Le (1968–), a younger male poet. Themes in the works of these ethnic poets range from modernist self-exploration to hymns of ethnic identity, cultural loss, acculturation, and environmental issues.

Yet the lineup on May 12 consisted not of ethnic poets reading their Chinese-language poetry, but of ethnic poets reading what has become known as "mother tongue" poetry.

The first act was Shi Ying, a transplanted Han folk singer from Yunnan. After the stage was set with music, Wangxiu Caidan (1967–), a Tibetan poet from Gansu (north of Sichuan), read a Tibetan poem entitled "Fate of a Tiger" as the audience followed along with the Chinese translation in the program. The poem opens with the metaphor of an endangered creature, an image not uncommon in poems from the southwest: "A tiger, strode forth from the lines of a poem, walking right to here. / She wore a lovely striped skin, moving with confident steps, her bloody tongue wagging, and arched tail waving." A beast that was once king of the forest becomes a plaything for people to gawk at in the zoo, controlled by the whims of humans. As the poem develops, the speaker engages with the wavering, dreamlike images of a female tiger, until he himself dissolves within the imagery of the tiger's fate.

Next on the program was the Mongol poet Ha Sen (1971–), who writes in both Mongolian and Standard Chinese. Since she was unable to attend, reading in her place was a young Mongol woman from Eastern Inner Mongolia who is fluent in both Mongolian and Daur, the language of another northeastern ethnic group. The crisply enunciated sounds of Ha Sen's poems read in Mongolian made her words come alive as poetry that is felt and experienced, though no one in the audience could understand the literal meaning. It was this phenomenon of poetry as pure, heightened sound that seemed to appeal to the audience, who could get a sense of the words from the translation in the program. One poem spoke of snowflakes that turned out to be pear blossoms, which were in turn soon transformed into a metaphor for love.

These tranquil, lilting lyrics were followed by a crash of thunder from Yi poet Lama Yizuo (1987–), a disciple of Aku Wuwu (1964–), the first poet to write in the modern Yi script. Lama's poem, entitled "Last Night Someone Died of Drinking," was delivered in screeching Nuosu, a major Yi dialect, and accompanied by soul-rending conniptions as the author belted out a litany of "deaths" visited on the inhabitants of the city, beginning with, "Last night someone in this city died of drinking, / right here in this city," a reference to the social ills that befall some vulnerable ethnic migrant workers in urban areas around China. Only an English translation accompanied the Yi words in the program.

The last poet to perform was Aku Wuwu, who coined the term "mother tongue literature" and serves as an inspiration to younger advocates of native-tongue writing. Aku (whose Han name is Luo Qingchun) is a professor and dean of Yi studies at the Southwest University for Nationalities, a large ethnic minority university in Chengdu. Having learned Standard Chinese only at age seven, he is a speaker of the Nuosu dialect of Yi. His clarion call for ethnic revival, "Calling Back the Soul of Zhyge Alu," written in the mid-1980s, was the first major poem written in the modern Yi script, and remains his signature work today. As he took center stage, he paused and seemed to gather himself before roaring out passages of the poem, which calls for the return of the soul of the ancient culture-hero who shot down the extra suns burning the earth and who tamed lightning. The poem implicitly calls for a revival in spirit and direction for the Yi people, who are struggling with issues of identity and acculturation. Modeled in part on chants used by Yi shamans to call back the wandering souls of ill children, the poem is an example of Aku's technique of combining the cultural knowledge gained in his youth and in his research with the ecstatic reveries of his poetic vision. Despite the barrier of language (mitigated by a small print version in English provided by the event organizers), the recital electrified the room. Encouraged to join in the chorus, the multiethnic crowd cried out together, "O la, Come back! O la, come back!" The production of such energy is a natural result of Aku's philosophy on "mother tongue" writing, which can be summed up in one quote: "My mother tongue and my life are the same, inseparable. Without it I am like a living corpse." In order to promote the use of minority languages and the writing of "mother tongue" poetry, Aku often reads at rural schools and community events. Several of his Yi-language poems, including one recalling memories of his mother, are reprinted in textbooks used by rural Yi children.

Once the room had settled down after Aku's performance, the petite emcee leaned forward and asked for poems from the audience. After a few moments of hesitation, an editor of *MIND* offered a poem by Thomas Hardy (1840–1928) that she had found inspiring while in England. Once the ice was broken, another audience member recited a moving poem commemorating the anniversary of the 2008 earthquake that wiped out nearly 80 percent of the population of the Qiang ethnic group in northern Sichuan. Reading in both Qiang language and Chinese, the poet moved the room to silence. After a few moments, the room again returned to normalcy. A young man in the audience then read a poem written in Tibetan off of his cell phone, not willing to have his ethnic group upstaged by the high voltage of the Yi poets. Finally, several poets were called on to explain their work and answer audience questions.

At the end, books and addresses were exchanged and autographs inscribed. Once the chairs were rearranged and the electronic equipment was stored, the poets and editors of *MIND* retired to a nearby eatery to chat over beer and spicy noodles about the night's events and plan for a number of upcoming readings that would involve even more ethnic poets reciting in an even greater number of mother tongues.

The reading on May 12, 2013, was unusual only in its stress on the use of native languages as a medium for the writing and performance of poetry. In a metropolitan setting, with a diverse audience of urban sophisticates, a new form of agency is possible for ethnic minority poets and writers. Ethnic poets increasingly appear at regional and national poetry readings throughout the country, and local poetry readings given by resident poets are even more common. As ethnic poets proactively interact with their peers from the Han majority and take advantage of the commercial value of displaying their works in bookstores and at cultural events, new horizons emerge for the growth of ethnic culture in both rural and urban contexts, even as traditional languages and distinctive cultural attributes are in many cases under siege. As more ethnic writing appears in Chinese and minority languages, more writing is being translated into other languages. One example is Ewenki novelist Chi Zijian's novel *Last Quarter of the Moon*, recently published in English translation, which depicts one of the last herding peoples in China's northeast. In turn, urban audiences cultivate their literary tastes by encountering once-unfamiliar cultures, languages, perspectives, and idioms that have grown out of Chinese soil, contributing to new understandings of minority and majority literature and the cultural interaction between the two.

MARK BENDER

2066

Mars over America

Chinese Science Fiction Presents the Posthuman Future

In 2066, China dominates the world as its sole superpower. A team of Chinese Go players is sent to the poverty-stricken United States to show off China's cultural superiority. This is the setting upon which Han Song's (1965–) 2000 science fiction novel *Mars over America* opens. That China will rise to become a world power has been a central motif of Chinese science fiction since the genre's appearance in the first decade of the twentieth century. Known then as *kexue xiaoshuo*—literally "science fiction"—it was one of the new genres promoted by Liang Qichao (1873–1929) when he launched the magazine *New Fiction* in 1902. Through the efforts of Liang and his contemporaries, late Qing science fiction was established as a genre consisting mainly of utopian narratives that projected the political desire for China's reform onto an idealized, technologically more advanced world. Liang's own novel, *The Future of New China* (1902), is structured to outline the late Qing reformer's blueprint for China's self-strengthening, national rejuvenation, and eventual ascendancy to become a world power. Although Liang never finished his novel, its splendid vision of China's future was immediately appropriated by numerous late Qing science fiction novelists. As a result, Chinese science fiction as a genre was closely associated with the discourse of an emerging nationalism, and the image of a politically and technologically transformed future China functioned as the engine responsible for the genre's cultural dynamism.

Nearly a century later, the utopian vision of China's rise is again a prominent theme, recapitulated as well as parodied in contemporary Chinese science fiction. Since the beginning of the twenty-first century, the genre has undergone a sudden revival in China. This is occurring at a time when the Chinese government seeks a "peaceful rise" and nationalism within China is again becoming popular. Yet China's future direction is far from certain. Heightened aspirations for change and profound anxieties about China's future have characterized a new wave of Chinese science fiction.

The new wave has a dark and subversive side. It dismantles utopianism by including dystopian anomalies, and questions some of the key concepts of Chinese modernity, such as progress, development, nationalism, and scientism. At its most radical, the new wave embraces an avant-garde cultural spirit that encourages the reader to question reality and think beyond conventions. The three most important authors of the new wave are Wang Jinkang (1948–), Han Song, and Liu Cixin (1963–), whose writings have influenced younger writers such as Chen Qiufan (1981–), Fei Dao (1983–), Bao Shu (1981–), Xia Jia (1984–), Chi Hui (1984–), and Chang Jia (1984–).

The novel that signaled the arrival of a new wave in Chinese science fiction was Liu Cixin's *China 2185*, a political cyberpunk novel that he began to write in spring 1989. Without any reference to the student movement on the square, the novel nevertheless begins with a scene in Tiananmen: a young computer engineer crosses the deserted square on a dark night in 2185 and approaches the still-standing Mao Mausoleum. He manages to scan Mao Zedong's (1893–1976) dead brain cells and creates a simulated, cybernetic version of the great man. Combining political fantasy with science fiction, *China 2185* describes a cybernetic popular uprising triggered by the resurrection of Mao in cyberspace, an uprising that paralyzes the authorities in the real world. Liu does not seem to either glorify the cybernetic uprising or discredit Mao's political legacy, but instead he concentrates on experiments of conceiving "alterity" for the future of humanity, which is not only "post-Mao," but also "posthuman."

China 2185 remains unpublished. Liu waited for ten years to begin publishing stories and novels, and he quickly became the best-selling author in science fiction. His magnum opus, *The Three-Body Trilogy*, has sealed his reputation as China's foremost science fiction writer. The trilogy tells an epic story that begins in the Cultural Revolution, when a Chinese astronomer secretly establishes contact with a hostile alien civilization living in an unstable star system, and it concludes with the end of the universe. What Liu presents in the novel is clearly not an ideal world; on the contrary, it is the worst possible world. But in this novel, as well as in his other short stories, Liu again envisions a posthuman future and challenges the conventional ideas of humanity, reason, science, technology, progress, and governance.

The end of the solar system is the climax of Liu's trilogy. The main characters witness the disappearance of the human world from Pluto, where they construct a last monument to the human civilization. At this moment, all is lost. China's rising, eternal peace on Earth—all the most splendid utopian dreams are gone. But by bringing the reader to this moment, Liu has truly led them to encounter the unknown. His literary imagination transcends the "obsession with China," as C. T. Hsia (1921–2013) famously described the moral burden that has dominated modern Chinese literature. In *The Three-Body Trilogy*, Liu directly speaks to the infinity of the universe.

In Liu's fictional world, human society is often treated as a minor problem when compared to the extravagant and grandiose scale of the universe. Human survival is made possible merely through the mercy of a supreme alien species, and the extinction of humanity does not have much of an impact on the universe. Most of Liu's work can be called "posthuman" because of its highly technologized and omnipotent perspective. Experimenting with ideas of changing physical reality, he creates entire new universes and depicts them. His master plot is humankind's encounter with the unknown dimensions of the universe, a place that remains largely alien to human understanding. Populated by grandiose superhuman, transhuman, or posthuman figures or visions, Liu's science-fictional imagination is fiercely lofty, sublime, and awe inspiring.

Han Song's *Mars over America* is another pivotal novel in the new wave of science fiction. Han's narrative presents a future world based on posthuman technologies. On the surface, it centers on a sublime image of the future China, but the novel reveals a hideous side to this success story. As described in the novel, by the middle of the twenty-first century, the Chinese have control of the most advanced technology in the world: a superpowerful AI network called Amanduo, which connects everyone to a central processor that dictates what people think, feel, and do. Compared with Liang's unfinished *The Future of New China*, Han's novel presents a much more palpable image of China's future approach to wealth and power. It is a rather disheartening image, however: with Amanduo controlling China, the superpower is now manipulated by a machine. A substantial difference has become clear in the transformation from Liang's Confucian New China to Han's Amanduo-programmed China. The late Qing reformer's ideal of national rejuvenation and self-strengthening is sabotaged by the entire nation's loss of sovereignty and submission to a system that manipulates the consciousness, sensibilities, and sensations of every one of its citizens.

The novel presents a paradoxical vision that combines a futuristic showcase of national pride with a strong sense of self-reflection that critiques Chinese politics and culture. In Han's version of China's 2066, the ideology of "strengthening the nation" is treated with poignant parody as China's rise is built on the systematic manipulation of its citizens. Nothing is voluntary; submission is the only rule.

The irony may appear even stronger when Mao's legacy is taken into consideration. For 2066 is not a randomly chosen number: 2066 will mark the one hundredth anniversary of the outbreak of the Cultural Revolution that put Maoist utopianism into practice. Actually, the entire title of the novel, consisting of two parts, contains a clear allusion to Mao's story. The first part, *Mars over America*—which can also be translated as *Fire Star over America*, for the word for Mars in Chinese literally translates as "fire star"—is a reference to the most influential book about Mao's rise, *Red Star over China*, written by the American journalist Edgar Snow (1905–1972). Snow's 1937 reportage gave Western readers their first positive glimpse of Mao and his Red Army. The Chinese translation of Snow's book was released in 1938 under the title *Random Sketches on a Journey to the West*, which was borrowed by Han for the second part of his own title.

The "journey to the West" refers to Snow's trek to China's north-western provinces, where Mao's revolutionary regime was based. But its implied meaning—seeking "truth" from the West—is a reference to the classic Chinese fantasy novel *Journey to the West*, a fictionalized account of the monk Xuanzang's (ca. 602–664 CE) famous westward pilgrimage to Buddhist India. For traditional Chinese readers, "the journey to the West" means the search for an ultimate truth that will guide the Chinese people to Buddha's spiritual realm. In the context of the remapping of global politics since the late Qing, the "journey to the West" signifies the reorientation of Chinese intellectual thought toward concepts and ideas from the modern West. Mao's Communist Revolution, the "red star over China" was also the result of a westward pilgrimage in this modern context.

These diverse meanings are carefully appropriated in Han's *Mars over America*. While "the journey to the West" is no longer oriented toward ancient India, it remains a journey toward truth and a journey closely linked to the nationalist urge for China's self-strengthening. More importantly, Han's *Mars over America* also skews the meaning of the westward journey. Instead of seeking "truth" in the West, the Chinese Go players are expected to bring "truth" *to* the West. Go, as China's national game, is said in the novel to contain the ultimate key to peace and harmony, which the future Chinese government wishes to ensure through introducing the game to other nations. What unfolds in the novel, however, is the story of an unexpected discovery by the novel's young Chinese protagonist of a more authentic "truth." For the duration of the young Go player's journey through the United States, he is disconnected from Amanduo and has to learn about the true nature of the Real. The narrative becomes a bildungsroman of how this young man acquires a self-consciousness independent from the consciousness provided by AI technology. Ultimately, when the Amanduo system backfires, reality sinks in—the protagonist begins to see the chaos in the third millennium that was previously excluded from the harmonious world image created by the AI.

China's future in Han's novel appears even more dystopian when the narrative is revealed as being framed by an eerie vision. The protagonist recounts his life story retrospectively, when he is already seventy-six years old, which means that his journey to the United States has taken place sixty years in the past. Jumping back to the future's future—2126—it is implied that both China and the United States have been wiped out by a superior alien species that landed on Earth in 2066 and turned the entire planet into a *fudi*, a "land of happiness." In Chinese, *fudi* is a euphemism for the land of the dead, referring to an afterlife of eternal rest or "happiness." Through this twist of the narrative, China's future ends in uncertainty.

In the short story "My Fatherland Does Not Dream," which has never been published, Han depicts the nightmarish side of China's rise: the entire Chinese population "sleepwalks" at night, unconsciously participating in the creation of the country's economic miracle and helping to realize the nation's dream of wealth and power. The story reveals that the Chinese government has been secretly using "communal microwaves," a marvelous new technology, to create a new nation of disciplined and hardworking sleepwalking citizens. In the story, the national leader proudly announces, "Sleepwalking has awakened 1.3 billion Chinese people," which sounds like an ironic reprisal of Lu Xun's (1881–1936) famous call to awaken China's sleeping population. The entire nation is now going back to sleep, or worse, sleepwalking; restless, senseless, and dreamless, they are deprived of the right to see reality, not to mention the right to dream of an alternative. Han's story was written ten years before the Chinese government began to promote the "Chinese dream"—a collective dream for the entire nation. In the story, sleepwalkers act out the uncanny unconscious of the Chinese dream dictated by the very few "sleepless" national leaders on a "committee of darkness." The sleepwalking population turns the Chinese dream into a reality that they do not see, living in a dream that is not theirs.

When science fiction becomes a popular genre again in China, Han, like Liang a century earlier, sees in science fiction a magical power that could inspire a nation: "Science fiction is a sort of literature that dreams, and it is itself a utopia." But Han, together with Liu Cixin and others, reenergizes the genre by consolidating and reinventing a variety of generic conventions, cultural elements, and political visions—ranging from space opera to cyberpunk fiction, from utopianism to posthumanism, and from parodied visions of China's rise to deconstructions of the myth of national development. In a peculiar way, Chinese science fiction has entered its golden age at the same time that it generates a new wave of subversion of the genre. Chinese science fiction enlivens the dream for the future of a new China, and the contemporary new wave also unleashes its night-marish shadows.

BIBLIOGRAPHY: Mingwei Song, ed., "Chinese Science Fiction: Late Qing and the Contemporary," special issue, *Renditions* 77/78 (2012). David Der-wei Wang, *Fin-de-Siècle Splendor: Repressed Modernities of Late Qing Fiction, 1849–1911* (Stanford, CA, 1997). Yan Wu and Veronica Hollinger, eds., "Chinese Science Fiction," special issue, *Science Fiction Studies* 40, no. 1 (2013).

MINGWEI SONG

CONTRIBUTORS

Nick ADMUSSEN is an assistant professor of Chinese literature at Cornell University. His first book is *Recite and Refuse: Contemporary Chinese Prose Poetry*. He is also a translator of contemporary Chinese poetry, most recently of the Sichuan poet Ya Shi.

Joseph R. ALLEN is professor of Chinese literature and cultural studies, and founding chair of the Department of Asian Languages and Literatures, at the University of Minnesota, Twin Cities. His publications include *Taipei: Cities of Displacements*, winner of the 2014 Joseph Levenson Book Prize from the Association of Asian Studies.

Andrea BACHNER teaches comparative literature at Cornell University. Her research explores comparative intersections between Chinese, Latin American, and European cultural productions in dialogue with theories of interculturality, sexuality, and mediality. She is the author of *Beyond Sinology: Chinese Writing and the Scripts of Culture* and coeditor of *The Oxford Handbook of Modern Chinese Literatures*.

Mark BENDER teaches traditional Chinese folk literature at The Ohio State University. He specializes in traditional oral literature of Han and ethnic minority local cultures, contemporary ethnic minority poetry, and translation. Among his works is the coedited volume *The Columbia Anthology of Chinese Folk and Popular Literature*.

Michael BERRY is professor of Asian languages and cultures at the University of California, Los Angeles. He is the author of *Speaking in Images: Interviews with Contemporary Chinese Filmmakers; A History of Pain: Trauma in Modern Chinese Literature and Film; Jia Zhangke's Hometown Trilogy;* and *Boiling the Sea: Hou Hsiao-hsien's Memories of Shadows and Light*. Berry is also coeditor of *Modernism Revisited* and *Divided Lenses* and the translator of several contemporary Chinese novels.

959

Yomi BRAESTER is Byron and Alice Lockwood Professor in the Humanities and professor of comparative literature, cinema, and media at the University of Washington in Seattle. His books include *Witness against History: Literature, Film, and Public Discourse in Twentieth-Century China* and *Painting the City Red: Chinese Cinema and the Urban Contract*. His book project on cinephilia in the People's Republic of China is supported by a Guggenheim Fellowship.

Clint CAPEHART is a PhD candidate in the Department of East Asian Languages and Civilizations at Harvard University. His research interests include modern and contemporary Chinese literature as well as the literature, history, and philosophy of early China, with a focus on excavated texts and the reconstruction of pre-Qin intellectual history.

Kwok Kou Leonard CHAN teaches classical Chinese literature and Hong Kong literature at the Education University of Hong Kong. His fields of interest are Chinese poetry and poetics, literary historiography, and Hong Kong literature. His works include *The Conception of Lyrical China* and *Hong Kong in Its History of Lyricism*.

Kang-i Sun CHANG, the inaugural Malcolm G. Chace 1956 Professor of East Asian Languages and Literatures at Yale University, is a scholar of classical Chinese literature with an interest in comparative studies of poetry, literary criticism, gender studies, and cultural theory and aesthetics. Her works include *Journey through the White Terror: A Daughter's Memoir*.

Sung-sheng Yvonne CHANG received her PhD from Stanford University and is a professor of Chinese and comparative literature at the University of Texas at Austin. She is interested in reexamining modern literary developments in East Asia through sociologically informed conceptual frameworks. Her major publications include *Modernism and the Nativist Resistance: Contemporary Chinese Fiction from Taiwan; Literary Culture in Taiwan: Martial Law to Market Law;* and *The Columbia Sourcebook of Literary Taiwan*.

Pheng CHEAH is professor of rhetoric and chair of the Center of Southeast Asia Studies at the University of California, Berkeley. He has published widely on the theory and practice of cosmopolitanism, including *What Is a World? On Postcolonial Literature as World Literature*. A book on globalization and the Three Chinas from the perspective of the films of Jia Zhangke, Tsai Ming-liang, and Fruit Chan is forthcoming.

Guangchen CHEN is a PhD candidate in comparative literature, and a recipient of the Frederic Sheldon Traveling Fellowship at Harvard University. He was a junior fellow at the network "Principles of Cultural Dynamics" at Freie Universität Berlin. His research interests include writers as collectors, the history of emotions, Sino-Czech cultural relations, and the phenomenology of music. He translated Albert Schweitzer's *Bach* into Chinese, and his translation of David Damrosch's *How to Read World Literature* is in progress.

Jianhua CHEN received his PhD in Chinese literature from Fudan University and Harvard University. He taught at Hong Kong University of Science and Technology and is Zhiyuan Chair Professor of Humanities at Shanghai Jiao Tong University. His research interests cover Chinese literary culture from the thirteenth to twentieth century. His works include "Popular Literature and Visual Culture in Early Modern China" and "Linguistic Turns and Literary Fields in Twentieth-Century China."

Jingling CHEN received her PhD from Harvard University and teaches at Middlebury College. Her interests include Chinese and Greek comparative literature, modern and contemporary Chinese narrative, and modern Chinese intellectual history. She is completing a book on the Greek imaginary and Chinese intellectual and cultural modernity.

Lingchei Letty CHEN teaches modern Chinese literature and comparative literature at Washington University in Saint Louis. She specializes in modern and contemporary Chinese literature, Sinophone studies, and Chinese diaspora studies. She is particularly interested in identity politics and memory. Her works include "When Does Diaspora End and Sinophone Begin?" and *Memory's Shores: Remembrance of the Mao Years*.

CHEN Pingyuan is a native of Teochew in Guangdong, and a professor of Chinese at Peking University. From 2008 to 2012, he served as the chair of the Chinese Department. He has been named as a Changjiang Scholar by the Chinese Ministry of Education and is a researcher at the Central Research Institute of Culture and History. He has published over thirty books, including *The Transformation of Narrative Form in Chinese Fiction, Literati Dreams of the Knight-Errant through the Ages, The Founding of Modern Chinese Scholarship, Touching History and Entering the May Fourth Era,* and *Literary History as a Discipline.*

CHEN Sihe is a Changjiang Scholar, named by the Chinese Ministry of Education, at Fudan University, Shanghai, China, and director of Fudan Libraries. He specializes in modern and contemporary Chinese literature, and the Sino-Western literary relationship. His major publications include *The Conception of Entirety of China's New Literature; A Development of a Personality: A Biography of Ba Jin; A New History of Contemporary Chinese Literature* (chief editor); and *Fifteen Lectures on Modern and Contemporary Chinese Literature.*

Xiaomei CHEN teaches modern Chinese literature, film, and theater at the University of California, Davis. She is the author of *Occidentalism; Acting the Right Part* and *Staging Chinese Revolution: Theater, Film, and the Afterlives of Propaganda.* She is the editor of *Reading the Right Text* and *Columbia Anthology of Modern Chinese Drama.*

Eileen J. CHENG teaches Chinese language and literature at Pomona College. She specializes in modern Chinese literature and culture. Her work includes *Literary Remains: Death, Trauma, and Lu Xun's Refusal to Mourn,* and she is working on *Jottings under Lamplight: Essays on Life and Modern Culture,* a coedited volume of translations of Lu Xun's essays.

CHONG Fah Hing teaches Sinophone Malaysian literature and modern Chinese fiction at Universiti Putra Malaysia. His research focuses on Sinophone and Malay literary writings in Malaysia and Singapore, and literature, nation, and literary migration in Southeast Asia and East Asia. He is specifically interested in the Sinophone leftist literary movement in Malaysia from the 1920s till the beginning of Cold War era. His work includes *National Literature: Hegemony and Response.*

Katherine Hui-ling CHOU teaches theater at National Central University in Taiwan. She has published widely in the fields of cultural anthropology, gender and performances, Chinese film history, and performance culture; her research focuses on performing arts in creative industry and cultural economy. Her artistic credits include *He Is My Wife and He Is My Mother* and *President's Invitation 3.0*. She is also the editor in chief of *Performing Taiwan: Script, Design and Stagecraft, 1943–*.

Eileen Cheng-yin CHOW's research and teaching at Duke University (where she codirects Story Lab) center on serialized storytelling, press practices and publics, transcultural fandoms, and the origins and articulations of Chinatowns around the world. As director of the Cheng Shewo Institute at Shih Hsin University in Taipei, Chow oversees multiple projects on the history of Chinese journalism, social media's role in protest politics, and the building of a large-scale oral historical archive.

Rey CHOW is Anne Firor Scott Professor of Literature and the current director of the Program in Literature at Duke University. She is the author of *Not Like a Native Speaker: On Languaging as a Postcolonial Experience* and coeditor of *Sound Objects* (forthcoming). In 2016 Chow was elected to the American Academy of Arts and Sciences.

CHU T'ien-hsin was born into a famous literary family in Taiwan. Her father, Chu Hsi-ning, an established writer, fostered a group of writers from the younger generation, among whom are his three daughters, with T'ien-hsin as the second. She started publishing works as early as high school, and is the author of more than twenty books. Her works have been translated into English, French, and Japanese, including the novella *The Old Capital*.

Tarryn Li-Min CHUN is a postdoctoral fellow at the University of Michigan's Lieberthal-Rogel Center for Chinese Studies. Her research and teaching areas include modern and contemporary Chinese theater, literature, and media culture, with a focus on the relationship between performance and technology. She has contributed scholarly articles and reviews to *Asian Theatre Journal*; *TDR: The Drama Review*; *Wenxue*;

and an edited volume entitled *Staging China: New Theatres in the Twenty-First Century.*

Claire CONCEISON is Quanta Professor of Chinese Culture and a professor of theater arts at the Massachusetts Institute of Technology. She is a scholar, translator, and director. Her publications include *Significant Other: Staging the American in China,* Ying Ruocheng's autobiography *Voices Carry: Behind Bars and Backstage during China's Revolution and Reform,* and the anthology *I Love XXX and Other Plays* by Meng Jinghui.

John A. CRESPI is the Henry R. Luce Associate Professor of Chinese in the Department of East Asian Languages and Literatures at Colgate University. He researches modern and contemporary Chinese poetry, as well as China's mid-twentieth-century illustrated satire magazines. His publications include *Voices in Revolution: Poetry and the Auditory Imagination in Modern China* and an online unit for the Massachusetts Institute of Technology's Visualizing Cultures project on the 1930s satire magazine *Modern Sketch.*

Susan DARUVALA works in modern Chinese literature and film. She is a fellow of Trinity College, University of Cambridge, and has retired from her teaching post in the Department of East Asian Studies. She is the author of *Zhou Zuoren and an Alternative Chinese Response to Modernity.* Her research interests focus on Chinese aesthetic discourses, as well as the modern Chinese essay, the literary scene in Republican China, and Chinese film.

Gloria DAVIES is a literary scholar and historian of China at Monash University in Australia. Her research covers several areas including Chinese intellectual and literary history, contemporary Chinese thought, comparative literature and critical theory, and studies of cultural flows in the digital age. Her works include *Lu Xun's Revolution: Writing in a Time of Violence.*

Darrell William DAVIS is a film historian who has published on Japanese, Taiwan, and East Asian media. Now based in Hong Kong, he taught for eight years in Australia, and before that in Japan, California, and Hawaii.

He continues to research and publish in media industry, ethnicity, and film consumption in East Asia.

Kirk A. DENTON is professor of modern Chinese literature at The Ohio State University. He is the author of *Exhibiting the Past: Historical Memory and the Politics of Museums in Postsocialist China* and editor of *The Columbia Companion to Modern Chinese Literature* and the journal *Modern Chinese Literature and Culture*.

Alexander DES FORGES teaches Chinese and comparative literature at the University of Massachusetts Boston. He is the author of *Mediasphere Shanghai: The Aesthetics of Cultural Production* and numerous articles on early modern and modern literature, culture, and film. His book project is a critical reading of the civil service examination essay as a key mode of literary practice in the Ming and Qing dynasties.

Amy DOOLING teaches Chinese literature at Connecticut College. She specializes in modern women's writing and feminist culture. Her publications include *Writing Women in Modern China: An Anthology of Women's Literature from the Early Twentieth Century* and *Women's Literary Feminism in Twentieth-Century China*.

Kai-cheung DUNG is a Hong Kong novelist. He started writing in the early 1990s and has published more than twenty works in Chinese, among which *Atlas: The Archeology of an Imaginary City* has been translated into English.

Susan Chan EGAN grew up in the Philippines. An early retirement from finance allows her to indulge in the ancient arts of observing, reading, and writing. Currently based in California, she is the author of *A Latterday Confucian* and its Chinese version *Hong Ye Zhuan*, coauthor of *A Pragmatist and His Free Spirit*, and cotranslator of *The Song of Everlasting Sorrow*.

Benjamin A. ELMAN is Gordon Wu 1958 Professor of Chinese Studies, professor of East Asian studies and history, and formerly chair of the Department of East Asian Studies at Princeton University. He works at the intersection of several fields including history, philosophy, literature, religion, economics, politics, and science. Elman's books include *Classicism, Examinations, and Cultural History* and *A Cultural History of Modern Science in China.*

Géraldine FISS teaches modern Chinese literature and film at the University of Southern California. Her research focuses on transcultural practice and innovation in modern and contemporary Chinese literature and thought, especially Chinese-German literary and intellectual encounters. She also works on Chinese and transnational modernisms, Chinese women's fiction and film, and East Asian ecocriticism. Her book manuscript is entitled *Textual Travels and Traveling Texts: German Culture and Ideas in Early Twentieth Century China.*

Grace S. FONG is professor of Chinese literature in the Department of East Asian Studies, McGill University, and director of the Ming Qing Women's Writings digital archive and database project (http://digital .library.mcgill.ca/mingqing/). Her research interests encompass classical Chinese poetry and poetics, gender and the theory and practice of life writing, and women writers in late imperial China. Her works include *Herself an Author: Gender, Agency, and Writing in Late Imperial China.*

Natascha GENTZ is chair of Chinese Studies at the University of Edinburgh and teaches modern Chinese cultural studies in transnational perspectives. Her research interests include the history of Chinese journalism and Chinese media concepts, global conceptual history and transnational knowledge production, and the evolution of modern Chinese drama in theory and practice.

Alison M. GROPPE teaches modern Chinese literature, film, and popular culture at the University of Oregon. She specializes in literary and cinematic representations of identity, Sinophone studies, and world literature. Her publications include *Sinophone Malaysian Literature: Not Made in China.*

HA Jin teaches fiction writing and literature at Boston University. He has published sixteen books in English, including the novel *The Boat Rocker.* His work has been translated into more than thirty languages.

John Christopher HAMM teaches modern Chinese literature in the Department of Asian Languages and Literature at the University of Washington, Seattle. His areas of research include popular literature, genre fiction, and print culture. His publications include *Paper Swordsmen: Jin Yong and the Modern Chinese Martial Arts Novel.*

Patrick Dewes HANAN (1927–2014) was the Victor S. Thomas Professor Emeritus of Chinese Literature at Harvard University. He was a Sinologist, literary historian, and translator. He specialized in pre-twentieth-century vernacular fiction. His scholarly works include *The Chinese Shorty Story; The Invention of Li Yu;* and *Chinese Fiction of the Nineteenth and Early Twentieth Centuries.*

Kristine HARRIS, an associate professor of history and Asian studies at the State University of New York, New Paltz, specializes in modern Chinese cultural history with an emphasis on cinema, media, and gender studies. Her work has appeared in *The Oxford Handbook of Chinese Cinemas* and *History in Images: Pictures and Public Space in Modern China.*

Lauran R. HARTLEY is Tibetan Studies Librarian for the C. V. Starr East Asian Library at Columbia University and also serves as an affiliated lecturer in Tibetan literature for the Department of East Asian Languages and Cultures. She received her PhD in Tibetan studies from Indiana University in 2003, and is coeditor of the book *Modern Tibetan Literature and Social Change.* Her research focuses on Tibetan literary production and intellectual discourse from the eighteenth century to present.

Satoru HASHIMOTO is assistant professor of modern Chinese and Sinophone literature and culture at the University of Maryland, College Park. His research interests include transregional history of East Asian literatures from antiquity to the present, comparative aesthetics, critical theory, and world literature. Among his publications is "World of Letters: Lu Xun, Benjamin, and *Daodejing*," which appeared in *Journal of World Literature.*

Man HE teaches Chinese literature and language at Williams College. She specializes in modern and contemporary Chinese literature, visual culture, and performance study. Her article "When S / He Is Not Nora: Hong Shen, Cosmopolitan Intellectuals, and Chinese Theaters in 1910s China and America" was published in *Modern Chinese Literature and Culture*. She is working on her first manuscript, *At the Backstage of Chinese Play-Making: From Overseas Students to Workers Ensembles, 1910s–1990s*.

Ari Larissa HEINRICH teaches Chinese literature and cultural studies at the University of California, San Diego. He is the translator of Qiu Miaojin's *Last Words from Montmartre*. His books include *The Afterlife of Images: Translating the Pathological Body between China and the West* and *Chinese Surplus: Biopolitical Aesthetics and the Medically Commodified Body*.

Michael Gibbs HILL is visiting associate professor of Chinese at the College of William and Mary. He is the author of *Lin Shu, Inc.: Translation and the Making of Modern Chinese Culture* and the translator of *China from Empire to Nation-State* by Wang Hui and *What Is China?* by Ge Zhaoguang (forthcoming).

Michel HOCKX is professor of Chinese literature and director of the Liu Institute for Asia and Asian Studies at the University of Notre Dame. His research deals with modern and contemporary Chinese literary communities, their organizations and publications, and their relationship with the state. He also works on modern Chinese poetry and poetics. His books include *Internet Literature in China*.

Tze-ki HON is a professor in the Department of Chinese and History at City University of Hong Kong. He specializes in the commentaries of the *Yijing* (*I Ching*, Book of Changes) and the cultural history of twentieth-century China. He recent works include *The Yijing and Chinese Politics*, *Revolution as Restoration*, *Teaching the I Ching*, and *The Allure of the Nation*.

Hu Ying teaches modern Chinese literature and culture at the University of California, Irvine. She specializes in late Qing literature, feminist theory, and translation studies. Her works include *Burying Autumn: Poetry, Friendship and Loss* and *Beyond Exemplar Tales: Women's Biography in Chinese History* (coedited).

Alexa HUANG teaches in East Asian languages and literatures, English, theater, and international affairs at George Washington University in Washington, DC, where she is founding codirector of the Digital Humanities Institute. She was former vice president of the Association for Asian Performance and specializes in Sinophone and Chinese intercultural film and theater.

Hsinya HUANG is professor of American and comparative literature and former dean of the College of Arts and Humanities, National Sun Yat-Sen University, Taiwan. She is the author or editor of books and articles on Native American and indigenous literatures, ecocriticism, and postcolonial and ethnic studies. Her research projects respectively investigate radiation ecologies in Native American and Pacific Islanders' literatures and Chinese railroad workers in North America.

Theodore HUTERS is emeritus professor of Chinese at University of California, Los Angeles, and editor of the translation journal *Renditions*. His work is focused on modern Chinese literature and literary history of the period between 1890 and 1925, as well as the intellectual background to that writing. He is working on the crisis of modernity in early twentieth-century China.

Wilt L. IDEMA taught Chinese literature at Leiden University and Harvard University. He specializes in the study of traditional vernacular literature (drama, fiction, and narrative ballads) and late imperial women's literature. His publications include *The Metamorphosis of "Tianxian pei": Local Opera under the Revolution (1949–1956)*.

Heather INWOOD is university lecturer in modern Chinese literature and culture and a fellow of Trinity Hall at the University of Cambridge. Her research focuses on interactions between contemporary Chinese literature, popular culture, and media. She is the author of *Verse Going Viral: China's New Media Scenes*.

Tsuyoshi ISHII researches Chinese modern intellectual history and philosophy at the University of Tokyo. His publications include *Dai Zhen and Chinese Modern Philosophy: From Philology to Philosophy* and *Philosophy of the Equalization of Things: Zhang Taiyan and the Experience of East Asia in Early Modern Chinese Thought*.

David JIANG is a stage director. He also teaches and researches theater. He has worked in mainland China, Taiwan, Hong Kong, the United States, and the United Kingdom. He was the dean of the School of Drama at the Hong Kong Academy for Performing Arts (2001–2009). His directing works include classics, contemporary plays, musicals, and Chinese drama.

Hui JIANG teaches critical theory, modern Chinese literature, and African literature at Peking University. He specializes in the novel theory, Marxism, and African literary movement and thought.

Huan JIN teaches at the City University of Hong Kong. She received her PhD from Harvard University and specializes in late imperial and early Republican Chinese literature (ca. 1500–1930), as well as the history of the book. She is working on a project entitled *Writing the Taiping Civil War (1851–1864): Propaganda, Testimony, and Literary Mediation.*

Andrew F. JONES is professor of Chinese at the University of California, Berkeley. He is the author of *Developmental Fairy Tales: Evolutionary Thinking and Modern Chinese Culture.*

Har Ye KAN is a lecturer in the Geography Department at Dartmouth College. She specializes in modern and contemporary urbanism in China and the broader East Asian region. Coauthored works include *China's Urban Communities* and *Urban Intensities: Contemporary Housing Types and Territories.*

Paize KEULEMANS teaches early modern Chinese literature at Princeton University. He specializes in the interaction between the medium of text and the sense of sound, as well as the relationship between literature and other media, including film and video games. His works include *Sound Rising from the Paper: Nineteenth-Century Martial Arts Fiction and the Chinese Acoustic Imagination.*

Richard KING teaches Chinese literature, film, language, and popular media at the University of Victoria, Canada. His research is on fiction, theory, and visual arts, particularly in the Mao era. Publications include *Milestones on a Golden Road: Writing for Chinese Socialism 1945–1980* and several volumes of translated fiction.

Jeffrey C. KINKLEY is a courtesy professor of history and of world languages and literatures at Portland State University. Author of *The Odyssey of Shen Congwen* and translations of Shen's and other modern Chinese writers' works, he has turned his attention to historical and social aspects of contemporary Chinese fiction. His works include *Visions of Dystopia in China's New Historical Novels.*

Faye Yuan KLEEMAN teaches modern Japanese literature and comparative literature at the University of Colorado. She specializes in modern and contemporary Japanese and Taiwanese literature, Japanophone studies, film, gender, and (post)colonial theory. Her works include *In Transit: The Formation of an East Asian Culture Sphere* and the articles "Chain Reactions—Japanese Colonialism and Global Cosmopolitanism in East Asia" and "Body, Identity, and Social Order: Japanese Crime Fiction in Colonial Taiwan."

Lucas KLEIN is an assistant professor at the University of Hong Kong. He is the translator of *Notes on the Mosquito: Selected Poems of Xi Chuan,* winner of the 2013 Lucien Stryk Prize, and of *October Dedications,* poetry by Mang Ke. His work has appeared in *Jacket, Rain Taxi, CLEAR, Comparative Literature Studies,* and *PMLA,* and in publications from Fordham University Press, Black Widow, Zephyr, and New Directions.

Uganda Sze Pui KWAN is associate professor of the Chinese Division at Nanyang Technological University, Singapore, where she teaches translation studies at both graduate and undergraduate levels. She specializes in late imperial Chinese history, modern Chinese literature, and Sino-Japanese comparative literary studies. Her research is about the making of Chinese studies by the British interpreters who came to Asia between the nineteenth century and the early twentieth century.

John T. P. LAI is an associate professor in the Department of Cultural and Religious Studies, Chinese University of Hong Kong. His research revolves around the interdisciplinary study of religion, literature, and translation, with a focus on Chinese Christian literature. His books include *Negotiating Religious Gaps: The Enterprise of Translating Christian Tracts by Protestant Missionaries in Nineteenth-Century China* and *A Critical Study of the Late-Qing Chinese Translations of "The Pilgrim's Progress."*

Charles A. Laughlin is Ellen Bayard Weedon Chair Professor of East Asian Studies at the University of Virginia. He has published extensively on Chinese literature from the 1920s to the 1960s, including two books: *Chinese Reportage: The Aesthetics of Historical Experience* and *The Literature of Leisure and Chinese Modernity*. Laughlin also edited *Contested Modernities in Chinese Literature*. His current research is on the engagement with desire from Chinese revolutionary literature to the literature and film of socialism.

Casey Lee is a PhD candidate in Chinese literature at Harvard University. Her research focuses on the relationship between contemporary media cultures and cultural modernity. Her dissertation considers how creative production by Chinese fans of Japanese animation, comics, and games (ACG) culture engages the People's Republic of China's shifting position in the world through unruly articulations of sociopolitical and interpersonal life.

Haiyan Lee is an associate professor of Chinese and comparative literature at Stanford University. She is the author of *Revolution of the Heart: A Genealogy of Love in China, 1900–1950*, which won the 2009 Joseph Levenson Prize (post-1900 China) from the Association for Asian Studies, and *The Stranger and the Chinese Moral Imagination*.

Leo Ou-fan Lee is currently a chair professor at the Chinese University of Hong Kong. His publications in English include *Shanghai Modern* and *City between Worlds: My Hong Kong*. He has also published more than twenty volumes of cultural criticism in Chinese, including two books on Eileen Chang.

Jie Li is assistant professor of East Asian languages and civilizations at Harvard University. Her research and teaching interests include East Asian cinema and modern Chinese literary, media, and cultural studies. She is the author of *Shanghai Homes: Palimpsests of Private Life* and coeditor of *Red Legacies in China: Cultural Afterlives of the Communist Revolution*.

Li Juan was born to a family in the Xinjiang Production and Construction Corps, and she grew up in both Sichuan and Xinjiang. Li lived for a time in a region of China inhabited by Kazakh nomads. In her works, she strives to write in a purely nonfictional style. Her published works include *A Corner of Altay; My Altay; When Walking the Road at Night, Please Sing with All Your Might; The Sheep Path;* and *Winter Pasture.*

Li Ruru teaches both Chinese language and culture at Leeds University in England. Her works are about Chinese theater and Shakespeare on the Chinese stage, including *Staging China: New Theatres in the Twenty-First Century* (editor); *The Soul of Beijing Opera: Theatrical Creativity and Continuity in the Changing World; Cao Yu: Pioneer of Modern Chinese Drama* (photographic exhibition); and *Shashibiya: Staging Shakespeare in China.* She regards regular contact with theater as essential to her academic work.

Sher-shiueh Li is a research fellow at the Institute of Chinese Literature and Philosophy, Academia Sinica, Taiwan. He is also on the faculty of the Cross-Cultural Studies Institute, Fu Jen University, and the Graduate Institute of Foreign Languages and Literatures, Taiwan University. A Chinese-Western comparatist, Li had published numerous papers before his *European Literature in Late Ming China* and *Transwriting: Translated Literature and Late Ming Jesuits,* both in Chinese, saw their appearances in this century. Li's publications include a coauthored English book entitled *Jesuit Chreia in Late Ming China: Two Studies with an Annotated Translation of Alfonso Vagnone's "Illustrations of the Grand Dao."*

Wai-yee Li teaches Chinese literature at Harvard University. She focuses on early China and the late imperial period. Her publications include *Women and National Trauma in Late Imperial Chinese Literature* and an annotated translation of *Zuozhuan.*

Ping-hui Liao is Chuan Lyu Endowed Chair Professor in Taiwan Studies and head of Cultural Studies at the University of California, San Diego. He is the author of a dozen of books in Chinese—including *Keywords 200 in Literary and Critical Studies*—and hundreds of articles in English, which cover a wide array of areas such as postmodernism, postcolonialism, music and culture, and modern Taiwanese literature and film. He is coeditor of *Taiwan under Japanese Colonial Rule, Comparatizing Taiwan,* and several other critical volumes in Chinese, Japanese, and English.

Pei-yin LIN teaches at the School of Chinese, University of Hong Kong. She obtained her PhD from the School of Oriental and African Studies, University of London, and was a visiting scholar at Harvard Yenching Institute (2015–2016). Her primary research interest is modern Chinese literature and culture, with a focus on Taiwan. Her *Colonial Taiwan: Negotiating Identities and Modernity through Literature* is forthcoming.

Perry LINK, retired from Princeton University, is Chancellorial Chair for Teaching across Disciplines at the University of California, Riverside. He publishes on modern Chinese language, literature, popular culture, intellectual history, and politics. His books include *An Anatomy of Chinese: Rhythm, Metaphor, Politics*.

LIU Jianmei is professor of Chinese literature and comparative literature in the Division of Humanities at Hong Kong University of Science and Technology. She is the author of *Zhuangzi and Modern Chinese Literature; Revolution Plus Love: Literary History, Women's Bodies;* and *Thematic Repetition in Twentieth-Century Chinese Fiction*.

Petrus LIU is associate professor of humanities at Yale-NUS (National University of Singapore) College. He is the author of *Queer Marxism in Two Chinas* (a finalist for the 2016 Lambda Literary Award in LGBT Studies) and *Stateless Subjects: Chinese Martial Arts Literature and Postcolonial History*. He also coedited "Beyond the Strai(gh)ts," a special issue of *positions*. He is writing a new book on the aesthetics of the Cold War in queer Asia.

Christopher LUPKE (PhD, Cornell University) is professor and chair of East Asian Studies at the University of Alberta. His books include *The Sinophone Cinema of Hou Hsiao-hsien: Culture, Style, Voice, and Motion*. His research focus is modern and contemporary Chinese culture, including Taiwan.

N. Göran D. MALMQVIST is professor emeritus in Sinology at Stockholm University and a member of the Swedish Academy. He has published works in the fields of Chinese linguistics and literature and some fifty volumes of translations of Chinese literature, ancient, medieval, premodern, and contemporary.

Bonnie S. McDougall is honorary associate in Chinese studies at the University of Sydney and professor emeritus at the University of Edinburgh. She has spent long periods in China, as well as Europe and America, writing on modern Chinese literature and translating poetry, fiction, drama, letters, essays, and film scripts by Bei Dao, Gu Cheng, Ah Cheng, Chen Kaige, Lu Xun, Mao Zedong, Kai-cheung Dung, and many others.

Mo Yan's writing career began when he was a soldier (he enlisted in the People's Liberation Army in 1976). He made a breakthrough as a novelist with *Red Sorghum* in 1986. He studied literature at Beijing Normal University and received a master's degree in 1991. He left the army in 1997 and later became a professional writer. His other major novels include *The Gallic Ballads, The Republic of Wine, Big Breasts & Wide Hips, Sandalwood Death, Life and Death Are Wearing Me Out,* and *Frog.* He has received numerous awards and honors, including the Fukuoka Asian Culture Prize, the Newman Prize for Chinese Literature, and the Mao Dun Literature Prize. In 2012, he received the Nobel Prize in Literature.

Stephen Owen is the James Bryant Conant University Professor at Harvard University, where he teaches classical Chinese literature and comparative literature. He specializes in classical poetry and lyric, premodern literary theory, and world literature. His books include a complete translation of the poetry of Du Fu for the Library of Chinese Humanities.

Peng Hsiao-yen is research fellow at the Institute of Chinese Literature and Philosophy, Academia Sinica. She specializes in transcultural studies, using as methodology the concept of transcultural lexicon to shed light on the global significance of local events. Her works include *Dandyism and Transcultural Modernity: The Dandy, the Flâneur, and the Translator in 1930s Shanghai, Tokyo, and Paris.*

Qian Liqun has roots in Hangzhou, but was born in Chongqing. He is professor emeritus of Chinese at Peking University. Qian specializes in modern Chinese literature, particularly the works, lives, and perspectives on literature of Lu Xun, Zhou Zuoren, post–May Fourth Chinese intellectuals, and Mao Zedong. His representative works include *The Search for the Soul; The Life of Zhou Zuoren; An Encounter with Lu Xun;* and *The Mao Era and the Post-Mao Era: Writing Another Kind of History,* and he has edited the three-volume *A Chronicle of Modern Chinese Literature: Using Literary Advertisements as an Index.*

Ying QIAN teaches Chinese cinema and visual culture at Columbia University. Her research interests include documentary cinema in comparative perspectives, China's revolution and socialism, and ethnic minority writing and filmmaking. She is completing a book manuscript entitled *Visionary Realities: Documentary Cinema in China's Revolutionary Century,* which investigates documentary cinema's capacities to mediate between the visible and the visionary in a society engineering its own radical transformation.

Andy RODEKOHR works at Wake Forest University, where he teaches Chinese literature, film, and culture. He is completing a book manuscript on the imagination, representation, and dissemination of crowds in modern China. His next project compares the emergence of the "new waves" of cinema in Hong Kong, Taiwan, and the People's Republic of China.

Carlos ROJAS is professor of Chinese cultural studies; gender, sexuality, and feminist studies; and arts of the moving image at Duke University. His research focuses on issues of gender and visuality, corporeality and infection, and nationalism and diaspora studies. His works include *Homesickness: Culture, Contagion, and National Transformation in Modern China* and the coedited volume *The Oxford Handbook of Modern Chinese Literatures.*

Andrew SCHONEBAUM is associate professor of Chinese literature at the University of Maryland, College Park. He specializes in traditional Chinese culture, literature, and the history of daily life. His works include *Novel Medicine: Healing, Literature and Popular Knowledge in Early Modern China.* His next book project focuses on curiosity and the unseen in China.

Shuang SHEN teaches comparative literature and Chinese literature at Penn State University. Her books include *Cosmopolitan Publics: Anglophone Print Culture in Semi-colonial Shanghai* and *Eileen Chang: Degree Zero,* an edited volume of critical essays on Eileen Chang. Her areas of specialization include modern Chinese literature, postcolonial literature and theory, Asian American literature, and Chinese diaspora history and literature. She is working on a project focused on literary cultural circulation in the Asia Pacific during the Cold War period.

Kyle SHERNUK is a PhD candidate in modern and contemporary Chinese literature at Harvard University. His research focuses on contemporary Sinophone and Chinese-identified literatures and cultures, with specific attention to disenfranchised populations, including ethnic, sexual, and socioeconomic minorities.

Yunzhong SHU teaches modern Chinese and modern Chinese literature at Queens College, City University of New York. His research is focused on modern Chinese fiction. He has published *Buglers on the Home Front: The Wartime Practice of the Qiyue School* and articles on modern Chinese literature in English and Chinese.

Brian SKERRATT received his PhD from Harvard University. He has taught at the Chinese University of Hong Kong, and is a Fulbright Postdoctoral Researcher at National Chengchi University in Taiwan, where he is carrying out research and translation projects involving contemporary Taiwanese poetry and culture.

Norman SMITH teaches modern Chinese history at the University of Guelph in Canada. He specializes in the history of northeast China. His books include *Intoxicating Manchuria: Alcohol, Opium and Culture in China's Northeast* and *Resisting Manchukuo: Chinese Women Writers and the Japanese Occupation.*

Richard Jean So is assistant professor of English at the University of Chicago. He works on modern American and Chinese literatures, as well as the digital humanities. His books include *Transpacific Community: America, China and the Rise and Fall of a Cultural Network.*

Mingwei SONG teaches modern Chinese literature at Wellesley College. He has written and published about youth discourse, science fiction, and other topics in modern and contemporary Chinese literature. His works include *Young China: National Rejuvenation and the Bildungsro-man, 1900–1959.*

Weijie SONG teaches modern Chinese literature and film at Rutgers University, New Brunswick. His research interests include urban studies, martial arts and popular culture, comparative imagology, environmental imagination, and Sinophone and diaspora studies. His works include *Mapping Modern Beijing: Space, Emotion, and Literary Topography.*

Dylan SUHER is a PhD candidate in modern and contemporary Chinese literature at Harvard University. His research focuses on pop culture ide-ologies and the influence of film and television on literature in the People's Republic of China during the 1990s. He also serves as a contributing editor for *Asymptote*, a journal that focuses on literature in translation.

E. K. TAN is associate professor in the Department of Cultural Studies and Comparative Literature at Stony Brook University. He specializes in modern and contemporary Chinese literature, Sinophone studies, Southeast Asian studies, queer Asia, and postcolonial theory. His works include *Rethinking Chineseness: Translational Sinophone Identities in the Nanyang Literary World* and "In Search of New Forms: The Impact of Bilingual Policy and the 'Speak Mandarin' Campaign on Sinophone Singa-pore Poetry" in *Interventions: International Journal of Postcolonial Studies.*

Xiaobing TANG teaches modern Chinese literary and cultural studies at the University of Michigan. His publications include *Visual Culture in Contemporary China: Paradigms and Shifts.* A research area of partic-ular interest to him is representations of sound and the human voice in various media.

Emma J. TENG is the T. T. and Wei Fong Chao Professor of Asian Civi-lizations at the Massachusetts Institute of Technology, where she teaches courses in Chinese culture, Chinese migration history, and Asian American studies. Her interests include travel writing, race and ethnic studies, and gender studies. Teng is the author of various works, including *Taiwan's Imagined Geography: Chinese Colonial Travel Writing and Pictures, 1683–1895* and *Eurasian: Mixed Identities in the United States, China and Hong Kong, 1842–1943.*

Stephen Teo is associate professor at the Wee Kim Wee School of Communication and Information, Nanyang Technological University, Singapore. His research deals mainly with Asian cinemas, and he is the author of *Hong Kong Cinema: The Extra Dimensions; Wong Kar-wai; King Hu's "A Touch of Zen"; Director in Action: Johnnie To and the Hong Kong Action Film; Chinese Martial Arts Cinema: The Wuxia Tradition;* and *The Asian Cinema Experience: Styles, Spaces, Theory.*

Karen L. Thornber is Victor and William Fung Director of the Harvard University Asia Center, chair of the Harvard Council on Asian Studies, and director of the Harvard Global Institute Environmental Humanities Initiative. She is also professor of East Asian languages and civilizations and of comparative literature. Her extensive publications focus on comparative and world literature, trauma, postcolonialism, East Asian literatures, literatures of the Indian Ocean Rim, and the environmental and medical humanities, among other topics.

Xiaofei Tian is professor of Chinese literature at Harvard University. Her publications include *Visionary Journeys: Travel Writings from Early Medieval and Nineteenth-Century China* and *The World of a Tiny Insect: A Memoir of the Taiping Rebellion and Its Aftermath.*

Q. S. Tong is university professor of English at Sun Yat-sen University, China. Before he joined Sun Yat-sen University, he worked at the University of Hong Kong. He has published, in both English and Chinese, on issues of critical significance in literary and cultural studies, with special attention to the historical interactions between China and the West. His work focuses on the Chinese-language reform movement in the early twentieth century and its sociopolitical consequences.

Chien-hsin Tsai is associate professor of modern Chinese society and culture in the Department of Asian Studies at the University of Texas at Austin. He is coeditor of *Sinophone Studies: A Critical Reader* and author of *A Passage to China: Literature and Loyalism in Colonial Taiwan.*

Jing Tsu, a literary critic and cultural historian of modern China, is professor of East Asian languages and literatures and comparative literature at Yale University. Her works include *Sound and Script in Chinese*

Diaspora, and she is working on a book on what happened to the Chinese script in the age of the alphabet.

Maghiel VAN CREVEL teaches Chinese literature at Leiden University. He specializes in poetry from the People's Republic of China. His publications include *Chinese Poetry in Times of Mind, Mayhem and Money.*

Nicolai VOLLAND teaches Chinese literature and comparative literature at Penn State University. His research focuses on modern Chinese literature in its transnational dimensions, as well as visual culture and print culture. He is the author of *Socialist Cosmopolitanism: The Chinese Literary Universe, 1945–1965* (forthcoming) and editor of *The Business of Culture: Cultural Entrepreneurs in China and Southeast Asia, 1900–1965.*

Rudolf G. WAGNER is senior professor of Chinese studies at the Cluster Asia and Europe, Heidelberg University, and Fairbank Center Research Associate, Harvard University. He specializes in Chinese intellectual history and China's cultural interaction with the world. His works include *Joining the Global Public: Word, Image, and City in Early Chinese Newspapers* (editor); *Chinese Encyclopaedias of New Global Knowledge (1870–1930)* (coeditor); and *Modernity's Classics* (coeditor). He is coeditor of *Transcultural Studies.*

WANG Anyi is a writer of more than thirty books, including thirteen novels such as *The Song of Everlasting Sorrow* and *Anonymous.* Her works have won multiple literary awards and have been translated into more than twelve languages. She is also a professor at Fudan University, Shanghai, China, where she teaches contemporary Chinese literature and creative writing.

Ao WANG is an assistant professor of Asian languages and literatures at Wesleyan University. His main academic interest is classical Chinese poetry. He has published five books of his own poetry, and has been the recipient of prizes such as the Anne Kao Poetry Prize and the New Poet Prize from *People's Literature.*

Ban WANG is William Haas Professor in Chinese Studies at Stanford University. His major publications include *The Sublime Figure of History,*

Illuminations from the Past, and *History and Memory.* He has written widely on East-West cultural relations, aesthetics, Chinese cinema, and international politics and edited six books on Chinese film, revolution, socialism, and the New Left. His recent work has been on international culture and world politics.

Chih-ming WANG is associate research fellow at Academia Sinica, Taipei, Taiwan. He also teaches cultural studies at National Chiao-Tung University, Hsinchu, Taiwan. He guest-edited a special issue on "Asian American Studies in Asia" for *Inter-Asia Cultural Studies* and is the author of *Transpacific Articulations: Student Migration and the Remaking of Asian America.* His research focuses on Asian American literature and cultural studies in diasporic and transpacific contexts.

David Der-wei WANG is Edward C. Henderson Professor of Chinese and Comparative Literature at Harvard University. He specializes in modern and contemporary Chinese literature, Sinophone studies, and literary theory. His works include *The Lyrical in Epic Time: Chinese Intellectuals and Artists through the 1949 Crisis.*

WANG Hui is a professor of literature and history at Tsinghua University. In 1990, Wang published his first book, *Resisting Despair: Lu Xun and His Literary World,* in Taiwan and later in Shanghai. Afterward, he moved to the study of Chinese intellectual history and has engaged in a series of intellectual debates since 1990. His main works include *The Rise of Modern Chinese Thought* (four volumes); *The Depoliticized Politics;* and *From an Asian Perspective: The Narrations of Chinese History.* Many of his works have been translated into different languages, including English, such as *China's New Order, The End of the Revolution, China from Empire to Nation-State,* and *China's Twentieth Century.*

Pu WANG is assistant professor of Chinese literature and culture and the Helaine and Alvin Allen Chair in Literature at Brandeis University. He has finished a book manuscript on Guo Moruo, translation, and the Chinese Revolution. He is also a poet writing in Chinese.

Xiaojue WANG teaches modern Chinese literature, film, and comparative literature at Rutgers University, New Brunswick. Her research interests include modern Chinese and German literatures, film and media studies, the cultural Cold War, literary theory, and comparative literature. She is the author of *Modernity with a Cold War Face: Reimagining the Nation in Chinese Literature across the 1949 Divide.*

WEI Yan teaches modern Chinese literature at Lingnan University of Hong Kong. She specializes in modern and contemporary Chinese literature, popular literature, and Sinophone studies. Her PhD dissertation is "The Rise and Development of Chinese Detective Fiction: 1900–1949."

John B. WEINSTEIN is the dean of the Early Colleges at Bard College, principal of Bard High School Early College–Newark, and associate professor of Chinese and Asian studies at Bard College at Simon's Rock. A theater scholar, director, and translator, he specializes in modern and contemporary Chinese and Taiwanese plays. He is the editor and cotranslator of *Voices of Taiwanese Women: Three Contemporary Plays.*

Ellen WIDMER teaches Ming and Qing literature at Wellesley College. Her research specialties are women's literature of the Ming and Qing, missionary studies, and the classical Chinese novel. Among her books are two about the Qing: *The Beauty and the Book: Women and Fiction in Nineteenth-Century China* and *Fiction's Family: Zhan Xi, Zhan Kai and the Business of Women in Late-Qing China.*

Martin WOESLER is professor of literature and communication in China at Witten / Herdecke University, Germany; visiting professor at the Literature Institutes, Beijing Normal University and Nanjing Normal University; and visiting scholar at the Literature Institute, Nanjing University, China. He specializes in modern and contemporary Chinese literature, the Chinese essay, *Hongloumeng* translation studies, comparative literature, and literary theory. His studies include the canonization process of Chinese literature and early translations between Chinese and Western literature.

WONG Ain-ling is a film critic and independent researcher. Previously, she was a programmer at the Hong Kong International Film Festival and research officer at the Hong Kong Film Archive. She is guest lecturer at Chinese University of Hong Kong. She is particularly interested in the

Chinese cinema of the 1930s and 1940s. Her publications include *An Affair with Film; Dreamy Talks; Fei Mu—Poet Director* (editor); and *Fei Mu's Confucius* (editor).

Lawrence Wang-chi WONG is professor of humanities at the Department of Translation, Chinese University of Hong Kong. He specializes in modern Chinese literature and politics, the translation history of modern China, and Hong Kong studies. He is chief editor of the *Journal of Translation Studies* and *Studies in Translation History*. His books include *Between Translation and Literature* and *Translation and Modern China*.

Mary Shuk-han WONG is associate professor in the Chinese Department at Lingnan University. She received her PhD in the Department of Comparative Literature at the University of Hong Kong. She is the author of *Feminine Writing: Cinema, Literature and Everyday Lives* and *Hong Kong Cinema: Writer, Literature and Cinema*. Her major edited books include the *Hong Kong Literature and Culture of the 1950s* series (six volumes) (coeditor) and *Liu Yichang and Hong Kong Modernism* (coeditor).

Shengqing WU teaches modern Chinese literature at the Division of Humanities of the Hong Kong University of Science and Technology. Her research interests include classical-style poetry written in the modern era, emotion studies, and the relationship between image and text. She is the author of *Modern Archaics: Continuity and Innovation in the Chinese Lyric Tradition, 1900–1937*.

XIA Xiaohong is a native of Beijing and a professor of Chinese literature at Peking University. Her main focus is on literary trends, the lives of women, and society and culture during the late Qing and early Republican era. Her works include *Enlightenment and Patrimony:Liang Qichao's Literary Road; The Perspectives of Literary Women of the Late Qing; Late Qing Women and Fin-de-Siècle China; Liang Qichao: Between Politics and Scholarship;* and *The Late Qing Construction of a Female Civic Sensibility*.

Lanjun XU is associate professor of modern Chinese literature and cultures at the National University of Singapore. Her main research interests include the cultural history of children in modern China and the Cold War cultural networks between China, Hong Kong, and Southeast Asia.

Her works include a book manuscript, *The Child and Chinese Modernity: Culture, Nation and Technologies of Childhood in Modern China*, and a Chinese monograph, *Chinese Children and War*.

Steven YAO is Edmund A. LeFevre Professor of Literature at Hamilton College. His research interests include global modernisms and transpacific literature. He is the author of *Translation and the Languages of Modernism* and *Foreign Accents: Chinese American Verse from Exclusion to Postethnicity*. He has earned fellowships from the Stanford Humanities Center, the American Council of Learned Societies, and the American Council on Education.

Catherine Vance YEH is professor of modern Chinese literature and transcultural studies at Boston University. Her research focuses on the global migration of literary forms, the transformation of theater aesthetics in transcultural interaction, and entertainment culture as an agent of social change. Her publications include *Shanghai Love: Courtesans, Intellectuals, and Entertainment Culture, 1850–1910* and *The Chinese Political Novel: Migration of a World Genre*.

Emilie Yueh-yu YEH is professor and director of the Academy of Film at Hong Kong Baptist University. Her publications include *Staging Memories: Hou Hsiao-hsien's "A City of Sadness"* (coauthor) and *Beyond Shanghai: New Perspectives on Early Chinese Cinema*.

Michelle YEH is distinguished professor in East Asian languages and cultures at the University of California, Davis, where she teaches classical and modern Chinese poetry, as well as Taiwanese literature and film. Her major publications on modern Chinese poetry include books and articles in English and Chinese, as well as translations and edited anthologies in English. She coedited *The Columbia Sourcebook of Literary Taiwan*.

YING Lei is a PhD candidate in modern Chinese literature and Presidential Scholar at Harvard University. Her research explores the nexus between Buddhism and modern Chinese literary and intellectual history. She is completing her dissertation, "Our Shared Karma: Buddhism, Literature, and the Modern Chinese Revolution."

Wai-lim YIP, retired University of California, Davis, professor of literature, has been creating and critiquing poetry in a cross- and intercultural context with equal impact on both the Chinese and the English worlds. Chief among his sixty-plus books are *Fifth Years of Poetry*; *Ezra Pound's "Cathay"*; *Diffusion of Distances*; *Chinese Poetry: Major Modes and Genres*; *Hiding the Universe: The Poetry of Wang Wei*; *Comparative Poetics*; *Chinese Poetics*; *Reading the Modern and the Postmodern*; and his recent *Gemlike Flame: Essays on Modern Poetry from China, Hong Kong, and Taiwan*, as well as a book of translations of modern European and Latin American poets entitled *And All the Trees Sing*. His influence abroad is significant and extensive.

Helen Praeger YOUNG is a visiting scholar at the Center for East Asian Studies, Stanford University. She is the author of *Choosing Revolution: Chinese Women Soldiers on the Long March* and has published many essays based on her interviews of Red Army women soldiers. She continues to pursue research, writing, and lecturing on the experience of women in modern Chinese history.

YU Hua worked as a dentist for over five years before becoming a writer in 1983. To date he has published five full-length novels, six short- and medium-length story collections, and five prose collections. His major works include *To Live, Chronicle of a Blood Merchant, Cries in the Drizzle, Brothers, The Seventh Day, China in Ten Words, Boy in the Twilight*, and *The Past and the Punishments*. His works have been translated into thirty languages and published in over thirty countries. He is the winner of Italy's Premio Grinzane Cavour (1998) and Giuseppe Acerbi Literary International Prize (2014), and France's Chevalier de L'Ordre des Arts et des Lettres (2004) and Prix Courrier International (2008).

Yingjin ZHANG is distinguished professor and chair of the Department of Literature at the University of California, San Diego. His books include *The City in Modern Chinese Literature and Film*; *Cinema and Urban Culture in Shanghai*; *Screening China*; *Chinese National Cinema*; *From Underground to Independent*; *Cinema, Space, and Polylocality in a Globalizing China*; *A Companion to Chinese Cinema*; *New Chinese-Language Documentaries*; and *A Companion to Modern Chinese Literature*.

ILLUSTRATION CREDITS

INDEX

A TIMELINE

of

LITERARY

HISTORY

of

MODERN

CHINA

THE REFORM MOVEMENT 1898

1895 ⊢

FIRST SINO-JAPANESE WAR 1894 – 1895 ■

1891 ⊢

1881 ⊢

1875 ⊢ QIU JIN

1873 ⊢ LIANG QICHAO

1858 ⊢ KANG YOUWEI

1857 ⊢ LIU E

1852 ⊢ LIN SHU

1850 – 1864 TAIPING REBELLIO

● *Dream of the Red Chamber*   1839 – 1842 FIRST OPIUM WAR

1792

⊢ GONG ZIZHEN ⊣ 1841